International Financial Reporting and Analysis

A Contextual Emphasis

Mark E. Haskins
The University of Virginia

Kenneth R. Ferris
The American Graduate School of International Management

Thomas I. Selling
The American Graduate School of International Management

IRWIN

Chicago • Bogotá • Boston • Buenos Aires • Caracas
London • Madrid • Mexico City • Sydney • Toronto

Irwin Book Team
Publisher: *Mike Junior*
Executive editor: *Jeff Shelstad*
Editorial coordinator: *Kelly Williams*
Marketing manager: *Heather L. Woods*
Production supervisor: *Pat Frederickson*
Manager, graphics and desktop services: *Kim Meriwether*
Project editor: *Karen J. Nelson*
Designer: *Larry J. Cope*
Compositor: *Wm. C. Brown Publishers*
Typeface: *10/12 Times Roman*
Printer: *R. R. Donnelley & Sons Company*

Times Mirror
Higher Education Group

Library of Congress Cataloging-in-Publication Data
Haskins, Mark E.
   International financial reporting and analysis : a contextual emphasis/Mark E. Haskins, Kenneth R. Ferris, Thomas I. Selling.
      p. cm.
   Includes index.
   ISBN 0–256–13998–9
   1. Accounting.   2. Financial statements.   3. Comparative accounting.   I. Ferris, Kenneth R.   II. Selling, Thomas I.
III.   Title.
HF5635.H35   1996
657—dc20   95–23622

Preface

The globalization of financial markets has increased the value of knowledge about how business is conducted in other countries. One important aspect of that understanding is an awareness of the way in which international financial results are reported. Indeed, understanding the measurement and reporting process has a special urgency when considered as part of the capital formation and allocation process. Thus, one of the principal objectives of this book is to explore and understand the financial reporting practices used by companies from various countries around the world.

The book is intended for graduate students and upper-level undergraduates. In an undergraduate setting, the book assumes an intermediate-level accounting background. In an MBA setting, the book assumes student proficiency in a strong introductory financial accounting course prerequisite. In either instance, the book (1) provides an opportunity for students to learn about diverse financial reporting practices from around the world, (2) provides students with sufficient understanding of contextual factors so that they may understand the reasons for diverse financial reporting practices across countries, and (3) in achieving (1) and (2), a meaningful

decision context, namely the review and analysis of firm performance by analysts, investors, and managers, is offered.

In the pursuit of these objectives, this book adopts a threefold emphasis. First, like some other international financial reporting books, it chronicles and discusses some of the more significant similarities and differences in generally accepted accounting practices found in a selected number of countries. Unlike other books, however, this book posits the importance of understanding country context as a necessary prerequisite to comprehending the story being told by the specific accounting practices used by a particular company domiciled in a particular country. Indeed, the importance of and insights into the cultural, governmental, and business contexts of the book's focal countries is a constant theme throughout. Last, and in contrast to other books on international financial reporting, this book emphasizes a user's perspective, explicitly devoting four chapters to financial analysis issues and highlighting such pertinent issues within each of the country-specific chapters. These four chapters are set apart with a bold border on each page, thus highlighting their distinctiveness and allowing instructors to incorporate them into varied course sequences and to varying extents.

The book is divided into four parts:

I. International Financial Reporting and Standard Setting
II. Financial Statement Analysis
III. Financial Reporting Practices and Contexts in Selected Countries
IV. Harmonization of International Accounting and Reporting Standards Revisited

The first chapter presents Geert Hofstede's framework for analyzing the significant cultural contexts present in a country. This framework is referred to throughout the country-specific chapters. Chapter 1 also highlights the pertinent legal/political and business environment factors likely to influence the practice and developments of financial reporting. Chapters 2 and 3 provide background on the major international alliances working toward large-scale geographic harmonization of financial reporting: the International Accounting Standards Committee and the European Economic Union.

Part II of the book is devoted to the fundamentals of financial statement analysis as well as some of the special challenges presented by a desire to analyze annual reports of non–U.S. companies. In the latter section of this part of the book, the special challenges in financial reporting for multinational companies is considered.

The third part of the book takes the reader on a macro-level journey to the financial reporting contexts of seven countries: Great Britain, Germany, Japan, Sweden, Brazil, South Korea, and Italy. The emphasis in these chapters is on country context and the major similarities/differences in financial reporting practices across these seven countries and the United States. Included in these chapters are numerous annual report excerpts, highlighting particular financial reporting practices prevalent in a country's corporate annual reports. These seven countries were chosen because of the comparative differences and similarities they exhibit between each other and the United States.

The final section of the book consists solely of a chapter that is an edited transcript of a February 1995 speech given by Mr. Arthur Wyatt, former chair of the International Accounting Standards Committee. This chapter is titled "Harmonization's Future." Mr. Wyatt has been at the heart of many of the key financial reporting debates during the past 20 years. His thoughtful and provocative views on the future of global accounting harmonization provide a powerful capstone to the book, immediately following the country-specific chapters.

As an additional avenue for learning about the evolving, dynamic, fascinating world of international financial reporting, the end-of-chapter materials provide a series of varied and provocative forums for further exploration. First, as a service to our readers, Richard D. Irwin, Inc., has agreed, on an annual basis, to make available a set of recent corporate annual reports from the seven countries presented in the book. These reports, bound in book format, can be used with the annual report assignment presented at the end of each country chapter, thereby maintaining a freshness and recency not found in most books of this sort. We hope you avail yourself of this service and find it valuable. Second, each chapter presents some study opportunities in a unique section titled Issues and Information for Further Inquiry. The assignments presented in this section are drawn from the business press and/or recent academic business literature. They are intended to cultivate a heightened awareness that a variety of international business issues affect or are affected by international financial reporting concerns. Moreover, these assignments often require a bit of library research that serves to deepen and broaden a student's understanding of various topics while facilitating their familiarity with useful resources. Third, the end-of-chapter materials frequently focus on a specific international financial reporting practice in the Exercises, as well on more extensive or comprehensive financial reporting practices in the Cases sections. The accompanying instructor's manual is intended to assist instructors in identifying the key and/or provocative insights imbedded in each student assignment.

We would like to draw your attention to two other subtle, but valuable, features of the text. Throughout the text, the first appearance of a key word, name, or phrase is highlighted by bold type. These bolded words or phrases then appear in the glossary that can be found at the end of the text. Also, at the end of the text is an extensive set of tables summarizing comparative accounting and reporting practices for 11 additional countries (in addition to the text's 7 focal countries). Together, these end-of-text materials are intended to be a resource for students of international financial reporting.

It is important to note that the book is about generalized tendencies and attributes. Generalizations make comparisons possible, and the comparisons we make are intended to be purely informative, not verdicts of better versus worse. It is in that spirit that we undertake this investigation of international financial reporting.

This book has been in process for five years. During that time numerous students and colleagues have contributed in large and small ways. We thank them all, especially Chris Wenger and Lynna Martinez. We would like, however, to acknowledge the encouragement and patience of Jeff Shelstad at Richard D. Irwin, Inc.; the tireless manuscript processing of Lee Pierce, Dot Govoruhk, Bessie Truzy, and Kathleen Collier; and our colleagues Bob Sack, Brandt Allen, and E. Richard Brownlee II who continuously bring their insights in international financial reporting to the classroom.

Mark E. Haskins
Kenneth R. Ferris
Thomas I. Selling

Contents in Brief

Contents

ix

**3   Financial Reporting and the European
Union   66**

PART II

Financial Statement Analysis

**4   Financial Statement Analysis:
An Overview   109**

PART III

Accounting Standards and Practices in Selected Countries

8   Great Britain   413

9   Germany   479

PART IV

**Harmonization of International
Accounting and Reporting Standards
Revisited**

15   Harmonization's Future   833

PART I

International Financial Reporting and Standard Setting

International financial reporting is a dynamic, evolving field of inquiry. Powerful new technologies and communications devices have opened the world for an explosion in cross-border commerce and capital creation. Never before has there been so much pressure on, and opportunity for, leaders of financial reporting thought to help shape the most useful ''language'' by which suppliers of capital and seekers of capital communicate across companies, industries, countries, and cultures.

The first three chapters of this text set the stage for our inquiries into country-specific financial reporting practices and the fine art of financial analysis. Students of international financial reporting need to be aware of the forces that shape financial reporting as well as the progress to date on the harmonization of contemporary accounting practices. Toward that end, Chapters 1 through 3 provide the backdrop for all subsequent chapters and discussions.

ACCOUNTING AND ITS GLOBAL CONTEXTS

Accounting reporting and disclosure standards and practices do not develop in a vacuum but reflect the particular environment in which they are developed.[1]

Accounting cannot be culture free.[2]

Introduction

The importance of putting data in a context is no secret. Educators and psychologists have long known that people learn and retain information more easily if they integrate it with what they already know. This process of contextualizing data contributes to the creation of meaning from data. Indeed, managers, investors, and analysts constantly strive to contextualize the financial data with which their desks are strewn daily. Consequently, one of the main goals of this book is to highlight and elaborate on a set of analytical considerations that readers of international financial statements should be aware of as they seek to interpret the data contained therein for the purpose of making informed decisions.

Accounting is often called the *language of business.* Although not every financial information user must be able to create the "language," all users must be able to "read" it fluently and appreciate the assumptions and complexities that condition its production. As the intricacy of financial reporting increases, those who can use financial information adroitly will find themselves in possession of an increasingly valuable skill. Those who are deficient run greater risk of being victimized by their ignorance.

---

[1]A. Adhikari and R. H. Tondkar, "Environmental Factors Influencing Accounting Disclosure Requirements of Global Stock Exchanges," *Journal of International Financial Management and Accounting,* Summer 1992, p. 76.

[2]M. H. B. Perera, "Toward a Framework to Analyze the Impact of Culture in Accounting," *The International Journal of Accounting* 24, no. 1 (1989), p. 43.

With the advent of a global economy, characterized by electronically accessible stock exchanges and multinational enterprises operating in scores of countries, the production, dissemination, and use of financial information are no longer restricted by national borders. Understanding the context within which information from other nations is generated often imposes special demands on both managers and investors. More specifically, the premises on which financial data are constituted in other parts of the world are now a matter of crucial importance. For financial reporting, a new imperative for interpretation has begun.

The knowledge that one needs to interpret and understand financial statements from other countries goes beyond merely acquainting oneself with what financial reporting methods and practices were used in preparing the documents (although this is, of course, important). Even if complete harmonization of international financial reporting standards were achieved—which is not likely to happen for some time to come—one would still need important contextual information to assess the significance of the financial data.

Accordingly, the chapters that follow are designed to familiarize the reader with some of the contextual and analytical issues surrounding financial reporting in a variety of countries. They discuss how cultural, legal, political, and economic contexts shape financial information. Because each chapter presents a number of issues, they are necessarily broad in their approach. The aim is not to make readers expert analysts or masters of technical detail; rather, the objective is to enlighten readers as to the various key questions germane to just about any set of foreign financial statements that come under review: What is the relationship of financial reporting to tax law in this country? What role, if any, does a country's accounting profession play in the creation of local reporting and disclosure standards? Who are the primary users of the financial statements—investors, unions, legal authorities? The concern for and understanding of these and other sociocultural issues will make the reader a more intelligent consumer of international financial information.

The content of this book is organized as follows. Chapters 1 through 3 provide the reader with a background of some of the larger, more important institutional issues: Along what dimensions and to what extent do country contexts differ and potentially influence the development of financial reporting practices? Who is responsible for international accounting principles, and how are they set? What is the European Union and how has it assisted in the harmonization of accepted accounting practice across a diverse set of nations? From these broad, macrolevel considerations, the text then moves to a review of microlevel issues in Chapters 4 through 7. For example, how do analysts, investors, and managers make economic decisions, and how are those decisions impacted by diverse and inconsistent international accounting practices? How do the decisions of these individuals change when dealing with international, as opposed to domestic, companies? Chapters 8 through 14 focus on seven countries selected because they represent a varied set of economic, political, and social dimensions. Finally, Chapter 15 revisits the subject of harmonization.

Although only seven countries are specifically considered, the potential benefits of this book are more extensive than such a small sample would immediately suggest.

As readers become more familiar with financial reporting around the world, they will find a considerable amount of similarity among particular nations, for reasons both cultural and historical. These transnational similarities make it possible to develop classifications of key international financial reporting characteristics. For example, a basic understanding of British financial reporting will help one understand financial reporting in numerous other Commonwealth countries such as Australia, Hong Kong, and New Zealand. Becoming familiar with the Brazilian system of monetary correction should yield general insights about financial reporting in other inflationary economies (especially South American ones). The presence of common themes helps not only to situate whole systems in relation to each other but also to gauge the importance of particular variations. The goal is to highlight and discuss some of the key contextual factors pertinent to understanding a variety of international financial reporting practices.

As the more or less common structure of the country-specific chapters implies, the framework used here makes rough distinctions among cultural, legal, political, and business influences. These categories are not meant to be definitive by any means; other approaches might have been used as well. The important point about the framework adopted here is that it implicitly proposes a set of long-term factors—national culture, statutory and tax law, labor, capital markets, role of the accounting profession—that affect the structure and use of financial accounting information. Any such list, of course, is hardly likely to be either exhaustive or universal; hence, the reader will notice that the structure of the country-specific chapters will vary somewhat, but the basic sections remain the same throughout. The following is a description of the general approach used in the country-specific chapters of this book.

Cultural Environment

Information is more than words; it is words that fit into a cultural framework.[3] Familiarization with a language is, by itself, necessary but not sufficient. Language is but a "means of communication within a particular culture."[4] Indeed, the "language" of financial reporting is conditioned by a nation's cultural influences.

Accounting, the language of business, is the handling of symbols that have meaning to those initiated in business.[5] Universally speaking, however, the same symbols may mean different things to financial information users of different cultures. What should we conclude, for example, if we find that the shareholders' equity of a Japanese steelmaking firm is 10 percent of its total capitalization and its current ratio is .75 as compared to 40 percent and 1.2, respectively, for a U.S. steelmaker? Is this cause for alarm or applause?

---

[3]G. Hofstede, *Cultures and Organizations: Software of the Mind* (Berkshire, England: McGraw-Hill, 1991), p. 217.

[4]V. Terpstra and K. David, *The Cultural Environment of International Business* (Cincinnati: South-Western, 1985), p. 18.

[5]Hofstede, *Cultures and Organizations,* p. 155.

The cultural analysis in the country-specific chapters begins by drawing on the work of Geert Hofstede, director of the Institute for Research on Intercultural Cooperation, at the University of Limburg, Maastricht, The Netherlands. Defining *culture* as a kind of "collective mental programming" that affects the way people perceive and act in the world, Hofstede discusses five important cultural "dimensions": power distance, individualism, long-term orientation, uncertainty avoidance, and masculinity.[6] These five cultural dimensions serve to identify the core values that explain the general similarities and differences in cultures around the world. These dimensions reflect the different ways in which societies answer basic questions about the organization and the conduct of their institutions. The distinctive cultural dimensions that Hofstede discusses, although subject to criticisms of simplification, have been time tested[7] and found to be associated with nations' economic growth, management accounting systems in use, support for global financial accounting harmonization, and business failures.[8]

Large Power Distance versus Small Power Distance

The concept of **power distance** (PD) refers to the degree to which people are willing to live with unequally distributed power within and across their institutions and organizations. *Institutions* are the basic elements of society such as the family, school, and the community; *organizations* are the places where people work. A notion of PD helps typify the behavior of the less powerful as well as the more powerful members of a society. A high score on the PD index indicates that a national culture has a high tolerance for inequality. In such a society, people accept a hierarchy that has a place for everyone, and such positions are justified by those in power and by the historical

---

[6]The cultural dimension of masculinity (MAS) is a construct that describes the extent to which social gender roles tend to be distinct in a given society. Although interesting and important for understanding some aspects of societal attitudes, we believe that it does not bear on financial reporting attitudes and it is therefore not a part of subsequent discussions.

[7]G. Hofstede and M. Bond, "Hofstede's Culture Dimensions: An Independent Validation Using Rokeach's Value Survey," *Journal of Cross-Cultural Psychology,* December 1984, pp. 417–33. See also R. Hodgetts, "A Conversation with Geert Hofstede," *Organizational Dynamics,* Spring 1993, pp. 53–61, and The Chinese Culture Connection, "Chinese Values and the Search for Culture-Free Dimensions of Culture," *Journal of Cross-Cultural Psychology,* June 1987, pp. 143–64.

[8]See S. Ueno and U. Sekaran, "The Influence of Culture on Budget and Control Practices in the USA and Japan: An Empirical Study," *Journal of International Business Studies,* 4th Quarter 1992, pp. 659–74; and G. L. Harrison, "The Cross-Cultural Generalizability of the Relation between Participation, Budget Emphasis, and Job-Related Attitudes," *Accounting, Organizations, and Society* 17, no. 1 (1992), pp. 1–15. See also R. H. Franke, G. Hofstede, and M. H. Bond, "Cultural Roots of Economic Performance: A Research Note," *Strategic Management Journal* 12 (1991), pp. 165–73; and A. Smith, D. R. Deis, Jr., and R. Holland, "Cultural Mapping of Attitudes toward International Harmonization Efforts: A Cross-National Study," paper presented at annual meeting of the American Accounting Association, San Francisco, 1993, and J. Li and S. Guisinger, "How Well Do Foreign Firms Compete in the United States?" *Business Horizons,* November–December 1991, pp. 49–53.

tradition of those positions. In contrast, people from societies scoring low on the PD index are interested in a leveling of power and require justification for power inequalities.

The basic issue addressed by this cultural dimension is how a society handles inequalities among people. In large PD societies, the

> political spectrum . . . is characterized by strong right and left wings with a weak center. Incomes in these countries are very unequally distributed, with a few very rich and many very poor people. Moreover, taxation protects the wealthy, so that incomes after taxes can even be more unequal than before. Labor unions tend to be government controlled; where they are not, they are ideologically based and involved in politics. . . . The political spectrum in [small PD] countries usually shows a powerful center and weaker right and left wings. Incomes are less unequally distributed than in large power distance countries. Taxation serves to redistribute income, making income after taxes less unequal than before. Labor unions are independent and less oriented to ideology and politics than to pragmatic issues on behalf of their members.[9]

The relevance of a PD notion to financial reporting is twofold.[10] First, large PD countries are likely to tend toward greater statutory control over financial reporting practices to achieve and maintain a uniformity in reporting that is not likely to be achieved if financial reporting practices predominantly emanate from the deliberative processes of a professional organization that airs ideas for debate and seeks consensus from a diverse constituency. Indeed, the national statutes pertaining to financial reporting that exist in Brazil and Japan exert a much greater influence over external financial reporting than those in the United States, Great Britain, or Germany (all of which have substantially lower PD scores than Brazil or Japan), where professional organizations more actively shape practice.[11] Second, the PD concept suggests important implications for understanding a society's attitude toward access to and availability of information. It seems likely that high PD societies may be characterized by the restriction of information to preserve secrecy, power, and/or role inequalities. Thus, in terms of financial reporting providing a more or less full and open view of a business entity, high PD societies are likely to provide fewer financial disclosures than small PD societies. Results from at least one broad-based study that ranked countries according to the extensiveness of the financial disclosures made by their companies identify Brazil, Korea, and Italy (relatively high PD countries) as providing less extensive disclosures than Sweden, Great Britain, and the United States (relatively low PD countries).[12] The extent to which such a tendency facilitates an understanding of root causes for

---

[9]Hofstede, *Cultures and Organizations,* pp. 38–39.

[10]See S. J. Gray, ''Towards a Theory of Cultural Influence in the Development of Accounting Systems Internationally,'' *Abacus* 24, no. 1 (1988), pp. 9–11.

[11]See F. D. S. Choi, *Handbook of International Accounting* (New York: John Wiley, 1991), and Price Waterhouse, *Doing Business in Brazil* (New York: Price Waterhouse, 1986), esp. p. 63.

[12]Center for International Financial Analysis and Research, *International Accounting and Auditing Trends* (Princeton, N.J.: CIFAR, 1991), esp. p. 201.

differences in particular financial reporting practices from around the world is useful to consider. For example, might differences in PD factors explain, at least in part, why Italian companies are not required, and generally choose not, to disclose segmental information whereas Swedish companies must and do?[13] One objective of this book is to introduce such thought-provoking possibilities.

Some examples of the key differences between small and large PD societies are presented in Exhibit 1–1. The PD scores of the countries discussed in the following chapters are shown here.

Hofstede's Power Distance (PD) Scores (higher scores = larger PD)	
Country	*PD Score*
Brazil	69
South Korea	60
Japan	54
Italy	50
Great Britain	35
Germany	35
Sweden	31
United States	40

Of primary importance is the relative position of the countries, not the absolute values of the scores.

Individualism versus Collectivism

Societies that exemplify the **individualism** (IDV) construct tend to be those in which the ties between individuals are loosely coupled (i.e., people are expected to look after themselves and their immediate family). In contrast, a low score on the IDV index corresponds to a collectivist society. **Collectivism** pertains to societies in which people are integrated into strong, cohesive in-groups, which throughout peoples' lifetimes continue to protect them in exchange for unquestioning loyalty. The fundamental issue addressed by the IDV cultural dimension is the degree of interdependence that a society maintains among individuals. For example, employees of organizations in individualistic societies tend to place great value on the freedom to adopt their own approach to their work assignments. In contrast, employees of collectivist societies place less

---

[13]Coopers & Lybrand, *International Accounting Summaries* (New York: John Wiley, 1991).

EXHIBIT 1–1

Key Differences between Large and Small Power Distance Societies

Small Power Distance	*Large Power Distance*
• Inequalities among people should be minimized.	• Inequalities among people are both expected and desired.
• There should be, and there is to some extent, interdependence between less and more powerful people.	• Less powerful people should be dependent on the more powerful; in practice, less powerful people are polarized between dependence and counterdependence.
• Hierarchy in organizations means an inequality of roles, established for convenience.	• Hierarchy in organizations reflects the existential inequality between higher-ups and lower-downs.
• Decentralization is popular.	• Centralization is popular.
• There is a narrow salary range between top and bottom of organization.	• Salary range between top and bottom of organization is wide.
• Subordinates expect to be consulted.	• Subordinates expect to be told what to do.
• The ideal boss is a resourceful democrat.	• The ideal boss is a benevolent autocrat or good father.
• Privileges and status symbols are frowned upon.	• Privileges and status symbols for managers are both expected and popular.
• All should have equal rights.	• The powerful have privileges.
• Powerful people try to look less powerful than they are.	• Powerful people try to look as impressive as possible.
• Power is based on formal position, expertise, and ability to give rewards.	• Power is based on family or friends, charisma, and ability to use force.
• The way to change a political system is by changing the rules (evolution).	• The way to change a political system is by changing the people at the top (revolution).
• The use of violence in domestic politics is rare.	• Domestic political conflicts frequently lead to violence.
• Pluralist governments based on outcome of majority votes.	• Autocratic or oligarchic governments are based on cooptation.
• Political spectrum shows strong center and weak right and left wings.	• Political spectrum, if allowed to be manifested, shows weak center and strong wings.
• Small income differentials in society are further reduced by the tax system.	• Large income differentials in society are further increased by the tax system.
• Prevailing religions and philosophical systems stress equality.	• Prevailing religions and philosophical systems stress hierarchy and stratification.
• Prevailing political ideologies stress and practice power sharing.	• Prevailing political ideologies stress and practice power struggle.
• Native management theories focus on role of employees.	• Native management theories focus on role of managers.

Source: G. Hofstede, *Cultures and Organizations: Software of the Mind* (Berkshire, England: McGraw-Hill, 1991).

value on freedom to do their work their way; instead, they place a higher value on training and opportunities to improve their work skills so they become full-fledged members of the team, making their expected contribution. Other examples of some key differences between individualist and collectivist societies can be examined in Exhibit 1–2. The IDV scores of the countries discussed in the following chapters are shown here.

EXHIBIT 1–2

Key Differences between Individualist and Collectivist Societies

Individualist	*Collectivist*
• Everyone grows up to look after him- or herself and his or her immediate family only.	• People are born into extended families or other in-groups that continue to protect them in exchange for loyalty.
• Identity is based in the individual.	• Identity is based on the social network to which one belongs.
• Children learn to think in terms of ''I.''	• Children learn to think in terms of ''we.''
• Speaking one's mind is a characteristic of an honest person.	• Harmony should always be maintained and direct confrontations avoided.
• Purpose of education is learning how to learn.	• Purpose of education is learning how to do.
• Employer-employee relationship is a contract supposed to be based on mutual advantage.	• Employer-employee relationship is perceived in moral terms, like a family link.
• Hiring and promotion decisions are supposed to be based on skills and rules only.	• Hiring and promotion decisions take employees' in-group into account.
• Management is management of groups.	• Management is management of individuals.
• Task prevails over relationship.	• Relationship prevails over task.
• Individual interests prevail over collective interests.	• Collective interests prevail over individual interests.
• Everyone has a right to privacy.	• Private life is invaded by group(s).
• Everyone is expected to have a private opinion.	• Opinions are predetermined by group membership.
• Laws and rights are supposed to be the same for all.	• Laws and rights differ by group.
• Restrained role of the state in the economic system.	• Dominant role of the state in economic system.
• Economy is based on individual interests.	• Economy is based on collective interests.
• Political power is exercised by voters.	• Political power is exercised by interest groups.
• Native economic theories are based on pursuit of individual self-interests.	• Imported economic theories are largely irrelevant because unable to deal with collective and particularist interests.
• Ideologies of individual freedom prevail over ideologies of equality.	• Ideologies of equality prevail over ideologies of individual freedom.
• Self-actualization by every individual is an ultimate goal.	• Harmony and consensus in society are ultimate goals.

Source: G. Hofstede, *Cultures and Organizations: Software of the Mind* (Berkshire, England: McGraw-Hill, 1991).

Hofstede's Individualism Scores
(higher scores = greater IDV)

Country	*IDV Score*
Great Britain	89
Italy	76
Sweden	71
Germany	67
Japan	46
Brazil	38
South Korea	18
United States	91

Of primary importance is the relative position of the countries, not the absolute values of the scores.

It has been hypothesized that societies with less IDV exhibit tendencies toward greater statutory control over financial reporting, leading to less flexibility accorded companies in the application of specific financial reporting practices than in societies with greater IDV.[14] Furthermore, such a tendency also suggests the likelihood of financial information being more closely held by the companies domiciled in societies with less IDV. Together, such tendencies lead one to expect more conservative financial reporting from companies in societies with less IDV.

The merits of such hypothesized relationships warrant continued testing and refinement. Results from two recent studies, however, provide evidence of a profile of conservative financial reporting that ranks Japan as more conservative than Germany, which is more conservative than Italy, which is more conservative than Great Britain.[15] As the reader will note, these four countries are more or less IDV in the same order.

Uncertainty Avoidance versus Uncertainty Acceptance

The concept of **uncertainty avoidance** (UAV) can be thought of as the extent to which the members of a society feel threatened by uncertain or unknown situations. This feeling is usually expressed through a need for predictability expressed in written and unwritten rules. Uncertainty-avoiding cultures generate, nurture, and uphold explicit codes of belief and behavior and tend to be unaccepting of behaviors, attitudes, and ideas opposite to the group norms. The emotional need for laws and rules in a strong UAV culture often leads to the establishment of rules or rule-oriented behavior that sometimes is nonsensical or dysfunctional. Consider, for example, Japan (UAV score = 92), which has a law stating that before a merchant can open a business in a given locale, existing merchants—including competitors—must first approve the merchant's entrance.[16] Another characteristic of a strong UAV culture is that its citizens tend to be pessimistic about their possibilities to influence authorities. Few citizens are ready to protest decisions made by authorities; they depend on the government's expertise and believe that this is how things should be. The authorities and the citizens share the same norms about their mutual roles.[17] In contrast, low UAV cultures tend to be flexible, prefer fewer rules, and are willing to, and often do, participate in politics, even if only at the lowest local level.

---

[14]Gray, ''Towards a Theory of Cultural Development of Accounting Systems.''

[15]See S. J. Gray and L. H. Radebaugh, *International Accounting and Multinational Enterprises* (New York: John Wiley, 1993), esp. pp. 386–90. It should be noted that the United States was included in these studies and was found to be more conservative than Great Britain but less conservative than Germany or Japan.

[16]Interview with Brian Rawson in summer 1992. Mr. Rawson lived and worked in Japan as a business consultant for seven years.

[17]Hofstede, *Cultures and Organizations: Software of the Mind.*

Another example of the differences between high and low UAV cultures is that low UAV countries tend to be innovative and high UAV cultures tend to focus on full-scale implementation of innovations, requiring a considerable sense of detail and punctuality. Hofstede cites as an example Great Britain (UAV score = 35), which has produced more Nobel Prize winners than Japan (UAV score = 92), which has put more new products on the world market.[18] One other aspect of low UAV cultures is that they are not as focused on trying to craft the future and extend greater tolerance to those members of society who hold different ideas and attitudes.

From a financial reporting perspective, it has been posited that relatively higher UAV societies exhibit greater tendencies toward conservatism than do lower UAV societies, due to the caution with which the former approach the uncertainty of future events.[19] Moreover, to avoid conflict and preserve security—both attributes of higher UAV societies—secrecy (i.e., more limited disclosures) is likely to be an attitude underlying financial reporting practices in high UAV countries. As one might expect, therefore, uniformity rather than flexibility in reporting practices is the preference imposed on the companies residing in relatively higher UAV societies. In a recent study of preferences for the international harmonization of accounting principles, preliminary evidence suggests that higher UAV societies do exhibit stronger preferences in support of current international harmonization efforts than do low UAV societies.[20]

Exhibit 1–3 provides additional examples of some of the general differences between uncertainty-avoiding cultures and uncertainty-accepting cultures. The following are UAV scores for the countries discussed at length later in this book:

Hofstede's Uncertainty Avoidance Scores
(higher scores = greater UAV)

Country	UAV Score
Japan	92
South Korea	85
Brazil	76
Italy	75
Germany	65
Great Britain	35
Sweden	29
United States	46

Of primary importance is the relative position of the countries, not the absolute values of the scores.

---

[18]Ibid.

[19]Gray, ''Towards a Theory of Cultural Development of Accounting Systems.''

[20]Smith, Deis, and Holland, ''Cultural Mapping of Attitudes.''

EXHIBIT 1–3

Key Differences between Uncertainty-Avoiding Cultures and Uncertainty-Accepting Cultures

Uncertainty Avoiding	*Uncertainty Accepting*
• The uncertainty inherent in life is felt as a continuous threat that must be fought.	• Uncertainty is a normal feature of life, and each day is accepted as it comes.
• High stress and a subjective feeling of anxiety are prevalent.	• Low stress and a subjective feeling of well-being are prevalent.
• There is an acceptance of familiar risks and fear of ambiguous situations and of unfamiliar risks.	• Society is comfortable in ambiguous situations and with unfamiliar risks.
• What is different is dangerous.	• What is different is curious.
• Students are comfortable in structured learning situations and concerned with the right answers.	• Students are comfortable with open-ended learning situations and concerned with good discussions.
• Emotional need for rules, even if these will never work, is characteristic.	• There should not be more rules than are strictly necessary.
• Time is money.	• Time is a framework for orientation.
• Society feels an emotional need to be busy and an inner urge to work hard.	• Society feels comfortable when lazy and hard-working only when needed.
• Precision and punctuality come naturally.	• Precision and punctuality have to be learned.
• Deviant ideas and behavior resistance to innovation are suppressed.	• Tolerance of deviant and innovative ideas and behavior exists.
• Society is motivated by security and esteem or belongingness.	• Society is motivated by achievement and esteem or belongingness.
• Many and precise laws and rules exist; if rules cannot be respected, members are sinners and should repent.	• Few and general laws and rules exist; if rules cannot be respected, they should be changed.
• Citizens are negative toward institutions.	• Citizens are positive toward institutions.
• Conservatism, extremism, and law and order prevail.	• Tolerance and moderation prevail.
• Nationalism, xenophobia, and repression of minorities prevail.	• Regionalism, internationalism, and attempts at integration of minorities are common.
• There is a belief in experts and specialization.	• There is belief in generalists and common sense.
• There is only one Truth, ours.	• One group's truth should not be imposed on others.
• Religious, political, and ideological fundamentalism and intolerance characterize society.	• Human rights—nobody should be persecuted for beliefs—are respected.
• In philosophy and science, the tendency is toward grand theories.	• In philosophy and science, the tendency is toward relativism and empiricism.

Source: G. Hofstede, *Cultures and Organizations: Software of the Mind* (Berkshire, England: McGraw-Hill, 1991).

Long-Term Orientation versus Short-Term Orientation

In practical terms, a society with a **long-term orientation** (LTO) values persistence, ordering of relationships by status and observing this order, thrift, and having a sense of shame, whereas a society with a **short-term orientation** (STO) values personal stability, protecting face, and respect for tradition.[21] Hofstede notes that the attributes akin to an LTO are more oriented toward the future (especially perseverance and thrift); they are more dynamic and support entrepreneurial activity. For example, perseverance or tenacity in the pursuit of goals is an important attribute for both intrapreneurs and entrepreneurs. Similarly, thrift leads to savings and the accumulation of capital for reinvestment. Moreover, having a sense of shame contributes to a sensitivity to social contacts and keeping one's commitments (a Japanese example of this, *dantai ishiki,* or group consciousness, is discussed in more detail in Chapter 10).

The societal attributes more closely aligned with a STO tend to focus on the past and present, and they tend to be more static. At the STO end of the spectrum, personal stability and saving face, if overemphasized, tend to dampen initiative and risk taking. Also, too much respect for tradition impedes innovation. Part of the reason for the economic success of the Five Dragons (i.e., Japan, Taiwan, Singapore, South Korea, and Hong Kong) is the apparent ease with which these countries have accepted Western technological innovations.[22] Exhibit 1–4 summarizes key differences between countries with long-term orientation versus short-term orientation.

The relationship between LTO values and economic growth (gross national product—GNP—per capita) provides evidence that certain LTO values (as opposed to STO values) show a strong positive relationship with economic growth (see Exhibit 1–5). This may explain, in part, the fast-paced growth of the Five Dragons over the past three decades. The LTO scores for two of the Five Dragons (Japan and South Korea) as are those available for the other countries discussed later in this book follow.

Hofstede's Long-Term Orientation Scores
(higher scores = greater LTO)

Country	LTO Score
Japan	80
South Korea	75
Brazil	65
Sweden	33
Germany	31
Great Britain	25
Italy	Not available
United States	29

Of primary importance is the relative position of the countries, not the absolute values of the scores.

---

[21]G. Hofstede and M. Bond, ''The Confucius Connection: From Cultural Roots to Economic Growth,'' *Organizational Dynamics,* 1988; and Hofstede, *Cultures and Organizations: Software of the Mind.*
[22]Holstede, *Cultures and Organizations: Software of the Mind,* p. 169.

EXHIBIT 1–4
Key Differences between Long-Term Orientation and Short-Term Orientation

Long-Term Orientation	*Short-Term Orientation*
• Adaptation of traditions to a modern context.	• Respect for traditions.
• Respect for social and status obligations within limits.	• Respect for social and status obligations regardless of cost.
• Thrift, sparing resources.	• Social pressure to "keep up with the Joneses" even if it means overspending.
• Large savings, funds available for investment.	• Small savings, little money for investment.
• Perseverance toward slow results.	• Quick results expected.
• Willingness to subordinate oneself for a purpose.	• Concern with "face."
• Concern with respecting the demands of Virtue.	• Concern with possessing the Truth.

Source: G. Hofstede, *Cultures and Organizations: Software of the Mind* (Berkshire, England: McGraw-Hill, 1991).

Because an LTO orientation emphasizes thrift, perseverance toward steady results, and the willingness to subordinate oneself to a purpose, a positive linkage to financial reporting tendencies of conservatism and uniformity is likely. In general, Japan and South Korea tend to exhibit strong LTO orientations and, indeed, their financial reporting tends to manifest these traits.

To briefly summarize, then, Hofstede's cultural dimensions have been introduced as a way to think about the possible cultural root causes of differences in financial reporting practices across countries. The Hofstede scores are useful not in the sense that they are absolute measures of anything but because they indicate the relative extent to which certain attributes typify various countries' "collective programming."

A limited number of countries are discussed in this text. For those interested, the scores for all the countries Hofstede studied are presented in Appendix 1A. The seven countries discussed in this text share some similarities and exhibit some differences. To the extent that "a picture is worth a thousand words," consider Exhibits 1–6 and 1–7 as descriptive of the similarity and dissimilarity in a cultural context of this text's seven focal countries.

Legal and Political Environment

One of the fundamental aspects of any financial reporting system is its relationship to tax law. In the United States and Great Britain, the influence of tax provisions on the calculation of accounting income is minimal: Companies may report one set of figures in their financial statements and a substantially different set on their tax returns. In many other countries, however, taxable income is more closely related to accounting income. In Japan and Germany, for example, expenses must be recorded on the books of accounts—hence, included in financial statements—to qualify for deduction on a company's tax return. The requirement that accounting and taxable income be substantially the same naturally prompts companies to measure income as conservatively

EXHIBIT 1-5   LTO Score versus Average Annual Growth Rate per Capita

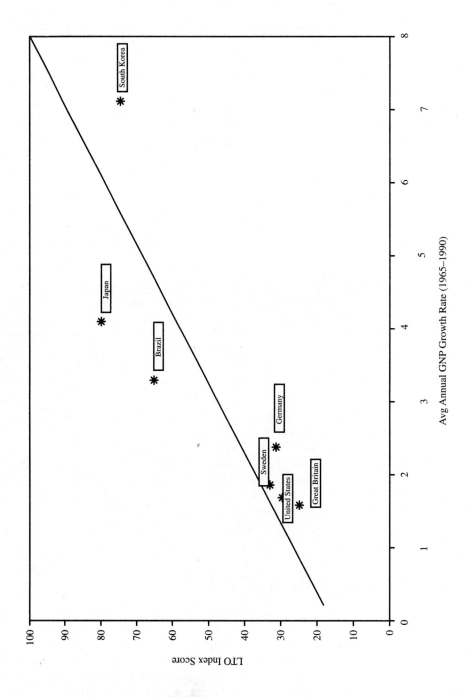

Exhibit 1–6
Relative Positions of Various Countries on an IDV by PD Grid

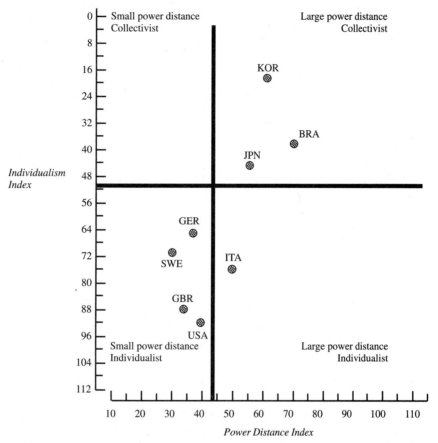

Source: G. Hofstede, *Cultures and Organizations: Software of the Mind* (Berkshire, England: McGraw-Hill, 1991).

as legally possible. Certain expenses, most notably depreciation, are calculated according to legislative requirements and incentives instead of sound business experience. As a consequence, accountants and auditors become less concerned with fair presentation than with legal compliance. And because tax law is formulated by national legislative bodies in response to varying political and economic agendas, its influence on financial reporting is one of the most obvious and immediate hindrances to establishing a common set of international reporting standards.

Although corporate tax law and its relationship to financial reporting have a more direct effect on financial reporting standards, individual tax law also plays a role. Tax incentives for individuals are some of the tools that governments use to encourage or discourage share ownership among small investors, which in turn has an impact on the nature and orientation of corporate financial reporting. Nations eager to develop

Exhibit 1–7
Relative Positions of Various Countries on an IDV by UAV Grid

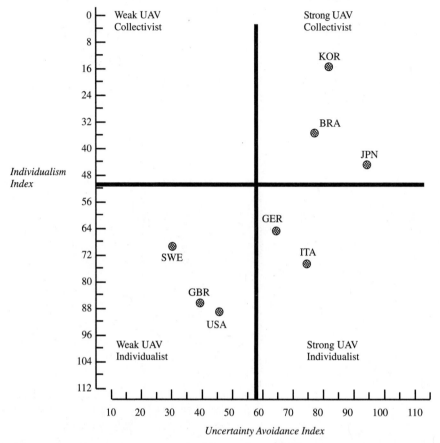

Source: G. Hofstede, *Cultures and Organizations: Software of the Mind* (Berkshire, England: McGraw-Hill, 1991).

stronger stock exchanges—Italy is a good example—are not only adjusting government regulation in an attempt to ensure fair and free markets but also are implementing tax incentives to encourage their citizens to buy and hold stocks. If this trend persists, it is likely to move financial reporting standards in the direction of the market-driven practices of Anglo-American countries.

Tax law is a factor in the development and practice of specific countries' financial reporting norms as is the general nature of a country's legal system. For example, the 13-category hierarchical classification scheme for the world's legal systems presented in Exhibit 1–8 has been found to be useful in identifying clusters of countries

Exhibit 1–8

A Hierarchical Classification of Legal Systems

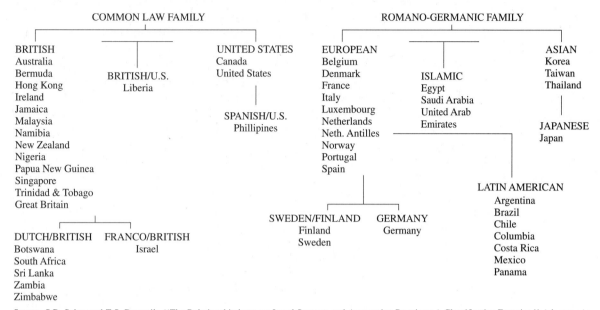

Source: S.B. Salter and T.S. Doupnik, ''The Relationship between Legal Systems and Accounting Practices: A Classification Exercise,'' *Advances in International Accounting* 5 (1992), pp. 3–22.

employing similar accounting practices.[23] Other legal and political factors impinge on financial reporting systems as well: the role of government in formulating principles and standards, the volatility of the political system (which may affect the frequency of reform), as well as the existence of external pressures (such as European Union membership) on governments to revamp systems. Such matters are considered in subsequent chapters.

Business Environment

Because modern financial reporting springs from the development of the publicly held corporation (with its separation of ownership and management and its limitation on liability exposure), the dominant form of business in an economy can have a material effect on the sophistication of financial reporting standards in a country. In Italy, for example, the continuing prominence of small, family-owned companies (and large ones

---

[23]S. B. Salter and T. S. Doupnick, ''The Relationship between Legal Systems and Accounting Practices: A Classification Exercise,'' *Advances in International Accounting* 5 (1992), pp. 3–22.

as well) has undoubtedly contributed to the slow development of public-minded financial reporting standards in that country. Every developed nation recognizes some version of the publicly owned corporation as a primary business entity, but the reporting requirements imposed on such companies can vary widely. Company law in most countries distinguishes between publicly and closely held corporations and between "large" and "small" companies (however they may be defined) and adjusts financial reporting requirements accordingly. Moreover, the prevalence of, or the desire to build, world-class multinational corporations may also influence a country's willingness to accommodate financial reporting practices amenable to interested parties in other countries. In terms of the number of major multinational companies propagated by the economies of this text's focal countries, Exhibit 1–9 depicts quite a variation. We might at times find it insightful to posit a company's, if not a country's, adoption of internationally accepted accounting standards to be consistent with that company's expressed desire to elevate its overall international image and awareness (e.g., Fiat and Bayer). These matters are considered in the Form of Business section of each chapter dealing with a focus country.

Closely related to the forms of business in a country is the state of its capital markets (i.e., stock and bond markets). The nature of financial reporting standards and the fundamental purpose of the entire financial reporting system depend on customary sources of capital. In such countries as Germany and Japan, where banks have long played a very powerful role in stoking economic growth, disclosure tends to be de-emphasized because lenders (who are usually major investors as well) generally have ready access to internal corporate information. In addition to the banking system, the development of stock exchanges—the distribution of share ownership, the mix of domestic and international listings, the effectiveness of regulation, the stringency of listing requirements—has a powerful effect on financial reporting standards and the quality of disclosure. Exhibit 1–10 provides some recent data exhibiting the disparity among nations in some of these areas.

A sophisticated and modern system of financial disclosure requires an accounting profession that is well educated and numerous enough to ensure its proper functioning. One certainly sees this in countries such as Great Britain and the United States, where the accounting profession shares responsibility for creating financial reporting standards. But even in nations where financial reporting standards are largely a matter of central legislation, the sophistication and training of the accounting profession (usually because it serves as an adviser to the legislature and is itself charged with developing auditing standards) noticeably affect the quality of financial reporting. For example, Swedish multinationals under the guidance of a professional elite able and willing to debate reporting practices consistently publish some of the most comprehensive annual reports throughout the world even though Swedish accounting standards are dictated by commercial law.

The final major element discussed in the business environment section of the country chapters is the influence of organized labor on financial reporting practices. This influence has rarely been a matter of labor unions changing the way income is measured or assets are valued; rather, it generally has taken the form of ancillary disclosures—compensation of directors and top management, employment figures by

EXHIBIT 1–9

Number of Countries in 1993 Fortune Global 500

United States	159
Japan	135
Great Britain	41
Germany	32
Korea	12
Sweden	12
Italy	7
Brazil	1

Source: ''Guide to the Global 500,'' *Fortune,* July 25, 1994, pp. 137–96.

EXHIBIT 1–10

Various International Securities Exchange Information

Panel A: Number of Companies Listed on Primary Securities Exchange*

Country and Exchange	Domestic	International
Brazil (Rio de Janeiro)	612	0
Italy (Milan)	220	0
Great Britain (International Stock Exchange)	2,006	553
Japan (Tokyo)	1,627	125
South Korea (Korea Stock Exchange)	669	0
Sweden (Stockholm)	121	11
Germany (Frankfurt)	389	354
United States (New York)	1,673	96

*Source: ''The International Stock Exchange Directory,'' *Institutional Investor,* international ed., April 1991.

Panel B: Number of European Companies, by Country, Registered with the U.S. Securities and Exchange Commission (SEC) and Thereby Meeting the SEC's Reporting Standards‡

Great Britain	**52**
Italy	**7**
Sweden	**6**
Germany	**1**
Netherlands	10
France	8
Spain	7
Ireland	6
Norway	3
Portugal	2
Denmark	2

Source: P. Gumbel and G. Steinmetz, ''German Firms Shift to More-Open Accounting,'' *The Wall Street Journal,* March 15, 1995, pp. C1, C17.

region and business sector, and so on—and an increase in social reporting. European firms are much more apt to use their annual reports as a platform for responding to public concerns on a variety of social issues, employment being one of the most prominent. Most of these companies respond to labor-related and other social concerns by including a statement of policies and programs or some other form of narrative presentation. Some, however, go beyond this to include a value-added set of financial statements designed to measure a company's creation of wealth and show its distribution among major stakeholders: employers, investors, and government. The growth of the labor movement, with its demands for more socially responsible corporate behavior, has undoubtedly helped to create a social climate that requires such disclosure from companies.

Selected Financial Reporting Practices and Illustrations

Each chapter includes a number of illustrations taken from the annual reports (English-language versions) of companies headquartered in the country under consideration. The illustrations are offered in the belief that whatever explanations are provided here will be inadequate without the experience of actually confronting foreign financial statements, with all the bafflement that may attend such a confrontation. Accordingly, readers should take sufficient time to peruse additional complete sets of financial statements from various countries to discover points of differences as well as common themes and practices within the various reports. The Selected Financial Reporting Practices section of each country-specific chapter (i.e., in Chapters 8–14) includes a list of significant practices that extend the narrative part of the chapter. Readers should not consider these practices as carved in stone because financial reporting practices are changing rapidly in many parts of the world to accommodate the emerging global economy. Nevertheless, this section should supplement a discussion that may at times seem theoretical and speculative with useful detail, and it should give the reader some idea of practices around the world with regard to such items as, say, research and development expenditures.

Summary

Context is critical for interpreting and understanding financial data. This chapter and, indeed, this book posit that financial reporting practices are a consequence of various contextual factors that include a country's (1) dominant culture, (2) system of taxation, (3) role of capital markets, and (4) business-government relations. The financial reporting differences that are exhibited around the world are rooted in nationalistic preferences, attitudes, and systems. The following chapters attempt to highlight the international and country-specific forces influencing the financial reporting practices employed by publicly held companies around the world. Generally accepted accounting practices do differ across countries to varying degrees. Reasons for their similarity and their differences can be explained and understood, to a large extent, by understanding the context within which the practices exist.

Suggested Readings

Choi, F. D. S., and R. M. Levich. "Behavioral Effects of International Accounting Diversity." *Accounting Horizons,* June 1991, pp. 1–13.

Dixon, M. "Where International Relations Break Down." *Financial Times,* November 10, 1989, p. 18.

Franke, R.; G. Hofstede; and M. Bond. "Cultural Roots of Economic Performance: A Research Note." *Strategic Management Journal* 12 (1991), pp. 165–73.

Gray, S. "Cultural Influences and the International Classification of Accounting Systems." Presented at EIASM Workshop on Accounting and Culture. Amsterdam, 1985.

———. "Towards a Theory of Cultural Influence on the Development of Accounting Systems Internationally." *ABACUS* 24, no. 1 (1988).

Hofstede, G. *Culture's Consequences: International Differences in Work-Related Values.* Sage Publications, 1980.

———. *Cultures and Organizations: Software of the Mind.* Berkshire, England: McGraw-Hill, 1991.

———, and M. Bond. "Hofstede's Culture Dimensions: An Independent Validation Using Rokeach's Survey." *Journal of Cross-Cultural Psychology* 15, no. 4 (December 1984), pp. 417–33.

———. "The Confucius Connection from Cultural Roots to Economic Growth." *Organizational Dynamics,* Spring 1988, pp. 4–21.

Meek, G.K., and S. Sandagaran. "A Survey of Research on Financial Reporting in a Transnational Context." *The Journal of Accounting Literature* (1990), pp. 145–82.

Nobes, C., and R. Parker. *Comparative International Accounting.* Englewood Cliffs, NJ: Prentice-Hall, 1991.

Raimond, P.; M. Hinard; and J. Weitkamp. "Comparing European Companies." *European Management Journal* 6, no. 4 (1988), pp. 367–74.

The Chinese Culture Connection. "Chinese Values and the Search for Culture-Free Dimensions of Culture." *Journal of Cross Cultural Psychology* 18, no. 2 (1987). The Chinese Culture Connection is the name given to an international network of 23 colleagues orchestrated by Michael Bond.

APPENDIX 1A
A LISTING OF HOFSTEDE'S CULTURAL DIMENSION SCORES BY COUNTRY

Country or Region	IDV Score	PD Score	UAV Score	MAS Score	LTO Score
United States	91	40	46	62	29
Australia	90	36	51	61	31
Great Britain	89	35	35	66	25
Canada	80	39	48	52	23
Netherlands	80	38	53	14	44
New Zealand	79	22	49	58	30
Italy	76	50	75	70	—
Belgium	75	65	94	54	—
Denmark	74	18	23	16	—
Sweden	71	31	29	5	33
France	71	68	86	43	—
Ireland	70	28	35	68	—
Norway	69	31	50	8	—
Switzerland	68	34	58	70	—
Germany	67	35	65	66	31
South Africa	65	49	49	63	—
Finland	63	33	59	26	—
Austria	55	11	70	79	—
Israel	54	13	81	47	—
Spain	51	57	86	42	—
India	48	77	40	56	61
Japan	46	54	92	95	80
Argentina	46	49	86	56	—
Iran	41	58	59	43	—
Jamaica	39	45	13	68	—
Brazil	38	69	76	49	65
Arab countries	38	80	68	53	—
Turkey	37	66	85	45	—
Uruguay	36	61	100	38	—
Greece	35	60	112	57	—
Philippines	32	94	44	64	19
Mexico	30	81	82	69	—
East Africa	27	64	52	41	—
Portugal	27	63	104	31	—
Malaysia	26	104	36	50	—
Hong Kong	25	68	29	57	96
Chile	23	63	86	28	—
West Africa	20	77	54	46	—
Singapore	20	74	8	48	48
Thailand	20	64	64	34	56
Salvador	19	66	94	40	—
South Korea	18	60	85	39	75
Taiwan	17	58	69	45	87
Peru	16	64	87	42	—
Costa Rica	15	35	86	21	—
Pakistan	14	55	70	50	0
Indonesia	14	78	48	46	—
Colombia	13	67	80	64	—
Venezuela	12	81	76	73	—
Panama	11	95	86	44	—
Ecuador	8	78	67	63	—
Guatemala	6	95	101	37	—

Source: G. Hofstede, *Cultures and Organizations: Software of the Mind* (Berkshire England: McGraw-Hill, 1991).

INFORMATION AND ISSUES FOR FURTHER INQUIRY

I.1.1 An International Accounting Conceptual Framework

In a November 25, 1993, *Financial Times* article (p. 12), "Standard Setters Try to Hammer Out Differences—Encouraging Signs of a Move towards Harmonization of Financial Reporting," author Kate Atchley notes that "the function of accounting is perceived as serving different needs in different social and economic environments [and] what constitutes economic reality depends upon where you live: is it the tax collector's reality, the stock market's reality or that of the creditors?"

Required:

Obtain a copy of the International Accounting Standards Committee's "Framework for the Preparation and Presentation of Financial Statements." Discuss how that document manifests (or fails to manifest) the perspective put forth by Atchley.

I.1.2 American Depositary Receipts

In an October 6, 1993, *Financial Times* article (p. 28), "Kaufhof Holding Plans Sponsored ADR Scheme," writer David Waller notes that there are "three ways that shares in non-U.S. companies can be traded in North America." At one end of the spectrum, a company can list on a U.S. stock exchange just as any U.S. company might. At the other end of the spectrum is the unsponsored American depositary receipt (ADR) mechanism. Between these two is the third option utilizing sponsored ADRs.

Required:

Investigate and report on the two types of ADR programs, making sure to note how they work, their pros and cons, and their financial reporting requirements. Why might a non-U.S. company choose a sponsored ADR plan versus a full listing?

I.1.3. Audit Reports

In a December 15, 1994, *Financial Times* article (p. 20), "Accountancy: Cookbook May Be Put on the Back Burner," author Jim Kelly asserts that "the role of auditors, the scope of their duties and responsibilities, are issues too long left to the almost glacial pace of change in the accountancy profession."

Required:

Choose any two of the seven focal countries in this text and obtain a copy of an annual report of a company from each of those countries. Compare and contrast the audit report noting such things as to whom the report is addressed, the date of the report relative to the company's fiscal year-end, the scope of work noted, the conclusion rendered, and any other interesting features. As a potential investor in those companies, what is your conclusion about the auditors' reports?

I.1.4. Culture-Based Business Propositions

In a 1993 *Journal of Business Ethics* (vol. 12, pp. 753–60) article, "The Effects of Culture on Ethical Decision-Making: An Application of Hofstede's Typology," S. J. Vitell, S. L. Nwachukwu, and J. Barnes present a number of propositions related to Hofstede's cultural dimensions of uncertainty avoidance, individualism, and power distance. Those propositions are as follows:

a. *Proposition:* Business practitioners in countries that are high on individualism (i.e., the United States) will be less likely to consider professional, industry, and organizational norms (formal and informal) when forming their own [moral] norms than business practitioners in countries that are high on collectivism (i.e., Japan).

b. *Proposition:* Business practitioners in countries with a small power distance (i.e., the United States) are likely to consider informal professional, industry, and organizational norms as more important than formal codes of ethics when forming their own [moral] norms.

c. *Proposition:* Business practitioners in countries that are high in uncertainty avoidance (i.e., Japan) will be more likely to consider formal professional, industry, and organizational codes of ethics when forming their own [moral] norms than business practitioners in countries that are low in uncertainty avoidance (i.e., the United States).

d. *Proposition:* Business practitioners in countries that are high on individualism (i.e., the United States or Canada) will be likely to consider themselves as more important stakeholders than owners/stockholders and other employees while business practitioners in countries that are high on collectivism (i.e., Japan) will be likely to consider the owners/stockholders and other employees as more important stakeholders than themselves.

e. *Proposition:* Business practitioners in countries with high uncertainty avoidance (i.e., Japan) will be likely to consider the owners/stockholders and other employees as more important stakeholders than themselves while business practitioners in countries with low uncertainty avoidance (i.e., the United States or Canada) will be likely to consider themselves as more important stakeholders than the owners/stockholders and other employees.

f. *Proposition:* Business practitioners in countries that are high in uncertainty avoidance (i.e., Japan) will be less likely to perceive ethical problems than business practitioners in countries that are low in uncertainty avoidance (i.e., the United States).

Required:

Prepare a brief summary of the financial reporting issues/concerns/considerations that spring from each proposition. Are the conclusions contained in your summary important to you as a potential user of financial statements from around the world? Why or why not?

CHAPTER 2

Harmonization of International Accounting and Reporting Standards

The objective of harmonization is the comparability of accounts.[1]

Comparable financial statements would bring benefits to U.S. and foreign companies in three main areas of business and finance: conducting competitive surveillance; managing relationships with customers, suppliers, and others; and raising capital abroad or investing in foreign securities.[2]

A growing number of countries are working to harmonize their accounting practices with the international norms, and many developing countries have adopted the international standards in their entirety.[3]

Introduction

Even a brief survey of the financial press from the last 10 years reveals that articles on the **harmonization** of world accounting standards have appeared with ever-increasing frequency. Everyone, it seems, is talking about it—academics, standards setters, securities regulators, analysts, columnists, and practitioners alike. Its ramifications—economic, political, cultural, technical—are routinely examined and debated. Once deemed by many to be little more than a utopian fantasy, harmonization has become a major theme in almost any discussion of international business.

More important, the talk is increasingly being followed with action. With the promulgation of standards by the **International Accounting Standards Committee**

---

[1]K. Van Hulle, "Harmonization of Accounting Standards in the EC," *European Accounting Review,* November 2, 1993, p. 387.

[2]S. F. O'Malley, "Accounting across Borders," *Financial Executive,* March/April 1992, p. 28.

[3]C. Frost, "International Accounting," *Export Today,* February 1995, p. 35.

(IASC), harmonization has in the last two decades moved from the realm of theoretical debate to the arena of practical experimentation. In the 1990s, as **European Union** (EU) member countries complete their implementation of the Fourth and the Seventh Directives—the EU policies regarding the presentation of annual accounts and consolidated accounts of companies (discussed at length in Chapter 3)—and as more firms voluntarily adopt IASC standards, the possibilities and limitations of harmonization will be tested as never before. But what exactly does harmonization mean, and why has it become such an important issue?

On the simplest level, *harmonization* is the process of bringing international accounting standards into some sort of agreement so that the financial statements from different countries are prepared according to a common set of principles of measurement and disclosure. To the uninitiated, this might seem to be a rather straightforward matter, requiring perhaps four to five years (or less) for study and a few more for implementation. In fact, harmonization is an amazingly complex process fraught with political and technical pitfalls.

As is true of any transnational effort, harmonization must address the issue of national sovereignty and its changing role in a world community that is continually becoming more economically and technologically interdependent. National governments have a vested interest in the financial information produced by private companies, frequently using these data as the basis for tax collection, statistics gathering, and implementation of macroeconomic policy. Governments are understandably reluctant to allow international agencies to influence the shape of financial information in ways that could disrupt the basic legal and fiscal structures of their countries. Because international financial reporting agencies (such as the IASC) generally have no means to force national governments to accept their recommendations, they must rely on the delicate arts of negotiation and persuasion. Success requires the achievement of a widespread consensus, which takes considerable time and patience.

Moreover, would-be harmonizers must weigh these national sovereignty political problems against technical and conceptual issues. For example, what degree of uniformity in financial reporting practices is most useful and desirable? Many scholars and practitioners believe that complete uniformity would not necessarily yield the best results; it might actually distort financial statements by stressing form over substance. In fact, many differences in financial reporting methods are far from arbitrary, reflecting divergences in economic "infrastructures" as well as cultural habits. To understand these differences, one must appreciate something of the diversity of business practices around the world.

International accounting standards must therefore maintain a delicate balance between counterproductive rigidity and confusing and needless diversity. For such standards to be viewed as worthwhile, they must be comprehensive and detailed enough to provide positive guidance for the well-educated provider of the financial data, yet simple enough to be comprehensible to the consumer with relatively little training who relies on the financial data for important insights. International standards must be useful in many different cultural and economic contexts. These and other problems ensure that harmonization will be a long and difficult process, requiring careful consideration at every step.

Exhibit 2–1
Partial Listing of Non-U.S. Equity Securities Traded on the New York Stock Exchange*

Country	Company	New York Stock Exchange Symbol
Africa	ASA Ltd.	ASA
Australia	Broken Hill Proprietary Ltd.	BHP
Bermuda	ADT Ltd.	ADT
British West Indies	Club Med, Inc.	CMI
Canada	Placer Dome, Inc.	PDG
Chili	Compania de Teléfonos de Chile	TCH
Denmark	Novo-Nordisk A/S	NVO
France	Rhone-Poulenc S.A.	RPV
Hong Kong	Hong Kong Telecommunications Ltd.	HKT
Ireland	Allied Irish Banks Plc	AIB
Israel	Elscint Ltd.	ELT
Italy	Benetton Group S.p.A.	BNG
Japan	Hitachi Ltd.	HIT
Mexico	Teléfonos de Mexico S.A.	TMX
Netherlands	Phillips N.V.	PHG
Netherlands Antilles	Schlumberger Ltd.	SLB
New Zealand	Telecom Corp. of New Zealand Ltd.	NZT
Norway	Norsk Hydro a.s.	NHY
Philippines	Benguet Corporation	BE
Spain	Repsol S.A.	REP
Great Britain	British Petroleum Plc	BP

*Foreign securities traded on the NYSE represent either actual equity securities or ADRs (American depositary receipts).

Market Forces

The process of harmonization continues, propelled by the profound economic forces of international trade and capital movements. In spite of all the obstacles created by widely divergent financial reporting methods, the adoption of global financing strategies by multinational corporations and of global investment strategies by institutional and individual investors is causing the flow of financial information to increase among nations and continents. The search for less costly capital on the one hand, and higher returns on the other, has transformed securities markets into international marketplaces with listings and buyers from all corners of the globe. As the final decade of the 20th century began, more than 500 companies were listed on at least one stock exchange outside their home country. These listings are in many cases quite important in meeting the capital needs of companies, as well as in raising their visibility in strategically significant markets. From the viewpoint of investors, the listing of foreign companies on domestic exchanges provides the opportunity to buy shares in enterprises that they may have previously admired only from afar. Exhibit 2–1, for example, provides a partial listing of the non-U.S. companies whose equity securities trade on the New York Stock Exchange.

The trend toward globalization in the world's securities markets has created formidable challenges in the areas of communications and investor relations, however, especially for those firms listing their securities on exchanges in several countries. Multinationals are having to determine how to communicate with current and prospective foreign investors in terms that they can readily understand. Prudent investors quite naturally expect a premium from companies that seem ''risky,'' a perception that is more likely to haunt firms with less than totally understood financial reporting practices. As a result, many companies listed on major securities exchanges voluntarily exceed minimum disclosure requirements. For a company seeking capital in two or three countries with different financial reporting standards and practices, the necessity of keeping investors informed is burdensome; for one pursuing it in six or eight, it can be a serious and costly matter indeed. Timely, informative, comprehensive financial reporting becomes a major effort requiring considerable planning and coordination.

With no universally accepted set of international financial reporting and disclosure guidelines, multinationals have responded with a variety of strategies: (1) translating the text of home-country annual reports into the reader's language (**convenience translations**); (2) translating the text of home-country annual reports into the reader's language and into the reader's currency (**convenience statement**); (3) preparing several sets of statements that report results in different languages and currencies according to different countries' accounting principles (**multiple reporting**); (4) providing reconciliations in annual reports and filing forms with a foreign country's equivalent of the Securities and Exchange Commission to meet its minimum financial reporting requirements based on local GAAP (**reconciliation report**); and (5) preparing financial reports in accordance with IASC accounting standards (**world standards report**).[4]

Exhibits 2–2 through 2–6 present examples of these five strategies. Obviously, reporting strategies that ignore differences in local accounting principles present problems for local analysts and investors; on the other hand, those reports that consider them require considerably more time and expense on the part of the preparer. Either way, someone absorbs the costs of divergent principles and standards of financial reporting; generally, the multinational preparers do so. It is not surprising, then, that multinationals are supporting harmonization, in part, because it promises to reduce differences in reporting requirements and that analysts and investors are supporting it because it promises to provide a more comparable basis from which well-informed investing decisions can be made.

Unquestionably, market forces are providing a much-needed impetus for harmonization of financial reporting standards. However, the influence of the market on international financial reporting standards should not obscure the importance of political and professional initiatives in this area. This point sometimes escapes the financial press, which has an unfortunate tendency to ascribe progress to the demands of the

---

[4]G. Meek, ''Competition Spurs Worldwide Harmonization,'' *Management Accounting,* August 1984, pp. 47–49.

EXHIBIT 2–2

Convenience Translation: Income Statement—Bayer Group

Language: Reader's   **Currency:** Home Country's   **GAAP:** Home Country's

	1991 In Millions of DM	1992 In Millions of DM
Net sales	**42,401**	**41,195**
Cost of goods sold	24,849	23,864
Gross profit	**17,552**	**17,331**
Selling expenses	9,455	9,476
Research and development expenses	3,007	3,096
General administration expenses	1,919	1,858
Other operating income	1,773	1,383
Other operating expenses	1,766	1,508
Operating result	**3,178**	**2,776**
Income from investments in affiliated companies—net	74	53
Interest income (expense)—net	(251)	(180)
Other non-operating income (expense)—net	205	44
Nonoperating result	**28**	**(83)**
Income before income taxes	**3,206**	**2,693**
Income taxes	1,353	1,130
Income after taxes	**1,853**	**1,563**
Minority interests	29	47
Net income	**1,824**	**1,516**

Auditors' Opinion Excerpt
The financial statements of the Bayer Group comply with the German statutory provisions.

Stock Exchange Listings
German stock exchanges, plus the stock exchanges in Basel, Geneva, Zurich, Tokyo, London, Vienna, Paris, Madrid, Milan, Barcelona, Amsterdam, Antwerp, Brussels, Luxembourg, and Stockholm.

---

financial industry and to blame inevitable difficulties on the governments and professional groups that first began pushing for harmonization. For example, a headline in the May 8, 1985, edition of *The Wall Street Journal* boldly proclaimed: "Where Boards and Governments Have Failed, the Market Could Internationalize Accounting." Likewise, *Forbes* reported that the internationalizing of capital markets was producing results when public and professional groups such as the IASC and the EU supposedly had failed.[5] Perhaps such descriptions simply indicate the ideological predilections of journal editors, showing the forces of free enterprise succeeding when the efforts of everyone else (most notably "boards and governments") have failed. However, this is simply no longer a fair characterization. The fact of the matter is that market forces are speeding up a process that has been underway for some time—one that has been created, nurtured, and guided by the farsightedness of several political and professional

---

[5]"Take the Cash and Let the Standards Go," *Forbes,* July 2, 1984.

Exhibit 2–3
Convenience Statement: Income Statement—Japan Airlines

Language: Reader's   **Currency:** Reader's and Home Country's   **GAAP:** Home Country's

	Millions of Yen		Thousands of U.S. Dollars (Note 2)
Income statement excerpt	1992	1991	1992
Operating revenues			
Passenger:			
Domestic	¥ 286,437	¥ 272,076	$ 2,169,977
International	613,368	621,134	4,644,727
Cargo:			
Domestic	29,864	29,975	226,242
International	159,191	172,709	1,205,992
Incidental and other	292,146	257,464	2,213,227
	1,381,008	1,353,361	10,462,181
Operating expenses			
Flying operations	284,968	277,614	2,158,848
Maintenance	101,943	102,974	772,295
Passenger services	188,385	174,057	1,427,159
Aircraft and traffic servicing	228,278	207,883	1,729,378
Reservation sales and advertising	203,256	195,119	1,539,818
General and administrative	81,686	70,855	618,833
Depreciation and amortization	115,149	116,787	872,340
Cost of incidental revenue	184,969	172,531	1,401,280
	1,388,637	1,317,824	10,519,977
Operating (loss) income	¥ (7,629)	¥ 35,536	$ (57,795)

Footnote Excerpt

Japan Airlines Company, Ltd. (the "Company") and its consolidated domestic subsidiaries maintain their accounting records and prepare their financial statements in accordance with accounting principles and practices generally accepted in Japan, and its consolidated foreign subsidiaries in conformity with those of the country of their domicile. The accompanying consolidated financial statements have been compiled from the consolidated financial statements filed with the Minister of Finance as required by the Securities and Exchange Law of Japan and include certain additional financial information for the convenience of readers outside Japan.

U.S. Dollar Amounts

Amounts in U.S. dollars are included solely for the convenience of readers. The rate of ¥132 = $1, the approximate exchange rate prevailing on March 31, 1992, has been used. The inclusion of such amounts is not intended to imply that yen have been or could be readily converted, realized or settled in U.S. dollars at that or any other rate.

Stock Exchange Listings

Tokyo Stock Exchange, Osaka Securities Exchange, Nagoya Stock Exchange
Depositary receipts traded through the NASDAQ System and SEAQ International

EXHIBIT 2–4

Multiple Reporting: Income Statement—Omron Corporation

Language: Reader's   **Currency:** Reader's and Home Country's   **GAAP:** Reader's

	Millions of Yen		Thousands of U.S. dollars (Note 2)
	1992	1991	1992
Net sales	¥483,247	¥464,376	$3,633,436
Costs and expenses:	319,589	295,124	2,402,925
Cost of sales			
Selling, general and administrative	103,463	93,622	777,917
Research and development	33,587	29,952	252,534
Interest expense (income), net (Note 6)	3,995	(2,099)	30,038
Foreign exchange loss (gain)	(312)	1,372	(2,346)
Other, net	3,122	2,856	23,474
Total	¥463,444	¥420,827	$3,484,542
Income before income taxes, minority interests and extraordinary item	¥ 19,803	¥ 43,549	$ 148,894

Footnote Excerpt

The accompanying consolidated financial statements, stated in Japanese yen, include certain adjustments, not recorded on the books of account, to present these statements in accordance with accounting principles as generally accepted in the United States. The principal adjustments include accrual of certain expenses, recognition of the value of warrants issued with bonds, accounting for termination and retirement benefits, accrual of deferred income taxes relating to these adjustments and other timing differences, and accounting for prior years' stock dividends at market value.

Certain reclassifications have been made to accounts previously reported in order to conform to 1992 classifications.

Translation into United States Dollars

The accounts of the Companies are maintained in or translated into Japanese yen. The U.S. dollar amounts included herein are solely for convenience. The translations should not be construed as representations that Japanese yen amounts have been, could have been or could in the future be converted into U.S. dollars. As the amounts shown in U.S. dollars are for convenience only, the approximate exchange rate at March 31, 1992, of ¥133 = U.S. $1 has been used to translate all figures presented in the consolidated financial statements.

Stock Exchange Listings

Kyoto Stock Exchange, Osaka Securities Exchange, Tokyo Stock Exchange, Nagoya Stock Exchange, Luxembourg Stock Exchange, Frankfurt Stock Exchange

organizations. Harmonization efforts not only currently depend on the groundwork laid by these groups over the last 20 years but also will continue to look to them for guidance and coordination in years to come. The vigorous growth of the IASC, which claimed members from nine nations in 1973 as compared with more than 75 twenty years later, indicates that its efforts are gaining recognition and credibility as capital markets become more international. Following are brief descriptions of the international organizations that to a greater or lesser extent have been promoting the cause of harmonization. A more extensive discussion of the impact of the EU is included in Chapter 3.

EXHIBIT 2–5

Reconciliation Report: Income Statement—Hanson Plc

Language: Reader's   **Currency:** Reader's   **GAAP:** Reconciled

	1992 £ million	1991 £ million
Sales turnover		
Continuing operations	7,808	7,555
Acquisitions	903	
	8,711	7,555
Discontinued operations	87	136
	8,798	7,691
Costs and overheads less other income	7,730	6,736
Operating profit		
Continuing operations	978	927
Acquisitions	80	
	1,058	927
Discontinued operations	10	28
	1,068	955
Continuing operations		
Profit on disposal of fixed asset investments	39	211
Costs of closures	(23)	(57)
Profits on disposal of discontinued operations	156	19
	172	173
Net interest income	46	88
Profit on ordinary activities	1,286	1,316
Taxation	197	258
Profit on ordinary activities after taxation	1,089	1,058

Footnote Excerpt

The accounts have been prepared in accordance with applicable accounting standards [as provided in the Companies Act of 1985], including Financial Reporting Standards 2 and 3, using the historical cost convention adjusted for revaluations of certain fixed assets. The following is a summary of the estimated material adjustments to profit which would be required if U.S. generally accepted accounting principles (U.S. GAAP) had been applied.

	Years Ended September 30			
	£ million		$ million	
	1992	*1991*	*1992*	*1991*
Profit available for appropriation as reported in the consolidated profit and loss account	1,089	1,058	1,940	1,885
Estimated adjustments				
Goodwill amortization	(95)	(93)	(169)	(166)
Foreign currency translation	(11)	(22)	(20)	(39)
Pensions	52	59	93	105
Timberlands depletion and reforestation	(36)	(24)	(64)	(43)
Taxation	(96)	(22)	(171)	(39)
	(186)	(102)	(331)	(182)
Estimated profit available for appropriation (net income) as adjusted to accord with U.S. GAAP	903	956	1,609	1,703
Arising from				
Continuing operations	737	928	1,313	1,653
Discontinued operations	166	28	296	50
	903	956	1,609	1,703

Stock Exchange Listings

London, Zurich, Basel, Geneva, Paris, and New York

EXHIBIT 2–6

World Standards Report: Income Statement—Fiat Group

Language: Reader's   **Currency:** Reader's and Home Country's   **GAAP:** IASC

In Millions of Dollars 1992		In Billions of Lire	
		1991	*1992*
	Revenues and other income Net sales and revenues		
34,096	Industrial activities	48,300	50,291
1,700	Financial services	2,486	2,507
1,226	Insurance	1,579	1,809
3,050	Retailing	4,123	4,499
40,072	**Total net sales and revenues**	**56,488**	**59,106**
571	Other income, net	972	842
40,643	**Total sales and revenues**	**57,460**	**59,948**
	Costs and expenses		
20,279	Purchases	26,971	29,911
9,524	Labor and related costs	13,411	14,048
7,334	Other operating expenses	9,788	10,817
2,025	Depreciation and amortization	3,083	2,987
195	Change in inventories	683	(288)
(1,113)	Capitalized construction cost of plant and equipment	(1,330)	(2,231)
911	Interest expense and other charges—financial services	1,496	1,343
1,251	Insurance claims and other technical expenses	1,668	1,846
40,006	**Total costs and expenses**	**55,770**	**59,009**
637	**Income before taxes and minority interest**	**1,690**	**939**

Footnote Excerpt

The consolidated financial statements have been prepared from the statutory financial statements approved or prepared by the Boards of Directors for approval by the stockholders of the individual consolidated companies, adjusted, where necessary, to conform with Group accounting principles, which are consistent with those issued and adopted (International Accounting Standards) by the accounting profession in Italy and recommended in Italy by the Consob (the Italian Regulatory Commission for the Stock Exchange).

Stock Exchange Listings

Milan (and 9 others in Italy), Frankfurt (and 7 others in Germany), Paris, London, New York

Political Organizations

United Nations

The interest of the United Nations (U.N.) in financial disclosure is primarily motivated by its desire to control the impact of **multinational enterprises** (MNEs)—including **multinational corporations** (MNCs)—on the economies and quality of life in newly industrialized countries. Accordingly, since 1972 the U.N. has formed a variety of councils and study groups, such as the Centre on Transnational Corporations, that have examined the international activities of MNEs and developed a code of conduct to encourage socially responsible behavior. In 1977, the Group of Experts on International Standards of Accounting and Reporting, an ad hoc study group formed by the U.N. Centre, created a list of minimum financial and nonfinancial disclosures that should be included in the annual reports of MNEs.[6] Recommended financial reporting disclosures on the list include financial statements for individual firms within consolidated groups, segment information by line of business, research and development expenditures, employment information, and transfer pricing policies. In addition, the U.N. group pointed out that useful disclosure would be facilitated by the preparation of comparable reports regardless of national origin. Because the U.N. has no jurisdiction over MNEs, it cannot enforce these disclosure recommendations, and its attempts to influence governments to enact them as law have met with little success.

Obviously, the approach to standard setting taken by the U.N. is highly politicized and more concerned with curbing exploitation than with ensuring the efficient allocation of capital. The primary user groups envisioned by the U.N. initiatives are national governments. As a result, the main beneficiaries of the U.N.'s efforts have been those governments that have used its guidelines as an unofficial framework for regulating MNEs. Thus, the needs of investors and multinationals have generally been subordinated.

OECD

The **Organization for Economic Cooperation and Development** (OECD), formed in 1960, is an association of 24 governments of industrialized nations from the noncommunist world. Its purpose, as its title suggests, is to promote cooperation among industrialized nations by serving as a forum in which member countries can consult each other with regard to important policy matters such as exchange rates or the balance of trade. It also facilitates the circulation of economic information by compiling statistics and preparing forecasts.

---

[6]United Nations Centre on Transnational Corporations, "International Standards of Accounting and Reporting" (New York: U.N. Publications, 1984), E/C.10/1982/8/Rev.1.

In 1976, the OECD issued a code of conduct for MNEs that included guidelines for disclosures in annual reports.[7] Because the OECD has taken a relatively moderate line on multinationals, stressing voluntary restraint instead of national regulation, its views have been granted a hearing among industrialized nations. Although the OECD has been promoting harmonization and hosted a major conference in 1985 that examined the issue from a variety of perspectives, it does not actually propose specific accounting standards and does not intend to do so.

Professional Organizations

International Accounting Standards Committee

The **International Accounting Standards Committee** (IASC), founded in 1973 by a group of professional accounting organizations from nine countries, has since grown to include more than 100 professional accounting bodies (e.g., the American Institute of Certified Public Accountants) from over 75 nations. Headquartered in London, the IASC is the most widely recognized professional group in charge of developing and issuing international accounting and reporting standards. The committee is governed by a board of 14 members representing 13 countries (as of 1994 these were: United States, United Kingdom, South Africa, the Nordic Federation of Public Accountants, India, Netherlands, Italy, Jordan, Japan, Germany, France, Canada, and Australia) and the International Association of Financial Analysts. It takes 11 of 14 votes to issue a reporting standard. The IASC's objectives are:

(a) To formulate and publish accounting standards to be used in the presentation of financial statements and to promote their worldwide acceptance;

(b) To work for the improvement and harmonization of regulations, accounting standards, and procedures relating to the presentation of financial statements.

Lacking some of the political and technical barriers that must inevitably slow the harmonization process, the IASC has made considerable headway, at least on paper, issuing more than 30 **international accounting standards** (each known as an IAS) since its founding. Appendix 2A provides a list of the IASs as of January 1995, as well as the IASC's other active projects.

Lacking the authority to enforce observance of its standards, the IASC has had to exercise a great deal of diplomacy and discretion both in formulating standards and in urging their adoption by national standard-setting bodies. The IASC must continually weigh the benefits of greater uniformity (i.e., less diversity) in financial reporting practices against the social and economic costs of retooling accounting systems, and it must remember that many financial reporting practices arise from legitimate local

---

[7]"Declaration on International Investment and Multinational Enterprises," *The OECD Guidelines for Multinational Enterprises* (Paris: OECD, 1986).

needs. Consequently, the typical IAS attempts to build in a certain amount of flexibility. It may mix levels of conformity, prescribing a particular accounting method in one instance while allowing alternative treatments in another so long as the one selected is adequately disclosed and its effects noted.

This approach by the IASC has won some important endorsements for IASC pronouncements. Today many prominent multinational firms make a point of mentioning in their annual reports that they prepare their statements in conformity with international accounting standards (e.g., Fiat and Nestlé).[8] Moreover, the International Stock Exchange in London allows foreign firms seeking a listing to do so if they follow IASC guidelines.

The IASC has, until now, focused on obvious targets—financial reporting practices that are clearly arbitrary or unsound—in the belief that filtering out such practices is an important first step toward harmonization. In countries that have not yet issued financial reporting standards or that allow more than one accounting treatment of a given transaction, the IASC has urged local officials to adopt uniform practices consistent with existing IASs. In short, rather than immediately pushing toward complete uniformity, it has instead sought to reduce or prevent excessive diversity. This pluralistic approach has won a hearing for IASC standards in the private as well as the public sector, from multinational corporations as well as developing countries.

In early 1987, the IASC began a significant move toward a new level of international harmonization. At that time, a steering committee on comparability of financial statements was appointed to review existing international accounting standards with the objective of reducing the number of alternative treatments permissible—a movement spearheaded by the International Organization of Securities Commissions and Similar Organizations (IOSCO) (discussed later in this chapter).

In January 1989, the IASC released Exposure Draft 32, *Comparability of Financial Statements* (E32). It dealt with 29 accounting issues for which the choice of alternative accounting treatments permitted by IASs may have a material effect on the definition, recognition, measurement and display of income, expenses, assets, liabilities, or shareholders' equity in the financial statements of an enterprise. The objectives of the E32 proposals were to

(a) Eliminate all but one accounting method for which the alternative methods represent an unrestricted choice for like transactions and events.

(b) Ensure that the appropriate method is used where the alternatives represent different methods that should be used in different circumstances.

In deciding which alternative treatments should be required, preferred, or eliminated, the IASC invoked a multifaceted set of criteria:

(a) Current worldwide practice and trends in national accounting standards, law, and generally accepted accounting principles.

---

[8]According to Frost, approximately 190 companies from around the world disclosed the fact that their financial statements were in conformity with IASC standards. See C. Frost, ''International Accounting,'' *Export Today,* February 1995, p. 35.

(b) Conformity with the Framework for the Preparation and Presentation of Financial Statements (which was in exposure draft form at the time E32 was issued).

(c) The views of regulators and their representative organizations, such as IOSCO.

(d) Consistency within an international accounting standard and with other international accounting standards.

In these circumstances, E32 identified a preferred treatment and an allowed alternative. E32 proposed that an enterprise that presents financial statements using allowed alternative treatments and that purport to conform with IASs should reconcile its reported net income and shareholders' interests to those amounts determined using the preferred treatments. The original E32 proposals are listed in Appendix 2B.

The IASC received more than 160 comment letters on the proposals in E32. The letters were virtually unanimous in supporting the objective of greater comparability of financial statements and the exposure draft as a whole. Inevitably, however, many respondents disagreed with one or more of the detailed proposals in E32.

In some instances, the consequence of adopting the E32 revisions would have a significant impact on the financial reporting results of corporations in certain countries. For example, if the United States chose to follow the IASC's recommendations as outlined in E32, the net income reported by U.S. companies would be significantly affected by at least two of these revisions: IAS 2, *Valuation and Presentation of Inventories in the Context of the Historical Cost System,* and IAS 22, *Accounting for Business Combinations.*

IAS 22

IAS 22, *Accounting for Business Combinations,* deals with goodwill (among other things). Prior to E32, IAS 22 allowed positive goodwill to be recognized as an asset and amortized to income *or* to be adjusted immediately (i.e., written off) to shareholders' equity (it was silent on the issue of the length of the amortization period). The proposed treatment of positive goodwill eliminated one acceptable approach—the immediate adjustment (write off) to shareholders' equity—a method widely used by corporations in Great Britain and other countries.[9] The E32 treatment proposed that positive goodwill be recognized as an asset and that it usually be amortized over a 5- (but not to exceed a 20-) year period. This change would have had a profound effect on the reported net income of U.S. companies since U.S. GAAP recognizes positive goodwill as an asset and amortizes it to income over as long as a 40-year period. The proposed shorter amortization period would significantly increase reported expenses

---

[9]See Chapter 8 on Great Britain for an example of the effect on reported net income if the proposed IAS 22 were adopted in lieu of current British standards regarding goodwill.

and dampen net income. Should countries decide to adopt the proposed IAS 22 as a worldwide norm, the effects on financial reporting results could have other repercussions throughout the international business community:

> The implication of the revised IAS 22 for potential corporate buy-outs cannot be overlooked. The higher annual goodwill charges implied by IAS 22's five-year amortization period in countries permitting a longer period could drive down the amount in excess of fair value of net assets which purchasers would be willing to pay. In order to keep goodwill amortization charges to income as low as possible, buyers are likely to pay less for purchased goodwill. Thus prices are likely to decline.[10]

In finalizing its Comparability Project in November 1993, the IASC passed the E32 suggested revision to IAS 22. Thus, the IASC narrowed the acceptable alternative treatments for positive goodwill.

IAS 2

IAS 2, *Valuation and Presentation of Inventories in the Context of the Historical Cost System,* deals with the type of cost-flow assumption used in valuing inventories. Prior to the revisions to E32 proposed in the *Statement of Intent,* IAS 2 recommended using FIFO or a weighted-average cost formula but also allowed LIFO, specific identification, and the base stock formula. The proposed amended treatment would eliminate LIFO as an alternative. Under the LIFO cost-flow method, costs are assigned to units sold on the basis that inventories represent the earliest purchases or production. As a result, the use of this method usually results in a material difference in both the carrying value of inventories and the cost of sales when compared with that obtained using the FIFO or weighed-average cost formulas. Since the LIFO cost-flow approach does not assign the most current costs to ending inventories, the IASC argued that its use may distort the balance sheet. Be that as it may, there was so much public sentiment to keep LIFO as an allowed alternative that the IASC reversed its E32 position and has continued to pose LIFO as an allowed alternative in IAS 2.[11]

In November 1993, after six years of debate and reconsideration, the final versions of the 10 IAS revisions springing from the Comparability of Financial Statements Project were approved by the IASC board. The revised IASs (see Appendix 2A) are effective for fiscal years beginning on or after January 1, 1995. In the end, of 24 accounting alternatives available in the original versions of the 10 IASs, 16 were eliminated.[12] Thus ends one of the most ambitious IASC undertakings. The relative speed with which it was accomplished and the broad-based debate it sparked may portend a new era of IASC importance.

---

[10]R. Brunovs and R. Kirsch, "Goodwill Accounting in Selected Countries and the Harmonization of International Standards," *ABACUS* 27, no. 2 (1991), pp. 135–61.

[11]V. Pereira, "Fewer Alternatives Permitted," *Accountancy,* July 1994, pp. 121–22.

[12]Ibid.

As with anything that attempts to change or coordinate products of culture, albeit in an effort to benefit all parties concerned, the IASC has drawn considerable criticism from various quarters. It has been accused of allowing industrialized nations to dominate the standard-setting process, of legislating from on high with little regard for the needs of practitioners and financial analysts, and of serving multinationals and ignoring smaller domestic enterprises. At a conference on harmonization held by the OECD in 1985, John L. Kirkpatrick, then IASC chairman, addressed some of these criticisms. The IASC, he pointed out, owes no allegiance to any nation and makes a point of including developing nations on its governing board. It consults analysts, executives, managerial accountants, and industry groups as standards are developed, and it recognizes that the acceptance of each IAS depends on its usefulness to users and preparers of statements. Small domestic companies as well as giant multinationals are included in its jurisdiction, a fact that the IASC implicitly recognizes by trying to make its standards concise, clear, and simple enough to be useful around the world.

Two other complaints, somewhat broader in scope than those mentioned, are sometimes leveled against the IASC. The first and most common is that the IASC is ineffectual. The truth of this charge depends largely on how one chooses to measure effectiveness. The lack of an enforcement mechanism has undoubtedly slowed progress toward harmonization, but one can hardly blame the IASC itself for the limitations imposed on it by the politics of national sovereignty. In the endeavor in which the IASC may properly be held accountable—winning acceptance of its standards by dint of negotiation and consultation—studies indicate that the committee is making significant progress. Although it is still relatively rare for a government or a company to endorse international accounting standards en masse, they are frequently being used as models by national standard-setting bodies. A study conducted in 1988 found that most of the 54 nations studied substantially conform to international accounting standards.[13] A recent follow-up study found that "the number of countries where either national requirements or national practice generally conform with IAS, has risen for the vast majority of IASC's current standards."[14] Perhaps the most important contribution of the IASC in this respect is that it has provided a focus for debate and has created what has been referred to as an *international subculture* for accounting standards that is beginning to have a visible impact on the formation of accounting policy around the world.[15]

The second charge, less frequently made but more serious, is that the IASC is too concerned with technical conformity and is not sensitive enough to the cultural and economic issues underlying national accounting systems. This is a troubling charge, one that ultimately calls into question the feasibility of harmonization. It implicitly asks us to consider what level of engagement and reform is necessary for the

---

[13]H. Gernon, S. E. C. Purvis, and M. A. Diamond, *An Analysis of the Implications of the IASC's Comparability Project* (Los Angeles: University of Southern California, 1990).

[14]IASC, "International Accounting Harmonisation—Steady Progress," *Insight,* June 1993, p. 17.

[15]J. Gaertner and N. Rueschhoff, "Cultural Barriers to International Accounting Standards," *CA Magazine,* May 1980, pp. 36–39.

creation of meaningful international standards. Is it enough to change an accounting system alone, or must legal systems, economic habits, and basic cultural attitudes be altered as well to achieve financial reporting harmonization? This is a difficult question to answer because the interaction between cultural contexts and accounting norms is not understood fully. In this regard, the IASC, like the European Union, can be regarded as a large-scale experiment that will, as time goes on, yield valuable information about harmonization.

International Organization of Securities Commissions and Similar Organizations

In February 1985, the U.S. Securities and Exchange Commission (S.E.C.) published a document calling for comments on eased requirements for multinational securities offerings and the use of a common prospectus by companies in the United States, Great Britain, and Canada. Two distinct approaches for multinational securities offerings were considered: (1) *reciprocal*—the prospectus used by an issuer in its own country would be accepted for offerings in each of the other countries and (2) *common prospectus*—all three countries would agree on disclosure standards for an offering document (prospectus) that would then be usable in more than one country. More than 70 responses were received from issuers, securities exchanges, and industry representatives: 50 favored the reciprocal approach and 21 (including the IASC) favored the common prospectus approach.[16] At the time, however, the S.E.C. could not decide how to proceed, partly due to the desire to extend the arrangement to other countries, especially Japan.[17] The desire to include countries outside the Americas and Europe in multinational securities offerings led, in part, to the transformation of the Interamerican Conference of Securities Agencies and Similar Organizations from a regional group to a global body in 1987 and renamed the **International Organization of Securities Commissions and Similar Organizations** (IOSCO).[18] This new and influential organization has more than 115 securities regulatory agencies (or securities exchanges if a country has no government regulatory agency) from around the world as members, representing coverage of 85 percent of the world's capital markets.[19] IOSCO members have resolved to

    a. cooperate together to ensure a better regulation of the markets, on the domestic as well as on the international level in order to maintain just and efficient securities markets;

[16]C. Sampson, "Facilitation of Multinational Securities Offerings," in *Research in Accounting Regulation,* ed. Gary J. Previts (Greenwich, CT: JAI Press, 1988), p. 216.

[17]In June 1991, the United States and Canada agreed on a multijurisdictional disclosure system (MJDS), which allows companies in one jurisdiction to file home-country documents in the other's jurisdiction. The British were not included. As of July 1992 there were 21 filings, 19 issuers, and $3 billion in debt capital moved from Canada to the United States as a result of a reciprocity agreement between the U.S. S.E.C. and the Ontario S.E.C.; fewer have gone from the United States to Canada. Information based on phone interview in July 1992 with an attorney at the International Affairs Dept., S.E.C.

[18]R. S. O. Wallace, "Survival Strategies of a Global Organization: The Case of the International Accounting Standards Committee," *Accounting Horizons,* June 1990, pp. 1–22.

[19]*IOSCO Annual Report 1994* (Montreal: IOSCO, undated).

   b. exchange information on their respective experiences in order to promote the development of domestic markets;

   c. unite their efforts to establish standards and an effective surveillance of international securities transactions; and

   d. provide mutual assistance to ensure the integrity of the markets by a rigorous application of the standards and by effective enforcement against offenses.[20]

IOSCO has set up six working committees to review and propose solutions to regulatory problems related to international securities transactions. One committee works with the IASC to identify accounting standards that securities regulators might be ready to accept in the case of multinational offerings. In 1987, IOSCO accepted an invitation to join the IASC consultative group. IOSCO's membership has meant that it can influence the work of the IASC, and IOSCO is credited with having spearheaded the movement to reduce options in IASs (i.e., IOSCO informed IASC that it would enforce the IASC's standards if the IASC would reduce the number of acceptable treatments in its existing standards and if it would buttress the existing set of IASs to meet the needs of capital markets and the international business community). With an eye toward harmonization, two noted authorities have stated that "the acceptability of the IASC's accounting rules eventually will be determined by IOSCO as well as the individual securities exchanges making up IOSCO."[21] Indeed, to this end, in October 1993, IOSCO endorsed the IASC's standard on cash flow statements stating:

> the President's Committee recommends that the members of IOSCO take all steps necessary and appropriate in their respective home jurisdictions to accept cash flow statements prepared in accordance with IAS 7, as amended, as one alternative to statements prepared in accordance with the regulator's domestic accounting standards relating to cash flow statements in connection with cross-border offerings and continuous reporting by foreign issues.[22]

At about the same time that IOSCO endorsed IAS 7, it also promulgated a list of core accounting issues (see Exhibit 2–7) that it asserted must be included in IASC pronouncements for IOSCO to endorse those pronouncements for use by issuers in connection with cross-border securities offerings and multiple listings. The IASC was very optimistic about an imminent, comprehensive, significant endorsement of the IASC's pronouncements by IOSCO since IAS 7 had just been endorsed and because all of IOSCO's core issues, except one (interim reporting), were addressed in existing IASs or were being addressed in its active projects. In 1994, such optimism was soon dashed when the IASC received written communication from IOSCO concerning the

---

[20]*IOSCO Annual Report 1991* (Montreal: IOSCO, undated).

[21]A. R. Wyatt and J. F. Yospe, "Wake-up Call to American Business: International Accounting Standards Are on the Way," *Journal of Accountancy,* July 1993, p. 82.

[22]IASC, "Agreement on Cash Flow Statements and Core Standards," *IASC Insight,* December 1993, p. 4.

EXHIBIT 2–7

<h2 style="text-align:center">IOSCO List of Desired Core International
Accounting Standards</h2>

General

Disclosure of accounting policies
Changes in accounting policies
Information to be disclosed in financial statements

Income Statement

Revenue recognition
Construction contracts
Production and purchase costs
Depreciation
Impairment
Taxes
Extraordinary items
Government grants
Retirement benefits
Employee benefits
Research and development
Interest
Hedging

Balance Sheet

Balance sheet impact of income statement items listed above
Property, plant, and equipment
Leases
Inventories
Deferred taxes
Foreign currency
Investments
Financial instruments/off-balance-sheet transactions
Joint ventures
Contingencies
Events occurring after the balance sheet date
Current assets and current liabilities
Business combinations (including goodwill)
Other intangibles

Cash Flow Statements

Cash flow

Other Standards

Consolidated financial statements
Subsidiaries operating in hyperinflationary economies
Associates/Equity accounting
Segments
Interim reporting
Earnings per share
Related-party disclosures
Discontinued operations
Fundamental errors
Changes in estimates

Source: *IASC Insight*, December 1993.

Exhibit 2–8

IOSCO's Position on the IASC's Existing IASs, as of December 1994

Standards Acceptable to IOSCO

IAS2   Inventories
IAS7   Cash Flow Statements (*endorsed by IOSCO, 1993*)
IAS8   Net Profit or Loss for the Period, Fundamental Errors and Changes in Accounting Policies
IAS11   Construction Contracts
IAS16   Property, Plant and Equipment
IAS18   Revenue
IAS20   Accounting for Government Grants and Government Assistance
IAS21   The Effects of Changes in Foreign Exchange Rates
IAS22   Business Combinations
IAS23   Borrowing Costs
IAS24   Related Party Disclosures
IAS27   Consolidated Financial Statements and Accounting for Investments in Associates
IAS29   Financial Reporting in Hyperinflationary Economies
IAS31   Financial Reporting of Interest in Joint Ventures

Standards Unacceptable to IOSCO

IAS9   Research and Development Costs
IAS10   Contingencies and Events Occurring after the Balance Sheet Date
IAS17   Accounting for Leases
IAS19   Retirement Benefits Costs

Standards Subject to Review by IASC

IAS1   Disclosure of Accounting Policies
IAS5   Information to be Disclosed in Financial Statements
IAS13   Presentation of Current Assets and Current Liabilities (*All covered by Presentation of Financial Statements*)
IAS12   Accounting for Taxes on Income
        (*E49, Income Taxes*)
IAS14   Reporting Financial Information by Segment
        (*Draft Statement of Principles for Revised Standard*)
IAS25   Accounting for Investments (*To be reviewed following the Financial Instruments Project*)

Standards Not Considered by IOSCO

IAS4   Depreciation Accounting
IAS15   Information Reflecting the Effects of Changing Prices
IAS26   Accounting and Reporting by Retirement Benefit Plans
IAS30   Disclosures in the Financial Statements of Banks and Similar Financial Institutions

---

Source: *IASC Insight,* December 1994.

acceptability of 24 other existing IASs (see Exhibit 2–8). As noted in the exhibit, IOSCO judged 14 as acceptable and 4 as unacceptable, delayed judgment on another 6 pending the outcome of the IASC's in-process review of them, and did not consider 4 others. To the dismay of the IASC, IOSCO endorsement of the acceptable 14 was not forthcoming, and it was made clear that "IOSCO will not endorse further Standards [beyond the endorsement of IAS 7], including the 14 acceptable IASs, until IASC has completed all the core standards to IOSCO's satisfaction.''[23] According to the IASC chairman, IOSCO's position raises two fundamental questions: Should IOSCO endorse the process of setting international accounting standards in the same way that its members endorse the process of setting national standards? Or should it review, in detail, each international accounting standard? IOSCO is currently following the second approach, something that most of its members do not do in their own jurisdiction.[24] Moveover, the IASC chairman has described the approach that he believes would be most appropriate for IOSCO to adopt in the pursuit of the shared objective of multinational companies being able to use one set of financial statements for listing shares and raising capital on any stock exchange. His recommendation is for IOSCO to

- Accept international accounting standards as a comprehensive set of standards.
- Acknowledge that international accounting standards may require different treatments from those preferred by individual IOSCO members.
- Endorse the process of setting international accounting standards rather than review each standard in detail.
- As an interim step, pending endorsement of the process, endorse those international accounting standards that it accepts and those that have recently been revised through an extensive due process in which IOSCO played an important part—this will drastically reduce the need for restatement or reconciliation by foreign issuers.[25]

It will be interesting to see how this fundamentally divergent view on process is resolved. Both groups have expressed a shared commitment to ''a programme to develop a set of accounting standards by mid-1999 for companies seeking a listing in global markets.''[26]

International Federation of Accountants

An important ally of the IASC in the harmonization process is the **International Federation of Accountants** (IFAC), an association of professional accounting organizations from more than 70 nations. Headquartered in New York, IFAC was formed in 1977 to encourage a consistently high standard of professionalism among accountants around the world. IFAC has largely devoted itself to providing international guidelines for the accounting profession in the areas of auditing, ethics, and professional education. It has become the primary source of statements on international auditing standards, having issued almost 30 international auditing guidelines that attempt to codify a body of acceptable auditing practices for all independent examinations of financial statements.

---

[23]E. Shiratori, ''Time for a Different Approach from IOSCO,'' *IASC Insight,* December 1994, p. 10.
[24]Ibid.
[25]Ibid., p. 11.
[26]J. Kelly and R. Lepper, ''Plan for Global Accounting Standards,'' *Financial Times,* July 12, 1995, p. 3.

In 1982, the IFAC and the IASC entered into an agreement under which IFAC recognized IASC as the sole official source of international accounting standards, affirmed the autonomy of IASC in their development, and promised to promote the use of international standards in all IFAC member countries. In return, IASC recognized IFAC as the authorized representative of the accounting profession worldwide, accepted all members of IFAC as members of IASC, and gave IFAC authority to nominate candidates for membership on the governing board of IASC The cooperation of the two organizations effectively enlists the accounting profession in the promotion of international accounting standards issued by IASC and should help to win favor for them among the international business community as a whole.

Summary

Undoubtedly, today's world markets and cross-border economies are anything but static. Certainly, the reunification of the two Germanys, the fall of communism in the former Soviet Union, the passage of Italy's first-ever antitrust law in this decade to complement European Union legislation, and the advent of a Eurocheque-writing system designed to facilitate cross-border payments are but a few examples that change, when desired and needed, can come quickly. Moreover, such changes are testimony to diverse interests working toward shared objectives and finding ways mutually satisfying to all. Never before have there been such promising precedents against which the possibility for generally accepted international financial reporting practices has been sought and anticipated. It seems clear that the desire, willingness, and need for such principles exist; the issues now involve priorities, time, and enforcement. A recent chairman of the U.S.–based Financial Accounting Standards Board has gone on record stating that the ''FASB would support an objective that seeks to create superior international standards that would gradually supplant national standards as the superior standards become universally accepted.''[27]

---

[27]D. R. Beresford, ''Internationalization of Accounting Standards: The Role of the Financial Accounting Standards Board,'' *Financial Accounting Standards Board Status Report,* series 065, no. 195, June 1988, p. 4.

Suggested Readings

Beresford, D. R. "Internationalization of Accounting Standards." *Accounting Horizons,* March 1990, pp. 99–107.

Choi, F.D. "Economic Effects of Multinational Accounting Diversity." *The Journal of International Financial Management and Accounting,* Summer 1989, pp. 105–29.

————, and R. Levich. *The Capital Market Effects of International Accounting Diversity.* Homewood, IL: Dow Jones-Irwin, 1990.

Gray, S. J. "The Impact of International Accounting Differences from a Security Analysis Perspective." *The Journal of Accounting Research,* Spring 1980, pp. 64–76.

International Accounting Standards Committee. *International Accounting Standards 1991/ 1992.* London, England: IASC, 1991.

Park, J., and K. Park. *Global Equity Markets.* Chicago: Probus Publishing, 1991.

Roll, R. "Industrial Structure and the Comparative Behavior of International Stock Market Indices." *The Journal of Finance,* March 1992, pp. 3–41.

Tay, J., and R. Parker. "Measuring International Harmonization and Standardization." *ABACUS,* January 1990, pp. 71–88.

U.S. Securities and Exchange Commission. "Internationalization of Securities Markets." *Report to the U.S. Senate Committee on Banking, Housing, and Urban Affairs.* Washington, D.C.: Government Printing Office, 1987.

Wallace, R. S. O. "Survival Strategies of a Global Organization: The Case of the International Accounting Standards Committee." *Accounting Horizons,* June 1990, pp. 1–22.

Wyatt, A.R., and J.F. Yospe. "Wake-Up Call to American Business: International Accounting Standards Are on the Way." *Journal of Accountancy,* July 1993, pp. 80–85.

APPENDIX 2A

INTERNATIONAL ACCOUNTING STANDARDS IN FORCE
as of January 1995

		Issuance Date
IAS 1	Disclosure of Accounting Policies	January 1975
IAS 2*	Valuation and Presentation of Inventories in the Context of the Historical Cost System	October 1975
IAS 4	Depreciation Accounting	October 1976
IAS 5	Information to be Disclosed in Financial Statements	October 1976
IAS 7	Statement of Changes in Financial Position, as amended to become Cash Flow Statements	October 1977, December 1992
IAS 8*	Unusual and Prior Period Items and Changes in Accounting Policies	February 1978
IAS 9*	Accounting for Research and Development Activities	July 1978
IAS 10	Contingencies and Events Occurring After the Balance Sheet Date	October 1978
IAS 11*	Accounting for Construction Contracts	March 1979
IAS 12	Accounting for Taxes on Income	July 1979
IAS 13	Presentation of Current Assets and Current Liabilities	November 1979
IAS 14	Reporting Financial Information by Segment	August 1981
IAS 15	Information Reflecting the Effects of Changing Prices	November 1981
IAS 16*	Accounting for Property, Plant and Equipment	March 1982
IAS 17	Accounting for Leases	September 1982
IAS 18*	Revenue Recognition	December 1982
IAS 19*	Accounting for Retirement Benefits in the Financial Statements of Employers	January 1983
IAS 20	Accounting for Government Grants and Disclosure of Government Assistance	April 1983
IAS 21*	Accounting for the Effects of Changes in Foreign Exchange Rates	July 1983
IAS 22*	Accounting for Business Combinations	November 1983
IAS 23	Capitalization of Borrowing Costs	March 1984
IAS 24	Related Party Disclosures	July 1984
IAS 25	Accounting for Investments	March 1986
IAS 26	Accounting and Reporting by Retirement Benefit Plans	January 1987
IAS 27	Consolidated Financial Statements and Accounting for Investments in Subsidiaries	April 1989
IAS 28	Accounting for Investments in Associates	April 1989
IAS 29	Financial Reporting in Hyperinflationary Economies	July 1989
IAS 30	Disclosures in the Financial Statements of Banks and Similar Institutions	August 1990
IAS 31	Financial Reporting of Interests in Joint Ventures	December 1990

IASC WORK IN PROGRESS
as of January 1995

Proposed new international accounting standards
   E48 (supercedes E40) Financial Instruments (addresses some of the issues in IAS 25 and 30)
   E49 (supercedes E33) Income Taxes
Published preliminary proposals
Earnings per share
Intangible assets
Segment information
Framework for the preparation and presentation of financial statements

---

*Revised as a part of IASC's Comparability of Financial Statements Project. Revisions to the standard approved November 1993, with an effective date of January 1, 1995.

APPENDIX 2B

PROPOSALS IN EXPOSURE DRAFT 32, *COMPARABILITY OF FINANCIAL STATEMENTS*

Issues	Required or Benchmark Treatment	Allowed Alternative Treatment	Treatment Eliminated
1. Correction of fundamental errors and omissions; adjustments resulting from accounting policy changes	Adjust opening retained earnings (subject to certain exceptions)	Include in income of the current period	
	Amend comparative information	Present amended pro forma comparative information	
2. Recognition of revenue and net income on construction contracts	Percentage of completion method		Completed contract method
	When the conditions for profit recognition are not met, recognize revenue to the extent of related costs		
3. Measurement of property, plant, and equipment	Measure at cost	Measure at revalued amounts	
4. Measurement of property, plant, and equipment acquired in exchange for another asset	Fair value for dissimilar assets acquired		Net carrying amount of asset given up for dissimilar assets acquired
	Net carrying amount of asset given up for similar assets acquired		Fair value for similar assets acquired
5. Recognition of a revaluation increase relating to a revaluation decrease previously charged to income	Recognize in income of the current period		Recognize in shareholders' interests
6. Recognition of revenue on transactions involving the rendering of services	Percentage of completion method		Completed contract method
7. Determining the cost of retirement benefits	Accrued benefit valuation methods	Projected benefit valuation methods	
8. Use of projected salaries in determining the cost of retirement benefits	Incorporate an assumption about projected salaries		Do not incorporate an assumption about projected salaries

APPENDIX 2B   (continued)

Issues	Required or Benchmark Treatment	Allowed Alternative Treatment	Treatment Eliminated
9. Recognition of past service costs, experience adjustments, and the effects of changes in actuarial assumptions	Recognize systematically over a period approximating the average of the expected remaining working lives of participating employees		Recognize in income of the current period as they arise
10. Recognition of foreign exchange gains and losses on long-term monetary items	Recognize in income of the current period unless hedged		Defer and recognize in income of current and future periods
11. Recognition of foreign exchange losses on the acquisition of an asset that result from a severe devaluation against which there is no practical means of hedging	Recognize in income of the current period	Recognize as part of the cost of the asset	
12. Exchange rate for use in translating income statement items of foreign entities	Exchange rates at the dates of the transactions (or average rate)		Closing exchange rates
13. Treatment of differences on income statement items translated at other than the closing rate	Recognize in shareholders' interests		Recognize in income of the current period
14. Subsidiaries operating in hyperinflationary economies	Restate financial statements in accordance with IAS 29, *Financial Reporting in Hyperinflationary Economies,* before translation		Translate financial statements without prior restatement
15. Exchange differences on foreign operations integral to those of the parent	Recognize in income of the period unless hedged	Recognize as part of the cost of an asset when they result from a severe devaluation against which there is no practical means of hedging	Defer and recognize in income of current and future periods
16. Accounting for business combinations	Purchase method for acquisitions Pooling of interests method for uniting of interests		Pooling of interests method for acquisitions Purchase method for uniting interests

APPENDIX 2B   (continued)

Issues	Required or Benchmark Treatment	Allowed Alternative Treatment	Treatment Eliminated
17. Positive goodwill	Recognize as an asset and amortize to income on a systematic basis over its useful life. The amortization period should not exceed 5 years unless a longer period can be justified which should not, in any case, exceed 20 years		Adjust immediately to shareholders' interests
18. Negative goodwill	Allocate over individual nonmonetary assets. After such an allocation, if negative goodwill remains, treat as deferred income and recognize in income on a systematic basis as for positive goodwill	Treat as deferred income and recognize in income on a systematic basis as for positive goodwill	Adjust immediately to shareholders' interests
19. Measurement of minority interest arising on a business combination	Measure at preacquisition carrying amounts	Measure at postacquisition fair values	
20. Measurement of investment properties	Measure at cost with depreciation	Measure at revalued amounts	Measure at cost without depreciation
21. Recognition of a realized gain previously recognized in revaluation surplus	Transfer to retained earnings		Recognize in income of the current period
22. Assignment of cost to inventories	FIFO and weighted average cost formulas	LIFO formula	Base stock inventories
23. Recognition of development costs	Recognize immediately as expenses	Recognize as assets when they meet specified criteria	
24. Recognition of borrowing costs	Recognize immediately as expenses	Recognize as part of the cost of an asset if it takes a substantial period of time to get it ready for its intended use or sale	
25. Measurement of long-term investments	Measure at cost	Measure at revalued amounts	

APPENDIX 2B   (concluded)

Issues	Required or Benchmark Treatment	Allowed Alternative Treatment	Treatment Eliminated
26. Measurement of marketable equity securities held as long-term investments	Measure at cost recognizing declines in value that are other than temporary on an individual investment basis	Measure at revalued amounts	Measure at the lower-of-cost-or-market value on a portfolio basis
27. Measurement of current investments	Measure at market value	Measure at the lower-of-cost or market value on an individual investment basis	Measure at the lower-of-cost-or-market value on a portfolio basis
28. Recognition of increases and decreases in market values of current investments	Recognize in income of the current period		Recognize in revaluation surplus
29. Recognition of finance income on finance leases by a lessor	Net investment method for finance leases other than leveraged leases Net cash investment method for leveraged leases		Net cash investment method for finance leases other than leveraged leases Net investment leases method for leveraged leases

Source: *International Accounting Standards 1991/1992* (London: IASC, 1991), pp. 20–21.

INFORMATION AND ISSUES FOR FURTHER INQUIRY

I.2.1 Harmonization

a. In a November 2, 1993, *European Accounting Review* (pp. 387–96) article, K. Van Hulle asserted that harmonization of financial reporting can probably be achieved in one of three ways:

   (1) Development of uniform rules (similar to U.S. practice).
   (2) Compromises allowing different financial reporting options that are viewed as equivalent as long as appropriate disclosures are made in the notes (this is the current EU approach).
   (3) Allowance of options but clearly labeling them as *preferred, not preferable but allowed,* and *not allowed;* use of a method other than that labeled *preferred* requires a reconciliation of the method used to the preferred one (this is the IASC approach).

Required:

Assuming that harmonization is a worthy goal, write an essay discussing the pros and cons of each of these approaches. Begin your essay with a statement as to which approach you endorse.

      b. In the same article, Van Hulle reported the views on financial reporting harmonization expressed by the CFOs of two major international companies:

Hugh Collum of Smith Kline Beecham: There are only two major stock exchanges in the world: London and New York. The accounting standard setting bodies of the UK and the US should therefore get together and develop the accounting standards. The rest of the world should merely follow their lead.

    Gerhard Liener of Daimler-Benz: During the last few decades the English language has become the world language without a resolution of the UN or any other institution. It just happened. Well, something very similar is happening in international accounting. The Anglo-Saxon principles are gaining more ground and thus getting nearer and nearer to becoming the world's accounting language.

    The expression ''Anglo Saxon'' . . . as used by Mr. Liener . . . does not include the UK . . . [it] is clearly an option for US GAAP.

Required:

Write an essay discussing your agreement or disagreement with these statements. Do not devote space in your essay summarizing or paraphrasing these comments. Your thoughts and rationale are important.

      c. Van Hulle ended the same article with a series of questions posited to encourage thinking on the need for/role of the international harmonization of financial reporting practices.

        Question 1: Do capital markets ''need'' harmonization of accounting standards?

        Question 2: What does comparability mean? Is absolute comparability possible or desirable?

        Question 3: Does reconciliation of different accounting methods serve to provide useful information or is it likely to confuse the user?

Required:

Write an essay presenting your well-reasoned thinking for each of these questions.

I.2.2 Twenty Years of Harmonization

In a July 1, 1993, *Financial Times* article (p. 9), ''Elusive Harmony: Assessing 20 Years of Progress Towards Global Standards,'' E. Emenyonu and S. Gray state that ''progress towards harmonization over the last 20 years has been mixed.'' They based this statement on a study of 293 large publicly held company annual reports. The sample comprised 25 French, 42 German, 54 Japanese, 82 British, and 96 U.S. companies. They constructed a "harmony index" for each of 26 accounting practices to assess the extent of international harmonization. The index ranges from zero (complete diversity in practices) to 1 (absolute uniformity in practices). For purposes of this assignment, accept the validity of their harmony measurements as reported below.

Uniformity: Twenty Years Apart Across 293 Companies (0–1 in Increasing Harmony)

Issue	1971–72	1992–93	Percentage of Change
Consolidation method	0.0963	0.9269	862.5%
Investments in associates	0.7784	0.9376	20.4
Treatment of goodwill	0.6865	0.5441	−20.7
Rate for translating income statement of subsidiaries	0.5417	0.7039	29.9
Treatment of translation differences	0.5377	0.5063	−5.8
Treatment of exchange differences	0.2323	0.8136	250.2
Method used to assign cost to inventories	0.3853	0.2825	−26.7
Measurement basis for recording inventories	0.6781	0.7564	11.5
Definition of market value	0.6164	0.6990	13.4
Cost basis for recording property, plant, equipment	0.7629	0.7906	3.6
Gains/losses on disposal of property, plant, equipment	0.7093	0.9777	37.8
Method of accounting for depreciation	0.3294	0.2295	−30.3
Method of valuing long-term investments	0.8471	0.6088	−28.1
Gains/losses on disposal of long-term investments	0.5803	0.9889	85.9
Method of valuing current investments	0.5731	0.7662	33.7
Gains/losses on disposal of current investments	0.6999	0.9914	41.6
Method of accounting for borrowing costs	0.9426	0.3843	59.2
Basis for providing for deferred taxes	0.7732	0.2321	−70.0
Method of treating deferred taxes	0.4005	0.3953	−1.3
Accounting for extraordinary and exceptional items	0.9401	0.9950	5.8
Treatment of research expenditures	0.3592	0.9465	163.5
Treatment of development expenditures	0.4125	0.9098	119.5
Determination of the cost of pension	0.9524	0.4882	−48.7
Treatment of past service costs/experience adjustments	0.9439	0.8501	−9.9
Method of accounting for long-term contracts	0.6670	0.5933	−11.0
Method of treating government grants	0.7300	0.6300	−16.0
Average harmony index score	0.6230	0.6903	10.8

Required:

Do you agree with the authors' conclusion regarding the progress toward harmonization? Why or why not? Moreover, if you could eliminate three obstacles to increased harmonization, what would those obstacles be and how would you propose they be overcome?

EXERCISES

E.2.1 Standard-Setting Roles

Write a one- to two-page brief, spelling out what you believe _____ role should be in the international standard-setting process. The blank is to be filled in according to the following:

Letter Beginning Your Last Name	File in Blank with
A to D	the Financial Accounting Standards Board's
E to K	the Security and Exchange Commission's
L to N	the New York Stock Exchange's
O to Z	multinationals'

E.2.2 Comparative Assumptions

What underlying assumptions make it possible to compare/contrast the financial statements of two U.S. companies such as Ford and General Motors? Do such assumptions hold for similar cross-border comparisons? Why or why not?

E.2.3 Has Harmonization Worked?

The Centre for International Financial Analysis and Research (CIFAR) publishes an annual survey of global accounting practices. Some of the highlights of CIFAR's latest survey include the following:

- German and Japanese financial data tend to underreport earnings and book values (because of depreciation policies and use of unrestricted provisions).
- The most comprehensive and relevant financial data come from Australia, Canada, France, Ireland, New Zealand, Scandinavia (except Denmark), South Africa, the United Kingdom, and the United States.
- Below average disclosure of financial data occurs most often in Austria, Belgium, Denmark, Germany, Italy, Japan, the Netherlands, and Spain.
- The accounting policies with the least consistency worldwide are depreciation (i.e., the same asset may be written off over 5 years in one country and 20 years in another) and accounting for goodwill (i.e., goodwill is capitalized and amortized in some countries while it is charged to equity in others).

CIFAR also restates the income of various companies from a selection of countries to a common set of accounting methods (usually the current IASC standards). The purpose of the restatement is to assess how far removed are the reported earnings of a representative set of firms from a common standard. The percentage change in net income to the common standard was as follows:

Company Location	Percentage Change in Reported Earnings to IASC Earnings
Belgium	9
France	6
Germany	44
Italy	11
Japan	12
Sweden	60
Switzerland	–8
Great Britain	4

Required:

What conclusions do you draw from CIFAR's survey with respect to the success of harmonization to date? What conclusions do you draw from the data in regard to harmonization within the EU?

E.2.4 MNCs: What Nationality?

One of the consequences of the globalization of corporate entities has been the creation of what is commonly called the *multinational corporation* (MNC). For example, Exxon Corporation, founded in the United States, now generates more sales (78 percent) and holds more assets (58 percent) outside the United States than it does within it. This phenomenon is happening all over the world as companies expand beyond their original national borders. (See the following chart.)

The development of domestic companies into MNCs raises important accounting, economic, legal, and political issues. For example, how does an MNC determine which accounting principles to follow, those of the country of its incorporation or those of the country in which it generates the most income or sales? In what country should it pay taxes? To what country does it owe its allegiance?

Required:

How should an MNC determine which country's accepted accounting practices it should follow for financial reporting purposes? Be prepared to justify your position.

The Largest 20 Nonfinancial Transnational Corporations Ranked by Foreign Assets, 1990 (Dollars, Billions)

Rank	Corporation	Country	Foreign Assets	Total Assets	Foreign Sales	Total Sales
1	Royal Dutch Shell	GB/Netherlands	69.2	106.4	47.1	106.5
2	Ford	United States	55.2	173.4	47.3	97.7
3	GM	United States	52.6	180.2	37.3	122.0
4	Exxon	United States	51.6	87.7	90.5	115.8
5	IBM	United States	45.7	87.6	41.9	69.0
6	British Petroleum	Great Britain	31.6	59.3	43.3	59.3
7	Asea Brown Boveri	Switzerland	26.9	30.2	25.6	26.7
8	Nestlé	Switzerland	—	28.0	35.8	36.5
9	Philips Electronics	Netherlands	23.3	30.6	28.8	30.8
10	Mobil	United States	22.3	41.7	44.3	57.8
11	Unilever	GB/Netherlands	—	24.7	16.7	39.6
12	Matsushita Electric	Japan	—	62.0	21.0	46.8
13	Fiat	Italy	19.5	66.3	20.7	47.5
14	Siemens	Germany	—	43.1	14.7	39.2
15	Sony	Japan	—	32.6	12.7	20.9
16	Volkswagen	Germany	—	42.0	25.5	42.1
17	Elf Aquitaine	France	17.0	42.6	11.4	32.4
18	Mitsubishi	Japan	16.7	73.8	45.5	129.3
19	GE	United States	16.5	153.9	8.3	57.7
20	Du Pont	United States	16.0	38.9	17.5	37.8

E.2.5 U.S. versus Non-U.S. GAAP

In a comparison of reported earnings and shareholders' equity using U.S. and home-country GAAP, the following results were obtained:

	U.S. GAAP		Home-Country GAAP	
	Net Income	*Shareholders' Equity*	*Net Income*	*Shareholders' Equity*
SmithKline Beecham (GB) (pounds, millions)	474	4,113	638	743
Volvo (Sweden) (kronor, millions)	816	29,494	682	33,864

Required:

What generalizations would you draw from these data with respect to (1) U.S. versus British GAAP and (2) U.S. versus Swedish GAAP?

E.2.6 U.S. versus Japanese GAAP

A survey of the reported performance of eight Japanese electronics companies revealed an average profit margin (i.e., net income/net sales) of 6.31 percent using Japanese GAAP and an average price-earnings ratio of 41.4. Using U.S. GAAP, these same eight companies reported an average profit margin of 9.03 percent and an average price-earnings multiple of 26.33.

Required:

    (a) Based on these data, what generalizations would you draw about the reported earnings and price-earnings ratios of U.S. companies (using U.S. GAAP) versus comparable Japanese companies (using Japanese GAAP)?

    (b) How should an efficient worldwide equity market respond to differences in accepted accounting practice between countries?

E.2.7 Economic Consequences of Harmonization

In May 1994, Swiss pharmaceutical company Roche Holdings Ltd. acquired Syntex Corporation (a U.S. company) for $5.3 billion. One month later, Sandoz Ltd., another Swiss pharmaceutical company, offered $3.7 billion for Gerber Products Co.

According to analysts familiar with the two transactions, the purchases were motivated by two factors. The first is a strong Swiss franc relative to the U.S. dollar, which made the acquisition of Syntex and Gerber appear relatively inexpensive despite the high U.S. dollar price tag. The second is a dramatic change in IASC accounting standards with respect to the accounting for goodwill that would become effective year-end 1994. Goodwill refers to the amount paid for a company in excess of its fair market value. For example, Roche's offer price exceeded Syntex's fair market value by approximately $3.0 billion, and Sandoz's offer for Gerber exceeded that company's fair market value by about $2.0 billion.

Prior to 1995, most European companies had a choice as to how they accounted for goodwill: They could either capitalize goodwill to the balance sheet and then amortize it against earnings, or they could write it off in total against existing shareholders' equity. Most European firms, including Roche and Sandoz, chose the latter method. Beginning in 1995, the charge-to-equity method is no longer available for many European companies as part of the IASC's harmonization efforts.

Required:

    (a) What is the advantage of the charge-off method of accounting for goodwill to companies such as Roche and Sandoz? Why would they prefer it to the alternative of capitalizing and amortizing goodwill?

    (b) How do U.S. companies account for goodwill?

    (c) Which method do you prefer, and why?

CASES

CASE 2.1
ANALYZING THE FINANCIAL EFFECTS OF INTERNATIONAL
REPORTING PRACTICES

Harmonizing International Accounting Standards

To facilitate the orderly flow of capital among and between international capital markets, the International Accounting Standards Committee (IASC) is attempting to harmonize the reporting practices followed in different countries. To understand why harmonization is important, it is first necessary to understand the financial effects produced by differing disclosure and reporting practices. This case focuses on three controversial areas: the accounting for goodwill, inventory, and research and development costs.

The following are three different case scenarios. Analyze each scenario independently and identify the financial statement effect of each alternative accounting or reporting practice.

Goodwill   Throughout the world, it is commonly accepted that *goodwill* results when an acquiring company (the acquiror) purchases another company (the acquiree) and pays more than the fair market value for the acquiree's identifiable net assets. How this excess purchase price—or goodwill—is accounted for varies considerably from country to country. In the United States, for example, goodwill is capitalized to the acquiror's balance sheet and then is amortized against earnings over the goodwill's expected useful life (but not in excess of 40 years). In Great Britain, however, goodwill is frequently charged in total against an equity reserve account (usually the Profit and Loss account) at the time of an acquisition. Contrary to both of these treatments, the IASC has proposed that when goodwill arises as a consequence of a merger or acquisition, it should be capitalized to the acquiror's balance sheet and then amortized against earnings over a period not to exceed 20 years, preferably over only 5 years.

Scenario:

During 1991, American Telephone and Telegraph Company (AT&T) made a successful acquisition bid for the NCR Corporation. The initial bid of $6.12 billion (U.S.) came at a time when NCR's net assets were reportedly worth $1.77 billion (U.S.).

Required:

Calculate the effect on AT&T's annual earnings of accounting for the NCR goodwill under each of the three approaches (i.e., those of the United States, the British, and the IASC). Does the accounting treatment for goodwill affect the price that an acquiror would (or should) be willing to pay for an acquiree in a merger or acquisition?

Inventory   Throughout the world, the accounting for inventories is usually limited to such well-known methods as LIFO (last-in, first-out), FIFO (first-in, first-out), and weighted average. Occasionally, methods such as NIFO (next-in, first-out) or HIFO (highest-price-in, first-out) may be encountered. In the United States, LIFO accounting is the inventory method preferred by most publicly held companies.

Since FIFO is the most prevalent inventory method permitted worldwide (probably because it depicts the actual flow of inventory in the vast majority of settings), the IASC seriously considered eliminating LIFO as an acceptable method to account for inventories.

Scenario:

The 1990 financial statements of the Goodyear Tire & Rubber Company report that its inventories are valued using the LIFO method. The footnotes also reveal the following:

> The total cost of inventories on hand at year-end 1990, 1989, and 1988, were $1,346.0 million, $1,642.0 million, and $1,702.0 million, respectively. The cost of inventories using the LIFO method was less than the approximate current cost of inventories by $335.4 million at December 31, 1990, $330.6 million at December 31, 1989, and $306.6 million at December 31, 1988.

Goodyear's financial statements also disclosed that income before taxes was $55.9 million, $470.9 million, and $490.0 million in 1990, 1989, and 1988, respectively.

Required:

Assume that the IASC decided to eliminate the use of LIFO for inventory valuation purposes. How much net income after tax (assume a 50 percent tax rate) would Goodyear have disclosed in 1989 and 1990? If this proposal were also implemented by the U.S. Internal Revenue Service, how would this affect the income taxes paid by Goodyear in 1989 and 1990 and by how much?

Research and Development Costs   The accounting for research and development (R&D) costs around the world is quite diverse. In some countries, such as the United States, all R&D costs must be expensed against earnings in the year in which they are incurred. In other countries, however, R&D costs may be capitalized to the balance sheet and then amortized against earnings over the expected period of benefit. Currently, the IASC has proposed to permit the capitalization of R&D costs if a company can prove that a market does (or will) exist for its proposed product.

Scenario:

The 1990 financial statements of Goodyear Tire & Rubber Company reveal that R&D costs deducted against earnings totaled $331.3 million, $303.3 million, and $304.8 million in 1990, 1989, and 1988, respectively.

Required:

Assume that the IASC proposal for R&D is implemented and that Goodyear is able to demonstrate that a market will exist for its proposed products. Calculate the after-tax dollar effect on Goodyear's 1989 and 1990 earnings, assuming the capitalization of R&D costs and a 50 percent tax rate.

CASE 2.2
EVALUATING THE EFFECTS OF ALTERNATIVE INTERNATIONAL ACCOUNTING PRACTICE ON MERGER AND ACQUISITION DECISIONS

International Acquisitions, Inc.

Katherine Miller, director of mergers and acquisitions for International Acquisitions, Inc. (IAI), was sitting in her office evaluating what appeared to be a significant stumbling block for a deal that had been brought to her for approval by the company's U.S. subsidiary. IAI is an international holding company for a group of independent hotel chains and resorts located around the world. Headquartered in Phoenix, Arizona, IAI has significant operations in Germany, Japan, the United Kingdom, the United States, Mexico, and five Caribbean countries.

Organizationally, the company is structured into 10 largely autonomous operating companies based on geographical location and country boundaries. Holding company-level executives encourage executives of the various operating companies to operate independently, even to the point of competing for convention business. This philosophy is believed to be the best way to keep the various units at peak operating efficiency, a characteristic considered essential in the highly competitive hotel and resort industry. The only area in which operating company-level executives are required to seek holding company-level approval involve the acquisition (or divestiture) of hotels and resorts.

The Deal   The proposal that Miller was reviewing involved the acquisition of a chain of six resort hotels, located in Florida, California, and Hawaii. The properties were very desirable, and holding company-level executives were highly enthusiastic about the prospects of acquiring the resorts. The resort hotels were being sold as a package, and Miller expected that they would also be of considerable interest to such well-known companies as Hilton, ITT-Sheraton, and Marriott. In fact, Miller's current concern over the deal evolved from her expectation that a number of foreign hotel companies would, in all likelihood, also be bidding on the six-hotel package.

Since the properties were all located within U.S. boundaries, the acquisition proposal had originated within IAI's U.S. operating company (IAI-U.S.). As Miller reviewed the proposed acquisition price data (see Exhibit 1), she realized that U.S. accounting and tax regulations might cause IAI-U.S. to lose this acquisition opportunity. Miller was concerned that if a foreign bidder for the properties emerged, the more lenient treatment of goodwill for accounting or tax purposes in other countries might permit such a company to outbid IAI-U.S. for the resort package.

In anticipation of this possibility, Miller decided to evaluate the bid price that IAI might be able to pay if the acquisition were handled through its German, Japanese, and British operating companies. As a first step in this process, she developed a table comparing the prevalent accounting and tax treatments for goodwill in each of the four countries (see Exhibit 2).

Required:

   (a) Using the assumptions and valuation approach described in Exhibit 1, calculate the maximum bid price that IAI could offer for the six-hotel package through its German, Japanese, and U.S. subsidiaries.

   (b) Is Miller's concern about losing the properties to a foreign bidder justified? Why or why not?

   (c) How will harmonization affect this type of problem for IAI in the future?

EXHIBIT 1

Comparative Acquisition Bid Price Data
Source: IAI-U.S.

I. Maximum Bid Price Based on Projected Accounting Earnings (after goodwill amortization and taxes) of $4 Million per Year for a 20-Year Horizon, Discounted at Various Hurdle Rates

Hurdle (discount) rate	10%	15%	20%
Maximum bid price (000's)	$21,547	$16,384	$13,016
Goodwill	6,547	1,384	(1,984)

Assumptions

1. Constant tax rate of 34 percent.
2. Fair market value of the resort properties is $15 million.
3. Acquisition price is that price (P) that would render the purchase a zero net present value (NPV) project; that is, if the hurdle rate equals 10%, then

$$NPV = PV - P = 0$$
$$= PV - [15,000 + GW]$$

where

GW = Goodwill
PV = [PV factor for $n = 20$, $i = 10\%$ ×
      Projected Annual Accounting Earnings]

4. Projected Annual Accounting Earnings are calculated as follows:

	(000s)
Accounting earnings before goodwill amortization and income taxes	4,000
Less: Amortization of goodwill (GW)	− GW/40
Accounting earnings before income taxes	[4,000 − GW/40]
Less: Income taxes (@ 0.34)	1,360 − (GW/40)(.34)
Projected Annual Accounting Earnings	[2,640 − (GW/40)(.66)]

II. Maximum Bid Price Based on After-Tax Cash Flow, Discounted at 10%

Hurdle (discount) rate	10%
Maximum bid price (000's)	$24,019
Goodwill	9,019

EXHIBIT 1   (concluded)

Assumptions

1. Constant tax rate of 34 percent.
2. Fair market value of the resort properties is $15 million.
3. Acquisition price is that price (P) that would render the purchase a zero net present value (NPV) project; that is,

$$NPV = PV - P = 0$$
$$= PV - [15,000 + GW]$$

where

GW = Goodwill
$PV = [PV$ factor of $n = 20$, $i = 10\% \times$ After-Tax Cash Flow]

4. After-Tax Cash Flow is calculated as follows:

	Years 1–15	Years 16–20
Earnings before goodwill amortization and income taxes	$4,000	$4,000
Less: Amortization of goodwill (GW)	-0-	GW/15
Taxable earnings	4,000 − (GW/15)	$4,000
Less: Income taxes (@ 0.34)	[1360 − (GW/15)(.34)]	(1,360)
Taxable earnings after tax	2,640 − (GW/15)(.66)	$2,640
Add: Noncash amortization of goodwill	GW/15	-0-
After-Tax Cash Flow	$2,640 + (GW/15)(.34)	$2,640

EXHIBIT 2

Alternative Accounting and Tax Treatment of Goodwill

Country	Acounting Treatment	Tax Treatment
Germany	Goodwill capitalized to the balance sheet and amortized against earnings over 5 years	Goodwill capitalized and amortized over 15 years
Japan	Goodwill capitalized to the balance sheet and amortized against earnings over 5 years	Goodwill capitalized and amortized over 5 years
Great Britain	Goodwill charged (in total) against equity reserve at the time of acquisition	Goodwill not tax deductible
United States	Goodwill capitalized to the balance sheet and amortized against earnings over 40 years	Goodwill capitalized and amortized over 15 years

CHAPTER

3

Financial Reporting and the European Union

It is a fundamental objective of the European Union (EU) that a common economic market be achieved which allows for free mobility of capital, labour and enterprise, as well as trade, across the borders between member countries. This requires that the infrastructure of markets be harmonized, and financial accounting is a part of that infrastructure.[1]

The quality of financial reporting in the EU has considerably improved with the implementation of the accounting directives.[2]

Introduction

Founded in 1957 when six nations—France, West Germany, Italy, Belgium, the Netherlands, and Luxembourg—signed a series of international treaties, the **European Union** (EU) includes three cooperative alliances intended to improve the efficiency and competitive ability of its members: the European Coal and Steel Community, the European Atomic Energy Commission, and (the best known and most important) the European Economic Community (E.E.C.). From its tentative and experimental beginnings, the European Union has grown in size and ambition, attracting nine new members—the United Kingdom, Ireland, and Denmark in 1973; Greece in 1981; Portugal and Spain in 1986; and Sweden, Austria, and Finland in 1995—eager to avail themselves of the benefits of belonging to a large trading bloc. Ultimately, the 15 member[3]

---

[1]P. Thorell and Whittington, G., "The Harmonization of Accounting within the EU," *The European Accounting Review* 3, no. 2 (1994), p. 216.

[2]K. Van Hulle, "Harmonization of Accounting Standards in the EU," *The European Accounting Review* 2, no. 2 (1993), p. 390.

[3]In November 1994, Norway voted not to join the European Union. Moreover, many expect membership to continue to grow with an eye toward central and eastern Europe; in particular, the Czech Republic, Poland, Hungary, Slovakia, Bulgaria, and Romania are likely candidates.

66

nations of which the European Union is currently composed intend to create the world's largest free market economy, comprising nearly four hundred million people, by removing all physical, technical, and fiscal barriers that hinder the free movement of capital, goods, and people within the EU.

Although as of 1995, the Union represented a single market, significant changes would be still needed before a unified Europe would be achieved. Prior to the admission of Sweden, Austria, and Finland to the EU, implementation of the EU's "Single Internal Market" directives by the other 12 nations was mixed. As of February 1993, implementation into national law of these directives ranged from 72 percent in Greece to 92 percent in Denmark.[4] Moreover, complete implementation of other E.E.C. policies has been formally pushed back. For example, three major policies have revised deadlines for full implementation: (1) implementation of a single monetary unit called the **European Currency Unit** (ECU), now slated for 1997–1999; (2) integration of agricultural policies, reslated for 1996; and (3) the "single passport" for stockbrokers and banks to deal shares across the EU, now slated for 1996. The economic union of these nations has proven to be a gargantuan and multifaceted task involving debate and compromise on a staggering array of issues: trade policy, company and tax law, product regulation, labor relations, monetary policy, financial markets, and legal and financial reporting requirements. Inevitably, the arduous process of negotiating these issues has forced member nations not only to confront the laws and traditions separating their respective economies but also to consider in a new light the economic structures— their history and purpose, their implicit cultural values—that have been responsible for these barriers. In the broadest terms, the existence of the European Union is prompting a reevaluation of the place of national sovereignty and cultural diversity in an increasingly supranational and transcultural economic order.

Several cases in point typify this basic need for reconsidering long-standing national positions in attempting to comply with specific EU rules. For example, Luxembourg has had to reevaluate its role as a haven for holding companies as it seeks to adhere to EU rules regarding consolidated financial statements. In hammering out an agreement on insider trading laws, the Italians have had to examine the prominence of close-knit groups (i.e., families) in their economy and to revise their notions of acceptable business behavior. Similarly, the British have had to defend their rigid notion of fair play rather than simply to assume its universal applicability. Even many apparently "objective" guidelines, such as technical standards concerning product quality, may express essentially cultural preferences. A German law requiring a minimum alcohol content in alcoholic beverages, for example, was struck down by EU officials in 1979 because it prevented the import of French alcoholic beverages. It was ruled that a product legally produced and marketed in one member country has the right to be sold in other member countries, barring genuine public health or safety concerns. (This principle, incidentally, is forcing the International Stock Exchange in London to

---

[4]B. Straetz, "A Top Priority for the EU in 1993: Implementing the Single Internal Market," *Business America,* March 8, 1993, pp. 11–15.

grant listings to European continent–based companies that might not otherwise qualify for exchange membership. For further information, see the following section on Securities Exchanges.) In effect, the ruling implied that the German "technical" standard was an arbitrary cultural preference, expressing a German idea of "purity" and "quality" among alcoholic beverages that could not be used to restrict the import of goods meeting different but legitimate standards.

Despite the fact that financial statements prepared in one member state must be accepted in all other member states for purposes of cross-listing shares on stock exchanges, the EU continues to be a major force in (and a major forum for) the international movement to harmonize financial reporting practices. The efficient movement of capital within the European Union depends to a great extent upon an acceptable level of comparability among financial statements assembled in different member nations. While the goal of comparability does not require absolute uniformity in the reporting systems of all member nations, it does call for a considerable degree of coordination and the elimination of needlessly diverse reporting practices. Even this more limited goal presents a formidable challenge, however, for the roughly 3 million EU companies that must comply with EU financial reporting harmonization goals (this is in contrast to the roughly 10,000 companies in the United States that must comply with S.E.C. reporting requirements). The European Union includes countries with extremely diverse economies, ranging from the highly concentrated industrial base of the Netherlands to the prevalent agrarian economy of Portugal. Even the highly industrialized members, such as the United Kingdom and Germany, provide sharp contrasts in the style and orientation of their financial reporting practices, the surface variations often indicating deeply rooted divergences in philosophy and purpose. Indeed,

> In most Continental countries, the accountant's goal is to comply with strict rules and to hold down tax liabilities—and not to impress investors. In Britain, the Netherlands, the U.S. and other countries with more of an Anglo-Saxon business tradition, reports to shareholders are distinct from tax calculations and accounting rules are much more flexible; accountants use lots of judgment and don't let rigid rules get in the way of presenting a "true and fair view" of the company . . . [Continental] and Anglo-Saxon accountants don't even share the same basic aims.[5]

Whatever the difficulties facing the EU harmonization efforts, the consequences of its success or failure will reach far beyond its borders. Users and preparers of financial statements around the world are watching intently for a number of reasons. First, the ultimate success of global harmonization requires that everyone in the movement be aware of what everyone else is doing. Otherwise, harmonization will merely create new layers of reporting requirements on top of existing national practices, exacerbating the problem that it is intended to solve. Second, while proponents and skeptics have long debated the possibility of harmonization, the European Union is actually putting the question to a major test. Its efforts, uniting the political assent of 15 national governments with the international economic forces drawing Europe and the world together, constitute

---

[5]B. Haggerty, "Differing Accounting Rules Snarl Europe," *The Wall Street Journal,* September 4, 1992, pp. A3C.

a large-scale experiment that should give a clearer notion of harmonization's feasibility. Third, the financial reporting requirements developed and approved by the European Union directly affect a large number of foreign multinationals who operate in member countries. Fourth, the European Union is becoming such a formidable member of the world economy that foreign managers and regulators will feel increasingly obliged to conform to its standards. In a very real sense, then, much of the world has a stake in what is decided in the EU's headquarters in Brussels. To appreciate its true significance, one must see European harmonization in a global context.

The European Commission (one of the governing bodies of the European Union, along with the Board of Ministers) demonstrated its awareness of the global implications of the European experiment when it announced in January 1990 that it would join the International Accounting Standards Committee's Consultative Group. In addition, in 1991 the European Union created an Accounting Advisory Forum of financial statement regulators, preparers, and users. (This forum will merely discuss standards, not set them.) By taking these steps, the European Commission hopes to accomplish two important objectives. First, by actively coordinating its efforts with the IASC, it will avoid duplication of effort and the needless proliferation of reporting requirements. Second, it hopes to take advantage of the IASC's more detailed treatment of accounting issues not currently addressed by EU directives, thereby improving the comparability of financial statements within the European Union without itself having to formulate further standards.[6] From the viewpoint of users, the linkage between the EU and the IASC holds the promise that the two most active and influential players in the harmonization movement will create compatible standards.

The other uniquely important element of European harmonization resides in the Union's ability, unlike that of the Organization for Economic Cooperation and Development and the United Nations, to enforce its pronouncements on financial reporting. Under the terms set out by the Treaty of Rome (1957) that formed the European Union, the European Union's ruling bodies may issue regulations, which are specific and immediately binding on members of the Union, or directives, which are broad and must be incorporated by members into national law by a given deadline. (It should be noted that these deadlines may be, and often are, pushed back or missed.) Members that fail to incorporate directives in a timely fashion may be brought before the European Court of Justice and ordered to comply. To date, the EU Council of Ministers has issued two major directives that bear directly on accounting matters. The Fourth Directive, adopted by the European Union in 1978, establishes acceptable formats for financial statements as well as basic reporting requirements for companies operating in EU territory, and the Seventh Directive, adopted in 1983, promulgates standards governing the preparation of consolidated statements for business groups. As a matter of political necessity, some latitude has been granted to member nations as to the precise mode of implementation and enforcement of these two directives. Hence, their objective has been mutual recognition based on minimum rules rather

---

[6]Forums addressing these issues are held three times a year to improve the comparability of financial statements.

than uniformity. Indeed, a representative from the German Ministry of Justice was recently paraphrased along these lines:

> mutual recognition of financial statements is not dependent on harmonization . . . Mutual recognition is guaranteed in EU Member States for general purposes and listings at stock exchanges for all financial statements drawn up under the requirements of the Fourth [and] Seventh Directives.[7]

More specific discussion of each of these directives follows.

The Fourth Directive

Purpose

The Fourth Directive (a summary of its contents is presented in Appendix 3A) was adopted by the European Union on July 25, 1978, after 15 years of gestation, debate, and revision. The text of the directive calls for member states to incorporate its requirements into their respective legal systems within two years, a target date that proved to be altogether too ambitious. Not a single member country was able to meet the deadline; however, the United Kingdom and Denmark were the first to comply when they passed amended Companies Acts in 1981, with the Netherlands following in 1983. Since 1991, compliance has been met by all member-nations, except the three most recent additions where its compliance is in progress.

The Fourth Directive has two strategic objectives. First, by coordinating company law in member nations, it seeks to eliminate needless legal and bureaucratic obstacles to economic activity within the Union. Second, by establishing basic reporting requirements and acceptable financial statement formats, it attempts to create a minimum level of comparability among financial statements throughout the European Union. In pursuit of these objectives, the directive not only sets out minimum auditing and disclosure requirements but also enjoins particular auditing and accounting principles on examiners and preparers of financial statements. The directive applies to all public and private limited liability companies, with the exception of banks and insurance companies. In addition, it allows some concessions such as abridged statement formats and more lenient audit requirements to small and medium-sized companies. Small and medium-sized companies are defined as those that do not exceed two of the following three limits[8]:

	Small	*Medium*
1. Balance sheet total assets	2 million ECU[9]	8 million ECU
2. Net sales	4 million ECU	16 million ECU
3. Average employees during year	50	250

---

[7]IASC, ''Mutual Recognition of Financial Statements in International Capital Markets,'' *Insight*, December 1993, p. 11.

[8]In an effort to simplify obligations of small and medium companies, the original limits set in 1978 were doubled by an amendment to the Fourth and Seventh Directives in November 1990. The limits shown above reflect those set out in the 1990 amendment. Limits 1 and 2 were the only ones raised in 1990; the limits regarding the number of employees remains unchanged since 1978.

[9]At the end of January 1995, one ECU (European currency unit, a basket currency that serves as the monetary unit of the European Union) was worth approximately $1.22.

Audit and Public Filing Requirements

Under EU law, each member state must establish and maintain a public registry of companies operating in that nation. Each company must submit to this registry an annual report that includes a balance sheet, a profit-and-loss statement, explanatory footnotes, and a report of an independent and professionally qualified auditor. (A statement of changes in financial position is *not* required under the Fourth Directive. Acceptable qualifications for auditors are set forth in the Eighth Directive.) The auditor must not only examine the financial statements themselves but also verify their consistency with the annual report in which they appear. Small companies (as defined previously) may be exempted from the audit requirement at the discretion of the member state.

True and Fair View

An important and much-discussed feature of the Fourth Directive is its adoption of the **true and fair view** as the ultimate criterion for financial reporting in the European Union. According to Article 2 of the directive, preparers should ignore any provision therein if compliance with that provision would conflict with presentation of a true and fair view of a company's financial position and income. (Any such departure and the reason for it must be disclosed in the notes.) To understand the full significance of this choice of policy, one must appreciate something of the implicit cultural values lurking behind it, as well as its relation to accounting practices of various countries in the Union, especially Great Britain and Germany.

The phrase *true and fair view* has long been included in British audit reports; it represents a concept analogous to *fair presentation* in U.S. auditing. Fraught with philosophical implications, it signifies a particular approach to financial reporting in which financial statements are valued not so much for their compliance with particular rules as their ability to create an overall picture of a company's financial affairs. At least in theory, the true and fair view criterion ensures that statements are not only correct but also are useful indicators of a company's financial health. The fulfillment of this criterion requires a concern for *substance over form* and the application of professional judgment. The independent auditor, according to this view, serves as a referee as well as a reporter/preparer. Ultimately, the true and fair view suggests a culturally conditioned distrust of rules—a skepticism of their efficacy unless they are subordinated to human judgment—and a belief in an abstract fairness that can never be completely codified.

German audit reports (see Exhibit 3–1), on the other hand, have traditionally emphasized technical conformity of financial statements, with the auditor expressing an opinion that they fulfilled all legal requirements set out by existing company and tax law. (It is worth noting that in Great Britain, as in the United States, financial reporting is separated from tax compliance, while in Germany the two are linked.) Until the adoption of the Fourth Directive, such concepts as true and fair view or fair presentation held relatively little importance in German auditing. Now, however, German audit reports must express an opinion not only on the correctness of company accounts and their compliance with appropriate laws but also on whether they render a true and fair view. Unfortunately, the mere presence of a phrase in the audit report does not guarantee that

---

EXHIBIT 3–1

Comparison of an Audit Report from British and German Annual Reports

A British Audit Report	*A German Audit Report*

Report of the Auditors to the members of the BOC Group Plc

We have audited the financial statements on pages 50 to 77.

Respective responsibilities of directors and auditors

As described on page 47, the Company's directors are responsible for preparation of financial statements. It is our responsibility to form an independent opinion, based on our audit, on those statements and to report our opinion to you.

Basis of opinion

We conducted our audit in accordance with Auditing Standards issued by the Auditing Practices Board. An audit includes examination, on a test basis, of evidence relevant to the amounts and disclosures in the financial statements. It also includes an assessment of the significant estimates and judgements made by the directors in the preparation of the financial statements, and of whether the accounting policies are appropriate to the Company's circumstances, consistently applied and adequately disclosed.

We planned and performed our audit so as to obtain all the information and explanations which we considered necessary in order to provide us with sufficient evidence to give reasonable assurance that the financial statements are free from material misstatement, whether caused by fraud or other irregularity or error. In forming our opinion we also evaluated the overall adequacy of the presentation of information in the financial statements.

Opinion

In our opinion the financial statements give a true and fair view of the state of affairs of the Company and the Group at 30 September 1994 and of the profit, total recognised gains and cash flows of the Group for the year then ended and have been properly prepared in accordance with the Companies Act 1985.

Coopers & Lybrand

Chartered Accountants and Registered Auditors
London, 28 November 1994

Independent auditors' report for Volkswagen AG

The consolidated financial statements, which we have audited in accordance with professional standards, comply with the German legal provisions. With due regard to the generally accepted accounting principles, the consolidated financial statements give a true and fair view of the Group's assets, liabilities, financial position and profit or loss. The Group management report is consistent with the consolidated financial statements.

Hanover, February 23, 1994

C & L TREUARBEIT
DEUTSCHE REVISION
Aktiengesellschaft
Wirtschaftsprüfungsgesellschaft
Steuerberatungsgesellschaft

Siepe   Dr. Heine
Wirtschaftsprüfer   Wirtschaftsprüfer

the concept will (or can) be similarly applied in various countries. Time will tell whether the gap between the German and British approaches has actually been narrowed.

Valuation Principles

The Fourth Directive adopts several general principles of valuation that must be adhered to in the preparation of financial statements. Among the key ones are the following:

- The company must be presumed to be a *going concern.*
- Methods of valuation must be *consistent* from year to year.
- Profit calculations must be based on the concept of *prudence* (including only profits earned as of the balance sheet date while also including all foreseeable losses).
- Income and expenses must conform to the *matching* principle and be calculated on the *accrual basis.*

As in the case of the true and fair view, one should remember that these concepts are broadly stated and may be applied rather differently in different countries.

Other Reporting Practices

The Fourth Directive also sets out a number of other minimum standards for reporting covering a variety of areas. The following are some of the highlights:

- Companies generally must use *historic cost* as the basis for asset valuation, but member states may allow *replacement value accounting* for certain fixed assets so long as there is full disclosure of the impact on the financial statements.
- Companies need not disclose the effects of *inflation* on financial statements unless required by the member state. Any revaluation reserve created by the application of methods of accounting for inflation may not be distributed as dividends unless realized.
- If a member nation allows the *capitalization* of research and development expenses, any capitalized amount should be written off in five years or less. Longer periods may be allowed under exceptional circumstances if appropriate disclosure is made in the notes.
- Taxes on ordinary profit and extraordinary items should be disclosed separately, though the two may be combined on the face of the profit and loss statement. When income tax expense differs materially from income tax payable, the difference must be disclosed. *Deferred income tax* accounting is not required.
- Pension costs charged against income must be disclosed. However, the directive contains no detailed guidance for determining *pension expenses or liabilities.*

- Subscribed capital, paid-in capital, revaluation reserve (if applicable), other reserves, and retained earnings must be disclosed on the balance sheet. The number and par value of shares issued during the year, the number and par value of each class of stock outstanding, and a description of convertible debentures, stock rights, or other such instruments must be disclosed in the notes.

- The Fourth Directive makes no specific requirements with regard to accounting for leases, related-party transactions, or foreign currency translation. The only segment reporting requirements are net sales broken down by line of business and geographical market, and average number of employees by category.

As these examples suggest, the Fourth Directive concerns itself with broad issues rather than detailed guidance, an approach that has the advantage of making the document politically palatable but one that also has the drawbacks of leaving many important accounting issues unresolved and perhaps allowing too much flexibility in accounting method selection.

Statement Formats

The Fourth Directive allows two formats for balance sheets, horizontal and vertical, and four formats for profit and loss statements, two that present results by type of expenditure (e.g., all salaries and wages shown as personnel expense) and two that present them by type of operation (e.g., all salaries and wages distributed across cost of goods sold, marketing expense, and administration expense). Member nations may require any one of these formats or allow companies to choose among them. Some of the formats look similar to U.S. statements; others differ markedly. Exhibits 3–2 and 3–3 present the income statements and balance sheets of Beiersdorf Group, a German medical products company, and BOC, a British industrial gases concern. Note that Beiersdorf's balance sheet employs a horizontal format similar to U.S. balance sheets but presents assets and liabilities by increasing liquidity instead of decreasing liquidity, as is the U.S. custom. Unlike U.S. practice, Beiersdorf's income statement is organized by type of expenditure. On the other hand, BOC's balance sheet employs a vertical format, one that balances net assets with shareholders' equity. Note that BOC's income statement employs a format similar to that used by U.S. companies.

Amendments

In November 1990, the EU council amended the Fourth and Seventh directives. With the intent to simplify financial reporting obligations of small and medium-sized companies, the council increased the minimum requirements used to define small and medium-sized companies. Another purpose of this amendment was to promote the use of ECUs as the primary currency in the annual reports of those companies required to file annual reports.[10]

---

[10]"Council Directive of 8 November 1990 Amending: Directive 78/660/EEC on Annual Accounts, and Directive 83/349/EEC on Consolidated Accounts, as Concerns the Exemption for Small and Medium-sized Companies and the Publication of Accounts in ECUs," *Official Journal of the European Communities*, No. L 317/57, 16. 11. 90.

EXHIBIT 3–2

Beiersdorf AG
Balance Sheet
(000s DM)

	31.12.1993		*31.12.1992*	
Assets				
Intangible assets		101,879		92,343
Tangible assets				
Land and buildings	169,528		172,131	
Machinery, technical installations, factory and office equipment	142,679		246,893	
Assets under construction and payments on account	11,701	323,908	31,213	350,237
Financial assets				
Shares in affiliated companies and participations	879,639		857,284	
Other financial assets	1,276	880,915	1,297	858,581
Fixed assets		1,306,702		1,301,161
Stocks				
Raw materials and supplies	64,642		71,169	
Work in progress	43,479		51,834	
Finished goods, merchandise	133,631		134,588	
Payments on account	431	242,183	457	258,048
Accounts receivable and other current assets				
Trade debtors	109,190		88,309	
Accounts receivable from affiliated companies and participations	191,862		122,132	
Other accounts receivable and current assets	35,760	336,812	49,414	259,855
Securities, liquid funds				
Securities	463		459	
Liquid funds	45,213	45,676	32,593	33,052
Current assets		624,671		550,955
Prepaid expenses		1,720		404
		1,933,093		1,852,520
Equity and Liabilities				
Subscribed capital	210,000		210,000	
Capital reserves		301,830		301,830
Revenue reserves				
Legal reserve	7,000		7,000	
Other retained profits	540,805	547,805	469,360	476,360
Unappropriated profit		71,445		54,600
Shareholders' equity		1,131,080		1,042,790
Untaxed special reserves		6,100		22,220
Provisions				
Provisions for pensions and similar obligations	499,200		477,750	
Provisions for taxes	32,075		18,160	
Other provisions	130,848	662,123	129,160	625,070
Liabilities				
Liabilities to banks	13,029		22,452	
Trade creditors	57,488		62,420	
Accounts payable to affiliated companies and participations	22,671		37,363	
Other liabilities	40,602	133,790	40,205	162,440
Outside capital		795,913		787,510
		1,933,093		1,852,520

EXHIBIT 3–2 (concluded)

Beiersdorf AG
Income Statement
(000s DM)

	1.1.-31.12.1993		1.1.-31.12.1992	
Sales		4,763,438		4,552,254
Changes in stocks of finished and unfinished				
goods		19,862		26,561
Own work capitalized		25,157		23,069
Other operating income		90,898		75,530
		4,859,631		4,624,292
Material costs				
Cost of raw materials, supplies and merchandise	1,395,618		1,363,147	
Cost of external services	50,238		49,904	
Personnel costs				
Wages and salaries	997,066		1,009,807	
Social security contributions and assistance costs	200,342		195,115	
Pension costs	50,512		61,543	
Depreciation on intangible and tangible assets	199,417		199,810	
Other operating expenses	1,563,884	4,457,077	1,377,517	4,256,843
Operating result		402,554		367,449
Net income from participations		+ 9,798		+ 6,547
Depreciation on financial assets and current asset				
securities		29		242
Net interest		48,807		45,309
Result from ordinary activities		363,516		328,445
Extraordinary profit		—		+ 9,282
Profit before taxes		363,516		337,727
Taxes on income and profit		160,550		155,895
Other taxes		23,561		23,288
Profit for the year		179,405		158,544
Profit due to minority shareholders		3,289		2,818
Transfer to reserves		104,671		101,126
Unappropriated profit		71,445		54,600

Status

Although more than 17 years have passed since the adoption of the Fourth Directive, its effects are still being debated because of the amount of time that has been required for EU members to incorporate it into their national laws. Reviews at this point appear to be favorable but mixed. The directive unquestionably has had a major impact on reporting standards around Europe, even in countries outside the European Union, and it has reduced the diversity of national reporting practices. For example, a survey conducted by the Fédération, des Experts–comptables Européens (FEE)—an organization representing European accounting bodies—compares various forms of accounting and reporting practices between three groups of countries: (1) those in the European Union that must comply with the Fourth Directive, (2) those for which this was not compulsory (in 1989), and (3) non-EU (EFTA) countries. On aggregate, the survey found that more similarities than differences exist between EU and non-EU

EXHIBIT 3–3

BOC Group
Balance Sheet
Years Ended September 30, 1993 and 1994

	£ Million	
	1994	*1993*
Fixed assets		
Tangible assets	2,374.3	2,295.5
Intangible assets	38.4	44.9
Investments	191.9	190.2
	2,604.6	2,530.6
Current assets		
Stocks	328.1	317.8
Debtors due within one year	752.0	678.5
Deposits and cash due within one year	132.8	158.8
Assets due beyond one year	92.6	99.7
Current assets	1,305.5	1,254.8
Current liabilities		
Creditors: *amounts falling due within one year*		
Borrowings and finance leases	(247.9)	(475.0)
Other	(805.1)	(710.2)
Current liabilities	(1,053.0)	(1,185.2)
Net current assets	252.5	69.6
Total assets *less* current liabilities	2,857.1	2,600.2
Long-term liabilities		
Creditors: *amounts falling due after more than one year*		
Borrowings and finance leases	(855.0)	(659.2)
Other	(50.7)	(26.6)
Provisions for liabilities and charges	(220.7)	(218.4)
	(1,126.4)	(904.2)
	1,730.7	1,696.0
Capital and reserves		
Called-up share capital		
Equity capital	119.5	118.9
Nonequity capital	2.5	2.5
Share premium account	243.5	237.4
Revaluation reserve	81.2	80.2
Profit and loss account	993.2	1,009.1
Related undertakings reserves	69.9	40.7
Shareholders' funds	1,509.8	1,488.8
Minority shareholders' interests	220.9	207.2
	1,730.7	1,696.0

countries' accounting in Europe and that listed companies disclose more detailed information than do unlisted ones. It also notes that, strikingly enough, Italy, Spain, and the E.F.T.A. countries surveyed disclose more information in certain instances than companies from the other countries.[11] In summary, the results of the survey indicate

---

[11]"FEE European Survey of Published Accounts 1991," press release; copy provided by Fédération des Experts Comptables European.

EXHIBIT 3–3 (continued)

BOC Group
Income Statement
Years Ended September 30, 1993 and 1994

	£ Million			
	Before Restructuring Costs	Exceptional Restructuring Costs	1994 Total	1993
Turnover				
Continuing operations	3,462.3		3,462.3	3,235.5
Acquisitions	20.8		20.8	—
Turnover, including share of related undertakings	3,488.1		3,483.1	3,235.5
Less related undertakings' turnover	190.8		190.8	168.0
Turnover	3,292.3		3,292.3	3,067.5
Cost of sales	(1,852.3)	(30.2)	(1,882.5)	(1,687.7)
Gross profit	1,440.0	(30.2)	1,409.8	1,379.8
Net operating expenses	(1,004.6)	(54.8)	(1,059.4)	(959.0)
Operating profit				
Continuing operations	432.7	(85.0)	347.7	420.8
Acquisitions	2.7	—	2.7	—
Operating profit	435.4	(85.0)	350.4	420.8
Exceptional losses on disposal of businesses			(16.6)	—
Profit on ordinary activities before interest			333.8	420.8
Interest (net)			(80.7)	(83.2)
Profit on ordinary activities before tax			253.1	337.6
Tax on profit on ordinary activities			(121.7)	(115.4)
Profit on ordinary activities after tax			131.4	222.2
Minority interests			(17.8)	(18.3)
Profit for the financial year			113.6	203.9
Dividends			(110.6)	(110.1)
Surplus for the financial year			3.0	93.8
Earnings per share, per 25p				
Ordinary share, net basis, undiluted				
On published earnings			23.82p	42.97p
Exceptional items			20.05p	—
Before exceptional items			43.87p	42.97p

that a high level of basic harmonization has been achieved. Yet critics argue that the directive allows too much latitude on important issues such as leases, pensions, taxation, and currency transactions, and they are calling for further reform. EU officials are undoubtedly hoping that the Union's recent affiliation with the IASC will enable them to effectively address any remaining accounting issues without having to endure the arduous negotiations and lengthy delays that issuing a new directive would entail.

The Seventh Directive

Purpose

The **Seventh Directive** (a summary of its contents is presented in Appendix 3B), adopted by the European Commission and Board of Ministers in 1983 after eight years of sometimes heated debate, establishes basic rules for preparing consolidated statements in EU nations. To comply with the directive, member states were required to enact legislation by the end of 1987 that would take effect no later than 1990. Hence, EU parent companies falling under the provisions of the Seventh Directive were to begin (if they were not already doing so) preparing consolidated statements for fiscal years beginning in 1990 and thereafter.

Until the formulation of the Seventh Directive, many EU countries had few if any regulations requiring consolidated accounts or governing their preparation; others had devised sophisticated guidelines. Because of this wide variation, the process of negotiation and compromise leading up to the directive's adoption involved a number of difficult issues, such as which forms of business should be covered by its provisions, whether entities should be defined by legal control or economic integration, and how the technical process of consolidation should be handled. In the end, the directive's mandatory provisions, which were intended to provide a minimum level of disclosure and comparability, generally followed the Anglo-American approach with its emphasis on legal control.

Who Must Consolidate?

As a matter of political necessity, the Seventh Directive allows member states considerable latitude in deciding who must prepare consolidated statements. Each state decides whether the directive should apply to all groups that include a limited liability company as a member or only to groups whose parent firm is a limited liability company. In addition, member states may exempt financial holding companies from consolidation requirements if the company to be exempted can show that it has not influenced the management decisions of its subsidiaries for the past year and has not influenced the appointment of any directors or management personnel for the past five years. Finally, member states may also exempt firms that meet the criteria for a medium-sized company stated in the Fourth Directive, unless any of the companies to be consolidated is listed on a securities exchange in an EU nation. A transitional clause, effective only for 10 years pursuant to 1990, expands the size limits for a medium-sized firm (for this purpose only) to a maximum amount of up to 2.5 times the criteria expressed in ECUs (see the section covering Fourth Directive), thus, a maximum amount of 20 million ECU ($24.4 million) for the balance sheet total asset amount, maximum sales of 40 million ECU ($48.8 million), and an average of 500 employees.

Intermediate-size parent companies (i.e., heads of a subgroup) that are at least 90 percent owned by another EU company need not prepare consolidated financial statements if minority shareholders do not request them and their parent company prepares consolidated statements. Member nations may also grant exemptions to subgroups owned by non-EU enterprises if these non-EU parents provide consolidated statements prepared and audited in a manner consistent with the provisions of the Seventh Directive. This last exemption avoids placing an undue burden (i.e., two different sets of consolidated statements) on groups headquartered in such countries as the United States or Canada.

Scope of Consolidation

In general, parent companies must consolidate all domestic and foreign subsidiaries. (This represents a significant departure for German groups, which had previously been required to consolidate only domestic subsidiaries.) Certain exceptions may apply, as in the case of subsidiaries held for resale, those whose activities are so different from other members that their inclusion would not give a true and fair view of the group, or those whose results are immaterial relative to the consolidated group.

Definition of Control

A parent is deemed to have *control* if one of the following applies:

- It owns or controls the majority of the voting rights in another undertaking (including those voting rights held by a subsidiary or a nominee).
- It is a shareholder or member in another undertaking and has the right to appoint or remove a majority of the members of its administrative, management, or supervisory body.
- It is a member or shareholder in another undertaking and exercises control over it by virtue of a contract.
- It is a member or shareholder in another undertaking and exercises control by virtue of an agreement with other shareholders (this provision being at the discretion of each member state).

In addition, member states may require consolidation if a parent holds a "participating interest" in another firm and either exercises a dominant influence over the affiliate or shares a common management with it. A "participating interest" is a long-term shareholding exceeding a statutory percentage set by each nation: 10 percent in France and Belgium and 20 percent in Denmark, the Netherlands, and Great Britain. This option is a concession to those countries—primarily Germany and France—that have tended to emphasize *de facto* rather than *de jure* control in their consolidation requirements.

Member states may also require horizontal groups to consolidate if they share a common management or a majority of directors even if they are not linked by share ownership. One example of this arrangement is Unilever, which is an association of a British company with a Dutch company, both of which have the same board of directors.

Methods of Consolidation

Consolidated statements, like those prepared for individual companies, must include (at least) a balance sheet, an income statement, and explanatory footnotes, and they must present a true and fair view of the group's activities and financial position. As in the case of the Fourth Directive, if any provision of the Seventh Directive conflicts with a true and fair view, preparers should depart from it, disclosing the divergence and the reason for it in a note. The format of group statements must be chosen from those described in the Fourth Directive and must remain consistent from year to year. Likewise, the method of consolidation must remain consistent from year to year.

If group members have been using different valuation methods in their own statements, the differences must be adjusted so that all assets and liabilities are valued consistently in the group statements. This requirement covers not only those cases in which a subsidiary has employed replacement cost or some other method of restating fixed assets, but also methods of inventory costing. Thus, *all* inventory in the group must be restated according to the same method, be it LIFO, FIFO, weighted average, or some other method.

Accounts must be consolidated line by line, with all intercompany balances and transactions eliminated. *Goodwill,* defined as the excess of acquisition price over the fair market value of the assets purchased, must be identified separately in the consolidated accounts and amortized. Member states are allowed to choose the precise manner of the amortization: they may require companies to amortize goodwill over a period of five years or less (a procedure recommended, but not required, by the directive), they may allow companies to write it off over some longer period not to exceed its useful economic life, or they may allow companies to write it off immediately against reserves without charging it against income (a method commonly used in the United Kingdom but currently being reconsidered there). Negative goodwill, or a bargain purchase, is not discussed in detail in the directive and remains open to a variety of treatments. (A primer on consolidated accounting practices is presented in Appendix 6A).

Equity Method

Under Article 33 of the Seventh Directive, companies must use the equity method to account for the profits and losses of unconsolidated affiliates in which they hold a participating interest (defined by national statute previously noted) and over which they exercise significant influence.[12] The parent company must calculate goodwill arising from the purchase of its share of the affiliate (i.e., the excess of the cost of the

---

[12]A company is considered to exercise a "significant influence" over another company when it has 20 percent or more of the shareholders' voting rights in that company.

investment over the fair market value of the investor's share of the affiliate's net assets) and amortize it according to the guidelines mentioned. The parent company also records its share of the affiliate's income or loss in the investment account, as well as any dividends received. (The mechanics of the equity method are considered in detail in Chapter 6.)

Proportionate Consolidation Method

The Seventh Directive provides jointly owned entities the option of using the proportionate consolidation method in lieu of the equity method. Under proportionate consolidation, an investor consolidates with its financial statements its proportionate share of each asset, liability, revenue, and expense item of an investee. (This topic is discussed in detail in Appendix 6A.)

Audit Requirements

Until the adoption of the Seventh Directive, consolidated financial statements, if and when they were prepared, were not always audited in many European countries. The directive, however, requires all consolidated statements to be examined by an auditor, authorized by the applicable national laws. (The Eighth Directive requires auditors to be professionally competent and independent.) The auditor of the parent company's consolidated accounts need not audit each subsidiary (which in many cases will be located in another country); instead, they may rely on the opinion of the subsidiary's auditor as to the information passed on to the parent corporation. As is the case with auditors of single-company financial statements, the auditors of group statements must ascertain that the annual report and the analyses contained therein are consistent with the consolidated financial statements.

Status

The provisions of the Seventh Directive provide a radical departure for many EU member states, some of whom (e.g., Greece, Luxembourg, Italy, Portugal) have had few or no requirements for companies to publish consolidated statements. Others that do require consolidated statements (e.g., Belgium, France, Germany) have had to include many more companies under the new laws and to change significantly the methods by which consolidation is carried out. The F.E.E. survey (referred to earlier in this chapter) found that companies in some countries tend to use internationally harmonized accounting policies in consolidated accounts rather than in the single accounts. This relates to those countries where the application of Article 29 of the Seventh Directive makes possible the use of different accounting policies in the consolidated accounts than those used in the single accounts. This plays an important role in those countries, such as Germany and France, where the single accounts are used for tax purposes, and, thus, the accounting methods and valuation methods are strongly influenced by legal and taxation requirements. Progress toward the improvement of the comparability of financial information may therefore lie with the consolidated accounts rather than the single accounts. Although it is too early to tell precisely what the outcome of these reforms will be, the large disparity between the consolidation requirements and practices that existed before the adoption of the Seventh Directive ensures that it will represent a major improvement in reporting standards.

As even this brief review of the Fourth and Seventh Directives should indicate, the guidance they offer tends to be broad, leaving some issues untouched and others open to a variety of interpretations and practices. While the two directives represent a major step forward in the effort to harmonize accounting methods and reporting practices within the EU, comparability remains something of an unreached ideal. Union members have begun to wonder whether directives, which involve years of negotiation, are too cumbersome to achieve the desired ends. Thus, as the EU enters the next phase of integration, it may have to face the broader question of an appropriate regulatory mechanism.

Securities Exchanges

In their quest to facilitate the free movement of capital among member nations, EU leaders have spent considerable time thinking about the form and regulation of securities exchanges. The Union contains 35 stock exchanges, in contrast to eight in the United States, with those in London, Milan, Frankfurt, Madrid, Amsterdam, and Paris seeking center stage.[13] Each exchange is locally regulated, with its own legal and cultural peculiarities. In the face of this diversity, the challenge facing Union officials is twofold. The first and most immediate is to harmonize local regulations so that companies may cross-list their shares and investors can expect reasonable protection of their interests on any exchange in any member nation. This in itself will be a major task requiring the achievement of consensus on such issues as listing requirements and insider trading.[14] The second and more strategic concern is to consider what system of securities exchanges will ultimately best serve European interests: a group of regional markets with similar regulations but still basically competing with each other for listings and investors, or a fully integrated electronic network that would list all major European securities and provide investors with the greatest possible variety and liquidity.

---

[13]"Too Many Trading Places," *The Economist,* June 19, 1993, pp. 21–23. The three newest members of the EU have one securities exchange each.

[14]As previously noted, member states must accept financial statements prepared in accordance with the standards of other member states. Thus, the listing requirement issues pertain to such things as number of shareholders, discussed later in this chapter.

Listing Requirements

To accomplish the first job—harmonization of exchange regulations—the EU has issued a series of directives covering listing requirements. The first directive, issued in 1980, established minimum standards for a local exchange to qualify as an EU stock exchange. Although exchanges in member countries could not offer more lenient listing rules, they were free to exceed the basic requirements. This arrangement made compliance for more developed and sophisticated exchanges, notably the **International Stock Exchange** (I.S.E.) in London, a fairly simple matter involving only minor adjustments.

The next logical step is for an EU plan in which a company meeting the listing requirements of one EU–approved local exchange will be entitled to a listing on all of them. This so-called Eurolist plan is moving ahead.[15] Thus, it would be possible for an Italian company listed only in Milan to gain a listing on the I.S.E. in London. In effect, the higher standards of the I.S.E. are being struck down as impediments to trade. As noted earlier, goods (in this case, securities) that meet the minimum standards of the EU cannot be prevented from entering particular countries because of higher national standards. Although the European Commission has taken the position that mutual recognition does not imply that regulators must lower standards for domestic as well as foreign applicants, many in London expect that the I.S.E., as a matter of political necessity, will have to lower its listing standards for all new applicants, domestic as well as foreign. I.S.E. officials are particularly concerned that the more lenient requirements will reduce their ability to maintain secondary and tertiary securities markets since applicants would find it almost as easy to gain an official listing on the primary exchange.

Insider Trading

Another EU directive, whose deadline for implementation was mid-1992, requires member nations to enact laws banning insider trading on securities exchanges. Few issues have so effectively illustrated the cultural obstacles to EU integration as this one, highlighting as it does not only differences in practice but also divergences in values. Specifically, the debate surrounding insider trading has exposed widely varying attitudes toward secrecy (i.e., the ownership of information), commercial fairness, and insider status.

At one extreme is Great Britain, with its toughly worded insider trading laws and its cultural ideals of fair play and sportsmanship. (This is not to assert that the cultural ideals are scrupulously observed but that they exist.) In Great Britain, perhaps because so many corporations are owned by thousands of shareholders, the general public (investors and potential investors) is deemed to have certain informational rights that insider trading laws are intended to safeguard. At the other extreme is Italy, where the family is the more dominant social unit, economically as well as

---

[15]*The Economist,* June 19, 1993.

culturally. Large financial empires are still controlled by families. This fact and the belief that group membership (i.e., insider status) should confer advantages have led Italians, until very recently, to accept insider trading as a legitimate activity. Between these two extremes fall most of the other EU nations, including Germany, which until now has depended on voluntary agreements rather than legal sanctions to prevent insider trading.

As a consequence of these disparate attitudes and widely varying business practices, the EU directive has rather vaguely defined *insider information* as any knowledge that would have a significant effect on share prices if it were to become publicly known. Thus, trading on inside information will be a crime not only for those who work for or advise the company in question but also for those who learn it second-hand, such as journalists. The main questions at this point concern whether the law will be enforceable, given its broad definition of insiders and inside information, and whether in any case it will be vigorously enforced by national authorities. The effect of a law, like the effect of other norms, depends to a large extent on how it is handled within its sociocultural setting.

A European Equity Market?

In 1989, the Federation of Stock Exchanges in the European Community (F.S.E.E.C.), a collection of high-level stock exchange officials from around the European Union, began to discuss the possibility of creating a single, electronically linked equity market for Europe's most prominent companies. As presently envisioned, it would include not only the EU nations but also Switzerland, the fourth largest equity market in Europe. The result would be a massive league of securities exchanges, lightly regulated and more extensively used by professional traders than individual investors. Prices for the securities of hundreds of European multinationals could be quoted both in ECUs (the Union's basket currency) and each company's domestic currency.

The idea is being championed by the British, who believe that the I.S.E.'s own international electronic quotation system (called *SEAQ International*) provides a workable model. Their enthusiasm has been generally supported by the French, who nevertheless favor retaining some competition. But it is opposed by the Germans, who suspect that London wants to consolidate its position as the leading financial center of Europe with the Continental bourses playing subordinate roles. That particular course of events would leave Frankfurt, the German candidate for European financial dominance, at a distinct disadvantage. The Germans propose instead a scenario in which a number of regional exchanges continue to compete for business. Obviously, the emotionally charged issue of national prestige easily insinuates itself into these arguments, though national pride is usually couched in the language of reason. Whatever the merits and motivations of the respective sides, the idea of a pan-European securities market is alive and well and sure to contribute urgency to the cause of accounting harmonization.

Corporate Taxation

One of the thorniest issues still facing the European Union is that of corporate taxation. Proposals for tax harmonization, as is true of every EU measure, must balance respect for national sovereignty with the need for economic rationalization. For more than 20 years, EU negotiators have struggled to achieve a satisfactory compromise, but only recently has real progress begun to be evident.

The divergences in tax law facing EU negotiators fall into three categories: tax rates, tax bases, and tax systems. Tax rates are perhaps the most similar of the three: all member nations have a corporate tax rate between 25 and 40 percent, except Germany, whose rate is closer to 45 percent. The equation becomes more complex, however, because nations charge this rate against different tax bases, which they manipulate by granting such allowances as accelerated depreciation and investment credits. Finally, countries may employ a classical tax system, in which corporate profits are taxed in the hands of shareholders as well as in the hands of the corporation (e.g., the Netherlands and Luxembourg); an imputation system, in which profits are taxed once at the same rate regardless of whether they are retained in the business or distributed to shareholders (e.g., Great Britain); or a split-rate system, in which distributed profits are subject to a lower corporate tax rate than those retained in the business (e.g., Germany).

The case for tax law harmonization is usually cast in terms drawn from classical economics, stressing the efficiency of the markets and the need for investment decisions based on economic, not legal, criteria. Analysts have pointed out, for example, that variations in tax codes distort the competitive ability of corporations (specifically, their ability to achieve a given after-tax rate of return) and their decisions concerning the location of new investments. But it should also be remembered that variations in tax law are often responsible for major differences in financial reporting practices as well. Particularly in those nations in which financial reporting is linked to macroeconomic and tax policies—that is, most EU nations except Great Britain and the Netherlands—calculation of financial net income and the valuation of assets may be materially affected by tax considerations. Thus, harmonization of tax law has the potential to facilitate the harmonization of financial accounting standards. But whether this proves to be the case with EU deliberations remains to be seen.

Summary

Whatever difficulties and disagreements remain to be overcome, one message emerges consistently from EU member states: We've come too far to turn back now. Too much is at stake. An EU-sponsored study, The European Challenge 1992 (usually referred to as the *Cecchini Report*),[16] attempted to gauge the economic

---

[16]Paolo Cecchini, *The European Challenge, 1992: The Benefits of a Single Market* (Aldershot, England: Wildwood House Limited, 1988), summary of the *Cecchini Report*. The *Cecchini Report* (Brussels, Belgium: The Commission of the European Communities, 1988).

benefits of achieving the single market. Its authors estimated that, in the medium term, the aggregate gross domestic product of EU nations would grow approximately 4.5 percent per year (representing about $200 to $300 billion of economic benefits annually), that an additional 1.8 million jobs would be created in the European Union (representing a 1.5 percent reduction in unemployment), and that the consumer price index would fall 4.5 percent. Over the long term, the report estimates, aggregate gross domestic product could rise 7 percent, 5.7 million new jobs could be created, and prices could fall 6 percent. All of this is expected to result from the increased efficiencies of a single market.

Economic incentives of this magnitude simply cannot be ignored—neither by the EU officials who are working to make them real nor by outsiders watching the process happen. Everyone will be affected; there will be no casual bystanders. Regulators in nonmember countries—especially in Europe, but in other parts of the world as well— are already feeling the pressure to coordinate their requirements with those of the European Union. U.S. banks, it has been suggested, will be hard pressed to compete with larger European counterparts globally unless the patchwork of state and federal regulations that govern their domestic operations is reformed and brought into line with EU regulations. Governments and businesses that fail to respond to the challenges and opportunities presented by European unification may find themselves shouldered to the margins of the global marketplace.

Inevitably, the prospect of dealing with this new economic colossus has inspired some nervousness among nonmember states and multinational businesses headquartered in other countries. The most persistent fear is that the European Union will turn out to be a new trading bloc, an economic fortress that will close its markets to imports and use its power to subordinate old trading partners. Essentially, this thinking fuels fears that a unified Europe will damage the all-important transatlantic alliance that has provided an anchor for the Free World since 1945. European business leaders have discounted this scenario, pointing out that many EU members depend heavily on exports to overseas markets, especially the United States. (The United States and the European Union are each other's largest trading partner.) To ensure continued access to these markets, they will keep the European market open to imports. Although European nations will undoubtedly gain leverage in trade negotiations by presenting a united front, the door to Europe will by no means be nailed shut. The more likely scenario, then, is continued—probably increasing—international trade, with the benefits of the single market being diffused around the globe.

Most U.S. multinationals currently operating in Europe seem to be adopting an attitude of cautious optimism toward the European Union, regarding the fundamental changes underway as more of an opportunity than a threat. While new EU regulations may create unprecedented problems by redefining trade restrictions with regard to the rest of the world, many companies will use the emergence of a unified European market as the opportunity (or justification) to enter new markets and consolidate their European operations. Since Europe will no longer be a patchwork of conflicting regulations and trade barriers, U.S. companies will be freer to move plants and people to more efficient and profitable locations without losing access to established markets. In addition, previously restricted markets, especially in such areas as financial services, will be open for the first time. U.S. multinationals, like their European and Japanese counterparts, are increasing their investment in Europe to take advantage of these new possibilities.

Far from resulting in intercontinental isolation, then, European unity is likely to result in even stronger ties with the rest of the world, including Europe's old ally and trading partner, the United States. It is true that the United States will be less able to take the lead than formerly, a change that will require some adjustment in attitudes, and, as is ever the case in cross-cultural communication, forbearance. Likewise, in the development of workable international financial reporting standards, the United States will have to share more of the limelight with European standard setters. But the opportunities for reciprocal and mutually beneficial influence between the European Union and the United States will be—already are—unprecedented. What is made of these opportunities will, in large part, depend on a willingness to learn to speak a common financial language. Indeed,

> one of the most important strategic questions facing the EU in the area of harmonization of accounting [is]: should it concentrate on harmonization *within* the EU or should it also attach importance to harmonization between the EU and the rest of the world?[17]

With such a question framing the macro issue and because there are no additional EU financial reporting directives planned for the foreseeable future,

> there is still scope for confusion and still a need for care and expertise when making [intra-] European accounting comparison.[18]

Suggested Readings

Alexander, D. "A European True and Fair View?" *European Accounting Review* 1 (1993), pp. 59–80.

Cecchini, P. *The European Challenge, 1992: The Benefits of a Single Market.* Aldershot, England: Wildwood House Limited, 1988.

Choi, F. D. "Financial Disclosure and Entry to the European Capital Market." *Journal of Accounting Research,* Autumn 1973, pp. 159–75.

Diggle, G., and C. Nobes. "European Rule-Making in Accounting: The Seventh Directive as a Case Study." *Accounting and Business Research* 24, no. 96 (1994), pp. 319–33.

"The Economics of European Disintegration." *The Economist,* May 22, 1993, p. 56.

"The European Single Market." *Financial Times,* January 19, 1993, survey section.

---

[17]Thorell and Whittington, "The Harmonization of Accounting within the EU," p. 228.

[18]C. Nobes, "EC Group Accounting: Two Zillion Ways to Do It," *Accountancy,* December 1990, p. 85.

Gumbel, P. "Customs of the Countries." *The Wall Street Journal,* September 30, 1994, p. R10.

Hegarty, J. "Accounting Integration in Europe—Still on Track." *Journal of Accountancy,* May 1993, pp. 92–95.

Hopwood, A. G. "The Future of Accounting Harmonization in the Community." *European Accounting* (1991), pp. 12–21.

Nobes, C. "EC Group Accounting: Two Zillion Ways to Do It." *Accountancy,* December 1990, pp. 84–85.

———, and S. Zambon. "Piano, Piano: Italy Implements the Directives." *Accountancy,* July 1991, pp. 84–85.

"A Survey of the European Community." *The Economist,* July 11, 1992, pp. 1–30.

"Too Many Trading Places." *The Economist,* June 19, 1993, pp. 21–23.

Tully, S. "Europe 1992: More Unity Than You Think." *Fortune,* August 24, 1992, pp. 136–42.

Wilson, A. "Harmonisation: Is It Now or Never for Europe?" *Accountancy,* November 1994, p. 98.

APPENDIX 3A
A BRIEF SUMMARY OF THE EU'S FOURTH DIRECTIVE

- Article 1 states that the directive relates to public and private companies throughout the European Union, except that member states need not apply the provisions to banks, insurance companies, and other financial institutions.

- Article 2 defines the annual accounts to which it refers as the balance sheet, profit and loss account, and notes.

- Articles 3–7 contain general provisions about the consistency and detail of the formats for financial statements; there is a specified order of items, some items cannot be omitted, and corresponding figures for the previous year must be shown.

- Articles 8–10 detail two formats for balance sheets: horizontal or vertical; one or both may be allowed by member states.

- Articles 11 and 12 allow member states to permit small companies to publish considerably abridged balance sheets.

- Articles 13 and 14 concern details of disclosure, particularly contingent liabilities, which were shown in the United Kingdom but not in some other countries.

- Articles 15–21 concern the definition and disclosure of assets and liabilities.

- Articles 22–26 specify four formats for profit and loss accounts that member states may choose.

- Article 27 allows member states' medium-sized companies to avoid disclosure of the items making up gross profit.

- Articles 28–30 contain definitions relating to the profit and loss accounts.

- Articles 31 and 32 provide general rules of valuation.

- Article 33 is a lengthy explanation of the directive's stance toward accounting for inflation or for specific price changes.
- Articles 34–42 relate to detailed valuation and disclosure requirements for various balance sheet items.
- Articles 43–46 concern the disclosures that are obligatory in the annual report, including the notes to the accounts. Small companies may be partially exempted.
- Articles 47–51 relate to the audit and publication of accounts. Member states may exempt "small companies" from publishing profit and loss statements; "medium-sized companies" can abridge their balance sheets and notes.
- Articles 52–62 deal with the implementation of the directive and with transitional problems, particularly those relating to consolidation, which await the seventh directive.

   Source: Student report.

APPENDIX 3B
A BRIEF SUMMARY OF THE EU'S SEVENTH DIRECTIVE

- Articles 1–4 require undertakings (which member states may restrict to mean limited companies) to draw up consolidated accounts that include subsidiaries and subsubsidiaries, and so on, irrespective of their location.
- Article 5 allows member states to exempt financial holding companies that neither manage their subsidiaries nor take part in board appointments.
- Article 6 allows member states to exempt medium-sized and small groups, using the criteria of the Fourth Directive and assuming that no listed company is included.
- Articles 7–11 exempt a company from the requirement to consolidate its own subsidiaries if it is itself a wholly owned subsidiary of an EU company.
- Article 12 allows member states to require consolidation when companies are managed by the same persons.
- Articles 13–15 allow various subsidiaries to be excluded from the consolidation if they are immaterial.
- Article 16 requires that consolidated accounts shall be clear and shall give a true and fair view.
- Article 17 requires the Fourth Directive's formats to be used, suitably amended.
- Article 18 requires consolidation to be 100 percent.
- Article 19 requires there to be a once-and-for-all calculation of goodwill based on fair values at the date of first consolidation or at the date of purchase.
- Article 20 allows merger accounting when any cash payment represents less than 10 percent of the nominal value of shares issued.
- Articles 21–23 require minority interest to be shown separately, and 100 percent of income of consolidated companies to be included.

- Articles 24–28 require consistency, elimination of intragroup items, use of the parent's year-end as the group's year-end, and disclosure of information to enable meaningful temporal comparisons when the composition of the group has changed.
- Article 29 requires the valuation rules of the Fourth Directive to be used and uniform rules to be used for the consolidation of all subsidiaries.
- Articles 30 and 31 require positive goodwill on consolidation to be depreciated or to be immediately written off against reserves and that negative goodwill only to be taken to profit if it is realized or when it was due to the expectation of future costs or losses.
- Article 32 allows member states to require or permit proportional consolidation for joint ventures.
- Article 33 requires associated companies to be recorded as a single item, initially valued at cost or at the proportion of net assets.
- Articles 34–36 specify the number of disclosures relating to group companies and consolidation methods.
- Articles 37 and 38 deal with publication and audit.
- Articles 39–51 deal with transitional and enabling provisions.

    Source: Student report.

ISSUES AND INFORMATION FOR FURTHER INQUIRY

I.3.1 Institutional Plumbing

In a *Financial Times* article titled "Stock Markets Slow Down on Road to Convergence" (January 4, 1993, p. 29), author Peter Martin asserts that "the institutional plumbing necessary for an integrated European stock market was lacking [due in part to the belief that] substantial national differences in accounting and tax practice remained." Given such a situation, he reports that European securities markets cope by "using valuation measures that minimize the differences between national accounting and tax policies."

Required:
Through inquiries to investment banking houses and/or library research, report on some of the valuation measures used to "minimize the differences."

I.3.2 Outdated EU Directives?

In a *Financial Times* article titled "Why Figures Do Not Add Up" (January 20, 1995, p. 42), Andrew Jack notes that "there is a feeling of frustration that the European [accounting] directives are now becoming extremely outdated."

Required:
Do you agree with Jack? Why or why not?

EXERCISES

E.3.1 Mutual Recognition

K. Van Hulle, a member of the EU Commission, recently posed the following question:

> What are the prerequisities (i.e., shared objectives, not political concerns) necessary for a mutual recognition of accounting practices between the EU and the US?[1]

Required:
Prepare a short essay presenting your answer to this question.

E.3.2 Consolidated Reporting: The Seventh Directive

In November 1993, Akzo NV of the Netherlands agreed to acquire Sweden's struggling Nobel Industrier AB. The merger would create one of Europe's largest specialty chemical concerns. Akzo agreed to pay 16.7 billion Swedish kronor (or approximately $2.06 billion) in cash and stock and to assume an estimated 8 billion kronor in debt for Nobel's core chemical operations. To help finance the purchase, Akzo also disclosed a proposed 1.3 billion Dutch guilder (about $684.1 million) stock offering.

In response to the news release, the price of Akzo shares tumbled 6 percent, from 197.2 to 185.1 guilders, and Nobel's share price rose 23 percent. Akzo's bid price of 29.6 kronor was 35 percent above Nobel's most recent closing share price.

Required:
1. Under the Seventh Directive, how should Akzo account for its pending merger with Nobel Industrier? Prepare the entry for Akzo's investment in Nobel.
2. Summarize the financial statement effects on Akzo of a merger with Nobel; be sure to consider the related equity offering.
3. What inferences would you draw from the market price movements in the shares of Akzo and Nobel? Why did Akzo offer a 35 percent premium above Nobel's recent share price?

---

[1]K. Van Hulle, "Harmonization of Accounting Standards in the EU: Is It the Beginning or Is It the End?" *European Accounting Review* 2 (1993), p. 396.

E.3.3 Countertrade

Countertrade refers to a group of international trade arrangements based on the concept of "barter," or the exchange of equivalent goods and services. Consider, for example, the following EU countertrade transactions:

- An EU beverage company in the United Kingdom exchanged £10 million of soft drink syrup for an equivalent value of Stolichnaya vodka from Russia. The exchange of goods was prompted by Russian government restrictions on the use of "hard" currency to finance that country's international trade; that is, Russian purchases of EU goods and services could be paid for only with rubles, not with pounds, marks, or guilders.[1]

- An EU manufacturer in Germany agreed to provide steel pipe to a Russian energy company to build a natural gas pipeline from Russia to Germany. Compensation for the steel pipe would be made in the form of significantly discounted natural gas transported by the pipeline.

- An EU aircraft manufacturer provided £225 million in airplanes and parts to a Yugoslavian air transport company in exchange for £175 million in currency and £50 million in Yugoslavian goods (e.g., foods, wines) to be imported over the next five years.

Required:

1. What are the risks and rewards of countertrade?
2. How would you account for each of these transactions?

E.3.4 Mergers, Acquisitions, and State-Controlled Companies

In mid-1993, AB Volvo of Sweden and Renault of France announced plans to merge and create the world's sixth largest automobile manufacturer. The merger was hailed as a milestone for consolidation of Europe's fragmented auto industry, as well as an important display of the kind of economic cooperation that was expected to emerge in the wake of the formation of the European Union. By early December 1993, however, AB Volvo announced that the merger had been canceled. According to a Volvo spokesperson, Volvo's big institutional shareholders challenged the merger agreement because of "suspicion about Renault as a state-owned French company." The large investor groups felt that any kind of control by a state or local government was simply incompatible with the need to make business decisions based on economic or industrial logic.

---

[1]A currency is considered *hard* if it is expected to appreciate relative to major trading currencies; conversely, a currency is considered *soft* if it is expected to depreciate relative to major trading currencies or if its exchange rate is artificially maintained (e.g., by government decree).

Following the merger cancellation announcement, Volvo's benchmark Class B shares surged to 458 kronor, up more than 3 percent. Shortly thereafter, Volvo's president and chairman of 22 years, Pehr Gyllenhammar, resigned.

Required:

1. Unlike those in the United States, many EU companies are controlled and supported, in whole or in part, by national, state, or local governments. What risks does this control and support pose for foreign investors?

2. How might the risks identified in question 1 be reflected in a company's financial statements?

E.3.5 EU Accounting Practices

An article in *The Financial Times* ("Report Calls for Accounting Harmonization," February 16, 1993) expressed concern over the lack of conformity in accepted accounting practices among EU member-nations. Specifically, the writers expressed concern about the following divergent practices:

- Upward revaluation of assets on the balance sheet (e.g., in Italy and the United Kingdom).
- Excess or special depreciation on the income statement to reduce taxable earnings (e.g., in Germany and Switzerland).
- Capitalization of certain intangible assets, such as interest costs and R&D costs, on the balance sheet (e.g., in France and Italy).
- Goodwill written off to reserves and negative goodwill credited to retained earnings (e.g., Italy and Netherlands).
- Creation of discretionary provisions and reserves to help smooth reported earnings (e.g., Germany).

Required:

Consider the preceding list of accounting policies and try to identify parallel practices under U.S. GAAP. Consider also how you might overcome such differences in accounting practice to generate comparative financial data in companies from different countries.

E.3.6 Harmonization of EU Equity Markets

As the European Union matures, an expectation held by many is that the securities markets of EU-member nations will converge to form, in essence, a pan-EU marketplace. Preliminary evidence indicates that this is already happening to some extent:

in 1991, the equity markets of the member nations all moved in the same direction, with only one market (Italy) diverging in performance by more than 10 percent from the average. Currently, such administrative issues as common listing requirements and regulations for brokers-dealers are being determined. But more fundamental problems remain. For example, in 1992, currency devaluations by Britain, Italy, Sweden, Spain, Portugal, Finland, and Norway led to significant share price changes in those countries, causing the average performance of five of the eight largest securities markets to diverge from average by more than 10 percent. Thus, currency stability is seen as one factor preventing full EU market harmonization.

Required:

Prepare a list of the factors that you believe are important in establishing a common EU equity market. Be prepared to discuss how those factors affect equity markets.

E.3.7 Comparing Auditors' Reports

One element of published financial data that financial statement users have come to take for granted is the independent auditors' report. Although an audit examination by a licensed independent professional is not required in every country nor by all companies (i.e., the requirement is often linked to the issuance of publicly held securities or to firm size—small companies that can least afford the cost of an audit examination are often permitted to waive the requirement), sophisticated financial statement users have come to expect the issuance of an unqualified or "clean" auditors' opinion.

The presence of an independent audit report provides assurances to the statement user that the reasonableness and reliability of the financial information, as well as the integrity of the system that generated the information, have been evaluated. Standards of integrity and reasonableness, however, are very much culturally dependent, and, thus, it is quite likely to find the presence of cultural diversity reflected in both the form and content of the auditors' report.

Required:

Following are the auditors' report of five international companies. Compare and contrast their form and content, and when possible, identify the presence of cultural diversity.

1. L'Oreal

L'Oréal is a leading manufacturer of cosmetics, consumer and pharmaceutical products, and perfumes, headquartered in Clichy, France. The company's 1990 auditor's report contained the following:

REPORT OF THE AUDITORS ON THE CONSOLIDATED FINANCIAL STATEMENTS

Ladies, Gentlemen,

In accordance with the terms of our appointment at the General Meeting of June 20, 1986, we hereby submit our report on:

- the examination of the consolidated financial statements of L'Oréal S.A., as attached to this report,
- the review of the Report of the Board of Directors on the management of the Group,

for the year ended December 31, 1990.

1—Opinion on the consolidated financial statements

We have examined the consolidated financial statements and performed all the tests and procedures that we considered necessary in the circumstances, in accordance with professional standards.

In our opinion, the consolidated financial statements have been properly prepared and give a true and fair view of the assets, financial position and results of the consolidated Group.

2—Specific tests and information

We have also performed the specific verifications required by law, in accordance with professional standards.

In our opinion, the information given in the Report of the Board of Directors on the management of the Group is correct and agrees with the information contained in the consolidated financial statements.

Paris, April 16, 1991

The Statutory Auditors

Pierre FEUILLET   Albert PAVIE

2. Procordia

Procordia is a Swedish conglomerate with significant operations in beverages, consumer products, food products, health care, and various service industries. The company's 1991 auditors' report contained the following:

Auditors' Report

We have examined the Annual Report, the consolidated financial statements, the accounting records and the administration by the Board of Directors and the President for 1991. Our examination was made in accordance with generally accepted auditing standards.

Parent Company

The Annual Report has been prepared in accordance with the Swedish Companies Act. We recommend to the Annual Meeting

- that the income statement and the balance sheet be adopted;
- that the unappropriated profits be dealt with in accordance with the proposal in the report of the Board of Directors; and
- that the members of the Board of Directors and the President be discharged from liability for the 1991 fiscal year.

The Procordia Group

The Consolidated financial statements have been prepared in accordance with the Swedish Companies Act.
We recommend that the consolidated income statement and the consolidated balance sheet be adopted.

Stockholm March 24, 1992

Hans Karlsson	Göran Tidström
Authorized Public Accountant	Authorized Public Accountant

---

3. Rolls-Royce Plc

Rolls-Royce Plc is a U.K. company principally involved in the manufacture and sale of automobiles and industrial engines. The company's 1991 auditors' report contained the following:

Report of the auditors

To the members of Rolls-Royce Plc

We have audited the accounts on pages 4 to 19 in accordance with Auditing Standards.

In our opinion the accounts give a true and fair view of the state of affairs of the Company and the Group at December 31, 1991 and of the profit and source and application of funds to the Group for the year then ended and have been properly prepared in accordance with the Companies Act 1985.

KPMG Peat Marwick
Charted Accountants   London
Registered Auditor   March 4, 1992

---

4. Shiseido Company, Ltd.

Shiseido is one of Japan's leading manufacturers of cosmetics, beauty and skincare products, fitness and fashion products, health food, and pharmaceuticals. The company's 1990 auditors' report contained the following:

To The Board of Directors of
Shiseido Company, Limited

We have examined the Consolidated Balance Sheets of Shiseido Company, Limited and its subsidiaries at March 31, 1990 and 1989 and the related Consolidated Statements of Income, Shareholders' Equity, and Cash Flows for the year ended March 31, 1990, for the four-month period ended March 31, 1989 and for the year ended November 30, 1988, expressed in yen. Our examinations were made in accordance with generally accepted accounting principles in Japan, and accordingly, included such tests of the accounting records and such other auditing procedures as we considered necessary in the circumstances.

In our opinion, the consolidated financial statements referred to above, stated in yen, present fairly the consolidated financial position of Shiseido Company, Limited and its subsidiaries at March 31, 1990 and 1989 and the consolidated results of their operations and the changes in shareholders' equity and cash flows on a consolidated basis for the year ended March 31, 1990, for the four-month period ended March 31, 1989, and for the year ended November 30, 1988, in conformity with generally accepted accounting principles in Japan applied on a consistent basis, except for the change, with which we concur, in the method of accounting for write-off of unsold merchandise returned, as described in Note 2 (10) of the Notes to the Consolidated Financial Statements.

The amounts expressed in U.S. dollars have been translated on the basis set out in Note 3 of the Notes to the Consolidated Financial Statements.

Tokyo, Japan
June 28, 1990

Chuo Shinko Audit Corporation
Independent Certified Public Accountants

5. Statoil

Statoil (or Den norske stats oljeselskap a.s.) is the largest oil and gas producer in the North Sea, headquartered in Stavanger, Norway. The company's 1991 auditors' report contained the following:

AUDITORS' REPORT FOR 1991

To the shareholder of Den norske stats oljeselskap a.s.:

We have audited the annual report and accounts of Den norske stats ojeselskap a.s. for 1991. The annual report and accounts, which comprise the Board of Directors' report, the profit and loss account, balance sheet, cash flow statement and notes to the accounts, are presented by the company's Board of Directors and its President.

Our responsibility is to examine the company's annual report and accounts, it accounting records and other related matters.

We have conducted our audit in accordance with relevant laws, regulations and Norwegian generally accepted auditing standards. We have performed those audit procedures which we considered necessary to confirm that the annual report and accounts are free of material misstatement. In accordance with Norwegian generally accepted auditing standards, we have examined selected parts of the evidence supporting the accounts and assessed the accounting principles applied, the estimates made by management, and the content and presentation of the annual report and accounts. To the extent required by Norwegian generally accepted auditing standards, we have reviewed the company's internal control and the management of its financial affairs.

The Board of Directors' proposal for the appropriation of net profit is in accordance with the requirements of the Norwegian Companies Act.

In our opinion, the annual report and accounts, which show a net profit for the year of NOK 2,782 million for the parent company and a consolidated net profit for the year of NOK 2,741 million, have been prepared in accordance with the requirements of the Norwegian Companies Act and with Norwegian generally accepted accounting principles.

STAVANGER, 27 FEBRUARY 1992
ERNST & YOUNG & CO. AS

ERNST ALSAKER
STATE AUTHORISED PUBLIC ACCOUNTANT (NORWAY)

CASES

CASE 3.1
HARMONIZATION OF ACCOUNTING AND REPORTING POLICIES

A Comparison of Three EU Companies

An important goal of the International Accounting Standards Committee (IASC) is the harmonization of accounting and reporting practices throughout the world. It has long been thought that the formation of the European Union (EU) would significantly assist the IASCs harmonization efforts by bringing conformity to the accepted accounting practices of a significant set of countries that have historically maintained rather diverse accounting procedures. Indeed, mandatory implementation of the Fourth and Seventh Directives, involving the form and content of financial statements and standards regarding the preparation of consolidated accounts, respectively, *should* have brought the accounting and reporting practices of EU companies into greater conformity.

Whether (or not) this increased conformity has indeed been achieved and whether the attained conformity is sufficiently adequate are matters of opinion and speculation. Many securities market analysts complain even now that the generally accepted accounting practices of the EU-member nations are still far too disparate to make the reported accounting results of EU companies "transparent." Some of the divergences in practice noted by analysts include the following:

- Some EU countries permit the upward revaluation of assets; others do not. This causes distortions not only in asset values but also in earnings (due to differences in depreciation charges) for essentially equivalent companies.
- Some EU companies require conformity between book and tax income; others do not. This causes earnings to be depressed in some countries and inflated in others.
- Asset capitalization policies are not consistent between EU-member countries. This causes dramatic differentials in reported earnings and assets.
- Some EU countries permit, and even encourage, the use of discretionary provisions and reserves to help "smooth" reported earnings; others do not.

Required:

Compare and contrast the reported accounting policies of the three EU companies whose summary of significant accounting policies follow (each represents a different EU-member nation). Identify those policies that you believe cause the greatest differentials in reported earnings and assets. Sequence the three companies according to their relative (i.e., standardized) profitability.

AB Electrolux
Summary of Significant Accounting Policies
Selected Excerpts

(a) Principles of consolidation

The consolidated financial statements include the accounts of the Company and all of its majority owned subsidiary companies. Significant intercompany transactions have been eliminated.

As from 1992, investments in those associated companies in which the Group controls 20–50% of the voting rights have been accounted for using the equity method. The cumulative effect adjustment for 1991 and prior years was not material and was recorded directly to stockholders' equity. Years prior to 1992 were not restated for this accounting change. Other investments are carried at cost.

(b) Goodwill

Goodwill arising in connection with acquired businesses is amortized over a ten-year period except for the 1986 acquisitions of White Consolidated Industries, Inc. (''White'') and Industrie Zanussi S.p.A (''Zanussi'') and the 1989 acquisition of American Yard Products, for which forty-year periods are used.

(e) Research and development costs

Research and development costs are expensed as incurred.

(f) Inventories

Inventories are stated at the lower of cost, determined on a first-in, first-out (FIFO) basis, or market. Cost includes material, labor and manufacturing overhead.

(g) Deferred taxes and special reserves

Deferred taxes have been provided on special reserves; by foreign subsidiaries in certain countries; in connection with the acquisition of companies and for other significant temporary differences.

As from the first quarter in 1993, the United States subsidiaries have adopted FAS 109. The initial effect of the adoption has been recorded against equity in conformity with Swedish accounting principles.

(h) Property, plant and equipment

Property, plant and equipment are stated at cost except for revaluations of certain land and buildings, which under certain circumstances are allowed under accounting principles generally accepted in Sweden.

Property, plant and equipment are depreciated for financial reporting purposes (''depreciation according to plan'') on the straight line method over their respective estimated useful lives. The principal lives are: land improvements—20 years, buildings—25–50 years, machinery and equipment—3–14 years, rental equipment—3–5 years, and production tools and computer hardware—3 years. Land is not depreciated, while computer software is expensed as incurred.

British Biotech Plc
Summary of Significant Accounting Policies
Selected Excerpts

The consolidated financial statements have been prepared in accordance with applicable Accounting Standards in the UK. The significant accounting policies adopted in arriving at the consolidated financial statements are as follows:

(a) Accounting convention

The consolidated financial statements have been prepared under the historical cost convention.

(b) Basis of preparation

The consolidated financial statements are based on the financial statements of British Biotech Plc and its principal subsidiary undertakings, British Biotech Pharmaceuticals Limited and British Biotech Inc. (together ''the Group'').

On March 17, 1989 the Group legal structure was reorganized with British Biotech Plc becoming the Group holding company following the issue to British Biotech Pharmaceuticals Limited shareholders of one fully paid Ordinary share in British Biotech Plc for each fully paid Ordinary share held in British Biotech Pharmaceuticals Limited and one fully paid Preferred Ordinary share in British Biotech Plc for each fully paid Preferred Ordinary share held in British Biotech Pharmaceuticals Limited. As there has been no change in ownership or control and the exchange of shares involved companies under common control, the pooling of interest method has been applied in preparing these consolidated financial statements. The period from inception, as shown in the consolidated financial statements, commences at the date of incorporation, February 4, 1986, of British Biotech Pharmaceuticals Limited which predates the incorporation of British Biotech Plc on October 13, 1988. British Biotech Plc did not trade during the period from October 13, 1988 to March 16, 1989.

(e) Research and development

Expenditure on research and development is written off in the period in which it is incurred.

(f) Intangible assets

Patents and trade marks in respect of potential products in research and development are not capitalized.

(g) Purchased goodwill

Purchased goodwill is written off against reserves (accumulated deficit) as it arises.

(h) Property, plant and equipment

Freehold land and assets in the course of construction are not depreciated. Depreciation is calculated to write off the cost less residual value of other property, plant and equipment in equal annual installments over their estimated useful lives as follows:

Freehold buildings	-Fifty years
Buildings—internal works	-Five to fifty years
Leasehold buildings	-Period of lease
Plant and machinery	-Four or five years
Fixtures and fittings	-Five years

(j) Inventories

Inventories are stated at the lower of cost and net realisable value. Cost is determined on a first in, first out basis and comprises the cost of direct materials and labour plus attributable overheads.

(k) Deferred taxation

Deferred taxation is recognised to the extent that it is probable that a tax liability will become payable or an asset will be recoverable in the foreseeable future.

Peugeot S.A.
Summary of Significant Accounting Policies
Selected Excerpts

(a) Consolidation

The financial statements of significant subsidiaries in which Peugeot S.A. holds directly or indirectly a majority interest are consolidated, with the exception of banking and finance subsidiaries, which are included in the consolidated financial statements on an equity basis.

Companies in which Peugeot S.A. holds directly or indirectly an interest of 20 to 50% and exercises significant influence over operating and financial policies, as well as banks and finance subsidiaries, are included in the consolidated financial statements on an equity basis (note 4).

Certain companies meeting the above criteria have not been consolidated as considered not significant in relation to the consolidated financial statements (note 5).

According to the US "Financial Accounting Standard Board" (FASB) statement no. 94 banks and finance companies in which Peugeot S.A. holds directly or indirectly a majority interest should have been consolidated in the financial statements. The Group provides the presentation required by the

FASB in note 23 and continues as in prior years to carry banks and finance subsidiaries on the equity basis in its main financial statements. There is no difference between the financial statements presented in note 23 and the main financial statements in respect of consolidated net income and stockholders' equity.

Investments in nonconsolidated companies are valued at cost except in the case of permanent decline in the value of the investment.

All significant intercompany transactions are eliminated.

(b) Property

Land, plant and equipment are carried at cost, including capitalized interest expense. The French legal revaluations and foreign revaluations are not reflected in the consolidated financial statements.

Maintenance and repair costs are expensed as incurred, except for those which enhance the productivity or prolong the useful life of an asset.

Depreciation is calculated on a straight-line basis over the estimated useful lives of the respective assets as follows:

	Useful lives, in numbers of years
Buildings	16 to 20
Material and equipment	6.66 to 16
Data processing equipment	3 to 4
Transport and handling equipment	4 to 7
Furniture and fixtures	10
Land improvements	25

(c) Intangible assets

Goodwill, representing the excess of purchase price over the fair value of net tangible assets at the date of acquisition of businesses purchased, is amortized on a straight-line basis over a period not exceeding 20 years. Other intangible assets consisting principally of patents and trademarks are amortized on a straight-line basis over the estimated periods benefitted, not in excess of 20 years. Intangible assets are included in the balance sheet in "other assets."

(d) Inventories

Finished goods and work-in-progress are valued at the lower of cost and replacement value (for goods purchased from third parties) or present manufacturing cost (for goods manufactured by the group), not in excess of net realizable value. Cost is determined by the First-In, First-Out (FIFO) method.

(h) Research and development costs

All research and development costs are expensed as incurred. These costs amounted to FF 5,531 million in 1993 and FF 5,245 million in 1992.

(i) Deferred income taxes

Deferred income taxes are provided in respect of differences between reported and taxable income recognised in different time periods (note 18).

No provision has been made for withholding and other taxes on undistributed earnings of subsidiaries and affiliated companies which are considered to be permanently invested.

CASE 3.2
THE SEVENTH DIRECTIVE

Equity Method versus Proportional Consolidation

The Seventh Directive, adopted in 1983, established the basic principles and standards for EU companies to follow in preparing consolidated financial statements. The key aspects of the directive are

- A parent company must consolidate all subsidiaries unless the subsidiary is held for resale, the subsidiary's results are immaterial relative to the group, or the subsidiary's principal line of business is sufficiently different from that of the group that consolidation would result in misleading data.
- Consolidation is to be effected by purchase accounting unless certain circumstances exist (e.g., a 90 percent or more shareholding is achieved by means of an exchange of shares), in which case pooling of interests accounting may be used *if* permitted by the EU-member nation.
- Associated companies are to be accounted for using the equity method, and joint ventures may be accounted for using either the equity method or proportional consolidation.

This case concerns the later issue.

Background   On January 1, 1995, Global Enterprises Ltd. (GE) formed a joint venture with European Investments SpA. Each of the venture partners was to hold a 50 percent shareholding in the new company, which was to be called Global J.V., Inc., and consequently each contributed the equivalent of 500,000 British pounds (about $780,000 U.S.) in exchange for its one-half ownership interest.

Immediately *prior* to the formation of the joint venture, Global Enterprises' balance sheet appeared as follows:

	£000s
Assets	9,000
Liabilities	1,500
Shareholders' equity	7,500
	9,000

GE financed its investment in Global J.V. by a EuroBond offering of £500,000.

During the joint venture's first year of operations, business was not very robust, as expected, and costs exceeded revenues for a net loss of £100,000. At year-end 1995, Global J.V.'s auditors approved the balance sheet as "true and fair."

Global J.V., Inc.
Balance Sheet
As of 31 December, 1995
[£000s]

Assets	1,300
Liabilities	400
Shareholders' equity	
Share capital	1,000
Profit & loss	(100)
	1,300

As usual, 1995 was a very successful year for GE, producing a net profit (excluding the joint venture's results) of £600,000.

Required:

    (a) Prepare GE's year-end earnings statement and balance sheet, including the results of Global J.V. assuming the use of (a) the equity method and (b) proportionate consolidation. (Ignore tax considerations.)

    (b) Which method do you prefer, and why?

PART II

Financial Statement Analysis

The objective of any financial statement analysis is ultimately to make an informed decision—to invest or divest, to lend or call a loan, to expand or to contract. The information necessary to make an informed decision may be self-generated or obtained from second- or third-party sources. In either case, much, if not most, of the needed information will be provided by a process known as **financial statement analysis.**

In this section, the fundamentals of financial statement analysis are introduced. The limitations and constraints of this process are considered, as well as the considerable problem of translating the results of foreign operations into a domestic currency. The objective of this section is to provide the reader with a foundation in financial statement analysis *before* considering the eccentricities of financial data found in the financial disclosures of companies operating in specific foreign countries.

CHAPTER 4

FINANCIAL STATEMENT ANALYSIS: AN OVERVIEW

[T]here is much to learn from the financial ratios of a business enterprise.[1]

Financial statement analysis is the process of reviewing and interpreting financial information for the purpose of appraising the financial health and operating performance of a company. Many individuals associate financial statement analysis exclusively with an activity commonly known as **ratio analysis,** or the process of analyzing ratios formed from two or more financial statement numbers (e.g., the return on sales is the ratio of net income to net sales). This book adopts a broader perspective, however, in which financial statement analysis is seen to include not only the development and interpretation of ratios using historical accounting data but also the preparation of pro forma financial data and the critical evaluation of the accounting measurement rules used in the presentation of the financial data being analyzed. This broader perspective on financial statement analysis is necessary for two reasons.

First, it is widely recognized that almost all financial decisions—e.g., to merge or acquire, to expand operations, to invest, or to lend—are based largely on *expectations* about the future. Thus, when buying shares of stock in a company, for example, it is frequently said that "an investor pays for future, not past earnings." Hence, the price that an informed investor should be willing to pay for an interest in a company will depend substantially on his or her projections of the future state of the firm: its earnings, cash flow, liquidity, and so on. One important source of information to aid in the development of such expectations is the recent *historical* performance of a company, particularly when combined with informed assessments about industry-specific and general economic trends. Thus, the value of historical financial statements can be seen to derive from their contribution in helping analysts and managers predict the future on the basis of the recent past.

---

[1]J. E. Kristy, "Striking the Right Balance and Proportion," *Business Credit,* February 1993, p. 20.

109

Second, one of the principal conclusions reached in the first section of this book was that harmonization of accounting and reporting practices throughout the world is unlikely to occur in the near future. As a consequence, financial statement users will continue to face the difficult analytical problem of interpreting financial data from different countries prepared using accounting concepts and measurement approaches reflective of those unique business, cultural, and legal environments. Even if international harmonization of accounting principles was attainable in the foreseeable future, there would undoubtedly still exist a diversity of practice in applying generally accepted accounting principles and, thus, the need to be able to analyze, interpret, and perhaps restate the diverse set of practices to a common benchmark. Thus, before an informed analysis of financial data—either domestic or international—can occur, the analyst or manager must first understand the specific accounting concepts and measurement rules in use. A second thing the analyst or manager must understand is the country context in which the financial data are grounded. For example, is the cultural context such that secretive approaches to accounting disclosure and conservative judgment are the norm? Do local tax laws, as in the case of Germany and Japan, drive the principal financial reporting practices? An understanding of these unique country-specific considerations will facilitate the user's interpretation of reported financial data.

To summarize, in this book *financial statement analysis* is seen to include the following:

- Preparation and interpretation of ratios and other summary measures of financial performance using data from accounting reports and other sources.
- Development of financial forecasts, primarily in the form of pro forma financial statements.
- Understanding the country-specific context in which the financial data are prepared.
- Critical evaluation of accounting methods used in the presentation of the financial data being analyzed. The objective of this aspect of financial statement analysis is to make the fullest use of accounting data in a given set of circumstances.

Uses of Financial Statement Analysis

The uses of financial statements are many and varied. Senior corporate executives and boards of directors analyze internal financial statements to assess the performance of operating divisions and their managers. Money lenders such as banks, insurance companies, pension funds, and others analyze statements to assess the ability of potential borrowers to repay principal and interest. Merger and acquisition specialists analyze financial statements to determine the desirability of acquiring a given takeover target and the purchase price that should be paid. Brokerage house analysts review financial statements to arrive at buy, sell, or hold recommendations for their clients. For these analysts, and others, the contents of a company's financial statements are often the key input in arriving at their financial decisions.

Not all elements of a company's financial statements, however, are relevant to the decisions of the varied financial statement users. Thus, the credit review manager whose job it is to review the creditworthiness of applicants for working capital loans is likely to pay particular attention to an applicant's recent and projected cash-generating ability, whereas a long-term credit assessment is likely to focus on a company's potential for profitability and its capital structure. Just which elements of the financial statements will be most informative depends on the goals and objectives of the financial statement user.

The common link to virtually all reasons for financial statement analysis, however, is that analysts form assessments of (1) the expected future returns from courses of action (e.g., to invest, divest, or do nothing) and (2) the degree of risk that some return other than the expected one from a course of action will occur. A business decision, at its most basic level, often reduces to the question of whether expected returns are worth the attendant risks, and financial statement analysis is one important way to assess these dimensions of a business decision.

Financial Health and the Basic Financial Statements

The Content of a Financial Report

Although the format, style of presentation, and terminology may differ dramatically from one country to the next, almost all countries require companies with publicly traded securities to issue two basic financial statements: the **balance sheet** and the **income statement.** Many countries also require that additional statements be presented, principally a **statement of changes in financial position,** although this statement may take a variety of formats. In the United States, for example, it takes the form of a **statement of cash flows,** whereas in Korea it takes the form of a **statement of funds flow.**

The analysis of foreign-based companies is often impeded by a diverse set of factors, one of which has historically been the lack of disclosure of a statement of cash flows. Other differences include those related to language, financial disclosure standards for information to supplement the basic financial statements, and accounting methods. Frequently, however, these differences are mitigated when a foreign-based company desires access to the capital markets of another country. Foreign issuers are usually required to prepare and submit various accounting and legal documents that comply with the securities laws of that country, and this is the case in the United States.

Since the United States is one of the two largest capital markets in the world (the other is Japan), it is an obvious candidate for companies needing or desiring foreign investment. The U.S. capital markets, however, are the most strictly regulated markets in the world; and consequently, foreign companies seeking access to U.S.

investors often find compliance with U.S. disclosure regulations a considerable burden, as well as quite costly.[2]

Public offerings by foreign companies in the United States are regulated by the U.S. Securities and Exchange Commission (SEC), and the reporting requirements for foreign issuers are essentially the same for domestic companies. In reality, however, the SEC frequently grants accommodations to foreign issuers, for example by waiving requirements such as the disclosure of salaries and shareholdings of individual officers and major shareholders. Initial public offerings by non-U.S. companies are registered with the SEC on Form F-1, whereas secondary public offerings are registered via Forms F-2 or F-3. Non-U.S. companies whose securities are publicly held must file periodic financial reports with the SEC, although these statements need not be prepared according to U.S. GAAP so long as they contain a reconciliation of significant variations in net income and shareholders' equity from U.S. GAAP. U.S. domestic companies are required to make an annual filing via Form 10-K; non-U.S. companies make such filings via Form 20-F. When non-U.S. companies sell their securities in the United States through means of a **private placement,** the disclosure requirements of the SEC do not apply; thus, no reconciliation with U.S. GAAP is required.

To make a well-informed financial analysis, we believe that analysts need, at a minimum, the following basic data: a balance sheet, an income statement, *and* a statement of cash flows, all for at least three consecutive years, preferably longer. Thus, when a statement of cash flows is not presented, the analyst must have the requisite skills (or computer software) to develop such a statement—a topic that is the focus of Appendix 4A to this chapter.

The Balance Sheet

A major determinant of financial health is financial position—the nature and extent of a company's resources, as well as the claims by nonowners on those resources—and, this information can be found principally in a company's balance sheet. The balance sheet is similar to a photograph of the financial health of a company in that the statement describes the assets and equities of a company *as of* a particular point in time. By comparing a sequence of consecutive balance sheets, it is possible to assess the growth (or decline) in a company's financial position.

Exhibit 4–1 contains consecutive (or ''comparative'') financial statements for Mitsui & Company, Ltd., a prominent Japanese industrial company whose principal lines of business include chemical products, food stuffs, machinery, petroleum, and steel products manufacturing. Mitsui principally operates in Asia, Canada, Central and South America, Europe, the Middle East, and the United States through its 250

---

[2]Foreign stock traded publicly in the United States is usually done through trades of **American depositary receipts** (ADRs) or **stock depositary receipts** (SDRs). ADRs and SDRs do not represent actual shareholdings in a foreign company but are securities *backed* by actual shareholdings wherein the actual shares are held in trust for the investor by a bank or other recognized trustee. These beneficial ownership shares are issued to avoid such problems as the collection of dividends denominated in a foreign currency and to facilitate rapid ownership transfer.

EXHIBIT 4–1

Mitsui & Company, Ltd.
Comparative Balance Sheets
As of March 31
(in billions of yen)

	1992	*1991*	*1990*	*1989*	*1988*
Assets					
Cash and short-term investments	2,117	2,984	3,092	1,242	692
Accounts receivable	2,730	3,056	2,894	2,548	2,255
Inventories	484	428	496	385	318
Other current assets	462	578	594	274	200
Total current assets	5,793	7,046	7,076	4,449	3,465
Fixed assets					
Fixed assets	630	749	531	480	416
Depreciation and amortization	(214)	(230)	(175)	(164)	(146)
Net fixed assets	416	519	356	316	270
Investments and advances—equity	284	278	230	126	153
Investments and advances—other	894	954	893	616	429
Other assets	1,120	1,040	1,061	822	785
Total assets	8,507	9,837	9,616	6,329	5,102
Liabilities					
Long-term debt due in one year	528	462	215	215	182
Short-term borrowings	2,606	3,145	3,446	1,995	1,384
Short-term borrowings—total	3,134	3,607	3,661	2,210	1,566
Accounts payble/creditors—trade	1,936	2,238	2,116	1,865	1,652
Current liabilities—other					
Accrued expenses & deferred income	87	112	84	60	51
Income taxes payable	29	24	23	24	25
Current liabilities—sundry	462	664	646	140	125
Total other current liabilities	578	800	753	224	201
Total current liabilities	5,648	6,645	6,530	4,299	3,419
Deferred income taxes	12	20	18	–0–	–0–
Long-term debt	2,127	2,480	2,399	1,607	1,362
Minority interest	31	16	14	14	13
Provision for pensions	67	56	50	28	27
Liabilities—total	7,885	9,217	9,011	5,948	4,821
Shareholders' Equity					
Common stock capital	177	176	172	87	65
Capital surplus/share premium reserve	276	275	270	186	145
Retained earnings	278	262	232	204	170
Cumulative translation adjustment	(110)	(93)	(69)	(94)	(99)
Shareholders' equity—total	622	620	605	381	281
Total liabilities and shareholders' equity	8,507	9,837	9,616	6,329	5,102

EXHIBIT 4–1 (continued)

Mitsui & Company, Ltd.
Comparative Income Statements
Years Ended March 31
(in billions of yen)

	1992	1991	1990	1989	1988
Sales/turnover (net)	17,818	20,833	19,507	16,764	15,779
Operating revenues—other	16	14	12	11	11
Net revenues—total	17,834	20,847	19,519	16,776	15,790
Operating Expense					
Cost of goods sold	17,182	20,218	18,957	16,278	15,373
Selling, general and administrative	459	427	387	341	281
Operating expense—other	17	12	9	10	15
Operating expense—total	17,658	20,657	19,353	16,629	15,669
Depreciation and amortization	51	47	37	28	37
Operating income	125	143	130	119	84
Interest and related expense	391	470	312	207	185
Nonoperating income (expense)					
Interest and dividend income	337	413	272	171	146
Nonoperating income (expense)—other	9	(4)	(15)	6	19
Nonoperating income (expense)—total	346	409	257	177	164
Income (loss) before income taxes and appropriations	81	83	75	89	63
Income taxes					
Current	67	45	26	46	35
Deferred	(10)	5	19	6	4
Other	–0–	–0–	–0–	–0–	–0–
Income taxes—total	57	50	45	53	39
Net items					
Equity in earnings—after tax	3	9	6	4	(1)
Preacquisition profits	–0–	–0–	–0–	–0–	–0–
Net items—other	–0–	–0–	–0–	–0–	–0–
Net items—total	3	9	6	4	(1)
Net income	27	41	36	40	23

EXHIBIT 4–1 (continued)

Mitsui & Company, Ltd.
Comparative Statements of Cash Flows
For Years Ended March 31
(in billions of yen)

	1992	*1991*	*1990*	*1989*
Operating Activities				
Income before extraordinary items	27	41	36	40
Depreciation and amortization	51	47	37	28
Deferred taxes	(9)	3	22	12
Sale of fixed assets and sale of investments	(21)	(44)	(29)	(12)
Funds from operations—other	35	120	48	16
Accounts receivable/debtors—dec. (inc.)	350	(223)	(403)	(250)
Inventories/stocks—dec. (inc.)	(61)	59	(89)	(24)
Accounts payable/creditors and accrued liabilities—inc. (dec.)	(379)	224	224	217
Income taxes—accrued—inc. (dec.)	–0–	–0–	–0–	–0–
Assets and liabilities—other (net change)	(127)	(14)	171	(23)
Operating activities—net cash flow	(134)	213	18	4
Investing Activities				
Investments—increase	(194)	(548)	(485)	(338)
Investments—decrease	276	297	129	130
Short-term investments	128	27	(977)	–0–
Capital expenditures	(154)	(139)	(73)	(84)
Sale of fixed assets—tangible	12	37	21	19
Investing activities—net cash flow	69	(325)	(1,385)	(272)
Financing Activities				
Equity stock—reduction	–0–	–0–	–0–	–0–
Equity stock—addition	1	4	123	33
Cash dividends	(11)	(11)	(8)	(6)
Long-term debt—issuance	573	719	1,160	555
Long-term debt—reduction	(692)	(297)	(466)	(345)
Current debt—change	(522)	(262)	1,382	535
Financing activities—other	–0–	–0–	–0–	19
Financing activities—net cash flow	(651)	154	2,191	791
Exchange rate effect	(17)	(97)	13	(10)
Cash and cash equivalents—inc. (dec.)	(733)	(55)	837	512

subsidiaries and associated companies outside Japan. With operations in cement, chemicals, commerce, construction, energy, engineering, finance and insurance, food, machinery, mining, paper, plastics, real estate, steel, and transportation, few, if any, companies, can claim to be as diversified as Mitsui.

One way to begin an analysis of the balance sheet of such a company is the same as we might approach a picture in a museum. Standing at a distance, we see the broadest features: total assets, total liabilities, and shareholders' equity.

- Mitsui's total assets measured in accordance with Japanese GAAP were ¥ 8,507 billion as of March 31, 1992. Using the current dollar exchange rate at that date, this would be approximately $64 billion. By this rough measurement, which ignores differences between U.S. and Japanese GAAP, it would place Mitsui eighth among the nonfinancial companies comprising the Fortune 500 at that date. Also, over the last five years, total assets have grown about 67 percent. Japanese inflation over the same five-year period was about 70 percent. As you will see in Chapter 10, major differences exist between U.S. and Japanese reporting practices with respect to intercorporate investments, depreciation of fixed assets, and inventory measurement. Without additional information, it is difficult to establish whether our estimate of total assets is high or low in relation to the U.S. Fortune 500 firms to which we are comparing Mitsui.

- Total liabilities are well over 20 times more than shareholders' equity! In the United States, only financial services firms such as banks would carry such a large amount of liabilities relative to shareholders' equity. If these balance sheets were issued by a U.S. industrial firm, no doubt many analysts would judge that the firm was exposed to a very high level of *financial risk.* Mitsui's level of total liabilities is considered normal for a Japanese company, however, and relative to shareholders' equity it has decreased substantially in recent years. Chapter 10 also discloses that Japanese companies have traditionally relied on bank-related debt as their principal source of external financing, and, as a consequence, they appear to be substantially more leveraged than their U.S. counterparts.

A closer look at Mitsui's assets reveals that a substantial amount of the company's assets are classified as current, and the amount of other assets is two to three times higher than fixed assets. What could those other assets be? Most probably they represent intangible assets. Is it significant that Mitsui's fixed assets are less than one-tenth the reported amount of its current assets and less than one-half of its other assets? Definitely; information as to the relative mix of a company's assets reveals to the analyst the dominant line of business of the company. Mitsui's emphasis on trading, as opposed to manufacturing, is revealed by its relatively large investment in inventories and receivables versus its investment in capital assets.

As you can see, an analysis of the balance sheet at this broad level may raise more questions than are answerable without knowledge of the other basic financial statements, the notes accompanying the financial statements, and other data. That is not to say that our overview to this point would be valueless: an analyst would be getting some idea as to where to focus a search for more information and what types of accounts contain material balances.

The Income Statement

The income statement, or statement of earnings, summarizes the events and transactions that produce revenues for a company as a consequence of selling a product or providing a service, as well as the events and transactions that result in expenses for the company. Unlike the balance sheet, which reflects the financial health of a company as of a particular point in time, the income statement summarizes the recent *operating performance* of a company *for* a given period of time, usually a quarter or a year.

When analyzing the income statement, one of the key analytical activities involves the identification of (1) recurring and nonrecurring income or loss and (2) nonoperating items. As noted earlier, financial decisions should be predicated largely on expectations about the future: the ability to pay *future* dividends, the ability to deliver *future* innovative products, and the ability to repay *future* incremental interest and principal. Nonrecurring and nonoperating items usually provide few insights about a company's future operations and, thus usually have little information value for financial analysts.

An analysis of Mitsui's income statements could also begin by viewing them from a distance and then moving closer to see some of the detail:

- Net income increased substantially in the fiscal year ending March 31, 1989 (FY89). It remained steady for two years and dipped sharply in FY92.
- Net sales grew fairly steadily through FY91 but dropped about 13 percent in FY92. The decline in income, however, was much greater, about 35 percent.
- Cost of goods sold is by far the largest expense item. As a consequence, an important consideration is how, and in what proportion, the cost of goods sold varies with sales activities. Is a high level of fixed costs the reason for the disproportionate decrease in net income relative to net sales, or have prices for production inputs increased faster than Mitsui's sales prices?
- Interest and dividend income have grown at a faster rate than net income. Is this income derived from nonoperating assets or from interest-bearing trade receivables?

The Statement of Cash Flows

The statement of cash flows reveals how a company has obtained and utilized its most liquid assets: cash and cash equivalents.[3] The statement summarizes and categorizes the inflows and outflows of cash from various sources for a given period of time. Under

---

[3]**Cash equivalents** refer to short-term government securities that are readily converted to cash or have a very short maturity period.

both U.S. and IASC GAAP, the cash inflows and outflows are usually categorized into three areas of activity: cash flows from *operations* (CFFO), cash flows for *investing activities,* and cash flows from *financing activities.* In some countries, the presentation of a statement of cash flows is not a required financial statement disclosure. Nonetheless, a financial analysis of any company would be seriously deficient without a consideration of where cash came from and where it has gone. Thus, financial statement users must have the requisite skills to prepare such a statement when it has been omitted, is inadequate, or is not a required disclosure. In fact, Exhibit 4–1 presents comparative statements of cash flows for Mitsui for only four years because of formatting differences in FY88 and earlier years.

The analysis of a company's cash flows usually involves the identification of several key measures. At the broadest definitional level are the *net cash flows* for the period. This figure represents the increase (or decrease) in a company's overall cash position; it is a summation of the cash inflows and outflows from all sources.

- Mitsui's cash balance has varied considerably over the last four fiscal years. Where does Mitsui get its cash, and how is it used?

Although each of the subcomponents of cash flow is important, greatest emphasis is usually placed on the **cash flows from operations.** The CFFO is considered to be a highly significant indicator of a company's short-term financial health; it is essentially equivalent to a company's net income measured on a cash basis instead of an accrual basis.

- Relative to FY91, Mitsui's CFFO for the previous two years was approximately at a break-even level. Thus, an important question is what constitutes the Funds from Operations—Other in FY91?
- In FY92, the collection of cash on receivables was ¥350 billion higher than revenues for the year. This increase to CFFO was more than offset by the decrease in accounts payable of ¥379 billion. Both of these significant amounts are related to the decline in net sales for FY92.

Ideally, a company generates substantially all of its cash needs from operating activities, but this is seldom, if ever, the case. Usually, a company must borrow, generate new equity capital, and sometimes even liquidate revenue-producing assets to support its cash-consuming operations. An analyst needs to answer the following question: When are these other cash-generating activities appropriate? Do they create excess risk under the circumstances? Are they the result of poor management decisions in past periods?

- Mitsui's negative CFFO in FY92 was partially offset by positive net cash flow from investing activities. Investing activities consisted of payments for capital expenditures and a net liquidation of investments.
- In the previous three years, Mitsui's debt increased considerably to finance its capital expenditures and additions to investments. In FY92, significant amounts of cash were used to reduce both long-term and current debt.

- Since operations did not generate any cash in FY92, the debt reduction was entirely accomplished by drawing down cash balances that existed at the beginning of the year. If FY93 is another ''down'' year for Mitsui, will it be able to raise additional cash at reasonable interest rates?

When the CFFO is negative, a company is likely to be forced to borrow, generate new equity capital, or sell its revenue-producing assets to support its cash-consuming operations. Obviously, a prolonged period of negative CFFO can be disastrous for a company, often leading to bankruptcy. However, the CFFO must be analyzed carefully. A financially sound company undertaking a significant growth or expansion effort is very likely to experience a negative CFFO largely as a consequence of the significant cash investment in receivables and inventory that is necessary to support such expansionary efforts. Thus, of primary concern to analysts are those companies experiencing a negative CFFO in a nongrowth period or in ways that indicate that growth is not being managed properly.

A final key measure of cash flows is **discretionary cash flow** or **free cash flow**. Although not specifically defined in official accounting literature or expressly reported in financial statements, discretionary cash flow is generally viewed as that portion of a company's CFFO available to finance discretionary corporate activities (e.g., the acquisition of another company, the early retirement of debt or equity, or some form of capital asset expansion). Thus, a company's free cash flow is usually measured as its CFFO less any nondiscretionary cash disbursements or payments in the subsequent period (e.g., ''regular'' dividends, currently maturing debt payments, replacement of productive capacity, and the like). Free cash flow is important to analysts because it represents a source of cash for growth, and to lenders because it is a source of cash for principal and interest repayment relating to any new (incremental) debt agreements. Clearly, the greater a company's free cash flows, the greater will be the company's ability to undertake new opportunities when they arise.

It should be noted that the concept of free cash flows is futuristic in perspective (i.e., the current period CFFO less any required disbursements in the following period). As a consequence, analysts frequently treat a company's free cash flows as if they were a *permanent* stream, particularly if the time frame of analysis is relatively short-term (e.g., the next three to five years). Thus, as with the income statement, an important aspect of the analysis of cash flows involves the identification of the permanent and transitory cash flows. As always, permanent cash (or income) flows are valued more highly than transitory (nonrecurring) cash (or income) flows.

Methods of Financial Statement Analysis

Effective financial statement analysis involves obtaining information from financial statements. Unfortunately, being human, analysts usually reach a point of information overload: the point at which adding to current knowledge is counterproductive in terms of making the most efficient decision. Financial analysts can cope with complexity effectively by adding information and, thus complexity, slowly. Much of the art of financial statement analysis involves the development of methods for adding layers of complexity gradually and for judging when a sufficiently coherent picture of a company has emerged. To add more complexity beyond such a point is either unnecessary for the decision at hand, or is likely to do more to cloud one's impression than to sharpen it. The techniques described in this section and in the next chapter can be broadly viewed as ways of dealing with complexity.

Format Standardization

Anyone who has read even a few annual reports knows that apart from major categories, financial statements are not presented in a standardized format. Differences in presentation occur across companies within a given country, across years for a given company, as well as across countries (as we will see beginning in Chapter 8).

The financial statements of Mitsui in Exhibit 4–1 were placed in a standard format by a data services company and were presented in this book with minor modifications to aid in their readability. Beginning with Chapter 8, we will begin analyzing company data in its original country-specific format; however, at this stage, to control the level of data complexity encountered, as well as to illustrate how foreign financial data can be and are reformatted, we will focus on the *process* of financial analysis using the more familiar North American format for financial data. If we had wanted to present Mitsui's original financial statements and did not have a database service available, clear presentation would have required a compilation of as many as four different annual reports, all of which may have been prepared in a different format. An additional advantage of financial databases is that all other industrial companies in the database are presented in the same format, facilitating comparisons across companies as well as across time.

The principal disadvantage of standardized formatting is that some information may be lost through overaggregation of account balances or may lose its meaning through the use of standardized categories. For example, a more detailed presentation of the Other Assets category on Mitsui's balance sheets would be useful. The label Other Assets can mean many different things to different companies in different countries. An analyst may need at least to scan the original financial reports to verify that the standardized format of the database service is not too highly aggregated for the purpose of his or her analysis.

Restatement

Data complexity attributable to differing accounting methods arises because of a number of reasons:

- Countries have not uniformly adopted one set of generally accepted accounting standards.
- Accounting standards vary in the flexibility afforded preparers with respect to the choice of accounting methods to be used.

- The unit of measurement may differ across entities (e.g., the use of different currencies in different countries or adjusting for the effects of inflation on a single currency).

Sometimes, differences in accounting methods are fully attributable to differences in underlying cultural, legal, and/or economic circumstances, but in many cases, new information may be revealed by a restatement of the original reporting methods to a common benchmark.

Restatement of financial data is often a laborious and inexact process. It should, however, be considered by an analyst when:

- A sufficiently high probability exists that restatement will materially affect the results of the financial analysis and when the effort of restatement is apparently worth the cost (in terms of computer or personal time and effort).
- When the financial statements do not adequately reflect the economic substance of transactions or events.
- When different accounting methods have been used to report similar transactions or events.
- When sufficient information is available to accomplish an informative restatement.

Chapter 6 considers the issue of restatement in greater detail.

Trend and Cross-Sectional Analysis

One way to cut through the complexity of financial statements, related disclosures, and other available information is to think of the starting point as seeking answers to the following two broad questions:

1. What significant patterns and relationships exist in the financial statements?
2. What is observed that explains any patterns and relationships or that may cause the observed patterns or relations to change in the future?

(The answers to these two questions, are, of necessity, quite lengthy, and we will approach them sequentially. Readers desiring first to obtain a flavor of the answer to the second question may wish to skim the subsequent section, ''Behind the Ratios: Investigating Cause and Effect.'')

Trend analysis and **cross-sectional analysis** are methods by which to answer the first question. Trend analysis involves the identification of patterns within financial statements across time; cross-sectional analysis involves identification of relationships within the same time period. Informative cross-sectional relationships are usually sought across financial statements from firms within the same industry or by comparing one or more sets of financial statements with industry averages.

The level of analysis that is most comprehensive is that of the *consolidated entity.* This is because disclosures and financial statements tend to be most detailed at this level for public companies from all around the world. Depending upon the disclosure standards of a given country, however, an informative financial analysis could occur at any one of the following levels as well:

Business segment.

Geographic sales region.

Product line.

Interim reporting dates (e.g., by quarter) during the fiscal year.

Two popular analysis methods for investigating trend and cross-sectional relationships are common-size financial statements and financial statement ratios.

Common-Size Financial Statements.   In **common-size financial statements,** all amounts are expressed as a percentage of some base financial statement item. For example, a **common-size balance sheet** might express all asset (equity) account balances as a percentage of total assets (equities); a **common-size income statement** might express all revenue and expense account balances as a percentage of net revenues, gross revenues, or total assets. Trend analysis of common-size balance sheets permits the analyst to determine, for example, how the relative composition (or mix) of total assets or total equities is changing over time, whereas a trend analysis of common-size income statements reveals the changing relation of various expense accounts to the reported revenues of a company.

Exhibit 4–2 presents common-size balance sheets for Mitsui & Co., Ltd., for 1988 through 1992 and reveals that a significant shift in the composition of the company's assets took place: the level of cash and short-term investments increased from an aggregate 13.6 percent to 32.2 percent of total assets and then declined somewhat. From FY89 to FY90, the largest relative increase in this category occurred, and it was accompanied by a decline in accounts receivable. It appears that much of the growth in the company's total assets (i.e., an increase of ¥3,406 billion) occurred as growth in its liquid current assets (i.e., an increase of ¥1,425 billion). Noncurrent assets, on the other hand, remained relatively stable on a percentage basis, with no one category accounting for a major portion of the remainder of the change. Although some changes occurred in the composition of current liabilities, the relative mix of current and noncurrent liabilities and shareholders' equity was relatively stable. Trade credit declined somewhat while short-term borrowings increased, and total liabilities also declined slightly. Overall, the percentages suggest that Mitsui may have embarked on a strategy during 1990 to accumulate liquid resources. Just why that strategy may have been adopted is not directly ascertainable from the available financial data and thus points out one of the common frustrations of financial analysis: the data often raise more questions than they answer. Nonetheless, what is important to note is that our basic common-size analysis has identified a rather significant trend in the mix of Mitsui's assets. One possible explanation is that the company is about to embark on a significant expansion effort, either in the form of one or more corporate acquisitions or in the form of additional sales (i.e., increased market share) and has chosen to finance this expansion with its liquid assets. Another explanation is that the increased liquidity may indicate that the company is positioning itself for a significant stock buy-back or debt reduction.

EXHIBIT 4–2

Mitsui & Company, Ltd.
Common-size Comparative Balance Sheets
For Years Ended March 31

	1992	1991	1990	1989	1988
Assets					
Cash and short-term investments	24.9	30.3	32.2	19.6	13.6
Accounts receivable	32.1	31.1	30.1	40.3	44.2
Inventories	5.7	4.4	5.2	6.1	6.2
Other current assets	5.4	5.9	6.2	4.3	3.9
Total current assets	68.1	71.6	73.6	70.3	67.9
Fixed assets					
Fixed assets	7.4	7.6	5.5	7.6	8.1
Depreciation and amortization	0.0	0.0	0.0	0.0	0.0
Net fixed assets	4.9	5.3	3.7	5.0	5.3
Investments and advances—equity	3.3	2.8	2.4	2.0	3.0
Investments and advances—other	10.5	9.7	9.3	9.7	8.4
Other assets	13.2	10.6	11.0	13.0	15.4
Total assets	100.0	100.0	100.0	100.0	100.0
Liabilities					
Long-term debt due in one year	6.2	4.7	2.2	3.4	3.6
Short-term borrowings	30.6	32.0	35.8	31.5	27.1
Short-term borrowings—total	36.8	36.7	38.1	34.9	30.7
Accounts payable/creditors—trade	22.8	22.8	22.0	29.5	32.4
Current liabilities—other					
Accrued expenses & deferred income	1.0	1.1	0.9	1.0	1.0
Income taxes payable	0.3	0.2	0.2	0.4	0.5
Current liabilities—sundry	5.4	6.8	6.7	2.2	2.5
Total other current liabilities	6.8	8.1	7.8	3.5	3.9
Total current liabilities	66.4	67.6	67.9	67.9	67.0
Deferred income taxes	0.1	0.2	0.2	0.0	0.0
Long-term debt	25.0	25.2	25.0	25.4	26.7
Minority interest	0.4	0.2	0.1	0.2	0.3
Provision for pensions	0.8	0.6	0.5	0.4	0.5
Liabilities—total	92.7	93.7	93.7	94.0	94.5
Shareholders' Equity					
Common stock capital	2.1	1.8	1.8	1.4	1.3
Capital surplus/share premium reserve	3.2	2.8	2.8	2.9	2.9
Retained earnings	3.3	2.7	2.4	3.2	3.3
Cumulative translation adjustment	0.0	0.0	0.0	0.0	0.0
Shareholders' equity—total	7.3	6.3	6.3	6.0	5.5
Total liabilities and shareholders' equity	100.0	100.0	100.0	100.0	100.0

EXHIBIT 4–2 (continued)

Mitsui & Company, Ltd.
Common-size Comparative Income Statements
For Years Ended March 31

	1992	1991	1990	1989	1988
Sales/turnover (net)	99.9	99.9	99.9	99.9	99.9
Operating revenues—other	0.1	0.1	0.1	0.1	0.1
Net revenues—total	100.0	100.0	100.0	100.0	100.0
Operating expense					
Cost of goods sold	96.3	97.0	97.1	97.0	97.4
Selling, general and administrative	2.6	2.0	2.0	2.0	1.8
Operating expense—other	0.1	0.1	0.0	0.1	0.1
Operating expense—total	99.0	99.1	99.1	0.1	0.1
Depreciation and amortization	0.3	0.2	0.2	0.2	0.2
Operating income	0.7	0.7	0.7	0.7	0.5
Interest and related expense	2.2	2.3	1.6	1.2	1.2
Nonoperating income (expense)					
Interest and dividend income	1.9	2.0	1.4	1.0	0.9
Nonoperating income (expense)—other	0.0	0.0	−0.1	0.0	0.1
Nonoperating income (expense)—total	1.9	2.0	1.3	1.1	1.0
Income (loss) before income taxes and appropriations	0.5	0.4	0.4	0.5	0.4
Income taxes					
Current	0.4	0.2	0.1	0.3	0.2
Deferred	−0.1	0.0	0.1	0.0	0.0
Other	0.0	0.0	0.0	0.0	0.0
Income taxes—total	0.3	0.2	0.2	0.3	0.2
Net items					
Equity in earnings—aftertax	0.0	0.0	0.0	0.0	0.0
Preacquisition profits	0.0	0.0	0.0	0.0	0.0
Net items—other	0.0	0.0	0.0	0.0	0.0
Net items—total	0.0	0.0	0.0	0.0	0.0
Net income	0.2	0.2	0.2	0.2	0.1

Answers to these speculations may be available from company officials, press releases, or from the commentaries accompanying Mitsui's financial data.

In the preparation of the common-size income statements for Mitsui in Exhibit 4–2, all figures are presented as a percentage of net revenues. Throughout the five years ended March 31, 1992, Mitsui's net income was a fairly constant 0.2 percent of total sales (or "total trading transactions"), which is surprisingly low for a company of Mitsui's size and maturity. As will be seen in Chapter 10, the profitability of Japanese companies is systematically depressed relative to those of U.S. companies as a consequence of the institutional setting in Japan, namely, that reporting practices tend to be driven by existing tax regulations. Note also the consistently large relation (i.e., approximately 96 to 97 percent) between sales and cost of goods sold, a relation no doubt significantly influenced by the fact that in Japan only those expenses reported on a company's financial reports may be deducted for tax purposes. The relationships between net revenues and expense categories are remarkably stable throughout the five years. The only notable exceptions are parallel increases in interest expense and interest and dividend income. The amount of interest and related expense has almost doubled in its relationship to sales over the five years examined. If interest had remained a constant percentage of sales, the pre-tax profit margin would have been three times higher in 1992.

Common-size financial statements can help the analyst form impressions about the direction of a company's financial health or operating performance over time and the relative importance of any given account within a given period. The other principal use is to aid in predicting the future financial performance of a company. Most companies prepare projections or **pro forma financial statements** based on assumptions about the future for their own *internal* planning purposes, but very few companies issue those projected financial statements publicly.[4] Analysts, however, may prepare pro forma financial statements based on published history and carefully constructed assumptions about a company's future. For example, based on expected product demand, an analyst can formulate an estimate of a company's future sales under various selling price scenarios. From this estimate of revenues, a pro forma income statement can be prepared after identifying those expenses that vary as a function of sales level (e.g., cost of goods sold) and those that are relatively fixed (e.g., depreciation and certain overhead costs). Thus, with a reasonable estimate of revenues and knowledge of the relationship between the various expense categories and revenues that can be gained from common-size statements, a pro forma income statement can be prepared.

For example, based on Mitsui's financial statements in Exhibit 4–1 and the common-size statements in Exhibit 4–2, an analyst might feel safe in predicting that

---

[4]The one exception to this general rule in the United States involves the distribution of a prospectus in conjunction with a merger or an initial public offering. The acquiring (or offering) company often issues pro forma statements to reflect the current (or pending) period results as if the merger (public offering) had already transpired.

overall net income will remain a relatively constant percentage of net revenues if net revenues fluctuate in the same range as it has over the previous four years; however, such an analysis would be too superficial to warrant such a definitive statement. Given the importance of estimated revenues to pro forma income statements (i.e., almost all other numbers are derived from it), a more in-depth analysis is warranted. A consideration of expected inflation rates, population growth, and market demand for Mitsui's products would, at a minimum, also be necessary. The topic of pro forma statements will be revisited in greater detail in Chapter 5.

Ratio Analysis.   Ratio analysis is a powerful method for coping with the volume and complexity of data presented in most financial statements. Ratio analysis effectively summarizes multiple financial statement categories into one or a few relative indices of performance and financial position. Conversion of financial statement categories into relative measures is also important because it helps to control for differences in scale (the denominator of a ratio) across companies and/or across time.

The numerator of a financial ratio can usually be interpreted as the financial statement element being measured and the denominator as the scale, or units of measure. For example, consider a firm with $100 of cash and $1,000 of total assets. The ratio of cash to total assets is 0.1; consequently, it can be said that, as of one point in time, the amount of cash per dollar of total assets was 10 cents. If this ratio decreased over time, even while the total cash balance was increasing, one might investigate whether the firm's actual cash balance needs were changing disproportionately to the change in the size of the firm, or whether there was some other reason for the change in the value of the ratio of cash to total assets.

The **return on common equity** (ROCE) is an example of a ratio that summarizes a large amount of information in one number as well as controlling for scale. ROCE is often expressed as net income available to common shareholders for a given period divided by average total shareholders' equity for the same period. It is the amount of net income of a period per average dollar of total shareholders' equity invested during the period. A richer description of this ratio is that it is a summary indicator of the degree to which a company achieved the goal of maximization of common (or ordinary) shareholder wealth.

The preceding calculation of ROCE also illustrates the dilemma of how to combine numbers that represent "flows" over an interval of time (e.g., net income, revenues, expenses) with numbers that represent "stocks" at a particular point in time (e.g. assets, liabilities, owners' equity). When flows and stocks are combined to form a single ratio, the following conventions are adopted throughout this book:

- When flows and stocks are combined to form a single ratio, the *average* level of stocks for the relevant time period is used. This averaging process can usually be well approximated by the arithmetic mean of the beginning and ending value of stocks for the period. The principal benefit of this approach is to lessen any distortions in a ratio caused by a significant contraction or expansion of stocks during a given period.

- When data availability restricts calculation of arithmetic means, the level of stock as of the end of the relevant time period is used.

Numerous ratios have been developed to assist in the analysis of financial statements, and they typically fall into five principal categories:

Financial Health
1. Liquidity
2. Solvency

Operating Performance
3. Asset management
4. Profitability
5. Return to investors

For each of these categories, we have selected for discussion a representative set of ratios that professional analysts have found useful when analyzing a company. In Chapter 5, we introduce additional ratios as we explore the topic of ratio analysis in further detail.

Liquidity.   **Liquidity** refers to the ability of a company to satisfy its short-term obligations as they fall due; it is an assessment of the short-term **default risk** of a company.[5] These debt-exposure ratios typically associate the liquid resources of a company with its currently maturing obligations. In general, current obligations may be satisfied by drawing on existing current assets, from new asset flows provided by current operations, or by refinancing with other short-term or new long-term debt. Three such ratios follow:

$$\text{Current ratio} = \frac{\text{Current assets}}{\text{Current liabilities}}$$

$$\text{Quick ratio} = \frac{\text{Cash + Marketable securities + Accounts receivable}}{\text{Current liabilities}}$$

$$\text{CFFO to current liabilities ratio} = \frac{\text{Cash flow from operations}}{\text{Average current liabilities}}$$

These three ratios are examples of *coverage* ratios in that they indicate the ability of a particular set of current assets or cash flows to "cover" or satisfy a company's current liabilities. The **current ratio,** for example, indicates the extent to which the available current assets cover existing current liabilities; the **quick (or acid test) ratio** indicates the coverage of current liabilities by a company's highly liquid, or quick assets. The **CFFO to current liabilities,** on the other hand, examines the coverage provided by a company's operations, as measured by its CFFO.

   Historically, some rules of thumb have been used in the United States to judge the adequacy of these ratios (e.g., 2:1 for the current ratio and .5:1 for the quick ratio);

---

[5]*Default risk* refers to the ability of a company to satisfy its currently due and future obligations. Short-term default risk is usually referred to as the degree of *liquidity,* whereas long-term default risk is referred to as the degree of *solvency.*

however, these rules of thumb have no foundation in reality here or abroad, and it is far better for an analyst to use currently developed industry averages or a company's ratio for a prior period when making evaluative judgments.

The quick ratio is a more conservative measure of a company's short-term debt exposure. It refers to only the liability coverage provided by a company's **quick assets,** namely those highly liquid current assets such as cash and cash equivalents, short-term investments, and receivables. The current ratio, on the other hand, includes the coverage provided by inventories, prepaid expenses, and other current assets. A frequent concern of analysts is that these latter current assets may not be particularly liquid and possibly more susceptible to accounting measurement errors, and, thus, the current ratio may overstate a company's true liquidity. The quick ratio, however, reflects only coverage by a company's most liquid assets and, for this reason, may be preferred over the current ratio.[6] Analysts who prefer the current ratio also consider that liquidation of inventories generally results in cash inflows that exceed the book value of inventory.

The CFFO to current liabilities ratio relates a company's ability to generate cash from operations to its currently due obligations. This ratio focuses on a company's ability to repay current liabilities from operations rather than from existing current assets or additional financings.

To illustrate these liquidity measures, consider the Mitsui financial data presented in Exhibit 4–1. Mitsui's CFFO for 1989 and 1990 was ¥4,188 and ¥17,929 million, respectively:

	FY92	*FY91*	*FY90*	*FY89*	*FY88*
Current ratio	1.03	1.06	1.08	1.04	1.01
Quick ratio	0.86	0.91	0.92	0.88	0.86
CFFO to current liabilities	−0.02	0.03	0.00	0.00	N/A

These ratios reveal that, in 1992, for every yen of current liabilities, Mitsui had ¥1.03 of current assets and ¥0.86 of quick assets. The trend of these ratios has been declining in recent years, but whether they indicate an acceptable level of risk can only be judged by comparing them to industry averages for, say, the top quartile of comparable Japanese firms. Mitsui's CFFO is minuscule relative to its balance of current liabilities. Thus, short-term creditors must depend on the level of current resources plus any additional future financings to cover Mitsui's current liabilities because it is clear that the company's operations are providing insignificant amounts of cash relative to its current liabilities.

---

[6]Classified balance sheets, which clearly identify a company's current and noncurrent assets and liabilities, are not required of all companies in the United States or abroad. When nonclassified balance sheets are permitted, it is usually because a segmentation of assets (and liabilities) on a basis of liquidity (expected duration to maturity) is not meaningful. When this is the case, an analysis of liquidity, particularly using the current or quick ratio, is seldom performed.

Solvency. **Solvency** refers to a company's long-term debt repayment ability; it is a measure of the firm's long-term default risk. In general, a highly leveraged (or debt-laden) company is usually characterized by a lower level of solvency, whereas a less leveraged company is usually considered to be more solvent. In many Commonwealth countries, the concept of leverage is referred to as *gearing*. Solvency, or gearing, is often evaluated in two ways: (1) the amount of debt and (2) the ability of a company's operations to support its current level of debt.

The *amount* of debt carried by a company is usually assessed by two ratios, the **debt to equity ratio** and the **debt to total capitalization ratio:**

$$\text{Debt to equity ratio} = \frac{\text{Long-term debt}}{\text{Shareholders' equity}}$$

$$\text{Debt to total capitalization ratio} = \frac{\text{Long-term debt}}{\text{Long-term debt + Shareholders' equity}}$$

These ratios highlight the portion of a company's capital structure that is represented by its long-term borrowings. The ability of a company's operations to support its current level of debt servicing (i.e., interest plus principal payments) is indicated by a series of *coverage* ratios that typically include the **interest coverage ratio,** the **CFFO to interest charges ratio,** and the **CFFO to total liabilities ratio:**

$$\text{Interest coverage ratio} = \frac{\text{Net income before income taxes + Interest expense}}{\text{Interest expense}}$$

$$\text{CFFO to interest charges ratio} = \frac{\text{Cash flow from operations}}{\text{Interest expense}}$$

$$\text{CFFO to total liabilities ratio} = \frac{\text{Cash flow from operations}}{\text{Average total liabilities}}$$

In applying these ratio formulas to Mitsui's financial statements, at least two calculational issues have to be considered: the definition of long-term debt and how to approximate net income before taxes. *Long-term debt* generally refers to liabilities that are the result of a contract in which the amount and timing of future cash flows for both principal and interest are specified. Such a strict definition might exclude pension liabilities, for the amount and timing of future cash outflows to pensioners depends on future uncertainties such as employee turnover rates, mortality, and the future returns on plan assets. Actuarially determined estimates of much of the future uncertainties related to future pension costs tend to be very reliable, however, and it seems unreasonable to treat long-term debt issuances differently from pension liabilities.[7]

---

[7]Although *minority interest* and *deferred income taxes* will be described more fully in Chapter 6, neither is a legal liability that would be paid in the event of a firm's liquidation. The accounting concepts underlying these items also vary greatly across countries in ways that affect its comparability to long-term debt agreements. In the calculations of Mitsui's ratios, *long-term debt* is defined to include pension liabilities and to exclude minority interest and deferred income taxes.

With respect to calculating net income before taxes, Mitsui's income statement discloses the following items:

- Net income before taxes and equity in earnings of unconsolidated subsidiaries.
- Equity in earnings of unconsolidated subsidiaries net of taxes.
- Current and deferred components of income tax expense.

In the following ratio calculations, net income before taxes has been approximated as the sum of the first two items above, although it would be theoretically correct to "gross up" the equity in earnings of unconsolidated subsidiaries by the amount of taxes in that line item. To perform the gross up accurately requires using the average tax rates of all of Mitsui's unconsolidated subsidiaries. The following are Mitsui's solvency indicators using the data from Exhibit 4–1:

	FY92	FY91	FY90	FY89	FY88
Debt to equity	3.53	4.09	4.06	4.29	4.93
Debt to total capitalization	0.26	0.26	0.25	0.26	0.27
Interest coverage	1.21	1.19	1.26	1.45	1.34
CFFO to interest charges	−0.34	0.45	0.06	0.02	NA
CFFO to total liabilities	−0.02	0.02	0.00	0.00	NA

The debt to equity and the debt to total capitalization ratios indicate that the level of Mitsui's debt declined steadily from 1988 to 1992 as compared to its shareholders' equity but remained a relatively constant proportion of total capitalization. The results with respect to the company's debt coverage from operations is somewhat mixed, however. The interest coverage ratio declined slowly, suggesting that Mitsui's ability to support its current debt service level with earnings declined; however, on a CFFO basis, the company's ability to pay its interest charges from operations-related cash flows increased substantially. Whether the FY92 ratio of −0.34 is a reliable predictor of the future should be evaluated through additional research. In summary, the coverage ratios reveal that, while Mitsui's CFFO has provided some limited coverage of its debt service, it may not be counted on to significantly reduce its debt exposure. Why this is the case may be explained by reference to the cultural and business setting in Japan. As will be noted in greater detail in Chapter 10, many of Japan's large companies are members of a **keiretsu,** or confederation of companies (usually with interlocking directorates and intercompany shareholdings), that provide economic support to one another. Mitsui, for example, is a member of one of Japan's six largest keiretsu, which includes, among other companies, various banks and insurance companies. Given Mitsui's virtually direct access to external liquidity via its keiretsu members, the company may feel less compelled to maintain a high level of internal liquidity.

A final word on solvency and leverage is warranted. The concept of solvency and the thrust of these debt-level and coverage ratios suggests a negative connotation as though debt is to be avoided and reduced whenever possible. Debt is not always bad, and in fact can be quite healthy for a company. A widely accepted financial maxim is that a company *should* borrow so long as (1) its after-tax cost of borrowing is less than its cost of equity funds *and* (2) so long as its rate of return on borrowed funds exceeds its cost of borrowing. Under these conditions, borrowing adds value to the firm; it enables the company to increase its return to its owners. Borrowing can also be detrimental, however, because excessive debt levels can drain a company of its earnings and cash flow. Consequently, the decision to borrow is an important strategic one requiring careful consideration of the traditional trade-off of risk and return.

Asset Management.   **Asset management** refers to how efficiently a company utilizes its available resources. A company with superior asset management usually experiences superior earnings and profitability relative to its competitors in its industry; it is also usually characterized by lower default risk.

Asset management is usually investigated from two perspectives: (1) the level of *turnover* or activity experienced by various critical assets, such as inventory and receivables, and (2) the *efficiency* or *effectiveness* of that activity. Three prominent activity ratios are:

$$\text{Receivable turnover ratio} = \frac{\text{Net sales}}{\text{Average receivable balance}}$$

$$\text{Inventory turnover ratio} = \frac{\text{Cost of goods sold}}{\text{Average inventory level}}$$

$$\text{Total asset turnover ratio} = \frac{\text{Net sales}}{\text{Average total assets balance}}$$

The **receivable turnover ratio,** for example, indicates the rate at which a company's receivables are converted to cash, whereas the **inventory turnover** ratio indicates the number of times that the available stock of inventory was "turned" or sold during a given period. In general, a higher turnover rate is preferred to a lower one. In the case of receivables, a high turnover indicates effective receivable management, whereas a low rate may indicate serious problems in the sales-receivable-collection cycle. With respect to inventory, a high turnover rate helps reduce the potential loss due to product obsolescence or deterioration, but if the rate is too high, it may also indicate that a company is losing sales opportunities because inventory levels are inadequate to satisfy customer tastes or demand.[8] Unfortunately, there is no ideal turnover rate for either inventory or receivables, and, as always, it is important to compare these ratios with those of prior periods, industry averages, and competitor-company ratios.

The **total asset turnover ratio** is unlike the prior two turnover ratios, which focused on current asset management effectiveness in that this indicator focuses on *all* of the assets at management's disposal. This ratio can be particularly revealing for

---

[8]The importance and interpretation of inventory turnover indicators must be evaluated in light of the increasing use of just-in-time (JIT) inventory management systems.

capital-intensive companies (i.e., those companies having a large investment in non-current fixed assets); conversely, it could be meaningless for the evaluation of professional service firms whose principal asset—people—is not reflected on the balance sheet. As before, a higher ratio is to be preferred, indicating that management is effective in generating a significant level of sales from its available asset base. A high turnover rate can also be problematic, however, if the reason for the high rate is the liquidation of the company's revenue-producing assets. Similarly, a declining ratio may not necessarily indicate poor asset utilization if the reason for the decline is an increase in capital investment.

Two efficiency ratios, derived from the turnover ratios, are as follows:

$$\text{Average receivable collection period ratio} = \frac{365 \text{ days}}{\text{Receivable turnover ratio}}$$

$$\text{Average number of days' inventory on hand ratio} = \frac{365 \text{ days}}{\text{Inventory turnover ratio}}$$

The **average receivable collection period ratio** indicates the average number of days that a receivable is outstanding before the amount is collected; the **average number of days' inventory on hand ratio** refers to the average number of days required to liquidate the existing stock of inventory based on current sales volume. In both cases, a low ratio is preferred. A high average collection period can reflect problems in either a company's credit-granting policy or its credit-collection policy (or both). A high number of days' inventory on hand can reflect an excessive quantity of inventory on hand, suggesting that current production should be curtailed. Like the turnover ratios, there is no ideal ratio for either the average collection period or the number of days' inventory on hand. The following are Mitsui's asset management indicators using the data from Exhibit 4–1:

	FY92	*FY91*	*FY90*	*FY89*
Receivable turnover	6.16	7.00	7.17	6.98
Inventory turnover	37.66	43.72	43.02	46.32
Total asset turnover	1.94	2.14	2.45	2.94
Average receivable collection period	59.27	52.13	50.91	52.28
Average number of days' inventory on hand	9.69	8.35	8.48	7.88

Overall, Mitsui's asset management appears to be deteriorating. The company's receivable collection period is approaching 60 days, and although its inventory turnover is quite rapid, it declined from 46 times in FY89 to 38 times in 1992. One explanation for the very high inventory turnover is Mitsui's use of just-in-time (JIT) inventory management techniques; a second explanation is the company's high proportion of trading-related versus manufacturing-related sales. Mitsui's total asset turnover ratio also declined from 2.94 in FY89 to 1.94 in FY92. This result can be seen to be caused by two factors: (1) a significant growth (over 50 percent) in assets and (2) a modest growth (approximately 16 percent) in sales. Quite often, a growth in sales, earnings, and cash flow lag a company's growth in revenue-producing assets, which could be the case here. A review of this ratio for FY93 and thereafter will be a key in forming an assessment of whether the company's asset management is deteriorating or not.

Profitability.   **Profitability** refers to a company's overall ability to generate earnings and, by extension, cash flows from operations. As observed earlier, of greatest importance to any financial decision is the level of a company's permanent or recurring earnings. **Transitory earnings (cash flows)** by their very nature have little value because they cannot be expected to recur in future periods.

The principal source of information regarding a company's profitability is, of course, its income statement; however, informative performance indicators can also be formed by using various balance sheet accounts, as we will see shortly. As a first step in analyzing a company's operating performance, consideration should be given to the trend in historical revenue, sometimes called *turnover* or *transactions,* which may reveal important firm-specific or industrywide trends. These data can help identify where a company is in its normal **life cycle.** Is it, for example, in a growth state, or alternatively, in a very mature stage of decline? (The topic of product/corporate life cycles is considered further in Chapter 5.) Moreover, comparing company sales data against industry data will help reveal whether the entity under review is an industry leader or an industry laggard.

A series of profitability ratios can also be constructed for comparison purposes with prior years' data or against industry averages. Three widely examined profitability ratios are the **return on total assets** (sometimes called the *return on investment* or ROI), the **return on equity,** and the **return on sales:**

$$\text{Return on assets ratio } = \frac{\text{Net income}}{\text{Average total assets}}$$

$$\text{Return on equity ratio} = \frac{\text{Net income}}{\text{Average shareholders' equity}}$$

$$\text{Return on sales ratio } = \frac{\text{Net income}}{\text{Net sales}}$$

The **return on total assets** (ROA) ratio measures a company's overall effectiveness in generating earnings from its available resources. This widely utilized indicator can be used to assess not only a company's profitability but also its overall asset management effectiveness. The **return on equity** (ROE) ratio also measures a company's performance in using its assets to generate income; however, unlike the ROA, this measure evaluates operating performance only in relation to the resources provided by the shareholders of a company. Finally, the **return on sales** (ROS) ratio indicates the percentage of sales that is earned as net income and that may be retained in the company to support operations or be paid to shareholders as a dividend. It is noteworthy that each of these ratios indicates not only how well the entity generates earnings but also implicitly how well it controls its costs. In general, for each of these return ratios, a higher ratio indicates greater profitability and operating performance; it also indicates a greater ability to generate permanent earnings and cash flows.

To illustrate these ratios, consider their values for Mitsui & Co., Ltd:

	FY92	FY91	FY90	FY89	FY88
Return on assets	0.3%	0.4%	0.5%	0.7%	NA
Return on equity	4.3	6.7	7.4	12.2	NA
Return on sales	0.2	0.2	0.2	0.2	0.1%

These results highlight a number of points. First, despite Mitsui's rather significant growth in assets and sales, no parallel growth in profitability occurred. In fact, the level of profitability, both in an absolute sense and relative to total assets, shareholders' equity, and sales, declined from 1989 to 1992. Second, with the exception of the ROE, Mitsui's return ratios are all quite low when compared to the ratios that one might expect to see from comparable U.S. companies. As will be discussed in Chapter 10, published Japanese financial statements are largely expected to conform to the existing tax code in Japan. Thus, net income and other measures of profitability can naturally be expected to be depressed as Japanese managers attempt to minimize their income tax obligation to their governmental taxation authorities. In the United States, however, with few exceptions, published financial statements need not conform to Internal Revenue Service (IRS) regulations but to GAAP as promulgated by the FASB Consequently, the level of profitability reported by U.S. firms can (and usually does) substantially exceed the level of taxable income reported to the IRS, thereby yielding profitability indicators to shareholders that are significantly above those evident to the IRS and above those reported by their Japanese counterparts.

Return to Investors.   For publicly owned companies, the return to investors holding common stock is one of the most frequently evaluated areas of firm performance.

Perhaps the most often examined measure of shareholder return is a company's **earnings per share,** or EPS (although in some countries, such as Germany and Italy, there is no disclosure of EPS whatsoever). There is considerable diversity throughout the world regarding the measurement of EPS, and the procedures followed in the United States are probably the most complex. In many countries (e.g., Brazil, Japan, and Sweden), the reported EPS is simply a company's **raw (or basic) EPS:**

$$\text{Raw EPS} = \frac{\text{Net income} - \text{Preferred dividends}}{\text{Weighted average number of common shares outstanding}}$$

Note that the divisor is not merely the actual number of common (ordinary) shares outstanding at the end of a given accounting period but an average of those outstanding shares, weighted by the proportion of time in the period that the shares were actually held by shareholders. This weighting process ensures that the EPS is not artificially distorted by an end-of-period event such as a public offering or a share repurchase. For example, at the beginning of FY90, Mitsui had 1.369 billion common shares outstanding, and, by year-end, this total had grown to 1.530 billion; however, the weighted average number of shares was only 1.496 billion.

In the United States and elsewhere (e.g., Korea), a more complex calculation is often undertaken to recognize the *potential* dilution (i.e., reduction) of future EPS that might occur if existing convertible (e.g., convertible preferred stock and bonds) or exchangeable (e.g., stock options and warrants) securities are converted to or exchanged for new shares of stock. When such securities exist, two EPS calculations may be required:

$$\text{Primary EPS ratio} = \frac{\text{Earnings applicable to common stock}}{\text{Weighted average common stocks} + \text{Common stock equivalents}}$$

$$\text{Fully diluted EPS ratio} = \frac{\text{Earnings applicable to common stock}}{\text{Weighted average common shares} + \text{Common stock equivalents} + \text{Other potentially dilutive securities}}$$

Common stock equivalents (CSEs) are a subset of those securities that enable the holder to become a common stockholder by exercising various rights inherent in the CSE. For example, for purposes of calculating **primary EPS** and **fully diluted EPS,** common stock options and warrants are usually considered to be CSEs, and thus are treated *as if* the securities had already been exercised. Further, in the calculation of fully diluted EPS, those convertible securities that fail to achieve CSE status may nonetheless be included on an *as-if-converted* basis in an effort to portray a conservative scenario for future EPS. Note that both primary and fully diluted EPS contain pro forma characteristics: they attempt to reflect the potentially dilutive effects on EPS of various securities that might, at some future date, cause additional shares of common stock to be issued. The International Accounting Standards Committee has recommended that firms disclose only basic and fully diluted EPS, and it is expected that the U.S. Financial Accounting Standards Board will affirm that recommendation.

The following table contains Mitsui's fiscal year-end common shares outstanding and reported EPS for the years 1988 through 1992. Since both the number of common shares outstanding and EPS increased for the first four years, net income must have grown at a faster rate than the number of shares used in the denominator of the EPS calculation. The decline in EPS for FY92 is largely a result of reduced net income.

The basic EPS calculation is consistently higher than Mitsui's reported EPS, indicating that the denominator (i.e., outstanding shares) in Mitsui's calculation is greater than the weighted average number of common shares outstanding. Mitsui's supplemental notes to the financial statements (not presented here) disclose that Mitsui has convertible bonds and warrants outstanding, causing a potentially dilutive effect on earnings. This potential dilution has been reflected by the company in its reported EPS, even though disclosure of diluted EPS is not required under Japanese GAAP.

	FY92	FY91	FY90	FY89	FY88
Common shares outstanding (millions)	1,547	1,543	1,530	1,369	1,306
Reported EPS (¥ per share)	16.75	25.15	24.35	28.60	18.01
Basic EPS (¥ per share)	17.46	26.68	25.12	30.16	

The multitudes of investors have a diverse set of preferences regarding the traditional trade-off of the reinvestment of cash flows versus dividend payments. Firms that generate roughly the same level of earnings but that pay no dividends are able to fund growth internally to a greater extent than those that do pay dividends. To those investors who invest principally for dividend returns, the **cash dividend yield** is a key financial indicator. This measure reveals the current rate of cash return on a common (ordinary) share, based on its current selling price, and exclusive of any cash returns that *could* be realized if the stock were sold:

$$\text{Cash dividend yield ratio} = \frac{\text{Cash dividend per common share}}{\text{Average market price per common share}}$$

The following data illustrate that Mitsui's dividend rate per share increased over the five years presented, but the cash dividend yield ratio indicates that it is a minuscule amount compared to market price. Investors in Mitsui common stock are evidently trading on future share price appreciation and/or the prospect of significantly higher dividends. Given Mitsui's meager cash flow from operations, price appreciation appears more likely to occur in the near term than increased dividend yield.

The **cash dividend payout** is a measure of the return actually paid to shareholders as a percentage of current distributable income; it is a measure of the actual earnings distributed to shareholders in the form of dividends:

$$\text{Cash dividend payout ratio} = \frac{\text{Cash dividend to common shareholders}}{\text{Net income applicable to common shareholders}}$$

From an investor's perspective, a higher cash dividend payout ratio results in immediate increased cash inflows. On the other hand, from management's perspective, a growth-oriented company would want to maintain minimal payout levels to retain as much cash as possible to support continued growth.

For Mitsui, the cash dividend per share, yield, and payout were as follows:

	FY92	FY91	FY90	FY89	FY88
Cash dividend per share	7.0%	7.0%	6.5%	5.5%	4.9%
Cash dividend yield	1.1	0.9	0.6	0.6	0.7
Cash dividend payout	40.1	26.3	26.3	18.1	26.8

Mitsui kept the level of dividends paid constant over the most recent two years while earnings declined. As a consequence, the payout ratio increased from 26.3 to 40.1 percent. Whether this payout level is acceptable or not must be judged relative to the investor's income needs and relative to the payouts of comparable companies.

Company-Specific Ratios.   The financial ratios discussed here are but a limited sampling of a larger set of potentially useful ratios. Many companies, in fact, devise and present ratios that are often unique to their corporate settings. These company-specific ratios are usually designed to highlight aspects of their particular businesses or industries. Analysts should give special consideration to these indicators because they often provide special insights into what a company regards as important when assessing its financial health and operating success. Mitsui, a worldwide, highly diversified company, for example, presents its total sales broken down by the type of sale (i.e., export, import, offshore, and domestic), as well as by the commodity sold (i.e., iron and steel, nonferrous metals, machinery, chemicals, foodstuffs, textiles, energy, general merchandise, and property/service business). This financial data enables Mitsui to emphasize to investors the extent of its diversification and, thus, the lower risk associated with investing in such a company. (A basic tenet of financial management is to minimize systematic risk through diversification.) As you work your way through the financial reports of companies, try to identify those financial metrics that a company selects to portray its financial strengths.

Behind the Ratios: Investigating Cause and Effect

At the beginning of our discussion of trend and cross-sectional analysis we posed two questions. The first question concerned the trends and patterns in financial statement numbers; the second question was: What is observed that explains any patterns and relationships in the financial statement numbers, or that may cause the observed patterns and relations to change in the future?

Four types of items should be investigated when addressing this question:

Country/industry factors.

External economic events.

Internal economic events.

Accounting policies and changes in those policies.

Country/Industry Factors.   The nature of regulation, competition and ownership structure, and other country- and/or industry-specific factors can have a profound effect on the way financial results are interpreted. Much of the remainder of this book is devoted to a discussion of these considerations. For Mitsui, consider how the previously mentioned keiretsu form of industrial organization can effect its financial results:

- Mitsui's high leverage ratios relative to those for U.S. companies are attributable in large part to financial conditions in Japan: the keiretsu has caused the relationship between banks and member manufacturing concerns to be highly interdependent. As a result, bankruptcy of keiretsu members has been extremely low.

- Banks may hold significant equity interest in firms while also lending funds to these same firms. Therefore, the distinction between interest and dividend payments is less important in Japan than in the United States. Interest coverage ratios tend to be low in Japan but are not viewed with much concern.

- Liquidity ratios also tend to be low because short-term debt is frequently used when U.S. firms would normally consider long-term financing. This allows member banks to minimize exposure to interest rate fluctuations because the opportunity to set new rates occurs frequently. Short-term debt in Japan serves much the same function as long-term variable rate debt in the United States.

- Average collection periods on receivables tend to be longer in Japan. During business downturns, credit extensions are frequently granted to accommodate a customer's need to maintain a stable workforce. In return, a loyal customer helps the seller maintain its own workforce stability.

- Higher levels of management job security make management less concerned about profitability, perhaps explaining Mitsui's low profit margins. It has been said that sales growth is the primary objective of Japanese management, for maximum market share provides the greatest assurances of long-run stability and profitability.

External Events.   Changes in the *legal environment* occur frequently, often in the form of changes in tax rates and tax rules. In general, changes in statutes and regulations may change the way sales and marketing are conducted, products are designed and manufactured, or the prospects for enterprise success. For example, the success of many ventures in communications depends highly on the outlook for favorable governmental regulation. In addition, many ongoing enterprises, particularly manufacturing concerns, may depend highly on their exposure to changes in legislation pertaining to product and environmental liabilities (e.g., air and water contamination).

Macroeconomic events and trends, however, do not affect all industries or companies to the same degree, or even in the same direction. Analysts often evaluate a company's exposure to general economic or specific industry cycles, inflation, interest rate changes, and foreign currency exchange rate fluctuations. This latter factor is particularly important when considering foreign competitors, prices on imported goods, receivable and payable balances denominated in a foreign currency, and the performance of foreign subsidiaries.

For example, Mitsui's recent financial results should be evaluated in light of recent external events in Japan. At the time of this writing, Japanese real estate and securities prices were severely depressed from recent record highs. How will these events be reflected according to Japanese GAAP in the financial statements of affected companies?

To what extent has there been an economic effect on Mitsui that will not be reflected in their financial statements until future periods?

Internal Events.   Some internal events are the result of recent management decisions (e.g., the curtailment of repairs and maintenance expenditures); others are the result of decisions that often occurred long ago. The following are some examples of significant internal events that should be considered in any financial analysis:

- Recent business combinations, creations, or disposals.
- Product introductions and terminations.
- Changes in business practices.
    - —Sales and marketing.
    - —Product design.
    - —Manufacturing inputs or processes.
    - —Credit policies.
- Changes in discretionary expenditures such as advertising, R&D, capital improvements, maintenance, and implementation of JIT for inventories.
- Legal uncertainties.
    - —Litigation.
    - —Unasserted claims on a product known to be defective.
- Financial uncertainties.
    - —Issuance of redeemable or convertible securities.
    - —Maturity of long-term debt.
    - —Debt covenant violations.
    - —Sales with significant service commitments remaining.
    - —Warranties, guarantees, and commitments.
    - —Receipt of payments "in kind."
    - —Insurance reimbursement.
    - —Restricted assets of foreign subsidiaries.
- Dependencies.
    - —Major customers.
    - —Major suppliers.
    - —Related parties.
    - —Patents or copyrights that are threatened or may expire.

Information regarding many of these internal events can be obtained by reading the written company documentaries that accompany publicly disclosed financial data. In other cases, analysts may need to investigate any legislatively mandated nonfinancial disclosures. For example, in the United States, companies with publicly traded securities (either debt or equity) are required to include a discussion and analysis of the effect of past and future internal and external events on financial results and liquidity in annual reports, quarterly reports, and public offerings of securities. For example, it would be interesting to learn the causes for the decline in Mitsui's 1992 sales: how much of the decline was due to (1) changes in prices of goods, (2) volume of goods sold, or (3) unfavorable exchange rate movements for foreign sales. U.S. SEC disclosure requirements mandate a discussion of these factors, but in Japan such disclosures are not required. U.S. public companies must also file a Form 8-K report with the SEC when any of the following types of events occur:

- A change in control of the company,
- An auditor change or disagreement,
- An acquisition or disposition of a significant amount of assets not in the ordinary course of business,
- A resignation of one (or more) member(s) of the board of directors due to a disagreement,
- A bankruptcy filing.

Finally, analysts should avail themselves of the industry- and company-specific commentaries provided by such investment services as Moody's, Standard and Poor's, and Value Line, among others.

Accounting Policies and Changes. Accounting policies, and changes in those policies, usually do not have a direct effect on a company's cash flows, but they can have a significant effect on managerial incentives and decisions, and the way in which financial statement information is analyzed. At the time of this writing, for example, U.S. financial statements have been profoundly affected by changes in accounting standards for income taxes, nonpension benefits granted to employees upon retirement (e.g., health care coverage), marketable securities, loans receivable, granting of stock options to employees, and more. Similarly, in the United Kingdom, the recent adoption of Financial Reporting Standards Nos. 1–3 have had a dramatic effect on the format of British financial statements, requiring (among other things) the presentation of a statement of cash flows. The effect of these changes in accounting standards undoubtedly will have a significant impact on financial statements, as well as on the internal decisions made by management.

A company's management team has significant discretion in the choice of accounting policies from year to year. Significant sources of changes in accounting policies to consider include the following:

- Classification.
  - —Continuing versus discontinued operations.
  - —Performing versus nonperforming loans.
  - —Foreign currency translation gains and losses.
- Changes in accounting principles, such as switching from LIFO to FIFO inventory cost-flow assumptions.
- Changes in accounting estimates.
  - —Useful lives of fixed assets.
  - —Actuarial assumptions for pension liabilities.
  - —Allowances for bad debts or sales returns.

- "Hidden reserves."
  —Liabilities established for business combinations, restructuring charges, discontinued operations, deferred tax asset allowances, and inventory valuation allowances.
  —Peculiar assumptions for pension plans, depreciation, and amortization periods.
- Revenue recognition.
  —Premature revenue or gain recognition, such as for "bill and hold" arrangements.
- Delayed expense recognition.
  —Inadequate accruals of liabilities for litigation, environmental cleanup costs, and unasserted claims.
  —Excess capitalization of expenses such as R&D, interest, advertising, and preopening costs.

In most (but not all) countries, a change in accounting policy or estimate that produces a material financial effect is usually detailed in the notes accompanying the financial statements. Thus, a careful review of a company's footnotes should reveal the magnitude and direction of these managerial decisions. Nonetheless, the effects of some decisions, such as the use of hidden reserves to manage a company's reported performance, are often difficult, if not impossible, to identify. Strategies for investigating these internal policy actions will be discussed in subsequent chapters.

Summary

The purpose of this chapter was to overview the process of financial statement analysis. This process may involve both trend and cross-sectional analysis and the search for the causes of trends and patterns. Frequently, the process involves the use of common-size financial statements that help identify changes in asset or equity mixes or changes in the various income statement account relationships. Ratio analysis is also a key element of any financial statement review, and Exhibit 4–3 illustrates the ratios discussed in this chapter. In the next chapter, we introduce additional ratios, consider some of the limitations of these analytical processes, and explore some of the more sophisticated aspects of financial statement analysis.

EXHIBIT 4–3

Summary of Financial Statement Ratios

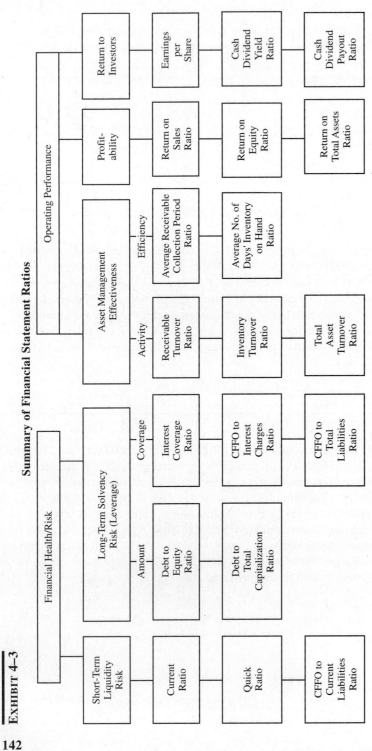

Suggested Readings

Bernstein, L. *Financial Statement Analysis: Theory, Application, and Interpretation.* Burr Ridge, IL: Richard D. Irwin, 1989.

Casey, C., and N. Bartczak. "Cash Flow—It's Not the Bottom Line." *Harvard Business Review,* July/August, 1984, pp. 61–67.

Choi, F. M. Hino, S. Min, S. Nam, J. Vjiie, and A. Stonehill. "Analyzing Foreign Financial Statements: The Use and Misuse of International Ratio Analysis." *Journal of International Business Studies,* Spring/Summer, 1985, pp. 113–31.

Dyckman, T. R., and D. E. Morse. *Efficient Capital Markets and Accounting.* Englewood Cliffs, NJ: Prentice-Hall, 1986.

Ferris, K., K. L. Tennant, and S. I. Jerris. *How to Understand Financial Statements: A Nontechnical Guide for Financial Analysts, Managers, and Executives.* Englewood Cliffs, NJ: Prentice-Hall, 1992.

Giacommo, D., and D. Mielke. "Using the Statement of Cash Flows to Analyze Corporate Performance," *Management Accounting,* May 1988, pp. 54–57.

Hussein, H., V. Bavishi, and T. Gangolly. "International Similarities and Differences in the Auditor's Report." *Auditing: A Journal of Practice and Theory,* Fall 1987, pp. 124–33.

Lev, B. *Financial Statement Analysis: A New Approach.* Englewood Cliffs, NJ: Prentice-Hall, 1974.

O'Glove, T. L. *Quality of Earnings.* New York: Free Press, 1987.

Stickney, C. P. *Financial Statement Analysis: A Strategic Perspective.* Harcourt Brace Jovanovich, 1990.

APPENDIX 4A
CASH FLOW STATEMENT PREPARATION

Since a *statement of cash flows* (SCF) is not currently a required financial statement disclosure in all countries, analysts must be prepared to develop the data for it themselves. This appendix presents a simplified approach to the preparation of a statement of cash flows, using the IASC *Statement No. 7* format as a fundamental model (which conforms to that of *SFAS No. 95* in the United States).[1]

At a minimum, to prepare a basic single-period SCF from available public documents, the following data are needed: (1) the income statement for the current period and (2) the balance sheets from the beginning and the end of the accounting period. With only these three items, it is possible to prepare a rudimentary statement of cash flows using the four-step process outlined below.

To begin, recall that the fundamental accounting equation for the balance sheet is given as

$$Assets = Liabilities + Owners' equity$$

or

$$A = L + OE \tag{1}$$

---

[1]*IAS Statement No. 7* (revised 1992) requires that a statement of cash flows be presented as part of a company's financial statements.

Substituting the major components of a company's assets, liabilities, and owners' equity into expression (1) yields the following:

$$CA + NCA = CL + NCL + CS + RE \qquad (2)$$

where

$$CA = \text{Current assets}$$
$$NCA = \text{Noncurrent assets}$$
$$CL = \text{Current liabilities}$$
$$NCL = \text{Noncurrent liabilities}$$
$$CS = \text{Capital stock}$$
$$RE = \text{Retained earnings}$$

Decomposing the current assets into cash (C) and all other current assets (OCA), yields yet another version of the fundamental accounting equation:

$$C + OCA + NCA = CL + NCL + CS + RE \qquad (3)$$

At this juncture, it is necessary to accept one concept on faith: a statement of cash flows is nothing more than a formal explanation of the positive and negative changes to the cash account as it appears on the balance sheet; that is, the SCF merely lists where a company's cash inflows came from and how the various cash amounts were used. Clearly, then, having access to a company's internal accounting records would make it a simple matter to produce a statement of cash flows by merely listing the various debits (inflows) and credits (outflows) to the company's cash account. But it is highly unlikely that such access would be available and, thus, a process is needed by which to estimate these data from publicly available documents.

As noted above, the SCF is simply a listing of the various changes in a company's cash account and, thus, can be expressed by the following equation:

$$\text{Cash}_B - \text{Cash}_E = \Delta\text{ Cash} \qquad (4)$$

where

$$B = \text{Beginning of the accounting period}$$
$$E = \text{End of the accounting period}$$
$$\Delta = \text{The change in}$$

Using a few basic algebraic concepts, it is possible to redefine equation (4) in terms of equation (3). Putting the subscripts B and E on the elements of equation (3) yields

$$C_B + OCA_B + NCA_B = CL_B + NCL_B + CS_B + RE_B \qquad (3')$$

and

$$C_E + OCA_E + NCA_E = CL_E + NCL_E + CS_E + RE_E \qquad (3'')$$

Isolating C_B and C_E on the left-hand side of the equation yields

$$C_B = CL_B + NCL_B + CS_B + RE_B - (OCA_B + NCA_B) \qquad (5)$$

and

$$C_E = CL_E + NCL_E + CS_E + RE_E - (OCA_E + NCA_E) \qquad (6)$$

Subtracting expression (6) from (5) yields

$$C_B - C_E = (CL_B - CL_E) + (NCL_B - NCL_E) + (CS_B - CS_E) + (RE_B - RE_E) \qquad (7)$$
$$- (OCA_B - OCA_E) - (NCA_B + NCA_E)$$

Expression (7), then, is a more explicit, formalized version of expression (4), and, thus, both are representations of the statement of cash flows. More important, expression (7) gives us a very simple approach to the preparation of an SCF. In words, expression (7) tells us that the SCF is merely a listing of the changes in all of the balance sheet accounts.

From this, we can now formulate a four-step method to create a very useful but basic SCF:

1. Calculate the changes in all balance sheet accounts by subtracting the ending balance from the beginning balance for each account.

2. Identify the total change in the cash account. This figure represents the ''bottom line'' of the SCF: all increases and decreases in the cash account *must* net to this figure. It is, in essence, a check figure to verify the accuracy of the analysis.

3. Identify each balance sheet account with the activity most closely related to it: operations, investing, and financing. As a general rule, the following associations are usually made:

    Operations: RE, OCA, CL
    Investing: NCA
    Financing: NCL, CS

4. Place each of the individual balance sheet accounts (except Cash) under one of three categories of activities and identify whether the change in the account involved a source or use of cash. (Recall that the total sources and uses must aggregate to the check figure identified in step 2.)

An Illustration

To illustrate the four-step process, consider the financial statements of Global Enterprises, Inc. (GE) presented in Exhibits 4A–1 and 4A–2. Exhibit 4A–1 presents GE's comparative balance sheets for 1994 and 1993, whereas Exhibit 4A–2 presents GE's income statement for 1994.

Following the four-step procedure:

1. Calculate the change in all the balance sheet accounts, as shown in Exhibit 4A–1.

2. The check figure for the SCF is a decrease of $15.2 million. Thus, GE's uses of cash must have exceeded its sources of cash by $15.2 million.

3. The last column of Exhibit 4A–1 identifies the activity category associated with each individual balance sheet account. It is important to note that judgment calls are necessary at this step. For example, even though current liabilities (e.g., accounts payable and accrued liabilities payable) are typically associated with a company's operations, certain current liabilities (e.g., notes payable and the current portion of long-term debt) are more commonly considered to be financing related. Similarly, marketable securities, a current asset, may be considered principally operations related in some settings and investing related in others. Oftentimes, without specific knowledge of the transactions that gave rise to a particular account, it is difficult to be certain as to an account's proper classification. A misclassification, however, does

EXHIBIT 4A–1

Global Enterprises, Inc.
Comparative Balance Sheets
(in millions)

As of December 31

	1994	1993	Δ	Activity Category*
Assets				
Cash and cash equivalents	$ 11.5	$ 26.7	(15.2)	—
Marketable securities	33.6	0.3	33.3	I
Receivables	99.9	80.1	19.8	O
Inventories	95.4	255.3	(159.9)	O
Total current assets	$ 240.4	$ 362.4		
Investments	516.5	624.1	(107.6)	I
Property and equipment (net)	194.2	190.4	3.8	I
Goodwill	5.9	6.0	(0.1)	I
Other assets	68.1	167.3	(99.2)	I
Total assets	$1,025.1	$1,350.2		
Liabilities and Shareholders' Equity				
Notes payable and current long-term debt	$ 54.2	$ 145.1	(90.9)	F
Other current liabilities	152.5	276.1	(123.6)	O
Total current liabilities	206.7	421.2		
Long-term debt	363.4	584.2	(220.8)	F
Deferred income taxes	49.6	35.7	13.9	O
Other debt	8.2	9.1	(0.9)	F
Total noncurrent liabilities	421.2	629.0		
Shareholders' capital	294.6	287.4	7.2	F
Retained earnings	102.6	12.6	90.0	O
Total shareholders' equity	397.2	300.0		
Total equities	$1,025.1	$1,350.2		

*O = operations; I = investing; F = financing.

EXHIBIT 4A–2

Global Enterprises, Inc.
1994 Income Statement
(in millions)

Operating revenues	$ 579.3
Less: Operating expenses	472.3*
Net income†	$ 107.0

*Includes depreciation expense of $10.0 million.
†Dividends paid out of net income in 1994 amounted to $17.0 million.

EXHIBIT 4A–3

Global Enterprises, Inc.
Simplified Statement of Cash Flows
(in millions)

Operations	Source/(Use)
Retained earnings	$ 90.0
Receivables	(19.8)
Inventories	159.9
Other current liabilities	(123.6)
Deferred income taxes	13.9
Cash flows from operations	$ 120.4
Investments	
Marketable securities	$ (33.3)
Investments	107.6
Property and equipment (net)	(3.8)
Goodwill	0.1
Other assets	99.2
Cash flows from investing	$ 169.8
Financing	
Notes payable and current long-term debt	$ (90.9)
Long-term debt	(220.8)
Other debt	(0.9)
Contributed capital	7.2
Cash flows for financing	$(305.4)
Decrease in cash and cash equivalents	$ 15.2

not lead to an unbalanced cash flow statement but merely a misspecification of the relative amounts in the three activity categories.

4. Exhibit 4A–3 contains the changes in the balance sheet accounts placed under the three activity categories. Note that the total of the three activity categories equals the change in the cash account (i.e., a decrease of $15.2 million), and this ensures that the analysis was performed correctly.

We can conclude based on the simplified SCF in Exhibit 4A–3 that Global Enterprises generated positive cash flows from operations of $120.4 million and from investing of $169.8 million, while spending $305.4 million on financing activities (principally the retirement of debt). For many financial analyses, the simplified SCF is sufficient; however, in other circumstances, a more exacting SCF is required, and can be generated by using other available information. In the preparation of Exhibit 4A–3, only GE's balance sheet data were utilized, and, thus, a refinement of this exhibit is possible by also incorporating the income statement data from Exhibit 4A–2. For example, Exhibit 4A–2 reveals that the 1994 earnings for GE were $107.0 million, and dividends paid amounted to $17.0 million. Note that these two amounts net to the change in the retained earnings account on the balance sheet (i.e., $107 − $17 = $90.0). Thus, by substituting these two new figures for the retained earnings figure in our initial SCF, we are able to produce a refined measure of the company's cash flows. The restated figures are as follows:

	Original	Adjustment	Revised
Operations	$ 120.4	−90.0 in retained earnings + 107.0 1994 net income	$ 137.4
Investing	169.8		169.8
Financing	(305.4)	− 17.0 1994 dividend payments	(322.4)
Decrease in cash	$ 15.2		$ 15.2

Notice that the inclusion of the additional income statement data did not change the check figure—a decrease in cash and cash equivalents of $15.2 million—but did result in a restatement of the cash flows from operations and for financing. Our restated figures suggest that the cash flows from operations were actually $137.4 million, as opposed to $120.4 million, and the cash flow for financing was a negative $322.4 million, instead of a negative $305.4 million.

Another common refinement that should usually be made to a simplified SCF involves depreciation (and any other cost allocation accounts such as amortization and depletion). It is well known that depreciation is an accrual accounting concept in which the original cost to acquire a depreciable asset is allocated over the many periods expected to benefit from the asset. Thus, depreciation expense is the portion of an asset's cost allocated to a given accounting period; it represents neither a current cash inflow nor a current cash outflow.

Given that depreciation is frequently one of the largest expense items deducted in arriving at periodic net income, it is usually necessary to adjust net income for this item to avoid understating the actual cash flows from operations. Exhibits 4A–2 and 4A–3 reveal the change in property and equipment, net of the current depreciation expense, and the current depreciation expense, respectively. Using T-accounts to help visualize the events that happened, we can assess the cash flow effects of these accounts as follows:

	Property Equipment (net)		1994 Depreciation Expense
12-31-93 Balance	$190.4		$10.0
1994 Purchases	13.8		
		$10.0	
12-31-94 Balance	$194.2		

Without reference to the current depreciation charge of $10.0 million, our initial conclusion was that $3.8 million was spent to acquire new property and equipment (i.e., a use of cash). By including the depreciation expense, we see that the actual cash expended for new capital equipment was $13.8 million; with these two figures, we are able to further refine our SCF from Exhibit 4A–3:

	Revised	*Adjustment*	*Final*
Operations	$ 137.4	+10.0 1994 Depreciation expense	$ 147.4
Investing	169.8	−10.0 Additional 1994 purchases	159.8
Financing	(322.4)		(322.4)
Decrease in cash	$ 15.2		$ 15.2

At this juncture, we have utilized all available information; thus, we are unable to refine our SCF further. These two examples involving retained earnings (net income and dividends) and property and equipment (depreciation and purchases) readily illustrate the benefit of extending the simplified SCF when additional data are available.

Direct versus Indirect Methods

Although no additional information is available to further refine our SCF, one final consideration involves the presentation format of the *operations* section of the SCF. Two alternative approaches exist for presenting the cash flow from operations: the direct and indirect methods.

Although these two approaches to formatting the operations section of the SCF originated in the United States, they are gaining widespread acceptance in countries that require the presentation of an SCF as a basic financial statement. The choice of which method to use does not affect either the total cash flow from operations ($147.4 million) or the total change in cash and cash equivalents ($15.2 million). Most companies that present an SCF usually prefer the indirect method, which is essentially used in Exhibit 4A–3; however, many professional analysts prefer to use the direct method because of the additional insights that it provides regarding a company's operations.

To illustrate how a direct method version of the cash flow from operations is constructed, we begin with the major elements of the income statement (see Exhibit 4A–2) and then adjust these elements for the various balance sheet accounts that relate to them. Thus, for example, operating revenues are adjusted for the change in receivables, and operating expenses are adjusted for the change in inventory, deferred income taxes, other current liabilities, and of course, the depreciation expense:

Accrual Income Statement		*Adjustment*	*Cash Flow Effect*
Operating revenues	$ 579.3		
	(19.8)	Increase in receivables	$ 559.5
Operating expenses	$ 472.3		
	(159.9)	Decrease in inventory	
	123.6	Decrease in other current liabilities	
	(13.9)	Increase in deferred income taxes	
	(10.0)	Depreciation expense	(412.1)
Cash flow from operations			$ 147.4

Note that under either the direct or the indirect method, the cash flow from operations remains the same (i.e., $147.4 million); however, under the direct method, the rearrangement of data allows us to identify two additional cash flow items:

Cash flow from operating revenues	$ 559.5
Cash flow for operating expenses	(412.1)

These two figures can be quite revealing about a company's internal operations. For example, the relationship of cash operating revenues to accrual operating revenues (i.e., $559.5/$579.3) reveals the rate at which cash is produced for each dollar of sales: in this case, about 96.6 percent. The measure also is often used to assess the quality of a company's revenue recognition policies. In general, the higher the relationship between cash and accrual revenues, the better the quality of a company's revenue recognition policies. In this case, the relationship is quite strong, and, thus, we would conclude that GE's revenue recognition policies were appropriate. Where the relation is quite low, it usually indicates that the company is using revenue recognition policies that are too liberal and, consequently, may be recording accrual sales well in advance of the receipt of cash on those sales. When this occurs, it is often referred to as **front-end loading.**

The relationship between cash operating expenses and accrual operating expenses also can be used to evaluate a company's accounting policies, specifically its expense recognition policy. For most companies, the relation of its cash to accrual operating expenses (i.e., $412.1/$472.3) will be less than 1, in large measure due to the adjustment for such noncash expenses as depreciation, amortization, and the change in deferred income taxes; however, when this relation is substantially greater than 1, it may be indicative of **rear-end loading.** Rear-end loading occurs when a company incurs significant cash expenditures that are accounted for as assets, rather than as expenses. In some instances, the capitalization to the balance sheet of such expenditures is well justified; in others, it may not be. In any case, when the relation of cash to accrual operating expenses is large, most professional analysts regard this as a red flag requiring further investigation.

Summary

The purpose of this appendix was to review a simple four-step procedure to prepare a statement of cash flows. A thorough financial analysis would be incomplete without considering a company's cash flows, and international financial analysts frequently find it necessary to prepare such an analysis themselves since it is not required in all countries. In subsequent chapters, we will return to the cash flow techniques developed in this appendix when we address the issue of preparing pro forma financial statements and assessing a company's free cash flows.

ISSUES AND INFORMATION FOR FURTHER INQUIRY

I.4.1   Credit Reporting Agencies

In an October 13, 1993, *Financial Times* article, "FT Exporter" (p. XIV), Paul Melly reported that "it is not easy to obtain accurate information on the recent financial performance of [companies] in many parts of the world [due in large measure to the fact that there is] no central collection point [and because] company accounts are hard to compare [since] accounting requirements vary from country to country." Melly does note that a few leading agencies, such as Graydon and Dun & Bradstreet, maintain databases on many companies and, for a fee, provide "reports in a standard format with standard principles for assessing creditworthiness."

Required:

Investigate via phone calls and/or library research the nature of the information available from Dun & Bradstreet pertaining to the creditworthiness of the many European companies it monitors. In particular, you should note the financial ratios it uses. Comment on the coverage and usefulness of those ratios.

I.4.2   The Best Ratios

In a February 1993 *Business Credit* article (pp. 20–22), "Striking the Right Balance and Proportion," James Kristy asserts that of 100 or so possible financial ratios, the following ratios are "the most useful of all for assessing the financial strength of a business enterprise":

- Current.
- Quick.
- Liquidity (cash and cash equivalents divided by current liabilities).
- Equity/debt (shareholders' equity divided by total debt).
- Return on equity.

Required:

(a) Do you agree that these five are "the most useful"? Why or why not?
(b) Identify and discuss at least two financial reporting choices whose use would affect the five ratios Kristy identifies.

EXERCISES

E.4.1   Interpreting Ratios

One day at work at the Valley National Bank, a co-worker from the international lending division approaches you for assistance. This credit analyst has made a number of calculations and notes, but is obviously puzzled by what the results mean: ''None of this makes any sense to me; I just don't understand what's going on with this British borrower!'' Her numerical analysis included the following data:

	1994	1993
Return on equity	22%	19%
Working capital	£ 20,000	£ 5,000
Current ratio	1.25	1.07
Quick ratio	0.50	0.50
Average days' receivable outstanding	73	81
Inventory turnover	1.25×	1.69×
Times interest earned	3.75×	4.17×
Long-term debt to equity ratio	0.80	0.60
Dividends paid to shareholders' equity ratio	22%	19%
Shares outstanding	5,000,000	5,000,000

Required:

Try to help your co-worker develop an understanding of this borrower by identifying the important financial trends suggested by these data.

E.4.2   Interpreting Ratios

One day at work at the Valley National Bank, a co-worker from the international lending division approaches you for assistance. The fellow credit analyst has made a number of calculations and notes, but is obviously puzzled by what the results mean: ''None of this makes any sense to me; I just can't seem to understand what's going on with this Japanese borrower!'' Her numerical analysis included the following data:

	1994	1993
Return on sales	6.23 %	8.23%
Sales increase (in dollars)	(2.00)%	18.30%
Gross margin percent	35 %	37.5%
Research and development expenses as a percent of sales	6.67 %	8.17%
General and administrative expenses as a percent of sales	12.50 %	10.62%
Total asset turnover	1.08×	0.95×
Return on total assets	5.75 %	8.68%
Return on equity	13.84 %	20.98%
Effective tax rate	42.50 %	40.00%
Average selling price per unit	¥ 4.80	¥ 5.10

Required:

Try to help your co-worker develop an understanding of this borrower by identifying the significant financial trends suggested by this data.

E.4.3   Receivable Analysis

The following are selected summary financial data for two international beverage companies:

	1993	1992
Net sales (in millions)		
CCE, Inc.	$ 4,852.5	$ 4,843.75
PCO, Inc.	19,052.5	15,666.25
Average trade receivables (in millions)		
CCE, Inc.	371.25	367.5
PCO, Inc.	1,550.0	1,223.75

Required:

Using the financial data, calculate the receivable turnover ratio and average number of days' collection period ratio for each company. What conclusions would you draw from these data regarding the credit management policy of each company?

E.4.4   Inventory Analysis

Following are selected summary financial data for two international beverage companies:

	1993	1992
Cost of goods sold (in millions)		
CCE, Inc.	$2,891.25	$2,835.00
PCO, Inc.	9,335.00	7,446.25
Average inventory on hand (in millions)		
CCE, Inc.	$ 160.00	$ 156.25
PCO, Inc.	681.25	552.50

Required:

Using the above financial data, calculate the inventory turnover ratio and the average number of days' inventory on hand for each company. What conclusions would you draw from these data regarding the inventory management policy of each company?

E.4.5   Ratio Analysis and Alternative GAAP

Ratios may be influenced by real changes in the operating performance of a company, as well as by artificial changes in a company's reported accounting numbers. Consider, for example, the case of FIFO Company and LIFO Company, which are identical in every respect except the method used to value inventory: LIFO Company uses the LIFO method, FIFO Company uses the FIFO method. The following are the most recent income statement data and balance sheets for the two Japanese companies:

Income Statement Data

	FIFO Company	LIFO Company
Sales	¥ 40,000,000	¥ 40,000,000
Less: Cost of sales	(18,400,000)	(22,560,000)
Gross margin	21,600,000	17,440,000
Less: Operating expenses	(10,000,000)	(10,000,000)
Net income	¥ 11,600,000	¥ 7,440,000

Balance Sheet Data

	FIFO Company	LIFO Company
Quick assets	¥ 18,000,000	¥ 18,000,000
Inventory	7,600,000	3,440,000
Total current assets	¥ 25,600,000	¥ 21,440,000
Noncurrent assets (net)	40,000,000	40,000,000
Total assets	¥ 65,600,000	¥ 61,440,000
Current liabilities	¥ 8,400,000	¥ 8,400,000
Noncurrent liabilities	18,000,000	18,000,000
Total liabilities	¥ 26,400,000	¥ 26,400,000
Total shareholders' equity	39,200,000	35,040,000
Total equities	¥ 65,600,000	¥ 61,440,000

Required:

Using the preceding financial data, calculate the following financial indicators for each firm:

  a. Current ratio.

  b. Inventory turnover ratio.

  c. Average number of days' inventory on hand.

  d. Return on total assets ratio.

  e. Total debt to total assets ratio.

  f. Long-term debt to shareholders' equity ratio.

  g. Gross margin ratio.

  h. Return on sales ratio.

  i. Return on equity ratio.

  j. Earnings per share (assume 2 million shares outstanding).

Based on these ratios, which company represents the following:

  k. The best investment opportunity?

  l. The best acquisition opportunity?

  m. The best lending opportunity?

E.4.6   Cash Flow Analysis

It was early 1994, and Pam Herberger was sitting at her desk staring at a set of financial statements. The statements, which follow, were those of the HFS Corporation, a British corporation. They represented the raw materials for Pam's first assignment as a credit analyst in the international lending division of Valley National Bank.

Herberger's immediate supervisor, Katherine Miller, had received the HFS statements as part of a loan application package. Because HFS was a privately-held company, the statements did not have to conform to existing FASB or SEC disclosure standards; however, the only significant omission that Miller had noticed was the absence of a cash flow statement. Rather than ask the new customer to provide one, which might delay the loan review process, she decided to ask Pam to derive one from the available financial data.

Required:

  (a) Prepare a statement of cash flows for HFS for 1993.
  (b) On the basis of your answer to part (a), and any other analysis that you believe is necessary, prepare an evaluation of the creditworthiness of HFS, assuming that the company is interested in (1) a short-term loan of £15 million for working capital purposes and (2) a £75 million five-year loan for capital asset purchases.

HFS Corporation
Statement of Income
(in thousands)

	As of December 31	
	1993	*1992*
Net revenue	£22,733	£60,095
Less: Costs and expenses		
Cost of operations	28,250	13,818
General and administrative	5,777	2,541
Interest	9,901	5,389
Depreciation and amortization	22,708	7,118
	66,636	28,866
Net income before income taxes	56,097	31,229
Provision for income taxes:		
Current	203	
Deferred	24,266	12,804
Total	24,469	12,804
Net income after income taxes	31,628	18,425
Dividends paid	9,134	4,268
Transferred to retained earnings	£22,494	£14,157

HFS Corporation
Comparative Balance Sheets
(in thousands)

	As of December 31	
	1993	*1992*
Assets		
Current assets		
Cash	£ 14,696	£ 16,390
Receivables		
Trade	20,378	10,808
Other	324	866
Inventories	15,967	3,843
Prepaid expenses	197	2,414
Total current assets	£ 51,562	£ 34,321
Noncurrent assets:		
Property, plant, and equipment (at cost)	258,908	152,145
Less: Accumulated depreciation	(34,224)	(11,516)
Total noncurrent assets	224,684	140,629
Deferred charges and other assets	2,041	1,666
Total assets	£278,287	£176,616
Liabilities and Shareholders' Equity		
Current liabilities		
Accounts payable	£ 20,160	£ 16,710
Accrued expenses payable	2,901	1,077
Income taxes payable	203	–0–
Current maturities on long-term debt	6,826	5,301
Total current liabilities	30,090	23,088
Long-term liabilities		
Convertible subordinated debentures	10,056	10,061
Notes payable	123,949	79,900
Deferred income taxes	44,730	20,464
Total long-term liabilities	178,735	110,425
Shareholders' equity		
Capital stock	1,380	912
Additional paid-in capital	19,949	16,552
Retained earnings	48,133	25,639
Total shareholders' equity	69,462	43,103
Total liabilities and shareholders' equity	£278,287	£176,616

E.4.7   Debt versus Equity

In October 1993, Henderson Land Ltd. issued a new type of convertible debt instrument called a SIREN (step-up income redeemable equity note). Under the new offering, the Hong Kong–based real estate development company agreed to pay an escalating coupon rate of 4 percent in Year 1, 4.5 percent in Year 2, and 5 percent in Year 3. In addition, the debt instrument was convertible into shares of Henderson China Ltd. *when* (and if) the mainland China subsidiary ultimately went public. Like the coupon rate, the conversion price (rate) varied as a function of the duration of time until Henderson China issued shares to the public. If the subunit went public within one year, the conversion price would be 5 percent *less* than the subsidiary's initial public offering (IPO) price, 6 percent less if the IPO occurred in Year 2, and 7 percent less if the IPO occurred in Year 3. Analysts familiar with the company predicted that the IPO would occur in 1996, at which time the convertible debt holders would be required to convert to stock. If the IPO were canceled or failed to occur within three years, Henderson agreed to redeem the debentures at 107 percent of face value. At the time of the convertible debt offering, Henderson China was a wholly owned subsidiary of Henderson Land Ltd. Henderson China's principal assets were land investments in mainland China. The $400 million debt offering was oversubscribed by $1.6 billion.

Required:

    (a) From an analytical perspective, should the $400 million of convertible debt be treated as debt or as equity on Henderson's financial statements? Why? And, does it really matter how the convertible debt is treated?

    (b) Why do you think that the convertible debt offering was oversubscribed?

E.4.8   Basic Financial Statement Analysis

The Charter Company was organized in 1959 as a consolidation of several existing corporations. The company's primary line of business was petroleum production and marketing, although it also maintained a significant equity investment in the Charter Security Life Insurance Company.

In 1983, the Charter Company was listed by *Fortune* magazine among the 100 largest U.S. industrial companies. For the year ended December 31, 1983, revenues totaled $5.7 billion, and income from continuing operations was $50.4 million. For 1982, revenues were $4 billion, and earnings from continuing operations were $29.8 million.

In spite of the continuing worldwide glut in crude oil and petroleum products, Charter had maintained its quarterly dividend of $.25 per share from the second quarter of 1980 through the first quarter of 1984. During 1983 and early 1984, Charter's common stock traded in a range of $8.00 to $13.75. In the latter half of 1983, however, a number of adverse articles began appearing in the financial press, questioning the quality of Charter's reported earnings. Nonetheless, the company's 1983 financial

---

statements, released in early 1984, indicated no particular financial concerns. Moreover, the firm's "Big Eight" auditing firm, Peat, Marwick, Mitchell & Co., had issued a "clean" opinion, subject only to a consistency qualification (to which they concurred).

During the first week of April 1984, however, Charter reported a substantial first quarter loss and announced plans to cut oil production and lay off employees. The company's common stock dropped in price from $9.50 per share on April 3 to $6.625 on April 5. The price then steadily decreased to $3.25 by the end of April.

On April 20, 1984, the Charter Company and 43 of its subsidiaries filed voluntary petitions for relief under Chapter 11 of the Bankruptcy Act.

Required:

(a) Calculate the following ratios for each year during the period 1980–1983. Comment on the trend indicated by each ratio with respect to the financial performance and condition of the Charter Company:

(1) Profitability:
Return on average total assets (assume a 46 percent income tax rate).

(2) Turnover:
1. Accounts receivable (based on average gross trade receivables).
2. Inventory (based on average total inventory).
3. Total assets (based on average total assets).

(3) Liquidity:
1. Current ratio.
2. Quick ratio.

(4) Solvency:
1. Total liabilities to total equities.
2. Total long-term debt to total long-term debt plus owners' equity.

(b) The Charter Company had a number of nonrecurring and/or noncash components of income from continuing operations in 1983. Beginning with the 1983 earnings from continuing operations, adjust this figure for nonrecurring and/or noncash items. (Information for these adjustments is included in Exhibits 1, 3, and 4.)

(c) Calculate the cash provided by (used in) operations for each year during the period 1980–1983, starting with the amount of working capital provided by operations shown in Exhibit 3 and adjusting for changes in current asset and current liability accounts on the balance sheet (Exhibit 2), which are related to operations.

(d) Based on the information presented in the case, discuss the extent to which the stock market, in the aggregate, anticipated Charter's problems and priced its common stock accordingly. (See Exhibit 5.)

(e) Comment on the extent to which operating current assets and operating current liabilities represented sources or uses of cash for the Charter Company for the years 1980–1983. Comment on how the pattern of operating cash flows was similar (or dissimilar) to the operating cash flows for the 18 oil companies in Exhibit 6.

EXHIBIT 1

THE CHARTER COMPANY
Consolidated Statements of Earnings
Years Ended December 31
(in thousands)

	1983	1982	1981	1980	1979
Revenues	$5,656,770	$4,017,161	$4,966,171	$4,563,011	$4,296,370
Equity in net earnings of Charter Security Life and other affiliates	117,958	43,402	14,080	661	2,357
	$5,774,728	$4,060,563	$4,980,251	$4,563,672	$4,298,727
Expenses:					
Cost of sales and operating	$5,364,820	$3,744,462	$4,512,215	$4,193,275	$3,624,619
Selling, general and administrative	99,987	101,968	190,656	112,694	154,608
Interest	80,886	69,879	89,196	77,133	44,000
Depreciation, depletion, and amortization	37,939	36,074	32,511	35,085	28,851
Write-off of certain units at Bahamas refinery	49,428	—	—	—	—
Write-down of tanker	7,772	—	—	—	—
Total expenses	$5,640,832	$3,952,383	$4,824,578	$4,418,187	$3,852,078
Earnings before income taxes, etc.	$ 133,896	$ 108,180	$ 155,673	$ 145,485	$ 446,649
Income taxes	83,514	78,350	99,727	95,248	78,923
Earnings from continuing operations	$ 50,382	$ 29,830	$ 55,946	$ 50,237	$ 367,726
Discontinued operations, net	(1,950)	5,430	(48,229)	—	—
Extraordinary charge	—	—	—	—	(2,388)
Earnings before cumulative effect	$ 48,432	$ 35,260	$ 7,717	$ 50,237	$ 365,338
Cumulative effect on prior years of a change in accounting principle	5,463	—	—	—	—
Net earnings	$ 53,895	$ 35,260	$ 7,717	$ 50,237	$ 365,338

EXHIBIT 2

THE CHARTER COMPANY
Consolidated Balance Sheets
December 31
(in thousands)

	1983	1982	1981	1980	1979
Assets					
Current assets					
Cash and cash equivalents	$ 64,031	$ 59,939	$ 69,283	$ 94,112	$ 95,632
Receivables					
Trade accounts	294,715	262,646	343,862	322,237	296,344
Other	22,756	18,736	25,967	32,142	41,488
Affiliates	31,030	30,106	11,479	16,312	499
Short-term notes and current installments of long-term receivables	2,868	24,744	8,815	3,133	8,745
	351,369	336,232	390,123	373,824	347,076
Less: Allowance for doubtful receivables	10,951	8,622	14,464	56,062	14,005
Net receivables	340,418	327,610	375,659	367,762	333,071
Inventories					
Petroleum	352,162	228,462	111,313	270,094	319,001
Other	17,554	11,287	25,374	25,477	29,179
Total inventories	369,716	239,749	136,687	295,571	348,180
Assets held for sale	15,260	—	—	—	—
Prepaid expenses	12,302	14,578	27,316	16,217	16,971
Total current assets	$ 801,727	$ 641,876	$ 608,945	$ 773,662	$ 793,845
Investments					
Bahamas refinery affiliates	311,151	374,913	389,060	407,402	408,635
Charter Security Life & other affiliates	261,115	125,955	76,751	83,190	55,060
Other	4,237	41,515	41,160	39,990	44,342
Total investments	576,503	542,383	506,971	530,582	508,037
Property, plant, and equipment	426,415	407,814	403,187	468,851	395,188
Less: Accumulated depreciation and depletion	152,343	140,977	124,409	122,225	92,889
Net property, plant, and equipment	274,072	266,837	278,778	345,626	302,299
Net assets of discontinued operations	—	26,282	2,717	—	—
Intangibles from acquisitions (net)	61,877	59,110	74,115	44,293	73,023
Other assets	99,020	91,558	69,800	51,097	51,481
Total assets	$1,813,199	$1,628,046	$1,541,326	$1,746,260	$1,728,694

EXHIBIT 2

THE CHARTER COMPANY (continued)
Consolidated Balance Sheets
December 31
(in thousands)

	1983	1982	1981	1980	1979
Liabilities and Stockholders' Equity					
Current liabilities					
Notes payable	$ 144,000	$ 3,250	$ 50,500	$ 76,563	$ 858
Current installment of long-term debt	28,317	29,342	17,192	21,402	23,363
Accounts payable	419,967	416,924	309,275	348,312	374,387
Payable to affiliates	39,143	21,257	—	—	—
Accrued expenses	54,579	48,261	54,939	71,747	74,499
Income taxes	14,749	21,625	27,217	17,433	28,208
Total current liabilities	700,755	540,659	459,123	535,457	501,315
Long-term debt excluding current installments	111,134	133,086	251,425	404,631	416,087
Long-term debt payable to unconsolidated, wholly owned subsidiaries	94,000	91,000	—	—	—
Subordinated debt, net of discount, excluding current installments	189,261	154,200	81,673	81,316	84,412
Net liabilities of discontinued operations	20,554	—	—	—	—
Deferred income taxes	32,504	16,068	43,820	27,377	41,728
Deferred credits and other	50,864	52,242	50,704	19,793	36,828
Stockholders' equity					
Preferred stock[a]	129,312	114,787	117,608	117,917	125,372
Common stock[b]	16,587	21,570	21,592	21,592	20,166
Additional paid-in capital on common stock	35,635	53,721	67,233	67,202	57,268
Retained earnings	429,298	448,924	447,555	470,476	449,629
Net unrealized gain on investment securities of unconsolidated subsidiaries, net of income taxes	3,295	1,789	593	499	(4,111)
	614,127	640,791	654,581	677,686	648,324
Total liabilities and stockholders' equity	$1,813,199	$1,628,046	$1,541,326	$1,746,260	$1,728,694

[a]Aggregate liquidation preference: $134,972,000 in 1983 and $112,572,000 in 1982.
[b]Shares outstanding: 16,587,051 in 1983 and 21,570,101 in 1982.

EXHIBIT 3

THE CHARTER COMPANY
Schedules of Working Capital Provided by Operations
Years Ended December 31
(in thousands)

	1983	1982	1981	1980	1979
Working capital provided by operations					
Earnings from continuing operations	$ 50,382	$ 29,830	$ 55,946	$ 50,237	$367,726
Charges (credits) to earnings affecting working capital					
Depreciation, depletion, and amortization	37,939	36,074	32,511	35,085	28,851
Gain on exchange of investment in St. Joe Paper Company	(17,125)	—	—	—	—
Deferred income taxes and other	7,850	(7,631)	4,254	1,928	4,843
Equity in net earnings of Charter Life and other affiliates	(117,958)	(43,402)	(14,080)	(661)	(2,357)
Equity in net losses of Bahamas refinery affiliates included in cost of sales	12,511	18,542	27,548	16,775	10,376
Write-off of certain units in Bahamas refinery	49,428	—	—	—	—
Write-down of tanker	7,772	—	—	—	—
Total working capital provided by operations	$ 30,799	$ 33,413	$106,179	$103,364	$409,439

EXHIBIT 4

THE CHARTER COMPANY
Selected Notes to 1983 Financial Statements

1. Significant Accounting Policies

A. Basis of Financial Presentation. The accompanying consolidated financial statements include the accounts of The Charter Company and its majority-owned subsidiaries ("Charter") other than Charter Security Life Insurance Company (Louisiana) and subsidiaries ("Charter Security Life"), COFI Credit Corporation ("COFI") and First Charter Savings Bank ("First Charter") which are accounted for by the equity method. Charter's Bahamas refinery affiliates and other affiliated companies, all 31% to 50% owned, are also accounted for by the equity method. All significant intercompany accounts and transactions for Charter have been eliminated in consolidation.

B. Inventories. Inventories are stated at the lower of cost or market. Certain petroleum inventories aggregating $115,242,000 at December 31, 1983 and $83,664,000 at December 31, 1982 were determined under the last-in, first-out method ("LIFO"). Such petroleum inventories, if stated at current costs, would have been $41,554,000 and $48,051,000 higher, respectively. If the first-in, first-out method ("FIFO") of inventory valuation had been used for such inventories, reported net earnings would have been lower by $6,497,000 ($.28 primary and fully diluted earnings per share) for 1983, $6,015,000 ($.21 primary and fully diluted earnings per share) for 1982 and $12,750,000 ($.45 primary and fully diluted earnings per share) for 1981. The cost of the remaining petroleum and other inventories is determined under the FIFO method. Crude oil and product exchange balances are reflected in petroleum inventories.

EXHIBIT 4 (continued)

THE CHARTER COMPANY
Selected Notes to 1983 Financial Statements

Certain petroleum inventories at December 31, 1983 were less than inventory levels at December 31, 1982 or the date of acquisition resulting in a liquidation of LIFO layers which were carried at lower costs. If such inventories had been replaced at current costs, net earnings for 1983 would have been lower by approximately $12,803,000 ($.56 primary and fully diluted earnings per share). Certain petroleum inventories at December 31, 1981 were less than prior year levels resulting in a liquidation of prior years' LIFO layers which were carried at lower costs. If such inventories had been replaced at current costs, net earnings for 1981 would have been lower by approximately $15,686,000 ($.56 primary and fully diluted earnings per share).

F. Change in Accounting Principle. Effective January 1, 1983, Charter changed its accounting method of expensing the cost of spare parts at the Houston refinery to inventorying the spare parts and charging the cost to operations as utilized. This change was made to improve the matching of costs of spare parts to the benefits derived from their usage and establish financial control over these items. Net earnings for the first quarter of 1983 have been restated by $5,463,000 to reflect the cumulative effect of the change on prior years. The effect of this change was not material to 1983 earnings from continuing operations. The pro forma and cumulative effects on net earnings of prior years is not determinable because the necessary data is unavailable.

G. Miscellaneous Policies. Refining, marketing and other facilities are depreciated principally by the straight-line method over their estimated useful lives. During 1983, Charter revised the estimated useful lives of certain property, plant and equipment. The effect of this change in accounting estimate was an increase in net earnings of $3,003,000 ($.13 primary and fully diluted earnings per share). During the fourth quarter of 1983, Charter renegotiated a contract and recorded a gain of $33,600,000.

5. Investment in Bahamas Refinery Affiliates

Charter's investment in the Bahamas refinery affiliates includes three 50% owned joint ventures: Bahamas Oil Refining Company ("BORCO"), BORCO Desulfurization Company ("BODCO") and BORCO Marine Company ("MARCO"). These joint ventures receive fees from the partners for use of the refinery and related facilities. The operations of these joint ventures do not reflect the partners' purchases of crude oil, sales of refined products and processing or storage agreements with third parties. Charter's share of the net operating losses of these ventures was $12,511,000, $18,542,000 and $27,548,000, for 1983, 1982 and 1981, respectively, including depreciation and amortization related to the excess of the appraised value over the historical cost of the assets allocated to property, plant and equipment at the time of the acquisition. Charter's share of the losses of these ventures is recorded as cost of sales and operating expenses in its consolidated statements of earnings because these joint ventures are part of Charter's crude oil refining system. In addition, BORCO and BODCO wrote off certain units during 1983 since use of such units is not anticipated in the foreseeable future. Charter's share of the write-off plus the write-off of the related excess of the appraised value over the historical cost of these assets was $49,428,000.

EXHIBIT 5

THE CHARTER COMPANY
Quarterly Earnings per Share, Cash Dividends, and Common Stock Prices
For the Fiscal Year 1983 and the First Two Quarters of 1984

| | 1983 | | | | 1984 | |
	First Quarter	Second Quarter	Third Quarter	Fourth Quarter	First Quarter	Second Quarter
Fully diluted earnings per share						
From continuing operations	$ (0.31)	$ 0.51	$ 1.34	$ 0.23	$ (1.49)	$ (2.84)
Net earnings	(0.05)	0.43	1.34	0.23	(2.38)	(35.14)
Common dividend per share	0.25	0.25	0.25	0.25	0.25	0.00
Market price						
High	$13.375	$13.750	$12.500	$12.250	$12.875	$ 9.750
Low	11.125	10.750	10.250	8.000	8.500	2.000

EXHIBIT 6
Net Income, Working Capital, and Operating Cash Flows of Fortune Top 100 Industrial Oil Companies (*n* = 18) for Fiscal Years Ending December 31, 1979 to 1983

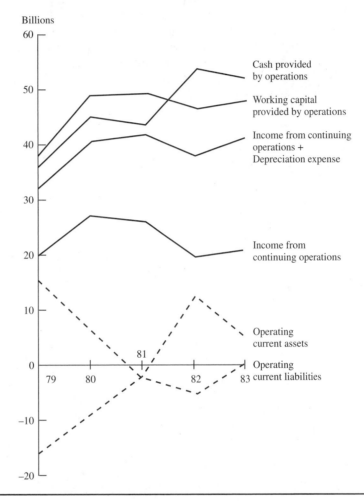

E.4.9   Ratios Tell a Story—International (A)

Corporate financial positions, results of operations, and cash flows vary substantially among companies. One of the principal reasons for the variation can be traced to the characteristics of the industries within which the companies operate. Some industries require large investments in property, plant, and equipment, whereas other industries do not. In some industries, the product-pricing structure allows companies to earn

This exercise was prepared by Robert M. Conroy and E. Richard Brownlee II. Copyright © 1992 by the Darden Graduate Business School Foundation, Charlottesville, Virginia.

significant profit margins, while in other industries the profit margins are low. In most low-margin industries, however, companies often experience a relatively high volume of product throughput. Credit terms also vary among industries, with companies in some industries relying heavily on cash sales.

A second reason for corporate financial statement variation is due to different management philosophies and competencies. Some managements try to maintain a close relationship between production or service capacity and current demand, while others are more intent on building capacity in anticipation of demand. Some managements prefer a low debt-to-equity relationship, while others rely heavily on borrowed funds. Certainly the nature of the industry also affects managements' willingness to incur debt. Financial statement differences among competing companies that follow similar operating policies result, at least in part, from different management capabilities.

A third reason for corporate financial statement variation is attributable to the use of alternate accounting principles and to different estimates and judgments made in applying specific accounting principles. Comparisons of the financial statements of companies from different countries need to be made with the understanding that the generally accepted accounting principles used in their preparation are not uniform around the world.

These differences in industry characteristics, company policies, management philosophies and competencies, and accounting principles can be highlighted through the analysis of financial ratios. Exhibit 1 presents balance sheets, in percentage form, and selected ratios computed from the 1990 balance sheets and income statements of the following 11 companies:

A. Advertising agency (Europe).

B. Airline (North America).

C. Automobile manufacturer (Europe).

D. Commercial bank (North America).

E. Department store (North America).

F. Electronic game manufacturer (Asia).

G. Food and convenience stores (Asia).

H. Oil company—refining and production (Europe).

 I. Pharmaceuticals (North America).

 J. Public utility—gas (Asia).

K. Steel producer (Asia).

Using the data presented in Exhibit 1, identify each of the 11 companies represented. Give your reasons for associating a particular company with a particular column of data. The ratios in Exhibit 1 are based on the following formulae:

1. Current ratio $= \dfrac{\text{Total current assets}}{\text{Total current liabilities}}$

2. Acid test (quick ratio) $= \dfrac{\text{Quick assets (usually, Current assets} - \text{Inventory)}}{\text{Total current liabilities}}$

EXHIBIT 1

Companies' Data

	1	2	3	4	5	6	7	8	9	10	11
Assets											
Cash & equivalents	1.0%	2.1%	27.7%	22.1%	10.0%	19.8%	6.4%	7.1%	17.2%	61.6%	14.9%
Accounts receivable	16.5	16.2	2.8	27.4	52.7	12.3	5.3	87.7	14.3	7.7	16.8
Inventory	23.7	11.3	6.3	11.7	1.8	3.4	0.5	0.0	19.5	15.9	11.1
Other current assets	1.7	1.4	2.3	2.6	0.5	2.5	1.7	0.0	1.0	1.9	4.1
Total current assets	42.9	31.0	39.1	63.8	65.0	38.0	13.9	94.8	52.0	87.1	46.9
Net property & equip.	53.1	56.9	44.4	28.8	7.5	54.1	80.0	2.2	18.0	11.5	33.9
Other assets	4.0	12.1	16.5	7.4	27.5	7.9	6.1	3.0	30.0	1.4	19.2
Total assets	100.0%	100.0%	100.0%	100.0%	100.0%	100.0%	100.0%	100.0%	100.0%	100.0%	100.0%
Liabilities											
Notes payable	4.1%	5.6%	2.5%	17.2%	12.0%	7.4%	4.5%	2.0%	24.1%	0.0%	9.8%
Accounts payable	14.9	9.4	17.8	26.2	35.0	0.0	4.6	83.4	7.0	20.5	14.2
Accrued taxes	1.9	4.9	7.5	2.0	0.0	0.0	4.2	0.0	0.3	14.0	11.2
Other current liabs.	7.5	11.4	2.5	5.9	24.9	37.4	4.5	0.0	16.3	6.9	0.0
Total current liabs.	28.4	31.3	30.3	51.3	71.9	44.8	17.8	85.4	47.7	41.4	35.2
Long-term debt	43.2	17.0	7.8	10.0	1.7	18.5	31.7	3.3	6.4	0.0	1.5
Other liabilities	4.1	15.1	0.7	26.9	4.2	15.0	16.4	5.5	11.0	0.7	8.7
Total liabilities	75.7%	63.4%	38.8%	88.2%	77.8%	78.3%	65.9%	94.2%	65.1%	42.1%	45.4%
Equity											
Preferred stock	0.3%	0.0%	0.0%	0.0%	0.0%	0.0%	0.0%	0.6%	0.0%	0.0%	0.0%
Cap. stock & surplus	1.3	12.2	27.1	9.0	14.6	1.5	27.6	2.0	23.7	3.3	8.9
Retained earnings	22.7	24.4	34.1	2.8	7.6	20.2	6.5	3.2	11.2	54.6	45.7
Total equity	24.3%	36.6%	61.2%	11.8%	22.2%	21.7%	34.1%	5.8%	34.9%	57.9%	54.6%
Total liabs. & equity	100.0%	100.0%	100.0%	100.0%	100.0%	100.0%	100.0%	100.0%	100.0%	100.0%	100.0%
Ratios											
Current ratio	1.51	0.99	1.29	1.25	0.91	0.85	0.78	1.11	1.09	2.10	1.33
Acid test	0.68	0.63	1.08	1.02	0.88	0.77	0.76	1.11	0.68	1.72	1.02
ROS	4.83%	5.46%	6.75%	0.38%	2.20%	4.50%	2.15%	0.84%	−1.23%	16.60%	22.18%
Asset turnover	1.73	1.08	1.79	0.90	1.90	1.36	0.46	0.11	0.81	1.14	0.96
ROA	8.36%	5.87%	12.09%	0.35%	4.18%	6.11%	0.99%	0.09%	−1.00%	18.87%	21.96%
Financial leverage	4.11	2.73	1.64	8.45	4.50	4.60	2.93	17.18	2.87	1.73	1.83
ROE	34.37%	16.40%	19.77%	2.93%	18.79%	28.12%	2.00%	1.61%	−2.87%	32.59%	38.82%
Debt to capital	64.00%	31.70%	11.03%	45.80%	7.20%	46.00%	48.20%	36.10%	15.50%	0.00%	2.8%
Inventory turnover	5.28	7.04	18.89	6.40	—	—	—	—	3.46	4.09	1.71
Receivables collection	34.84	55.01	5.78	111.12	101.07	33.10	42.25	2875.96	64.29	24.87	64.00

3. ROS (return on sales) $= \dfrac{\text{Net income}}{\text{Net sales}}$

4. Total asset turnover $= \dfrac{\text{Net sales}}{\text{Average total assets}}$

5. ROA (return on total assets) = ROS × Asset turnover

$\qquad = \dfrac{\text{Net income}}{\text{Average total assets}}$

6. Financial leverage $= \dfrac{\text{Average total assets}}{\text{Average total stockholders' equity}}$

7. ROE (return on equity) = ROA × Financial leverage

$\qquad = \dfrac{\text{Net income}}{\text{Average total stockholders' equity}}$

8. Long-term debt to capital $= \dfrac{\text{Long-term debt}}{\text{Long-term debt} + \text{Total stockholders' equity}}$

9. Inventory turnover $= \dfrac{\text{Cost of goods sold}}{\text{Average inventory during the period}}$

10. Receivables collection (days) $= \dfrac{\text{Average accounts receivable during the period}}{\text{Net sales/365 days}}$

E.4.10   Ratios Tell a Story—International (B)

Corporate financial positions, results of operations, and cash flows vary substantially among companies. One of the principal reasons for the variation can be traced to the characteristics of the industries within which the companies operate. Some industries require large investments in property, plant, and equipment, whereas other industries do not. In some industries, the product-pricing structure allows companies to earn significant profit margins, while in other industries the profit margins are low. In most low margin industries, however, companies often experience a relatively high volume of product throughput. Credit terms also vary among industries, with companies in some industries relying heavily on cash sales.

A second reason for corporate financial statement variation is due to different management philosophies and competencies. Some managements try to maintain a close relationship between production or service capacity and current demand, while others are more intent on building capacity in anticipation of demand. Some managements prefer a low debt-to-equity relationship, while others rely heavily on borrowed funds. Certainly the nature of the industry also affects management's willingness to incur debt. Financial statement differences among competing companies that follow similar operating policies result, at least in part, from different management capabilities.

This exercise was prepared by Robert M. Conroy and E. Richard Brownlee II. Copyright © 1992 by the Darden Graduate School of Business Foundation, Charlottesville, Virginia.

EXHIBIT 1

Automobile Manufacturers' Financial Data

	Europe	North America	Asia
Assets			
Cash & equivalents	17.2%	3.2%	13.8%
Accounts receivable	14.3	18.6	11.5
Inventory	19.5	20.7	4.5
Other current assets	1.0	0.4	24.6
Total current assets	52.0	42.9	54.4
Net property & equip.	18.0	28.7	22.3
Other assets	30.0	28.4	23.3
Total assets	100.0%	100.0%	100.0%
Liabilities			
Notes payable	24.1%	25.2%	7.4%
Accounts payable	7.0	6.5	7.7
Accrued taxes	0.3	0.0	1.7
Other current liabs.	16.3	30.7	12.7
Total current liabs.	47.7	62.4	29.5
Long-term debt	6.4	27.3	16.6
Other liabilities	11.0	2.5	3.2
Total liabilities	65.1%	92.2%	49.3%
Equity			
Preferred stock	0.0%	0.0%	0.0%
Cap. stock & surplus	23.6	0.6	6.0
Retained earnings	11.3	7.2	44.7
Total equity	34.9	7.8	50.7
Total liabs. & equity	100.0%	100.0%	100.0%
Ratios			
Current ratio	1.09	0.69	1.85
Acid test	0.68	0.36	1.69
ROS	−1.23%	−2.63%	4.84%
Asset turnover	0.81	0.84	1.11
ROA	−1.00%	−2.21%	5.35%
Financial leverage	2.87	12.80	1.97
ROE	−2.87%	−33.67%	9.53%
Debt to capital	15.50%	77.70%	24.70%
Inventory turnover	3.46	3.53	20.36
Receivables collection	64.29	80.69	37.96

A third reason for corporate financial statement variation is attributable to the use of alternate accounting principles and to different estimates and judgments made in applying specific accounting principles. Comparisons of the financial statements of companies from different countries need to be made with the understanding that the generally accepted accounting principles used in their preparation are not uniform around the world.

Exhibits 1 through 4 present balance sheets, in percentage form, and selected ratios computed from the 1990 balance sheets and income statements of companies in

EXHIBIT 2

Airlines' Financial Data

	Europe	North America	Asia
Assets			
Cash & equivalents	5.2%	19.8%	29.3%
Accounts receivable	15.2	12.3	10.0
Inventory	0.9	3.4	3.1
Other current assets	3.3	2.5	4.5
Total current assets	24.6	38.0	46.9
Net property & equip.	72.9	54.1	36.9
Other assets	2.5	7.9	16.2
Total assets	100.0%	100.0%	100.0%
Liabilities			
Notes payable	3.4%	7.4%	5.5%
Accounts payable	13.9	0.0	9.7
Accrued taxes	1.7	0.0	1.3
Other current liab.	18.2	37.4	11.8
Total current liab.	37.2	44.8	28.3
Long-term debt	37.8	18.5	41.1
Other liabilities	2.7	15.0	5.4
Total liabilities	77.7%	78.3%	74.8%
Equity			
Preferred stock	0.0%	0.0%	0.0%
Cap. stock & surplus	5.9	1.5	21.5
Retained earnings	16.4	20.2	3.7
Total equity	22.3	21.7	25.2
Total liabs. & equity	100.0%	100.0%	100.0%
Ratios			
Current ratio	0.66	0.85	1.66
Acid test	0.64	0.77	1.55
ROS	2.21%	4.50%	1.09%
Asset turnover	1.15	1.36	0.76
ROA	2.54%	6.11%	0.82%
Financial leverage	4.49	4.60	3.97
ROE	11.39%	28.12%	3.27%
Debt to capital	62.90%	46.00%	62.00%
Inventory turnover	117.76	0.0	0.00
Receivables collection	48.35	33.10	48.28

EXHIBIT 3

Oil Companies' Financial Data

	Europe	North America	Asia
Assets			
Cash & equivalents	2.1%	2.7%	43.8%
Accounts receivable	16.2	17.1	19.2
Inventory	11.3	10.3	6.0
Other current assets	1.4	1.6	2.4
Total current assets	31.0	31.7	71.4
Net property & equip.	56.9	58.8	17.1
Other assets	12.1	9.5	11.5
Total assets	100.0%	100.0%	100.0%
Liabilities			
Notes payable	5.6%	7.3%	15.0%
Accounts payable	9.4	17.1	22.0
Accrued taxes	4.9	6.6	6.7
Other current liabs.	11.4	1.8	6.5
Total current liabs.	31.3	32.8	50.2
Long-term debt	17.0	10.3	20.8
Other liabilities	15.1	15.8	2.9
Total liabilities	63.4%	58.9%	73.9%
Equity			
Preferred stock	0.0%	0.1%	0.0%
Cap. stock & surplus	36.6	1.8	13.0
Retained earnings	0.0	39.2	13.1
Total equity	36.6	41.1	26.1
Total liabs. & equity	100.0%	100.0%	100.0%
Ratios			
Current ratio	0.99	0.97	1.42
Acid test	0.63	0.65	1.30
ROS	5.46%	4.48%	1.05%
Asset turnover	1.08	1.39	1.14
ROA	5.87%	6.22%	1.20%
Financial leverage	2.73	2.43	3.82
ROE	16.04%	15.12%	4.58%
Debt to capital	31.7 %	20.1 %	44.3 %
Inventory turnover	7.04	7.72	17.00
Receivables collection	55.01	45.04	61.39

EXHIBIT 4

Pharmaceuticals' Financial Data

	Europe	North America	Asia
Assets			
Cash & equivalents	22.5%	14.9%	40.5%
Accounts receivable	17.1	16.8	22.7
Inventory	18.4	11.1	7.7
Other current assets	7.3	4.1	0.7
Total current assets	65.3	46.9	71.6
Net property & equip.	33.7	33.9	21.4
Other assets	1.0	19.2	7.0
Total assets	100.0%	100.0%	100.0%
Liabilities			
Notes payable	9.9%	9.8%	3.2%
Accounts payable	7.6	14.2	9.6
Accrued taxes	0.0	11.2	3.8
Other current liab.	10.8	0.0	6.3
Total current liab.	28.3	35.2	22.9
Long-term debt	5.2	1.5	18.6
Other liabilities	8.5	8.7	6.7
Total liabilities	42.0%	45.4%	48.2%
Equity			
Preferred stock	0.0%	0.0%	0.0%
Cap. stock & surplus	50.5	8.9	15.2
Retained earnings	7.5	45.7	36.6
Total equity	58.0	54.6	51.8
Total liabs. & equity	100.0%	100.0%	100.0%
Ratios			
Current ratio	2.31	1.33	3.13
Acid test	1.66	1.02	2.79
ROS	7.54%	22.18%	6.51%
Asset turnover	0.96	0.96	0.61
ROA	7.28%	21.19%	3.98%
Financial leverage	1.72	1.83	1.93
ROE	12.53%	38.82%	7.69%
Debt to capital	8.2 %	2.8 %	8.2 %
Inventory turnover	2.58	1.71	2.58
Receivables collection	64.61	64.00	64.61

the same industries but from three different continents—Asia, Europe, and North America. The four industries represented are:

Exhibit 1—Automobile manufacturers.
Exhibit 2—Airlines.
Exhibit 3—Oil companies.
Exhibit 4—Pharmaceutical companies.

EXHIBIT 5

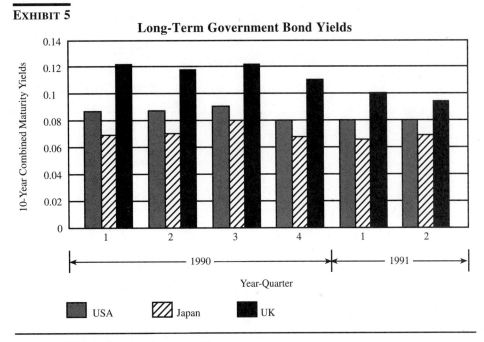

Source: *World Financial Markets,* September 1991.

For analysis purposes, Exhibit 5 contains data on the yields of long-term government bonds for 1990 through the first half of 1991.

Required:

Study the exhibits and then answer the following questions:

    (1) Does a clear industry "footprint" appear for each of the four industries?

    (2) Does a clear geographic "footprint" appear for each of the three continents?

    (3) What general conclusions can be drawn from the data?

The ratios presented in Exhibits 1–4 are based on the following formulae:

    1. Current ratio $= \dfrac{\text{Total current assets}}{\text{Total current liabilities}}$

    2. Acid test (quick ratio) $= \dfrac{\text{Quick assets (usually, Current assets} - \text{Inventory)}}{\text{Total current liabilities}}$

    3. ROS (return on sales) $= \dfrac{\text{Net income}}{\text{Net sales}}$

    4. Total asset turnover $= \dfrac{\text{Net sales}}{\text{Average total assets}}$

5. ROA (return on total assets) = ROS × Asset turnover = $\dfrac{\text{Net income}}{\text{Average total assets}}$

6. Financial leverage = $\dfrac{\text{Total assets}}{\text{Total stockholders' equity}}$

7. ROE (return on equity) = ROA × Financial leverage
    $= \dfrac{\text{Net income}}{\text{Average total stockholders' equity}}$

8. Long-term debt to capital = $\dfrac{\text{Long-term debt}}{\text{Long-term debt + Total stockholders' equity}}$

9. Inventory turnover = $\dfrac{\text{Cost of goods sold}}{\text{Average inventory during the period}}$

10. Receivables collection (days) = $\dfrac{\text{Average accounts receivable during the period}}{\text{Net sales/365 days}}$

CASES

CASE 4.1
BASIC FINANCIAL STATEMENT ANALYSIS

Oracle Systems Corporation

> The company has experienced phenomenal growth, having doubled in size, year after year, for most of its 13-year history. Lawrence J. Ellison is known for his almost fanatical aggressiveness and take-no-prisoners attitude regarding competitors. "It is not sufficient that I succeed; all others must fail," he once said, paraphrasing Genghis Khan. But now the picture could be changing.[1]

Until 1990 Oracle Systems Corporation had logged a nearly unparalleled record of sustained rapid growth: 118 percent compound annual sales growth from 1982 to 1989. Competitors, investors, and customers had searched the financial results of the company for clues to its success. These searches, however, tended to generate more questions than answers. Now, in the first half of 1990, the company had disclosed unsettling news that triggered a *66 percent drop* in the company's share price. About $2 billion in market value of equity simply vanished. This event renewed efforts of outsiders to understand the company: Was the company *healthy?* Had management made the right choices in running the company? Was management doing a good

---

[1]Andrew Pollack, "Fast Growth Oracle Systems Confronts the First Downturn," *New York Times,* September 10, 1990.

This case was prepared by Robert F. Bruner from public information with the assistance of Fadi Micaelian. Copyright © 1992 by the Darden Graduate Business School Foundation, Charlottesville, VA.

EXHIBIT 1

ORACLE SYSTEMS CORPORATION
Income Statements, 1984–1990
(in thousands except per share amounts)

| | Fiscal Year Ended May 31 | | | | | | | 1990 Qtr. Ended | |
	1984	*1985*	*1986*	*1987*	*1988*	*1989*	*1990*	*Aug. 31*	*Feb. 28*
Revenues									
Licenses	$12,282	$21,902	$44,657	$101,264	$205,435	$417,825	$689,898		
Services	433	1,257	10,726	30,007	76,678	165,848	280,946		
Total revenues	12,715	23,159	55,383	131,271	282,113	583,673	970,844	$214,799	$245,561
Operating expenses									
Sales and marketing	6,431	14,542	27,171	65,651	124,148	272,812	465,074		
Cost of services			5,644	18,661	51,241	100,987	160,426		
Research and development	2,009	3,886	7,478	9,949	25,708	52,570	88,291	20,615	21,685
General and admin.	1,673	1,989	4,248	8,603	17,121	34,344	67,258	230,187	174,673
Total operating expenses	10,113	20,417	44,541	102,864	218,218	460,713	781,049		
Operating income	2,602	2,742	10,842	28,407	63,895	122,960	189,795	(36,003)	49,203
Other income (expense)	(305)	(157)	(367)	(509)	1,084	(2,715)	(17,135)	7,516	5,342
Income before taxes	2,297	2,585	10,475	27,898	64,979	120,245	172,660		
Taxes	908	1,034	4,579	12,275	22,093	38,479	55,250	(14,796)	14,035
Net income	$ 1,389	$ 1,551	$ 5,896	$ 15,623	$ 42,886	$ 81,766	$117,410	(28,723)	29,826
Earnings per share	$0.11	$0.12	$0.11	$0.12	$0.32	$0.61	$0.86		
Number of shares outstanding	12,340	12,770	54,864	125,028	132,950	135,066	136,826		

Source: Company annual reports.

job? What represented the real source of value in this company? Investors also wondered exactly what was happening in the company that warranted such a dizzying drop in share price.

The Company.   Oracle Systems Corporation was founded in 1979 by Lawrence J. Ellison to commercialize an innovative database management system (DBMS) that he had just developed for a U.S. intelligence agency. The company produced a broad product line of systems, tools, and applications, which by 1990 were portable across all major computing platforms, from personal computer to mainframe. Under Ellison's aggressive leadership, Oracle more than doubled its sales every year from 1980 to 1989; it became the fastest growing software company in the world and, with sales of $971 million in the fiscal year (FY) ended May 31, 1990, was the dominant software producer in its specialty. Exhibits 1, 2, and 3 present the firm's income statements, balance sheets, and financial ratios for 1985–1990.

An extremely aggressive business strategy distinguished Oracle from its peers. Outside observers cited four main elements to this strategy:

1. **Sell aggressively.** Oracle distributed its products through a proprietary sales force and had 44 offices in the United States alone. This approach allowed close

EXHIBIT 2

ORACLE SYSTEMS CORPORATION
Balance Sheets, 1985–1990
(in thousands)

| | Fiscal Year Ended May 31 | | | | | | August 31, |
	1985	1986	1987	1988	1989	1990	1990
Assets							
Current assets							
Cash and cash equivalents	$ 599	$12,524	$ 37,557	$ 48,610	$ 49,393	$ 49,828	$ 50,198
Trade receivables	9,032	26,554	65,205	129,999	261,989	468,071	394,648
Other current assets	331	2,393	6,376	13,218	25,551	51,358	76,428
Total current assets	9,962	41,471	109,138	191,827	336,933	569,257	521,274
Property, net	4,491	14,152	26,896	47,554	94,455	171,945	203,887
Computer software develop.	0	0	4,818	6,920	13,942	33,396	41,707
Other assets	1,010	1,805	2,940	3,267	14,879	12,649	12,245
Total assets	$15,463	$57,428	$143,792	$249,568	$460,209	$787,247	$779,113
Liabilities and Stockholders' Equity							
Current liabilities							
Notes payable	$ 694	$ 3,164	$ 5,196	$ 6,507	$ 23,334	$ 42,501	$ 34,970
Accounts payable	1,432	4,835	10,645	23,502	51,582	64,922	57,281
Accrued expenses	3,360	11,301	28,737	62,627	88,014	134,028	82,135
Customer advances	897	2,993	3,847	9,547	15,403	42,121	70,011
Total current liabilities	6,383	22,293	48,425	102,183	178,333	283,572	244,397
Long-term debt	1,373	5,641	9,025	5,363	39,208	94,065	165,643
Deferred income taxes	340	843	3,686	7,379	12,114	22,025	10,397
Stockholders' equity	7,367	28,651	82,656	134,643	230,554	387,585	358,676
Total liabilities and stockholders' equity	$15,463	$57,428	$143,792	$249,568	$460,209	$787,247	$779,113

Note: Accounts receivable (A/R) are net of these allowances for doubtful accounts:

		Percent of A/R	Percent of A/R (restated)
1987	$ 6,628,000	10.2	
1988	$10,102,000	7.8	
1989	$16,829,000	6.4	
1990	$28,445,000	6.1	14.2

The 1990 allowance for doubtful accounts was restated to $66,445,000.

Source: Company annual reports.

management and control of the field sales force. Sales representatives were given ambitious objectives each quarter. Typically, a quota almost doubled on a yearly basis, while the representative's territory often was reduced. The firm was particularly generous to representatives who achieved or exceeded their objectives. Those who fell short of their quotas were summarily fired. Sales representatives, perceived by some as arrogant and aggressive, often sold Oracle software that was not yet available to achieve their quotas. Outsiders attributed the company's marketing style to its founder.

EXHIBIT 3

ORACLE SYSTEMS CORPORATION
Analytical Financial Ratios, 1985–1990

	Fiscal Year Ended May 31					
	1985	*1986*	*1987*	*1988*	*1989*	*1990*
Current ratio	1.56	1.86	2.25	1.88	1.89	2.01
Quick ratio	1.51	1.75	2.12	1.75	1.75	1.83
Debt/total assets	13.37%	15.33%	9.89%	4.76%	13.59%	17.35%
Days' sales outstanding	142	175	181	168	164	176
Debt/equity	0.28	0.31	0.17	0.09	0.27	0.35
Times interest earned	17.46	29.54	55.81	58.94	45.29	11.08
Inventory turnover	69.97	23.14	20.59	21.34	22.84	18.90
Asset turnover	1.50	0.96	0.91	1.13	1.27	1.23
Operating profit margin	11.84%	19.58%	21.64%	22.65%	21.07%	19.55%
Net profit margin	6.70%	10.65%	11.90%	15.20%	14.01%	12.09%
Return on total assets	10.03%	10.27%	10.86%	17.18%	17.77%	14.91%
Return on equity	21.05%	20.58%	18.90%	31.85%	35.47%	30.29%

Source: Company annual reports.

2. **Maintain technology and product leadership.** Oracle's current technological leadership benefited from an early lucky decision to use the SQL computer language. Eventually adopted by IBM, this language became the industry standard. Continued development efforts had widened the use of Oracle's software to virtually all types and brands of computer systems. Oracle was the first to offer networking capabilities with its database, and Oracle had aggressively expanded its range of products.

   To maintain its leadership, Oracle recruited aggressively from what it believed were the top five computer schools in the United States (Harvard, Massachusetts Institute of Technology, Stanford, the University of California at Berkeley, and Carnegie Mellon). Engineers in research and development enjoyed flexible work schedules, higher salaries than the industry average, sizable bonuses, and stock purchase plans. In 1990 the company built a large headquarters complex in Belmont, California, that included the largest and most modern corporate gymnasium in northern California.

3. **Diversify into related fields.** The company had expanded out of the production of software and into computer consulting services and then into the area of system integration. As the range of Oracle's product line expanded, these compatible services expanded as well.

4. **Expand internationally.** Oracle had established subsidiaries and close exclusive distributors in more than 70 countries around the world. Oracle ranked among the top 50 U.S. exporters.

Oracle Systems went public on March 12, 1986, at an issue price of $2.00. Three years later, the share price peaked at $28.375.

The Software Industry.   The broad business sector referred to as computing had, until the 1980s, been dominated by equipment manufacturers. With the advent of personal computers and

EXHIBIT 4

**Oracle Systems Corporation—Percentage Shares of Market for Database
Management Systems Expected in 1991**

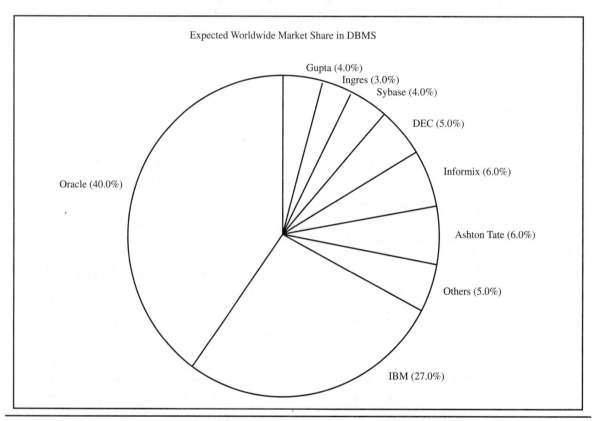

Expected Worldwide Market Share in DBMS

Gupta (4.0%)
Ingres (3.0%)
Sybase (4.0%)
DEC (5.0%)
Informix (6.0%)
Oracle (40.0%)
Ashton Tate (6.0%)
Others (5.0%)
IBM (27.0%)

Source: Datamation.

the increasing competition among hardware vendors, however, the software vendors had become
significant players in the computing sector. In the 1980s, customers increasingly made hardware
decisions based on software availability. This trend drove the hardware manufacturers to integrate
forward into software development, a step with comparatively low capital requirements.

By 1990 the DBMS segment of the software industry included three types of competitors:
(1) hardware producers that had integrated forward (e.g., IBM, DEC), (2) specialized database
vendors (e.g., Oracle, Ingres, Informix, Sybase, Ashton Tate, Gupta Technologies) whose
software could work on a variety of hardware platforms, and (3) many small software houses
providing highly specialized DBMS products. One analyst estimated that the market demand
for DBMS exceeded $10 billion.[2] The major buying segment of this market consisted of large
corporations that had heterogeneous computing environments. Oracle permitted these firms to
link their machines together and share the data. Exhibit 4 reveals that IBM and Oracle dominated

[2]S. M. Smith et al., ''Oracle Systems'' (Los Angeles, CA: Donaldson, Lufkin, and Jenrette, 1991).

the DBMS market. Oracle's revenues had grown faster than IBM's because of Oracle's multiple-platform operating ability.

Disclosures in March 1990.   On March 20, Oracle reported quarter earnings essentially unchanged from the same quarter a year earlier. The company attributed the zero growth results to the disallowal by auditors of about $15 million in sales. Many Oracle software contracts were sold on a trial basis, which raised questions about when revenue could be recognized.[3] For the first time, the auditors opined that some of these ''sales'' would never actually be realized. This surprise triggered rumors about declining product quality, increases in accounts receivable (and doubtful accounts), and reports of sales representatives leaving the company. Upon this revelation, the company's stock price plunged 31 percent from its all-time high of $28.375 per share (achieved just days before the announcement). Journalists reported the following comments by securities analysts:

> There is a credibility issue on the part of management . . . are these random and fragmentary items constrained to this one quarter, or are they symbolic of a longer-term problem? [David Readermann, analyst with Shearson Lehman Hutton]

> Management is stretching harder and harder to make their growth objectives. The disallowal of some sales by auditors tells you that the growth is not sustainable; that the business is just not there. [Rick Sherlund, analyst with Goldman, Sachs]

> There is a lot of controversy still swirling around Oracle. Most people would consider the first bit of bad news a big red flag and stand clear. I'm still a big fan of the strategy and how well they've done to date. [Mark Findlay, analyst with Soundview Financial Group][4]

Following the announcement and price drop, 20 lawsuits were filed against Oracle. Essentially, these suits alleged fraud and misrepresentation. Investors vented more outrage when it was disclosed that six Oracle officers profited by selling 645,000 shares before the March earnings disclosure. The company denied any wrongdoing.

---

[3]Accountants acknowledge that *when* revenue can be recognized is a matter of some judgment. Typically, revenues represent not only cash sales but also credit sales. The key point of judgment is when revenue has been earned, or ''realized.'' Once it has been realized, it can be ''recognized'' in the income statement. Realization depends on (a) management's being able to *measure* the revenue (i.e., knowing with fair certainty how much revenue has been earned) and (b) the occurrence of a *critical event* at which there is fair certainty that the revenue-generating transaction will be completed. For instance, consider at which moment revenue should be recognized: the ''handshake'' deal, receipt of a formal order, shipment of the order, receipt of cash? The crucial phrase here is ''fair certainty,'' and it is an important focus of the auditor's work. There are many revenue-recognition methods. Special industries (e.g., consulting, project management, contracting, mining and petroleum, land sales, franchising, and entertainment) have unique recognition techniques.

One prominent accounting textbook—E. R. Brownlee II, K. R. Ferris, and M. E. Haskins, *Corporate Financial Reporting* (Burr Ridge, IL: Richard D. Irwin, 1990), pp. 80–81—states:

> A misconception about reported numbers is that they are exact or precise. In spite of the best efforts of managers and internal and external auditors, this is rarely if ever the case. There are many reasons for the lack of precision in accounting measures; some may be attributed to necessarily arbitrary cost allocations or alternative reporting procedures, while others may be a function of the intentional manipulation of reported accounting numbers.

[4]All quotations are from Lawrence M. Fisher, ''Surprise Hurts Oracle Systems,'' *New York Times,* April 5, 1990.

Announcement in September 1990.   On September 25, 1990, Oracle announced its first-ever quarterly loss, $36 million (versus a profit of $11.7 million for the same quarter a year earlier). Ellison told investors that the loss came mainly from a $45 million shortfall in U.S. sales, plus a $25 million write-down resulting from a restructuring of the firm. Oracle's U.S. finance department, which was responsible for the faulty third- and fourth-quarter 1990 financial statements, was merged into the corporate finance department to ensure strict accounting standards. The company also announced that 10 percent of its domestic workforce (about 400 persons) would be laid off. Ellison said,

> Oracle is shifting its strategy to emphasize profitability and product quality, instead of market share and sales growth, to meet demands in the maturing market for database applications. . . . Implementation of the reorganization just took too long. Several managers responsible for the restructuring have been fired.[5]

Oracle also indicated that its revenue growth for the first fiscal quarter would be only 30 percent, rather than the 50 percent the company had projected. Finally, the company reduced its growth projections for the rest of the year from 50 percent to 25 percent.

At this September announcement, the company's stock price dropped to $8.125. One journalist commented:

> [I]nvestors had been becoming increasingly wary of Oracle, if only because it was inevitable that the company's breakneck growth would have to slow eventually. Some analysts have also said the company had angered customers, in part by promising more product features than it could deliver in its rush for sales. . . . If the suspicions are correct, it would indicate that the company's problems run deeper. . . . But Oracle paints a rosier picture, saying it continues to gain market share. "As we adjust to a more conventional growth rate, our company will be stronger than ever," Mr. Ellison said. Some other providers of database software have also seen some softening of business.[6]

Conclusion

Because about $3.5 billion in Oracle Systems' market value of equity evaporated between the end of February and the end of September 1990, analysts wondered whether this change in value was, in fact, associated with changes in financial performance in the recent past. The company's share price performance had been outstanding (as shown in Exhibit 5). What had changed? What was the rate of change? Was the company *unhealthy?* For comparison purposes, Exhibit 6 gives financial ratios for a portfolio of other software companies, and Exhibit 7 presents comparative financial ratio information on the 11 leading producers of relational DBMSs.

---

[5]Quoted from Reuters financial report, September 25, 1990.
[6]Andrew Pollack, "Fast-Growth Oracle Systems Confronts First Downturn," *New York Times,* September 10, 1990.

EXHIBIT 5

Oracle Systems Corporation—Oracle Systems' Month-End Share Prices, Adjusted for Stock Splits

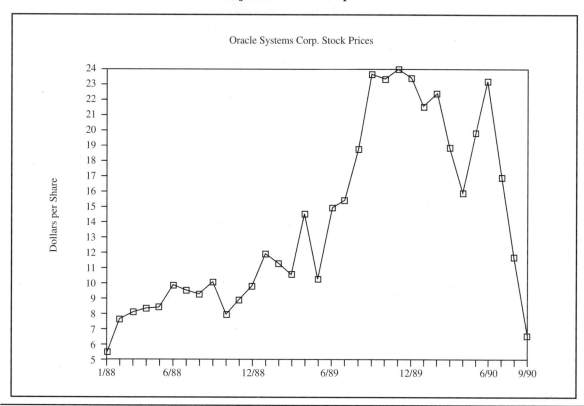

Source: Standard and Poor's Corporation.

EXHIBIT 6

ORACLE SYSTEMS CORPORATION
Common-Sized Financial Statements of Computer Software
Producers' Averages, 1986–1990
(in percentages)

	1986	*1987*	*1988*	*1989*	*1990*
Income Statement					
Sales	100.0%	100.0%	100.0%	100.0%	100.0%
Costs and expenses	80.6	79.9	79.0	78.9	82.3
Operating income	19.4	20.1	21.0	21.1	17.7
Depreciation	6.1	6.1	5.9	5.3	5.2
Interest	1.0	1.1	0.8	1.0	1.1
Special items	0.9	−0.7	0.0	0.0	0.0
Income taxes	4.9	5.4	5.2	4.7	4.1
Net income	6.5	8.2	9.1	10.1	7.3
Common dividends	1.6	1.2	1.1	1.5	1.3
Balance Sheet: Assets					
Cash and equivalents	28.8	24.2	20.1	17.2	19.2
Receivables	22.9	26.0	27.9	32.4	31.8
Inventories	1.3	1.7	1.7	1.7	1.5
Other current assets	6.1	4.3	3.3	3.7	3.5
Total current assets	59.2	56.2	53.0	55.0	55.9
Net property, plant, and equipment	26.8	19.5	20.0	19.1	17.5
Intangibles	9.7	8.5	9.2	10.0	9.1
Other assets	4.3	15.9	17.7	15.8	17.5
Total assets	100.0	100.0	100.0	100.0	100.0
Balance Sheet: Liabilities and Equity					
Notes payable	0.8	0.8	0.8	0.9	3.3
Current long-term debt	1.4	1.4	1.4	0.7	0.9
Accounts payable	3.3	3.8	3.8	4.5	3.9
Taxes payable	6.6	6.2	5.7	5.9	5.7
Accrued expenses	5.1	3.7	3.2	5.0	5.8
Other current liabs.	8.5	9.2	9.8	9.0	9.8
Total current liabs.	25.7	24.6	24.6	26.1	29.4
Long-term debt	18.7	12.2	11.0	11.2	5.8
Deferred taxes	1.4	2.6	3.7	3.4	3.5
Investment tax credit	0.9	0.0	0.0	0.0	0.0
Other liabs.	2.4	2.3	1.8	1.9	1.7
Common stock	1.1	1.0	0.9	2.1	2.0
Capital surplus	12.0	23.1	22.8	19.4	19.0
Retained earnings	38.6	37.6	41.0	43.9	46.6
Less treasury stock	−0.8	−3.3	−5.8	−8.0	−8.1
Total liabilities and equity	100.0	100.0	100.0	100.0	100.0

Note: The companies on which this exhibit is based are Autodesk, Automatic Data, Computer Associates, Computer Sciences, Lotus Development, Novell, Oracle, Shared Medical Systems, and Cullinet.

Source: Standard & Poor's Corporation.

EXHIBIT 7

ORACLE SYSTEMS CORPORATION
Financial Ratios for Competitors in Database Management Software

Ratio	Ask Computer (FY 6/90)	BMC Software (FY 3/90)	Borland Int'l. (FY 3/90)	Computer Assoc. (FY 3/90)	Informix Corp. (12/89)	Lotus Devel'p. (12/89)	Microsoft Corp. (FY 6/90)	Oracle Systems (FY 5/90)	Platinum Technol. (12/89)	Progress Software (11/89)	Software Publish. (FY 9/90)	Sybase, Inc. (12/89)
Business focus	DBMS	DBMS	Broad Line	Broad Line	DBMS	Broad Line	Broad Line	DBMS	DBMS	DBMS	Broad Line	DBMS
Previous four quarters' sales	$112 mm	$110 mm	$262 mm	$1.25 bn	$14.9 mm	$652 mm	$1.3 bn	$980 mm	$11.1 mm	$26.9 mm	$140 mm	$89 mm
Liquidity ratios												
Quick ratio	1.88	2.97	2.54	2.13	2.68	3.39	3.37	1.51	1.99	1.54	3.64	2.00
Current ratio	2.01	3.26	2.92	2.20	2.94	3.73	3.85	1.75	1.99	1.67	3.95	2.07
Sales/cash	0.35	1.66	8.79	11.32	5.76	2.02	2.63	18.39	12.93	3.61	1.78	3.43
Activity ratios												
Receiv. turnover	3.42	9.53	27.20	2.11	2.00	5.69	6.54	2.18	2.57	4.24	7.38	2.23
Days' sales out.	105	38	13.23	170	180	63	55	165	140	85	48.8	161
Inventory turn.	53.6	NA	290	49.16	27.46	24	21.3	NA	NA	46.23	73.4	NA
Days' inv. out.	6.67	NA	1.24	7.32	13.11	15	16.9	NA	NA	7.8	4.9	NA
Sales/net working capital	40.5	1.86	8.87	3.14	2.05	1.85	2.22	3.90	4.32	4.5	1.77	2.54
Sales/plant and equip.	20.18	4.64	18.63	3.90	6.68	3.55	3.64	5.33	37.7	9.62	11.83	4.79
Sales/curr. assets	2.03	1.29	5.78	1.72	1.35	1.36	1.64	1.68	2.15	1.80	1.32	1.31
Sales/assets	1.25	1.00	4.36	0.86	1.01	0.92	1.07	1.20	2.03	1.48	1.17	1.01
Sales/employees	220,028	205,396	649,407	180,348	122,570	198,583	210,017	134,546	NA	NA	214,033	105,385
Leverage ratios												
Liabilities/assets	0.32	0.34	0.38	0.32	0.48	0.54	0.17	0.56	0.48	0.54	0.25	0.49
Liabilities/capital	0.47	0.52	0.51	0.46	0.86	0.68	0.20	1.00	0.90	1.08	0.34	0.97
Liabilities/equity	0.47	0.52	0.61	0.47	0.93	1.17	0.20	1.27	33.47	1.15	0.34	0.97
Times int. earned	37.8	NA	NA	NA	NA	NA	NA	10.77	NA	31.66	NA	7.76
Total debt/equity	0.01	NA	0.19	0.03	NA	0.73	NA	0.30	NA	0.11	NA	NA
Assets/equity	1.47	1.52	1.61	1.47	1.93	2.17	1.20	2.27	1.90	2.15	1.34	1.97
Profitability ratios												
Net income/sales	0.02	0.19	−0.04	0.10	0.04	0.12	0.24	0.09	0.06	0.09	0.14	0.06
Net income/assets	0.03	0.19	−0.19	0.08	0.04	0.11	0.25	0.11	0.12	0.13	0.16	0.06
Net income/capital	0.04	0.29	−0.26	0.12	0.08	0.14	0.30	0.19	0.23	0.25	0.22	0.12
Net income/equity	0.04	0.29	−0.31	0.12	0.09	0.24	0.30	0.24	8.66	0.27	0.22	0.12

Source: Disclosure Incorporated.

CASE 4.2
BASIC FINANCIAL STATEMENT ANALYSIS

MiniScribe Corporation

As a research analyst for the prestigious Alexander & Ferris brokerage firm, Paula Perry knew the value of not accepting representations, either expressed or financial, by company officials. All too often a thorough examination of the firm and its industry would tell a different story. Sometimes there would only be a slight difference, while at other times very drastic differences would be identified.

In early October 1988, Paula's manager requested that she analyze the latest financial results of MiniScribe Corporation, a disk-drive manufacturer. Rumors abounded in the financial community that MiniScribe was experiencing cash flow and inventory problems. Alexander & Ferris had just received the company's third quarter results (Exhibit 1), and Paula had been asked to analyze those results to determine if Alexander & Ferris should continue to retain MiniScribe on its "Buy" recommendation list.

After conducting a thorough investigation of MiniScribe and the disk-drive industry, Paula prepared the following background report.

Background

The Company.   In July 1980, Terry Johnson started MiniScribe Corporation, a manufacturer of disk drives[1] for personal computers, from his basement in Longmont, Colorado. By the third quarter of 1988, MiniScribe had become the second largest producer of disk drives in the United States. MiniScribe also reported its 13th consecutive quarter of increased revenue and profits, a record unmatched by any other disk-drive maker. Further, company officials expected MiniScribe to be listed among the Fortune 500 by year-end 1988. This continued success had made MiniScribe one of Wall Street's favorite stocks, and it was recommended by many investment analysts on Wall Street.[2]

Terry Johnson's basement adventure of building a multimillion-dollar company took off with the first shipment of full-heighted 5-¼ inch, 12.8 megabyte Winchester-technology disk drives in October of 1981. Using an innovative rack-and-pinion actuator of its own design, MiniScribe had entered a fledgling industry. Technology was new and untested, and market acceptance was a major concern. Fortunately, the company grew rapidly from $81,000 in sales for 1981 to $77 million in 1983 sales. A large order from IBM accounted for 61 percent of 1983 sales. In November 1983, MiniScribe issued its first public stock offering at $11.50 per share.

No sooner had the stock issuance hit the market than the future turned bleak. In January 1984, IBM decided to manufacture its own disk drives and canceled or rescheduled its orders

---

*This case was prepared by Philip D. Drake from publicly available information. Copyright © 1992 by Philip D. Drake. All rights reserved to the author.

[1]A disk drive is to a computer as a turntable is to a stereo. The disk drive is used by the computer operator to store and retrieve information. Two basic types of drives exist. The hard-disk drive, which reads from and writes to an aluminum-coated rigid platter stored inside the computer, is basically used for storage. The floppy-disk drive, which reads from and writes to a flexible diskette, allows the user to import and export information from various sources.

[2]MiniScribe was the 10th most actively traded stock on NASDAQ during 1987.

EXHIBIT 1

MINISCRIBE CORPORATION
Unaudited Interim Financial Statements
Consolidated Income Statement
(in thousands, except per share data)

	Nine Months Ended 10/2/88	Six Months Ended 7/3/88	Three Months Ended 4/3/88
Sales	$486,645	$309,028	$138,562
Cost of sales	375,017	240,776	110,298
Gross profits	111,628	68,252	28,264
Selling, general, and administrative	45,780	27,535	10,798
Research and development	13,408	8,096	3,724
Income from operations	52,440	32,621	13,742
Other income (expenses), net	(4,592)	(2,882)	(1,153)
Income before taxes and extraordinary credit	47,848	29,739	12,589
Provision for income taxes	11,125	6,536	2,938
Income before extraordinary credit	36,723	23,203	9,651
Extraordinary credit	3,732	2,222	1,124
Net income	$ 40,445	$ 25,425	$ 10,775
Income per share			
Income before extraordinary credit	$ 0.93	$ 0.59	$ 0.25
Extraordinary credit	0.10	0.06	0.03
Net income per share	1.03	0.65	0.28
Weighted average of common and common equivalent shares outstanding	39,532	39,390	38,990

Consolidated Balance Sheet
(in thousands)

	10/2/88	7/3/88	4/3/88	1/3/88
Assets				
Current assets				
Cash	$ 26,404	$ 35,829	$ 47,008	$ 48,956
Account receivable	172,832	108,580	77,897	57,144
Inventories	141,283	92,585	83,182	85,172
Other current assets	2,590	1,638	1,292	976
Total current assets	343,109	238,632	209,379	192,248
Property and equipment, net	103,334	91,715	78,352	71,540
Other assets	12,020	11,698	10,271	9,818
Total assets	$458,463	$342,045	$298,002	$273,606
Liabilities and Stockholders' Equity				
Current liabilities				
Accounts payable and short-term borrowings	$179,438	$ 94,303	$ 63,308	$ 60,527
Accruals and other liabilities	32,348	18,680	21,693	12,398
Current portion of long-term debt	462	668	1,117	1,250
Total current liabilities	212,248	113,651	86,118	74,175
Long-term debt	100,601	99,775	98,838	98,220
Stockholders' equity				
Preferred stock	66	67	69	69
Common stock	304	298	295	291
Capital in excess of par value	73,108	71,296	70,380	69,245
Notes receivable from officers	(97)	(245)	(251)	(172)
Retained earnings	72,233	57,203	42,553	31,778
Total stockholders' equity	145,614	128,619	113,046	101,211
Total liabilities and stockholders' equity	$458,463	$342,045	$298,002	$273,606

with MiniScribe. Simultaneously, the growth of the microcomputer industry slowed significantly. Because of reduced sales and the resulting large losses during the second half of 1984 through the first half of 1985, combined with heavy spending on research and development and major capital expenditures incurred in connection with the development of a manufacturing facility in Singapore, MiniScribe faced a severe liquidity crisis during the first four months of 1985.

In May 1985, an investor group led by the venture-capital firm of Hambrecht & Quist provided a $20 million capital infusion. In conjunction with the investment, Q. T. Wiles, chairman of the board of Hambrecht & Quist, became chairman of the board and CEO of MiniScribe. Following Mr. Wiles' appointment, the company's senior management and organization structure was realigned.

Mr. Wiles was widely regarded as a successful turnaround artist, particularly of high-tech companies. Referred to as Dr. Fix It, Q. T. Wiles was credited for rescuing over 12 high-tech companies, including Adobe Systems, Silicon General, and Granger Associates. Mr. Wiles was known as an autocratic leader who advocated his own management style, known as "Q. T.'s Disciplines." His collection of 13 principles included a requirement that managers keep weekly market and profit reports for each of their product lines. In a 1987 *Business Week* interview, Wiles said of himself, "It's easier to produce the numbers than put up with Q. T.'s reaction."

The reorganization of MiniScribe focused on arranging the firm into five divisions, each focusing on a specific market, product segment, or research effort. This resulted in the entire company operating with a renewed entrepreneurial spirit. According to Jim Steger, vice president of manufacturing, MiniScribe was literally a series of one-man budgets. "We charge a robot operator for the floor space he occupies, and he runs his part of the operation as his own business. It gives the right mind-set to people to say, 'I own this little business; I must make it as cost-effective as I can.' " As a result, financial results became the sole determinant for employee incentives and bonuses.

To facilitate the imposition and acceptance of individual responsibility, MiniScribe's books were closed weekly. Thus, a manager would know within seven days how successfully his area or division was performing. With such rapid feedback, managers could quickly respond to problems before they could cause significant damage. (Most companies access their financial progress on a monthly basis.) So impressive were these tactics that Japanese managers visited MiniScribe's Singapore facility to study the company's approach.

Under Mr. Wiles' leadership, MiniScribe introduced several new product lines, including the 380-megabyte high-performance drive. The new products were quickly accepted by the market and, coupled with a general recovery in the microcomputer industry, led to a resurgence in MiniScribe's sales. By the third quarter of 1985, the company was again profitable.

Technical reviews of MiniScribe's products were generally quite favorable. Sales were made to both just-in-time distributors and major computer companies such as Apple, Digital Equipment, and CompuAdd. To maintain their market share, MiniScribe emphasized their research and development commitment, and in 1987, *Electronic Business,* a leading trade journal, ranked MiniScribe second in R&D spending increases with a 131.7 percent increase over 1986.

MiniScribe's stock price reflected this positive information. The share price rebounded from a low of $1 in 1985 to over $13 in July of 1988 (Exhibit 2). However, the price declined to a little over $8 in October 1988, as industry competition increased. Similar stock decreases also occurred for MiniScribe's primary competitors (Exhibit 3).

From all outward appearances, MiniScribe had made the turnaround and was well on its way to becoming a billion-dollar company. Sales and net income were increasing each quarter, and the company's market share was roughly 16 percent of the world's disk-drive market, with

EXHIBIT 2

MiniScribe Corporation: Common Stock Prices, 1986–1988

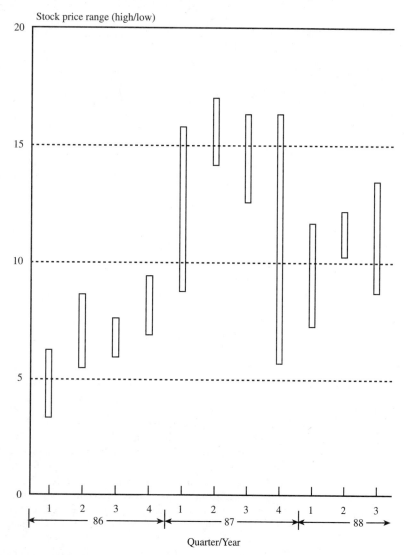

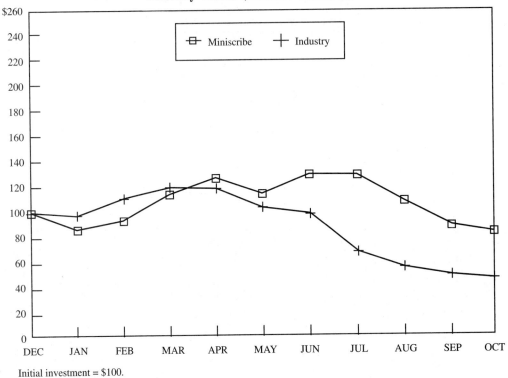

Monthly Values (12/31/87–10/31/88)

Initial investment = $100.

MiniScribe dominating the 3½-inch disk-drive segment. The 3½-inch disk drives accounted for nearly 45 percent of MiniScribe's sales.

Employing more than 8,350 people worldwide, MiniScribe maintained production facilities in Colorado, Singapore, and Hong Kong. The Singapore facility, which accounted for 80 percent of company sales, was completely automated with 53 robots, making it one of the largest and most sophisticated plants in that country. In Hong Kong, where MiniScribe made printed circuit boards, officials anticipated this segment to generate over $300 million in 1989 sales, thereby making MiniScribe that country's largest electronic manufacturer.

The Industry.   In 1988, the disk-drive industry was dominated by Seagate Technology with sales over $1.3 billion. The other major competitors—Computer Memories, Micropolis, Maxtor, Quantum, and Priam—had combined 1987 sales of less than $1 billion. Four new companies entered the industry in 1987 and 1988, marking the first entrants, with the exception of Conner Peripherals, since a 1984 industry shake-out. Industry financial results are presented in Exhibit 4.

Competition for sales was intense as the industry was frequently locked in a heated price war. Due to overcapacity throughout the industry, the average cost of a megabyte of memory— a common standard of measure—had fallen approximately 25 percent during the first 10 months of 1988. Dataquest, a research firm which tracks computer-related companies, estimated world

---

EXHIBIT 4

Disk-Drive Manufacturers Industry Ratios
(for the first three quarters of 1988)

	1st Qtr.	*2nd Qtr.*	*3rd Qtr.*
Liquidity Ratios			
Quick	2.50	2.00	1.67
Current	3.54	3.12	3.00
Current liabilities to net worth	0.52	0.58	0.59
Total liabilities to net worth	0.95	1.00	1.02
Efficiency Ratios			
Inventory turnover	68 days	67 days	75 days
Accounts receivable turnover	43 days	54 days	55 days
Accounts payable turnover	41 days	41 days	46 days

production capacity to be over 17 million disk drives. However, Dataquest anticipated that only 14 million drives would be purchased in 1988. As a consequence of this overcapacity, price competition was expected to be intense and write-offs of inventory high. "We're in for another shake-out by next summer," said a Dataquest analyst.

The market's tastes were also changing from 5¼-inch disk drives to the 3½-inch drives. For 1988, Dataquest expected orders to total nearly 10 million 3½-inch drives, compared to only 4 million 5¼-inch disk drives. Forecasts for 1989 demand were 12 million 3½-inch drives, and less than 4 million 5¼-inch drives. While MiniScribe dominated the 3½-inch-drive market, the industry was subject to rapid technological change, which exerted considerable pressure on a company to turn inventory as quickly as possible.

Recent market entrants utilized a modified second-generation design that involved one-half the number of parts as compared to first-generation designs that characterized such firms as MiniScribe. The fewer parts would result in lower production costs, making these entrants a potential threat to the established leaders.

Paula learned that established firms—like MiniScribe—were constantly looking for new markets for the smaller disk drives. For example, one proposed new use involved the installation of a disk drive in fax machines, thereby enabling them to store incoming messages if their machine ran out of paper. Laser printer and photocopiers were also possible candidates to store boilerplate documents which could be reproduced as desired. These additional markets would be needed since Dataquest had forecasted that growth in the U.S. PC market would decline from 29 percent in 1987 to 17 percent in 1988 and 9 percent in 1989.

Required:

    (a) Using the data in Exhibit 1, prepare a statement of cash flows for MiniScribe for each quarter of 1988.

    (b) Calculate the liquidity and efficiency ratios for MiniScribe for each quarter during 1988.

    (c) What "red flags" or concerns can you identify?

    (d) What recommendation would you make to Paula's manager? Explain.

CASE 4.3
BASIC FINANCIAL STATEMENT ANALYSIS:

The Regina Company

On April 26, 1989, Regina Company, a manufacturer of vacuum cleaners for home use, filed for protection from creditors under Chapter 11 of the Federal Bankruptcy Code. This filing came after negotiations for the sale of the company and attempts to arrange interim financing had been terminated. Although there was mention of Regina's quality-control problems and testy relationships with suppliers, warning signs of Regina's financial troubles were scarce. Less than six months before the bankruptcy filing, Regina was still receiving positive reviews from stock market analysts.

Management.   Donald Sheelen was what many people call a "born leader." He graduated from the University of Dayton in 1968 as president of his class. He received his MBA from Syracuse University in 1973 and took a marketing position with Jelco, Inc., Johnson & Johnson's medical equipment unit. In 1980, Sheelen joined Regina Company, then a subsidiary of General Signal Corp., as executive vice president. By 1983, he had become president of Regina.

In April 1984, General Signal Corp. began negotiating the sale of several of its appliance units, including Regina. Regina was profitable, but the appliance segment did not fit the parent's long-term plans. Although other companies in Regina's industry were given the opportunity to bid, they did not, and Sheelen led a management buyout financed primarily with debt.

Financing of Management Buyout.   On June 29, 1984, Sheelen's management group acquired all the stock of Regina Company at a cost of approximately $38.1 million, including approximately $6.7 million of assumed liabilities. The net cost of $31.4 million included:

- $22.8 million cash to General Signal.
- $5.0 million subordinated note to General Signal.
- $1.1 million warrant to Midlantic. (The warrants were exercisable at $375,000 for 20 percent of the stock.)
- $1.8 million in rights to future tax reductions.
- $700,000 in other costs.

The cash paid was funded with:

- $14.0 million bank term loan.
- $7.5 million bank revolving demand loan (borrowing based on eligible receivables and inventory up to $16.0 million).
- $1.5 million from the sale of 4 million shares of common stock at $0.375 per share.

The acquisition was accounted for as a purchase in accordance with U.S. generally accepted accounting principles, and the assets and liabilities were stated at their fair market values as of

---

This case was prepared by Thomas I. Selling, with assistance from Lisa Carothers. Copyright © 1991 by Thomas I. Selling. All rights reserved.

the acquisition date. In October 1984, Regina received the proceeds from the issuance of $14.8 million in industrial revenue bonds, and the cash was used to reduce the company's bank debt.

In November 1985, Regina Company went public at $10.50 per share. The offering consisted of 800,000 shares offered for sale by Regina, and 910,000 shares currently owned by officers (Exhibit 1). Net proceeds to Regina were $7.8 million.

Marketing Campaign.   In an effort to surpass Hoover Co., the dominant company in the market, Regina began an aggressive marketing and product development campaign after going public. In 1987–88, Regina nearly doubled its expenditures for advertising, primarily through increased use of television. In an industry where companies usually spend 12 percent of sales on advertising, Regina was spending over 20 percent. The television ads were a primary vehicle for Sheelen to become a very visible, colorful spokesperson for Regina. He was known for spilling corn flakes on the floor to demonstrate Regina's superior cleaning ability.

Sheelen's management team also emphasized fast-paced product introductions, low prices, and generous rebates. Regina was metamorphosed from a producer of light-weight vacuum cleaners, where it was dominant in its niche, to a marketer of a broad line of appliances. New product introductions included the Steemer, a low-cost household carpet cleaner; the House-keeper, a low-cost upright vacuum cleaner; and Home-Spa, an inexpensive portable unit that converted a bathtub into a whirlpool. By the beginning of 1987, sales of Regina's base business of electric brooms had shrunk to 10 percent of total revenues whereas the Housekeeper and Home-Spa constituted 70 percent.

Sheelen's aggressive marketing strategy evidenced significant returns in terms of sales and earnings growth. Sales grew from $67 million in 1985 to $181 million in 1988. Earnings jumped from 90 cents per share in 1986 to $2 per share in 1988. Market analysts appeared impressed by the transformation. A *Business Week* article gave credit to ''. . . the skilled management team [that] has turned the company around.'' Also in 1987, Regina was singled out as a smart stock pick in a *Barron's* ''roundtable'' discussion with three top money managers. And, in June 1988, Shearson Lehman Hutton added Regina to its Growth Stocks Recommended List. The September 1988 issue of *OTC Review* also gave Regina positive reviews.

Reversal of Fortune.   On September 21, 1988, Regina Company stunned analysts by announcing that sales for the first fiscal quarter (ending September 30) would be substantially lower than expected and the company would show a loss for the quarter. Regina attributed the lower sales estimate to a ''recent order slowdown'' and a larger than anticipated number of returns.

Defective equipment and high rates of return contributed significantly to Regina's financial problems. Sheelen bypassed proper product testing, and about 16 percent of the Housekeeper vacuums were returned. K mart, which accounted for 20 percent of Regina's total sales, reported that 20 percent of the Housekeeper 1000 model were returned. And Target Stores, another major retailer of Regina products, reported that at least 50 percent of the Housekeeper Plus 5000 line were returned. In contrast, Hoover and Eureka experienced rates of return of less than 1 percent.

The market's reaction to management's quarterly earnings forecast was severe. Regina's stock plunged from $17 to $10 a share. Within days Sheelen, who now owned 40 percent of the company, resigned. Regina then asked its accounting firm, Peat Marwick Main & Co., to conduct a full-scale investigation of the company's accounting records. Subsequently, Peat Marwick withdrew its opinion on the fiscal year ended June 30, 1988 financial statements because the statements were found to be materially incorrect. It was discovered that Sheelen

---
EXHIBIT 1

Public Offering

As part of Regina's 1985 public offering the company sold 800,000 shares of stock and shareholders sold 910,000 shares. Following the public offering, 4,528,400 shares of stock were outstanding.

	Before Offering	*After Offering*
Officers Holding Stock		
Donald D. Sheelen,		
Chairman and President	2,000,000 (53.6%)	1,800,000 (39.8%)
James A. Flynn,		
Vice Chairman, Executive Vice		
President—Marketing, and Treasurer	618,400 (16.6%)	518,400 (11.4%)
John Gerbeth,		
Vice President—Operations,		
Secretary, and Director	700,000 (18.8%)	500,000 (11.0%)
Jonathan Leaver,		
Director	410,000 (11.0%)	–0–
All officers and directors	3,728,400 (100%)	2,818,400 (62.2%)

---

had ordered his chief financial officer to manipulate the reported figures on product returns and sales.

Electrolux Purchases Regina.   Malcolm Sherman, newly elected chairman, president, and chief executive officer, tried to revive Regina in the aftermath of the falsified financial statements and after many previous officers pleaded guilty to fraud charges. However, following numerous attempts to secure additional financing or find a buyer failed, Regina filed for bankruptcy on April 26, 1989.

On June 7, 1989, Regina confirmed that it had agreed to be acquired by a unit of Electrolux Corp., an Atlanta floor-care company.

Required:

    (a) Exhibits 2, 3 and 4 contain comparative income statements, balance sheets, and selected supplementary notes for Regina. What indications of possible trouble, if any, are provided by the financial data?

EXHIBIT 2

REGINA COMPANY
Comparative Statements of Income: 1985–1988
(in thousands)

	Year Ended June 30			
	1985	*1986*	*1987*	*1988*
Net sales	$67,654	$76,144	$128,234	$181,123
Operating costs and expenses*				
Cost of goods sold	43,988	46,213	70,756	94,934
Selling, distribution, and administration	9,121	10,366	14,621	21,870
Advertising	9,416	8,557	26,449	39,992
Research and development	673	1,182	1,530	2,423
Total operating costs	63,198	66,318	113,356	159,219
Operating income	$ 4,456	$ 9,826	$ 14,878	$ 21,904
Interest expense	2,930	1,930	1,584	3,189
Income before income taxes	$ 1,526	$ 7,896	$ 13,294	$ 18,715
Income tax expense	405	3,807	6,189	7,761
Net income	$ 1,121	$ 4,089	$ 7,105	$ 10,954

*Depreciation and amortization of fixed assets.	**6–30–85**	**6–30–86**	**6–30–87**	**6–30–88**
	$1,497	$2,001	$2,016	$1,601

(b) Prepare comparative statements of cash flows for fiscal years 1985 through 1988 using the indirect method. What do these statements indicate about how the company financed its growth and managed its financial affairs?

(c) Given the case facts it will be more difficult to prepare comparative statements of cash flows using the direct method, but do so anyway and state the additional assumptions you had to make. What additional insights, if any, are provided by this alternative format?

(d) How should Regina have accounted for its product return problems on its financial statements?

(e) Were Regina's independent auditors negligent in their responsibilities? If so, in what way?

EXHIBIT 3

REGINA COMPANY
Comparative Balance Sheets: 1984–1988
(in thousands)

	Years Ended June 30				
	1984	*1985*	*1986*	*1987*	*1988*
Assets					
Current assets					
Cash	$ 328	$ 36	$ 63	$ 514	$ 885
Accounts receivable, net	8,551	11,719	14,402	27,801	51,076
Inventory	11,109	6,325	9,762	19,577	39,135
Other	6	475	708	1,449	3,015
Total current assets	$19,994	$18,555	$24,935	$49,341	$ 94,111
Property, plant, and equipment cost	17,219	18,486	19,523	19,736	27,884
Less accumulated depreciation	–0–	(1,304)	(3,140)	(4,948)	(6,336)
Other assets	1,118	1,776	1,884	1,112	2,481
Total assets	$38,331	$37,513	$43,202	$65,241	$118,140
Liabilities and Stockholders' Equity					
Current liabilities					
Short-term borrowings	$ 7,500	$ 3,732	$ 2,707	$ –0–	$ –0–
Current portion of term loan	1,400	1,400	–0–	900	1,250
Accounts payable	3,082	4,724	7,344	15,072	13,288
Accrued liabilities	3,800	3,091	3,127	5,468	4,710
Income taxes payable	2,349	1,145	1,554	2,619	3,782
Total current liabilities	$18,131	$14,092	$14,732	$24,059	$ 23,030
Long-term debt					
Term loan	12,600	–0–	–0–	–0–	–0–
Industrial revenue bonds	–0–	14,800	14,800	13,900	12,650
Subordinated note	5,000	5,000	–0–	–0–	–0–
Bank debt	–0–	–0–	–0–	5,941	47,432
Mississippi state debt	–0–	–0–	–0–	–0–	1,975
Total long-term debt	$17,600	$19,800	$14,800	$19,841	$ 62,057
Deferred income taxes	–0–	118	685	1,254	1,881
Stockholders' equity					
Common stock, $.0001 par value	1	1	1	1	1
Common stock purchase warrant	1,100	1,100	–0–	–0–	–0–
Additional paid-in capital	1,499	1,473	8,010	8,018	8,149
Retained earnings	–0–	1,121	5,210	12,315	23,269
Less: treasury stock, cost	–0–	(192)	(236)	(247)	(247)
Total stockholders' equity	$ 2,600	$ 3,503	$12,985	$20,087	$ 31,172
Total liabilities and shareholders' equity	$38,331	$37,513	$43,202	$65,241	$118,140

EXHIBIT 4

Selected Notes to Financial Statements

Allowance for Doubtful Accounts
June 30, 1985: $191,000
June 30, 1986: $200,000
June 30, 1987: $476,000
June 30, 1988: $426,000

Loans 1986

Short-term borrowings	Bank's prime rate plus 1% per annum (9.5% on June 30, 1986).
Industrial revenue bonds	Interest due monthly, based on a floating rate computed by appointed indexing agents, up to a maximum of 18%. Annual fee of 1.75% of balance of the bonds.

Loans 1987

Short-term borrowings	Bank's prime rate plus 1% per annum. On June 29, 1987 the Company terminated this agreement and replaced it with long-term bank debt at a lower interest rate.
Industrial revenue bonds	No changes on calculation of monthly interest charge. Annual fee lowered to 1.5% in July 1986.
Bank debt	Three-year revolving credit facility totaling $25,000,000 at the bank's prime interest rate. Secured with eligible trade receivables and inventories. Borrowing used primarily to pay down short-term loan.

Loans 1988

Industrial revenue bonds	Interest rate calculation and annual fee remained the same.
Mississippi state debt	Loan for $3,000,000 bears no interest for the first three years and 3% interest over the remaining twelve years. Loan is secured by expanded facilities. Principal is payable in twelve equal, annual installments of $250,000 beginning December 1990 through 2002.
Bank debt	Arrangement with two banks which enables Regina to borrow up to $50,000,000. Revolving credit facility expiring June 1990. Has various interest rate options approximating the banks' prime interest rate. Commitment free of $\frac{1}{8}$ of 1% on unused portion. Secured by trade receivables and inventories.

CASE 4.4
FINANCIAL STATEMENT ANALYSIS

Bayern Brauerei

In early January 1993, Maria Ober arrived at Bayern Brauerei[1] to participate in her first meeting of the board of directors. She had recently joined the board at the behest of her uncle, the managing director of the company. August Ober had told her that the board could use her financial expertise in addressing some questions that would come up in the near future, but he would not be specific as to the nature of those questions. The company was owned entirely by 16 uncles, aunts, and cousins in the Ober family. Maria had received an MBA degree from a well-known business school and had worked for the past six years as a commercial loan officer for a leading bank in Frankfurt, Germany. With the permission of the bank, she agreed to join the Bayern Brauerei board.

The agenda for the January meeting of the directors consisted of three items of business: (1) approval of the 1993 financial budget, (2) declaration of the quarterly dividend, and (3) approval of the compensation scheme for Max Leiter, the company's sales and marketing manager. Because she knew little about the company, Maria decided to visit it for a day before the first board meeting.

The Company.   Bayern Brauerei produced two varieties of beer, dark and light, for which it had won quality awards consistently over the years. Its sales and profits in 1992 were DM102.3 million and DM2.6 million, respectively.[2] (See Exhibit 1 for historical and projected financial statements.) Founded in 1737, the Bayern Brauerei had been in the Ober family for 12 generations. An etching of Gustav Ober, the founder, graced the label of each bottle of beer.

The company was located in a village just outside Munich, Germany. Its modern equipment was capable of producing 700,000 hectoliters of beer per year, and in 1992 the company sold 667,000 hectoliters. This equipment was acquired in 1987 following a fire that destroyed the old equipment.

Because of its efficiency improvements and slightly larger size, the new equipment increased the potential output of the brewery. This additional capacity remained unused, however, until late 1989. In that year, the Berlin Wall fell, and Germans were permitted to move freely between the eastern and western portions of Germany. August Ober envisioned a significant new market for high-quality beer in eastern Germany and resolved to penetrate that market. Accordingly, in 1990 he hired Max Leiter away from a major beer producer to rejuvenate the Bayern Brauerei sales staff and to move aggressively to position Bayern's beer in *die neuen Bundesländer* (the new federal states, *Länder*)[3] that joined with West Germany in the unification of 1990.

This case was prepared by Professor Robert F. Bruner. Copyright © 1992 by the University of Virginia Darden School Foundation, Charlottesville, VA. All rights reserved. Revised 6/93.

[1]In English, Bayern Brauerei (BI-ern BROY-reye) means Bavarian Brewery.

[2]In January 1993, the Deutsche mark could be exchanged for about US$0.63.

[3]Five new federal *Länder* emerged from the former German Democratic Republic, commonly known as East Germany. This region included an area of 106 thousand square kilometers and a population of about 15.1 million. The region was dominated by Berlin, which added a population of about 3.4 million. Emigration from the eastern *Länder* was expected to reduce population slightly over the next few years. At the time of unification, manufacturing industry in this region was plagued by badly outdated premises, plant, and equipment. Shortly thereafter, industrial production and incomes fell dramatically as enterprises in the region closed their doors. In January 1993, the economic recovery of the eastern *Länder* was proving to be painfully slow.

EXHIBIT 1

BAYERN BRAUEREI
Historical and Projected Income Statements and Balance Sheets
(fiscal year ended December 31; all figures in DM thousands)

Historical and Projected Income Statements

		Actual				Projected	
		1989	*1990*	*1991*	*1992*	*1993*	*1994*
1	Sales: Western *Länder*	78,202	78,984	80,959	83,476	85,981	88,560
2	Sales: Eastern *Länder*	—	3,113	12,825	18,879	27,375	35,587
3	Net sales	78,202	82,097	93,784	102,356	113,355	124,147
	Operating expenses						
4	Production costs and expenses	40,667	43,390	50,159	56,298	65,410	71,292
5	Admin. and selling expenses	15,734	15,967	18,663	20,164	21,000	24,000
6	Depreciation	4,550	5,439	7,367	7,650	7,650	8,530
7	Excise duties	11,526	11,174	11,734	11,949	12,211	12,566
8	Total operating expenses	(72,477)	(75,970)	(87,923)	(96,061)	(106,271)	(116,388)
9	Operating margin	5,725	6,127	5,861	6,294	7,084	7,759
10	Allowance for doubtful accounts	(9)	(6)	(28)	(19)	(188)	(46)
11	Interest expense	(841)	(778)	(2,260)	(2,085)	(2,421)	(2,711)
12	Earnings before taxes	4,884	5,349	3,574	4,191	4,476	5,002
13	Income taxes	(1,647)	(1,845)	(1,412)	(1,634)	(1,566)	(1,751)
14	Net earnings	3,237	3,504	2,162	2,557	2,909	3,251
15	Dividends to all common shares	2,428	2,628	1,622	1,917	2,182	2,439
16	Retention of earnings	809	876	541	639	727	813

In early 1993, German consumers accounted for all of the company's sales, of which 81 percent were in western Germany (mainly the states of Baden and Bavaria) and 19 percent in the new federal states. Despite their relatively small portion of total sales, however, the eastern *Länder* had accounted for most of the unit growth in Bayern's sales over the past three years.

Bayern served its markets through a network of independent distributors. In western Germany, these distributors purchased Bayern's beer, stored it temporarily in their own refrigerated warehouses, and ultimately sold it to *their* customers at the retail end of the distribution chain (e.g., stores, restaurants, and hotels). Max Leiter had adopted a different distribution strategy with regard to the eastern *Länder*.

Lunch with Uncle August.   After driving down from Frankfurt, Maria's visit began with a luncheon meeting with August Ober. Now age 57, August had worked at the brewery for his entire career. His experience had been largely on the production side of the brewery, where he had risen to the position of brewmaster before assuming general management of the company upon the retirement of his father. He said,

EXHIBIT 1 (continued)

Historical and Projected Balance Sheets

		Actual				Projected	
		1989	*1990*	*1991*	*1992*	*1993*	*1994*
Assets							
1	Cash	6,764	10,040	11,254	12,283	13,603	14,898
2	Accounts receivable						
	Western *Länder*	8,740	9,004	9,104	9,477	9,658	9,948
	Eastern *Länder*	–0–	310	2,987	4,505	6,750	8,775
	Allowance for doubtful						
	accounts	(87)	(93)	(121)	(140)	(328)	(374)
3	Inventories	7,732	7,853	8,965	14,330	15,870	17,381
4	Total current assets	23,149	27,114	32,189	40,454	45,552	50,627
5	Investments and other						
	assets	3,911	3,913	3,918	3,914	3,000	3,000
6	Gross property, plant, and						
	equipment	73,667	73,667	76,500	76,500	85,300	93,933
7	Accumulated depreciation	(29,505)	(34,944)	(42,311)	(49,961)	(57,611)	(66,141)
8	Net property, plant, and						
	equipment	44,162	38,723	34,189	26,539	27,689	27,792
9	Total assets	71,222	69,750	70,296	70,908	76,242	81,419
Liabilities and Stockholders' Equity							
10	Bank borrowings (short						
	term)	3,765	7,166	7,633	7,884	12,785	17,267
11	Accounts payable	4,511	4,607	4,705	5,328	5,668	6,207
12	Other current liabilities	9,325	9,031	10,316	11,259	12,469	13,656
13	Total current liabilities	17,601	20,804	22,654	24,471	30,922	37,131
14	Long-term debt, bank						
	borrowings	20,306	14,755	12,911	11,066	9,222	7,378
15	Stockholders' equity	33,315	34,191	34,732	35,371	36,098	36,911
16	Total liabilities and						
	stockholders' equity	71,222	69,750	70,296	70,908	76,242	81,419

Over the long history of this company, the Obers have had to be brewers, not marketers or finance people. As long as we made an excellent product, we always sold our output at the price we asked. Then, in 1989, I realized that we needed more than just production know-how. I wanted to enter the eastern Länder because it had traditionally been a good market for our beer before the partition in 1949. Returning to eastern Germany was, for me, reclaiming a lost market. Thus I hired Max Leiter to lead this initiative.

I'm quite pleased with what Max has been able to accomplish. He has organized 5 distributorships, taken us from 0 to 211 customer accounts, and set up warehousing arrangements—in 30 months, and on a small budget! He really produces results. I am afraid I will have to pay him a lot more money next year, if I am to keep him. As it is, I paid him DM122,860 in 1992, consisting of a base salary of DM80,000 and an incentive payment of DM42,860, which is calculated as 0.5 percent of the annual sales increase. As you know from my letter to the board of directors, I am proposing increases in both his base salary (to DM95,000) and incentive payment (to 0.8 percent of the annual sales increase).

EXHIBIT 2

BAYERN BRAUEREI
Sources and Uses of Funds Statements
(fiscal year ending December 31; all figures in DM thousands)

		Actual			Projected	
	1990	*1991*	*1992*	*1993*	*1994*
Sources of Funds						
1 Net income	3,504	2,162	2,557	2,909	3,251
2 Increases in allowance for doubtful accounts	6	28	19	188	46
3 Depreciation	5,439	7,367	7,650	7,650	8,350
4 Increases in short-term debt	3,401	467	251	4,901	4,482
5 Increases in accounts payable	96	98	623	340	540
6 Increases in other current liabilities	(294)	1,286	943	1,210	1,187
7 Total sources of funds	12,152	11,408	12,042	17,198	18,036
Uses of Funds						
8 Dividend payments	2,628	1,622	1,917	2,182	2,439
9 Increases in cash balance	3,276	1,214	1,029	1,320	1,295
10 Increases in accts. receivable (W. Ger.)	264	100	373	181	290
11 Increases in accts. receivable (E. Ger.)	310	2,677	1,518	2,245	2,025
12 Increases in inventories	121	1,112	5,365	1,540	1,511
13 Increases in other assets	2	5	(4)	(914)	–0–
14 Reductions in long-term debt	5,551	1,844	1,844	1,844	1,844
15 Capital expenditures	–0–	2,834	–0–	8,800	8,633
16 Total uses of funds	12,152	11,408	12,042	17,198	18,036

Max was very helpful in pulling together the financial plan for 1993 [see Exhibit 1]. It shows handsomely rising sales and profits! Also, he prepared various analytical presentations, including a sources and uses of funds statement [Exhibit 2] and a detailed ratio analysis [Exhibit 3]. One very helpful analysis was the breakeven chart[4] Max prepared [Exhibit 4]. It shows that, as we increase our volume above the breakeven volume, our profits rise disproportionately faster.

If we keep on this growth course, we'll exhaust our existing unused productive capacity by late 1993. The budget for 1993 calls for investment of DM8.8 million in new plant and equipment. Max has proposed that in 1994 we invest DM8.6 million in a state-of-the-art warehouse and distribution center in Berlin. He argues that we won't be able to sustain our growth in the eastern Länder without these major investments. I haven't even begun thinking about how we will finance all this growth. In recent years, we have depended more on short-term bank loans than we used to. I don't know whether we

---

[4]This chart shows the relationship between revenues, costs, and volume of output. For instance, revenues are calculated as the volume of hectoliters of beer sold times the unit price of DM153.46 per hectoliter. Fixed costs (DM27.814 million) remain constant as unit output varies and are the sum of administration and selling expense plus depreciation. Variable costs are the sum of production costs, excise duties, and allowance for doubtful accounts, or DM102.29 per hectoliter. At any given level of output, total costs are the sum of variable and fixed costs. Profits or losses are illustrated as the difference between the revenue and total-cost lines, but note carefully that "profit" here is implicitly defined as earnings before interest and taxes (EBIT). This analysis identifies the breakeven volume, where revenues just equal total costs. Bayern Brauerei's breakeven volume was 540,600 hectoliters.

EXHIBIT 3

BAYERN BRAUEREI
Ratio Analyses of Historical and Projected Financial Statements
(fiscal year ended December 31)

		Actual				Projected	
		1989	*1990*	*1991*	*1992*	*1993*	*1994*
Profitability							
1	Operating profit margin (%)	7.3	7.5	6.2	6.1	6.2	6.3
2	Average tax rate (%)	33.7	34.5	39.5	39.0	35.0	35.0
3	Return on sales (%)	4.1	4.3	2.3	2.5	2.6	2.6
4	Return on equity (%)	9.7	10.2	6.2	7.2	8.1	8.8
5	Return on net assets (%)	6.7	7.9	7.8	8.5	9.8	11.0
6	Return on assets (%)	4.5	5.0	3.1	3.6	3.8	4.0
Leverage							
7	Debt/equity ratio (%)	0.72	0.64	0.59	0.54	0.61	0.67
8	Debt/total capital (%)	41.9	39.1	37.2	34.9	37.9	40.0
9	EBIT/interest (×)	6.8	7.9	2.6	3.0	2.9	2.9
Asset Utilization							
10	Sales/assets	1.10	1.18	1.33	1.44	1.49	1.52
11	Sales growth rate (%)	4.0	5.0	14.2	9.1	10.7	9.5
12	Assets growth rate (%)	6.0	−2.1	0.8	0.9	7.5	6.8
	Receivables growth rate (%)						
13	Germany	4.0	6.6	29.8	15.6	17.4	14.1
14	Western *Länder*	4.0	3.0	1.1	4.1	1.9	3.0
15	Eastern *Länder*	0.0	NMF	863.5	50.8	49.8	30.0
	Days in receivables						
16	Germany	40.8	41.4	47.1	49.9	52.8	55.0
17	Western *Länder*	40.8	41.6	41.0	41.4	41.0	41.0
18	Eastern *Länder*	NMF	36.3	85.0	87.1	90.0	90.0
19	Payables to sales (%)	5.8	5.6	5.0	5.2	5.0	5.0
20	Inventories to sales (%)	9.9	9.6	9.6	14.0	14.0	14.0
Liquidity							
21	Current ratio	1.32	1.30	1.42	1.65	1.47	1.36
22	Quick ratio	0.88	0.93	1.03	1.07	0.96	0.90

Notes: These financial ratios show the performance of the firm in four important areas:

Profitability is measured both in terms of *profit or expense margins* (lines 1–3) and as *investment returns* (lines 4–6). Investors will focus on the latter measures of profitability.

Leverage ratios measure the use of short-term and long-term debt financing by the firm. In general, higher usage of debt increases the risk of the firm. Higher ratios of debt to equity and to capital (lines 7 and 8) suggest higher financial risk. The ratio of EBIT to interest expense measures the ability of the firm to "cover" its interest payments; lower levels of this ratio suggest higher risk (line 9).

Asset-utilization ratios measure the efficiency of asset use. For instance, the sales-to-assets ratio (line 10) shows how many DM of sales are generated per DM of assets; a higher figure suggests more efficiency, and a lower figure suggests less efficiency. Over the long term differences in the growth rates of sales (line 11) and assets (line 12) can lead to production problems of over- or undercapacity. Days in receivables (lines 16–18) shows how many days it takes to collect the average credit sale; the longer it takes, the greater the investment in receivables.

Liquidity ratios measure the resources available to meet short-term financial commitments. The current ratio (line 21) is the ratio of all current assets to all current liabilities. The quick ratio (line 22) is the ratio of only cash and receivables (i.e., those assets that can be liquidated quickly) to all current liabilities.

EXHIBIT 4

BAYERN BRAUEREI

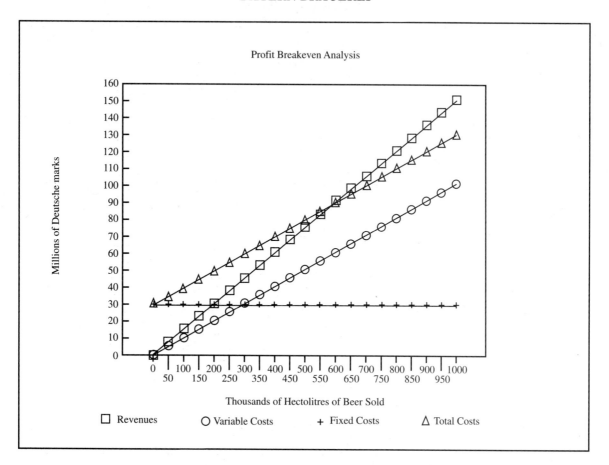

should continue to rely on them to the extent we have. Right now, we can borrow from our long-standing Hausbank at an 11 percent rate of interest.[5] Our banker asked me to meet with him next week to discuss our expansion plans; I'm guessing that he can't wait to get more of our business!

With the improved profits, I am proposing an increase in dividends for this quarter to a total of DM545,500, one-fourth of the projected dividends to be paid in 1993. This should keep the Ober family happy. As you know, half of our family stockholders are retirees and rely on the dividend to help make ends meet.

We have traditionally aimed for a 75 percent dividend payout from earnings each year, to serve our older relatives.

---

[5]In January 1993, the annual rate of return on short-term German government debt was 8.25 percent.

August Ober had been quite talkative during the meal, allowing Maria little opportunity to ask questions or offer her own opinions. She was disquieted by some of the statements she heard, however, and resolved to study the historical and forecasted financials in detail. Then, quite abruptly, Uncle August announced that lunch was done and he would take her to meet Max Leiter.

Meeting with Max Leiter.   After the introductory pleasantries, Maria asked Max to describe his marketing strategy and achievements in the eastern *Länder*. Max said,

> Our beer almost sells itself; discount pricing and heavy advertising are unwarranted. The challenge is getting people to try it and getting it into a distribution pipeline, so that when the consumer wants to buy more, she can do so. But in 1990 and 1991, the beer distribution pipeline in eastern Germany was nonexistent. I had to go there and set up distributorships from nothing; there were willing entrepreneurs, but they had no capital. I provided the best financing I knew how, in the form of trade credit concessions. First, I extended credit to distributors in the East who could not bear the terms we customarily gave our distributors in western Germany. I relaxed the terms to these new distributors from 2 percent 10, net 40 to 2 percent 10, net 80.[6] Even on these terms, our distributors are asking for more time to pay; I plan to relax the payment deadline to 90 days. I am confident that we will collect on all of these receivables; my forecast assumes that bad debts as a percentage of accounts receivable will amount to only 2 percent.
>
> These distributors are real entrepreneurs. They started with nothing but their brains. They have great ambitions and learn quickly. Some of them have gotten past due on their payments to us, but I suspect that they will catch up in due course. Virtually all the retailers and restaurateurs we supply are expanding and enhancing their shops, buying modern equipment, and restocking their own inventories—all without the support of big banks like yours in Frankfurt! Most of these retailers can't get bank credit; their "bootstrap" financing is ingenious and admirable. A little delay in payment is understandable.
>
> I should add that the other parts of my marketing strategy involved field warehousing, to permit rapid response to market demand, and quite a lot of missionary activity, to see that our beer received the proper placement in stores and restaurants. My policy on field inventories has been to support the fragile distributor network by carrying a substantial part of the inventory on behalf of the distributor. This resulted in a sizable increase in inventory for the company in 1991 and 1992.
>
> These new marketing policies have paid off handsomely in terms of our unit growth in the new federal states. Sales in the eastern Länder grew 47 percent in 1992—a rate of increase that I aim to sustain for the foreseeable future. Without my changes in credit and inventory policy, we would have realized only a small fraction of our current level of sales there. In 1993 I hope to establish 5 more distributors and place our beer in 100 more stores and restaurants.

Maria inquired about the signs of economic recession in Germany and the deep recession in the eastern *Länder*. Max seemed relatively unconcerned and said confidently that unit sales in the new federal states would rise significantly in 1993. At the close of their meeting, Maria asked for information on Bayern's credit customers. Max supplied several files from which she extracted the summary information in Exhibit 5.

---

[6]2 percent 10, net 40 means that Bayern's customer can take a 2 percent discount if payment is made within 10 days of invoice, and that otherwise the full payment is due within 40 days.

EXHIBIT 5

BAYERN BRAUEREI
Selected Information on Bayern's Distributors in the Eastern *Länder*

Bayern Distributors by City	Magdeburg	Chemnitz	Dresden	Gera	Berlin	Composite Ratios, German Beer-Distribution Industry
Income Data						
Net sales, 1992	DM4,500,000	DM3,600,000	DM3,100,000	DM1,500,000	DM6,179,000	NA
Operating profit/sales	1.8%	2.2%	3.0%	1.1%	3.5%	3.7%
Pretax profit/sales	1.7	1.9	2.3	0.7	3.1	3.5
Assets (as % of total)						
Trade receivables	12.9	13.5	16.5	19.5	13.0	12.0
Inventory	15.1	19.0	30.0	25.0	22.0	31.0
Fixed assets	33.1	29.1	25.0	21.0	28.0	24.0
Total	100.0%	100.0%	100.0%	100.0%	100.0%	100.0%
Liabilities						
ST bank borrowings	0.1%	2.1%	1.5%	2.5%	4.0%	15.0%
Trade payables	29.2	32.2	28.7	37.5	19.0	16.3
Total curr. liabs.	35.0	41.0	33.2	43.2	27.0	39.4
LT debt	2.5	0.0	3.0	0.0	5.0	16.0
Net worth	32.5	59.0	63.8	56.2	68.0	44.6
Total	100.0%	100.0%	100.0%	100.0%	100.0%	100.0%
Ratios						
Current ratio	1.1	1.2	1.1	0.9	1.6	1.4
Days' sales outstanding	27.7	25.9	27.4	39.5	19.8	19.4
Sales/assets	2.0	1.9	2.2	1.8	2.4	2.3
Pretax profit/assets	2.9%	3.6%	5.1%	1.3%	7.4%	8.0%
Debt/equity	8.0%	3.6%	7.1%	4.4%	13.2%	69.5%

Conclusion

After a lengthy dinner that evening, at which she met the other directors, Maria returned to the information she had gathered that day. She would need to form an opinion on the three matters coming before the board the next day (the financial plan, the dividend declaration, and the compensation plan for Max). She also wanted to study the company's reliance on debt financing. The other directors would be interested to know why, if the company was operating so profitably above its breakeven volume, it needed to borrow so aggressively? Maria also wondered about the wisdom of Bayern's aggressive penetration of the eastern *Länder:* did rapid sales growth necessarily pay off in terms of more profits or dividends? All this would take more study. She yawned and then poured herself a cup of coffee before returning to scrutinize the numbers.

FINANCIAL ANALYSIS: FURTHER CONSIDERATIONS

International financial statement analysis is in an early stage of development, but it is evolving rapidly in response to increasing cross-border investments by portfolio managers.[1]

Among the key themes developed in Chapter 4 were that (1) an important use of historical financial statements is to help analysts and managers predict the future and (2) effective financial statement analysis involves obtaining information in such a way that the process of obtaining the information itself aids the process of forming judgments and making decisions. In this chapter, we return to those themes by continuing our development of a systematic approach to ratio analysis, and by introducing pro forma financial statements. In Chapters 8–14, we will return to the third key theme of Chapter 4, namely, that effective financial statement analysis must consider not only the specific accounting methods in use but also the cultural context within which financial data are prepared.

A Fundamental Framework for Ratio Analysis[2]

In response to the need to control an increasingly diverse set of businesses, F. Donaldson Brown of the Du Pont Powder Company, one of the world's first conglomerates, is commonly acknowledged to have developed the first systematic approach to ratio

---

[1]R. Todd and R. Sherman, "International Financial Statement Analysis," in *Handbook of International Accounting* ed., F. D. S. Choi (New York: John Wiley, 1991), p. 939.

[2]The contents of the first two sections are based substantially on articles coauthored by T. I. Selling and C. P. Stickney: "The Effects of Business Environment and Strategy on a Firm's Rate of Return on Assets," *Financial Analysts Journal,* January-February 1989, and "Disaggregating the Rate of Return on Common Shareholders' Equity: A New Approach," *Accounting Horizons,* December 1990.

analysis.[3] His approach centered on two financial concepts—profit margin and asset turnover—that were considered at the time to be the two key elements for controlling a company's operations. As discussed in Chapter 4, profit margin refers to the ability of a company to generate profit from a given level of revenues, while asset turnover refers to the effective (or ineffective) utilization of a company's investment in assets.

Brown observed that for capital-intensive operations, such as manufacturing or mining, expenditures for long-lived assets were quite significant albeit infrequent, and the effectiveness of day-to-day decisions could be better measured by a company's profit margin than its asset turnover. Retailers, on the other hand, typically added less value to the goods they sold than did manufacturers, and, frequently, they had relatively little control over the purchase and sales prices of their merchandise. Thus, for these firms, profit margin would be less crucial than asset (principally receivables and inventory) turnover as an element of control. Brown's insight was to link the concepts of profit margin and asset turnover together to form one overall index of corporate performance that a firm could use to evaluate any of its diverse operating segments. Brown's overall index of profitability became known as the **Du Pont formula,** and is given as follows:

$$\text{Du Pont formula} = \text{Profit margin} \times \text{Asset turnover} \tag{1}$$

$$= \frac{\text{Net income after tax}}{\text{Net sales}} \times \frac{\text{Net sales}}{\text{Average total assets}}$$

Multiplying the formula's components yields the well-known indicator ROA (or ROI):

$$\text{Return on assets} = \frac{\text{Net income after tax}}{\text{Average total assets}} \tag{2}$$

The return on assets, as used in the original Du Pont formula, embodies all of the components of the balance sheet (i.e., average total assets) and the income statement (i.e., net income after tax) and indicates management's success in generating a return on the resources placed at its disposal by owners. The Du Pont formula demonstrates that a response to the question of how the return on assets changed over time could be made in terms of either changes in profit margin, asset turnover, or both.

A more detailed analysis of the components inherent in the Du Pont formula would entail an examination of the ratios that are themselves components of profit margin and asset turnover. For example, receivables turnover, inventory turnover, and fixed asset turnover are all components of a company's total asset turnover. Similarly, the relationship of cost of goods sold to net sales and administrative expenses to net sales are components of a company's profit margin. Thus, it is possible to identify factors causing changes in either of the formula's two elements by investigating subcomponents of the two ratios themselves. An example of this type of decomposition analysis is illustrated in Exhibit 5–1 for Cray Electronics Holdings Plc. Cray Electronics Holdings is a British company engaged in the manufacture of communications software products and the provision of information systems consulting services. Panels A and B

[3]H. T. Johnson and R. S. Kaplan, *Relevance Lost: The Rise and Fall of Management Accounting* (Boston, MA: Harvard Business School Press), 1987, p. 84.

EXHIBIT 5–1

Cray Electronics Holdings Plc
Panel A—Comparative Balance Sheets as of April 30
(in thousands)

	1992	1991	1990
Assets			
Cash and short-term investments	£ 2,637	£ 324	£ 600
Accounts receivable	29,583	24,823	31,258
Inventories	18,092	18,059	21,175
Prepaid expense and accrued income	1,625	1,271	1,725
Current assets—sundry	1,737	6,597	2,145
Total current assets	£53,674	£51,074	£56,903
Fixed assets	24,507	23,093	45,478
Depreciation and amortization	(13,532)	(10,712)	(15,160)
Fixed assets—net	£10,975	£12,381	£30,318
Investments and advances	82	1,472	2,457
Total assets	**£64,731**	**£64,927**	**£89,678**
Liabilities			
Short-term borrowings	£ 8,134	£18,772	£32,973
Accounts payable/creditors—trade	10,824	6,974	12,047
Current liabilities—other	15,634	10,685	15,005
Total current liabilities	£34,592	£36,431	£60,025
Long-term debt	9,360	9,146	11,482
Total liabilities	**£43,952**	**£45,577**	**£71,507**
Shareholders' equity			
Common/ordinary capital	13,451	10,492	9,411
Share capital—other	400	400	400
Capital surplus/share premium reserve	3,234	2,113	2,113
Revaluation reserve	1,252	4,656	4,498
Retained earnings	2,442	568	(1,075)
Equity reserves—other	–0–	1,121	2,824
Total shareholders' equity	**£20,779**	**£19,350**	**£18,171**
Total liabilities and shareholders' equity	**£64,731**	**£64,927**	**£89,678**

contain balance sheets and income statements; panel C depicts a traditional Du Pont decomposition analysis based on these reported numbers.

Enhancements to the Du Pont Formula

The development of modern financial management theory has focused increased attention on management's ability to generate returns to shareholders, and, consequently, managerial attention to financing decisions (e.g., the use of debt versus equity capital) is ever more intense. This led to the identification of a shortcoming in the Du Pont formula as a basis for modern financial statement analysis, namely that the formula's

Exhibit 5–1 (continued)
Panel B—Income Statements for Years Ended April 30
(in thousands)

	1992	1991
Sales/Turnover (net)	**£84,786**	**£ 107,286**
Operating expense		
Cost of goods sold	51,233	68,255
Selling, general and administrative	24,039	27,004
Operating expense—total	75,272	95,259
Depreciation of fixed assets	2,117	2,621
Operating Income	**£ 7,397**	**£ 9,406**
Interest and related expense	2,745	6,076
Nonoperating income (expense)—total	135	179
Net income before income taxes	£ 4,787	£ 3,509
Income taxes		
Current	978	1,027
Deferred	331	146
Other	24	(94)
Income taxes—total	1,333	1,079
Net income before extraordinary items	3,454	2,430
Extraordinary items net of tax effects	(542)	(769)
Net income	£ 2,912	£ 1,661

inability to conveniently distinguish between the effects of management's operating decisions from those of its financing decisions on the return on invested capital.

For example, consider two firms that are identical in every respect, except that Firm A financed its asset acquisitions using only equity capital, while Firm B is financed with a debt to equity ratio of 25 percent. (In Commonwealth countries such as Australia, Canada, New Zealand, and Great Britain, the use of debt financing is referred to as *gearing;* in the context of these illustrations, we use the more common U.S. rubric of *leverage*.)[4] Although Firms A and B are equally profitable before considering interest expense, Firm A's ROA is higher than that of Firm B.[5] A refinement of ROA, **unleveraged ROA** (UROA), that overcomes this shortcoming and reflects the equality of operating performance for both firms, is given by the following:

$$\text{UROA} = \frac{\text{Net Income} + \text{Interest expense} \times (1 - \text{Incremental tax rate})}{\text{Average total assets}} \qquad (3)$$

$$= \frac{NI + I(1 - TR)}{ATA}$$

---

[4]In general, $\text{Gearing} = \dfrac{\text{Interest-bearing debt}}{\text{Owners' equity}}$; $\text{Leverage} = \dfrac{\text{Total assets}}{\text{Owners' equity}}$.

[5]Implicit to this argument is that both debt and equity capital bear an opportunity cost. In the case of debt, this opportunity cost is explicitly captured by the deduction of "interest expense" on the income statement, whereas no parallel charge for equity capital is reflected in a firm's net income.

EXHIBIT 5–1 (continued)

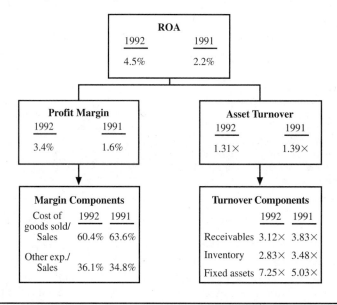

**Panel C—Du Pont Decomposition Analysis for
Cray Electronics Holdings Plc**

This diagram depicts a traditional Du Pont decomposition analysis for Cray Electronics Holdings Plc. As the analysis reveals, the increase in Cray's ROA from 1991 to 1992 was largely due to a significant increase in the company's profit margin, which in turn was attributable to a decline in the cost of goods sold to sales ratio over that same period. The increase in ROA was partially offset by a marginal decline in the total asset turnover; the nominal effect of asset turnover on ROA could be attributed to substantial but offsetting effects among its various components.

Because interest expense is subtracted in calculating the numerator (i.e., net income) in the traditional measurement of ROA, it should be added back if the numerator is to exclude the effects of debt financing. The amount added back, however, must also reflect the deductibility of interest expense in computing taxable net income; thus, interest expense is multiplied by 1 minus the incremental tax rate to arrive at the after-tax effect of excluding interest expense from net income after taxes.

The reformulation of UROA into unleveraged profit margin and asset turnover can be seen as follows:

$$
\begin{aligned}
\text{UROA} &= \frac{NI + I(1 - TR)}{ATA} \\
&= \frac{NI + I(1 - TR)}{S} \times \frac{S}{ATA} \\
&= \text{Unleveraged profit margin} \times \text{Asset turnover}
\end{aligned}
\tag{4}
$$

EXHIBIT 5-2

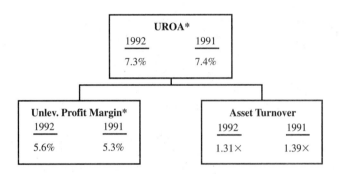

**Unleveraged ROA Analysis for
Cray Electronics Holdings Plc**

Although the ROA for Cray Electronics Holdings increased from 2.2 to 4.5 percent from 1991 to 1992, UROA can be seen to decrease slightly. The difference must be due to interest expense, generally viewed to be a nonoperating item. The data reveal that unleveraged profit margin improved but not sufficiently to offset the decline in asset turnover.

UROA*	
1992	1991
7.3%	7.4%

Unlev. Profit Margin*			Asset Turnover	
1992	1991		1992	1991
5.6%	5.3%		1.31×	1.39×

* The U.K. corporate tax rate for the year ended March 31, 1992, was 33 percent. For the previous year, the rate was retroactively reduced from 35 percent to 34 percent. In these calculations, a 33 percent incremental tax rate was used.

where *S* refers to a company's net sales and *ATA* refers to its average total assets. Exhibit 5.2 illustrates the decomposition of UROA for Cray Electronics.

Now that ROA has been ''deleveraged,'' a remaining refinement is to reinsert the effects of financial leverage in the Du Pont formula in such a way that it can be separately identified. The objective of this refinement is to develop an analytical framework that portrays some overall index of profitability as a multiplicative function of UROA and the effects of management's financing decisions on profitability. The general form of the framework should be as follows:

$$\text{Overall index of profitability} = UROA \times \text{Financial leverage} \qquad (5)$$

We begin developing the framework by designating the **return on common equity** (ROCE) as the new overall index of corporate performance:

$$\text{ROCE} = \frac{NI - PD}{ACEQ} \qquad (6)$$

PD in Equation (6) represents the dividends paid to preferred shareholders, and *ACEQ* is the average common equity for the period. The quantity (*NI* − *PD*) is referred to as *net income available to common shareholders.* Notice that since preferred dividend distributions are not tax deductible in the United States, there is no after-tax effect to consider. (In other countries such as Germany, preferred dividends are treated like interest expense for tax purposes, and thus the tax effect must be incorporated in Equation (6) by multiplying *PD* by 1 minus the incremental tax rate.) By excluding required distributions to preferred shareholders, ROCE reflects a measure of real returns to a company's true (i.e., voting) owners. It reflects the commonly held view that the principal goal of management should be to maximize shareholder wealth. Equation 5 can now be restated as follows:

$$\text{ROCE} = \textit{UROA} \times \text{Financial leverage} \qquad (7)$$

Intuitively, financial leverage has the effect of magnifying operating results: a positive UROA should translate into an even higher ROCE when financial leverage is present. A useful ratio that portrays the extent of a company's financial leverage is the **common shareholders' capital structure leverage ratio** (CSL):

$$\text{Common shareholders' capital structure leverage ratio} = \frac{\text{Average total assets}}{\text{Average common equity}} \qquad (8)$$

CSL measures the extent to which common shareholders, as opposed to other suppliers of capital, have financed a company's investment in assets. In the context of this ratio, average common equity (ACEQ) is the average of total shareholders' equity excluding preferred shareholders' equity and minority interest.[6] CSL is commonly greater than or equal to 1 (so long as ACEQ is greater than zero) and can therefore be viewed as a leveraging factor; it has the effect of magnifying UROA.

CSL alone, however, does not fully explain the effects of financial leverage on the computation of ROCE. In the following equation, we develop the ROCE decomposition further by (1) incorporating CSL into the ROCE analysis framework, (2) separating UROA into its unleveraged profit margin and asset turnover components, and (3) creating a new variable, *Z,* to denote the remaining unexplained multiplicative component of ROCE:

$$\text{ROCE} = \frac{\text{Unleveraged}}{\text{profit margin}} \times \frac{\text{Asset}}{\text{turnover}} \times \frac{\text{Capital}}{\text{structure}} \times Z \qquad (9)$$
$$\text{leverage}$$

Substituting the formulas for ROCE, unleveraged profit margin, asset turnover, and capital structure leverage into equation (9), and then solving for *Z,* we obtain an expression for *Z* that we interpret as **common equity's share of operating earnings** (CSOE):

$$Z = \frac{NI - PD}{NI + I(1 - TR)} = \text{Common equity's share of operating earnings} = \text{CSOE} \qquad (10)$$

---

[6]For simplicity, this section assumes ''minority interest'' of zero. If it were greater than zero, minority interest in earnings of subsidiaries would be treated as interest expense. The topic of minority interest is covered in detail in Appendix 6A.

We then substitute CSOE in Equation (9) to obtain our completed ROCE analysis framework:

$$\text{ROCE} = \frac{NI + I(1 - TR)}{S} \times \frac{S}{ATA} \times \frac{ATA}{ACEQ} \times \frac{NI - PD}{NI + I(1 - TR)} \quad (11)$$

$$= \frac{\text{Unleveraged}}{\text{profit margin}} \times \frac{\text{Asset}}{\text{turnover}} \times \frac{\text{Capital structure}}{\text{leverage}} \times \frac{\text{Common equity}}{\substack{\text{share of} \\ \text{operating earnings}}}$$

Common equity's share of operating earnings (CSOE) measures the proportion of a company's operating earnings (i.e., earnings before payments to creditors and preferred shareholders) allocable to the common shareholders. If net income after all payments to preferred shareholders—that is, the numerator in Equation (10)—is positive, the denominator of Z will be greater than its numerator. And, since the value of Z must range between zero and 1, the effect of CSOE on ROCE is to dampen the effect of capital structure leverage because the value of CSOE is similarly between zero and 1.

ROCE, like ROA and UROA, can be expressed by various levels of subcomponents, and this decomposition is illustrated in Exhibit 5–3 for Cray Electronics Holdings.[7] Exhibit 5–4 diagrammatically summarizes the development of the enhanced Du Pont formula.

UROA and Financial Leverage: A Closer Look

Exhibit 5–5 presents two plots for the purpose of studying international patterns in UROA. Each point in the plot represents five-year (1988–1992) industry averages of unleveraged profit margin and asset turnover, aggregated by one of five industries and five countries studied.[8] In panel B, the data points are labeled by country of origin of the companies; and in panel C, these same data points are labeled by industry. Each plot contains a reference line, or isoquant, representing the infinite number of ways that a UROA of 5 percent is achievable. All points above and to the right (below and to the left) of this reference line represent UROAs greater (less) than 5 percent.

Panel B largely confirms broad views of the accounting practices and management cultures in the countries studied. Excluding the utilities (the four left-most points),

---

[7]To gain a better understanding of how operating, investing, and financing decisions affect ROCE, Selling and Stickney (1990, op. cit.) decomposed the annual percentage change in ROCE for a sample of U.S. firms into the portions attributable to changes in UROA, CSOE, and CSL. The results of that study demonstrate that most of the variability in ROCE is due to changes in UROA. In general, firms did not appear to make significant changes in their capital structure to compensate for annual changes in UROA. Such a result makes intuitive sense since major changes in capital structure require a new debt or equity issue or substantial repurchases of outstanding debt or stock, both of which take time and are costly to execute. Their findings, however, do not rule out the definite possibility that CSL and CSOE may play a more important role in explaining the change in ROCE for particular firms in particular years. Cray Electronics Holdings is illustrative of this point.

[8]Industries were defined by two-digit SIC codes. Two of the five industries used are represented only in four countries because of limitations on data availability. Specifically, the food industry is not included for Italy, and the electrical industry is not included for the United Kingdom.

EXHIBIT 5–3

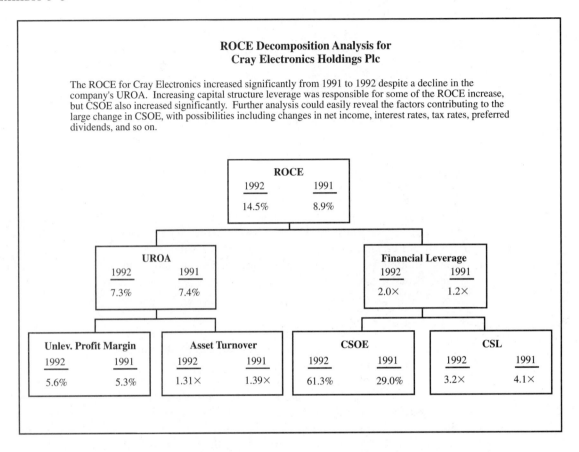

**ROCE Decomposition Analysis for
Cray Electronics Holdings Plc**

The ROCE for Cray Electronics increased significantly from 1991 to 1992 despite a decline in the company's UROA. Increasing capital structure leverage was responsible for some of the ROCE increase, but CSOE also increased significantly. Further analysis could easily reveal the factors contributing to the large change in CSOE, with possibilities including changes in net income, interest rates, tax rates, preferred dividends, and so on.

which is a heavily regulated industry throughout the world, the data points of each country form remarkably tight clusters with surprisingly little overlap between countries:

- U.K. companies have the highest UROAs, probably because goodwill is not capitalized; therefore, assets are understated relative to the other countries.

- German and Italian companies have relatively low ROAs because of reserve accounting that gives management broad discretion.

- U.S. and Japanese data points are most widely dispersed because companies in these countries have less ability to "manage" reported earnings. U.S. companies may have slightly higher UROAs on average because of less conservative depreciation methods; Japanese depreciation expense conforms with its tax code, which allows for accelerated depreciation; U.S. companies predominantly use straight-line depreciation for financial reporting purposes.

EXHIBIT 5–4

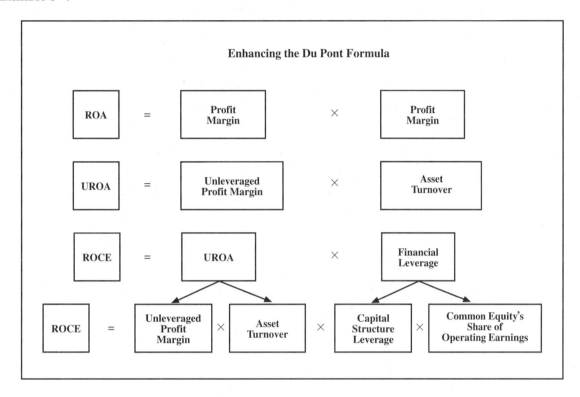

It is much more difficult to interpret industry differences in panel C of Exhibit 5–5 across countries because of the confounding effect of each country's accounting practices. (This is just one more demonstration of the need to make data more comparable via restatement!) However, the two industries with the most extreme financial statement characteristics seem to overcome country differences:

- Because of their capital intensity, utilities have the lowest asset turnover. UROA varies widely because of regulation, which in large part determines what constitutes a "fair" return on invested capital for these companies.
- The commodity-like nature of food products and their perishability may dominate actual differences in quality and brand-name effects. As such, this industry is dominated by relatively low profit margins (lowest in three of four countries) and relatively high asset turnover.

In general, two explanations for differences in UROA have been found to aid in the development of a coherent and succinct financial analysis, and they are the extent of a company's **operating leverage** and its **product life cycle.**[9]

---

[9]Selling and Stickney, "The Effects of Business Environment and Strategy."

EXHIBIT 5–5

International Patterns of UROA
Panel A: Countries and Industries in the Sample

Countries	Industries
Germany	Electronic Equipment (except computers)
Italy	Electrical and Gas Utilities
Japan	Chemical Products
United Kingdom	Food Products
United States	Industrial and Commercial Machinery

Panel B: Margin and Turnover by Country

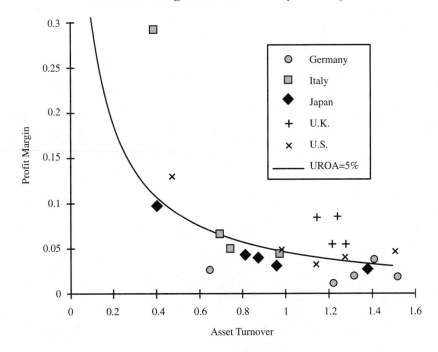

Operating Leverage.   Firms operate with different mixtures of fixed and variable operating costs. Capital intensive companies, for example, incur relatively large amounts of depreciation expense, which is more or less fixed for any given period. Most retailers and wholesalers, by contrast, incur a high proportion of variable costs. Firms with a high proportion of fixed costs usually experience significant increases in operating income as their volume of sales increase. This occurs because fixed costs are being spread over a larger number of units sold, resulting in a decrease in the average unit cost.

The process of operating with a high proportion of fixed costs is referred to as **operating leverage.** Firms with high levels of operating leverage usually experience

EXHIBIT 5–5 (continued)
Panel C: Margin and Turnover by Industry

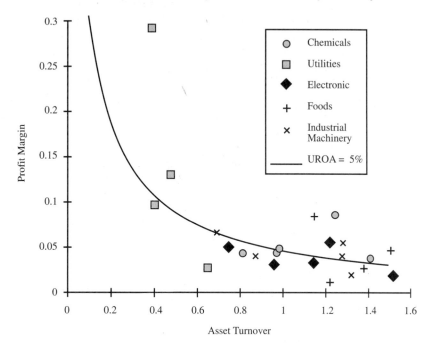

greater variability in their UROAs than firms with lower levels of operating leverage. The proportion of total assets composed of fixed (or plant) assets—the **capital intensity ratio**—indicates the degree of a company's operating leverage. Higher levels of the capital intensity ratio are associated with high levels of UROA variability. Data also indicate that, consistent with modern financial theory, industries with high UROAs tend to have a high variability in UROAs, as measured by its standard deviation.

Product Life Cycle.   Product life cycle theory posits that products (and therefore the companies that produce them) move through four identifiable phases: introduction, growth, maturity, and decline. During the introduction and growth phases, a firm's focus is on product development (product R&D spending), market development (advertising and other promotional spending), and capacity enlargement (capital spending). The objective of these activities is to gain market acceptance and market share. During the maturity phase, as competition becomes more intense, emphasis shifts to reducing costs through improved capacity utilization (in gaining economies of scale) and more efficient production. During the decline phase, firms exit the market as sales decline and profit opportunities diminish.

During the introduction and early growth phases, expenditures on product development and marketing, coupled with relatively low sales levels, usually lead to negative

ROAs and/or UROAs. As sales accelerate during the high-growth phase, operating income and UROAs turn positive. The rate of growth in UROAs is dampened during this phase, however, as extensive product development, marketing, and depreciation expenses moderate operating income, but heavy capital expenditures to build capacity for higher future sales increase the denominator of UROA. UROA usually increases significantly during the maturity phase because of the benefits of economies of scale and learning curve phenomena, as well as the general curtailment of capital expenditures. Finally, UROA deteriorates during the decline phase as operating income decreases, but it may remain positive or even increase for some time into this phase.

The concept of product life cycle can be applied most effectively to financial statements generated for a firms' **strategic business units (SBUs)**—independent, autonomous business segments that could be managed as viable and isolated concerns. The concept can be extended, however, to an entire firm by assessing the mix of products within the firm. For example, a computer firm often produces products that range from their introduction phase to their decline phase, although most computer firms are today probably in the later part of their high-growth phase. Other firms may be in a bipolar position: they have few mature products but many products in the other three categories. The food-processing industry is fully mature, although new products are continually being introduced. The U.S. steel industry might be viewed as being in the decline phase, although some companies have modernized production sufficiently to stave off decline. The Japanese steel industry, on the other hand, is generally viewed as being in the maturity phase.

Profit Margin–Asset Turnover Mix.   Possible explanations for differences in the profit margin–asset turnover mix also come from the disciplines of economics and business strategy. Economic theory helps to explain how capacity and competitive constraints affect the profit margin and asset turnover mix, and business strategy helps to explain how product differentiation and cost leadership strategies affect the mix.

Capacity and Competitive Constraints.   Exhibit 5–6 depicts the ideas of capacity and competitive constraints in the context of UROA analysis. The two curves in Exhibit 5–6 represent two levels of UROA; the curve farthest from the origin of the graph represents the higher of the two UROA levels. Both UROA levels depicted can be achieved by an infinite number of total asset turnover and unleveraged profit margin combinations. Managers seeking to maximize UROA (i.e., to be on a curve as far as possible from the origin) face constraints that limit the strategies that they can implement to increase their UROA.

Managers in industries that have heavy fixed capacity costs and require lengthy periods to add new capacity operate under a *capacity constraint.* As a consequence, there is an upper limit on the level of asset turnover that they can achieve. To attract sufficient capital, these managers must generate relatively high profit margins. The high profit margins usually are achieved through some form of entry barrier (e.g., large capital requirements, high risk, or regulation) and the attainment of economies of scale (i.e., spreading the fixed capacity costs over a large number of units sold). Examples of industries that operate under a capacity constraint are telecommunications, real

Exhibit 5–6

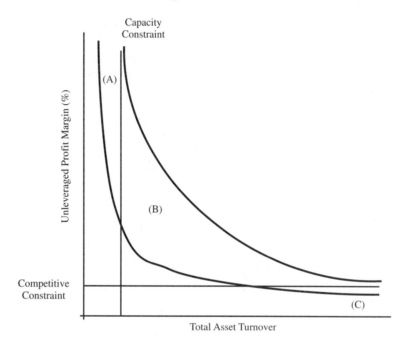

Constraints on
Profit Margin–Asset Turnover Mix

estate, and oil exploration. These firms tend to operate in the area of section (A) of Exhibit 5–6.

Managers in industries whose products are commodity like in nature, that have few entry barriers, and have intense competition operate under a *competitive constraint;* that is, there is an upper limit on the profit margin that they can achieve. To attract sufficient capital, these managers must strive for higher asset turnover. High asset turnover might be achieved by minimizing fixed costs, purchasing in sufficient quantities to realize discounts, or integrating vertically or horizontally to obtain cost savings. Such actions to control costs are also usually matched with aggressively low prices to gain market share and drive out marginal firms. Most retailers and wholesalers operate under a competitive constraint and thus are usually found to operate in section (C) of Exhibit 5–6.

Managers of firms that operate in section (B) of Exhibit 5–6 are not affected to a significant degree by either capacity or competitive constraints, at least as compared to those that operate in the tails of the curves. Thus, they have more latitude to take actions that will increase profit margin, asset turnover, or both, to achieve a higher UROA.

Product Differentiation versus Cost Leadership. The thrust of a *product-differentiation strategy* is to create a product that is perceived industrywide to be unique and to therefore earn a higher profit margin by charging a higher price. The differentiation could relate to product capabilities, product quality, service, channels of distribution, or some other factor. The thrust of a *cost-leadership strategy* is to become the lowest-cost producer in a market to be able to charge the lowest prices and achieve the highest volume. The low-cost position can be achieved through economies of scale, production efficiencies, outsourcing or similar factors, or asset parsimony (maintaining strict controls on investments in receivables, inventories, and plant and equipment).

The product-differentiation strategy may be viewed as profit-margin focused, whereas the cost leadership strategy is primarily asset-turnover focused. Note that movements toward (A) of Exhibit 5–6 are product-differentiation oriented, and movements in the direction of (C) from any point along the UROA curves are cost-leadership oriented. Thus, although grocery stores will likely cluster around (C), some grocery stores will place heavy emphasis on specialty products (e.g., bakery, delicatessen, fresh flowers, VCR rentals, prescription drugs) that have higher profit margins than most grocery products.

Flexibility in trading off profit margin versus asset turnover is important when a firm considers its strategic alternatives (product differentiation versus cost leadership). Consider, for example, a firm with a profit margin–asset turnover mix marked as (A) in Exhibit 5–6. This firm will have to give up significant profit margin to obtain a meaningful increase in asset turnover. To increase UROA, therefore, it should emphasize actions that increase profit margin. Firms in section (C), on the other hand, will have to give up considerable asset turnover to obtain much of an increase in profit margin. To increase UROA, these firms should emphasize actions that increase asset turnover. For firms operating in section (B), however, trade-offs of margin for turnover are more equal. Such firms would seem to have greater flexibility to design strategies that promote profit margin or asset turnover, or some combination (and/or some particular element[s] of these two components) when striving to increase UROA.

In summary, microeconomic and business strategy concepts are useful in understanding the behavior of UROA over time and across firms and industries. UROA variability differs across firms and industries, for example, according to their levels of operating leverage. UROA also differs across firms as products pass through different stages in their life cycles. Shortly we will investigate how forecasts of financial variables such as UROA can be transformed into pro forma financial statements.

The Du Pont Formula: A Final Comment

The Du Pont formula represents a powerful analytical framework to evaluate the financial health of most firms. A key assumption inherent in the formula is that financial accounting provides relevant and reliable measurements of management performance and changing business conditions. In countries such as Germany and Japan, where management strategies purportedly have much longer time horizons and where there is closer conformity between accounting and taxable income, the Du Pont formula may not so clearly capture the year-to-year financial effects of management performance and the dynamics of business environments. One modification to the framework used in this chapter to accommodate different time horizons is to compute ratios over longer time periods, say three to five years. For example, it may be more valid to compare ROCEs for a five-year period when comparing the ROCE of Cray Holdings to those of a Japanese firm in the same industry.[10]

In countries outside the United States, management objectives are explicitly different than simply maximizing common shareholder wealth. Consequently, alternative approaches may be superior to the Du Pont formula for evaluating management's progress toward achieving objectives that are not captured by ROA or ROCE. However, an investor's interest in the company may still remain simple: to choose a portfolio of investments that maximize return on investment given a target level of risk. Thus, a focus on ROA and ROCE may still be appropriate for the investor, even if management does not evaluate themselves the same way. Some alternatives to the Du Pont formula will be discussed in Chapters 8–14, as we consider the unique environmental setting of the individual countries.

Pro Forma Financial Statements: Projecting Financial Results

The purpose of projected or **pro forma financial statements**[11] is to aid analysts and managers in the formation of explicit, detailed forecasts of future profitability, financial health, and cash flow. As noted earlier, the historical financial statements prepared under the GAAP of any country in the world are not intended to be forecasts of the future. For the most part, the reported accounting data reflect only past cash flows and reasonably certain future cash flows that are the result of past events. For example, costs of inventory and equipment measure past cash flows, whereas principal amounts of receivables and debt measure highly probable future cash flows resulting from past transactions.

Pro forma analysis can enhance the analysis of historical financial statements by incorporating forecasts of future events into the traditional accounting framework. At one extreme, a set of pro forma financial statements can be prepared by projecting one determinant of a company's financial results and holding all other historical results constant; or at the other extreme, by forecasting changes in all determinants of financial

---

[10]Comparing financial ratios over extended horizons is sometimes sufficient to overcome differences in cultural context as reflected in accounting methods; in other cases, it is not, and some restatement is necessary (see Chapter 6).

[11]For the purposes of this book, the terms *projected* and *pro forma* financial statements are used interchangeably. However, the reader should be aware that the term *pro forma financial statements* has a more general meaning in practice, referring to either projected financial statements *or* restatements of historical financial statements to reflect hypothetical events. For an example of the latter, SEC regulations state in regard to acquisitions of significant subsidiaries that took place during the most recent fiscal year: ''Pro forma financial information should provide investors with information about the continuing impact of a particular transaction by showing how it might have affected historical financial statements if the transaction had been consummated at an *earlier* [emphasis supplied] time.'' See SEC Regulation S-X, Rule 11–02.

results. The fundamental accounting equation is used as an organizing framework in preparing projected financial statements for the same reason that it is used for presentation of historical financial statements: to reduce the possibilities for reflecting the economic impact of transactions to those that conform to the simple and familiar logic of the fundamental accounting equation. A second reason is that if projections are prepared on the same basis as historical financial statements, it is easier to compare the projections to historical results. Projections are frequently extrapolations of patterns exhibited in the financial statements of past periods because historical patterns frequently can reasonably be presumed to recur in future periods.

Projected financial statements have many uses. Company management generates projected financial statements as part of the budgeting process: to set goals for profitability, anticipate future cash needs, evaluate opportunities for expansion, control the rate of growth, or perform sensitivity analyses on key determinants of financial results. Outside financial analysts may generate forecasts for many of the same reasons, and they may use projected financial statements to evaluate the feasibility of business acquisition opportunities, opportunities to provide debt or equity financing, or, in general, to value a business. The final section of this chapter (see pp. 230–37) illustrates the use for pro forma financial statements in valuation decisions.

Developing Projected Financial Statements

Even the simplest set of projected financial statements requires numerous forecasts, assumptions, and simplifications. After all, historical financial statements for a period are a summarization of thousands of events, prices, quantities, and so on. Usually with the aid of commonly available and popular electronic spreadsheet software, an analyst or manager can make judgments as to how to express these many details as a manageable number of determinants of projected financial results. Major determinants usually include such items as sales forecasts, cost structure, interest rates, tax rates, and capital expenditures. The care with which an analyst or manager expresses these determinants depends on their significance, available information, and the desired level of complexity and detail in the pro forma financial statements. For example, forecasted sales may reflect not only historical sales patterns but also industry and economywide trends, stage of products in their life cycles, and known product R&D projects.

The analyst must also be aware of assumptions that are inherent in the preparation of projected financial statements that are both subtle and unnecessary in the preparation of historical financial statements. For example, in forecasting interest expense, the analyst must consider the timing of financing events within a period and the timing of operating events that will either generate or use cash. In forecasting changes in fixed assets, the analyst must be aware of the interactions between depreciation expense, purchases of new fixed assets, and dispositions of existing fixed assets.

The simple example to follow examines the types of forecasting and modeling choices that can be made and, with the aid of personal computer spreadsheet software, illustrates procedures by which these forecasts can be reflected in projected financial statements. We begin in Exhibit 5–7 with the condensed historical income statements and balance sheets of Kaufmann & Hess, GmbH (K&H) in the first numerical column. K&H is a hypothetical German manufacturing firm with sales totaling 1,000,000 DM

EXHIBIT 5–7

KAUFMANN & HESS, GmbH
Historical and Projected Financial Statements
Projection of Operating Results and Asset Mix

	Historical Amounts (1995)		Projected (1996)
Income Statement			
Sales	DM1,000.0		DM1,100.0
Cost of goods sold	550.0	55%	605.0
Other operating expenses	200.0	20%	220.0
Operating income	DM 250.0		DM 275.0
Interest	26.0		
Net income before taxes	DM 224.0		
Taxes	89.6		
Net income	DM 134.4		
Less: dividends	10.0		
Change in retained earnings	DM 124.4		
Balance Sheet			
Cash	DM 10.0	2%	DM 11.0
Accounts receivable	100.0	20	110.0
Inventory	50.0	10	55.0
Fixed assets, net	340.0	68	374.0
Total assets	DM 500.0	100%	DM 550.0
Accounts payable—trade	DM 45.0		
Short-term debt	210.0		
Long-term debt	50.0		
Total liabilities	DM 305.0		
Paid-in capital	30.0		
Beginning retained earnings	40.6		165.0
Add: Net income	134.4		
Less: Dividends	10.0		
Ending retained earnings	DM 165.0		
Total equities	DM 500.0		DM 550.0

for the most recently completed fiscal year (1995) and a historical growth rate in sales of 10 percent per year. The task at hand is to generate projected financial statements for the upcoming fiscal year (1996). In practice, an analyst would ordinarily prepare financial statements for more than one period into the future (perhaps as much as three to five years) and base those projections on financial statements going back more than one year, but the simple circumstances portrayed in Exhibit 5–7 should be sufficient for our purposes at this point. (We will consider projections for additional future periods later in Exhibit 5–11.)

Exhibit 5–7 also includes a partial forecast for 1996 for K&H. The following steps were undertaken to create this partial forecast. Shaded areas of the projected income statement and balance sheet will be completed in later steps.

Step 1. *Forecast sales growth.* This is frequently the most crucial assumption since, as we will soon see, many other elements of both the pro forma income statement and balance sheet will be based on this number. For simplicity, we assume a sales growth equal to the historical average of 10 percent.

Step 2. *Forecast operating expenses (excluding interest).* We assume that operating expenses are a constant percentage of sales, but this assumption is almost certainly unrealistic. Expense behavior is usually modeled by fixed and variable components. Fixed expenses remain at the same level over relatively wide fluctuations in sales; variable expenses move in proportion to changes in sales.

Step 3. *Forecast the change and composition of total assets.* We assume that total assets vary in direct proportion to sales. This is roughly equivalent to assuming a constant total asset turnover ratio. In addition, the composition of projected total assets is assumed to follow the most recent common-size balance sheet. (A more refined analysis could focus on individual asset categories. For example, it is quite reasonable to expect that fixed asset turnover would decrease with small increases in sales and that current asset turnover would remain relatively constant. Moreover, the analyst would certainly want to review the most recent annual report to see if management has made any explicit statements about planned capital acquisitions or divestitures that would assist in forecasting the composition of total assets.)

Step 4. *Set total equities equal to total assets, and beginning retained earnings equal to ending retained earnings of the previous period.*

The shaded areas of the balance sheet of Exhibit 5–7 can be thought of as projections of financing decisions to be made by management, and the shaded areas on the income statement can be thought of as the consequences on net income of these financing decisions. These management actions can be partitioned into those that are part of long-term plans, and those that are in response to short-term cash surpluses and deficits. Exhibit 5–8 reflects the following steps to project long-term financing policies:

Step 5. *Forecast net proceeds from the issuance and purchase of capital stock.* We assume that no new issuances or repurchases will occur during the period; hence, paid-in capital is unchanged.

Step 6. *Forecast issuances and retirement of long-term debt.* We assume that no new issuances or retirements will occur during the period; hence, total long-term debt is unchanged.

Step 7. *Forecast dividends for the period.* We assume that management policy is to maintain a constant dividend.

For each of steps 5–7, it would be wise to review a firm's most recent annual report to see whether management has made any explicit statements about anticipated stock sales or repurchases, new debt issuances or retirements, or dividend payment policy. These explicit statements can be used to verify or modify the analyst's assumptions.

Step 8. *Forecast changes in noninterest bearing liabilities.* We will assume, for simplicity, that management's policy is to maintain accounts payable at 9 percent of

EXHIBIT 5–8

KAUFMANN & HESS, GmbH
Historical and Projected Financial Statements
Projection of Operating Results, Asset Mix and
Long-Term Financing Policy

	Historical Amounts (1995)		Projected (1996)
Income Statement			
Sales	DM1,000.0		DM1,100.0
Costs of goods sold	550.0	55%	605.0
Other operating expenses	200.0	20%	220.0
Operating income	DM 250.0		DM 275.0
Interest	26.0		
Net income before taxes	DM 224.0		
Taxes	89.6		
Net income	DM 134.4		
Less: dividends	10.0		10.0
Change in retained earnings	DM 124.4		
Balance Sheet			
Cash	DM 10.0	2%	DM 11.0
Accounts receivable	100.0	20	110.0
Inventory	50.0	10	55.0
Fixed assets, net	340.0	68	374.0
Total assets	DM 500.0	100%	DM 550.0
Accounts payable—trade	DM 45.0	9%	49.5
Short-term debt	210.0		
Long-term debt	50.0		50.0
Total liabilities	DM 305.0		
Paid-in capital	30.0		30.0
Beginning retained earnings	40.6		165.0
Add: Net income	134.4		
Less: Dividends	10.0		10.0
Ending retained earnings	DM 165.0		
Total equities	DM 500.0		DM 550.0

total assets, as reflected by the common-size balance sheet. A more refined analysis might focus on forecasting the future accounts payable turnover ratio.

The projected income statement and balance sheet can be completed by considering the effect of short-term cash surpluses and deficits. This is necessary because we have fixed the amount of cash on the projected balance sheet to be 11.0 million DM, without any idea as to how much cash will actually be generated by the next period's operating, investing and, financing activities. A simple way to handle the problem of cash surpluses (deficits) relative to the projected ending cash balance of 11 million DM is to assume purchases (issuances) of capital stock during the period sufficient to affect the surplus (deficit); however, in reality, capital stock is rarely manipulated in this manner by management. A more complex but realistic method that can be used is to adjust the amounts of short-term interest-bearing debt for cash deficits and surpluses. This method is more complex because the level of debt on the balance sheet reflects the level of interest expense on the income statement and, hence, the amount of cash used to pay interest. However, it is more realistic because many companies maintain bank lines of credit or similar types of revolving short-term debt arrangements to handle exactly these circumstances.

The following steps describe the completion of the projected income statement and balance sheet as shown in Exhibit 5–9:

Step 9. *Project an average tax rate.* We assume a flat rate of 40 percent.

Step 10. *Create an equation for the calculation of interest expense.* We assume that cash receipts and disbursements will occur evenly over the period. Hence, interest expense will be a function of both the beginning and ending amounts of debt. We also assume that the interest rates on short- and long-term debt are 10 percent and 12 percent, respectively. Thus, our algebraic expression for interest expense is

$$\text{Interest expense} = .1 \frac{STD_1 + STD_2}{2} + .12 \frac{LTD_1 + LTD_2}{2} \tag{12}$$

where the subscripts 1 and 2 denote the beginning and end of the period, respectively, and *STD* and *LTD* are short- and long-term debt, respectively.

Step 11. *Create an equation for the calculation of end-of-period short-term debt.*

$$STD_2 = \text{Total equities} - \text{Retained earnings} - \text{Paid-in capital} \tag{13}$$
$$- \text{Long-term debt} - \text{Accounts payable}$$

where all amounts in Equation (13) are as of the end of the period to be forecast.

Calculation of short-term debt using Equation (13) is not as straightforward as it may first appear. The problem is one of circular logic in the equations caused by double-entry accounting. Although not shown explicitly, STD_2 is in both sides of the equation: retained earnings is a function of net income for the period, which is in turn a function of interest expense for the period, which is in turn a function of STD_2, which is what we are trying to solve for! Circular logic creates a calculational problem that is best handled by iterative calculations on a spreadsheet program.

The amounts added by steps 9 through 11 remain shaded in Exhibit 5–9.

The final step in the process of preparing projected financial statements for K&H is to prepare a statement of cash flows. This is a fairly mechanistic process that does not differ from the preparation of historical cash flows once the income statement and balance sheet have been prepared. In essence, the pro forma statement of cash flows is not independently prepared but is derived from the pro forma income statement and balance sheet just prepared (using the methods described in Appendix 4A). The statement of cash flows in Exhibit 5–10 has only one "twist": operating and investing cash flows are combined into one category.

EXHIBIT 5–9

KAUFMANN & HESS, GmbH
Historical and Projected Financial Statements
Completed with Amounts Added by Steps 9–11 Shaded

	Historical Amounts (1995)		Projected (1996)
Income Statement			
Sales	DM1,000.0		DM1,100.0
Cost of goods sold	550.0	55%	605.0
Other operating expenses	200.0	20%	220.0
Operating income	**DM 250.0**		**DM 275.0**
Interest	26.0		21.2
Net income before taxes	**DM 224.0**		**DM 253.8**
Taxes	89.6		101.5
Net income	**DM 134.4**		**DM 152.3**
Less: dividends	10.0		10.0
Change in retained earnings	**DM 124.4**		**DM 142.3**
Balance Sheet			
Cash	DM 10.0	2%	DM 11.0
Accounts receivable	100.0	20	110.0
Inventory	50.0	10	55.0
Fixed assets, net	340.0	68	374.0
Total assets	**DM 500.0**	**100%**	**DM 550.0**
Accounts payable—trade	DM 45.0	9%	DM 49.5
Short-term debt	210.0		113.2
Long-term debt	50.0		50.0
Total liabilities	**DM 305.0**		**DM 212.7**
Paid-in capital	30.0		30.0
Beginning retained earnings	40.6		165.0
Add: Net income	134.4		152.3
Less: Dividends	10.0		10.0
Ending retained earnings	**DM 165.0**		**DM 307.3**
Total equities	**DM 500.0**		**DM 550.0**

See Appendix 5A for a printout of the formulas used to calculate the figures in this exhibit using Microsoft *Excel*.

There are two reasons for not distinguishing between operating and investing cash flows. First, there may not be enough information to make the distinction accurately in a projected statement of cash flows. In analyzing the change in fixed assets, it is necessary to know the amount of depreciation expense for the period, an operating item, versus net fixed asset acquisitions/dispositions, an investing item. In historical financial statements, depreciation expense is often aggregated with cost of sales. Second, the distinction between operating and investing cash flows is not always informative. For example, fixed asset acquisitions to maintain existing productive capacity are arguably operating cash flows, even though no accounting standard requires preparers to distinguish in the statement of cash flows between fixed asset expenditures for expansion versus maintenance of productive capacity. For purposes of preparing projected financial statements,

Exhibit 5–10

KAUFMANN & HESS, GmbH
Projected Statement of Cash Flows
1996

Operations		
Net income		DM 152.3
Adjustments		
Change in accounts receivable	(10.0)	
Change in inventory	(5.0)	
Change in fixed assets	(34.0)	
Change in accounts payable	4.5	(44.5)
Cash provided by operations		**DM 107.8**
Financing		
Additions (reductions) in short-term debt	(96.8)	
Additions (reductions) in long-term debt	0.0	
Additions (reductions) in paid-in capital	0.0	
Dividends	(10.0)	
Net cash from financing		**(106.8)**
Change in cash		**DM 1.0**

we believe that capital expenditures made to maintain existing product capacity should be classified as operating cash flows (as in the calculation of free or discretionary cash flows). An investing category is informative when a major asset expenditure or divestiture is planned that significantly changes the firm's productive capacity.

In summary, although the use of K&H as an illustration emphasizes an organizing framework for preparing projected financial statements, analysts should not lose sight of the applicability of various financial analysis techniques discussed thus far as aids in projecting financial results. Ratio analysis and common-size financial statements are used to analyze trends in relationships among numbers on the financial statements. In making projections, the analyst must forecast how certain trends and relationships will change (or not change, as the case may be) with time. In the next section, we illustrate how to use financial statement projections to value a firm (or other investment opportunity) for sale or acquisition, which is just one way in which pro forma statements can be used by professional analysts and managers.

Valuing Ownership Interests

Financial analysis does not always involve business valuation, but it frequently does. The two most common reasons that business valuation is an important aspect of financial analysis are (1) illiquid markets for trading the stock of a company to be bought or sold and (2) identification of mispriced securities. Before discussing the common approaches to business valuation, these two motivations are explored.

Illiquid Markets

Many companies, even large ones, are not publicly traded. For example, in the United States, Hughes Aircraft was a privately held corporation until purchased by General Motors over 10 years ago. Mars, Inc. (the U.S. candy company) is still privately owned, and E. Merck, Germany's largest pharmaceuticals company, made its initial public offering of shares as recently as 1995.

The market for corporate control is also illiquid, and prices may differ from the market for noncontrolling interests in a company's stock (e.g., quoted prices on stock exchanges). For example, it is well known that successful tender offers almost always require that the purchaser pay a substantial premium over the trading price per share of a target firm, whereas no premium is required to purchase, say, 100 shares. Financial projections and valuation methods help to determine how a change in control would affect a corporation's financial results and how much of a premium over the current share price is justified.

Market Mispricing

Although many financial theorists argue that securities markets are efficient in the sense that all publicly available information is reflected in an unbiased manner in stock prices, legions of analysts persist in applying the tools of financial analysis for the purpose of identifying over- and underpriced stocks. Analysts seek opportunities to create insights into financial information that they believe are not noticed by others, or to incorporate information in their analysis that they believe other market participants have not discovered or have improperly valued. In addition, some markets may be less informationally efficient than others: smaller companies may not be followed as closely as larger companies by the market, and in some countries (e.g., Germany), actual "information asymmetries" exist. For example, larger shareholders may have access to information that small shareholders do not have, and in some countries (e.g., Italy), trading on inside information is much less restrictive than in the United States.

Valuation Methods

Theoretically, the valuation of an ownership interest in a business entails the calculation of the present value of expected future cash flows to owners for all future periods. The details and variants of the discounted cash flow (DCF) method are described in many finance textbooks. The problem is that direct application of financial theory to valuation often yields results that appear unreasonable. This is usually due to the lack of accuracy of assumptions that generate projected future cash flows into the too distant future. Therefore, the best method of determining value depends on the circumstances: every business has its own unique characteristics, and available information relevant to its valuation can vary considerably. In addition to the DCF approach to valuation, other methods to be discussed in this section are based on direct comparison with the market price of similar businesses, or adjustments to balance sheet and income statement numbers for the relationship between observed market prices of "comparable" businesses and their accounting numbers.

Discounted Cash Flow Methods.   Under the DCF method, a potential buyer (or seller) analyzes a company's operations using the techniques discussed in Chapter 4 and the current chapter. On the basis of that analysis, which usually includes the preparation of pro forma financial statements, estimates of the amount and timing of the future cash flows that are expected to accrue to the potential buyer are then developed. The degree of **nondiversifiable risk** is assessed,[12] and is usually incorporated into the analysis via the selection of a discount rate. The process of discounting future cash flows is captured by the following equation:

$$V = \sum_{t=1}^{n} \frac{D_t}{(1 + r)^t}$$

where

V = The net present value of the future cash flows to the owners

D_t = The dividend payment (or any cash distribution) at time t (14)

r = The risk-adjusted required rate of return

As mentioned earlier, the most critical issue in applying this equation is the forecast horizon or, more specifically, the number of periods (months, quarters, or years) for which pro forma financial statements are prepared. There is no widely accepted answer, although most analysts agree that forecasts beyond five to seven years are highly suspect because of the uncertainties that may arise. One way to mitigate these uncertainties is to substitute so-called discretionary or free cash flows for dividend flows. By definition, discretionary cash flows are greater than dividends, since dividends are themselves a discretionary cash outflow. This substitution has the effect of increasing V, implicitly by the present value of cash flows used to sustain the business for a longer period of time than explicitly considered in the DCF calculation. Other variants include substituting a company's cash flow from operations (*CFFO*) for D. However, neither method may be an adequate substitute for an estimate of the "terminal value" of the business (i.e., the value at the end of the time period over which expected dividend or cash flows have been forecast).

A related issue is whether future dividend streams adequately describe the benefits of ownership in a company. The following equation portrays the additional benefits to be derived through ownership of a target company by another business:

$$V_{sub} = \sum_{t=1}^{n} \frac{(D_s + P_{is} + MSC_s)}{(1 + r)^t}$$ (15)

where for simplicity, time subscripts are excluded and

V_{sub} = The parent's net present value of subsidiary cash flows

D_s = The dividend payment from subsidiary

---

[12]*Nondiversifiable risk* refers to the unique, nonsystematic risk associated with an investment. Most risk can be hedged by investing in a diverse set of assets (e.g., a portfolio of securities), whereas nondiversifiable risk usually cannot be effectively, or completely, hedged.

P_{is} = The profit on intracompany sales

MSC_s = The miscellaneous payments from the subsidiary (fees, royalties, interest and principal repayments, income tax credits)

Market Comparables.   This method of valuing a firm assesses value through a process of comparison with similar, recently sold (or purchased) businesses. This process is quite common in the real estate industry, particularly in real estate transactions involving a single asset, but it is somewhat difficult to apply to businesses involving a bundle of diverse assets, largely because of the difficulty of finding recently sold businesses with comparable bundles of assets. Nonetheless, for asset-dependent businesses, this approach may provide an approximate basis for assessing firm value. For example, companies involved in the oil and gas industry are often valued relative to the market value of their oil and gas reserves. This rough approximation of value may be useful in those situations in which only the reserves (or assets) of the company are being purchased, not the liabilities, and in which the costs of extraction are nominal. When differences in cost structure or asset composition are material, comparables enhanced by accounting values may be an alternative approach for valuation. This is the rationale for the balance sheet and income statement–based valuation methods to be described next.

Balance Sheet Valuation Methods.   Balance sheet–based valuation methods are essentially grounded in the notion that a buyer (seller) purchases (sells) the net assets of a company, and the economic value of the net assets bears some relationship to their book values. Before the U.S. savings and loan debacle of the 1980s, the purchase price of an S&L was typically quoted as a multiple of the institution's net book value (e.g., 1.5 times net book value). This valuation approach was followed for many years because of the relative stability of interest rates and the stability of the markets in which S&Ls provided financing. Investors who paid a price in the range of 1.5 times net book value generally earned an adequate return for the risks taken.

A significant limitation of the balance sheet valuation approach arises, however, when interest rates shift or other changes in business conditions cause the market value of assets (and liabilities) to differ from their recorded balance sheet values. One way to deal with this limitation is to "adjust" individual balance sheet values for an estimate of the amounts by which accounting valuations misstate fair values. This approach is often used today to evaluate the reasonableness of selling prices for banks, insurance companies, securities firms, and other financial institutions, whose principal assets are primarily driven by interest rates. For example, industry analysts suggest that insurance companies in the United States usually sell for 1.4 times adjusted book value and securities firms for 1.5 times adjusted book value. Although these adjustments are appealing because of their simplicity, they also have limitations. First, multiples of book values are usually not transferable across borders because of differences in governmental regulations and risk profiles. Second, adjustment to net asset book values is not ordinarily undertaken as a valuation method when large portions of a company's assets are nonfinancial: it is much more difficult for an external analyst to accurately estimate the fair values of assets other than financial assets.

It is also possible to combine balance sheet valuation methods with the DCF method. For example, projected dividend cash flows for five to seven years are estimated, and the terminal value of the business is estimated as a multiple of net worth from the projected balance sheet as of the terminal date. This procedure is reflected in the following valuation equation:

$$V = \sum_{t=1}^{n} \frac{D_t}{(1 + r)^t} + \frac{(NW_n)(X)}{(1 + r)^n} \tag{16}$$

where

NW_n = Book value of net worth at the terminal date, n

X = A multiple of book value based on market prices of comparable companies

Earnings-Based Methods.   Under this approach, the value of a company is assumed to be a multiple of its operating earnings or operating cash flow. For example, the value of a newspaper company might be quoted as 14 times operating cash flow. The advantage of this approach is its simplicity and the use of widely available data. Price/earnings ratios are also widely quoted in the financial press, and it is a simple matter to calculate an average P/E ratio for companies in the same industry that are otherwise comparable. The particular limitations of this approach involve the possibility that a single earnings number may not represent a company's worth; it may be distorted by uncharacteristically good (or poor) recent company performance. Also, earnings for a period are particularly sensitive to a company's accounting policies and may not be comparable with earnings numbers for companies that have available market prices. Finally, as will be seen in Chapters 8–14, P/E ratios vary dramatically across borders as a consequence of cultural, business, and legal factors.

Evaluating International Investment Opportunities

The use of DCF analysis in conjunction with pro forma financial statements is a powerful tool for evaluating the value of almost any firm or investment opportunity. In this section, we illustrate this approach in the context of an international investment opportunity.

The process of evaluating *international* investment opportunities involves greater complexity than evaluating purely domestic ones.[13] Although the fundamental approach is similar for both domestic and international opportunities, the number of factors to be considered increases substantially when projects cross national borders. In this section, we explore the process of multinational capital budgeting and show how the DCF framework discussed above can be implemented in the face of such additional concerns as foreign currency risk, country (or political) risk, foreign taxes, and repatriation laws, among others.

---

[13]We are indebted to T. H. Woodland for her input on this topic.

Multinational Capital Budgeting: Project versus Parent Cash Flows.   A primary difference between evaluating domestic versus foreign investments involves the risks associated with a project's cash flows. For domestic investments, the parent's and the project's cash flows are equivalent, whereas for a foreign investment, the parent's cash flow stream rarely equals that of the project. The cash flows between a parent and its foreign subsidiary are exposed to the additional considerations of foreign income (or withholding) taxes, exchange rate fluctuations, and restrictions on the movement of capital (e.g., the repatriation of profits from the subsidiary's domicile to that of the parent).

Thus, multinational capital budgeting usually involves the added complexity of generating *two* sets of pro forma statements, one for the parent and one for the project (or subsidiary). *Project cash flows* are usually computed in the **functional currency** of the subsidiary: the inflows are the after-tax funds received from the parent and the outflows are the after-tax profits generated by the project.[14] Project cash flows, however, must be considered in light of two special risks: the risk of expropriation and the risk of blocked funds. **Expropriation risk** refers to the probability that a project's assets and operations will be taken over by a foreign government, with or without compensation to the parent.[15] **Blocked funds risk,** on the other hand, refers to existing or pending foreign laws that restrict the flow of funds out of a given locale. Although blocked funds cannot be repatriated, they can usually be reinvested in the foreign country and at some point in the future may be transferable.

Parent cash flows are usually computed twice, once in the functional currency of the subsidiary and then translated into the functional currency of the parent. This latter computation requires an assumption with respect to the movement of exchange rates and thus requires an explicit consideration of exchange rate exposure.[16] For the parent, the outflows are represented by the pre-tax dollars sent to (or paid for) the subsidiary, whereas its inflows are represented by the subsidiary's after-tax profits, adjusted to reflect profit repatriation limitations and exchange rate fluctuations. The parent's inflows usually take the form of dividends, although some multinational companies also use interest and principal repayments, transfer pricing, management fees, rents, and royalties to shift income across national boundaries (or from a subsidiary to a parent). Sophisticated international tax law writers, however, have adopted the position that

---

[14]The ''functional currency'' of a company is the currency in which it primarily conducts its business operations. For example, a British company, headquartered in London and with shares traded on both the London Stock Exchange and the New York Stock Exchange, but whose principal operations involve trading in Hong Kong (in transactions denominated in Hong Kong dollars), would have a functional currency of Hong Kong dollars, not British pounds or U.S. dollars.

[15]When expropriation is uncompensated, the parent company can usually seek some form of recompensation (i.e., a tax loss deduction or insurance recovery) in its own domicile. Alternatively, the parent may seek recovery from the Overseas Private Investment Corporation (OPIC), which provides insurance coverage against currency inconvertibility by law, expropriation, civil war or revolution, and wrongful or improper calling of a guarantee. These payments, of course, must be considered when evaluating an international investment opportunity.

[16]The topics of foreign exchange exposure and accounting for exchange rate fluctuations are addressed in detail in Chapter 7.

virtually *all* forms of repayment to a parent company constitute dividends and thus are subject to local income tax laws.

A measure of the net present value of cash flows received by a parent from a foreign subsidiary can be modeled by the following equation:

$$V_{sub} = \sum_{t=1}^{n} \frac{(D_s + P_{is} + MSC_s)\ FX - (D_s + P_{is} + MCS_s)(FX)(T_d)}{(1 + r)^t} + \frac{(NW_n)(X)}{(1 + r)^n} \quad (17)$$

where

FX = The foreign exchange rate
T_d = The domestic tax rate

Reinvestment versus Repatriation.   The desirability of embarking on a foreign investment may, in large measure, be linked to local repatriation laws. Consider, for example, the decision by McDonald's in the early 1990s to invest $40 million in a restaurant in Moscow. This multimillion dollar investment in the former Soviet Union was made with the full realization that existing (and current) Soviet laws prevented the repatriation of any of the restaurant's profits. Obviously, McDonald's Moscow investment was predicated on market growth objectives, not on cash flow repatriation.[17]

In the absence of repatriation constraints, an issue often arises as to where (i.e., in what country) a parent should invest its scarce resources. This decision is usually resolved using the following investment maxim: invest in that locale with the highest rate of return, adjusted for foreign exchange risk and political risk.

Blocked funds—either partially or fully—may have considerable value to a parent company, depending on its cash needs. Blocked funds, particularly those that can be reinvested at rates of return that equal or exceed those experienced by the parent company, can have considerable value if the objectives of the parent are market share oriented, as in the case of McDonald's. Blocked funds, however, also can be quite costly when the local rates of return are low and prospects for future repatriation of the blocked funds are negligible. When these conditions exist, alternative payment schemes from the subsidiary to the parent (i.e., intracompany loans, management fees, transfer prices) should be considered to reduce the magnitude of blocked funds.

Multinational Capital Budgeting: A Process Approach.   The analysis of international investment opportunities presents a challenge to most analysts. The complexity of this challenge can be managed, however, by sequentially addressing the problem in a stepwise fashion, as follows:

Step 1. *Develop rational assumptions.* The backbone of any DCF analysis is the forecasted cash flow data and, hence, pro forma financial statements. The key to

---

[17]Since McDonald's original investment of $40 million, the exchange rate of the ruble relative to the U.S. dollar has fallen by more than 1,000 percent, causing a parallel decline in the value of this foreign investment as reflected on the parent's financial statements. This type of foreign exchange exposure can be hedged against in a variety of ways—a topic for consideration in Chapter 7.

meaningful pro forma data is the use of rational, well-reasoned assumptions regarding the subsidiary's future performance, local political risk, and the general economic conditions. Examining the local and regional business and political environment (i.e., country risk analysis), as well as the structure of a subsidiary's industry, provide a useful starting point.[18] Assumptions as to market growth, inflation, changes in market share, and changes in costs must be incorporated in a project's pro forma analysis. The parent must also provide a rough business plan that identifies and quantifies the value and effects that can be obtained by putting the project under new, foreign ownership, as well as the effects of any restructuring activities, technology upgrades, and synergy exploitation. These plans should represent an important input to the project pro formas.

Step 2. *Develop project forecasts.* The parent should always first develop a set of profitability projections for the venture assuming status quo. This enables the investor to estimate the value of the project in its current state to the parent. A second set of projections should then be prepared incorporating the effects of any proposed reorganization or restructuring, infusion of capital, expertise, or technology, and the exploitation of any economies of scale or other synergies. This allows the parent to carefully consider the value of changes to the existing project.

As part of this phase, scenarios regarding changes in exchange rates and governmental regulations should be drafted. Also, at this stage, these scenarios, as well as all assumptions previously developed, should be subjected to **sensitivity analysis,** which refers to evaluating how changes in a given assumption or scenario will affect a project's operating performance or cash flows. This type of analysis is useful for two reasons. First, it highlights those assumptions or scenarios that create the greatest risk for project success; these assumptions and scenarios must be reevaluated for their reasonableness (i.e., if it is unlikely that a purchaser for an asset exists, assuming

---

[18]The use of country risk analysis has increased in recent years in both its importance and its sophistication. Interested readers should consider the related readings in the Suggested References at the end of this chapter. On a regular basis, *Euromoney* provides a country risk ranking. Its rankings for this text's focal countries are

Country Risk Ratings (1 = least risky)

	1990	*1995*
Japan	2	2
United States	11	5
Germany	19	7
United Kingdom	18	10
Sweden	8	21
Italy	17	22
S. Korea	20	26
Brazil	67	58
*No. of countries ranked	133	187

Source: *Euromoney,* September 1990, pp. 87–90 and March 1995, pp. 376–81.

that an asset will be sold is an unrealistic scenario). Second, it identifies for parent management those assumptions that need to be most closely tracked after a project begins. Tracking the most influential factors will enable management to control, as much as humanly possible, the success of a foreign project.

Step 3. *Determine the appropriate discount rate.* Determining the appropriate discount rate (*r*) for any capital budgeting analysis is, at best, a tenuous science. In the typical domestic DCF analysis, the discount rate is usually set equal to the firm's weighted-average cost of capital (WACC) or some desired (or required) rate of return (in essence, a hurdle rate of return). For international investment opportunities, however, additional considerations are necessary.

In theory, the discount rate should be the *risk-adjusted* required rate of return on invested funds for a given company.[19] Thus, if the net cash flows for a given investment opportunity are less certain than would normally be the case for a firm (i.e., the probable distribution of returns is more dispersed than usual), the discount rate must be adjusted to reflect this uncertainty. Thus, increasing the discount rate is a fairly straightforward mechanism to capture the additional risk exposure that tends to characterize international investment projects. One disadvantage to the approach of adding a risk premium to the discount rate is that it assumes that the degree of risk is uniform over the life of the project. Due to the exponential nature of discounting, a uniformly higher discount rate (because of an add-on risk premium) substantially penalizes early cash flows and may not adequately reflect the risk in later periods.

Step 4. *Selecting an appropriate investment horizon and terminal value.* The final decisions to be made before undertaking a project analysis concern the likely time horizon of the project and the identification of any residual or terminal value. The time horizon of a project should be tied to the expected useful life of the asset or investment being purchased, whereas the terminal value should be determined with reference to rational assumptions regarding the value of the assets at the time of their disposal. In general, most professional analysts work with time horizons of five to seven years. Investment horizons longer than seven years are usually so difficult to predict with any reasonable degree of certainty that analysts try to avoid doing so. Moreover, adopting a shorter time horizon (e.g., three to five years) is another means to reflect additional risk exposure in one's analysis.

The terminal value of a project represents the expected cash flows, if any, to be received on termination or abandonment of a project. Terminal values are usually difficult to predict, particularly when the investment horizon exceeds five years, although we suggested the use of balance sheet–based approaches in the previous section.[20]

---

[19]This rate may actually be less than the parent's WACC if the funds can be borrowed elsewhere at a lower cost of capital.

[20]For those investments expected to continue in perpetuity, a terminal value can be estimated using any number of available growth models. For example, see F. J. Weston and T. E. Copeland, *Managerial Finance* (New York: Harcourt, Brace, Jovanovich, 1989), pp. 696–712.

An Illustration. A U.S.–based trading company is considering the acquisition of Kaufmann & Hess, GmbH (K&H). With respect to this investment, the following facts have been gathered:

German tax rates	
Corporate income tax	40%
Withholding tax on dividends	15%
U.S. tax rates	
Corporate income tax (with credit given for foreign withholding taxes paid)	36%
Exchange rate	1.6 DM/$1 U.S.

To determine an appropriate purchase price, executives of the U.S. company have agreed on the following assumptions for purposes of preparing pro forma data regarding the investment:

- Sales dollar volumes will increase in response to new export markets at the rate of 10 percent per annum through 1997 and 7 percent per annum thereafter through 2000. Asset levels and cost structure assumptions are identical to those made earlier.
- The German DM is projected to depreciate 2 percent per annum against the U.S. dollar.
- The residual value at the end of year 2000 is approximately 110 percent of the December 31, 2000, projected net worth. Since the U.S. company plans to hold K&H indefinitely, tax effects of the terminal value are ignored.
- In 1996, all excess cash will be used to pay down short-term debt. Thereafter, all excess cash will be remitted to the parent company in the form of dividends.

The U.S. executives have determined that they will be willing to pay a price equal to the present value of the project. For purposes of the analysis, the executives have decided to use a discounted cash flow approach over a five-year time horizon with a 14 percent discount rate. The risks of expropriation and of blocked funds were both considered to be negligible.

Analysis. Exhibit 5–11 presents projected financial statements for K&H over the five-year time horizon. Note that, except for minor reformatting for the purpose of conciseness, the first column of Exhibit 5–11 is identical to the projections in Exhibits 5–9 and 5–10. Exhibit 5–12 illustrates the value calculation using Equation (17). The analysis reveals that the U.S. company should be willing to pay $409,700 U.S. (DM655,520) on December 31, 1995, to acquire the German operations (see also Appendix 5A).

EXHIBIT 5–11

KAUFMANN & HESS, GmbH
Projected Financial Statements

	1996	1997	1998	1999	2000
Income Statement					
Sales	DM1,100.0	1,210.0	1,294.7	1,385.3	1,482.3
Cost of goods sold	605.0	665.5	712.1	761.9	815.2
Other operating expenses	220.0	242.0	258.9	277.0	296.4
Operating income	DM 275.0	**302.5**	**323.7**	**346.4**	**370.7**
Interest	21.2	26.1	21.7	22.2	22.6
Net income before taxes	DM 253.8	**276.4**	**302.0**	**324.2**	**348.1**
Taxes	101.5	110.6	120.8	129.7	139.2
Net income	DM 152.3	**165.8**	**181.2**	**194.5**	**208.9**
Balance Sheet					
Cash	DM 11.0	12.1	12.9	13.8	14.8
Accounts receivable	110.0	121.0	129.5	138.6	148.3
Inventory	55.0	60.5	64.7	69.2	74.0
Fixed assets, net	374.0	411.4	440.2	471.0	504.0
Total assets	DM 550.0	**605.0**	**647.4**	**692.7**	**741.2**
Accounts payable—trade	DM 49.5	54.5	58.3	62.4	66.8
Short-term debt	113.2	113.2	113.2	113.2	113.2
Long-term debt	50.0	50.0	50.0	50.0	50.0
Total liabilities	DM 212.7	**217.7**	**221.5**	**225.6**	**230.0**
Paid-in capital	30.0	30.0	30.0	30.0	30.0
Retained earnings	307.3	357.3	395.9	437.1	481.2
Total equities	DM 550.0	**605.0**	**647.4**	**692.7**	**741.2**
Statement of Cash Flows					
Net income	DM 152.3	165.8	181.2	194.5	208.9
Adjustments					
Change in net working capital	(10.5)	(11.5)	(8.9)	(9.5)	(10.1)
Change in fixed assets	(34.0)	(37.4)	(28.8)	(30.8)	(33.0)
Cash provided by operations	DM 107.8	**116.9**	**143.5**	**154.2**	**165.8**
Add. (dec.) in short-term debt	(96.8)	0.0	0.0	0.0	0.0
Add. (dec.) in long-term debt	0.0	0.0	0.0	0.0	0.0
Add. (dec.) in paid-in capital	0.0	0.0	0.0	0.0	0.0
Dividends	(10.0)	(115.8)	(142.6)	(153.3)	(164.8)
Net cash from financing	DM (106.8)	**(115.8)**	**(142.6)**	**(153.3)**	**(164.8)**
Change in cash	DM 1.0	**1.1**	**0.9**	**0.9**	**1.0**

EXHIBIT 5–12

KAUFMANN & HESS, GmbH
Valuation by U.S. Firm

	Total	1996	1997	1998	1999	2000
Dividends remitted by K&H		DM 10.0	DM 115.8	DM 142.6	DM 153.3	DM 164.8
Less: 15% withholding		1.5	17.4	21.4	23.0	24.7
Net dividends		DM 8.5	DM 98.4	DM 121.2	DM 130.3	DM 140.1
Foreign exchange rate		1.632	1.665	1.698	1.732	1.767
Dollar value of dividends net of German withholding taxes		$ 5.2	$ 59.1	$ 71.4	$ 75.2	$ 79.3
Less: U.S. taxes		1.9	21.3	25.7	27.1	28.5
Net cash flow from dividends		$ 3.3	$ 37.8	$ 45.7	$ 48.1	$ 50.8
Terminal net worth						$ 511.2
Adjustment factor						1.1
						562.3
Net cash flows		$ 3.3	$ 37.8	$ 45.7	$ 48.1	$ 613.1
Interest factor		0.8772	0.7695	0.6750	0.5921	0.5194
Present value	$ 409.7	$ 2.9	$ 29.1	$ 30.8	$ 28.5	$ 318.4

Summary

Disaggregations of financial statement ratios are useful when they capture, or measure, in a convenient format, important factors of interest in managing a firm. The variant of the Du Pont formula described in this chapter captures in one equation the impact of both operating and financing decisions on financial statements. The commonly encountered problem of mixing financing costs with operating costs is solved by assigning the financing costs and capital structure to a separate component of ROCE. One important outcome of this modification is to create a pure measure of operating performance, UROA. A firm's business environment and the strategies it uses to deal with that environment affect its ability to increase UROA. The extent to which a firm is subject to capacity or competitive constraints, for instance, may determine whether it can pursue a higher ROA by increasing profit margin via product differentiation strategies or by increasing asset turnover via cost leadership strategies.

Firm valuation concepts and pro forma financial statements are very closely linked. Reference to financial statement numbers are often a reference point for estimates of firm value (e.g., multiples of book assets, book net worth, operating income) and pro forma financial statements are an important way to explicitly consider the impact of future events on firm value.

Valuation of international investment opportunities are significantly more complex than domestic ones. Investors face additional sources of risk, including repatriation risk and foreign exchange risk.

Suggested References

Andriole, S. J., and G. W. Hopple. "An Overview of Political Instability Research Methodologies: Basic and Applied Recommendations for the Corporate Analysts." In *Global Risk Assessment,* ed. J. Rogers, vol. 3, 1988.

Copeland, T., T. Koller, and J. Murrin. *Valuation: Measuring and Managing the Value of Companies.* New York: John Wiley, 1990.

De la Torre, J. and D. H. Neckar. "Forecasting Political Risks for International Operations." *International Journal of Forecasting* (1988).

Haendel, D. *Foreign Investment: The Management of Political Risk.* Hartford, CN: Westview Press, 1979.

Heymann, H., R. Bloom, and R. Auster, "Cost-Volume-Profit Analysis Applied to Cash Management," *Cashflow,* July–August, 1984.

Li, R. P. "Investment and Political Risk Analyses: Framework and Strategies." In *Global Risk Assessment,* ed. J. Rogers, vol. 3, 1988.

Meek, G. "U.S. Security Market Responses to Alternate Earnings Disclosures of Non–U.S. Multinational Corporations." *The Accounting Review,* April 1983.

Rappaport, A. *Creating Shareholder Value: The New Standard for Business Performances.* New York: The Free Press, 1986.

Roll, R. "Industrial Structure and the Comparative Behavior of International Stock Market Indices." *The Journal of Finance,* March 1992.

Weston, F. J., and T. E. Copeland. *Managerial Finance.* New York: Harcourt Brace Jovanovich, 1989.

APPENDIX 5A
KAUFMANN & HESS, GmbH:
DISPLAYED FORMULAS FOR EXCEL™ SPREADSHEET

		A	B	C	D
1		Interest rate on STD	0.1		
2		Interest rate on LTD	0.12		
3		Tax Rate	0.4		
4		Sales growth rate	0.1		
5					
6					
7			Historical Amounts		Projected
8		Income Statement			
9		Sales	1000		=B9*(1+$B$4)
10		Cost of goods sold	550	=B10/$B$9	=C10*$D9
11		Other operating expenses	200	=B11/$B$9	=C11*$D9
12		Operating Income	=B9-B10-B11		=D9-D10-D11
13		Interest	27		=B1*(B28+D28)/2+B2*(B29+D29)/2
14		Net income before taxes	=B12-B13		=D12-D13
15		Taxes	=B14*$B$3		=D14*$B$3
16		Net Income	=B14-B15		=D14-D15
17		Less: dividends	10		=B17
18		Change in retained earnings	=B16-B17		=D16-D17
19					
20		Balance Sheet			
21		Cash	10	=B21/$B$25	=B21/$B$25*$D$25
22		Accounts receivable	100	=B22/$B$25	=B22/$B$25*$D$25
23		Inventory	50	=B23/$B$25	=B23/$B$25*$D$25
24		Fixed assets, net	340	=B24/$B$25	=B24/$B$25*$D$25
25		Total assets	=SUM(B21:B24)	=SUM(C21:C24)	=B25/B9*D9
26					
27		Accounts payable—trade	45	=B27/B25	=C27*D25
28		Short-term debt	210		=D37-D36-D32-D29-D27
29		Long-term debt	50		=B29
30		Total liabilities	=SUM(B27:B29)		=SUM(D27:D29)
31					
32		Paid-in capital	30		=B32
33		Beginning retained earnings	41.2		=B36
34		Add: Net income	=B16		=D16
35		Less: Dividends	=B17		=D17
36		Ending retained earnings	165		=D33+D34-D35
37		Total equities	=B30+B32+B36		=D25

ISSUES AND INFORMATION FOR FURTHER INQUIRY

I.5.1   ROE

In a Spring 1991 *Journal of Accounting, Auditing & Finance* article (pp. 233–54), ''An Evaluation of Accounting Rate-of-Return,'' Stephen Penman concludes that ''ROE is best interpreted as a profitability measure, not a risk measure [but] it is not sufficient for distinguishing future profitability and thus is not a satisfactory summary measure for financial statement analysis.''

Required:

Obtain a copy of Professor Penman's article, study it, and provide a one- to two-page discussion of its significance to financial statement users. Be sure to address the following question: ''Is ROE's shortcoming a function of accounting conventions?'' Why or why not?

I.5.2   Valuation

In a January 4, 1993, *Financial Times* article (p. 29), ''Stock Markets Slow Down on Road to Convergence,'' Peter Martin reports that financial analysts endeavor to use ''valuation measures that minimize the differences between national accounting and tax policies such as the ratio of a company's share price to its net cash flow.'' Pertinent to this point, the investment banking firm Morgan Stanley reports the following aggregate information for all the companies listed on several of this text's focal countries' primary securities exchanges:

	P/BV		P/CE		P/E	
	12/91	*3/94*	*12/91*	*3/94*	*12/91*	*3/94*
Japan	2.42	2.13	9.9	10.7	35.3	74.2
United States	2.32	2.53	9.9	9.7	21.7	19.7
United Kingdom	1.81	2.33	8.4	10.6	15.2	17.2
Sweden	1.51	2.35	7.9	13.8	15.8	439.1
Italy	1.07	1.77	2.5	8.9	14.0	loss
Germany	1.82	2.18	4.6	5.8	15.1	31.7

Source: *Morgan Stanley Capital International Perspective* (1st Quarter 1992 and 2nd Quarter 1994)

P/BV = Share market price to company reported book value
P/CE = Share market price to cash earnings (Net income + Depreciation)
P/E = Share market price to net income

Required:

(a) What do you perceive as the relative advantage/disadvantage of each of the three measures? Opine as to what sorts of financial reporting conventions might be influencing the denominators of the three measures.

(b) As a prelude to the country-specific chapters that follow, review the data table and identify at least two paired-country comparisons that you find most interesting across the three measures. What makes each pair interesting to you? What country contextual factors might be significant explanations of the similarity/dissimilarity in the pair's measures?

EXERCISES

E.5.1   Du Pont Formula Analysis

One day while at work at Venture Capitalists, Inc., a co-worker from the acquisitions department came to you for assistance. He was evaluating the financial results of two potential acquisition opportunities that were quite comparable in a number of respects. Both Japanese firms manufactured equivalent quality (and competing) products, controlled about the same market share, and earned the same ROE of 21 percent. His analysis had also identified the following financial differences:

	Firm X	Firm Z
ROS	2%	7%
ROA	7%	10.5%
Asset turnover	3.4×	1.5×
Total assets to shareholders' equity	3.0×	2.0×

Required:

Assist your co-worker in reaching a conclusion as to which company (X or Z) Venture Capitalists, Inc., should prefer to acquire.

E.5.2   Leverage Analysis

The following are condensed 1994 financial statement data for the Gear-Up Company Plc. Gear-Up's sales (or "turnover") have been as high as £60 million and as low as £40 million during the past five years; however, its interest coverage (i.e., times interest earned) has always been in excess of 4.5 during that same period. Gear-Up maintains an open line of credit with its lead lender, the Bank of Westminster, which would allow the company to borrow up to £10 million for a five-year term at 10 percent.

Gear-Up Co., Plc
Condensed Balance Sheet
As of December 31, 1994
(in thousands of pounds)

Noncurrent assets	18,000
Current assets	9,000
Intangible assets	5,000
Total assets	32,000
Current liabilities	6,000
Debentures (8%)	16,000
Shareholders' equity	10,000
Total equity	32,000

Gear-Up Co., Plc
Condensed Income Statement
For the Year Ended December 31, 1994
(in thousands of pounds)

Turnover	50,000
Less: Cost of sales	(32,500)
Selling and admin. expenses	(12,200)
Interest expense	(1,280)
Pre-tax net income	4,020
Less: Income taxes	(1,608)
Net income	2,412

Required:

(a) Using these data as a base, prepare at least four different sets of pro forma financial statements to demonstrate the effect of an increase in leverage on the company's ROE. Two of your pro forma presentations should assume the same sales and operating expenses but different levels of borrowing. The other pro forma presentations should assume an increase in debt and increased and decreased levels of sales. (You will need to make assumptions about the relationship between sales and the various expenses.)

(b) What can you infer from your analysis about the effect of leverage on shareholder returns, as measured by ROE?

E.5.3   Pro Forma Income Statements

HFS Corporation is in the latter stages of its principal product life cycle. The CEO has proposed that the company invest $10 million in a new product that has been under development for some time. Although the new product has received a good response in limited test markets, the board of directors is not convinced that this would be in the best interests of shareholders or the company. The following are HFS's income statements for 1992–1994.

HFS Corporation
Comparative Income Statements

	1992	1993	1994
Sales of old product	$ 10,000	$8,000	$7,000
Cost of sales—old product	6,000	5,000	4,550
Marketing costs—old product	1,500	1,280	1,225
Depreciation—old product	500	450	400
Interest—old product	200	180	150
Contribution—old product	$ 1,800	$1,090	$ 675
Sales of new product	$ 1,000	$3,000	$4,000
Cost of sales—new product	750	2,175	2,800
Marketing costs—new product	200	600	800
Depreciation—new product	100	110	150
Interest—new product	50	55	75
Contribution—new product	$ (100)	$ 60	$ 175
Corporate expense	$ 450	$ 475	$ 500
Income before taxes	1,250	675	350
Income taxes	$ 500	$ 270	$ 140
Net income	$ 750	$ 405	$ 210
Net assets employed—old product	$ 5,000	$4,800	$4,600
Net assets employed—new product	1,000	1,100	1,500
Owners' equity	3,600	3,800	3,900

Required:

Using these data, prepare two sets of pro forma income statements for HFS for 1995 and 1996, assuming that (1) $10 million will be invested in the new product, and (2) the new product is abandoned. List the assumptions that you made to prepare the pro formas. On the basis of your pro formas, what recommendation would you make to the board of directors?

E.5.4   Analysis of Unlevered Return on Assets

GTE Corporation is the fourth largest publicly owned telecommunications company in the world and is the largest local telephone company in the United States. GTE's two major product segments are Telephone Operations (Telephone) and Telecommunications Products and Services (Telecommunications).

Telephone provides a wide variety of communications services ranging from local telephone service for the home and office to highly complex voice and data services for industry. Telephone serves 17.1 million access lines in 33 states with the largest number of lines in California. Five million access lines are served in five foreign countries.

Results for 1993 include a one-time pre-tax restructuring charge of $1.8 billion provided to implement a reengineering plan to take place over the next three years. When fully implemented, the plan is expected to consolidate many areas of GTE and reduce the number of Telephone employees by 17,000.

Telecommunications develops and markets a wide variety of telecommunications systems and services, including mobile-cellular communications, government and defense communications systems and equipment, satellite and aircraft passenger communications (e.g., telephones for passengers in commercial aircraft), and yellow pages. Telecommunications revenues declined 5 percent in 1993; lower government communication sales resulting from the wind-down of a large contract more than offset higher revenues from the growth in mobile-cellular business. In 1993, 495,000 cellular telephone customers were added, an increase of 45 percent over 1992. Total cellular service revenues were $1.1 billion, a 27 percent improvement over 1992.

Exhibits 1, 2, and 3, present income statements, balance sheets, and statements of cash flow for GTE. Exhibit 4 presents additional segment data, and Exhibit 5 presents selected financial ratios for 1992.

Required:

    (a) Compute the missing financial ratio amounts in Exhibit 5 for 1993. Assume that GTE's income tax rate for all years presented to be 34 percent. (*Note:* You must decide how to deal with 1993 restructuring and merger costs and extraordinary charge—early retirement of debt.)

    (b) To the maximum extent possible given the data, interpret the change in GTE's unleveraged ROA from 1992 to 1993.

EXHIBIT 1

GTE Corporation and Subsidiaries
Consolidated Statements of Income
(millions of dollars)

	1993	*1992*
Revenues and Sales		
Telephone operations	$ 15,829	$ 15,862
Telecommunications products and services	3,919	4,122
Total	$ 19,748	$ 19,984
Costs and Expenses		
Telephone operations	$ 11,765	$ 11,828
Telecommunications products and services*	3,578	3,940
Restructuring costs	1,840	
Total	$ 17,183	$ 15,768
Operating income	$ 2,565	$ 4,216
Other (Income) Deductions		
Interest expense	1,197	1,332
Other	(190)	130
Total	$ 1,007	$ 1,462
Income before taxes	$ 1,558	$ 2,754
Income tax provision	568	967
Income from continuing operations	$ 990	$ 1,787
Discontinued operations		(48)
Extraordinary charge—early retirement of debt	(90)	(52)
Cumulative effect of accounting changes†		(2,441)
Net income (loss)	$ 900	$ (754)
Prefered stock dividends of parent	(18)	(26)
Net income (loss) applicable to common stock	$ 882	$ (780)

---

*Includes cost of sales as follows: $ 3,036 $ 3,143

† A one-time noncash charge made on January 1, 1992, to adopt *SFAS 106* on postretirement benefits. *FAS 106* requires that these benefits be recorded during the years that employees render service.

EXHIBIT 2

GTE Corporation and Subsidiaries
Consolidated Balance Sheets
(millions of dollars)

	1993	1992	1991
Assets			
Current assets			
Cash and temporary investments	$ 322	$ 354	$ 517
Receivables	3,900	3,565	3,663
Inventories	659	814	910
Other current assets	1,067	1,563	2,476
Total	$ 5,948	$ 6,296	$ 7,566
Property, plant and equipment	28,720	29,820	29,323
Goodwill	2,102	2,167	2,180
Investment in unconsolidated companies	1,431	1,361	1,374
Deferred charges	2,462	1,683	1,114
Other non-current assets	912	817	880
Total	$35,627	$35,848	$34,871
Total assets	$41,575	$42,144	$42,437
Liabilities and Shareholders' Equity			
Current liabilities			
Short-term loans	$ 1,644	$ 2,692	$ 2,291
Accounts payable	1,968	1,917	1,895
Accrued taxes	1,108	571	621
Accrued restructuring costs	540		
Dividends payable	469	447	431
Other current liabilities	2,204	1,884	1,988
Total	$ 7,933	$ 7,511	$ 7,226
Long-term debt	13,019	14,182	16,049
Reserves and deferred credits			
Deferred taxes	2,808	3,071	3,184
Other	6,960	6,053	3,339
Total	$ 9,768	$ 9,124	$ 6,523
Total liabilities	$30,720	$30,817	$29,798
Minority interests in equity of subsidiaries	1,106	1,077	1,123
Preferred stock, subject to mandatory redemption	156	174	153
Shareholders' Equity			
Preferred stock	111	112	509
Common stock	48	47	46
Additional paid-in capital	7,309	7,134	6,232
Reinvested earnings	2,769	3,621	5,977
Guaranteed ESOP obligation	(644)	(657)	(673)
Treasury stock		(181)	(728)
Total	$ 9,593	$10,076	$11,363
Total liabilities and shareholders' equity	$41,575	$42,144	$42,437

EXHIBIT 3

GTE Corporation and Subsidiaries
Consolidated Statements of Cash Flows
(millions of dollars)

	1993	*1992*
Cash Flows from Operations		
Income from continuing operations	$ 990	$1,787
Depreciation and amortization	3,419	3,289
Restructuring costs	1,840	
Deferred taxes	(864)	37
Change in current assets and current liabilities, excluding the effects of acquisitions and depositions	(13)	(268)
Other—net	(95)	(13)
Net cash from operations	$ 5,277	$ 4,832
Cash Flows from Investing		
Capital expenditures	(3,893)	(3,909)
Acquisitions and investments	(46)	(84)
Sale of assets	2,267	662
Other—net	(66)	55
Net cash used in investing	$(1,738)	$(3,276)
Cash Flows from Financing		
GTE common stock issued	383	1,513
Long-term debt issued	2,325	590
Long-term debt and preferred stock retired	(4,836)	(2,002)
Dividends to shareholders of parent	(1,744)	(1,572)
Increase (decrease) in short-term obligations, excluding current maturities	304	(254)
Other—net	(3)	6
Net cash from (used in) financing	$(3,571)	$(1,719)
Change in cash and cash equivalents	$ (32)	$ (163)

EXHIBIT 4

GTE Corporation and Subsidiaries
Geographic and Operating Segment Data
(millions of dollars)

	1993	1992
Foreign Segment Data		
Revenues	$ 2,482	$ 2,369
Operating income	328	244
Total assets	6,096	5,963
Domestic Segment Data		
Revenues	$17,266	$17,615
Operating income	572	(998)
Total assets	35,479	36,181
Telephone Operations Data		
Revenues	$15,829	$15,862
Operations and maintenance	8,796	8,979
Depreciation and amortization	2,969	2,849
Restructuring costs	1,370	–0–
Operating income	2,694	4,034
Total assets	33,746	33,154
Access minutes of use (in millions)	55,616	51,976
Access lines (in thousands)		
Total	22,065	21,440
United States	17,073	16,819
Employees (in thousands)		
Total	95	104
United States	73	81
Telecommunications Data		
Revenues	$ 3,919	$ 4,122
Depreciation and amortization	450	440
Restructuring costs	398	
Other operating costs	3,128	3,500
Operating income	(57)	182
Total assets	5,973	6,204

EXHIBIT 5

GTE Corporation and Subsidiaries
Selected Financial Ratios

	1993	*1992*
Consolidated		
Unlevered rate of return on assets		6.3%
Profit margin for UROA		13.3%
Total assets turnover		0.47×
Depreciation and amortization expense percentage		16.5%
Other operating expenses percentage		62.4%
Income tax expense percentage (excluding tax effects of interest expense)		7.1%
Accounts receivable turnover		5.53×
Inventory turnover		3.65×
Fixed asset turnover		0.68×
Foreign Operations		
Rate of return on assets		4.1%
Profit margin		10.3%
Asset turnover		0.40×
Domestic Operations		
Rate of return on assets		−2.8%
Profit margin		−5.7%
Asset turnover		0.49×
Telephone Products Segment		
Rate of return on assets		12.2%
Profit margin		25.4%
Asset turnover		0.48×
Telecommunications Segment		
Rate of return on assets		2.9%
Profit margin		4.4%
Asset turnover		0.66×

E.5.5   Analysis of Return on Common Equity:
Short- and Long-Term Risk Factors

Refer to the data for GTE Corporation in Exercise 5.4.

Required:

(a) Compute the missing financial ratio amounts in the following table for GTE for 1993.

(b) To the maximum extent permitted by the data, interpret the change in ROCE that occurred from 1992 to 1993. You need not explain reasons for the changes in UROA.

(c) Evaluate the changes in GTE's short-term and long-term risk factors.

GTE Corporation and Subsidiaries
Selected Financial Ratios

	1992	1993
Rate of return on common equity	16.4 %	
Common earnings leverage	0.66	
Capital structure leverage	3.95	
Current ratio	0.84	
Quick ratio	0.52	
Cash flow from operations to current liabilities	65.6 %	
Long-term debt to total assets	33.7 %	
Cash flow from operations to total liabilities	11.4 %	
Interest coverage	3.07	

E.5.6   Interpreting ROCE and Its Components

Listed below are five possible scenarios occurring during 1993 that may fully explain a change in ROCE and/or its components

Scenario 1

The interest rate on debt increased. Cash normally used to pay dividends is now used to pay the increased interest costs to lenders.

Scenario 2

A significant purchase of fixed assets was funded by debt. For the current period, incremental depreciation was exactly offset by reductions in the cost of sales. It is expected that cost savings in excess of incremental depreciation will occur in future years.

Scenario 3

Sales decreased. Operating expenses did not decrease at the same rate because of the presence of fixed costs. The diminished profitability is offset by reduced dividends.

Scenario 4

The company spun off a subsidiary to shareholders. The subsidiary made no contribution to operating revenues or expenses during either 1992 or 1993.

Scenario 5

The company purchased its own shares on the open market as a defense against a hostile takeover. The purchase was funded by issuing bonds.

Required:

Match each of these five scenarios with the five firms (i.e., A–E) in the following table. (Each case is based on actual company data, and there may be inaccuracies due to rounding.)

Changes in ROCE for Five Disguised Firms

	ROCE	=	ROA	×	Adjusted Leverage	=	Profit Margin	×	Asset Turnover	×	Common Earnings Leverage	×	Capital Structure Leverage
Firm A													
1992	15.5%		9.2%		1.7		5.4%		1.7		0.9		1.9
1993	13.5		9.2		1.5		5.4		1.7		0.8		1.9
Firm B													
1992	2.7		2.5		1.1		2.1		1.2		0.7		1.6
1993	0.5		0.9		0.6		0.9		1.0		0.4		1.6
Firm C													
1992	21.6		13.6		1.7		18.5		0.7		0.9		1.7
1993	23.0		13.6		1.7		18.5		0.7		0.8		2.0
Firm D													
1992	7.6		4.6		1.7		7.4		0.6		0.8		2.0
1993	3.3		0.6		5.5		7.4		0.1		0.8		6.7
Firm E													
1992	6.2		4.9		1.3		3.4		1.5		0.9		1.5
1993	8.1		6.0		1.3		3.4		1.8		0.9		1.5

E.5.7   Preparing Pro Forma Income Statements

Waterloo Furniture Components, Ltd. (WFC) is a manufacturer of office equipment and related products. The company is headquartered in Kitchener, Ontario, Canada, but is a wholly owned subsidiary of a U.S.–based conglomerate. WFC sells primarily to North American markets, and is increasing its sales to Asian and European markets.

Ron Simmons, president of WFC, is faced with a dilemma and requests your advice. Among the WFC product lines are office couches, whose markets have been steadily eroded by full-line U.S. furniture manufacturers selling similar products at significant price discounts. The mark-up on these products is, however, substantial and even at reduced volume levels make a significant contribution to WFC's pre-tax profits (in part because they absorb significant amounts of WFC's overhead).

In 1991, WFC was one of the first North American office equipment manufacturers to introduce a personal computer wrist rest in response to medical reports diagnosing large numbers of computer keyboard operators as having Carpal tunnel syndrome—an inflammation of the wrist apparently caused by extended computer keyboard use. Although the wrist rest product line had lost money in its first year, sales growth had been substantial, and by 1993, the new product line was showing a modest contribution to profit. Ron felt that the wrist rest product line had substantial profit opportunities in the short term (i.e., the next three to five years), but he was concerned about recent developments in the area of voice-activated computers, which would substantially reduce the amount of keyboard-related activities of computer users. According to recent computer industry surveys, voice-activated computers could be mass marketed as early as 1996. In the interim, however, industry sales of wrist rest type products were projected to exceed $200 million in each of 1994 and 1995. Analysts were reluctant to forecast 1996 sales due to uncertainties associated with the introduction of voice-activated personal computers.

Ron has been given the OK from holding company executives to invest up to $5 million in new plant and equipment for the wrist rest product line. He was concerned, however, that demand for the product could dramatically erode once voice-activated computers became available at reasonable prices. Ron's dilemma was as follows: Should he invest the available $5 million in an expansion of the wrist rest product line or instead ask headquarters for an increase in his R&D budget to begin the development of a new product line of office equipment compatible with voice-activated computers?

Required:

The following are selected income statement data for WFC for the period 1991–1993. To help you advise Ron, you should begin by developing pro forma income data for 1994–1996.

Clearly identify all assumptions used in preparing your pro formas. What recommendation would you make, and why?

Waterloo Furniture Components, Ltd.
Selected Income Data
(000s omitted)

	Year Ended December 31		
	1991	*1992*	*1993*
Offices couches			
Sales	$15,000	$12,000	$10,500
Less: cost of sales	(9,000)	(7,500)	(6,825)
depreciation	(750)	(675)	(600)
marketing costs	(2,250)	(1,920)	(1,838)
interest charges	(300)	(270)	(225)
Contribution to income	$ 2,700	$ 1,635	$ 1,012
Wrist rests			
Sales	$ 2,000	6,000	$ 8,000
Less: cost of sales	(1,500)	(4,350)	(5,600)
depreciation	(200)	(220)	(300)
marketing cost	(400)	(1,200)	(1,600)
interest charges	(100)	(110)	(150)
Contribution to income	$ (200)	$ 120	$ 350
Corporate overhead	$ 720	$ 760	$ 800
Income before taxes	$ 1,780	$ 995	$ 562
Less: Income taxes	(712)	(398)	(225)
Net income	$ 1,068	$ 597	$ 337
Contribution to cash flow*			
Couches	$ 3,450	$ 2,310	$ 1,612
Wrist rests	–0–	340	650
Net assets employed			
Couches	$ 5,000	$ 4,800	$ 4,600
Wrist rests	1,000	1,100	1,500
Owners' equity	3,600	3,800	3,900

*Contribution to cash flow = Contribution to income + Depreciation.

E.5.8   Pro Forma Financial Statements

SANTOS Ltd. is an oil and gas exploration and production company headquartered in Adelaide, Australia. SANTOS maintains exploration and/or production operations in Australia (principally South Australia, Queensland, and the Northern Territory), Southeast Asia (principally Cambodia, Papua New Guinea, and Indonesia), the United States (principally Texas, Oklahoma, and Louisiana) and Europe (principally in the North Sea and the Irish Sea).

During 1994, SANTOS expects to embark on a significant drilling program in the Pierce oil and gas field of the North Sea (blocks 22/22C, 22/27a, and 23/27). According to the company's managing director, SANTOS will drill 10 wells at an average cost of $4 million per well and that six of those wells will yield aggregate crude oil reserves (or gas equivalents) of approximately 10 million barrels. The remaining four wells are expected to be commercially unproductive.

The company's production plan calls for a maximum exploitation effort to earn the highest financial return. Consistent with this goal, the company's managing director developed the following production scenario:

Year	Number of Barrels (or gas equivalents thereof) to Be Produced	Estimated Lifting Cost per Barrel*
1994	1,000,000	$5
1995	1,500,000	5
1996	1,500,000	6
1997	2,500,000	7
1998	3,500,000	8
	10,000,000	

*Excludes depreciation, depletion, and amortization costs.

Because of the relatively calm political atmosphere in the Middle East and expectations that conditions would remain so for the foreseeable future, oil and gas analysts have predicted substantial price increases in crude oil. The most recent projections call for an estimated selling price of $30, $30, $35, $50, and $45 per barrel in 1994 through 1998, respectively.

Because of the relatively low interest rates prevailing during 1993, SANTOS decided to seek syndicated bank financing for the exploration program. While organizing her presentation for bank representatives, the managing director realized that the perceived economic feasibility of the exploration program might appear different, depending on whether the company elected to use the full cost method or the successful efforts method. Consequently, she sent an immediate request to the controller: ''Prepare pro forma statements showing the alternative accounting effects on cash flow, profit before tax, and financial position if we elect to use the successful efforts method or the full cost method.''

For purposes of pro forma statement preparation, assume that the $40 million loan will be repaid as follows: (1) interest payments of 10 percent per year on the balance of the loan outstanding as of the beginning of the year and (2) $10 million principal repayment annually, to be paid at year end, beginning December 31, 1995.

Required:

Based on your pro forma statements for the period 1994 through 1998, what accounting method (successful efforts or full cost) recommendation would you make to the managing director, and why?

Cases

CASE 5.1
VALUATION OF A COMPANY

American Pharmaceuticals, Inc.

European Chemical and Drug, Ltd. (EUROCAD), a major international corporation operating primarily in the chemical industry, has decided that it wishes to expand its operations to penetrate both the American pharmaceutical market (which includes prescription and over-the-counter medications) and the household products market (cleaning agents, air fresheners, and the like). The EUROCAD management team assigned to this task targeted American Pharmaceuticals, Inc. (AMPHARM), a leading U.S. manufacturer of pharmaceuticals and household products with international markets and production facilities, as a synergistic complement to EUROCAD's product lines. Characteristic of EUROCAD's business style, the expansion is to be accomplished by outright purchase of AMPHARM stock. In addition, EUROCAD had commissioned Kidder Company, a major financial consulting firm, to prepare an in-depth investigative report on the target company.

AMPHARM had not been looking to be acquired, nor, to its knowledge, had anyone been seeking to acquire it. Thus, EUROCAD's proposal came as quite a surprise. Upon studying their suitor, however, AMPHARM's management came to realize that EUROCAD had a reputation for getting what they wanted and were usually willing to pay for it, within reason. Moreover, during the preliminary negotiations, EUROCAD had guaranteed AMPHARM's senior management that they would be retained in their current positions (or better) for at least five years after the acquisition. Accordingly, AMPHARM's management and board have become increasingly receptive to EUROCAD's offers.

It is now February 5, 19X6, and the negotiations between EUROCAD and AMPHARM are about to enter their final stage. All that remains is to settle on the total price for AMPHARM. The transaction will be an exchange of cash for all (100 percent) of the outstanding stock. The acquiring company will assume all assets and liabilities present on the books as of December 31, 19X5, and will account for the transaction as a purchase. You have been engaged to present a formal report identifying and justifying the price(s) which should be deliberated by the negotiating parties. You will receive a copy of the executive summary and pertinent financial information contained in the Kidder Report; your report should be based only on that information and, at a minimum, should include the following:

1. A discussion of your overall opinion of, and outlook on, AMPHARM, including the main reasons and/or assumptions supporting your overall opinion.
2. A description of the types and results of analysis performed on AMPHARM's financial data, and your justification for using these approaches. You should also

---

This case was prepared by Phillip Ricci, Leon J. Hanouille, and Gregg J. Jarrell. Copyright © 1993 by the American Accounting Association. Reprinted with permission from the American Accounting Association.

discuss other approaches that you considered and rejected, and explain your reasons for rejecting them. Examples of analysis could include (among others): trends; dollar and percent changes; ratios; price/earnings; growth rate of dividends; weighted cost of capital; rate of return.

3. A discussion of the various prices that could be offered for AMPHARM, their relative significance and applicability to the situation, and your opinion as to which is the most realistic and appropriate.

Kidder Report (Executive Summary)

Introduction.   American Pharmaceuticals, Inc. (AMPHARM) has divisions and subsidiaries engaged domestically in development, manufacture, and marketing of pharmaceutical specialties, proprietary products, household products, cosmetics, toiletries, chemicals, and other products. The foreign division manufactures and markets certain of these products abroad; it operates exclusively outside the U.S. and does not include any operations relating to products produced in the U.S.

Report of the Chairman of the Board and Chief Executive Officer.   In 19X5 sales grew 13 percent to $1,990,434,000 from $1,753,724,000 in 19X4. Income from continuing operations for 19X5 rose 12 percent to $1.715 million. Income per share on this basis increased 14 percent to $2.91 from $2.56 a year earlier. There were fewer shares outstanding at the end of 19X5 as a result of a company stock purchase program.

Net income for 19X5 was 56 percent above that of the previous year. Net income in 19X4 had been decreased by a $44.3 million one-time after-tax charge for the company's planned divestiture of the Milton Davies Chemical Co. The sale of this business was completed late in 19X5 with no effect on the year's financial results.

In addition to taking actions to expand its sales base, the company has also implemented a number of programs to increase profits and generate the funds needed to finance growth. As a result of an expansion and strengthening of worldwide tax planning activities, the company's effective corporate tax rate (federal, state, and foreign combined) has declined to 42.8 percent from 48 percent four years ago.

During this period, stringent manufacturing cost reduction programs have resulted in cost of goods as a percent of sales declining to 34 percent from 39 percent. A worldwide administrative cost reduction program is now beginning to yield positive results. Savings from these programs are being reinvested to provide advertising and promotional support for AMPHARM products throughout the world. In the last four years, advertising and promotion spending has increased to $413 million from $266 million.

In 19X5 the company's expenditures for new plant and equipment totaled $68 million. Funds continue to be spent for upgrading of facilities to achieve operating efficiencies and to maximize production in countries with lower tax rates. A further enlargement of the pharmaceutical production facility in Mexico is under way. Additionally, a plant currently under construction in France is expected to begin production early next year.

Despite having to borrow to finance recent acquisitions, a stock purchase program, and higher investment spending in advertising and promotion, the company continues in very strong financial condition. Effective asset management has been successful in controlling inventories and accounts receivable. Internally generated funds are also being channeled into a more focused and fruitful research and development program. Expenditures for discovery and development of new medicinal compounds and other company products have risen from $68 million in 19X2 to $103 million in 19X5, with a further 15 percent increase planned for 19X6.

The company remains committed to the discovery and development of new therapeutically superior compounds in specific medical areas. Close coordination between the company's research group and worldwide marketing management has resulted in a sharper focus on the development and commercialization of these pivotal compounds. The research group's resources are being concentrated on therapeutic categories consistent with the overall strategic plan.

Based on the company's strong financial condition and heightened optimism, the Board of Directors voted last April to increase the quarterly dividend by 10 percent to 33 cents (or $1.32 annually), the largest increase in eight years.

The cornerstone upon which the company's strategic plan for accelerated growth is built has been and continues to be its skilled and dedicated people. Through the efforts of its 22,100 employees, 19X5 was a year of accomplishment. With their continued support, the company will record even more significant achievements in 19X6 and beyond.

Key Personnel.   The company has an excellent management team with a number of years, experience. They are known for their expertise in the pharmaceutical industry. Among the Vice-Presidents, James Star and Frazer Gillan are of key importance. Mr. Star oversees the marketing and sales department, which also works closely with the research and development group in the creation of new products. Mr. Gillan oversees the manufacturing department and has been instrumental in the implementation of the cost cutting procedures and increased efficiency in the manufacturing department. Below is the complete listing.

Top Officers	Title	Yrs of Service	Age
George M. Cohen	Chariman of the Board and CEO	25	61
Samuel E. Lands	President and Chief Operating Officer	21	54
Luke Skies	Senior V-P & General Counsel	27	60
R. J. Walker	Senior V-P Finance	19	51
Eugene F. McCarty	Group Vice-President, Foreign Markets	24	53
Josh Meeks	Group Vice-President, R & D	12	47
James Star	Group Vice-President, Marketing	29	57
Frazer Gillan	Group Vice-President, Manufacturing	27	58
John Wells	Group Vice-President, Information Mgmt.	16	52

Company Strengths.   Investors should consider the following factors in their evaluation of the company:

Strong Reputation: The AMPHARM name is one of the most highly regarded in the industry. The company has been a major presence in the pharmaceutical and household product markets for over 80 years, and has developed a strong reputation as a high-quality, low-cost manufacturer. Because of this, certain of the company's products enjoy the largest market share in their respective market segments.

Longstanding Relationships: The company has longstanding relationships with the medical profession. These relationships, coupled with the company's reputation, afford the company extensive opportunities to introduce new products into the marketplace.

Management: The company has an experienced and dedicated management team. The company's management has a reputation within the industry for expertise and the ability to remain consistently profitable.

Future Growth Potential: The current demand for pharmaceutical products is very strong and expected to remain strong in the future. The market is expanding due to a number of factors, including the increasing human life span on a worldwide basis and the accompanying increased medical attention; the increased number of individuals covered by health care plans; and the increased health care consciousness in many countries. In addition the company introduced a number of successful new products in 19X5 and has received patents on several other new products.

Financial Statements. Financial Statements and other information for AMPHARM are presented in Appendix A of this report.[1] Other significant financial information is presented in Appendix B; key industry data appear in Appendix C.

APPENDIX A
FINANCIAL INFORMATION

AMPHARM
Income Statement and Other Information
(in thousands of dollars except per share amounts)

	For the Year Ended December 31,				
	19X5	*19X4*	*19X3*	*19X2*	*19X1*
Net sales	1,990,434	1,753,724	1,725,600	1,756,810	1,653,871
Cost of goods sold	673,501	611,523	620,456	655,446	647,259
Marketing & administrative	915,341	799,063	772,008	776,237	689,653
Research & development	102,863	85,118	85,374	77,499	67,993
Other, net	−1,109	−19,715	−7,400	2,931	2,228
Total costs & expenses	1,690,596	1,475,989	1,470,438	1,512,113	1,407,133
Income from continuing operations before taxes	299,838	277,735	255,162	244,697	246,738
Provision for taxes	128,331	124,425	113,722	112,289	118,556
Income from operations	171,507	153,310	141,440	132,408	128,182
(Loss) income from discontinued operations	–0–	−43,601	1,920	4,436	3,788
Net income	171,507	109,709	143,360	136,844	131,970
Income per share from continuing operations	2.91	2.56	2.34	2.17	2.11
Net income per share	2.91	1.83	2.37	2.24	2.17
Dividends paid	76,200	71,409	69,705	67,583	64,318
Dividends per share	1.29	1.19	1.15	1.11	1.06
Working capital	622,560	644,572	639,627	642,834	589,470
Shareowners' equity	973,548	936,445	924,196	912,700	860,912
Total assets	1,723,781	1,617,790	1,458,871	1,470,485	1,332,957
Property before depreciation	687,705	616,465	639,407	632,741	604,688
Long-term debt	208,489	87,530	79,543	87,659	72,362
Capital expenditures (continuing operations)	67,881	67,102	61,942	55,233	71,775
Number of employees	22,100	21,330	22,455	23,447	24,062
Number of shareowners	32,932	36,514	38,657	42,557	43,193
Average common shares outstanding (in thousands)	59,015	59,969	60,585	61,168	60,879

---

[1]Arrangements can be made with the case authors to obtain the information on disk in electronic spreadsheet format.

APPENDIX A (continued)

Consolidated Balance Sheet
(in thousands of dollars)

	As of December 31,	
	19X5	*19X4*
Assets		
Current Assets:		
Cash	13,329	10,849
Short-term investments	370,002	436,931
Accounts receivable	378,541	359,872
Inventories	261,629	236,556
Prepaid expenses	75,292	73,299
Net assets held for sale	0	45,268
Total current assets	1,098,793	1,162,775
Property, Plant & Equipment:		
Land	17,914	19,492
Buildings	288,230	260,872
Machinery & equipment	381,561	336,101
	687,705	616,465
Less accumulated depreciation	290,549	258,275
Net property, plant & equipment	397,156	358,190
Trademarks & Goodwill	99,236	28,799
Other Assets and Deferred Charges	128,596	68,026
Total Assets	1,723,781	1,617,790
Liabilities & Shareholders' Equity		
Current Liabilities:		
Notes and loans payable	139,681	234,251
Accounts payable	99,158	84,307
Accrued expenses	202,614	172,857
Accrued income taxes	34,780	26,788
Total current liabilities	476,233	518,203
Long-term debt	208,489	87,530
Deferred income taxes	65,511	75,612
Shareowners' equity	973,548	936,445
Total liabilities & shareowners' equity	1,723,781	1,617,790

APPENDIX A (continued)
Consolidated Statement of Cash Flows
(in thousands of dollars)

	Years Ended December 31,		
	19X5	*19X4*	*19X3*
Net Cash Flow from Operating Activities			
Income from continuing operations	17,1507	153,310	141,440
Adjustments for differences between income and cash flows from operating activities:			
Depreciation & amortization expense	43,944	34,740	33,342
Increase in deferred income taxes	2,012	1,035	6,794
Increase (Decrease) in current payables	50,607	10,788	−19,294
(Increase) Decrease in accounts receivable	−18,669	−15,843	13,960
(Increase) Decrease in inventories	−25,073	38,009	10,372
Net assets held for sale	45,268	−45,268	0
Decrease for the effect of exchange rate changes	−12,526	−2,961	−28,846
Other	2,446	1,577	2,342
(Loss) Income from discontinued operations	0	−43,601	1,920
Discontinued operations, non-cash expenses	0	50,503	7,136
Net cash provided by operating activities	259,516	182,289	169,166
Cash Flows from Investing Activities			
Additions to property, plant & equipment	−67,881	−74,176	−73,158
Proceeds from sales—property, plant & equipment	6,377	12,242	11,321
(Increase) Decrease in other assets and deferred charges	−54,449	−37,997	9,764
Net assets of acquired companies	−94,469	0	0
Net cash used for investing activities	−210,422	−99,931	−52,073
Cash Flows from Financing Activities			
(Decrease) Increase in short-term debt	−94,570	99,812	19,549
Increase (Decrease) in long-term debt	108,871	7,298	−5,320
Purchase of treasury stock	−52,180	−39,023	−25,866
Payments of dividends to shareowners	−76,200	−71,409	−69,705
Other	536	13,407	−14,371
Net cash (used) provided by financing activities	−113,543	10,085	−95,713
Net (decrease) in cash and short-term investments	−64,449	92,443	21,380

APPENDIX A (continued)

Business by Industry Segments
(in thousands of dollars)

	Years Ended December 31,		
	19X5	*19X4*	*19X3*
Sales			
Pharmaceutical specialties	303,797	268,865	268,203
Proprietary products	329,381	279,987	273,019
Household and other products	594,097	566,374	516,296
International	780,971	656,638	690,919
Intersegment sales	−17,812	−18,140	−22,837
Consolidated sales	1,990,434	1,753,724	1,725,600
Operating profit			
Pharmaceutical specialties	65,985	61,250	53,228
Proprietary products	54,900	40,490	26,916
Household and other products	97,785	98,985	89,083
International	82,191	67,536	78,509
Segment operating profit	300,861	268,261	247,736
Net Unallocated income (expense)	−1,023	9,474	7,426
Income from continuing operations before taxes	299,838	277,735	255,162
Assets			
Pharmaceutical specialties	402,918	348,589	359,571
Proprietary products	117,972	115,910	122,987
Household and other products	249,017	170,204	150,117
International	694,916	606,453	580,133
Corporate, including short-term investments	258,958	331,366	138,909
Discontinued operations	0	45,268	107,154
Consolidated assets	1,723,781	1,617,790	1,458,871

APPENDIX B

OTHER FINANCIAL INFORMATION

Short-term debt: Notes and loans payable consist of the following:

	December 31,	
(in thousands of dollars)	*19X5*	*19X4*
Bank loans	$ 47,908	$ 38,528
Commercial paper	86,797	171,957
Current portion of LT debt	4,976	23,766
	$139,681	$234,251

APPENDIX B (continued)

The worldwide weighted average interest rates on short-term debt were 11.1 percent during 19X5, 16.1 percent during 19X4, and 24.1 percent during 19X3. The interest rates were influenced by borrowing in highly inflationary countries. The highest amounts of short-term debt outstanding during 19X5, 19X4, and 19X3 were $336,858,000, $327,225,000, and $201,574,000, respectively. The average amounts of short-term debt outstanding during 19X5, 19X4, and 19X3 were $222,849,000, $244,594,000, and $140,358,000, respectively.

Long-term debt outstanding December 31, 19X5, was $208,489,000, comprised of:
  (1) $44,400,000 10 7/8% pound notes maturing in four years.
  (2) $6,195,000 capitalized lease obligations.
  (3) $27,200,000 10% Industrial Revenue Bonds due to mature in six years.
  (4) $14,944,000 other debt.
  (5) $15,750,000 Industrial Revenue Bonds, maturing in 27 years.
  (6) $100,000,000 8 7/8% Eurobonds to mature in 10 years.

Capital Stock: common, par $2.50. Authorized 100,000,000 shares; outstanding December 31, 19X5, 59,015,000 shares, including 3,500,000 shares in treasury of which 2,100,000 shares are reserved for options.

			Stock Price	
Almanac:	*Year*	*Dividend*	*High*	*Low*
	19X1	$1.02	29 5/8	19 3/4
	19X2	1.11	29 5/8	22 1/8
	19X3	1.15	30	23 1/2
	19X4	1.19	41 3/8	26 3/4
	19X5	1.29	52	36 3/8

Other: — The number of shareowners at December 31, 19X5, was 32,932.
  — Except for trademarks and goodwill, the asset values on the balance sheet are a close approximation of fair market values. Market price per share on December 31, 19X5, was 50 1/8.
  — Companies in the pharmaceutical and household product markets with approximately the same capital structure have a stock beta of 0.90.
  — On the average, long-term debt for the company trades at 150 basis points premium over comparable long-term government bonds.
  — AMPHARM has consistently maintained a minimum overall Aa rating on its debt.

APPENDIX C
KEY INDUSTRY INFORMATION

Average Balance Sheets for the Pharmaceutical and Household Products Industry (in percents of totals)	19X5	19X4	19X3
Cash	14.6	13.5	13.3
Accounts Receivable	17.8	19.1	20.0
Notes Receivable	0.6	0.3	0.1
Inventory	21.9	23.0	23.5
Other Current	8.9	8.9	7.3
Total Current Assets	63.8	64.8	64.2
Fixed Assets	17.5	18.1	18.7
Other Non-Current	18.7	17.1	17.1
Total Assets	100.0	100.0	100.0
Accounts Payable	9.5	10.1	11.9
Bank Loans	1.2	2.2	2.2
Notes Payable	3.0	4.2	1.6
Other Current Liabilities	14.7	12.9	14.1
Total Current Liabilities	28.4	29.4	29.8
Other Long-Term Debt	15.5	12.1	14.6
Deferred Credits	0.2	0.3	0.5
Net Worth	55.9	58.2	55.1
Total Liabilities and Net Worth	100.0	100.0	100.0
Other averages			
Net Sales	100.0	100.0	100.0
Gross Profit	47.2	47.2	42.6
Net Profit after Tax	5.3	7.0	7.8

Ratios—by Quartiles	19X5 Quartiles			19X4 Quartiles			19X3 Quartiles		
	upper	median	lower	upper	median	lower	upper	median	lower
Solvency									
Quick Ratio (times)	2.4	1.2	0.7	2.0	1.3	0.6	2.2	1.1	0.7
Current Ratio (times)	4.8	2.2	1.7	4.3	2.4	1.6	4.3	2.4	1.6
Current Liabilities to Net Worth (%)	15.0	41.3	81.4	21.4	40.7	76.5	24.3	44.8	95.7
Current Liabilities to Inventory (%)	72.6	116.8	182.7	74.8	121.4	187.4	66.2	123.6	166.2
Total Liabilities to Net Worth (%)	22.8	67.2	147.8	26.6	62.8	119.3	29.0	68.4	132.5
Fixed Assets to Net Worth (%)	22.4	44.9	91.7	18.1	39.1	69.3	23.3	45.6	70.4
Efficiency									
Collection Period (days)	29.6	50.7	72.6	31.2	52.4	71.1	30.6	52.5	69.4
Sales to Inventory (times)	8.6	6.8	5.0	8.4	6.3	4.7	9.5	6.3	4.8
Assets to Sales (%)	53.8	80.5	125.3	50.2	70.0	105.0	46.3	65.8	91.6
Sales to Net Working Capital (times)	6.4	3.7	1.8	6.3	4.2	2.7	7.2	4.3	2.8
Accounts Payable to Sales (%)	3.2	5.6	9.4	2.9	5.4	10.0	3.4	5.8	9.0
Profitability									
Return on Sales (%)	14.0	7.1	0.3	13.7	7.8	2.2	12.4	8.1	4.5
Return on Assets (%)	14.3	9.2	0.5	14.6	9.1	2.8	15.4	10.6	6.6
Return on Net Worth (%)	24.5	16.9	1.5	25.2	15.3	5.7	28.3	19.2	11.9

Source: Dun & Bradstreet Credit Services, *Industry Norms and Key Business Ratios.*

APPENDIX C (continued)
INDUSTRY SURVEYS EARNINGS SUPPLEMENT: PHARMACEUTICALS AND HOUSEHOLD PRODUCTS

| Company | Yr. | Qtr. | F.Y. | Revenues | | | | Income | | | | Profitability | | |
				Latest qtr. (mil.$)	Chng from prior yr.(%)	Latest 12mos (mil.$)	Chng from prior yr.(%)	Latest qtr. (mil.$)	Chng from prior yr.(%)	Latest 12mos (mil.$)	Chng from prior yr.(%)	Latest qtr. ret. on rev.(%)	12mos ret. on rev.(%)	12mos ret. on equity (%)
American Home Prod. Corp	X5	JUN	DEC	1,113	3.7	4,594	6.4	167	10.3	688	11.0	15.0	15.0	32.4
AMPHARM	X5	JUN	DEC	454	0.8	1,806	−4.2	33	2.8	147	2.5	7.3	8.1	15.8
Bristol Myers Co	X5	JUN	DEC	1,080	1.9	4,236	3.2	126	13.3	502	13.6	11.7	11.8	23.3
Lilly (Eli) & Co	X5	JUN	DEC	757	4.6	3,156	2.5	110	−3.4	501	4.3	14.5	15.9	22.4
Merck & Co	X5	JUN	DEC	877	−1.6	3,553	4.7	138	5.0	506	7.6	15.7	14.2	19.3
Pfizer Inc	X5	JUN	DEC	1,002	1.2	3,903	1.8	138	15.6	547	14.8	13.7	14.0	22.3
Schering Plough	X5	JUN	DEC	480	0.8	1,879	2.5	52	8.1	182	4.6	10.8	9.7	13.8
Smithkline Beckman Corp	X5	JUN	DEC	771	8.0	3,058	5.7	121	1.0	503	1.5	15.8	16.4	24.0
Squibb Corp	X5	JUN	DEC	475	7.7	1,944	7.6	52	11.1	208	13.0	11.0	10.7	16.1
Upjohn Co	X5	JUN	DEC	543	7.6	2,059	3.4	52	8.4	168	−9.7	9.6	8.2	14.4
Warner-Lambert Co	X5	JUN	DEC	811	1.7	3,198	2.0	67	8.0	235	9.1	8.2	7.3	15.9
American Home Prod Corp	X6	JUN	DEC	1,198	7.6	4,827	5.1	181	8.5	747	8.7	15.1	15.5	32.4
AMPHARM	X6	JUN	DEC	489	13.5	1,840	4.6	37	10.3	160	9.0	7.5	8.7	16.8
Bristol Myers Co	X6	JUN	DEC	1,172	8.5	4,648	9.7	119	−3.8	545	9.3	10.2	11.7	22.1
Lilly (Eli) & Co	X6	JUN	DEC	879	16.2	3,473	10.0	126	14.2	545	8.9	14.3	15.7	21.7
Merck & Co	X6	JUN	DEC	1,005	14.5	3,740	5.2	173	25.5	602	18.9	17.2	16.1	21.8
Pfizer Inc	X6	JUN	DEC	1,118	11.6	4,221	7.8	156	13.5	620	12.9	14.0	14.7	21.8
Schering Plough	X6	JUN	DEC	585	12.8	2,159	10.2	72	30.1	230	21.3	12.3	10.7	15.0
Smithkline Beckman Corp	X6	JUN	DEC	883	14.5	3,462	13.2	123	1.6	501	−0.4	14.0	14.5	21.8
Squibb Corp	X6	JUN	DEC	585	23.2	2,258	16.1	68	29.3	255	22.5	11.6	11.3	17.5
Upjohn Co	X6	JUN	DEC	594	9.4	2,129	11.2	65	23.9	224	23.1	10.9	10.5	17.3
Warner-Lambert Co	X6	JUN	DEC	761	−6.1	3,103	−3.0	121	80.3	−257	—	15.8	−8.3	−20.9

Source: Standard & Poor's Compustat Services, Inc.

CASE 5.2
IPO VALUATION

The Talbots, Inc.

Initial public offerings (IPOs) of companies whose products are well-liked and easily recognized often attract higher than average interest among investors. The IPO of The Talbots, Inc. (Talbots) in late 1993 was no exception. Talbots is a leading U.S. specialty retailer of women's classic apparel, shoes, and accessories. The company's net sales during 1992 were $642 million, of which retail store sales were $495 million and catalog sales were $147 million. By the end of 1992, there were 286 retail store outlets. In that same year, Talbot issued 25 separate catalogs with a combined circulation of more than 60 million.

Company Background.   The first Talbots store opened in 1947 in Hingham, Massachusetts, when Rudolf and Nancy Talbot, who had inherited a small women's apparel shop, put their name on the store. The couple painted the door of that first store red, a tradition that continues at Talbots' stores today. One year later, the first Talbots catalog was issued, with a circulation of approximately 3,000. After twenty-five years of operation, the chain had expanded to only five stores, located in Massachusetts and Connecticut. The catalog side of the business, however, had grown rapidly.

General Mills Corporation purchased Talbots in 1973 and began to invest heavily to expand the company. Talbots grew to 126 stores and $350 million in sales per year by 1988, at which time General Mills, in an effort to scale back its diversification program, decided to sell Talbots. The buyer, Jusco USA, paid approximately $325 million. Jusco USA is a holding company and a wholly-owned subsidiary of Jusco Co., Ltd., a Japanese conglomerate with interests in real estate, retailing, and supermarkets.

The expansion of Talbots proceeded at an even more rapid pace under Jusco by refocusing catalog operations, adding new stores and developing new complementary store concepts that capitalized on the strength of Talbots' name and loyal customer base. By August 1993, Talbots operated 313 stores in 44 states, the District of Columbia, and Canada. Exhibit 1 contains a tabulation of store openings by year from 1982 through August 1993. Exhibit 2 contains summary financial information for Talbots from approximately the date of acquisition of Talbots by Jusco to July 31, 1993. Exhibit 3 contains financial statements and selected notes that were supplied with the IPO prospectus.

Talbots' Strategic Positioning.   In addition to Talbots' flagship ''Misses'' stores, the company expanded into other niche specialty store concepts after its acquisition by Jusco. These included Talbots ''Petites'' (specializing in smaller-sized women's clothing), Talbots ''Kids'' (clothing for boys and girls), and Talbots ''Intimates'' (sleepwear and lingerie items). The company also operated Talbots ''Surplus'' stores, in which excess merchandise inventory was sold at discounted prices. The merchandising strategy in all store concepts focuses on achieving a ''classic look,'' emphasizing simple, timeless styles. Over 90 percent of store merchandise consists of styles that are sold exclusively under the Talbots label.

This case was prepared by Mitchell W. Slape under the supervision of Thomas I. Selling. Copyright © 1995 by Thomas I. Selling. All rights reserved.

EXHIBIT 1

The Talbots, Inc.
Store Openings by Year and Kind

	Number of Stores						
	Talbots Misses	Talbots Petites	Talbots Kids	Talbots Intimates	Talbots Surplus	Annual Total	Cumulative Total
End of 1982	29					29	29
Opened 1983	7					7	36
Opened 1984	12				2	14	50
Opened 1985	26	1			2	29	79
Opened 1986	21				1	22	101
Opened 1987	18					18	119
Opened 1988	18					18	137
Opened 1989	19[a]					19	156
Opened 1990	31	3	2			36	192
Opened 1991	34	5	6		3	48	240
Opened 1992	26	13	6	1		46	286
Opened 1993	12	9	6			27	313
Totals	253	31	20	1	8	313	

[a] 20 stores opened and 1 store closed during year through August 31, 1993.

Talbots' business strategy is to maintain its strong competitive position in private label classic apparel and to capitalize on the strength of the Talbots name and loyal customer base through geographic expansion and development of new business concepts. Specifically, key elements of the company's strategy include:

1. To maintain a strong competitive position as a full-price retailer of private label classic apparel offering personalized customer service;
2. To continue to capitalize on its complementary store and catalog operations;
3. To capitalize on its strengths through the development of new business concepts (such as Talbots Petites and Talbots Kids); and
4. To continue expansion at the rate of 45 to 50 new stores per year for the foreseeable future.

Each of these key elements are described in greater detail below:

Full Price, Private Label Retailer. There are only four sales events a year in all stores (with the exception of the Surplus stores), consisting of two end-of-season sales and two mid-season sales, each scheduled in conjunction with catalog sales events. There are no other promotional events during the year. This strategy is designed to project Talbots as a high quality, reasonably priced brand that may be purchased at regular price. Following each sale event, all remaining merchandise, other than shoes, is sent to Talbots Surplus stores for final clearance.

The focus on private label merchandise is designed to provide Talbots with a higher gross margin than would be obtained on other merchandise, and establishes Talbots' identity as a brand of women's classic wardrobe apparel. Talbots' private label merchandise features the

EXHIBIT 2

The Talbots, Inc.
Summary Financial Information
(dollars in thousands, except per share amounts)

	Fiscal Year Ended				Twenty-Six Weeks Ended	
	Jan. 27, 1990	Jan. 26, 1991	Jan. 25, 1992	Jan. 30, 1993	July 25, 1992	July 31, 1993
Statement of Earnings Information:						
Net sales	$452,772	$473,614	$521,212	$641,839	$292,231	$334,431
Cost of sales, buying and occupancy	285,031	309,416	332,445	397,762	179,184	203,680
Selling, general and administrative expenses	139,779	144,153	157,149	189,816	85,295	96,090
Royalty expense to related party	8,784	8,730	9,063	10,510	4,915	5,351
Operating income	19,178	11,315	22,555	43,751	22,837	29,310
Interest expense, net	18,888	18,077	12,207	8,313	4,450	3,339
Equity in investee loss	–0–	281	–0–	–0–	–0–	–0–
Income taxes	816	–0–	4,726	15,021	7,794	10,649
Income (loss) before extraordinary item ..	(526)	(7,043)	5,622	20,417	10,593	15,322
Extraordinary item	541	–0–	1,911	–0–	–0–	–0–
Net income (loss)	$ 15	$ (7,043)	$ 7,533	$ 20,417	$ 10,593	$ 15,322
Other Financial Information:						
Capital expenditures	$ 23,164	$ 25,171	$ 22,676	$ 26,032	$ 10,500	$ 12,756
Depreciation and amortization	19,523	22,517	25,217	26,250	12,902	13,532

					At July 31, 1993	
					Actual	As Adjusted(a)
Balance Sheet Information:						
Working capital (deficit)	$ 29,174	$ 22,172	$ 24,009	$ 37,929	$(2,741)(b)	$(2,741)(b)
Goodwill, net	51,640	50,297	48,953	47,608	46,937	46,937
Total assets	309,839	333,523	342,220	354,726	379,186	474,556
Total debt	205,832	209,058	190,998	169,000	177,500	144,000
Stockholders' equity	57,204	80,161	87,584	108,069	123,407	252,277

building blocks of a classic wardrobe, including such items as the classic blazer, white blouse, and turtleneck sweater, as well as other complementary fashion items and accessories to create the company's signature "classic look."

Complementary Store and Catalog Operations.   Talbots operates its stores and catalogs as an integrated business and provides the same personalized service to its customers regardless of whether merchandise is purchased through its stores or catalogs. The company has a single-price strategy throughout its catalogs and U.S. stores.

Talbots' catalog operations also provide important demographic information about potential store locations and serve as an integral part of its expansion strategy. Catalogs are also used to test new business concepts such as Talbots Kids and Talbots Intimates before building new

EXHIBIT 2 (continued)

	Fiscal Year Ended				Twenty-Six Weeks Ended	
	Jan. 27, 1990	Jan. 26, 1991	Jan. 25, 1992	Jan. 30 1993	July 25, 1992	July 31, 1993
Store Operating Information:						
Net store sales (in thousands)	$306,189	$335,474	$387,356 .	$494,953	$223,800	$ 260,790
Percentage increase (decrease) in comparable store sales	5.2%	(5.4)%	(2.4)%	11.7%	13.3%	4.6%
Selling square footage at end of period ..	602,498	705,893	857,772	979,495	908,185	1,041,323
Weighted average net sales per selling square foot	$ 548	$ 510	$ 494	$ 536	498	506
	(dollars in thousands, except per catalog)					
Catalog Operating Information:						
Net catalog sales	$146,583	$138,140	$133,856	$146,886	$68,431	$73,641
Sales per catalog	$ 1.88	$ 1.86	$ 2.14	$ 2.44	$ 2.35	$ 2.35
Number of catalogs distributed	78,108	74,370	62,582	60,159	29,136	29,557
Number of catalog orders filled	2,170	1,962	1,840	1,829	899	937
Number of catalog customers at end of period	5,685	6,249	6,528	6,835	6,661	6,937

(a) Adjusted to reflect the sale by the Company of 11,000,000 shares of Common Stock and the application of $103.0 million of net proceeds therefrom to purchase the Trademarks in the territory, $25.0 million to repay indebtedness incurred to finance the Dividend Payment and approximately $33.5 million to repay a portion of the Term Loan.
(b) Includes $45.0 million of indebtedness incurred under the Revolving Credit Facility which expires June 20, 1994.

stores. The catalogs are also used to communicate Talbots' classic image, to provide customers with fashion guidance in coordinating outfits, and to generate store traffic.

Introduction of New Business Concepts.   In 1984, Talbots began offering merchandise in petite sizes in its catalogs. In 1985, it opened the first Talbots Petites store. Talbots plans to continue to open Petites stores adjacent to its Misses stores and to expand the space within selected Misses stores for Petite merchandise.

In 1990, based on a successful response to a separate catalog dedicated to apparel for boys and girls, the first Talbots Kids store was opened. Talbots implemented a similar strategy to introduce Talbots Intimates, which offers classic sleepwear, daywear (principally underwear), and loungewear.

Expansion.   Talbots intends to open approximately 20 Misses stores per year in the United States and three to four Misses stores per year in Canada into the foreseeable future. Additionally, the chain plans to grow its specialty store concepts, adding 12 to 14 Petites stores, 8 to 10 Kids stores, and up to 6 Intimates stores per year. The company is also exploring opportunities for expansion into international markets in Canada and the United Kingdom.

EXHIBIT 3

The Talbots, Inc.
Consolidated Statement of Earnings
For the Fifty-Two Weeks Ended January 26, 1991 and January 25, 1992
And the Fifty-Three Weeks Ended January 30, 1993
(dollar amounts in thousands except per share data)

	Year Ended		
	January 26, 1991	*January 25, 1992*	*January 30, 1993*
Net Sales	$473,614	$521,212	$641,839
Costs and Expenses			
Cost of sales, buying, and occupancy	309,416	332,445	397,762
Selling, general and administrative expenses	144,153	157,149	189,816
Royalty expense to related party	8,730	9,063	10,510
Operating Income	11,315	22,555	43,751
Interest expense, net	18,077	12,207	8,313
Equity in Investee Loss	281		
Income (Loss) Before Taxes and			
Extraordinary Item	(7,043)	10,348	35,438
Income Taxes		4,726	15,021
Income (Loss) Before Extraordinary Item	(7,043)	5,622	20,417
Extraordinary Item—Utilization of a net			
operating loss carryforward		1,911	
Net Income (Loss)	$ (7,043)	$ 7,533	$ 20,417
Pro Forma Information (Unaudited):			
Net income			$ 26,994
Net income per share			$ 0.81
Weighted average number of shares of			
common stock outstanding (in thousands)			33,286

The cost to Talbots of opening a new Misses store, which vary in size from 3,500 to 6,500 gross square feet (a typical Misses store averages approximately 4,800 square feet), generally ranges from $600,000 to $700,000. In smaller markets, however, these stores may be scaled down to 3,800 to 4,000 gross square feet. The cost of a new Petites, Kids, or Intimates store generally ranges from $350,000 to $400,000. The stores average 1,800, 2,500, and 2,500 gross square feet, respectively. Approximately 75 percent of the floor area of all Talbots stores is devoted to selling space (including fitting rooms), with the balance allocated to stockroom and other non-selling space. Included in the cost of opening any store are its working capital requirements. The majority of Talbots' store properties are leased. As of August 31, 1993, the company owned the property for only 9 of its 313 stores.

Talbots stores have been renovated from time to time, in many cases in connection with expansion in size and/or lease renewals. In 1992, Talbots undertook 15 major renovations of its stores at a total cost of approximately $2.5 million. Talbots also expanded the selling space in seven of its existing Misses stores at a total cost of approximately $1 million. These store expansions resulted in an aggregate increase of 7,400 square feet of net selling space.

EXHIBIT 3 (continued)

The Talbots, Inc.
Consolidated Balance Sheets
January 25, 1992 and January 30, 1993
(dollar amounts in thousands except per share data)

Assets	January 25, 1992	January 30, 1993
Current Assets:		
Cash and cash equivalents	$ 10,198	$ 6,193
Customer accounts receivable—less allowance for doubtful accounts of $987 and $767	37,783	45,023
Merchandise inventories	72,839	85,366
Deferred catalog costs	5,402	7,386
Due from affiliate	1,808	1,646
Deferred income taxes	2,267	2,755
Prepaid and other current assets	9,582	10,822
Total current assets	139,879	159,191
Property and equipment, net	130,458	127,777
Goodwill—Net of accumulated amortization of $4,807 and $6,151	48,953	47,608
Intangibles—Net of accumulated amortization of $13,167 and $16,829	18,835	15,173
Deferred income taxes	4,095	4,977
Total Assets	$342,220	$354,726

Liabilities and Stockholders' Equity		
Current Liabilities:		
Notes payable to banks	$ 48,000	$ 42,000
Accounts payable	28,467	35,019
Accrued liabilities	28,121	33,925
Income taxes payable	2,787	2,818
Current maturities of long-term obligations	8,495	7,500
Total current liabilities	115,870	121,262
Long-term obligations	134,503	119,500
Deferred rent under lease commitments	4,263	5,895
Commitments	–0–	–0–
Stockholders' Equity:		
Common stock, $.01 par value; 40,000,000 shares authorized, 22,122,450 shares issued and outstanding	221	221
Additional paid-in capital	89,779	89,779
Retained earnings (deficit)	(2,306)	18,111
Translation adjustment	13	97
Deferred pension cost	(123)	(139)
Total stockholders' equity	87,584	108,069
Total Liabilities and Stockholders' Equity	$342,220	$354,726

EXHIBIT 3 (continued)

The Talbots, Inc.
Consolidated Statements of Cash Flow
For the Fifty-Two Weeks Ended January 26, 1991 and January 25, 1992
And the Fifty-Three Weeks Ended January 30, 1993
(dollar amounts in thousands)

	Year Ended		
	January 26, 1991	January 25, 1992	January 30, 1993
Cash Flows from Operating Activities:			
Net income (loss)	$ (7,043)	$ 7,533	$ 20,417
Adjustments to reconcile net income (loss) to net cash provided by (used in) operating activities:			
Depreciation and amortization	22,517	25,217	26,250
Deferred rent	1,567	1,538	1,632
Loss on disposal of property and equipment	451	807	2,235
Deferred income taxes	(694)	(4,958)	(1,370)
Changes in current assets and liabilities:			
Customer accounts receivable	(6,357)	(6,078)	(7,251)
Merchandise inventories	(9,497)	(3,388)	(12,600)
Deferred catalog costs	(759)	(388)	(1,984)
Due from affiliate	(862)	(872)	162
Prepaid and other current assets	(3,297)	497	(1,050)
Accounts payable	(514)	5,490	6,570
Accrued liabilities	(2,125)	9,408	5,843
Income taxes payable	(1,248)	2,787	31
Net cash provided by (used in) operating activities	(7,861)	37,593	38,885
Cash Flows from Investing Activities:			
Additions to property and equipment	(25,171)	(22,676)	(26,032)
Proceeds from disposal of property and equipment	177	157	709
Decrease in acquisition liabilities	(180)		
Net cash used in investing activities	(25,174)	(22,519)	(25,323)
Cash Flows from Financing Activities:			
Borrowings (payments) under notes payable to banks	24,000	(12,000)	(6,000)
Payments of borrowings: long-term debt and capital lease	(20,967)	(8,503)	(11,495)
Capital investment from Jusco (Europe) B.V.	30,000		
Net cash provided by (used in) financing activities	33,033	(20,503)	(17,495)
Effect of Exchange Rate Changes on Cash	–0–	(21)	(72)
Net Decrease in Cash and Cash Equivalents	(2)	(5,450)	(4,005)
CASH AND CASH EQUIVALENTS, BEGINNING OF YEAR	15,650	15,648	10,198
CASH AND CASH EQUIVALENTS, END OF YEAR	$15,648	$10,198	$ 6,193

EXHIBIT 3 (continued)

The Talbots, Inc.
Selected Notes to Consolidated Financial Statements
(dollar amounts in thousands except per share data)

2. Summary of Significant Accounting Policies

Deferred Catalog Costs—Catalog costs, including costs of production and mailing, are deferred and
amortized over the estimated productive selling life of the catalog, generally three to five months.
Merchandise Inventories—Inventories are stated at the lower of average cost or market using the retail
inventory method on a FIFO (first-in, first-out) basis.
Finance Charge Income—Finance charge income on customer accounts receivable is treated as a
reduction of selling, general and administrative expense. For the year ended January 26, 1991, January
25, 1992 and January 30, 1993, the amount was $4,053, $4,641, and $5,393 respectively.

6. Property and Equipment

Property and equipment consists of the following:

	January 25, 1992	January 30, 1993
Land	$ 11,522	$ 11,522
Buildings	37,351	37,189
Fixtures and equipment	55,154	57,668
Software	3,115	3,511
Leasehold improvements	62,219	64,792
Leasehold interests	12,427	12,191
Construction in progress	4,196	5,054
	185,984	191,927
Less accumulated depreciation and amortization	(55,526)	(64,150)
Property and equipment—net	$130,458	$127,777

7. Long-term debt at January 30, 1993 matures as follows:

1993	7,500
1994	52,500
1995	7,500
1996	7,500
1997	$ 52,000
Total long-term obligations	$127,000

Key Aspects of Talbots' Operations

Purchasing.   Talbots' private-label merchandise is designed through coordinated efforts of
its merchandising and manufacturing team. Styles are developed based upon prior years' sales
history and current fashion trends for each of the six merchandising periods (winter, resort,
spring, summer, transition, and fall).

Talbots staffs a Hong Kong office that acts as a liaison with manufacturers. Approximately one-
half of private-label merchandise is manufactured offshore. Talbots does not own or operate its own
manufacturing facilities. Most of Talbots' foreign purchases are denominated in U.S. dollars.

EXHIBIT 3 (continued)

Loan and Revolving Credit—Interest terms on the loan agreement and the revolving credit agreement are negotiable, at the Company's option, for periods of one, three, and six months. The interest rates are set at an adjusted **LIBOR** plus a spread of .375%. Under these agreements, the interest terms were fixed at January 30, 1983 until April 29, 1993 and July 29, 1993, respectively. The loan and revolving credit agreements are guaranteed by JUSCO Co., Ltd. Subsequent to year end, these guarantees were lifted.

Notes Payable to Banks—The Company has available an unsecured line-of-credit facility of $90,000, of which notes totaling $42,000 are outstanding at January 30, 1993, and are due between February 2, 1993, and July 29, 1993. The notes bear interest at rates ranging from 3.8125% to 4.4375%.

Interest Expense—Interest expense for the years ended January 26, 1991, January 25, 1992, and January 30, 1993 was $18,861, $12,858 and $8,754, respectively. Interest paid on a cash basis for the years ended January 26, 1991, January 25, 1992, and January 30, 1993 was $20,154, $10,839, and $10,698, respectively.

10. Leases

The Company conducts the major part of its operations in leased premises with lease terms expiring at various dates through 2010. Most store leases provide for base rentals plus contingent rentals which are a function of sales volume and provide that the Company pay real estate taxes, maintenance, and other operating expenses applicable to the leased premises. Additionally, most store leases provide renewal options and contain rent escalation clauses. The total base rental obligation for a lease is expensed on a straight-line basis over the term of the lease.

Additionally, during the year ended January 30, 1993, the Company entered into a noncancellable operating lease for computer equipment.

The aggregate minimum future rental commitments under noncancellable operating leases totaled $231,189 at January 30, 1993, and amounts due for each of the next five years are summarized as follows:

1994	$28,861
1995	28,812
1996	27,528
1997	25,160
1998	22,624

Rent expenses for the years ended January 26, 1991, January 25, 1992 and January 30, 1993 was $17,984, $22,261, and $26,770 respectively, which includes $827, $827, and $1,226, respectively, of contingent rental expense.

Advertising.   To strengthen its classic image, Talbots launched a national advertising campaign in the fall of 1991 with the positioning line, "Talbots IS the Classics." The single- and double-page advertisements have appeared in national magazines such as *Vogue, Vanity Fair, Harper's Bazaar,* and *Bon Appetit.* Talbots spent $9.2 million on advertising in 1992 compared to $6.4 million in 1991 and $5.6 million in 1990.

Customer Credit.   Talbots' customers may pay for merchandise with the Talbots credit card, major third-party credit cards, cash, or check. Credit card sales were 80.5% of net sales in 1992, 80.8% in 1991, and 80.1% in 1990. In 1992, 28.7% of net sales were made with the

Talbots' credit card and 51.8% were made with third-party credit cards. Accounts written off in 1992 totaled $561,000.

Staffing and Compensation.   As of August 31, 1993, Talbots had 4,808 employees, of whom 1,321 were full-time salaried employees, 904 were full-time hourly employees, and 2,583 were part-time hourly employees. Store management receives compensation in the form of salaries and performance-based bonuses based on store sales, expenses, and shrinkage. Sales associates are paid on an hourly basis and receive performance incentives, but not commissions.

During 1992, Talbots adopted Statement of Financial Accounting Standards No. 106, "Employers' Accounting for Postretirement Benefits Other Than Pensions." In connection with the adoption of SFAS No. 106, Talbots recorded an expense of $809,000, which included a transition obligation of $676,000.

Catalog Operations.   Beginning in 1989, Talbots implemented a program to improve the productivity of its catalog operations by broadening its merchandise assortment and by targeting its catalog circulation toward better established and prospective buyers. During the period 1989 to 1992, catalog mailings were reduced by 23.0%, while sales per catalog increased by 29.8%.

Talbots attempts to make around-the-clock catalog shopping as convenient as possible. Sales associates at telemarketing centers in Hingham, Massachusetts, and Knoxville, Tennessee, utilize on-line computer terminals to enter customer orders and to retrieve information about merchandise and its availability. These sales associates also offer suggestions and help customers to select merchandise. They can also provide detailed information regarding merchandise features. All catalog items are displayed in sample stores at the telemarketing sites, thereby allowing sales associates to view merchandise as they assist customers.

Talbots' Competition.   The women's retail apparel industry is highly competitive. Talbots' direct competitors include certain departments of national specialty department stores like Lord & Taylor, Sak's Fifth Avenue, Neiman Marcus, and Nordstrom as well as strong regional department store chains such as Macy's, Marshall Field's, and Dillard's. Other competitors include specialty retailers such as The Limited, Ann Taylor, Eddie Bauer, and The GAP, as well as catalog companies such as L.L. Bean, Lands' End, J. Crew, and Spiegel. Exhibit 4 contains selected financial data for three of Talbots' principal competitors: Dillard's, The Limited, and Spiegel.

Details of the Initial Public Offering.   There were 33,122,450 total shares of outstanding common stock prior to the IPO, which were owned by Jusco USA. Jusco was offering to sell 11,000,000 shares for between $15 and $17 per share. The proceeds of the offering were to be used as follows:

- $103 million to Jusco in exchange for Talbots' trademarks currently owned by Jusco's European subsidiary.

- $25 million to repay indebtedness incurred by Talbots to finance a dividend to Jusco. The dividend was declared on August 19, 1993, and was paid on or about November 15, 1993.

- The remaining proceeds were to be used to repay approximately $33.5 million of a Talbots' term loan. The term loan is payable by Talbots and was incurred to finance

EXHIBIT 4

Data for Competitors of Talbots
(dollar amounts in millions except for per share data)

Selected Company Data	The Limited			Dillard's			Spiegel		
	1993	*1992*	*1991*	*1993*	*1992*	*1991*	*1993*	*1992*	*1991*
Net Sales	$7,245	$6,944	$6,149	$5,131	$4,714	$4,036	$2,596	$2,218.73	$1,976.32
Cost of Goods Sold	5,286	4,954	4,356	3,307	3,043	2,566	1,537	1,345	1,174
SG&A Expense	1,250	1,183	1,069	1,293	1,173	1,039	900	724	691
Interest Expense	64	62	64	131	122	109	72	76	80
Tax Expense	254	280	257	158	139	116	39	30	14
Net Income	391	465	403	241	236	206	49	43	17
Current Assets	2,221	1,784	1,604	2,457	2,367	2,089	1,593	1,303	1,302
Accounts Receivable	1,057	837	736	1,097	1,090	989	999	817	894
Inventory	734	804	730	1,300	1,179	1,053	439	411	307
Fixed Assets	1,667	1,814	1,657	1,921	1,689	1,338	289	205	177
Total Assets	4,135	3,846	3,419	4,430	4,107	3,499	2,211	1,785	1,725
Current Liabilities	707	721	520	796	690	737	627	495	366
Long-Term Debt	650	642	714	1,238	1,255	875	972	764	841
Total Liablilties	1,694	1,579	1,542	2,349	2,275	1,915	1,643	1,307	1,271
Owners' Equity	2,441	2,268	1,877	2,082	1,832	1,583	567	478	454
Cash Flow from Operations	448	754	476	315	359	176	20	139	108
Capital Expenditures	76	490	542	317	355	332	204	114	57
Present Value of Leases	3,406	2,875	2,452	193	186	157	386	340	300
Shares Outstanding (millions)	357.81	362.65	361.79	112.99	112.52	111.57	107.74	104	103.96
Price per Share—High	$ 30.00	$ 32.90	$ 31.60	$ 52.80	$ 51.50	$ 45.60	$ 23.40	$ 9.00	$ 10.50
—Low	$ 16.60	$ 19.30	$ 17.60	$ 33.10	$ 30.00	$ 25.50	$ 7.80	$ 5.00	$ 5.40

Jusco's acquisition of Talbots. Seven annual principal payments of $7.5 million began on June 28, 1991. After applying the proceeds of the IPO to repay a portion of the indebtedness under the term loan, Talbots will be requested to continue annual principal payments of $7.5 million, plus interest, with a final payment of $7.0 million on June 30, 1998.

The financial statement impact of the use of the proceeds and certain other arrangements between Jusco and Talbots are made explicit in the pro forma financial statements contained in Exhibit 5.

Dividend Policy.   Other than the $25 million debt-financed dividend payment to be repaid from the proceeds of the IPO, Talbots has never paid dividends on its common stock. Upon completion of the IPO, Talbots intends to declare quarterly dividends of $.03 per share, beginning for the fiscal quarter ended January 29, 1994.

Exhibit 4 (continued)

Ratio Analysis	The Limited			Dillard's			Spiegel		
	1993	1992	1991	1993	1992	1991	1993	1992	1991
Return on Assets	10.90%	13.90%	14.20%	7.70%	8.30%	8.60%	4.80%	5.30%	4.00%
Profit Margin	5.98%	7.30%	7.24%	6.38%	6.72%	6.90%	3.71%	4.21%	3.51%
Total Asset Turnover	1.82	1.91	1.96	1.2	1.24	1.24	1.3	1.26	1.14
Return on Common Equity	8.30%	11.20%	11.70%	6.20%	6.90%	7.00%	4.70%	4.60%	1.90%
Return on Assets	10.90%	13.90%	14.20%	7.70%	8.30%	8.60%	4.80%	5.30%	4.00%
Common Earnings Leverage	0.9	0.92	0.91	0.74	0.75	0.74	0.51	0.46	0.24
Capital Structure Leverage	1.69	1.75	1.83	2.18	2.23	2.21	3.82	3.77	3.82
Cost of Goods Sold/Sales	72.96%	71.33%	70.83%	64.45%	64.56%	63.57%	59.19%	60.61%	59.43%
Interest Expense/Sales	0.88%	0.90%	1.04%	2.55%	2.59%	2.71%	2.78%	3.43%	4.03%
Income Taxes/Sales	3.51%	4.03%	4.18%	3.09%	2.95%	2.87%	1.49%	1.36%	0.70%
Accounts Receivable Turnover	7.65	8.83	8.75	4.69	4.54	4.23	2.86	2.59	2.18
Inventory Turnover	6.88	6.46	6.62	2.67	2.73	2.64	3.62	3.75	3.65
Fixed Asset Turnover	4.16	4.00	4.03	1.95	2.18	2.35	10.52	11.61	11.96
Current Ratio	3.14	2.48	3.08	3.09	3.43	2.83	2.54	2.63	3.56
Quick Ratio	2.10	1.36	1.68	1.45	1.72	1.41	1.84	1.80	2.72
Operating Cash Flow/Total Liab.	26.50%	47.80%	30.30%	13.40%	15.80%	9.20%	1.20%	10.60%	8.50%
Total Liab./Total Assets	41.00%	41.00%	45.10%	53.00%	55.40%	54.70%	74.30%	73.20%	73.70%
Long Term Debt/Total Assets	15.70%	14.10%	20.90%	28.00%	30.50%	25.00%	44.00%	42.80%	48.80%
Long Term Debt/Owners' Equity	26.60%	23.90%	38.00%	59.50%	68.50%	55.30%	171.20%	159.80%	185.40%
Interest Coverage Ratio	11.10	12.95	11.33	4.05	4.08	3.95	2.21	1.97	1.39
Operating Cash Flow/Cap. Expen.	5.93	1.54	0.88	0.99	1.01	0.53	0.10	1.21	1.89
Comp. Store Sales (% Change)	NA	NA	NA	9.00%	17.00%	12.00%	11.00%	17.00%	NA
Sales per Square Foot	$289	$285	$278	$147	$142	$138	NA	NA	NA

Required:

1. What makes Talbots an attractive or unattractive investment? Part of your analysis should include a comparison, to the extent permitted by the data in the case, of Talbots' financial performance and risk relative to its competitors.

2. Prepare annual forecasted balance sheets, income statements, and statements of cash flows for the five years subsequent to the IPO. For simplicity, assume that Talbots' fiscal year end subsequent to the IPO will be changed to July 31.

3. Is the public offering of Talbots' common stock at a price of $16 per share an attractive investment opportunity? For simplicity, assume that the IPO will take place on July 31, 1993.

EXHIBIT 5

The Talbots, Inc.
Pro Forma Consolidated Statements
(unaudited)

	Fiscal Year Ended January 30, 1993		
	Actual	Pro Forma Adjustments	Pro Forma
Consolidated Statement of Earnings		*(dollars in thousands, except per share amounts)*	
Net Sales	$641,839		$ 641,839
Cost of Sales, Buying and Occupancy	397,762		397,762
Selling, General and Administrative Expenses	189,816	$ 1,298[a]	191,114
Royalty Expense to Related Party	10,510	(10,510)[b]	0
Operating Income	43,751	9,212	52,963
Interest Expense, net	8,313	(1,411)[c]	6,902
Income Before Income Taxes	35,438	10,623	46,061
Income Taxes	15,021	4,046[d]	19,067
Net Income	$ 20,417	$ 6,577	$ 26,994
Net Income per Share of Common Stock			$ .81
Weighted Average Number of Shares of Common Stock Outstanding			$33,285,900

[a]Net increase in selling, general and administrative expenses as follows: Because the purchase of the Trademarks in the territory is from a related party, the trademarks are recorded at the related party's historical cost of $95.4 million. Amortization of $2.4 million will be recognized annually over forty years.

[b]Termination of royalty fee payments for use of Trademarks.

[c]Incremental interest due to the replacement of the guarantees with letters of awareness. Increase in interest of (1) 0.125% on average outstanding revolving credit balance of $45.0 million and (2) 0.25% on average outstanding term loan balances of $86.6 million, and $80.4 million for the period ended January 30, 1993, July 25, 1992, and July 31, 1993, respectively.

[d]Tax effect of the above transactions using a 40% incremental tax rate, net of a $203,000 annual tax benefit due to the difference in the tax and book bases of the Trademarks.

EXHIBIT 5 (continued)

The Talbots, Inc.
Pro Forma Consolidated Statements
(unaudited)

	At July 31, 1993		
Consolidated Balance Sheet	*Actual*	*Pro Forma Adjustments (dollars in thousands)*	*Pro Forma*
Assets			
Current Assets	$183,349		$183,349
Property and Equipment	129,468		129,468
Goodwill, net	46,937		46,937
Trademarks	–0–	$ 95,370[(a)]	95,370
Intangibles, net	13,342		13,342
Deferred Income Taxes	6,090		6,090
Total Assets	$379,186	$ 95,370	$474,556
Liabilities and Stockholders' Equity			
Current Liabilities	$186,090		$186,090
Long-Term Obligations	63,000	$(33,500)[(b)]	29,500
Deferred Rent under Lease Commitments	6,689		6,689
Stockholders' Equity:			
Common stock	221		331
Additional paid-in capital	89,779	128,760[(c)]	218,539
Retained Earnings	33,433		33,433
Translation adjustment	113		113
Deferred pension cost	(139)		(139)
Total stockholders' equity	123,407	128,870	252,277
Total Liabilities and Stockholders' Equity	$379,186	$ 95,370	$474,556

[(a)] Because the purchase of the Trademarks in the Territory is from a related party, the Trademarks are recorded at such related party's historical cost of $95.4 million. The excess of the purchase price over the related party's historical cost reduces additional paid-in capital by $7.6 million.

[(b)] Repayment of a portion of the Term Loan.

[(c)] Gross proceeds of the Offerings net of estimated expenses of approximately $14.5 million, $25.0 million for the Dividend Payment and $7.6 million excess of the Trademarks purchase price over historical cost (see (a) above).

Special Issues in Financial Analysis

[E]arnings are distorted by accounting conventions that make it hard to compare values from one [securities exchange] to the next. But compare one must, if one has any hope of applying rationality to picking stocks.[1]

In the previous two chapters, the fundamentals of financial statement analysis were considered. Implicit to that discussion was the important assumption of data comparability, both over time for a given firm, as well as between firms. As we will see in Chapters 8–14, however, this assumption is unlikely to be valid when comparing the financial data of companies from different countries and often within the same country. Even if a high degree of harmonization is achieved by the International Accounting Standards Committee (IASC), comparability concerns will continue to persist because of the inherent variability of financial data permitted under acceptable IASC reporting alternatives.

In this chapter, we consider a variety of data comparability issues, as well as some techniques that might be used to make adjustments to available data for the purpose of attaining improved comparability:

- Alternative revenue recognition policies.
- Alternative inventory valuation approaches.
- Alternative depreciation and amortization policies.
- Alternative asset capitalization policies.
- Asset impairment and revaluation.
- Off-balance sheet debt.
- Balance sheet reserves.

---

[1]P. Fuhrman, ''Parlez-vous P/E?'' *Forbes,* June 27, 1988, p. 276.

Alternative Revenue Recognition Policies

Generally accepted revenue recognition policies are likely to vary significantly within the various industries of a given country as well as between countries. Thus, the problem of alternative revenue recognition practices will be encountered when analyzing the financial results of almost any multinational company, regardless of the origin of the accounting principles used by the company in its financial statements. For example, consider the variability of revenue recognition practices among some typical industries within the United States:

- Retail concerns typically recognize revenue at the point of sale.
- Original equipment manufacturers (OEMs) frequently recognize revenue at the point of shipment.
- Oil and gas companies may recognize revenue from the sale of crude oil and condensate prior to its extraction. This is accomplished through the sale of carved-out production contracts.
- Companies producing goods or providing services under long-term contracts frequently recognize revenue on a percentage-of-completed work basis.

The following examples of non–U.S. revenue recognition practices illustrate some of the differences that can occur across countries:

- In Hong Kong, profit on installment sales contracts is generally recognized in proportion to cash payments received, whereas the more common practice in the United States is to recognize all revenues—except for amounts attributed to financing activities—at the point of sale.
- In Germany, the accepted practice is to delay revenue recognition until a right of return period has expired.
- German companies rarely recognize revenue under long-term contracts on a percentage-of-completed work basis. Revenue recognition is usually delayed until a contract is completed.

When evaluating the revenue recognition policy of a given company, regardless of its national reporting origins, it is always wise to begin by comparing the policy in use to accepted industry norms. The use of an industry-accepted method, however, does not guarantee that a company's revenue (and thus cash flow) streams will be risk free. Consider, for example, OEMs that recognize revenue at the industry-accepted norm of point of shipment. Because of highly competitive marketplaces, these companies frequently offer customers a right-of-return option that may last up to six months. As a consequence, the revenue (and cash) streams of such companies are often quite unpredictable, particularly when economic conditions are less than robust.

Aside from unexpected economic downturns that are usually accompanied by significant increases in sales returns and bad debts, the most often encountered concern with corporate revenue recognition policies is overly aggressive (or early) recognition, which is often referred to as front-end loading. **Front-end loading** occurs when sales are prematurely recognized, perhaps before a firm offer to buy is received or, if producing under contract, before sufficient completion levels have been attained.[2] The consequence of this is that revenues and net income, as well as receivables and total current assets, are overstated relative to more conservative and reasonable revenue recognition. These overstatements naturally are translated into somewhat overly optimistic assessments of corporate profitability, liquidity, and solvency; only a firm's cash flow and asset management indicators will indicate its true situation.

Thus, front-end loading has the effect of improving the appearance of current period results, usually at the expense of future periods. If front-end loaded revenues are used as a basis for projecting future corporate revenues, there is some risk that an analyst's projections of revenues, earnings, and cash flow will be excessively optimistic. Of concern to the analyst, then, is the need to assess the reasonableness, and riskiness, of a company's revenue recognition policy.

In general, two types of risk are associated with revenues: (1) risk that the revenues have been booked too early and that a final sale will not be consummated and (2) risk that, once consummated, the sale will not yield the anticipated level of cash inflows. The first type of risk can be minimized by adopting a conservative revenue recognition policy (e.g., recognition at the point of sale) or when an aggressive (liberal) recognition policy is adopted, by establishing a sufficient reserve to cover any future sales returns.

The second type of risk (i.e., cash collection risk) can be minimized by adopting a conservative credit-granting policy or by establishing a sufficient reserve to cover any future uncollectible accounts. The need for this reserve is estimated at the end of each accounting period, usually on the basis of a process known as **aging of accounts receivable,** which assumes that the older a receivable is, the lower the probability of collection. This process of estimating future uncollectible receivables enables management to deduct from current revenues an amount (i.e., the ''provision for bad debts'') representing the cost of extending credit during the current period. A parallel reserve account, the allowance for uncollectible accounts, appears on the balance sheet as a contra receivable account.[3]

When either type of risk is high, both the quality of the reported revenues and trade receivables will be low, and, as a consequence, the expected cash flows from

---

[2]In a recent example of front-end loading, Kendall Square Research Corporation (a U.S. company) disclosed that it would restate its 1992 results downward because the company had recognized during 1992 certain computer sales to universities that had inadequate funding to make future installment payments. In response to the news announcement, the company's stock price fell 33 percent. See *The Wall Street Journal,* November 30, 1993.

[3]It is always instructive for an analyst to evaluate the reasonableness of a company's allowance for uncollectible accounts. Consider, for example, the case of Urcarco, Inc., which operates a chain of used car lots in the United States. According to the company's prospectus for its initial public offering, 22.7 and 18.4 percent of the cars sold in 1988 and 1989, respectively, were repossessed. For those same years, the allowance for uncollectible accounts relative to the outstanding receivable balance amounted to only 6.9 and 8.9 percent, respectively. In July 1990, two shareholder lawsuits were filed against Urcarco alleging that the company's financial statements were not prepared in conformity with GAAP on grounds that revenue recognition occurred prematurely and that allowances for sales returns and uncollectible accounts were inadequate.

operations uncertain. Evidence regarding the presence of these risks can be obtained in several ways:

- *Reviewing the footnote "Summary of Significant Accounting Policies" adopted by management in the preparation of the financial statements.* While the extent of accounting policy disclosure varies from country to country, a presentation of such information is required in most countries, as well as by *IAS No. 1.* This footnote can provide the analyst with information concerning just how and when revenues are being recognized. Hopefully, the adopted method will be an industry-accepted practice, and where it is not, the analyst should investigate whether special circumstances exist to warrant deviation from industry norms. Exhibit 6–1 (panel A), for example, presents the footnote disclosures of British Airways Plc (BA), American Airlines (AMR Corporation), and Lufthansa in regard to their accounting for operating revenues.

- *Comparing the cash collections from sales with sales recognized on the income statement.* Although there is frequently a lag between sale recognition and cash collection, the lag period should not exceed the normal cash collection cycle of a company or its industry (e.g., 30 to 60 days). However, when the lag period is excessive (or growing), it usually indicates the use of an aggressive revenue recognition policy, a substandard credit-granting policy, poor credit management, or some combination of these. Exhibit 6–1 (panel B) presents a comparison of accrual and cash revenues for British Airways Plc and two of its principal international competitors; that exhibit reveals that BA's cash sales lag its accrual sales in all but one year. Comparison to Lufthansa and American Airlines suggests, however, that its industry-accepted revenue recognition policy is not overly aggressive. The analysis could be extended further to include a time-series and cross-sectional comparison of bad debt allowances.

- *Examining such asset-based quality indicators as the average receivable collection period.* This ratio indicates the average time required to collect an outstanding receivable and can provide important insights regarding not only the quality of receivables and the quality of the credit-granting policies employed by a company but also the quality of its revenue recognition policy. A growing or excessive receivable collection period is usually a very good predictor of pending cash flow problems.[4] Exhibit 6–1 (panel C) presents the average receivable collection period for the same three airlines. BA's collection period seems to be improving slightly over time while Lufthansa's is eroding; however, BA still substantially lags Lufthansa. American's collection period may reflect a higher proportion of domestic service revenues in its sales mix, which may tend to include more cash sales.

---

[4]To illustrate the value of this tool, consider the case of Cardillo Travel Systems, Inc., a receivables-intensive travel service company. As of September 1985, Cardillo's receivables accounted for over 40 percent of the company's total assets. According to an SEC complaint issued on July 27, 1987, the company had experienced serious liquidity problems that had not been publicly disclosed. To the insightful analyst, however, Cardillo's liquidity problems could have been identified early in 1985 by examining the average receivable collection period, which had escalated to over 563 days. (The average collection period for most companies ranges between 30 and 90 days.)

EXHIBIT 6–1

Financial Statement Footnote Disclosures: Revenue Recognition

Panel A. Revenue Recognition Policy

British Airways

Operating revenues comprise the revenue from airline traffic carried during the year and revenue from other airline service and package holidays provided or delivered during the year. Operating revenues exclude sales based taxes and intragroup sales.

American Airlines

Passenger ticket sales are initially recorded as a current liability. Revenue derived from the sale is recognized at the time transportation is provided.

Lufthansa

No disclosure.

Panel B. Comparison of Cash and Accrual Sales for British Airways and Two Competitors

	1992	*1991*	*1990*	*1989*	*1988*
British Airways					
Total operating revenues	£5,566	£5,224	£4,937	£4,838	£4,257
Add (subtract) decrease (increase) in trade receivables	(65)	(107)	138	(90)	(73)
Cash revenues	£5,501	£5,117	£5,075	£4,748	£4,184
Percentage difference	**1.2%**	**2.0%**	**−2.8%**	**1.9%**	**1.7%**
American Airlines					
Total operating revenues	$14,396	$12,887	$11,720	$10,480	$8,824
Add (subtract) decrease (increase) in trade receivables	(144)	148	(65)	(53)	(104)
Cash revenues	$14,252	$13,035	$11,654	$10,427	$8,720
Percentage difference	**1.0%**	**−1.2%**	**0.6%**	**0.5%**	**1.2%**
Lufthansa					
Total operating revenues	DM18,495	DM17,219	DM15,827	DM14,314	DM12,570
Add (subtract) decrease (increase) in trade receivables	(125)	(279)	(69)	(512)	(253)
Cash revenues	DM18,369	DM16,940	DM15,758	DM13,802	DM12,317
Percentage difference	**0.7%**	**1.6%**	**0.4%**	**3.6%**	**2.0%**

Panel C. Average Receivable Collection Period (365 ÷ Receivable Turnover)

British Airways	52.1 days	49.5 days	53.4 days	56.3 days	57.0 days
American Airlines	22.2	24.8	28.6	29.9	32.3
Lufthansa	48.1	47.3	47.5	45.1	40.3

Companies that fail to present a statement of cash flows or that present an indirect method statement of cash flows necessitate a calculation of cash revenues as above.

Alternative Inventory Valuation Policy

The list of generally accepted inventory valuation approaches (or cost flow assumptions) varies greatly between countries. Although LIFO, FIFO, and weighted average are the most commonly used methods in the United States, LIFO is not permitted for use by companies in Great Britain or other British Commonwealth countries. Some countries (e.g., Australia, France, Hong Kong, Japan, and Germany) permit LIFO valuation for consolidated foreign subsidiaries but not for domestic company reports. Japan is one of the few countries permitting the use of highest-price-in, first-price-out (HIFO).

This diversity in accepted practice makes it essential for the financial analyst to carefully evaluate a company's chosen inventory valuation policy. The inventory valuation decision affects not only the inventory account on the balance sheet and, thus, a firm's liquidity and asset management indicators but also the cost of goods sold on the income statement, hence, a firm's reported profitability and solvency.

An analyst should consider a number of issues when evaluating the cost of goods sold and ending inventory. First, it is essential to remember that the various alternative inventory costing approaches are merely cost allocation methods. Each requires that a different assumption be made regarding the flow of costs from a firm's inventory of unsold goods to the cost of goods sold, and only one (i.e., specific identification) attempts to pattern the flow of costs after the actual flow of products. When inventory prices vary over time, these methods produce very different effects on the balance sheet and the income statement. Consequently, they also produce (possibly substantially) different effects on the typical balance sheet and income statement ratios used by analysts.

Consider, for example, Exhibit 6–2, which presents the income statement and selected financial ratios for two economically identical multinational companies from Japan—FIFO Company and LIFO Company—which differ only in regard to the accounting method used to value the cost of goods sold and ending inventory. A review of these financial data reveals that since inventory costs are rising, FIFO Company appears to be financially better off than LIFO Company: Earnings are higher by ¥7.8 million, the liquidity indicators of working capital and the current ratio are higher, the borrowing capacity (as measured by the debt-to-equity ratio) is greater, and the profitability indicators of return on sales, return on equity, and return on assets are superior. Only the inventory turnover ratio appears to be better for the LIFO Company. But are these indicators really depicting economic reality?

Holding the question of taxes aside, the answer to this question is an emphatic "No!" The companies are economically identical, in spite of what the financial ratios indicate. In effect, the different cost allocation assumptions inherent in LIFO and FIFO mask the real economic performance of the two companies, which happens to be equivalent. If we now add the dimension of taxes and assume that each company uses the same costing approach for both tax purposes and financial statement purposes, the conclusion is even more startling: the LIFO company is actually superior in economic performance to the FIFO Company because greater cash flow is preserved in the LIFO Company due to its lower taxable earnings. Thus, contrary to the financial indicators, the LIFO Company would be a superior investment.

A second analytical consideration concerns those companies using the LIFO method or other similar valuation methods (e.g., HIFO) that tend to or are designed to

---

EXHIBIT 6–2
Inventory Costing Methods and Financial Statement Analysis

The following are the income statements and selected financial ratios for two companies that are
identical in every respect except with regard to the method of inventory costing and the cost of goods
sold:

	FIFO Company	LIFO Company
Sales	¥75,000,000	¥75,000,000
Less: Cost of goods sold	(34,500,000)	(42,300,000)
	¥40,500,000	¥32,700,000
Less: Other operating expenses	(15,000,000)	(15,000,000)
Net income before tax (NIBT)	¥25,500,000	¥17,700,000
Earnings per share	¥2.55	¥1.77
Current ratio	1.67:1	1.57:1
Working capital	¥10,800,000	¥3,000,000
Inventory turnover	2:1	3:1
Debt-to-equity ratio	1:5.17	1:4.91
Return on assets	10.8%	8.0%
Return on equity	14%	12.1%
Return on sales	34%	24%

assign the highest costs to cost of goods sold and the lowest costs to ending inventory.
One adverse outcome of these methods concerns the quality of the ending inventory
valuation as reported on the balance sheet. Under LIFO and HIFO, the most recent
(highest) inventory costs are assigned to the cost of goods sold, while the older, usually
lower inventory costs are assigned to the ending inventory on the balance sheet. When
inflation is present, the cost values reflected in the Inventory account may be substantially undervalued relative to their actual replacement cost. Thus, not only will the
Inventory account be understated, but so also will be the level of working capital and
such ratios as the current ratio, which includes the undervalued Inventory account.

The problem of inventory value misstatement is particularly prevalent among U.S.
firms because of their propensity to use LIFO to obtain the income tax sheltering
provided by this method. It is also a problem in Japan and, to a lesser extent, Germany,
where higher-costing inventory is charged to net income in an effort to constrain taxable (and consequently book) income. In countries such as Great Britain and Italy,
where asset revaluations are permitted and/or LIFO is not permitted, inventory value
understatement is rarely encountered.[5]

---

[5]Some countries, such as the United States, do not permit the upward revaluation of inventories;
these countries usually restrict inventory adjustments to write-downs under the lower-of-cost-or-market
approach. Given the propensity for most economies to experience some degree of price inflation, the
lower-of-cost-or-market adjustments for most companies tend to be relatively immaterial in amount.
Occasionally, however, in commodity-related industries, such as the oil and gas industry, these
downward revaluations may be quite significant. Essentially every country in the world permits the
downward revaluation of inventory, but only a few, such as Brazil, Italy, and Great Britain, also permit
the upward revaluation of inventory.

EXHIBIT 6–3
Results of Worldwide LIFO Inventory Valuation Study

Country of Incorporation	Firms with Inventory	Firms with Inventory Methods Disclosure	Firms with Inventory Valued at LIFO	Percentage of LIFO-Disclosed Firms
Belgium	56	22	6	27%
Canada	328	191	14	7
France	240	129	7	5
Germany	247	54	18	33
Great Britain	607	102	2	2
Italy	140	114	57	50
Japan*	698	553	53	10
South Africa	141	119	4	3
Switzerland	112	26	1	4
United States	2,582	1,965	753	38
Total	**5,151**	**3,275**	**915**	**28%**

*Global Vantage does not distinguish between HIFO and LIFO. Consequently, Japanese firms reported as LIFO in the database may actually measure their inventory using HIFO.

To gain some perspective on the frequency with which LIFO accounting may be encountered worldwide, we conducted a study of the Compustat Global Vantage database of industrial companies. Exhibit 6–3 lists, by country,[6] the number of Global Vantage firms that report inventory, the number of those firms that disclose their method(s) of inventory valuation, and the number of firms that disclose that at least some of their inventory is valued using LIFO. The last column indicates, as expected, great variation in the incidence of LIFO firms across countries.

Concerned that the LIFO inventory values reported by companies listed on U.S. stock exchanges may be substantially undervalued, the FASB and the SEC adopted a requirement in 1978 that audited financial statements using LIFO disclose the firm's LIFO reserve in the inventory footnote.[7] The **LIFO reserve** measures the difference between the current (or replacement) cost of ending inventory and its calculated LIFO cost. Thus, by adding the LIFO reserve to the LIFO cost of ending inventory, the analyst can obtain a more reliable assessment of the economic value of ending inventory. Similarly, a more realistic value for working capital and the current ratio may also be obtained. Finally, for those analysts interested in comparing LIFO earnings to FIFO earnings, the LIFO reserve is a useful tool for such comparisons. By adding the change in the LIFO reserve from one year to the next to the net income before tax (NIBT) under LIFO, the analyst can approximate the FIFO NIBT.

[6] We omitted countries that had relatively few industrial companies on the database.

[7] *IAS No. 2*, as revised, permits the use of FIFO, weighted or average cost, specific identification, or LIFO for purposes of valuing inventories. Where LIFO is used, the impact on ending inventory, as compared to using either FIFO or weighted-average cost, should also be disclosed (i.e., the equivalent of the LIFO reserve).

A third analytical concern, also relating to companies using LIFO, involves LIFO liquidations. A **LIFO liquidation** occurs when inventory stock levels of a LIFO company decline below stock levels existing at the beginning of the fiscal period. When this occurs, cost of goods sold consists of two components: (1) cost of inventory acquired or manufactured during the period and (2) cost of inventory acquired or manufactured during past periods, going as far back in time possibly as the company's inception. These latter costs may be much lower than the current manufacturing costs, causing net income before tax to be overstated relative to non–LIFO liquidation periods. This increase in NIBT is purely a "paper profit" in that the cash flows from operations are not equivalently increased. In fact, the cash flows from operations are actually decreased under a LIFO liquidation in that the paper profits are usually subject to corporate income taxation. Consequently, in the eyes of most analysts, LIFO liquidation profits are of questionable quality.[8]

As a final point, the analyst should note that LIFO liquidations largely occur in the context of *unit or quantity* LIFO. Because of the extensive clerical effort associated with maintaining unit LIFO cost data for hundreds, and perhaps thousands, of different inventory items each year, many companies find it cost advantageous to use *dollar-value* LIFO. Under dollar-value LIFO, cost data are maintained for "pools" of inventory items, rather than for individual inventory items. One positive outcome of this approach is that the cost decreases experienced by some inventory items in a pool are offset by cost increases in others, consequently decreasing the likelihood of LIFO liquidation profits within a given pool.

Dollar-value LIFO, however, is not without its own limitations. For example, the U.S. SEC has, at times, charged companies (e.g., Stauffer Chemical Company) with overstating earnings, in part by improperly structuring dollar-value LIFO "puddles." The SEC alleged, for example, that Stauffer Chemical occasionally tailored its inventory pools selectively into very small inventory groups called *puddles* to maximize the earnings increase effect of certain product LIFO liquidations. To resolve the issue, the SEC required Stauffer to recombine a number of its 288 inventory pools, thereby lowering its reported earnings.

The issues raised above suggest that reported earnings and ratios based thereon can often be misleading. When inventory costs are rising, FIFO yields higher reported earnings than does LIFO, HIFO, or the weighted-average method. From a lender's or investor's perspective, however, higher earnings are not necessarily the most important performance criteria. Indeed, the level of cash flow is likely to be far more important to credit or investment analysts than are accrual earnings. Thus, when evaluating the financial health of a company, it is important to ascertain how the company is valuing its inventory for tax purposes, as well as for financial statement purposes.

Although it is always dangerous to make generalizations, particularly involving accounting methods, the following statement appears justified: During a period of rising materials and manufacturing costs, a company is best off if it can utilize the

---

[8]On the other hand, excess accumulations of inventory resulting from a desire to avoid the adverse tax consequences of LIFO liquidation are also undesirable and diminish the quality of liquidity ratios and turnover ratios that involve inventory.

LIFO or HIFO inventory costing method for both taxes and financial statement purposes. Not only will the cash flows of the company be preserved, but the methods also permit superior managerial decision making. In spite of these obvious advantages, some managers nonetheless adopt the FIFO or weighted-average approach (perhaps because neither LIFO nor HIFO is permitted in their particular locale). When this is the case, the analyst should investigate any special circumstances (e.g., expiring tax credits, local accounting standards) that might justify this inventory costing decision. When no special circumstances exist, a lower quality of earnings may be implied.

Amortization and Depreciation Policy

Amortization (depreciation) refers to a company's current period allocation of intangible asset cost (fixed asset cost) against its revenues. Following the cost of goods sold and income taxes, depreciation and amortization often represent the next largest deduction against revenues on the income statement. Similarly, on the balance sheet, the capitalized values of property, plant, and equipment and of intangible assets frequently represent the largest categories of a company's total assets.

Most countries around the world permit the use of such traditional depreciation methods as straight line, double-declining balance, and sum-of-the-years' digits; goodwill, if capitalized, is amortized on a straight-line basis worldwide (although other methods are permitted but are rarely used). Despite this worldwide consistency among accepted amortization and depreciation methods, the international financial analyst must be sensitive to the following considerations:

- In countries such as the United States and Great Britain where tax and book income may substantially diverge, the prevalent depreciation treatment for published financial statements is straight line; however, in countries such as Germany and Japan where tax and book income are substantially alike, the prevalent depreciation treatment is double-declining balance or sum-of-the-years' digits. Restatement for these systematic depreciation differences is difficult, if not impossible. Consequently, the analyst must look to comparisons of cash flow data to overcome these cost allocation differentials.

- Despite the presence of essentially identical assets, the depreciable life of assets may vary significantly between international companies. For example, Lufthansa, the German airline, depreciates its fleet of aircraft over an average estimated life of 10 years, whereas British Airways, its British competitor, depreciates its fleet over an estimated life of approximately 17 years. This systematic difference in depreciation policy reflects the institutional setting faced by each firm (see Chapters 8 and 9). To obtain increased data comparability between such firms, the analyst needs to adjust the depreciation expense on the income statement and accumulated depreciation on the balance sheet for such estimate differences or alternatively focus principally on cash flow data, which inherently adjust for such cost allocation differentials. For example, in the case of Lufthansa and British Airways, to place the two airlines on a common amortization basis, Lufthansa's depreciation charges could be reduced by an average of 41 percent (i.e., 1 minus (10/17)) to reflect that company's faster depreciation write-off schedule as compared to that of British Airways. Alternatively, since the cash flow from operations is inherently adjusted for depreciation charges, comparing the two airlines' performance on this financial indicator naturally overcomes any differences in reported profits attributable to such variances in cost allocation methods.

- The accounting for goodwill may vary not only in terms of method but also in terms of amortization period. Exhibit 6–4 (panel A), for example, reveals that Lufthansa amortizes its goodwill at a rate of 25 percent per year (i.e., over four years), whereas Imperial Chemical Industries Plc, a British conglomerate, immediately charges off its goodwill directly against its balance sheet reserves. Although most countries require that goodwill be capitalized to the balance sheet and then be amortized against earnings over the asset's expected economic life, in some countries (principally Germany, Italy, Japan and Great Britain), goodwill may be written off immediately against shareholders' equity (see Appendix 6A for an illustration of this approach). The charge-to-equity approach is preferred by some firms because it avoids the drag on future earnings caused by periodic goodwill amortization.[9] Analysts desiring to achieve greater data comparability between a firm using the charge-to-equity method and one using capitalization and amortization will find it easiest to restate the latter firm to a charge-to-equity basis (i.e., determine in which year restatement will be assumed to start and then write off the outstanding balance of goodwill against retained earnings, adjusting deferred income taxes for any tax effects).

- When goodwill is capitalized to the balance sheet, the acceptable period for amortization can vary dramatically. For example, most companies in Canada and the United States adopt a 40-year write-off, but in Japan and Korea, a 5-year write-off is the norm (see Exhibit 6–4, panel B). Restatement for alternative amortization periods is a relatively straightforward process, and it is usually easiest to restate from a longer period to a shorter one.[10] To execute the restatement, obtain $n + 1$ periods of historical data, where n equals the numbers of periods of comparative data desired for analytical purposes (e.g., if $n = 5$, $n + 1 = 6$).

---

[9]While the charge-to-equity method is not considered GAAP in the United States, the practice is remarkably similar to the restatement procedures followed by most U.S. lending institutions. That is, because goodwill, unlike most tangible assets, lacks a readily accessible resale market, lending institutions usually reduce a borrower's "borrowing base" (i.e., collaterizable assets) by the quantity of its goodwill. This restatement is usually executed by writing off any goodwill (and other intangibles with questionable resale value) against the borrower's net worth. As a consequence, most lending institutions modify the debt-to-equity ratio to become the debt-to-tangible-equity ratio.

[10]Most analysts find it intuitively easier to restate from longer to shorter amortization periods, and there is another reason for doing so. Given the uncertainty associated with the expected life of most intangibles, the strong preference of most professional analysts is to write intangibles off over shorter periods of time. In essence, the quality of reported earnings is generally perceived to be higher when shorter amortization and depreciation periods are in use.

Exhibit 6–4

Financial Statement Disclosures: Goodwill

Panel A. Alternative Accounting Approaches for Goodwill

Deutsche Lufthansa AG

Acquired concessions and similar rights are generally depreciated at a rate of 20 percent. Goodwill resulting from the consolidation
is depreciated at a rate of 25 percent.

Imperial Chemical Industries Plc

On the acquisition of a business, fair values are attributed to the net assets acquired. Goodwill arises where the fair value of the
consideration given for a business exceeds such net assets. UK Accounting Standards require that purchased goodwill be
eliminated from the balance sheet either upon acquisition against reserves or by amortization over a period. Elimination against
reserves has been selected as appropriate to the goodwill purchases made during recent years.

Panel B. Alternative Amortization Periods

AMR Corporation

The excess of the purchase price over the fair value of the net assets acquired (goodwill), aggregating $296.5 million at December
31, 1990, net of accumulated amortization of $22.4 million, is being amortized on a straight-line basis over 40 years.

Mitsui & Co. Ltd.

The consolidated financial statements include the accounts of the Company and its majority-owned domestic and foreign subsidiaries
(together ''the companies''). The excess of the cost of investments in subsidiaries over the equity in net assets at dates of
acquisition is being amortized over periods of five to twenty years using the straight-line method.

Panel C. Negative Goodwill

Volvo

Acquisitions of companies are accounted for using the purchase method. Shareholders' equity in the subsidiaries at date of
acquisition, including Equity in untaxed reserves, is eliminated in its entirety. Accordingly, only income arising after the date of
acquisition is included in shareholders' equity. The difference between the cost of shares in a subsidiary and the shareholders'
equity of the subsidiary at date of acquisition is, if the cost of the company's shareholding represents a higher amount (excess
value), allocated to the assets to the extent considered appropriate. The remaining excess is included in the consolidated balance
sheets as Goodwill. Negative goodwill is included in Shareholders' equity (Restricted reserves) or in Current liabilities. In the
latter case, the negative goodwill is amortized over a maximum period of five years to cover losses and/or reconstruction costs in
the acquired company.

Measure the change in the goodwill balance from $n + 1$ to n to assess the
quantity of periodic amortization and average estimated life. (Be sure to
review the footnotes to determine if there were any additions to goodwill
during this time frame.) Using the $n + 1$ balance of goodwill, recalculate the
amortization for the shorter write-off period and calculate the increase to the
expense account. It should be observed that this process is merely an
estimation process and likely to be imprecise. Depending on the availability of

historical data, a more accurate spreadsheet of the amortization process, and adjustments thereto, can be developed. As always, the accuracy of the restatement process is dictated by the availability of data and the desired level of accuracy.

- Regardless of the home country of the company under analysis, the analyst must carefully review the accompanying footnotes and supplemental schedules to see if any amortization (depreciation) policy changes were effected during the period of comparison. For example, in 1991 Union Camp, a large U.S. pulp and paper manufacturer, changed its estimate of the expected useful life of its mill equipment from 16 to 20 years. This policy change added $51 million to the company's 1991 net income and was disclosed in the footnotes. The comparability of Union Camp's financial data during this period relative to, say, Mitsubishi Paper Mills would have been dramatically altered by this policy change, unless, of course, the change brought Union Camp's policies into greater conformity with those of Mitsubishi. Since Union Camp's cash flows were unaffected by this decision (it was not undertaken for tax purposes), the statement of cash flows represents a ''safe haven'' for analysts seeking a consistent source of reliable data for analytical purposes. In effect, analysts can safely circumvent the data comparability issues created by this type of policy change by focusing on a company's CFFO or discretionary cash flows. This strategy would be particularly useful in those cases in which the level of intangibles or fixed assets is large relative to total assets.

Alternative Asset Capitalization Policies

World accounting policies with respect to the capitalization of asset values differ dramatically. Consider, for example, the array of accounting practices regarding the capitalization of interest and for research and development costs as depicted in Exhibit 6–5. For R&D costs, accepted policy runs the gamut from full expensing in the United States, to limited capitalization in Japan, to full capitalization in Brazil.

Once capitalized, the period of amortization also varies from a fixed five-year period in Japan and Sweden to a variable period of ''expected benefit'' in Brazil. Similarly, accepted policy regarding the capitalization of interest for self-constructed assets varies from ''not permitted'' in Japan to ''required'' in Brazil and the United States.

These divergences raise a number of analytical issues. First, with the exception of companies domiciled in Germany and Japan, where accepted accounting policies are driven by tax policy, the analyst must always investigate for the presence of **rear-end loading.** A basic tenet of international GAAP, commonly referred to as the *matching principle,* stipulates that when revenues are recognized on the income statement, all of the expenses associated with generating those revenues also should be recognized. Some companies, however, elect to postpone the recognition of some of these expenses through a process of rear-end loading.

EXHIBIT 6–5

Asset Capitalization Policies

Country	R&D Costs	Interest on Borrowings
United States	Expensed currently (except for software development companies).	Capitalization required for self-constructed assets.
Great Britain	Research costs expensed, but some development costs capitalized.	Capitalization permitted but not widely practiced.
Germany	Expensed currently.	Capitalization permitted but not required.
Italy	May be expensed or, if capitalized, written off over five years; practice is dictated by tax laws.	Interest on debt obtained specifically for the acquisition or construction of an asset must be capitalized (as required by tax law).
Japan	R&D for existing products expensed currently, but capitalized for new products (with five-year write-off).	Capitalization not permitted (except for real estate development companies).
Korea	Should be capitalized if the costs (1) relate to specific products or technology, (2) are identifiable, and (3) are reasonably expected to be recovered; otherwise they should be expensed.	Capitalization required.
Sweden	Capitalization is permitted (with five-year write-off).	Capitalization permitted on self-constructed assets.
Brazil	Capitalized; amortized over expected period of benefit.	Capitalization required for self-constructed assets.

Under rear-end loading, an expenditure (which may involve either an actual cash outflow or the incurrence of a liability for future cash outflows) is accounted for as an asset on the balance sheet rather than as an expense on the income statement. As a consequence, current period expenses are understated, causing net income and total assets to be overstated. Eventually, the deferred expenses pass through to the income statement and, when that occurs, the future period expenses are overstated, causing net income to be understated. Thus, rear-end loading effectively involves trading off future earnings for higher current period earnings.

Identifying that a company has engaged in rear-end loading usually involves making a subjective assessment on the part of the analyst; in effect, the analyst must be willing to conclude that, contrary to management opinion, a higher level of costs should have been deducted against current and/or past earnings than in fact were. Perhaps the best example of this involves the relatively ill-defined long-term asset account Deferred Charges. This account frequently contains a host of expenditures whose accounting treatment is ambiguous, at least in the eyes of management. Because of the uncertainty associated with the recoverability (or revenue-generating capacity) of these ''assets,'' professional analysts often take a conservative view and restate the financial statements by writing off any deferred charges against retained earnings (and adjusting the deferred income taxes to reflect the fact that the costs have probably already been expensed for tax purposes). This restatement approach is also routinely followed by most lending institutions who justify the write-off on grounds that the resale market for deferred charges (and similar intangible assets) is limited or nonexistent.

To illustrate this problem, consider the 1980s case of CUC International, Inc., a consumer shop-at-home company. Under U.S. GAAP at the time, the costs of obtaining new CUC customers could be either expensed immediately when customers signed up, or deferred and amortized over the expected life of the new membership. CUC elected the latter approach and amortized new membership costs over a three-year period. By 1988, however, the level of deferred expenses exceeded the company's reported income, and in March 1989, CUC took a $51 million write-off to eliminate not only its 1988 earnings but also those of the prior three years as well.

A second analytical concern relates to the divergence of accepted practice regarding such high profile expenditures as interest and research and development costs. U.S. GAAP, as well as that of Brazil and many other countries, requires that all costs incurred in the acquisition of an asset and the preparation for its intended use be capitalized into the asset's balance sheet valuation. A natural extension of this general philosophy is to require the capitalization of interest on funds borrowed during the period of an asset's preparation or construction. Under this practice, the amount of interest to be capitalized is based on the interest charges actually incurred for a specific project or, if unknown, the firm's weighted average cost of capital and the average construction account will ultimately be written off in the form of higher futu redepre-

ciation charges, the analyst should be concerned with the fact that current earnings will appear to be higher than anticipated because borrowing costs are being capitalized rather than expensed. Similarly, although earnings appear to be currently improved, actual cash flows are reduced by the current payments for debt service charges. Thus, under capitalization of interest, current earnings and cash flows are moving in an opposite, rather than parallel, direction.

Many professional analysts view the capitalization of interest to be an approved form of rear-end loading, arguing that since the cash outflow for interest charges occurs currently, it is inappropriate to defer the expense deduction until depreciation of the capitalized expenditure occurs at a later date. As a consequence, these professionals scan the footnotes to assess the level of currently capitalized interest[11] and then charge those amounts off against retained earnings (net of the related deferred income tax effect under the assumption that the interest charges were probably immediately expensed for tax purposes).

Exhibit 6–6, for example, presents the financial statements of a (unnamed and figures scaled) real estate development company. The data reveal that in the absence of interest capitalization, the company would have reported a pre-tax loss of $16,577 in 1992, instead of a gain of $6,130. The company was so debt-laden that current debt service charges exceeded its total revenues, as well as its existing balance in cash and cash equivalents.

---

[11]*SFAS No. 34* in the United States and *IAS No. 23* require that when interest is capitalized, the capitalized amount be disclosed in the footnotes to the financial statements.

EXHIBIT 6–6

Capitalization of Interest

	For the Six Months Ended June 30,	
Panel A. Consolidated Statement of Income	1992	1991
Total Revenues	$19,538	$18,072
Cost and expenses		
Cost of land sold	5,592	3,325
Development service expense	3,712	9,145
Interest expense	22,707	19,569
Interest capitalized	(22,707)	(19,569)
Selling, general, and administrative expenses	4,104	3,216
Total	$13,408	$15,686
Income before taxes	$6,130	$2,386
Income taxes	2,820	1,098
Adjustment from parent company	(2,820)	(1,098)
Net income	$6,130	$2,386
Panel B. Consolidated Balance Sheet	June 30, 1992	December 31, 1991
Assets		
Cash and investments	$14,313	$29,877
Accounts and notes receivable	30,852	21,659
Inventories of land	519,197	500,115
Rental real estate	13,244	13,438
Property and equipment	2,812	3,127
Other assets	4,421	3,811
Total	$584,839	$572,027
Liabilities and Shareholders' Equity		
Accounts payable and accrued liabilities	$20,908	$23,817
Notes payable	420,047	410,455
Total liabilities	$440,955	$434,272
Common stock	100	100
Additional paid-in capital	30,475	30,475
Retained earnings	113,309	107,180
Total shareholders' equity	143,884	137,755
Total	$584,839	$572,027

Obviously, a cash flow analysis would reveal that in spite of the positive accrual net earnings, the cash flow from operations was significantly negative. A second important distortion caused by the capitalization of interest involves the balance sheet valuation of "inventories of land." During the period 1991 to 1992, land values in the company's principal area of operations were substantially depressed and falling. Note, however, that as a consequence of the capitalization of interest to this account, the value of the land appears to be rising, contrary to reality. In fact, the company should probably have written down the value of its real estate holdings to their fair market value but had not as yet done so. Why the asset write-down (and the associated loss) had not yet been recognized in the financial statements is a topic we consider shortly.

A final analytical concern involves the divergence in practice relating to R&D costs. *IAS No. 9* prescribes that all R&D costs be expensed as incurred, with the exception of those development costs that must be capitalized if they meet the following criteria:

- The product or process is clearly defined, and attributable costs can be clearly identified therewith.
- The technical feasibility of the product or process has been demonstrated.
- Management has indicated its intention to produce, market, or use the product or process.
- There is clear evidence of the utility or marketability of the product or process.
- Adequate resources exist, or are reasonably expected to be available, to complete and market the product or process.

As Exhibit 6–5 reveals, however, existing GAAP for R&D varies greatly, with some countries permitting the capitalization of some (e.g., Japan) or all (e.g., Brazil) of a company's research and development outlays, and others (e.g., Germany) not permitting capitalization. In the United States and Great Britain, the accounting for such intangibles is largely dictated by whether the ''asset'' was internally or externally developed. Internally developed intangible assets are expensed immediately, whereas those intangible assets acquired from other entities (i.e., externally developed) may be capitalized to the balance sheet. This treatment produces two significant analytical concerns. First, for a company actively involved in a research and development program, little (if any) of this investment will ever appear on its balance sheet. Consequently, these companies may have significant unreported intangible asset values. Second, since little of the initial development cost is ever capitalized to the balance sheet, current earnings may be relatively understated due to R&D write-offs, with future earnings relatively overstated due to the absence of any R&D expenses to be matched with future revenues.

Several types of R&D costs have been exempted from the general treatment in the United States. Computer software development companies, for example, are permitted to capitalize R&D costs once a commercially viable prototype has been developed; however, all original or new product development costs must be expensed as incurred. Similarly, the natural resource industry is permitted to capitalize all R&D costs under the full cost method, but only some under the successful efforts method.

Asset Impairment and Revaluation

The capitalization of interest, deferred charges, and R&D costs permitted in some countries presents excellent examples of the large differences in accepted accounting practice that can exist between nations. It clearly reinforces the notion that restatement is often necessary to put financial analysis at the international level on a level playing field. The extreme positions also raise doubts about the ability of international standard setters to achieve effective harmonization. These differences must be acknowledged as challenges to effective international financial analysis, and the analyst must respond to this challenge by equipping himself or herself with the necessary tools to overcome these impediments.

Thus far, the question of *which* expenditures should be capitalized (versus expensed) was considered. We now address the related issue of valuation adjustments, either upward (revaluation) or downward (**impairment**), of expenditures that were previously recognized as assets.

Impairment

It is widely accepted around the world that if the economic value of an asset has been permanently impaired, the value of the asset should be currently written down by a charge against earnings to reflect the expected diminishment in future earnings and cash flows.[12] Just when an asset is ''permanently'' impaired, however, is a matter of professional judgment. And, in most cases, corporate management is reluctant to adjust the value of its corporate assets downward, hoping that the observed decline in value is only temporary. From an accounting standpoint, an asset write-down is unpopular for two reasons: not only are total assets and net worth reduced but also current earnings are similarly reduced.

Consider, for example, the case of Trafalgar House Plc, a British property, construction, and transportation company. In 1993, Trafalgar concluded that the economic conditions in Great Britain had deteriorated sufficiently to place in jeopardy the recoverability of certain of the company's investments. As a consequence, Trafalgar took a write-down of £397.3 million for property impairments and restructuring costs, declaring in effect the value of these assets to be ''permanently'' impaired.

Consider also the case of Southland Corporation, the struggling owner of the 7-Eleven convenience store chain. In 1987, Southland had been taken private in a $4.9 billion leveraged buyout. Unfortunately, intense competition from convenience store operators put severe pressure on Southland's earnings, which were insufficient to meet the substantial interest payments resulting from the huge debt incurred to effect the change in ownership. To reflect this diminished earnings power of its assets, Southland took a one-time write-down of $947 million in the fourth quarter of 1989. In addition, the company began negotiations with 7-Eleven Japan Co. in an effort to obtain a cash infusion for the ailing U.S. company.

Of concern to the analyst in regard to the question of permanent impairment is the vagueness inherent in existing international accounting standards, which effectively provide corporate management with considerable leeway in the timing and amount of asset write-downs. These issues are also of concern to the FASB and the IASC, which are attempting to construct guidelines that would delineate when, and by what

---

[12]If an asset has been previously revalued upward using a revaluation reserve account, the write-down should first be taken against the reserve account; and in the event that the write-down exceeds the reserve balance, the excess should be charged against current earnings.

amount, asset write-downs should occur. According to a recent FASB exposure draft on the impairment question, an asset impairment should be presumed to have occurred when any of the following conditions are found to exist:[13]

- A substantial reduction in the extent to which a plant (or other material asset) is used.
- A dramatic change in the manner in which an asset is used.
- A substantial drop in the market value of an asset.
- A significant change in the existing law or business environment, adversely affecting the utility of an asset or group of assets.
- A forecast indicating the lack of long-term profitability for an asset or group of assets.
- Costs capitalized in association with an asset, which exceed the cost to acquire or construct the asset.

While a particular set of guidelines has not as yet been accepted by the IASC or other country standard-setting organizations, the FASB exposure draft represents an excellent starting point for an analyst to evaluate whether a company's assets should be written down. It is commonly expected that these criteria will soon be adopted at an international level in response to the impairment issue.

Revaluation

The revaluation of assets is undertaken annually by companies in Britain and other Commonwealth countries and periodically (i.e., when mandated by the government) in Italy (see Exhibit 6–7, panels A and B). In Brazil, asset values are revalued and indexed for that country's high rate of inflation (Exhibit 6–7, panel C), and in Germany and Sweden, revaluation is permitted, but only in unusual circumstances (see Chapters 9 and 11). In Japan and the United States, however, a strict application of the historical cost rule is followed, and consequently revaluations are not permitted (except for marketable securities).

Although professional analysts applaud the efforts of Japan and the United States to secure *objective* asset values, they readily point out that the financial statements of companies from these countries can be very misleading, particularly in regard to long-lived, appreciating assets such as property and long-term investments. These analysts correctly observe that Japanese and U.S. financial statements often transfer the burden of obtaining up-to-date asset values from the data-presenting company (which

---

[13]Financial Accounting Standards Board exposure draft, "Accounting for the Impairment of Long-Lived Assets" (Stamford, CT, November 29, 1993). Exposure drafts are proposed accounting standards on which the public is invited to provide comments to the FASB prior to the issuance of an official statement of financial accounting standards.

EXHIBIT 6–7

Financial Statement Disclosures: Asset Revaluation

Panel A. British Airways Plc
Tangible fixed assets

(a) Basis

Tangible fixed assets are stated at cost except for certain aircraft fleets and properties that are included at valuation. Depreciation is calculated to write off the cost or valuation, less residual value, on the straight-line basis.

(b) Fleet

Cost/valuation. Apart from the Concorde fleet, which remains at a zero book value, the majority of the owned aircraft fleets were professionally valued on a market value basis at March 31, 1988, and are included in the financial statements on the basis of that valuation, with subsequent expenditure at cost, less depreciation.

The cost of the aircraft that have been financed in part by loans, finance leases, and hire purchase arrangements in foreign currency is adjusted at each year-end to take account of the sterling cost of related repayments during the year and the translation of outstanding liabilities on such foreign currency borrowings at the year-end rate of exchange, or the appropriate forward rate where liabilities have been covered forward.

Panel B. Fiat
Plant, property, and equipment are recorded at purchase or construction cost. These values are adjusted where specific laws of the country in which the assets are located allow revaluation to reflect, even if only partially, the changes in the purchasing power of the local currency or when a revaluation is obligatory. Plant, property, and equipment as of December 31, 1991 and 1990, comprise the following (in billions of lire):

| | 1991 | | | 1990 |
	Gross	*Accumulated Depreciation*	*Net*	*Net*
Land and buildings	9,497	2,121	7,376	5,588
Plant and machinery	23,504	15,184	8,320	7,677
Other equipment	3,457	—	2,559	1,705
Construction in progress	39,017	19,431	19,586	16,386

In 1991, Italian legislation (law 413/91) imposed on companies the compulsory revaluation of industrial and civil buildings and land to be developed by using coefficients established by the same law. The effect of the compulsory revaluations on consolidated fixed assets is approximately 1,600 billion lire. Depreciation on revalued amounts will be calculated beginning in 1992.

presumably is in the best position to know those values) to the financial statement user, who may be ill-equipped to assess such information. At the extreme, this situation may lead to mispriced securities in the Japanese and U.S. stock markets.

The systematic revaluation of assets in some countries, and the absence of revaluation in others, is another source of data differentials. Unless an analyst has a particular vantage point that would permit him or her to know the underlying asset values of a U.S. or Japanese firm, it is usually best not to try to revalue those assets to achieve comparability with, say, a British firm. Instead, since the revaluation reserve is publicly disclosed in the shareholders' equity section of the balance sheet, it is a simpler task to readjust the British firm's asset values downward to achieve parity. If the goal of the financial analysis, however, is acquisition, the use of historical cost values may limit the usefulness of the financial analysis.

Exhibit 6–7 (continued)
Financial Statement Disclosures: Asset Revaluation

Panel C. Cruzeiro do Sul S.A.—Property and Equipment
Thousands of Cruzeiros

	12/31/91		12/31/90		
	Monetarily Corrected Cost	*Accumulated Depreciation*	*Monetarily Corrected Cost*	*Accumulated Depreciation*	*Depreciation Rates —% p.a. Jan./Dec.*
Flight equipment					
B-727/100	33,074,826	(19,145,174)	33,074,826	(13,048,407)	20[a]
B-737/200	67,596,296	(35,675,823)	72,758,427	(24,921,020)	16.6
Spare and repair parts	33,407,662	(28,659,379)	26,042,902	(20,752,220)	[b]
Ground equipment	7,190,724	(7,084,783)	6,453,936	(6,268,781)	10.0–20.0
Real estate	7,401,335	(4,173,830)	3,110,627	(1,692,185)	4.0
	148,670,843	(94,783,989)	141,440,718	(66,682,613)	

[a]In accordance with the service life of the equipment which, in the case of flight equipment, was established based on an appraisal report of October 1988.
[b]Depreciated at the same rates as the related equipment.

As a result of the flight equipment revaluation made in October 1988, depreciation expense and cost of goods written off were charged to results of operations in 1991 in the amounts of Cr$16,232,228 thousand and Cr$513,716 thousand, respectively. The amount of Cr$42,509,046 thousand remains in Property and equipment and will be recorded in the results of operations of future years when realized. The revaluation reserve made that year is Cr$7,017,432 thousand lower than the remaining balance in Property and equipment due to partial compensation with losses determined in prior years.

This year, in accordance with article 2 of Law 8200/91, a special monetary correction was calculated for the items classified in Property and equipment. The calculation was based on the IGP-DI (General price Index) variation since the acquisition or revaluation date of the items through January 1991. The positive difference in relation to the individual value of each item was added to the cost of such item with contra entries to the Capital reserve denominated "special monetary correction."

Off-Balance Sheet Debt

The problem of **off-balance sheet debt**—obligations not reported on the face of the balance sheet—plagues the accounting of every country in the world, to a greater or lesser extent. In this section, the more common forms of off-balance sheet debt are considered, as well as techniques to compensate for their impact.

Unconsolidated Debt

Accepted practice with respect to the consolidation of controlled subsidiaries varies greatly between nations (see Appendix 6A). In the United States, all majority-controlled subsidiaries (except those in bankruptcy or in the process of being sold) must be consolidated with the financial results of the parent company; however, in Japan, controlled subsidiaries may remain unconsolidated and, instead, are accounted for by the equity method. This presents the anomalous situation in Japan (and other countries) that debt obligations legally attributable to the parent company may remain unconsolidated.[14] Even in the United States, however, the debt of a joint venture that is guaranteed by the venture partners (i.e., the parent companies) may remain off-balance sheet to the partners because joint ventures are accounted for by the equity method.[15] As a consequence, the debt position of the parent, as revealed by its balance sheet, appears less highly leveraged than in fact it really is. To overcome this, it is a simple matter to adjust (increase) both the assets and the liabilities of the parent for the quantity of the debt, carried on the books of the unconsolidated subsidiary or joint venture, but accruing to the parent by virtue of legal guarantees. This permits the analyst to obtain a truer assessment of the parent's effective level of gearing.

To illustrate, consider the case of General Motors, a large U.S. automaker, and its wholly owned financing subsidiary, General Motors Acceptance Corporation. Prior to 1988, GM accounted for GMAC on an unconsolidated basis using the equity method. Beginning in that year, as a consequence of the adoption of *SFAS No. 94* by the FASB, GM consolidated the operations of GMAC, and the effect of this accounting change can be illustrated by comparing the total debt-to-equity ratio for GM in 1992 both with and without the operations of GMAC:

	1992
Total debt-to-equity: without consolidation	18.5%
Total debt-to-equity: with consolidation	29.7%
Change	61%

These figures clearly illustrate the dramatic effect on solvency metrics that results when a parent is able to off-load debt on an unconsolidated subsidiary or joint venture.

---

[14]Frequently, when a subsidiary or affiliate company undertakes a bank lending agreement, additional guarantees for the loan may be sought from a parent company or a majority shareholder. Like a cosigner on a note, the parent company effectively assures the lender that if the subsidiary is unable to fulfill the debt contract, it will assume responsibility for the debt servicing and repayment. From the perspective of a parent company, this type of guarantee is an executory contract—no obligation arises until some future event (i.e., default by the subsidiary) occurs—and thus must be disclosed in the parent company's footnotes if the commitments are material in amount.

[15]In the United States, for example, *SFAS No. 94,* "Consolidation of All Majority-Owned Subsidiaries," does not cover joint ventures. Thus, if a parent company is involved in a number of joint ventures that have significant outstanding lines of credit guaranteed by the parent, the debt will appear only on the financial statements of the joint venture. In the view of many analysts, it is imperative to consider a worst-case scenario in which the joint venture fails and the parent is legally obligated to assume the guaranteed debt. Obviously, the worst-case scenario may never arise; however, if the investment or lending opportunity appears viable even under the worst-case conditions, the analyst can gain a certain degree of confidence through such information. Under *IAS No. 5,* the preferred accounting for joint ventures is proportionate consolidation, although the equity method is also allowed. When proportionate consolidation is adopted, the problem of unconsolidated off-balance sheet debt is avoided.

Contingent Liabilities

Contingencies, or **contingent liabilities,** represent a category of potential liabilities. Whether a contingent liability is reported in the footnotes or not, however, is largely determined by management's assessment of the probability of the liability's expected occurrence. Under *SFAS No. 5* in the United States and *IAS No. 10,* if a contingent loss is "probable" and can be reasonably estimated, a liability should be formally accrued on the balance sheet, along with a loss on the income statement. If, on the other hand, the loss is only "reasonably possible" or if probable but the amount cannot be reasonably estimated, only footnote disclosure is required (see Exhibit 6–8, panels A and B). Finally, if realization of the loss and, hence liability, is judged only to be "remote," then no disclosure whatsoever is required.

The "probable" threshold for purposes of applying *SFAS No. 5* or *IAS No. 10* is not explicit in the accounting literature. It is generally considered to be well above a 50 percent probability, somewhere between a probability of 70 to 90 percent, depending on the source. But just what conditions indicate a probable liability versus a reasonably possible liability vary between managers and often between auditors. More often than not, "probable" liabilities end up being reported only in the footnotes or, unfortunately, not at all.

Consider, for example, the case of Bristol-Myers Squibb, Dow Corning, and Merck, three international pharmaceutical companies involved in the manufacture of silicon breast implants. In the late 1980s, medical tests revealed that the implants were capable of leaking and that silicon could be linked to various health problems experienced by implant patients. Because of uncertainty regarding the extent of company liability associated with the defective implants, none of the companies accrued losses (or liabilities) for the class action lawsuits filed against them until early 1994, at which time the firms agreed to contribute various sums to a trust fund on behalf of the implant patients.

This case illustrates the all-too-often reluctance by management to recognize a loss and the related liability associated with contingent future events. Although the desire to avoid unpleasant news is quite natural, it suggests that analysts should be prepared to take an aggressive stance in regard to restating published financial statements with respect to contingent liabilities.

Leveraged Employee Stock Option Plans

Another important source of off-balance sheet (but guaranteed) debt involves the increasingly popular leveraged employee stock ownership plan (ESOP). ESOPs are usually established to provide a company's rank-and-file employees with a means to obtain an ownership interest in the company that employs them. The employing company may donate shares of stock to the ESOP annually as a function of the company's profitability or make shares available for purchase by the ESOP. A twist on this basic theme is for the ESOP to borrow funds to buy additional shares of stock. Since the ESOP's only asset is usually the company's previously contributed shares, such borrowings must be guaranteed by the ESOP sponsor.

EXHIBIT 6–8
Financial Statement Disclosures: Commitments and Contingent Liabilities

Panel A. Mitsui & Co., Ltd.

The companies customarily enter into long-term purchase contracts for certain items, principally iron ore, copper ore, machinery and equipment, and aluminum ingots, either at fixed prices or at basic purchase prices adjustable to market. In general, customers of the companies are also parties to the contracts or by separate agreements are committed to purchase the commodities from the companies; such customers are large Japanese industrial companies. Long-term purchase contracts at fixed or basic purchase prices amounted to approximately ¥890,300 million ($5,634,810 thousand) at March 31, 1990. Scheduled deliveries are at various dates through 2001.

The companies had financing commitments totaling ¥68,985 million ($436,614 thousand) at March 31, 1990, principally for financing, on a deferred-payment basis, the cost of equipment to be purchased by their customers through 1993.

In the furtherance of their trading activities, it is a customary practice for the companies to guarantee, severally or jointly with others, indebtedness of certain of their customers and suppliers and of certain associated companies, as well as to guarantee the performance of contracts by such entities. At March 31, 1990, the aggregate amount of such guarantees was ¥256,584 million ($1,623,949 thousand), including ¥64,479 million ($408,095 thousand) relating to associated companies.

Various claims and legal actions are pending against the Company and its subsidiaries in respect of contractual obligations and other matters arising out of the conduct of the companies' business. Provision has been made for estimated liabilities under certain claims. In the opinion of management, based upon the advice of counsel, any additional liability will not materially affect the consolidated financial position or results of operations of the Company and its subsidiaries.

Panel B. Volvo

	1991	1990
Discounted bills	520	308
Guarantees		
Bank loans and trade bills—associated companies	80	182
Bank loans—customers and others	565	79
Export credits	29	—
Other contingent liabilities	3,497	2,701
Total	4,691	3,270

The amount for guarantees to customers and others, pertaining to bank loans, 565, includes the unutilized portion of approved credit facilities, 170.

Other contingent liabilities include repurchase guarantees in the amount of 1,394 (984) pertaining to leasing vehicles.

In accordance with a price clause in the agreement with Renault, the payments made for Volvo's and Renault's car operations can to a certain extent be adjusted depending on the companies' future profit levels, not to exceed FRF 1 billion.

As of January 1, 1993, Volvo's subsidiaries in the United States will apply the new American accounting rules (FAS 106), regarding health-care and other post-retirement benefits for personnel leaving the company, which becomes effective on that date. The total amount pertaining to commitments made through December 31, 1991, has been estimated at between 490 and 770. This amount is not included in Total contingent liabilities shown above.

The leveraged ESOP creates a particularly incestuous set of relations if the ESOP's only source of cash is the company sponsor (which is often the case). Note that if the sponsor experiences financial difficulties, not only is the sponsor's own debt placed in jeopardy, but so too is the debt of the ESOP if the dividend payments on the sponsor's stock (and thus the ESOP's assets) are impaired. If the ESOP holds investments (and hence cash flow sources) other than the sponsor's stock, there is clearly a greater margin for error; but, if the ESOP's only asset is the sponsor's stock, the analyst would be wise to treat the debt of the ESOP as that of the company sponsor.

Executory Contracts

A final category of off-balance sheet debt involves a group of contractual agreements called **executory contracts.** These contractual commitments are accounted for off the balance sheet because the event triggering the commitment has usually not yet occurred. As a consequence, executory contracts are disclosed principally through the footnotes, much like a contingent liability. Examples include operating leases, purchase or supply agreements, loan guarantees on the borrowings of related companies, take-or-pay contracts, and working capital maintenance agreements, to name only a few.

To illustrate the accounting conundrum created by these contracts, consider the following two contractual relationships:

1. A company borrows $1 million from a bank, agreeing to repay the borrowed amount, plus interest of $150,000 over a 12-month period.
2. A company signs a noncancellable, nontransferable lease on retail space, agreeing to pay $1.15 million in rent payments over the next 12 months.

In both cases, the company has incurred an economic liability of approximately equivalent amounts (i.e., $1.15 million over the one-year period, ignoring the small differential associated with the time value of money); however, only in the first relationship is the company obligated to record an accounting liability for future payments.

The second relationship depicts a typical operating lease, which in many countries (including the United States) requires no balance sheet recognition of the future lease payments. Instead, the lease payments are recognized only on the income statement as a lease expense, when paid. When operating leases are carried off the balance sheet, existing international GAAP (i.e., *IAS No. 17*) usually requires that the minimum future lease payments be disclosed in the company's footnotes.

It is often difficult for cash flow minded analysts to understand why the accounting profession differentiates operating leases (and similar executory contracts) from other accounting liabilities. Perhaps the best explanation of this can be seen by examining the similarities and differences in the two preceding relationships. Although both contracts involve approximately equivalent cash outflows, they differ as to the amount of consideration received at contract signing. With the bank loan, consideration of $1 million was immediately received, and, thus, a liability for the repayment of that

---
EXHIBIT 6-9

Accounting for Leases

Country	Operating Leases	Capital Leases
Brazil	All leases, regardless of economic substance, are treated as operating leases. If capital leases are treated as operating leases, footnote disclosure of the asset and liability is required.	Not applicable.
Germany	Leases are carried off the balance sheet but must be disclosed in footnotes if material.	Accounting treatment follows complex tax rules.
Great Britain	Treatment and criteria are similar to those in the United States.	Criteria are similar to those in the United States; however, capitalized leases are carried at face value.
Italy	All leases, regardless of economic substance, are treated as operating leases. No footnote disclosures required.	Not applicable.
Japan	Substantially all leases are treated as operating but no disclosures are required.	Not applicable.
Korea	Treatment and criteria are similar to those in the United States.	Treatment and criteria are similar to those in the United States. Present value of lease obligation is reported if significantly different from face value.
Sweden	Leases are carried off the balance sheet unless the lease contract requires acquisition of the leased asset at some point during the lease period.	If a lease agreement provides for a deferred acquisition, at terms specified in the lease contract, balance sheet disclosure is recommended. Leases are valued at face value of obligation.
United States	Leases are carried off the balance sheet, with footnote disclosure of future minimum, noncancelable lease payments.	Capitalized asset and liability are carried at present value of minimum future lease payments.

---

amount must be recorded. With the operating lease, however, only a *promise* of future consideration (i.e., the opportunity to utilize the retail space) was received.

For many analysts, this subtle distinction is irrelevant; what matters is that the company has a noncancelable obligation to make future cash payments. Similarly, in the eyes of many financial statement users, this condition alone is sufficient justification to merit inclusion of the economic liability in the accounting statements. Given this particular viewpoint, it is a simple matter to restate a company's financial statements for these unreported obligations if adequate information disclosures exist. As Exhibit 6–9 reveals, many countries (e.g., Brazil, Italy, and Japan) fail to capitalize any type of lease, and for those countries that do (e.g., Germany, Korea, and Sweden), the level of financial disclosures is quite limited. Thus, despite the IASC recommended treatment, only Great

Britain and the United States appear to adequately conform to the reporting expectations of *IAS No. 17.* Consequently, for both British and U.S. companies and those foreign companies that do provide adequate footnote disclosure, the restatement of financial statements to depict noncapitalized leases on the balance sheet is relatively straightforward.

To illustrate how this restatement can be undertaken, consider the financial data of Global Enterprises, Inc., a multinational company headquartered in the United States and presented in Exhibit 6–10.

Exhibit 6–10 reveals that GE leases substantial quantities of retail space, all via operating leases. To assess the impact of these operating leases on the financial statements of GE, we adopt an approach of treating all operating leases as capital leases, which involves capitalizing the present value of the future lease payments on GE's balance sheet as both a liability and an asset. Assuming that GE's incremental cost of borrowing at July 30, 1993, is 10 percent (the company's footnotes revealed that GE's short-term weighted average cost of capital was 9.3 percent and its long-term notes carried interest rates of approximately 9.75 percent), an estimate of the present value of the minimum future lease payments after 1993 total approximately $350.8 million. Using this estimated figure, the analyst then increases GE's long-term assets (i.e., leased property) by $350.8 million and its liabilities by an equivalent amount.[16]

Another executory contract deriving its existence from banking relations is the **working capital maintenance agreement.** Instead of guaranteeing the full performance of a debt contract, a parent company may guarantee only certain aspects of a contract. For example, since most debt contracts specify that the existing financial condition of a borrower be maintained, a working capital maintenance agreement (WCMA) may be negotiated wherein a parent or affiliate company commits to maintaining the level of working capital of the borrower. Note the executory aspect of this agreement: In the event that the borrower's working capital falls below the level specified by the debt agreement, the guarantor is obligated to provide the necessary cash infusion to maintain the working capital level for the remaining life of the contract.

Most managers view a WCMA as a bottomless ''black hole'' in that there are seldom any limits (other than the life of the debt contract) on the required cash infusions. On more than one occasion, a guarantor has found it less costly to merely pay off the debt contract as a means to escape the perpetual cash flow drain created by a WCMA. Thus, analysts would be wise to note this view, and given that current GAAP disclosures for some countries require the presentation of the basic elements of an existing WCMA in the guarantor's footnotes, it is important to consider the impact of such commitments on the future cash flows of a company.

---

[16]More specifically, the accounting entry would appear as follows:

Dr. Leased assets	$350.8 million	
Cr. Short-term lease obligation		$50.8 million
Cr. Long-term lease obligation		$300.0 million

The analyst should note that restating the balance sheet with this entry also requires a consideration of the effect of the restatement on the income statement. With capitalization, the lease expense needs to be replaced by depreciation expense (on the newly capitalized asset) and interest expense on the lease liability. Hence, capitalization requires that the analyst make certain assumptions regarding depreciation on the newly capitalized asset (i.e., method, salvage value, expected life).

EXHIBIT 6–10

GLOBAL ENTERPRISES, INC.

Panel A. Consolidated Balance Sheet (July 30, 1993)

Assets	
Total current assets	$529,544
Net property, plant, and equipment	264,118
Excess of cost over net assets of subsidiaries acquired, less applicable amortization	60,597
Other assets and deferred charges, at cost less applicable amortization	10,626
Total assets	$864,885
Liabilities and Stockholders' Equity	
Total current liabilities	$271,293
Deferred federal and state income taxes	14,167
Long-term debt, excluding current installments	11,133
Stockholders' equity	
Common stock of $.10 par value. Authorized 100 million; issued 37,461,475	3,746
Capital in excess of par value	108,971
Retained earnings	455,575
Total stockholders' equity	$568,292
Total liabilities and stockholders' equity	$864,885

Panel B. Footnote Disclosures: Leases

The company conducts the major portion of its retail operations from leased store premises under leases that will expire within the next 25 years. Such leases generally contain renewal options exercisable at the option of the company. In addition to minimum rental payments, certain leases provide for payment of taxes, maintenance, and percentage rentals based upon sales in excess of stipulated amounts.

	1993
Total rental expense was as follows:	
Minimum rentals	$55,980
Percentage rentals	10,735
	$66,715

At July 30, 1993, minimum rental commitments under non-cancellable leases were as follows:

Year	
1994	$ 55,892
1995	54,884
1996	53,434
1997	52,107
1998	50,606
1999–2003	210,166
2004–2008	129,807
2009–2013	54,572
after 2013	4,918
	$666,386

A final example is the **take-or-pay contract,** sometimes called a *thru-put contract.* Under a take-or-pay contract, one company agrees to make specific future cash payments to another for a predetermined minimum quantity of products or services. Payment for the minimum quantity is required regardless of whether a buyer desires, or is even able to accept, the product. Hence, if a buyer ceases operations, either temporarily or permanently, the cash outflow required by the take-or-pay contract must be maintained. Existing GAAP in the United States and elsewhere requires that a company disclose the existence of and the minimum cash flows required under such contracts, thereby enabling the financial statement user to more accurately project the future cash flows of a company under various operating scenarios. *IAS No. 10* requires only that when such contracts may lead to contingent losses, those losses be accrued if their occurrence is probable, or footnoted if occurrence is reasonably probable.

Balance Sheet Reserves

In the United States, the shareholders' equity section of the balance sheet is commonly segmented into three principal parts. *Contributed capital* includes the par or stated value of any issued common or preferred shares, as well as any contributed capital in excess of par or stated value. *Earned capital* includes retained earnings, both appropriated and unappropriated. Lastly, there are the *adjustments to shareholders' equity* that include any shares held in treasury, the cumulative foreign currency translation adjustment (to be discussed in Chapter 7), and any unrealized gains and losses on a company's long-term portfolio of investments (see Appendix 6A).

In the financial statements of many non–U.S. companies, however, a fourth category is often observed as part of shareholders' equity, namely one or more ''reserve'' accounts.[17] These equity reserve accounts may arise for a variety of reasons, and some of the most common are as follows:

Account	Purpose or Source of Origination
Revaluation reserve	The cumulative (credit) balance resulting from the periodic (e.g., as in Brazil and Italy) revaluation of noncurrent assets to reflect their changing market values, which is usually unavailable for distribution
Legal (or statutory) reserves	The cumulative balance of retained profits (usually 5–10 percent of annual earnings) that must be legally reinvested in the operations of a company and that is usually unavailable for distribution (e.g., as in Japan and Sweden)
Restricted reserves	The cumulative balance of retained earnings whose retention is required by a company's charter of association or incorporation and that is usually unavailable for distribution (e.g., as in Italy and Sweden)

---

[17]Usually, retained earnings is considered to be a reserve account (e.g., Profit and Loss Reserve).

From an analytical perspective, these reserves create a variety of financial effects, including these:

- Restricting, to a greater extent, the ability of a company to pay dividends.
- Preserving, on average, a higher portion of retained profits.
- Creating a form of legally or statutorily enforced corporate reinvestment.

Not unexpectedly, one outcome of the use of equity reserves is a somewhat lower return on equity, at least as compared with the United States as the following data for 1993 reveal:

	Average ROE
United States	14.9
Great Britain	13.5
Japan	11.2
Sweden	8.0

Available Reconciliations to U.S. GAAP

The U.S. SEC grants foreign firms whose securities trade on national exchanges in the United States, and thus that are required to file financial statements with the agency, the alternative of presenting financial statements prepared in accordance with U.S. GAAP or of presenting financial statements according to the accounting principles of their home country. If the latter alternative is chosen, additional disclosures reconciling net income and shareholders' equity under home country GAAP to U.S. GAAP must accompany financial statements filed with the SEC. Arguably, the most famous of such reconciliations was made in 1993 by Daimler-Benz AG of Germany, which is reproduced in Exhibit 6–11.

Daimler-Benz, the largest manufacturer in Germany, was widely acknowledged to be experiencing financial problems in 1993. Despite these problems, Daimler had a long record of consistently healthy earnings under German GAAP. Due to its urgent need to gain access to U.S. financial markets, Daimler became the first German company to seek listing on a major U.S. stock exchange and, as a result, subjected itself to U.S. GAAP disclosure requirements. The reconciliation to U.S. GAAP revealed what many had expected: that German accounting techniques had effectively hidden Daimler's inability to generate a profit—Daimler's German GAAP net income for the first six months of 1993 was DM168 million versus a net loss of DM949 million under U.S. GAAP!

The Daimler disclosures effectively vindicated the SEC for its tough stance on foreign companies that were unwilling to disclose U.S. GAAP results in exchange for full access to U.S. investors. However, Exhibit 6–11 does contain one element of compromise: the reconciliation disclosures fail to facilitate a restatement of a foreign company's assets and liabilities to U.S. GAAP.

EXHIBIT 6–11

DAIMLER-BENZ AG
Notes to Unaudited Interim Condensed Consolidated Financial Statements
(in millions, except per share amounts)

The following is a summary of the significant adjustments to net income for the six-month periods ended June 30, 1993 and 1992, and to stockholders' equity at June 30, 1993 and December 31, 1992, which would be required if U.S. GAAP had been applied instead of German GAAP.

	Six Months Ended June 30,	
	1993	*1992*
Net income as reported in the consolidated income statements under German GAAP	DM168	DM1,073
Less: Income and losses applicable to minority shareholders	(51)	84
Adjusted net income under German GAAP	117	1,157
Add: Changes in appropriated retained earnings—provisions, reserves, and valuation differences	(1,615)	(169)
	(1,498)	988
Other adjustments required to conform with U.S. GAAP		
Long-term contracts	30	70
Goodwill and business acquisitions	(33)	(35)
Business dispositions		337
Pensions and other postretirement benefits	(135)	80
Foreign currency translation	(7)	161
Financial instruments	(293)	(199)
Other	67	(130)
Deferred taxes	920	(255)
Net income (loss) in accordance with U.S. GAAP before cumulative effect of a change in accounting principle	(949)	1,017
Cumulative effect of change in accounting for postretirement benefits other than pensions as of January 1, 1992, net of tax of DM 33		(52)
Net income (loss) in accordance with U.S. GAAP	**(949)**	**965**
Earnings (loss) per share in accordance with U.S. GAAP	DM(20.37)	DM20.73*
Earnings (loss) per American depositary share in accordance with U.S. GAAP†	DM(2.04)	DM2.07*

*Includes the negative effect of change in accounting for postretirement benefits other than pensions of DM 1.12 per share (DM 0.11 per American depositary share).
†Earnings per American depositary share are calculated on the basis of 10 American depositary shares for every ordinary share.

A General Framework for Restatement

Given sufficient information for an informative restatement, how should one go about it? The approach taken in this section assumes that the analyst simulates an "opening" of a company's accounting ledger for a given period and debits and credits various accounts. The purpose is to achieve a cost-effective and preferable representation of financial results for the purposes the analyst has in mind. The approach also retains the

Exhibit 6–11 (continued)

	At June 30, 1993	At Dec. 31, 1992
Stockholders' equity as reported in the consolidated balance sheets under German GAAP	DM18,938	DM19,719
Less: Minority interest	(1,260)	(1,228)
Adjusted stockholders' equity under German GAAP	17,678	18,491
Add: Appropriated retained earnings—provisions, reserves, and valuation differences*	8,316	9,931
	25,994	28,422
Other adjustments required to conform with U.S. GAAP		
Long-term contracts	161	131
Goodwill and business acquisitions	1,844	1,871
Pensions and other postretirement benefits	(1,347)	(1,212)
Foreign currency translation	203	(342)
Financial instruments	287	580
Other	(1,672)	(1,708)
Deferred taxes	761	(138)
Stockholders' equity in accordance with U.S. GAAP	26,231	27,604

*The adjustment to stockholders' equity of DM8,316 and DM9,931 would have reduced other provisions at June 30, 1993, and December 31, 1992, by DM5,945 and DM8,105, respectively. The remainder of the adjustments would have increased inventories and other receivables under U.S. GAAP.

logic of the double-entry accounting model and thereby imposes a discipline on the analyst to fully consider the effects of restatement on financial reports.

To describe this approach to restatement and to discuss some of the issues an analyst may encounter when attempting to achieve a useful restatement, we adapt an actual analyst's evaluation of a major German conglomerate, which we will call *Blauweiss AG*. Comparative balance sheets and an income statement for one recent year is presented in Exhibit 6–12.

The objective of the restatement is to reflect U.S. GAAP to the maximum extent practicable on the financial statements of *Blauweiss* to make them more comparable. The following is a summary of some important differences between German and U.S. GAAP identified by the analyst (see also Chapter 9). For some of these differences, the analyst has explicitly estimated their effects on a comparison of *Blauweiss'* financial statements with those of U.S. companies. For other differences, sometimes the best an analyst can do is merely note their existence and subjectively incorporate their impact on financial ratios and other measures of risk and return. For still others, the analyst may find it beneficial to undertake a partial restatement.

Excess Depreciation.   Most deductions claimed for tax purposes must also be booked for accounting purposes by German companies. Consequently, items such as accelerated depreciation claimed for taxes are also reported as expenses for shareholder reporting purposes. Had the straight-line method been used for book purposes, which is common in the United States and most other countries, the analyst estimated that the

EXHIBIT 6–12

BLAUWEISS AG

Panel A. Condensed German GAAP Balance Sheet, December 31, 19x9 (DM millions)

Current Assets

Cash and short-term investments	DM3,574	
Accounts receivable	4,704	
Inventories	2,898	
Total current assets		DM11,176

Current Liabilities

Debt	(607)	
Payables	(2,654)	
Accruals and provisions	(4,444)	
		(7,705)
Net Current Assets		3,471
Fixed assets	13,089	
Accumulated depreciation	(9,216)	
		3,873
Intangible assets	449	
Other assets	721	
		1,171
		8,515
Pension provision		(3,472)
Other liabilities		(50)
		DM4,993

Shareholders' Equity

Common ordinary capital	2,446	
Retained earnings	2,547	
Total shareholders' equity		**DM4,993**

Panel B. German GAAP Income Statement, Year Ended December 31, 19x9 (DM millions)

Sales	DM22,330	
Inventory change/capitalized work	1,559	
Operating output	23,889	
Other operating income	688	
Cost of materials	(12,361)	
Staff costs	(7,830)	
Other operating expenses	(2,653)	
Income from participations	95	
Depreciation & amortization	(995)	
Value adjustments	(21)	
Net interest	292	
Profit on ordinary activities		DM1,104
Extraordinary results		(98)
Taxes		(501)
Net income		**DM505**

fixed assets would have been DM1,450 million higher as of the most recent balance sheet date. It is also estimated that straight-line depreciation was less than German tax basis depreciation in 19x9 by DM56 million.

The following journal entry gives recognition to these facts:

Ref.	Account Titles	Debit	Credit
a	Accumulated Depreciation	1,450	
	Depreciation and Amortization		
	(Retained Earnings)		56
	Retained Earnings		1,394

The effect on retained earnings is seen to consist of two components: the effect on the *current* period's earnings and the effect on *prior* periods' earnings. Thus, an entry similar to this one would be made for all periods that the analyst chose to restate.

Both U.S. and German GAAP provide for a proper matching of income tax expense to the book income before taxes for a period (however, the numerous book/tax conformity rules in the German tax code reduce the materiality of deferred taxes in that country). The following entry is made to capture the effect of the timing difference between book and tax income due to different depreciation methods:

Ref.	Account Titles	Debit	Credit
b	Taxes (Retained Earnings)	28	
	Retained Earnings	770	
	Deferred Taxes		798

Deferred Taxes is credited for the cumulative timing difference of DM1,450 multiplied by an assumed incremental tax rate of 55 percent.[18] The effects on income of current and prior periods is identical in concept to the adjustments made for excess depreciation.

Contingency Reserves.   Contingency reserves are a principal means used by German companies to smooth earnings. As evidence of the contingent nature of these reserves, the other income caption in German profit and loss statements usually includes write-backs of prior year reserves no longer considered necessary. The analyst estimated that at least DM900 million of the amounts included in Accruals and Provisions would not be allowable under U.S. GAAP. New accruals in 19x9 are roughly estimated at DM50 million and are thought to be a component of Other Operating Expenses.

---

[18]The normal German federal tax rate for corporations subject to unlimited tax liability is 50 percent. The incremental effect of local income taxes can vary widely.

The following journal entries recognize these facts. It is assumed that the first entry creates a timing difference between book income before taxes and taxable income, thus necessitating the second entry.

Ref.	Account Titles	Debit	Credit
c	Accruals and Provisions	900	
	Other Operating Expenses (Retained Earnings)		50
	Retained Earnings		850
d	Taxes (Retained Earnings)	28	
	Retained Earnings	467	
	Deferred Taxes		495

Goodwill.   *Blauweiss's* present accounting policy is to capitalize and amortize goodwill from acquisitions over a period of four years. Considering that (1) common U.S. practice is to amortize goodwill over a 40-year amortization period and (2) *Blauweiss* has not recently acquired major subsidiaries, the analyst estimates that goodwill is understated as of December 31, 19x9, by DM285 million and that earnings for 19x9 are overstated by DM79 million.

The entry to record the adjustment to goodwill and shareholders' equity accounts is identical in concept to the depreciation adjustments made earlier:

Ref.	Account Titles	Debit	Credit
e	Intangible Assets	285	
	Depreciation and Amortization (Retained Earnings)		79
	Retained Earnings		206

However, the recognition of deferred taxes on differences between the financial statement carrying amount and the tax basis of goodwill depends on whether (and over what period) the amortization of goodwill is deductible for tax purposes. For U.S. federal income tax purposes, amortization of goodwill is currently deductible, but only over an amortization period of 15 years. German tax law similarly provides for the deductibility of goodwill from taxable income but over much shorter periods. Thus, the after-tax effect of this restatement should give rise to recognition of a deferred tax liability:

Ref.	Account Titles	Debit	Credit
f	Taxes (Retained Earnings)	43	
	Retained Earnings	114	
	Deferred Taxes		157

Minority Interest.   As is customary in Germany, *Blauweiss* considers minority interest to be part of shareholders' equity, and, consequently, there is no deduction in earnings for the minority interest's share in subsidiary earnings. In the United States, minority interest is classified separately from equity, and the minority interest's share of a subsidiaries' earnings are treated as a deduction from income. Minority interest in subsidiaries is estimated to be DM395 million as of the balance sheet date, and the income effect for the year is estimated to be DM41 million. The prior years' cumulative effect on income is estimated to be DM100 million.

The following entry accomplishes three things: (1) it reduces income of the current period by the amount of minority interest in earnings of consolidated subsidiaries, (2) it reduces retained earnings as of the beginning of the period by the effect of Minority Interest in Earnings from prior periods, and (3) it transfers the difference between DM395 million and the amounts from (1) and (2) from Common Ordinary Capital to a new balance sheet account titled Minority Interest in Subsidiary.

Ref.	Account Titles	Debit	Credit
g	Minority Interest in Earnings	41	
	Retained Earnings	100	
	Common Ordinary Capital	254	
	Minority Interest in Subsidiary		395

There is no deferred tax provision because minority interest in earnings is not deductible for tax purposes in Germany.

Provision for Pensions.   German pension plans are normally unfunded, and significant pension liabilities appear on the balance sheet. Pension expense, which is tax deductible, is based on changes in an actuarial pension obligation at the balance sheet date discounted at prescribed rates of interest. Income on pension assets is not separately identified because the pension assets themselves are not legally segregated from other company assets. Past service costs (i.e., retroactive grants of pension benefits to current or retired employees as a result of establishing a pension plan or "sweetening" an existing pension plan) are generally recognized immediately.

U.S. companies, on the other hand, fund their pension plans during periods of employee service (because if there is no funding, no tax deduction is permitted), and, in general, the company permanently forgoes access to plan assets. The pension plan is treated as a separate entity for accounting purposes and is not consolidated. Pension expense for financial reporting purposes is based on changes in actuarial liabilities (similar to the practice in Germany) but is reduced by actuarial estimates of income generated by pension plan assets. Past service costs are amortized over an extended period of time.

The most significant difference between U.S. and German plans is generally thought to relate to the issue of consolidation or, stated more plainly, whether the pension liability should be netted on the balance sheet against assets that will be used to pay retirees. To make German and U.S. financial statements more comparable, either reversing the offset on U.S. company financial statements or offsetting pension liabilities with pension assets could be appropriate.

In fact, neither solution is fully satisfactory because the divergence between U.S. and German GAAP in the area of pension accounting is in large part related to substantive differences in the pension plans themselves. Since German companies do not separately fund their actuarial pension liabilities, there is no legal segregation of pension plan assets, and the company determines how the assets will be utilized. Since U.S. companies establish separate legal entities for pension assets that are governed by trustees who are independent of the funding corporation, U.S. companies relinquish control of the assets.

Analysts may either make no restatement for pension accounting differences between the United States and Germany, or they may restate U.S. company balance sheets. Reasons to support the latter approach are the following:

- No information is available on German companies that would help an analyst identify which assets, if any, are earmarked to pay pension liabilities.
- Supplemental disclosures in U.S. company reports are usually sufficient to effect a disaggregation of pension assets and liabilities on the balance sheets of U.S. companies.
- U.S. companies do, in fact, have some control of pension plan assets: They select the plan trustees, and funding is usually not irrevocable. It is possible for any over funded pension plan assets to revert to the full control of the plan sponsoring company.

Extraordinary Results. In Germany, extraordinary or unusual items that arise outside of ordinary operations are separately disclosed. The United States does not permit the segregation of extraordinary items from income from continuing operations unless the event that gave rise to the gain or loss recognition was both unusual and nonrecurring.

Since one objective of financial analysis is often to estimate a future stream of permanent income flows, an analyst frequently excludes extraordinary or unusual items from income. In doing so, however, a full restatement of both income statements and balance sheets is often not possible and/or desirable. For instance, the ''extraordinary results'' of DM98 million for *Blauweiss* probably resulted in a net outflow of cash or the incurrence of a future obligation. Although the analyst might want a better measure of permanent income than the net income reported, future profitability and riskiness are functions of the firm's level of cash and its future obligations, regardless of the type of event—unusual or ordinary—that gave rise to the change in assets and/or liabilities.

Ref.	*Account Titles*	*Debit*	*Credit*
h	Retained Earnings	98	
	Extraordinary Results (Retained		
	Earnings)		98
i	Taxes (Retained Earnings)	54	
	Retained Earnings		54

The two entries taken together adjust the income statement for the after-tax effect of the extraordinary results on income. There is no balance sheet effect because retained earnings is both debited and credited for equal amounts.

Summary of *Blauweiss* Restatements.   The exercise of identifying areas for restatement can lead to actual changes in the appearance of financial statements in preparation for conducting an analysis or, as in the case of pension accounting, can alert the analyst to differences that are difficult to quantify but could be explicitly considered when evaluating accounting measures of profitability and financial position.

With respect to *Blauweiss,* the application of German GAAP has created a conservative bias that understates both net assets and earnings. Earnings trends likely tend to be very smooth because of the broad discretion of German financial statement issuers to manipulate provisions and reserves through valuation allowances and provisions for contingencies. The effect of restatement on the income statement and balance sheet are summarized in two worksheets that compose Exhibit 6–13. In general, restatement increases income dramatically, as anticipated. It also reduces liabilities and increases shareholders' equity, increasing the "strength" of *Blauweiss'* already strong balance sheet.

Exhibit 6–14 illustrates the effects of these restatements on selected financial ratios. Although liquidity and solvency ratios improve materially, the dramatic effect on profitability is reflected in the increased ROA, ROE, and ROS ratios.

A number of other German accounting differences limit comparability to U.S. companies and understate *Blauweiss's* shareholders' equity under German GAAP relative to U.S. GAAP:

- As is customary in Germany, *Blauweiss* classifies its income statement items by nature of expense (materials, personnel, and so on) rather than by function (cost of sales, advertising). Reformatting would be useful but extremely difficult. For example, we have no way of knowing how to allocate personnel expenses among product and period cost categories. As a result, normal U.S. profitability measures such as gross profit margin, the relationship of advertising to sales, and so forth are not calculable.
- Asset write-downs (e.g., for inventory or fixed assets) are more conservative under German GAAP.
- Foreign currency translation losses are recognized, but gains are deferred under German GAAP. This approach is more conservative than either of the two permissible approaches under U.S. GAAP.
- Less overhead is generally included in inventory under German GAAP, and direct costing is permissible.

Summary

General purpose financial statements satisfy some of the needs for financial information, but it is not infrequent for an analyst to be dissatisfied with some of the accounting methods that have a significant impact on objective analytical measures. Much of this dissatisfaction stems from a lack of comparability across companies being analyzed:

- Use of different, albeit permissible, accounting alternatives for similar circumstances. For example, one company may cost its inventory on a FIFO basis, but another may use a LIFO basis.

EXHIBIT 6–13

The Effect of Restatement for Blauweiss AG

Panel A. Restatement Worksheet for Balance Sheet, December 31, 19x9 (DM millions)

	Original	Debit	Ref.	Credit	Ref.	Restated
Current assets						
Cash and short-term investments	DM 3,574					DM 3,574
Accounts receivable	4,704					4,704
Inventories	2,898					2,898
Total current assets	DM 11,176					DM 11,176
Current liabilities						
Debt	DM (607)					DM (607)
Payables	(2,654)					(2,654)
Accruals and provisions	(4,444)	900	c			(3,544)
Total current liabilities	(7,705)					(6,805)
Net current assets	DM 3,471					DM 4,371
Fixed assets	13,089					13,089
Accumulated depreciation	(9,216)	1,450	a			(7,766)
	3,873					5,323
Intangible assets	449	285	e			734
Other assets	721					721
	1,171					1,456
	DM 8,515					DM 11,150
Pension provision	(3,472)					(3,472)
Other liabilities	(50)					(50)
Deferred taxes				798	b	
				495	d	
				157	f	(1,450)
Minority interest in subsidiary				395	g	(395)
	DM 4,993					DM 5,783
Shareholders' equity						
Common/ordinary capital	DM 2,446	254	g			DM 2,192
Retained earnings	2,547	798	b	1,450	a	
		495	d	900	c	
		157	f	285	e	
		141	g			3,591
Total shareholders' equity	DM 4,993					DM 5,783

- Different accounting standards for the same economic events, as, for example, the difference in accounting for contingencies between the United States and Germany.

- Differences in economic circumstances that motivate a difference in accounting standards, as, for example, the difference in accounting for pensions between the United States and Germany.

It is extremely rare that financial statements perfectly match the needs of an analyst performing an in-depth evaluation of a company. Restatement connotes the ad hoc

Exhibit 6–13 (continued)

Panel B. Restatement Worksheet for Income Statement, Year Ended December 31, 19x9 (DM millions)

	Original	Debit	Ref.	Credit	Ref.	Restated
Sales	DM 22,330					DM 22,330
Inventory change/capitalized work	1,559					1,559
Operating output	DM 23,889					DM 23,889
Other operating income	688					688
Cost of materials	(12,361)					(12,361)
Staff costs	(7,830)					(7,830)
Other operating expenses	(2,653)			50	c	(2,603)
Income from participations	95					95
Depreciation & amortization	(995)			56	a	
				79	e	(860)
Value adjustments	(21)					(21)
Minority interest in earnings		41	g			(41)
Net interest	292					292
Profit on ordinary activities	DM 1,104					DM 1,248
Extraordinary results	(98)			98	h	–0–
Taxes	(501)	28	b			
		28	d			
		43	f			
		54	i			(348)
Net income	**DM 505**					**DM 900**

Exhibit 6–14

Effects of Restatement on Ratios for Blauweiss AG

Comparative Ratio Analysis

	Originally Reported	Restated	Percentage Difference
Current ratio	1.45	1.64	13.2%
Quick ratio	1.07	1.22	13.2
Debt to equity ratio	70.5%	60.9%	−13.7
Interest coverage ratio	4.78	5.27	10.3
Receivables turnover ratio	4.75	4.75	0.0
Total asset turnover ratio	1.38	1.24	−9.7
Return on assets ratio	3.1%	5.0%	61.0
Return on equity ratio	10.1%	15.6%	53.9
Return on sales ratio	2.3%	4.0%	78.2

adjustments undertaken by an analyst to alter the content and appearance of company-prepared financial statements. The purpose is to enhance the comparability, relevance, and reliability of accounting information in a specific decision context. At least *some* restatement is almost always undertaken, ranging from as simple as rearranging and combining items to as complex as modifying accounting methods.

APPENDIX 6A
A PRIMER ON CONSOLIDATED REPORTING PRACTICES

Consolidated Reporting Practices

In many countries throughout the world, when one company obtains a "controlling" interest in another, the parent company is required to present the financial results of the subsidiary company on a consolidated or combined basis. The preparation of consolidated financial statements (i.e., statements reflecting the financial results of a parent company and its controlled subsidiaries) becomes, however, problematic when the parent company operates in one country and thus maintains its financial results in the currency of that country but its subsidiaries operate principally in other countries, maintaining their financial data in the currency of those other countries. It would be meaningless, for example, to consolidate the U.S. dollar-denominated results of a U.S.–based parent company with the Italian lira-denominated results of an Italian-based subsidiary. Thus, before the financial results of the combined entities can be prepared, the data of the foreign subsidiary must first be translated into U.S.–dollar equivalents. Following this translation process, which is the focus of Chapter 7, the consolidated financial results can then be tabulated.

But how are consolidated financial statements prepared? What accounting alternatives exist, and when are those alternative methods likely to be used? Unfortunately, the prevalent reporting practices used throughout the world are quite diverse, and the purpose of this appendix is to briefly overview those practices.

Control: Passive versus Active Investments.   A key determinant used to identify the appropriate consolidation practice in almost every country involves the extent of *control* exercised by a parent company over its subsidiaries. Control is usually indicated by the quantity of voting shares held by the parent company and thus refers to the capacity of one entity to dominate the decision making of a second entity in regards to its operating policies. In most instances, a shareholding of less than 5 percent usually indicates a low degree of control, whereas a shareholding of 50 percent or more indicates a high degree of control. Between 5 and 50 percent, however, is a substantial gray area in which local accounting practices may differ dramatically. Even in those apparently clear-cut circumstances in which the level of ownership interest exceeds 50 percent, variation in consolidation practices may exist between countries, as will be seen shortly.

In the United States, for example, a shareholding of from 0 to 20 percent is generally interpreted as a low degree of control. For investments of this size, it is assumed (unless evidence to the contrary exists) that the parent company is unable (or unwilling) to exercise control over the operating policies of such subsidiaries. These *passive* investments are usually accounted for on a portfolio basis at their market value. Under this approach, an investment in a subsidiary is carried on the books of the parent company at its original cost, unless market fluctuations indicate the need for an upward *or* downward revaluation. Under U.S. GAAP (i.e., *SFAS No. 115*), the unrealized gains or losses due to revaluation are reflected in the income statement for portfolios of trading securities and on the balance sheet (in owners' equity) for portfolios of securities that are "available for sale" (i.e., are not considered to be trading securities). This treatment essentially parallels the accounting practice followed in such countries as Great Britain, wherein annual revaluation is the norm; however, in other countries, such as Germany and Japan, where assets are valued at historical cost applied conservatively, only downward revaluation (i.e., lower of cost or market) is permitted. *IAS No. 25* permits such investments to be valued at their original cost (without regard to market fluctuations), at the lower of cost or market, or at revalued amounts in excess of original cost.[19] Exhibit 6A–1 presents the footnote disclosures for several international companies illustrating the accounting treatment adopted for their investments.

When the level of parent shareholding exceeds 20 percent or when there is evidence that a parent company can exercise significant decision-making influence over the operations of a subsidiary (e.g., when the parent company has placed one or more of its executives or directors on the board of directors of the subsidiary), the parent will usually be required to account for its investment using the **equity method.**

Investments accounted for under the equity method are called *active* investments and usually involve associate or affiliate companies that may also be major suppliers to, or buyers from, the parent company or one of its various controlled subsidiaries. Although the equity method is a form of *un*consolidated reporting, it is often referred to as a *one-line consolidation.* To understand why this is the case, consider an illustration in which Global Enterprises S.p.A. (GE) purchases a 20 percent shareholding in Foreign Subsidiary, Inc. (FS), for L100,000. Immediately prior to this purchase, the balance sheets of the two companies appeared as follows:

	Assets	= Liabilities	+ Shareholders' Equity
GE S.p.A.	L1,000,000	= L0	+ L1,000,000
FS, Inc.	L700,000	= L200,000	+ L500,000

In the year following GE's investment in FS, FS earned net income of L25,000 and paid cash dividends of L10,000. In terms of FS's balance sheet, these events would appear as follows:

	Assets	= Liabilities	+ Shareholders' Equity
	L700,000	= L200,000	+ L500,000
Net income	+ 25,000		+ 25,000
Dividends	− 10,000		− 10,000
	L715,000	L200,000	L515,000

---

[19]When an investment (or other long-term asset) is revalued above its original cost, the corresponding credit entry is usually to an equity reserve account carried under shareholders' equity on the balance sheet (e.g., Reserve for Asset Revaluations).

Exhibit 6A–1
Financial Statement Disclosures: Accounting for Investments

Panel A. Fiat

Investments

Investments in unconsolidated companies over which the group has significant influence (generally
between 20 percent and 50 percent of voting capital) are stated on an equity basis. Less significant
investments (generally companies in which the group holds less than 20 percent of voting capital) are
valued at cost. Provision is made for the write-down of investments where there is a permanent loss in
value.

Panel B. Mitsui & Co., Ltd.

Investments and marketable securities

Investments in associated companies (generally companies owned 20 percent to 50 percent and corporate
joint ventures) are, with minor exceptions, stated at cost adjusted for the company's equity in earnings
or losses since dates of acquisition, after appropriate adjustments for intercompany profits, dividends,
and amortization (over periods of 5 to 20 years using the straight-line method) of differences between
the cost of such investments and the equity in net assets at dates of acquisition.

The current and noncurrent portfolios of marketable equity securities (included in marketable securities
and other investments, respectively, in the accompanying consolidated balance sheets) are each stated
at the lower of aggregate cost or market.

Marketable securities and other investments (exclusive of marketable equity securities) are stated at the
lower of cost or market and at cost or less, respectively.

Panel C. Volvo

The Volvo Group comprises the parent company, all subsidiaries—defined as companies in which AB
Volvo holds more than 50 percent of the voting rights—and associated companies that are not
subsidiaries but in which AB Volvo has long-term holdings equal to at least 20 percent of the voting
rights.

Acquisitions of companies are accounted for using the purchase method. Shareholders' equity in the
subsidiaries at date of acquisition, including equity in untaxed reserves, is eliminated in its entirety.
Accordingly, only income arising after the date of acquisition is included in shareholders' equity. The
difference between the cost of shares in a subsidiary and the shareholders' equity of the subsidiary at
date of acquisition is, if the cost of the company's shareholding represents a higher amount (excess
value), allocated to the assets to the extent considered appropriate. The remaining excess is included in
the consolidated balance sheets as goodwill.

Effective in 1989, holdings in associated companies are reported in accordance with the equity method.
The group's share of reported income in such companies, before allocations and taxes, is included in
the consolidated income statement, reduced in appropriate cases by amortization of excess values. The
group's share of reported taxes in associated companies and estimated taxes in allocations are included
in the group's tax expense.

As a consequence of these events, FS's total and net assets increased by L15,000; and, since GE holds a 20 percent ownership interest in FS, it can logically be argued that the underlying value of GE's investment in FS has increased by L3,000 (i.e., .20 × L15,000).

This logic is inherent in the equity method, and, consequently, GE values its year-end investment in FS as follows:

Original investment	L100,000
Ownership interest in	
Net income (.2 × L25,000)	5,000
Dividends (.2 × L10,000)	(2,000)
Year-end value	L103,000

The equity method is appealing in that it values the parent's investment in a subsidiary on a basis consistent with the operations of the subsidiary. The parent's investment account is increased (decreased) as a function of the subsidiary's earnings (losses). Similarly, the parent is entitled to report its proportionate interest in the subsidiary's earnings (and losses) as part of its own net income. Thus, the equity method provides a one-line summary of the operations-related activities of the subsidiary on the financial statements of the parent company. *IAS No. 22* recommends the use of the equity method for investments in associated companies except when they are held exclusively for sale.

Consolidated Reporting.   In most countries, when a company obtains more than 50 percent of the voting shares of another company, accepted accounting practice dictates the use of consolidated reporting practices. In Germany and Japan, among others, however, this is not necessarily the case (see Chapters 9 and 10); when a controlled subsidiary is not consolidated, the equity method is the appropriate method of accounting for such investments.

Consolidated reporting may involve either a *full* or *partial* combination of financial data. When a company acquires a 100 percent shareholding in another, the consolidated results under either full or partial consolidation are exactly equivalent. When an acquired investment is less than 100 percent, however, full and partial consolidation yields different consolidated results.

To illustrate, consider a simple acquisition between two independent companies. Assume, for example, that Global Enterprises S.p.A. purchased 90 percent of the voting stock of Foreign Subsidiary, Inc., for L243,000.

Immediately prior to the acquisition, the balance sheets of the two companies appeared as follows:

	GE S.p.A.	FS, Inc.
Assets	L700,000	L312,000
Liabilities	L150,000	L100,000
Shareholders' equity	550,000	212,000
Total equities	L700,000	L312,000

Assume also that according to GE's financial analysts, the fair market value of FS's net assets was L267,000, or L55,000 more than its net book value of L212,000. This increase in value is attributable to several long-term assets whose reported book values were below current estimates of their fair market value. After considering this additional information, the analysts concluded that GE had purchased goodwill in the amount of L2,700 from FS as follows:

Fair Market Value of 90 Percent Shareholding in FS	
L267,000 × .90 =	L240,300
Purchase price	L243,000
Less: Fair market value	(240,300)
Goodwill	L2,700

GE may have been willing to pay a premium in excess of the appraised value of FS's net assets for several reasons: the presence of a loyal customer base for FS's product, a competent management group, an efficient distribution system, and anticipated cost savings and other synergies between the operations of GE and FS.

Immediately following the acquisition, GE's balance sheet would appear as follows:

Assets	
Investment in FS	L243,000
Other assets	457,000
Total assets	L700,000
Liabilities	L150,000
Shareholders' equity	550,000
Total equities	L700,000

Full vs. Partial Consolidation.   At this juncture, GE's preparation of consolidated financial statements is predicated on the firm's decision to use full or partial consolidation. Under partial consolidation, only 90 percent of FS's reported values are transferred to GE's financial statements.[20]

---

[20]Partial consolidation is usually executed by taking a percentage of the subsidiary's assets and liabilities on a line-by-line basis. *IAS No. 31,* "Financial Reporting of Interests in Joint Ventures," specifically identifies the use of the partial (or proportionate) consolidation for jointly controlled entities.

Thus, the journal entry to transfer the purchased net assets of FS to GE's books appears as follows:

Dr. Assets (from FS)	L280,800	
Dr. Revaluation of FS's Assets	49,500*	
Dr. Goodwill	2,700	
Cr. Liabilities (from FS)		L 90,000
Cr. Investment in FS		243,000

*.90 (L55,000) = L49,500. This represents GE's ownership share of the increase in the fair market value of FS's net assets.

In effect, GE's Investment in FS is replaced with the assets and liabilities from FS that GE now controls, which must also be revalued to reflect their acquisition cost (or fair market value), and the goodwill that GE purchased as part of the acquisition. GE's consolidated balance sheet then appears as:

Assets	
Assets (acquired from FS)	L330,300*
Other assets	457,000
Goodwill	2,700
Total Assets	L790,000
Liabilities (from GE)	L150,000
Liabilities (from FS)	90,000
Shareholders' equity	550,000
Total equities	L790,000

*(L280,800 + L49,500).

Partial consolidation assumes that the parent's consolidated balance sheet should reflect only its *proportionate* interest in the net assets of the acquired company. For this reason, partial consolidation is also sometimes called *proportionate* consolidation. *Full consolidation,* however, assumes that since the parent company is the majority shareholder of the subsidiary, the parent effectively controls *all* of the subsidiary's net assets despite the fact that it might not own them all. Thus, under full consolidation, all of the subsidiary's net assets are consolidated with those of the parent. This practice, however, necessitates the creation of a new account— Minority Interest—to reflect the portion of the subsidiary's net assets not in fact owned by the parent company.

To illustrate, consider again GE's 90 percent acquisition of FS. Under full consolidation, the journal entry to transfer 100 percent of FS's net assets to GE appears as follows:

Dr. Assets (from FS)	L312,000	
Dr. Revaluation of FS's Assets	49,500	
Dr. Goodwill	2,700	
Cr. Liabilities (from FS)		L100,000
Cr. Minority Interest		21,200*
Cr. Investment in FS		243,000

*.10 (L212,000) represents the portion of FS's net assets not owned by GE.

Note that under this approach, 100 percent of the value of FS's assets and liabilities are transferred to GE's consolidated financial statements despite the fact that GE owns only 90 percent of FS. GE's consolidated balance sheet then appears as:

Assets	
Assets (acquired from FS)	L361,500*
Other assets	457,000
Goodwill	2,700
Total assets	L821,200
Liabilities (from GE)	L150,000
Liabilities (from FS)	100,000
Minority interest	21,200
Shareholders' equity	550,000
Total equities	L821,200

*(L312,000 + L49,500).

The Minority Interest account, which represents the value of FS's net assets *not* owned by GE, appears as a credit balance on GE's consolidated balance sheet, although it is neither a debt obligation nor a shareholders' equity account. It is, in effect, merely a balancing account required under the full consolidation approach. As a consequence, this account is frequently ignored by financial analysts when calculating such ratios as the debt-to-equity ratio or the debt-to-total capitalization ratio.

As a concluding observation, it is noteworthy that the full consolidation approach results in a higher level of total (but not net) assets being reported by the parent company on its consolidated balance sheet (e.g., L821,200 versus L790,000). Since the consolidated net income of the parent may reflect only those earnings attributable to the parent and its ownership interest in its subsidiaries (i.e., the portion of the consolidated net earnings attributable to the minority shareholders are excluded and added to the Minority Interest account), some distortions in calculated ratios may result. For example, assume that in the year following GE's investment in FS, the consolidated net earnings before minority interest totaled L100,000, with L40,000 of that amount attributable to FS's operations. The calculation of GE's consolidated earnings *after* minority interest appears as follows:

Consolidated earnings before minority interest	L100,000
Less: Earnings attributable to minority interest	4,000*
Consolidated earnings	L 96,000

*.10 (L40,000).

GE's consolidated balance sheet appears as follows:

Assets	
Assets (acquired from FS)	L401,500
Other assets	517,000
Goodwill	2,700
Total assets	L921,200
Liabilities (from GE)	L150,000
Liabilities (from FS)	100,000
Minority interest	25,200
Shareholders' equity	646,000
Total equities	L921,200

Under full consolidation, GE's year-end assets total L921,200, whereas under partial consolidation, they total only L886,000 (i.e., L790,000 + L96,000). The return on total assets (ROA) ratio is calculated as follows:

Full Consolidation

$$\frac{L96,000}{(L821,000 + L921,200)/2} = 11.0\%$$

Partial Consolidation

$$\frac{L96,000}{(L790,000 + L886,000)/2} = 11.5\%$$

In this instance, GE's ROA is numerically higher under partial consolidation than under full consolidation (i.e., 11.5 versus 11.0, respectively). To avoid the analytical problems that may result if inappropriate comparisons are made, the analyst should always verify that comparable consolidation (and other accounting) practices have been used.

Goodwill.   A final consideration in our review of consolidated reporting practices involves goodwill. **Goodwill** arises when one entity acquiring another pays more than the fair market value of the acquired company. In the preceding illustration, GE was found to have paid L2,700 more than the appraised value of a 90 percent interest in FS:

Purchase price (of 90 percent shareholding)	L243,000
Fair market value	(240,300)
Goodwill	L 2,700

In accounting language, GE's acquisition of its 90 percent shareholding in FS is called a *purchase* because the transaction involved an exchange of one asset (i.e., cash) for another (i.e., the voting stock of FS). But not all acquisitions are executed in this manner. In some instances, the acquiror company may exchange its voting stock for the stock of the acquiree company. When such stock exchanges occur, IASC standards permit the acquiror to utilize the **pooling-of-interests** method of accounting.[21]

---

[21]*IASC Exposure Draft No. 45* (1992) requires that purchase accounting be used in all business combinations except when it is not possible to identify the acquiror firm, in which case the pooling-of-interests method should be used. *ED No. 45* also requires that any goodwill inherent in the purchase price be capitalized to the balance sheet and amortized against earnings over a period of 5 years (with the possibility of extending the write-off period to 20 years).

Under the pooling-of-interests method, the value assigned to the acquiror's shares exchanged in an acquisition is *not* their fair market value but the book value of the investment as carried on the acquiree's financial statements. For example, if GE had acquired 100 percent of FS's voting shares by exchanging its own shares for the voting shares of FS, the value assigned to GE's investment in FS would be L212,000. FS's book value would be used to value the GE investment even if the fair market value of the GE shares given up in the exchange exceeded L212,000. An important consequence of the pooling method is that goodwill *never* occurs under this approach. Thus, if goodwill is reported on the balance sheet of a company, it can be inferred that the company has engaged in various acquisition activities involving the purchase method.

Even if the purchase method is used to account for an acquisition, however, some local accounting practices enable the acquiror to avoid disclosing the amount of goodwill incurred in an acquisition. For example, in Germany, Italy, Japan, and Great Britain, goodwill incurred as a consequence of an acquisition may be written off directly against various equity reserve accounts. To illustrate, consider again GE's acquisition of a 90 percent shareholding in FS, wherein goodwill in the amount of L2,700 was incurred. Assuming partial consolidation, GE's consolidated balance sheet following the acquisition appears as follows:

	Goodwill Capitalized to Balance Sheet	*Goodwill Charged Against Reserves*
Assets		
Assets (acquired from FS)	L330,300	L330,300
Other assets	457,000	457,000
Goodwill	2,700	—
Total assets	L790,000	L787,300
Liabilities (from GE)	L150,000	L150,000
Liabilities (from FS)	90,000	90,000
Shareholders' equity	550,000	547,300
Total equities	L790,000	L787,300

Note that under the charge-to-equity approach of accounting for goodwill, GE's total and net assets are reduced by the amount of goodwill (i.e., L2,700) written off.

In most countries, if goodwill is capitalized to the balance sheet under purchase accounting, it must be periodically amortized against earnings, although the amortization period varies greatly from country to country. In Canada and the United States, for example, the typical amortization period is 40 years, whereas in Japan and Korea, a 5-year amortization period is prevalent. In any case, the presence of goodwill on the consolidated balance sheet of the parent company represents a "drag" on the company's future earnings. In the case of GE, the reduction in earnings would be L540 per year (i.e., L2700/5) if a 5-year amortization period is used, or only L67.50 per year if a 40-year amortization period is adopted. (*Note:* Although straight-line amortization of goodwill is the most prevalent amortization approach, other methods are acceptable and vary by location.)

Companies that elect to write goodwill off immediately against existing equity reserve accounts do so primarily to avoid the reduction in future earnings associated with the amortization of goodwill. Why this election might be made by management can be explained with reference to existing stock market theories. As noted in Chapter 4, it is widely accepted in the financial community that a company's share price today is a reflection of investor expectations regarding the company's future earnings. Hence, to maximize a company's share price, it follows that management should adopt those policies that maximize future earnings. One way to maximize the future accounting earnings of a company is to minimize the write-offs taken against future earnings (e.g., goodwill amortization). Whether in fact the charge-to-equity method of accounting for goodwill results in a higher share price is unclear.

Finally, although goodwill is most commonly found as an asset account on the balance sheet (e.g., when the purchase price of an investment exceeds its fair market value), on occasion an acquiror may find that its purchase price of an investment is *less* than the investment's recorded book value. When this occurs, **negative goodwill**—a credit balance—is said to arise (see Exhibit 6–4, panel C). Not surprising, the accounting for negative goodwill is quite diverse. In Germany, for example, negative goodwill is carried on the balance sheet as a credit balance and may be amortized to (i.e., an increase in) earnings over time. Under U.S. GAAP, however, negative goodwill may not be carried on a company's balance sheet and instead is usually written off against the remaining depreciable cost basis of an acquiree's long-term depreciable assets. Finally, in those countries such as Italy and Great Britain where the charge-to-equity method is permitted, negative goodwill may be added immediately to the acquiror's equity reserves. Each of these approaches produces a different effect on the acquiror's balance sheet and income statement; however, whether the cash flow effect is equivalent is a function of local tax regulations regarding the tax deductibility of goodwill.

Summary

Consolidation accounting practices vary greatly from one country to the next. In most locations, the prevalent accounting treatment is the purchase method, although the pooling-of-interests method is also permitted by IASC standards. In some settings, despite a majority shareholding, a parent company may account for a controlled subsidiary using the equity method, which is essentially an abbreviated form of consolidated reporting. When an investment in a subsidiary is significant but does not constitute a controlling interest, the investment may be accounted for at its original cost, using the lower-of-cost-or-market method, at its revalued amount, or using the equity method. As always, the analyst should first identify accepted local accounting practice before embarking on any financial review.

Suggested Readings

Comiskey, E., and C. Tritschler. ''On or Off the Balance Sheet—Some Guidance for Credit Analysts.'' *Journal of Commercial Bank Lending,* August 1984.

Dawson, J. P., P. M. Neupert, and C. P. Stickney. ''Restating Financial Statements for Alternative GAAP: Is It Worth the Effort?'' *Financial Analysts Journal,* November/December 1980.

Ferris, K. R., K. L. Tennant, and S. Jerris. *How to Understand Financial Statements: A Nontechnical Guide for Financial Analyst Executives and Managers.* New York: Simon and Schuster, 1992.

Hector, G. ''Cute Tricks on the Bottom Line.'' *Fortune,* April 24, 1989.

Heian, J., and J. Thies. ''Consolidation of Finance Subsidiaries: $230 Billion in Off-Balance Sheet Financing Comes Home to Roost.'' *Accounting Horizons,* March 1989.

Means, K., and P. Kazenski. ''SFAS 34: A Recipe for Diversity?'' *Accounting Horizons,* September 1988.

Sannella, A. ''The Capitalization of Operating Leases: The Discounted Cash Flow Approach.'' *Journal of Commercial Bank Lending,* October 1989.

Wang, P. ''The Unlevel Accounting Field.'' *Forbes,* November 28, 1988.

ISSUES AND INFORMATION FOR FURTHER INQUIRY

I.6.1   U.S. GAAP Reconciliation

In a September 23, 1993, letter to *The Wall Street Journal* (p. A17), Mary Shapiro, an SEC commissioner, strongly defended the U.S. position that foreign companies seeking securities listings in the United States should continue to be required to comply with U.S. GAAP because ''reconciliation provides significant information that is not made public in a foreign company's home jurisdiction.''

Required:

Obtain a form 20-F filing for an overseas company from your business library or from the Securities and Exchange Commission. In addition, obtain a form 10-K filing from a U.S. company in the same industry. Prepare a side-by-side listing of the sections contained in each filing. For the similar section headings, prepare a notation as to whether the section content is similar or dissimilar and in what ways (e.g., breadth of information, level of detail, tone of presentation).

   On a scale of 1 to 10 (with 10 being exactly similar and 1 having no similarity), rate the similarity of the two filings and comment on your rating.

I.6.2   Alternative International GAAP and Financial Ratios

In a February 16, 1993, *Financial Times* article (p. 25), ''Report Calls for Accounting Harmonisation,'' Andrew Jack notes that a NatWest Securities research report ''warns that until standards are more uniform, investors need to be wary of differing accounting practices.'' He cites the report as highlighting several accounting practices of note that differ between countries including:

1. Revaluation upward of assets on the balance sheet (e.g., Olivetti and Philips).
2. Accelerated depreciation (e.g., Germany).
3. Substantial goodwill write-downs.
4. Long-term contracts.
5. Provisions and reserves used to help smooth profits.
6. Definition of extraordinary items.

Required:

Explain how each of these six items might affect the ROA, ROS, and ROE ratios.

EXERCISES

E.6.1   Restating Financial Statements: Inventory

Following are the balance sheet and income statement of Global Enterprises, Inc. as of December 31, 1993. The footnotes to GE's financial statements included the following statement regarding inventories:

> Inventories are valued on a FIFO basis. If LIFO has been used, inventories would have been valued at ¥889,000 on January 1, 1993, and at ¥1,270,000 on December 31, 1993.

Required:

(a) Assume that the tax rate is 50 percent and that Global Enterprises had been using FIFO for tax purposes. Restate the company's balance sheet and income statement for 1993 to reflect the use of LIFO instead of FIFO. (Would you recommend such a method change for income tax purposes also?)

(b) Calculate the following ratios for 1993 under both LIFO and FIFO:

(1) Current ratio.

(2) Inventory turnover.

(3) Average number of days' inventory on hand.

(4) Total debt-to-equity ratio.

(c) Which method do you think Global Enterprises should use, and why?

GLOBAL ENTERPRISES, INC.
Income Statement
For the year ended December 31, 1993

Sales revenue		¥4,950,000
Less: Cost of sales		
Beginning inventory	¥1,205,000	
Cost of production	3,665,000	
Goods available for sale	4,870,000	
Less: Ending inventory	1,720,000	
		(3,150,000)
Gross margin		1,800,000
Less: Research and development expenses	350,000	
Licensing fees	100,000	
Selling and administrative expenses	400,000	
		(850,000)
Net income before taxes		950,000
Less: Income taxes	475,000	
Investment and research tax credits	(60,000)	
		(415,000)
Net income after taxes		¥ 535,000

GLOBAL ENTERPRISES, INC.
Balance Sheet
As of December 31, 1993

Assets		*Equities*	
Current assets		Current liabilities	
Cash	¥ 436,000	Accounts payable	¥ 820,000
Trade receivables (net of allowance for		Accrued expenses payable	80,000
uncollectible accounts)	828,000	Total current liabilities	900,000
Inventories	1,720,000		
Prepared expenses	30,000		
Total current assets	3,014,000		
Noncurrent assets		Noncurrent liabilities	
Property, plant, and equipment	¥ 3,940,000	Notes payable	2,320,000
Less: Accumulated depreciation	(1,360,000)	Deferred federal Income taxes	800,000
	2,580,000	Total liabilities	4,020,000
Land	560,000	Owners' equity	
Deferred research and development cost	1,150,000	Common stock ¥ 1 par	2,000,000
Total assets	¥ 7,304,000	Retained earnings	1,284,000
		Total equities	¥ 7,304,000

E.6.2 Restating Financial Statements: Depreciation

The 1993 financial statements of Global Enterprises, Inc., included the following statement regarding the company's depreciation of property, plant, and equipment:

> Property, plant, and equipment is depreciated on a straight-line basis. If an accelerated method had been used, the depreciation expense for 1993 would have been ¥230,000 higher, and the end-of-year balance in Accumulated Depreciation ¥450,000 higher.

Required:

(a) Using the 1993 financial statements presented in Exercise 6.1 and assuming a 50 percent tax rate, restate Global Enterprises' financial statements for 1993 to reflect the use of accelerated depreciation (instead of straight line). GE reports all depreciation as a component of cost of goods sold. Would you recommend this policy change for income tax purposes?

(b) Calculate the following ratios for 1993 under both straight-line and accelerated depreciation:

    (1) Return on sales.

    (2) Return on total assets.

    (3) Noncurrent asset turnover.

    (4) Total asset turnover.

(c) Which method do you think GE should use, and why?

E.6.3   Restating Financial Statements: Research and Development Costs

The 1993 financial statements of Global Enterprises, Inc., included the following statement regarding the company's treatment of research and development costs:

> The research and development expense for 1993 represented one-half of the actual R&D expenditure for 1993; the remaining balance had been capitalized. The company's policy is to begin amortization of these capitalized costs once a commercially productive asset has been developed. To date, no productive assets have resulted from the research program represented by the currently capitalized R&D costs.

Required:

(a) Using the financial statements presented in Exercise 6.1 and assuming a 50 percent tax rate, restate Global Enterprises' financial statements for 1993 to reflect the full current expensing of all R&D costs. (What recommendation would you make for income tax purposes?)

(b) Calculate the following ratios for 1993 under the old and new policies regarding expensing R&D expenditures:

(1) Return on sales.
(2) Return on total assets.
(3) Noncurrent asset turnover.
(4) Total asset turnover.

(c) Which method do you think Global Enterprises should adopt, and why?

E.6.4   Restating Balance Sheets: Leases

Global Telecommunications, Plc, leases a substantial portion of its noncurrent assets. For example, as of year-end 1993, GT had leased over one-third of its total noncurrent assets, and the capitalized obligations associated with those leases represented nearly 50 percent of the company's total reported long-term debt (see condensed balance sheet). In addition, the footnotes to the company's statements revealed that some of those leased assets were accounted for as "operating leases":

At December 31, 1993, the aggregate minimum rental commitments under noncancellable operating leases were as follows:

Year Ending 12/31	Amount
1994	£ 16,610,000
1995	15,443,000
1996	14,441,000
1997	12,669,000
1998	10,580,000
1999 and thereafter	49,220,000
Total minimum lease payments	£118,963,000

GLOBAL TELECOMMUNICATIONS, Plc
Condensed Balance Sheets
As of December 31
(in thousands)

	1993	1992
Assets		
Current assets	£228,428	£ 48,946
Noncurrent assets (net)	631,970	417,946
Total	£860,398	£466,892
Equities		
Current liabilities	£185,540	£ 23,729
Long-term debt	206,494	44,665
Capitalized lease obligations	227,582	250,451
Shareholders' equity	240,782	148,047
Total	£860,398	£466,892

Required:

(a) Assume that the implicit interest rate on GT's operating leases is 12 percent. Restate the balance sheet at year-end 1993, assuming that all of the operating leases should be capitalized.

(b) Calculate the following ratios both before and after your restatement in part (a):

(1) Long-term debt-to-shareholders' equity.

(2) Total debt-to-total assets.

(c) In an efficient marketplace, what should happen to GT's debt rating following the capitalization of all operating leases?

E.6.5   Alternative GAAP: FIFO versus LIFO

The following information is taken from the 1993 financial statements of Cifra, SA, a major Mexican retailing company:

Inventories are valued on a LIFO basis; the year-end balances (in millions, new pesos) at 30 June were

	1993	1992
Inventory	3,158	3,029

If FIFO had been used, inventory would have been 2,152 million higher than reported on June 30, 1993 (2,266 million higher on June 30, 1992). During 1993, net reductions in inventory levels resulted in liquidations of LIFO bases of 114 million in 1993 (163 million in 1992).

The condensed financial statements of Cifra are as follows:

CIFRA, SA
Balance Sheet
As of 30 June
(in millions, new pesos)

	1993	1992
Assets		
Quick assets	7,754	7,327
Inventories	3,158	3,029
Total current assets	10,912	10,356
Noncurrent assets	12,376	11,259
Total assets	23,288	21,615
Equities		
Current liabilities	8,688	8,153
Long-term liabilities	3,162	3,099
Total liabilities	11,850	11,252
Owners' equity	11,438	10,363
Total equities	23,288	21,615

CIFRA, SA
Statement of Earnings
For the year ended 30 June
(in millions, new pesos)

	1993	1992	1991
Sales of products and services rendered	26,797	26,500	27,240
Cost of goods sold	(24,248)	(24,095)	(24,793)
Other income & expenses	450	312	167
Provision for income taxes	(975)	(900)	(962)
Net earnings	2,024	1,817	1,652

Required:

(a) If Cifra had used FIFO instead of LIFO in all prior years, how would the company's 1992–1993 financial statements differ? (Ignore income tax considerations.)

(b) Compare the income tax consequences of using LIFO instead of FIFO in 1993 for Cifra.

(c) Assuming a tax rate of 33 percent, estimate the total tax savings received by Cifra in all years as a consequence of using LIFO instead of FIFO.

(d) Calculate the following ratios for 1993 under both LIFO and FIFO:
   (1) Current ratio.
   (2) Quick ratio.
   (3) Inventory turnover.
   (4) Average number of days' inventory on hand.

E.6.6   Restating Financial Statements: Pooling versus Purchasing Accounting

In 1978, Carlton Brewing Co. (Melbourne, Australia) acquired the net assets of its chief competitor, the United Brewing Co., by issuing 1,891,678 shares of Carlton ordinary stock to the owners of United, forming the largest brewery in Australia (now the Carlton-United Brewing Co. or CUB). Carlton had accounted for the transaction as a pooling of interests and, accordingly, included in its consolidated balance sheet only $32 million of new net assets (i.e., the book value of United's net assets in 1978).

The merger was recorded on Carlton's books as follows:

Dr. Net assets (from United)	$32.0 million	
Cr. Ordinary capital		$ 3.0 million
Cr. Retained earnings		29.0 million

At the time of the merger, Carlton's shares traded on the Melbourne Stock Exchange at approximately $50 per share. Following are the consolidated financial statements for the Carlton-United Brewing Co. as of June 30, 1992 and 1993:

CARLTON-UNITED BREWING CO.
Consolidated Balance Sheet
As of 30 June, 1992 and 1993
(in millions)

	December 31,	
	1993	*1992*
Assets		
Cash and cash equivalents	$ 104	$ 147
Debtors	912	693
Inventories	1,750	1,670
Land	81	66
Building and equipment (net)	2,928	2,572
Long-term investments	103	85
Other assets and goodwill	220	146
Total	$6,098	$5,379
Liabilities and Shareholders' Equity		
Short-term creditors	$1,067	$ 790
Income tax payable	198	133
Notes payable	430	404
Deferred income tax	23	(24)
Long-term creditors (total)	948	1,011
Total	2,666	2,314
Ordinary capital	180	177
Retained earnings	3,252	2,888
Total	$6,098	$5,379

CARLTON-UNITED BREWING CO.
Consolidated Income Statement
For the Year Ended June 30, 1993 and 1992
(in millions)

	1993	1992
Turnover	$8,598	$7,613
Cost of goods sold	6,957*	6,172*
Other expenses (net)	844	715
Income taxes	232	234
Total expenses	8,033	7,121
Income	$ 565	$ 492
Note		
Depreciation for year	370	312
Dividends	201	182

*This figure includes depreciation allocable to cost of goods sold.

Required:

(a) Restate the CUB financial statements for 1992 and 1993 to reflect the use of purchase accounting instead of pooling of interests.

(b) How would CUB's reported net income change under purchase accounting? What conclusion, in general, would you draw from this about the effect of pooling versus purchasing accounting on reported net income?

(c) Calculate the following ratios for CUB in 1992 and 1993 under the two methods of consolidated reporting:

   (1) Total debt-to-total assets.
   (2) Book value per share. (Assume that 86.5 million shares are outstanding.)
   (3) Earnings per share.
   (4) Return on equity.

   What conclusion, in general, would you draw about the effect of pooling versus purchasing accounting on ratio analysis?

E.6.7   Restating Financial Statements: Depreciation

The 1993 annual report of the Carlton-United Brewing Co. (CUB), headquartered in Melbourne, Australia, reported the following statement about the company's depreciation policy:

> Depreciation is computed principally using accelerated methods . . . for both income tax and financial reporting purposes. If the straight-line method had been in use, Buildings, machinery, and equipment (net) would have been $504 million, $430 million, and $370 million higher than reported at June 30, 1993, 1992, and 1991, respectively, and the depreciation expense for 1993, 1992, and 1991 would have been, respectively, $74 million, $60 million, and $48 million less.

Required:

(a) Using the CUB financial statements presented in Exercise 6.6 and assuming a 35 percent tax rate, restate the company's balance sheets for 1992 and 1993 to reflect the use of straight-line depreciation. Assume that straight line is used for both financial and tax reporting purposes.

(b) By how much would the company's reported net income change in 1992 and 1993 as a consequence of using straight-line depreciation?

(c) Calculate the following ratios for 1992 and 1993 under both depreciation methods:

(1) Return on sales.

(2) Return on total assets.

(3) Noncurrent asset turnover.

(4) Total asset turnover.

Under which method do the ratios look best?

E.6.8   Restating Financial Statements: Inventory

The 1993 annual report of the Carlton-United Brewery Co. (CUB), disclosed the following statement about the company's inventory (or ''stock'') policy:

> If FIFO had been in use, stocks would have been $1,960 million, $1,654 million, and $1,388 million higher than reported at June 30, 1993, 1992, and 1991, respectively. . . . The company has used LIFO for both tax and financial reporting purposes since 1978 when the merger of the Carlton and United companies occurred.

Required:

(a) Assume a tax rate of 35 percent and that CUB had adopted the FIFO method in 1978 and had been consistently used since that time. Restate the CUB balance sheets presented in Exercise 6.6 as of year-end 1992 and 1993 to reflect the use of the FIFO method.

(b) Assess the effect on net income in 1992 and 1993 assuming the use of FIFO instead of LIFO.

(c) Calculate the following ratios for 1992 and 1993 under both FIFO and LIFO:

(1) Current ratio.

(2) Inventory turnover.

(3) Average number of days' inventory on hand.

(4) Total debt-to-shareholders' equity.

Under which method do the ratios look best?

E.6.9   Analysis of Doubtful Accounts

In late 1993, T2 Medical, Inc., restated its earnings for the first and second quarters of 1993 sharply downward after the company discovered ''accounting irregularities and errors.'' The disclosure of the accounting problems was accompanied by the resignation of the company's chief executive officer and its chief financial officer. According to a company spokesperson, the earnings restatements stemmed largely from inadequate provisions for doubtful accounts. In the case of T2 Medical, a provider of intravenous drug therapy and other medical services in the home, doubtful accounts represent billings that neither insurance companies nor patients are likely to pay. In early 1994, the SEC began an investigation of the company's accounting practices.

Required:

    (a) Why would a company or its management intentionally understate its provision for doubtful accounts?

    (b) How could an analyst identify that a company had underprovided for its doubtful accounts?

E.6.10   Accounting for Goodwill

During 1993, both QVC Network, Inc., and Viacom, Inc., made competitive acquisition bids for Paramount Communications, Inc. Both bids placed a value on Paramount of approximately $10 billion, and both offers involved a substantial amount of cash, as well as stock; thus, regardless of which firm won the bidding for Paramount, the acquiror would be required to account for the investment on a purchase method basis. Industry analysts speculated that Paramount's fair market value was approximately $7.5 billion, as compared to its book value of approximately $4.5 billion, at the time of the tender offers.

Required:

    (a) How much goodwill is inherent in the acquisition bids for Paramount? Over what period of time would you recommend that the Paramount goodwill be written off? (*Hint:* Paramount is in the film production and sports business.) Calculate the annual "drag" on earnings caused by the goodwill, based on your estimate of the life of the Paramount goodwill.

    (b) Why would QVC Network or Viacom be willing to pay in excess of the fair market value of Paramount?

    (c) As we will see in Chapters 8–14, the accounting for goodwill differs dramatically around the world. In Japan, for instance, goodwill is written off over 5 years, and in Germany over 15 years. In Great Britain, goodwill may be written off as a lump sum against retained earnings on the date of acquisition. Given the disparities of these practices, it is difficult to compare the performance of companies from different countries. What measure (or measures) of performance would you prefer to evaluate as a means to overcome this lack of comparability?

E.6.11   Restatement of Restructuring Charges

Refer to the data in Exercise 5.4. GTE's 1993 $1,840 million pre-tax ($1,173 million after-tax) restructuring charge primarily reflects the development of alternative transmission methods through technological advances and increased competition. It includes $1,400 million at Telephone Operations, primarily to implement the company's reengineering plan. This plan will redesign and streamline processes to improve customer responsiveness and product quality, reduce the time necessary to introduce new products and services, and further reduce costs. The reengineering plan will be implemented over the next three years, with expected reductions of approximately 17,000 Telephone Operations employees during that time. The reengineering effort is expected to result in savings of approximately $1 billion annually after full implementation in 1996.

The restructuring charge also includes a $400 million reduction in the carrying value of satellite communication assets (and certain other assets) to estimated net realizable value, primarily reflecting technological advances and increased competition.

The Telephone Operations reengineering plan includes $680 million to upgrade or replace existing customer service and administrative systems and enhance network software, $410 million for employee separation benefits associated with workforce reductions, and $210 million primarily for the consolidation of facilities and operations and other related costs.

Required:

    (a) Describe as fully as possible the effects of the restructuring charge on the financial statements.

    (b) Prepare a journal entry that would eliminate the effects of the restructuring charge from GTE's 1993 financial statements.

    (c) Is full restatement by an analyst for the effect of the 1993 restructuring charge advisable? Discuss the pros and cons, and, if appropriate, recommend an alternative to full restatement.

E.6.12   Restating Financial Statements

Global Electronics, Inc. (GE) produces airborne navigation systems, military and civilian communication systems, and multimedia systems and equipment that are marketed internationally largely to governmental customers. In early 1994, GE decided to modify several of its accounting and reporting policies to bring the company into closer compliance with existing IASC accounting proposals. This decision was reached because company executives felt that the company would have a better chance of winning governmental contracts around the world if GE were perceived to be more an international company and less a U.S. company. GE was headquartered in Chicago, Illinois.

Accounting Policy Changes

Since the company was founded in 1972, GE had used the LIFO method of accounting for its inventories. This decision was largely driven by GE's desire to minimize its current U.S. income taxes and the LIFO compliance regulation that required U.S. companies adopting LIFO for tax purposes to also use LIFO for financial reporting purposes. Consistent with a 1992 IASC proposal to eliminate the use of LIFO inventory accounting, GE had decided to switch to the FIFO method effective January 1, 1993. Company executives recognized that this accounting policy change would, of necessity, affect the company's tax position as well.

Prior to 1994, GE's policy with respect to research and development costs had been to capitalize all such costs applicable to specific product lines (or government contracts) to the extent that the costs were thought to be recoverable from existing or expected orders; all other R&D costs were charged to expense as incurred. Although company executives felt that this policy was substantially in compliance with IASC guidelines, they decided, nonetheless, to adopt a policy in which all R&D costs would be expensed when incurred. This change appeared warranted because of the changing environment of government contracting. Although in the past, GE could be certain that all R&D costs would be reimbursed by government clients, this was becoming less the case. Increasingly, government clients were expecting companies to spend their own risk capital on projects with little or no guarantee of reimbursement. GE decided to implement this policy change effective January 1, 1993.

Finally, prior to 1994, GE had followed an amortization policy for its various patents and license agreements under which these assets were amortized against earnings using a straight-line approach, with an estimated life of 15 years. GE executives realized, however, that with the de-escalation of the Cold War, many of their patented and licensed military products would face a rapidly declining marketplace. This fact, among others, suggested that patents and licenses be written off over a substantially shorter period. Thus, effective January 1, 1993, GE executives decided to amortize any remaining balances in those asset accounts over a 5-year period.

The following Exhibits 1 and 2 are GE's comparative financial statements for 1992 and 1993. These statements do *not* reflect the accounting policy changes reached by GE executives in early 1994.

Required:

   (a) Restate GE's 1993 statement of earnings to reflect the use of FIFO inventory accounting. If GE had used FIFO since 1972, by how much would the company's retained earnings have increased (relative to the use of LIFO) by year-end 1993? If GE had been using FIFO throughout all of 1993, what would the specific dollar effect have been on the company's net working capital?

   (b) Restate GE's 1993 financial statements to reflect the new R&D policy effective January 1, 1993. Using an adjusting entry, illustrate how this change would be implemented. Should this policy be implemented for tax purposes also? Why or why not?

   (c) Restate GE's 1993 financial statements to reflect the adoption of the new patents and licensing amortization policy. Using an adjusting entry, illustrate how this change could be implemented. Should this policy be implemented for tax purposes also? Why or why not?

   (d) Explain how an efficient securities market should respond to these accounting policy changes vis-à-vis GE's stock price.

EXHIBIT 1

GLOBAL ELECTRONICS, INC.
Partial Consolidated Balance Sheets
(000s)

	As of December 31,	
Assets	*1992*	*1993*
Current assets		
Cash	$ 17,700	$ 21,416
Receivables (net)	56,532	58,114
Inventories—At current cost (approximates FIFO)	120,295	137,614
Less: Allowance to reduce value to LIFO basis	(28,052)	(31,261)
Total current assets	$ 166,475	$ 185,883
Investments in and advances to unconsolidated and		
50%-owned companies	21,144	23,524
Property, plant, and equipment	100,089	110,068
Less: Accumulated depreciation	(53,796)	(55,925)
Goodwill	9,950	9,000
Patent and license agreements	1,268,254	1,265,611
Less: Accumulated depreciation	(230,717)	(383,223)
Deferred research and development costs	1,061,726	2,140,445
Less: Accumulated amortization	(562,174)	(1,127,586)
Total assets	$1,780,951	$2,167,797

EXHIBIT 2

GLOBAL ELECTRONICS, INC.
Consolidated Statement of Earnings
(000s)

	As of December 31,	
	1992	*1993*
Revenues	$993,533	$1,070,990
Costs and expenses		
Cost of goods sold (including depreciation and		
amortization)	924,648	985,043
Selling and administrative	52,281	59,140
Interest and financing charges (net of interest earned)	8,187	12,424
	$985,116	$1,056,607
Earnings before taxes and extraordinary items	8,417	14,383
Provision for income taxes	(3,702)	(6,332)
	4,715	8,051
Equity in earnings of unconsolidated and 50%-owned		
companies	1,746	2,372
Earnings before extraordinary items	6,461	10,423
Extraordinary items	(1,266)	–0–
Net earnings	$ 5,195	$ 10,423

CASES

CASE 6.1
RESTATING FINANCIAL STATEMENTS

Waterloo Office Products International, Inc.

Waterloo Office Products International, Inc., is a U.S.–based manufacturer of office equipment and related products. Presented in Exhibits 1 and 2 are Waterloo's condensed income statements and balance sheets for 1992 and 1993. Assume that you are an analyst working for a leading institutional investor. Your assignment is to recast Waterloo's financial statements to reflect the use of alternative accounting practices. Consider each issue independently, and assume a tax rate of 35 percent.

1. **Inventory Accounting**

    A review of Waterloo's footnotes revealed the following:

    • The company used LIFO to value all of its inventory.
    • The LIFO reserve was $1.96 billion, $1.654 billion, and $1.388 billion, respectively, as of December 31, 1993, 1992, and 1991.

    Required:

    (a) Assume that Waterloo had used LIFO since its founding in 1973; restate its income statements and balance sheets as of year-end 1992 and 1993 to reflect the use of FIFO.

    (b) Calculate the following ratios for Waterloo for 1992 and 1993 under both LIFO and FIFO:

    (1) Current ratio.
    (2) Inventory turnover.
    (3) Average number of days' inventory on hand.
    (4) Total debt-to-equity ratio.

    Under which method do the ratios look their best?

2. **Depreciation Accounting**

    A review of Waterloo's footnotes revealed that the company had used accelerated depreciation methods for both tax and financial reporting purposes. Moreover, information with respect to the age of Waterloo's depreciable assets suggests that if straight-line depreciation had been used instead, the depreciation expense for 1993, 1992, and 1991, would have been $74 million, $60 million, and $48 million less, respectively, and the account Building and Equipment (net) would have been $504 million, $430 million, and $370 million higher than originally reported, respectively.

    Required:

    (a) Restate Waterloo's income statements and balance sheets for 1992 and 1993 assuming that straight-line depreciation is used for financial reporting purposes but that accelerated depreciation continues to be used for tax purposes.

(b) Calculate the following ratios for Waterloo for 1992 and 1993 under both the original financial statements and the restated financial statements:

(1). Return on sales.

(2) Return on total assets.

(3) Noncurrent asset turnover.

(4) Total asset turnover.

Under which set of financial statements do the ratios look their best?

3. Consolidation Accounting

The footnotes accompanying Waterloo's consolidated financial statements reveals that at year-end 1991, Waterloo acquired the net assets of Pundra Industries (a Canadian manufacturer of office products) by issuing 1.9 million shares of Waterloo common stock in exchange for all of the voting shares of Pundra Industries. Because of the nature of the transaction, Waterloo accounted for the acquisition as a pooling of interests and, accordingly, included in its consolidated balance sheet the book value of Pundra's net assets (i.e., $32 million).[1] At the time of the transaction, Waterloo's common stock traded over-the-counter at approximately $50 per share, giving the stock exchanged an implicit total value of $95 million.

Required:

(a) Restate Waterloo's 1992 and 1993 financial statements to reflect the use of purchase accounting for the Pundra acquisition. Assume that the fair market value of Pundra's identifiable net assets is $32 million and that any capitalized goodwill is amortized over 40 years.

(b) Calculate the following ratios for Waterloo for 1992 and 1993 under both purchase accounting and the pooling-of-interests method:

(1) Total debt-to-total assets.

(2) Book value per share (assuming that 86.5 million shares are outstanding following the acquisition).

(3) Earnings per share.

(4) Return on equity.

Under which method do the ratios look their best?

4. Cash Flow Accounting

A review of Waterloo's financial statements revealed that an indirect method statement of cash flows (not included here) was presented along with the consolidated income statements and consolidated balance sheets.

Required:

Prepare a direct method statement of cash flows for Waterloo for 1993.

---

[1]The transaction was recorded on Waterloo's books as follows:

Dr. Net Assets (from Pundra Industries)	$32 million	
Cr. Common Stock		$3 million
Cr. Retained Earnings		29 million

EXHIBIT 1

WATERLOO OFFICE PRODUCTS INTERNATIONAL, INC.
Condensed Consolidated Statement of Income
For the Years Ending December 31, 1993 and 1992
(in millions)

	1993	1992
Sales	$8,598	$7,613
Cost of goods sold	6,957*	6,172*
Other expenses (net)	844	715
Income taxes	232	234
Total expenses	8,033	7,121
Income	$ 565	$ 492
Note		
Depreciation for year	370	312
Dividends	201	182

*This figure includes depreciation allocable to cost of goods sold.

EXHIBIT 2

WATERLOO OFFICE PRODUCTS INTERNATIONAL, INC.
Condensed Consolidated Balance Sheets
As of December 31, 1993 and 1992
(in millions)

	December 31,	
Assets	1993	1992
Cash and cash equivalents	$ 104	$ 147
Receivables (net)	912	693
Inventories	1,750	1,670
Land	81	66
Building and equipment (net)	2,928	2,572
Long-term investments	103	85
Other assets and goodwill	220	146
Total	$6,098	$5,379
Liabilities and Owners' Equity		
Payables and accruals	$1,067	$ 790
Income tax payable	198	133
Notes payable	430	404
Deferred income tax	23	(24)
Long-term debt (total)	948	1,011
Total	2,666	2,314
Common stock	180	177
Retained earnings	3,252	2,888
Total	$6,098	$5,379

CASE 6.2
CONSTRUCTIVE CAPITALIZATION OF LEASES

Apple Computer

Of all the success stories of the personal computing industry, perhaps none is as impressive as that of Apple Computer. Founded in a garage in 1975 by college drop-out Steve Jobs, it took just six years for Apple to achieve net sales of $334 million and assets of $254 million. By 1991, Apple produced net income of $310 million on net sales of $6.3 billion, with total assets of $3.5 billion, and had become the first personal computing company to reach the Fortune 100.

From a financial standpoint, what was most striking about Apple's success was the complete absence of any long-term debt (other than deferred income taxes) in the company's capital structure. This apparent absence of financial leverage was in significant contrast to other major computer companies (see Exhibit 1):

The footnotes to Apple's financial statements, however, reveal a somewhat different story. Specifically, Apple's footnotes detail that the company had entered into substantial amounts of operating leases:

> The company leases various facilities and equipment under noncancelable lease arrangements. The major facilities leases are for terms of 5 to 10 years and generally provide renewal options for terms of up to 10 additional years. Rent expense under all operating leases was approximately $163 million, $139 million, and $106 million in 1991, 1990, and 1989, respectively. Future minimum lease payments under these noncancellable operating leases as of September 27, 1991, are as follows (in thousands):

Year	
1992	$107,580
1993	103,629
1994	79,565
1995	55,166
1996	33,903
Thereafter	60,143
Total minimum lease payments	$439,986

This case was prepared by William J. R. Wilson and Kenneth R. Ferris. Copyright © 1993 by Kenneth R. Ferris. All rights reserved to the authors.

EXHIBIT 1

COMPARATIVE CAPITAL STRUCTURE OF
Major Computer Companies
(as of December 31, 1991)

Company	Long-Term Debt (millions)	Long-Term Debt to Capital Ratio (percent)
AST Research	$ 30.1	9%
Commodore International	71.9	19
Compaq	73.9	4
Digital Equipment	150.0	2
Hewlett-Packard	190.0	3
IBM	11,191.0	24
Sun Microsystems	351.4	22
Unisys	2,997.7	60

Apple's footnotes further detail that, in 1991, a subsidiary of the company formed a partnership with a local real estate developer for the purpose of constructing a campus-type office facility, which was then to be leased to Apple and to be held by the partnership as a long-term investment. Under this arrangement, Apple executed noncancellable leases with the partnership for the buildings for terms of 12 to 17 years.[1] Lease payments were to commence at various dates in 1993 and 1994. Under the leases, the future minimum lease payments were as follows (in thousands):

Year	
1992	$ —
1993	10,119
1994	19,136
1995	19,136
1996	19,844
Thereafter	294,193
Total minimum lease payments	$362,428

[1] Apple accounts for this subsidiary under the equity method. Accordingly, a portion of the partnership's earnings that include the lease payments are allocated back to the company based on its ownership percentage.

Lease Accounting.   In the United States, the accounting for leases is governed by FASB *Statement No. 13.* Under this statement, leases are classified into two categories: capital and operating. Capital leases are considered to be the equivalent of a purchase contract, consequently requiring the lessee to record a lease asset and a lease liability on its balance sheet. Operating leases, on the other hand, require no balance sheet disclosure (except via the footnotes) because they transfer no rights, risks, or rewards of ownership from the lessor to the lessee.

The criteria used to distinguish between the two types of leases are well defined:

1. The lease transfers ownership of the leased asset to the lessee by the end of the lease period.
2. The lease agreement contains a bargain purchase option under which the lessee is entitled to purchase the leased asset at a substantial discount from its fair market value.
3. The lease term is equal to 75 percent or more of the estimated economic life of the leased asset.
4. The present value of contractual lease payments is equal to or greater than 90 percent of the leased asset's fair market value at the inception of the lease agreement.

If any one of these criteria is satisfied, the lease must be treated as a capital lease; if none are satisfied, the lease must be treated as operating. If the lease is accounted for as a capital lease, the minimum lease payments (excluding those payments contingent on future sales or income) are discounted at the lower of the interest rate implicit in the lease or the lessee's incremental borrowing rate. The decision as to how to amortize the associated lease asset is a management decision. Generally, if the capital lease transfers ownership of the asset to the lessee or contains a bargain purchase option, the asset should be depreciated over its estimated economic life. Otherwise, the lease asset should be depreciated in such a way that it is fully amortized when the lease expires. If, on the other hand, a lease is classified as operating, no balance sheet disclosure of either the lease asset or the lease liability is required; however, footnote disclosure of the minimum future lease payments, in total and for each of the successive five years, is required.

Analytical Considerations.   To cash flow-oriented financial analysts, such as loan officers and credit analysts, the distinction between a capital lease and an operating lease may exist only in the minds of the accounting standard setters. After all, both involve, at a minimum, a fixed set of noncancellable future cash outlays.

That a distinction exists at all reflects the balance sheet orientation of accounting regulators, in that both types of leases have essentially equivalent effects on the other principal financial statements (i.e., the income statement and the statement of cash flows). The distinction does, however, reinforce the belief held by some corporate managers that the total borrowing capacity of a company can be increased by keeping some (or all) leases off-balance sheet.

Required:

Consider Apple's balance sheet (Exhibit 2) and income statement (Exhibit 3).

(a) Has the exclusive use of operating leases increased Apple's borrowing capacity?

(b) Restate the company's financial statements to reflect the capitalization of all operating leases in 1991 and then compare the company's leverage position, both before and after restatement, by calculating the following ratios:

(1) Total liabilities/total assets.
(2) Total liabilities/total equity.
(3) Long-term debt/cash flows from operations.

Your analysis should assume discount rates of both 6 and 10 percent.

EXHIBIT 2

APPLE COMPUTER, INC.
Consolidated Balance Sheets
September 24, 1991, and September 28, 1990
(in thousands of dollars)

Assets	1991	1990
Current assets:		
Cash and cash equivalents	$ 604,147	$ 374,682
Short-term investments	288,572	622,409
Accounts receivable, net of allowance for doubtful		
accounts of $53,933 ($49,426 in 1990)	907,159	761,868
Inventories	671,655	355,473
Prepaid income taxes	222,980	125,535
Other current assets	169,097	163,359
Total current assets	$2,863,610	$2,403,326
Property, plant, and equipment:		
Land and buildings	$ 198,107	$ 117,350
Machinery and equipment	485,872	402,168
Office furniture and equipment	146,433	137,485
Leasehold improvements	205,602	187,868
	$1,036,014	$ 844,871
Accumulated depreciation and amortization	(588,036)	(446,706)
Net property, plant, and equipment	$ 447,978	$ 398,165
Other assets	$ 182,009	$ 174,216
	$3,493,597	$2,975,707

EXHIBIT 2 (continued)

APPLE COMPUTER, INC.
Consolidated Balance Sheets
September 24, 1991, and September 28, 1990
(in thousands of dollars)

Liabilities and Shareholders' Equity	*1991*	*1990*
Current liabilities		
Notes payable	$ 148,566	$ 122,630
Accounts payable	357,084	340,575
Accrued compensation and employee benefits	119,468	115,513
Income taxes payable	14,857	33,241
Accrued marketing and distribution	136,712	164,713
Accrued restructuring costs	162,365	—
Other current liabilities	277,999	250,383
Total current liabilities	$1,217,051	$1,027,055
Deferred income taxes	$509,870	$501,832
Commitments		
Shareholders' equity:		
Common stock, no par value; 320,000,000 shares authorized; 118,385,899 shares issued and outstanding in 1991 (115,358,922 shares in 1990)	278,865	136,555
Retained earnings	1,492,024	1,312,156
Accumulated translation adjustment	(2,377)	4,142
	$1,768,512	$1,452,853
Notes receivable from shareholders	(1,836)	(6,033)
Total shareholders' equity	$1,766,676	$1,446,820
	$3,493,597	$2,975,707

EXHIBIT 3

APPLE COMPUTER, INC.
Consolidated Statements of Income
Three Fiscal Years Ended September 27
(in thousands, except per share amounts)

	1991	*1990*	*1989*
Net sales	$6,308,849	$5,558,435	$5,284,013
Costs and expenses			
Cost of sales	$3,314,118	2,606,223	2,694,823
Research and development	583,046	478,019	420,083
Selling, general and administrative	1,740,293	1,728,508	1,534,794
Restructuring costs and other	224,043	33,673	—
	$5,861,500	$4,846,423	$4,649,700
Operating income	$ 447,349	$ 712,012	$ 634,313
Interest and other income, net	52,395	66,505	110,009
Income before income taxes	$ 499,744	$ 778,517	$ 744,322
Provision for income taxes	189,903	303,622	290,289
Net income	$ 309,841	$ 474,895	$ 454,033
Earnings per common and common equivalent share	$ 2.58	$ 3.77	$ 3.53
Common and common equivalent shares used in the calculations of earnings per share	$ 120,283	$ 125,813	$ 128,669

CASE 6.3
RESTATING FINANCIAL STATEMENTS

Australasian Technology, Inc. (A)

In February 1994, Joe Fisher began working as a credit analyst in the International Lending Department of the National Bank of Texas, the lead bank of a large regional bank holding company. He had spent his first few months on the job in the bank's training program and had just been assigned to the International Lending Department.

His first assignment concerned Australasian Technology, Inc. (ATI), a Pacific Rim–based company that primarily manufactured electronic components for computers under licensing agreements with several Japanese companies. In addition, however, the company maintained a small research and development staff that occasionally provided improvements on the foreign-designed products.

Joe learned that ATI, like many of the companies that he would be asked to analyze, was not publicly held. As a consequence, the financial statements that he had been given to analyze (see Exhibits 1 and 2) had probably not been audited by an independent certified public accountant and, in all likelihood, would not have been prepared in conformity with U.S. generally accepted accounting principles.

Concerned about the possibility that the financial statements might have been prepared in a manner that would make the firm look its very best and possibly even overstate the prior performance of the company, Joe had been instructed by his supervisor to restate ATI's balance sheet and income statement in a manner consistent with ''conservative U.S. generally accepted accounting principles.'' Because the company's financial statements had no accompanying explanatory footnotes, Joe proceeded by first contacting by telephone (and later by facsimile letter) the controller of ATI. From this conversation, he learned the following:

1. The financial statements he received were stated in U.S. dollar equivalents, and although the company's primary source of sales were international, all operations were headquartered in Sydney, Australia.

2. Inventories (or ''stocks'') were stated on a FIFO basis. If LIFO had been utilized, the value of inventories would have been $889,000 at January 1, 1993, and $1,270,000 at December 31, 1993.

3. Property, plant, and equipment had been depreciated on a straight-line basis. If an accelerated method had been utilized, the depreciation expense for 1993 would have been $230,000 more, and the balance in the accumulated depreciation account as of December 31, 1993, would have been $450,000 higher.

This case was prepared by Kenneth R. Ferris. Copyright © 1993 by Kenneth R. Ferris. All rights reserved to the author.

EXHIBIT 1

AUSTRALASIAN TECHNOLOGY, INC.
Balance Sheet
As of December 31, 1993

Assets			*Equities*	
Noncurrent assets			Creditors	
Property, plant, and equipment $3,940,000			Accounts payable	$ 820,000
Less: Accumulated depreciation (1,360,000)			Accrued expenses payable	80,000
		$2,580,000	Total current liabilities	900,000
Land		560,000		
Deferred research & development costs		$1,150,000		
Total noncurrent assets		$4,290,000		
Current assets			Noncurrent liabilities	
Cash		$436,000	Notes payable	$2,320,000
Trade debtors (net of allowance for			Deferred income taxes	800,000
uncollectible accounts)		828,000	Total liabilities	$4,020,000
Stocks		1,720,000	Shareholder capital	
Prepaid expenses		30,000	Ordinary share capital	$2,000,000
Total current assets		$3,014,000	Profit & loss reserve	1,284,000
Total assets		$7,304,000	Total equities	$7,304,000

EXHIBIT 2

AUSTRALASIAN TECHNOLOGY, INC.
Income Statement
For the Year Ended December 31, 1993

Turnover		$4,950,000
Less: Cost of sales		
Beginning stock	$1,205,000	
Cost of production	3,665,000	
Goods available for sale	4,870,000	
Less: Ending stock	(1,720,000)	
		(3,150,000)
Gross profit		$1,800,000
Less: Research and development expenses	350,000	
Licensing fees	100,000	
Selling and administrative expenses	400,000	
		(850,000)
Profit before taxes		$950,000
Less: Income taxes	475,000	
Investment and research tax credits	(60,000)	
		(415,000)
Profit set aside to reserves		$535,000

4. The research and development expense for 1993 represented one-half of the actual R&D expenditure for 1993; the remaining balance had been capitalized. The company's policy with respect to capitalized R&D costs was to begin amortization only after a commercially productive asset had been developed. To date, no productive assets had resulted from the research program represented by the currently capitalized R&D costs.

5. During 1993, investment and research tax credits of $60,000 had been earned; no credits had been earned prior to 1993. The tax credits had been accounted for using the flow-through method.

6. The company had no contributory pension plan for its employees and, hence, no unfunded pension obligation.

7. For tax purposes, the company had utilized accelerated depreciation, FIFO, and had fully expensed all research and development expenditures.

Joe realized that, overall, ATI had utilized a relatively liberal set of accounting methods to prepare its financial statements and that, in at least one instance (i.e., the capitalization of R&D), the company had not followed U.S. generally accepted accounting principles. Accordingly, Joe decided to restate the financial statements using the following accounting practices:

1. LIFO inventory valuation.
2. Accelerated depreciation.
3. Expensing of R&D as incurred.
4. Deferral of investment and research tax credits.

With respect to the tax credits, Joe decided to write the credits off over a period of 10 years and to assume that the credits had been earned on June 30, 1993.

Required:

(a) Restate ATI's balance sheet and income statement using the accounting methods and assumptions selected by Joe.

(b) As part of the credit analysis, compute the following:
   (1) The LIFO inventory reserve at January 1, 1993, and December 31, 1993.
   (2) The current ratio at December 31, 1993, for both the original and revised financial statements.
   (3) The debt-to-tangible-net-worth ratio at December 31, 1993, for both the original and revised financial statements.

(c) Compare the creditworthiness of ATI as revealed by the original versus revised financial statements.

CASE 6.4
RESTATING FINANCIAL STATEMENTS

Australasian Technology, Inc. (B)

In January 1994, Australasian Technology, Inc. (ATI), had approached the National Bank of Texas about the possibility of obtaining a $680,000 loan for the acquisition of new electronic component production equipment. The new equipment was part of a major capital investment program designed to enable the company to manufacture the latest technology in component parts. ATI manufactured electronic components for computers under licensing agreements with several Japanese companies.

On the strength of the company's financial history and on the condition that the owners of ATI also invest at least $2 million of their own capital in the expansion program, the loan was approved in late March 1994. Because the acquisition and installation of the equipment would take approximately 18 months and, hence, would not be generating revenue for some time, the 10-year loan was so structured that only debt service payments were required the first three years; thereafter, payments would include both principal and interest.

In February 1996, ATI provided the bank with its 1995 year-end financial statements. The loan agreement required the company to periodically submit its financial reports to the bank to enable the bank to monitor its financial condition and determine how adequately the loan covenants were being met. Joe Fisher, the analyst who had worked on the initial credit review in 1994, was given the 1995 statements and instructed to undertake the current loan review (Exhibits 1 and 2).

Joe immediately observed several major changes in the company's financial statements and disclosure practices. Unlike the initial set of reports that he had analyzed, the 1995 statements contained explanatory footnotes and had been audited by an independent certified public accountant. Not only were these latest financial statements prepared on a basis consistent with U.S. generally accepted accounting principles but also Joe soon learned that they had been prepared using relatively conservative accounting practices. Joe recalled that, as part of the initial loan review, his supervisor had instructed him to restate the financial statements because the company had utilized such liberal accounting methods in their statement preparation. He also noted that during 1994, the company had adopted a pension plan for its employees and had undertaken appropriate funding of the plan.

In developing his strategy for the loan review, Joe mentally noted that, for comparison purposes, it might be useful to restate the 1995 financial statements to an accounting basis consistent with that of the 1993 and 1994 reports. This would provide him with several bases to evaluate the company's performance.

This case was prepared by Kenneth R. Ferris. Copyright © 1993 by Kenneth R. Ferris. All rights reserved to the author.

AUSTRALASIAN TECHNOLOGY, INC.
Income Statement
For the Year Ended December 31, 1995

Turnover		$10,588,000
Less: Cost of sales		
Beginning stock	$ 2,640,000	
Cost of production	8,470,000	
Goods available for sale	$11,110,000	
Less: Ending stock	(3,800,000)	
		(7,310,000)
Gross profit		$ 3,278,000
Less: Research and development expense	514,000	
Licensing fees	200,000	
Selling and administrative expense	1,400,000	
		(2,114,000)
Profit before taxes		$ 1,164,000
Less: Income taxes	$ 582,000	
Investment and research tax credits	(20,000)	
		(562,000)
Profit set aside to reserves		$ 602,000

AUSTRALASIAN TECHNOLOGY, INC.
Balance Sheet
For the Year Ended December 31, 1995

Noncurrent assets			Creditors	
Property, plant, and equipment	$ 7,880,000		Accounts payable	$ 2,760,000
Less: Accumulated depreciation	(3,250,000)		Accrued expenses payable	160,000
	$ 4,630,000		Total current liablities	$ 2,920,000
Land	1,020,000			
Total noncurrent assets	$ 5,650,000			
Current assets			Noncurrent liabilities	
Cash	872,000		Notes payable	$ 2,320,000
Trade debtors (net of allowance for			Bank loan	680,000
uncollectible accounts)	1,656,000		Total liabilities	$ 5,920,000
Stocks	3,800,000		Deferred investment and research tax	
Prepaid expenses	60,000		credits	$ 400,000
Total current assets	$ 6,388,000		Shareholder capital	
Total assets	$12,038,000		Ordinary share capital	4,000,000
			Profit and loss reserve	1,718,000
			Total equities	$12,038,000

From reading the accompanying footnotes, Joe learned that the 1995 statements had been prepared using the following accounting methods:

1. Inventories were stated on a LIFO basis.

2. Property, plant, and equipment was depreciated on an accelerated basis.

3. Research and development costs were expensed as incurred.

4. Investment and research tax credits were deferred and written off over the life of the related asset (or a maximum of 10 years).

5. The firm reported no deferred income taxes because its tax return and accounting statements had been prepared on a consistent basis.

6. Pension costs, reported as part of selling and administrative expenses, included a $200,000 payment into the firm's pension fund.

He decided to restate the financial statements as follows:

1. FIFO inventory.

2. Straight-line depreciation.

3. Capitalization of one-half of R&D expenditures (effective January 1, 1995).

4. Flow through of the investment and research tax credits.

5. No funding or accruing of the past service pension cost (effective January 1, 1995).

A conversation with the controller of ATI provided him with the following additional information: (1) the FIFO value of ATI's stocks (i.e., inventory) was $3,640,000 at January 1, 1995, and $5,200,000 at December 31, 1995, respectively; (2) if straight-line depreciation had been used, the depreciation expense for 1995 would have been $105,000 *less* and accumulated depreciation at December 31, 1995, would have been $950,000 *less;* and (3) investment and research tax credits of $100,000 were earned in 1995.

Joe realized that some of these accounting changes (e.g., the LIFO to FIFO switch) would create real tax effects and, hence, decided to assume that any additional tax liabilities for prior years would be immediately paid in cash. In addition, however, he recognized that most of the other changes were only for accounting purposes but nonetheless would have to be accounted for through a deferred income tax account.

Required:

(a) Restate the 1995 ATI balance sheet and income statement using the accounting methods and assumptions selected by Joe.

(b) Calculate the following:

(1) The LIFO inventory reserve at January 1, 1995, and December 31, 1995.

(2) The current ratio at December 31, 1995, for both the original and revised set of financial statements.

(3) The debt-to-tangible-net-worth ratio at December 31, 1995, for both the original and revised set of financial statements.

(c) Compare the creditworthiness of ATI as revealed by the original versus restated financial statements.

Accounting for Foreign Operations

[C]ross-border business has been driven forward by three main things: falling regulatory barriers to overseas investment; tumbling telecommunications and transport costs; and free domestic and international capital markets in which companies can be bought, and currency and other risks can be controlled.[1]

When a company operates exclusively within a single domestic market, it faces a set of conventional but nonetheless substantial business risks. These risks include those that characterize any competitive business situation and can typically involve new capital formation, product identity, quality, pricing, and obsolescence. When a company operates in a variety of marketplaces—domestic and foreign—representing diverse cultural, ethnic, and national contexts, however, its business risks are magnified both in number and in complexity. The question of how the Kellogg Company, a U.S. maker of breakfast cereals, can market a new product in the United States is far less complex than the question of how it can market Frosted Flakes™ or Cheerios™ in Italy or Brazil. Kellogg must identify and respond to differences in language, consumer preferences, and issues relating to product distribution, manufacturing, packaging, and advertising. Without question, many new concerns and problems arise when a company expands its base of operations beyond its own domestic market and begins operating in international markets as well.

From an accounting perspective, the principal source of complexity relates to differences in a company's *local currency* (in accounting parlance, its **reporting currency**) and the other currencies in which it may transact its business. For example,

---

[1]"A Survey of Multinationals," *The Economist,* March 27, 1993, p. 6.

Kellogg, as a U.S.–based corporation, uses the U.S. dollar for its reporting currency; however, Kellogg must translate currency in several situations:

- Contracts for sales and purchases of goods and services between Kellogg and other companies may specify that payment is to be made in a foreign currency (e.g., the lira or the cruzeiro real). To give accounting recognition to these transactions in its dollar-based accounting records, Kellogg must translate these foreign currency–denominated transactions into U.S. dollars using prevailing foreign currency exchange rates.

- Kellogg may hold or acquire foreign currency or enter into a forward contract or option to sell or acquire foreign currency. Kellogg must translate the units of foreign currency it holds in bank accounts into U.S. dollars using appropriate foreign currency exchange rates. This is also true for foreign currency futures and options contracts it has chosen to enter into.

- Kellogg may present its financial statements on a consolidated basis with one or more foreign subsidiaries whose accounting records are based in a foreign currency. To combine the financial statements of these foreign subsidiaries with Kellogg, they must first be translated into U.S. dollars.

The purposes of this chapter are to explore the role of foreign currency in business transactions and to consider how multinational companies account for international operations. Financial reporting policies with regard to foreign exchange can frequently have a material impact on financial statements—and related ratios—when exchange rates between a reporting currency (i.e., the U.S. dollar for Kellogg) and other currencies fluctuate. The following are just a few examples:

- In a case to be described more fully in the section on hedging, one analyst who was following Dell Computer recently claimed that deferred losses on investments in foreign currency options amounted to as much as 50 percent of Dell's net income. The analyst suspected that these losses were improperly deferred and should have been reflected in the income of the current period.

- Nissan reported foreign exchange income of ¥45 billion for the year ended March 31, 1993. The firm reported a loss of ¥55 billion for the year. In this chapter, we will describe how foreign exchange accounting policies can effect net income.

- Michelin reported reductions in shareholders' equity resulting from ''cumulative translation adjustments'' of FRF 4 billion, roughly twice total shareholders' equity. In this chapter, we shall also describe the cause and nature of cumulative translation adjustments as a separate component of shareholders' equity.

The challenge to analysts in situations such as those described is to evaluate the appropriateness of management's accounting policies with respect to investments in foreign currencies and foreign subsidiaries. This may entail distinguishing between the real effects of foreign currency movements on income for a period and what may be the result of income manipulation by management, or the application of ''form-driven'' accounting standards. The analyst must have sufficient technical knowledge of this complex area of accounting to gather relevant additional data to make appropriate assumptions and well-reasoned inferences. An intermediate product of the analysis may include a restatement of reported results.

Before discussing these analytical challenges, we begin with some background on foreign exchange. Foreign exchange presents a complex set of problems as companies and analysts try to determine the real effect of foreign exchange fluctuations on the earnings, cash flows, and net worth of a business.

Foreign Exchange

One principal source of complexity in conducting business across borders arises because each country in the world operates with its own form of currency or **exchange.** For example, the United States has the dollar ($); in Japan, the yen (¥); and in Great Britain, the pound (£). One potential simplification, for at least some European countries, results from the formation of the European Monetary Union, in which some members of the European Union (EU) are trying to encourage their fellow member-nations to conduct their business transactions using a single currency, the European currency unit (ECU), as mandated by the Maastricht Treaty of November 1991. Whether a single EU currency will emerge is uncertain, but such a proposal will surely make accounting for EU financial activities less complex.

Since the end of World War II, the level of international business activity by multinational firms has grown exponentially. Further, the increase of multinational companies (MNCs) and other publicly traded firms has created worldwide demand for financial reporting standards regarding the presentation of foreign operations in local currency. Generally accepted accounting principles (GAAP) governing foreign currency transactions and the translation of foreign currency financial statements in the United States are, for the most part, found in *SFAS No. 52.*[2] The existing world standard may be found in *IAS No. 21,* which is substantially consistent with *SFAS No. 52.* Current accounting practice in Korea, Sweden, and Great Britain is also substantially in compliance with *IAS No. 21,* while accounting treatment in Brazil, Germany, Italy, and Japan is not (although each of these four countries is likely to attain compliance in the near future).

Foreign exchange information is publicly available from a variety of sources. Exhibit 7–1, for example, presents a list of eight major countries with their related currency. The currency symbols in the exhibit are used as a quick method to indicate monetary denominations used by foreign exchange traders and information services and are part of a de facto world standard used to indicate over 100 currencies.

Exchange rates express the amount it costs to purchase one unit of currency with another currency. Rates can be quoted directly (i.e., in units of *local* currency) or indirectly (i.e., in units of a *foreign* currency). To illustrate the difference between direct and indirect quotation, consider the exchange rate between the USD as local

---

[2]*SFAS No. 52,* ''Foreign Currency Translation'' (Stamford, CT: FASB, 1981).

EXHIBIT 7–1

Selected Major Foreign Currencies

Country	Currency	Symbol
Brazil	Cruzeiro real	BCR
Germany	Deutsche mark	DEM
Great Britain	Pound sterling	GBP
Italy	Lira	ITL
Japan	Yen	JPY
South Korea	Won	SKW
Sweden	Krona	SEK
United States	Dollar	USD

currency and the DEM as the foreign currency. A direct quotation of the exchange rate indicates the number of USD it would cost to purchase one DEM, say 0.5741 USD on January 28, 1994. An indirect quotation is the reciprocal of this amount, or DEM 1.7420. This is the number of DEM required to purchase one USD.

To promote economic stability, the major currencies of the world were at one time fixed. Occasionally, large changes (called **devaluations** or **revaluations**) in the exchange rates were required when substantial value changes occurred between two or more currencies. Today, value swings—appreciation or depreciation—caused by changes in the demand for, or in expectations regarding the value of, the various currencies, occur so often that a floating exchange rate system has been adopted in which all major currencies are free to move against all other currencies according to market demand and expectations. Not all exchanges of foreign currency take place, however, at market rates. Many countries still control the flow of capital over their borders by establishing ''official'' exchange rates. Frequently, official exchange rates for inflows (outflows) of foreign currency are more (less) favorable than market rates.

Foreign Exchange Risk

Presented in Exhibit 7–2 are the prevailing market exchange rates (called **spot rates**) as of January 1 and January 2, 1995 for several major currencies. These rates and those for a large number of currencies are quoted in the financial press on a daily basis and generally reflect the exchange rate among banks for amounts equivalent to 1 million USD or more. Rates for smaller transactions, such as when a traveler exchanges money at the airport when entering a new country, are usually less favorable.

Note that for some major currencies, such as the pound sterling and Deutsche mark, rates (**forward exchange rates**) are also quoted for future delivery of currency in 30, 90, or 180 days. As we will soon see, most international trade involves a delay between setting the price of a transaction (e.g., the sale or purchase of goods between Kellogg and a foreign customer or supplier), and receiving (making) payment for those goods. Consequently, at least one of the participants in such a transaction faces the risk of losing

EXHIBIT 7-2

Selected 1995 Foreign Currency Exchange Rates

	USD Equivalent		Currency per USD	
Country (currency)	January 1	January 2	January 1	January 2
Brazil (BCR)	1.1758	1.1758	0.8500	0.8500
Britain (GBP)	1.5650	1.5595	0.6390	0.6412
30-day forward	1.5647	1.5593	0.6391	0.6413
90-day forward	1.5646	1.5591	0.6392	0.6414
180-day forward	1.5644	1.5589	0.6392	0.6415
Germany (DEM)	0.5741	0.5772	1.7420	1.7326
30-day forward	0.5727	0.5758	1.7462	1.7367
90-day forward	0.5703	0.5734	1.7536	1.7441
180-day forward	0.5677	0.5708	1.7615	1.7519

Source: *The Wall Street Journal,* January 3, 1995.

some amount of local currency purchasing power because the exchange rate may fluctuate before payment is made or received; this type of risk is called currency risk or foreign exchange risk. Entering into a forward exchange contract to receive or pay foreign currency at a future date is one way for companies to limit or eliminate the risk associated with adverse fluctuations of exchange rates on commitments to pay or receive foreign currency. Put another way, a multinational company holding a receivable (payable) in a foreign currency can **hedge** all or part of its exposure to fluctuation in foreign exchange spot rates by entering into a forward contract to pay (receive) foreign currency at or around the due date of the receivable (payable).[3] The decision to hedge, however, involves real transaction costs and hence certain risks itself (to be discussed shortly).

Foreign exchange risk thus refers to the potential gain or loss that may arise from holding receivables or payables denominated in a foreign currency when a movement in the exchange rate between the two currencies occurs. As noted, this exposure can be limited through the purchase of foreign exchange contracts (to be discussed shortly), as well as in other ways. One approach is for the counterparty to an exchange to agree on an effective price, as of a given day, that is *not* subject to exchange rate movements. This is normally accomplished by fixing or ''denominating'' the price of the goods or services in units of local currency of the company that does not wish to bear foreign exchange risk. For example, if it purchased goods from a German distributor, Kellogg could eliminate its exposure to foreign currency exchange rate fluctuations if the price of the goods were denominated in USD. In this way, all risk related to fluctuations in the DEM/USD exchange rate prior to settlement of the transaction would be borne by the German supplier. The USD to be received by the German supplier would be convertible into more or fewer DEM, depending on the movement of foreign exchange rates.

---

[3]A *hedge,* or *hedging,* refers to the process of attempting to reduce or eliminate a firm's exposure to a particular type of risk (e.g., foreign exchange risk).

In accounting parlance, risk of adverse foreign exchange movements as a result of the settlement of purchases or sales of goods and services is called **transaction risk.**[4]

Accounting versus Economic Foreign Exchange Transaction Risk

Transaction risk arises because receivables and payables that are denominated in foreign currencies are reported on balance sheets at their parent company's currency equivalents as of the balance sheet date. The restatement of these receivables and payables using balance sheet date spot exchange rates typically results in income statement gains and losses. For example, a receivable denominated in a foreign currency that was outstanding at two balance sheet dates would give rise to a *transaction gain* (*loss*) on two income statements if the foreign currency devalued (revalued) against the home currency.

To illustrate, consider a U.S. company that sold goods to a British customer for 100,000 GBP on December 15, 19x5. At the date of the transaction, the exchange rate was 2.00 USD. On December 31, 19x5, the end of the U.S. company's fiscal year, the exchange rate was 2.10 USD, and on January 15, 19x6, the date payment was received from the British customer, the exchange rate was 2.15 USD. Journal entries for the U.S. company (keeping its books in USD) related to this transaction follow:

12/15/x5	Accounts Receivable	200,000	
	Sales Revenue		200,000
12/31/x5	Accounts Receivable	10,000	
	Foreign Currency Transaction Gain		10,000
1/15/x6	Cash	215,000	
	Foreign Currency Transaction Gain		5,000
	Accounts Receivable		210,000

In general, transaction gains (or losses) occur on foreign currency receivables and payables that are measured at spot exchange rates on balance sheets. Under existing U.S. and IASC GAAP, these gains (or losses) are reported on a company's income statement in the period in which the gain (or loss) arose. Note in the preceding example that the U.S. company's total transaction gain of 15,000 USD was spread between 19x5 and 19x6. Obviously, managers prefer to avoid any unpleasant surprises, such as a transaction loss, and thus regularly monitor their company's accounting transaction exposure or net receivable/payable position denominated in foreign currencies.

Accounting transaction exposure, however, may not necessarily equate to economic exposure. Whereas **accounting exposure** is the risk of reporting income statement

---

[4]*Transaction risk* (or *exposure*) refers to the likelihood that a company will experience a real cash flow gain (or loss) on an individual transaction as a direct consequence of an exchange rate movement. This economic risk is frequently distinguished from a second type of risk that results from currency movements: **translation risk** (or **accounting exposure**), which generally reflects the likelihood of experiencing an unrealized valuation gain (or loss) on the net assets of a company located in another country when exchange rate changes occur between balance sheet dates. Under both FASB and IASC accounting standards, the effects of transaction risk are reflected on the income statement, whereas the effects of translation risk are most commonly reflected on the balance sheet.

gains and losses for a period, **economic exposure** is the risk of real wealth changes—or changes in purchasing power—resulting from uncertain future events. In the case of foreign exchange transaction risk, the uncertain future events in question cause movements in foreign exchange rates. The following are some examples of exchange rate movements when recognition of accounting gains or losses may not correspond to real economic gains or losses:

- The same economic events that caused a movement in exchange rates also affect the purchasing power of the reporting currency, and, hence, the price that a company will pay and receive for various goods and services. Although accounting recognition is given immediately to changes in the fair value of foreign exchange and foreign currency–denominated receivables and payables, recognition of cost and revenue increases due to changing prices is postponed until realized in actual transactions.

- A company does not intend to convert the foreign exchange received in settlement of a sale into the home currency but will use it to purchase other goods and services in the foreign country. Inventory measured in historical home country currency may be a natural hedge against foreign currency payables if the inventory is to be sold for foreign currency, yet the timing of income recognition on these items differ. Recognition of profits on investments in inventory is delayed until the period in which the inventory is sold; losses in foreign currency–denominated trade payables are recognized as soon as exchange rates fluctuate.

Forward Foreign Currency Contracts as Hedges

Strategies for reducing transaction exposure are commonly referred to as *hedges,* as previously noted, and they can take many forms. One form just described is to agree to settle a transaction in one's home currency. In exchange for such an accommodation, however, the counterparty to the transaction is likely to charge a fee in the form of a less favorable price on the goods or services exchanged.

When a transaction is denominated in the home currency of one of the parties to a transaction, no additional hedging activity by the party receiving the accommodation is usually needed. However, the party granting the accommodation may wish to hedge its currency risk exposure. One way for the accommodating company to limit its foreign currency risk is by entering into a transaction with an exchange broker to purchase or sell foreign currency for future delivery at a fixed exchange rate. To illustrate, assume that on January 2, 1995, a U.S. company sells and delivers goods to a German company. The agreement between the two companies stipulates that the U.S. company shall be paid 10 million DEM on February 1, 1995. To hedge its foreign currency exposure of 10 million DEM (or $5,772,000 = 10 million DEM × 0.5772 USD), the U.S. company could sell a 10 million DEM, 30-day forward contract. Given the forward exchange rates in Exhibit 7–2, such a contract would obligate the U.S. company to provide 10 million DEM in exchange for 5,758,000 USD (10 million DEM × 0.5758 USD). To demonstrate how the forward contract functions to eliminate accounting exposure,

---

EXHIBIT 7–3
Foreign Exchange Contract Illustration (Current Spot Rate is $.5772; 30-Day Forward Rate is $.5758)

	Possible February 1 DEM/USD Spot Rates		
	$0.6772 *(revaluation)*	*$0.5772* *(no change)*	*0.4772* *(devaluation)*
Effect of DEM–denominated receivable on pre-tax net income	**(1,000,000) USD**	**–0–USD**	**1,000,000 USD**
Effect of forward contract on pre-tax net income:			
Contract premium	(14,000)*	(14,000)	(14,000)
Gain (loss) on forward contract	1,000,000	–0–	(1,000,000)
Potential net gain (loss) with forward contract	**(14,000) USD**	**(14,000) USD**	**(14,000) USD**

*14,000 USD is the difference between the value of the receivable in dollars as of January 2 (10 million DEM × 0.5772 USD = 5,772,000 USD) and the value of the forward contract as of January 2 (10 million DEM × 0.5758 USD = 5,758,000 USD). In theory, the $14,000 premium contains two components. The first is a charge (or compensation, as the case may be) for interest gained (or lost) due to the difference between risk-free interest rates on the two currencies. The second component is the transaction costs, or fee, paid to the exchange broker. According to *SFAS 52*, exchange premiums or discounts on forward contracts accounted for as hedges are amortized on a straight-line basis to income over the life of the forward contract.

Exhibit 7–3 shows how the U.S. firm's net income is affected under the three basic future spot rate scenarios (no change, a revaluation, and a devaluation) and with (line 4) and without (line 1) a forward exchange contract used as a hedge.

The first line of Exhibit 7–3 indicates that the U.S. company is exposed to a change in reported profits of ±1,000,000 USD with each 10 cent change in the DEM exchange rate from its January 2 spot rate. The investment in the forward exchange contract costs 14,000 DEM, and its effect on net profit is to reduce profits by the amount of the "premium." However, changes in the value of the forward contract mirror changes in the value of the receivable, thereby eliminating any variability in future profits due to changes in the DEM exchange rate. Thus, with a forward contract as a hedge, the company's profit is fixed, but at a marginally lower level (i.e., by 14,000 USD) than if the exchange rate were stable for the 30 days to settlement.

Other Forms of Hedging

Foreign exchange risk can also be altered by means of **option contracts.** The most fundamental difference between forward contracts and option contracts is that forward contracts require an exchange of currency at the settlement date. An option contract grants one party to the contract the right to choose whether (and sometimes when) an exchange will actually take place. Option contracts are often described as one-sided hedges because they are a form of "currency insurance." When structured properly, they pay a return only when foreign currency exchange rates move unfavorably relative to a company's unhedged position in a foreign currency. Using options to hedge foreign currency positions has one principal disadvantage, however: they cost significantly more than forward contracts. Accounting for options as hedges will be discussed in the following section.

The final form of hedging considered here is *enterprise risk management.* As previously stated, certain operating assets and obligations that are the result of operating activities can be viewed as natural hedges of foreign currency positions. Some companies manage their multinational business by limiting their exposure to unfavorable movements in foreign currency exchange rates without incurring the cost of forward contracts or options. For example, a company might hold inventory to be sold in a foreign country as a **natural hedge** against its payables exposure. Or changes in the value of long-term debt denominated in a foreign currency may be naturally hedged by real estate investments in foreign countries.

The topic of risk management is quite broad and complex and deserves attention beyond the space available in this book. The interested reader is referred to the list of Suggested Readings at the end of this chapter.

Accounting for Foreign Exchange Gains and Losses

When companies engage in international business operations, the nature and extent of the business risk faced changes.[5] For example, Exhibit 7–4 is an excerpt from the Management Discussion and Analysis section of Occidental Petroleum's recent SEC filing, which describes its view of the risks associated with its foreign operations.

EXHIBIT 7–4

Excerpt from the Management Discussion and Analysis of Occidental Petroleum Company's Annual Report

FOREIGN INVESTMENTS

Portions of Occidental's oil and gas assets are located in countries outside North America, some of which may be considered politically and economically unstable. These assets and the related operations are subject to the risk of actions by governmental authorities and insurgent groups. Occidental attempts to conduct its financial affairs so as to protect against such risks and would expect to receive compensation in the event of nationalization. At December 31, 1992, the carrying value of Occidental's oil and gas assets in countries outside North America aggregated approximately $900 million, or approximately 5 percent of Occidental's total assets at that date. Of such assets, approximately $460 million was located in Latin America, and most of the rest were located in the Middle East and Pakistan.

---

[5]Expansion into international markets *does* increase a firm's exposure to risk; however, it is noteworthy that such expansion may also represent a form of risk reduction through diversification into new markets.

Accounting standards for reporting foreign currency transactions focus on the timing of recognition of foreign currency exchange gains and losses. The issues involve three classes of transactions:

1. Foreign currency–denominated receivables/payables arising from a company's operating activities.
2. Speculative investments in foreign currency spot markets, forward contracts, and options.
3. Hedges of future commitments that have created foreign currency risk.

Accounting for the first two classes of transactions is fairly straightforward and noncontroversial. Investments in foreign currencies, foreign currency forward and option contracts, and foreign currency–denominated receivables/payables are measured at their fair values. Unrealized gains and losses are recognized as income/loss through the process of revaluing related balance sheet assets and liabilities. Accounting for hedges, on the other hand, is highly controversial and in a state of flux throughout the world. The nature of the controversy and its effects on financial statements is discussed in the next section.

Hedge Accounting

Hedge accounting is an attempt to resolve measurement and recognition inconsistencies in accounting. The undesirable effects of the inconsistencies principally manifest themselves in income statement numbers that some argue do not adequately measure performance in a given period.

In general, *hedge accounting* refers to methods that defer all or some of the gains or losses in the fair value of hedging instruments to a point in time when they can be offset by gains or losses on hedged items; in essence, it is a form of **income smoothing.** Most of the controversy in accounting for foreign currency transactions involves whether hedge accounting should be permitted and, if so, under what conditions. No accounting standard-setting organization has fully and satisfactorily dealt with the question, although the Financial Accounting Standards Board and the International Accounting Standards Committee are both actively trying to resolve problems presented by existing practice.

Measurement inconsistencies addressed by hedge accounting arise from differences in the bases of measurement applied to **hedged items** and **hedging instruments.** For example, inventories held by U.S. companies are generally reflected on balance sheets at their historical costs. The fair value of inventory to be sold for a foreign currency may fluctuate considerably, however, as expressed in the foreign currency. A hedging instrument such as a foreign currency futures or option contract is normally measured at its fair value as of each balance sheet date. If hedge accounting were applied, gains or losses on the hedging instrument would be deferred until the hedging instrument no longer functions as a hedge—usually the time at which the inventory is sold.

Recognition inconsistencies addressed by hedge accounting arise when the hedged item is not recognized or does not even come into being until after the hedging instrument is acquired or created. Without some form of hedge accounting, changes in the value of the hedging instrument may occur and be recognized before the hedged item is recognized. For example, a German food processor desires to hedge its price risk from a firm purchase commitment to buy a fixed amount of wheat at the spot price, denominated in a foreign currency. Under hedge accounting, gains or losses in the market value of a hedging instrument designed to reduce some aspect of the exposure to foreign currency fluctuations would be deferred until the wheat is physically delivered to the German baker.

Some of the most important questions to be resolved by standard setters and analysts are illustrated by a recent dispute between Dell Computer Corporation and David R. Korus, a computer industry analyst. The dispute was first publicized in *The Wall Street Journal* on November 30, 1992, and was also the subject of an investigation by the Securities and Exchange Commission into Dell's accounting practices. The dispute centered around Dell's accounting for losses on investing in foreign currency options. Dell's second quarter financial statements in 1992 disclosed deferred unrealized currency losses through hedge accounting of $38 million—more than half of Dell's pretax profits for the year to date. At the end of the 1991 fiscal year, Dell disclosed in its annual report that it had sold currency option contracts worth $435 million. In contrast, Dell's international sales for 1991 were only $200 million; it appears that many of these option contracts were accounted for as hedges of future, uncommitted sales.

The primary issue in the Dell-Korus dispute was whether foreign currency option contracts sold by Dell were properly accounted for as hedges of exposure to foreign currency fluctuations or as speculations in foreign currencies. To add concreteness to the issues, assume that Dell anticipated sales of computers nine months in the future in the country of Grabem (a mythical country). These anticipated sales were expected to yield an economic and accounting profit of $24,500 at the date of sale—so long as the exchange rate between the U.S. dollar and the "grabule" (symbol ₵) remained at $1:₵1. To ensure the realization of the profit on the anticipated sales, Dell hedged the value of its anticipated sales with a purchased put option (e.g., an option to sell grabules to a counterparty for $1 per grabule). The premium on the put option was $1,650, which entitled Dell to sell ₵24,500 for $24,500 on September 30.

Proponents of hedge accounting would argue that the $1,650 premium was insurance against the event that the value of the future sales would be less than $22,850 ($24,500 − $1,650) and that the net cost of the hedge (premium plus gain or loss on the market value of the option until exercised) should be matched against the profits on the sales of the computer in the period in which the computer sales occur. Under this approach, gains or losses in the value of the foreign currency put option that would have occurred in interim periods would be deferred until the period in which the computer sales occur. Hedge accounting has many practical and theoretical problems that potentially impair its relevance to users of financial statements. The following three questions address these problems.

1. *Is an option an appropriate hedging instrument?* Some would argue that options should not qualify as hedging instruments because, as pointed out in the previous section, they always cost more than forward contracts at inception. It is logical to conclude that the decision not to use the least

costly hedging instrument is a form of speculation. In addition, the hedging instrument is effective only as a hedge if no other hedges exist. Perhaps Dell has payables or purchase commitments denominated in grabules. Or perhaps sales prices of personal computers in Grabem are responsive to changes in exchange rates between the grabule and the U.S. dollar.

2. *Should transactions that are not given accounting recognition qualify as hedged items?* For example, firm commitments to purchase/sell goods or services are not given accounting recognition until performance by one or both parties to the commitment has occurred. U.S. GAAP clearly allows gains and losses on foreign currency *forward* contracts to be deferred if management specifically designates the purpose of the contracts as hedges of *firm* commitments. However, some U.S. companies have applied hedge accounting to other less probable anticipated transactions by using foreign currency options as the hedging instrument. In Dell's case, the hedged item is not even a commitment but a subjective forecast of future sales *and* their profitability. Some would argue that hedge accounting has gone too far when it allows preparers of financial statements to apply hedge accounting to highly uncertain future profits.

3. *What criteria should be used to distinguish between hedging and speculative activities?* Currently, the distinction is largely governed by management intent. If a Dell competitor entered into the exact same transactions and had the exact same prospects for sales in Grabem *but* did not designate the put options as hedges, radically different measures of income could result for substantially identical economic circumstances.

To illustrate another company's accounting for hedging activities, Exhibit 7–5 presents the footnote disclosure relating to Occidental Petroleum's hedging activities. The footnote reveals that Occidental has both purchased and sold foreign currency exchange contracts and that the gains and losses on those contracts are being deferred and recognized at maturity. It is not clear, however, how much of the value of these contracts involves forward contracts and how much involves options. No disclosure is

---

EXHIBIT 7–5
Occidental Petroleum Corporation Foreign Currency Exchange Contract Disclosures

FOREIGN CURRENCY EXCHANGE CONTRACTS

Occidental enters into foreign currency exchange contracts to hedge foreign currency denominated debt. Market value gains and losses are deferred and recognized at maturity. At December 31, 1992, Occidental had foreign exchange contracts, most of which mature in 1993, totaling $34 million of purchases and $20 million of sales. At December 31, 1991, Occidental had foreign exchange contracts, most of which matured in 1992, totaling $135 million of purchases and $30 million of sales. The decrease from 1991 to 1992 reflected amounts on contracts, that matured, which were included in 1991 to hedge future interest and principal payments associated with a foreign currency denominated debt obligation that matured in 1992.

made of the amount of losses or gains that have been deferred as a result of the application of hedge accounting.

Accounting for Foreign Subsidiaries

A significant problem for a multinational company is how to present its financial statements on a consolidated basis when one or more of its foreign subsidiaries maintain accounting records in a foreign currency. A significant problem for analysts is to evaluate the consolidated financial statements of companies with significant foreign subsidiaries. Considerable latitude is available to these companies, and that may lead to important differences in financial statement presentation.

To combine the financial statements of foreign subsidiaries with a parent company, the financial statements of the subsidiaries must first be translated into the reporting currency of the parent. To facilitate the translation process, two key translation method issues must be resolved:

1. Which assets and liabilities should be translated at the exchange rate existing at the balance sheet date (i.e., the *current* rate) versus the rates existing when the assets and liabilities were originally measured for financial statement purposes (i.e., *historical* rates)?

2. How should variances in the value of translated assets and liabilities (i.e., the effects of differences between the current and historical rates) be characterized on financial statements: as gains and losses on the income statement or as some component of shareholders' equity on the balance sheet?

SFAS No. 52 provides for two methods of foreign currency translation, depending on the circumstances faced by a company; these alternatives are also effectively permitted under *International Accounting Standard (IAS) No. 21*. A description of these two methods will help to clarify just how these issues can have a significant and predictable impact on consolidated financial statements.

How SFAS No. 52 *Works*

SFAS No. 52 provides a set of criteria that, when evaluated by management, allows a determination of the appropriate translation method to be used: the temporal method or the all-current method. Under the **all-current** (or **current rate**) **method,** all assets and liabilities are translated at the *current* exchange rate. If the all-current method is used, translation gains and losses must be excluded from income and instead accumulated as a component of shareholders' equity, and all income statement events must be translated at the rate that prevailed when the revenue or expense was recognized. This rate can be approximated by using the weighted-average exchange rate for the period.

All income statement events and balance sheet items can be quantified either in terms of past transactions (e.g., inventory, plant and equipment, common stock, depreciation, cost of goods sold) or in terms of future transactions (e.g., cash, receivables, short-term payables). Under the **temporal method** of translating foreign financial statements, items quantified in terms of future events are translated at the current exchange rate, whereas items quantified in terms of past events are translated at historical rates. This approach preserves existing accounting logic, which argues that if it is proper to quantify an item in terms of a past event, it would also seem proper to quantify that item at the exchange rate that existed when the past event took place. *SFAS No. 52* also specifies that if the temporal method is used, immediate recognition of translation gains and losses on the income statement is mandatory.

Why should the income statement treatment of translation gains and losses depend on the accounting approach under *SFAS No. 52?* The answer to this question lies in the criteria for method selection. *SFAS No. 52* introduced the concept of the *functional currency* to determine the appropriate recognition of foreign currency translation gains, losses, and adjustments. In most cases, the functional currency is either the local currency of the foreign subsidiary or the U.S. dollar.

Management must designate a functional currency for each foreign subsidiary, using the criteria suggested in *SFAS No. 52.* If the functional currency is determined to be the U.S. dollar, the temporal method is used, and gains or losses resulting from translation are included in income for the period. Alternatively, if the functional currency is the local currency, the all-current method is applied; translation gains or losses are not recognized in the income statement but are included in shareholders' equity as translation adjustments.

In general, the criteria for selecting a company's functional currency establish whether the foreign subsidiary is an independent, cash-generating center; if it is, the local currency is considered the functional currency. In coming to this determination, the following factors must be weighed:

- The degree to which cash flows related to the foreign entity's individual assets and liabilities are in the foreign currency or affect the parent's cash flows.
- The responsiveness of sales prices of the foreign entity's products on a short-term basis to changes in exchange rates.
- The existence of an active local market for the foreign entity's product, even though there may be significant amounts of exports.
- Whether labor, materials, and other costs for the foreign entity's products are incurred locally or elsewhere.
- The denomination of debt and the extent to which funds generated by the foreign entity's operations are sufficient to service existing and normally expected debt obligations.
- The volume of intercompany transactions and the extent of the interrelationship between the operations of the foreign entity and the parent company.

These criteria seek to assess the degree to which the exposure of cash flows from the foreign subsidiary to the parent are a principal source of foreign business risk for the parent. If so, the accounting exposure represented by the temporal method with immediate recognition of translation gains and losses would more closely match the economics of a situation in which the foreign subsidiary was not an independent generator of cash. The rationale underlying the all-current method is that it is merely an arithmetic procedure for restating the financial statements of the foreign subsidiaries, and any gain or loss has no economic interpretation; it is merely a *residual* of a mechanical arithmetic procedure.

Illustrating and Comparing the Methods

To illustrate the differences between the temporal and all-current methods in terms of their effects on reported earnings and financial position, consider an example in which the functional currency of the foreign subsidiary is identified as the local currency. We'll call this local currency the "grabule" (symbol ₵) and assume, for simplicity and with no loss in generality, that the exchange rate is fixed at $1:₵1 until January 19X1, the beginning of the current accounting period, and that the dollar devalues during 19X1 so that the exchange rate becomes $2:1 by the end of the period, December 31, 19X1.

Balance Sheet Results. Exhibit 7–6 illustrates the differences in balance sheet amounts under the all-current and temporal translation methods. Only monetary items (cash and payables, in this case) are translated at the same rate under both methods. The all-current method calls for the translation of inventory and equipment at the current rate, whereas the temporal method requires the use of historical rates. Because FIFO inventory accounting is used and the cost of goods sold equals the beginning inventory balance (see Exhibit 7–7), the ending inventory value must consist of 100 percent of the period's purchases. The appropriate historical rate for inventories valued using FIFO is the average rate for the period (1.5), assuming that the purchases took

---

EXHIBIT 7–6

Balance Sheet Translation

	Local Currency		All-Current Method		Temporal Method	
	1/1/19x1	*12/31/ 19x1*	*12/31/ 19x1*	*Note*	*12/31/ 19x1*	*Note*
Assets						
Cash	₵ or $ 100	₵ 150	$ 300	(1)	$ 300	(1)
Inventory (FIFO)	500	750	1,500	(1)	1,125	(2)
Property, plant, & equipment (net)	800	700	1,400	(1)	700	(3)
Total assets	₵ or $ 1,400	₵1,600	$3,200		$2,125	
Equities						
Payables	₵ or $ 200	₵ 200	$ 400	(1)	$ 400	(1)
Common stock	900	900	900	(3)	900	(3)
Retained earnings	300	500	1,900		825	
Total equities	₵ or $ 1,400	₵1,600	$3,200		$2,125	

Notes:

(1) Translated at current exchange rate of $2:₵1.

(2) Since the ending inventory was purchased ratably throughout the period, it is translated at the average exchange rate of $1.5:₵1.

(3) Translated at historical exchange rate of $1:₵1.

EXHIBIT 7–7

Income Statement Translation

	Local Currency	All-Current Method		Temporal Method	
	12/31/x1	12/31/x1	Note	12/31/x1	Note
Sales	₵1,000	$1,500	(1)	$1,500	(2)
Cost of goods sold	(500)	(750)	(1)	(500)	(3)
Depreciation	(100)	(150)	(1)	(100)	(4)
Taxes	(200)	(300)	(1)	(300)	(1)
Operating income	₵ 200	$ 300		$ 600	
Translation gain (loss)				(75)	(5)
Net income	₵1,600	$ 300		$ 525	
Translation adjustment		$1,300	(5)		

Notes:
(1) Translated at average exchange rate for the period of $1.5:₵1.
(2) Same as (1), assuming sales occurred evenly throughout the period.
(3) Consists of beginning inventory acquired prior to December 31, 19X1, when exchange rate was $1:₵1.
(4) Translated at rate in effect when related assets were acquired—$1:₵1.
(5) See Exhibit 7–8 for derivation of these amounts.

place at a constant rate over the period. The retained earnings balances under both methods are, for now, "plug figures"; hence, we will ignore for the moment the translation adjustment disclosure required by the all-current method.

In general, the application of the all-current method results in higher (lower) values for assets (and hence net worth) if the U.S. dollar devalues (revalues) against a foreign currency (e.g., the grabule). The effect of this change on conventional financial ratios may increase the likelihood that some firms will become in technical default of certain indenture provisions. The dividend-paying ability of a firm may or may not be affected, depending on whether applicable laws consider the shareholders' equity account available for the payment of dividends.

Alternatively, the balance sheet (and income) numbers provided under the temporal method may be relatively easy to interpret. Under temporal method translation, a historical cost in grabules is multiplied by the exchange rate prevailing at the time of the transaction to yield a dollar-denominated amount that is easy to interpret. It is simply a description of the actual cash flow that occurred to acquire the asset, translated at the dollar equivalent of that time period. The same local currency–denominated historical cost multiplied by the current exchange rate (per the all-current method) yields a number that defies interpretation: it is not a meaningful description of past cash flows, nor is it a description of future flows. Because changes in exchange rates are critically affected by comparative changes in prices, fluctuations in the exchange rate probably reflect some change in the underlying structure of asset prices. This, in turn, probably means that the mix and quantity of assets held has changed.

Income Statement Results. Exhibit 7–7 shows how reported net income is significantly affected under the all-current method because of the deferral of translation gains

EXHIBIT 7–8
Translation Adjustment versus Translation Gain (Loss)

	12/31/x1		
	Local Currency	All-Current Method	Temporal Method
Beginning net assets	₡1,200	$1,200	$1,200
Ending net assets	1,400	2,800	1,725
Difference to be accounted for	₡ 200	$1,600	$ 525
Operating income	₡ 200	$ 300	$ 600
Translation gain (loss)	—	—	(75)
Net income	₡ 200	$ 300	$ 525
Translation adjustment	—	1,300	—
Change in owners' equity	₡ 200	$1,600	$ 525

and losses, as well as other factors. Under the temporal method, the cost of goods sold (using FIFO) and the depreciation expense are translated at historical rates, whereas sales and other items are translated at the current rate. The leverage provided by the fixed element of expense creates substantial variation in income—200 percent in our example—compared with the actual average foreign currency fluctuation for the period of only 50 percent.

Under the all-current method, on the other hand, all income statement items, including depreciation and the cost of goods sold, are translated at the average current rate. The fluctuation in income due to translation is thus 50 percent. Therefore, as this example illustrates, the fluctuation of operating income due to changes in the exchange rate is always less under the all-current method than under the temporal method.

Translation Adjustment. As Exhibit 7–8 indicates, the total translation adjustment under the all-current method is significantly larger than, and in the opposite direction of, the translation gain or loss under the temporal method. The fluctuation in income is significantly less under the all-current method because (1) the fluctuation of operating income is reduced (as described above) and (2) translation gains and losses are not reflected in income.

The all-current method leads to smaller fluctuations in operating income and much smaller fluctuations in net income in response to changes in exchange rates but much greater changes in shareholders' equity because of translation adjustments. Everyone who uses financial ratios and income and equity numbers needs to be aware of those differences.

Systematic Ratio Effects

Exhibit 7–9 summarizes the effect on some key financial ratios as a result of statement translation using the temporal method versus the all-current method. For example, under a devaluation, operating income using the all-current method is lower than

EXHIBIT 7–9
Temporal versus All-Current Methods: Key Financial Statement Ratios

	Dollar Devaluation	*Dollar Revaluation*
Current ratio	Increase	Decrease
Quick ratio	No change	No change
CFFO to current liabilities	Decrease	Increase
Debt to equity	Indeterminate	Indeterminate
Debt-to-total capitalization	Indeterminate	Indeterminate
Interest coverage*	Decrease	Increase
CFFO to interest expense	Decrease	Increase
CFFO to total liabilities	Decrease	Increase
Receivable turnover	No change	No change
Inventory turnover	Indeterminate	Indeterminate
Total asset turnover	Decrease	Increase
Average collection period	No change	No change
Average number of days' inventory on hand	Indeterminate	Indeterminate
Return on assets*†	Decrease	Increase
Return on equity	Indeterminate	Indeterminate
Return on sales*	Decrease	Increase

*Assuming that net income used in the ratio calculation excludes translation gains and losses; otherwise indeterminate.
†Assuming the numerator of the ratio is less than the denominator.

operating income under the temporal method because all expenses translated at the current rate are larger. (If revaluation occurs, the opposite result is produced.) Net income differences, including translation gains and losses, cannot be predicted, however. Although operating income under the all-current method is lower, a translation loss probably results under the temporal method if, as is likely, the firm is in a net translation liability position (i.e., total liabilities exceed its total monetary assets of cash, receivables, and marketable securities). The change in net income, therefore, depends on the relative magnitude of the decrease in operating income under the all-current method compared with the translation loss under the temporal method.

All asset categories and net worth are higher under the all-current method, which provides for the translation of all assets at the current devalued rate rather than under the temporal method, which requires that only some of these assets be translated at the current rate. All liability and debt items are translated at the same rate under both methods; hence, there is no change in liabilities and debt. The translation of sales is also unaffected.

Summary

Foreign operations, whether isolated transactions or those involving controlled foreign subsidiaries, possess attributes of risk that can be distinctly different from domestic operations. An important question for analysts to address is whether the

---
EXHIBIT 7–10

Risk Concepts

Currency risk: The degree of stability (or lack thereof) in the exchange rates between foreign currencies. Also known as **foreign exchange risk.**

Transaction risk: The likelihood of experiencing a cash flow gain or loss on an individual transaction as a direct consequence of an exchange rate movement.

Translation risk: The likelihood of experiencing an unrealized valuation gain or loss on the net assets of an entity located in a foreign country as a direct consequence of an exchange rate movement occurring between balance sheet preparation dates. Also known as **accounting risk.**

Political risk: The degree of stability (or lack thereof) among political groups and the established government in a given country; a significant contributor to currency risk.

Expropriation risk: The likelihood that a company's assets located in a foreign domain will be involuntarily appropriated by the government, with or without compensation.

---

accounting for foreign operations adequately portrays the impact of these risks on income and financial position.

Management has considerable latitude in its choice of accounting for foreign operations, and these choices often have a material impact on financial statements. Related issues include the following: (1) whether investments in foreign currency contracts (forward contracts and options) should be accounted for as speculations or as hedges of other exposures to foreign currency fluctuations, (2) which asset and liability account balances should change as a result of foreign currency exchange rate movements, and (3) how such changes in asset and liability balances should be reflected in owners' equity and income of past, current, and future periods.

An important and pervasive theme of this chapter has been the identification of a company's exposure to various sources of business risk, the measurement and subsequent reporting of that risk in a firm's consolidated financial statements, and ways to minimize the adverse consequences of those risk factors to the financial health and welfare of a company. Exhibit 7–10 summarizes the principal risk factors encountered by a business when conducting business on an international level.

In the next section of this book, we consider the specific business, cultural, and legal environments of seven different countries. Our goal is to become sufficiently familiar with the contextual environments of those countries so as to permit a fuller, more complete financial analysis of companies operating therein.

APPENDIX 7A

The European Currency Unit

The European Union (EU established the European Monetary System and created a composite currency unit, the European currency unit (ECU), on March 13, 1979. The ECU combines a

---

EXHIBIT 7A–1

The ECU and Its Components

Currency	(A) Fixed Unit per ECU	(B) Current Exchange Rate	(A*B) Currency Contribution
Belgian franc	3.301	$0.02841	$0.093781
British pound	0.08784	1.4769	0.129731
Danish krone	0.1876	0.1493	0.028009
Dutch guilder	0.2198	0.5209	0.114494
French franc	1.332	0.17095	0.227705
German mark	0.6242	0.5847	0.364970
Greek drachma	1.44	0.00399	0.005746
Irish punt	0.008552	1.4358	0.012279
Italian lira	151.8	0.0006126	0.092993
Portuguese escudo	1.393	0.00572	0.007968
Spanish peseta	6.885	0.007194	0.049531
Dollars per ECU			**$1.2259**

basket of currencies in fixed proportions, or weights, in accordance with each country's economic ranking. These weights are used daily by the European Union in Brussels together with the current exchange rates for individual currencies to yield a value for the ECU. Exhibit 7A–1 illustrates this calculation for a recent set of exchange rates and weights.

Intervention Mechanism.   The individual currencies' exchange rates are maintained within preset bands through the EU's exchange rate mechanism (ERM). When fluctuations become greater than these specified boundaries, the ERM provides for different types of intervention in currency markets, depending on the circumstances, such as whether a currency has moved against all ERM currencies or a single ERM currency. Intervention steps that can be taken include the following:

1. Diversified intervention or intervention using numerous currencies rather than the single currency that deviates most from the currency of the country concerned. This presumably allows the burden of intervention to be shared by various EU currencies.

2. Central rate change, which may be required to reflect real rate disparities.

3. Fiscal and income policies.

Why Use the ECU?   The ECU is the proposed vehicle to create a single European currency. Currently, it is widely used in international bond issues and, to a lesser extent, in banking and hedging transactions. In most countries, its private use, except as a denomination currency for bond issues, has been very limited. Informed observers believe its full implementation planned for 1997 is more likely to be 1999.

The effect of universal use of the ECU would eliminate national currencies, creating greater convenience for travelers and buyers of small amounts of goods. Small companies would recoup their competitive disadvantage as compared to larger companies that can engage in currency and banking transactions at lower rates. Some also believe that inflation can be more easily managed from a central bank than numerous national central banks, and politics would be a step removed from management of the economy through monetary means.

Others believe that universal adoption of the ECU is too great a sacrifice for individual countries, which would lose the ability to stave off recessions through exchange rate intervention or, in general, through government management of monetary policy. The presence of a single currency administered by an independent central bank would not be a panacea for economic recession. Member countries would still make fiscal policy that would substantially affect the economies of other member countries.

Suggested Readings

Agmon, T., and D. Lessard. "Investor Recognition of Corporate International Diversification." *Journal of Finance,* September 1972, pp. 1049–55.

Brewer, T.L. "Political Risk Assessment for Foreign Direct Investment Decisions." *Columbia Journal of World Business,* Spring 1981, pp. 5–13.

Bierman, J., Jr., L.T. Johnson, and D. S. Peterson. *Hedge Accounting: An Exploratory Study of the Underlying Issues.* Norwalk, CT: FASB, 1991.

Canto, Victor A. "Everything You Always Wanted to Know about the European Monetary System, the ECU and ERM, but Didn't Know Who to Ask." *Financial Analysts Journal,* November–December 1991, pp. 49–55.

Crawford, M. *One Money for Europe?* New York: Macmillan Press, 1993.

Doukas, J., and N. Travles. "The Effect of Corporation Multinationalism on Shareholders' Wealth: Evidence from International Acquisitions. *Journal of Finance,* December 1988, pp. 1161–76.

Errunza, V., and L. Senbet. "The Effects of International Operations on the Market Value of the Firm: Theory and Evidence." *Journal of Finance,* May 1981, pp. 401–17.

Fatemi, A. "Shareholder Benefits from Corporate International Diversification." *Journal of Finance,* December 1984, pp. 1325–44.

Fitzpatrick, M. "The Definition and Assessment of Political Risk in International Business: A Review of the Literature." *Academy of Management Review* 8, 1992, pp. 249–54.

Haner, F. T., and J. S. Ewing. *Country Risk Assessment: Theory and World-Wide Practice.* New York: Praeger, 1985.

Howell, L. D. "Political Risk in Southeast Asia: A Perspective through the Economist Model." *Journal of Asian Business,* Spring 1993, pp. 19–36.

Kohrin, S. J. "Political Risk: A Review and Reconsideration." *Journal of International Business,* Spring 1979, pp. 67–80.

Leavy, B. "Assessing Country Risk for Foreign Investment Decisions." *Long Range Planning* 17, 1993, pp. 141–50.

Marsh, D. "EMU Strain Begins to Show." *Financial Times,* January 17, 1995, p. 13.

ISSUES AND INFORMATION FOR FURTHER INQUIRY

I.7.1   U.N. World Investment Report

In a July 21, 1993, *Financial Times* article (p. 3), "An Open Door Alone Is Not Enough to Attract Cash," David Dodwell cites the U.N.'s 1993 World Investment Report as stating that "governments keen to attract foreign investment '. . . should go beyond general, broad based efforts and focus on particular functions (e.g., regional head-quarters, research and development, *accounting* [emphasis added]) for which they believe they have certain advantages'."

Required:

Discuss, being as specific as you can be, accounting principles that could be viewed by shareholders as providing a country with "a certain advantage" in attracting foreign direct investment. Do you perceive that the push toward the harmonization of accounting standards is conflicting with a nation's possible accounting "advantage"? Why or why not?

I.7.2   The Big Six as Multinationals

The March 27, 1993, issue of *The Economist* contained a special feature, "A Survey of Multinationals." The survey provides the following food for thought:

> The world's six biggest accountancy firms are in the top rank in virtually every country in the world, except where they are barred by law. Yet auditing and accounting are intensely local affairs, requiring detailed knowledge of local rules and regulations. Arthur Andersen or Price Waterhouse ought not, in theory, to have an advantage over domestic competitors except with multinational clients—which, though large, are almost always a minority. Why, then, have these firms themselves become such successful multinationals?
>
> One answer may lie in their ancillary businesses such as consulting, in which they have special skills; another may lie in their ability to buy and organise information technology. But these are not enough to explain such widespread dominance. Reputation, the power of the brand name, must play the biggest part. The market for accounting and auditing is an imperfect one: buyers lack the information to tell a good accountant from a bad one, or find it costly to find out, which comes to the same thing. They also seek the accountant's brand name as a means to convince others about their own worth, especially investors and creditors, who are similarly short of information.

Required:

Prepare an overview of the various organizational structures used by the Big Six in becoming multinational firms. Highlight some of the firms' key international statistics (e.g., clients, revenues, partners). Do you agree with the writer's assertions in the second paragraph? Why or why not?

EXERCISES

E.7.1   Foreign Currency Translation Effects

In mid-October, 1993, Digital Equipment Corporation reported a greater-than-expected loss and a 9 percent decline in revenue for the first quarter of its 1993 fiscal year (i.e., July 1–June 30). According to analysts familiar with the company, adverse foreign currency translations accounted for approximately half of the decline in sales for the period. In response to the adverse news, Digital's share price declined nearly 10 percent to $35.125.

According to a company spokesperson, Digital's revenues fell from $3.31 billion in 1992 to $3.0 billion in 1993. Currency translations apparently aided reported revenues in 1992 but reduced them in the first quarter of 1993 when the U.S. dollar strengthened against most foreign currencies. Digital generates approximately 50 percent of its sales in Europe.

Required:

(a) Did the decline in Digital's revenues that resulted from the adverse foreign currency movement represent a *real* economic loss to the company? If so, why? If not, why not?

(b) How could Digital's managers have avoided the revenue loss created by the adverse currency movement?

(c) Assuming that the stock market is efficient, what can we infer about the currency-related revenue loss from the movement of Digital's share price?

E.7.2   Foreign Currency Translation Adjustments

All developed countries in the world require that when a company conducts operations in a foreign location, the results of those foreign operations be included with those of the parent company.[1] What differs between each country is the specific mechanical process that is followed to translate the foreign operating results into the reporting currency of the parent company. Regardless of the mechanical process used, one account is common to the balance sheets of all countries: the Cumulative Currency Translation Adjustment account. This shareholders' equity account summarizes the unrealized foreign currency adjustments that occur from one period to the next.

---

[1]Not all countries require that the results of foreign subsidiaries be *consolidated* with those of the parent company and where consolidated reporting is not utilized, some other method of accounting (usually equity method accounting) is used. Thus, regardless of the specific method employed, the results of a company's foreign operations are reflected in some manner on the parent's financial statements.

The following are the account balances for the cumulative currency adjustment account taken from the financial data of four international companies:

	Cumulative Foreign Currency Translation Adjustment Account Balance	
	1993	*1992*
Company A	$ 564	$ 72
Company B	132	(189)
Company C	(456)	(309)
Company D	(39)	(474)

Required:

Assume that the underlying balance sheets of the four companies' foreign subsidiaries have not materially changed from 1992 to 1993. Explain what might have happened to cause the changes in the cumulative currency translation adjustment account for each company.

E.7.3   Managing Foreign Exchange Risk

JAS Industries was founded in 1974 by Jason A. Smith. Smith was a mechanical engineer working in the aerospace industry in 1973 when cutbacks in government funding of the space program caused his layoff. When he was laid off, Smith had been working on quality control problems involving the computer processing of data received from "down range" radar tracking stations. Most of the problems seemed to center on the card-sorting machines that frequently jammed or failed to read the cards properly. Smith believed that these problems could be overcome with relatively minor modifications in the machines.

Although Smith was offered jobs in other states and other sectors of the aerospace industry, he did not want to leave his home in Florida. With borrowed money he formed JAS Industries to produce card-sorting machines. The first few machines produced by JAS Industries were actually built in Smith's garage. With Smith's contacts with the major aerospace contractors, he was able to gain access to a large market that could readily appreciate the superior qualities of his product. He was also able to gain access to a large pool of young, eager, and talented engineers who were more than willing to forgo the vicissitudes of the space race to join a rapidly expanding firm that promised them "a piece of the action."

During the 1970s, JAS Industries grew rapidly based on innovations in card sorters, printers, terminals, and other peripheral computer equipment. Also during this period JAS Industries expanded overseas, following a well-established pattern of firms entering international markets. In 1978, some of JAS Industries' products had come to the attention of a major European defense contractor, and by the summer of that year the firm had begun exporting two of its product lines to France. During the same year, the firm entered into a contract with a Japanese firm to supply it with transistors and diodes for computer terminals. Although neither contract represented a large portion of JAS Industries' sales or purchases, it was the firm's first brush with the issues of international finance. It was also this experience that was to set the tone for future financial arrangements involving exchange rate risk.

Rick Fredericks became the treasurer for JAS Industries when the firm moved from Smith's garage to its first manufacturing facility in a rented warehouse. Fredericks was an industrial engineer who excelled in cost accounting. In fact, it was Fredericks's keen attention to detail that had enabled JAS Industries to win several particularly profitable bids from defense contractors. When Fredericks assumed his responsibilities as treasurer for JAS Industries, he enrolled in an evening master of accountancy program at a local college. It was during the course of his studies that he was introduced to and became convinced of the truth of the efficient market hypothesis. If exchange markets were efficient, he reasoned, the cost of hedging was money needlessly spent. In both of the foreign contracts concluded in early 1978, Fredericks acted on his beliefs. Unfortunately, both contracts were unsuccessful from the viewpoint of exchange rate risk.

On large orders, such as that of the French defense contractor, it was customary for JAS Industries to require one-third of the contract price (denominated in the foreign currency) to be paid in advance and the balance on delivery. In February 1978, when the contract was signed, the French franc was trading at approximately $1 = Fr 4.2575. By August 1978, when the printers and card sorters had arrived in the port of Le Havre, the spot rate for the French franc was $1 = Fr 4.9570. Needless to say, the anticipated margin of 15 percent was not reached. Likewise, the contract with the Japanese sup- plier encountered similar problems. In May 1978, JAS Industries agreed to pay ¥2,995,750,000 upon delivery of the electronic components it had ordered from its Japanese supplier. In May, the spot rate for the yen was $1 = ¥260.50, and by October, when the parts arrived in Jacksonville, Florida, the spot rate was $1 = ¥249.25. Jason Smith was not pleased with the results of the company's first venture into the world of floating exchange rates. Following a somewhat heated meeting with Fredericks, he told the treasurer to "do whatever is necessary to see that the company doesn't suffer this kind of loss again."

During the next three years, the company continued to expand and to become more deeply involved in foreign contracts. By 1981, 24 percent of the firm's sales were to European companies, and 9 percent were to Latin American companies. That year the firm's total sales topped the $100 million mark. Imports of Japanese electronic components also increased proportionately. Although Fredericks was uncomfortable with the costs involved, he used forward contracts to hedge all but the smallest transactions, keeping in mind Smith's dictum.

By 1982, JAS Industries was seriously considering opening a final assembly plant in Europe and was actively looking for a plant site. During that same year, Jason Smith's daughter graduated from a well-respected university with a master's degree in international business. Jody Smith joined the firm that summer and was given the responsibility of coordinating the financial planning for the new facility, tentatively sited in Cornwall, England. It was not long before the subject of exchange risk management came up. Jody Smith strongly recommended in a preliminary report that a comprehensive strategy be developed to address JAS Industries' exchange risk management problems. Rick Fredericks (to whom she reported on the project) readily agreed for several reasons: first, he felt that the cost of hedging with forward contracts was becoming burdensome, and second, he recognized that in fiscal year 1983 the company would have to adopt the provisions of *FASB Statement No. 52.* Jason Smith also readily agreed that such a strategy should be developed, but for somewhat different reasons. He hoped that JAS Industries would be in position to make its first public stock offering in 1984. With so much of the firm's business being done overseas, he was concerned with the impact of foreign exchange fluctuations on the future stock price.

Jody Smith was assigned the further responsibility of developing and recommending a foreign exchange risk management strategy for JAS Industries. This task was to be undertaken with the support of the Treasury department, the project team working on the new plant, and the firm's auditors.

Required:

- (a) Could JAS Industries have avoided the use of forward contracts and still have projected its exposure to exchange rate risk?
- (b) Would the use of other techniques (if any) affect the contract prices? How?
- (c) Is the exposure to exchange rate risk affected by opening the new plant in England? Is this exposure different from the exposure created by the foreign buyers and suppliers?
- (d) What techniques are available to handle the exposure created by the new plant?
- (e) Does the existence of a Japanese supplier, who will presumably supply some parts to the plant in England, make available any exposure management techniques that would not exist otherwise?
- (f) How will the adoption of *FASB 52* affect the exposure to exchange risk? Is hedging as important under *FASB 52?* Would the same hedging techniques be used under *FASB 52* as under *FASB 8?*
- (g) Do you believe that the way JAS Industries manages its exchange risk could have any effect on its stock price? Why or why not?
- (h) Based on your answer to part (g), what objectives do you think JAS Industries should pursue in the area of exchange risk?

E.7.4   Determining the Functional Currency

In late December 1981, Mr. John Hughes, corporate controller of Data-Chip Technology Corporation (DCTC), a U.S.–based multinational firm, was considering adopting *FASB Statement No. 52* for 1981. In the past, the company's financial statements had been prepared in accordance with *FASB Statement No. 8,* reflecting trans-

---

EXHIBIT 1

DATA-CHIP TECHNOLOGY CORPORATION OF FRANCE
Income Statement for the Year Ended December 31, 1981
(amount in thousands)

			FASB 8 Translation	
		Francs	*Exchange Rate*	*Dollars*
Sales		29,000	0.190*	$5,510
Cost of goods sold	14,500		0.200†	$2,900
Selling and administrative expenses	6,000		0.190	1,140
Depreciation expense	2,500		0.222‡	555
Interest expense	500	23,500	0.190	95 4,690
		5,500		820
Other income principally interest		500	0.190	95
Earnings before income taxes		6,000		915
Income taxes		2,400	0.190	456
Operating income before translation		3,600		459
Translation gain				113
Net operating income		3,600		572
Retained earnings	1/1/81	10,100		2,491
Dividends paid		1,200	0.170§	204
Retained earnings	12/31/81	12,500		2,859

*Average exchange rate during 1981.
†Average exchange rate during period when inventory was acquired.
‡Exchange rate on the date when property was acquired.
§Exchange rate when dividends were paid.

---

lation gains or losses in the income statement. Mr. Hughes was aware of *FASB 52*'s provision for excluding translation gains or losses from net income which would reduce the volatility in the company's future earnings, but he was uncertain what the impact on DCTC's reported earnings in current and future years might be. He asked Mr. Chris Brown, manager of the international accounting department, to recommend by the afternoon of Tuesday, January 4, 1982, whether or not the company should adopt *FASB 52* for 1981.

Background

DCTC was established in the United States in 1970 and was well known in the industry for its electronic innovations. The firm had experienced a growth rate of 25 percent in the first five years of its operations. To maintain this high rate of growth and to capture the vast European market, a wholly owned subsidiary had been established in France in 1975. The French subsidiary catered to the entire European market, and the business was largely carried out in French currency—the franc. The company's product for the European market was primarily produced in France. The volume of intercompany

EXHIBIT 2

DATA-CHIP TECHNOLOGY CORPORATION OF FRANCE
Balance Sheet as of December 31, 1981
(amount in thousands)

Assets	*Francs*	*FASB 8* Translation — Exchange Rate	*FASB 8* Translation — *Dollars*
Cash assets:			
Cash	500	.174*	$ 87
Marketable securities	1,500	.174	261
Accounts receivable	4,000	.174	696
Inventories	2,800	.195†	546
Prepaid expenses	700	.220‡	154
	9,500		$1,744
Plant and other property	30,000	.222§	6,660
Less: Accumulated depreciation	13,000	.222	2,886
	17,000		3,774
Total assets	26,500		5,518

Liabilities and stockholders' equity			
Current liabilities:			
Accounts payable	1,000	.174	174
Loans payable	500	.174	87
Taxes payable	1,500	.174	261
Obligations under warranties	400	.174	70
Accrued expenses and liabilities	1,600	.174	278
	5,000		870
Long-term debt	3,000	.174	522
Deferred income taxes	1,000	.212‖	212
Stockholders' equity	5,000	.211§	1,055
Retained earnings	12,500		2,859
Total liabilities and stockholders' equity	26,500		5,518

*Exchange rate December 31, 1981.
†Average exchange rate during period when inventory in the December 31, 1981, balance sheet was acquired.
‡Exchange rate on date when prepaid expenses were incurred.
§Exchange rates on date property acquired, capital stock issued.
‖Historical rate applicable to deferred income taxes.

transactions and cash flows had been low, and the subsidiary had little need for long-term debt because of its ability to generate sufficient funds from operations. Most of its expansion since 1975 was internally financed.

The subsidiary's financial statements for fiscal year 1981, presented in francs, and the *FASB 8* translation are shown in Exhibits 1 and 2.

The parent company had been quite satisfied with the subsidiary's operating results. For the past six years, as in 1981, the French franc operating profit margin (before translation) was 12.4 percent. The sales volume had grown at an average rate of 30 percent over the last six years. However, the exchange rate movements during the last six years had resulted in reporting increasing or decreasing operating margins and net income.

The average exchange rates for the French franc for the past 10 years are shown in Exhibit 3. The franc started weakening in 1979. It was trading at the rate of 5.748 francs per dollar in 1981, below its previous historical low rate of 5.558 in 1969. The French government made a desperate and vigorous attempt in September 1981 to defend the franc, which caused a serious loss of foreign exchange and forced the government to devalue the franc in October 1981. The government of François Mitterrand was pressing ahead with nationalization plans, and its attempts to stimulate the sluggish French economy produced such a large budget deficit that the government had to impose a price freeze. The consumer price index had risen to 162 in 1981 from 118 in 1978, and the prime interest rate had risen to 15.6 percent.

EXHIBIT 3

Average Exchange Rates for Franc

Year	Francs per U.S. Dollar	Percent Variation	Year	Francs per U.S. Dollar	Percent Variation
1972	5.125		1977	4.705	+5.31
1973	4.708	+8.14	1978	4.180	+11.16
1974	4.444	+5.61	1979	4.020	+4.26
1975	4.485	−0.92	1980	4.516	−12.34
1976	4.969	−10.79	1981	5.263	−16.54

Required:

(a) What would be the appropriate functional currency for the French subsidiary if *FASB Statement No. 52* were adopted? What translation gains or losses would be reflected in current income under *FASB 52?*

(b) What would be the impact on current income if *FASB 52* were adopted? What would be the translation adjustment under *FASB 52,* and how would it be reported? Would the current and future income of the company be completely insulated from changes in the exchange rate of the French franc?

(c) What is the nature of accounting exposure in the subsidiary? What would be the result of this exposure on income under increasing and decreasing exchange rates?

(d) What appears to be the future outlook for the franc, and how will it affect the subsidiary's position under *FASB 52?*

(e) What considerations will be pertinent in making a decision about the adoption of *FASB 52?* Do you recommend that *FASB 52* be adopted for 1981?

E.7.5   Translating Foreign Financial Statements

Graham International, Inc. (GI), is a subsidiary of a Canadian-based conglomerate, The Graham Group, headquartered in Vancouver, Canada. GI, Inc., is headquartered in Mexico City, Mexico, although it represents the parent company worldwide.

Exhibits 1 & 2 present GI's financial statements for fiscal year 1993, expressed in new pesos. In late 1992, the Mexican government replaced its old currency—the peso— with a new currency, the new peso; 1 new peso equals 1,000 old pesos.

GI had existed since 1987 when it was capitalized with an investment of 3,000,000 pesos (or 3,000 new pesos). At that time, the exchange rate was approximately 1,800 pesos to the Canadian dollar. Since then, the company has earned (after taxes and dividends) 15,000,000 pesos, with a translation value of $7,500 Canadian.

During 1993, the exchange rate between the new Mexican peso and the Canadian dollar was as follows:

01/01/1993	$.40 (1 new peso = $.40 Canadian)
12/31/1993	.36
1993 average	.38

Required:

(a) Prepare the translated (in Canadian dollar equivalents) financial statements of Graham International, Inc., at December 31, 1993.

(b) Determine the balance (if any) required in the cumulative translation adjustment account for the owners' equity section of The Graham Group's 1993 balance sheet.

(c) Prepare a translated statement of cash flows for Graham International, Inc., as of December 31, 1993.

EXHIBIT 1

GRAHAM INTERNATIONAL, INC.
Statement of Income
For the Year Ended December 31, 1993
(in new pesos)

Sales	82,000
Less: Costs and expenses	
Costs of sales	42,000
Depreciation	4,050
Selling, general and administrative expenses	7,250
Interest	2,500
	55,800
Net income before taxes	26,200
Less: Income taxes	13,300
Net income	12,900
Dividends paid to parent (12/31/91)	1,500

EXHIBIT 2

GRAHAM INTERNATIONAL, INC.
Balance Sheet
As of December 31
(in new pesos)

	1992	1993
Assets		
Cash	2,000	3,000
Accounts receivable	6,000	7,400
Inventory	7,000	10,000
Total current assets	15,000	20,400
Plant and equipment	39,000	42,000
Less: Accumulated depreciation	(4,950)	(9,000)
Net plant and equipment	34,050	33,000
Total assets	49,050	53,400
Equities:		
Liabilities		
Accounts payable	6,050	4,000
Long-term debt	25,000	20,000
Total	31,050	24,000
Owners' equity		
Capital stock	3,000	3,000
Retained earnings	15,000	26,400
Total	18,000	29,400
Total equities	49,050	53,400

E.7.6   Translating Financial Statements Denominated in a Foreign Currency

Salem Electronics Company produces various types of household electronic equipment, which it sells primarily through retail store chains in the United States. On October 1, 19X0, Salem established a wholly owned subsidiary in South Korea, called Salem-Korea, for the purpose of assembling a small home version of a video arcade game that Salem had been licensed to produce. The Korean subsidiary sells its output directly to the U.S. retailers that carry the game (as opposed to selling its output to its U.S. parent for resale to U.S. retailers).

The following are the subsidiary's condensed balance sheets as of September 30, 19X1 and 19X2 (fiscal year-end) and an income statement for the year ended September 30, 19X2. Salem's controller, Marion Francis, asked a member of the accounting staff to translate these statements into U.S. dollars, following *FASB Statement No. 52*. The controller was particularly interested in how the choice of the functional currency—Korean or U.S.—would affect the translated financial statements.

The accounting staff person assembled the following information to assist in preparing the two sets of translated statements:

1. The South Korean unit of currency is the won. As of October 1, 19X0, the exchange rate was 1,000 won = $1.50; as of September 30, 19X1, the rate was 1,000 won = $1.30; as of September 30, 19X2, the rate was 1,000 won = $1.20.

2. All fixed assets were acquired on October 1, 19X0. All depreciation is considered a cost of producing inventory.

3. The video game has been so popular that Salem-Korea has been shipping them as fast as it can make them. As a result, no inventory was on hand at the end of either fiscal year.

4. The capital stock of Salem-Korea was issued to Salem Electronics on October 1, 19X0; no additional capital stock transactions had taken place. Dividends were paid by Salem-Korea for the first time in its history on September 30, 19X2.

SALEM-KOREA
Comparative Balance Sheets
(in millions of won)

Assets	9/30/19X1	9/30/19X2
Cash	800	1,176
Receivables	500	900
Fixed assets	1,800	1,600
Total assets	3,100	3,676
Equities		
Total liabilities	2,200	2,300
Capital stock	1,000	1,000
Retained earnings	(100)	376
Total equities	3,100	3,676

Income Statement
For the Year Ended 9/30/X2
(in millions of won)

Revenues	7,090
Cost of sales	4,415
Other expenses	1,399
Operating income	1,276
Translation gain (loss)	–0–
Net income	1,276
Less dividends	800
Change in retained earnings	476

Required:

    (a) Prepare translated year-end statements for Salem-Korea under the two functional currency assumptions.

    (b) Explain why the translation adjustment under the all-current method differs from the translation gain or loss under the temporal method.

E.7.7 Estimating the Effects of Accounting Exposure on FinancialStatements to Foreign Currency Movements

Contessa Hotels is one of the larger hotel chains in the United States. Its wholly owned subsidiary, Contessa International, builds and operates hotel properties in Europe.

To establish a hotel in Europe, Contessa International typically obtains financing denominated in the new hotel's local currency for up to about 80 percent of the hotel's cost. The remaining start-up funds are obtained through equity financing and U.S. dollar–denominated intercompany loans. The hotel is built with materials and labor primarily sourced from within the country of operation. Hotel operating expenses are paid in the foreign currency of the country of operation, and hotel revenues are collected in the same currency. Net foreign currency operating flows above these amounts are used to repay the construction loan and intercompany loans and to pay dividends.

At the end of a recent fiscal year, the balance sheet of Contessa International was as follows:

Assets		
Cash and receivables	$ 2,777	
Inventory	317	
Plant and equipment, net	35,434	
Deferred costs	1,490	
Total		$40,018
Equities		
Short-term payables		$ 3,091
Long-term debt		
Swedish kronors	$ 5,465	
German marks	16,090	
French francs	2,751	
Belgian francs	5,026	
Total		29,332
Paid-in capital		7,595
Total		$40,018

Required:

(a) Prior to *SFAS No. 52,* Contessa used the current/noncurrent method of foreign currency translation. Calculate foreign currency translation exposure under this method as well as for the two methods that *SFAS No. 52* comprises.

(b) Assuming the average of all foreign currencies in which Contessa's European subsidiary has invested devalues 10 percent during the next year, approximate the translation gain/loss or translation adjustment that would occur under all three methods.

(c) Demonstrate the equivalence of the following two statements:

   (1) Translation gain/loss on an account translated at the current exchange rate is equal to the balance of the account measured in *foreign* currency units at the beginning of the period multiplied by the change in exchange rates.

   (2) Translation gain/loss on an account translated at the current exchange rate is equal to the balance of the account measured in *local* currency units at the beginning of the period multiplied by the *relative* change in exchange rates.

(d) Contrast the current/non-current method with the other two methods.

E.7.8 Accounting for Foreign Currency Risk Exposure

The January 5, 1995, issue of *The Wall Street Journal* carried a news piece with the following headline: "U.S. Firms Feel the Pain of Peso's Plunge." According to the article, because of the Mexican pesos' 37 percent decline in value relative to the U.S. dollar, many U.S. companies with significant operations in Mexico would be taking substantial asset write-downs. The following are examples:

- Ford Motor Co. executives reported that the cost of Ford autos "in peso terms has gone up enormously." In 1994, Ford exported over 27,000 vehicles to Mexico in addition to manufacturing some 200,000 vehicles there.

- Mattel, Inc., the toy maker, reported that it would take a "significant" charge against fourth quarter earnings because "the peso's decline has reduced the value of its Mexican inventory and receivables."

Prior to the pesos' devaluation, the exchange rate was $1.00: 3.45 NP (or new peso); following the devaluation, the exchange rate was approximately $1.00: 4.75 NP.

Required:

(a) Ignoring the specific dollar amounts involved, construct the journal entries for Ford and Mattel necessary to reflect the effects of the peso's decline in value.

(b) For both Ford and Mattel, explain why the fall in the peso necessitated an asset write-down.

E.7.9   Hedging and Accounting Effects

In April 1988, the Walt Disney Corp. entered into a series of transactions that, as a press release stated, ''Effectively monetizes a substantial portion of the expected royalties from certain Tokyo Disneyland operations.''

The company sold 20 years of Tokyo Disneyland royalties to a group of Japanese institutions for approximately 90 billion yen (about $725 million after conversion to U.S. dollars on foreign currency markets). The Japanese institutions have no recourse to Walt Disney Corp. if the actual royalty payments are less than expected. Likewise, Walt Disney Corp. does not participate in any royalty payments that are greater than expected.

''With this approach, we transferred some of the risk of the forecast for 20 years of revenues,'' said a Walt Disney Corp. executive. ''Firms that have a series of identifiable flows from trademarks, royalties, license fees, franchises and the like might look at it.''

Required:

(a) What risks did Walt Disney Corp. hedge by this transaction? What did it cost the company to do it?

(b) Describe the effect of the transaction on financial statements for 1988 and beyond.

(c) If (a) the exchange rate today were ¥100:$1, (b) interest rates were substantially lower, and (c) royalty payments to date corresponded to expected amounts, which party to the transaction would have gained to date and which would have lost by this transaction?

E.7.10   Hedge Accounting

Easter Company is based in the United States and has historically sold most of its output domestically. However, on November 1, 1992, Easter received a firm commitment to purchase a large quantity of merchandise from a Japanese company. The agreement between Easter and its new customer provided for delivery of merchandise on or before January 1, 1993, for payment to Easter of ¥100 million at the earlier of January 31, 1993, or 30 days from the date of delivery of the merchandise.

Easter had considered actions to limit its exposure to risk from fluctuations in the exchange rate between the Japanese yen and the U.S. dollar for a number of reasons. Primarily, this was a significant exposure given its cash situation. Second, it was believed that exchange markets could become particularly volatile around the time of a U.S. presidential election. Easter considered two hedging alternatives:

Alternative 1: Enter into a forward contract on November 1, 1992, to deliver ¥100 million 60 days hence (January 31, 1993).

Alternative 2: Purchase U.S. put options to sell an aggregate value of ¥100 million for $810,000 (price per yen of $0.008100). Easter would sell the option, which would expire on March 31, 1993, on the open market on January 31, 1993.

Easter has a calendar fiscal year-end. Relevant currency exchange data covering the period from the inception of the purchase commitment with the Japanese company and receipt of cash payment by Easter are as follows:

	Spot Rate	Forward Rate		Price of Put Option
November 1, 1992	$0.008106	$0.008103	60 days	$0.0107
December 31, 1992	0.008026	0.008020	30 days	0.0162
January 31, 1993	0.008055	—	—	0.0057

Required:

(a) Assume that the merchandise was delivered to the Japanese customer on January 1, 1993. Assess the effect on profitability that each of the two alternatives would have had for both 1992 and 1993. Consider that hedge accounting may, or may not, be available.

(b) Should hedge accounting be allowed in these, or similar, circumstances?

CASES

CASE 7.1
ALTERNATIVE HEDGING STRATEGIES AND THE EFFECTS ON EARNINGS AND CASH FLOWS

Advance Technologies, Inc.

On October 1, 1992, Eileen Harrison, Vice President Finance for Advance Technologies, was contemplating the effects that a weakening Canadian dollar would have upon the company's projected 1993 financial results. The upcoming Canadian Constitutional Referendum was having marked effects on the value of the Canadian dollar, which had fallen 3.56 cents in value relative to the U.S. dollar since the first of September. Advance had recently entered into a loan agreement with a major Canadian bank to finance its expansion into manufactured specialty plastics. To remain in compliance with the covenants of the loan, Advance was required to generate a minimum level of profitability throughout the term of the loan. In light of the recent volatility in currency markets worldwide, Harrison knew it was important to understand the effects that an ever-weakening dollar would have on Advance's income and cash flows, and the tools available to manage them.

The Company.   Advance Technologies was engaged in the manufacture and sale of a wide range of engineered plastic products in the Canadian marketplace. A decision was made in 1990 to pursue a strategy focused on specialty, proprietary products. Management believed this approach to the Canadian marketplace was essential for Advance to build a lasting competitive advantage. After a long search, Advance entered into a licensing agreement with Hart Industries, a large plastic resin manufacturer based in New York, on September 30, 1991. The agreement granted Advance exclusive Canadian manufacturing and distribution rights to a revolutionary new plastic called Cryolac. While Cryolac was a premium product it faced competition from Canadian produced plastics. In exchange, Advance was required to pay an upfront sum, a monthly licensing fee of US $250,000, and was required to purchase raw materials necessary to the manufacture of Cryolac from Hart. All such purchases were made in U.S. dollars at prices negotiated annually.

To finance the upfront investment in Cryolac and the purchase of specialty manufacturing equipment, Advance obtained financing from two sources—a Canadian bank and Hart Industries. Contained in the Canadian loan agreement were several covenants regarding profitability. Advance was required to generate, at a minimum, a before tax profit of $9 million. Hart agreed to accept a US $1 million note from Advance as partial payment of the upfront licensing fee. The note was payable in full ten years from the date of the agreement.

The Situation

Advance was exposed to significant foreign exchange risk as a result of the Hart agreement. While all of the company's revenues were denominated in Canadian dollars, a large part of its expenses were paid in U.S. funds. Thus, Advance had to regularly convert its Canadian dollar cash flows to cover expenses in the United States. As the Canadian dollar weakened, Advance's cash flow and profitability were adversely affected.

Harrison was faced with a great deal of uncertainty regarding the relative exchange rate of the Canadian and U.S. dollars over the next twelve months. The historical relationship between these two currencies is illustrated graphically in Exhibit 1. Both domestic and international events were creating unprecedented levels of volatility in currency markets, and the Canadian dollar was dropping rapidly in response. A *Globe and Mail* article (September 29, 1992) discussing the situation is presented in Exhibit 2.

Harrison's concerns were compounded by the loan covenants regarding profitability. While Advance's projected income before tax of $12.5 million was more than acceptable, Advance's budget was based on a U.S. dollar equal to CDN $1.2195 and the dollar was currently trading at $1.2536. Exhibit 3 outlines the multi-currency budgeted financial statements for the current fiscal year.

EXHIBIT 1

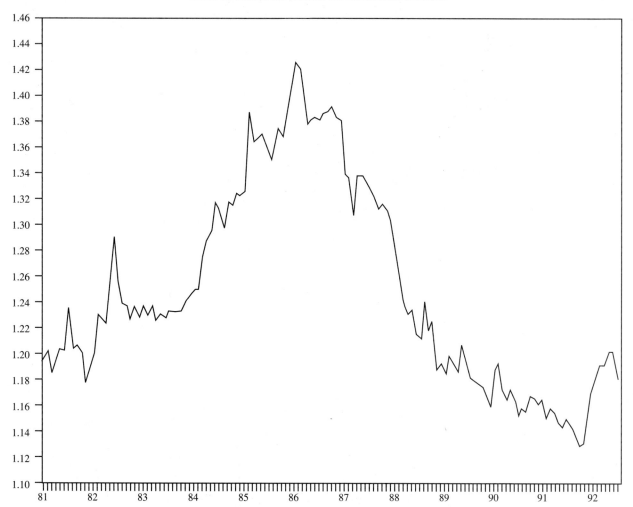

Cost of One U.S. Dollar in Canadian Dollars

Hedging Vehicles

Harrison had investigated various alternatives for hedging Advance's foreign exchange risk. They included: (1) call options, (2) put options, and (3) forward contracts. The purchase of a call option grants the buyer the right, but not the obligation, to purchase foreign currency from the seller at a fixed strike price, on or before a specified date. The amount paid for this privilege is called the option premium.

The purchaser of a put option has the option to sell foreign currency at a set price for a particular time period. The writer of a put option must be prepared to purchase the foreign currency if the holder of the option decides to exercise the right.

EXHIBIT 2

ADVANCE TECHNOLOGIES
The *Globe and Mail* Article

The Canadian dollar plunged yesterday to its lowest point in more than four years, amid massive selling sparked by fears that the No side had gained ground in the referendum campaign and by last week's report suggesting there will be economic devastation if the country breaks up.

Despite aggressive intervention by the Bank of Canada, the dollar came perilously close to falling below 80 U.S. cents, a level it has not seen since April of 1988, tumbling 0.51 cents to close at 80.15. It came under heavy selling pressure at noon, and then again about two hours later. Selling began in Tokyo early in the trading day, and continued in North America.

Investors have begun examining their Canadian holdings after recent polls in Quebec and Western Canada showing diminished support for the Charlottetown constitutional accord, along with Friday's Royal Bank report that Canada's standard of living would drop and the jobless rate would soar to 15 per cent if the country broke apart.

"The No side has been getting most of the attention, and there has been a lack of progress by the Yes side," said Andrew Pyle, economist with MMS International, a financial market information service. "The situation is looking more dismal."

Although the Royal Bank report appeared to support the Yes camp, in Quebec it was viewed as a scare tactic by an "anglo institution," Mr. Pyle said. With "the Yes side in tatters," he added investors have decided to sell Canadian holdings.

The selling pressure on the currency has been increasing since Labour Day, when turmoil in currency markets over European unity and the French referendum on the Maastricht Treaty sent the British pound, the Italian lira and other weak European currencies reeling. Since the vote a week ago, attention has focused on North America and Canada's Oct. 26 referendum on the constitutional agreement.

U.S. press reports on the weekend speculated about a victory for the No forces. One story dubbed the Canadian dollar the "British pound of North America," referring to the 10 per cent drop in value of the pound against the German mark in the past two weeks. That conjures up memories of the mid-1980s, when the currency was being labelled the "Hudson Bay peso."

With no end to the market turmoil in sight, the dollar could lose another 1.5 cents in value by the time of the referendum, said Marc Chandler, a New York-based currency analyst with IDEA Inc., a financial market information service. Even after the referendum it is expected to fall further, because the Canadian economy is behind the U.S. recovery by about six months, Mr. Chandler said.

Some of the recent selling of Canadian investments by Japanese institutions relates to adjusting their portfolios halfway through their financial year.

The Canadian dollar has fallen 4.2 per cent in value against its U.S. counterpart since Sept. 1. Since peaking at 89.29 cents last November, it has tumbled 10.2 per cent.

Interest rates on money-market instruments rose dramatically, pointing to a sharp increase in the Bank of Canada rate this week, and a potential jump of half a percentage point in the prime lending rate from its current 19-year low of 6.25 per cent.

Marian Stenson, "Fears Torpedo Canadian Dollar," *Globe and Mail,* September 29, 1992.

EXHIBIT 3

ADVANCE TECHNOLOGIES
Pro Forma Income Statement
Year Ended September 30, 1993
(CAD $000s, USD 1.00 = CAD 1.2195)

	USD Component	CAD Component	Total
Revenue	—	$160,000	$160,000
COGS	$ 45,760	67,935	113,695
Gross margin	(45,760)	92,065	46,305
License fee	3,658	—	3,658
Depreciation	—	9,640	9,640
Selling & admin.	—	19,232	19,232
Interest	91	1,191	1,282
Total	3,749	30,063	33,812
EBT	(49,509)	62,002	12,493
Tax (40%)	—	4,997	4,997
Net income	$(49,509)	$ 57,005	$ 7,496

ADVANCE TECHNOLOGIES
Pro Forma Balance Sheet
As at September 30, 1993
(CAD $000'S, USD 1.00 = CAD 1.2195)

	USD Component	CAD Component	Total
Cash	—	$ 678	$ 678
A/R	—	17,280	17,280
Inventory	—	11,555	11,555
Net fixed assets	—	30,065	30,065
Total		59,578	$59,578
A/P	$6,668	$ 9,492	$16,160
Debt	1,220	13,233	14,453
Equity	—	28,965	28,965
Total	$7,888	$51,690	$59,578

Two types of options were available—American and European. American-style options could be exercised any time between the date of purchase and the maturity date, whereas European-style options could only be exercised on the maturity date.

Forward contracts obligate the buyer to purchase a specific amount of foreign currency at a specified date in the future at a locked-in exchange rate. The exercise of a forward contract is not optional.

Alternative Hedging Strategies.   Harrison was considering a number of strategies including the purchase of a call option, the simultaneous purchase of a call option and sale of a put option, and the purchase of a forward contract.

Advance could purchase U.S. dollar call options only. This strategy involves the purchase of a number of call options in amounts equal to the anticipated monthly U.S. dollar cash outflow.

EXHIBIT 4

ADVANCE TECHNOLOGIES
At-the-Money Option
Strike Price = 1.2536

Expiry Date	Put Premium (% of CDN$)	Call Premium (% of CDN$)
Oct. 31, 1992	1.14	1.25
Nov. 30, 1992	1.44	1.52
Dec. 31, 1992	1.65	1.74
Jan. 31, 1993	1.73	1.82
Feb. 28, 1993	1.82	1.90
Mar. 31, 1993	1.90	1.99
Apr. 30, 1993	1.98	2.09
May 31, 1993	2.06	2.20
June 30, 1993	2.14	2.31
July 31, 1993	2.24	2.42
Aug. 31, 1993	2.35	2.53
Sept. 30, 1993	2.45	2.64
Average	1.908	2.034

The result of this strategy would be to set an upper limit to the cost of future purchases of U.S. dollars. The call premiums for options with a strike price equal to the current exchange rate (i.e., 1.2536) are provided in Exhibit 4.

A second strategy that Advance could follow would be to purchase a number of call options as noted above and simultaneously sell a number of put options for equivalent dollar amounts. The impact of this strategy would be to set an upper limit to the cost of future purchases of U.S. dollars and generate some money for the firm from the put premiums. However it would also limit the benefit that would accrue to Advance of any increase in the value of the Canadian dollar. This strategy is called a "collar." Since Advance would be committing to the potential purchase of foreign currency at some future date it would be required to put up "margin" equal to 4 percent of the face value of the option. This margin might take the form of a guaranteed line of credit at the bank.

The third strategy considered by Harrison was similar to the second. In this case, the firm would purchase calls and sell an equivalent dollar amount of puts, but the strike price of each contract would be set in such a way that the cost of the call premium would be just offset by revenue from the sale of the put. The advantage of setting up this "zero cost tunnel" is that there is no net cash outlay to create the position. On the other hand, the "protection" afforded by this strategy varies somewhat through time. An overview of the arrangements for a zero cost tunnel is seen in Exhibit 5.

Finally, Advance could purchase forward contracts and lock in the cost of future purchases of foreign currency. Since Advance is committing to the purchase of a fixed amount of foreign currency at some future date, it must put up "margin" equal to 8 percent of the face amount of the purchase. Forward contract rates are seen in Exhibit 6. Advance would be expected to pay the offer price.

Advance's U.S. dollar cash flow requirements are relatively stable throughout the course of the year. Therefore, any hedging strategy would involve the purchase of twelve monthly contracts or options of equal amount, to match Advance's cash requirements.

EXHIBIT 5

ADVANCE TECHNOLOGIES
Zero Cost Tunnel
Strike Prices

Expiry Date	Puts	Calls
Oct. 31, 1992	$1.2491	$1.2690
Nov. 30, 1992	1.2508	1.2749
Dec. 31, 1992	1.2541	1.2799
Jan. 31, 1993	1.2541	1.2821
Feb. 28, 1993	1.2542	1.2842
Mar. 31, 1993	1.2542	1.2863
Apr. 30, 1993	1.2553	1.2880
May 31, 1993	1.2564	1.2897
June 30, 1993	1.2575	1.2915
July 31, 1993	1.2580	1.2927
Aug. 31, 1993	1.2585	1.2938
Sept. 30, 1993	1.2590	1.2950
Average	1.2551	1.2856

EXHIBIT 6

ADVANCE TECHNOLOGIES
Forward Contract Rates[1]

	Bid	Offer
1 month	1.2590	$1.2598
2 months	1.2628	1.2639
3 months	1.2669	1.2686
4 months	1.2681	1.2695
5 months	1.2692	1.2706
6 months	1.2703	1.2718
7 months	1.2716	1.2736
8 months	1.2731	1.2750
9 months	1.2745	1.2765
10 months	1.2753	1.2775
11 months	1.2762	1.2784
12 months	1.2770	1.2794
Average	1.2703	1.2719

[1]Advance expected to pay the offer rate.

Conclusion

Harrison was unsure which hedging alternative to suggest to Advance management. She wanted to show the other managers the effect on projected income and cash flow of a Canadian dollar at 1.2395, 1.2595, 1.2795, and 1.2995 without the use of a hedging strategy. Then she intended to show the costs and benefits of each of the proposed hedging vehicles. In order to show the worst case scenario she decided to assume that any movement in the exchange rate would occur on the first day of the 1993 fiscal year. Harrison's counterparts would be very interested in the results of her analysis, since if the company did not earn $9 million before taxes, the company would be in violation of the Bank's covenants.

CASE 7.2
ACCOUNTING FOR FOREIGN OPERATIONS

National Cabinet Lock of Canada, Inc.

National Cabinet Lock of Canada, Inc. (NCLC), is a manufacturer of locks and cabinet hardware headquartered in Toronto, Canada. NCLC was 95 percent acquired by a U.S. company, Valcor, Inc., on January 1, 1986.

This case concerns the accounting for NCLC's operations during fiscal year 1992 and its subsequent consolidation into Valcor's consolidated financial statements. Exhibits 1 and 2 present Valcor's 1992 year-end financial statements *excluding* the operations of NCLC. Exhibit 3 presents a summary of NCLC's transactions during 1992, and Exhibit 4 is NCLC's beginning balance sheet in U.S. dollars where the functional currency is (1) the U.S. dollar and (2) the Canadian dollar. As of January 1, 1992, NCLC's trial balance contained the following accounts (in Canadian dollars):

	Balance	
Account	*Dr.*	*Cr.*
Cash	$ 9,000	
Trade receivables (net)	5,000	
Inventory	1,000	
Equipment (net)	200,000	
Trade payables		$ 3,000
Long-term debt		100,000
Common stock		75,000
Retained earnings		37,000
	$215,000	$215,000

This case was prepared by Kenneth R. Ferris and Barbara L. Reed. Copyright © 1993 by Kenneth R. Ferris. All rights reserved.

EXHIBIT 1

Valcor, Inc.*

Panel A. Unconsolidated Income Statement for the year ended December 31, 1992 (000s omitted; in U.S. dollars)

Sales	$ 6,000.00
Less: Cost of goods sold	(5,000.00)
Gross profit	$ 1,000.00
Less: Selling/administrative expenses	(300.00)
Depreciation	(200.00)
Profit before subsidiary earnings	$ 500.00
Add: Equity in earnings of unconsolidated Canadian subsidiary	26.65
Profit before income taxes	$ 526.65

Panel B. Unconsolidated Balance Sheet as of 12/31/92 (000s omitted, in U.S. dollars)

Assets		*Equities*	
Cash	$1,000.00	Trade payable	$ 100.00
Receivables	211.60	Long-term debt	900.00
Inventory	100.00	Common stock	1,100.00
Investment in subsidiary	151.90	Retained earnings	528.90
Equipment (net)	1,000.00	Cumulative translation adjustment account	34.60
Land	200.00		
Total assets	$2,663.50	Total equities	$2,663.50

*The functional currency is assumed to be the Canadian dollar.

EXHIBIT 2

Valcor, Inc.*

Panel A. Unconsolidated Income Statement for the year ended December 31, 1992 (000s omitted, in U.S. dollars)

Sales	$ 6,000.00
Less: Cost of goods sold	(5,000.00)
Gross profit	$ 1,000.00
Less: Selling administrative expenses	(300.00)
Depreciation	(200.00)
Profit before subsidiary earnings	$ 500.00
Add: Equity in earnings of subsidiary	23.28
Net Income before taxes	$ 523.28

Panel B. Unconsolidated Balance Sheet as of 12/31/92 (000s omitted, in U.S. dollars)

Assets		*Equities*	
Cash	$1,000.0	Trade payable	$ 100.00
Receivables	211.60	Long-term debt	900.00
Inventory	100.00	Common stock	1,100.00
Investment in subsidiary	85.39	Retained earnings	496.99
Equipment (net)	1,000.00		
Land	200.00		
Total assets	$2,596.99	Total equities	$2,596.99

*The functional currency is assumed to be the U.S. dollar.

EXHIBIT 3

NATIONAL CABINET LOCK OF CANADA, INC.
Transaction Data for 1992*

1. Sales of $100,000*(C) occurred evenly throughout the year.
2. NCLC uses the FIFO method of accounting for inventory; thus, assume that any ending inventory was purchased on 8/04/92. Purchases of inventory were as follows:

04/25/92	$20,000 (C)
08/04/92	$24,000 (C)

All purchases of inventory are on account, and $5,500 (C) remained in the inventory account at year-end. The beginning inventory was purchased at the beginning exchange rate.
3. Expenses were incurred evenly throughout the year. Expenses other than depreciation and cost of goods sold amounted to $15,000 (C) for the year. Equipment is being depreciated on a straight-line basis over the 10-year remaining life.
4. On October 6, 1992, NCLC purchased undeveloped land in Mississauga (a suburb of Toronto) for $50,000 (C), financed by debt provided by the Bank of Montreal.
5. On June 30, 1992, NCLC paid dividends totalling $2,000 (C) to its shareholders.
6. At year-end, NCLC had the following ending account balances (in Canadian dollars):

Trade receivables (net)	$ 4,000
Trade payables	2,000
Long-term debt	100,000
Common stock	75,000

*Figures followed by (C) represent Canadian dollars.

EXHIBIT 4

NATIONAL CABINET LOCK OF CANADA, INC.

Beginning Balance Sheet in $ (functional currency = C)

Cash	$ 9,450	
Trade receivable	5,250	
Inventory	1,050	
Equipment (net)	210,000	
Trade payables		$ 3,150
Long-term debt		105,000
Common stock		60,000
Retained earnings		37,600
Cumulative translation adjustment		20,000
	$225,750	$225,750

Beginning Balance Sheet in $
(functional currency = U.S. $)

Cash	$ 9,450	
Trade receivable	5,250	
Inventory	1,050	
Equipment (net)	160,000	
Trade payables		$ 3,150
Long-term debt		105,000
Common stock		60,000
Retained earnings		7,600
	$175,750	$175,750

Exchange rates between the Canadian and U.S. dollars during 1992 were as follows:

Date	Rate
01–01–92	$1.00 C = $1.05 U.S.
04–25–92	1.00 = $1.09
06–30–92	1.00 = $1.11
08–04–92	1.00 = $1.16
09–03–92	1.00 = $1.14
10–06–92	1.00 = $1.15
12–31–92	1.00 = $1.18
Weighted average	1.00 = $1.10
01–01–86 (when acquisition occurred and when equipment was acquired)	1.00 = $0.80

Required:

(a) Using the information in the case, prepare NCLC's 1992 balance sheet and income statement in Canadian dollars.

(b) Prepare NCLC's 1992 balance sheet and income statement in U.S. dollars, assuming the functional currency is the Canadian dollar (i.e., the current method). Refer to Exhibit 4 for NCLC's beginning balance sheet in U.S. dollars where the functional currency is the Canadian dollar.

(c) Prepare Valcor's consolidated financial statements for 1992, using the information from Exhibit 1 and assuming that the functional currency is the Canadian dollar. When NCLC was acquired on January 1, 1986, the book value and market value of all the assets and liabilities were equivalent. There was no goodwill implicit in the NCLC purchase.

(d) Prepare NCLC's 1992 financial statements in U.S. dollars, assuming that the functional currency is the U.S. dollar (i.e., the temporal method). Refer to Exhibit 4 for NCLC's beginning balance sheet in U.S. dollars where the functional currency is the U.S. dollar.

(e) Prepare Valcor's consolidated financial statements for 1992, using the information from Exhibit 2 and assuming the functional currency is the U.S. dollar. Follow the same assumptions in part (c).

CASE 7.3
FOREIGN CURRENCY TRANSLATION

Computers International, Inc.

William Dodenhoff has just returned from a trip to his company's corporate headquarters in the United States. Dodenhoff is the general manager of Computers International, Inc.'s (CI) German subsidiary. Both CI and its German subsidiary are involved in the manufacture and distribution of computer parts.

Not only is Dodenhoff suffering from jet lag but also he had received some disturbing news from his U.S. boss, Wallace Smith, that was giving him more of a headache than the jet lag. Smith had informed him that on the advice of the firm's independent accountants, management was considering a change in the functional currency of the German subsidiary from the U.S. dollar to the German mark.

Corporate management had originally selected the U.S. dollar as the functional currency for several reasons. First, approximately 36 percent of the subsidiary's sales were intercompany sales to other subsidiaries located in Europe. Moreover, all of these sales were denominated in U.S. dollars under company policy that called for all intercompany transactions to be U.S. dollar denominated. Second, royalty payments, which represented approximately 22 percent of the subsidiary's total expenses, were paid to various research and development divisions of the company located worldwide. Again, these payments are denominated in U.S. dollars under existing company policy. Third, the subsidiary generally remits about 15 percent of its profits to headquarters. When dividends and royalties are combined, a significant portion of the subsidiary's cash outflows are in U.S. dollars. Last, and perhaps the most important reason, management was accustomed to the U.S. dollar being the functional currency and was happy with the results. Management was uncertain how the change in functional currency would affect reported results and, consequently, internal performance measures. In particular, they were concerned how the change would affect trends in expenses measured in U.S. dollars. The company had recently adopted a total quality management (TQM) approach to improve profits. TQM focuses on reducing expenses while improving the quality of a company's products.

Management was not concerned about the unexpected swings in income that could result from exchange gains and losses when the functional currency is the U.S. dollar. It was not anticipated that these gains and losses would have a material effect on the consolidated income because corporate headquarters hedged against such gains and losses. Even if the functional currency were the foreign currency and the translation gains and losses not recognized in consolidated income, headquarters would probably hedge the translation gains and losses because should the company decide to sell part or all of their foreign operations, the cumulative translation gain or loss would be recognized in consolidated income at the time of the sale.

While still in the United States, Dodenhoff had called Frederick Sauer, his assistant in Germany, and asked him to prepare a report that would show how the proposed change in the functional currency would affect the subsidiary's financial statements. He had just finished reading the report and the results were worse than he had anticipated.

Dodenhoff's thoughts were interrupted by the buzzer on his desk. It was his secretary informing him that his call to the United States had been completed and that Wallace Smith was on the line. He picked up the phone: ''Hi, Wally; I'm glad I was able to reach you. I realize it is still early morning in the States.''

''Good to hear from you; I hope your return trip to Germany was not too exhausting. What can I do for you?''

''Well, ever since I left headquarters I have been mulling over this idea about changing the functional currency, and the more I contemplate the change the more I feel confident that it is not the best way to go.''

''I am interested in hearing your thoughts about the change because earlier today I talked with our independent auditors, and they are pushing hard for the change. To be quite honest, Bill, some of the points they brought up were very convincing.''

''Wally, I was just reviewing *FASB Statement No. 52,* and, as you know, it lists several economic indicators to be used when determining the functional currency of a foreign subsidiary. According to these indicators, the functional currency should be the currency of the country in which a subsidiary primarily generates and expends cash. And, as you well know, a substantial portion of our sub's operations involves intercompany sales to our other affiliates located throughout Europe. Moreover, our firmwide policy is that the transfer price for all intercompany sales is to be denominated in U.S. dollars. In addition, we maintain extensive research and development divisions located around the world that do fundamental and advanced research in computer technology. Royalty payments made to the research and development divisions are denominated in U.S. dollars, and these royalty payments represent a substantial share of the German subsidiary's total expenses. Also, all of the dividends that we remit to headquarters are in U.S. dollars. Although we retain about 85 percent of our profits for future growth in Germany, when we do send cash to headquarters, it is company policy that the cash be denominated in U.S. dollars.''

''What you say may be true, Bill; however, the auditors contend that *FASB No. 52* concludes that the functional currency should be the foreign currency when the foreign operations are relatively self-contained and integrated within a particular country. You may make sales to entities outside of Germany, but 45 percent of the subsidiary's sales are within Germany; and, generally, the sales outside of Germany are denominated in marks except for intercompany sales. Moreover, 90 percent of the piece parts and raw materials used by your subsidiary are supplied by German companies. And, as a final point, all labor and most costs—with the exception of those you mentioned—are denominated in marks, which is a key point since the subsidiary generates enough marks to cover most of its mark expenses and debt obligations. All in all, these factors have convinced the auditors that the German subsidiary is relatively self-contained and, consequently, that the functional currency should be the mark.'' (See Table 1 for a list of the FASB's economic indicators to be used in determining the functional currency of a foreign subsidiary.)

''Nonetheless, Wally, it is our responsibility to determine the functional currency of our subsidiaries. *Statement No. 52* clearly indicates that management's judgment is paramount in determining the functional currency of a subsidiary in those instances in which the indicators are mixed and the functional currency is not obvious. My best judgment is that the functional currency should be the U.S. dollar. Besides, in the past, we have used the U.S. dollar as the functional currency, and the auditors have given us a clean opinion! *Statement No. 52* states that once a determination of the functional currency is made, the decision should not be changed unless there are significant changes in economic facts and circumstances. And, in my opinion, there haven't been any significant changes. To switch the functional currency now could lead to the erroneous inference that we were wrong in the past and that our previously issued financial statements were misleading—a fact that could very likely lead to a shareholder lawsuit against the company, as well as the auditors.''

TABLE 1

FASB STATEMENT NO. 52
Economic Indicators for Determining the Functional Currency

Cash Flow Indicators

Foreign currency: Cash flows related to the foreign entity's individual assets and liabilities are primarily in the foreign currency and do not impact the parent company's cash flows.

Parent's currency: Cash flows related to the foreign entity's individual assets and liabilities directly impact the parent's cash flows on a current basis and are readily available for remittance to the parent company.

Sales Price Indicators

Foreign currency: Sales prices for the foreign entity's products are not primarily responsive on a short-term basis to changes in exchange rates but are determined more by local competition or by local government regulation.

Parent's currency: Sales prices for the foreign entity's products are primarily responsive on a short-term basis to changes in exchange rates; for example, sales prices are determined more by worldwide competition or by international prices.

Sales Market Indicators

Foreign currency: There is an active local sales market for the foreign entity's products, although there might also be significant amounts of exports.

Parent's currency: The sales market is mostly in the parent's country or sales contracts are denominated in the parent's currency.

Expense Indicators

Foreign currency: Labor, materials, and other costs for the foreign entity's products or services are primarily local costs, even though there might also be imports from other countries.

Parent's currency: Labor, materials, and other costs for the foreign entity's products or services, on a continuing basis, are primarily costs for components obtained from the country in which the parent company is located.

Financing Indicators

Foreign currency: Financing is primarily denominated in foreign currency, and funds generated by the foreign entity's operations are sufficient to service existing and normally expected debt obligations.

Parent's currency: Financing is primarily from the parent or other dollar-denominated obligations, or funds generated by the foreign entity's operations are not sufficient to service existing and normally expected debt obligations without the infusion of additional funds from the parent company. Infusion of additional funds from the parent company for expansion is not a factor, provided funds generated by the foreign entity's expanded operations are expected to be sufficient to service that additional financing.

Intercompany Transactions and Arrangements Indicators

Foreign currency: There is a low volume of intercompany transactions and there is not an extensive interrelationship between the operations of the foreign entity and the parent company. However, the foreign entity's operations may rely on the parent's affiliates' competitive advantages, such as patents and trademarks.

Parent's currency: There is a high volume of intercompany transactions and there is an extensive interrelationship between the foreign entity and the parent company. Additionally, the parent's currency generally would be the functional currency if the foreign entity is a device or shell corporation for holding investments, obligations, intangible assets, etc., that could readily be carried on the parent's or an affiliate's books.

Reprinted with the permission of Financial Accounting Standards Board, Stamford, Connecticut.

TABLE 2

COMPUTERS INTERNATIONAL, INC.
German Subsidiary
Balance Sheets*
19X1
(marks in thousands)

	Beginning Actual	*Ending Pro Forma*
Cash	50	95
Accounts receivable, net	201	198
Inventories	81	72
Prepaid expenses	62	65
Total current assets	394	430
Property, plant, and equipment	390	405
Other assets	240	240
Total assets	1,024	1,075
Accounts payable	88	90
Accrued liabilities	294	290
Total current liabilities	382	380
Long-term debt	163	163
Other liabilities	50	54
Common stock	88	88
Retained earnings	341	390
Total liabilities and stockholders' equity	1,024	1,075

*See notes to Table 3.

"You've brought up some good points, Bill, and I promise to discuss them with the auditors. I'm having a meeting with them next week, and one of the topics on the agenda is changing the functional currency of the German subsidiary. I'll present your arguments to them and, after the meeting, I'll give you a call to let you know their reaction. In the meantime, if you think of anything else you would like for me to discuss with them, give me a call."

"Thanks for being so open to my suggestions, and I will certainly give you a call if there is anything else I feel should be brought to their attention."

Dodenhoff slowly put down the phone and began reflecting on the events of the past three years. It was almost three years ago that he had been promoted to general manager of the German subsidiary. Corporate management in the United States had been dissatisfied with the prior financial performance of the German subsidiary, and he had been given the charge to reduce costs since they were higher than comparable costs in any of the company's other manufacturing facilities around the world. Headquarters had also indicated that they thought the German subsidiary had the potential to generate higher sales. They had realized that it would take some time to get things turned around and had given him five years to accomplish this task.

For the past three years, Dodenhoff and his staff had worked hard to improve the sales and the cost structure of the German subsidiary. Finally, this year, it appeared that all of their efforts were going to pay off. The budgeted results indicated that profits were to be at an all-time high due to increased sales and reduced costs from a more efficient use of fixed assets. So far this year, the subsidiary's results were at budget and in some cases better than budget. (See Table 2 for last year's actual balance sheet and the budgeted (pro forma) balance sheet for this year prepared in marks and Table 3 for the budgeted (pro forma) income statement prepared in marks.)

TABLE 3

COMPUTER INTERNATIONAL, INC.
German Subsidiary
Pro Forma (Budgeted) Income Statement*
19X1
(marks in thousands)

Sales	600
Cost of sales	252
Gross profits	348
Selling, general & administrative	200
Depreciation expense	52
Operating income	96
Taxes	38
Net income	58

ROA = 58 ÷ 668.5 = 8.68%.
Average net assets = ((1024 − 382) + (1075 − 380))/2 = 668.5.

*Statements in Tables 2 and 3 were prepared according to CI's budgeted activities as follows:
1. Dividends—9,000 marks, paid evenly over the year.
2. Fixed assets—67,000 marks, purchased evenly over the year. It is company policy to take no depreciation in the year an asset is purchased and take a full year's depreciation in the year an asset is sold or scrapped. No assets were sold or scrapped this year.
3. Manufacturing costs—243,000 marks; assume that all costs are incurred evenly over the year.
4. Beginning inventory—81,000 marks; all purchased at the beginning exchange rate.
5. Ending inventory—72,000 marks; all purchased at the ending exchange rate.
6. Included in selling general and administrative expenses are 64,000 marks of prepaid expenses. These resulted from Beginning prepaid (62,000) + Purchased prepaid (67,000) − End prepaid (65,000) = 64,000.
7. Inventories and prepaid expenses assume a FIFO flow of costs and were purchased evenly over the year.
8. Assume no beginning and ending raw materials and work in process inventories.

In addition, return on net assets (ROA)—a key performance indicator used by top management to evaluate subsidiary performance—was anticipated to be much higher than previous years. Management defined ROA as income before transaction gains and losses divided by the average of total assets minus current liabilities. Transaction gains and losses were eliminated from the calculation since headquarters hedges these gains and losses.

Dodenhoff was aware that the company's top executives used ROA for a variety of decision-making purposes, including the determination of bonuses for all of the firm's managerial level employees. For the first time in many years, management of the German subsidiary was anticipating decent bonuses, and, consequently, morale was high.

When Dodenhoff had called his assistant, Frederick Sauer, from the United States, he had asked him to survey the firm's international bankers to obtain a forecast of expected movements in the exchange rate between the mark and the U.S. dollar for the coming year. He had instructed Sauer to use these estimates to prepare U.S. dollar pro forma financial statements for the German subsidiary under various scenarios: (1) that the U.S. dollar was the functional currency and the value of the U.S. dollar would appreciate relative to the mark, (2) that the U.S. dollar was the functional currency and the value of the U.S. dollar would depreciate relative to the mark, (3) that the mark was the functional currency and the value of the U.S. dollar would appreciate relative to the mark, and (4) that the mark was the functional currency and the value of the U.S. dollar would depreciate relative to the mark. In each scenario that Sauer had developed,

Dodenhoff found that the income (before transaction gains and losses) of the German subsidiary was higher when the functional currency was the U.S. dollar, largely due to the lower costs. Also, the ROA was considerably higher, as was the gross margin and return on sales percentages when the functional currency was the dollar.

Dodenhoff was concerned that the morale of his employees would be adversely affected if their bonuses were lower than anticipated. He was also concerned about the effect that the change in functional currency would have on costs. One of his primary responsibilities had been to reduce costs, and he felt that he would have a harder time convincing top management that the cost structure had improved significantly if the functional currency were the mark. When the functional currency is the dollar, many of the subsidiary's costs are remeasured using historical exchange rates and are unaffected by exchange rate fluctuations; but, when the functional currency is the foreign currency, all costs are remeasured using current exchange rates and, thus, tend to fluctuate more. In the past, top management's philosophy was that they were primarily concerned about the impact that foreign operations had on the consolidated financial statements. Therefore, their main emphasis in the evaluation process was on the financial results of the foreign subsidiaries in dollars and very little, if any, attention was devoted to the financial results calculated in the foreign currency. Dodenhoff doubted that this philosophy would change in the future. Hence, any change that affected the financial results in dollars could potentially have a large effect on the evaluation of foreign subsidiaries and their managers, and, based on Sauer's report, a change in the functional currency would not bode well for the evaluation of the German subsidiary.

In addition, management was used to evaluating him and the subsidiary when the functional currency was the dollar, and he was comfortable with things as they were. Sauer's report illustrated how the choice of functional currency affected the budgeted financial statements for the coming year. He also felt unsure how the change would affect the overall evaluation of the subsidiary. Currently, headquarters was responsible for hedging the transaction gains and losses that were reported on the income statement. If the functional currency were the mark, translation gains and losses would be reported in stockholders' equity. Would headquarters continue to hedge the gains and losses if they were not reported on the income statement? If they were not hedged, would the translation gains and losses be used in the evaluation of foreign subsidiaries? These questions and others needed to be answered before Dodenhoff could feel comfortable with the change in the functional currency.

Dodenhoff decided to contact Sauer to inform him of the meeting between Smith and the auditors. Sauer and his staff could surely generate some additional arguments for not changing the functional currency. Perhaps one argument they could emphasize was that the choice of the functional currency did not really affect cash flows or the economic consequences of the underlying transactions. Any differences were simply the result of bookkeeping gains and losses. So, why not use the choice that gives the subsidiary the best reported results? Dodenhoff decided to discuss this argument, and others, with his staff before calling Smith.

He looked at his watch. It was later than he thought and he had to prepare for his next appointment. He wanted to brief his staff as soon as possible about the proposed accounting change and get their feedback. He decided to have his secretary set up a meeting for tomorrow morning.

Required:

    (a) Based on the economic indicators listed in Table 1 and the information given in the case, should the functional currency of CI's German subsidiary be the U.S. dollar or the mark? Why?

(b) If you were advising Dodenhoff, would you recommend that he confront the auditors with the argument that any differences in net income and ROA that result from the choice of functional currency are nothing more than bookkeeping gains and losses; therefore, a company is justified in choosing the functional currency that gives the best reported results? Why or why not?

(c) Assume that the functional currency is the U.S. dollar. Using the following exchange rates, calculate the expected net income of the German subsidiary in U.S. dollars (use the pro forma statements in Tables 2 and 3 as a starting point). Assuming that the German subsidiary does not include transaction gains and losses in calculating its return on net assets, calculate the expected ROA.

Spot Rates	
Beginning exchange rate	US$ = 1.58DM
Average exchange rate	US$ = 1.35DM
Ending exchange rate	US$ = 1.32DM
Purchased PP&E on beginning balance sheet	US$ = 2.40DM
Issued common stock	US$ = 3.60DM
Purchased other assets	US$ = 2.10DM
Purchased beginning prepaid expenses	US$ = 1.90DM
Purchased prepaid expenses during year	US$ = 1.35DM
Ending prepaid expenses	US$ = 1.35DM

(d) Assume that the functional currency is the mark and that the beginning cumulative translation adjustment was a gain of $47,000 and beginning retained earnings totaled $200,000. Using the exchange rates from part (c), calculate the expected net income of the German subsidiary and the expected ROA.

(e) Assume that the functional currency is the U.S. dollar. Using the following exchange rates, calculate the expected net income of the German subsidiary in U.S. dollars (use the pro forma statements in Tables 2 and 3 as a starting point). Assuming that the German subsidiary does not include transaction gains or losses in the calculation of return on net assets, what is the expected ROA?

Spot Rates	
Beginning exchange rate	US$ = 1.58DM
Average exchange rate	US$ = 1.70DM
Ending exchange rate	US$ = 1.90DM
Purchased PP&E on beginning balance sheet	US$ = 2.40DM
Issued common stock	US$ = 3.60DM
Purchased other assets	US$ = 2.10DM
Purchased beginning prepaid expenses	US$ = 1.90DM
Purchased prepaid expenses during year	US$ = 1.70DM
Ending prepaid expenses	US$ = 1.70DM

(f) Assume that the functional currency is the mark and that the beginning cumulative translation adjustment was a gain of $47,000, and the beginning retained earnings totaled $200,000. Using the exchange rates from part (e) above, calculate the expected net income of the German subsidiary and the expected ROA.

(g) Why is the ROA consistently higher when the functional currency is the U.S. dollar? Is the ROA a good indicator for purposes of evaluating the performance of the subsidiary management (and when determining employee bonuses)? Should ROA be calculated in the foreign currency or in U.S. dollars for purposes of evaluating foreign subsidiary performance? Explain your reasoning.

PART III

Accounting Standards and Practices in Selected Countries

In this section of the book, the unique contexts of and the financial reporting practices in seven major countries around the world are compared and contrasted. As you will see, despite all of the efforts directed toward harmonization, reporting practices remain widely divergent from country to country. This is all the more interesting because each of the seven countries has a highly developed capital market. The cultural, business, and legal explanations for these divergences are also considered. Perhaps an alternative title for this section should be "a global guide to disharmony."

A principal objective of the following section is to compare and contrast not only the financial reporting practices of the seven countries but also the business, cultural, and legal setting of each country to identify the presence of any systematic effects that might be manifested in financial indicators. Consider, for example, the following 1993 fiscal-year data:[1]

Country	Quick Ratio	Interest Coverage Ratio	Inventory Turnover	Return on Assets
Great Britain	0.86	4.72	5.22	0.05
Germany	1.27	3.25	5.11	0.02
Japan	0.98	2.74	5.42	0.02
Sweden	0.99	1.56	2.58	0.01
South Korea	0.49	1.35	6.40	0.01
Italy	0.94	1.92	3.70	0.02
United States	1.00	2.90	4.84	0.03

---

[1]Data were obtained from the Compustat International file and reflects the median ratio of all listed firms.

Although it is tenuous to draw firm conclusions at this stage, some observations are nonetheless noteworthy. For example, German companies appear to maintain the highest quick ratios, with South Korean companies the lowest. For this latter group, liquidity appears to be enhanced by maintaining the highest inventory turnover. British companies appear to maintain the highest interest coverage ratio and, thus, appear somewhat debt averse as compared to South Korean or Swedish companies. These results, however, may be less related to debt aversion than to relative profitability—the return on assets is highest for British firms and lowest for South Korean and Swedish firms.

As you approach the next seven chapters, one of your educational missions is to focus on those institutional and cultural differences and similarities that may explain these data.

CHAPTER
8

Great Britain[1]

The ASB's [Accounting Standards Board] proposals implicitly make the balance sheet the central plank of the financial statements, with the profit and loss account dependent upon it. The ASB appears to favor current valuations in preference to historical costs. Their approach seems to be to try to make the balance sheet more like a statement of wealth, with the movement in net assets being the primary measure of performance.[2]

Financial reporting in the U.K. remains in a state of some turmoil.[3]

Introduction

As the first great industrial power of the modern era, Great Britain has had a broad and enduring influence on financial reporting practices around the world. The historical importance and geographical reach of British financial reporting practices grow directly out of Great Britain's former role as a world power and pioneer of capitalism, and its continuing influence on international accounting standards is more that of an elder partner than a ruler. This shift in the dynamics of power is reflected in Great Britain's changing trade patterns, which have moved away from its colonies and dependencies

---

[1]In Chapter 1, Hofstede's cultural studies involving Great Britain were introduced. We have titled this chapter to be consistent with his focus. In fact, Great Britain includes England, Wales, and Scotland, whereas the United Kingdom includes Great Britain and Northern Ireland. We draw no distinctions for financial reporting purposes between Great Britain and the United Kingdom.

[2]R. Paterson, ''In Support of the Profit and Loss Account—Balance Sheets Should Show the Results of the Company's Transactions,'' *The Financial Times,* September 16, 1993, p. 15.

[3]A quote attributed to another party by J. Kelly, ''A Sector in Turmoil Needs a Guiding Hand—A Recent Study into U.K. Accounting Practice Has Mixed Feelings about the ASB,'' *The Financial Times,* October 27, 1994, p. 30.

413

of the 19th century to its current membership in the European Union (EU) and close ties with the United States.

Despite the dissolution of its empire, Great Britain continues to be a major factor in developing international financial reporting standards. It is not only a member of the European Union but also is prominently represented in other bodies that are attempting to develop workable international accounting standards, such as the Organization for Economic Cooperation and Development (OECD) and the International Accounting Standards Committee (IASC), of which the latter is headquartered in London. (For more information on these and other groups promoting harmonization of accounting standards, see Chapter 2.) Given the prominent role of Great Britain in international financial reporting circles, it is not surprising that British company law and reporting standards have exerted a heavy influence on EU directives affecting reporting practices. But Britain's influence comes from private sources as well: British multinationals are a major presence throughout the industrialized and developing world, and the international prestige of London's capital markets ensures that British financial reporting and disclosure requirements remain a prominent issue for major multinational firms around the world.

Environmental Factors

Cultural Environment

Although U.S. and British financial reporting have in many respects gone their own ways over the last 200 years, the exchange of ideas that has characterized Anglo-American relations has maintained a fundamental cultural bond between the two systems and the people that operate them. This bond can be illustrated by comparing the scores of U.S. subjects in Hofstede's study with those of their British counterparts. In three of the focal cultural dimensions, the scores of the two countries are separated by only five points or less. In power distance (PD), the British group registered a 35, and the U.S. group scored 40; in individualism (IDV), the British subjects scored 89, and the U.S. subjects 91; and in long-term orientation (LTO), the British scored 25 and Americans scored 29. In the only category in which the group scores were more than five points apart—uncertainty avoidance (UAV)—the British group scored 35 and the U.S. group 46.

In the context of Gray's analysis of the dimensions of the financial reporting subculture (outlined in chapter one), the UAV scores reported for the British in fact reflect the slightly lower degree of conservatism found in British financial reporting as compared to practices in the United States. For example, the treatment of goodwill differs significantly between the United States and Great Britain: the United States requires the capitalization and amortization of goodwill, whereas preferred practice in Great Britain involves an immediate write-off of goodwill against shareholder reserves (a practice not allowed in the United States or under the IASC's recently revised *IAS 22*). Research on the differences in profits reported under U.S. GAAP versus those reported under British GAAP indicate that profits under the latter were 10–15 percent higher than under U.S. GAAP as a result of the difference in treatment of just goodwill.[4] This reflects a more optimistic, less conservative approach in the measurement practices used in Great Britain versus those used in the United States. Other less conservative practices that differ between the United States and Great Britain, and that have a material effect on profit, include the treatment of inventories, deferred taxation, and the revaluation of long-lived assets. These and other financial reporting differences are discussed in detail in a subsequent section.

The 11-point spread in UAV, suggesting that the British have slightly more tolerance for ambiguity than do Americans, runs counter to a popular stereotype that contrasts a supposedly British love of order and propriety with a supposedly American love of unabashed freedom. No doubt it is true that the stereotype accurately reflects one side of the British national character. However, it is equally true that the British have long cherished liberty as a distinctive feature of their society and culture—so much so that forms of social enforcement now taken for granted (e.g., police forces, standing armies) met with vehement opposition on their introduction in England. Inevitably, the preservation of liberty has often entailed accepting a measure of disorder, a trade-off the British have been willing to make more often than is commonly appreciated. Perhaps, then, there is a cultural reason that the British output in the area of accounting regulation has lagged well behind that of the United States. Prior to its demise in August 1990 the main British accounting regulatory body, the **Accounting Standards Committee,** issued only one pronouncement—these pronouncements were called **Statements of Standard Accounting Practice** (SSAPs)—for approximately every four issued by the Financial Accounting Standards Board in the United States. Another interesting observation recently made regarding the financial reporting subculture in Great Britain is that when British auditors were surveyed regarding their attitudes about the true and fair view audit opinion, several respondents volunteered that fair was more important than true; none suggested the reverse.[5] Such a response is perhaps not surprising given the British penchant for relatively small PD (e.g., all should have equal rights) and relatively low UAV (e.g., ambiguity of fair versus true is quite acceptable).

Whatever the cultural differences between Great Britain and the United States may mean, they should be kept in perspective. For example, they diminish considerably when we contrast U.S. and British scores with those of Latin America, the Far East, or even continental European groups in Hofstede's study. The cultural dimension scores for both Great Britain and the United States reflect a society characterized by flexible rules, the absence of an all-powerful hierarchy, and the solution of problems through negotiation. These characteristics seem a fairly accurate description of accounting policy formation and application in both Great Britain and the United States.

---

[4]P. Weetman and S. Gray, ''A Comparative International Analysis of the Impact of Accounting Principles on Profits: The U.S.A. versus the U.K., Sweden and The Netherlands,'' *Accounting and Business Research,* Fall 1991, pp. 363–79. In order to provide a fair comparison, the researchers reconciled the profits reported by British companies with earnings that would have been reported under U.S. GAAP.

[5]R. Parker and C. Nobes, '' 'True and Fair': U.K. Auditors' View,'' *Accounting and Business Research,* Fall 1991, p. 353.

Legal and Political Environment

Corporation Law.   With very few exceptions, such as formation by Royal Charter, British companies are incorporated under the Companies Act currently in force. (The most recent one at this writing is the **Companies Act of 1985,** as amended in 1989 to incorporate the EU's Seventh Directive.) The act requires all corporations to maintain accounting records that include sufficient information to give a **true and fair view** of a company's financial position and operations. The phrase *true and fair view,* first introduced in the 1947 Companies Act, is important in British accounting and auditing. Even though its meaning is difficult to ascertain with precision (as is likely to be the case with any standard of "fairness"), it is the key phrase by which auditors express an opinion on a set of corporate financial statements. Companies must present audited financial statements in a stipulated format and a directors' report to shareholders at the annual meeting. In addition, they must file these documents with the Registrar of Companies.

In 1990, John Major, former foreign secretary and chancellor of the exchequer under Margaret Thatcher, became prime minister. Aside from his soft-spoken manner, Mr. Major differed significantly from Mrs. Thatcher in at least one area: he wanted Britain in the mainstream of the European Union. In fact, during the latter weeks of Mrs. Thatcher's government, Mr. Major led the way for Britain's full membership into the European Monetary System. Even in the face of turmoil in September 1992, as the British pound sank against the German mark, thereby forcing the pound out of the **European Exchange Rate Mechanism** (ERM), Mr. Major, who was then president of the European Union, reaffirmed his commitment to European cooperation. As prime minister, he eased the long-standing tensions between Britain and its EU colleagues and proved a steadfast ally to the United States during the war in the Persian Gulf. Mr. Major's first priority, however, was to reduce inflation: he believed that inflation was Britain's main economic and social poison and he made significant progress in bringing it down. This was no small task given that:

> Under-investment, as an attitude of mind among managers and officials, generation after generation, has been by far the most debilitating British Disease. [An observation borne out by the fact that] since 1975, British companies have retained an average 45% of their earnings for reinvestment [as compared to] French and American firms [which] have retained 54%, Japanese firms 63% and German firms 67%.[6]

Individual Tax Law—Investor Incentives.   The investor orientation that has traditionally dominated British financial reporting is clearly reinforced by British tax law, which gives individuals several important incentives to invest in stocks. Although capital gains are taxable, they are eligible for tax breaks favoring small investors: net gains, less losses carried forward, are indexed to eliminate the effects of inflation. An annual exemption, which currently amounts to £5,800, further decreases the taxable

---

[6]"A Survey of Britain—Too Good a Job," *The Economist,* October 24, 1992, pp. Surveys 4 and 5.

portion of any gain. (At January 1995 exchange rates—$1.57 to £1—the exemption excluded the first $9,100 of capital gains from income.) Amounts in excess of the annual exemption are taxed at the marginal rate applicable to the highest portion of an individual's income. Tax rates on ordinary income range from 20 percent on the first £3,000 of taxable income, to a basic rate of 25 percent on income between £3,000 and £23,700, with a 40 percent rate applied to income over £23,700.

Interest and dividend income is treated as ordinary income and thus is subject to tax rates as high as 40 percent. Under the imputation system adopted by Great Britain in 1973, however, shareholders are granted partial relief from double taxation on corporate profits. When a British corporation pays dividends, it must also make an advance payment on its income taxes for the year. The current amount of this advance payment is 25 percent of the dividends paid. The advance payment, officially known as the **Advance Corporation Tax** (ACT), is paid by the company to the Inland Revenue Service and is imputed to shareholders as a tax credit to be applied against their personal income tax for the year. Thus, if a company pays a dividend of £100,000 and an advance tax payment of £25,000, a shareholder with a 1 percent holding would receive a dividend of £1,000 and a tax credit of £250 to be applied against his or her individual income tax obligation. The taxpayer must report £1,250 of income, which at a tax rate of 20 percent creates an additional £250 of tax liability. Thus, the imputed tax credit eliminates the marginal tax liability generated by the dividend payment—but only if the taxpayer is in the lowest income bracket. Taxpayers whose income falls in a higher bracket owe a tax liability larger than the credit they receive. For example, a taxpayer in the 40 percent bracket receives the same £250 tax credit, but the dividend income generates an additional tax liability of £500 (£1,250 × 40 percent), creating a net tax liability of £250 (£500 − £250) from the £1,000 dividend payment—an effective tax rate of 25 percent on the dividend income. The corporation also receives a credit of £25,000 which it can use, subject to certain limitations, to offset its tax liability on its next return.

Corporate Tax Law—Effects on Financial Statements.   Great Britain is one of a number of nations in the world (like the United States) in which corporate tax law does *not* serve as the basis for financial reporting. In many countries, such as Germany, Japan, and Sweden, firms must keep their books of account in accordance with the dictates of tax regulations, a practice that subjects financial reporting standards to the actions of legislators and greatly hinders comparability across national boundaries. In Great Britain, however, the process is reversed. Income statements are prepared according to British GAAP and then are adjusted to arrive at taxable income. Typical adjustments include such items as substituting statutory "capital allowances" for financial depreciation and applying to current income any tax losses carried forward from a previous period. Because these adjustments are restricted to the tax return and are not entered on a company's books, readers of British financial statements escape the burdensome task of having to make adjustments and reclassifications to eliminate the effects of tax regulations to obtain more comparable measures of firm performance.

SSAP No. 15 requires companies to adopt for financial reporting purposes a modified version of the liability method of accounting for income taxes. Basically, this

---

EXHIBIT 8–1

RTZ Plc
Deferred Tax Disclosure

Deferred tax is provided using the liability method in respect of all timing differences to the extent that, in the opinion of the directors, they are expected to reverse in the foreseeable future. Advance corporation tax is deducted in arriving at the net deferred tax provision to the maximum extent possible. Any remaining advanced corporation tax is written off in the profit and loss account. The provision for deferred taxation and the amount for which provision has not been made are as follows:

	U.K. Tax	Overseas Tax	Total (£m) 1992	Total (£m) 1991
Provided in Accounts				
Accelerated capital allowances	16	228	244	299
Other timing differences	34	64	98	19
	50	292	342	318
Deduct: Advance corporation tax recoverable	(37)	—	(37)	(31)
Overseas tax credits recoverable	—	(55)	(55)	(37)
	13	237	250	256
Amount Unprovided				
Accelerated capital allowances	12	50	62	72
Other timing differences	—	4	4	5
	12	54	66	77
Deduct: Advance corporation tax recoverable	(9)	—	(9)	(13)
	3	54	57	64

---

standard requires British companies to account for timing differences between tax and financial reporting only to the extent that management believes that a tax liability or asset will actually materialize. According to the standard, management should base its judgment on reasonable assumptions and on all relevant information available up to the date on which the financial statements are approved. Companies must also disclose the amount of the potential deferred tax liability that is not reflected on the balance sheet. Exhibit 8–1, extracted from the footnotes to the financial statements of RTZ Plc, illustrates the typical disclosures for a firm's deferred tax liability, both recorded and unrecorded.

As can be seen from this schedule, accelerated tax depreciation (called *accelerated capital allowances* in Great Britain) and other timing differences account for a total of £307 million (i.e., £250 + £57) in deferred taxes. Of this, however, only £250 million is carried on the company's financial statements (or *provided in accounts,* to use British parlance). This number is lumped into a balance sheet figure called *provisions for liabilities and charges* (not shown on this schedule, but see the RTZ balance sheet presented in Exhibit 8–6). The directors of RTZ have estimated that only the former, larger (£250) amount is likely to materialize as a tax liability. According to British GAAP, the advance corporation tax recoverable figure represents that portion of the firm's ACT payments (see the preceding section) that the firm will be able to net against its tax liability for the year.

The current corporate tax rate in Britain is 33 percent; however, a "small companies rate" of 25 percent applies to companies that earn less than £250,000. Taxable profits between £250,000 and £1,250,000 are taxed at a slightly higher rate, but if a company's taxable profits exceed £1,250,000, all of it is taxed at 33 percent.

Business Environment

Form of Business.   The dominant business entity in Great Britain is the limited liability company, also referred to as a *company limited by shares.* A limited liability company may be incorporated as either a private or a public concern, the latter having the right to issue securities to the public. Both public and private companies must have at least two stockholders, and public companies must have at least two directors as well, but private companies need have only one director. For a limited liability company to be incorporated as a public entity, it must have a minimum share capital of £50,000 and include **Public Limited Company** (or **Plc**) in its name. A private company is subject to no minimum capital requirement and must include the word *Limited* (or **Ltd.**) at the end of its name.

Value Added.   British attitudes toward business and its social responsibilities are well documented. In a recent survey of corporate annual reports from nine countries, the British reports rated the best on disclosure of corporate social information.[7] Indeed, the belief that corporations must look beyond the maximization of profit has become a permanent if oft-debated element in British public opinion.

A by-product of this belief is the search for progressive ways to report the results of business operations—new methods that depict the corporation as a locus of cooperation rather than as a unit of competition. One of the most widespread and best known experiments in this direction is the **value-added statement,** which a significant minority of European firms began to include in their corporate reports in the 1970s. (See Exhibit 8–2 for an example of a value-added statement, which is taken from the annual report of the BOC Group, a British conglomerate.) Although the popularity of value-added statements has declined in recent years because questions have been raised about their usefulness, a number of prominent British firms continue to present them along with more traditional documents.

Devised by a U.S. Treasury official in the 18th century, the concept of value added has since been used by governments as a measure of national income. In the 1970s it was embraced by corporations—on the recommendation of the British government and

---

[7]A. Jack, "Survey Reveals Variety in Accounts," *The Financial Times,* October 5, 1992, p. 17.

Exhibit 8–2

BOC Group
Value-Added Statement

	1991		1990	
	£million	%	*£million*	%
Value Added				
Turnover	2,718.5		2,643.9	
Bought-in materials, services, & depreciation	(1,639.3)		(1,590.1)	
Value added	1,079.2		1,053.8	
Application				
To employees as pay or for pensions & welfare schemes	711.8	66.0	658.2	62.5
To banks & other lenders as interest	79.9	7.4	71.9	6.8
To governments as tax on profits	90.1	8.3	89.7	8.5
To partners in partly owned companies	7.3	0.7	5.0	0.5
To group shareholders	96.0	8.9	88.8	8.4
	985.1	91.3	913.6	86.7
Retained within the group	94.1	8.7	140.2	13.3
	1,079.2	100.0	1,053.8	100.0

the accounting profession—to provide additional information to shareholders, serve as the basis of employee incentive programs, and improve public and employee relations by showing what a company does with the wealth it creates. In short, a value-added statement provides a measure of wealth created by the operations that a company performs on inputs, and it shows the distribution of that wealth among major constituent groups: employees, investors, and the government. Such operations may involve constructing or manufacturing goods, assembling them, or simply making them more available.

The basic numerical definition of *value added* is sales less purchases. A refinement of this definition distinguishes gross value added (as just defined) from net value added, which subtracts depreciation as well as purchases from sales. Depending on who's doing the calculating, depreciation may be figured on a historical cost basis or a current cost basis. Governments typically attempt to calculate depreciation using the latter. The interest in value added has also spawned a variety of ratios, such as value added/ payroll costs and operating profit/value added, designed to provide company planners with a new perspective on operations and to express the efficiency of a company in terms that are more easily understandable to the general public.

Accounting Profession and Policy Formulation. The accounting profession in Great Britain is rich in tradition, well trained, and influential. Just as Great Britain is the cradle of modern capitalism, it is also the founding place of modern financial reporting and of the independent audit. The professional British title corresponding to certified public accountant in the United States is **chartered accountant,** and the best known professional associations are the English and Scottish and, in the larger context of the United Kingdom, the Irish Institute of Chartered Accountants. Along with the members of the Chartered Association of Certified Accountants, members of the three bodies just mentioned are recognized by the Department of Trade and Industry as qualified to carry out the required annual audit of British companies. The education and experience requirements for public practice include successful completion of special institute examinations, a minimum three years of training in an authorized training office, and two years of approved experience after completing the other qualification requirements.

These professional associations not only regulate entry into the profession but also governed the formulation of accounting and auditing standards until mid-1990. Although corporate financial statements must adhere to the basic requirements and format prescribed by national legislation, the promulgation of specific accounting and auditing standards was controlled by private committees formed by six associations of professional accountants (including the four bodies noted above). The Accounting Standards Committee (ASC) issued statements of standard accounting practice (SSAPs) in a manner similar to the process used by the Financial Accounting Standards Board in the United States on topics ranging from the accounting treatment of government grants to current cost accounting.

In 1990, however, responsibility for standard setting passed from the ASC to the newly formed **Financial Reporting Council** (FRC). The mission of the FRC, which is both better financed and more powerful than the ASC, is to tighten accounting rules in Great Britain and to develop a broader, more strategic outlook on financial reporting. In effect, the formation of the FRC streamlines and centralizes accounting policy formation, taking it out of the hands of Great Britain's numerous accountancy bodies and giving it to a council that includes industry and stock market representatives as well as professional accountants. The primary deliberative body of the FRC on accounting matters is its *Accounting Standards Board.* The key characteristic of the FRC is its radical expansion of the constituencies involved in the accounting standard-setting process: users, preparers, and auditors are all involved.[8] The fundamental nature of the first several FRSs indicates the basic, hard look being directed toward British financial reporting. For example, the FRC's first **financial reporting standard** (*FRS No. 1*) created the requirement for presentation of a statement of cash flows in lieu of a statement of sources and application of funds, *FRS No. 2* dealt with the accounting for subsidiaries, and *FRS No. 3* revisits the reporting of financial performance (i.e., income statement presentation issues), all but doing away with a previously overused income statement category—extraordinary items.

---

[8]R. Dearing, "Accounting Standards the New Approach," *Accountancy,* June 1990, pp. 86–87.

Within three years of its formation, informed observers of the ASB ascertained a clear orientation being articulated and pursued. Specifically, it appeared that a key aspect of the ASB's actions was a

> Desire to move the attention of readers of accounts away from a single number—earnings— towards a wider range of indicators of a company's performance.[9]

> [This] approach [, in the minds of some,] puts undue emphasis on the balance sheet. Financial reporting, from this standpoint, is essentially an exercise in valuation.[10]

To this end, some of the ASB's more recent standards (e.g., *FRS Nos. 4–7*) also exhibited a very clear focus on the identification, recording, and valuing of balance sheet items. Consider also that in a 1993 published *statement* (as opposed to a published *standard*), the ASB set voluntary guidelines for companies for including an Operating and Financial Review (OFR) section in their annual reports. The OFR is similar to the Management Discussion and Analysis (MD&A) section found in U.S. annual reports. The OFR's aim is to provide a narrative of company performance ''with analysis and a balance of good and bad while providing some element of a projection of the business into the future.''[11] Such guidance is again evidence of the ASB's predilection to try to provide financial statement users with a multifaceted view of a company.

Capital Markets.   London has long been one of the financial capitals of the world, with a market capitalization that makes it Europe's largest equity market. Market capitalization is 98.5 percent of the British gross domestic product, meaning that equities are more representative of that country's economy than of any other European market.[12] The main securities exchange in Great Britain is officially designated as The International Stock Exchange of the United Kingdom and the Republic of Ireland, but it is traditionally and familiarly known simply as The Stock Exchange. Since 1973, The Stock Exchange has been electronically integrated with the securities exchanges of a number of other cities across England, Scotland, and Ireland, making it in fact not a single exchange but a network. The Stock Exchange lists around 7,000 securities, many of which are issued by foreign companies, and it has developed and maintained sophisticated mechanisms of disclosure to protect the interests of both large and small investors.

Companies must fulfill a number of stringent requirements to be granted a full listing on The Stock Exchange. The securities to be listed must have a minimum initial capitalization of £700,000, and at least 25 percent of any class of issued equity capital must be held by the public. (In practice, the initial capitalization usually exceeds £5,000,000.) With its application for listing, the company must submit a variety of

---

[9]A. Jack, ''Accounting Review Brings Mixed Results,'' *The Financial Times,* September 23, 1992, p. 19.

[10]Paterson, ''In Support of the Profit and Loss Account,'' p. 15.

[11]A. Jack, ''Broad-Brush Approach for a Truer Picture,'' *The Financial Times,* July 8, 1993, p. 2.

[12]''Guide to European Equity Markets 1992: United Kingdom,'' *Euromoney: European Equity Markets Supplement,* January 1992, pp. 52–55.

financial data, including audited financial statements. These should consist of the company's most recent balance sheet, its income statement, and a statement of cash flows (this latter statement is a recent requirement imposed by *FRS No. 1*). After it is granted a listing, the company must publish audited annual financial statements within six months of its year-end and unaudited interim statements semiannually. It must also release on a timely basis important ancillary information, such as preliminary profit announcements, details of major transactions, explanation of departures from standard accounting practices, and particulars concerning borrowings. The Stock Exchange reserves the right to publish information itself or to suspend a listing if it deems a company's public financial disclosures to be inadequate.

Since 1980 The Stock Exchange has provided an unlisted securities market (USM) whereby smaller, less established companies unable to meet the requirements for full listing may offer securities to the public. Companies seeking entry to this market need present only operating results from the last three years and place at least 10 percent of their securities in the hands of the public. No initial minimum capital requirement is stipulated, but most securities quoted on the USM are initially capitalized at £3,000,000 or more. In addition to full listing and USM, in 1987 The Stock Exchange opened the Third Market for capital-hungry new firms that did not have a sufficient trading history to qualify for the other two markets; however, the Third Market was subsequently absorbed into the USM. Although these alternative markets have been active, their viability may diminish if, as the result of EU negotiations, The Stock Exchange is required to ease its requirements for full listing.

Small companies may also offer their securities via over-the-counter (OTC) markets. Britain's OTC market, which quotes more than 200 companies, provides capital for risk-oriented firms that desire greater flexibility than The Stock Exchange can provide. Requirements for entry into the OTC market are determined by the particular dealer handling the new issue.

Great Britain has recently begun deregulating various aspects of its capital markets to encourage competition and broaden share ownership. The most profound alterations took effect in October 1986 in what was popularly heralded, with wry anxiety, as the "Big Bang." The Big Bang included a broad range of measures: abolishing minimum commission rates, admitting international firms to membership on The Stock Exchange, abandoning the mandatory separation of brokering and jobbing functions, and introducing an electronic trading system that allows off-floor trading. It was hoped that these changes would improve London's competitive edge as a trading center and that what the financial services industry would lose in lower commissions it would more than recoup in extra volume as small investors entered the market in larger numbers. As the new system began, the market's capacity rose fivefold, costs doubled, and fee levels halved. For the first year, turnover (i.e., sales) and profits stayed high. Then came the crash of Black Monday, and turnover collapsed. Though it is now back to 1987 levels, the market still has too much capacity.[13] Five years after the Big Bang, the winners are the institutional investors who have seen commission rates on large

---

[13]"Five Years Since Big Bang," *The Economist,* October 26, 1991, p. 24.

EXHIBIT 8–3

British Share Ownership Profile

Share Owner	1969	1989	1993
Pension funds	9.0%	30.6%	34.2%
Insurance companies	12.2	18.6	17.3
Other financial institutions	14.7	9.3	10.3
Individuals	49.5	22.9	19.3
Public sector	2.6	2.0	1.3
Commercial sector	5.4	3.8	1.5
Overseas	6.6	12.8	16.3
Total	100.0%	100.0%	100.0%

Source: *The Financial Times,* December 2, 1994.

bargains in well-traded shares pared sharply; the losers are the individual investors. For them, commissions, with no cross-subsidy from big deals, have risen slightly.

Another big winner has been the overseas investors. In 1993, foreign investors were the single largest category of British share buyers. Moreover,

> It is U.S. investors which form the largest single non-U.K. presence, accounting for 54.2 percent of all non-U.K. money in the U.K. stock market. Investors based in the EU hold a paltry-by-comparison 19.5 percent of all non-U.K. owned shares in Britain.[14]

With a diminishing role for the British individual direct investor and an increased presence for British institutional investors as well as overseas investors (see Exhibit 8–3), the tumultuous state of British financial reporting alluded to at the beginning of this chapter might be partly grounded in a changing presence of potentially powerful shareholders.

The Big Bang and subsequent changes have sparked an important debate over the best way to ensure that the markets remain fair. Traditionally self-regulating, The Stock Exchange is now overseen by a group of self-regulatory organizations (SROs) that must answer to the newly formed Securities and Investments Board (SIB), a watchdog agency with an ambiguous legal status. Observers expect, however, that the SIB will evolve into an extension of the national government with broad powers to regulate financial reporting as well as securities trading. Some commentators speculate that the SIB may even become directly involved in setting accounting and auditing standards. Paradoxically, the deregulation of the British capital markets has created the prospect of increased regulation of financial reporting. One remaining issue for the regulators is whether the system would function better with fewer regulatory bodies. Overlap between watchdogs creates confusion over who is responsible for what. It also increases the risk of a small, weak regulatory body becoming too close to those it is supposedly policing.[15]

---

[14]N. Cohen, "U.S. Dominates Investment Growth," *The Financial Times,* December 2, 1994, p. 8.

[15]"Regulatory Woes," *The Economist,* March 14, 1992, pp. 92, 94.

Labor Relations. Despite the 1980s decade of Thatcherism, organized labor still exerts a significant if somewhat diminished influence over British society. Whereas membership in U.S. labor unions has never reached 40 percent and currently stands at less than 20 percent, British trade unions represent around 45 to 50 percent of the workforce, or about 11 million people (down from 13.5 million members in 1979). Traditional union concerns, such as protection from arbitrary dismissal and the right to reasonable working conditions, are now institutionalized in the legislative framework in which British business operates.

Although labor relations have had little direct impact on accounting methods and conventions, they have undoubtedly affected several of the disclosure requirements imposed on British corporations. For example, the Companies Act of 1985 requires certain disclosures pertaining to directors' fees and management salaries exceeding £30,000. Specifically, the company must reveal the amount paid to the chairman and (if not the same person) to the highest paid director, and it must indicate where remuneration paid to other directors and to management falls on a pay scale broken into £5,000 increments. The company must also disclose wage and salary expenses, social security costs, and pension costs paid to or on behalf of employees. All of this information may be of interest to union negotiators as well as investors. The Exhibit 8–4 note, taken from the financial statements of Hanson Plc, an industrial management company that lists Smith Corona and Jacuzzi among its holdings, illustrates the form that these disclosures typically assume.

British law does not mandate employee representation on company boards (as is the case in Sweden); however, a firm employing 250 or more workers must disclose its policy concerning employee consultation programs. Many individual companies and the Confederation of British Industry (an association of employers) have responded to the legal requirement by publicly supporting voluntary programs for employee participation at the firm level. In addition, many firms encourage share ownership among employees. Grand Metropolitan, for example, the international food and drink conglomerate, touches on these themes in its 1992 annual report (see Exhibit 8–5). Although Grand Metropolitan would undoubtedly like to be considered progressive, its policy statement is typical of those found in the annual reports of other British multinational firms.

Selected Financial Reporting Practices

Retrospectively, it has been argued that contemporary British financial reporting practices are the result of 20 years of two countervailing forces—preferences for and against the standardization of practice.[16] The pressure for standardization is attributed to senior members of the accounting profession, interested government agencies, and the financial press. General preferences for more accounting choice and flexibility tend to be articulated most consistently by corporate managers.

---

[16]C. Nobes, "Cycles in U.K. Standard Setting," *Accounting and Business Research* 21, no. 83, (1991), pp. 265–74.

EXHIBIT 8–4

Hanson Plc
Labor-Related Disclosures
(£ millions)

	1993	1992
Employment costs		
Aggregate gross wages and salaries	**1,360**	1,248
Employers' social security costs	**107**	100
Employers' pension contributions	**33**	27
	1,500	1,375

Employment costs included above relating to directors amounted to £9mm (£8mm) including bonuses of £265,000 (£550,000), directors' fees of £203,000 (£171,000), and pension contributions of £1.8mn (£1.7mn). Emoluments of the chairman representing salary and benefits amounted to £1,363,000 (£1,350,000). Emoluments of the chairman and the other directors (except where duties were discharged wholly or mainly outside Great Britain) for the year fell within the following ranges:

	1993	1992		1993	1992
£0 –£5,000	—	1	£215,001–£220,000	**1**	1
£5,001–£10,000	—	2	£245,001–£250,000	**1**	1
£25,001–£30,000	**2**	1	£315,001–£320,000	**1**	—
£30,001–£35,000	**2**	2	£405,001–£410,000	—	1
£40,001–£45,000	**1**	1	£430,001–£435,000	**1**	—
£110,001–£115,000	—	1	£535,001–£540,000	**1**	—
£125,001–£130,000	**1**	—	£605,001–£610,000	—	1
£165,001–£170,000	—	1	£730,001–£735,000	—	1
£195,001–£200,000	**1**	—	£770,001–£775,000	**1**	—
£200,001–£205,000	—	1	£1,345,001–£1,350,000	—	1
£210,001–£215,000	**1**	—	£1,360,001–£1,365,000	**1**	—

	1993	1992
The average number of persons employed during the year		
U.K.	**18,000**	21,000
U.S.	**48,000**	50,000
Others	**5,000**	4,000
	71,000	75,000

A case in point has to do with accounting for business combinations. The chart on page 428 is a summary of the swings in sentiment as expressed in various ASC and FRC statements. As noted by informed observers,

> The use of merger accounting [i.e., the pooling of interests method] will generally lead to higher reported group profits . . . than acquisition accounting [i.e., the purchase method]. Therefore, it can be said that to restrict the use of merger accounting is income-reducing. The [force for a high degree of standardized practice] is provided by senior policymakers

---

EXHIBIT 8–5

Grand Metropolitan Employee Involvement

GrandMet seeks to ensure that, wherever it operates, its businesses have high quality employment policies which benefit both employees and the company. Whilst they vary in detail around the world according to cultural and legislative requirements, these policies cover such areas as employee involvement, respect and equality of opportunity for individuals, and communications.

Employee Involvement

Employee involvement remains a high priority at GrandMet. Various businesses in the group engage in team building on departmental and cross functional bases to improve employees' understanding of various functions and businesses.

In 1992 the company was authorized to introduce a U.S. Employee Stock Purchase Plan to allow and encourage employees to purchase GrandMet stock. Shareholders' approval is being sought at the Annual General Meeting to an International Savings-Related Share Option Plan. If approved, the concept of gaining involvement through share ownership will be extended in 1993 to a number of continental European operations.

The savings-related share option scheme was again actively promoted in the United Kingdom.

Cultural Diversity

For the past year GrandMet senior management has been introduced, through awareness training, to the increasing issues in the workplace and society affecting women, ethnic minorities, people with disability and other groups. The Chairman's Committee and other senior management have participated in workshops designed to create a working environment that encourages all different groups to develop their full potential based on their ability alone.

Depending on their skills and abilities, disabled people are given the same consideration as others when applying for jobs and have the same opportunities for promotion, career development and training as other employees. Employees who become disabled and unable to continue in their existing jobs are given the opportunity to be retrained for suitable alternative employment.

Communications

In 1992 GrandMet surveyed its 900 most senior managers on the effectiveness of communications and how improvements could be made to achieve higher commitment and motivation. The results of this audit have enabled GrandMet to make a number of changes to its communications strategy that will make information more relevant to the intended audiences.

The company also communicates with employees through internal publications and briefing meetings.

---

supported by the Department of Trade and Industry and by criticism from the press. The force opposing standardization and the control of merger accounting, is provided by managers.[17]

Such a case in point is not all that different from certain U.S. experience (e.g., deferred taxes). The fact of the matter is that British accounting standards are the result of a process of debate, lobbying, and change just as U.S. standards are. As will be seen in subsequent chapters, however, this is not the predominant process in other countries (e.g., Japan and Germany).

---

[17]Ibid., p. 269.

	Consolidation Accounting Sentiments	*Degree of Standardization Sought*
Late 1960s	Merger accounting is used for some large U.K. business combinations.	Low
1971	*ED 3* would demand merger accounting for mergers and acquisition accounting for acquisitions, although the rules might be avoidable.	High
1973	*ED 3* lapses after suggestions of illegality under the Companies Act 1948.	Low
1980	*Shearer* v. *Bercain.* This tax case held, *obiter dicta,* that merger accounting was illegal.	Low
1981	Companies Act grants merger relief (subsequently in s.131 of Companies Act 1985).	
1982	*ED 31* would impose standard practice similar to *ED 3.*	High
1985	*SSAP 23* allows acquisition accounting to be used for mergers and continues to have rules that can be evaded.	Low
1990	*ED 48* would demand merger accounting for mergers and acquisition accounting for acquisitions. Also the rules would be much tighter and mergers would be very rare.	High
1994	*FRS 6* adopts the intentions of *ED 48.*	High

ED = Exposure draft of a proposed accounting standard.
FRS = Financial reporting standard.
Source: C. Nobes, "Cycles in U.K. Standard Setting," *Accounting and Business Research* 21, no. 83 (1991), pp. 265–74.

Terminology

Several terms used in British financial statements may confuse or mislead unwary foreign readers. *Fixed assets,* for example, refers to *all* assets retained for continuous use in the business, not just to property, plant, and equipment (which the British call *tangible fixed assets*). The word *stocks,* on the other hand, generally refers to inventory, not shareholders' equity. Receivables are often lumped under the laconic heading "debtors," whereas payables of different sorts may simply be listed as "creditors." On the income statement, often called the *profit and loss account,* sales are referred to as *turnover.* Alternatively, *profit and loss account,* along with *reserves* or *retained profits,* may refer to retained earnings or some component thereof. As these examples suggest, the financial statement user must cultivate a judicious suspicion of familiar terminology; it may camouflage a distinctively British usage.

Format

Although the format of British financial statements varies in a number of ways from that used in typical U.S. statements, the most noticeable difference is in the arrangement of the balance sheet. Some British balance sheets, following the horizontal format, resemble U.S. balance sheets but run from low liquidity to high liquidity; hence, fixed assets appear above current assets and shareholders' equity above liabilities. Companies adopting the alternative vertical format offset current assets against current liabilities and then offset total assets against current liabilities, balancing this figure against long-term liabilities and stockholders' equity. The balance sheet of B.A.T. Industries (see Exhibit 8–6) provides an example of the horizontal format, whereas the RTZ balance sheet illustrates the vertical format (see Exhibit 8–7).

Consolidation

The Companies Act of 1985 requires companies with subsidiaries to prepare ''group accounts.'' Under current practice, there is a substantial degree of subjectivity in the choice between accounting for a business combination via ''acquisition accounting'' (similar to the purchase method in the United States) versus ''merger accounting'' (equivalent to the pooling-of-interests method in the United States). Even though specific criteria exist for using merger accounting, managers can usually satisfy these criteria by careful structuring of a business deal. Similar to practice in the United States, *Financial Reporting Standard No. 6,* issued in September 1994, restricts the use of merger accounting to those business combinations in which one party does not control another but in which the entities come together to equally share in future risks and benefits. The new criterion set forth is that merger accounting be permitted only in those instances when acquisition accounting would not give a true and fair view of the nature of the business combination. The essence of this change is to have the substance of a business combination rather than the particular details of its execution dictate the method of accounting for it.

Valuation of Assets

A British company may choose to value its assets according to historical cost principles or alternative valuation rules, or it may choose to use different methods for different assets. According to historical cost rules, current assets should be carried at the lower of cost or net realizable value; fixed assets should be carried at cost less accumulated depreciation (if applicable) and any permanent decline in value. (A permanent decline in value must be recognized as a loss on the income statement.) LIFO and the base stock method are generally considered unsuitable for inventory valuation.

The alternative valuation rules allow assets to be written up above historical cost as follows:

- Tangible and intangible fixed assets (except goodwill) may be written up to current cost.
- Long-term investments may be written up to market value as of the date of the last valuation (even if it differs from the balance sheet date).
- Investments of 20 percent or more in an affiliate's share capital may be accounted for under the equity method.

Exhibit 8–6

B.A.T. INDUSTRIES
Horizontal Format Balance Sheet
(millions of pounds)

	Group		Company	
Assets	*1992*	*1991*	*1992*	*1991*
Commercial and Corporate Activities				
Tangible fixed assets	**1,352**	1,050	**6**	6
Investments in group companies			**2,036**	1,930
Other investments and long-term loans	**103**	87		
Fixed assets	**1,455**	1,137	**2,042**	1,936
Stocks	**1,849**	1,401		
Debtors	**710**	569	**2,610**	1,968
Current investments	**227**	225		
Short-term deposits	**416**	377		
Cash and bank balances	**105**	43	**1**	1
	4,762	3,752	**4,653**	3,905
Financial Services—General Business				
Interest in underwriting associations	**1,548**	1,039		
Investments	**3,492**	2,981		
Associates	**34**	37		
Tangible fixed assets	**341**	334		
Other assets	**1,068**	907		
Cash and bank balances	**20**	20		
	6,503	5,318		
Financial Services—Life Business				
Interest in life businesses	**1,026**	912		
Investments	**18,507**	16,398		
Associates	**7**	12		
Tangible fixed assets	**106**	103		
Other assets	**1,076**	844		
Cash and bank balances	**136**	107		
	20,858	18,376		
Investments in associates	**570**	431		
Total assets	**32,693**	27,877	**4,653**	3,905

EXHIBIT 8–6 (continued)

	Group		Company	
Liabilities and Capital	*1992*	*1991*	*1992*	*1991*
Capital and Reserves				
Share capital	**370**	369	**370**	369
Share premium account	**177**	173	**177**	173
Capital redemption reserves	**26**	26	**26**	26
Capital reserves	**220**	242		
Deferred investment gains	**120**	120		
Profit and loss account	**3,062**	2,149	**900**	704
Interest of B.A.T. Industries' shareholders	**3,975**	3,079	**1,473**	1,272
Interest of minority shareholders	**367**	289		
Shareholders' funds	**4,342**	3,368	**1,473**	1,272
Commercial and Corporate Activities				
Provisions for liabilities and charges	**661**	575		
Borrowings	**2,801**	2,091	**314**	314
Creditors	**2,096**	1,655	**2,866**	2,319
	5,558	4,321	**3,180**	2,633
Financial Services—General Business				
General business insurance funds	**2,970**	2,673		
Borrowings	**235**	138		
Other liabilities	**602**	591		
	3,807	3,402		
Financial Services—Life Business				
Long-term assurance funds	**17,834**	15,744		
Borrowings	**47**	46		
Other liabilities	**1,105**	996		
	18,986	16,786		
Total funds employed	**32,693**	27,877	**4,653**	3,905

EXHIBIT 8–7

RTZ Plc
Vertical Format Balance Sheet
(millions of pounds)

			1992		1991
Fixed assets					
Intangible assets			**109**		68
Tangible assets			**2,514**		2,465
Investments			**1,261**		1,031
			3,884		3,564
Current assets					
Stocks/inventories	**620**			677	
Debtors and prepayments/accounts receivable	**861**			735	
Investments	**117**			159	
Cash at bank and in hand	**588**			508	
	2,186			2,168	
Creditors due within one year					
Short-term debt	**386**			194	
Creditors and accruals/accounts payable	**679**			694	
	1,065			888	
Net current assets			**1,121**		1,280
Total assets less current liabilities			**5,005**		4,844
Creditors due after one year					
Medium and long term loans			**1,360**		1,321
Advance receipts against sales contracts			**—**		132
Provisions for liabilities and charges			**623**		564
Outside shareholders' interests			**123**		283
			2,899		2,544
Capital and reserves					
Called-up share capital			**112**		112
Share premium account			**1,025**		1,011
Other reserves	**155**			140	
Profit and loss account	**1,607**			1,281	
			1,762		1,421
RTZ shareholders' funds			**2,899**		2,544

It is not uncommon for a firm to revalue its land and buildings periodically, taking the surplus to a revaluation reserve account in the shareholders' equity section of the balance sheet. This reserve is not available for distribution to shareholders.[18] Companies are required to disclose the bases of valuation for inventories, investments, and fixed assets. In light of the valuation options open to British companies and their possible impact on the balance sheet, a careful reader will surely want to check this information.

Goodwill

Purchased *goodwill* is defined as the difference between the fair value of consideration given and the aggregate fair values of the assets received in an acquisition. Normally, neither goodwill nor negative goodwill is carried on the balance sheet; both are written off immediately against (or to) retained earnings. This practice has given British companies something of an advantage over U.S. firms in takeover battles in that U.S. firms, unlike their British counterparts, must consider how the amortization of a large amount of purchased goodwill may affect their future profitability and, hence, share price.[19] In early 1990, however, the ASC issued an exposure draft proposing that British firms be required to capitalize goodwill and amortize it over 20 years. The proposal spawned considerable controversy, but as of this writing, no final decision regarding the standard has been made.

Research and Development

Research expenditures are generally written off immediately against current earnings, whereas development costs may be capitalized to the balance sheet if they fulfill a number of requirements concerning the technical and commercial feasibility of the project to which they are related. Deferred development expenditures must be reviewed at the end of each period and be written off immediately if they no longer meet these feasibility requirements.

Leases

SSAP No. 21 distinguishes between operating and finance leases, requiring the latter to be capitalized by lessees in financial statements for years beginning on or after July 1, 1987. (Capitalization requirements for lessors came into effect three years earlier.) Finance leases are deemed to be those that essentially transfer the benefits and risks of ownership to the lessee (as evidenced by the fact that the present value of the minimum

---

[18]As the revalued amounts are written off (i.e., depreciated) against earnings, a proportionate transfer is made annually from the revaluation reserve account to retained earnings, at which time the revaluation reserve becomes distributable to shareholders.

[19]When a previously purchased subsidiary is sold, any goodwill originally charged off to equity reserves must then be charged against retained earnings; the effect of this practice is to reduce the amount of gain recognized on a subsequent sale of a subsidiary.

lease payments equals 90 percent or more of the leased asset's fair market value, evaluated at the inception of the lease agreement). Lessees should record an asset to be depreciated over the shorter of the lease term (including likely renewals) or the asset's useful life, record a liability for future payments to the lessor, and apportion lease payments between interest expense and repayment of principal. The lessor should record a receivable for the total minimum lease payments plus any residual value, less any provision for bad debts. The lessor should likewise apportion payments received between interest income and repayment of principal.

Owners' Equity

In Great Britain, owners' equity is usually reflected under the heading Capital and Reserves on the balance sheet. The principal elements of this heading (and their U.S. counterpart in parentheses) include:

- Called-up share capital (common and preferred stock).
- Share premium account (paid-in capital in excess of par value).
- Revaluation reserve.
- Other reserves.
- Capital redemption reserve (treasury stock, at par).
- Reserves provided by the articles of association.
- Profit and loss account (retained earnings).

Under the Companies Act of 1985, dividends may be paid out of the Profit and Loss account only, although the Revaluation Reserve and the Capital Redemption Reserve may be used to issue additional share capital, for example, in the form of a share dividend.

Segment Reporting

Until 1990, British companies had only to disclose sales by geographic area. *SSAP No. 25*—one of the last issued by the ASC—requires companies to report sales, pretax profits, and operating assets by both geographic area and line of business.

Earnings per Share

Contrary to U.S. practice, basic earnings per share (called *primary earnings per share* in the United States) is calculated without regard to common stock equivalents. The basis for calculating earnings per share must be disclosed in the footnotes.

Cash Flow Statements

One of the final acts of the ASC prior to its disbanding was the publication of *Exposure Draft No. 54,* "Cash Flow Statements." It proposed to replace *SSAP No. 10,* "Statements of Source and Application of Funds," with a statement of cash flows similar to what is now required in the United States. *SSAP No. 10* had long been criticized for its failure to define *funds* and for permitting a wide variety of formats. The new proposal tackled these criticisms head on, defining *cash* and *cash equivalents* and proposing a standard statement format. Indeed, the first act of the FRC was to issue *FRS No. 1,* which substantially adopted the ASC's cash flow exposure draft, and simultaneously brought British cash flow reporting into conformity with *SFAS No. 95* in the United States. The cash flow statement became mandatory for fiscal years ending after March 23, 1992.

Reconciliation of U.S. and British GAAP

Because British firms are frequently listed on U.S. securities exchanges,[20] some publish a reconciliation of net income and shareholders' equity calculated according to the accounting principles of the two countries.[21] Exhibits 8–8 and 8–9, excerpted from the Hanson Plc annual report, present a reconciliation and explanatory notes that illustrate how the differences between U.S. and British accounting methods may affect net income and shareholders' equity. Notice that the treatment of goodwill is particularly important in Hanson's case, accounting for most of the difference between the net income figures and the shareholders' equity figures. Exhibit 8–10 presents a summary comparison of selected British and U.S. financial reporting standards.

Analytical Considerations

The analysis of British financial statements can be problematic for foreign analysts, not only because of terminology and format differences but also because of significant method differences.[22] The reporting differences of principal concern include

- The revaluation of assets above historical cost.
- The charge-to-equity treatment of goodwill.
- Off-balance-sheet financing.

---

[20]In a recent report, it was noted that 52 British companies, more than from any other European country, were registered with the U.S. Securities and Exchange Commission and therefore had to file U.S. GAAP financial statements or provide a reconciliation of their results based on British GAAP to U.S. GAAP. See P. Gumbel and G. Steinmetz, ''German Firms Shift to More-Open Accounting,'' *The Wall Street Journal,* March 15, 1995, pp. C1, C17.

[21]A recent study revealed that the reconciliation between U.S. and British GAAP provided investors with incremental information above and beyond the information content of just British GAAP-based financial results. Consequently, the finding supports the disclosure of such reconciliations for the benefit of foreign investors. See M. E. Barth (Harvard University) and G. Clinch (University of New South Wales), ''International Accounting Differences and Their Relation to Share Prices: Evidence from U.K., Australian, and Canadian Firms,'' working paper, June 1993.

[22]Despite these differences, a recent study reveals that the earnings disclosures by British companies are at least as informative and timely for investors as are U.S. corporate earnings disclosures. See A. Alford, T. Jones, R. Leftwich, and M. Zmijewski, ''The Relative Informativeness of Accounting Disclosures in Different Countries,'' working paper, University of Chicago, July 1993.

EXHIBIT 8–8

Hanson Plc and Subsidiaries
Reconciliation to U.S. GAAP

The following is a summary of the estimated material adjustments to profit and ordinary shareholders' equity which would be required if U.S. Generally Accepted Accounting Principles (U.S. GAAP) had been applied.

	£ million Years Ended September 30,			
Profit Available for Appropriation	*1993*	*1992*	*1993*	*1992*
Profit available for appropriation as reported in the consolidated profit and loss account	**734**	1,089	**1,098**	1,628
Estimated adjustments:				
Goodwill amortization	**(94)**	(95)	**(141)**	(142)
Foreign currency translation	**(7)**	(11)	**(10)**	(16)
Pensions	**34**	52	**51**	78
Timberlands depletion and reforestation	**(32)**	(36)	**(48)**	(54)
Taxation	**(22)**	(96)	**(33)**	(144)
	(121)	(186)	**(181)**	(278)
Estimated profit available for appropriation (net income) as adjusted to accord with U.S. GAAP arising from:	**613**	903	**917**	1,350
Continuing operations	**561**	701	**839**	1,048
Discontinued operations—income (loss) from operations	**19**	44	**29**	66
—gain (loss) on disposals	**33**	158	**49**	236
	613	903	**917**	1,350

	Per share		Per ADR	
Earnings	p	p	$	$
Undiluted—continuing operations	˙**11.6**	14.5	**0.87**	1.09
—discontinued operations	**1.1**	4.2	**0.08**	0.31
—profit available for appropriation	**12.7**	18.7	**0.95**	1.40
Diluted —continuing operations	**11.6**	14.4	**0.87**	1.08
—discontinued operations	**1.1**	4.2	**0.08**	0.31
—profit available for appropriation	**12.7**	18.6	**0.95**	1.39

	At September 30,			
Ordinary Shareholders' Equity	*1993*	*1992*	*1993*	1992
Ordinary shareholders' equity as reported in the consolidated balance sheet	**3,953**	4,224	**5,912**	6,317
Estimated adjustments:				
Goodwill and other intangibles	**4,379**	3,340	**6,549**	4,995
Revaluation of land and buildings	**(166)**	(166)	**(248)**	(248)
Pensions	**223**	189	**333**	283
Timberlands depletion and reforestation	**(105)**	(60)	**(157)**	(90)
Taxation	**(320)**	(102)	**(479)**	(153)
	4,011	3,201	**5,998**	4,787
Estimated ordinary shareholders' equity as adjusted to accord with U.S. GAAP	**7,964**	7,425	**11,910**	11,104

The exchange rate used to translate the above figures was that ruling at the 1993 balance sheet date ($1.4995 to £).

EXHIBIT 8–9

Hanson Plc and Subsidiaries
U.S. vs. British GAAP

The following are the main U.S. accounting principles which differ from those generally accepted in the United Kingdom as applied by Hanson in its financial statements:

Goodwill and Other Intangibles

Goodwill and other intangible assets arising on the acquisition of a subsidiary are written off in the year in which that subsidiary is acquired. Under U.S. GAAP such goodwill is capitalized and is amortised through the profit and loss account over its estimated useful life, not exceeding 40 years.

Taxation

Deferred taxation is not provided where, in the opinion of the directors, no liability is likely to arise in the foreseeable future. However, under U.S. GAAP, deferred taxation would be provided on a full deferral basis.

U.K. GAAP permits the reduction of the tax charge by the use of tax losses available at the time of acquisition. However, U.S. GAAP requires that the benefit of such losses is adjusted through goodwill and tangible fixed assets.

Revaluation of Land and Buildings

Periodically land and buildings are revalued on an existing use basis by professionally qualified external valuers and such assets are written up to the appraised value. Depreciation is, where applicable, calculated on these revalued amounts. When revalued properties are sold, the gain or loss on sale is calculated based on revalued carrying amounts and reflected in income and any revaluation surplus thus realized is reclassified directly to retained earnings. Under U.S. GAAP such revaluations would not be reflected in financial statements and the gain or loss on sale would be calculated based on original cost and reflected in income. The amount of additional depreciation charged in respect of the revalued properties is not material.

Timberlands

Reforestation costs are charged to the profit and loss account when incurred and depletion of timberlands is only provided to the extent that the amount of timber harvested exceeds the estimated growth of standing timber. Under U.S. GAAP depletion on a unit of production basis is charged to profit and loss account and reforestation costs are capitalized as part of the carrying cost of timberlands.

Foreign Currencies

Revenues, expenses, assets and liabilities relating to overseas subsidiaries are translated at the year-end rate. Under U.S. GAAP assets and liabilities are translated as under U.K. GAAP; however, revenues and expenses are translated at average rates for the year.

Pension

The accounting policy of the group has not been to account for exceptional past pension surpluses, when surpluses do not revert to the employer. Under U.S. GAAP, such surpluses are recognized and credited over an appropriate future period.

EXHIBIT 8–10

Comparison of Accounting and Reporting Standards

Item	Great Britain	United States
Asset valuation	Historical cost with revaluation adjustments permitted (either upward or downward)	Historical cost with selected revaluation (principally downward)
Inventory: valuation	Principally FIFO and average cost methods; LIFO not permitted for tax purposes, hence rarely used	Principally LIFO (because of tax considerations); also FIFO and average cost methods
Inventory: year-end	Lower of cost or net realizable value	Lower of cost or replacement cost
Depreciation	Principally straight line with accelerated methods permitted	Principally straight line with accelerated and production methods permitted
Goodwill	Principally charged off against equity reserves but capitalization permitted	Capitalized to balance sheet, with amortization (principally straight line) over a maximum of 40 years; negative goodwill not permitted (i.e., eliminated against noncurrent assets)
Research and development costs	Research costs expensed as incurred; development costs may be capitalized under limited situations	Research costs expensed currently; development costs expensed currently except in certain industries (i.e., software, oil and gas)
Capitalized interest costs	Capitalization permitted, but not widely practiced	Capitalization required for self-constructed assets
Intercorporate Investments:		
Marketable securities (current asset: trading securities)	Lower of cost or market value (portfolio basis) with revaluation permitted	Mark to market (on an individual security basis) with unrealized gains and losses taken to income
Long-term investments:		
0–20% ownership (available-for-sale securities)	Historical cost with revaluation permitted	Mark to market (on an individual security basis) with unrealized gains and losses taken to shareholders' equity
20–50% ownership	Equity method	Equity method
51–100% ownership	Consolidated, using pooling or purchase accounting	Consolidated, using pooling or purchase accounting
Debt valuation	All debt valued at face or settlement value	Long-term debt (except deferred income taxes) valued at present value; all other debt valued at face value
Leases	Financing leases capitalized to balance sheet; operating lease disclosed in footnotes	Capital leases reflected in balance sheet; operating leases disclosed in footnotes
Deferred income taxes	Computed under liability method	Computed under liability method
Pension liabilities	Reflected on balance sheet	Reflected on balance sheet
Discretionary reserves	Specific reserves permitted	Restricted to identifiable operational losses
Statement of cash flows	Required	Required

The revaluation of assets, along with the parallel creation of an equity revaluation reserve, causes a systematic upward bias in the balance sheet valuation (i.e., total assets and net worth) of British firms. Although revaluation leaves the statement of cash flows relatively unaffected, largely because revaluation is not permitted for tax purposes and the higher depreciation charges on the revalued assets are netted out, future reported earnings may nonetheless be somewhat depressed as a consequence of the additional depreciation charges resulting from any upward asset revaluation. These affects may also be manifested in financial ratios as follows:

Ratio	*Effect on British Firm Relative to U.S. Firm*
Profitability ratios (i.e., ROA, ROE)	Understated
Solvency ratios (i.e., debt-to-total assets, debt-to-equity)	Understated

The charge-to-equity method of goodwill permits a company to immediately write off any goodwill resulting from an acquisition against its existing (or future) shareholders' equity reserves. Although this treatment tends to produce a lower level of total assets and shareholders' equity as compared to U.S. firms, which must capitalize purchased goodwill, the effect on the *future* earnings of a British firm is usually quite positive. Since goodwill is fully written off, the future earnings stream of the company is not burdened with the regular amortization charges that U.S. firms face. As a consequence, this accounting treatment causes the following systematic ratio effects:[23]

Ratio	*Effect on British Firm Relative to U.S. Firm*
Profitability ratios (i.e., ROS, ROA, and ROE)	Overstated
Solvency ratios (i.e., debt to total assets, debt to equity, times interest earned)	Overstated

The distortive effects of the charge-to-equity method of accounting for goodwill are sometimes partially offset when a company acquires a well-established brand name or trademark as part of an acquisition. When this occurs, some British firms partially restore the written-off goodwill by capitalizing a portion of it as a brand or trademark on the balance sheet, usually under the account heading Other Intangible Assets. This

---

[23]Despite the distortions caused by the charge-to-equity method, British investment analysts essentially use the same ratios as U.S. analysts for technical analysis purposes. See, for example, R. Pike, T. Meerjanssen, and L. Chadwick, ''The Appraisal of Ordinary Shares by Investment Analysts in the U.K. and Germany,'' *Accounting and Business Research,* Autumn 1993, pp. 489–99.

practice, however, is not yet widespread, largely because capitalized intangibles must be amortized against future earnings.

A final analytical concern involves off-balance sheet financing, which has been the focus of a number of accounting standards in recent years in the United States. The ambiguity of *SSAP No. 21,* the British leasing standard, for example, enables most British firms to treat their lease agreements as operating leases, despite the fact that under U.S. GAAP comparable leases would be capitalized to the balance sheet as a capital lease. A recent accounting exposure draft currently being evaluated in Great Britain, however, would eliminate many of the off-balance-sheet techniques currently employed by British companies by requiring that auditors consider the substance, not just the form, of financing contracts when evaluating whether an asset and liability should be recognized. Thus, auditors may be called on, for example, to require companies to book sale and repurchase agreements as de facto loans, rather than as a sale of an asset.

In recent years, British accounting standard setters have taken significant steps to eliminate some of the previously material divergences between British and U.S. GAAP. For example, *Financial Reporting Standard (FRS) No. 1,* adopted in 1992, requires the presentation of a statement of cash flows along lines similar to *SFAS No. 95,* and *FRS No. 2* requires the consolidation of substantially all controlled subsidiaries in a manner similar to *SFAS No. 94.* This latter FRS effectively eliminated the off-balance-sheet accounting of finance subsidiaries and their typically massive debt. Most recently, the ASB adopted *FRS No. 3,* which

- Limits those items that are reported as ''extraordinary'' on the profit and loss statement.
- Requires that earnings per share be calculated *after* all exceptional and extraordinary items.
- Excludes any realized revaluation surplus (associated with the retirement of a revalued asset) from reported profits.

The efforts of the FRC to improve the disclosure practices in Great Britain already appear to have had a positive impact on securities prices. Projected price-earnings ratios for the 12-month period beginning March 1994 (as reported by *The Wall Street Journal*) indicate increasing market efficiency among British securities as evidenced by the close proximity of the average P-E ratios for the leading U.S. (15.1) and British (14.6) companies. This relatively small discrepancy—it is less than for any of the other G-7 nations—is interpreted by financial economists as indicating an increasing availability of high-quality financial information in Great Britain.

Summary

In fall of 1990, then-Prime Minister Margaret Thatcher spoke to Parliament pledging ''more of the same.'' Specifically, she promised that income tax rates would be cut again, more government-owned companies would be privatized (including British

Rail), and the number of citizen shareholders would continue to increase. Shortly after this speech, the Thatcher era, marked by deregulation, reduced union influence, support for small businesses, and hard-nosed notions of free trade came to an end.

A number of Mrs. Thatcher's policies and preferences have been embraced by Mr. John Major's Tory government through the first half of the 1990s. Of particular note is the issue of broadened public ownership of equity securities. In 1990 approximately one in four British adults owned shares as compared to one in five in 1989. Individual share ownership accounted for only 20 percent of the stock market, however, as compared to 28 percent in 1980. Thus, share ownership has broadened but not significantly deepened. Moreover, according to a February 1990 survey conducted by the Confederation of British Industry, 60 percent of shareholders owned shares in only one company, with two in five respondents reported having no idea where to go to buy securities.[24] Such insights reveal a rather unsophisticated public involvement in the equity market. Thus, to date, financial reporting has not needed to be particularly responsive or even concerned with the investing public.

Great Britain has become a major international business center creating growth *and* interdependencies. To whit, approximately 42 and 39 percent of U.S. and Japanese, respectively, corporate investment in the EU is placed in Great Britain.[25] Moreover, "one of the most encouraging things about Britain today is that people are asking questions. Nothing is off-limits."[26] Perhaps an increased international interdependency and a willingness to question long-standing thinking and ways of doing things may portend a reinvigorated opportunity for change and leadership in the world business community for Great Britain.

Suggested Readings

"A Survey of Britain." *The Economist,* October 24, 1992.

Arthur Andersen & Co. *The Accounting Profession in the U.K.* Chicago, IL: Arthur Andersen & Co., 1991.

Bruce, R. "The Analysts We Deserve." *Accountancy,* August 1994, p. 48.

Dearing, R. "Accounting Standards: The New Approach." *Accountancy,* June 1990, p. 86.

Ernst & Young. *U.S./U.K. GAAP Comparisons: A Comparison between U.K. and U.S. Accounting Principles.* New York, NY: Ernst & Young, 1990.

Garside, L. "What Should We Tell Them?" *Accountancy,* August 1994, p. 83.

Nobes, C. "Cycles in U.K. Standard Setting." *Accounting and Business Research,* Summer 1991, pp. 265–74.

Price Waterhouse & Co. *Doing Business in the United Kingdom.* New York, NY: Price Waterhouse, 1990.

Smith, T. *Accounting for Growth.* London: Century Business, 1992.

---

[24]R. Waters, "Seeking a Nation of Shareholders," *The Financial Times,* March 23, 1990, p. 7.

[25]"A Survey of Britain—In the Tracks of Nissan," *The Economist,* October 24, 1992, Surveys 15 and 16.

[26]Ibid., Survey, 3.

ISSUES AND INFORMATION FOR FURTHER INQUIRY

I.8.1   Property Valuations

One important feature of British accounting is the option to revalue property on corporate balance sheets upward to its market value. In a September 3, 1993, *Financial Times* article (p. 25), ''A Tough Value Judgment,'' Vanessa Houlder reports that a leading British properties company ''recently produced a discussion paper on accounting treatment for investment properties [wherein it] concluded that the current basis of valuation did not work well for certain types of property.''

Required:
(a) Research and report on British companies' current practices of reflecting property values in their balance sheets.
(b) Report on the current valuation debate, taking care to detail the issues and the relevant pros and cons.

I.8.2   Goodwill

In a November 16, 1993, *Financial Times* article (p. 23), ''Open Season on the Fate of Goodwill,'' Andrew Jack asserts that goodwill is ''one of the most controversial topics in [British] financial reporting.'' He predicts that the debate on reforming current British goodwill accounting practices ''will be rife and reforms strongly contested.''

Required:
Research and report on the issues and options at the heart of the goodwill accounting debate in Great Britain. Be sure to be as up-to-date as possible in your research.

EXERCISES

E.8.1   Preparing Financial Statements under British GAAP

The following is the post-closing general ledger data from the accounts of Rolls-Royce Plc:

ROLLS-ROYCE Plc
Post-Closing Ledger Accounts
December 31, 1991
(millions of £)

	Dr.	Cr.
Short-term deposits and cash	410	
Debtors	931	
Stocks	924	
Investments—subsidiaries	—	
Investments—other	49	
Tangible assets	721	
Creditors: due within one year		23
Other creditors: due within one year		1,201
Creditors: due after one year		335
Other creditors: due after one year		160
Provision for liabilities/charges		167
Minority interest in subsidiaries		27
Called-up share capital		193
Share premium account		242
Revaluation reserve		128
Other reserves		20
Profit and loss account		539
Turnover		3,515
Income from interests in associated companies		6
Attributable to minority interest in subsidiaries		5
Dividends	24	
Exceptional items	58	
Cost of sales	2,959	
Commercial, marketing, and product support costs	96	
General and administrative costs	216	
Research and development costs	125	
Interest expense (net)	16	
Taxation	32	
	6,561	6,561

Required:

Using the ledger account data, prepare an income statement and balance sheet (using vertical format) for Rolls-Royce for the year ended December 31, 1991.

E.8.2   Comparative Balance Sheets

The following are the 1990 balance sheets of two entertainment industry companies, Thorne EMI of the United Kingdom and Time Warner of the United States.

THORNE EMI
Balance Sheet
At March 31

	1990 *£m*
Fixed assets	
Music publishing copyrights	216.8
Tangible fixed assets	1,126.3
Investments	109.6
Net assets of retail financing subsidiaries	19.2
	1,471.9
Current assets	
Stocks	363.5
Debtors	693.7
Investments: cash equivalents	45.3
Cash at bank and in hand	83.6
	1,186.1
Creditors: Amounts falling due within one year	
Borrowings	(125.6)
Other creditors	(1,137.9)
	(1,263.5)
Net current liabilities	(77.4)
Total assets less current liabilities	1,394.5
Creditors: Amounts falling due after more than one year	
Borrowings	(319.4)
Other creditors	(16.2)
	(335.6)
Provisions for liabilities and charges	
Deferred taxation	(36.2)
Other provisions	(146.6)
	(182.8)
	876.1
Capital and reserves	
Called-up share capital	96.6
Share premium account	55.6
Other reserves	646.1
Goodwill	(653.6)
Profit and loss reserve	498.6
Shareholders' funds	643.3
Minority interests	232.8
	876.1

TIME WARNER
Balance Sheet
At December 31
(in millions of dollars)

	1990
Assets	
Current asset	
Cash and equivalents	$ 172
Receivables, less allowances for doubtful receivables and returns of $761	2,071
Inventories	1,239
Other current assets	464
Total current assets	3,946
Receivables due after one year	552
Noncurrent inventories	1,759
Investments	1,874
Land and buildings	776
Cable television equipment	2,585
Furniture, fixtures, and other equipment	1,180
	4,541
Less accumulated depreciation and amortization	(1,415)
Property, plant, and equipment, net	3,126
Excess of cost over net assets acquired	9,073
Cable television franchises	3,097
Music copyrights, record catalogues, and other assets	1,910
Total assets	**$25,337**
Liabilities and Shareholders' Equity	
Current liabilities:	
Accounts payable and accrued expenses	$3,601
Debt due within one year	31
Accrued income taxes	19
Total current liabilities	3,651
Long-term debt	11,184
Deferred income taxes	2,637
Unearned portion of paid subscriptions	521
Other liabilities	1,030
Shareholders' equity:	
Preferred stock, $1 par value, 250 million shares authorized, 117.9 million shares issued, $5.954 billion liquidation preference	118
Common stock, $1 par value, 750 million shares authorized, 70.4 million shares issued	70
Paid-in capital	6,919
Retained earnings	499
Treasury stock, at cost, 12.9 million common shares and .7 million preferred shares in 1990	(1,292)
Total shareholders' equity	6,314
Total liabilities and shareholders' equity	**$25,337**

Required:

    (a) Compare and contrast the balance sheet presentations of the two companies, including the titles used to describe the various balance sheet accounts. Prepare a list of the differences that you observe.

    (b) Which presentation do you prefer, and why?

E.8.3   Revaluation of Assets

Under British GAAP, the basic financial statements are normally prepared using the historical cost convention; however, the Companies Act of 1985 also permits the revaluation of certain assets:

- Intangible fixed assets (i.e., leased fixed assets) may be valued at current cost, defined as the lower of an asset's net replacement cost or recoverable value.
- Tangible fixed assets (i.e., freehold property, leasehold property, plant and equipment) may be valued at current cost or market value (defined as the value as of the most recent revaluation date).
- Fixed asset investments (i.e., investments in controlled subsidiaries) may be reported at their market value as of their latest valuation or at a value determined by the board of directors if market values are not available (or are significantly out of date).
- Current investments (i.e., marketable securities) may be valued at current cost (i.e., current replacement cost or net realizable value).
- Stocks (i.e., inventory) may be valued at current replacement cost.

The following are selected excerpts from the 1992 footnotes of Dunlop Plc, a British manufacturer. The company follows British GAAP and annually revalues its assets by independent appraiser and/or by the company's officers and directors. Any changes in the asset values are credited to a shareholders' equity reserve account, Reserve for Asset Revaluations.

		1992	1991
Leased land, plant, and equipment	At cost	179,328	91,726
	(amortization)	(29,552)	(28,144)
		149,776	63,582
Plant and equipment	At cost	1,918,036	1,804,436
	Independent		
	valuation	—	200
	Officer valuation	9,830	9,830
		1,927,866	1,814,466
	(depreciation)	(854,860)	(750,928)
		1,073,006	1,063,538
Freehold land	At cost	30,996	33,074
	Independent		
	valuation	165,748	182,766
	Officer valuation	1,216	1,608
		197,960	217,448
Leasehold land and buildings	At cost	35,370	19,926
	Independent		
	valuation	19,322	24,762
	Officer valuation	2,214	2,384
		56,906	47,072
	(amortization)	(8,968)	(6,890)
		47,938	40,182

The independent and officer valuations were reported as of June 30, 1992.

Required:

(a) What are the advantages and disadvantages of the British practice of permitting annual revaluations of assets?

(b) Contrast this policy with that followed in the United States.

(c) Do you think the IASC should adopt the U.S. or British position? Why?

(d) Prepare the journal entry necessary to record

(1) the revaluation of plant and equipment,

(2) the annual transfer of depreciation on revalued amounts from the revaluation reserve to the profit and loss account, and

(3) the retirement of revalued plant and equipment that has not been fully depreciated.

E.8.4   Accounting for Shareholder Accounts

Rolls-Royce Plc is one of the world's most recognized and respected manufacturers. According to the company's year-end 1991 annual report, the shareholders' equity section of its balance sheet appeared as follows (in millions of £):

	1991	1990
Capital and reserves		
Called-up share capital	193	192
Share premium account	242	239
Revaluation reserve	128	132
Other reserves	20	22
Profit and loss account	539	579
Shareholders' funds	1,122	1,164

The related footnotes to the company's capital and reserves were presented as follows:

Share capital

	Special share of £1	Ordinary shares of 20p each	Nominal value £m
Authorized			
At January 1 and December 31, 1991	1	1,282,000,000	256
Issued and fully paid			
At January 1, 1991	1	960,903,654	192
Exercise of share options	—	788,801	—
In lieu of paying 1990 dividends in cash	—	1,309,758	1
At December 31, 1991	1	963,002,213	193

Subject to the provisions of the Companies Act 1985, the special rights redeemable preference share (special share) may be redeemed by the Treasury Solicitor at par at any time.

Reserves

	Non-distributable			
	Share premium £m	Revaluation reserve £m	Other reserves £m	Profit and loss account £m
Group				
At January 1, 1991	239	132	22	579
Arising on share issues	3	—	—	—
Transfers between reserves	—	(4)	(2)	6
Loss for the year	—	—	—	(46)
At December 31, 1991	242	128	20	539
Company				
At January 1, 1991	239	127	263	440
Arising on share issues	3	—	—	—
Transfers between reserves	—	(4)	(2)	6
Loss for the year	—	—	—	(68)
At December 31, 1991	242	123	261	378

Goodwill, written off against other reserves, cumulatively amounts to **£243m** (1990 £243m).

The undistributed profits of overseas subsidiary and associated undertakings may be liable to overseas taxes and/or U.K. tax (after allowing for double tax relief) if remitted as dividends to the U.K.

Required:

    (a) Using journal entries, explain the changes in Rolls-Royce's capital and reserve accounts during 1991.

    (b) If Rolls-Royce followed U.S. GAAP, how would the company's capital and reserves accounts be different?

E.8.5   Valuation of the Firm: Accounting for Goodwill

In late 1994, Browning-Ferris Industries (BFI) launched a hostile takeover bid for Attwoods Plc, a British waste service company. The BFI offer of £364 million (or approximately $570 million) was flatly rejected by Attwoods' management on grounds that it was grossly underpriced. BFI executives, on the other hand, argued that the offer represented a premium of more than 115 percent above Attwoods' current value.

According to the BFI offer document, if Attwoods followed U.S. GAAP for goodwill, Attwoods' 1993 reported earnings of 5.3 pence per share would be halved to 2.5 pence per share. Based on average price-earnings multiples for waste companies in the United States, the value of one ordinary Attwoods share would be approximately 50 pence, or 19 times earnings. Hence, BFI's offer of 109 pence for each ordinary share could be seen to be quite generous. (Just prior to the BFI offer, Attwoods' ordinary shares had traded at 105 pence on the London Stock Exchange.)

BFI executives expressed concern that Attwoods' earnings were inflated when considered under U.S. accounting standards. In Great Britain, goodwill is written off directly against retained earnings, whereas in the United States it is capitalized to the balance sheet and typically amortized off against earnings over a 40-year expected life. Through 1993, Attwoods had written off against owners' equity over £179 million in goodwill.

Required:

Evaluate the merits of BFI's offer for Attwoods. Is it generous, as BFI executives claim, or grossly underpriced as Attwoods' management argue? Justify your position.

E.8.6   Merger Accounting

In December 1993, the Granada Group Plc announced a takeover bid for LWT Holdings Plc. The tender offer came amidst a consolidation of the British television industry. Both Granada and LWT are independent broadcasting companies.

According to the tender offer, Granada would exchange six of its ordinary shares for every five of LWT. The Granada offer valued LWT at approximately £600 million, or approximately 1 percent below LWT's prior day aggregate market value of £606 million. Directors of LWT unanimously voted to reject the Granada offer.

Required:

    (a) Why would the directors of LWT vote to reject the Granada offer?

    (b) Assuming that the tender offer is eventually successful, how should Granada account for its investment in LWT? (Assume that LWT's book value is £525 million.)

    (c) Assume that the tender offer is successful in its original form (i.e., not subsequently modified). How much goodwill is inherent in the Granada offer? How should this goodwill be accounted for?

E.8.7   Acquisition Accounting

On November 30, 1993, Carlton Communications Plc announced a £624 million tender offer (or £26 per share) for the outstanding shares of Central Independent Television that it didn't already own. Carlton and Central are the two largest British independent television companies; the British government owns the largest broadcasting company, the British Broadcasting Corporation (or BBC). Together, Carlton and Central will represent about 22 percent of the British television ad revenue market.

Carlton, which already owns 19.1 percent of Central, agreed to pay £204 million in cash, with the remainder in ordinary and convertible preference shares for Central. For every 100 Central shares, Carlton indicated that it would pay £850.62 cash, 114 new Carlton ordinary shares, and 875 new Carlton preference shares. Carlton also agreed to retire all of Central's 6.5 percent convertible subordinated debentures due in 2008. The value of Carlton's bid was placed at 20 percent above Central's market value prior to the offer.

Required:

    (a) How should Carlton account for its acquisition of Central, and why?

    (b) If the fair market value of Central's net assets and shares not previously owned by Carlton were equivalent on the day *prior* to the Carlton tender offer, how much goodwill would be inherent in the transaction?

    (c) How would the transaction be recorded on Carlton's financial records?

    (d) How should Carlton account for the goodwill inherent in the tender offer?

    (e) Why would Carlton be willing to pay a 20 percent premium for Central's shares?

E.8.8   Statement of Cash Flows

The Body Shop International Plc (TBS) produces and sells skin, hair care, and other health-related products through 727 stores worldwide. The company owns or has franchised 210 retail outlets in Great Britain and 517 retail outlets in 40 different countries.

TBS is headquartered in West Sussex, England, and consequently issues financial statements conforming to accepted accounting practice in Great Britain. Until 1994, the presentation of a statement of cash flows was not required under British GAAP.

Required:

The following are the group financial statements of TBS for the years ending February 29, 1992 and February 28, 1991. Using these data, prepare a statement of cash flows for 1992, identifying the cash flows from (for) operations, investing, and financing activities. What observations can be drawn from these data with respect to TBS during 1992?

THE BODY SHOP INTERNATIONAL Plc
Balance Sheets
As of February 1992

	Group	
	1992	*1991*
	£000	*£000*
Fixed assets		
Tangible assets	56,359	43,484
Investments	2,298	2,114
	58,657	45,598
Current assets		
Stocks	38,457	33,484
Debtors	36,061	26,895
Cash at bank and in hand	483	344
	75,001	60,723
Creditors: amounts falling due within one year	54,060	36,143
Net current assets	20,941	24,580
Total assets less current liabilities	79,598	70,178
Creditors: amounts falling due after more than one year	(2,669)	(2,924)
Provisions for liabilities and charges		
Deferred tax	(2,459)	(553)
Minority interests	(292)	(1,552)
	74,178	65,149
Capital and reserves		
Called up share capital	9,361	9,262
Share premium account	33,502	32,289
Profit and loss account	31,315	23,598
Shareholders' funds	74,178	65,149

THE BODY SHOP INTERNATIONAL Plc
Consolidated Profit and Loss Account
For the Year Ended February 29, 1992

	1992 £000	1991 £000
Turnover	**147,441**	115,599
Cost of sales	**68,210**	50,393
Gross profit	**79,231**	65,206
Selling and distribution costs	**32,021**	27,494
Administrative expenses	**19,335**	15,725
	51,356	43,219
Trading profit	**27,875**	21,987
Interest receivable	**539**	541
	28,414	22,528
Interest payable	**3,211**	2,491
Profit on ordinary activities before tax	**25,203**	20,037
Tax on profit on ordinary activities	**8,688**	7,311
Profit for the financial year	**16,515**	12,726
Minority interests	**120**	623
Profit attributable to members of holding company	**16,395**	12,103
Dividends paid and proposed	**2,995**	2,261
Amount transferred to reserves	**13,400**	9,842
Earnings per ordinary share	**8.8p**	6.7p

THE BODY SHOP INTERNATIONAL Plc
Consolidated Statement of Source and Application of Funds
For the Year Ended February 29, 1992

	1992		*1991*	
	£000	*£000*	*£000*	*£000*
Source of funds				
Group profit before tax		**25,203**		20,037
Adjustments for items not involving the movement of funds:				
Group share of profit on acquisition of minority interest		**(1,380)**		(45)
Depreciation		**4,711**		3,500
Loss on disposal of fixed assets		**61**		4
Other goodwill written off		**(284)**		—
Exchange differences		**(240)**		257
Generated from operations		**28,071**		23,753
Proceeds on disposal of fixed assets		**398**		164
Issue of shares		**1,312**		29,623
		29,781		53,540
Application of funds				
Purchase of fixed assets		**18,213**		18,220
Purchase of investments		**184**		2,114
Corporation tax paid		**7,627**		5,723
Dividends paid		**2,570**		1,818
Purchase of goodwill		**5,439**		291
Redemption of variable rate loan stock		**1,000**		1,000
		35,033		29,166
Increase (decrease) in net working capital:				
Stocks	**4,973**		10,124	
Debtors	**8,718**		8,320	
Creditors	**(2,739)**		(2,319)	
		10,952		16,125
		45,985		45,291
Increase (decrease) in net liquid funds		**(16,204)**		8,249

THE BODY SHOP INTERNATIONAL Plc
Notes on the Accounts
For the Year Ended February 29, 1992

Accounting Policies

Basis of accounting
The accounts are prepared under the historical cost convention and in accordance with applicable Accounting Standards. The principal accounting policies which affect these accounts are as follows:

Consolidation
The consolidated accounts incorporate the accounts of the holding company and its subsidiary undertakings. All of these accounts have the same financial year end. Where subsidiaries are acquired during the year their results are included in the consolidated profit and loss account from the effective dates of acquisition. The holding company's accounting policies have been applied consistently in dealing with items which are considered material in relation to the consolidated accounts.

Stocks
Stocks are included at the lower of cost and net realizable value. Finished stocks are usually valued at the cost of the raw materials, plus the cost of productive labour and with the addition of an appropriate proportion of factory overheads. However, where net realisable value is lower than cost then this lower figure is used. The cost of materials is calculated on the ''first in, first out'' basis whereby, as materials are used, the value of stock is adjusted by the cost of the oldest relevant materials. Net realizable value means the anticipated sale proceeds less the anticipated costs of selling the goods.

Depreciation and amortization
No depreciation is provided in respect of the cost of freehold land.
The cost of other fixed assets is written off by equal annual installments over their expected useful lives, using the following estimates of useful life:
Freehold buildings—Over 50 years
Leasehold property—Over the periods of the respective leases
Plant and equipment—Over 3 to 10 years

Accounting for finance leases
Gross earnings from finance leases are allocated to accounting periods on a straight-line basis over the lives of the respective leases, a basis which approximates to a constant periodic return on the net cash investment in finance leases.

Research and development
Research and development expenditure is usually charged to the profit and loss account in the year in which it is incurred. However, for development expenditure on future products, where the viability of the project is reasonably certain, the costs are carried forward as prepayments in the balance sheet to be written off within one year of the product launch.

Translation of foreign currencies
The trading results and balance sheets of foreign subsidiaries are converted into sterling at the rates of exchange ruling at the year-end. Any difference which arises as a result of converting the opening balance sheets at the year-end rate is taken straight to reserves. Other conversion differences are dealt with in the profit and loss account.

Deferred tax
Deferred tax is provided on differences arising from the inclusion of items of income and expenditure in taxation computations in periods different from those in which they are included in the accounts. The provision for deferred tax is provided at anticipated tax rates and to the extent that it is likely that a liability or asset will crystallize in the future.

Where advance corporation tax is expected to be recoverable it is deducted from the provision for deferred tax.

Goodwill
Purchased goodwill represents the amount by which the price paid for a business or company exceeds the fair value of the assets and liabilities acquired. Where goodwill arises it is written off immediately to reserves.

Turnover
Turnover represents the total amount receivable in the ordinary course of business for goods sold and services provided and excludes sales between companies in the Group, discounts given and Value Added Tax.

E.8.9   Financial Analysis: Great Britain versus United States

The following are the 1993 summary results (i.e., earnings summaries as they appeared in *The Wall Street Journal*) for four pharmaceutical companies; three are U.S.–based companies (American Home Products Corporation, Bristol-Myers Squibb Co., and Pfizer, Inc.) and the fourth is an Anglo-American company based in London (SmithKline Beecham Plc):

AMERICAN HOME PRODUCTS		
Quar Dec 31:	*1993*	*1992*
Sales	$2,116,304,000	$2,002,463,000
Net income	382,748,000	361,553,000
Avg shares	310,509,000	3,125,881,000
Shr earns:		
Net income	1.23	1.16
Year:		
Sales	8,304,851,000	7,873,687,000
Income	1,469,300,000	1,150,738,000
Acctg adj	. . .	a310,104,000
Net income	1,469,300,000	1,460,842,000
Avg shares	310,668,000	314,201,000
Shr earns:		
Income	4.73	3.66
Net income	4.73	4.65

a-Cumulative effect on prior periods of accounting changes.

BRISTOL-MYERS SQUIBB CO.		
Quar Dec 31:	*1993*	*1992*
Sales	$2,992,838,000	$2,823,811,000
aInc ct op	225,825,000	(43,081,000)
Inco dis op	. . .	c626,081,000
Net income	255,825,000	583,000,000
Avg shares	512,171,000	517,763,000
Shr earns:		
Inc ct op	.50	(.08)
Net income	.50	1.13
Year:		
Sales	11,412,675,000	11,155,879,000
aInc ct op	1,959,128,000	1,537,853,000
Inco dis op	. . .	c669,857,000
Income	1,959,128,000	2,207,710,000
Acctg adj	. . .	b(246,012,000)
Net income	1,959,128,000	1,961,698,000
Avg shares	515,246,000	517,967,000
Shr earns:		
Inc ct op	3.80	2.97
Income	3.80	4.26
Net income	3.80	3.79

a-Includes net non-recurring charges of $310,000,000 in 1993 and $570,000,000 in 1992.

b-Cumulative effect of an accounting change. c-Includes $605,116,000 net gain on disposal of discontinued operations.

PFIZER, INC.

Quar Dec 31:	1993	1992
Sales	$1,989,200,000	$1,947,100,000
Net income	288,900,000	b278,800,000
Shr earns:		
Net income	.90	.83
Year:		
Sales	7,477,700,000	7,230,200,000
bIncome	657,500,000	1,093,500,000
Acctg adj	. . .	a(282,600,000)
Net income	657,500,000	810,900,000
Shr earns:		
Income	2.05	3.25
Net income	2.05	2.41

a-Cumulative effect of an accounting change. b-Includes non-recurring pre-tax charges of $752,000,000 in the 1993 year, compared with gains of $15,300,000 in the quarter and $110,500,000 in the 1992 year.

SMITHKLINE BEECHAM

Quar Dec 31:	1993	a1992
bSales	1,660,000,000	1,406,000,000
Net income	218,000,000	c196,000,000
Year:		
bSales	6,040,000,000	4,924,000,000
dNet income	813,000,000	711,000,000

a-Restated. b-From continuing operations. c-Includes non-recurring charge. d-Includes non-recurring charges of 35,000,000 in 1993 and 36,000,000 in 1992.

Amounts in British pounds.

The shares of each of the U.S.–based drug companies, as well as the ADRs of SmithKline, trade on the NYSE; closing share prices on the day of these earnings releases were as follows:

American Home Products	$64.24
Bristol-Myers Squibb	$58.75
Pfizer	$62.875
SmithKline Beecham	$30.125

(*Note:* SmithKline Beecham had approximately 390 million equivalent shares [including ADRs] outstanding.)

Required:

   (a) Compare the financial results of the four companies; calculate the P-E ratio for each.

(b) What conclusions can you draw about the perceived investment potential of each company?

(c) What do you think happened to the share price of each company in response to the earnings release?

E.8.10   Asset Impairment and Restructuring

In December 1993, Trafalgar House Plc reported its 1993 year-end (i.e., October 1– September 30) results. The British property, construction, and transportation company disclosed that it had experienced a £347.2 million pre-tax loss for the year, after a £397.3 million charge for property write-downs and restructuring costs. As a consequence, the London-based Trafalgar House disclosed that its dividend would be cut 46 percent, from 6 to 3.25 pence per share. The company also indicated that it expected no significant improvement in operating results until 1995.

To strengthen its balance sheet, the company also announced its intention to raise approximately £400 million through a rights issue and a placement of new convertible preference shares. According to a company spokesperson, the proceeds would be used to repay debt, to provide an equity and liquidity base for its engineering and construction businesses, to finance improvements of its Cunard fleet of cruise ships and hotels, and to replenish residential loan associations.

Required:

(a) What accounting journal entries (ignoring amounts) are required to execute: (1) an asset write-down, (2) an asset restructuring, (3) a rights issue, and (4) a placement of new convertible preference shares?

(b) What is the likely effect of the four events identified in part (a) on the following ratios for Trafalgar House: (1) current ratio, (2) long-term debt-to-equity ratio, (3) asset turnover ratio, and (4) return on assets ratio?

E.8.11   Accounting Information, Stock Prices, and Market Efficiency

On December 3, 1993, Hanson Plc reported that its pre-tax profit for the year ended September 30 fell by 21 percent to £1.02 billion. In response to the news announcement, Hanson's ordinary shares fell by 16 pence (to 268.5 pence) in London, and in the United States, where the company's shares trade as ADRs on the NYSE, Hanson fell $1.375 to $19.625 per share. The nearly 7 percent drop in the ADR share price was attributed to investor surprise over the disappointing earnings and shareholder unhappiness that the company failed to raise its dividend. According to a Hanson company spokesperson, this was the first time since the company's founding two decades earlier that a dividend increase had not been announced in conjunction with the release of year-end results.

Derrick Bonham, CEO of Hanson, blamed the lower profits on a coal strike in the United States and recessionary environments in both the United States and Britain. Bonham estimated that the continuing coal strike had already cost the company approximately £125 million during fiscal year 1993.

Stock market analysts familiar with Hanson noted other concerns, however, about the company. In early 1993, Hanson acquired Quantrum Chemical, and as part of that transaction assumed over $2.5 billion in debt of the U.S.–based chemical company. As a consequence, Hanson's debt-to-equity ratio stood at 86 percent at year-end 1993. Hanson's finance director, William Landryt, warned analysts that Hanson's net interest cost for 1994 would increase by approximately £275 million as a result of the higher debt loading. Within two trading days of Hanson's news announcement, the company's ADRs had fallen to $19, a total decline of nearly 10 percent.

Required:

    (a) Based on the information available, how much of Hanson's 1993 earnings drop could be attributed to factors other than the U.S. coal strike?

    (b) On the basis of the Hanson case, what factors affect security prices, and why?

    (c) Assume the role of Derrick Bonham. What actions might you take to reverse Hanson's trend of declining earnings?

E.8.12   Financial Data and Security Prices

Just what type of information causes stock prices to move upward and downward, and why, is a subject of considerable debate among security analysts. Consider, for example, the case of Eurotunnel, the Anglo-French company that will operate the long-awaited tunnel (or "Chunnel") under the English Channel between France and Britain. During the period December 10, 1993, to January 10, 1994, the price of Eurotunnel shares rose about 40 percent, from 460 pence to 644 pence (or approximately $9.56) per share. During that same period, the following information was released to the public in regards to the Chunnel:

- On December 10, Eurotunnel took possession of the Chunnel from building contractors.

- In mid-December, the British government acted to lower interest rates.

- On December 20, the French and British governments jointly disclosed that they had extended Eurotunnel's right to operate the Chunnel for an additional 10 years.

- In early January, Eurotunnel's lead banking syndicate approved the company's funding plan, which included a commitment by the lenders to provide up to £500 million in new loans and paved the way for a long-awaited £500 million (or approximately $742.5 million) stock rights issue.

- On January 10, Eurotunnel started selling tickets for its "Le Shuttle" car transport service, at prices ranging from £160 to £300, depending on the season; at those prices, Chunnel travel would be slightly more expensive, although faster, than travel by ferry boat. The £10 billion project was scheduled to begin service on May 6, 1994.

Analysts familiar with the project were reportedly skeptical about its prospects for success, despite recent share price increases. Their concerns focused on the project's heavy debt load and its ability to generate sufficient revenues in an already highly competitive marketplace.

Required:

(a) Explain why each of the preceding news events was associated with a positive share price movement.

(b) What do these events and their related stock market response suggest about the anticipatory behavior of securities markets?

(c) What kind of news or events would you expect to cause an adverse (or downward) share price reaction for Eurotunnel?

E.8.13   MTNs and Interest Rate Swaps

Historically, a company's source of debt financing usually has been tied to the expected duration of its expected borrowing. For example, banks have traditionally been the source of short- (1–3 years) and medium-term (3–5 years) financing, whereas the public debt market has been the principal source of long-term (6–20 years) financing, and insurance companies and pension funds have been the primary source for very long-term (20–30 years) borrowings. These traditional boundaries, however, have become blurred with increased competition among lending sources, as well as the advent of new types of debt securities. One such example is the emergence of medium-term notes, or MTNs, which have grown to more than one-third of the U.S. public corporate debt market. Most MTNs are noncallable, unsecured, senior debt instruments, with fixed coupon rates, investment-grade credit ratings, and maturities of three to five years.

To illustrate, consider the 1993 MTN offering by SmithKline Beecham Plc. The British pharmaceutical company desired to borrow $1 billion in the three- to five-year maturity range and consequently launched two MTN programs, one in Europe and one in the United States. The funds were to be used principally on behalf of SmithKline's U.S. operations.

The European MTN offering consisted of three separate fixed-rate, Eurosterling issues of varying maturities and coupon rates, totaling £100 million (approximately $450 million). The U.S. program, on the other hand, consisted of 14 separate issues, between $20 and $200 million each, and totaling $590 million. Depending on their maturity date, the U.S. offerings paid between 7.75 and 8.125 percent, which was about 15 to 25 basis points above comparable debt instruments. (A *basis point* is equivalent to one-hundredth of 1 percent.) Shortly after the two MTN offerings, SmithKline "swapped" the fixed-rate instrument for floating-rate dollar-based obligations.

Required:

- (a) How should SmithKline account for the interest rate swap? How do interest rate swaps affect the financial statements of the swap parties?
- (b) Why would SmithKline want to execute an interest rate swap? What advantages does a swap provide the company?

E.8.14   Accounting for Capital and Reserves

The following table contains selected financial information from the 1993 annual report of Carlton Communications Plc.

Required:

Using the available information, prepare journal entries to explain the changes in the company's Capital and Reserves accounts for 1993.

	(£000)	
Selected Financial Information	*1993*	*1992*
Capital and Reserves		
Called-up share capital	18,190	18,143
Share premium account	7,880	3,228
Revaluation reserve	2,346	11,977
Other reserves	30,659	40,214
Profit and loss account	365,658	309,730
Total	424,733	383,292
Selected Footnote Information	*1993*	*1992*
Called up Share Capital	*£000*	*£000*
Authorized:		
272,000,000 Ordinary shares of 5p each (1992—272,000,000)	13,600	13,600
170,000,000 6.5p (net) Cumulative Convertible Redeemable Preference		
shares of 5p each (1992—170,000,000)	8,500	8,500
	22,100	22,100
Issued and fully paid:		
198,811,194 Ordinary shares of 5p each (1992—197,844,477)	9,941	9,893
164,986,887 6.5p (net) Cumulative Convertible Redeemable Preference		
shares of 5p each (1992—164,993,528)	8,249	8,250
	18,190	18,143

The following changes have taken place in the issued share capital of the Company:

Share Premium Account, Revaluation and Other Reserves	Share Premium Account £000	Revaluation Reserve £000	Other Reserves £000
(a) The Group			
At 1 October 1992	3,228	11,977	40,214
Premium on the issue of shares	4,652	—	—
Goodwill written off in the year	—	—	(9,839)
Share of associated undertakings' other reserve movements	—	—	284
Transfer to profit and loss account	—	(401)	—
Exchange differences	—	215	—
Revaluation in the year	—	(9,445)	—
At 30 September 1993	**7,880**	**2,346**	**30,659**
(b) The Company			
At 1 October 1992	3,228	9,479	993,374
Premium on the issue of shares	4,652	—	—
Transfer to profit and loss account	—	(289)	(179,480)
Revaluation in the year	—	(6,941)	—
At 30 September 1993	**7,880**	**2,249**	**813,894**

At 30 September 1993, other reserves of the Company, which were non-distributable, comprised (a) £369.1 million being the remaining balance of special reserves created on the cancellation of the share premium account in previous years, and (b) £272.2 million being the amounts arising on the application of section 131(2) of the Companies Act 1985 not yet realised. Transfers from other reserves to the profit and loss account represent section 131(2) amounts realized on disposals. The cumulative goodwill written off to Group reserves at 30 September 1993 amounted to £1,026,640,000.

Profit and Loss Account	The Group £000	The Company £000
At 1 October 1992	309,730	78,516
Retained profit for the year	46,091	443,575
Transfer from revaluation reserve	401	289
Transfer from other reserves	—	179,480
Goodwill reinstated on disposal of subsidiary	1,188	—
Exchange differences	8,248	—
At 30 September 1993	**365,658**	**701,860**

Exchange differences in the Group are net of the movement on foreign currency borrowings and balance sheet hedging of £33,104,000. Included within the Company's profit and loss account at 30 September 1993 was an amount of £507,485,000 which was not distributable at that date. On 14 January 1994, £101,490,000 of such amount was realized and became distributable.

CARLTON COMMUNICATIONS Plc
Reconciliation of Movements in Shareholders' Funds

	1993 *£000*	*1992* *£000*
Profit for the financial year	**94,028**	74,807
Ordinary and preference dividends	**(47,937)**	(45,564)
Other recognized gains and losses	**(982)**	587
New share capital issued	**4,699**	72,893
Goodwill written off	**(9,839)**	(71,569)
Goodwill reinstated in respect of disposal of business	**1,188**	—
Share of associates' other reserves movements	**284**	(96)
Net additions to shareholders' funds	**41,441**	31,058
Shareholders' funds at beginning of the year	**383,292**	352,234
Shareholders' funds at the end of the year	**424,733**	383,292

CASES

CASE 8.1
GREAT BRITAIN VERSUS U.S. GAAP

SmithKline Beecham Plc

SmithKline Beecham Plc (SKB) discovers, manufactures, and markets pharmaceuticals, over-the-counter (OTC) medicines, and other health-related products. The company manufactures its products in 27 different countries and markets them in most countries throughout the world. Although the company is headquartered in Middlesex, England, the vast majority of its sales occur in the United States, Italy, France, Germany, Japan, Spain, and Belgium.

SKB, a public limited company incorporated in 1989, was formed for the purpose of effecting the combination of the pharmaceutical and OTC medicine business of SmithKline Beckman Corporation, a Pennsylvania corporation, and Beecham Group Plc, a public limited company incorporated under the laws of England; Beecham also manufactured consumer health products.

Although the shares of SKB trade principally on the London Stock Exchange, they are also readily available to U.S. investors in the form of American depositary shares (ADRs), which trade on the New York Stock Exchange. Each ADR represents five ordinary SKB shares, which are held in trust for U.S. investors by Morgan Guaranty Trust Company of New York. Foreign companies issuing ADRs in the United States are required to file form 20-F with the Securities

---

This case was prepared by Kenneth R. Ferris from publicly available documents. Copyright © 1993 by Kenneth R. Ferris. All rights reserved to the author.

Eᴄʜɪʙɪᴛ 1

SMITHKLINE BEECHAM Plc
Consolidated Profit and Loss Account
For the Year Ended December 31, 1990

	£m	
	1990	*1989*
Sales		
Continuing operations	**4,501**	4,264
Discontinued operations	**263**	633
	4,764	4,897
Cost of goods sold	**(1,703)**	(1,889)
Gross profit	**3,061**	3,008
Selling, general and administrative expenses	**(1,701)**	(1,790)
Research and development expenditure	**(393)**	(400)
Trading profit of continuing operations	**938**	725
Trading profit of discontinued operations	**29**	93
Share of profits of associated companies	**3**	8
Profit before interest and taxation	**970**	826
Interest	**(110)**	(102)
Profit on ordinary activities before taxation	**860**	724
Tax on profit on ordinary activities	**(286)**	(244)
Profit on ordinary activities after taxation	**574**	480
Minority interests	**(9)**	(4)
Auction Rate Preference Share dividends	**(21)**	—
Profit before extraordinary items	**544**	476
Extraordinary items	**303**	(346)
Profit attributable to shareholders	**847**	130
Dividends payable	**216**	80
Earnings per Ordinary Share	**41·0p**	36·5p
Earnings per Equity Unit	**205·0p**	182·5p

and Exchange Commission. This registration statement presents the company's foreign financial statements prepared in accordance with U.S. GAAP or presents a reconciliation of the company's foreign GAAP statements to U.S. GAAP.

Required:

Exhibits 1 to 5 present the SKB 1990 financial statements prepared in accordance with British GAAP, a statement of SKB's accounting policies, and a reconciliation of the SKB statements to U.S. GAAP. Using these data, prepare a comparative financial analysis of SKB for 1990 using the British GAAP statements and the reconciliation data to U.S. GAAP. Calculate any financial ratios using both the British GAAP data and the reconciled data, and highlight any significant differences. As part of this analysis, construct a statement of cash flows from the SKB statements presented.

EXHIBIT 2

SMITHKLINE BEECHAM Plc
Balance Sheets
For the Year Ended December 31, 1990

	£m	
	1990	*1989*
Fixed Assets		
Tangible assets	**1,433**	1,473
Investments	**45**	91
	1,478	1,564
Current Assets		
Stocks	**488**	515
Debtors	**1,150**	1,275
Assets held pending disposal	**—**	166
Investments	**459**	5
Cash	**314**	229
	2,411	2,190
Creditors: amounts falling due within one year		
Loans and overdrafts	**(1,108)**	(986)
Other	**(1,306)**	(1,556)
	(2,414)	(2,542)
Net current (liabilities) assets	**(3)**	(352)
Total assets less current liabilities	**1,475**	1,212
Creditors: amounts falling due after more than one year		
Loans	**(341)**	(999)
Other	**(31)**	(31)
Provisions for liabilities and charges	**(284)**	(457)
	(656)	**(1,487)**
Net Assets	**819**	(275)
Capital Employed		
Capital and reserves		
Called up share capital	**349**	351
Reserves	**939**	348
SB Shareholders' equity before elimination of goodwill	**1,288**	699
Goodwill reserve	**(915)**	(995)
SB Shareholders' equity after elimination of goodwill	**373**	(296)
Auction Rate Preference Shares of subsidiary	**415**	—
Minority interests	**31**	21
Total Shareholders' Funds	**819**	(275)

EXHIBIT 3

SMITHKLINE BEECHAM Plc
Source and Application of Funds
For the Year Ended December 31, 1990

	£m	
	1990	*1989*
Funds generated from trading		
Trading profit	967	818
Beecham trading profit for the first quarter 1989	—	(143)
Depreciation	151	134
Miscellaneous items, including exchange	(7)	(16)
	1,111	793
Changes in working capital		
Stocks—(increase) decrease	(19)	4
Debtors—(increase)	(53)	(87)
Creditors and provisions—increase	109	96
	37	13
Changes in fixed assets		
Purchases of tangible assets	(264)	(209)
Sales of tangible assets	30	14
	(234)	(195)
Cash flow from operations	914	611
Interest	(110)	(113)
Tax paid	(276)	(199)
Dividends received from former SmithKline subsidiaries	—	56
Dividends paid	(210)	(203)
Free cash flow after financing costs and tax	318	152
Shares issued	4	191
Auction Rate Preference Shares issued, less expenses	409	—
Sale of investments	3	8
Acquisitions, including deferred payments	(123)	(34)
Disposal of business	526	95
Extraordinary items paid	(246)	(145)
Special dividend paid to former shareholders of SmithKline Beckman Corporation	—	(431)
Net inflow (outflow) of funds	891	(164)
Net funds		
Net (borrowings) at the beginning of the year	(1,748)	(163)
Exchange restatement	181	(87)
Issue of Loan Stock 1990/92	—	(1,334)
Net inflow (outflow) of funds	891	(164)
Net (borrowings) at the end of the year	(676)	(1,748)
Net (borrowings) in continuing businesses	(676)	(1,751)
Net surplus funds in businesses in the course of disposal	—	3
	(676)	(1,748)

The movement in net borrowings for the year represents the difference between the amounts shown in the opening and closing balance sheets. Movements in other items do not correspond to the change in balance sheet amounts primarily due to the effects of translating opening currency balances of overseas subsidiaries at closing exchange rates.

Net borrowings comprise loans and overdrafts less cash and short-term investments.

EXHIBIT 4

SMITHKLINE BEECHAM Plc
Accounting Policies

The financial statements are prepared under the historical cost convention, modified for the revaluation of land and buildings. Certain comparative figures have been amended to reflect changes in presentation.

Basis of Consolidation
The consolidated accounts include the accounts of the Company and its subsidiaries to 31 December. The results of businesses sold are included up to the date of disposal. As permitted by the Companies Act of 1985, the Company has not presented its own profit and loss account.

Currency translation
Profit and loss accounts of companies operating outside Great Britain are translated to sterling using average rates of exchange for the period. The net assets of such companies are translated to sterling at the rates of exchange ruling at the balance sheet dates.

Exchange differences which relate to the translation of net assets of overseas companies and to foreign currency borrowings are taken directly to reserves. All other exchange differences are taken to the profit and loss account.

The costs and benefits arising from hedging arrangements to mitigate the effect of exchange rate fluctuations on profits are dealt with in the profit and loss account in the year in which the related exposure arises.

Research and development expenditure
Laboratory buildings and equipment used for research and development are included as fixed assets and written off in accordance with the Group's depreciation policy. Other research and development expenditure is written off in the year in which it is incurred.

Deferred taxation
Deferred taxation is provided on timing differences using the liability method where it is probable that tax liabilities or assets will crystallize within the foreseeable future.

Goodwill
Goodwill, representing the excess of the purchase consideration over the fair value of the net tangible assets acquired, is eliminated in the Group balance sheet against reserves in the year of acquisition.

Tangible fixed assets and depreciation
Tangible fixed assets are stated at cost (or professional valuation in the case of certain land and buildings) less depreciation. Depreciation is charged on the cost or valuation of fixed assets, except freehold land, in equal annual instalments over their estimated useful lives. The range of average lives for each major asset category are:

Freehold buildings	20 to 50 years	Plant and equipment	10 to 20 years
Leasehold land and buildings	Term of lease	Vehicles	5 to 7 years

Stocks
Stocks are stated at the lower of cost or net realizable value. The cost of finished goods and work in progress comprises raw materials, direct labor and related production overheads.

Retirement benefits
The cost of providing pension benefits is charged to the profit and loss accounts over the periods benefitting from the employee's services. The difference between the charge to the profit and loss account and the contributions paid to the retirement plans is included as an asset or liability in the balance sheet. The costs of providing other retirement benefits is charged to the profit and loss account when paid.

EXHIBIT 5

SMITHKLINE BEECHAM Plc
Additional Information for U.S. Investors

The Group prepares its consolidated accounts in accordance with generally accepted accounting principles (''GAAP'') in the U.K.

U.K. are explained on pages 30 and 31. U.K. GAAP differs in certain respects from U.S. GAAP. The effect of such differences of a material nature is set out below. There is a fundamental difference between U.K. and U.S. GAAP in the accounting for the merger. Under U.K. GAAP the combination is accounted for using merger accounting principles, whereas under U.S. GAAP the transaction is accounted for using the purchase accounting method. For the purposes of this reconciliation to U.S. GAAP, it has been assumed that SmithKline is the acquiree.

	Year ended 31 December,	
	1990 *£m*	*1989* *£m*
Income Statement Data		
Net income after extraordinary items per U.K. GAAP	847	130
U.S. GAAP adjustments (net of taxation):		
Elimination of SmithKline results prior to merger	—	(144)
Merger transaction and SmithKline restructuring costs	—	281
Goodwill—Beecham	(88)	(26)
Deferred taxation	(3)	(30)
Purchase accounting:		
Amortization of intangible assets	(85)	(60)
Amortization of goodwill	(67)	(28)
Depreciation and other	(7)	(42)
Other, net	32	6
Net income per U.S. GAAP	629	87
Represented by:		
Income before non-recurring charges and taxes on income	680	349
Non-recurring credits (charges)	124	(115)
Taxes on income	(300)	(162)
Income from continuing operations	504	72
Income from discontinued operations (net of taxes)	125	15
Net income per U.S. GAAP	629	87
Per Share Data		
Average number of A and B Ordinary Shares in issue	1,326m	952m
Per Ordinary Share per U.S. GAAP		
Income from continuing operations	38·0p	7·5p
Net income	47·4p	9·1p
Per Equity Unit per U.S. GAAP		
Income from continuing operations	190·0p	37·5p
Net income	237·0p	45·5p

EXHIBIT 5 (continued)

SMITHKLINE BEECHAM Plc
Additional Information for U.S. Investors

	31 December,	
	1990 *£m*	*1989* *£m*
Balance Sheet Data		
Shareholders' equity per U.K. GAAP	373	(296)
U.S. GAAP adjustments:		
Goodwill—Beecham	344	461
Capitalization of interest	38	37
Dividends	58	50
Deferred taxation:		
due to timing differences	(80)	(66)
due to ACT	14	5
Revaluation reserve	(140)	(156)
Other, net	20	(13)
Purchase accounting:		
Property, plant and equipment	52	69
Intangible assets	551	754
Goodwill	2,598	2,665
Other, net	27	35
Shareholders' equity per U.S. GAAP	3,855	3,545

(a) Goodwill

Under U.K. GAAP, goodwill may be amortised over its useful life through the profit and loss account or eliminated directly against reserves. Under U.S. GAAP, goodwill is capitalised and amortised by charges against income over the period which, it is estimated, is to be benefited. Goodwill eliminated directly against reserves in the U.K. accounts has been reinstated and amortised over a 40 year period, which is the estimated useful life for the purpose of U.S. GAAP.

(b) Capitalisation of interest

Under U.K. GAAP, the capitalisation of interest is not required and the Group does not capitalise interest in its financial statements. U.S. GAAP requires interest incurred as part of the cost of acquiring fixed assets to be capitalised and amortised over the life of the asset.

(c) Deferred tax

Under U.K. GAAP, provision is made for deferred tax under the liability method where it is probable that a tax liability will become payable or a tax asset will crystallise within the foreseeable future. In the U.S., Accounting Principles Board Opinion No. 11 requires deferred tax to be provided in full under the deferral basis.

Under U.K. GAAP, the Group writes off any Advance Corporation Tax (''ACT'') which is not considered to be recoverable. However, if deferred taxation is provided, such ACT may be available for offset against the balance on the deferred taxation account. As deferred taxation is provided under U.S. GAAP on all timing differences, the deferred tax account has been reduced by the appropriate amount of ACT.

(d) Extraordinary items

Under U.K. GAAP, the costs or credits relating to the restructuring of the Group, including the disposal of operations, may be classed as extraordinary items. Under U.S. GAAP, such disposals and one-time charges are treated as non-recurring items or as discontinued operations.

EXHIBIT 5 (continued)

(e) Discontinued operations

Under U.K. GAAP, income earned from both continuing operations and discontinued operations up to the date of sale is aggregated in the consolidated income statement; material gains and losses arising on the sale of discontinued operations may be shown as extraordinary items. Under U.S. GAAP, gains or losses on the sale of those activities which comply with the U.S. GAAP definition of discontinued operations are not shown as extraordinary items but are shown under the heading ''discontinued operations,'' and income from continuing operations and discontinued operations normally is disclosed separately for each year presented.

(f) Ordinary dividends

Under U.K. GAAP, dividends are provided for in the fiscal year in respect of which they are declared by the Board of Directors. Under U.S. GAAP, such dividends are not provided for until formally declared by the Board of Directors.

(g) Property revaluation

Under U.K. GAAP, properties are carried either at original cost or a subsequent valuation, less related depreciation, calculated on the revalued amount where applicable. Any surplus on the revaluation of a property is taken directly to shareholders' equity. Under U.S. GAAP revaluations of properties are not permitted.

(h) Purchase accounting adjustments

Under U.K. GAAP, the combination is being accounted for using merger accounting principles, pursuant to which the assets and liabilities of the Group are the sum of the historical net assets of Beecham and SmithKline. Under U.S. GAAP, the combination has been accounted for using the purchase method. For the purposes of this reconciliation, SmithKline has been treated as the acquiree. Under the purchase method, the aggregate purchase price was allocated to the assets and liabilities of SmithKline based upon their independently appraised fair values, with the remainder allocated to goodwill. Goodwill arising of £2,693 million is being amortised over 40 years.

(i) Future developments

Statement of Financial Accounting Standards (''SFAS'') No. 96, ''Accounting for Income Taxes,'' was issued in December 1987 and subsequently amended in December 1989. The Standard, which becomes effective no later than the 1992 fiscal year, requires a change in accounting for income taxes from the deferral method to the liability method, for the purposes of U.S. GAAP.

SFAS No. 106, ''Employer's Accounting for Post-Retirement Benefits other than Pensions'' was issued in December 1990 with adoption required by 1993. This statement requires, among other things, the recording of post-retirement benefits on the accrual basis, the disclosure of the components of annual costs and the assumptions utilised to develop such costs.

The Group is currently studying these U.S. Accounting Standards to determine the effect they may have on its reconciliation of net income and shareholders' equity between U.K. and U.S. GAAP.

CASE 8.2
CONSOLIDATING INTERNATIONAL ACQUISITIONS

Hanson Plc

On July 1, 1993, *The Wall Street Journal* carried the following news release:

U.K.'s Hanson to Buy Maker of Polyethylene

Hanson Plc, betting on a cyclical rebound in plastics prices, said it agreed to buy troubled Quantum Chemical Corp., the U.S.'s largest polyethylene maker, in a stock swap valuing Quantum at $20 a share, or $720 million.

Hanson, a London–based conglomerate whose products range from tobacco, coal, and chemicals to pots, pans, and jacuzzis, also agreed to assume loss-plagued Quantum's $2.5 billion in debt. Based on Quantum's closing share price of $12.50 as of June 30, 1993, the buyout offer represented a 60 percent premium over Quantum's current market value. The proposed tax-free swap of 1.176 newly issued Hanson ADRs for each Quantum share required approval by two-thirds of Quantum's shareholders.

Wall Street analysts familiar with the chemical industry expressed concern that Quantum's willingness to sell may indicate that Quantum executives do not expect a rebound in plastics prices in the foreseeable future. At the peak of the last plastics cycle in 1988, Quantum's operating profit totaled nearly $760 million, or 12.5 times 1992 operating profit of $61 million.

Quantum saddled itself with the $2.5 billion debt load in a 1989 restructuring when plastics prices were near their peak. Massive debt service requirements, along with the cyclical slump in polyethylene prices, left the company with a 1992 loss before accounting charges of $118.4 million (or $3.98 per share), compared with a 1991 loss of $123 million (or $4.26 per share).

Required:

   (a) Presented in Exhibits 1 and 2 are the abbreviated 1992 financial statements for Quantum Chemical Corporation and Hanson Plc. Using this information, prepare the consolidated financial statements for Hanson, assuming that the acquisition was effected on December 31, 1992, using the following methods:

      (1) Pooling of interests.
      (2) Purchase accounting with goodwill capitalized to the consolidated balance sheet.
      (3) Purchase accounting with goodwill charged against retained earnings on the consolidated balance sheet.

      For methods 2 and 3, assume that Quantum's fair market value is equal to its net worth.

   (b) Calculate the following ratios under each of the three consolidation approaches:
      (1) Profitability:
         (*a*) Return on sales.

   (*b*) Return on total assets.

   (*c*) Return on equity.

  (2) Solvency

   (*a*) Total debt to owners' equity.

   (*b*) Total debt to total assets.

 (c) Under which consolidation approach to the ratios appear their best?

EXHIBIT 1

1992 Condensed Balance Sheets*
(000s omitted)

	Hanson Plc	Quantum
Current assets	$11,077,000	$ 961,800
Property, plant & equipment (net)	9,146,000	1,972,500
Other long-term assets	318,000	219,600
Total assets	$20,541,000	$3,153,900
Current liabilities	$ 6,386,000	$ 438,300
Long-term debt	5,069,000	2,504,000
Other long-term liabilities	4,862,000	682,700
Total liabilities	$16,317,000	$3,625,000
Common stock†	$ 2,368,000	261,100
Revaluation reserves	166,000	—
Other appropriate reserves	65,000	—
Retained earnings	1,625,000	(732,200)
Total shareholder equity	$ 4,224,000	$ (471,100)
Total liabilities and shareholder equity	$20,541,000	$3,153,900

*Hanson's fiscal year-end is September 30, but for Quantum is December 31. For simplicity, however, assume that the fiscal year-end for both companies is December 31.
†Quantum had 30.1 million shares outstanding in 1992. Assume that Hanson's par value is $1 per ADR.

EXHIBIT 2

1992 Condensed Income Statements
(000s omitted)

	Hanson Plc	Quantum
Net sales	$ 8,798,000	$ 2,367,400
Less: Cost of goods sold	(5,752,000)	(2,103,600)
Depreciation/amortization	(252,000)	—
Other operating expenses	(1,765,000)	(202,400)
Operating income	$ 1,029,000	$ 61,400
Add: net interest income (expense)	239,000	(252,200)
Pre-tax net income (loss)	$ 1,268,000	$ (190,800)
Less: Income taxes	(187,000)	72,400
Income (loss) before accounting changes	$ 1,081,000	$ (118,400)
Less: Cumulative effect of accounting changes	—	(169,100)
Net income (loss)	$ 1,081,000	$ (287,500)

CASE 8.3
ASSET VALUATION AND THE FOURTH DIRECTIVE

British Airways Plc

The EU's Fourth Directive, passed in 1978, is generally viewed as *the* significant breakthrough in the harmonization of EU company accounting. It represented an important compromise between the legalistic approach to financial reporting typified by Germany and the professional judgment approach characterized by the British. This compromise is apparent in the flexibility that the Fourth Directive permits in the implementation of its articles.

Consider, for example, the valuation of assets. The Fourth Directive indicates that companies must use historical cost as the basis for asset valuation but also allows member-states to permit (or require) companies to revalue certain assets to reflect the effects of inflation, so long as the departure from historical cost is necessary to give a true and fair view and so long as the departure is disclosed in the financial statements. Examples of such departures include these:

- The valuation of property, plant, equipment, and inventories at replacement cost.
- The revaluation of tangible fixed assets and financial fixed assets (i.e., investments and loans) to fair market value.
- The valuation of *all* financial statement items by a method designed to recognize the effects of inflation.

An Illustration

To illustrate the functioning and effects of the Fourth Directive, the following information was excerpted from the 1991 financial statements of British Airways Plc:

- Footnote Disclosure of Accounting Policies
  Accounting Convention—The accounts have been prepared under the historical cost convention modified by the inclusion of certain assets at valuation as stated below and in accordance with all applicable British accounting standards.

This case was prepared by Kenneth R. Ferris from publicly available documents. Copyright © 1993 by Kenneth R. Ferris. All rights reserved.

Tangible Fixed Assets—Tangible fixed assets are stated at cost except for certain aircraft fleets and properties that are included at valuation. Depreciation is calculated to write off the cost or valuation, less residual value, on the straight-line basis.

Apart from the Concord fleet, which remains at nil book value, the majority of the owned aircraft fleets were professionally valued on a market value basis on 31 March 1988 and are included in the accounts on the basis of that valuation, less depreciation.

All properties, other than those of a specialized use nature such as hangars and aircraft maintenance buildings, were professionally valued at open market value for existing use or open market at 31 March 1984 and are included in these accounts on the basis of that valuation, less depreciation.

• Footnote Disclosure of Financial Effects

	(£ Millions)		Net Book Value	
	Valuation	*Depreciation*	*1991*	*1990*
Revalued fleet and properties are included in the accounts at the following amounts:				
Property (valued in 1984)	100	27	73	63
Fleet (valued in 1988)	1,044	719	325	414
Total—31 March 1991	1,144	746	398	477
If these assets had not been revalued they would have been included at the following amounts:				
31 March 1991	955	684	271	—
31 March 1990	1,066	706	—	300

• Footnote Disclosure of Reconciliation to U.S. GAAP
Property and Fleet Valuation. Under U.S. GAAP, tangible assets must be stated at cost less accumulated depreciation. The valuation of properties at 31 March 1984 and fleet at 31 March 1988 incorporated by British Airways in its financial statements would not therefore have been included in financial statements prepared in accordance with U.S. GAAP and the subsequent charges for depreciation would have been correspondingly lower. When such assets are sold, however, any revaluation surplus thus realized would be reflected in income.

The estimated effect of the significant adjustments to net income and to shareholders' equity that would be required if U.S. GAAP were to be applied instead of accounting principles generally accepted in Great Britain are

	(£ millions)	
	1991	*1990*
Net income (after tax)		
Depreciation		
Fleet	61	83
Property	3	—
Surplus arising on disposal of revalued aircraft	33	28
Shareholders' equity		
Fleet	(264)	(299)
Property	(23)	(25)

Required:

Presented in Exhibits 1 and 2 are British Airways' 1990 and 1991 group profit and loss statements and balance sheets. Using this information and that contained in the case, consider the following questions:

(a) Under British and EU GAAP, are British Airway's net worth and net income overstated? If so, why (and by how much)? If not, why not?

(b) As an investment analyst, which data—the U.S. GAAP or the British/EU GAAP— would you prefer to use for your investment decisions? Why?

(c) When comparing the financial results for British Airways to a U.S.–based airline (e.g., American or Delta), how is your analysis likely to be affected? (*Hint:* Provide specific examples of ratios or other financial indicators that will be affected by the differences in GAAP.)

EXHIBIT 1

BRITISH AIRWAYS Plc
Group Profit and Loss Account
For the Year Ended 31 March
(in £ millions)

	Group	
	1991	*1990*
Turnover	4,937	4,838
Cost of sales	(4,653)	(4,339)
Gross profit	284	499
Administrative expenses	(117)	(115)
Operating Surplus	167	384
Other income and charges	112	18
Net interest payable	(29)	(57)
Profit before Exceptional Item	250	345
Exceptional item	(120)	
Profit on Ordinary Activities before Taxation	**130**	345
Taxation	(35)	(100)
Profit on Ordinary Activities after Taxation	95	245
Minority interests		1
Profit Attributable to Shareholders	95	246
Dividends paid and proposed	(64)	(64)
Retained Profit for the Year	31	182
Earnings per share		
—Basic	13.2p	34.1p
—Fully diluted	13.4p	31.2p
Dividends per share	8.85p	8.85p

EXHIBIT 2

BRITISH AIRWAYS Plc
Balance Sheet
As of March 31
(in £ millions)

	Group	
	1991	*1990*
Fixed Assets		
Tangible assets		
Fleet	2,513	1,917
Property	392	339
Equipment	229	208
	3,134	2,464
Investments	108	108
Current Assets		
Stocks	37	40
Debtors	795	923
Short-term loans and deposits	203	300
Cash at bank	22	32
	1,057	1,295
Creditors: amounts falling due within one year	(1,600)	(1,816)
Net Current Liabilities	(543)	(521)
Total Assets Less Current Liabilities	2,699	2,051
Creditors: amounts falling due after more than one year	(1,366)	(755)
Provisions for Liabilities and Charges	(55)	(64)
	1,278	1,232
Capital and Reserves		
Called up share capital	180	180
Reserves		
Revaluation	82	121
Other	(11)	(18)
Profit and loss account	707	629
	958	912
Convertible Capital Bonds 2005	320	320
	1,278	1,232

ANNUAL REPORT ANALYSIS

Imperial Chemical Industries (ICI)

An interesting and important challenge for students of international financial reporting is to study the published annual reports of various companies from different countries. Your instructor will provide you with appropriate a recent copy of the ICI annual report. To facilitate your delving into the annual report, undertake the following endeavors.

Required:

  (a) List the key differences between the ICI annual report and what you would expect to see for a U.S. company like Dow Chemical.

  (b) Calculate the following ratios for ICI, taking care to note the assumptions you found necessary to make and where you found the appropriate pieces of data in the annual report.

$$(1) \text{ Current ratio} = \frac{\text{Total current assets}}{\text{Total current liabilities}}$$

$$(2) \text{ Quick ratio} = \frac{\text{Cash + Marketable securities + Accts. Rec.}}{\text{Total current liabilities}}$$

$$(3) \text{ Operating cash flow to current liabilities} = \frac{\text{Operating cash flow}}{\text{Average total current liabilities}}$$

$$(4) \text{ Debt-to-equity ratio} = \frac{\text{Long-term debt}}{\text{Owners' equity}}$$

$$(5) \text{ Debt-to-total capitalization ratio} = \frac{\text{Long-term debt}}{\text{Long-term debt + Owners' equity}}$$

$$(6) \text{ Interest coverage ratio} = \frac{\text{Net income before interest and income taxes}}{\text{Interest expense}}$$

$$(7) \text{ Operating cash flow to interest charges} = \frac{\text{Operating cash flow}}{\text{Interest expense}}$$

$$(8) \text{ Operating cash flow to total liabilities} = \frac{\text{Operating cash flow}}{\text{Average total liabilities}}$$

$$(9) \text{ Receivables turnover ratio} = \frac{\text{Net sales}}{\text{Average accts. receivable}}$$

$$(10) \text{ Inventory turnover} = \frac{\text{Cost of goods sold}}{\text{Average inventory}}$$

$$(11) \text{ Asset turnover} = \frac{\text{Net sales}}{\text{Average total assets}}$$

$$(12) \text{ Average collection period ratio} = \frac{365 \text{ days}}{\text{Receivables turnover ratio}}$$

(13) Average number of days'
      inventory on hand ratio $=$ $\dfrac{365 \text{ days}}{\text{Inventory turnover ratio}}$

(14) Return on assets (ROA) $=$ $\dfrac{\text{Net income}}{\text{Average total assets}}$

                        OR $=$ ROS × Asset turnover

(15) Return on equity (ROE) $=$ $\dfrac{\text{Net income}}{\text{Average total owners' equity}}$

                        OR $=$ ROA × Financial leverage

(16) Return on sales (ROS) $=$ $\dfrac{\text{Net income}}{\text{Net sales}}$

(17) Financial leverage $=$ $\dfrac{\text{Average liabilities + average owners' equity}}{\text{Average owners' equity}}$

(18) Basic earnings per share (EPS) $=$ $\dfrac{\text{NI applicable to common shareholders}}{\text{Weighted average common shares}}$

(19) Cash dividend yield $=$ $\dfrac{\text{Cash dividend per common share}}{\text{Market price per common share}}$

(20) Cash dividend payout $=$ $\dfrac{\text{Total cash dividend to common shareholders}}{\text{Net income}}$

(c) What do you conclude about the availability of the appropriate data in the annual report for calculating these ratios?

(d) What does this financial analysis tell you about ICI?

(e) What analytical metrics did ICI choose to report for itself? What do those choices say about the message the company is striving to tell and the audience it is addressing?

Germany

The German accounting "system is so flexible that it is easily abused."[1]

It is an illusion to believe that the financial statements of a German public limited company would be fully comparable with those of a U.S. corporation if both were drawn up under U.S. GAAP. The economic, social, and legal environment of those enterprises may be so different that the accounting figures can be assessed only taking into account the divergent environments.[2]

Introduction

Although the infrastructure of Germany[3] lay in ruins at the end of World War II, the country currently boasts the third largest economy in the Free World. With the help of the United States, Germany accomplished its *Wirtschaftwunder* (economic miracle) and has again taken a prominent place in the community of nations. Moreover, Germany maintains a powerful position in the European Union. Indeed, it is already the case that the European Monetary Institute (EMI) has moved its headquarters to Frankfurt and the European Monetary System exchange rate mechanism is pegged to the strong German currency, the deutsche mark, or D-mark.[4]

---

[1]G. Steinmetz, "German Shares Are Easy to Buy, But Analysts Warn of Pitfall," *The Wall Street Journal,* March 20, 1995, p. C1.

[2]H. Biener, "What Is the Future of Mutual Recognition of Financial Statements and Is Comparability Really Necessary?" *The European Accounting Review* 3, no. 2 (1994), pp. 335–42.

[3]This chapter primarily reflects the long-standing West German environment. With the unification of the two Germanies, experts believe the West German model of business will dominate; indeed, indications since unification are of a dramatic East German embrace of West German modes. The unification has, however, created certain challenges that are discussed later in this chapter.

[4]The purpose of the EMI is "to strengthen the coordination of monetary policy among EU [member countries'] central banks and promote economic convergence among member [countries] so they can meet the tough criteria which the treaty has prescribed for Emu [European monetary union] membership." See P. Norman, "Chrysalis of a Bank of Europe," *Financial Times,* November 21, 1994, p. XV.

In spite of this country's remarkable economic resurgence and its wealth and power today, Germans as a group are not known for free-wheeling optimism (prior remarks notwithstanding). On the contrary, they are a highly prudential people with a tendency to discourage or suppress excessive risk-taking and speculative behavior. Hostile corporate takeovers, for example, are virtually impossible in Germany in the face of restrictions on equity voting rights and the opposition of banks, which are themselves major corporate shareholders. Likewise, German financial reporting practices have become (along with Japanese financial reporting practices, which were influenced by German principles in the late 19th and early 20th centuries) some of the world's foremost examples of conservatism in measuring profits and valuing assets. Unlike professionals in most other countries, German accountants have been reluctant to even consider the merits of price-level accounting over the last 20 or 30 years. Some of the reasons for this conservatism, historical as well as cultural, are discussed in the next section.

Environmental Factors

Cultural Environment

Hofstede's study of cultural attitudes recorded similar scores by German and U.S. subjects in the areas of power distance (PD) (35 by the Germans, 40 by the Americans) and long-term orientation (LTO) (31 by the Germans, 29 by the Americans). However, the scores in Hofstede's other two areas showed greater discrepancies: the German subjects' score of 67 in individualism (IDV) sharply contrasts with the Americans' score of 91, and the Germans' 65 in uncertainty avoidance (UAV) is considerably higher than the Americans' 46.

What light can these results shed on German financial reporting? The relatively low score in individualism highlights the German consensus-building tendencies. Indeed, "the concept of *Mitbestimmung* or co-determination is deeply ingrained in the national mentality."[5] Such a strong orientation to group consensus building often impedes change, slows decision making, and builds vast webs of rules and regulations. The relatively high score in uncertainty avoidance is manifested in the virtual nonexistence of venture capital and a predilection for investment safety.[6] Together, these two dimensions suggest that the German national culture places a premium on safety, predictability, and adherence to an established system of reasoned, somewhat entrenched, rules. The Germans' low score in the area of PD, which concerns the centralization of power, suggests that authority is primarily vested in systems rather than in individuals. The relatively low LTO score highlights a tendency for thrift, large

---

[5]"Mighty Leap out of Recession," *Financial Times,* September 30, 1994, p. XXII.

[6]See A. Fisher, "Afraid of a Flutter," *Financial Times,* November 21, 1994, p.V and J. Templeman, G. Edmondson, and L. Miller, "Finally, Germany Is Paring the Fat," *Business Week,* October 17, 1994, pp. 64–66.

savings, and a preference for slow and steady progress. Indeed, German companies report interim financial results on a semiannual basis, not a quarterly basis as required in the United States. Based on this configuration of scores, Hofstede typifies German organizations in the cultural paradigm of the ''well-oiled machine,'' which he describes as embodying a technocratic orientation that depends heavily on rules and established procedures instead of on personal command or individual initiative. In fact, German managers tend to believe that their authority with subordinates and their standing with colleagues is earned by their expertise, not their organizational position.[7]

Such scores could also lead one to expect that German financial reporting systems tend to be more static and rigid than U.S. systems. Indeed, German financial reporting practices tend to deemphasize the role of professional judgment, which by its nature must entail a certain amount of individual creativity, subjectivity, and, hence, unpredictability. Most commentators would probably agree with this description, noting the higher degree of uniformity and the greater importance of rules in German financial reporting. This insight, useful as it may be, should not be allowed, however, to create the misconception that German financial reporting is therefore unsophisticated or unprofessional. On the contrary, it is highly sophisticated and requires considerable insight in its application. German accountants and auditors are among the world's most highly trained. The fundamental point is that their training and ability are channeled differently than those of accountants in Anglo-Saxon nations. German accountants are less likely (and, because of the legalistic nature of German accounting, less able) to experiment or innovate than their British or American counterparts. Naturally, the German financial reporting system, characterized as it is by cultural and structural rigidity, changes less frequently than the U.S. or British systems, which are constantly evolving.

Given the cultural predispositions just described, it should not be a surprise that German accounting principles are essentially the product of legislation, created by specific provisions in both tax law and company law. (The legislative process creates the centralized system of rules to which all must adhere.) The cultural importance of this mode of accounting policy formation is that it concerns accountants and auditors primarily with correctness and compliance rather than fairness and disclosure. To illustrate this orientation, one need only examine the traditional German auditor's report, which has only recently been superseded in the pursuit of EU conformity. The orientation it reveals to a large extent persists today in German auditing and accounting. The accepted form reads: ''According to our legally required audit, the accounting, the financial statements, and the annual report comply with statutory provisions and the Company's articles of association.'' The terseness of this statement suggests a rather simple situation: either the law is being complied with or it is not. The sentence conveys little sense that professional judgment is being exercised in the audit or that these financial statements must communicate information to other people, such as investors.

---

[7]C. Lorenz, ''Styles of Execution,'' *Financial Times,* February 23, 1994, p. 9.

Whatever cultural biases German financial reporting (and social policy in general) may have in the direction of uniformity and stability, they have surely been reinforced by German history—specifically the interwar period, with its disastrously high rates of inflation and unemployment. (It is interesting to note that German accounting was in an important formative stage during this time with a uniform chart of accounts appearing for the first time in 1930.) Even now, Germany continues to be perhaps the most inflation-conscious nation in the world. Although inflation indices in Germany have rarely exceeded 5 percent per year in the last 15 years, even these relatively low rates are sometimes sufficient to trigger public anxiety and send officials scurrying to tighten the money supply. Indeed, one of the major reasons that the German business community has consistently and vehemently opposed any form of current cost accounting is its fear that such a scheme might reinforce inflationary expectations among businesspeople and the public at large.

Legal and Political Environment

Individual Tax Law.   Tax laws in Germany are currently designed to encourage individual investors to buy and hold equity shares. Although nominal rates on individual income range from 22 percent to 52 percent and dividends are included in taxable income, the government has adopted an imputation system that grants partial relief from double taxation of corporate profits. The individual taxpayer who receives dividends from a corporation is granted a credit amounting to 36 percent of the sum of the dividend payment plus the credit. For instance, shareholders receiving DM4,000 in dividends would also receive a credit of DM2,250 and would declare income of DM6,250 (4,000 + 2,250) on their tax return. For taxpayers in a 36 percent tax bracket, the credit would exactly offset the extra tax liability generated by the income (6,250 × 36 percent = 2,250). Those in a higher bracket would find the marginal liability attributable to the dividend payment somewhat higher than the credit.

Long-term capital gains on private assets are not taxed in Germany, and securities must be held only six months to qualify as long term. Exceptions to the capital gains exclusion include the sale of a significant interest (25 percent or more) in a business (in which case special rules apply) and the sale of securities held as business assets. Short-term capital gains, net of a DM1,000 exclusion, are included in taxable income.[8]

Corporate Tax Law.   Even though tax rates are relatively high, companies are permitted very generous deductions in reporting taxable income. Corporate tax is levied according to a split-rate system under which undistributed corporate profits are taxed at 45 percent and distributed profits at 30 percent. In Germany, as in a number of other nations (such as Japan and Sweden), book and tax income are required to be substantially the same. This linkage between fiscal and financial reporting has the predictable effect of reinforcing the extreme conservatism with which German companies measure income. For example, the financial depreciation taken by most companies is generally

---

[8]$1 U.S. = DM1.55, as of January 1, 1995.

the maximum allowable under tax law, which in some cases may be triple declining balance (or even more if special incentives apply).

Some differences between book income and taxable income are permitted, one of the most common being the accrual of losses or write-down of assets deemed appropriate for financial reporting purposes but not permissible as a tax deduction. (The willingness to write book income even lower than necessary to procure tax benefits indicates the powerful hold that conservatism has on the German psyche. Tax law is not its only motivation.) A form of deferred tax accounting may be employed when book income diverges from taxable income. If taxable income exceeds book income, giving rise to a potential deferred tax asset, a German company may record the asset on its financial statements only if it blocks an equivalent amount of retained earnings from distribution until the asset is reversed, however, it need not record the asset at all. If, on the other hand, book income exceeds taxable income, giving rise to a potential deferred tax liability, the company must record the liability on the books. In this regard, the recent financial statements of the Hoechst Group, a German chemicals concern, include a footnote stating that it is the policy of the company to record deferred tax liabilities but not deferred tax assets.

One also may locate untaxed reserve accounts on German balance sheets between shareholders' equity and long-term liabilities. These reserves function in a manner very similar to the untaxed reserves on Swedish financial statements (see Chapter 11), allowing firms to defer the recognition of income (i.e., income smoothing) for a stated period of time in accordance with special tax provisions. One such provision encourages overseas investment by allowing German companies to defer the capital gains tax on assets transferred to certain foreign countries; another encourages takeovers of troubled companies by allowing the buyer to place up to 40 percent of the purchase costs in an untaxed reserve. For example, Hoechst includes a footnote in its financial statements (see Exhibit 9–1) regarding untaxed reserves of DM692 million that appear on the parent company's balance sheet.

The preponderance of obscure legal reference versus actual explanation in Exhibit 9–1 reveals what is perhaps the most important effect of tax law on German accounting: an orientation toward compliance instead of disclosure.

EU Membership.   As a founding member of the Common Market and the country with the largest economy in the EU, Germany has continued to push for a broadening and deepening of the European Union.[9] In particular, Germany is in favor of admitting Poland, the Czech Republic, Slovakia, and Hungary by the year 2000. Moreover, Germany strongly favors the single currency (ECU) and an elevated role for the European Parliament. Germany sees itself at the nexus of the European Union and indeed, some commentators have noted that "as Germany goes, so goes Europe."[10]

---

[9]M. M. Nelson, "Kohl's Re-Election Bestows Added Clout in Setting a Course for European Union," *The Wall Street Journal,* October 18, 1994, p. A14.

[10]J. Templeman, "Not What the Doctor Ordered," *Business Week,* October 31, 1994, p. 60.

EXHIBIT 9–1

Hoechst AG Untaxed Reserves Note
Special Reserve Items Subject to Future Taxation

The special reserve items subject to future taxation in Hoechst AG include amounts under Article 6b EStG and section 35 EStR. These amount overall to DM 55 million (DM 26 million in the previous year, also including amounts under Article 52 para 8 EStG). In addition, the special reserve items subject to future taxation also include adjustments which arose under income tax regulations pursuant to Articles 6b, 7D EStG, Article 1 EntwHStG, Article 3 ZonenRFG, Articles 80, 82d EStDV, Article 14 BerlinFG, section 35 EStR, Article 4 FördergebietsG and the former provisions of Article 7C EStG and Articles 79, 82, 82de EStDV. Of the total adjustments of DM 637 million (DM 704 million in the previous year), DM 567 million relates to tangible fixed assets (DM 634 million in the previous year), DM 67 million to investments (DM 67 million in the previous year) and DM 3 million to current assets (DM 3 million in the previous year). Figures for the Hoechst Group are not required since adjustments allowable for tax purposes only and special reserve items subject to future taxation are not shown in the Group balance sheet.

The net income for the year of Hoechst AG increased by DM 14 million (by DM 45 million in the previous year), owing to measures taken solely in accordance with tax regulations. These measures, in the financial year or in previous years, were certain depreciation and write-offs of assets or the setting-up of special reserve items subject to future taxation.

As a result of tax measures, in subsequent years there will be earnings subject to an average tax burden of DM 43 million.

Germany has been deeply involved in the process of harmonizing financial reporting practices among EU member states. In December 1985, the government instituted wide-ranging reforms of the nation's accounting laws to bring them into compliance with both the Fourth and Seventh Directives, as well as with international standards issued by the International Accounting Standards Committee, making Germany one of the first nations to incorporate both directives in its national legal system.

One potentially important effect of EU harmonization is the introduction of the true and fair view criterion into German accounting and auditing. (For more on this criterion, see Chapter 8.) Instead of merely ascertaining that financial statements comply with all relevant provisions of company and tax law, German auditors are now required to express an opinion on the fairness of the documents under examination, including the management report. Changes in the wording of the auditor's report reflect the evolving understanding of the auditor's role. Whereas earlier auditor's reports consisted only of a brief statement on the legality and propriety of the financial statements, since 1987 they have been suggesting that a more complex process of judgment is at work (see Exhibit 9–2).

The movement away from legal compliance toward fair presentation as the proper standard of financial reporting is a direct result of EU negotiations on the Fourth Directive. Some commentators have questioned, however, whether the importation of the true and fair criterion will have much of a practical effect on the extremely conservative valuation and measurement habits of the Germans. As long as tax law continues to

---

EXHIBIT 9–2

German Audit Report: Hoechst Group

The auditors have issued the following opinion:

According to our audit, performed in conformity with our professional duties, the Group financial statements comply with German legal requirements. The Group financial statements present a true and fair view of the net worth, as well as the financial and earnings position of the Group in accordance with the generally accepted German accounting principles. The notes to the Group accounts and the Group management report have been combined with the notes to the accounts and the management report of the parent company, Hoechst AG. The Group management report is in conformity with the Group financial statements.

Frankfurt am Main, 3 March 1994

C&L TREUHAND-VEREINIGUNG
DEUTSCHE REVISION

Wirtschaftsprüfungsgesellschaft
Steuerberatungsgesellschaft

Dr. Kroneberger   Seif
Wirtschaftsprüfer   Wirtschaftsprüfer

---

have a significant influence on financial reporting, the commentators argue that the role of professional judgment in auditing and accounting will be limited.

Business Environment

Form of Business.   German law recognizes two types of limited liability companies as legal entities in their own right: the *Aktiengesellschaft* (AG) and the *Gesellschaft mit beschränkter Haftung* (GmbH). The first of these, the AG, is analogous to the publicly held corporation in the United States and the Plc in Great Britain. It is the only business entity in Germany whose shares may be traded on a stock exchange. The second, the GmbH, is analogous to a privately held corporation. It is generally selected by those owners, such as families, who wish to retain a measure of privacy and close personal control over their business.

An AG must have at least five shareholders at the time of its formation (although afterwards a smaller number of shareholders is permissible). It must possess a minimum share capital of DM100,000 (about $65,000) with at least 25 percent of this amount paid in. The AG is governed by two bodies: a *board of management,* which oversees the day-to-day operations, and a *supervisory board,* which advises company managers on behalf of the shareholders. Although the views of the supervisory board carry considerable weight with management, it usually does not possess the legal power to direct the company. All supervisory board members are appointed by the shareholders (unless a company has more than 500 employees, in which case employee representatives must be included on the board as well).

A GmbH need have only one shareholder at the time of its formation and share capital of at least DM50,000 (about $32,500), with the higher of 25 percent of the capital or DM25,000 paid in. Apart from these numerical differences, a GmbH differs from an AG in other important respects: its shares are not freely transferable, and the responsibility for managing it is usually assumed by one or more individual directors instead of a management board. A GmbH employing fewer than 2,000 employees is not required to form a supervisory board.

Reporting and Audit Requirements.   German businesses must keep accurate and up-to-date business records designed in such a way that an audit may be performed with reasonable dispatch; however, German companies are not required to have their records audited. Firms may avoid the trouble and expense of an audit if they qualify as ''small companies'' by meeting two of the following three criteria: a balance sheet total of less than DM3.9 million (about $2.5 million), annual revenue of less than DM8 million (about $5.2 million), and fewer than 50 employees. (Note that these exemptions follow those set out by the European Union in the Fourth Directive as described in Chapter 3.) All other companies must subject their records to examination by a statutory auditor. In Germany, a statutory audit must be performed by an independent auditor who is a professionally qualified member of the accounting profession. A statutory audit is therefore a good deal more than a mere formality.

In addition, firms that qualify as large companies must publish a complete set of financial statements, along with directors' and auditors' reports, in the *Federal Gazette.* A *large company* is deemed to be one that meets two of the following three criteria: total assets of more than DM15.5 million (about $10 million), annual sales of more than DM32 million (about $20.8 million), and more than 250 employees. Medium-sized firms (i.e., those that qualify neither as large nor as small companies) must file their audited financial statements with the *Trade Register* (where they are open to public examination) but are not required to publish them.

Accounting Profession.   The accounting profession in Germany is well trained and widely respected. The professional title that qualifies one to audit financial statements—***Wirtschaftsprüfer*** (WP)—requires a university degree in economics, law, or a related subject, five years of experience in practice (four of which are in auditing), and successful completion of a rigorous examination. Few candidates manage to achieve full qualification before their early thirties.

Although accounting principles and the duties of auditors are closely legislated in Germany (at least as compared to U.S. standards), the accounting profession provides advice and acts as unofficial interpreter with regard to these areas. The profession also regulates entry into the main professional body, the *Wirtschaftsprüferkammer,* and it investigates and punishes violations of professional ethics and discipline. In addition, it bears primary responsibility for developing standards for audit fieldwork.

The stringent requirements for admission into the accounting profession in Germany have kept the number of WPs low—about 7,000 practitioners serving a nation of over 80 million people—and have created a special difficulty in implementing EU accounting directives. The directives have dramatically increased the number of German companies that must be audited beyond the profession's ability to perform the task. Yet WPs fear that opening the attest function to less qualified practitioners would put both the quality of audits and the profitability of the profession at risk. Consequently, a compromise has been worked out under which medium-sized companies may be audited by less qualified accountants and the requirements for qualification as a WP have been temporarily reduced.

Banks.   Banks play a strong central role in providing capital to German companies, not only by granting loans but also by purchasing shares. When a German company seeks financing, its bank may lend money or buy shares, depending on the immediate financial position of the venture as well as its long-term outlook. Consequently, many German banks have built up sizable shareholdings in nonfinancial companies. A recent annual report of Deutsche Bank, for example, discloses significant equity interests in a number of public companies outside of the banking industry, including a 24 percent stake in Daimler-Benz. In the same report, Deutsche Bank also discloses significant interests in several dozen privately held companies.

Needless to say, the extent of these equity holdings enable German banks to wield an unusual amount of influence over the policies of their clients.[11] The degree of this influence is reflected in the composition of the supervisory boards of many companies. The supervisory board of a large German company typically includes at least one member from a major bank; many include more. A recent annual report of Daimler-Benz, for example, reveals that its supervisory board includes no less than four members from Germany's three major commercial banks: Deutsche Bank, Dresdner Bank, and Commerzbank. (The total membership of the board is 21, including about half a dozen employee representatives as required by law.)

The power of German banks and the presence of their representatives on the supervisory boards of major companies have important implications for financial reporting in Germany. Most important, banks have access to inside information on company operations and therefore do not have to depend on published financial statements as their major source of data. Because their largest shareholders also tend to be both their lenders and to some extent insiders, German companies have relatively little incentive to develop the extensive—and expensive—financial reporting systems that firms in English-speaking countries find necessary to attract and hold investors. Although the disclosure standards governing German financial reporting are more sophisticated than those in countries still dominated by family-owned business cartels (such as Italy), they are simply not as detailed and extensive as those in countries with strong public capital markets and a long tradition of financial stewardship (such as

---

[11]Recent proposed federal legislation has sought to limit a bank's shareholdings to no more than 5 percent of companies' shares. The legislation is not likely to pass. See J. Templeman, ''Suddenly, Germans Love to Hate Their Banks,'' *Business Week,* February 20, 1995, p. 56.

Great Britain). Given this fact, combined with the fact that "under German corporate law, the principle is to protect the creditors and not the shareholders,"[12] it is not surprising that the German "equity markets are underdeveloped by international standards."[13]

Stock Exchanges.   Germany has eight stock exchanges. The Frankfurt exchange, with about 70 percent of the volume of all trading throughout Germany, is the largest, with the other seven operating as regional exchanges. In a move to create a world-class, primary exchange, the Deutsche Borse was created in early 1993. It serves as a holding company for the eight exchanges and has thrust the Frankfurt exchange to center stage. In spite of the global importance of the German economy, it is surprising that the total capitalization of the German stock market is only 27 percent of its gross domestic product, as compared to 61 percent in the United States, 62 percent in Japan, and 143 percent in the United Kingdom. As late as 1993, less than 700 companies were listed on German exchanges (as compared to about 6,500 in the United States, 1,300 in Japan, and 1,400 in the United Kingdom) and only about 6 percent of German adults directly owned company shares (in spite of an average household savings rate of 13 percent, well beyond that of the average U.S. household), as compared to 35 percent in the United States and 20 percent in the United Kingdom.[14] It is also surprising to note that only as recently as 1994 did Germany make insider trading a criminal offense and set up its first Securities and Exchange Commission–like governing body, the Federal Supervisory Agency.[15]

Germany's commercial banks dominate the securities brokerage business, contributing to the lack of a strong equity culture in the country. To this end, the banks have historically focused on brokering for their large investors (e.g., institutions or other corporations), not small investors. Moreover, it is only recently, with a concern for investor fairness protection in mind, that the banks are required to establish "Chinese walls" between their trading and corporate finance departments.[16]

As a consequence of its secondary role, the German capital market has had little impact on financial reporting standards. The notion of shareholder value as a prime concern of German corporations traditionally has simply not existed.[17] Listed companies must supply the stock exchange with copies of their annual reports, but they need not fulfill any other substantial disclosure requirements. The influence of outside investors on financial disclosure is not likely to increase until small investors (or other outsiders) enter the German stock market in greater numbers, or more German

---

[12]Templeman, "Suddenly, Germans Love to Hate Their Banks."

[13]"Frankfurt's Role Consolidated," *Financial Times,* May 31, 1994, p. I.

[14]See G. Whitney, "Big Frankfurt Banks Concentrate Power," *The Wall Street Journal,* May 12, 1994, p. A10; and D. Waller, "Slow Birth of a Watchdog," *Financial Times,* October 25, 1993, p. VII; and A. Fisher, "Afraid of a Flutter," *Financial Times,* November 21, 1994, p. V.

[15]A. Fisher, " 'Tally-ho' Sounds for an Elusive German Breed," *Financial Times,* December 23, 1994, p. 17.

[16]See "Commerzbank AG," *The Wall Street Journal,* November 15, 1994, p. A18; S. Ascarelli, "Germany's Law on Insider Trading Takes Effect Today," *The Wall Street Journal,* August 1, 1994, p. A12; and A. Fisher, "Perturbation in the Boardrooms," *Financial Times,* November 21, 1994, p. IV.

[17]See D. Waller, "Wooing the Shareholders," *Financial Times,* November 27, 1992, p. 15.

companies seek listings on overseas exchanges.[18] (In 1988 Bayer became the first German company to have its shares quoted on the Tokyo exchange, and in 1993 Daimler-Benz became the first German company listed on the New York Stock Exchange—NYSE.) The major change most likely to evolve if such a phenomenon were to occur (and it appears that it will), is an increased level of corporate transparency (i.e., clearer, more extensive, and more timely financial disclosures).[19]

It is also worth noting that in Germany, equity holdings by a pension fund or an insurance company are restricted to 15 percent of their total investment portfolio. Moreover, to the extent that companies in these two industries do make equity investments, they are allowed to invest only in companies with ''respectable'' financial leverage. Many business leaders believe that these restrictions have provided a German business environment that is more conducive to allowing companies to adopt long-term profit orientations rather than short-term profit policies and tactics.

Reunification and Capital Markets.   The reconstruction of the East German economy poses a major challenge for unified Germany that will require a great deal of expensive development capital. No one questions the overall strength of the German economy and its ability to absorb the necessary costs, but some observers have wondered whether German capital markets are modernized and efficient enough to effect a smooth transfer of funds and to capture the confidence of international investors. Critics note such disadvantages as the modest capitalization of the German stock exchanges (mentioned above), outdated procedures for issuing bonds, provincial business practices (e.g., the lack of insider trading safeguards until recently), a low rate of equity investment by the German public, and the resistance of many bankers and financial executives to change. When German officials have demonstrated a willingness to modernize, it has often been the result of external pressures.

By confronting German capital markets with an unprecedented challenge that could strain their resources, reunification has the potential to drive Germany even further into the global mainstream as German companies scramble for investment capital at home and overseas, and German officials reconsider the role of domestic stock and bond markets in the German economy as a whole. The basis for such a reassessment already exists, thanks to the creation of the European Union and Frankfurt's long-range goal of challenging London as Europe's preeminent financial center. Far from prompting a retreat into an isolated nationalism, reunification may well create further impetus for reform and, in the end, draw Germany even further into the complicated and sticky web of international finance.

---

[18]In 1994, the German government passed legislation recommending that publicly held companies lower the nominal value of their capital stock from the traditional DM50 (about $32.50) to DM5 (about $3.25). The purpose of the legislation was to lower the average per share price of German companies in an effort to increase share investments by small investors. Indeed, A. Fisher, ''Afraid of a Flutter,'' reports a recent, slightly positive change in German's preference for investing in shares versus bonds, and A. Sharpe, ''Germany Starts to Open Up,'' *Financial Times,* September 21, 1994, p. IV notes this may be a long-term trend.

[19]See ''Frankfurt's Role Consolidated,'' and A. Fisher, ''Frankfurt Brushes Up Its Act,'' *Financial Times,* December 9, 1994, p. 12.

Labor.   Trade unions have long exerted a powerful influence on German politics and economics that appears in a variety of ways. For example, German industrial workers can boast of the world's highest wages and most restricted working hours.[20] But on the other hand, German industry has a solid commitment to employee consultation and participation; the works council (*Betriebsrat*), for example, is a permanent feature in most companies. In addition, the supervisory boards of companies with more than 500 employees must include employee representatives. For companies with 500 to 2,000 employees, one-third of the board members must be employee representatives; for companies with more than 2,000 employees, the proportion of employee representatives rises to one-half. Thus, German labor relations law grants a measure of real power to employee groups, an arrangement that both management and labor have praised publicly and privately.

Parallel with this commitment to employee consultation is the belief that employees (as stakeholders in an enterprise) are entitled to reasonably clear and complete information about their company. This belief (along with EU guidelines) has had some effect on the financial disclosures that companies must include in their annual reports. Firms are required to provide footnotes revealing total remuneration paid to management and supervisory board members, and they must disclose the average number of employees in each area of the business. Exhibit 9–3 presents notes from the financial statements of the Hoechst Group illustrating a typical format for these disclosures.

In addition to these legally required disclosures, pressure from unions and various political groups has made German companies sensitive to public opinion and encouraged them to experiment with various types of social reporting. Although some companies have included value-added statements (see Chapter 8 on Great Britain) or social accounts statements in their annual reports, the most popular alternative usually involves some form of narrative presentation. The excerpts depicted in Exhibit 9–4 were taken from the annual report of Preussag Group, a transport and plant engineering company; they illustrate the way in which union pressure and public opinion have prompted German companies to provide some form of social reporting. As you examine these pages, be sure to notice the attention paid to newer issues such as gender and parental leave. Fair employment practices and training are also common themes in German social reporting; another issue that frequently appears is protection of the environment.

Perhaps the most troublesome aspect of German unification involves labor. At the end of 1993, unemployment in the 11 states formerly composing West Germany had risen to 8.3 percent while in the five former East German states, unemployment stood at 17.6 percent.[21] Predictions for the next several years forecast that these rates would

---

[20]See Steinmetz, ''German Shares Are Easy to Buy, But Analysts Warn of Pitfall,'' and G. E. Schares, ''Germany's Mighty Unions Are Being Forced to Bend,'' *Business Week,* March 1, 1993, pp. 52–53. The latter reports average hourly industrial wages of about $29 per hour as compared to those in the United States of $24 per hour and in Japan of $21 per hour.

[21]''Germany Survey,'' *The Economist,* May 21, 1994, pp. 3–34.

EXHIBIT 9–3

Hoechst Personnel Disclosures

Personnel Costs

	Hoechst Group		Hoechst AG	
	1993	*1992*	*1993*	*1992*
Wages and salaries	11,677	11,724	4,277	4,422
Compulsory social security contributions and expenses related to pensions and benefit	2,766	2,661	1,140	1,114
of which for pensions	(1,002)	(908)	(499)	(475)
	14,443	14,385	5,417	5,536

Compulsory social security contributions include in particular the social security contributions paid by employers as well as contributions to employers' liability insurance associations. The expenses related to pensions and benefits include mainly pensions paid and allocations or provisions for pensions. Expenses related to provisions for severance and redundancy payments, transfers to external pension funds and insurance premiums for pensions are also shown under this item.

In Hoechst AG, pension payments amount to DM194 million (DM176 million in the previous year).

Average number of employees

Production, auxiliary plants	94,722	97,286	30,359	32,553
Sales	32,001	32,593	6,212	6,407
Research	15,200	15,300	7,057	7,514
Administration, other areas	30,560	32,489	10,627	11,411
	172,483	177,668	54,255	57,885

Information relating to the Board of Management and Supervisory Board of Hoechst AG

The total emoluments of the Supervisory Board amount to DM1,283,407 (DM1,537,250 in 1992).

The total emoluments of the Board of Management amount to DM10,883,466 for Hoechst AG and the Hoechst Group (1992: DM11,978,746).

Pensions for former members of the Board of Management or their surviving dependents amount to DM9,230,709 (1992: DM9,164,247). DM66,052,809 (1992: DM67,795,775) has been set aside for pension commitments vis-à-vis former members of the Board of Management and their surviving dependents.

Loans to members of the Supervisory Board under the general housing promotion scheme for employees amount to DM4,071 (1992: DM6,000). Interest is charged at up to 4.5% on these loans. Some amounts of up to DM10,000 are interest-free. In 1993 DM1,929 was repaid (1992: DM2,900).

At the end of 1993 loans to members of the Board of Management totaled DM49,220 (1992: DM63,380). Interest is charged on these at 4% or 6.5%. In 1993, DM14,160 was repaid (1992: DM25,800).

EXHIBIT 9–4

Preussag Group Employee Disclosures

At the end of the financial year 1992/93, the companies in the Preussag Group employed 73,319 people throughout the world. Weak markets and structural changes have forced some companies to take restructuring measures by way of social plans based on a balance of interests. On the other hand, more than 1,500 new jobs were created in the expanding areas of plant engineering and environmental technology.

Employee Structure

The employee structure was only affected by slight changes. The domestic Group companies reduced the number of employees by almost 2% to 64,099, whilst the share of foreign employees remained constant at 10%. Of these, around 60% were Turkish nationality and 14% came from member countries of the EU. The majority of our foreign employees have worked at Preussag for many years now and have made an important contribution to the Group's success.

The number of employees at our foreign Group companies increased by almost 15% to 9,220. The main reason for this was the reorganization of the international drilling contractor business. The EU accounted for just over 40% of these employees and North American for 18%.

Personnel Costs and Social Benefits

In the last financial year, the net value added of the Preussag Group was DM6,231 million. Of this amount, the employees represent the biggest share with 91.3%. Personnel costs and social benefits increased by a total of 3.7% to DM5,689 million. Of this amount, DM4,499 million was paid to employees in wages and salaries which increased in total by 3.6%. The employer's statutory social security contributions and payments for pensions and assistance increased by 4.1% and amounted to DM1,190 million.

The Group companies fulfilled their pension obligations to some 30,000 former employees or their dependents and more than 55,000 employees acquired vested pension rights, requiring DM295 million.

General and Specialized Training

Our long-term personnel policy is aimed toward investing in young people and training them to meet the ever-changing demands of industry. Group companies are training young people in more than 30 technical and commercial areas in 60 places, a growing number of which is the new Federal States. Traditionally the main areas of training lie in the steel, shipbuilding and coal sectors, but the industries of the future, environmental technology and plant engineering, are beginning to show their strength.

All in all, there are more than 2,100 trainees, most of them working toward a professional qualification. In the last financial year, more than 700 trainees successfully completed their final examinations, the majority of whom were then offered permanent employment at one of the companies of the Group.

Apart from attending specialized external courses, the central training program of the Group was also used intensively for the purpose of training our employees. More than 160 seminars and workshops were well attended. The work in quality circles and other specialist groups within the company under the leadership moderators also achieved increasing success.

Personnel Development

Cooperation throughout the Group has increased considerably in personnel development. This is true in particular of training in the junior management field and the individual promotion and preparation of potential managers for future responsibilities. New management development instruments met with positive response in the promotion programs. Numerous special events, foreign language tuition, local language courses and placements with foreign subsidiaries provided a variety of opportunities for preparing our personnel for new professional responsibilities.

Company Suggestion Scheme

More than 3,900 suggestions for improvements are proof of the commitment of our employees to the company, which benefitted not only the individuals concerned, but also their colleagues and the company as a whole. DM925 thousand was paid out in the form of bonuses and other benefits for the prize winning suggestions and is seen as a valuable investment in the rationalization of production processes, product improvements and increased health and safety.

Preussag Group Employee Disclosures

Health and Safety at Work

The overall positive trend in accident figures did continue. However, this development was overshadowed by tragic fatal accidents. Protecting the heath of our employees and designing trouble-free operating processes so that products and services can be made and provided safely is a major task which our companies are working on in cooperation with works doctors and health insurance companies. Efforts were mainly concentrated on measures to reduce the strain and risk of the working process, the investigation of the causes of sickness and the monitoring of health and safety programs.

The Preussag health insurance scheme is an increasingly important part of our social policy. With around 39,000 insured and more than 30,000 family members also insured, its membership has reached a new record. The continued increase in payments has had to be offset by an increase in the contribution to 12.4% at the moment, but this is still comparatively favorable.

Acknowledgment

Preussag has performed well under the unfavorable economic conditions prevailing in the financial year 1992/93. We would like to thank all our employees and managers who have provided the commitment and motivation to make this possible. We would also like to thank the elected employee representatives at the various companies and at Group level for their objective and conscientious cooperation in dealing with the problems we face.

Personnel of the Preussag Group	Sept. 30, 1993		Sept. 30, 1992		
	Number	*Percent*	*Number*	*Percent*	*Change Number*
Steel and non-ferrous metals production	**17,049**	**23.2**	17,736	24.1	−687
Energy	**13,475**	**18.4**	14,106	19.1	−631
Trading and transport	**7,778**	**10.6**	7,777	10.6	+1
Shipbuilding and rolling stock	**6,713**	**9.2**	7,123	9.7	−410
Plant engineering, environmental and information technology	**16,443**	**22.4**	14,888	20.2	+1,555
Building engineering and components	**10,695**	**14.6**	10,927	14.8	−232
Other companies	**1,166**	**1.6**	1,123	1.5	+43
Total	**73,319**	**100.0**	73,680	100.0	−361
Domestic	**64,099**	**87.4**	65,639	89.2	−1,540
Abroad	**9,220**	**12.6**	8,041	10.8	+1,179

increase. Moreover, the wage differentials between the two former Germanies are substantial. Real wages east of the former border are only about 30 to 40 percent of those west of the border. Clearly, those in the former East Germany do not want such a second-class position and without large increases, they are likely to head west. But if wages go up too fast in the east, companies will lose a major incentive for investing there. Such is but one dilemma springing from unification.

Selected Financial Reporting Practices

Succinctly stated, "the objectives of the German accounting system are to preserve equity, protect creditors, and facilitate the computation of taxable income."[22] In the pursuit of these objectives, the dominant principle imbedded in German accounting practices is that of **prudence** (*Vorsichtsprinzip*) wherein assets (liabilities) may be recorded at values less (higher) than the amounts that would be acceptable under U.S. GAAP.[23] Even with the 1986 Accounting Directives Law, which integrated the EU's Fourth, Seventh, and Eighth Directives into German legislation and, thus, the EU notion of true and fair, it has been "difficult to change decades of established practice merely by changing the law."[24]

Perhaps the most noted German practice in this regard is the use of *hidden reserves* (see subsequent discussion) to smooth earnings via the build up of liabilities and the decrease of earnings in good years and vice versa in so-called bad years. Such a practice has been linked to several contextual factors.[25] First, German law prohibits firms from retaining more than half of their annual earnings, thus, a sizable percent of earnings are potentially available for dividend payout. To minimize such outflows, companies have an incentive to minimize reported earnings in "good" years and to provide some stable level of dividends through "bad" years. Second, because of this dividend situation and given the banks' dominant role in financing and governing German companies, bankers' interests are protected by companies preserving cash (i.e., minimizing total dividend payouts) and, thus, preserving a strong debt-service capability. Third, because of the close link between tax and financial accounting, German management has incentive to minimize reported financial earnings. Fourth, as previously noted, labor unions are a powerful force in the German economy. Many believe that smoothing reported earnings serves to mitigate labor's demand for ever-increasing wages. Last, the devout adherence to the prudence (i.e., conservatism) principle is consistent with the German psyche that is relatively high on uncertainty avoidance.

If Germany seeks to improve its ability to draw on the world's financial resources, it must heed the call for greater transparency (i.e., fuller disclosures) in its companies' financial statements. As of March 1995, only one German company, Daimler-Benz, has met the U.S. financial reporting requirements that allowed it to achieve a NYSE listing. Thus, the world's most extensive equity market is virtually closed to German companies, in part, because of financial reporting practices that give "management the freedom to report what they want."[26] Since Daimler-Benz's 1993 financial reporting

---

[22]T. S. Harris, M. Lang, and H. P. Möller, "The Value Relevance of German Accounting Measures: An Empirical Analysis," *Journal of Accounting Research,* Autumn 1994, p. 190.

[23]T. S. Doupnik, "Recent Innovations in German Accounting Practice through the Integration of EC Directives," *Advances in International Accounting* 5 (1992), pp. 75–103.

[24]C. L. Corbridge, W. Austin, and D. J. Lemak, "Germany's Accrual Accounting Practices," *Management Accounting,* August 1993, p. 46.

[25]See Harris et al., "The Value Revelance of German Accounting Measures," and Doupnik, "Recent Innovations in German Accounting Practice through the Integration of EC Directives."

[26]"Company News," *Financial Times,* November 22, 1993, p. 17.

change of heart and NYSE listing, ''there has hardly been a rush [by other German companies] to follow.''[27]

Consolidation

German companies with domestic subsidiaries must prepare and publish audited financial statements if they meet two of the following three size criteria: have consolidated balance sheet total assets exceeding DM125 million (about $81.3 million), consolidated annual revenues exceeding DM250 million ($162.5 million), and more than 5,000 employees. If a German parent company is itself a subsidiary of another non-German, EU company that consolidates the German company according to EU directives, the German Commercial Code exempts the German parent from preparing consolidated financial statements. In preparing consolidated financial statements, both the purchase and pooling-of-interests methods are permitted; all domestic and foreign subsidiaries must be consolidated except if (1) a subsidiary is insignificant in relation to the group's net worth, total assets, and earnings; (2) the inclusion of the results of the subsidiary would be detrimental to a true and fair presentation of the group's results; or (3) the subsidiary is being held for sale. The equity method of accounting for interests of 20 percent or more in affiliates is also practiced.

Valuation

German accounting is fundamentally committed to a highly conservative application of historical cost as the most appropriate basis for valuation. (As discussed, both cultural bias and tax policy support this orientation.) All prospective losses are to be recognized via accruals and write-downs, but prospective gains and appreciation of assets may not be recorded until realized. Historical cost for fixed assets is the cost of acquisition; thus, extraordinary write-downs (appropriate if an impairment in value is expected to be permanent) may be reversed in future periods if an asset recovers its original value. However, an asset may never be written up above historical cost or, in the case of depreciable assets, not above net book value as though ''regular'' depreciation had continued to be charged. Historical cost for current assets operates somewhat differently. Because the historical cost of a current asset is defined as its book value at the beginning of a period, write-downs can never be reversed until the asset is disposed of. German companies are required to detail in their annual reports the increases and decreases to each of their long-term assets.

Inventories

Inventories are carried at the lower of cost or net realizable value. Manufacturing overhead costs may be treated as product costs or period costs. Cost must be allocated directly (i.e., specific identification), if possible; otherwise, the appropriate method is

---

[27]''More Capital, Less Privacy,'' *Financial Times,* March 29, 1995, p. 13.

usually the moving weighted average. FIFO is acceptable only if the corresponding physical flow can be demonstrated, and LIFO has been accepted only since 1990.

Goodwill

The purchase price paid for the assets of a business must be allocated among the individual assets acquired on the basis of their fair market values. Any excess is considered goodwill, which generally is amortized over four years on a straight-line basis.[28] A longer period may be used if appropriate under the circumstances. Goodwill arising from consolidation may be, and often is, charged directly against retained earnings. Negative goodwill is reported on the consolidated balance sheet as the difference arising on capital consolidation, usually under the classification heading deferred income; it may be amortized to current income only under certain conditions.

Research and Development

Research and development costs are expensed as incurred unless they are for a specific product and can be considered the beginning phase of that product's manufacturing process. Patents that are purchased are capitalized and amortized over their useful lives on a straight-line basis. Organization costs may not be capitalized.

Pensions and Postretirement Benefits

Beginning January 1, 1987, German companies were required to accrue all pension and postretirement benefits earned after that date. No accrual was required for benefits earned prior to 1987, although most German companies did so to take advantage of existing tax benefits.

In Germany, most pension plans are not funded via a third-party trustee as in the United States; the plans are in-house and the plan assets are essentially all the company's balance sheet assets. Because of this fact, the typical German company pension obligation reflected on its balance sheet is an amount similar to the accumulated benefit obligation. This is in contrast to a U.S. company that would report the liability as the difference between the accumulated benefit obligation and the fair market value of the plan assets held by the trustee.

Contingencies

Company law permits German companies to provide for estimated *future* expenses or losses so long as they are possible (as opposed to the more stringent notion of probable) and reasonable. Thus, under the principle of prudence, German companies may, for example, record accruals that, over time, equalize the annual expenses for (1) anticipated major repairs that have not, as of year-end, been undertaken; (2) research and

---

[28]For tax purposes, the amortization period for goodwill is fixed at 15 years.

development projects not yet started; and (3) advertising and promotional campaigns not yet executed.[29] Until the 1986 Accounting Directives Law, German law permitted an extreme application of the concept of prudence in which such liability reserves could be liberally used to stabilize earnings.[30] Although this activity was supposed to be attenuated beginning in 1986, traditional practice is often difficult to curtail, and as recently as 1993 (see Exercise 9.3), major German companies have publicly acknowledged the continued use of hidden reserves. Likewise, in 1989, Schering AG reported such accruals equal to 12 percent of total assets and an increase in the accruals that year equal to 45 percent of pre-tax earnings.[31]

Shareholder Capital and Reserves

Shareholder equity generally comprises minority interests, share capital, and reserve accounts, which may be either capital or revenue reserves. Both ordinary and preferred shares may be issued, and details as to voting rights (particularly when multiple voting rights are involved) must be disclosed, along with a stock's nominal or par value. Capital reserves include amounts received for the issue of shares in excess of their nominal (or par) value, payments by shareholders with respect to subscribed shares, and amounts paid for conversion rights on debentures. Revenue reserves, on the other hand, are prescribed by the Commercial Code and include the following:

- Reserves required by a company's articles of incorporation (e.g., appropriations of earnings for various purposes—company officers can transfer up to 50 percent of annual net profit to reserves without shareholder approval).
- Reserve for treasury stock (equivalent to the value of treasury stock held).[32]
- Legal reserve (i.e., 5 percent of each year's profits must be allocated to this reserve until the reserve reaches 10 percent of the par value of share capital, net of any loss carryforwards).

Dividends may be distributed from retained earnings and the excess of revenue reserves over any capitalized expenses.

Special Items with an Equity Component

This potentially confusing account represents income that has not yet been subject to income taxes. It usually represents the excess (or ''extraordinary'') depreciation, permitted by German tax law, used to currently shelter otherwise taxable income. As the

---

[29]See Corbridge et al., ''Germany's Accrual Accounting Practices.''

[30]These reserves can be created by underreporting revenues and cash inflows or by overstating expenses and cash outflows. During periods of reduced profitability, such reserves can be reversed as a mechanism to increase (i.e., smooth) reported earnings. The use of such reserves is often referred to as the ''creation of financial slack'' and ''hidden reserves.''

[31]See Doupnik, ''Recent Innovations in German Accounting Practice.''

[32]Treasury stock is usually accounted for as an asset under the account heading Temporary Investments.

name implies, the account reflects both an equity component (i.e., income) and a debt component (i.e., the future taxes owing on the sheltered income.)

Exhibit 9–5 presents a list of accounting principles taken from Preussag's 1993 annual report and reflects the influence of tax-driven accounting practices common to many German corporations. Exhibit 9–6 presents a summarized comparison of German and U.S. accounting and financial reporting standards.

EXHIBIT 9–5

Preussag Group Accounting Principles Disclosures

Notes on the Consolidated Financial Statements of the Preussag Group and on the Financial Statements of Preussag AG for the Financial Year 1992/93

The Consolidated Financial Statements of the Preussag Group and the Financial Statements of Preussag AG were prepared in accordance with the provisions of the Commercial Code, with due consideration of the supplementary regulations of the Companies' Act. In the balance sheets and the profit and loss statements of the Preussag Group and of Preussag AG, individual items have been grouped together for clarity of presentation; these items are referred to separately in these notes, together with the necessary explanations. The notes relating to the Consolidated Financial Statements and to the Financial Statements of Preussag AG are presented jointly.

The financial year of Preussag AG and of the Group runs from 1st October in any one year to 30th September of the following year.

Accounting and Valuation Methods

The same accounting and valuation methods as stipulated by Preussag AG were retained. Use was made of tax-related valuation options as in previous years.

Intangible and tangible assets were valued at cost of acquisition or manufacture, less scheduled depreciation. Manufacturing costs were determined on the basis of German tax regulations.

Depreciation was largely calculated on the basis of the following economic lives: 25–50 years for buildings; 5–20 years for plant and machinery including ships and railway cars; 3–10 years for other assets as well as for plant and office equipment.

Tangible fixed assets with a limited useful economic life were depreciated on the declining balance method, applying maximum rates allowable for tax purposes. Straight-line depreciation was then applied when the calculated amount based on this method exceeded that obtained by using the declining balance method. If use was made of tax-related extraordinary depreciation, assets were depreciated on the straight-line method. In accordance with tax simplification regulations, additions in the first half of the financial year were depreciated at the full rate for the year, whereas additions during the second half of the year were depreciated at half the annual rate. Low-value assets were written off in full in the year of acquisition.

For buildings and other real estate, depreciation was calculated either pro rata temporis on a straight-line basis, or, where permitted by tax regulations, on a declining balance basis.

If, at the financial year-end, the fixed asset was given a lower value, which was expected to be permanent, then the difference was offset by way of extraordinary depreciation expenses.

Use was made of tax-related options of depreciation methods and possibilities for transferring book profits. The resulting differences in relation to scheduled depreciation were included in the Financial Statements of Preussag AG under special non-taxed items. In the Consolidated Financial Statements, such special non-taxed items were dissolved and added to the revenue reserves while allowing for deferred taxation.

Investment allowances and subsidies received were absorbed without affecting results.

Fixed values have been established for reserve parts, factory equipment and rail installations. These accounted for 20–40% of the cost of acquisition or manufacture.

Successful crude oil and natural gas wells were generally depreciated on a declining balance basis, in accordance with the provisions of the State Ordinance (letter from the Federal Ministry for Finance dated 20th May 1980), whereas older wells were depreciated at reducing rates in line with the so-called Hanover Guidelines. Dry holes were written off in full.

EXHIBIT 9–5 (continued)
Preussag Group Accounting Principles Disclosures

Shares in Group companies and participation as well as other investments were valued at the cost of acquisition, or at the lower appropriate value. Non-interest or low-interest loans were discounted to their present values.

Inventories were valued on the basis of cost of acquisition or manufacturing costs, or at any lower appropriate value. Similar inventories were generally dealt with on the basis of the valuation simplification method (LIFO method).

Unfinished and finished goods and work in progress were valued on the basis of manufacturing costs, while observing the principle of the lower of cost or market value. They comprise direct material and production costs as well as proportions of indirect costs and depreciation as required by German tax laws and appropriate indirect cost surcharges for companies abroad. Coal stocks have been shown at the lower of production costs or the values determined in accordance with the guidelines of the Ruhr Mining Enterprises' Association. Where necessary, additional devaluation was applied. As far as risks in stock value were foreseeable, appropriate devaluations have been made. Advance payments received were fully offset against inventories.

In the case of receivables and other current assets, all identifiable individual risks and the general credit risk were taken into consideration by means of appropriate provisions.

Securities were shown at the rate of acquisition or the market rate as of the financial year-end, if lower.

Provisions for pensions, which also included coal-supply rights, early retirement and bridging payment rights, were itemized at the allowable value as per Section 6a of the Income Tax Law, calculated on actuarial principles based on an interest rate of 6%. In the case of personnel of foreign companies, the guidelines provided by national legislation have been observed.

Tax provisions and other provisions were valued in accordance with sound business principles.

Liabilities were shown at the repayable amount.

EXHIBIT 9–6
Comparison of German and U.S. Accounting and Reporting Standards

Item	Germany	United States
Asset valuation	Historical cost, applied conservatively (i.e., principally downward revaluation)	Historical cost, with selected revaluation (principally downward)
Inventory valuation	Principally specific identification or moving weighted average method; FIFO and LIFO permitted, although rarely used	Principally LIFO (because of tax considerations); also FIFO and average cost methods
Inventory: year-end	Lower of cost or replacement cost	Lower of cost or replacement cost
Depreciation	Straight line, accelerated methods, and production based methods permitted; excess (or extraordinary) depreciation based on tax code permitted and frequently used	Principally straight line, with accelerated methods permitted
Goodwill	Goodwill either capitalized and amortized over (preferably) 4 years (15 years for tax purposes), or charged directly to reserves; negative goodwill reported as ''difference arising on capital consolidation'' on balance sheet and may be taken to income under certain conditions	Capitalized to balance sheet, with amortization (principally straight line) over a maximum of 40 years; negative goodwill not permitted

---

EXHIBIT 9–6 (continued)

Comparison of German and U.S. Accounting and Reporting Standards

Research and development costs	Principally expensed as incurred	Research costs expensed currently; development costs expensed currently except in certain industries (i.e., software, oil and gas)
Capitalized interest costs	Capitalization permitted but not required	Capitalization required for self-constructed assets
Intercorporate investments:		
Marketable securities (current asset-trading)	Lower-of-cost-or-market value	Mark to market (on an individual security basis), with unrealized gains and losses taken to income
Long-term-investments:		
0–20% ownership (available for sale)	Lower-of-cost-or-market value	Mark to market (on an individual security basis), with unrealized gains and losses reported on balance sheet (i.e., owners' equity)
20–50% ownership	Lower-of-cost-or-market value; equity method principally used when a company, included in the consolidated statements of a group, has a significant shareholding in another unconsolidated company.	Equity method
51–100% ownership	Consolidated except when controlled subsidiary is held for resale, when value is immaterial relative to the group, or when consolidation would be detrimental to a true and fair view of the group; both pooling and purchase accounting permitted	Consolidated, using pooling or purchase accounting
Debt valuation	Principally face or settlement value, although present value permitted	Long-term debt (except deferred income taxes) valued at present value; all other debt valued at face or settlement value
Leases	Financing leases capitalized to the balance sheet; significant operating lease commitments disclosed in footnotes	Capital leases reflected in balance sheet; operating leases disclosed in footnotes
Deferred income taxes	Largely unnecessary due to close conformity of book and taxable income; when present, often not disclosed	Computed under liability method
Pension liabilities	Reflected on balance sheet and likely to be an amount equal to the accumulated benefit obligation	Reflected on balance sheet and equal to the accumulated benefit obligation less the fair market value of the plan assets
Discretionary reserves	General-purpose reserves permitted	Restricted to identifiable operational losses
Statement of cash flows	Not required	Required

Analytical Considerations

As noted, German financial reporting has an observable conservative bias that, not surprisingly, tends to understate the value of a firm's net assets and often its net earnings as well. The reasons for this, which are both cultural (historical) and institutional, include the following:

- *Legal requirements.* German accounting adheres strictly to company law, which results in an emphasis on legal form rather than economic substance.

- *Book-tax conformity.* Most deductions taken for tax purposes must also be recognized for accounting book purposes. As a consequence, excess depreciation claimed for tax purposes is also reflected in the accounting statements.

- *Creditor orientation.* German financial reporting tends to be principally oriented to creditor protection, rather than to investor returns.[33] As a consequence, greater attention is directed to provisions for asset write-downs and contingencies than would be found in, say, the United States or Great Britain.

The principal accounting factors causing the relative understatement of net worth and earnings of German companies include the following:

- *Excess depreciation of fixed assets.* German tax law permits accelerated depreciation at up to three times the straight-line rate; thus, German companies write off their fixed assets at a much faster rate than do U.S. companies. In addition, special tax allowances provided for investments in environmental protection equipment, R&D facilities, and equipment for R&D facilities effectively increase the tax basis, and thus, depreciation write-offs of these investments.

- *Contingency reserves.* Company law permits German companies to provide for estimated future expenses (or losses) so long as they are *possible* and *reasonable.* Under U.S. GAAP, the criteria to establish contingency reserves (i.e., a loss must be both *probable* and *measurable*) are more stringent. Thus, contingency reserves represent the primary means by which German companies smooth earnings. When general contingency reserves are created, they typically appear under the account rubric Other Provisions; and, when reserves created in prior years are no longer considered necessary, they are reported under Other Income on the income statement. The use of hidden or off-balance-sheet reserves adds further conversatism to reported results.

- *Accounting for long-term contracts.* The predominant treatment of long-term contracts in Germany is the completed-contract method, by which substantially all profits are deferred until the provisions of a contract are

---

[33]Additional evidence of a noninvestor orientation is the absence of a requirement for German companies to report earnings per share data.

EXHIBIT 9–7
German versus U.S. GAAP: A Comparison of the Financial Statement Effects

Item	Financial Statement Effect	Financial Ratio Effect
Excess depreciation	Fixed assets, total assets, and shareholders' equity understated	ROS understated*
		Leverage overstated
	Depreciation expense overstated; net income understated	Total and noncurrent asset turnover overstated
Contingency reserves	Liabilities overstated; shareholders' equity understated	ROA and ROS understated*
		Leverage overstated
	Net income understated	
Completed-contract accounting	Total assets, shareholders' equity, and net income understated	ROS understated*
		Leverage overstated
Goodwill write-off	Total assets, shareholders' equity, and net income understated	ROS understated*
		Leverage overstated

*Since both net income and shareholders' equity are understated, the effect of these German accounting treatments on return on equity cannot be systematically predicted.

---

essentially complete. In the United States, the prevailing accounting practice is the percentage-of-completion method. The completed-contract method tends to result in a lower reported earnings figure in all years except the year of contract completion. The method also causes substantial volatility in earnings (which may be controlled in German companies through the creation of general contingency reserves and hidden reserves).

- *Goodwill write-off.* Prior to 1987, the prevalent treatment of goodwill in Germany was the charge-to-equity method. Currently, prevalent practice is to capitalize goodwill to the balance sheet and amortize it against earnings over a 4- to 5-year period (to a maximum of 20 years). In the United States, the capitalization of goodwill is required, and amortization is normally over 40 years.

The relative financial statement effects in general, and on selected financial ratios in particular, of these accounting differences are summarized in Exhibit 9–7. A related issue is the extent to which the capital markets of Germany and the United States compensate for these accounting differences when pricing equity securities. Recent market data (i.e., as of year-end 1993) reveal the average price-earnings ratio of U.S. stocks to be 23; for German stocks it is 21. These P-E averages reflect, in part, the presence of a "bull" market in the United States and a "bear" market in Germany during 1993. That fact aside, however, the relative equality of the two P-E averages suggests that German securities may be somewhat *underpriced* as compared to U.S. securities. In the absence of differences in investor expectations regarding the strength of the German and U.S. economies, we normally expect the average P-E ratio for Germany to be substantially higher than that for the United States as a consequence of conservative German accounting practices.

Summary

October 3, 1990, marked the beginning of a new Germany "anchored in the west, while looking to the east, [that] may prove a source of stability in Europe."[34] Clearly, unification harbors as many challenges as it does opportunities. Helmut Kohl, former Chancellor of West Germany and the elected first chancellor of unified Germany has noted, however, that the very positive economic condition of West Germany in 1990 provided a fortuitous and sound base from which the economic challenges of unification could be tackled. Indeed, experts believe that German unity will result in only a modest change in the already successful position of the former West Germany. The joy with which the two Germanies embraced one another has been tempered, nonetheless, by the former East German's belief that the economic failures of the past 50 years were due to no fault of their own and that the (former) West Germans are willing to share their successes, but only to an extent. Living standards and productivity in the east, at the time of unification, were less than half that in the west. Thus, fears of counterproductive nationalistic feelings are well grounded, as are fears of growing unemployment in the east. The world is hoping for a successful German marriage, but with the world's highest labor costs, low and falling demand for its products, an overvalued currency, and an extremely burdensome social welfare system, its future holds significant challenges.

Suggested Readings

Abel, R. "A Comparative Simulation of German and U.S. Accounting Principles." *The Journal of Accounting Research,* Spring 1969, pp. 1–11.

Alexander, D., and S. Archer. *The European Accounting Guide.* London: Academic Press, 1991.

Berton, L. "No Comparisons: The Bottom Line Is that Accounting and Disclosure Rules Overseas Are a Minefield for the Uninitiated." *The Wall Street Journal,* September 22, 1989, p. 30.

Carson, I. "Accounting for Europe's Differences." *International Management,* June 1991, pp. 52–55.

Corbridge, C. L., W. W. Austin, and D. J. Lemak. "Germany's Accrual Accounting Practices." *Management Accounting,* August 1993, pp. 45–47.

Doupnik, T. S. "Recent Innovations in German Accounting Practice through the Integration of EC Directives," *Advances in International Accounting* 5 (1992), pp. 75–103.

"Germany Survey." *The Economist,* May 21, 1994, pp. 1–34.

Haller, A. "The Relationship of Financial and Tax Accounting in Germany: A Major Reason for Accounting Disharmony in Europe." *The International Journal of Accounting* 27, no. 4, 1992, pp. 310–23.

---

[34]"Germany's Third Chance," *Financial Times,* October 3, 1990, p. 14.

Harris, T. S., M. Lang, and H. P. Möller. "The Value Relevance of German Accounting Measures: An Empirical Analysis." *Journal of Accounting Research,* Autumn 1994, pp. 187–209.

Ordelheide, D. "True and Fair View: A European and a German Perspective." *European Accounting* Review 1 (1993), pp. 81–90.

Orsini, L., L. McAllister, and R. Parish. *World Accounting.* New York: Matthew Bender, 1992.

Price Waterhouse. *Doing Business in Germany.* New York: Price Waterhouse, 1991.

ISSUES AND INFORMATION FOR FURTHER INQUIRY

I.9.1   Deutsche Borse, AG

In a July 1, 1993, *Financial Times* article (p. 15), "Survey of German Banking and Finance," author David Waller muses, "Frankfurt is now the undisputed financial capital of Germany [but] is it on the verge of becoming the financial capital of Europe?" He cites one of the recent events that represents a giant step in that direction is the creation of the Deutsche Borse, the German stock exchange.

Required:

    (a) Research and chronicle the forces leading to the recent creation of the Deutsche Borse. What does this portend for the German and European equity markets?

    (b) Does this suggest an increased importance of the shareholder? Explain.

    (c) Detail the requirements for a listing on the Deutsche Borse. Do these seem shareholder oriented to you? Explain.

I.9.2   Change to a Core Level

In an April 29, 1993, *Financial Times* article (p. 18), "Daimler-Benz Gears Up for a Drive on the Freeway," author David Waller notes:

> German accounting differs from Anglo-American in a number of important areas. It is conditioned by tax laws and the requirement to put the interests of creditors above those of other users of accounts, for example shareholders. Although recent [EU] legislation has meant that group accounts have become more transparent, German accounting is still characterised by conservatism and a want of pertinent detail.
>
> The differences reflect contrasting styles of capitalism: the Anglo-American variety where the capital market plays an important role in the economy, and the Germanic, where there are only 665 listed companies and the stock market represents far smaller percentage of GDP than in the U.S. or the U.K.

As a partial but significant consequence of this fact, is the belief that:

> One of the ways in which the international investment community is ill-served [by German companies] is in the quality of accounting information.
>
> The poor quality of financial information available from many German companies makes it difficult for investors to buy a stock with confidence since valuations cannot be clearly established. . . . Few companies give any indication of divisional profits breakdown at the kind of level which would allow the investor to track margins over time and make comparison across companies.

Mr. Waller continues by noting that ''just as important as the impact on reported profits [of an adoption of U.S. accounting practices by German companies] are the longer-term cultural changes which are likely to be induced by greater accounting transparency.'' He goes on to cite the examples of segmental reporting and a U.S.-style statement of cash flows.

Required:

(a) How are these indicative of a ''cultural change''?

(b) Identify three other such changes likely to be experienced by German companies as a result of an entry into the U.S. capital markets.

EXERCISES

E.9.1   Accounting for Shareholders' Equity

The following is the shareholders' equity section of the 1993 balance sheet for Hoechst AG, a large German chemical and pharmaceutical company and parent company of the Hoechst Group.

Using journal entries, explain the changes in the company's shareholders' equity accounts from 1992 to 1993.

Required:

Selected Financial Information

Hoechst AG Stockholders' Equity

(DM, Millions)

	Notes	*31 Dec. 1993*	*31 Dec. 1992*
Subscribed capital	(9)	2,940	2,925
Capital reserves		3,898	3,880
Revenue reserves		3,243	3,226
Unappropriated retained earnings	(11)	412	527
Stockholders' equity	(8)	10,493	10,588

Selected Footnote Information

(8) Movement of equity

Hoechst Group	1.1.1993	Capital paid in	Net income for the year	Dividend payment	Currency translation	Other changes	31.12.1993
Subscribed capital of Hoechst AG	2,925	15					2,940
Capital reserves of Hoechst AG	3,880	18					3,898
Other revenue reserves	5,033		466	527	202	−847	4,327
Equity of Hoechst AG stockholders	**11,838**	**33**	**466**	**527**	**202**	**−847**	**11,165**
Shares of minority interests	2,018	37	290	150	65	115	2,375
	13,856	70	756	677	267	−732	13,540

Hoechst AG		Capital paid in	Net income for the year	Dividend payment	Transfer of net income for the year	
Subscribed capital	2,925	15				2,940
Capital reserves	3,880	18				3,898
Other revenue reserves	3,226				17	3,243
Unappropriated retained earnings	527	—	429	527	−17	412
	10,558	33	429	527	—	10,493

Goodwill of DM882 million was offset against the revenue reserves in the Hoechst Group under ''other changes.'' Subsidiaries and associated companies consolidated for the first time have generated a credit difference of DM67 million. Owing to the nature of this item, DM25 million was allocated to the revenue reserves and DM12 million has been shown in the 1993 income statement. A provision amounting to DM30 million has been set up for probable expenditures in the following years. The Group revenue reserves include the unappropriated retained earnings of Hoechst AG. In Hoechst AG, the increase in capital reserves by DM18 million relates to exercised option rights.

(9) Capital of Hoechst AG

The subscribed capital was increased by DM15 million (294,141 shares) from the unissued capital stock owing to the exercise of option rights.

Breakdown of the subscribed capital:

Number of shares	Nominal value in DM	Subscribed capital in DM
38,215,369	50	1,910,768,450
1,115,000	100	111,500,000
545,000	200	109,000,000
399,000	500	199,500,000
609,000	1,000	609,000,000
		2,939,768,450

Authorized capital:

Authorization until 5 June 1994	250
Authorization until 3 June 1996	500
	750

(10) Minority interests

This item comprises minority stockholders' interests in the equity of consolidated subsidiaries, in some cases after adjustment to the accounting principles of Hoechst AG.

(11) Unappropriated retained earnings of Hoechst AG

	DM
Net income for 1993	428,567,583
Profit brought forward from the previous year	—
	428,567,583
Transfer to revenue reserves	17,000,000
Unappropriated retained earnings	411,567,583
Proposed dividend payment	411,567,583
Profit brought forward	—

The Board of Management and Supervisory Board of Hoechst AG transferred DM17 million from the net income for the year to the revenue reserves. Their proposal to the Annual General Meeting will be that DM411567583 from the unappropriated retained earnings to distributed as dividend.

E.9.2   Special Items with an Equity Component

Under German tax laws, companies in certain industries are permitted (but not required) to depreciate their fixed assets at a rate in excess of normal historical cost-based depreciation. This special (or "extraordinary") depreciation is granted as an investment incentive and enables a company to currently shelter otherwise taxable income.

The following is selected financial information from the 1993 annual report of Deutsche Lufthansa, the national airline of Germany.

Required:

(a) Using journal entries, explain the change in Lufthansa's "special items with an equity portion" account in 1993.

(b) Based on a statutory tax rate of 45 percent (for undistributed profits), calculate Lufthansa's tax benefit from special depreciation in 1993 and in aggregate through year-end 1993.

(c) What comparable tax incentives exist for U.S. companies?

(d) For purposes of ratio analysis, how should the special items with an equity portion be classified: debt, equity, or neither?

Selected Financial Information

	(DM, thousands)	
	31 Dec. 1993	*31 Dec. 1992*
Net loss	91,614	391,123
Shareholders' equity	2,136,512	2,280,857
Special items with an equity portion	1,555,822	1,473,035
Provisions	4,429,370	4,192,7575
Liabilities	9,288,373	8,923,193
Total equities	17,410,077	16,869,842

Selected Footnote Information

Special items with an equity portion

Group	*Dec. 31, 93 (DM000)*	*Dec. 31, 92 (DM000)*
Value adjustments to fixed assets in accordance with §82f EStDV, §7d EStG, §14 BerlinFG and §2 DDR-IG	1,555,822	1,471,685
Reserves in accordance with §52(5) EStG	—	1,350
	1,555,822	1,473,035

Company		
Value adjustments to fixed assets in accordance with §82f EStDV and §7d EStG	1,343,288	1,378,768
Reserves in accordance with §52 (5) EStG	—	1,227
	1,343,288	1,379,985

The difference between the financial depreciation allowed under commercial law and that permitted by tax regulations appears under special items with an equity portion. §82f EStDV makes it possible to claim depreciation up to 30 percent of the acquisition costs on new aircraft in addition to normal depreciation. §7d EStG allows higher depreciation for measures which benefit environment protection.

The changes in special items with an equity portion have relieved the result from ordinary activities of the Company by DM37 million (previous year: DM476 million); Group's result has been charged with DM83 million (previous year: relief DM424 million). The tax on income resulting from the release of special items still existing will be spread over the course of the up to twelve-year release period (Group) or up to the ten-year release period (Company).

E.9.3   Analyzing Hidden Reserves

In December 1993, Volkswagen AG disclosed that the company was likely to report a consolidated loss of DM2.3 billion (or approximately $1.35 billion) for fiscal year 1993. Auto industry analysts in Europe, however, expressed skepticism that the company could achieve that level of earnings without drawing on hidden reserves. Analysts observed that the German auto market had steadily deteriorated in 1993, with VW sales down 24 percent.

In response to analysts' concerns, VW Chairman F. Piech denied that bookkeeping exercises would be used to enhance the company's profitability. Analysts familiar with German company accounting practices remained skeptical, however.

Required:

When analyzing a company's financial data, what information should be considered to help identify whether hidden reserves have been used to enhance reported results?

E.9.4   Analyzing Inventories

The last-in, first-out (LIFO) inventory valuation method is considered accepted accounting practice in only a few countries including Germany and the United States. According to the annual report of the BASF Group, a diversified German conglomerate, the company used LIFO to value a substantial portion of its inventory and average cost was used to value the remainder.

The following are selected financial data for the BASF Group as of year-end 1993, as well as the company's inventory footnote as it appeared in the annual report.

Required:

(a) Calculate the current value of the Group's inventory at year-end 1992 and 1993. (The LIFO reserve at year-end 1992 was DM534.3 million.)

(b) Calculate the Group's approximate net income (before tax) for 1993 assuming that FIFO (instead of LIFO) had been used to value its inventory.

(c) Compare the Group's inventory turnover ratio for 1993 under LIFO and FIFO.

(d) Comment on the decline in the Group's LIFO reserves from 1992 to 1993.

Selected Financial Data

	(DM, Millions)	
	31 Dec. 1993	*31 Dec. 1992*
Inventories	6,039.4	6,441.7
Sales (net)	40,568.4	41,932.8
Cost of sales	27,646.8	28,236.8
Net income (before tax)	1,057.6	1,239.4

Selected Footnote Information

Inventories

| | BASF Group | | BASF AG | |
	1993	*1992*	*1993*	*1992*
Raw materials and supplies			**305.9**	395.6
Work in process, finished				
goods and merchandise	**5,886.8**	6,293.8	**1,445.1**	1,627.0
Uncompleted contracts	**147.3**	136.7	**136.1**	190.5
Payment on account	**5.3**	11.2	**2.0**	0.3
	6,039.4	6,441.7	**1,889.1**	2,213.4

(DM, Millions)

For inventories valued on the LIFO basis, LIFO reserves approximated DM132 million for the BASF Group, and DM8 million for raw materials and DM72 million for work in process, finished goods and merchandise for BASF Aktiengesellschaft.

E.9.5   Accounting for Contingency Reserves

Under German GAAP, companies may provide for *future* expenses or losses currently, so long as the expenses or losses are *possible* and *reasonable*. When such events are provided for in the financial statements, they usually appear under the account Other Provisions and, when contingency reserves created in prior years are no longer considered necessary, they are usually reversed to Other Income on the income statement.

The following is selected financial information from the 1993 annual report of the Hoechst Group, relating to its Other Provisions account.

Required:

(a) Review the company's data relating to Other Provisions. Under U.S. GAAP, how would the various components be accounted for? (*Hint:* See *SFAS No. 5.*)

(b) Based on your analysis in part (a), restate Hoechst's Operating Income for 1993.

Selected Financial Information

	31 Dec. 1993	*31 Dec. 1992*
Total assets	39,112	36,911
Shareholders' equity	13,540	13,856
Other provisions	6,414	5,366
Operating income (before income taxes)	1,476	2,152

(DM, Millions)

Selected Footnote Information

Other provisions

	Hoechst Group		Hoechst AG	
	31.12.93	31.12.92	**31.12.93**	31.12.92
Taxes	1052	1096	353	505
Uncertain liabilities	4680	3687	1319	1090
Risks arising from transactions not yet settled	637	536	244	267
Maintenance	45	47	21	21
	6414	**5366**	**1937**	**1883**

The item ''uncertain liabilities'' includes many different types of provision. These relate in particular to expenditure on restructuring measures, holiday remuneration, compulsory social security contributions, environmental protection, anniversary allowances, discounts, bonuses and commissions.

The risks arising from transactions not yet settled are mainly risks arising from purchase and sales contracts, damage claims, plant engineering business and guarantees.

E.9.6. Statement of Cash Flows

Under German company law, corporations are required to present a balance sheet, an income statement, and relevant footnotes. Neither a statement of changes in financial position nor a statement of cash flows is required, although occasionally such information is presented as part of the report of the board of management and supervisory board to shareholders.

The following is the statement of changes in financial position of the Hoechst Group as it appeared in the company's 1993 annual report. Also presented are the company's balance sheet and statement of income.

Required:

Recast the 1993 statement of changes in financial position of the Hoechst Group into a statement of cash flows. What conclusions can you draw about the company from the cash flow data?

HOECHST GROUP
Statement of Changes in Financial Position

In DM Million			1993		1992
Net income for the year	+		756		1,182
Depreciation and write-offs of fixed assets and investments	+		3,322		3,180
Disposals of fixed assets and investments	+		414		369
Appreciation of fixed assets and investments	−		6		7
Increase in long-term provisions	+		899		699
Cash flow			**5,385**		**5,423**
Dividend payments (previous year and advance payments on dividends)	−		677		819
Funds from internal financing			**4,708**		**4,604**
Capital expenditure on tangible fixed assets	−	3,597		3,779	
Investments in participating interests	−	1,572		764	
Other additions to fixed assets and investments	−	222	5,391	315	4858
Change in inventories	−	−237		−7	
Change in receivables	−	1,174	937	115	108
Balance resulting from internal financing			**−1,620**		**−362**
Capital increases	+	70		127	
Change in long-term liabilities	+	1,424	1,494	576	703
Balance resulting from long-term financing			**−126**		**341**
Change in accounts payable, trade	+	31		−218	
Change in other liabilities	+	−331		−544	
Other changes	+	103	−197	−138	−900
Change in liquid assets			**−323**		**−559**

HOECHST GROUP
Statement of Income

		1993 DM (m)	1992 DM (m)
Net sales		**46,047**	**45,870**
Cost of sales	−	30,497	29,807
Gross profit from sales		**15,550**	**16,063**
Distribution/selling costs	−	9,969	9,973
Research costs	−	3,039	2,904
General administration costs	−	1,842	1,890
Other operating income	+	1,004	1,057
Other operating expenses	−	228	201
Operating profit		**1,476**	**2,152**
Income from investments	+	87	396
Net interest	−	449	488
Other financial income	+	113	48
Profit from ordinary activities/profit before taxes on income		**1,227**	**2,108**
Taxes on income	−	471	926
Net income for the year		**756**	**1,182**

HOECHST GROUP
Balance Sheet

Assets	*31 Dec. 1993* *DM (m)*	*31 Dec. 1992* *DM (m)*
Intangible fixed assets	323	300
Tangible fixed assets	15,778	14,794
Investments	3,188	2,839
Fixed assets and investments	**19,289**	**17,933**
Inventories	7,081	7,210
Accounts receivable, trade	8,212	7,452
Other receivables and other assets	1,943	1,742
Receivables and other assets	10,155	9,194
Marketable securities	564	1,198
Cheques, cash on hand, in the Bundesbank, the Postbank and in other banks	1,024	713
Liquid assets	1,588	1,911
Prepaid and deferred items	999	663
Current assets	**19,823**	**18,978**
	39,112	**36,911**
Stockholders' equity and liabilities		
Subscribed capital of Hoechst AG	2,940	2,925
Capital reserves of Hoechst AG	3,898	3,880
Revenue reserves	4,327	5,033
Minority interests	2,375	2,018
Stockholders' equity	**13,540**	**13,856**
Provisions for pensions and similar obligations	6,084	5,621
Other provisions	6414	5,366
Provisions	**12,498**	**10,987**
Corporate debt	7,280	6,765
Accounts payable, trade	2,715	2,637
Miscellaneous liabilities	3,009	2,597
Other liabilities	**13,004**	**11,999**
Deferred income	**701**	**69**
	39,112	**36,911**

E.9.7 Accounting for Negative Goodwill

Goodwill refers to the difference between the fair value of the identifiable net assets acquired in a business combination and the purchase price paid. On occasion, the purchase price paid for a company (or its net assets) may be less than its (their) current reported value. This might occur if a company is struggling financially or if the securities market perceives the future of the company to be limited or in doubt. Under these conditions, *negative goodwill* may arise as part of a business combination.

Under U.S. GAAP, negative goodwill may not be carried on the consolidated statements of the parent company, and instead is written off against the value of the noncurrent assets acquired in the combination. Under German GAAP, however, negative goodwill may be carried on the liability side of the consolidated balance sheet, usually under the account Difference Arising on Capital Consolidation.

The 1993 annual report of the BASF Group revealed the following information:

	DM, Millions	
	31 Dec. 1993	*31 Dec. 1992*
Goodwill (net)	17.8	88.0

In addition to amortization, the footnotes revealed that ''a difference of DM37.6 million on the liabilities side arising from the capital consolidation has been offset under goodwill.''

Required:

    (a) Prepare a hypothetical journal entry to show how negative goodwill might arise on the consolidated balance sheet of the BASF Group.

    (b) Prepare a journal entry to illustrate how the company offset its negative goodwill against its (positive) goodwill. What was the impact of this offset on the company's earnings?

E.9.8 Accounting for Shareholders' Equity

In January 1995, the *Wall Street Journal* carried a news release with the following headline: ''Pharmaceutical Firm Plans 10-for-1 Stock Split.'' The related article revealed that Schering AG, a German pharmaceutical company, planned to seek shareholder approval to split its ordinary shares (with nominal value of DM50) at a rate of 10 for 1 effective June 30, 1995. Prior to the announcement, the Schering shares had traded at DM1,005, or about $653, making them the second most expensive issue in the 30 security DAX blue-chip German stock index.

Required:

    (a) Using journal entries, explain how Schering might account for the 10-for-1 stock split on June 30, 1995.

    (b) Why do you think Schering management made the decision to undertake the split transaction?

    (c) Assuming an efficient capital market, what should happen to the price of the Schering shares on (1) June 30, 1995, immediately following the split, and (2) three to six months after the split?

E.9.9   Contingent Loss Recognition

In late 1993, Daimler-Benz AG disclosed that its projected net loss for the first nine months of 1993 would be substantially higher under U.S. GAAP than under German GAAP. According to the disclosure, Daimler's net loss under German GAAP would be DM180 million, whereas under U.S. GAAP it would reach DM2 billion (approximately $1.17 billion), a difference of over DM1.8 billion. According to a company spokesperson, the difference was largely attributable to the timing of the recognition of various contingent losses. During the third quarter, Daimler disclosed that it planned to lay off up to 35,000 employees by 1996 ''in response to mounting losses and shrinking markets.'' Provisions for all layoffs, including those for future periods, must be recognized currently under U.S. GAAP, whereas under German GAAP, they need not be recognized until the period in which the layoffs are actually expected to occur.

Required:

   (a) Prepare the accounting journal entry for Daimler-Benz for the layoffs as required under U.S. GAAP.

   (b) How would you expect the difference in accounting for loss contingencies between German and U.S. GAAP to affect Daimler's asset management, liquidity, and solvency ratios and its cash flows?

   (c) Daimler's shares are publicly traded in both the United States and Germany; how would you expect the company's share price to respond to the disclosure of the loss contingencies on the U.S. stock market (i.e., the NYSE)? On the German stock market?

E.9.10   Equity Transactions

In early 1994, Commerzbank AG announced that, after ''a very successful business year in 1993,'' the company would raise its dividend and hold a share offering for existing shareholders. Commerzbank, a German banking group, disclosed that it would raise its 1993 dividend from DM10 to DM12 (or approximately $6.88) per share. In addition, the company indicated that current shareholders would be given the opportunity to buy one new common share for every 10 previously held, at a price of DM315 (or approximately $180.53) per share, or over a 17 percent discount from the company's prior closing price of DM382.50. If the stock subscription is fully subscribed, the company would raise approximately DM945 million in new share capital.

Required:

   (a) How will these equity transactions be accounted for on Commerzbank's books?

(b) Why would the company price the new share offering to shareholders at a discount from current market price?

(c) What will the net effect of these equity transactions be on the company's total shareholders' equity?

E.9.11   Financial Restructuring

In late 1993, Metallgesellschaft AG, a German mining and industrial concern that was once considered one of Europe's "blue chip" investments, reported that expected earnings for the year ended September 30, 1993 would be a pre-tax loss of DM347 million. Following the earnings announcement, however, a report by *Spiegel,* one of Germany's leading news magazines, challenged the magnitude of the reported loss, citing insider sources who indicated that Metallgesellschaft may have lost billions of DM in oil futures trading. In response to the news items, Metallgesellschaft shares plunged more than 40 percent, losing over DM1 billion ($588 million) in market value. Analysts familiar with the company expressed concern that a substantial loss of the size rumored could be disastrous for the company, which was saddled with over DM8 billion ($4.63 billion) in short-term debt following a four-year acquisition spree. Foreign bank creditors might demand immediate payment of the loans, and there might be insufficient liquid assets available to cover the calls.

On January 7, 1994, Metallgesellschaft issued a revised statement of its 1993 results: the pre-tax loss would be DM1.8 billion ($1.0 billion), or nearly six times the original reported loss. The company also revealed that its potential exposure to other oil futures-related losses totaled DM1.5 billion. Kajo Neukirchen, the company's new CEO, indicated that Metallgesellschaft would be forced to file for bankruptcy unless bank creditors approved a restructuring package by January 12.

Later that same day, the company issued a second news release indicating that Metallgesellschaft and its bank creditors had agreed to raise DM2.7 billion ($1.6 billion) as part of a rescue plan for the troubled company. The elements of the plan were as follows:

- Metallgesellschaft would increase its equity by DM1.4 billion by issuing 5.6 million new shares for DM250 each (about $144 per share). This would increase the company's *nominal* equity capital by DM280 million from its current DM442 million. (German equity commonly carries a nominal face value, or par value, of DM50 per share.)

- Bank creditors would convert DM1.3 billion of Metallgesellschaft debt into subordinated convertible participation equity, a nonvoting equity instrument that could be converted into voting shares at a later date.

- Bank creditors would extend to the company a new DM500 million line of credit.

Analysts familiar with the company indicated that the company had approximately DM1.7 billion in retained earnings prior to the reported losses.

Required:

    (a) How would Metallgesellschaft account for the three elements of its rescue plan?

    (b) How will each of the elements affect the company's financial health?

E.9.12   Restructuring: Debt Forgiveness

In early 1994, German auto-maker Volkswagen AG agreed to forgive DM1.4 billion (approximately $819 million) in debt owed by its struggling Spanish subsidiary, SEAT SA. As part of the debt forgiveness agreement, SEAT would lay off more than 49 percent of its 22,400 employees and close a plant in Barcelona. The restructuring plan was anticipated to enable SEAT to return to profitability; SEAT posted an operating loss of DM1.2 million for 1993. A Volkswagen spokesperson indicated that the DM1.4 billion financing plan involved no cash transfer from VW to SEAT but was a forgiveness of part of the SEAT debt assumed by VW when it purchased SEAT in 1987.

Required:

    (a) How would you account for (1) the debt forgiveness on the books of Volkswagen and SEAT, (2) the anticipated layoff of approximately 9,000 SEAT employees on that company's books, and (3) the closing of the Barcelona plant on SEAT's books?

    (b) How are each of these events likely to affect Volkswagen's profitability ratios?

CASES

CASE 9.1
COMPARING GERMAN AND U.S. GAAP

Daimler-Benz (A)

Exhibits 1–5 present the 1991 consolidated financial statements of Daimler-Benz, the fourth largest company in Germany, and the report of its independent auditors. The company is composed of four principal operating divisions: Mercedes-Benz, a manufacturer of passenger cars and commercial vehicles; AEG, a manufacturer of domestic appliances, electrical systems, microelectronics, and rail systems; Deutsche Aerospace, a manufacturer of aircraft, defense and civil systems, propulsion systems, and space systems; and debis, a financial services company.

Required:

Using the following set of financial statements, compile a list of as many differences as you can identify between the Daimler-Benz financial report and what you would expect to find in a U.S. company annual report. You should try to identify both format and presentation differences, as well as accounting method differences. Be prepared to discuss (1) the significance of the differences in trying to come to an understanding of the financial profile of Daimler-Benz and (2) what the differences might tell you about the business environment and culture of Germany.

EXHIBIT 1

DAIMLER-BENZ
Consolidated Balance Sheet

Assets	Notes	*December 31, 1991* *(in millions of DM)*	*December 31, 1990* *(in millions of DM)*
Non-Current Assets			
Intangible Assets	(1)	774	304
Fixed Assets	(2)	16,574	15,057
Financial Assets	(3)	3,758	1,569
Leased Equipment	(4)	8,092	6,518
		29,198	23,448
Current Assets			
Inventories	(5)	20,732	18,855
Advance Payments Received	(6)	(5,827)	(5,727)
		14,905	13,128
Receivables	(7)	12,370	11,321
Other Assets	(8)	9,783	9,019
Securities	(9)	5,725	5,154
Cash	(10)	2,010	3,786
		44,793	42,408
Prepaid Expenses and Deferred Taxes	**(11)**	1,723	1,483
		75,714	67,339

Stockholders' Equity and Liabilities

Stockholders' Equity	(12)		
Capital Stock	(13)	2,330	2,330
Paid-In Capital	(13)	2,117	2,117
Retained Earnings	(14)	13,182	11,934
Minority Interests	(15)	1,214	881
Unappropriated Profit of Daimler-Benz AG		605	565
		19,448	17,827
Provisions			
Provisions for Old-Age Pensions and			
Similar Obligations	(16)	10,790	10,831
Other Provisions	(17)	17,239	16,536
		28,029	27,367
Liabilities			
Accounts Payable Trade	(18)	7,015	6,469
Other Liabilities	(19)	20,713	15,312
		27,728	21,781
Deferred Income		509	364
		75,714	67,339

EXHIBIT 2

DAIMLER-BENZ
Consolidated Statement of Income

	Notes	1991 *(in millions of DM)*	1990 *(in millions of DM)*
Sales	(20)	**95,010**	**85,500**
Increase in Inventories and Other Capitalized In-House Output	(21)	3,556	2,840
Total Output		**98,566**	**88,340**
Other Operating Income	(22)	3,545	3,598
Cost of Materials	(23)	(49,456)	(44,477)
Personnel Expenses of which for Old-Age Pensions DM1,511 million (1990: DM1,347 million)	(24)	(29,372)	(26,890)
Amortization of Intangible Assets, Depreciation of Fixed Assets and of Leased Equipment	(25)	(5,977)	(5,169)
Other Operating Expenses	(26)	(13,824)	(12,016)
Income from Affiliated, Associated and Related Companies	(27)	56	4
Net Interest Income	(28)	623	989
Write-Downs of Financial Assets and of Securities	(29)	(134)	(158)
Results from Ordinary Business Activities		**4,027**	**4,221**
Extraordinary Result	(30)	(544)	—
Income Taxes	(31)	(1,039)	(1,814)
Other Taxes	(31)	(502)	(612)
Net Income	(32)	**1,942**	**1,795**
Profit Carried Forward from Previous Year		8	5
Transfer to Retained Earnings		(1,275)	(1,124)
Income Applicable to Minority Shareholders		(99)	(145)
Loss Applicable to Minority Shareholders		29	34
Unappropriated Profit of Daimler-Benz AG		**605**	**565**

EXHIBIT 3

DAIMLER-BENZ
Consolidated Statement of Non-Current Assets

In Millions of DM
Acquisition/Manufacturing Costs

	1/1/1991*	Additions*	Reclassifications	Deductions	12/31/1991
Intangible Assets					
Franchises, Industrial Property Rights and Similar Rights, as well as Licenses to Such Rights	452	98	12	98	464
Goodwill	151	508	—	—	659
	603	606	12	98	1,123
Fixed Assets					
Land, Land Titles and Buildings including Buildings on Land Owned by Others	15,197	1,094	493	698	16,086
Technical Equipment and Machinery	19,962	1,600	674	1,582	20,654
Other Equipment, Factory and Office Equipment	14,884	1,746	389	1,433	15,586
Advance Payments Relating to Plant and Equipment and Construction in Progress	1,940	2,078	(1,568)	106	2,344
	51,983	6,518	(12)	3,819	54,670
Financial Assets					
Investments in Affiliated Companies	878	68	(4)	73	869
Loans to Affiliated Companies	8	5	—	2	11
Investments in Associated Companies	264	76	—	29	311
Investments in Related Companies	573	1,556	(3)	17	2,109
Loans to Related Companies	32	104	—	3	133
Investments in Long-Term Securities	246	341	—	36	551
Other Long-Term Receivables	623	333	7	91	872
	2,624	2,483	—	251	4,856
	55,210	9,607	—	4,168	60,649
Leased Equipment	9,444	4,191	—	1,782	11,853

*Including carryforward amounts of companies consolidated for the first time.

EXHIBIT 3 (continued)

DAIMLER-BENZ
Consolidated Statement of Non-Current Assets

	Amortization/Depreciation/Write-Downs					Net Book Value	
	1/1/1991*	Current Year	Reclassifications	Deductions	12/31/1991	12/31/1991	12/31/1990
Intangible Assets							
Franchises, Industrial Property Rights and Similar Rights, as well as Licenses to Such Rights	272	98	1	88	283	181	180
Goodwill	27	39	—	—	66	593	124
	299	**137**	**1**	**88**	**349**	**774**	**304**
Fixed Assets							
Land, Land Titles and Buildings including Buildings on Land Owned by Others	7,405	746	(7)	325	7,819	8,267	7,792
Technical Equipment and Machinery	17,017	1,649	12	1,349	17,329	3,325	2,945
Other Equipment, Factory and Office Equipment	12,472	1,672	(1)	1,225	12,918	2,668	2,412
Advance Payments Relating to Plant and Equipment and Construction in Progress	32	9	(5)	6	30	2,314	1,908
	36,926	**4,076**	**(1)**	**2,905**	**38,096**	**16,574**	**15,057**
Financial Assets							
Investments in Affiliated Companies	538	41	(5)	15	559	310	340
Loans to Affiliated Companies	2	—	—	—	2	9	6
Investments in Associated Companies	40	18	—	13	45	266	224
Investments in Related Companies	275	29	—	5	299	1,810	298
Loans to Related Companies	3	1	—	—	4	129	29
Investments in Long-Term Securities	38	1	—	17	22	529	208
Other Long-Term Receivables	159	25	5	22	167	705	464
	1,055	**115**	—	**72**	**1,098**	**3,758**	**1,569**
	38,280	**4,328**	—	**3,065**	**39,543**	**21,106**	**16,930**
Leased Equipment	**2,926**	**1,764**	—	**929**	**3,761**	**8,092**	**6,518**
						29,198	**23,448**

*Including carryforward amounts of companies consolidated for the first time.

EXHIBIT 4

DAIMLER-BENZ
Notes to the Consolidated Financial Statements

Principles and Methods

The consolidated financial statements have been prepared in accordance with regulations set forth in the Commercial Code; the amounts are shown in millions of D-marks. The items, which are summarized in the balance sheet and the statement of income, are separately shown in the notes and, where necessary, explained.

Accounting Principles and Valuation Methods

During the year under review, we have continued to apply the same accounting principles and valuation methods. Provisions for pensions have been calculated at the tax allowable interest rate of 6%; in this respect there exists a variance against the accounts of the parent company, which bases its provisions computation on an interest rate of 3.5%. Assets and liabilities presented in the consolidated balance sheet—in identical group circumstances—are uniformly valued. In 1991, as in previous years, provisions for approved conversion, reconstruction and maintenance projects have been set up, or have been systematically continued.

Intangible assets are valued at acquisition costs and written off over the respective useful lives. Goodwill resulting from the capital consolidation, if derived from the extension of the group, is in principle amortized over five years; goodwill relating to the restructuring of the group is charged to retained earnings. Goodwill which, for the first time in the year under review, arose from the creation of strategic alliances, is split. The portion relating to the group's expansion is written off over the relevant useful life, the one relating to the restructuring is charged to retained earnings.

Fixed assets are valued at acquisition or manufacturing costs. The self-constructed facilities comprise direct costs and applicable material and manufacturing overheads, including depreciation allowances.

The acquisition costs/manufacturing costs for fixed assets are reduced by scheduled depreciation charges. The opportunities for special tax-deductible depreciation allowances were fully utilized, i.e., in connection with Section 7d of the Income Tax Act and Section 82d of the Income Tax Regulations (environmental protection, and research and development investments), Section 14 of the Berlin Development Law, Section 3 of the Zone Border Area Development Law, Section 6b of the Income Tax Act and Subsection 35 of the Income Tax Guidelines.

Scheduled fixed asset depreciation allowances are calculated generally using the following useful lives: 17 to 50 years for buildings, 8 to 20 years for site improvements, 3 to 20 years for technical facilities and machinery, and 2 to 10 years for other facilities and factory and office equipment. Facilities used for multi-shift operations are depreciated using correspondingly lower useful lives. Buildings are depreciated using straight-line depreciation rates—and where allowable under the Tax Codes—declining rates. Movable property with a useful life of four years or more is depreciated using the declining-balance method. For movable property, we change from the declining-balance method to the straight-line method of calculating depreciation allowances when the equal distribution of the remaining net book value over the remaining useful life leads to higher depreciation amounts. Depreciation allowances on additions during the first and second half of the year are calculated using the full year or half-year rates, respectively. Low-value items are expensed in the year of acquisition.

Investments in *related companies,* and in *other long-term financial assets* are valued at the lower of cost or market; non-interest bearing or low-interest bearing receivables are shown at their present value. Major *investments in associated companies* are valued according to the book value method at equity.

Leased equipment is valued at acquisition or manufacturing costs, and is depreciated using the declining-balance method. We change from the declining-balance method to the straight-line method of calculating depreciation allowances when the equal distribution of the remaining net book value over the remaining useful life leads to higher depreciation amounts. The option to exercise tax-deductible depreciation, as per Section 14 of the Berlin Development Law, was used.

Raw materials and supplies as well as goods purchased *for resale* are valued at the lower of cost or market. Finished goods are valued at manufacturing costs which comprise, apart from direct material and direct labor, applicable manufacturing overheads including depreciation charges. To the extent that inventory risks are determinable, i.e., for reduced usability after prolonged storage or after design changes, reasonable deductions are made, which are calculated based on a free-of-loss-valuation.

Receivables and other assets—if non-interest bearing—are reduced to their present value at the balance sheet date, and are valued taking into account all known risks. A lump-sum allowance for doubtful accounts on a country-specific scale is deducted from the receivables in recognition of the general risk inherent in receivables.

Treasury stock is valued at the expected selling price to employees of the Daimler-Benz group. *Securities* are valued at the lower of cost or market value at the balance sheet date.

EXHIBIT 4 (continued)

DAIMLER-BENZ
Notes to the Consolidated Financial Statements

Provisions for old-age pensions and similar obligations are actuarially determined on the basis of an assumed interest rate of 6% using the Entry Age Actuarial Cost Method. The regulations of the 1992 Pension Reform Act have been taken into account in calculating the provision amount.

Provisions for taxes and other provisions are determined on the basis of fair and reasonable business judgments. The obligations in the personnel and social area are reflected in the financial statements at non-discounted values expected to be paid in the future as benefits are vested.

Liabilities are shown at their repayment amounts.

Companies Included in Consolidation

The companies included in consolidation encompass, apart from Daimler-Benz AG, 255 (1990: 269) domestic and foreign subsidiaries and 7 joint venture companies.

During the reporting year, 33 companies have, for the first time, been added to consolidation. Moreover, 7 joint venture companies were included pro rata, for the first time, pursuant to Section 310 of the Commercial Code. A total of 47 subsidiaries were deleted from consolidation.

The profit and loss accounts of 8 domestic and 19 foreign companies, which were deleted from the circle of consolidated companies at the end of the year, were still included in the consolidated statement of income.

The deletions from consolidation, resulting from the sale of the AEG Kabel Aktiengesellschaft, of AEG Elektrowerkzeuge GmbH and their subsidiaries, as well as the withdrawal from the office and communication field, do have consequences in the consolidated balance sheet. The material consequences are explained under the relevant balance sheet captions. In contrast, there are nearly no consequences in the consolidated statement of income because the expenses and income items of the above companies are still included.

Not included are 199 subsidiaries, whose effect on the consolidated financial statements is not material (their total sales volume is less than 1% of consolidated sales) and 11 companies administering pension funds whose assets are subject to restrictions.

In accordance with Section 296, Subsection 1, No. 1 of the Commercial Code, Deutsche Airbus GmbH is not consolidated because Messerschmitt-Bölkow-Blohm GmbH, in its relationship with this company, is restricted in exercising its rights, on account of agreements with the Federal Republic of Germany and of rules in the bylaws with regard to resolutions.

At the end of 1991, the helicopter activities of MBB and of the French Aerospatiale were merged into the newly founded Eurocopter group in order to form a strategic alliance. MBB holds 40% of the share capital in the new joint venture company Eurocopter Holding S.A., Paris. Because of the relatively short group affiliation, only the consolidated balance sheets, but not the statements of income of Eurocopter Holding S.A., and its subsidiaries, are included pro rata. The income and expenses for 1991 derived from the German helicopter activities are still included in the income statement of MBB. Comparability of the consolidated accounts against the previous year has not been impaired.

Principles of Consolidation

Capital consolidation was effected according to the book value method where the parent's acquisition costs are eliminated against the relevant share capital and retained earnings at the time of acquisition or first-time inclusion in consolidation. This applies analogously to the joint venture companies that are included pro rata. The differences resulting from the capital consolidation (debit balance) are, as far as possible, allocated to the relevant balance sheet items and are written off to income over their useful lives. For the treatment of the remaining differences (goodwill), see our explanations under ''accounting principles and valuation methods.'' The DM275 million goodwill resulting from the addition of the *joint venture* companies of the Eurocopter group is shown under ''intangible assets.'' Beginning in 1992, the portion applicable to the group's expansion will, analogously to the acquired goodwill in the individual financials, be written off to income over a useful life of 10 years. The remaining portion will be charged to retained earnings in 1992, without affecting income.

A difference (credit balance) resulting from the capital consolidation is shown under the balance sheet caption ''other provisions'' earmarked as ''difference from capital consolidation with reserve characteristics.''

Profits earned by subsidiaries after the date of acquisition are added to consolidated retained earnings. The unappropriated profit, as shown both in the separate financial statements of Daimler-Benz AG and in the consolidated financial statements, is the same. In connection hereto, we have charged the income-affecting consolidation adjustments and the profits earned by our subsidiaries to consolidated retained earnings.

EXHIBIT 4 (continued)

DAIMLER-BENZ
Notes to the Consolidated Financial Statements

The consolidated financial statements include 116 *associated companies.*

At year-end, twelve associated companies as well as our subsidiary Deutsche Airbus GmbH, Hamburg, have been included in our consolidated financial statements according to the *book value method* at equity. Goodwill of DM107 million, resulting from the purchase of additional shares of MBB, is charged to retained earnings, because it is connected with the restructuring of the group. In December 1991 we acquired a 35% stake in Sogeti S.A., Grenoble. On account of the short affiliation, we have included this investment at acquisition cost under the caption ''investments in related companies.'' Beginning in 1992, Sogeti will be accounted for under the equity method of accounting.

The remaining associated companies are shown under investments in affiliated companies at acquisition cost and in some instances less write-downs, as they are not material to the consolidated balance sheet, financial position and results of operations. Intercompany receivables and payables have been eliminated; the differences resulting from *debt consolidation* have been charged or credited to income.

All material *intercompany profits* resulting from the intercompany sales of goods and services have been eliminated, except items of minor importance. This also applies to sales of goods and services by associated companies to companies included in consolidation.

Intercompany sales and other intercompany earnings have been eliminated against the relevant costs, or reclassified to ''capitalized in-house output'' or to ''increase in inventories,'' respectively.

Deferred taxes (debit balance) shown in the consolidated balance sheet result from income-affecting consolidation adjustments.

Currency Translation

Foreign currency receivables are translated in the individual financial statements at the bid price on the day they are recorded or at the spot rate on the balance sheet date if lower. Foreign currency payables are translated at the asked price on the day they are recorded or the spot rate on the balance sheet date if higher.

The accounts of all foreign companies are translated to D-marks on the basis of historical exchange rates for non-current assets, and at year-end exchange rates for current assets, liabilities and unappropriated profit. Stockholders' equity in D-marks is the remaining difference between translated assets less translated liabilities and unappropriated profit. The difference resulting from the translation of balance sheet items is recorded in consolidated retained earnings.

Expense and income items are essentially translated at average annual exchange rates. To the extent that they relate to fixed assets (fixed asset depreciation, profit or loss from disposal of fixed assets), they are translated at historical costs. Net income, additions to retained earnings, and the unappropriated profit are translated at year-end rates. The difference resulting from the translation of annual net income, between annual average rates and the exchange rates at the balance sheet date, is reflected in other operating expenses.

The adjustments made in the income statements by our subsidiaries in Brazil for monetary devaluations have been retained in the consolidated statement of income without change, effectively preventing reflection of inflationary profits.

The income taxes, which were already geared to the balance sheet date in the national financial statements, have been translated at year-end rates.

Items from inflation-adjusted income statements of our Argentinian companies are translated at year-end exchange rates. Fictitious profits/losses resulting from the divergence between the inflationary trend and the changes in the currency's value have been eliminated.

Notes to the Consolidated Balance Sheet

1   Intangible Assets

Intangible assets, amounting to DM 774 million (1990: DM 304 million) comprise goodwill arising from the capital consolidation and from individual company financial statements, acquired EDP software, patents and, to a lesser extent, advance payments made. The increase against the previous year is largely due to the first-time pro rata inclusion of the Eurocopter group and relates to goodwill.

EXHIBIT 4 (continued)

DAIMLER-BENZ
Notes to the Consolidated Financial Statements

2   Fixed Assets

The increase in property, plant and equipment by DM 1,517 million to DM 16,574 million is derived from investments of DM 6,518 millions reduced by reclassifications of DM 11 million, disposals of DM 914 million, and depreciation of DM 4,076 million. The change in the circle of consolidated companies altogether reduced fixed assets by approximately DM 160 million. Special tax-deductible depreciation allowances amount to DM 77 million (1990: DM 95 million); depreciation in excess of scheduled depreciation amounts to DM 39 million (1990: DM 2 million).

3   Financial Assets

The increase in financial assets by DM 2,189 million to DM 3,758 million is largely due to the purchase of shares in Sogeti S.A., Grenoble, and Metallgesellschaft AG, Frankfurt am Main.

A complete listing of our stock ownership will be filed with the commercial registry office at the county court house in Stuttgart under the number HRB 173.

Investments in long-term securities totaling DM 529 million (1990: DM 208 million) are mostly accounted for by Daimler-Benz AG. Unscheduled write-downs, largely of investments in affiliated companies, of investments in associated companies, of investments in related companies and of other long-term receivables, totaling DM 115 million (1990: DM 110 million), had to be made.

Because of increased market values, investments in non-current assets should have been written up by DM 6 million in accordance with the value appreciation doctrine (Section 280 of the Commercial Code). However, such a write-up was omitted for tax reasons.

4   Leased Equipment

The increase in leased equipment—almost exclusively vehicles—by DM 1,574 million to DM 8,092 million, pertains largely to Mercedes-Benz Credit Corporation, Norwalk, Connecticut, U.S.A., and to Mercedes-Benz Leasing GmbH, Stuttgart. About 86% of the balance sheet total pertains to these two companies. Special tax-deductible depreciation allowances amount to DM 10 million (1990: DM 9 million).

5   Inventories

	In Millions of DM	
	12/31/1991	*12/31/1990*
Raw materials and supplies	3,041	3,468
Work in progress	8,160	7,553
Finished goods, parts and goods purchased for resale	8,557	7,083
Advance payments to suppliers	974	751
	20,732	18,855

AEG and Deutsche Aerospace account for nearly 50% of the consolidated inventories. The increase over last year is with DM 1,500 million derived from the Mercedes-Benz corporate division, particularly at Mercedes-Benz AG and its foreign sales companies, and with DM 800 million from the DASA corporate division, here almost exclusively through the first-time pro rata inclusion of the balance sheets of the Eurocopter group. The change in the circle of consolidated companies has reduced inventories by about DM 500 million.

6   Advanced Payments Received

Advance payments received amounting to DM 5,827 million (1990: DM 5,727 million) were almost exclusively for projects and long-term contracts at AEG, Dornier, MTU and MBB; they were deducted from inventories.

EXHIBIT 4 (continued)

DAIMLER-BENZ
Notes to the Consolidated Financial Statements

7   Receivables

8   Other Assets

	In Millions of DM	
	12/31/1991	*12/31/1990*
Receivables from sales of goods and services	10,625	9,077
of which maturing after more than one year	225	338
Receivables from affilitated companies	335	359
of which maturing after more than one year	11	113
Receivables from related companies	1,410	1,885
of which maturing after more than one year	596	659
Total receivables	12,370	11,321
of which maturing after more than one year	832	1,110
Other assets	9,783	9,019
of which maturing after more than one year	4,076	4,249

Approximately DM 0.3 billion (1990: DM 0.9 billion) of the receivables from related companies pertain mainly to fixed-interest debt instruments and securities.

Other assets include investments of liquid funds in debt instruments not traded on stock exchanges. They amount to DM 2,563 million (1990: DM 3,866 million).

Also shown here are receivables derived from the business activities of finance and leasing companies totaling DM 4.3 billion (1990: DM 3.2 billion).

9   Securities

	In Millions of DM	
	12/31/1991	*12/31/1990*
Treasury stock	16	61
Other securities	5,709	5,093
	5,725	5,154

During the year under review, we purchased 116,457 common shares (par value DM 5.8 million = 0.25% of total outstanding share capital) at an average price of DM 665 a share.

In October of 1991, we sold 184,754 shares to our employees (par value DM 9.2 million = 0.4% of total outstanding share capital) at a preferential price of DM 371 for each share (in the event that one share was purchased) or DM 412.50 for each share (in the event that two shares were purchased). On the balance sheet date, we held 42,766 ordinary shares (par value DM 2.1 million = 0.09% of total outstanding capital stock). They were all purchased during the year under review.

Other securities pertain mainly to fixed-interest-bearing debt instruments.

Within current assets, DM 26 million should have been written up according to the value appreciation doctrine, but such write-up was omitted for tax reasons.

10   Cash

Cash amounting to DM 2,010 million (1990: DM 3,786 million) consists of deposits in financial institutions, cash on hand, deposits at the Bundesbank (German Federal Bank), in post office accounts, and checks on hand.

Liquid funds, shown among various balance sheet captions, total DM 10.6 billion (1990: DM 13.7 billion).

EXHIBIT 4 (continued)

DAIMLER-BENZ
Notes to the Consolidated Financial Statements

11   Prepaid Expenses and Deferred Taxes

Deferred taxes on income-affecting elimination entries amount to DM 1,596 million (1990:1,363 million). Deferred taxes—a debit balance overall—shown in the consolidated individual balance sheets—are not included.

12   Stockholders' Equity

The changes in stockholders' equity are as follows:

	In Millions of DM
Balance at 12/31/1990	17,827
Dividends paid by Daimler-Benz AG for 1990	(557)
Amount transferred from 1991 net income to retained earnings	1,275
Write-off of goodwill	(107)
Unappropriated profit of Daimler-Benz AG 1991	605
Change in stock ownership of minority shareholders	333
Difference from currency translation	30
Other changes	42
Balance at 12/31/1991	19,448

13   Capital Stock and Paid-In Capital

Capital stock and paid-in capital pertain to Daimler-Benz AG.

14   Retained Earnings

Retained earnings comprise retained earnings allocated under statute of DM 160 million, retained earnings allocated for treasury stock of DM 30 million, and other retained earnings of DM 8,469 million of Daimler-Benz AG. Also reflected here are the company's share in the retained earnings and results of operations of consolidated subsidiaries, insofar as they have been earned by them since belonging to the group. Additionally, this caption takes into account the cumulative results from the elimination of intercompany earnings and from debt consolidation, as well as the difference arising from currency translations.

15   Minority Interests

The stock ownership of outside third parties in the subsidiaries included in consolidation pertain mostly to DASA AG, MBB, AEG, Mercedes-Benz of South Africa, Dornier and MTU. The increase against the previous year is largely due to the first time pro rata inclusion of the Eurocopter group.

16   Provisions for Old-Age Pensions and Similar Obligations

The pension provisions are unchanged from last year and amount to DM 10.8 billion. The change in the circle of consolidated companies has reduced pension provisions by DM 690 million. When the assets of the provident funds are added to the provisions for old-age pensions, the company's pension obligations are fully covered.

EXHIBIT 4 (continued)

DAIMLER-BENZ
Notes to the Consolidated Financial Statements

17   Other Provisions

	In Millions of DM	
	12/31/1991	*12/31/1990*
Provisions for taxes	1,248	1,649
Difference from capital consolidation with reserve characteristics	44	—
Other provisions	15,947	14,887
	17,239	16,536

The provisions for taxes include DM 645 million (1990: 1,139 million) which pertain, to a large extent, to Daimler-Benz AG for open years awaiting final assessment.

The difference amount with reserve characteristics resulting from the capital consolidation originates from the first-time consolidation of one subsidiary; this amount will be available to offset potential additional expenses during the start-up years.

Apart from existing worldwide warranty obligations, other provisions take into account, above all, obligations in the personnel and social area, risks from losses inherent in pending business transactions, and risks arising from contractual liabilities and pending litigation.

Additional provisions exist for expenditures which are based on approved change-over, alteration and some development projects, for possible additional costs in connection with completed contracts, and for maintenance which had been planned for the year under review but had to be deferred until the following year. In addition, provisions have been recorded for future obligations in connection with restructuring activities.

18   Accounts Payable Trade

19   Other Liabilities

	In Millions of DM	
	12/31/1991	*12/31/1990*
Accounts payable trade	7,015	6,469
of which due within one year	6,890	6,357
Financial liabilities		
Bonds	5,003	2,077
of which due within one year	634	—
in more than five years	1,534	842
Debentures	1,874	2,283
of which due within one year	1,874	2,283
Liabilities to financial institutions	5,380	4,123
of which due within one year	3,087	2,109
in more than five years	316	343
Notes payable	541	272
of which due within one year	521	83
in more than five years	7	7
Other liabilities		
Liabilities to affiliated companies	1,613	677
of which due within one year	1,580	677

EXHIBIT 4 (continued)

DAIMLER-BENZ
Notes to the Consolidated Financial Statements

19   Other Liabilities (continued)

	In Millions of DM	
	12/31/1991	*12/31/1990*
Liabilities to related companies	1,419	1,401
of which due within one year	1,095	1,005
in more than five years	86	54
Miscellaneous liabilities	4,883	4,479
of which due within one year	4,182	3,868
in more than five years	288	298
of which for taxes	891	907
of which for social benefits	823	758
Other liabilities	20,713	15,312
Total liabilities	27,728	21,781
of which due within one year	19,863	16,382
in more than five years	2,231	1,544

Of the liabilities to related companies, DM 430 million (1990: DM 270 million) pertain to liabilities to financial institutions. In addition, they pertain mainly to obligations due to project companies, incurred by MBB.

Debentures pertain to commercial paper issued in D-marks and U.S. dollars; they are shown at the issue price plus accrued interest up to December 31, 1991. In the previous year, U.S. dollar-denominated commercial paper of DM 2,283 million was shown under notes payable. The amount was reclassified for the purpose of comparability.

The increase in liabilities to affiliated companies is largely due to the take-over of the 1991 loss of AEG Olympia Office GmbH by AEG Aktiengesellschaft.

Miscellaneous liabilities largely comprise December 1991 accruals for wages and salaries as well as tax liabilities.

Total other liabilities include approximately DM 8.1 billion in connection with the refinancing of the strongly expanding leasing and sales financing activities for cars and commercial vehicles.

Liabilities to financial institutions, notes payable, liabilities to affiliated and related companies, miscellaneous liabilities, and advance payments received from customers (directly deducted from inventories) are materially secured, in the amount of DM 1,308 million (1990: DM 1,223 million) by mortgage conveyance or by assignment of receivables.

Contingent Liabilities

	In Millions of DM	
	12/31/1991	*12/31/1990*
Collateral	1,557	1,675
Discounted notes	218	156
Contractual guarantees	261	300
Pledges for indebtedness of others	7	12

In addition, we are liable for nonestimable compensatory payments, guaranteed by Deutsche Aerospace for 1992 and future years. For outside shareholders of AEG and of Deutsche Aerospace, there exist claims for nonestimable compensatory payments.

Moreover, there exist contractual performance guarantees that could not reasonably be estimated.

EXHIBIT 4 (continued)

DAIMLER-BENZ
Notes to the Consolidated Financial Statements

Other Financial Obligations

Other financial obligations arising from rental, property lease and leasing contracts average approximately DM 502 million annually; the average contract duration is 10 years. For companies not included in consolidation, we have other financial obligations amounting to DM 36 million; the average contract duration is 15 years. The remaining financial obligations, particularly purchase order commitments for capital investments, are within the scope of normal business activities. The obligation arising from stock subscriptions and from capital subscriptions in close corporations pursuant to Section 24 of the GmbH Act, amount to DM 11 million.

We are jointly and severally liable for certain non-incorporated companies, partnerships and joint venture work groups. In addition, there exist performance contracts and miscellaneous guarantees in connection with ongoing business transactions.

20 Sales

	In Millions of DM	
	1991	*1990*
Sales by corporate divisions:		
Mercedes-Benz	65,317	57,872
AEG	13,573	12,721
DASA	11,974	12,168
debis	4,146	2,739
	95,010	85,500
Sales by regions:		
Domestic	44,443	36,674
Foreign	50,567	48,826
Breakdown of foreign sales:		
EC countries	18,907	18,876
Other European countries	4,896	5,288
North America	12,969	12,820
Latin America	3,993	3,160
Other countries	9,802	8,682

21 Increase in Inventories and Other Capitalized In-House Output

	In Millions of DM	
	1991	*1990*
Increase in inventories of finished goods and of work in progress, including parts	2,111	1,514
Other capitalized in-house output	1,445	1,326
	3,556	2,840

EXHIBIT 4 (continued)

DAIMLER-BENZ
Notes to the Consolidated Financial Statements

22   Other Operating Income

The income amount included in this caption for the reversal of provisions totals DM 893 million. (1990: DM 792 million). Additional income is derived from exchange profits in connection with ongoing purchase and payment transactions, mostly earned abroad; exchange losses against such income are shown under other operating expenses. In addition, income is derived from costs charged to third parties, from security sales, and from rentals and leases.

DM 1,571 million of other operating income is attributable to prior years.

23   Cost of Materials

	In Millions of DM	
	1991	*1990*
Cost of raw materials and supplies as well as of goods purchased for resale	44,340	39,601
Cost of services purchased	5,116	4,876
	49,456	44,477

In relation to a total output of DM 98,566 million (1990: 88,340 million), the ratio to the cost of goods and services is unchanged at 50%.

24   Personnel Expenses/Employment

	In Millions of DM	
	1991	*1990*
Wages and salaries	23,813	21,881
Social levies and expenses for old-age pensions	5,559	5,009
	29,372	26,890
Employment (weighted annual average)	Number	Number
Wage earners	221,216	216,515
Salaried employees	144,101	141,631
Trainees/apprentices	16,194	16,071
	381,511	374,217

Both the increased average number of employees and the collective-bargaining wage and salary increases were the main reasons for the higher personnel expenses.

The average number of employees shown above does not yet include the employees of the Eurocopter Holding group, except for the employees of the German subsidiary.

25   Amortization of Intangible Assets, Depreciation of Fixed Assets and of Leased Equipment

	In Millions of DM	
	1991	*1990*
Amortization of intangible assets	137	112
Depreciation of fixed assets	4,076	3,558
Depreciation of leased equipment	1,764	1,499
	5,977	5,169

EXHIBIT 4 (continued)

DAIMLER-BENZ
Notes to the Consolidated Financial Statements

The depreciation of fixed assets pertains with more than 50% to Mercedes-Benz AG. The increase in depreciation of leasing equipment results from the growth of the leasing business of our domestic and foreign finance companies.

26   Other Operating Expenses

This caption comprises additions to provisions, maintenance expenses, administrative and selling expenses including sales commisions, rental and lease expenses, foreign exchange losses incurred in the normal course of business, freight-out, packaging, and expenses in connection with the currency revaluation at our Brazilian subsidiary companies. Overall, DM 85 million is applicable to prior years.

27   Income from Affiliated, Associated and Related Companies

	In Millions of DM	
	1991	*1990*
Income received from affiliated, associated and related companies	34	34
of which from affiliated companies	13	8
Income from profit and loss transfer agreements	15	20
Profit (loss) from companies included at equity	22	(31)
Loss from profit and loss transfer agreements	(15)	(19)
	56	4

28   Net Interest Income

	In Millions of DM	
	1991	*1990*
Income from other securities, and from long-term financial assets	125	54
Other interest and similar income	2,222	2,165
of which from affiliated companies	19	3
Interest and similar expenses	(1,724)	(1,230)
of which to affiliated companies	(18)	(5)
	623	989

29   Write-Downs of Financial Assets and of Securities

	In Millions of DM	
	1991	*1990*
Write-downs of financial assets	115	110
Write-downs of securities	19	48
	134	158

Exhibit 4 (continued)

DAIMLER-BENZ
Notes to the Consolidated Financial Statements

30   Extraordinary Results

	In Millions of DM	
	1991	*1990*
Extraordinary income	490	—
Extraordinary expenses	(1,034)	—
	(544)	—

The extraordinary income results from the sale of AEG KABEL Aktiengesellschaft and its subsidiaries.

Extraordinary expenses are in connection with the withdrawal from the office and communications technology business of AEG.

31   Taxes

	In Millions of DM	
	1991	*1990*
Income taxes	1,039	1,814
Other taxes	502	612
	1,541	2,426

The decline in tax expenses is largely due to the expansion of the circle of companies integrated for tax purposes, AEG Aktiengesellschaft and the Dornier companies belonging to DASA AG.

32   Net Income

Consolidated net income of DM 1,942 million has predominantely been earned by the Mercedes-Benz corporate division. Special tax depreciation of fixed assets and tax-allowable write-downs of current assets have reduced net income only slightly. Also, future charges in connection with such write-offs will not be material.

Other Information/Boards

Under the presumption that the proposed dividend is ratified by the shareholders at the Annual General Meeting on June 24, 1992, the remuneration paid by the Group companies to the members of the Board of Management and the Supervisory Board of Daimler-Benz AG amounts to DM 15,030,509 and DM 2,012,742, respectively. Disbursements to former members of the Board of the Management of Daimler-Benz AG and their survivors amount to DM 10,452,288. An amount of DM 87,815,046 has been provided for on the books of Daimler-Benz AG and of Mercedes-Benz AG for pension obligations to former members of the Board of Management and their survivors. As of December 31, 1991, advances and loans to members of the Board of Management of Daimler-Benz AG amount to DM 179,418. Home loans included herein are not subject to interest; other loans and advances bear interest averaging 5.5%. During the year, DM 129,784 was repaid. The stipulated maturities are ten years for home loans, and are not to exceed one year for other loans and advances.

EXHIBIT 5

Independent Auditors' Report

The accounting records and the consolidated accounts, which have been audited in accordance with professional standards, comply with the legal provisions. With due regard to the generally accepted accounting principles, the consolidated accounts give a true and fair view of the assets, liabilities, financial position and results of operations of the Daimler-Benz Group. The business review report, which summarizes the state of affairs of Daimler-Benz Aktiengesellschaft and that of the Group, is consistent with the financial statements of Daimler-Benz Aktiengesellschaft and the consolidated financial statements.

Frankfurt am Main, April 14, 1992

KPMG Deutsche Treuhand-Gesellschaft
Aktiengesellschaft
Wirtschaftsprüfungsgesellschaft

Zielke   Dr. Koschinsky
Wirtschaftsprüfer   Wirtschaftsprüfer
(Certified Public Accountant)   (Certified Public Accountant)

CASE 9.2
ACCOUNTING FOR RESERVES

Daimler-Benz (B)

On March 25, 1993, The *Wall Street Journal* carried an article with the following headline: "Daimler-Benz Discloses Hidden Reserves of $2.45 Billion, Seeks Big Board Listing." According to the article, Daimler-Benz AG, Germany's largest industrial company, would report $2.45 billion U.S. (or DM4 billion) as an unexpected addition to its 1992 balance sheet. The disclosure apparently came as part of Daimler's efforts to become the first German company to list its shares on the New York Stock Exchange (NYSE).

According to U.S. Securities and Exchange Commission representatives, many foreign companies would like to gain access to the huge U.S. equity and debt markets; however, a major stumbling block for those companies is complying with U.S. reporting and disclosure practices designed to protect investors. In a statement to financial analysts, Gerhard Liener, Daimler's chief financial officer, reported that the company had already adopted some U.S. accounting practices: it had been reporting quarterly data to shareholders for the past two years and its method of reporting cash flows had conformed to U.S. practice since 1992.

With respect to the previously undisclosed reserve of $2.45 billion, financial analysts observed that German companies "were notorious for squirreling away cash that never appears

---

This case was prepared by Kenneth R. Ferris from publicly available documents. Copyright © 1993 by Kenneth R. Ferris. All rights reserved to the author.

on their balance sheet." According to a Daimler spokesperson: "This is money that we've had in the back room, but it will be visible now. The company will continue to retain the cash as an internal cash reserve."

Analysts familiar with German accounting practice note that companies can create hidden or "silent" reserves in a variety of ways: understating revenues, overstating expenses, and overstating charges for "provisions for contingencies," among others.[1] With respect to Daimler's reserve, the $2.45 billion resulted from an inconsistent application of pension valuation methods throughout the company. Daimler's operating companies apparently discounted their pension fund commitments at 6 percent, whereas the holding company discounted those same commitments at 3.5 percent.

Daimler-Benz officials stated that they hope that the recent disclosures will help the company attain NYSE listing by year-end 1993. A remaining problem, however, may be the company's accounting for goodwill. Under U.S. practice, goodwill arising from a merger or acquisition must be capitalized to the balance sheet and then amortized off against earnings over the asset's expected useful life (but not to exceed 40 years). In recent years, Daimler acquisitions have produced over $2.0 billion in goodwill, which under German accounting practice has been charged off against retained earnings.

Required:

Exhibits 1 and 2 present the Daimler-Benz consolidated balance sheet and consolidated statement of income as of December 31, 1991. Recast the company's 1991 financial statements to reflect the previously hidden reserves and the goodwill charged to equity. Consider the ways that companies reporting their financial results under U.S. GAAP can smooth their reported earnings (e.g., create hidden reserves). List these methods and the reasons that a company might

---

[1]The provision for contingencies is analogous to the creation of a loss (or expense) reserve in the United States. The principal difference, however, is that in Germany, provisions for normally occurring expenses (e.g., maintenance) may be created often with the explicit purpose of smoothing reported earnings. Under U.S. practice, the creation of reserves is limited to specifically identifiable and estimable expected losses.

EXHIBIT 1

DAIMLER-BENZ AG
Consolidated Statement of Income

	In Millions of DM	
	1991	*1990*
Sales	**95,010**	**85,500**
Increase in Inventories and Other Capitalized In-House Output	3,556	2,840
Total Output	**98,566**	**88,340**
Other Operating Income	3,545	3,598
Cost of Materials	(49,456)	(44,477)
Personnel Expenses	(29,372)	(26,890)
of which for Old-Age Pensions DM1,511 million (1990: DM1,347 million)		
Amortization of Intangible Assets, Depreciation of Fixed Assets and of Leased Equipment	(5,977)	(5,169)
Other Operating Expenses	(13,824)	(12,016)
Income from Affiliated, Associated and Related Companies	56	4
Net Interest Income	623	989
Write-Downs of Financial Assets and of Securities	(134)	(158)
Results from Ordinary Business Activities	**4,027**	**4,221**
Extraordinary Result	(544)	—
Income Taxes	(1,039)	(1,814)
Other Taxes	(502)	(612)
Net Income	**1,942**	**1,795**
Profit Carried Forward from Previous Year	8	5
Transfer to Retained Earnings	(1,275)	(1,124)
Income Applicable to Minority Shareholders	(99)	(145)
Loss Applicable to Minority Shareholders	29	34
Unappropriated Profit of Daimler-Benz AG	**605**	**565**

want to smooth its reported results.

EXHIBIT 2

DAIMLER-BENZ AG
Consolidated Balance Sheet

	In Millions of DM	
Assets	*December 31, 1991*	*December 31, 1990*

Non-Current Assets		
Intangible Assets	774	304
Fixed Assets	16,574	15,057
Financial Assets	3,758	1,569
Leased Equipment	8,092	6,518
	29,198	23,448
Current Assets		
Inventories	20,732	18,855
Advance Payments Received	(5,827)	(5,727)
	14,905	13,128
Receivables	12,370	11,321
Other Assets	9,783	9,019
Securities	5,725	5,154
Cash	2,010	3,786
	44,793	42,408
Prepaid Expenses and Deferred Taxes	1,723	1,483
	75,714	67,339

Stockholders' Equity and Liabilities		
Stockholders' Equity		
Capital Stock	2,330	2,330
Paid-In Capital	2,117	2,117
Retained Earnings	13,182	11,934
Minority Interests	1,214	881
Unappropriated Profit of Daimler-Benz AG	605	565
	19,448	17,827
Provisions		
Provisions for Old-Age Pensions and Similar Obligations	10,790	10,831
Other Provisions	17,239	16,536
	28,029	27,367
Liabilities		
Accounts Payable Trade	7,015	6,469
Other Liabilities	20,713	15,312
	27,728	21,781
Deferred Income	509	364
	75,714	67,339

CASE 9.3
ACCOUNTING FOR LEASES

Deutsche Lufthansa AG

Deutsche Lufthansa AG is the parent company of the German national airline, Lufthansa. For most airlines, the largest single asset account is the investment in flight equipment. For example, at year-end 1990, nearly 60 percent of Lufthansa's total asset value was reflected in its fleet of over 200 aircraft. Comparable figures for American Airlines and British Airways were 52 and 64 percent, respectively.

Financing for the acquisition of fleet equipment is frequently provided externally in the form of leases. This case concerns the accounting for leases in Germany, the United Kingdom, and the United States.

Lease Accounting.   Most developed countries recognize the existence of two types of leases, capital and operating, but how that information is disclosed in financial statements and the extent to which capital leasing is utilized vary considerably between countries.

EU directives do not specify any required accounting treatment for leases, but *IAS No. 17* requires that the accounting for leases follow from the *substance* of the lease agreement. If a lease transfers substantially "all of the risks and rewards incident to ownership" to the lessee, it is considered to be a *capital* (or finance) *lease* under which the leased asset and a lease liability should be recognized on the lessee's balance sheet. The value assigned to the capitalized asset and liability is the lesser of the asset's (or liability's) fair market value or the present value of the minimum lease payments. If, on the other hand, a lease does not transfer substantially all of the risks and rewards of asset ownership to the lessee (i.e., those risks and rewards are retained by the lessor), the lease is considered to be an *operating lease* under which no balance sheet disclosure is required, but a lease expense should be reflected on the lessee's income statement.[1]

The fundamental concepts of *IAS No. 17* are likewise reflected in the generally accepted accounting practice of Germany, Great Britain, and the United States, but important differences nonetheless exist. In Great Britain, for example, a lease is usually considered to be a capital lease only when, as of the lease inception, the present value of the minimum lease payments equals (or exceeds) 90 percent of the fair market value of the leased asset. In the United States, however, a capital lease may exist when *any one* of the following four criteria is satisfied:

1. The lease agreement transfers ownership of the property to the lessee.
2. The lease agreement contains a bargain purchase option.
3. The lease term is at least 75 percent of the leased asset's useful economic life.

This case was prepared by Kenneth R. Ferris from publicly available documents. Copyright © 1993 by Kenneth R. Ferris. All rights reserved.

[1]*IAS No. 17* requires that, for both capital and operating leases, the footnotes to the financial statements disclose (1) the amount of assets held under capital or operating leases; (2) commitments for minimum lease payments under capital leases and noncancelable operating leases with a term of more than one year, giving the amounts and periods in which the payments are due; and (3) any significant financing restrictions, renewal or purchase options, and contingent rental payments arising from the lease agreement.

4. The present value of the minimum lease payments is at least 90 percent of the leased asset's fair market value.

In Germany, the primary criterion for determining the existence of a capital ease is the lease term in relation to the economic life of the leased asset: if the lease term is 90 percent or more of the leased asset's economic life, capitalization of the lease is required. Leases that are, in effect, installment sales, under which title passes after the final payment, are always considered to be capital leases.

The institutional setting in each country, however, may also influence prevalent GAAP. In Great Britain and the United States, for example, accounting standards and tax regulations rarely coincide. In Germany, however, prevailing GAAP is largely derived from the German Commercial Code, which in turn is dictated by tax court rulings and company law. Thus, lease accounting in Germany generally follows complex tax laws, and since depreciation deductions generally remain with the lessor, there is significant disincentive for German companies to use lease financing at all.

Required:

Exhibits 1–3 present selected financial data from the published annual reports of American Airlines, British Airways, and Lufthansa, respectively. Review these data and consider the following:

(a) Compare the amount of leasing, in total, and the proportion of capital to operating leases undertaken by each of the airlines. Also evaluate the extent of the financial statement disclosure regarding leases. What can you conclude from this regarding the institutional or cultural setting of each respective country?

(b) Calculate the total debt to total assets ratio and the total debt-to-equity ratio for the data in Exhibits 1–3. Restate Exhibits 1 and 2 to reflect the capitalization of operating leases for both American Airlines and British Airways and then recalculate these ratios. (Assume a discount rate of 8 percent.)

(c) Does the use of operating leases increase the ability of a company to lever itself? If so, are German companies at a competitive disadvantage in the world capital markets when competing for borrowed funds?

EXHIBIT 1

AMERICAN AIRLINES
Selected Financial Disclosures

Condensed Balance Sheet (31 December 1990)

($ millions)

Current assets	2,657.8
Equipment and property (net)	7,852.6
Equipment and property (net) under capital leases	1,295.0
Other assets	1,548.2
Total assets	13,353.6
Current liabilities	4,824.7
Long-term debt	1,674.2
Capital lease obligations	1,597.7
Other liabilities	1,529.6
Stockholders' equity	3,727.4
Total equities	13,353.6

Income Statement Data

Operating lease costs	580.5
Income before taxes	(33.3)

Footnote Disclosure: Lease Commitments

The future minimum lease payments required under capital leases (together with the present value of net minimum lease payments) and future minimum lease payments required under operating leases that have an initial or remaining non-cancelable lease term in excess of one year as of December 31, 1990, were as follows (in millions):

Year ending December 31,	Capital Leases	Operating Leases
1991	$ 185.1	$ 580.5
1992	184.7	612.1
1993	181.3	598.2
1994	179.4	584.9
1995	190.2	565.0
1996 and subsequent	2,275.6	11,817.0
	3,196.3[a]	14,757.7[a][b]
Less minimum sublease rentals	—	143.6
		$14,614.1
Less amount representing interest	1,539.5	
Present value of net minimum lease payments	$1,656.8[c]	

[a] Future minimum payments required under capital leases and operating leases include $451.1 million and $4.3 billion, respectively, guaranteed by AMR relating to special facility revenue bonds issued by municipalities. Minimum sublease rentals relative to capital leases are $26.0 million.

[b] American has 226 aircraft under operating lease. Other AMR subsidiaries operate 129 regional aircraft under operating leases. During 1990, 36 Boeing 727-100s, 20 Boeing 727-200s, 2 Boeing 747SPs and 6 Fairchild Metro IIIs which were previously owned were sold and leased back.

[c] Includes $140.5 million guaranteed by American.

The aircraft leases can generally be renewed at rates based on fair market value at the end of the lease term for one to five years. Most aircraft leases have purchase options at the end of the lease term at fair market value, but generally not to exceed a stated percentage of the defined lessor's cost of the aircraft. Of the aircraft American has under operating lease, 15 Boeing 767-300ERs and 25 Airbus A300-600Rs are cancelable upon 30-days' notice during the initial 10-year lease term. At the end of that term, the leases can be renewed for periods ranging from 10 to 12 years.

Rentals and landing fees for 1990, 1989 and 1988 include rent expense of $788.2 million, $621.9 million and $441.7 million, respectively.

EXHIBIT 2

BRITISH AIRWAYS Plc
Selected Financial Disclosures

Condensed Balance Sheet (31 March 1990)

	(£ millions)
Current assets	1,295
Fixed assets	
Fleet	3,438
Property and equipment	943
	4,381
Less: Accumulated depreciation	(1,917)
	2,464
Investments	108
Total fixed assets	2,572
Total assets	3,867
Current liabilities	1,816
Long-Term liabilities (excluding leases)	943
Finance lease obligations	132
Provisions for liabilities	64
Shareholders' equity	912
Total equities	3,867

Income Statement Data

Depreciation on finance-leased aircraft	30
Operating lease costs:	
Aircraft	179
Property and equipment	54
Income before taxes	345

Footnote Disclosure: Operating Lease Commitment

At March 31, 1991 future minimum rental payments under noncancelable operating leases were as follows:

	Fleet	Property and Equipment	Total
		(£ millions)	
Within one year	220	46	266
Between one and two years	178	27	205
Between two and three years	172	25	197
Between three and four years	137	24	161
Between four and five years	30	20	50
Over five years	2	231	233
	739	373	1,112

Exhibit 2 (continued)

BRITISH AIRWAYS Plc
Selected Financial Disclosures

Amounts payable within one year related to commitments expiring as follows:

Within one year	35	13	48
Between one and two years	14	6	20
Between two and three years	14	8	22
Between three and four years	102	12	114
Between four and five years	50	—	50
Over five years	5	7	12
	220	46	266

The fleet leasing commitments include the balance of rental obligations under operating leases in respect of 13 Boeing 747-400, seven Boeing 767-300, five Boeing 747-200, seven Boeing 757, 20 Boeing 737 and eight BAe ATP aircraft, but exclude nine Boeing 737 and three Boeing 757 aircraft which were converted from operating leases to finance leases with effect from March 31, 1991. In the case of most of these obligations, British Airways may be required to meet a small share of any loss on resale if options to renew the leases or convert them into finance leases are not exercised.

British Airways has extendible operating leases with two companies, which are affiliates of British Airways, for eight Boeing 747-400 and seven Boeing 767-300 aircraft.

Exhibit 3

DEUTSCHE LUFTHANSA AG
Selected Financial Disclosures

Condensed Balance Sheet (31 December 1990)

	(DM millions)
Current assets	3,139,483
Aircraft	7,828,706
Other assets	2,210,232
Total assets	13,178,421
Current liabilities	1,616,035
Long-term liabilities	3,636,729
Provisions	2,623,673
Special items with an equity portion	2,113,626
Shareholders' equity	3,186,535
Total equities	13,178,421

Income Statement Data

Income before taxes (DM millions)	142,446

Footnote Disclosure: Other Financial Commitments

The payments for long-term leasing contracts for aircraft amounted to DM105 million in the Group in 1990 (DM52 million in the AG). These contracts will involve payments in subsequent years of up to DM165 million (DM78 million in the AG).

ANNUAL REPORT ANALYSIS

Bayer AG

An interesting and important challenge for students of international financial reporting is to study the published annual reports of various companies from different countries. Your instructor will provide you with a recent copy of the Bayer annual report. To facilitate your delving into the annual report, undertake the following endeavors.

Required:

(a) List the key differences between the Bayer annual report and what you would expect to see for a U.S. company like Dow Chemical.

(b) Calculate the following ratios for Bayer, taking care to note the assumptions you found necessary to make and where you found the appropriate pieces of data in the annual report.

(1) Current ratio $=$ $\dfrac{\text{Total current assets}}{\text{Total current liabilities}}$

(2) Quick ratio $=$ $\dfrac{\text{Cash + Marketable securities + Accounts receivable}}{\text{Total current liabilities}}$

(3) Operating cash flow to current liabilities $=$ $\dfrac{\text{Operating cash flow}}{\text{Average total current liabilities}}$

(4) Debt-to-equity ratio $=$ $\dfrac{\text{Long term debt}}{\text{Owners' equity}}$

(5) Debt-to-total capitalization ratio $=$ $\dfrac{\text{Long term debt}}{\text{Long term debt + owners' equity}}$

(6) Interest coverage ratio $=$ $\dfrac{\text{Net income before interest \& income taxes}}{\text{Interest expense}}$

(7) Operating cash flow to interest charges $=$ $\dfrac{\text{Operating cash flow}}{\text{Interest expense}}$

(8) Operating cash flow to total liabilities $=$ $\dfrac{\text{Operating cash flow}}{\text{Average total liabilities}}$

(9) Receivables turnover ratio $=$ $\dfrac{\text{Net sales}}{\text{Average accts. receivable}}$

(10) Inventory turnover $=$ $\dfrac{\text{Cost of goods sold}}{\text{Average inventory}}$

(11) Asset turnover $=$ $\dfrac{\text{Net sales}}{\text{Average total assets}}$

(12) Average collection period ratio $=$ $\dfrac{\text{365 Days}}{\text{Receivables turnover ratio}}$

(13) Average number of days' inventory on hand ratio	=	$$\frac{\text{365 Days}}{\text{Inventory turnover ratio}}$$
(14) Return on Assets (ROA)	=	$$\frac{\text{Net Income}}{\text{Average total assets}}$$
OR	=	ROS × Asset turnover
(15) Return on equity (ROE)	=	$$\frac{\text{Net income}}{\text{Average total owners' equity}}$$
OR	=	ROA × Financial leverage
(16) Return on sales (ROS)	=	$$\frac{\text{Net income}}{\text{Net sales}}$$
(17) Financial leverage	=	$$\frac{\text{Avg. liabilities} + \text{Avg. owners' equity}}{\text{Avg. owners' equity}}$$
(18) Basic earnings per share (EPS)	=	$$\frac{\text{NI applicable to common shareholders}}{\text{Weighted average common shares}}$$
(19) Cash dividend yield	=	$$\frac{\text{Cash dividend per common share}}{\text{Market price per common share}}$$
(20) Cash dividend payout	=	$$\frac{\text{Total cash dividend to common shareholders}}{\text{Net income}}$$

(c) What do you conclude about the availability of the appropriate data in the annual report for calculating these ratios?

(d) What does this financial analysis tell you about Bayer?

(e) What analytical metrics did Bayer choose to report for itself? What do those choices say about the message the company is striving to tell and the

Japan

[Japanese] financial statements tend to distort results.[1]

Japanese companies have hidden profits in order to avoid social opprobrium. Window dressing is common and legal in Japan. . . . Japanese financial statements are not user-friendly and push individual investors out of the market.[2]

Introduction

When reviewing the major geopolitical developments of the latter half of the 20th century, historians will surely include among them the collapse of communism in eastern Europe, the formation of the European Union, and the establishment of Japan as an international economic power. In spite of its relatively small population (125 million people), tiny land mass, and relatively meager natural resources, Japan has developed one of the largest and fastest-growing economies in the world and has become a dominant force in international trade. It is tempting to ascribe the country's spectacular successes to the advantages of free markets, but Japanese economic prowess probably owes as much to Japanese discipline and social cohesiveness as to the "invisible hand." The Japanese have shown a remarkable ability to accommodate Western economic theory to traditional Japanese values, creating a unique way of conducting business and accounting for the results. The Japanese have a phrase to describe their ability to adapt foreign methods to their own needs and purposes: *wakon yosai,* which means "Japanese spirit, Western techniques."

Financial reporting practices, like so much else in modern Japan, represent a dynamic combination of foreign influence with indigenous attitudes and behavior

---

[1]H. Sender, "Why Japan's Financial Crisis Is So Scary," *Institutional Investor,* June 1992, p. 56.

[2]Akio Mikuni, former analyst at Nomura Securities quoted in J. Pickering, "National Audit Traditions Stall Global Standards," *Accounting Today,* November 23, 1992, p. 11.

patterns. Japanese law includes two major codes governing the preparation of financial statements: the German-influenced **Commercial Code,** the history of which dates back to 1899, and the **Japanese Securities and Exchange Law of 1948,** based on the U.S. Securities Exchange Acts of 1933 and 1934. Consequently, contemporary Japanese reporting practices consist of a curious amalgamation of Germanic conservatism and Anglo-American investor orientation, with the whole adapted to the distinctive cultural and economic structures governing Japanese business.

Like financial reporting in many other countries, Japanese reporting is moving toward a new internationalism as it responds to the development of global financial markets. Japanese multinationals are increasingly providing restated results for use by overseas investors. However, even as Japan's financial reporting practices move toward greater technical conformity with U.S. and international practices, well-informed interpretations of Japanese financial statements still require familiarity with its relevant cultural, legal, and economic contexts. For example, although differences in accounting rules are partly responsible for the low net income reported by most Japanese companies, a reader must bear in mind such confounding factors as the existence of the closely allied, legally independent corporate group known as *keiretsu;* the nature of Japanese capital markets; the relatively modest expectations of Japanese investors; and the often-cited long-run view that trades off short-term profitability in exchange for survival and ultimately market dominance.

Environmental Factors

Cultural Environment

Much has been written in recent years about the effect of Japanese culture on Japanese business practices, an influence that has created a striking contrast between the values and habits of Western capitalism and those of Asian capitalism. One may begin to grasp something of this cultural chasm by referring to Hofstede's series of indexes (introduced in Chapter 1) designed to measure the basic cultural attitudes: power distance (PD), individualism (IDV), uncertainty avoidance (UAV), and long-term orientation (LTO). In the first area, PD, the score for Japan indicated a high acceptance of power distance: 54 compared to 40 for the United States. In the area of IDV, Japan scored 46, and the United States had the highest score of any group included in the study, 91. In the area of UAV, the scores were reversed: the United States scored 46, and the Japanese registered a much higher 92. Finally, in the area of LTO, the Japanese scored 80, the third highest ranking in the group studied, and the United States scored a moderately low 29. Thus, we see dramatic divergences in the three categories of individualism, uncertainty avoidance, and long-term orientation, as well as a marked difference in power distance.

The difference between the U.S. and Japanese scores in IDV probably does not surprise anyone acquainted with Japanese culture. One of its most pervasive and influential features—one that has received extensive attention in the Western press and academic literature—is *dantai ishiki,* or group consciousness, and its related social values of interdependence and harmony. Group consciousness has been described as a *frame* orientation rather than an *attribute* orientation that sees the self in terms of affiliations with others rather than as a discrete individual with qualities and attributes all one's own.[3] This can be traced to the teachings of Confucius, specifically that the family is the model for all social organizations and a person is foremost a member of a family, not an individual.

In Japan, as well as in other East Asian societies influenced by Confucianism, the boundaries of freedom are defined much differently than in the West. Public duty, not individual rights, is the highest value. "Loyalty to the master," filial piety, and deference to authority—not freedom of expression or personal liberty—form the ethical foundations of society.[4] This cultural value profoundly affects the nature of Japanese business relationships and conditions attitudes toward external reporting of financial results.

It is often remarked in the West that Japanese group consciousness creates a level of loyalty within business organizations rarely seen in other cultures that results in extraordinary efforts by each individual for the good of the whole group. Although Westerners can certainly appreciate the importance and potential effectiveness of well-directed, cooperative action, they nevertheless place a high value on psychological (and, if possible, financial) independence and hence are not well equipped to understand the web of emotional and financial dependency that holds Japanese society together. It is normal and expected for Japanese workers to attach their careers—even their identities—to that of a corporate or personal patron. The West tends to stigmatize dependency, but the Japanese take it for granted as the natural and necessary condition of social existence.

Group membership is quite simply the dominant fact of Japanese economic life: people belong to companies, companies belong to groups, and everyone belongs to the nation.[5] This fact has resulted in some important alterations in economic practices imported from the West. Capitalism is still highly competitive in Japanese culture but is less a matter of creating individual opportunity than of fostering group security and harmony. Alliances and affiliations are not entered into lightly and are meant to last a very long time. These characteristics of Japanese business and culture are supported by the relatively high score for LTO. Within groups and alliances, the Japanese expect business relationships to proceed on the basis of mutual trust; as a result, disclosures tend to be personal and informal rather than routinized and mandatory. Thus, traditional Japanese managers may not see the point of creating and reviewing the kind of internal control systems that are so important for U.S. financial reporting. Moreover, because group membership involves a major emotional commitment, Japanese managers feel an unusually strong compulsion to screen corporate affairs—the routine as well as the potentially scandalous—from the view of outsiders. They are more disposed to maintain harmony and stability within the corporate household than to worry about the "rights" of outside parties, including small investors.

---

[3]J. McKinnon, "Cultural Constraints on Audit Independence in Japan," *International Journal of Accounting,* Fall 1984, pp. 17–43.

[4]N. Gardels, "East Beats West: Transforming Cultural Values into Economic Gains; The New World Order May Be Asian, Not Western, Replacing Liberalism With Conformity, Discipline," *The Washington Post,* January 5, 1992, p. C3.

[5]B. R. Schlender, "Japan: Is It Changing for Good?" *Fortune,* June 13, 1994, pp. 124–34.

Although the scores for IDV support the cultural differences discussed, the divergence of scores on the LTO index is equally supportive in explaining cultural differences between the United States and Japan. The divergence of scores on the LTO index, like that of IDV, probably does not surprise anyone acquainted with Japanese culture. Recall from Chapter 1 that LTO values are associated with the teachings of Confucius, teachings that are considered to be the roots of Eastern ethics and culture. Confucius was a teacher of practical ethics without any religious content—he dealt with virtue and harmony, but left the question of truth open. Hofstede posits that for this reason, questions concerning truth seem to be insignificant to Eastern cultures.[6] This cultural attitude toward truth may help to explain why true and fair accounting practices differ between Japan and, say, the United States or Britain. It may also help to explain why Japanese companies are allowed to have reserve accounts (not allowed in the United States) and how they may use these reserves. If in a given year a Japanese company expects a loss or extraordinarily low net income (compared to other years), it can, for example, draw from reserves to create a smoother, more consistent pattern of net income (financial reporting). This would seem to be supported by the idea that maintaining harmony, a key principle in Confucius's teachings, is more important than what is true and fair according to a Western mind-set.

In Chapter 1, the positive correlation between LTO and economic growth was discussed. In the case of Japan, as one would expect, the correlation is very strong. On the LTO index, Japan ranked third highest among the countries surveyed, and it ranked fifth highest in the average annual growth rate (for the 20-year period 1965 to 1985). The LTO values—perseverance, ordering relationships by status and observing this order, thrift, and having a sense of shame—are all related to Confucian teachings and therefore have undoubtedly played a significant role in the development of Japan's economic life over recent decades.

Recall from the discussion in Chapter 1 that a high UAV score and a low IDV score would support, in the case of Japan, a financial reporting subculture with a high degree of secrecy and low degree of professionalism. With respect to a professionalism versus statutory control orientation to financial reporting, it is true that changes in accounting standards or reporting requirements rarely work their way up from the professional grass-roots level in Japan; instead, the government acts as primary initiator and facilitator, not individual companies or the accounting profession.[7] As for secrecy, Japan's high UAV score and low IDV score, relative to those of the United States, explain, at least in part, a lower degree of disclosure in Japanese financial reporting than U.S. financial reporting.

Cultural attitudes, as described, may help to explain the remarkable reticence that characterizes the annual reports of Japanese companies: firms fulfill disclosure requirements, but they rarely volunteer information. Even Omron Corp., one of the world's

---

[6]G. Hofstede, *Cultures and Organizations: Software of the Mind,* London: McGraw-Hill (U.K.), 1991, p. 164.

[7]For example, most Japanese companies have a fiscal year-end of March 31, which coincides with the end of the Japanese government fiscal year.

premier manufacturers of automation components and a company that publishes an annual report espoused to be in accordance with U.S. GAAP, prefers to accept a qualified opinion from its auditor, Deloitte Touche Tohmatsu, rather than provide segment information (see Exhibit 10–1). Other disclosures that U.S. or European investors may take for granted—information concerning investments in subsidiaries and affiliates, employee and director remuneration, outstanding convertible debt, nonmonetary transactions, to name a few—rarely appear in Japanese reports. Although the Japanese government and the globalization of capital markets have been pressuring Japanese corporations toward greater disclosure, progress has been slower than many foreign investors would like.

Legal and Political Environment

Individual Tax Law. Japanese combined national and local individual tax rates range from 15 to 65 percent on taxable income of ¥4,600,000 ($46,000)[8] to ¥25,500,000 ($255,000) and above, respectively. Gains on the sale of corporate shares and convertible debentures are taxed at a preferential flat national plus local rate of 26 percent. The familiar notion of classifying capital gains as short term or long term is not applicable to gains on sales of securities, but it is a classification scheme imposed on the sale of real estate.

Corporate Tax Law. Japanese company law links financial income to taxable income by requiring that expenses claimed on a company's tax return be recorded on its books of account. With a statutory income tax rate of 37.5 percent on undistributed corporate income (and frequently an effective tax rate over 50 percent due to additional local income taxes), companies thus have a strong incentive to keep reported earnings down, chiefly by taking advantage of tax-deductible reserves and favorable depreciation provisions allowed by the Ministry of Finance. A few examples follow.

Many expense allowances familiar to U.S. managers, which are calculated on the basis of historical experience rates in the United States, must be recorded in Japanese financial statements at percentages provided by tax authorities and are usually calculated to be the maximum allowed by law irrespective of actual or expected experience rates. As a consequence, the amount deducted on a Japanese company's income statement as bad debts, sales returns, or sales warranties may have little to do with the actual economic conditions or prior experience of the firm. Other Japanese allowances, not so familiar to U.S financial statement readers, are also the product of tax regulations, even though that fact may never be disclosed. Kawasaki Steel's financial statements, for example, include an allowance of ¥42 billion for special repairs in the long-term liability section of its balance sheet. A characteristically laconic Japanese note "explains" the allowance without mentioning that it essentially represents a special tax benefit (see Exhibit 10–2).

---

[8]At January 1, 1995, $1 = ¥100.

EXHIBIT 10–1
Report of Omron Corporation's Independent Accountants

To the Board of Directors and Shareholders
of Omron Corporation

We have audited the accompanying consolidated balance sheets of Omron Corporation and subsidiaries as of March 31, 1994 and 1993, and the related consolidated statements of income, shareholders' equity and cash flows for each of the three years in the period ended March 31, 1994, all expressed in Japanese yen. These financial statements are the responsibility of the Company's management. Our responsibility is to express an opinion on these financial statements based on our audits.

We conducted our audits in accordance with auditing standards generally accepted in the United States. Those standards require that we plan and perform the audit to obtain reasonable assurance about whether the financial statements are free of material misstatement. An audit includes examining, on a test basis, evidence supporting the amounts and disclosures in the financial statements. An audit also includes assessing the accounting principles used and significant estimates made by management, as well as evaluating the overall financial statement presentation. We believe that our audits provide a reasonable basis for our opinion.

Certain information required by Statement No. 14 of the Financial Accounting Standards Board has not been presented in the accompanying consolidated financial statements. In our opinion, presentation of various segment information regarding operations is required for a complete presentation of the Company's consolidated financial statements in accordance with accounting principles generally accepted in the United States.

In our opinion, except for the omission of segment information as discussed in the preceding paragraph, the consolidated financial statements referred to above present fairly, in all material respects, the financial position of Omron Corporation and its subsidiaries as of March 31, 1994 and 1993, and the results of their operations and their cash flows for each of the three years in the period ended March 31, 1994, in conformity with accounting principles generally accepted in the United States.

As discussed in Note 1 to the consolidated financial statements, the company changed its method of accounting for income taxes effective April 1, 1993 to conform with Statement No. 109 of the Financial Accounting Standards Board.

Our audits also comprehended the translation of Japanese yen amounts into United States dollar amounts and, in our opinion, such translation has been made in conformity with the basis stated in Note 2. Such United States dollar amounts are presented solely for convenience.

(Signed) *Deloitte Touche Tohmatsu*

Source: Omron Annual Report, 1994.

This yearly special repair deduction is taken in addition to regular depreciation on equipment and allows the company to reap tax benefits before such costs are actually incurred. When the work is actually done, the account is zeroed out, with any variation between actual and estimated repair costs treated as current income or loss. Other allowances of this sort include employee retirement benefits and product warranty costs.

In addition, companies may create special reserves from retained earnings to secure special tax deferrals. For example, a company may obtain a tax deduction in the year

---

EXHIBIT 10–2

Footnote Excerpt from Kawasaki Steel's Annual Report

Allowance for special repairs

Blast furnaces and hot blast stoves, including related machinery and equipment, periodically require substantial component replacements and repairs. Such work normally occurs approximately every 7 to 10 years for blast furnaces and every 14 to 20 years for hot blast stoves. The estimated future costs of such maintenance are provided for and charged to income on a straight-line basis over the periods of the respective dates of such anticipated replacements and repairs. Difference between the estimated costs and actual costs are charged or credited to income as incurred.

Source: Kawasaki Steel Annual Report, 1994.

that it books a reserve as an appropriation of retained earnings; in some future period, the entry would be reversed, thereby restoring the amount to taxable income. The most common reserves of this type are for special depreciation (bonus or accelerated depreciation allowed in addition to regular depreciation), inventory price fluctuations, and overseas investment losses. All of these reserves and their related deductions are contingent on meeting specific Ministry of Finance requirements that are calculated to promote the Japanese national interest. Exhibit 10–3 presents a footnote from Kawasaki Steel's financial statements that illustrates and explains the nature of these reserves.

These reserves are often buried in retained earnings, with little or no reference to them on the financial statements themselves. Reserves of this sort do not conform to U.S. GAAP and result in a relative understatement of net income in Japanese financial statements vis-à-vis U.S. financial statements.

In addition, corporations must create a legal reserve, which is not a tax-deductible reserve; it is a requirement imposed by the Japanese Commercial Code. Corporations must appropriate to the legal reserve an amount of retained earnings equal to at least 10 percent of the cash dividends paid each period until the reserve equals 25 percent of stated capital (the par value of capital stock). The reserve (as well as surplus capital) is not available for dividends but may be used to reduce a corporate earnings deficit by a resolution of the shareholders or may be transferred to stated capital by a resolution of the board of directors. This legally mandated appropriation effectively requires corporations to maintain a proportionate level of capitalization by reinvesting a portion of earnings in the business; the deficit reduction provision allows companies to smooth income and create at least an appearance of stable, "harmonious" earnings over the long term.

Linking tax policy to financial reporting practices inevitably distorts the presentation of corporate performance in financial statements by encouraging managers to maximize tax benefits or requiring them to follow tax guidelines rather than striving to achieve a broader reporting objective akin to a true and fair representation of the business's economic substance. Predictably, the effect of tax law on Japanese financial statements has created some confusion among international investors. The artificially low earnings reported by Japanese companies and the strong performance of Japanese stocks on the Tokyo market during the 1980s resulted in extremely high price-earnings (P-E) ratios for many Japanese stocks, up to four or five times the average for U.S.

EXHIBIT 10-3

Footnote Excerpt from Kawasaki Steel
Annual Report

Retained earnings

Retained earnings include the reserves under the Special Taxation Measures Law. The schedule was as follows:

	Millions of Yen		Thousands of U.S. Dollars
As of March 31	*1994*	*1993*	*1994*
Reserve for accelerated depreciation	¥14,067	¥14,724	$136,375
Reserve for losses on overseas investments	149	214	1,450
Reserve for advanced depreciation of property	21,240	13,547	205,921
Total	¥35,457	¥28,486	$343,746

The Special Taxation Measures Law permits the Company to deduct for income tax purposes, transfers to certain reserves that are not required for financial accounting purposes, if recorded on the books as profit appropriations or charges to income, and to restore them to taxable income in future years.

Source: Kawasaki Steel Annual Report, 1994.

---

securities. Between 1984 and 1989, the Nikkei Index of Japanese stock prices rose at an average annual rate of 27.5 percent, and its P-E ratio increased from 37.9 to 70.9. Available evidence suggests that accounting differences explain about half of the long-run disparity between U.S. and Japanese P-Es. For example, if Japanese firms used U.S. GAAP, the average Japanese P-E ratio would have been 32.6, not 53.7, in 1989.[9] Accounting differences cannot, however, fully explain the doubling of this ratio in 1986 nor its decline between 1990 and 1992. During the 1980s, some Western analysts argued that the Tokyo securities market was impossibly overpriced. But others disagreed, pointing to the effect of tax law on financial reporting and suggesting that the price/net cash flow ratio was/is a more appropriate tool for comparing Japanese and U.S. equities. From December 1989, the Nikkei fell from a record high of 38,915.87 to a five and one-half–year low of 15,373.34 in July 1992. Despite this fall in securities prices, however, the market price-earnings ratio remained around 35, and analysts do not agree on the appropriate methods to evaluate Japanese stocks (more on this later).

National Economic Policy. Japanese firms also tend to report lower earnings than their U.S. counterparts because their managers are less interested in short-term profitability than in continuous long-term growth. (One reflection of this emphasis on the long run is Japanese managers' freedom from the quarterly earnings reports that publicly held U.S. companies must issue.) In this respect, they practice the macroeconomic strategy pursued by the nation's political and financial leaders. Market share,

---

[9]K. R. French and J. M. Poterba, "Were Japanese Stock Prices too High?" *Journal of Financial Economics,* October 1991, p. 337.

technological progress, and corporate harmony constitute the top priorities of Japanese managers and Japanese political culture. The sacrifice of immediate rewards and comforts for the sake of greater economic power in the future is a central tenet of the national consensus that has made possible the country's remarkable economic progress in the last few decades. Such an outlook fits well with the traditional Japanese commitment to lifetime employment, the fulfillment of which would naturally depend on continued economic growth and faith in the future. One could say, then, that the typically low net income reported by Japanese firms can be attributed in part to a social-political ethos that is less interested in short-term results than in long-term rewards.

Business Environment

Form of Business.   The dominant form of business organization in Japan is the *Kabushiki Kaisha* (KK), a type of limited liability company similar to a U.S. corporation. The Japanese Commercial Code requires that a KK elect at least one statutory auditor to examine the performance of its directors and report to shareholders annually. There is no requirement, however, that the statutory auditor be a certified public accountant.[10] A large KK—one with stated capital of ¥500 million (about $5.0 million, based on January 1995 exchange rates) or liabilities of ¥20 billion (about $200 million)—is required to appoint statutory auditors (usually members of the company organization) and is required to hire an independent outside auditor. The statutory auditors principally examine the managerial behavior of the directors and the performance of the independent auditor.[11] The duties and powers of the independent auditor are limited to the accounting records.

One reason that Japanese managers have historically been able to focus on long-term objectives without having to worry about takeovers is the pattern of stable shareholding established by the corporate families, or *keiretsu,* which dominate the Japanese economy. One might consider the *keiretsu* (literally, headless combines) a manifestation of group consciousness at the organizational level. These giant alliances of technically unaffiliated companies grew out of the U.S. attempt in the late 1940s to break up the great industrial conglomerations (known as *zaibatsu*) of prewar Japan. When the Allied Occupation ended in 1948, companies quietly and informally began to form new ties—generally under the aegis of a major bank or a large trading company—by lending each other money, establishing interlocking directorates, buying each other's stock, and creating helpful patterns of trade within the group.

Six large *keiretsu* dominate the Japanese business landscape. The Mitsui, Mitsubishi, and Sumitomo groups are the powerful trading company *keiretsu;* Fuji, Sanwa, and Dai-Ichi Kangyo are the dominant banking groups. One estimate places 12,000 companies, with sales equivalent to 25 percent of Japan's GNP, in the web of related companies headed by these six associations.[12] *Keiretsu* tend to be highly

---

[10]Coopers & Lybrand, *International Accounting Summaries,* New York: John Wiley & Sons, Inc., 1993, p. J-3.

[11]S. Sgromo, ed., *The Accounting Profession in Japan,* New York: American Institute of Certified Public Accountants, 1988.

[12]"Inside the Charmed Circle," *The Economist,* January 5, 1991, p. 54.

EXHIBIT 10–4
Number of Affiliated Companies in Some Japanese *Keiretsu*
(only a small fraction are consolidated)

Hitachi	688	Marubeni	378
Bridgestone	647	Honda	352
C. Itoh & Co.	628	Matsushita	340
Mitsui & Co.	513	Nissha Iwai	293
Mitsubishi Corp.	459	Sumitomo Corp.	287

Source: *The Economist*, January 5, 1991, p. 54.

diversified, each attempting to form within itself an economic microcosm to minimize risk and maximize benefit to individual members. One writer has summarized the principal characteristics of the *keiretsu* as follows:

- The members are all "independent" major firms in their own oligopolistic industries.

- The confederation pursues the one-set formula (i.e., excluding competitors but aimed at representing all lines within the confederation).

- Service firms (e.g., banking, trading, insurance, and shipping companies) from within the *keiretsu* perform special functions for industrial member firms in varying degrees (not usually to the complete exclusion of outsiders).

- Between the firms there are several cross-ties (e.g., borrowing from the same banks, mutual shareholdings, interlocking directors, using the same trademark and the same trading company, and liaison planning by presidents' clubs).

- Much interfirm business, horizontal and vertical, is done within the group of firms.

- Holding companies at the top (as in the prewar *zaibatsu*) have been eliminated so that the relationship between these groupings is now more cooperative than controlled.[13]

As Exhibits 10–4 and 10–5 illustrate, a vast number of group members typically do not purchase large enough blocks of stocks to trigger financial reporting consolidation requirements under Anglo-American rules. *Keiretsu* involve no holding company and no controlling board of directors as would be typical in European conglomerates, for example. The group as a whole often owns a significant percentage of the voting stock of each of its core members, but that ownership is dispersed among a number of companies. The quantitative aspect of share ownership is less important than the qualitative aspects of these relationships: planning and coordination, special trade and credit relationship, information sharing, and even occasionally rescuing a distressed firm.

---

[13]D. F. Henderson, *Foreign Enterprise in Japan: Law and Policies* (Chapel Hill, NC: University of North Carolina Press, 1973), pp. 131–32.

EXHIBIT 10–5

Mitsubishi Group: Major Shareholders in the Group's Financial Core (percentage of outstanding shares)

	Mitsubishi Bank	Mitsubishi Trust & Banking	Tokio Marine & Fire Insurance
Mitsubishi Bank	—	3.1	4.8
Mitsubishi Trust & Banking	1.8	—	3.5
Tokio Marine & Fire Insurance	4.3	1.9	—
Meiji Life Insurance	5.6	4.8	4.5
Mitsubishi (trading) Corporation	1.7	3.1	2.3
Mitsubishi Heavy Industries	3.0	2.7	1.8
Asahi Glass	—	2.3	1.7
Dai-ichi Life Insurance	3.7	—	—
Total	20.1	17.9	18.6

Source: *Japan Company Handbook, First Section* (Tokyo: Toyo Keizai Inc., 1990)

Keiretsu influence the capital structure of Japanese corporations by altering the relationship between debt and risk, and hence changing the way in which analysts should interpret a Japanese balance sheet. Until recently, when Japanese firms ventured more strongly into international equity markets, many of them carried a debt loading that would prove fatal to most U.S. or European businesses. Nippon Oil's balance sheet, for instance, shows that shareholders' equity accounts for only about 20 percent of its total assets. (By way of comparison, shareholders' equity in Shell was nearly 60 percent of total assets in the same year.) Commentators have offered a variety of explanations for this phenomenon: equity costs more and is scarcer in smaller Asian markets; Japanese workers tend to save rather than invest in stocks; and Japanese banks historically have played a central role in the economy because they were the primary sources of capital for post-war reconstruction. All of these explanations are valid, although some of the national characteristics they describe may be changing: the rise of investment trusts suggests that Japanese investors may be looking for equity investment vehicles, and the liquidity created by success in export markets has made some large trading companies less dependent on home-country banks for working capital. But such factors address necessities and constraints rather than the reasons that debt financing has worked well in Japan for so many years. In fact, many debt-laden Japanese corporations have survived and prospered because of the uniquely cooperative patterns of behavior between members of *keiretsu.*

Much of the debt on a typical Japanese corporate balance sheet has been provided by other members of its *keiretsu*—banks, insurance companies, trading companies—which means that less risk is attached to high levels of debt than would be the case elsewhere. Under normal circumstances, much of a firm's short-term bank debt is automatically rolled over, making it in fact a type of long-term debt. Trade credit, by virtue of extremely favorable terms of payment, also serves as a kind of semipermanent financing provided by major trading companies to its friends. And when a group member runs into trouble, its creditor affiliates—if it has properly maintained its alliances—will in fact extend additional credit, buy stock, and, if necessary, lend managerial expertise rather than abandoning it. What else would one expect since about 70 percent of the shares traded on the Tokyo exchange are in the hands of related firms?[14]

This kind of cooperative behavior, which would be difficult to characterize as strictly arm's length, not only changes the meaning and function of debt but also raises questions about the applicability of Western concepts of consolidated reporting to Japanese business. It has been argued rather persuasively that customary Anglo-American assumptions about stock ownership and legal control simply do not adequately explain the complexity of corporate relationships in Japan.[15] McKinnon suggests that there may be cultural limits to harmonization of accounting principles between countries, even though a measure of technical conformity to Western methods may be adopted by the Japanese. In essence, even if Japanese corporations prepare statements in accordance with U.S. GAAP, one's reading of them may yet be distorted simply by virtue of differing social and cultural factors. In spite of such questions, though, Japan continues to move toward consolidated financial statement guidelines similar to those practiced in the United States. As recently as 1991, the Ministry of Finance added disclosure requirements, some of which are very similar to those required by U.S. GAAP. For example, annual reports are now required to disclose related-party transactions among business entities belonging to the same financial group. The definition of *related parties* is similar to that adopted in the *Statement of Financial Standards No. 57* in the United States.[16]

Capital Markets.   The liberalization of Japanese financial markets and the explosive growth of the Tokyo Stock Exchange (TSE), now second in size in the world (using total market value as a measure) only to the New York Stock Exchange, has made Tokyo a major global financial center. The TSE is not the only stock exchange in Japan—there are eight others—but it is by far the largest in the country, routinely handling more than 80 percent of all shares traded. Although as recently as the early 1980s Japanese markets were reputed to be resistant to analysis and too geared to inside information, those opinions have become much less common as a wave of foreign involvement in the Japanese markets has dispelled misconceptions and lessened the likelihood of real abuses. The pressure exerted by an internationalized capital market may well turn out to be the single most effective agent for change in the evolution of Japanese accounting standards.

The securities markets in Japan are governed primarily by the Securities and Exchange Law of 1948, under the direction of the Ministry of Finance (MOF). Public offerings of more than ¥100 million (about $1 million) require the offering company

[14]*The Economist,* January 5, 1991.

[15]J. McKinnon, ''Application of Anglo-American Principles of Consolidation to Corporate Financial Disclosure in Japan.'' In *Frontiers of International Accounting,* ed. F. D. S. Choi and G. G. Mueller (Ann Arbor, MI: UMI Research Press, 1985), pp. 31–52.

[16]The Japanese Institute of Certified Public Accountants, *Corporate Disclosure in Japan* (Tokyo: JICPA, 1991), p. 68.

to file with the MOF a report including audited consolidated and parent-company financial statements for the last two fiscal years. Also, after an offering is completed, the company must file a report with the MOF, again including audited consolidated and parent-company financial statements, within three months of each fiscal year-end. In addition, eligibility for the TSE requires that a firm list at least 6 million shares if its main offices are located in or around Tokyo; if the company's main business is outside of Tokyo, companies must list at least 20 million shares. The number of shares held by the 10 largest and other specially related shareholders must not exceed 70 percent of the shares listed.

It is interesting to note that in Japan the "principal reason for holding shares is not to secure a financial return, but to further a business relationship."[17] Indeed, analysts estimate that "between 60 percent and 70 percent of listed shares in Japan are held by long-term investors for strategic purposes"[18] and that industrial companies hold about 25 percent of all shares while banks account for roughly 22 percent.[19] Such conditions create a situation in which freely traded and available shares are limited and trading volumes are far short of other major securities exchanges. For example, the 1993 value of securities traded in Japan totaled 21 percent of total capitalization; the same value for London, Paris, and New York were 60 percent, 56 percent, and 45 percent, respectively.[20] Stated in a slightly different way, the average daily trading volume in the foreign section of the exchange during the first quarter of 1995 was a mere 145,000 shares as compared to 2,750,000 shares in 1987.[21] Indeed, such circumstances, combined with the high cost of maintaining a Japanese listing have prompted a substantial number of foreign firms to exit the Japanese exchanges.[22] In fact, one recent account notes only 93 foreign companies listed on the Tokyo Exchange as compared to 127 at the end of 1991.[23] Among those exiting are General Electric, Scott Paper, Hewlett-Packard, and British Gas.

Generally, filing requirements similar to those applicable to Japanese companies apply to foreign companies desiring to make a public offering of shares in Japan. However, they need not file financial statements audited by Japanese auditors if the statements were examined by auditors deemed to be their equivalent. This provision has created an interesting situation: the Ministry of Finance will accept a U.S. audit

---

[17]G. Baker, "Trapped in Stagnant Waters," *Financial Times,* February 22, 1995, p. 19.

[18]J. Sapsford, "Cross-Holding System in Japan Shows Strains," *The Wall Street Journal,* August 25, 1994, p. A8.

[19]Baker, "Trapped in Stagnant Waters."

[20]Ibid.

[21]G. Baker and R. Waters, "Tokyo Exchange Hit by Departures of U.S. Companies," *Financial Times,* March 26, 1995, p. 1.

[22]According to Baker and Waters, "Tokyo Exchange Hit by Departures" and Baker, "Trapped in Stagnant Waters," the costs of being listed on a U.S. exchange are between $1 and $6 per 1,000 shares traded and between $6 to $10 on European exchanges. In Japan it is much more than the average cost on European exchanges. Moreover, investors in Japan must pay purchase fees eight times higher than the world's other major exchanges.

[23]"The Pressure Is Growing for Financial Deregulation," *The Wall Street Journal,* March 28, 1995, p. A21.

report, but the U.S. SEC will not necessarily accept a Japanese audit report. If the SEC is not familiar with the Japanese auditing firm providing the report, it will investigate the quality of the audit report before deciding whether to accept it.[24]

To stem the exodus of foreign companies from the Tokyo Exchange, a number of listing rules were relaxed effective January 1, 1995. Quite significantly, one change is that foreign companies will no longer have to translate full annual reports into Japanese; they may issue an abbreviated translated report for their Japanese investors.[25] It remains to be seen whether Tokyo can make enough changes quickly enough to solidify and build its potential as a major international equity center.

Because Japan's Commercial Code requires neither consolidated statements (in fact, it forbids them) nor comparative data,[26] securities laws have been the primary tool by which the Japanese government has propagated Anglo-American consolidation methods and the inclusion of prior year information. As a result of this approach, however, only those companies whose securities are registered with the Ministry of Finance are subject to consolidation rules, which require firms to publish both consolidated and parent-only financial statements. The MOF essentially accepts the U.S. definition of control, requiring companies to account for unconsolidated affiliates that are 20 to 50 percent owned using the equity method—but only in their consolidated statements. On unconsolidated (parent-only) financial statements, companies must show investments in other companies at the lower of cost or market.

During the 1980s, experts noted that the most dramatic growth in the TSE was not in original offerings but in the secondary stock market. This phenomenon suggests that the Japanese public has become more willing to invest in shares than they used to be. During the 1980s, individual investors and investment trusts (which get 80 percent of their funds from individuals) were undoubtedly encouraged to invest in the stock market by a variety of factors: the continuing gains posted by Japanese shares, the belief that the government would step in to support the market should that prove necessary, and the tax breaks available to individual investors in Japan. The early 1990s proved that Tokyo's stock market is not immune from drastic downturns. Although some individuals—as well as institutions—have realized substantial losses from investments in the stock market, others refuse to sell. In any case, the trend of increasing numbers of individual investors that began in the 1980s is not necessarily over. Perhaps what is over is the individual investor's complete dependence on brokers' advice and tolerance for little disclosure.[27] Recent events in the Japanese stock market may have initiated a basic shift in the financial habits of Japanese investors and, perhaps, in some of the reporting and disclosure habits of Japanese corporations.

The foregoing should not be construed, however, as a suggestion that the power of Japan's banks and financial institutions has been or is likely to be wrested away by

---

[24]An attorney at the SEC International Affairs Department, August 5, 1992.

[25]W. Dawkins, ''Tokyo Relaxes Listing Conditions,'' *Financial Times,* December 21, 1994, p. 15.

[26]Cooper & Lybrand, *International Accounting Summaries,* p. J-3.

[27]Comments by H. Ogasawara, a Japanese researcher visiting the University of Virginia, June 16, 1992.

individual equity investors with major consequences for financial reporting just around the corner. Japanese shareholders are generally less demanding than their U.S. counterparts. Today, even though loan defaults are up sharply and the stock market losses that have accrued to the banks' investment portfolios are inhibiting domestic lending, Japanese companies as a group still raise far more money from bank loans than from domestic equity markets. Change is happening, but it seems to be more attributable to the efforts and demands of foreign fund managers and analysts than to the requirements of a collection of individual Japanese investors. Nevertheless, a Japanese public that is becoming increasingly savvy in the ways of equity investment may create internal pressures for increased disclosure, if only by calling traditionally accepted roles and attitudes into question.

An increasing number of large Japanese corporations, primarily those that have aggressively pursued international financing in the past and that have become cash rich because of their success in export markets, are looking away from the traditionally powerful banks and placing more emphasis on foreign equity markets for meeting their capital needs. Sony, perhaps the most progressively international firm in Japan, was the first Japanese company to be listed on the New York Stock Exchange and often has more shares traded in New York than in Tokyo. The tendency of these companies to seek less expensive foreign capital, most recently in European markets, necessarily subjects them to more stringent disclosure requirements than would be the case at home. Consequently, internationally listed companies such as Sony, Sanyo, and Honda are becoming accustomed to the reporting practices of the West. As noted in Exhibit 10–6, many of these companies now provide results restated in accordance with U.S. GAAP for the use of U.S. investors.

Foreign investors and analysts have, in the past, characterized the Tokyo market as being too clubbish and susceptible to manipulation by insiders. The increasing involvement of foreign brokers and investment banks, however, has circumscribed the ability of anyone to "manage" the market or to conduct business as an insider. In addition, the Japanese government enacted tougher rules in January 1989, making insider trading a criminal instead of a civil offense. In late 1990, new regulations came into effect requiring investors with stakes of 5 percent or more in listed companies to file public reports detailing such holdings. Such moves are intended to make the market more transparent and less intimidating for small investors.

As Japan's stock exchanges grow and continue to attract foreign investment, power will inevitably be diffused among more sophisticated and heterogeneous investors who cannot be counted on to join in any informal collaboration. Moreover, as foreign fund managers observe and participate in the TSE over time, many are coming to understand it on its own terms rather than simply concluding that any apparently inexplicable quirk is the result of behind-the-scenes skulduggery. Foreign analysts are creating higher standards for securities analysis in Tokyo, and by doing so, they implicitly (and often explicitly) reiterate the case for fuller and fairer disclosure by companies. As these analysts and managers find their way, their successes encourage the Japanese to reexamine their accounting methods and disclosure practices and to improve them. At the time of this writing, the SEC and the Ministry of

Exhibit 10-6

Sony Corp. Footnote Excerpt from Financial Statements

Summary of Significant Accounting Policies

The parent company and subsidiaries in Japan maintain their records and prepare their financial statements in accordance with accounting principles generally accepted in Japan and its foreign subsidiaries in conformity with those of the countries of their domicile. Certain adjustments and reclassifications, including those relating to the tax effects of temporary differences, capitalization of stock purchase warrants, the appropriation for or reversal of special allowances, the accrual of certain expenses and the accounting for foreign currency translation, have been incorporated in the accompanying financial statements to conform with accounting principles generally accepted in the United States of America. These adjustments were not recorded in the statutory books of account.

Source: Sony Annual Report, 1994.

Finance are negotiating the possibility of reciprocating public stock offerings between the United States and Japan.

Banking. Modern Japanese banks were created by government fiat at the end of World War II to raise and distribute relatively inexpensive capital for Japan's industrial reconstruction. With such a mission, they have traditionally sought and earned very modest returns, and in turn have paid depositors a modest return on savings (of late, 3 percent as compared to 5 or 6 percent in Europe and the United States).[28] Because Japan has one of the highest personal savings rates at 15 percent,[29] it is not surprising to note that Japanese banks hold a higher proportion of their debt in the form of short-term demand deposits than most banks in Europe or the United States.[30] But after 50 years of such an environment and central role in "Japan Inc.", the banking system finds itself overpopulated, with several premiere banks at the heart of major *keiretsu* (e.g., Mitsubishi Bank) saddled with huge bad loan portfolios, and gradually losing ground to the bond and stock markets as providers of capital.

The mid-1990s are beginning to bear witness to a major (albeit slow) reconfiguration of the banking sector in Japan. The changes that are occurring were inevitable if the banks were to survive as viable, robust players in the world's financial sector. For example, in 1995 Sumitomo Bank wrote off $8 billion in bad loans, providing the most profound insight to date of the extent of nonperforming loans the banks possess.[31] Moreover, a merger between the Bank of Tokyo and Mitsubishi Bank was announced in 1995, thus setting the stage for creating the world's largest private bank.[32] It is anticipated that such a merger will finally ignite the winnowing

[28]G. Baker, "The Appeal of Foreign Climes," *Financial Times,* October 25, 1994, p. 15.

[29]"The Sun Also Sweats," *The Economist,* September 10, 1994, pp. 33–34.

[30]Baker, "The Appeal of Foreign Climes."

[31]R. Neff and W. Glasgall, "An $8 Billion Write-Off and a Celebration," *Business Week,* February 13, 1995, p. 56.

[32]J. Sapsford and R. Steiner, "Huge Japanese Merger Could Revitalize the Financial Sector," *The Wall Street Journal,* March 29, 1995, p. A1.

of the number of banks, leaving the truly strong ones that can compete on a global basis. Last, recent deregulation moves by Japan have opened the doors for the commercial banks to own their own securities companies that for the meantime are limited to issuing bonds.[33]

These and other changes portend some fundamental changes in the Japanese financial system. A traditional avoidance of uncertainty and a clear preference for long-term relationships may not be manageable in competing for a prominent position in the global financial market. Moreover, as industrial Japan shifts from market share goals toward a "more western-style stress on profitability and return on equity," banks will have to more carefully assess the creditworthiness and profit potential of its would-be customers.[34] Likewise, as the banks seek to be a more global source of funds, they will not be able to rely on relationships for garnering comfort regarding a customer's creditworthiness. Instead, more careful credit analysis will be necessary with an increased need for and reliance on financial disclosures. It is probable that Japanese banks will emerge as real consumers of financial information and thus catalysts for increased transparency in Japanese financial reports.

Accounting Profession and Policy Formulation.   Japanese accountants, like other Japanese professionals and workers, are highly educated and well trained. The enactment of the Certified Public Accountants Law in 1948 requires that Japanese accountants be as qualified as those of the United States and the United Kingdom; their status is comparable with Japanese lawyers.[35] To earn the designation of certified public accountant and to become eligible for membership in the Japanese Institute of Certified Public Accountants (JICPA), a candidate must pass three examinations covering mathematics, language competency, accounting, auditing, management, economics, business law, and other topics. After passing the second examination, the candidate may register as a junior CPA and begin to fulfill a two-year work experience requirement. Before applying for the third examination, the candidate must also complete a one-year course that covers all aspects of a CPA's duties. These stringent requirements have greatly limited the size of the profession in Japan: JICPA includes only about 10,000 members. Basic accounting principles and auditing standards are dictated by code law (specifically, the Commercial Code and the Securities and Exchange Law) or by the Business Accounting Deliberation Council, an agency of the Ministry of Finance. JICPA may issue supplementary guidelines for auditors.

Under the requirements of the Securities and Exchange Law of 1948, the auditors report expresses an opinion as to the fairness of presentation of a company's financial statements in accordance with Japanese GAAP. The opinion also refers to the consistent application of GAAP.

---

[33]G. Baker, "Ripple Effect of Tokyo's Big Bang," *Financial Times,* November 24, 1995, p. 15.

[34]"Japanese Corporate Strategy; New, Improved," *The Economist,* March 21, 1992, p. 72.

[35]JICPA, *The CPA Profession in Japan,* July 1987.

Selected Financial Reporting Practices

As noted earlier, tax accounting and financial reporting in Japan have a very close connection. Indeed, such a fact is but one manifestation of the dominant role that government ministries play in determining financial reporting practices. In sum, the essential difference between U.S. and Japanese GAAP is that the latter is determined in the public sector (principally by the Ministry of Finance), whereas the former is determined in the private sector (primarily the FASB).[36] Such a phenomenon has been described as the natural manifestation of the Japanese cultural belief in the moral basis of government and the belief in government's ''superior ability to formulate and implement the law.''[37] Moreover, group consciousness (i.e., low IDV) may be considered responsible for a Japanese corporate reluctance to make public disclosure of corporate financial activities.[38]

Given such a backdrop, it is useful to consider that

> Japanese accounting in the 1990s is descended from native medieval bookkeeping, overlaid by a commercial code modeled on late 19th century Franco-German precedents, rounded off with U.S.-inspired securities laws of the late 1940s.[39]

In particular, some of the German influence is manifested in a strict application of the historical cost concept, no provision for proposed dividends, only partial provision for pensions, and the dominance of form over substance (e.g., leases tend not to be capitalized). On the other hand, the U.S. influence can be seen in the preparation of funds flow statements, the amortization of goodwill, the sequence of balance sheet items (e.g., most to least liquid), and the frequent disclosure of earnings per share. A number of other similarities and nuances in Japanese reports are interesting, however, and important to note. These include valuation, consolidated reporting, doubtful accounts, liabilities, leases, deferred income tax, deferred charges, business enterprise tax, retirement and severance benefits, warrant bonds, director bonuses, depreciation expense, and shareholder capital and reserves.

Valuation

Japanese companies adhere closely to the historical cost principle applied conservatively. Inventories are valued at cost or at market if it is significantly lower and not expected to recover. Cost is determined by the following methods: individual cost, FIFO, LIFO, HIFO (i.e., highest price in), moving average, and/or adjusted selling price.

---

[36]T. Cooke, ''The Impact of Accounting Principles on Profits: The U.S. versus Japan,'' *Accounting and Business Research,* Autumn 1993, pp. 460–76.

[37]W. L. Harrison and J. L. McKinnon, ''Culture and Accounting Change: A New Perspective on Corporate Reporting Regulation and Accounting Policy Formulation,'' *Accounting, Organizations and Society* 11, no. 3, 1986, pp. 233–52.

[38]Ibid.

[39]C. Nobes, ''Japanese Practices Embody Radical Approach,'' *Financial Times,* February 14, 1991, p. 14.

Property, plant, and equipment are stated at cost less accumulated depreciation. (Current cost information is not used, even on a supplementary basis.) Depreciation, which is not applicable for land, is generally computed by the declining-balance method using rates prescribed under tax regulations, although the straight-line method may also be used. Special accelerated depreciation allowed under the tax laws is recorded either as a charge to income or as an appropriation of retained earnings.

In the case of marketable equity securities (other than shares in a subsidiary), lower of cost or market is applied to the securities on an individual basis, whereas in the United States, a mark-to-market approach is used on an individual security basis.

Consolidated Reporting

As in the United States, in Japan the financial results of majority-controlled subsidiaries must be consolidated with those of the parent unless (1) the voting control over the subsidiary is temporary (i.e., a sale is pending), (2) control is not effective (e.g., due to bankruptcy or reorganization), or (3) inclusion of the subsidiary's results would be misleading to shareholders. Consolidation may also be avoided if a subsidiary represents less than 10 percent of the consolidated group's total assets or sales (i.e., a materiality exclusion). Consolidation may be effected using either pooling-of-interests or purchase accounting, depending on how a parent's investment in a subsidiary was obtained.

Doubtful Accounts

A bad debt allowance is calculated in accordance with percentages of outstanding receivables as specified by tax law (e.g., retail companies—1%; manufacturing—0.8%; financial—0.3%; other—0.6%). It is considered generally accepted to charge the allowance to the legal limit, regardless of the dictates of sound business judgment and expected or actual past experience. In contrast, U.S. accounting practice stresses net collectible amounts in valuing accounts receivable—a long-standing tradition in accounting, stemming from the days when creditors were the major users of financial statements. In Japan, where a company's creditors are often members of the firm's own business group (and thus are privy to the group's detailed financial information), making the effort to determine and report exact or realistic collectible amounts has little significance because if the timely payment of an account is doubtful, it is likely to be given an extension or perhaps even forgotten.

Liabilities

Liabilities, both current and noncurrent, are recorded on the balance sheet at face value (as compared to present value under U.S. GAAP). Certain expenses (e.g., employee bonuses and repairs) and losses (e.g., sales returns and rebates) relating to future periods may be charged against current income by creating a reserve in the liabilities section of the balance sheet. Contingent losses on future sales, purchases, or product warranties must be accrued in the balance sheet if the liability is both probable and reasonably estimable.

Leases

Most leases are accounted for as operating leases by both the lessor and the lessee. Although in practice leases are rarely capitalized, a nonmandatory guideline issued by JICPA suggests the capitalization of some leases that contain a bargain purchase clause, those involving machinery that was built specifically for the lessee and cannot be leased to others, and those in which the leased property is land or buildings. As mentioned earlier, the general absence of lease capitalization is often cited as an example of one of several German-style features in Japanese accounting; it has been described as an example of the dominance of form over substance and the lack of an overriding fair principle.[40]

Deferred Income Tax

Because differences between taxable and financial income in Japan are minor, the deferral of income taxes is not as commonly found as it is in the United States. For example, in the United States, accelerated depreciation methods are frequently used for tax purposes, whereas straight-line depreciation is most commonly used for financial reporting purposes. This is not the case in Japan, where accelerated methods are typically used for both tax and reporting purposes. Japanese companies that restate results in accordance with U.S. GAAP, however, usually must make some provision for deferred income taxes.

Deferred Charges

Deferred charges permitted to be capitalized under the Japanese Commercial Code are as follows:

Deferred Charge	*Maximum Amortization Period*
Organization costs	5 Years
Preoperation costs	5 Years
Research and development costs	5 Years
New share issuance costs	3 Years
Bond issuance costs	3 Years or the redemption period, whichever is shorter
Bond discounts	The redemption period of debt

Goodwill may be recorded as a deferred charge only when it is acquired for consideration or through merger and consolidation and, if deferred, it is normally amortized against earnings over a five-year period. Research and development (R&D) expenses permitted to be capitalized are limited to those expenditures with respect to (1) research

---

[40]C. Nobes and S. Maeda, ''Japanese Accounts: Interpreters Needed,'' *Accountancy,* September 1990, pp. 82–84.

for new products and new techniques, (2) adoption of new techniques and new management structure, (3) development of resources, and (4) development of markets. The ability to capitalize R&D is a radical departure from U.S. GAAP, which requires R&D to be expensed when incurred. The effect of capitalizing R&D is to increase operating income; thus, in a year in which a Japanese company might expect especially low income, the ability to capitalize R&D allows for a smoothing of reported income.

Business Enterprise Tax

The local business enterprise tax (BET) is a tax that is normally about 12 percent of total corporate income. The BET is one of three corporate taxes and is the only one expensed on a cash basis. Thus, if net income and/or the BET rate increases year to year, the effective total Japanese corporate income tax rate for a given year will be several points lower than that year's combined nominal rate.

The BET is a cost-of-doing-business tax. Its rate schedule is determined by each prefecture (a local political subdivision) in which an entity operates. It has been observed that the BET is reported as a part of selling, general, and administrative costs in the statutory accounts filed in accordance with Japan's commercial code, but it is frequently aggregated with income tax expense in the convenience-translation financial statements issued for public consumption. As a result, the reported income before taxes differs for each of the two types of reports.[41]

Retirement and Severance Benefits

Japanese companies generally make lump-sum payments to retiring employees, the amount of which is calculated according to salary history and length of employment. Valuation of a company's retirement fund is required only every five years versus every year in the United States. There is no specific guidance on the discount rate to be used when valuing a retirement fund, and the long-term rate of return on plan assets is established by law. For comparison, under U.S. GAAP, the long-term rate is separately determined based on management's best estimate, and the discount rate is redetermined each year.

Although the full liability for retirement benefits consists of the benefits payable if all of a company's employees left as of the balance sheet date, many companies accrue only 40 percent of the full liability, the maximum allowed by tax law. Japanese companies rarely disclose the extent to which, if at all, their retirement obligations are funded. No minimum liability is recognized in Japan, as compared to the United States where a minimum liability based on the unfunded accumulated pension obligation is recognized. Exhibit 10–7 illustrates the pension disclosures for Japan Airlines.

Warrant Bonds

Warrant bonds are deep discounted bonds that are combined with a warrant and are typically sold on a 70/30 split (the warrant's value represents 30 percent of the

---

[41]Ibid.

EXHIBIT 10–7

Japan Airlines Footnote Excerpt

Accrued severance indemnities

An employee whose employment is terminated is entitled, in most cases, to a lump-sum severance payment, the amount of which is determined by reference to the basic rate of pay, length of service and the conditions under which the termination occurs. The Company has followed the accounting policy of providing for the liability for employees' severance indemnities to the extent to which they are deductible for income tax purposes. The rate of deduction permitted for income tax purposes is 40% of such liability.

In addition to the lump-sum payment plan, effective October 1, 1992, the Company and certain significant domestic subsidiaries established contributory funded defined benefit pension plans pursuant to the Welfare Pension Insurance Law of Japan to substitute for their non-contributory funded pension plans, while most other domestic subsidiaries maintained non-contributory funded pension plans. The cost of the pension plans are determined actuarially and the amortization of prior service cost is charged to income. Prior service cost is being amortized over a period of between 10 and 20 years.

Source: Japan Airlines 1994 Annual Report.

security's issue price, giving the bond an effective issue price of 70 percent of the security's total price). Warrant bonds act like zero coupon bonds, in which the full accrued value (unpaid interest plus principal) is paid at maturity; however, under Japanese GAAP, the discount on the bonds is not amortized. In effect, issuers derive an immediate, although illusionary, profit from issuing warrant bonds.

In theory, warrant bonds should be accounted for as two separate elements: (1) a warrant and (2) a low-coupon (coupon rates typically range from 2 to 4 percent), deep discount bond. Under U.S. GAAP, the issuer would recognize an amortization provision each year to account for the hefty payout at redemption, and the warrant element of the issue's proceeds would be taken into the capital surplus line of shareholders' equity.[42] Exhibit 10–8 presents the financial statement disclosures relating to warrant bonds under U.S. (Sony) and Japanese (Nippon Oil) GAAP; these disclosures provide for a comparison of the two disclosure practices.

Director Bonuses

Bonuses to directors and statutory auditors must be voted on by a company's shareholders and are treated as a distribution of profits rather than an expense. They are charged directly to retained earnings and are not tax deductible. In contrast, under U.S. GAAP, director bonuses are treated as an expense. This difference in treatment may explain, in part, the difference between the salaries of CEOs in the United States as

---

[42]E. Fingleton, ''The Black Magic Behind Warrant Bonds,'' *Institutional Investor: Japan Journal* Supplement (January 1990), p. 27.

EXHIBIT 10–8

Footnote Disclosures for Warrant Bonds

Nippon Oil

The 3% and 2.75% bonds in U.S. dollars, with separately transferable warrants to purchase common stock of the Company, were issued on August 25, 1987 and December 14, 1989, respectively. The warrants entitle the holders to subscribe for shares of common stock of the Company at ¥1,323.60 ($11.41) and ¥1,820.20 ($15.69) per share, respectively, subject to adjustment in certain circumstances. The rights under the warrants are exercisable up to and including August 14, 1992 and December 7, 1993, respectively.

Sony

On February 14, 1990, the company issued the 0.3% bonds of ¥100 billion, with detachable warrants. One warrant certificate is attached to each ¥1,000,000 bond and entitles the holders to subscribe ¥1,000,000 ($8,621) for shares of common stock of the company at ¥7,670 ($66.12) per share (subject to adjustment in certain circumstances). At March 31, 1993, warrants of ¥100 billion ($862,069 thousand) issued in 1990 were outstanding and will expire on February 10, 1994.

The estimated fair values of the warrants at the time of issuances were credited to additional paid-in capital with a corresponding charge to bond discounts. These discounts, which are netted against the face amount of the bond, are being amortized over the lives of the bonds. The effective annual interest rate with respect to the 0.3% bonds due 1994 is approximately 6.2%, after giving effect to the amount assigned to the warrants.

Source: Nippon Oil 1993 Annual Report and Sony Corp. 1993 Annual Report.

compared to those in Japan: executive compensation in Japan is substantially less than that in the United States.

Depreciation Expense

Depreciation expense is based on the accelerated depreciation method for both financial and tax reporting as required by Japanese tax regulations.

Shareholder Capital and Reserves

Owners' equity on the balance sheet is usually segmented into four accounts: Capital Stock, Capital Reserve, Legal Reserve, and Retained Earnings. Capital stock includes both common and preferred shares issued, with or without par value.[43] When shares are issued without a par value, not less than 50 percent of the proceeds of the sale price must be recorded as capital stock. The purchase of treasury stock is prohibited except to retire the stock or to facilitate a merger or acquisition.

The Capital Reserve account reflects any paid-in surplus from the sale of stock and any gain on the repurchase of treasury stock. The Legal Reserve account reflects appropriated retained earnings; an amount equal to at least 10 percent of each cash

---

[43]When common stock is issued with a par value, that value is most commonly ¥50.

dividend must be credited to the Legal Reserve account until the reserve equals 25 percent of the capital stock account. Finally, retained earnings is usually composed of both unappropriated and appropriated balances. Exhibit 10–9 presents a summary comparison of Japanese and U.S. accounting and reporting practices.

Analytical Considerations

The Center for International Financial Analysis and Reporting recently concluded that the accounting practices of Japan (and Germany) were the furthest removed from global norms and that this departure from global norms was manifested in substantially underreported earnings. Consider, for example, the average price-earnings ratio data for listed stocks reported in Exhibit 10–10. On the surface, these data appear to suggest that Japanese stocks are substantially overpriced relative to U.S. securities; however, when one considers the institutional setting in Japan, the high P-E multiple afforded Japanese securities can be seen to reflect, to a large extent, the underreporting of earnings characteristic of that country. Recall that conservative accounting practices in Japan are driven, in large part, by the legal requirement that expenses claimed for tax purposes correspond to those claimed for book purposes.[44] Thus, unlike their U.S. counterparts, Japanese managers are unable to effectively pursue the dual objectives of minimizing taxable income while maximizing book income. But what are the principal causes of income underreporting in Japan, and how are those factors likely to be manifested in financial indicators of performance? What are the key differences on the balance sheet under Japanese versus U.S. GAAP? With respect to the income statement, the primary determinants of income underreporting in Japan involve the use of discretionary tax-deductible reserves and higher depreciation provisions. With respect to the balance sheet, the key differences involve the valuation of liabilities, in general, and consolidation practices in particular.

As noted in Exhibit 10–9, Japanese companies value debt at its face, repayment, or settlement value. This treatment dramatically contrasts with U.S. practice by which long-term liabilities (except deferred income taxes) are valued at discounted (or present) value. All other things being constant, this difference in reporting practice generally causes Japanese companies to carry a lower book value (or net worth) than U.S. companies carry, since the repayment value of debt generally exceeds its present value. This practice may particularly distort financial analysis involving Japanese companies when one also considers the propensity of Japanese companies to finance via debt (versus equity). The lower book value of Japanese companies caused by their higher valuation of debt would, however, be partially offset by two other reporting considerations. First, many Japanese subsidiaries that would otherwise be consolidated under U.S. GAAP (i.e., *SFAS No. 94*) are equity accounted in Japan. An important consequence of this is that the debt of many unconsolidated Japanese

---

[44]This Japanese tax-book compliance requirement is somewhat akin to the LIFO tax-book compliance regulation that exists in the United States, although the origins of each are substantially different.

EXHIBIT 10–9

Comparison of Japanese and U.S. Accounting and Reporting Standards

Item	Japan	U.S.
Asset valuation	Historical cost (applied conservatively)	Historical cost, with selected revaluation (principally downward)
Inventory valuation	Specific identification, moving and weighted average, LIFO, FIFO, HIFO (i.e., highest purchase price)	Principally LIFO (because of tax considerations); also FIFO and average cost methods
Inventory: year-end	Lower of cost or replacement cost	Lower-of-cost or replacement cost
Depreciation	Principally accelerated methods, although production-based methods and straight-line also permitted	Principally straight line, with accelerated and production-based methods permitted
Goodwill	Capitalized and amortized, normally over 5 years; negative goodwill permitted	Capitalized to balance sheet, with amortization (principally straight-line) over a maximum of 40 years; negative goodwill not permitted
Research and development costs	Ordinary R&D expensed as incurred; R&D for new products, techniques, or markets deferred and amortized over 5 years	Research costs expensed currently; development costs expensed currently except in certain industries (i.e., software, oil and gas)
Capitalization of interest costs:	Generally not practiced except for real estate development companies	Capitalization required for self-constructed assets
Intercorporate investments		
Marketable securities (current asset-trading)	Lower-of-cost-or-market value	Market value (on an individual-security basis) with unrealized gains and losses to income statement
Long-term investments:		
0–20% ownership (available for sale)	Principally cost	Market value (on an individual-security basis) with unrealized gains and losses to balance sheet (i.e., owners' equity)
20–50% ownership	Equity method	Equity method
51–100% ownership	Consolidated, unless the subsidiary (1) composes less than 10% of total group assets or sales, (2) control is temporary, (3) is not a going concern, or (4) consolidation produces misleading results; unconsolidated subsidiaries equity method accounted; pooling and purchase accounting permitted	Consolidated, using pooling or purchase accounting
Debt valuation	All debt valued at face or repayment value	Long-term debt (except deferred income taxes) valued at present value; all other debt valued at face value
Leases	All leases treated as operating leases	Capital leases reflected in balance sheet; operating leases disclosed in footnotes
Deferred income taxes	Generally unrecorded due to close proximity of book and taxable income	Computed under liability method
Pension liabilities	Reflected on balance sheet	Reflected on balance sheet
Discretionary reserves	Specific reserves permitted	Restricted to identifiable operational losses
Statement of cash flows	Permitted under the Securities and Exchange Law but not subject to audit	Required

Exhibit 10–10
Average Price-Earnings Ratio Data of Companies Listed on the Tokyo Stock Exchange and the New York Stock Exchange

	Tokyo Stock Exchange*	*New York Stock Exchange†*
1984	27.4	10.7
1985	31.9	12.0
1986	49.8	16.2
1987	70.0	19.7
1988	63.8	14.2
1989	66.0	13.8
1990	52.7	14.7
1991	45.3	20.1
1992	44.8	25.4
1993	89.0	23.3
1994‡	73.1	15.1

*Financial Times, September 30, 1993.
†New York Stock Exchange Fact Book—1993.
‡The Wall Street Journal, March 17, 1994, where Japan's figure is for the Nikkei 225 and the NYSE column figure is for the Dow Jones Industrials.

subsidiaries is not reflected on the books of the consolidated entity, thereby causing the relative debt levels of U.S. conglomerates to exceed those of comparable Japanese companies. A final consideration relates to the treatment of leases. In Japan, few leases are capitalized to the balance sheet, suggesting that, *ceteris paribus,* there should be less leasing debt reported on the books of Japanese companies when compared to U.S. companies.

All in all, the conservative valuation of debt and the propensity to finance debt tend to cause Japanese companies to appear to be substantially less solvent than their U.S. counterparts. Recognizing that this may hurt their chances of obtaining foreign investment, many Japanese companies issue financial statements prepared according to U.S. GAAP, thereby enabling analysts and investors to make a more informed comparison of Japanese versus U.S. company results.

Profitability

A review of Japanese GAAP reveals that, relative to U.S. GAAP, numerous current income-reducing practices abound. For example, deductions for bad debts in Japan are prescribed by income tax regulations (usually about 1 percent of receivables) rather than actual corporate experience. In addition, interest costs relating to debt associated with the self-construction of assets cannot be capitalized and must be expensed as incurred. Of greater significance than either of these policies are the depreciation and reserve policies followed by Japanese companies.

In general, for purposes of calculating book depreciation, Japanese companies use the shorter estimated lives for depreciable assets specified by Japanese tax law,

EXHIBIT 10–11

Average ROE

	Listed Japanese Manufacturers*	Standard & Poor's Composite 500 U.S. Stocks†
1984	9.4%	13.1%
1985	8.5	11.0
1986	5.7	10.4
1987	6.5	11.8
1988	8.1	14.8
1989	8.3	13.5
1990	7.7	12.1
1991	5.6	8.6
1992	3.1	9.1‡
1993	2.5	10.3‡

*Financial Times, September 30, 1993.
†Standard & Poors Analyst's Handbook, 1993.
‡Fortune Industrials 500 median.

and declining-balance depreciation is the most prevalent method used. In contrast, most U.S. companies use straight-line depreciation and asset lives that exceed those permitted under the U.S. tax code. Not surprising, the net effect of these differences is that Japanese companies appear less profitable as a consequence of the larger depreciation deductions taken against earnings. This outcome is compounded by the fact that Japanese GAAP permits a company to establish contingency accounts for a variety of general future expenses, such as product warranties and various other business risks. In the United States, GAAP relating to the creation of contingent reserves is considerably more stringent, permitting reserves only for identifiable operating losses. Further, U.S. managers have little incentive to aggressively anticipate such charges against income, given the securities market's preference for higher (not lower) reported earnings and the preponderance of executive compensation plans linked to security prices.

The net effect of these practices is a relatively understated assessment of firm profitability. For example, consider the data presented in Exhibit 10–11. As a consequence of the understatement of profitability and the overstatement of debt, the average ROE for Japanese publicly listed companies was approximately 300 percent less than for U.S. publicly held companies. This distortion in reported financial indicators makes comparative cross-national financial analysis involving Japan a challenging exercise.

Analyzing Japanese Financial Data

It is widely acknowledged that significant accounting, economic, and cultural differences exist between Japan and the United States (and most other non-Asian countries) and that these differences should, and apparently are, reflected in security prices and such market-derived indicators as P-E ratios. But what are the implications of this for financial analysis? Should analysts, for example, attempt to restate Japanese financial data to conform to U.S.

Exhibit 10–12
A Comparison of Financial Data under Pure Japanese GAAP and U.S. GAAP
for Selected Companies in the Japanese Electronics Industry

	Fiscal Year 1990		Fiscal Year 1989	
	Japanese GAAP	*U.S. GAAP*	*Japanese GAAP*	*U.S. GAAP*
Depreciation expenses				
Depreciable assets/total assets	16.44%	16.80%	17.20%	16.52%
Accumulated depreciation/gross				
depreciable assets	59.90%	60.8%	61.67%	60.82%
Depreciation expense/COGS and SGA	5.28%	6.12%	4.97%	5.85%
Effective tax rate	54.87%	56.17%	53.17%	57.13%
Operating margin	5.87%	9.58%	5.21%	8.74%
Cumulative foreign currency adjustments				
to shareholders' equity	−0.72%	−1.09%	−1.11%	−2.08%
Return on assets	2.84%	3.93%	2.80%	3.53%
Return on equity	6.82%	9.28%	7.20%	8.39%
Price/earnings	107.28×	85.60×	59.49×	37.12×
Price/book value	2.8×	2.39×	2.75×	2.46×

Source: *International Accounting and Auditing Trends,* 2nd ed. (Princeton NJ: Center for International Financial Analysis & Research, Inc.), 1991, p. 236.

GAAP (some results from such efforts are shown in Exhibit 10–12) or should they evaluate less traditional financial indices, perhaps ones unique to the Japanese setting?

Until recently, the answers to these questions seemed clear. The preponderance of available evidence indicated that a majority of the difference between Japanese and U.S. financial measures could be reconciled by adjusting for the differences in accounting and business practices between the two countries.[45] More recently, however, the notion that analysts should attempt to restate Japanese financial data has been called into question. A recent study found that adjusting for different accounting principles explained very little of the difference in P-E ratios or rates of return on assets and common equity.[46] Subsequent research has revealed that neither country appeared to generate *systematically* higher profitability but that across time and for most industries, the ROA of U.S. companies exceeded those of Japanese companies primarily because of consistently higher asset turnover rates for U.S. firms.[47] The observed differences in profitability and rates of return have been primarily attributed

[45]See, for instance, K. R. French and J. M. Poterba, ''Were Japanese Stock Prices Too High?'' *Journal of Financial Economics* 29 (1991), pp. 337–63; and R. Officer and G. Isgro, ''The Relative Behavior of Price-to-Earnings Ratios in Australia, Japan, the U.S., and the U.K., and Implications Thereof,'' working paper, the University of Melbourne, Australia, 1990.

[46]P. Brown, V. Soybel, and C. Stickney, ''Achieving Comparability of U.S. and Japanese Financial Statement Data,'' *Japan and the World Economy* 5 (1993), pp. 51–72.

[47]P. Brown, V. Soybel, and C. Stickney, ''Comparing U.S. and Japanese Corporate-Level Operating Performance Using Financial Statement Data,'' *Strategic Management Journal,* January 1994, pp. 75–83.

to cultural (e.g., credit-granting policies and inventory management techniques) and structural (e.g., governmental controls over the supply of money) factors.

These findings appear to closely dovetail with the prevailing practice of professional mutual fund managers in the United States: instead of trying to restate foreign earnings to compare such traditional market indices as the P-E ratio for purposes of investment decisions, many mutual fund managers have opted for less traditional financial indexes, particularly those that are less sensitive to the differences in accounting practices that may exist between companies from different countries.[48] Consider, for example, the cash flow from operations (CFFO); this measure inherently removes many of the differences (e.g., depreciation accounting and other noncash or cost-allocation related factors) that exist between the accounting practices in different countries. Thus, some mutual fund managers now use the price-cash flow ratio and/or cash flow per share instead of the traditional P-E ratio as a benchmark to compare investments across national boundaries.

Summary

It would be unfair not to acknowledge that Japan is undergoing significant changes. During the early 1990s, the Nikkei stock average experienced a 48 percent drop (a decline of such magnitude not seen since 1950), a nine-year high in inflation, a rise in Tokyo housing costs to a level 10 to 12 times the average homebuyer's annual income, a sharp decline in banks' capital ratios necessitating many to market subordinated debt to their large corporate customers to replenish capital, an increase in interest rates, credit tightening by the Bank of Japan, saddling of the nation's financial institutions with billions of newly acknowledged bad debt, a decline in corporate profits by as much as 50 percent, the decrease in capital spending by as much as 30 percent, and the slowing of GNP growth to about 2 percent. Some analysts believe that these facts portend diminished future growth potential.[49] Indeed, "Japan, Inc." is reported by astute observers to be in the throes of a downward spiral that has managers settling for less quality, more top-down decision making, and the realization that *keiretsu* companies may not be as profitable as some of the independents.[50] Perhaps most telling of the demise of the Japanese mystique is a recent report noting that nearly one-third of the Japanese workforce would need to be laid off for Japanese employee productivity levels to reach those in the United States.[51]

Hard work, loyalty, education, and respect for traditional ways of doing things are still the foremost Japanese traits. The trend is clear, however, that Japan enters the last years of the 20th century more open to Western imports and investment than ever before,

---

[48]Morningstar Mutual Funds newsletter, December 10, 1993, p. 2; see also P. Martin, "Good Buys, but a Risky Business," *Financial Times,* August 22, 1992, p. 6.

[49]W. Dawkins, "Truly, Widely, and Deeply," *Financial Times,* October 17, 1993, p. 15.

[50]J. M. Schlesinger, M. Williams, and C. Forman, "Japan Inc., Wracked by Recession, Takes Stock of Its Methods," *The Wall Street Journal,* September 29, 1993, pp. 1 and A10.

[51]E. Thornton, "Japan's Struggle to Restructure," *Fortune,* June 28, 1993, pp. 84–88.

but with a realism that the 1980s formula for success needs serious modification. Currently, considerable concern exists in the West that Japan's recent bad economic trends will cause the Japanese government to become more insular (as before), not less, as a way to work out of this recession. For example, recent business news shows have talked about a proposal surfacing in Japan that would allow Japanese firms to copy, reproduce, and sell U.S. software in Japan. U.S. firms dominate the software market there because of copyright laws, but those laws may be removed! It is hoped that such actions would not be taken nor typify a revised Japanese approach to international business.

Perhaps more indicative of the subtle change in domestic priorities is the Ministry of International Trade and Industry's industrial policy paper for the 1990s. In lieu of the usual opening discussion of industrial goals, the paper dealt first with issues of worker vacations, increased consumer protection, higher imports, and better child care facilities.[52] Another example of change can be found in Japanese corporate goals. Japanese firms are being compelled to reconsider their traditional strategy of seeking maximum sales and market share. The nation's No. 2 automaker, Nissan, has formally abandoned its policy of giving top priority on increasing market share and has instead adopted a policy that emphasizes improving profitability.[53] This is not to say that Japanese executives are infected with the U.S. "short-term disease" of worrying about next quarter's earnings, but, stunned by what has happened to securities prices in recent months, some are starting to show more concern for shareholders. An aging workforce has also tightened Japan's labor supply. Companies are spending major sums to attract good personnel and are less prone to impose long work hours and less insistent on placing the company's interest above those of the individual. Increased disposable income is giving rise to more leisure-time pursuits on the part of many Japanese workers. Another avenue for change may come as a result of its prior economic successes and growing sense of economic confidence: Japan appears to be more willing to cooperate with other industrialized countries than to go its own way. Faced with a recently achieved economic maturity, Japan now finds itself needing to tend to issues previously subordinated to the one goal of world-class economic leadership.

Suggested Readings

Bildersee, J., J. Chek, and C. Lee. "The International Price-Earnings Ratio Phenomenon." *Japan and the World Economy* 4 (1990), pp. 263–82.

Campbell, N. "The Role of Japan's Top Managers." *Journal of General Management,* Winter 1994, pp. 20–28.

Choi, F. D. S. "Analyzing Foreign Financial Statements: The Use and Misuse of International Ratio Analysis." *The Journal of International Business Studies,* Spring 1983, pp. 113–31.

Cooke, T. E., and M. Kibruya. *Financial Reporting in Japan: Regulation, Practice, and Environment.* New York: Oxford Press, 1992.

---

[52]"How the Japanese are Changing," *Fortune,* September 24, 1990, pp. 15–22.

[53]P. Blustein, "When This Recession Is Over, Japan May Never Be the Same," *The Washington Post,* June 22, 1992, p. A1.

Coopers & Lybrand. *Executive Summary of Principal Differences between Accounting Principles in the United States and Japan.* New York: Coopers and Lybrand, 1989.

Dawkins, W. "Loosening of the Corporate Web." *Financial Times,* November 30, 1994, p. 13.

Fallows, J. "How the World Works." *The Atlantic Monthly,* December 1993, pp. 61–87.

Grant, C. "Information Sources for U.K. Investors and Financial Analysts Working in the Japanese Market." *Asian Review of Accounting* 1 (1992), pp. 12–30.

Lowe, H. D. "Shortcomings of Japanese Consolidated Financial Statements." *Accounting Horizons,* September 1990, pp. 1–9.

McDonald, J. "The *Mochiai* Effect: Japanese Corporate Cross-Holdings." *Journal of Portfolio Management* 9 (1989), pp. 90–94.

Schieneman, G. S. "Japanese P/E Ratios: Myth and Realty." *International Investment Review,* March 30, 1989.

Price Waterhouse & Co. *Doing Business in Japan.* New York: Price Waterhouse, 1990.

The Spicer and Oppenheim Guide to Financial Statements around the World. New York: Wiley, 1989.

ISSUES AND INFORMATION FOR FURTHER INQUIRY

I.10.1   Japanese Credit Analysis: Qualitative Aspects

In a January–February 1994 *Bankers Magazine* article (pp. 56–59), "Commercial Loan Decisions: The Japanese Way," S. Gupta, H. Roehm, and J. Castellano identify four important qualitative dimensions to Japanese bankers' commercial loan decisions: (1) the extent to which the applicant manages for the long term, (2) the applicant's commitment to employees, (3) the applicant's commitment to their community, and (4) the quality of the applicant's management.

Required:

Comment on the ways in which you see these considerations as consistent with or in contrast to what you understand to be the cultural context of doing business in Japan.

I.10.2   Stricter Disclosure

In a September 21, 1994 *Financial Times* article (p. V), "Overseas Investors Wooed," E. Terazono reports a Nippon Telegraph and Telephone official's rationale for its planned New York Stock Exchange listing: "By listing in the U.S., where the disclosure rules are stricter than in Japan, we hope to win trust from investors."

Required:

Identify several ways in which you believe the U.S. financial disclosure rules are stricter than those in Japan. Comment on whether meeting those stricter disclosures is likely to "win trust from investors."

EXERCISES

E.10.1   Accounting for Shareholders' Equity

The Honda Motor Co., Ltd., was incorporated in 1948 under the laws of Japan as Honda Giken Kogyo Kabushiki Kaisha. The company's stock began trading on the Tokyo Stock Exchange in 1957, on the NYSE in 1977, and on the London Stock Exchange in 1981. Today, Honda is one of the world's leading producers of motorcycles, automobiles, and related power products (e.g., portable generators, lawn mowers, tractors, ATVs).

The company's fiscal year-end (March 31) 1994 annual report disclosed the following balances in its shareholders' equity accounts:

	(¥, millions)	
	1993	*1994*
Stockholders' Equity		
Common stock, authorized 3,600,000,000 shares, par value ¥50 or without par value; issued 973,625,988 shares and 973,715,269 shares at March 31, 1993 and 1994, respectively (notes 5 and 8)	85,719	85,758
Capital surplus (notes 5 and 8)	171,952	171,948
Legal reserve (note 9)	23,537	24,173
Retained earnings (note 9)	1,130,226	1,139,658
Adjustments from foreign currency translation	(380,567)	(454,192)
Total stockholders' equity	1,030,867	967,345

In addition, the company's footnotes disclosed the following:

(8)   *Common Stock*

During the years ended March 31, 1992, 1993 and 1994, the Company issued approximately 159 thousand, 812 thousand and 89 thousand shares, respectively, of common stock in connection with the conversion of convertible debt. Conversions of convertible debt issued subsequent to October 1, 1982 into common stock and exercise of warrants were accounted for in accordance with the provisions of the Japanese Commercial Code by crediting one-half of the aggregate conversion price equally to the common stock account and the capital surplus account.

(9)   *Dividends and Legal Reserve*

The Japanese Commercial Code provides that earnings in an amount equal to at least 10% of all appropriations of retained earnings that are paid in cash, such as cash dividends and bonuses to directors, shall be appropriated as a legal reserve until such reserve equals 25% of stated capital. This reserve is not available for dividends but may be used to reduce a deficit or may be transferred to stated capital. Certain foreign subsidiaries are also required to appropriate their earnings to legal reserves under the laws of the respective countries of domicile.

Cash dividends and appropriations to the legal reserve charged to retained earnings during the years ended March 31, 1992, 1993 and 1994 represent dividends paid out during those years and the related appropriations to the legal reserve. The accompanying consolidated financial statements do not include any provision for the dividend of ¥7 per share aggregating ¥6,816 million to be proposed in June 1994 or the related appropriation to legal reserve.

Required:

Using journal entries, reconstruct the changes in Honda's shareholders' equity accounts for 1994.

HONDA MOTOR CO., LTD.
Consolidated Statements of Shareholders' Equity
Years Ended 31 March 1992, 1993, 1994

	Yen (millions)					
	Common Stock	*Capital Surplus*	*Legal Reserve*	*Retained Earnings*	*Adjustment from Foreign Currency Translation*	*Total Stockholders' Equity*
Balance at March 31, 1991	¥85,289	¥171,886	¥19,605	¥1,064,507	¥(253,580)	¥1,087,707
Net income for the year				59,731		59,731
Cash dividends ¥14 per share (note 9)				(13,617)		(13,617)
Transfer to legal reserve (note 9)			2,233	(2,233)		—
Common stock issued and capital surplus arising from conversion of debentures (note 8)	70	17				87
Adjustment from foreign currency translation					(36,245)	(36,245)
Balance at March 31, 1992	85,359	171,903	21,838	1,108,388	(289,825)	1,097,663
Net income for the year				37,157		37,157
Cash dividends ¥14 per share (note 9)				(13,620)		(13,620)
Transfer to legal reserve (note 9)			1,699	(1,699)		—
Common stock issued and capital surplus arising from conversion of debentures (note 8)	360	49				409
Adjustment from foreign currency translation					(90,742)	(90,742)
Balance at March 31, 1993	85,719	171,952	23,537	1,130,226	(380,567)	1,030,867
Net income for the year				23,699		23,699
Cash dividends ¥14 per share (note 9)				(13,631)		(13,631)
Transfer to legal reserve (note 9)			636	(636)		—
Common stock issued and capital surplus arising from conversion of debentures (note 8)	39	(4)				35
Adjustments from foreign currency translation					(73,625)	(73,625)
Balance at March 31, 1994	¥85,758	¥171,948	¥24,173	¥1,139,658	¥(454,192)	¥967,345

E.10.2. Accounting for Leases

Fuji Photo Film Co., Ltd., is Japan's largest producer of photographic films and papers and one of the world's leading manufacturers of imaging and information equipment and materials. Because the company's shares trade in the United States on the over-the-counter market, the company prepares an annual report for U.S. shareholders using U.S. accounting principles.

The following is selected information from Fuji's 1993 report to U.S. shareholders:

Selected Financial Information	
	(¥, millions)
Net income*	75,668
Shareholders' equity	1,103,851
Long-term debt†	146,409
Total assets	1,644,220

*Effective tax rate = 56 percent.
†Interest rates range from 3 to 10 percent.

Selected Footnote Information
Leases
The company leases office space, warehouses, and office and laboratory equipment. Leased property under capital leases at fiscal year-end amounted to ¥8,242 million with accumulated depreciation of ¥2,885 million.

Rental expenses for fiscal years 1993 and 1992 were ¥31,381 million and ¥30,350 million, respectively.

The minimum rental payments required under operating leases with initial or remaining noncancelable lease terms in excess of one year are as follows:

	(¥, millions)
1994	5,262
1995	5,060
1996	4,477
1997	2,872
1998	2,151
1999 and thereafter	2,577
Total minimum future rentals	22,399

Required:

(a) Calculate the present value of Fuji's minimum noncancelable future rentals assuming interest rates of 3, 5, and 10 percent.

(b) Assuming that all noncancelable leases should be capitalized to the balance sheet, determine the effect on Fuji's financial data.

(c) Explain how Fuji's financial data would differ if its financial results had been presented according to Japanese GAAP as opposed to U.S. GAAP.

E.10.3   Accounting for Marketable Securities

Under Japanese GAAP, marketable securities are carried at cost, or lower of cost, or market. In the United States, the accounting treatment depends on whether the securities are considered to be "trading securities" or "available for sale." Under *SFAS No. 115,* trading marketable securities are valued at market value, with any unrealized gains or losses reported as part of current earnings; available-for-sale securities are likewise carried at market value but any unrealized value adjustments are reported as part of owners' equity on the balance sheet.

The 1994 20-F filing by the Honda Motor Co., Ltd., whose shares trade on the NYSE via American Depositary Receipts, disclosed that as of fiscal year-end 1994 (i.e., March 31, 1994), the carrying value of its marketable securities had increased by ¥116,941 million. The company's year-end balance sheet, however, carried those investments at only ¥129,239 million, under the lower-of-cost-or-market method.

The following is additional financial data for the company as of fiscal year-end 1994:

Selected Financial Information	
	(¥, millions)
Total current assets	1,368,844
Total assets	3,012,896
Total shareholders equity	1,030,867
Net income*	23,699

*Effective tax rate = 52 percent.

Required:

(a) Assume that Honda's marketable securities are all trading securities. How would the company's financial results be affected?

(b) Assume that Honda's marketable securities are all available-for-sale securities. How would the company's financial results be affected?

E.10.4   Accounting for Special Tax Reserves

The Special Taxation Measures Law of Japan permits certain companies to create special equity reserves for the purpose of reducing their taxable income. For example, in addition to a deduction for ordinary depreciation based on an asset's statutory useful life, a company may be permitted also to deduct special depreciation. This excess, or additional depreciation, ranges from 6 to 30 percent of the first-year ordinary depreciation for qualifying assets. In addition to the special depreciation reserve, tax-deductible reserves may also be created to assist in the replacement of revenue-producing assets and for overseas investments. Special reserves must eventually be reversed to taxable income.

The following is selected information for Kobe Steel, Ltd., one of Japan's leading producers of ferrous and nonferrous metal products.

Selected Financial Information

	(¥, millions)	
	1991	*1990*
Shareholders' equity		
Common stock	213,610	212,710
Additional paid-in capital	132,253	129,741
Legal reserve	23,329	21,778
Retained earnings		
General reserve	16,007	14,893
Unappropriated	31,492	26,366
Total	416,691	405,488

Selected Footnote Information
General reserve

The Special Taxation Measures Law of Japan permits the company to take certain reserves as tax deductions. Such reserves are provided by appropriation of unappropriated retained earnings.

Such reserves at March 31, 1991 and 1990, were as follows:

	(¥, millions)	
	1991	*1990*
Reserve for replacement of properties	13,973	12,485
Reserve for special depreciation	344	311
Reserve for possible losses on overseas investments	1,690	2,097
	16,007	14,893

Required:

(a) Using journal entries, explain the changes in Kobe's general reserve accounts for 1991.

(b) Explain how the general reserves on the balance sheet can be used to reduce a company's taxable income. (Like many Japanese companies, Kobe Steel reported no deferred income taxes. The company's footnotes revealed that ''income taxes are based on taxable income, and are charged to income using the taxes payable method.'')

E.10.5.   Accounting for Research and Development Expenditures

The Commercial Code of Japan provides that certain research and development outlays may be capitalized to the balance sheet; however, such costs must be amortized against earnings at a rate of not less than 20 percent annually. The code provides that R&D expenditures for the following activities may be capitalized:

- New goods, services, or techniques.
- Exploitation of natural resources.
- Development of new or existing markets.

The following is selected information from the 1991 annual report of Kobe Steel, Ltd. The company's footnotes also disclosed that:

Expenses in respect of the development of new products and in respect of the research and application of new technologies are deferred and amortized over a five year period.

Selected Financial Information

	(¥, millions)	
	1991	*1990*
Deferred research and development expenses	17,847	15,744
Total assets	1,951,539	1,793,728
Total shareholders' equity	416,691	405,488
Net income*	23,380	23,035

*Tax rate of 49 percent.

Required:

Assume that Kobe wanted to restate its 1991 financial results to a basis consistent with U.S. GAAP in regard to R&D. What adjustment would you make and how would these adjustments affect the company's ROA and ROE? (For simplicity, assume the balance of deferred R&D in 1990 has all been incurred in that year.)

E.10.6   Free Share Distributions

Shareholders receive ''free'' shares when the board of directors declares either a stock dividend or a (forward) stock split. Under U.S. GAAP, the accounting for free share distributions varies considerably from company to company. It is generally thought, for example, that the most common way of accounting for a *stock split* is simply to adjust the par, stated, or nominal value of a stock proportionately downward to compensate for the increase in the number of shares outstanding. When a company prefers to avoid changing the par, stated, or nominal value of its stock, it can alternately transfer (or capitalize) an appropriate amount to reflect the increased shares outstanding from either retained earnings or additional paid-in-capital to the common stock at par (or stated) value account. With respect to *stock dividends,* multiple accounting treatments also exist, although it is believed that the most popular approach is to transfer from retained earnings or additional paid-in capital an amount reflecting either the par value (for ''large'' stock dividends) or the fair market value (for ''small'' stock dividends) of the freely distributed shares.

In Japan, a distinction between a stock split and a stock dividend is rarely made, with both events generally lumped together under the title free share distributions. The absence of a distinction appears warranted in that country for two reasons. First, only one accounting approach exists for both events. Second, the economic and accounting outcomes of both events are equivalent. Economically, the firm has not executed a wealth transfer of assets to its shareholders; it has merely increased the number of shares outstanding. Accountingwise, total shareholders' equity is unchanged.

Mitsui & Co., Ltd., is one of the world's largest conglomerates. It represents a network of over 900 companies, operating in all but a very few countries of the world. The following is selected financial information regarding the company's capital structure from its 1992 annual report:

Selected Financial Information

	(¥, millions)	
	1992	*1991*
Shareholders' equity (Note 6)		
Common stock ¥50 par value—authorized, 2,500,000,000 shares; issued and outstanding: 1992—1,546,839,182 shares; 1991—1,542,867,033 shares	177,355	175,803
Capital surplus	276,311	274,765
Retained earnings		
Appropriated for legal reserve	21,136	19,101
Unappropriated (Notes 4 and 13)	256,979	242,835
Foreign currency translation and other adjustments	(109,949)	(92,973)
Total shareholders' equity	621,832	619,531

MITSUI & CO., LTD.
Statement of Consolidated Shareholders' Equity
March 31, 1992, 1991, 1990

	Millions of Yen		
	1992	*1991*	*1990*
Common Stock (Note 6):			
Balance at beginning of year			
(1992—1,542,867,033 shares;			
1991—1,530,301,368 shares;			
1990—1,369,022,689 shares)	¥ 175,803	¥171,235	¥ 86,530
Common stock issued in public offering			
(1990—100,000,000 shares)	—	—	59,200
Common stock issued upon conversion of bonds			
(1992—2,698,539 shares;			
1991—5,433,141 shares;			
1990—54,409,079 shares)	1,149	2,314	23,307
Common stock issued upon exercise of warrants			
(1992—1,273,610 shares;			
1991—7,132,524 shares;			
1990—6,869,600 shares)	403	2,254	2,198
Balance at end of year			
(1992—1,546,839,182 shares;			
1991—1,542,867,033 shares;			
1990—1,530,301,368 shares)	¥ 177,355	¥175,803	¥171,235
Capital Surplus (Note 6):			
Balance at beginning of year	¥ 274,765	¥270,215	¥185,609
Public offering	—	—	59,200
Conversion of bonds	1,146	2,307	23,221
Exercise of warrants	400	2,243	2,185
Balance at end of year	¥ 276,311	¥274,765	¥270,215
Retained Earnings (Note 6):			
Appropriated for Legal Reserve:			
Balance at beginning of year	¥ 19,101	¥ 17,422	¥ 16,369
Transfer from unappropriated retained earnings	2,035	1,679	1,053
Balance at end of year	¥ 21,136	¥ 19,101	¥ 17,422
Unappropriated:			
Balance at beginning of year	¥ 242,835	¥214,277	¥187,178
Net income	26,981	40,990	36,414
Cash dividends paid at annual rate per share: 1992—¥7.0			
(5.3¢); 1991—¥7.0; 1990—¥6.0	(10,802)	(10,753)	(8,262)
Transfer to retained earnings appropriated for legal reserve	(2,035)	(1,679)	(1,053)
Balance at end of year (Notes 4 and 13)	¥ 256,979	¥242,835	¥214,277
Foreign Currency Translation and Other Adjustments:			
Balance at beginning of year	¥ (92,973)	¥(69,181)	¥(94,767)
Aggregate adjustment resulting from translation of foreign			
currency financial statements	(15,986)	(20,387)	25,586
Minimum pension liability adjustment	(990)	(3,405)	—
Balance at end of year	¥(109,949)	¥(92,973)	¥(69,181)

Selected Footnote Information

Significant Accounting Policies

Common Share Distribution

As permitted by the Commercial Code of Japan prior to April 1, 1991, Japanese companies, upon approval by the Board of Directors, could make a free distribution of shares to shareholders to the extent that the aggregate par value of the shares so distributed did not exceed the aggregate excess of (1) the proceeds from any previous sales of shares over the par value of the shares and (2) the conversion prices over the par value of shares issued in conversion of bonds or notes, which have been credited to either the common stock account or the capital surplus account (see Note 6). In Japan, a free distribution is clearly distinguished from a ''stock dividend'' paid out of earnings, which must be approved by the shareholders. In accordance with the accepted accounting practice in Japan, such free distribution of shares is accounted for by a transfer, as of the date of distribution, of an amount equal to the aggregate par value of the shares distributed from capital surplus to the common stock account, where the Company attributes the aggregate par value of the shares distributed to the excess proceeds that have been credited to the capital surplus account; where the Company attributes the aggregate par value of the shares distributed to the excess proceeds that have been credited to the common stock account, the free distribution does not give rise to any change in common stock or capital surplus. In either situation, the accepted Japanese accounting practice does not require any portion of retained earnings to be transferred to the common stock or capital surplus account in connection with such transactions.

Effective April 1, 1991, the Commercial Code of Japan was amended to permit Japanese companies, upon approval by the Board of Directors, to issue shares in the form of a ''stock split'' as defined, to shareholders to the extent that the aggregate par value of the shares to be distributed does not exceed the excess of the common stock amount over the par value of shares issued and outstanding (see Note 6).

Shareholders' Equity (Note 6)

Common Stock and Capital Surplus

Under the Commercial Code of Japan, certain issuance of common stock, including conversions of bonds and notes issued on and after October 1, 1982 are required to be credited to the common stock account for at least the greater of par value or 50% of the proceeds. The Commercial Code of Japan permits, upon approval of the Board of Directors, transfers of amounts from capital surplus to the common stock account.

In January 1990, the Company made a public offering in Japan of 100,000,000 shares of its common stock at ¥1,184 per share, the approximate market price at the time the offering price was established. Fifty percent of the proceeds of the shares, ¥59,200 million, was credited to common stock and the other 50% of the proceeds, ¥59,200 million, was credited to capital surplus.

At March 31, 1992, the holders of the warrants issued in March 1987 and February 1989 were entitled to subscribe to an aggregate of 6,283,461 shares and 113,385,076 shares, respectively, of the Company's common stock at the current exercise prices of ¥630.40 per share and ¥1,135.10 per share, respectively. The warrants are exercisable through the approximate due dates of the bonds with which the warrants were issued. The exercise prices and the number of shares of common stock that may be purchased upon the exercise of the warrants are subject to adjustments under certain conditions.

Pursuant to resolutions of the Board of Directors, the Company from time to time prior to March 31, 1989 issued new shares of its common stock to the existing shareholders without consideration. Such free share distributions did not result in a transfer of any portion of retained earnings to common stock or capital surplus (see Note 1). Publicly owned corporations in the United States issuing shares in similar transactions would be required to account for them as stock dividends as of the shareholders' record date by reducing retained earnings and increasing appropriate capital accounts by an amount equal to the fair value of the shares issued. If such United States practice had been applied to the cumulative free distributions of shares made during the 10 years to March 31, 1992, capital surplus at March 31, 1992 would have been increased by ¥87,860 million ($660,602) with a corresponding decrease in unappropriated retained earnings.

At March 31, 1992, 240,046,345 shares of common stock were reserved for the conversion of outstanding bonds and for the exercise of outstanding warrants.

Required:

   (a) Using journal entries, explain the changes in Mitsui's capital stock accounts from 1990 thru 1992.

   (b) Using journal entries, explain Mitsui's method of accounting for free share distributions. If U.S. GAAP had been followed for those distributions, how would the company's shareholders' equity accounts differ?

   (c) Why do companies execute free stock distributions?

E.10.7   Comparative Financial Analysis

The Shiseido Company Ltd. is one of the world's leading manufacturers of cosmetics and toiletries. (It also has operations in health foods, pharmaceuticals, and finance.) The Gillette Company, headquartered in the United States, is one of Shiseido's leading competitors.

Exhibit 1 presents the 1990 common-sized financial statements of Gillette, as well as selected financial ratios (Exhibit 2). Also presented are the 1990 consolidated balance sheet and income statement for Shiseido.

Required:

Use the 1990 Shiseido financial data to do the following:

   (a) Prepare common-size financial statements for the company.

   (b) Compute the necessary financial ratios to develop a comparative analysis of Gillette and Shiseido. Comment on any similarities and differences.

EXHIBIT 1

Shiseido versus Gillette
1990 Common-Sized Financial Statements

Panel A.   Income Statement

	Shiseido	Gillette
Net sales	100%	100%
Cost of goods sold		42.0
Gross profits		58.0
Operating expenses		40.2
Operating profits		17.8
Other income (expenses)		4.1
Pre-tax net income		13.7

Panel B.   Balance Sheet

	Shiseido	Gillette
Assets		
Cash and equivalents		2.2%
Receivables		27.7
Inventory		20.7
Other current assets	———	6.5
Total current assets	———	57.1
Investments		–0–
Fixed assets (net)		23.5
Intangible assets (net)		6.5
Other noncurrent assets	———	12.8
Total assets	100.00	100.00
Equities		
Bank loans—short term		7.3%
Currently due portion of long-term debt		2.8
Trade payables		22.9
Taxes payable/Expenses payable		2.6
Other current liabilities	———	–0–
Total current liabilities	———	35.6
Long-term debt		28.5
Deferred income taxes		3.2
Accrued employee costs		9.1
Other long-term liabilities		–0–
Minority interest		0.2
Shareholders' equity	———	23.6
Total equities	100.00	100.00

EXHIBIT 2

Shiseido versus Gillette
Comparative Financial Ratios (1990)

	Shiseido	*Gillette*
Liquidity		
Current ratio		1.60
Quick ratio		0.77
Solvency		
Total debt to equity		3.24
Long-term debt to total assets		.29
Times interest earned		4.57
Profitability		
ROA		.10
ROE		1.39
ROS		.08
EPS		$ 3.20
Asset Management		
Receivable turnover		4.09
Average number of days' receivables on hand		89.20
Inventory turnover		2.40
Average number of days' inventory on hand		151.70
Total asset turnover		1.18
Fixed asset (net) turnover		5.04

SHISEIDO COMPANY, LTD.
Consolidated Balance Sheets
March 31, 1990 and 1989

	Millions of Yen	
	March 31,	
Assets	*1990*	*1989*
Current Assets:		
Cash and time deposits	¥48,779	¥35,452
Marketable securities	9,502	14,254
Notes and accounts receivable:		
Trade	67,824	63,482
Unconsolidated subsidiaries and affiliates	5,908	4,359
	73,732	67,841
Less: Allowance for doubtful accounts	(1,103)	(780)
	72,629	67,061
Inventories (Note 4)	39,896	44,448
Short-term loans	32	1,909
Deferred taxes	12,953	11,993
Other current assets	6,296	13,250
Total current assets	190,087	188,367
Investments and Long-Term Receivables:		
Investments in securities	163,571	155,722

SHISEIDO COMPANY, LTD.　(continued)
Consolidated Balance Sheets
March 31, 1990 and 1989

	Millions of Yen	
	March 31,	
Assets	*1990*	*1989*
Investments in securities held under fund trust	74,000	33,000
Investments in and long-term loans to unconsolidated subsidiaries and affiliates	13,497	13,005
Other investments	9,503	6,023
	260,571	207,750
Property, Plant and Equipment, at Cost:		
Buildings and structures	83,086	79,930
Machinery and equipment	77,249	73,404
	160,335	
		153,334
Less: Accumulated depreciation	(110,258)	(103,081)
	50,077	50,253
Land	42,319	38,778
Construction in progress	6,984	984
	99,380	90,015
Intangible Assets (Note 5)	33,461	34,961
Adjustments on Foreign Currency Statement Translation	3,513	3,979
	¥ 587,012	¥ 525,072

Liabilities and Shareholders' Equity	*1990*	*1989*
Current Liabilities:		
Short-term bank loans	¥ 48,320	¥ 60,006
Current portion of long-term debt	—	2,576
Notes and accounts payable:		
Trade	67,238	62,367
Unconsolidated subsidiaries and affiliates	2,015	1,785
	69,253	64,152
Accrued income taxes	25,908	3,056
Accrued expenses	24,377	21,377
Other current liabilities	13,078	7,257
Total current liabilities	180,936	158,424
Long-Term Liabilities:		
Long-term debt (Note 6)	113,439	85,959
Accrued severance indemnities	5,259	6,597
Other long-term liabilities	4,203	3,651
Total long-term liabilities	122,901	96,207
Minority Interests in Consolidated Subsidiaries	24,577	22,741
Contingent Liabilities (Note 7)		

SHISEIDO COMPANY, LTD.   (continued)
Consolidated Balance Sheets
March 31, 1990 and 1989

| | Millions of Yen | |
| | March 31, | |
Liabilities and Shareholders' Equity	*1990*	*1989*
Shareholders' Equity:		
Common stock, par value ¥50 per share;		
Authorized; 800,000,000 shares at March 31, 1990 and 1989		
Issued; 283,069,860 shares, 280,265,354 shares at March 31, 1990		
and 1989, respectively	26,435	25,147
Capital surplus	24,214	22,927
Legal reserve	6,442	6,144
Retained earnings	201,507	193,482
	258,598	247,700
	¥587,012	¥525,072

SHISEIDO COMPANY, LTD.
Consolidated Income Statements
Millions of Yen

	For the Year Ended March 31, 1990
Net Sales	¥456,352
Cost of Sales	148,265
Gross profit	308,087
Selling, General and Administrative Expenses	273,725
Income from operations	34,362
Other Income (Expenses)	
Interest and dividend income	10,325
Interest expense	(3,937)
Others, net	5,158
	11,546
	45,908
Income Taxes	32,560
	13,348
Minority Interests in Net Income of Consolidated Subsidiaries	(2,033)
Amortization of Equity in Net Assets of Consolidated Subsidiaries over Investment Cost	47
Adjustments on Foreign Current Statement Translation	—
Net Income	¥ 11,362
Per Share:	
Net income	¥ 40.31
Dividend	11.00
Weighted Average Number of Shares (in thousands)	281,867

E.10.8   Profitability and Shareholder Return Analysis

The following are income statements from two electrical power companies, Kansai Electric Power Co. (serving Osaka, Japan) and Commonwealth Edison Co. (serving Chicago, Illinois).

Required:

(a) Perform a profitability analysis of the two statements.

(b) Perform an analysis of shareholder returns. (Assume an exchange rate of ¥140 = $1.)

(c) Estimate the cash flow from operations for each company.

THE KANSAI ELECTRIC POWER COMPANY, INCORPORATED
Statements of Income
Years ended March 31, 1991 and 1990

	Millions of Yen	
	1991	*1990*
Operating Revenues	¥2,245,007	¥2,075,296
Operating Expenses:		
Fuel	441,571	329,163
Purchased power	163,859	142,075
Maintenance	293,379	306,472
Depreciation	323,681	308,419
Taxes other than income taxes	140,383	132,957
Other	535,972	500,204
	1,898,845	1,719,290
Operating Income	346,162	356,006
Other (Income) Expenses:		
Interest expense	239,393	215,427
Exchange loss	—	14,369
Other, net	(2,953)	(1,722)
	236,440	228,074
Income before Provision for Reserve for Fluctuations in Water Level and Income Taxes	109,722	127,932
Provision for Reserve for Fluctuations in Water Level	1,668	6,525
Income before Income Taxes	108,054	121,407
Income Taxes (Note 8)	51,771	65,009
Net Income	¥ 56,283	¥ 56,398

	Yen	
Per Share of Common Stock:		
Net income—		
Primary	¥58	¥58
Assuming full dilution	¥57	¥56
Cash dividends applicable to period	¥50	¥49

COMMONWEALTH EDISON COMPANY AND SUBSIDIARY COMPANIES
Statements of Consolidated Income
(thousands except per share data)

		1990	1989
Electric Operating Revenues (Notes 2 and 3):	Operating revenues	$5,798,350	$5,782,850
	Provisions for revenue refunds	(536,364)	(31,800)
		$5,261,986	$5,751,050
Electric Operating Expenses and Taxes:	Fuel (Notes 1, 3 and 10)	$978,775	$951,350
	Purchased and interchanged power—net	(27,209)	(44,836)
	Deferred (under)/overrecovered energy costs—net (Notes 1 and 3)	8,415	(19,059)
	Operation	1,160,166	1,120,941
	Maintenance	489,463	435,664
	Depreciation (Note 1)	878,938	865,427
	Recovery of deferred plant costs	1,659	1,659
	Taxes (except income) (Note 14)	661,432	665,072
	Income taxes (Notes 1 and 13)—		
	Current—Federal	150,917	263,879
	—State	28,773	49,684
	Deferred—Federal—net	19,456	162,088
	—State—net	17,299	38,445
	Investment tax credits deferred—net (Notes 1 and 13)	(28,386)	(83,529)
		$4,339,698	$4,406,785
Electric Operating Income		$ 922,288	$1,344,265
Other income and Deductions:	Interest on long-term debt	$ (648,603)	(620,589)
	Interest on notes payable	(577)	(7,685)
	Allowance for funds used during construction (Note 1)—		
	Borrowed funds	13,840	17,898
	Equity funds	22,526	24,856
	Current income taxes applicable to nonoperating activities (Notes 1 and 13)	(5,932)	2,445
	Disallowed Byron Unit 1 plant costs (Note 3)	(133,661)	(52,808)
	Income tax effect of disallowed Byron Unit 1 plant costs (Note 3)	(1,288)	5,570
	Miscellaneous—net	(40,302)	(20,269)
		$(793,997)	$(650,582)
Net income		$ 128,291	$ 693,683
Provision for dividends on preferred and preference stocks		82,495	95,180
Net income on common stock		$ 45,796	$ 598,503
Average number of common shares outstanding		212,032	211,647
Earnings per common share		$0.22	$2.83
Cash dividends declared per common share		$3.00	$3.00

E.10.9 Foreign Investment Risks

The December 9, 1993, edition of *The Wall Street Journal* carried the following head-line: ''Bearish Japanese Incite Foreign Stampede of Bulls.'' The article reported that despite the fact that Tokyo share prices had fallen more than 19 percent since October 1993 and that Japanese analysts believed that further market declines were likely, foreign investors had begun buying Japanese securities at a record pace. The Nikkei 225 stock average, which closed at 16,508 on December 8, for example, was predicted to fall to as low as 12,000 by Nomura Securities, one of Japan's leading brokerage firms. Despite these dire warnings, foreign investors had purchased over $2.15 billion of Japanese equity securities in less than two months. During the same period, Japanese investors sold off shares valued at more than $3.85 billion. (On December 9, the U.S. dollar closed at 108.8 yen, and the 180-day forward spot rate closed at 107.8 yen.)

A related news story also carried in the December 9, 1993, edition of *The Wall Street Journal* attributed the latest drop in Japanese stock prices to growing concern among Japanese investors that the country's governing coalition might collapse, thereby jeopardizing efforts to rescue Japan's falling economy. According to the ar-ticle, the Tokyo markets had been ''spooked'' by signs that the Socialist Party, the largest party in Japan's ruling coalition, might not support Prime Minister Hasokawa's initiatives to accept some rice imports in a compromise to help conclude global trade-liberalization negotiations under the General Agreement on Tariffs and Trade (GATT).

Required:

   (a) Investing in foreign countries carries with it a number of risks beyond those likely to be encountered when investing in one's own domestic market. Based on the preceding information, identify the additional risks associated with investing in foreign opportunities.

   (b) Assuming that an investor desired to invest in Japanese securities, how might he or she limit the risk?

E.10.10 Valuation of the Firm

In 1989, Sony, the Japanese consumer electronics company, paid $3.4 billion for Co-lumbia Pictures. At the time of the acquisition, the price paid was approximately 340 times Columbia's 1989 net earnings of $10 million. Columbia Pictures was subse-quently renamed Sony Pictures Entertainment (SPE).

In late 1994, Sony announced that it would write off ¥265 billion (or approxi-mately $2.65 billion U.S., based on then-current exchange rates) of SPE's net worth. This disclosure followed a previous announcement that, for the first half of 1994, SPE's operations had lost ¥310 billion (or approximately $3.1 billion). Analysts familiar with Sony concluded that the SPE write-down was precipitated by a realization on the part of Sony executives that the original purchase price paid for SPE was significantly overvalued. According to Sony insiders, the original SPE acquisition price had been calculated on the basis of undiscounted future earnings.

Required:

   (a) Comment on Sony's valuation approach used in the acquisition of Columbia Pictures. If you disagree with Sony's method, what approach would you use?

   (b) On the basis of your approach, estimate how much Sony should have paid for Columbia Pictures.

E.10.11   Asset Impairment

In early 1994, a senior official with Hanwa Co. reported that the finance and trade company would take a ¥120 billion (about $1.2 billion) write-down of its portfolio of debt and equity investments. Hanwa had hoped that a recovery in the Japanese stock market would reduce the investment losses that it had been accumulating since 1990. A company spokesperson also indicated that although Hanwa had written down a substantial portion of its equity investments, the company still had over ¥150 billion in securities with as yet unrealized (and unbooked) losses of over 40 percent of their value. At the time of the announcement, Hanwa's stock had fallen to ¥450, about one-tenth of its 1990 all-time high of ¥4,460 per share. Hanwa's president resigned after the public announcement, stating, ''We apologize for the losses we have had to post.''

Required:

Comment on Hanwa's accounting for its security losses. Why hadn't the company taken the write-down sooner?

CASES

CASE 10.1
ANALYZING FINANCIAL DATA: U.S. VERSUS JAPANESE GAAP

Tanaguchi Corporation

I. Identifying Differences between U.S. and Japanese GAAP.   Dave Ando and Yoshi Yashima, recent business school graduates, work as research security analysts for a mutual fund specializing in international equity investments. Based on several strategy meetings, senior managers of the fund decided to invest in the machine tool industry. One international company under consideration is Tanaguchi Corporation, a Japanese manufacturer of machine tools. As staff analysts assigned to perform fundamental analysis on all new investment options, Ando and Yashima obtain a copy of Tanaguchi Corporation's unconsolidated financial statements (Appendix A) and set out to calculate their usual spreadsheet of financial statement ratios. Exhibit 1 presents the results of their efforts. As a basis for comparison, Exhibit 1 also presents the median ratios for U.S. machine tool companies for a comparable year. The following conversation ensues.

> *Dave:* Tanaguchi Corporation does not appear to be as profitable as comparable U.S. firms. Its operating margin and rate of return on assets are significantly less than the median ratios for U.S. machine tool operators. Its rate of return on common equity is only slightly less than its U.S. counterparts, but this is at the expense of assuming much more financial leverage and therefore risk. Most of this leverage is in the form of short-term borrowing. You can see this in its higher total liabilities to total assets ratio combined with its lower long-term debt ratio. This short-term borrowing and higher risk are also evidenced by the lower current and quick ratios. Finally, Tanaguchi Corporation's shares are selling at a higher multiple of net income and stockholders' equity than are those of U.S. machine tool companies. I can't see how we can justify paying more for a company that is less profitable and more risky than comparable U.S. companies. It doesn't seem to me that it is worth exploring this investment possibility any further.
>
> *Yoshi:* You may be right, Dave. However, I wonder if we are not comparing apples and oranges. As a Japanese company, Tanaguchi Corporation operates in an entirely different institutional and cultural environment than U.S. machine tool companies. Furthermore, it prepares its financial statements in accordance with Japanese generally accepted accounting principles (GAAP), which differ from those in the U.S.
>
> *Dave:* Well, I think we need to explore this further. I recall seeing a report on an associate's desk comparing U.S. and Japanese accounting principles. I will get a copy for us (Appendix B).

This case was prepared by Paul R. Brown and Clyde P. Stickney. Copyright © 1992 by the American Accounting Association. Reprinted with permission from the American Accounting Association.

EXHIBIT 1
Comparative Financial Ratio Analysis for Tanaguchi Corporation and U.S. Machine Tool Companies

	Tanaguchi Corporation	*Median Ratio for U.S. Machine Tool Companies*[a]
Profitability Ratios		
Operating Margin after Taxes (before interest expense and related tax effects)	2.8%	3.3%
× Total Assets Turnover	1.5	1.8
= Return on Assets	4.2%	5.9%
× Common's Share of Operating Earnings[b]	.83	.91
× Capital Structure Leverage[c]	3.8	2.6
= Return on Common Equity	13.3%[d]	13.9%[d]
Operating Margin Analysis		
Sales	100.0%	100.0%
Other Revenue/Sales	.4	—
Cost of Goods Sold/Sales	(73.2)	(69.3)
Selling and Administrative/Sales	(21.0)	(25.8)
Income Taxes/Sales	(3.4)	(1.6)
Operating Margin (excluding interest and related tax effects)	2.8%	3.3%
Asset Turnover Analysis		
Receivable Turnover	5.1	6.9
Inventory Turnover	6.3	5.2
Fixed Asset Turnover	7.5	7.0
Risk Analysis		
Current Ratio	1.1	1.6
Quick Ratio	.7	.9
Total Liabilities/Total Assets	73.8%	61.1%
Long-Term Debt/Total Assets	4.7%	16.1%
Long-Term Debt/Stockholders' Equity	17.9%	43.2%
Times Interest Covered	5.8	3.1
Market Price Ratios (per common share)		
Market Price/Net Income	45.0	9.0
Market Price/Stockholders' Equity	5.7	1.2

[a]Source: Robert Morris Associates, *Annual Statement Studies* (except price-earnings ratio).
[b]Common's Share of Operating Earnings = Net Income to Common/Operating Income after Taxes (before interest expense and related tax effects).
[c]Capital Structure Leverage = Average Total Assets/Average Common Stockholders' Equity.
[d]The amounts for return on common equity may not be precisely equal to the product of return on assets, common's share of operating earnings and capital structure leverage due to rounding.

Required:

Using the report comparing U.S. and Japanese accounting principles (Appendix B) and Tanaguchi Corporation's financial statements and notes (Appendix A), identify the most important differences between U.S. and Japanese GAAP. Consider both the differences in acceptable methods and in the methods commonly used. For each major difference, indicate the likely effect (increase, decrease, or no effect) (1) on net income, (2) on total assets, and (3) on the ratio of liabilities divided by stockholders' equity of converting Tanaguchi's financial statements to U.S. GAAP.

II. Comparing Profitability and Risk Ratios for U.S. and Japanese Firms.   Dave Ando and Yoshi Yashima spent the next several days converting the financial statements of Tanaguchi Corporation from Japanese to U.S. GAAP. Although their conversions required them to make several estimates, Dave and Yoshi felt comfortable that they had largely filtered out the effects of different accounting principles. Exhibit 2 presents the profitability and risk ratios for Tanaguchi Corporation based on Japanese GAAP (column 1) and as restated to U.S. GAAP (column 2). Column 3 shows the median ratios for U.S. machine tool companies (the same as those reported in Exhibit 1). After studying the financial statement ratios in Exhibit 2, the following conversation ensues.

> *Dave:* The operating profitability of Tanaguchi Corporation, as evidenced by the rate of return on assets, is still lower than comparable U.S. firms, even after adjusting for differences in accounting principles. Although Tanaguchi's rate of return on common equity is now higher than its U.S. counterparts, the higher return occurs at the expense of taking on substantially more debt and therefore more risk. A significant portion of the differences in price-earnings ratios between Tanaguchi Corporation and U.S. companies results from differences in accounting principles. However, large differences still remain. I'm still not convinced that investing in Tanaguchi Corporation makes sense. Yoshi, am I on track with my interpretations or am I missing something?
>
> *Yoshi:* I'm not sure we are yet to the point where we can recommend that our equity fund purchase shares of Tanaguchi Corporation. We need to develop a better understanding of why the restated financial ratios for Tanaguchi Corporation still differ so much from those for U.S. machine tool companies.
>
> One possible explanation might relate to the practice of many Japanese companies to operate in corporate groups, which the Japanese call *keiretsus.* Tanaguchi Corporation is a member of the Menji *keiretsu.* Each *keiretsu* typically comprises firms in eight or ten different industries (for example, one *keiretsu* might include firms in the steel, chemicals, forest products, retailing, insurance, and banking industries). The companies usually hold stock in each other; investments in the 25 percent to 30 percent range are common. These investments are not made for the purpose of controlling or even significantly

EXHIBIT 2
Comparative Financial Ratio Analysis for Tanaguchi Corporation and U.S. Machine Tool Companies

	Tanaguchi Corp (Japanese GAAP) (1)	Tanaguchi Corp. (U.S. GAAP) (2)	Median Ratio for U.S. Machine Tool Companies[a] (3)
Profitability Ratios			
Operating Margin after Taxes (before			
interest expense and related tax effects)	2.8%	2.9%	3.3%
× Total Assets Turnover	1.5	1.5	1.8
= Return on Assets	4.2%	4.5%	5.9%
× Common's Share of Operating			
Earnings[b]	.83	.83	.91
× Capital Structure Leverage[c]	3.8	4.0	2.6
= Return on Common Equity	13.3%[d]	14.8%	13.9%[d]
Operating Margin Analysis			
Sales	100.0%	100.0%	100.0%
Other Revenue/Sales	.4	.4	—
Cost of Goods Sold/Sales	(73.2)	(73.4)	(69.3)
Selling and Administrative/Sales	(21.0)	(20.6)	(25.8)
Income Taxes/Sales	(3.4)	(3.5)	(1.6)
Operating Margin (excluding interest and			
related tax effects)	2.8%	2.9%	3.3%
Asset Turnover Analysis			
Receivable Turnover	5.1	5.0	6.9
Inventory Turnover	6.3	6.5	5.2
Fixed Asset Turnover	7.5	7.2	7.0
Risk Analysis			
Current Ratio	1.1	1.0	1.6
Quick Ratio	.7	.7	.9
Total Liabilities/Total Assets	73.8%	74.5%	61.1%
Long-Term Debt/Total Assets	4.7%	5.1%	16.1%
Long-Term Debt/Stockholders' Equity	17.9%	18.3%	43.2%
Times Interest Covered	5.8	5.7	3.1
Market Price Ratios (per common share)			
Market Price/Net Income	45.0	30.9	9.0
Market Price/Stockholders' Equity	5.7	4.6	1.2

[a]Source: Robert Morris Associates, *Annual Statement Studies* (except price-earnings ratio).
[b]Common's Share of Operating Earnings = Net Income to Common/Operating Income after Taxes (before interest expense and related tax effects).
[c]Capital Structure Leverage = Average Total Assets/Average Common Stockholders' Equity.
[d]The amounts for return on common equity may not be precisely equal to the product of return on assets, common's share of operating earnings and capital structure leverage due to rounding.

influencing other members of the corporate group. Rather, they serve as a mechanism for providing operating links between the entities. It is common for one corporation in the *keiretsu* to source many of its raw materials from another group member and to sell a substantial portion of its products to entities within the group. Each *keiretsu* includes a bank that provides needed funds to group members. It is rare that the bank would allow a member of the group to experience significant operating problems or to go bankrupt due to lack of funds.

A second, but related, institutional difference between the U.S. and Japan concerns stock ownership patterns. Roughly one-third of Japanese companies' shares is held by members of its *keiretsu* and another one-third is held by financial institutions, typically banks and insurance companies not affiliated with the *keiretsu*. This leaves only one-third of the shares held by individuals. The large percentage of intercorporate stock holdings has historically lessened the concern about keeping investors happy by paying large dividends or reporting ever-increasing earnings per share, as seems to be the case in the U.S.

Instead, the emphasis of Japanese companies has been on serving new or growing markets, increasing market share, and strengthening the members of the *keiretsu*. The Japanese economy has grown more rapidly than that of the U.S. during the last several decades. In addition, Japanese companies have built their export markets and added operations abroad. The strategic emphasis has been on gaining market dominance in this growth environment and not on attaining particular levels of profit margin, rates of return, or earnings per share.

Finally, stock price changes in Japan appear related more to changes in real estate values than to the operating performance of individual companies. Real estate values and stock prices moved dramatically upward during the eighties, although significant decreases have occurred recently. The increasing stock prices appeared to keep investors happy, leading them to deemphasize the kinds of profitability performance evaluation common in the U.S. (*Note:* Your instructor may assign additional references in conjunction with this case that elaborate on strategic, institutional, and cultural differences between the U.S. and Japan.)

Required:

After studying the financial statements and notes for Tanaguchi Corporation, develop explanations for the differences in the profitability and risk ratios for Tanaguchi Corporation reported in column 2 of Exhibit 2 as compared to those reported in column 3 for U.S. machine tool companies.

APPENDIX A

UNCONSOLIDATED FINANCIAL STATEMENTS FOR TANAGUCHI CORPORATION

TANAGUCHI CORPORATION
Balance Sheet
(in billions of yen)

	March 31:	
Assets	*Year 4*	*Year 5*
Current Assets		
Cash	¥ 30	¥ 27
Marketable Securities (Note 1)	20	25
Notes and Accounts Receivable (Note 2):		
Trade Notes and Accounts	200	210
Affiliated Company	30	45
Less: Allowance for Doubtful Accounts	(5)	(7)
Inventories (Note 3)	130	150
Other Current Assets	25	30
Total Current Assets	¥ 430	¥ 480
Investments		
Investments in and Loans to Affiliated Companies (Note 4)	¥ 110	¥ 140
Investments in Other Companies (Note 5)	60	60
Total Investments	¥ 170	¥ 200
Property, Plant and Equipment (Note 6)		
Land	¥ 25	¥ 25
Buildings	110	130
Machinery and Equipment	155	180
Less: Depreciation to Date	(140)	(165)
Total Property, Plant and Equipment	¥ 150	¥ 170
Total Assets	¥ 750	¥ 850
Liabilities and Stockholders' Equity		
Current Liabilities		
Short-Term Bank Loans	¥ 185	¥ 200
Notes and Accounts Payable:		
Trade Notes and Accounts	140	164
Affiliated Company	25	20
Other Current Liabilities	40	50
Total Current Liabilities	¥ 390	¥ 434
Long-Term Liabilities		
Bonds Payable (Note 7)	¥ 20	¥ 20
Convertible Debt	20	20
Retirement and Severance Allowance (Note 8)	122	153
Total Long-Term Liabilities	¥ 162	¥ 193
Stockholders' Equity		
Common Stock, ¥10 par value	¥ 15	¥ 15
Capital Surplus	40	40
Legal Reserve (Note 9)	16	17
Retained Earnings (Note 9)	127	151
Total Stockholders' Equity	¥ 198	¥ 223
Total Liabilities and Stockholders' Equity	¥ 750	¥ 850

TANAGUCHI CORPORATION
Statement of Income and Retained Earnings for Fiscal Year 5
(in billions of yen)

Revenues

Sales (Note 10)	¥ 1,200
Interest and Dividends (Note 11)	5
Total Revenues	¥ 1,205

Expenses

Cost of Goods Sold	¥ 878
Selling and Administrative	252
Interest	13
Total Expenses	¥ 1,143
Income before Income Taxes	¥ 62
Income Taxes (Note 12)	(34)
Net Income	¥ 28

Retained Earnings

Balance, Beginning of Fiscal Year 5	¥ 127
Net Income	28
Deductions:	
Cash Dividends	(3)
Transfer to Legal Reserve (Note 9)	(1)
Balance, End of Fiscal Year 5	¥ 151

NOTES TO FINANCIAL STATEMENTS

NOTE 1: Marketable Securities
Marketable securities appear on the balance sheet at acquisition cost.

NOTE 2: Accounts Receivable
Accounts and notes receivable are noninterest bearing. Within 15 days of sales on open account, customers typically sign noninterest-bearing, single-payment notes. Customers usually pay these notes within 60 to 180 days after signing. When Tanaguchi Corporation needs cash, it discounts these notes with Menji Bank. Tanaguchi Corporation remains contingently liable in the event customers do not pay these notes at maturity. Receivables from (and payable to) affiliated company are with Takahashi Corporation (see Note 4) and are noninterest bearing.

NOTE 3: Inventories
Inventories appear on the balance sheet at lower of cost or market. The measurement of acquisition cost uses a weighted average cost flow assumption.

NOTE 4: Investments and Loans to Affiliated Companies

Intercorporate investments appear on the balance sheet at acquisition cost. The balances in this account at the end of Year 4 and Year 5 comprise the following:

	Year 4	Year 5
Investments in Tanaka Corporation (25%)	¥ 15	¥ 15
Investment in Takahashi Corporation (80%)	70	70
Loans to Takahashi Corporation	25	55
	¥110	¥140

NOTE 5: Investments in Other Companies

Other investments represent ownership shares of less than 20 percent and appear at acquisition cost.

NOTE 6: Property, Plant and Equipment

Fixed assets appear on the balance sheet at acquisition cost. The firm capitalizes expenditures that increase the service lives of fixed assets, while it expenses immediately expenditures that maintain the originally expected useful lives. It computes depreciation using the declining balance method. Depreciable lives for buildings are 30 to 40 years and for machinery and equipment are 6 to 10 years.

NOTE 7: Bonds Payable

Bonds payable comprises two bond issues as follows:

	Year 4	Year 5
12% semi-annual, ¥10 billion face value bonds, with interest payable on March 31 and September 30 and the principal payable at maturity on March 31, Year 20; the bonds were initially priced on the market to yield 10%, compounded semi-annually	¥11.50	¥11.45
8% semi-annual, ¥10 billion face value bonds, with interest payable on March 31 and September 30 and the principal payable at maturity on March 31, Year 22; the bonds were initially priced on the market to yield 10%, compounded semi-annually	¥ 8.50	¥ 8.55
	¥20.00	¥20.00

NOTE 8: Retirement and Severance Allowance

The firm provides amounts as a charge against income each year for estimated retirement and severance benefits but does not fund these amounts until it makes actual payments to former employees.

NOTE 9: Legal Reserve and Retained Earnings

The firm reduces retained earnings and increases the Legal Reserve account for a specified percentage of dividends paid during the year. The following plan for appropriation of retained earnings was approved by shareholders at the annual meeting held on June 29, Year 5:

Transfer to Legal Reserve	¥(1)
Cash Dividend	(3)
Directors' and Statutory Auditors' Bonuses	(1)
Elimination of Special Tax Reserve Relating to Sale of Equipment	1

NOTE 10: Sales Revenue

The firm recognizes revenues from sales of machine tools at the time of delivery. Reported sales for Year 5 are net of a provision for doubtful accounts of ¥50 billion.

NOTE 11: Interest and Dividend Revenue

Interest and Dividend Revenue includes ¥1.5 billion from loans to Takahashi Corporation, an unconsolidated subsidiary.

NOTE 12: Income Tax Expenses

The firm computes income taxes based on a statutory tax rate of 55 percent for Year 5.

APPENDIX B
COMPARISON OF U.S. AND JAPANESE GAAP

1. STANDARD-SETTING PROCESS

U.S.   The U.S. Congress has the legal authority to prescribe acceptable accounting principles, but it has delegated that authority to the Securities and Exchange Commission (SEC). The SEC has stated that it will recognize pronouncements of the Financial Accounting Standards Board (FASB), a private-sector entity, as the primary vehicle for specifying generally accepted accounting standards.

Japan   The Japanese Diet has the legal authority to prescribe acceptable accounting principles. All Japanese corporations (both publicly and privately held) must periodically issue financial statements to their stockholders following provisions of the Japanese Commercial Code. This Code is promulgated by the Diet. The financial statements follow strict legal entity concepts.

Publicly listed corporations in Japan must also file financial statements with the Securities Division of the Ministry of Finance following accounting principles promulgated by the Diet in the Securities and Exchange Law. The Diet, through the Ministry of Finance, obtains advice on accounting principles from the Business Advisory Deliberations Council (BADC), a body composed of representatives from business, the accounting profession, and personnel from the Ministry of Finance. The BADC has no authority on its own to set acceptable accounting principles. The financial statements filed with the Securities Division of the Ministry of Finance tend to follow economic entity concepts, with intercorporate investments either accounted for using the equity method or consolidated.

All Japanese corporations file income tax returns with the Taxation Division of the Ministry of Finance. The accounting principles followed in preparing tax returns mirror closely those used in preparing financial statements for stockholders under the Japanese Commercial Code. The Minister of Finance will sometimes need to reconcile conflicting preferences of the Securities Division (desiring financial information better reflecting economic reality) and the Taxation Division (desiring to raise adequate tax revenues to run the government).

2. PRINCIPAL FINANCIAL STATEMENTS

U.S.   Balance sheet, income statement, statement of cash flows.

Japan   Balance sheet, income statement, proposal for appropriation of profit or disposition of loss. The financial statements filed with the Ministry of Finance contain some supplemental information on cash flows.

3. INCOME STATEMENT

U.S.   Accrual basis.

Japan   Accrual basis.

4. REVENUE RECOGNITION

U.S.   Generally at time of sale; percentage-of-completion method usually required on long-term contracts; installment and cost-recovery-first methods permitted when there is high uncertainty regarding cash collectibility.

Japan   Generally at time of sale; percentage-of-completion method permitted on long-term contracts; installment method common when collection period exceeds two years regardless of degree of uncertainty of cash collectibility.

5. UNCOLLECTIBLE ACCOUNTS

U.S.   Allowance method.

Japan   Allowance method.

6. INVENTORIES AND COST OF GOODS SOLD

U.S.   Inventories valued at lower of cost or market. Cost determined by FIFO, LIFO, weighted average, or standard cost. Most firms use FIFO, LIFO, or a combination of the two.

Japan   Inventories valued at lower of cost or market. Cost determined by specific identification, FIFO, LIFO, weighted average, or standard cost. Most firms use weighted average or specific identification.

7. FIXED ASSETS AND DEPRECIATION EXPENSE

U.S. Fixed assets valued at acquisition cost. Depreciation computed using straight line, declining balance, and sum-of-the-years'-digits methods. Permanent declines in value are recognized. Most firms use straight line for financial reporting and an accelerated method for tax reporting.

Japan Fixed assets valued at acquisition cost. Depreciation computed using straight line, declining balance, and sum-of-the-years'-digits methods. Permanent declines in value are recognized. Most firms use a declining method for financial and tax reporting.

8. INTANGIBLE ASSETS AND AMORTIZATION EXPENSE

U.S. Internally developed intangibles expensed when expenditures are made. Externally purchased intangibles capitalized as assets and amortized over expected useful life (not to exceed 40 years). Goodwill cannot be amortized for tax purposes.

Japan The cost of intangibles (both internally developed and externally purchased) can be expensed when incurred or capitalized and amortized over the period allowed for tax purposes (generally 5 to 20 years). Goodwill is amortized over 5 years. Some intangibles (e.g., property rights) are not amortized.

9. LIABILITIES RELATED TO ESTIMATED EXPENSES (WARRANTIES, VACATION PAY, EMPLOYEE BONUSES)

U.S. Estimated amount recognized as an expense and as a liability. Actual expenditures are charged against the liability.

Japan Estimated amount recognized as an expense and as a liability. Actual expenditures are charged against the liability. Annual bonuses paid to members of the Board of Directors and to the Commercial Code auditors are not considered expenses, but a distribution of profits. Consequently, such bonuses are charged against retained earnings.

10. LIABILITIES RELATED TO EMPLOYEE RETIREMENT AND SEVERANCE BENEFITS

U.S. Liability recognized for unfunded accumulated benefits.

Japan Severance benefits more common than pension benefits. An estimated amount is recognized each period as an expense and as a liability for financial reporting. The maximum liability recognized equals 40 percent of the amount payable if all eligible employees were terminated currently. There is wide variability in the amount recognized. Benefits are deducted for tax purposes only when actual payments are made to severed employees. Such benefits are seldom funded beforehand.

11. LIABILITIES RELATED TO INCOME TAXES

U.S. Income tax expense based on book income amounts. Deferred tax expense and deferred tax liability recognized for temporary (timing) differences between book and taxable income.

Japan Income tax expense based on taxable income amounts. Deferred tax accounting not practiced. In consolidated statements submitted to the Ministry of Finance by listed companies (see No. 18), deferred tax accounting is permitted.

12. NONINTEREST-BEARING NOTES

U.S. Notes stated at present value of future cash flows and interest recognized over term of the note.

Japan Notes stated at face amount and no interest recognized over term of the note. Commonly used as a substitute for Accounts Payable.

13. BOND DISCOUNT OR PREMIUM

U.S.   Subtracted from or added to the face value of the bond and reported among liabilities on the balance sheet. Amortized over the life of the bond as an adjustment to interest expense.

Japan   Bond discount usually included among intangible assets and amortized over the life of the bonds. Bond discount and premium may also be subtracted from or added to face value of bonds on the balance sheet and amortized as an adjustment of interest expense over the life of the bonds.

14. LEASES

U.S.   Distinction made between operating leases (not capitalized) and capital leases (capitalized).

Japan   All leases treated as operating leases.

15. LEGAL RESERVE (PART OF SHAREHOLDERS' EQUITY)

U.S.   Not applicable.

Japan   When dividends are declared and paid, unappropriated retained earnings and cash are reduced by the amount of the dividend. In addition, unappropriated retained earnings are reduced and the legal reserve account is increased by a percentage of this dividend, usually 10 percent, until such time as the legal reserve equals 25 percent of stated capital. The effect of the latter entry is to capitalize a portion of retained earnings to make it part of permanent capital.

16. APPROPRIATIONS OF RETAINED EARNINGS

U.S.   Not a common practice in the U.S. Appropriations have no legal status when they do appear.

Japan   Stockholders must approve, each year, the ''proposal for appropriation of profit or disposition of loss.'' Four items commonly appear: dividend declarations, annual bonuses for directors and Commercial Code auditors, transfers to legal reserves, and changes in reserves.

   The income tax law permits certain costs to be deducted earlier for tax than for financial reporting and permits certain gains to be recognized later for tax than for financial reporting. To obtain these tax benefits, the tax law requires that these items ''be reflected on the company's books.'' The *pretax effect* of these timing differences *do not appear* on the income statement. Instead, an entry is made decreasing unappropriated retained earnings and increasing special retained earnings reserves (a form of appropriated retained earnings). When the timing difference reverses, the above entry is reversed. The *tax effects* of these timing differences do appear on the income statement, however. In the year that the timing difference originates, income tax expense and income tax payable are reduced by the tax effect of the timing difference. When the timing difference reverses, income tax expense and income tax payable are increased by a corresponding amount.

17. TREASURY STOCK

U.S.   Shown at acquisition cost as a subtraction from total shareholders' equity. No income recognized from treasury stock transactions.

Japan   Reacquired shares are either canceled immediately or shown as a current asset on the balance sheet. Dividends ''received'' on treasury shares are included in income.

18. INVESTMENTS IN SECURITIES

A. MARKETABLE SECURITIES (CURRENT ASSET)

U.S.   Lower of cost or market method.

Japan   Reported at acquisition cost, unless price declines are considered permanent, in which case lower of cost or market.

B. INVESTMENTS (NONCURRENT ASSET)

U.S.   Accounting depends on ownership: Less than 20%, lower of cost or market; 20% to 50%, equity method; greater than 50%, consolidated.

Japan   The principal financial statements are those of the parent company only (that is, unconsolidated statements). Intercorporate investments are carried at acquisition cost. Listed companies must provide consolidated financial statements as supplements to the principal statements in filings to the Ministry of Finance. The accounting for investments in securities in these supplementary statements is essentially the same as in the U.S.

19. CORPORATE ACQUISITIONS

U.S.   Purchase method or pooling of interests method.

Japan   Purchase method.

20. FOREIGN CURRENCY TRANSLATION

U.S.   The translation method depends on whether the foreign unit operates as a self-contained entity (all-current method) or as an extension of the U.S. parent (monetary/nonmonetary method).

Japan   For branches, the monetary/nonmonetary translation method is used, with any translation adjustment flowing through income. For subsidiaries, current monetary items are translated using the current rate, other balance sheet items use the historical rate, and the translation adjustment is part of shareholders' equity.

21. SEGMENT REPORTING

U.S.   Segment information (sales, operating income, assets) disclosed by industry segment, geographical location, and type of customer.

Japan   Beginning in 1990, sales data by segment (industry, geographical location) are required. No disclosure by type of customer.

Sources: The Japanese Institute of Certified Public Accountants, *Corporate Disclosure in Japan* (July 1987); KPMG Peat Marwick, *Comparison of Japanese and U.S. Reporting and Financial Practices* (1989).

Case 10.2
Identifying Industry Characteristics Through Financial Statements

The Case of the Unidentified Japanese Industries

Analyzing a company's financial statements requires an understanding of the environment in which a firm operates. Many characteristics of this environment are common to all firms in an industry and, to some extent, influence reported financial data. In addition, differences in accounting across countries may affect the power of accounting data to reflect industry characteristics.

Exhibit 1 presents condensed financial statement information for nine Japanese firms with principal operations in nine difference industries. Balance sheet and income statement items are expressed as a percentage of total net revenues. To improve "resolution" of these items, they have been calculated as four-year averages instead of annual figures.

The companies represented in the exercise operate primarily in the following industries:

Advertising agency services	Insurance underwriting
Automobile manufacturing	Metals mining
Consumer electronics	Pharmaceutical manufacturing
Discount retailing	Utilities
Distilling	

Required:

Using the data in Exhibit 1, match the companies (numbered 1 thru 9) with the industries listed above.

EXHIBIT 1

Common-Size Four-Year Average Financial Statements
(net sales or revenue = 100)

	1	2	3	4	5	6	7	8	9
Cash and cash equivalents	13.12	19.64	40.71	17.52	11.16	165.50	6.57	4.57	11.99
Net accounts receivable	9.87	24.64	41.00	39.17	29.07	16.70	7.27	11.81	12.56
Inventories	19.80	24.62	9.97	18.56	4.03	11.36	2.14	14.82	49.35
Total current assets	42.79	68.91	91.68	75.24	44.25	193.56	15.98	31.20	73.91
PPE at cost	36.58	66.89	81.83	125.97	20.08	39.58	401.62	74.02	69.63
Accumulated depreciation	10.91	39.78	34.16	48.84	4.57	17.60	134.04	29.35	31.75
Net property, plant, equipment	25.67	27.11	47.67	77.13	15.51	21.98	267.58	44.67	37.88
Other assets (net)	(1.74)	20.11	3.02	20.39	3.27	0.77	17.45	15.47	11.24
Total assets	66.72	116.13	142.37	172.76	63.04	216.31	301.02	91.34	123.03
Total current liabilities	16.05	62.40	29.47	60.56	20.16	144.20	173.55	32.07	62.62
Long-term debt	9.81	21.88	21.81	44.71	0.00	3.77	56.99	13.20	5.77
Other noncurrent liabilities	5.67	7.07	12.95	3.88	0.61	2.45	6.21	0.94	6.76
Total liabilities	31.53	91.35	64.22	109.14	20.77	150.42	236.75	46.21	75.15
Owners' equity	35.19	24.78	78.15	63.61	42.27	65.89	64.27	45.13	47.88
Total liabilities and equity	66.72	116.13	142.37	172.76	63.04	216.31	301.02	91.34	123.03
Net sales or revenue	100.00	100.00	100.00	100.00	100.00	100.00	100.00	100.00	100.00
Cost of goods sold	89.30	76.89	48.00	78.16	74.89	35.84	66.91	68.56	60.18
Depreciation expence	1.70	5.57	4.91	4.73	0.20	0.00	13.41	4.19	3.02
SG&A expense	0.57	1.08	1.11	3.98	19.66	7.92	10.72	0.97	4.22
R&D expense	0.00	6.64	13.20	0.00	0.00	0.00	0.00	4.65	0.00
Interest expense	7.62	2.64	13.54	9.11	0.00	23.35	0.00	24.33	32.50
Income taxes	0.48	1.91	8.00	2.86	1.66	1.56	3.09	1.30	1.21
Other (net)	(0.10)	1.34	2.46	(0.42)	1.96	30.94	1.91	(5.23)	(1.57)
Net income	0.43	3.92	8.79	1.57	1.63	0.38	3.96	1.24	0.46

ANNUAL REPORT ANALYSIS

Toyota

An interesting and important challenge for students of international financial reporting is to study the published annual reports of various companies from different countries. Your instructor will provide you with a recent copy of the Toyota annual report. To facilitate your delving into this annual report, undertake the following endeavors.

Required:

(a) List the key differences between the Toyota annual report and what you would expect to see for a U.S. company such as General Motors or Ford.

(b) Calculate the following ratios for Toyota, taking care to note the assumptions you found necessary to make and where you found the appropriate pieces of data in the annual report.

(1) Current ratio $= \dfrac{\text{Total current assets}}{\text{Total current liabilities}}$

(2) Quick ratio $= \dfrac{\text{Cash + Marketable securities + Accts. rec.}}{\text{Total current liabilities}}$

(3) Operating cash flow to current liabilities $= \dfrac{\text{Operating cash flow}}{\text{Average total current liabilities}}$

(4) Debt-to-equity ratio $= \dfrac{\text{Long-term debt}}{\text{Owners' equity}}$

(5) Debt-to-total capitalization ratio $= \dfrac{\text{Long-term debt}}{\text{Long-term debt + Owners' equity}}$

(6) Interest coverage ratio $= \dfrac{\text{Net income before interest \& income taxes}}{\text{Interest expense}}$

(7) Operating cash flow to interest charges $= \dfrac{\text{Operating cash flow}}{\text{Interest expense}}$

(8) Operating cash flow to total liabilities $= \dfrac{\text{Operating cash flow}}{\text{Average total liabilities}}$

(9) Receivables turnover ratio $= \dfrac{\text{Net sales}}{\text{Average accts. receivable}}$

(10) Inventory turnover $= \dfrac{\text{Cost of goods sold}}{\text{Average inventory}}$

(11) Asset turnover $= \dfrac{\text{Net sales}}{\text{Average total assets}}$

(12) Average collection period ratio $= \dfrac{\text{365 Days}}{\text{Receivables turnover ratio}}$

(13) Average number of days' inventory on hand ratio $= \dfrac{\text{365 Days}}{\text{Inventory turnover ratio}}$

(14) Return on assets (ROA) $= \dfrac{\text{Net income}}{\text{Average total assets}}$

      OR $= \text{ROS} \times \text{Asset turnover}$

(15) Return on equity (ROE) $= \dfrac{\text{Net income}}{\text{Average total owners' equity}}$

      OR $= \text{ROA} \times \text{Financial leverage}$

(16) Return on sales (ROS) $=$ $\dfrac{\text{Net income}}{\text{Net sales}}$

(17) Financial leverage $=$ $\dfrac{\text{Average liabilities} + \text{Average owners' equity}}{\text{Average owners' equity}}$

(18) Basic earnings per share (EPS) $=$ $\dfrac{\text{NI applicable to common shareholders}}{\text{Weighted average common shares}}$

(19) Cash dividend yield $=$ $\dfrac{\text{Cash dividend per common share}}{\text{Market price per common share}}$

(20) Cash dividend payout $=$ $\dfrac{\text{Total cash dividend to common shareholders}}{\text{Net income}}$

(c) What do you conclude about the availability of the appropriate data in the annual report for calculating these ratios?

(d) What does this financial analysis tell you about Toyota?

(e) What analytical metrics did Toyota choose to report for itself? What do those choices say about the message the company is striving to tell and the audience it is addressing?

Sweden

The interest in international accounting within Sweden seems to have increased over the last few years.[1]

Sweden, being a small country with several large international companies, has much to gain from harmonizing accounting standards with international practice, as far as the law permits.[2]

Introduction

The country of Sweden has long occupied a paradoxical place in the community of nations. One of the oldest continuous democracies in the world, it has carefully protected its autonomy politically by adhering to a policy of neutrality since 1815. However, the Swedes' insistence on their independence has hardly resulted in national isolation. Sweden has historically been a symbol of a progressive global order, of the need for nonviolent resolution of conflicts, and for international cooperation. Its leaders and politicians have always been active in promoting the cause of world peace.

It should be noted, however, that to date, during the 1990s, dramatic changes have occurred in Sweden.[3] Between 1989 and 1992, industrial production dropped 15 percent. Unemployment, never over 3.5 percent during the 1970s and 1980s, hit 14 percent in 1993. In 1991, the **krona** (the Swedish currency, frequently abbreviated as SEK or

---

[1]N. Hellman, ''A Comparative Analysis of the Impact of Accounting Differences on Profits and Return on Equity,'' *European Accounting Review,* December 1993, pp. 495–96.

[2]R. Rundfelt, ''Standard Setting in Sweden,'' *European Accounting Review,* December 1993, p. 589.

[3]For this background see ''Sweden: A Survey,'' *Financial Times,* December 21, 1993, pp. I–V; ''Ask the Devil,'' *The Economist,* March 13, 1993, p. 62; ''Join the Club,'' *The Economist,* February 22, 1992, pp. 44–45; ''This May Hurt,'' *The Economist,* January 16, 1993, p. 50; ''Worse and Worse,'' *The Economist,* October 9, 1993, pp. 58–59; and P. Klebnikov, ''The Swedish Disease,'' *Forbes,* May 24, 1993, pp. 78–79.

SKr) was pegged to the ECU (see Chapter 3) and was floated in 1992; within six months it had depreciated 21 percent against the ECU and a year later had depreciated 30 percent against the German mark. In 1990, Sweden ran a budget surplus, but by the middle of 1993, a budget deficit equal to 13.8 percent of gross domestic product (GDP) existed, the worst in the industrialized world (compare this rate to Italy's 10 percent, Great Britain's 8 percent, and the United States' 5 percent). Real estate prices dropped 50 percent in two years. An aggressive privatization program of Swedish companies had stalled due to a falling stock market. Experts believe, however, that Sweden's slide will begin to stop in 1995, and after, and out of the turmoil will emerge a reoriented, vigorous nation. Indeed, in November 1994, Sweden's populace voted to join the European Union (EU), making it the 15th country to do so and perhaps marking the beginning of a new era for Sweden.

The desire to balance national independence with international cooperation characterizes Sweden's place in the globalization of business. Although becoming more open, its capital markets restrict international influence and ownership. Comparatively few Swedish concerns are well known to foreign investors. Historically, the most important factor in determining financial reporting practices has been national tax and economic policy, not international capital markets. Yet Sweden's economy depends heavily on foreign trade; its exports account for approximately one-third of the nation's GDP. Swedish business and accounting professionals are active in the cause of harmonization: they participate in the activities of the International Accounting Standards Committee (IASC), award a prize each year to the Swedish company that produces the best annual report, and (in the case of large multinationals) pursue foreign investors by providing excellent and clear financial statements. A columnist for *The Wall Street Journal* has even suggested that the way to improve international financial reporting is to emulate Volvo, which takes pains to explain Swedish accounting methods to foreign investors and publishes a reconciliation of its financial results with U.S. GAAP.[4]

The Swedish, however, do not (overtly, at least) claim for themselves the leading role in developing international financial reporting guidelines that others have sometimes cast them in. On the contrary, Volvo's vice president of financial planning and control, Staffan Rydin, suggested in a recent interview that the Swedish business community looks to the United States for guidance in many areas.[5] Specifically, Rydin said that Volvo follows U.S. reporting standards as closely as it can while still meeting the requirements of Swedish law. It uses and promotes U.S. accounting practices that parallel international standards. Rydin adds that successful harmonization of accounting standards will depend largely on the willingness of Anglo-Saxon countries to assume leadership by bringing their existing standards into alignment and designing new ones with an eye toward their suitability for international use. In this manner, he says, a workable set of international standards can be created.

---

[4]J. N. Slipkowsky, "The Bottom Line in European Accounting," *The Wall Street Journal,* August 24, 1987, p. 22.

[5]J. N. Slipkowsky, "The Volvo Way of Financial Reporting," *Management Accounting,* October 1988, pp. 22–26.

Rydin's comments indicate that the attitudes and ideals that characterize Swedish society in general also shape the Swedish approach to the formulation of international financial reporting policy: a self-effacing pragmatism, a respect for technical expertise, a perspective that combines global awareness with a realistic assessment of national constraints, and a desire to build consensus through negotiation rather than to impose it through fiat.

Environmental Factors

Cultural Environment

Social Mandate and Individual Freedom.   One of the most intriguing and attractive aspects of Swedish culture is its ability to mediate between social welfare and individual privacy. On the one hand, Sweden is involved in one of the most far-reaching collectivist experiments ever attempted by a Western democracy. Almost 70 percent of its GDP goes for public expenditures, compared to an average of 45 percent for other OECD nations. On the other hand, Sweden is internationally famous as a bastion of individual freedom in which one's personal convictions and private morality are allowed considerable latitude. This concern for personal freedom may explain why a group of Swedish subjects in Hofstede's study of cultural attitudes scored a rather high 71 in individualism (compared to a score of 91 for U.S. subjects and 46 for the Japanese) in spite of the strongly collectivist elements in Swedish society.

It is important to remember this dual perspective of Swedish culture—the interplay between a strong tendency for individual preference and a genuine, pervasive social consciousness—to understand the place of financial reporting policy formation and regulation in Sweden. Even though financial reporting policy in Sweden is heavily influenced by the requirements of macroeconomic policy and tax law (more about this below), Swedish businesses and the national government nevertheless rely a great deal on the judgment of professionals in formulating and administering policy pronouncements. A well-regarded study of accounting regulation in Sweden found widespread agreement that auditors are a leading group in the process of policy formation and elaboration, indicating a healthy respect among the business community for auditor professionalism.[6] The study also found that although legislation is very important in setting boundaries, considerable debate takes place in the private sector about matters of method and theory. The professional judgment of private individuals and corporations does carry weight in Sweden. Impetus for discussion and change may be generated by a single firm's adoption of an innovation in its annual report or even by a single writer pursuing an issue in the press.

The willingness to engage in debate over policy rather than regarding it as engraved in stone implies a significant amount of tolerance for ambiguity on the part of the Swedish. Interestingly enough, the Swedish subjects in Hofstede's study scored low in the areas of uncertainty avoidance (29) and power distance (31), lower than the

---

[6]S. Jönsson, *Accounting Regulation and Elite Structures* (Chichester, England: Wiley & Sons, 1988).

United States (46, 40) and Great Britain (35, 35) in both categories. It has been argued that low scores in these areas, combined with a high score in individualism, indicate a bias toward professionalism in a national culture.[7] Indeed, the important role of the *Föreningen Auktoriserade Revisorer* (FAR), Sweden's counterpart to the U.S. American Institute of CPAs, in spearheading the creation in 1989 of a new standard-setting body, the *Redovisningsradet* (Financial Reporting Council), suggests that this hypothesis is borne out in the case of the Swedish accounting establishment.

Similar to the United States (29) and Great Britain (25), but in contrast to Japan (80) and Korea (75), Sweden scored a 33 on the long-term orientation cultural dimension. Such a relatively low score highlights a tendency for doing things the way they have always been done, a deemphasis of thrift, and a desire for more immediate results. Perhaps indicative of these traits is the historical role of global neutrality that Sweden has adopted and that was initially manifested in a fairly widespread opposition to joining the EU. Moreover, in recent history there has not been a need for personal savings and investment because the social welfare system provides unemployment and retirement incomes almost equal to one's working wages.

Auditor reports from two recent Swedish annual reports depict something of the commitment to tradition, a concern for the common good, the beginnings of an increased role for professional judgment, and a desire to embrace an EU sense of community. Exhibit 11–1 presents the 1993 auditor reports for Electrolux and Volvo. They both reflect a very Swedish orientation of the common good by attesting to the financial statement's conformity to the Swedish Companies Act; but only the auditors for Volvo express an opinion that the financial statements give a true and fair view of the company's income and financial position. The judgment of true and fair is a key phrase customarily employed by British audit reports that has now been adopted by members of the European Union (which Sweden joined in 1995 as well). A true and fair opinion criterion emphasizes the role of professional judgment in evaluating the financial statements of a company. This direct expression of an opinion was not expressly required under Swedish law in 1993, but its inclusion suggests that some Swedish auditors and multinationals want to convince foreign readers of their professional approach to financial reporting and their willingness to accommodate the needs of foreign investors, as well as their desire to fit into the European Union.

The Corporation in Society.   Europeans in general have a highly developed sense of the corporation as a public entity with social responsibilities, and nowhere is this more true than in Sweden. The Swedish people accept the need for corporate profitability, as long as the profits generated are reinvested in economic growth or otherwise used for the public good. The very nature of an extensive welfare state demands such an outlook. Beyond the immediate political imperatives, however, Hofstede's study suggests that there may be a more deeply rooted cultural basis in Sweden (and the other Nordic countries, for that matter) supporting a socially oriented view of business

---

[7]S. J. Gray, ''Towards a Theory of Cultural Influence on the Development of Accounting Systems Internationally,'' *Abacus* 24, no. 1 (1988), pp. 1–15.

EXHIBIT 11–1
Illustrative Swedish Audit Reports
AB Volvo

We have examined the Annual Report, the consolidated financial statements, the accounting records and the administration by the Board of Directors and the President for the year 1993.

In our opinion, the financial statements on pages 46 through 79 give a true and fair view of the income for the year 1993, and of the financial position at December 31, 1993.

Parent Company

The financial statements for the year have been prepared in conformity with the Swedish Companies Act.

We recommend that the Annual General Meeting:

adopt the Statement of income and the Balance Sheet, approve the disposition of earnings as proposed by the Board of Directors and the President, and discharge the members of the Board of Directors and the President from liability for their administration of the Company during 1993.

Group

The consolidated financial statements have been prepared in conformity with the Swedish Companies Act.

We recommend that the Annual General Meeting adopt the consolidated statement of income and the consolidated balance sheet.

March 22, 1994

Ragne Billing   Nils Brehmer
Authorized Public Accountant   Authorized Public Accountant

Electrolux

We have examined the annual report, the consolidated financial statements, the accounting records and the administration by the Board of Directors and the President for the accounting year 1993. Our examination was carried out in accordance with generally accepted auditing standards.

Parent Company

The annual report has been prepared in accordance with the Swedish Companies Act. We recommend that the Annual General Meeting
—adopt the income statement and the balance sheet,
—distribute the earnings as proposed by the Board of Directors and the President, and
—discharge the members of the Board of Directors and the President from liability for the financial year.

Group

The consolidated financial statements have been prepared in accordance with the Swedish Companies Act. We recommend that the Annual General Meeting adopt the consolidated income statement and the consolidated balance sheet.

Stockholm, March 1, 1994
Ernst & Young AB
Gunnargen Widhagen
Authorized Public Accountant

entities. On Hofstede's axis of masculinity, designed to measure the role of gender expectations in a society, Sweden scored the lowest of the 40 countries included in the survey.[8] In Hofstede's terms, Sweden has the most feminine culture of the countries surveyed (employing the term *feminine* in this context purely as a social construct). In other words, Hofstede's research indicates that Swedish culture elevates those values traditionally associated with femininity above those traditionally associated with masculinity—nurturance above competition, relationships above money, quality of life above public achievement.

Because of its emphasis on building and maintaining relationships, one might call it an *aptitude for solidarity,* this basic feature of Swedish culture may help to explain the relative importance of cooperation and conflict resolution in Swedish national culture. Likewise, it has undoubtedly contributed to certain features of Swedish corporate reporting, such as the required disclosure of employment and compensation information with potential ramifications for labor relations. Some firms (as many as 20 percent of those listed on the Stockholm Stock Exchange) have experimented with value-added statements as a social-reporting supplement to traditional financial statements. (For more on the value-added statement, see Chapter 8.) Moreover, it is not unusual for Swedish annual reports to focus at length on cooperative alliances with major competitors, the firm's sensitivity to the environment, and good relationships with workers.

Legal and Political Environment

Tax Law—General.   Corporate income, in Sweden as in the United States, is subject to double taxation. After income is taxed at the corporate level, cash dividends paid to shareholders are taxed again as ordinary income, or what is called *income from capital* in Sweden. (Companies not listed on the stock exchange, however, may deduct 70 percent of their dividends paid during the tax year.) Stock dividends are not taxable, and dividends received by a Swedish corporation from a second Swedish corporation in which it has an interest of 25 percent or more are also not taxable. Interest expense is fully deductible, and capital gains on the sale of equity shares are taxable at a flat rate of 25 percent.

Individual income tax rates in Sweden have been notoriously high. In recent times, the marginal tax rate reached as high as 85 percent, with most taxpayers falling into a bracket in the 40 to 50 percent range. The early 1990s, however, were a period of significant legislative reform for the Swedes, and currently the maximum individual tax rates are 31 percent for earned income up to SEK 201,600 ($26,800), and 51 percent on income levels above that.[9] In addition, however, Swedes pay a value-added tax (VAT) of 25 percent on most goods and services (although the rate is only 12 percent for food and beverages, passenger transportation, and hotel and restaurant services).

---

[8] In the other country-specific chapters included in this book, we have chosen not to address this cultural dimension, but because Sweden's score is so extreme, it is highlighted here.

[9] As of January 1, 1995, $1 = SEK 7.50.

Tax Law—Corporate.   As is the case in Japan, Swedish tax law prescribes essentially the same method of accounting for both tax and financial reporting. This requirement inevitably skews key figures on the financial statements because legalities and economic incentives built into the Swedish tax code take precedence over financial reporting practices that are generally accepted elsewhere.

The most important effect of Sweden's tax law on the financial statements of Swedish corporations is the creation of an untaxed reserve account called the *Special Tax Equalization Reserve* (SURV). Although corporate taxes in Sweden are levied nationally at a flat rate of 28 percent (as of 1994), corporations are able to lower their effective tax rate by allocating a portion of net income to the SURV account, which was designed by the Swedish government to encourage the reinvestment of corporate earnings. Not surprising, this opportunity creates an inherent fiscal conservatism, or fiscal bias, to the results of most Swedish companies.

A company makes an allocation by recording an increase (i.e., a credit) to the SURV account and a decrease (i.e., a debit) to the net income account. Because allocations to the untaxed reserve are eventually reversed and consequently increase income in later years, the SURV account essentially enables companies to defer a portion of their tax liabilities. As long as a company is able to make new allocations to the reserve to offset the reversal of previous allocations, it can continue to postpone a portion of its tax burden. However, to qualify for the tax deductions afforded by the use of untaxed reserves, companies must record allocations on their financial reports as well as on their tax returns. Conceptually, then, one could say that the untaxed reserve account is a hybrid account, containing elements of both debt and equity. Because it is a deferral of income that would have been taxed at a rate of approximately 28 percent, part of its balance represents a deferred tax liability, and the other represents stockholders' equity (specifically, retained earnings).

Untaxed reserves not only allow Swedish companies to reduce income in profitable years but also allow companies in cyclical industries to smooth income and maximize tax benefits over time. If a company records a net loss in one year, its management may elect in a later year to reverse a portion of its earlier allocations and include the reversal in income to avoid reporting the loss on its financial statements. Thus, the company gains a permanent tax advantage since no tax liability is created by reversing prior untaxed reserve allocations to cancel out a net loss. In effect, a company in this situation has been able to shift taxable income from a high-income period (in which income is taxed at 28 percent) to a low-income period (in which it is not taxed at all). The following table shows how a Swedish corporation can use untaxed reserves to allocate income between periods to maximize its tax benefits:

	Year 1	*Year 2*
Income before allocations & taxes	1000	(300)
Allocations to untaxed reserve	(400)	—
Reversal of reserve	—	300
Income before taxes	600	—
Taxes (28 percent)	168	—
Net income	432	—

By making a SEK 400 allocation to its untaxed reserve in Year 1, the company defers SEK 112 (400 × 28 percent) of its tax liability. By using SEK 300 of the reserve in Year 2 to cancel out a net loss, the company avoids reporting the net loss and eliminates SEK 84 (300 × 28 percent) of its deferred tax liability. SEK 100 remains in the reserve account, representing SEK 28 of deferred tax liability and SEK 72 of stockholders' equity.

Prior to 1991, Swedish companies could avail themselves of a variety of untaxed reserve accounts, including investment reserves, depreciation reserves, payroll reserves, and inventory reserves. Following is a more detailed description of each type.

- *Investment reserve.* Companies could, at their discretion, allocate up to 50 percent of their income before taxes to a general *investment reserve.* To obtain a tax deduction by making such an allocation, a company was required to deposit the amount of the allocation in a special noninterest-bearing account in the Bank of Sweden. On the balance sheet, these deposits were separated from current assets and carried just above ''fixed assets'' (which in Sweden refers to all long-term assets, not merely property, plant, and equipment). They are usually labeled *blocked accounts for investment and other reserves* or *restricted deposits in the Bank of Sweden.* These funds could be withdrawn only to make investments that were approved by an agency of the Swedish government.

When a company made a qualifying investment, the necessary portion of funds on deposit were released, and the investment reserve was decreased by the appropriate amount. On the balance sheet, the qualifying investment could be carried at its cost basis less the portion of funds released from the investment reserve used to acquire the investment, thereby decreasing the depreciable cost basis of the qualifying asset or preventing deduction of the qualifying expense. (*Remember:* The tax benefit has already been obtained.) In effect, the investment reserve allowed a tax deduction in the year in which a reserve was established instead of in the year in which a qualifying expenditure was made. Qualifying investments included, among other things, the construction or repair of buildings, purchase of new machinery or other tangible assets, expenditure on research and development, and costs incurred to develop export markets.

- *Depreciation reserve.* The *depreciation reserve* (also called the *accumulated accelerated depreciation reserve* or the *accumulated extra depreciation reserve*) arose from two sources. First, it included transfers from the investment reserve account when a company made an approved investment in depreciable property (essentially an initial write-off similar to additional first-year depreciation formerly allowed under the U.S. tax code). Second, the reserve included the annual excess (or deficiency) of tax depreciation over book depreciation. In the early years of an asset's life, the excess of tax over book depreciation increased the depreciation reserve, whereas in the later years when book depreciation exceeds tax depreciation, the excess decreased the depreciation reserve.

- *Payroll and inventory reserves.* The *payroll reserve* permitted companies to charge against current earnings an additional amount for employee costs, equivalent to a maximum of 20 percent of wage and salary expenses for the year, at the discretion of management. Companies could also allocate a portion of income to an *inventory reserve* in an amount not to exceed 50 percent of the value of ending inventory. This allocation was permitted in addition to normal write-downs for obsolescence or a decline in value. (A 5 percent writedown for obsolescence is generally allowed; Swedish GAAP requires that inventories be valued at the lower of cost, principally using FIFO, or replacement value.) If a company elected to make an allocation to the payroll reserve, however, it could allocate no more than 35 percent of the year-end inventory value to the inventory reserve. These two reserves effectively provided a ready source of interest-free, government-sponsored financing for business operations.

In 1991, the Swedish government undertook a significant legislative revamping to improve and update its tax laws. In essence, the inventory, payroll, depreciation, and investment reserves were eliminated in exchange for a significant reduction in Swedish corporate income tax rates (i.e., from 52 to 30 percent, effective January 1, 1991). The 1991 Swedish tax reform did not eliminate the excess depreciation allowance enjoyed by most companies, and it created the SURV account to replace the various prior untaxed reserve accounts. Corporations were permitted to allocate funds to the SURV account up to a maximum of 30 percent of a company's equity capital. The previously established untaxed reserve accounts were released to taxable income gradually, principally over the period from 1992 to 1995. Just as companies and investors became comfortable with the SURV account, it was abolished effective January 1, 1994. Companies may use one of two generally accepted ways to account for its abolishment:

- Take the full untaxed reserve account into income in 1994 and be taxed at 100 percent of the normal corporate rate; or,

- Take 20 percent of the reserve into income each year for five consecutive years (1994–1998) and be taxed at only 50 percent of the normal corporate rate.

Exhibit 11–2 presents data from Electrolux's 1993 financial statements and provides an overview of the activity in the company's reserve accounts. Notice that Electrolux's unrestricted reserves are equivalent to a U.S. company's retained earnings. It should also be noted that the SEK 183 in the Net Income column is the company's 1992 net income that is being closed to unrestricted reserves. Last, the restricted reserves are synonymous with the statutory reserves described above.

Because of the dramatic effect that allocations to untaxed reserves may have on net income, Swedish corporations argue, understandably, that consolidated net income under Swedish GAAP does not provide them with a useful basis for measuring financial performance and calculating per share data. As a consequence, they often prepare a reconciliation of their Swedish net income with net income as it would appear under U.S. GAAP using the latter as the basis for calculating earnings per share. Exhibit 11–3 presents such a reconciliation from the 1993 Electrolux financial statements. The exhibit reveals that the

EXHIBIT 11–2

Electrolux 1993 Reserves

Shareholders' equity, SEKm

	Share Capital	Restricted Reserves	Unrestricted Reserves	Net Income	Total
Opening balance	1,831	9,259	5,499	183	16,772
FAS 109 and *FAS 106,* etc.	—	—	−924	—	−924
Adjusted equity in compliance with *FAS 109 & 106*	1,831	9,259	4,575	183	15,848
Transfer of retained earnings, etc.	—	—	183	−183	—
Dividend payments	—	—	−458	—	−458
Transfers between restricted and unrestricted equity	—	−40	40	—	—
Translation differences, etc.	—	434	445	—	879
Net income	—	—	—	584	584
Year-end balance	1,831	9,653	4,785	584	16,853

Disposable consolidated earnings amount to SEK 5,369m. No allocation to statutory reserves is required. SEK 2,369m (2,733) referring to the share of equity in timing differences is reported under Statutory reserves in the balance sheet. This amount can be transferred to unrestricted reserves but will then be subject to taxation.

principal differences in Electrolux's net income relate to the accounting for acquisitions, pensions, and deferred income taxes. The company's shareholders' equity was also impacted by differences relating to the accounting for fixed assets and certain investments.

Business Environment

Form of Business.   The most common form of business organization in Sweden is the limited liability company (**Aktiebolag,** abbreviated AB), which is regulated by a national companies act. An AB may issue shares that carry voting or ownership restrictions. Class A shares carry greater voting power than class B shares: 10, 100, or even 1,000 times in some cases. Effectively, this equity structure concentrates voting power in the hands of a few investors and has created spheres of influence among Swedish multinationals. For example, the prominent Wallenberg sphere, controlled by Peter Wallenberg, controls 96 percent of the voting rights in Electrolux and 39 percent of the voting rights in Ericsson, while having provided under 7 percent of both companies' capital.[10] Moreover, it is estimated that the Wallenberg sphere accounts for 40 percent of the Stockholm exchange's market capitalization.[11] Its main rival, the Volvo-Skanska sphere, is controlled by Sören Gyll and includes Euroc, Opus, and Sandvik, as well as Volvo and Skanska. Other spheres play a supporting role in the Swedish economy.

---

[10]G. Dyer, ''Sweden: Europe's Most Powerful Families—The Wallenbergs,'' *Euromoney,* May 1994, p. 67.

[11]Ibid.

EXHIBIT 11–3

Electrolux Net Income Reconciliation

Consolidated financial statements according to US GAAP

The consolidated accounts have been prepared in accordance with Swedish accounting standards, which differ in certain significant respects from generally accepted US accounting principles (US GAAP). The most important differences are described below.

Changes in accounting principles

In the Electrolux consolidated accounts prepared in accordance with US GAAP, changes in accounting principles have been applied as of January 1, 1993 with regard to income taxes, pension benefits and employee benefits other than pensions. The accumulated effect of these changes after tax is reported separately in the income statement below under "Effect of changes in accounting principles." In accordance with Swedish accounting standards, the accumulated effect of changes in accounting principles is reported directly against opening Group equity. Changes have also been made in the principles for reporting holdings in securities. The effect of this change has been reported directly against shareholders' equity, in accordance with US GAAP. None of the changes in accounting principles has had any effect on liquidity.

The accumulated effects of changes in accounting principles that are reported directly in the income statement according to US GAAP amount to SEK 150m and comprises SEK 694m referring to income taxes, SEK 881m to employee benefits other than pensions, and SEK 37m to pensions.

Write-ups on assets

In certain situations, Swedish accounting principles permit write-ups of fixed assets in excess of acquisition cost. This does not normally accord with US GAAP.

Adjustment for acquisitions

In accordance with Swedish accounting principles, the tax benefit arising from application of tax-loss carry-forwards in acquired companies is deducted by the Group from the current year's tax costs. According to US GAAP, this tax benefit should be booked as a retroactive adjustment of the value of acquired assets.

Pensions

As of 1989, the American recommendation for pensions known as FAS 87 (Employers' Accounting for Pensions) is applied for pension plans outside the US. According to this recommendation, future salary increases, inflation and other factors must be taken into account for computation of the projected benefit obligation. The computed Swedish provision for PRI pensions is not adjusted for future salary increases, but this is offset by the lower discounting rate applied for computation of the provisions for PRI pensions in comparison with FAS 87. The initial difference arising from the first application of FAS 87 (January 1, 1989) is amortized over the future average employment period, so that the effect on net income is insignificant. Other significant differences have been adjusted in accordance with US GAAP.

Other benefits

In addition to pensions, some of the Group's subsidiaries, principally in the US, provide employees with benefits in the form of health care and life insurance subsequent to retirement. Recommendation No. 106 of the US Financial Accounting Standards Board (Employer's Accounting for Post-retirement Benefits Other Than Pensions), issued in 1990, requires that the estimated future commitment for these benefits be reported as a liability. This recommendation permits application of various types of transitional methods and must be introduced by 1993 at the latest for the Group's US subsidiaries and by 1995 for other companies. The Electrolux Group applied these recommendations as of 1993.

Securities

According to Swedish accounting principles, holdings of both debt and equity securities should be reported at the lower of acquisition cost or market value. According to FAS 115 (Accounting for Certain Investments in Debt and Equity Securities), these holdings should be classified with respect to intention, i.e., if they are intended to be traded, if they are to be retained until maturity, or in an intermediate category. Valuation as well as reporting of income differs according to the classification of the securities. For Electrolux, this means that certain securities must be reported at market value in the balance sheet, while the difference between market value and acquisition cost must be taken directly against equity, according to US GAAP. In connection with the sale of these securities, the change in value previously reported directly against equity will be reported in the income statement.

EXHIBIT 11–3   (continued)

Electrolux Net Income Reconciliation

Consolidated financial statements according to US GAAP

Deferred taxes

Taxation and financial reporting are affected during different periods by certain items. Electrolux reports deferred taxes on the most important timing differences, which refer mainly to untaxed reserves, with due consideration in certain cases for the future fiscal effects of tax-loss carry-forwards. US GAAP requires reporting of fiscal effects for all significant differences and tax-loss carry-forwards, with the proviso that deferred tax assets may be reported only if it is probable that the tax benefit will be utilized.

As indicated above, new accounting principles have been applied for taxes as of January 1, 1993. The new recommendation FAS 109 (Accounting for Income Taxes) differs from previously applied principles mainly in that fiscal effects are reported on the basis of the tax rate that will apply at the future date when taxation occurs. The principles applied previously involved reporting fiscal effects on the basis of the tax rates applicable on the date when the timing difference arose.

Application of US GAAP would have the following approximate effects on consolidated net income, shareholders' equity and the balance sheet.

A. Consolidated Net Income	1993 SEKm	1992 SEKm
Net income as reported in the consolidated income statement	584	183
Adjustments:		
Acquisitions	84	88
Pensions	−21	−18
Taxes	−123	−63
Approximate income according to US GAAP, before changes in accounting principles	524	190
Effect of changes in accounting principles	−150	—
Approximate net income according to US GAAP, after changes in accounting principles	374	190
Approximate income per share according to US GAAP, before changes in accounting principles	7.20	2.60
Approximate net income per share according to US GAAP, after changes in accounting principles (no. of shares in 1993 and 1992: 73,233,916)	5.10	2.60

B. Shareholders' Equity		
Shareholders' equity as reported in the consolidated balance sheet	16,853	16,772
Adjustments:		
Revaluation of fixed assets	−173	−178
Acquisitions	−1,211	−937
Pensions	−358	−194
Securities	235	—
Taxes	−357	−1,227
Total adjustments	−1,864	−2,536
Approximate shareholders' equity according to US GAAP	14,989	14,236

EXHIBIT 11–3   (continued)

C. Balance Sheet

The table below summarizes the consolidated balance sheets prepared in accordance with Swedish accounting principles and US GAAP.

| | SEKm | | | |
| | According to Swedish Principles | | According to US GAAP | |
	1993	*1992*	*1993*	*1992*
Current assets	47,670	44,251	50,738	47,113
Real estate, machinery and equipment	22,354	20,871	22,016	20,433
Shares and participations	1,120	818	1,355	818
Deferred taxes	455	—	140	—
Long-term receivables	530	399	810	399
Goodwill	5,108	4,443	4,020	3,766
Other assets	410	836	621	1,353
Total assets	77,647	71,618	79,700	73,882
Current liabilities	33,944	33,776	36,970	36,634
Long-term liabilities	26,460	20,382	27,351	21,097
Deferred taxes	—	373	—	1,600
Minority interests	390	315	390	315
Shareholders' equity	16,853	16,772	14,989	14,236
Total liabilities and shareholders' equity	77,647	71,618	79,700	73,882

The Swedish spheres resemble Japanese *keiretsu* in the mutual loyalty shown by member companies and in the protection they afford from hostile takeover. They also serve as a buffer against "excessive" foreign influence since most unrestricted shares—those that may be purchased or held by overseas investors—tend to be class B shares. Management teams among major Swedish multinationals have consequently been able to adopt long-term strategies with comparatively little regard for short-term profits, a behavior pattern that may be soon modified by the need to tap foreign capital markets, the deregulation of Sweden's own capital markets, and the tax reform package described above. Even so, the spheres are likely to remain a dominant factor in the Swedish economy for some time to come.

The Swedish Companies Act requires that the annual report of an AB—which must include a balance sheet, an income statement, a statement of changes in financial position, notes, an auditor's report, and various other management disclosures—be audited. The auditor must be either a *Godkand Revisor* (GR), a junior qualification requiring a two-year course of study in a university and five years of professional experience, or an *Auktoriserade Revisor* (AR), a senior qualification requiring a bachelor of commerce degree and five years of professional experience.

Capital Markets.   Sweden has only one securities exchange, located in Stockholm (the Stockholm Fondbörs). In this, as in other matters, the Swedish have shown their flair for technical innovation and their penchant for orderliness: replacing vocal bidding with a computerized trading system has made Stockholm's securities exchange one of the calmest trading arenas in the world. Although the Stockholm Exchange has generally performed impressively in the last decade (both in terms of prices and volume) and can trace its roots back more than 200 years, protectionist measures have restricted foreign access to Sweden's capital markets and prevented Stockholm from becoming an international financial center.

Securities listed on the Stockholm exchange are divided into two lists, AI and AII. The AI list, which accounts for more than 90 percent of the volume of equity trading, includes shares of the largest companies, those with more than SEK 10 million (approximately $1.3 million) in share capital and more than 1000 shareholders. An AII listing requires SEK 4 million (approximately $.5 million) in capital and more than 400 shareholders. A company wishing to list its shares on the exchange must file an application with the council of the exchange and submit audited annual reports for the last five years. Companies wishing to issue debt securities must provide financial statements for only the last two years.

The Swedish government has historically regulated the scope and manner of foreign involvement in Swedish securities markets to limit foreign competition for Swedish capital and foreign control of Swedish companies. Sweden recently, however, abolished a 1991 law limiting the number of shares available to foreign investors. Moreover, as of January 1, 1993, the last of the ownership restrictions limiting the kind and extent of shares foreigners may purchase and own was removed. In fact, the Companies Act now prohibits Swedish companies from designating certain types of shares (with certain types of rights) as restricted to Swedish citizens. Indicative also of Sweden's opening up of its capital markets are the regulations, effective January 1, 1994, that permit foreign companies (e.g., Credit Lyonnais of France and Unibank of Denmark) to become members of the Stockholm Stock Exchange. Clearly, Sweden is trying to open its financial markets so that it can become a global financial center. Exhibit 11–4 reports the foreign investment in Sweden, which has increased rapidly.

As a consequence of the Swedish government's historical insulation of its capital markets, international competition for capital does not yet exert the same kind of pressure on financial reporting in Stockholm as it does in New York, London, or Tokyo. Only a few large Swedish multinationals that have chosen to list on foreign exchanges—Volvo, Electrolux, and Ericsson are examples—have shaped their reporting methods and practices to attract foreign investors. The recently created Financial Reporting Council has, however, expressed an intention to promulgate Swedish accounting standards that are harmonious with IASC practices to the extent that the companies act allows.[12] Moreover, the progressive attitude adopted by the handful of

---

[12]Rundfelt, ''Standard Setting in Sweden.''

EXHIBIT 11–4

Stockholm Stock Exchange Foreign Investment

Year	Net Investment (SEK billion)	Foreign Share Ownership— % of Total Market Capitalization
1985	4.8	8.0
1986	2.4	8.0
1987	(4.1)	6.1
1988	(2.7)	6.6
1989	(1.9)	6.5
1990	1.2	7.7
1991	11.2	12.3
1992	13.3	18.0
1993 (11 months)	29.1	25.0

Source: *Investors Chronicle,* March 8, 1994.

Swedish-based international companies has affected the Swedish business community in general and has given Swedish companies a deserved reputation for high quality in international financial reporting. In particular, Volvo, which is listed (among other places) in London, Tokyo, and on the U.S. NASDAQ system, has provided leadership in promoting high accounting standards among Swedish companies. The international automaker's concern with quality financial reporting stems from its desire to tap international capital markets and its long-standing belief that ''shareholders are entitled to at least the same level of knowledge as tax inspectors.''

Relations with the European Union.   In May 1994, the European parliament voted in favor of admitting Sweden, Norway, Finland, and Austria into the European Union (EU). In November 1994, the Swedish populace voted its approval to join the European Union. Membership in it will have a considerable impact on the Swedish economy as both government and industry rethink their respective strategies with regard to the rest of Europe. Fear of EU retaliatory power prompted the Swedish government to deregulate banking and the capital markets as it edges toward harmonization with EU standards. Meanwhile Swedish multinationals, determined not to be left behind by EU competitors, have begun to invest heavily in member nations and to locate an increasing proportion of their manufacturing operations within EU borders. Membership in the European Union will also affect the country's financial reporting standards as well as other business practices.

Labor.   Sweden's strongly developed sensitivity to the social role of business is, to a large degree, reflected in the nation's approach to labor relations. Although membership in trade unions is not legally required of workers, Sweden is a highly unionized nation. At the close of 1993, 86 percent of the employed workforce belonged to a union as compared to 33 percent in the United Kingdom, 34 percent in Germany, and 15 percent in the United States.[13] Even so, relationships between management and employees are generally cooperative, and a number of labor relations laws in force since 1977 have tended to formalize attitudes and approaches that were already common. Employees participate in the operation of businesses; in companies with more than 100 employees, they have the right to place two members on the board of directors, one representing blue-collar employees and one representing white-collar employees. Management has praised this arrangement as an effective way for labor leaders to share responsibility for difficult personnel decisions.

This is by no means to say, of course, that labor-management friction is nonexistent. In a recent Volvo annual report, the letter to shareholders referred to a three-week strike by white-collar workers that cost the company an estimated SEK 1.1 billion, for which it received SEK 395 million in compensation from the Swedish Employers' Confederation and the Swedish Metal Trades Employers' Association. Nevertheless, Volvo's desire to depict itself publicly as a partner, not as an antagonist of labor, even in times of adversity, appeared throughout the letter. The chairman noted that in spite of the strike, the group increased its earnings thanks to ''a special and extraordinary effort on the part of all Volvo employees acting as a team.'' The chairman also stressed the company's commitment to providing employees with a pleasant and dignified work environment. Such a positive tone is all the more interesting because it came in a strike year.

Although there is no evidence of a significant, direct union influence on Swedish accounting practices, it would be naive to conclude that labor has no effect on Swedish financial reporting.[14] Even if unions themselves do not contribute directly to the formation of accounting policy, their relative prominence in Swedish politics and society affects the tone of management public relations (as we have just seen) and the ways in which government regulates the private sector. In fact, Swedish companies are required by law to disclose potentially sensitive employment information such as the average number of employees in each Swedish municipality and each foreign country, and total wages and salaries for the year with separate figures for senior management and other workers. (A copy of Volvo's personnel disclosure for 1993 is presented in Exhibit 11–5.) Such information could be particularly important in future management-labor disputes.

Selected Financial Reporting Practices

The primary objective of Swedish financial statements has historically been compliance with the law. Of late, and certainly now that Sweden must conform to the EU directives, true and fair financial reporting is the focus for listed companies. One aspect of the compliance objective that continues, however, is the:

---

[13]R. Taylor, ''Membership Still Growing,'' *Financial Times,* December 21, 1993, p. 111.

[14]Jönsson, *Accounting Regulation and Elite Structures.*

EXHIBIT 11–5
Volvo Personnel Disclosures (Unaudited)

At year-end 1993 the Volvo Group had 73,641 employees (60,115 at year-end 1992), of whom 43,977 were in Sweden and 29,664 in other countries. The acquisition of BCP Branded Consumer Products AB in November 1993 increased the number of Group employees by 17,320. Excluding acquisitions and divestments, the number of employees decreased by 3,183 in Sweden, and by 611 in other countries. Wages, salaries and social costs amounted to SEK 19,489M (16,857M in 1992).

Structure of workforce affected
The reduction in the number of Volvo Group employees continued during 1993. At year-end, 1,160 persons in Kalmar, Trollhättan, Arboga, and Köping had been notified of termination of employment. A certain amount of hiring has begun in the Göteborg car and truck plants, among other locations.

Since 1989, excluding acquisitions and divestments, the number of employees in Group companies has declined by 14,069, or 20%, with decreases of 7,804 employees in car operations and 4,731 in the truck sector.

In connection with the cutbacks in personnel, Volvo companies have faced problems in balancing such factors as length of employment and desired skills, equal opportunities for female employees, and age structures. The companies have undertaken comprehensive and costly measures to counteract imbalances in the employee structure. As a result, it has been possible to effect reductions in personnel with the agreement of the union organizations. Nevertheless, age distribution is affected adversely whereby the percentage of employees up to age 29 declined from 36 to 23% during the past five years. The percentage of employees in the 50–59 age interval has increased from 13 to 19%.

Lower absenteeism in Sweden
Absenteeism due to illness in the Group's Swedish sector—2.9% for short-term illnesses and 3.4% for longer illnesses—was the lowest in more than ten years. The figures for wage earners were 3.7 and 3.4%, respectively. The comparable figures for salaried employees were 1.5 and 1.4%. An initial evaluation of the changes in regulations pertaining to absenteeism due to illness shows that they have had no adverse effect on the health of employees. The BCP Group, which was acquired in November 1993, is not included in the above statistics.

Leadership-development programs
The development of employee skills is a basic element in the activities designed to achieve objectives established for the "Volvo 95" efficiency-improvement program. These objectives are to be achieved through focusing much of the management development effort on these issues. A special "Leadership and quality" Group staff unit was formed to coordinate and supervise leadership-training activities. Groupwide information has been produced to support a process a change that is keyed to Volvo's basic values. Group companies have developed various programs for executive development. The results of activities in this process of change are measured annually in an attitude survey.

Internationalization
None of the world's leading automotive groups has a domestic market as small as Volvo's. The combination of good products and the ability to operate in an international environment has been critical for Volvo's success. The basic internationalization strategy applicable to both manufacturing and marketing companies has always been to initially utilize local expertise in each market. Certain key positions have as a rule been filled by Swedish personnel, however. During 1993 an average of 430 Volvo employees were assigned to positions outside their home country.

New working methods
The reductions in personnel in recent years have accentuated the need for each employee's contribution to the earnings. It is important that the organization is developed parallel with working methods and individual competence.

Various projects related to the work environment, organizational development, and rehabilitation are being conducted, with the support of regional Work Life Funds, at a planned cost of more than SEK 1,000M. At year-end 1993 two-thirds of the projects had been carried out with good results.

Experience gained from the closed assembly plant in Uddevalla has been disseminated throughout Volvo to contribute to development of the organizational structure.

The work of harmonizing the terms of employment for wage earners and salaried employees continued during the year. A report submitted in April by a consultant for the employees supports earlier calculations of the economic advantages in organizations that do not make distinctions between wage earners and salaried employees. Group management and the union organizations have agreed that it should be possible to perform work within related areas as long as most of the tasks remain within the individual's trade union contract.

EXHIBIT 11–5   (continued)
Volvo Personnel Disclosures (Unaudited)

Work methods that utilize resources economically are a distinguishing feature of today's successful automotive manufacturers. There is widespread awareness of this within Volvo and improvements in the way resources are employed have been made throughout the organization. As a result of the cooperation with Mitsubishi in NedCar, Volvo has had an opportunity to learn how an efficient Japanese car producer develops and integrates products and production processes. The Japanese approach and method of working will result in greater productivity in the Born plant and is applicable generally within the Group.

Volvo's profit-related bonus system
During 1993, SEK 212M, representing the value of the 1987 contribution to the Volvo Employee Bonus Fund, was distributed. During the 1988–1993 period a total of SEK 1,403M was distributed to Volvo employees.

Senior executives' benefits
In accordance with a resolution adopted April 21, 1993, AB Volvo's Board of Directors appointed an Executive Development and Compensation Committee to serve for a trial period of one year.

During the year the Committee established rules governing bonuses and other benefits for senior executives within the group. The executives covered by these rules are the members of the Group Executive Committee, members of the executive committees of subsidiaries and a number of key persons.

Bonuses are based on the performance of the Volvo Group or of the executive's company. A bonus may, in principle, amount to a maximum of 35% of an executive's annual salary. In addition, SEK 25,000 may be paid in cases where individual-related goals have been met.

The employment contracts of certain senior executives contain provisions for severance payments when employment is terminated by the Company, as well as rules governing pension payments to executives who take early retirement.

The rules concerning severance payments provide that, when employment is terminated by the Company, an employee is entitled to severance pay equal to the employee's monthly salary for a period of 12 or 24 months, depending on age at the date of severance. In previously concluded contracts, an employee is entitled to severance pay equal to the employee's monthly salary for a period of 30 to 42 months. In agreements concluded after the spring of 1993, severance pay is reduced in the event the employee gains employment during the severance period, in an amount corresponding to 75% of income from new employment. An early-retirement pension may be received effective when the retiree reaches the age of 60. From that date until the retiree reaches normal retirement age, the retiree will receive 70% of the monthly salary.

In addition to the information provided pursuant to the Swedish Companies Act, the following information on benefits paid to the President and the Chairman is submitted in accordance with the recommendation of the Industry and Commerce Stock Exchange Committee.

In 1993 Sören Gyll, President and Chief Executive Officer, received a total of SEK 5.1M in compensation and other benefits.

Sören Gyll is eligible to retire at the age of 60. During the period between the ages of 60 and 65, his pension will amount to 70% of his final salary at date of retirement, and to 50% after he reaches the age of 65. AB Volvo and Sören Gyll have a mutual notice of termination period of 12 months. In the event of termination of employment at the request of the company, Sören Gyll receives a severance payment which amounts to a maximum of two years' salary and pension contributions from age 58 in an amount corresponding to 70% of final salary. The severance payment is to be made during the period up to the normal retirement age.

Bert-Olof Svanholm, Chairman of AB Volvo since January 19, 1994, will receive SEK 175,000 in director's fees during the period until the Annual General Meeting of shareholders on April 20, 1994. This amount constitutes part of the total directors' fees approved by the Special Meeting of shareholders on January 19, 1994.

In 1993, Pehr G Gyllenhammar, former Chairman of AB Volvo, received a total of SEK 11.2M in pension payments and other compensation. In addition, Pehr G Gyllenhammer received SEK 2.9M, representing payment of a bonus earned in 1987 but not previously paid out. Beginning in 1994 and until he reaches the age of 65, Pehr G Gyllenhammar will receive an annual pension that currently amounts to SEK 8.1M.

AB Volvo's current Board of Directors resolved on February 8, 1994 that in the future the issues previously addressed by the Executive Development and Compensation Committee would be handled directly by the Board. Accordingly, the committee was dissolved.

EXHIBIT 11–5   (continued)

Average Number of Employees by Municipality and Country

Sweden	1993	1992	1991	Outside Sweden	1993	1992	1991
Arboga	894	878	850	Norway	303	260	303
Bengtsfors	—	—	714	Denmark	375	204	198
Borås	287	308	330	Finland	599	647	668
Eskilstuna	35	37	19	Germany	476	470	527
Eslöv	151	—	—	Netherlands	898	1,007	397
Falkenberg	65	—	—	Belgium	5,162	5,230	5,014
Falköping	206	221	231	Great Britain	2,353	2,648	2,575
Flen	178	219	267	Ireland	22	—	—
Gävle	44	—	—	France	535	414	477
Göteborg	17,923	19,194	21,115	Switzerland	391	409	406
Hallsberg	86	—	—	Austria	279	213	217
Kalmar	791	809	937	Italy	370	428	444
Karlskrona	27	—	—	Spain	352	293	438
Karlstad	52	77	71	Portugal	20	—	—
Kristianstad	44	—	—	Hungary	85	—	—
Kungälv	61	77	131	United States	5,100	5,049	5,041
Köping	1,964	2,286	2,523	Canada	400	385	447
Lindesberg	508	632	709	Brazil	1,812	1,378	1,423
Malmö	155	78	83	Peru	270	287	363
Norrköping	20	—	—	Philippines	111	—	—
Olofström	3,708	3,929	4,104	Japan	426	448	447
Sigtuna	—	—	29	Singapore	70	72	75
Skellefteå	92	—	—	Malaysia	396	432	450
Skövde	4,415	4,668	4,887	Thailand	501	412	408
Sotenäs	83	—	—	Indonesia	20	—	—
Stockholm	994	722	222	Australia	470	453	405
Säffle	229	225	226	Countries with an average of less than 20 employees	38	49	39
Tanum	—	—	244				
Tidaholm	28	—	—	**Outside Sweden**	21,844	21,188	20,762
Trollhättan	2,606	3,899	3,466				
Uddevalla	345	822	872	**Group total**	59,490	60,635	64,368
Umeå	1,319	1,211	1,377				
Vara	89	143	173				
Örebro	32	—	—				
Municipalities with an average of less than 20 employees	215	12	26				
Sweden	37,646	39,447	43,606				

Women comprised 19% (18, 19) of the average number of employees in 1993.

Exhibit 11–5 (continued)

		December 31			
Number of employees by company group	*1989*	*1990*	*1991*	*1992*	*1993*
Volvo Car Group	34,607	33,629	29,570	28,453	26,803
Volvo Truck Group	25,117	24,242	23,344	22,097	20,386
Volvo Penta Group	2,547	2,186	2,036	1,539	1,417
Volvo Flygmotor Group	3,804	3,998	4,420	4,288	4,046
BCP Group	—	—	—	—	17,320
Provendor Group	8,300	—	—	—	—
Other companies	4,314	4,742	4,212	3,738	3,669
Group total	78,690	68,797	63,582	60,115	73,641

Wages, salaries and other remunerations (excluding social costs)

	SEK M		
	1993	*1992*	*1991*
AB Volvo			
Board of Directors and senior executives (of which, bonuses 1.3; 0; 0)	10.5	8.7	8.7
Other employees	145.3	127.0	123.8
Subsidiaries in Sweden			
Board of Directors and senior executives (of which, bonuses 4.4; 1.7; 1.9)	72.9	41.7	37.1
Other employees	7,883.6	7,514.2	7,578.4
Subsidiaries outside Sweden			
Board of Directors and senior executives (of which, bonuses 7.6; 2.0; 2.7)	191.1	130.0	109.6
Other employees			
Norway	88.3	55.4	64.2
Denmark	170.8	68.4	54.8
Finland	174.8	128.7	130.5
Germany	176.0	152.6	142.4
Netherlands	222.4	172.3	61.4
Belgium	1,308.7	1,003.7	928.1
Great Britain	594.3	466.1	469.0
France	132.3	89.3	111.2
Switzerland	143.4	117.4	120.6
Austria	78.7	51.0	44.2
Italy	88.5	98.9	96.3
Spain	88.2	71.8	88.1

EXHIBIT 11–5   (continued)

	SEK M		
	1993	*1992*	*1991*
United States	1,636.9	1,119.0	1,040.2
Canada	118.5	85.7	106.9
Brazil	237.8	143.0	154.5
Peru	32.5	22.2	42.9
Japan	203.0	122.9	107.5
Singapore	17.0	11.6	11.0
Malaysia	18.2	15.6	12.9
Thailand	31.3	17.0	14.9
Australia	78.0	62.3	63.8
Other countries	18.2	5.7	5.2
	5,657.8	4,075.6	3,870.6
Group total	13,961.2	11,897.2	11,728.2
Board of Directors and senior executives (of which, bonuses 13.3: 3.7; 4.6)	274.5	180.4	155.4
Other employees	13,686.7	11,716.8	11,572.8

---

[r]equirement that financial reporting should be in conformity with tax accounting. [Therefore,] in order to be able to show a more realistic profit figure, not totally destroyed by tax considerations, most [individual] Swedish companies account for deductions which are specifically made for tax purposes under the special heading of appropriations, with a corresponding entry under untaxed reserves in the balance sheet. For foreign readers this has proved to be confusing. The *Redovisningsrådet* therefore took the decision to abolish [this approach] in group accounts. Instead it introduced deferred tax accounting based on the U.S. system [and this practice] is limited to [only] group accounts.[15]

The *Redovisningsrådet*, often referred to as the Financial Reporting Council (FRC), is charged with establishing accounting standards. It includes nine part-time members representing the accounting profession, industry, and the government. As a body, it has no enforcement mechanism; corporate compliance is voluntary. To date, compliance has been generally high.

The underlying principles of Swedish GAAP are the widely embraced notions of historical cost, going concern, conservatism, and accrual accounting. Moreover, with an eye toward becoming a real player in the European Union and on the world corporate scene, the FRC work has exhibited a "strong influence from IASC standards."[16]

---

[15]Rundfelt, "Standard Setting in Sweden," p. 586.
[16]Ibid., p. 590.

Bad Debts

Receivables must be stated at the amount the company actually expects to collect (i.e., net realizable value). Bad debts are recorded by direct write-off or by creation of a reserve that reduces the asset; Swedish tax law does not permit bad debt deductions based on management estimates of uncollectible accounts.

Intercorporate Investments

Marketable securities considered to be current assets are valued at the lower-of-cost-or-market method applied individually or on a portfolio basis. Write-downs are included in current income, and reversals of previous write-downs are permitted. Long-term investments are carried at cost and written down only for permanent declines in value. Reversals of previous write-downs are not permitted, although in some cases, a write-down may be offset by the write-up of another noncurrent asset. Investments in 20 to 50 percent owned companies may be carried at cost or equity. If equity method accounted, the undistributed earnings of such affiliate companies should be classified as a restricted reserve (i.e., not available for distribution). A 50 percent share in a subsidiary (or an agreement that gives one company substantial control over another) requires the preparation of consolidated financial statements to be included with the parent-only statements in the annual report.

Inventories

As mentioned previously, inventories are carried at the lower of cost or net realizable value. Prior to 1991, inventories were frequently reported at an amount less than that permitted under the lower of cost or market due to existing tax incentives (i.e., ending inventory could be written down by as much as 50 percent to an *inventory reserve*); however, those incentives were rescinded effective January 1, 1991. Cost is principally determined using FIFO; use of the LIFO method is not permitted.

Fixed Assets

Fixed assets (defined as those for continuous use in or possession by the business) with values higher than net book value may be written up to reflect appreciated value if an offsetting entry is credited to a nondistributable shareholders' equity reserve or used to write down another fixed asset whose value has declined permanently. The current assessed value of real estate must be disclosed in the notes to the financial statements.

Long-Term Contracts

Construction contracts covering more than one accounting period are generally accounted for under the completed-contract method, although the percentage-of-completion method is also permitted.

Research and Development Costs

Under the Swedish Accounting Act (1974), R&D may be capitalized to the balance sheet and amortized to income over a period not to exceed five years. More recently, the *Redovisningsradet* has recommended that R&D be expensed as incurred unless the expenditure is recoverable with a high degree of certainty, the new product or process is technically feasible, and adequate resources exist to complete the project (and bring it to market if resale is intended).

Debt

The general accounting treatment applied to both current and long-term liabilities is the same; they are carried on the balance sheet at face or settlement value.

Leases

Most leases are accounted for as operating leases by both lessor and lessee even though the Swedish accounting profession has recommended that lease contracts containing an obligation to purchase should be capitalized to the balance sheet.

Interest Costs

Interest cost on debt associated with the construction of fixed assets is rarely capitalized, although the practice is permitted under Swedish GAAP.

Consolidations

Business combinations are usually accounted for under the purchase method, with any goodwill capitalized and amortized over a period not to exceed 10 years. Negative goodwill is permitted to be carried on the consolidated balance sheet and is usually classified as a current liability or as a restricted reserve in shareholders' equity. The pooling-of-interests method, permitted but rarely used, applies only if the acquiring company issues shares, the companies are approximately the same size, and both companies continue their particular business activities following the combination.

Extraordinary Items

Extraordinary items are defined more loosely by Swedish companies than is allowed under U.S. GAAP and may include such items as gains or losses on the sale of fixed assets, costs associated with plant closures, and foreign currency exchange gains or losses.

Segment Reporting

The Swedish Companies Act requires companies engaged in diverse lines of business to separately disclose the operating income (or loss) of each independent line of business, either on the income statement or in the footnotes. The Companies Act, however, does not require the disclosure of earnings per share data, although raw EPS can be calculated because disclosure of the number of shares outstanding is required.

Shareholders' Equity

Shareholders' equity is segmented into two categories: restricted and nonrestricted. Restricted equity (i.e., untaxed and unavailable for dividend distribution) includes capital stock, legal reserves, and revaluation reserves, whereas nonrestricted equity includes unrestricted reserves (principally retained earnings). Legal restricted reserves include the equity portion of the special tax equalization reserve, foreign currency exchange reserves,[17] and any amounts received in excess of the nominal value of issued shares. Revaluation reserves, on the other hand, arise in those rare circumstances when fixed assets are written up in excess of cost. Exhibit 11–6 presents a comparison of Swedish and U.S. accounting and reporting standards.

Analytical Considerations

In Sweden, like Germany and Japan, the financial statements of domestic companies tend to be systematically downwardly biased as compared to U.S. corporate financial data. As noted previously, the explanation for this is straightforward: Swedish tax law stipulates that taxable income be determined by reference to a taxpayer's accounting (or book) income. As a consequence, only those expenses appearing on a Swedish company's published financial statements may appear on its tax return (except for those additional deductions allowed under Swedish tax law). Given management's overriding desire to shelter income and cash flows from taxation, it stands to reason that Swedish companies would tend to report lower earnings than U.S. firms, on average. This expectation appears supported by the following country composite data for 1994:

	Return on Equity	Price-Earnings Ratio
Sweden	8.0*	20†
United States	13.7‡	15.1§

*Source: *The Wall Street Journal*, date unknown, p. C1.
†Source: *Reuter Textline*, August 15, 1994, Stockholm Exchange Companies.
‡Source: *Fortune*, May 15, 1995.
§Source: *The Wall Street Journal*, March 17, 1994, Dow Jones Industrials.

---

[17]This is a special situation in which unrealized foreign currency exchange gains arising from long-term receivables and payables are recorded (net of unrealized exchange losses) in an untaxed reserve.

EXHIBIT 11–6

Comparison of Swedish and U.S. Accounting and Reporting Standards

Item	Sweden	United States
Asset valuation	Principally historical cost, although revaluations are permitted under special circumstances	Historical cost, with selected revaluation (principally downward)
Inventory valuation	Principally FIFO, which is prescribed by tax law	Principally LIFO (because of tax considerations); also FIFO and average cost methods
Inventory: year-end	Lower of cost or net realizable value	Lower of cost or replacement cost
Depreciation	Principally straight line, but any ''appropriate depreciation plan'' permitted; excess depreciation permitted	Principally straight line, with accelerated and production-based methods permitted
Goodwill	Capitalized and amortized over a period not in excess of 10 years; exceptions, however, may be observed (e.g., the charge-to-equity method, a 40-year write-off, etc.); negative goodwill permitted and reported as either current liability or as shareholders' equity (restricted reserves)	Capitalized to balance sheet, with amortization (principally straight line) over a maximum of 40 years; negative goodwill not permitted (i.e., eliminated against noncurrent depreciable assets)
Research and development costs	Capitalization (and amortization over a 5-year period) or immediate expensing permitted	Research costs expensed currently; development costs expensed currently except in certain industries (i.e., software, oil and gas)
Capitalized interest costs	Permitted during construction and installation of assets but rarely practiced	Capitalization required for self-constructed assets
Intercorporate investments: Marketable securities (current asset trading)	Lower of cost or net realizable value, preferably on a portfolio basis	Market value (individual security basis), with unrealized gains and losses to income statement
Long-term investments: 0–20% ownership (available for sale)	Historical cost, adjusted for any permanent declines in value; upward revaluations permitted in rare cases	Market value (individual security basis only), with unrealized gains and losses to balance sheet (i.e., owners' equity)
20–50% ownership	Equity method	Equity method
51–100% ownership	Consolidated, using principally purchase accounting (although pooling permitted)	Consolidated, using pooling or purchase accounting
Debt valuation	Face or settlement value	Long-term debt (except deferred income taxes) valued at present value; all other debt valued at face value

---

EXHIBIT 11–6   (continued)

Comparison of Swedish and U.S. Accounting and Reporting Standards

Item	*Sweden*	*United States*
Leases	Principally operating leases (i.e., leases generally not capitalized)	Capital leases reflected in balance sheet; operating leases disclosed in footnotes
Deferred income taxes	Provided for in the balance sheet for (principally) untaxed reserves; otherwise generally unneeded because of book-tax consistency	Computed under liability method
Pension liabilities	Accrued on the balance sheet if not fully funded.	Reflected on balance sheet
Discretionary reserves	Fully permitted under Swedish tax laws but limited to excess depreciation and a special tax equalization reserve	Restricted to identifiable operational losses
Statement of cash flows	Not required, although statement of changes in financial position required and often presented on a cash basis (principally using indirect method)	Required

---

Despite Sweden's lower composite return on equity, the Swedish securities market appears to have compensated for the institutionalized downward income bias of that country as reflected in the relatively higher price-earnings multiples afforded Swedish companies.

What are the principal factors responsible for this downward biasing? Although there are many differences between U.S. and Swedish GAAP, the most important factors appear to be the following:

- *Depreciation.* In Sweden (as in the United States), fixed assets are normally valued at their acquisition cost less any depreciation taken to date. In certain circumstances, however, fixed assets may be written up to a higher carrying value if the assets are considered to have an ''enduring value'' in excess of acquisition cost. Assets whose values have been written up are then depreciated over their normal expected useful life, thereby creating depreciation deductions in excess of original historical cost. In any case, depreciation may be determined using either book or planned depreciation methods. Under *book depreciation,* the amount of depreciation claimed for tax purposes is equivalent to that taken for financial reporting (or book) purposes. Under *planned depreciation,* depreciation is limited to a deduction equivalent to straight-line amortization of the asset over its planned service life. Planned service lives, however, are determined by reference to the *minimum* service lives provided by Swedish tax law: machinery, 10 years; equipment, 5 years; and vehicles, 5 years. As a consequence, many Swedish firms depreciate their assets over the shortest lives permitted by Swedish law. In the United States, most firms adopt asset depreciation periods for book purposes that substantially exceed those permitted for tax purposes.

Swedish corporate managers may thus select whatever depreciation policy they so desire, subject to certain ceiling tests to avoid writing long-lived assets off too rapidly.[18] One outcome of this situation is that Swedish companies rarely deduct an amount that would be considered systematic under U.S. GAAP. More often than not, the amount deducted exceeds the systematic deduction, and, thus, a situation of excess depreciation is said to exist. As a consequence, the reported earnings of Swedish companies appear understated relative to their U.S. counterparts.

- *Untaxed Reserves.* Prior to 1991, Swedish companies were permitted to take reserve deductions against pre-tax operating income for a variety of purposes such as inventory, investment, and payroll. In 1991, however, a major tax reform eliminated most of these reserves in exchange for a substantial reduction in Sweden's corporate tax rate from 52 to 30 percent (28 percent beginning in 1994). As part of this reform effort, Swedish corporations were granted the right to allocate a portion of pre-tax earnings to a special tax equalization reserve (SURV), to a maximum of 30 percent of equity capital. In 1991, for example, Procordia, Sweden's fifth largest corporation (based on asset size), allocated SEK 600 million, or 17 percent, of pre-tax income to its SURV. These reserves may not be distributed as dividends until they are reversed to the income statement and included in taxable income. Swedish GAAP also provides that the untaxed reserves be segmented into its two components: a restricted equity reserve account (72 percent) and a deferred tax liability account (28 percent).

A significant consequence of the use of untaxed reserve accounts is the understatement of reported earnings and a parallel overstatement of assets (principally cash) and shareholders' equity (restricted reserves) relative to U.S. companies. With respect to traditional ratios, the profitability indicators of Swedish companies appear uniformly less positive than those of comparable U.S. companies. The liquidity and solvency indicators for Swedish companies, however, should (correctly) appear relatively more positive than for comparable U.S. firms. Finally, since the SURV is granted for tax purposes as

---

[18]Book depreciation is subject to two ceiling tests: (1) a 130 percent declining-balance rule and (2) a 20 percent straight-line provision. At the end of each year, a corporation has the option to select which of the two tests yields the highest depreciation charge. In all cases, however, the ceiling test selected must be consistently applied to all of a company's fixed assets.

well as book purposes, Swedish companies appear to be better cash flow generators than their U.S. counterparts. In effect, the SURV represented an interest-free loan, with an undefined payback period, from the Swedish government to its domestic corporations. As was noted earlier, however, the SURV was abolished effective January 1, 1994, and, consequently, this benefit will be eliminated as the SURV account balances are taken into income over the 1994–1998 time frame.

- *Capitalization of Asset Values.* Despite the fact that Swedish GAAP permits the capitalization of certain expenditures to the balance sheet as assets, most firms rarely avail themselves of this option. For example, while the capitalization of interest during the self-construction of assets is permitted in Sweden, most firms expense such interest costs to obtain current tax deductibility. Similarly, although most betterment expenditures are capitalized in the United States, they are expensed in Sweden, largely due to tax considerations. And despite the fact that under Swedish GAAP, R&D outlays can be capitalized, the practice is not widespread among Swedish firms. The consequence of this prevalent propensity to expense, rather than to capitalize, is a somewhat more conservative presentation of reported earnings.

Summary

Sweden is one of the most affluent countries in the world. It has had no significant underclass, virtually full employment (until recently), and relatively well-off retirees. It has the largest public service sector in the Western world: about 66 percent of its voters get their income from the government through jobs or welfare and over 70 percent of its GDP is devoted to public service expenditures. Such circumstances spring from the deeply held belief that the purpose of employers is to provide the financial resources that the state can use for the improvement of all citizens' standard of living via the provision of public services. During the first half of the 1990s, the vehicles for this welfare state—high tax rates and a dominant Social Democrat party—have been in flux. Recently tax rates have been lowered and then raised again; Swedish companies are pursuing a number of European alliances, some successfully (e.g., ASEA AB and BBC Brown Boveri Ltd.), some not (e.g., Volvo and Renault); and the Social Democrat party lost an election and then won the next one. It is generally conceded, however, that the "Swedish welfare state will be cheaper, leaner, and hopefully more efficient, but it will not disappear."[19] Time will tell how successful the Swedes will be in maintaining an enviable domestic prosperity and becoming a full-fledged player in the emerging EU community.

---

[19]D. Milbank, "Sweden's Welfare State Stares Down Reform Efforts," *The Wall Street Journal,* January 30, 1995, p. A15.

Suggested Readings

Cooke, T. E. "Disclosure in the Corporate Annual Reports of Swedish Companies." *Accounting and Business Research,* Spring 1989, pp. 113–24.

———. "Voluntary Corporate Disclosure by Swedish Companies." *The Journal of International Financial Management and Accounting,* Summer 1989, pp. 171–95.

Coopers & Lybrand. *Executive Summary of Principal Differences between Accounting Principles in the United States and Sweden.* New York: Coopers & Lybrand, 1989.

Davidson, S., and J. Kohlmeier. "A Measure of the Impact of Some Foreign Accounting Principles." *The Journal of Accounting Research,* Autumn 1966, pp. 183–212.

Hellman, N. "A Comparative Analysis of the Impact of Accounting Differences on Profits and Return on Equity: Differences between Swedish Practice and United States GAAP." *European Accounting Review* 3(1993), pp. 495–530.

Price Waterhouse. *Doing Business in Sweden.* New York: Price Waterhouse, 1991.

Rundfelt, R. "Standard Setting in Sweden." *European Accounting Review* 3 (1993), pp. 585–91.

Slipbrowsky, J. N. "The Volvo Way of Financial Reporting." *Management Accounting,* October 1988, pp. 22–26.

Weetman, P., and S. J. Gray. "A Comparative Analysis of the Impact of Accounting Principles on Profits: The U.S.A. versus the U.K., Sweden, and the Netherlands." *Accounting and Business Research,* Autumn 1991, pp. 363–79.

Issues and Information for Further Inquiry

I.11.1   Swedish Disclosure

In a Spring 1989 *Accounting and Business Research* article (pp. 113–24), "Disclosure in the Corporate Annual Reports of Swedish Companies," T. Cooke concludes that "disclosure by unlisted companies is lower than companies that are listed only on the Stockholm Stock Exchange. Furthermore, disclosure by companies listed only on the Stockholm Stock Exchange is lower than that for companies with multiple quotations."

Required:
Obtain a copy of this article and report on the nature of the disclosures investigated and the rationale(s) used to explain the reported disclosure differences.

I.11.2   Sweden versus the United States

In a December 1993 *European Accounting Review* article (pp. 495–530), "A Comparative Analysis of the Impact of Accounting Differences on Profits and Return on Equity: Differences between Swedish Practice and U.S. GAAP," N. Hellman reports that "the adjustments for U.S. GAAP requirements, on average, caused *lower* profits under U.S. GAAP, compared with profits in accordance with Swedish accounting practice. . . . These results were *not* in line with expectations.''

Required:

    (a) Obtain a copy of this article and report on the rationale for the initial expectations that Swedish GAAP would be more conservative than U.S. GAAP.

    (b) Summarize the author's rationale for the contrary results and comment on whether you see merit in that rationale or not.

Exercises

E.11.1   Recapitalization

In 1991, Trygg-Hansa Spp Holding AB, along with several other Swedish insurance companies, purchased the U.S.–based Home Insurance Co. for $970 million. At the time of the purchase, Home Insurance was experiencing large insurance losses and had recently missed a $410 million payment on some high-yield debt. The company's debt-to-equity ratio exceeded 70 percent at the time of the acquisition.

For nearly three years, Trygg-Hansa had been trying to restructure the U.S. insurance company's operations to return the company to profitability. In late 1993, Trygg-Hansa announced a recapitalization plan intended to speed up the restructuring effort by reducing the debt level and attendant interest costs of Home Insurance. According to the plan, Home Insurance would sell 7.5 million shares of common stock at a price of $17 per share and then issue $280 million in new lower interest rate debt. Assuming that the debt and stock sales were successful, Home Insurance's capitalization would increase from $941 million to $1.16 billion, its debt-to-equity ratio would fall to around 40 percent, and its interest charges would decline by about $35 million a year. After the debt and equity offerings, Trygg-Hansa would own approximately 47 percent of Home Insurance Series A common stock and approximately 65 percent of the company on a fully diluted basis.

Required:

    (a) Under Swedish GAAP, how should Trygg-Hansa account for its investment in Home Insurance?

    (b) Explain why Trygg-Hansa might own only 47 percent of Home Insurance's Series A common stock but 65 percent of the company on a fully diluted basis?

    (c) On the basis of the limited information in the case, explain how Home Insurance intends to utilize the proceeds of its debt and equity offerings.

E.11.2 Lease Capitalization

Volvo was founded in 1915 and has grown to be the largest industrial company (as measured by sales) in the Nordic area, including Sweden, Norway, Denmark, Finland, and Iceland. The company began assembling cars in 1926 and trucks in 1928. Today Volvo is engaged in a broad range of activities in the automotive and related industries (e.g., cars, trucks, and buses complemented by marine and industrial engines, aircraft engines, and construction equipment). The company also has substantial shareholdings in companies with operations in the branded consumer products field, as well as the pharmaceutical and biotechnology fields.

Volvo or its consolidated subsidiaries lease a significant number of assets. Under Swedish GAAP, lease contracts are accounted for as operating leases unless the lease agreement provides for the transfer of title from lessor to lessee at some point during the lease term.

In December 1984, Volvo shares began trading in the United States over the NASDAQ exchange in the form of American depositary shares (or ADSs). Each ADS represents one Class B Volvo share; each Class B share confers one-tenth (1/10) of one vote, whereas each Class A share confers one full vote. Accordingly, Volvo files an annual set of financial statements (form 20-F) with the U.S. Securities and Exchange Commission.

Volvo's year-end 1993 form 20-F revealed the following information:

Leasing

Future lease commitments are not generally capitalized but are accounted for as operating leases. Future minimum rental commitments, net of immaterial sublease rentals, at December 31, 1993, for non-cancelable operating leases are as follows:

	(in millions)
1994	SEK 605
1995	508
1996	419
1997	381
1998	267
1999 and thereafter	320
	SEK 2,498

Long-Term Debt

	1993
Bond loans	SEK 2,295
Convertible debenture loans	1,676
Other long-term loans	10,182
Total	SEK 14,153

The company's long-term debt carries a weighted average cost of capital of 12 percent.

Required:

    (a) Assume that all leases are capitalized to a company's balance sheet. What value would be assigned to Volvo's outstanding lease commitments on the company's balance sheet as of December 31, 1993?

    (b) Volvo's total assets at December 31, 1993, amounted to SEK 134,516 million. Calculate the company's long-term debt to total assets ratio *both* with and without the capitalization of Volvo's leases.

    (c) Are companies like Volvo able to leverage themselves to higher debt levels than would otherwise be the case (say, in the United States) as a consequence of Swedish GAAP, which does not require lease capitalization?

E.11.3   Converting Funds Flows to Cash Flows

In Sweden, limited companies are required to provide shareholders with an annual report containing an administration report, a balance sheet, an income statement, and a statement of changes in financial position. An increasing trend among Swedish companies is to present the statement of changes in financial position in the context of cash flow data. For example, the statement of changes in financial position for Esselte, as presented in the company's 1993 annual report and a brief description of that statement from the company's footnotes are presented here as an example. Esselte, headquartered in Solna, Sweden, is a worldwide supplier of office products.

Required:

    (a) Recast Esselte's statement of changes in financial position into a statement of cash flows (indirect method). (*Hint:* Refer to Esselte's balance sheet data in E.11.4 to assist your analysis.)

    (b) Comment on Esselte's financial health vis-à-vis its cash flows.

Excerpt from Esselte's Footnotes

STATEMENT OF CHANGES IN FINANCIAL POSITION

The Statement of Changes in Financial Position has been revised to better reflect cash flow, as well as the effects of exchange rate fluctuations, acquisitions and divestments. Accordingly, the terms used in the Statement of Changes in Financial Position correspond better to those used internally for controlling the divisions.

    Cash flow after financial items is the same as operating income, financial income and expense, taxes and dividends, as well as the change in capital employed in local currency translated into Swedish kronor using the average exchange rate for the period.

    The translation effects of exchange rate fluctuations during the year which have affected capital employed translated into Swedish kronor are shown as a separate item. Capital employed in the Group is defined as operating assets less operating liabilities. Capital employed includes tax receivables and tax liabilities, as well as appropriations for future costs.

    Unallocated capital employed includes mainly tax receivables and liabilities, certain real estate properties, as well as a reserve for future higher rental costs for the office building in Solna.

    The Group's net financial liabilities are defined as financial liabilities less financial assets.

ESSELTE
Statement of Changes in Financial Position
31 December, 1993 and 1992

	SEK Millions	
	1993	*1992*
Cash flow from divisions		
Operating income before depreciation	**1,054**	1,112
Change in working capital	**611**	62
Gross investments in machinery and equipment	**−297**	−398
Sales of machinery and equipment	**78**	46
	1,446	822
Cash flow from nonallocated items		
Nonallocated expenses	**−92**	−152
Nonrecurring costs	**−**	−270
Change in nonallocated capital employed	**3**	−89
	−89	−511
Cash flow before financial items	**1,357**	311
Cash flow from financial items		
Financial income and expense	**−152**	−271
Taxes	**−154**	−240
Dividends	**−86**	−180
	−392	−691
Cash flow after financial items	**965**	−380
Effects of exchange differences and acquisitions/divestments		
Exchange differences in capital employed, divisions	**−698**	−767
Acquired/divested capital employed, divisions	**39**	59
	−659	−708
Change in net financial liabilities	**306**	−1,088
Specification of change in net financial liabilities		
Change in liquid assets and short-term notes	**63**	−392
Change in blocked accounts in Central Banks	**−14**	2
Change in shares and other financial assets	**24**	−51
Change in financial assets	**73**	−441
Change in short-term borrowings	**89**	325
Change in long-term borrowings	**−160**	397
Change in pension liabilities	**−162**	−75
Change in financial liabilities	**−233**	647
Change in net financial liabilities	**306**	−1,088

E.11.4   Statement of Cash Flows

Esselte is a Swedish manufacturer of office products and supplies. Consistent with Swedish GAAP, the company did not present a statement of cash flows in its 1993 annual report. Esselte's balance sheet and footnotes are presented here.

Required:

   (a) Prepare a statement of cash flow for 1993 for Esselte using the company's balance sheet and footnotes.

   (b) Comment on the format of Esselte's balance sheet.

   (c) Based on your reading of the footnotes, what accounting policy differences exist between Swedish and U.S. GAAP?

ESSELTE
Consolidated Balance Sheet

			SEK Millions		
		December 31, 1993		*December 31, 1992*	
Operating assets					
Current operating assets					
Trade bills		**191**		177	
Accounts receivable		**2,061**		1,941	
Prepaid expenses and accrued income		**111**		118	
Other current receivables		**212**		209	
Inventories	Note 5	**2,000**	**4,575**	2,032	4,477
Long-term operating assets					
Long-term receivables			**94**		291
Goodwill	Note 6	**917**		891	
Other intangible assets	Note 7	**100**	**1,017**	97	988
Plants under construction		**1**		76	
Machinery and equipment	Note 8	**1,113**		1,162	
Buildings	Note 9	**758**		680	
Land and land improvements	Note 10	**114**	**1,986**	110	2,028
Operating assets			**7,672**		7,784
Financial assets					
Short-term financial assets					
Cash, bank and postal giro		**236**		260	
Short-term notes		**137**	**373**	50	310
Blocked account for investment reserve			**6**		20
Long-term financial assets					
Shares and other financial assets	Note 11		**66**		42
Financial assets			**445**		372
Total assets			**8,117**		8,156
Capital employed	Note 12		**5,153**		5,398
Assets pledged	Note 13		**202**		177

ESSELTE
Consolidated Balance Sheet
(continued)

		SEK Millions		
		December 31, 1993		*December 31, 1992*
Operating liabilities					
Current operating liabilities					
Trade bills		**94**		84	
Due to suppliers		**747**		652	
Accrued expenses and prepaid income		**841**		806	
Reserve for restructuring costs		**17**		49	
Other current liabilities		**439**	**2,138**	307	1,898
Long-term operating liabilities					
Deferred tax liability		**170**		170	
Other long-term liabilities		**211**	**381**	318	488
Operating liabilities			**2,519**		2,386
Financial liabilities					
Current financial liabilities	Note 14				
Utilized bank advances		**62**		59	
Short-term part of borrowings		**24**		38	
Other short-term borrowings		**1,512**	**1,598**	1,412	1,509
Long-term financial liabilities					
Long-term loans	Note 15	**1,182**		1,342	
Provisions for pensions	Note 16	**593**	**1,775**	755	2,097
Financial liabilities			**3,373**		3,606
Shareholders' equity					
Restricted shareholders' equity					
Share capital	Note 17	**428**		428	
Restricted reserves	Note 17	**351**	**779**	608	1,036
Unrestricted shareholders' equity					
Unrestricted reserves	Note 17	**1,299**		1,379	
Net income		**147**	**1,446**	−251	1,128
Shareholders' equity			**2,225**		2,164
Liabilities and shareholders' equity			**8,117**		8,156
Net financial liabilities	Note 18		**2,928**		3,234
Contingent liabilities	Note 19		**164**		205

Esselte Selected Footnotes
31 December 1993

Note 1   Costs of goods sold / Selling and administrative expenses

In the tables below, cost depreciation is distributed over cost of goods sold and selling and administrative expenses, as well as per type of asset.

	SEK m	
	1993	*1992*
Cost depreciation per type of cost		
Cost of goods sold	**−265**	−254
Selling and administrative expenses	**−249**	−184
Cost depreciation	**−514**	−438
Cost depreciation per type of asset		
Machinery and equipment	**−358**	−317
Buildings	**−48**	−35
Goodwill	**−89**	−73
Other intangible assets	**−19**	−13
Cost depreciation	**−514**	−438

Nonrecurring costs in the amount of SEK 270 m. are included in the Group's selling and administrative expenses in 1992. These costs were shown as extraordinary expenses in last year's Annual Report.

Write-down of receivables in finance companies	—	−10
Reserve for discontinuation costs	—	−179
Reserve for future rental costs	—	−51
Expenses related to demerger of the Group	—	−14
Unallocated restructuring costs	—	−16
Nonrecurring costs	—	−270

Note 2   Financial income and expense

	SEK m	
	1993	*1992*
Interest income		
Interest income	**24**	87
Interest income from hedging shareholders' equity in foreign subsidiaries	**95**	115
Interest income	**119**	202
Interest expense		
Interest portion of PRI pension cost in Sweden	**−24**	−38
Other interest expense	**−233**	−334
Interest expense	**−257**	−372
Other financial income and expense		
Capital gains/losses on listed shares	**2**	—
Capital gains/losses	**−2**	−92
Exchange differences in high-inflation countries	**−14**	−9
Other financial income and expense	**−14**	−101
Financial income and expense	**−152**	−271

	SEK m	
	1993	*1992*

Note 3   Tax

Corporate tax	−165	−276
Deferred tax	11	36
Full tax	−154	−240

Corporate taxes for the year totaling SEK 165 m. consist of SEK 0 m. (16) incurred in Sweden and SEK 165 m. (260) in other countries.

Note 4   Acquired and divested capital employed

	SEK m	
	1993	*1992*
Acquired capital employed		
Current operating assets, net	17	—
Long-term operating assets	2	—
Capital employed	19	—
Financial liabilities, net	13	—
Divested capital employed		
Current operating assets, net	—	569
Long-term operating assets	58	507
Capital employed	58	1,076

Divested capital employed in 1992 includes Scribona in an amount of SEK 923 m.

Note 5   Inventories

	SEK m	
	Dec. 31, 1993	*Dec. 31, 1992*
Raw materials	385	414
Work in progress	110	94
Semi-finished goods	64	101
Finished goods	1,441	1,423
Inventories	2,000	2,032

Note 6   Goodwill

Cost	1,438	1,638
Accumulated cost depreciation	−521	−747
Net value after cost depreciation	917	891

If goodwill written down in 1990 has been amortized instead according to plan over a period of 20 years, operating income for the year would have been SEK 37 m. lower and the net value of goodwill and shareholders' equity would have been SEK 614 m. higher at year-end 1993.

Note 7   Other intangible assets

Cost	240	208
Accumulated cost depreciation	−140	−111
Net value after cost depreciation	100	97

Other intangible assets comprise mainly acquired patent rights and capitalized expenses related to the development of software programs for commercial sale.

Note 8   Machinery and equipment

	SEK m	
	Dec. 31, 1993	*Dec. 31, 1992*
Cost	**3,241**	3,358
Accumulated cost depreciation	**−2,128**	−2,196
Net value after cost depreciation	**1,113**	1,162

Note 9   Buildings

Cost	**1,132**	997
Accumulated cost depreciation	**−374**	−317
Net value after cost depreciation	**758**	680
Taxation value, Swedish companies	**3**	3

Note 10   Land and land improvements

Cost	**128**	121
Accumulated cost depreciation	**−14**	−11
Net value after cost depreciation	**114**	110
Taxation value, Swedish companies	**2**	1

Note 11   Shares and other financial assets

	Type of security	*Book value SEK m*
Europeisk Luftcharter KB	participations	—
Sparess Datainvest KB	participations	—
Livia	participation note	5
Pension receivables		31
Promissory notes		6
Other financial assets		24
Shares and other financial assets		66

Note 12   Capital employed

	SEK m	
	Dec 31, 1993	*Dec 31, 1992*
Operating assets	**7,672**	7,784
Operating liabilities	**−2,519**	−2,386
Operating capital employed	**5,153**	5,398

Note 13   Assets pledged

	SEK m	
	Dec 31, 1993	*Dec 31, 1992*
Chattel mortgages	**42**	28
Real estate mortgages	**157**	138
Sundry assets in non-Swedish subsidiaries	**3**	11
Assets pledged	**202**	177

Note 14   Current financial liabilities

Of total Group short-term borrowings amounting to SEK 1,598 m., SEK 110 m. was secured.

Note 15   Long-term loans

	SEK m	
	Dec 31, 1993	*Dec 31, 1992*
Parent Company		
Bank loans	**1,075**	1,175
Foreign companies		
Mortgage loans	—	7
Other loans	**107**	160
Long-term loans	**1,182**	1,342

Of total Group long-term loans amounting to SEK 1,182 m., SEK 87 m. was secured.

    The Parent Company's long-term loans totaling SEK 1,075 m., consist of long-term credit facilities that become due for payment during the period 1995-1998 in accordance with the following payment structure: 1995 SEK 171 m., 1996 SEK 653 m., 1997 SEK 125 m. and 1998 SEK 126 m. These facilities were unutilized on December 31, 1993. Short-term borrowing corresponding to the value of the long-term credit facilities have been reclassified as long-term loans. The Group's long-term loan agreements contain commitments for maintaining certain financial key ratios.

Note 16   Provisions for pensions

	SEK m	
	Dec 31, 1993	*Dec 31, 1992*
Supplementary (PRI) pension obligation	**247**	455
Other pension obligations	**346**	300
Provisions for pensions	**593**	755

Note 17   Shareholders' equity

	SEK m				
	Share capital	*Restricted reserves*	*Unrestricted reserves*	*Net income*	*Total*
Balance					
January 1, 1993	428	608	1,128		2,164
Parent Company's dividend			−86		−86
Net income				147	147
Change in restricted reserves		−257	257		—
Change in translation differences		0			—
Balance Dec 31, 1993	428	351	1,299	147	2,225

The Group's unrestricted and restricted reserves at December 31, 1992 have been recalculated in accordance with the recommendation of the Swedish Financial Accounting Standards Council. The Group thus reports unrestricted reserves at year-end 1992 which are SEK 47 m. lower than the figure shown in the 1992 Annual Report. The Group's restricted reserves at December 31, 1992 have increased by an equivalent amount.

Note 18   Net financial liabilities

	SEK m	
	Dec 31, 1993	*Dec 31, 1992*
Financial assets	**445**	372
Financial liabilities	**3,373**	3,606
Net financial liabilities	**2,928**	3,234

Note 19 Contingent liabilities

Guarantees and contingent liabilities	**19**	71
Pension obligations	**2**	6
Other personnel commitments	**143**	128
Contingent liabilities	**164**	205

Note 20   Balance sheet exposure

The Group's Balance Sheet exposure consists mainly of the shareholders' equity of the foreign subsidiaries. Borrowing by the subsidiaries is as a rule raised in local currency.

At year-end 1993, the Esselte Group's Balance Sheet exposure corresponded to SEK 3,068 m. (2,874). Consolidated shareholders' equity in foreign currency is hedged by selling the respective currency on contract against Swedish kronor, or by borrowing the respective currency in the Parent Company. Each currency is normally hedged with forward exchange contracts but hedging can also be done in currency groups for currencies that fluctuate in a similar manner, and when each currency amounts to a maximum of one percent of the total shareholders' equity in foreign currency.

Exchange rates

Country	Currency	Code	Average rate		Year-end rate	
			1993	*1992*	*1993*	*1992*
Australia	1	AUD	**5.29**	4.28	**5.62**	4.87
Austria	100	ATS	**66.90**	52.95	**68.59**	62.48
Belgium	100	BEF	**22.52**	18.11	**23.22**	21.36
Canada	1	CAD	**6.04**	4.81	**6.24**	5.56
Denmark	100	DKK	**120.14**	96.45	**123.65**	113.25
Finland	100	FIM	**136.47**	130.00	**144.45**	134.30
France	100	FRF	**137.43**	110.00	**142.15**	128.53
Germany	100	DEM	**470.92**	372.67	**482.20**	437.48
Hong Kong	1	HKD	**1.01**	0.76	**1.08**	0.92
Italy	100	ITL	**0.50**	0.47	**0.49**	0.48
Japan	100	JPY	**7.03**	4.60	**7.45**	5.66
Malaysia	100	MYR	**302.90**	229.40	**311.00**	270.00
Netherlands	100	NLG	**419.21**	331.00	**430.85**	389.00
New Zealand	1	NZD	**4.22**	3.13	**4.65**	3.64
Norway	100	NOK	**109.79**	93.60	**111.25**	102.15
Portugal	100	PTE	**4.86**	4.36	**4.74**	4.91
Singapore	1	SGD	**4.83**	3.58	**5.20**	4.31
Spain	100	ESP	**6.14**	5.69	**5.86**	6.17
Switzerland	100	CHF	**526.99**	414.16	**568.00**	482.53
U.K.	1	GBP	**11.69**	10.22	**12.35**	10.68
U.S.A.	1	USD	**7.79**	5.82	**8.33**	7.05

E.11.5   Statement of Cash Flows

Under Swedish GAAP, public companies are required to provide shareholders with an annual report containing an administration report, balance sheet, income statement, and statement of changes in financial position (usually presented in terms of sources and uses of funds). There is an increasing tendency, however, for companies to present cash flow statements using the indirect method.

The following are the consolidated income statement and consolidated balance sheet for AGA for the year ended 31 December 1992 and 1993. AGA is headquartered in Stockholm and is one of the world's leading suppliers of industrial and medical gases.

AGA
Consolidated Income Statement

	SKr million	
	1993	*1992*
Sales	16,063	11,870
Other operating earnings	216	204
Operating expenses	−13,242	−9,820
Income before depreciation	3,037	2,254
Depreciation	−1,389	−965
Operating income	1,648	1,289
Dividends	32	28
Interest earnings	420	574
Interest expenses	−824	−640
Exchange rate adjustment	45	35
Share of income in Gullspångs Kraft	206	145
Share of income in other associate companies	35	46
Income after financial items	1,562	1,477
Nonrecurring items	—	−100
Income before tax	1,562	1,377
Paid tax	−275	−214
Deferred tax	−139	−152
Minority interests	−12	−4
Net income	1,136	1,007
Net income per share, SKr		
After paid tax, before nonrecurring items	26.65	26.40
After full tax, before nonrecurring items	23.75	22.60
After full tax, after nonrecurring items	23.75	21.15
Return, percent		
On capital employed, before tax	14.8	16.3
On total assets, before tax	10.2	11.5
On shareholders' equity, after full tax	14.3	14.8

AGA
Consolidated Balance Sheet

Assets	SKr million		*Liabilities and Shareholders' Equity*	SKr million	
	1993	*1992*		*1993*	*1992*
Current assets			**Current liabilities**		
Liquid assets and investments	**2,021**	2,828	Owed to suppliers	**1,107**	846
Accounts receivable, trade	**2,794**	2,199	Short-term loans	**2,316**	2,758
Prepaid expenses and			Accrued tax	**127**	123
accrued income	**253**	235	Accrued expenses and		
Other current accounts receivable	**244**	195	prepaid income	**2,170**	1,601
Inventories	**966**	967	Other current liabilities	**441**	325
Advance payments to suppliers	**28**	28	Advance payments from customers	**211**	159
Total current assets	**6,306**	6,452	**Total current liabilities**	**6,372**	5,812
Fixed assets			**Long-term liabilities**		
Shares and participations	**1,831**	2,254	Long-term loans	**3,880**	3,213
Long-term receivables	**200**	218	Provisions for pensions	**1,081**	1,123
Goodwill from acquisitions	**56**	9	Deferred tax	**2,188**	1,972
Land, buildings, machinery	**14,398**	11,619	Other long-term liabilities	**601**	572
Total fixed assets	**16,485**	14,100	**Total long-term liabilities**	**7,750**	6,880
Total assets	**22,791**	20,552	**Convertible loan**	**204**	204
			Minority interests	**155**	78
			Shareholders' equity		
			Restricted shareholders' equity		
			Share capital (26,008,531 A-shares		
			and 21,421,795 B-shares of SKr		
			25 each)	**1,186**	1,186
			Legal reserves	**5,064**	4,010
			Retained earnings		
			Free reserves	**924**	1,375
			Net income	**1,136**	1,007
			Total shareholders' equity	**8,310**	7,578
			Total liabilities and shareholders'		
			equity	**22,791**	20,552
Pledged assets			**Contingent liabilities**		
Real estate mortgages	**397**	105	Discounted bills receivable	**4**	6
Chattel mortgages, etc.	**81**	140	Guaranties and other		
Other assets	**97**	110	contingent liabilities	**273**	112

Note 15   Shareholders' Equity

Group	Share capital	Legal reserves	Retained earnings
Dec. 31, 1992	1,186	4,010	2,382
Dividend from Parent Company	—	—	−427
Currency translation differences	—	—	23
Transfers between legal reserves and retained earnings	—	1,054	−1,054
Net income in 1993	—	—	1,136
Dec. 31, 1993	1,186	5,064	2,060

Required:

(a) Using AGA's financial data, construct a statement of cash flows for 1993. Comment on the company's financial health vis-à-vis its cash flows.

(b) Of what use is the information on pledged assets and contingent liabilities presented at the bottom of AGA's consolidated balance sheet?

E.11.6   Accounting for Appropriations and Reserves

Atlas Copco AB is an international industrial company with operations in construction, mining, and the manufacture and sale of industrial tools and equipment. Although founded and headquartered in Stockholm, over 95 percent of the company's sales occur outside Sweden. Atlas Copco AB is the parent company of the Atlas Copco Group.

The following are the company's income statements and balance sheets for the years ended 31 December 1992 and 1993, as well as several excerpts from the notes to the financial statements.

Required:

(a) Using the following information, reconstruct the journal entries for 1992 and 1993 involving the Appropriations account.

(b) Calculate the company's return on investment (1) with and (2) without the use of the Appropriations and the Untaxed Reserves accounts.

ATLAS COPCO AB
Income Statement
(SEK, millions)

	1993	*1992*
Operating income	238	173
Operating expense	−85	−116
Operating profit before depreciation	153	57
Cost depreciation (NOTE 3)	−7	−8
Operating profit after depreciation	146	49

ATLAS COPCO AB
Income Statement
(SEK, millions)
(continued)

	1993	1992
Financial income and expense (NOTE 4)	**461**	282
Profit after financial income and expense	607	331
Appropriations (NOTE 5)	**−177**	−12
Profit before taxes	430	319
Taxes (NOTE 6)	**—**	0
Net Profit	**430**	319

ATLAS COPCO AB
Balance Sheet
(SEK, millions)

Assets		1993.12.31		1992.12.31	
Current assets	Cash, bank and short-term investments (NOTE 8)	**1,038**		1,174	
	Receivables (Note 9)	**1,673**	**2,711**	1,676	2,850
Fixed assets	Shares and participations (PAGE 27)	**3,816**		3,541	
	Other fixed assets (NOTE 13)	**415**	**4,231**	790	4,331
Total Assets			**6,942**		7,181

Liabilities and Shareholders' Equity					
Current liabilities	Non-interest-bearing liabilities (NOTE 17)	**326**		198	
	Interest-bearing liabilities (NOTE 17)	**1,692**	**2,018**	2,318	2,516
Long-term liabilities	Interest-bearing liabilities (NOTE 19, 21)		**446**		436
Total Liabilities			**2,464**		2,952
Convertible debenture loan (NOTE 22)			**—**		137
Untaxed reserves (NOTE 23)			**450**		458
Shareholders' equity	Share capital (36,703,184 shares, par value SEK 25) (NOTE 24)	**918**		855	
	Legal reserve (NOTE 25)	**1,737**		1,522	
	Retained earnings (NOTE 26)	**943**		908	
	Net profit	**430**	**4,028**	319	3,634
Total Liabilities and Shareholders' Equity			**6,942**		7,181
Assets pledged (NOTE 28)			**44**		5
Contingent liabilities (NOTE 28)			**636**		548

Excerpts: Notes to Financial Statements

Depreciation

The Atlas Copco Group uses three depreciation concepts: cost depreciation, book depreciation and current cost depreciation.

Cost depreciation is based on original cost and is applied according to the straight-line method over the economic life of the asset. Goodwill is amortized in accordance with a plan established for each specific case.

Book depreciation is used in each individual company in accordance with the maximum amount permitted by tax legislation in each country. The difference between book depreciation and cost depreciation is reported under "Appropriations" in the Income Statement. The total value is reported in the Balance Sheet among untaxed reserves under the heading "Accumulated additional depreciation." In the case of the Group, untaxed reserves and appropriations are eliminated.

5. Appropriations

Tax legislation in Sweden and in other countries allows companies to retain untaxed profits through tax-deductible allocations to untaxed reserves. By utilizing these regulations, companies can dispose and retain earnings within the business without being taxed. The untaxed reserves created through this means may not be used for dividends.

The untaxed reserves first become subject to tax when they are withdrawn. Should the company report a loss, certain untaxed reserves can be used to cover the loss without being taxed.

	Parent Company	
	1993	*1992*
Difference between book depreciation and cost depreciation (NOTE 23)	8	4
Allocation to tax equalization reserve	—	−206
Group contributions, net	−185	190
	−177	−12

Under certain circumstances, the transfer of earnings, in the form of Group contributions can be made between Swedish companies within the same Group. The contribution is a tax deductible expense for the donor and taxable income for the receiver. During 1993, the Parent Company received contributions from Atlas Copco Tools AB and made contributions to Atlas Copco Construction and Mining Technique AB and Uniroc AB.

23. Untaxed reserves

Untaxed reserves are reported in the Parent Company balance sheet as a compounded item. The distribution is shown below. These are totally eliminated in the consolidated accounts.

	Parent Company	
	1993	*1992*
Accumulated additional depreciation		
Machinery and equipment	12	20
Buildings	10	10
Tax equalization reserve	428	428
	450	458

	Accumulated Additional Depreciation	
	Machinery and equipment	*Buildings*
Opening value, Jan. 1, 1993	20	10
Dissolutions	−8	—
Closing value, Dec. 31, 1993	12	10

25. Restricted reserves

	Group	Parent Company
Restricted reserves, Dec. 31, 1992	3,429	1,522
Premium on conversion and non-cash issue	226	226
Less taxes	−11	−11
Transfers between restricted and unrestricted capital	773	
Restricted reserves, Dec. 31, 1993	4,417	1,737

The increase in restricted reserves for the Atlas Copco Group relates primarily to translation differences and the portion of shareholders' equity in allocations made to untaxed reserves in individual companies.

E.11.7   Accounting for Fixed Assets

The accounting for fixed assets in Sweden differs from that in the United States in two important respects. First, in certain circumstances (i.e., if an asset can be shown to have ''enduring value'' in excess of its acquisition cost), Swedish accounting principles permit fixed assets to be written up to values in excess of their historical cost, which in turn affects the depreciation that is charged on such revalued assets. Second, regardless of whether a company's fixed assets have been revalued or not, Swedish GAAP permits the level of reported (or ''booked'') depreciation charges to exceed normal cost-based depreciation. Under U.S. GAAP, fixed asset write-ups are not permitted and depreciation deductions are limited to the historical cost of an asset allocated over its expected economic life.

The Sandvik Group, headquartered in Sandviken, Sweden, is one of the world's leading manufacturers of specialty machine tools. Presented below are the income statement and balance sheet for the years ended 31 December, 1992 and 1993, for the parent company of the Sandvik Group. Also presented are selected excerpts from the company's notes to financial statements.

Required:

    (a) Using journal entries, explain the change in the Buildings account (see balance sheet) from SEK 312 in 1992 to SEK 304 in 1993.

    (b) Explain Sandvik's 1993 year-end valuation of SEK 304 for buildings.

    (c) In 1993, Sandvik incurred SEK 24 million in interest charges in connection with the financing of newly constructed fixed assets. Why wasn't this amount included in the valuation of the company's fixed assets (see Note 13, Fixed Assets)?

SANDVIK
Income Statement

		Amounts in SEK Millions	
		1993	*1992*
Invoiced sales	Note 2	**8,197**	7,047
Costs of production, selling and administration	Note 3	**−6,932**	−6,403
OPERATING PROFIT BEFORE DEPRECIATION		**1,265**	644
Scheduled depreciation	Note 4	**−343**	−300
OPERATING PROFIT AFTER DEPRECIATION		**922**	344
Financial items:			
Dividends received from subsidiaries		**603**	2,972
Interest received from subsidiaries		**19**	13
Other interest received	Note 5	**128**	171
Interest paid to subsidiaries		**−120**	−235
Other interest paid	Note 5	**−84**	−99
Exchange differences on loans	Note 6	**−10**	−78
PROFIT AFTER FINANCIAL INCOME AND EXPENSES		**1,458**	3,088
Non-recurring earnings	Note 8	**7**	1,017
Non-recurring expenses	Note 8	**−128**	−256
PROFIT BEFORE APPROPRIATIONS AND TAXES		**1,337**	3,849
Appropriations:			
Difference between book and scheduled depreciation	Note 18	**104**	124
Change in transitional reserve for inventory reserve, etc.	Note 19	**600**	300
Change in tax equalization reserve	Note 19	**−1,790**	−400
Other appropriations	Note 19	**−3**	14
Group contributions		**−33**	−115
PRE-TAX PROFIT		**215**	3,772
Accrued taxes	Note 21	**−75**	−0−
Estimated future taxes	Note 21	**79**	39
NET PROFIT		**219**	3,811

SANDVIK
Balance Sheet

		Amounts in SEK Millions	
Assets		*1993*	*1992*
CURRENT ASSETS			
Cash and bank balances		**70**	77
Short-term placements	Note 9	**1,374**	935
Receivables from subsidiaries		**1,395**	1,320
Trade accounts receivable		**498**	394
Prepaid expenses and accrued income		**177**	210
Other current receivables		**139**	118
Inventories		**1,906**	1,864
		5,559	4,918

SANDVIK
Balance Sheet
(continued)

		Amounts in SEK Millions	
		1993	*1992*
FIXED ASSETS			
Shares and participations in subsidiaries	Note 10	**5,675**	5,288
Shares and participations in other companies	Note 10	**419**	461
Receivables from subsidiaries		**171**	171
Other long-term receivables	Note 11	**15**	15
Construction in progress		**78**	63
Machinery and equipment	Note 13	**1,671**	1,688
Buildings	Note 13	**304**	312
		8,333	7,998
TOTAL ASSETS		**13,892**	12,916
Assets pledged	Note 14	**596**	581
Liabilities and Equity Capital			
CURRENT LIABILITIES			
Owed to suppliers		**423**	315
Tax debts		**152**	96
Accrued expenses and prepaid income		**672**	559
Short-term loans	Note 16	**6**	93
Other current liabilities to subsidiaries		**1,189**	1,035
Other current liabilities	Note 15	**168**	133
		2,610	2,231
LONG-TERM LIABILITIES			
Long-term loans	Note 16	**7**	13
Provision for pensions	Note 17	**787**	858
Latent tax liability	Note 20	**12**	91
Other long-term liabilities		**—**	42
		806	1,004
UNTAXED RESERVES			
Accumulated depreciation above schedule	Note 18	**1,129**	1,233
Tax equalization reserve	Note 19	**2,190**	400
Transitional reserve for inventory reserve, etc.	Note 19	**—**	600
Other untaxed reserves	Note 19	**8**	5
		3,327	2,238
EQUITY CAPITAL	Note 22		
Restricted equity capital:			
Share capital (278,476,380 shares of SEK 5			
nominal)	Note 23	**1,392**	1,366
Statutory capital reserve		**291**	286
Proposed new issue		**—**	25
		1,683	1,677
Unrestricted equity capital:			
Retained earnings		**5,247**	1,955
Net profit		**219**	3,811
		5,466	5,766
Total equity capital		**7,149**	7,443
TOTAL LIABILITIES AND EQUITY CAPITAL		**13,892**	12,916
Contingent liabilities	Note 24	**629**	1,005

SANDVIK
Excerpts from Footnotes

Valuation Principles

Fixed assets

Fixed assets are shown in the Accounts after the deduction of accumulated scheduled depreciation. Scheduled depreciation charges in the industrial operations are based on the historical cost of the assets and their estimated economic lives; for machinery and equipment this means normally between five and fifteen years, for buildings between ten and fifty years, and for site improvements twenty years. Degressive depreciation based on a life of from three to five years is applied to computer equipment. The difference between book and scheduled accumulated depreciation is shown as an untaxed reserve at the individual company.

Depreciation on the undepreciated portion of accumulated write-ups on buildings is charged at 2% of the original write-up.

NOTE 4. Depreciation

GROUP	Goodwill and other intangible assets		Machinery and equipment		Industrial and residential buildings		Site improvements		Total	
	1993	*1992*	*1993*	*1992*	*1993*	*1992*	*1993*	*1992*	*1993*	*1992*
Scheduled depreciation	**−82**	−48	**−874**	−741	**−146**	−86	**−2**	−2	**−1,104**	−877

PARENT COMPANY	Machinery and equipment		Industrial and residential buildings		Site improvements		Total	
	1993	*1992*	*1993*	*1992*	*1993*	*1992*	*1993*	*1992*
Scheduled depreciation	**−327**	−286	**−15**	−13	**−1**	−1	**−343**	−300
Difference between book and scheduled depreciation	**93**	115	**11**	9	—	—	**104**	124
Book depreciation	**−234**	−171	**−4**	−4	**−1**	−1	**−239**	−176

NOTE 13. Fixed assets

Machinery, equipment, buildings, land, site improvements and agricultural and forest properties are entered at their net value after scheduled depreciation and after accumulated write-ups not yet written off. Accumulated excess depreciation reported by the individual companies is entered among untaxed reserves under the heading "Accumulated depreciation above schedule."

GROUP	Machinery and equipment		Industrial and residential buildings		Agricultural and forest properties		Land and site improvements	
	1993	*1992*	*1993*	*1992*	*1993*	*1992*	*1993*	*1992*
Historical cost[1]	**11,689**	10,601	**3,545**	3,031	**1**	1	**548**	466
Accumulated scheduled depreciation	**−7,475**	−6,552	**−1,583**	−1,289	**—**	—	**−34**	−28
Scheduled remaining values	**4,214**	4,049	**1,962**	1,742	**1**	1	**514**	438
Accumulated write-ups not yet written off	**5**	8	**187**	186	**10**	10	**132**	130
Remaining values	**4,219**	4,057	**2,149**	1,928	**11**	11	**646**	568
Assessed valuations[2]	**—**	—	**916**	913	**34**	34	**135**	134
PARENT COMPANY								
Historical cost	**4,465**	4,166	**408**	403	**1**	1	**27**	27
Accumulated scheduled depreciation	**−2,794**	−2,478	**−177**	−164	**—**	—	**−5**	−5
Scheduled remaining values	**1,671**	1,688	**231**	239	**1**	1	**22**	22
Accumulated write-ups not yet written off	**—**	—	**—**	—	**10**	10	**40**	40
Remaining values	**1,671**	1,688	**231**	239	**11**	11	**62**	62
Accumulated depreciation above schedule	**−1,104**	−1,198	**−19**	−29	**—**	—	**−6**	−6
Book values	**567**	490	**212**	210	**11**	11	**56**	56
Assessed valuations	**—**	—	**197**	198	**34**	34	**42**	43

[1] The acquisition value of assets in acquired companies is based on the company's historical cost, regardless of whether the assets were acquired before or after the date when consolidation arose.

[2] The figures apply to the Swedish part of the Group. The book value of real estate held by foreign subsidiaries amounted to SEK 1,716 m. (1,658).

NOTE 18. Parent Company's accumulated depreciation above schedule

	Machinery and equipment	Industrial and residential buildings	Site improvements	Total
Reported at end of 1992	1,198	29	6	1,233
Difference between book and scheduled depreciation	−94	−10	—	−104
Reported at end of 1993	**1,104**	**19**	**6**	**1,129**

E.11.8   Accounting for Untaxed Reserves

Sandviken, Sweden, is the parent company of the Sandvik Group, which comprises over 200 companies operating in 60 countries worldwide. In 1993, the group had sales of approximately SEK 22 million, or about $165 million.

One of the unique features of generally accepted accounting practice in Sweden is the presence of untaxed reserves. Under Swedish GAAP, a company can smooth currently reported earnings by either appropriating a portion of pre-tax income (i.e., to lower current pre-tax profits) or by restoring to income appropriations from prior periods (i.e., to raise current pre-tax profits). Sandvik AB's income statement for 1992 and 1993 (see Exercise 11.7) reveals that both of these actions were undertaken by the company's management. The following excerpt from the company's income statement details those actions:

	(Amounts in SEK Millions)	
	1993	*1992*
Profit before appropriations and taxes	1,337	3,849
Appropriations:		
• Difference between book and scheduled depreciation	104	124
• Change in transitional reserve for inventory	600	300
• Change in tax equalization reserve	(1,790)	(400)
• Other appropriations	(3)	14
• Group contributions	(33)	(115)
Pre-Tax Profit	215	3,772

Additional information is available from the company's balance sheet (see Exercise 11.7):

	(Amounts in SEK Millions)	
	1993	*1992*
Untaxed Reserves		
• Accumulated depreciation above schedule	1,129	1,233
• Tax equalization reserve	2,190	400
• Transitional reserve for inventory	—	600
• Other untaxed reserves	8	5
	3,327	2,238

Finally, the company's footnotes provided additional detail:

NOTE 19. Parent Company's other untaxed reserves

	Tax Equalization Reserve (K)	*Transitional Reserve for Inventory*	*Other Untaxed Reserves*
Reported at end of 1992	400	600	5
Change during the year	1,790	−600	3
Reported at end of 1993	**2,190**	—	**8**

In compliance with a legal enactment concerning the reversal of untaxed reserves an allocation was made in 1991 to a transitional reserve for inventory reserve, etc. During 1993 the amount outstanding has been reversed to taxation.

Required:

    (a) Using journal entries, explain the changes in Sandvik's untaxed reserves for 1992 to 1993.

    (b) What is the maximum balance that Sandvik can carry in its tax equalization reserve at year-end 1992? at year-end 1993?

    (c) How much in income taxes did the company save in 1993 as a consequence of its large contribution to the tax equalization reserve?

E.11.9   Comparing U.S. and Swedish Balance Sheets

Although all developed countries essentially follow the same basic double-entry accounting system, there exist, nonetheless, subtle and occasionally substantial differences in the output (i.e., the basic financial statements) of that system. Sometimes the differences are classification related. For example, in France and Italy, it is considered proper GAAP to carry treasury stock as an asset on the balance sheet, rather than as a contra owners' equity item as is done according to U.S. GAAP. Other times the differences are terminology related. For example, in Commonwealth countries, *stock* refers to inventory; in the United States, *stock* is usually used in reference to shares of ownership in a company.

The following are two balance sheets from Electrolux, a Swedish company and one of the world's leading producers of household appliances. The balance sheet in the first table appeared in the company's 1993 20-F filing with the SEC. Electrolux shares trade on the NASDAQ over-the-counter exchange in the United States in the form of American depositary receipts. (Each Electrolux ADR equals one share of Class B stock.) The balance sheet in the second table appeared in the company's 1993 annual report to shareholders, as translated into English for international usage.

Required:

    (a) Reconcile the balance sheets presented in panels A and B.

    (b) Prepare a list of any particular classification-related or terminology-related differences between the two statements.

ELECTROLUX
Consolidated Balance Sheet
(per 20-F filing)

	(In Millions)	
Assets	*1992* *SEK*	*1993* *SEK*
Current assets		
Cash (Note 3)	1,980	2,415
Short-term investments (Note 3)	6,116	5,942
Trade accounts and notes receivable, net of allowances (Note 4)	16,509	18,522
Inventories (Note 5)	15,883	16,698
Other (Note 6)	3,763	4,093
Total current assets	44,251	47,670
Long-term assets		
Investments in associated companies (Notes 1a and 19)	818	1,120
Trade accounts and notes receivable, net of allowances	399	530
Goodwill, net of amortization (Note 8)	4,443	5,108
Deferred taxes (Note 11)	—	455
Other	836	410
	6,496	7,623
Property, plant and equipment (Notes 9 and 20)		
Cost	41,536	46,759
Less: Accumulated depreciation	(20,843)	(24,578)
	20,693	22,181
Revaluations, net of accumulated depreciation	178	173
Total assets	71,618	77,647
Liabilities and Stockholders' Equity		
Current liabilities		
Short-term borrowings (Note 10)	11,214	8,632
Current portion of long-term debt	4,327	3,970
Trade accounts and notes payable	8,281	9,486
Advances from customers	532	506
Income taxes (Note 11)	624	688
Other (Note 12)	8,798	10,662
Total current liabilities	33,776	33,944
Long-term debt less current portion (Note 13)	17,750	22,473
Deferred taxes (Note 11)	373	—
Deferred pension liability and other post retirement benefits (Note 14)	2,632	3,987
Minority interest	315	390
Stockholders' equity (Notes 16 and 24)		
Capital stock	1,831	1,831
Non-distributable reserves	9,259	9,653
Retained earnings	5,682	5,369
Total stockholders' equity	16,772	16,853
Total liabilities and stockholders' equity	71,618	77,647

ELECTROLUX
Consolidated Balance Sheet
(per annual report)

Assets	*1993-12-31*		*1992-12-31*	
Current assets (SEKm)				
Cash and bank deposits	2,415		1,980	
Shares and participations	5		—	
Bonds and other securities	5,937	8,357	6,116	8,096
Notes receivable	1,553		1,441	
Accounts receivable	16,969		15,068	
Prepaid expense and accrued income	1,539		1,277	
Other receivables	2,408	22,469	2,393	20,179
Inventories		16,698		15,883
Advances to suppliers		146		93
Total current assets		47,670		44,251
Blocked accounts for investment and other				
reserves		17		32
Fixed assets				
Share of equity in associated companies	389		266	
Shares and participations	731		552	
Bonds and other securities	208	1,328	597	1,415
Notes receivable	12		23	
Latent tax refund claims	455		—	
Long-term receivables	518	985	376	399
Leaseholds, patents, etc.	185		207	
Goodwill	5,108		4,443	
Advances to suppliers	142		158	
Construction in progress	736		704	
Machinery, equipment and tools	13,942		12,985	
Buildings	6,239		5,816	
Land and land improvements	1,241	27,647	1,208	25,521
Total fixed assets		29,960		27,335
TOTAL ASSETS		77,647		71,618
Assets pledged		1,882		2,118

Liabilities and Shareholders' (SEKm)				
Current liabilities				
Notes payable	896		845	
Accounts payable	8,590		7,436	
Tax liability	688		624	
Accrued expense and prepaid income	7,992		6,770	
Other current liabilities	2,670		2,028	
Advances from customers	506	21,342	532	18,235
Bank loans, etc.		12,602		15,541
Total current liabilities		33,944		33,776
Long-term liabilities				
Bond loans	9,768		7,004	
Mortgage loans, promissory notes, etc.	10,287	20,055	8,321	15,325
Deferred taxes	—		373	
Other long-term liabilities	2,418	2,418	2,425	2,798

ELECTROLUX   (continued)

	1993-12-31		1992-12-31	
Provisions for pensions				
PRI pensions (Pension Registration				
Institute)	1,313		1,947	
Other pensions	2,674	3,987	685	2,632
Total long-term liabilities		26,460		20,755
Minority interests		390		315
Shareholders' equity				
Restricted equity				
Share capital				
2,000,000 A-shares, par value SEK 25				
71,233,916 B-shares, par value SEK 25	1,831		1,831	
Statutory reserves	9,653	11,484	9,259	11,090
Unrestricted equity				
Unrestricted reserves	4,785		5,499	
Net income for the year	584	5,369	183	5,682
Total shareholders' equity		16,853		16,772
TOTAL LIABILITIES AND				
SHAREHOLDERS' EQUITY		77,647		71,618
Contingent liabilities		725		891

E.11.10   Cash Flow Analysis

Swedish generally accepted accounting practices require the presentation of a balance sheet, an income statement, and a statement of changes in financial position, but not a statement of cash flows. Exhibits 1 and 2 present the consolidated statements of income and the consolidated balance sheets for the Volvo Group for the years ended December 31, 1990 and 1991. Exhibit 3 presents selected information from Volvo's footnotes. (All amounts are SEK millions unless otherwise noted.)

Required:

   (a) Using the information in Exhibits 1–3, construct a consolidated statement of cash flows for 1991 for the Volvo Group. What conclusions can you draw about Volvo from your statement of cash flows?

EXHIBIT 1

VOLVO GROUP
Consolidated Statements of Income

		1991		*1990*
Sales		**77,223**		83,185
Costs and expenses				
Cost of sales	**(64,676)**		(68,756)	
Selling, general and administrative expenses	**(10,926)**	**(75,602)**	(11,241)	(79,997)
Depreciation and amortization		**(2,789)**		(2,621)
Operating income (loss)		**(1,168)**		567
Restructuring costs		**—**		(2,450)
Income from equity method investments		**1,218**		1,322
Financial income (expense)				
Dividends received	**15**		31	
Gain on sale of securities, net	**2,026**		116	
Interest income	**3,654**		3,777	
Interest expense	**(4,383)**		(3,731)	
Foreign exchange gain (loss)	**166**	**1,478**	41	234
Income (loss) after financial income (expense)		**1,528**		(327)
Extraordinary expense		**(725)**		—
Minority interests in (income) loss		**310**		40
Income (loss) before taxes		**1,113**		(287)
Taxes		**(431)**		(733)
Net income (loss)		**682**		(1,020)
Income (loss) per share, SEK		8.80		(13.10)
Approximate net income (loss) in accordance with U.S. generally accepted accounting principles		816		(23)
Approximate income (loss) per share in accordance with U.S. generally accepted accounting principles, SEK		10.90		(0.30)

(b) According to the supplementary information at the bottom of Exhibit 1, Volvo's earnings per share under U.S. GAAP were SEK 10.90 versus SEK 8.80 under Swedish GAAP. List those factors that might be responsible for that difference in reported earnings per share.

(c) Consider the supplementary information presented at the bottom of Exhibit 2. Why would a Volvo shareholder be interested in the amount of assets pledged, contingent liabilities, and capital expenditures approved?

EXHIBIT 2

VOLVO GROUP
Consolidated Balance Sheet

Assets	December 31, 1991		December 31, 1990	
Current assets				
Liquid funds	18,779		17,585	
Receivables	17,065		15,718	
Inventories	18,022	53,866	19,886	53,189
Investments in bonds		928		2,854
Restricted deposits in Bank of Sweden		41		2,072
Other assets				
Property, plant and equipment, net	17,232		18,327	
Investments in shares	30,399		21,530	
Long-term receivables and loans	3,909		3,807	
Intangible assets	373	51,913	318	43,982
Total assets		106,748		102,097
Liabilities and shareholders' equity				
Current liabilities				
Accounts payable	6,395		7,115	
Advances from customers	2,340		2,122	
Bank loans	17,127		14,954	
Other loans	5,952		9,667	
Other current liabilities	15,964	47,778	14,854	48,712
Long-term liabilities				
Bond loans	2,857		1,127	
Convertible debenture loans	1,679		1,679	
Other long-term loans	4,365		3,724	
Accruals for pensions	4,245		3,769	
Deferred tax liability in untaxed reserves	6,974	20,120	7,495	17,794
Minority interests		4,986		300
Shareholders' equity				
Restricted equity				
Share capital	1,940		1,940	
Restricted reserves	15,654	17,594	19,536	21,476
Unrestricted equity				
Unrestricted reserves	15,588		14,835	
Net income (loss) for the year	682	16,270	(1,020)	13,815
Total shareholders' equity		33,864		35,291
Total liabilities and shareholders' equity		106,748		102,097
Assets pledged		2,641		2,417
Contingent liabilities		4,691		3,270
Capital expenditures approved		5,900		7,000

EXHIBIT 3

Volvo Group
Selected Information from Footnotes
Accompanying 1991 Financial Statements

- Dividends paid by Volvo to shareholders in 1991: 1,203
- Transfers from restricted reserves to unrestricted reserves: 3,882
- Capital investments into property, plant, and equipment: 2,874
- Depreciation on property, plant, and equipment: 2,699; amortization on intangible assets: 90
- The write-off of property, plant, and equipment: 725 (see extraordinary expense on income statement)

CASES

CASE 11.1
SPECIAL TAX RESERVES

AB Volvo

Based on asset values, Volvo is the largest industrial company in Sweden. Founded in 1927 as a manufacturer of passenger cars, today the company's products include cars, trucks, buses, marine and industrial engines, and aerospace engines.

As is true in the United States and most other industrialized countries, the government of Sweden uses its tax laws to help achieve a wide variety of national goals. Unlike the United States, however, the effects of Sweden's tax laws and, by extension, its national goals can be observed in the financial statements of Swedish companies in that Swedish tax law stipulates that taxable income be assessed from a taxpayer's accounting statements. In essence, revenues and expenses may appear on a Swedish corporation's tax return only to the extent that they appear in the published financial statements. Thus, it is possible to examine the external financial statements of Swedish companies with the goal of identifying in what ways and to what extent the Swedish government has instituted economic incentives for its domestic companies.

In recent years, the use of tax incentives by the Swedish government has undergone a number of reforms. Prior to 1991, for example, companies could take significant pre-tax deductions from operating income by creating inventory, payroll, depreciation, and investment reserves.[1] Most of these untaxed reserves, however, were eliminated in 1991 in exchange for a significant reduction in Swedish corporate income tax rates (i.e., from 52 to 30 percent, effective January 1, 1991). The 1991 tax reform did not eliminate the excess depreciation allowance enjoyed by most companies and, in addition, created a special tax equalization reserve (SURV) that cannot

---

This case was prepared by Kenneth R. Ferris from publicly available documents. Copyright © 1993 by Kenneth R. Ferris. All rights reserved.

[1]The charge (a debit) against operating income was also credited to a nondistributable shareholders' equity reserve account.

EXHIBIT 1

AB VOLVO
1991 Financial Statements

Panel A. Statement of Income (SEK, millions)

	1991	*1990*
Sales	**530**	6,452
Costs and expenses	**(659)**	(6,405)
Depreciation	**(13)**	(32)
Operating income (loss)	**(142)**	15
Restructuring costs	—	(98)
Financial income (expense)		
Dividends received	**1,373**	817
Gain on sale of securities, net	**564**	3
Interest income	**251**	116
Interest expense	**(1,559)**	(1,221)
Foreign exchange gain	**518**	62
Income (loss) after financial income (expense)	**1,005**	(306)
Extraordinary income	**2,295**	3,750
Income before allocations and taxes	**3,300**	3,444
Allocations	**709**	809
Income before taxes	**4,009**	4,253
Taxes	**(250)**	—
Net income	**3,759**	4,253

exceed 30 percent of a corporation's equity capital. Further tax reform was enacted effective January 1994, lowering the corporate income tax rate to 28 percent and phasing out the SURV over the five-year period of 1994 to 1998.

Exhibit 1 presents the 1990 and 1991 income statements and balance sheets for AB Volvo, the parent company of the Volvo Group. Exhibit 2 contains selected footnote disclosures regarding those financial statements. Use these data to complete the following:

Required:

(a) What advantages and disadvantages arise for those firms that choose to employ (and most do!) the Swedish system of special reserves?

(b) What are the potential benefits of the system of untaxed reserves to the Swedish government?

(c) In what ways does the existence of the Swedish tax reserves system affect the ability of a financial statement user to evaluate a Swedish firm vis-à-vis a non-Swedish firm?

(d) Determine the financial effect of Sweden's tax equalization reserve on AB Volvo's financial statements for 1991. Show the journal entry used to create the 1991 reserve. If the tax equalization reserve did not exist in 1991, how would AB Volvo's key profitability ratios (ROA, ROE, and ROS) have changed?

EXHIBIT 1   (continued)

Panel B. Balance Sheet (SEK, millions)

	Dec. 31, 1991	Dec. 31, 1990
Assets		
Current assets		
Liquid funds	971	10
Accounts receivable from subsidiaries	2,241	917
Other receivables	40	668
Inventories	—	1,118
Total current assets	3,252	2,713
Restricted deposits in Bank of Sweden	—	266
Other assets		
Property, plant and equipment	143	253
Investments in shares—subsidiaries	6,484	10,499
Other investments in shares	23,906	16,300
Long-term loans to subsidiaries	1,400	834
Other long-term loans	74	157
Total other assets	32,007	28,043
Total assets	35,259	31,022
Liabilities and shareholders' equity		
Current liabilities		
Accounts payable	26	356
Advances from customers	—	19
Loans from subsidiaries	3,861	3,107
Other amounts due to subsidiaries	545	254
Other loans	778	4,870
Other current liabilities	792	1,471
Total current liabilities	6,002	10,077
Long-term liabilities		
Amounts due to subsidiaries	4,829	517
Bond loans	6	13
Convertible debenture loans	1,679	1,679
Other long-term loans	247	310
Accruals for pensions	785	794
Total long-term liabilities	7,546	3,313
Untaxed reserves	2,368	845
Shareholders' equity		
Restricted equity		
Share capital (77,605,009 shares par value		
SEK 25 each)	1,940	1,940
Reserves	1,242	1,242
Revaluation reserve	170	170
	3,352	3,352
Unrestricted equity		
Unrestricted reserves	12,232	9,182
Net income for the year	3,759	4,253
	15,991	13,435
Total shareholders' equity	19,343	16,787
Total liabilities and shareholders' equity	35,259	31,022
Assets pledged	216	199
Contingent liabilities	21,532	5,754
Capital expenditures approved	90	115

EXHIBIT 2

AB VOLVO
Selected Disclosures from 1991 Financial Report

Footnote 5. Foreign Exchange Gain (Loss)

Up to and including 1990, receivables and liabilities in foreign currencies were translated at rates of exchange which, in the case of receivables were the lower of the rate when the receivable was acquired and the year-end rate, and, in the case of liabilities, the higher of the rate when the liability was incurred and the year-end rate. Effective in 1991, receivables and liabilities in foreign currencies are translated at the year-end rate. Unrealized exchange gains on long-term receivables and liabilities are allocated to an exchange reserve. Exchange differences on borrowings and lendings, including forward contracts related to these loans, are reported as financial income. Other exchange differences are included in operating expenses. An application of this principle in prior years would have resulted in an increase of 1 on income before allocations and taxes during 1990 and a reduction of 360 on income in 1991.

Footnote 7. Allocations

	1991	*1990*
Group contributions received	2,528	782
Group contributions granted	(210)	—
Change in tax equalization reserve	(2,191)	—
Allocation to/Reversal of exchange reserve	(93)	—
Allocation to/Reversal of inventory reserve	335	(1)
Allocation to/Reversal of payroll reserve	63	(4)
Reversal of extra depreciation	10	(28)
Reversal of special investment reserve	189	—
Reversal of development reserve	77	—
Payment from Volvo Group Employee Educational Foundation	1	4
Total	709	809

EXHIBIT 2   (continued)

Footnote 17. Untaxed Reserves
The composition of, and changes in, untaxed reserves

	December 31, 1990	Transferred to subsidiaries	Allocations 1991	December 31, 1991
Tax equalization reserve	—	—	2,191	2,191
Exchange reserve	—	—	93	93
Inventory reserve	335	—	(335)	—
Payroll reserve	63	—	(63)	—
Special investment reserve	189	—	(189)	—
Development reserve	77	—	(77)	—
Accumulated extra depreciation				
Machinery and equipment	91	(66)	(6)	19
Buildings	63	—	(3)	60
Land improvements	6	—	(1)	5
Construction in progress	21	(21)	—	—
Total	845	(87)	1,610	2,368

Footnote 18. Shareholders' Equity

	Restricted equity				
	Share Capital	Legal Reserve	Revaluation Reserve	Unrestricted Equity	Total Shareholders' Equity
December 31, 1990	1,940	1,242	170	13,435	16,787
Cash dividend				(1,203)	(1,203)
Net income, 1991				3,759	3,759
December 31, 1991	1,940	1,242	170	15,991	19,343

CASE 11.2
PRO FORMA FINANCIAL STATEMENTS

Nordi-Sport AB

In July 1994, Anders Johannson, the CFO of Nordi-Sport AB, began preparing the annual loan renewal request for the company's revolving line of credit held with Swedbank in Stockholm. Because Mr. Johannson would be leaving on business for a few days, he asked one of the junior members of his accounting staff, Ms. Samuelsson, to complete the request. Specifically, he asked that she determine the required loan size and prepare a pro forma balance sheet, an income statement, and a cash budget that indicates the company's expected month-to-month cash balance and short-term credit needs over the next fiscal year.

This case was prepared by Thomas I. Selling and Mitchell W. Slape. Copyright © 1995 by Thomas I. Selling. All rights reserved.

"If sales projections are accurate, our short-term credit needs are definitely going to increase in the coming year," explained Mr. Johannson. "What we need to know, however, is when our peak borrowing is going to occur and how much the balance on the revolving line of credit is going to be."

Background of Nordi-Sport AB.   Nordi-Sport AB, a manufacturer of specialty winter sports equipment, was founded in 1982 in Stockholm, Sweden. The company rapidly developed a strong reputation in its home country for its high-quality cross-country and downhill skis. On the strength of that reputation, sales grew steadily throughout the 1980s. In 1989, in response to growing enthusiasm for snowboarding in Sweden and other Scandinavian countries, the company developed its first prototype snowboard. Following several months of testing and redesigning the product, it was introduced to the Swedish market in 1990. In spite of recessionary economic conditions in Sweden, coupled with a succession of mild winters, sales of the Nordi-Sport snowboard during the early 1990s were robust. The company's overall sales, while strong domestically, were further enhanced by product shipments to other Scandinavian countries. Exhibits 1 and 2 provide balance sheet and income statements for the preceding three fiscal years (fiscal year-end June 30). Exhibit 3 provides selected financial ratios calculated from the data.

Nordi-Sport had performed well in an increasingly competitive winter sports market in Sweden. The Swedish krona (SEK) 2.1 billion market (approximately $270 million) was dominated by a handful of larger Swedish companies. Several U.S. and European firms had also developed a strong presence in the market. Nordi-Sport had been successful by targeting the high-quality (and higher priced) upper end of the market. It was apparent that the industry would continue to grow rapidly in the coming years. In fact, sales growth for the company was expected to approach 15 percent through 1996.

In response to the rapid growth in sales, the company had found it necessary to increase the production capacity of its Stockholm plant. During the course of fiscal 1994 (ended June 30, 1994), plant expansion and new machinery were added. It was projected that these additions would increase capacity to a level sufficient to meet SEK 125 million in total sales. It was apparent that a large portion of this capacity would be absorbed by sales during fiscal year 1995. In fact, the marketing department projected sales of SEK 109 million during the coming fiscal year.

Nordi-Sport's revenues were largely composed of sales of snow skis and snowboards in the Swedish market. This created a high degree of seasonality over the year in terms of the firm's sales figures. Approximately 70 percent of Nordi-Sport's sales were made during the first six months of each fiscal year. Although revenues from international sales were steadily increasing each year, the majority of those sales were to neighboring Scandinavian countries, where monthly sales patterns resembled those in Sweden. Despite seasonal sales, the company chose to maintain a relatively steady production schedule throughout the year. This production scheduling was deemed necessary to retain the skilled workers who designed and manufactured the firm's products.

The company had maintained its revolving line of credit with Swedbank since the late 1980s. The revolver, which had a term of one year, was renewed each July. The bank had required that the revolver be structured to "rest," or be completely paid down, for a period of one month each year. Traditionally, Nordi-Sport began borrowing against the revolver in July and had repaid the balance by January of each year. During fiscal 1994, however, the company had been unable to pay down the balance of the bank line until late March. Furthermore, due to shortfalls in working capital, the company began borrowing against the revolver in April. By the end of fiscal year 1994, the outstanding balance on the revolver was SEK 10,109,000.

EXHIBIT 1

NORDI-SPORT AB
Balance Sheet as of June 30, 1992–1994
(in thousands of Swedish kronor)

	1992	*1993*	*1994*
Assets			
Current assets			
Cash	19,893	14,413	7,061
Accounts receivable	7,300	8,062	10,483
Inventories	12,305	14,227	16,470
Total current assets	39,498	36,702	34,014
Long-term assets			
Property, plant & equipment	54,567	60,024	78,031
Less: accumulated depreciation	(15,111)	(16,622)	(18,284)
Other assets	1,884	2,215	2,215
Total long-term assets	41,340	45,617	61,962
Total assets	80,838	82,319	95,975
Liabilities and Equity			
Current liabilities			
Short-term borrowing	–0–	–0–	10,109
Accounts payable	4,306	4,493	4,867
Current portion—long-term debt	999	1,101	1,214
Taxes due	147	601	1,151
Total current liabilities	5,452	6,195	17,341
Long-term debt	23,901	22,800	21,586
Total liabilities	29,353	28,996	38,927
Equity			
Share capital (500,000 shares)	31,825	31,825	31,825
Nonrestricted reserve	19,086	19,160	20,748
Result for the year	573	2,338	4,475
Total equity	51,485	53,323	57,048
Total liabilities and equity	80,838	82,319	95,975

Nordi-Sport's commercial banker at Swedbank had called Mr. Johannson during the spring of 1994 to express his concern about the company's usage of the revolving line of credit. Although the company had technically violated a loan covenant regarding a one-month "resting period," the banker indicated that he would be willing to work with the company to ensure that its credit needs were met. Along those lines, he had requested that Nordi-Sport prepare a detailed schedule of its short-term credit needs for the annual loan renewal to be completed in July.

Forecast Data: Fiscal Year 1995. To facilitate preparation of the requested schedule, Mr. Johannson had asked his staff to compile all relevant information regarding the firm's operations and cash flows for the coming fiscal year. That data included the following.

Credit Terms. Nordi-Sport's customers primarily consist of specialty sporting goods outlets, and all sales are made on credit. Terms extended on credit sales are net 30. To enhance sales revenues, however, the accounting department had allowed many accounts to exceed the 30-day payment requirement. In many cases, the inability of Nordi-Sport's customers

---

EXHIBIT 2

NORDI-SPORT AB
Income Statement as of June 30, 1992–1994
(in thousands of Swedish kronor)

Operating Revenue and Costs	1992	1993	1994
Operating revenue	72,047	79,816	92,489
Operating costs and expenses			
Materials purchases	27,729	30,523	34,741
Overhead and labor	33,891	37,306	42,460
Operating expenses	4,536	4,711	5,204
Depreciation of fixed assets	2,215	2,309	2,933
Change in stocks	(225)	(1,922)	(2,243)
Operating income	3,901	6,889	9,394
Currency exchange loss (gain)	132	444	(511)
Interest expenses	2,950	3,105	3,512
Result before tax	819	3,340	6,393
Income taxes	246	1,002	1,918
Net result	573	2,338	4,475

EXHIBIT 3

NORDI-SPORT AB
Selected Ratios

	1992	1993	1994
Return on common equity ratio	1.1%	4.4%	7.8%
Return on total assets	3.3%	5.5%	7.2%
Leverage	1.57	1.54	1.68
Common earnings leverage	21.7%	51.8%	64.5%
Profit margin	3.7%	5.7%	7.5%
Turnover	0.89	0.97	0.96
Gross profit margin	12.0%	14.8%	16.1%
Receivables turnover	9.87	9.90	8.82
Inventory turnover	6.56	6.44	6.52
Fixed asset turnover	1.74	1.75	1.49
Current ratio	7.24	5.92	1.96
Quick ratio	4.99	3.63	1.01
Debt-equity ratio	48.4%	44.8%	57.7%
Bank loan/(Cash + Accounts receivable)	0.0%	0.0%	57.6%

EXHIBIT 4

NORDI-SPORT AB
Estimated Monthly Sales and Month-End Accounts Receivable
Fiscal 1995
(in thousands of Swedish kronor)

	Net Sales	Accounts Receivable at Month End
July	7,509	16,538
August	10,595	21,557
September	14,951	30,996
October	15,436	37,475
November	17,250	39,488
December	9,751	33,335
January	8,111	21,620
February	6,782	17,903
March	3,871	11,001
April	3,629	8,579
May	3,813	8,652
June	7,267	12,978
	108,965	

to pay within 30 days was a result of the cash deficiencies experienced by these customers during Nordi-Sport's peak sales period. Monthly sales and month-end accounts receivable projections are provided in Exhibit 4.

Operating Costs and Expenses. Based on the marketing department's sales projections for fiscal 1995, Mr. Johannson's staff had estimated total operating costs and expenses.

• With the exception of two planned companywide vacation periods, the production schedule for fiscal 1995 would remain constant on a month-to-month basis. One of the vacation periods was planned for two weeks in December, the other for two weeks during May. Purchases of raw materials were scheduled for SEK 4,800,000 per month, with the exception of vacation months, when SEK 3,300,000 in purchases had been scheduled. All of the company's purchases were on account with terms extended to Nordi-Sport of net 30.

• Overhead and labor expenses associated with production (excluding depreciation) were expected to remain steady at SEK 3,175,000 per month throughout the fiscal year.

• Operating expenses (composed primarily of sales and general and administrative expenses) were expected to total SEK 5,690,000 and be incurred evenly over the year.

• Depreciation expenses of SEK 3,120,000 were forecasted for the year. Historically, 90 percent of depreciation could be attributed to manufacturing equipment and facilities.

• The company accounts for its inventory on a first-in, first-out basis. 20 percent of production in fiscal 1995 would be sold in 1996.

EXHIBIT 5

NORDI-SPORT AB
Loan Amortization Schedule

Date	Payment	Principal	Interest	Balance
6/30/92	—	—	—	24,900
12/31/92	1,732	487	1,245	24,413
6/30/93	1,732	512	1,221	23,901
12/31/93	1,732	537	1,195	23,364
6/30/94	1,732	564	1,168	22,800
12/31/94	1,732	592	1,140	22,208
6/30/95	1,732	622	1,110	21,586
12/31/95	1,732	653	1,079	20,934
6/30/96	1,732	685	1,047	20,248
12/31/96	1,732	720	1,012	19,528

Tax Disbursements. The corporate income tax rate applicable to Nordi-Sport was 30 percent. Sixty percent of taxes due at the end of a fiscal year are payable in two equal installments in the September and December following a fiscal year. Additionally, payments that are each equal to 20 percent of the total estimated corporate tax liability for the fiscal year are due in the months of March and June of a current fiscal year.
Capital Investment. Nordi-Sport has scheduled replacements of machinery of SEK 200,000 per month throughout fiscal 1995. In addition, Nordi-Sport was planning to install new labor-saving equipment and machinery in September of fiscal year 1995. The machinery, which cost SEK 2,000,000, would be paid for over the course of four months in equal monthly installments beginning in September.
Long-Term Debt. Nordi-Sport had financed its buildings and land with a fixed-rate, long-term loan through Swedbank. The principal balance of the debt as of June 30, 1994, was scheduled to be paid off over the next 11 years in equal semi-annual installments due on June 30 and December 31. Interest is calculated on the loan at 10 percent per annum on the unpaid balance. Exhibit 5 contains a portion of the loan amortization schedule.
Dividend Payments. Due to steadily rising profitability, the company had been increasing its dividends. It was projected that the board of directors would vote to further distribute SEK 1.0 per share dividends in August and February.

Preparing the Cash Budget and Pro Forma Statements

Ms. Samuelsson perused the data that had been gathered by the accounting staff. Given that her regular responsibilities included management of the firm's excess cash balances, she was aware that company practice was to maintain a cash balance of SEK 6,000,000 at all times. In the preparation of the cash flow schedule, Mr. Johannson had instructed his staff to indicate the principal and interest payments on the revolving credit as separate line items. Monthly interest on the revolving line of credit was calculated as 1 percent of the end-of-month balance.[1]

---

[1]For example, if the term loan balance was forecasted to be SEK 15,000 on July 31, the interest for July is SEK 150.

With these practices in mind, coupled with the detailed projections that she received for fiscal 1995, Ms. Samuelsson began to develop a spreadsheet for the cash budget and pro forma statements.

Required:

(a) Prepare the following items:

 (1) A monthly cash budget with the objective of calculating the monthly balances of the term loan.

 (2) A forecasted income statement for the year ended June 30, 1995, and a forecasted balance sheet as of the same date.

(*Hint:* Because of the ''circular'' interrelationships between the amount of the term loan, interest expense, and tax expense, you may want first to assume a zero tax rate and zero interest rate on the term loan.)

(b) Assume that Swedbank applies the following criteria in considering requests for seasonal borrowing:

- The loan should be fully paid off for at least 30 to 60 days at some point during the year.
- The loan balance should be at all times less than 60 percent of the sum of the company's cash balance and its accounts receivable balance.

Would you expect the bank to approve the loan request reflected in the monthly cash budget?

(c) What can Nordi-Sport do to reduce its use of the term loan?

ANNUAL REPORT ANALYSIS

Volvo

An interesting and important challenge for students of international financial reporting is to study the published annual reports of various companies from different countries. Your instructor will provide you with a recent copy of a Volvo annual report. To facilitate your delving into this annual report, undertake the following endeavors.

Required:

(a) List the key differences between the Volvo annual report and what you would expect to see for a U.S. company like General Motors or Ford.

(b) Calculate the following ratios for Volvo, taking care to note the assumptions you found necessary to make and where you found the appropriate pieces of data in the annual report.

(1) Current ratio $= \dfrac{\text{Total current assets}}{\text{Total current liabilities}}$

(2) Quick ratio $= \dfrac{\text{Cash + Marketable securities + Accts. Rec.}}{\text{Total current liabilities}}$

(3) Operating cash flow to current liabilities $= \dfrac{\text{Operating cash flow}}{\text{Average total current liabilities}}$

(4) Debt-to-equity ratio $= \dfrac{\text{Long-term debt}}{\text{Owners' equity}}$

(5) Debt-to-total capitalization ratio $= \dfrac{\text{Long-term debt}}{\text{Long-term debt } + \text{ Owners' equity}}$

(6) Interest coverage ratio $= \dfrac{\text{Net income before interest \& income taxes}}{\text{Interest expense}}$

(7) Operating cash flow to interest charges $= \dfrac{\text{Operating cash flow}}{\text{Interest expense}}$

(8) Operating cash flow to total liabilities $= \dfrac{\text{Operating cash flow}}{\text{Average total liabilities}}$

(9) Receivables turnover ratio $= \dfrac{\text{Net sales}}{\text{Average accts. receivable}}$

(10) Inventory turnover $= \dfrac{\text{Cost of goods sold}}{\text{Average inventory}}$

(11) Asset turnover $= \dfrac{\text{Net sales}}{\text{Average total assets}}$

(12) Average collection period ratio $= \dfrac{\text{365 Days}}{\text{Receivables turnover ratio}}$

(13) Average number of days' inventory on hand ratio $= \dfrac{\text{365 Days}}{\text{Inventory turnover ratio}}$

(14) Return on assets (ROA) $= \dfrac{\text{Net income}}{\text{Average total assets}}$

OR $= \text{ROS} \times \text{Asset turnover}$

(15) Return on equity (ROE) $= \dfrac{\text{Net income}}{\text{Average total owners' equity}}$

OR $= \text{ROA} \times \text{Financial leverage}$

(16) Return on sales (ROS) $= \dfrac{\text{Net income}}{\text{Net sales}}$

(17) Financial leverage $= \dfrac{\text{Average liabilities } + \text{ average owners' equity}}{\text{Average owners' equity}}$

(18) Basic earnings per share (EPS) $= \dfrac{\text{NI applicable to common shareholders}}{\text{Weighted average common shares}}$

(19) Cash dividend yield $=$ $\dfrac{\text{Cash dividend per common share}}{\text{Market price per common share}}$

(20) Cash dividend payout $=$ $\dfrac{\text{Total cash dividend to common shareholders}}{\text{Net income}}$

(c) What do you conclude about the availability of the appropriate data in the annual report for calculating these ratios?

(d) What does this financial analysis tell you about Volvo?

(e) What analytical metrics did Volvo choose to report for itself? What do those choices say about the message the company is striving to tell and the audience it is addressing?

Chapter 12

Brazil

Brazil conjures up nightmares of runaway inflation, with matching devaluation and interest rates, and enormous challenges to the simplest accounting tasks and business management.[1]

Introduction

Brazil has been called a sleeping giant, and with good reason. Encompassing 3.3 million square miles of mountains, plains, plateaus, rivers, and tropical rain forest, it boasts the world's fifth largest land mass, possesses extensive mineral and agricultural resources, and is the world's leading coffee producer. With a population of about 160 million and the largest economy in Latin America (10th in the free world), many observers expect that Brazil will eventually assume a prominent place in the community of nations.

Yet the road to modernization has been fraught with difficulty for Brazil. Hampered by a heritage of colonial exploitation and the effects of rapid development, the country has struggled to feed and educate its citizens, half of whom live on $800 (U.S.) or less per year. It is estimated that about 60 percent of Brazil's people effectively live outside its official economy. Its rural poor flock to urban slums, or *favelas,* making São Paulo one of the fastest growing cities in the world. In fact, the World Bank reports that as a nation, Brazil has the world's second largest gap between its rich and poor citizens.[2] Economically, the government wrestles with heavy foreign debt ($123 billion at mid-1993, the largest among developing nations) and chronic inflation (a record-setting 2,500 percent for 1993, but only 2 percent for the month of April 1995, the

---

[1]N. Cain, "Accounting in a Banana Republic," *Australian Accountant,* September 1991, p. 32.
[2]See *Brazil: Country Profile, 1989–90* (London: The Economist Intelligence Unit, 1989); and "Massacre by Rio's Police Terrorists," *Financial Times,* October 3, 1993, p. I.

lowest rate in 26 years). Politically, it is trying to escape the shadow of authoritarianism after two decades of military rule.

Brazil's economy is also one of the most centralized and protected among developing nations, characterized by a huge public payroll, tight restrictions on imports, and government ownership of strategic industries. Inevitably, these conditions have damaged the ability of Brazilian industries to compete internationally, preventing the nation from fully participating in the process of economic globalization. Although successive government administrations of late have attempted to stem inflation and redirect the economy toward freer markets and greater privatization, the historical resistance to such attempts has been powerful and entrenched. Even if a number of specific changes were to be implemented by the government, they are unlikely to succeed unless they win the support of the business community and the population at large, a dubious prospect in a society that has become accustomed to inflation and adept at thwarting or circumventing government austerity measures.

As a result, Brazil must overcome major obstacles if it is to secure the twin blessings of political freedom and economic prosperity. Crucial to this process in Brazil as elsewhere is the development of efficient capital markets, which in turn depend on investors having access to reliable and relevant financial information. Thus, corporate financial reporting has a role to play in the future of the nation. At present, accounting methods and reporting practices in Brazil are essentially dictated by the government via the Commercial Code, income tax laws, and the **Comissao de Valores Mobiliários** (CVM), the Brazilian equivalent of the Securities and Exchange Commission in the United States. Brazilian financial reporting has improved considerably in recent decades—a major reform package was passed in 1976—but the continuing economic instability that prevents Brazil's emergence as a global economic power is likely to hamper the development of sophisticated financial reporting standards as well.

Environmental Factors

Cultural Environment

The group of Brazilian subjects in Hofstede's study of cultural attitudes scored low in individualism (38), high in power distance (69), high in uncertainty avoidance (76), and moderately high in long-term orientation (65). (Recall that the U.S. scores were 91 in individualism, 40 in power distance, 46 in uncertainty avoidance, and 29 in long-term orientation.) The low score in individualism is not atypical for a developing country struggling to emerge from poverty and oligarchy; most Brazilians have simply never enjoyed the amount of wealth or personal freedom that characterize highly individualistic cultures.

The high scores in power distance and uncertainty avoidance place Brazil (along with Japan and other Latin American countries) in Hofstede's paradigm of the "pyramid." Organizations in pyramid cultures, according to Hofstede, tend to take the form of bureaucracies characterized by hierarchical personnel relations and codified work flow. Power tends to be centralized. This description seems to offer some insight into the Brazilian economy, major features of which include constant supervision by the central government and massive public monopolies in key industries. Accepted business practices—including financial reporting standards—generally radiate outward from centralized authorities.

Gray has drawn on Hofstede's findings to suggest that national cultures registering high scores in uncertainty avoidance and power distance and a low score in individualism tend to prefer rigid, codified financial reporting systems that leave relatively little room for the exercise of professional judgment.[3] The example of Brazil seems to support Gray's hypothesis. In Brazil, as in many European nations and in Japan, financial reporting standards are essentially legislated by a central authority. Although Brazil's accounting profession is well established, it does not boast the reputation for independent judgment and theoretical finesse that is considered desirable for accountants in more investor-oriented cultures. Accountants in Brazil do not, on the whole, take a leading role in setting standards or in addressing conceptual issues. (However, it should be noted that Brazilian auditors are required to express an opinion on the fairness of the financial statements examined, probably as a result of U.S. influence.) In terms of sheer numbers, Brazil has relatively few professionals fully qualified to serve as auditors—approximately 50,000. (By way of comparison, Great Britain has more than 160,000 accounting professionals.) Although the number of accountants in a given country is by no means a reliable indicator of the country's technical sophistication, a dearth of auditors usually indicates less developed equity markets, a less influential accounting profession, and greater government control of reporting standards. (Germany provides a good illustration of this.)

Legal and Political Environment

Government Ownership.   Because of its simultaneous and sometimes conflicting desires to promote economic development, limit foreign control, and curb inflation and foreign debt, the Brazilian government (even after the return to constitutional democracy in 1985) has consistently adopted an interventionist approach to economic policy. Several strategic industries—most notably petroleum, utilities, and telecommunications—consist of massive government-controlled monopolies. Petrobrás, Brazil's giant petroleum and petrochemical monopoly, illustrates the typical pattern of state ownership: 51 percent of its stock is held by the federal government, with the other 49 percent in the hands of other public entities (chiefly state governments) and outside investors.

Although recent government administrations have declared their intentions to sell state-owned enterprises and to decrease government interference in the economy at large, separating government from industry will be no easy task. Observers have noted that Brazil's 5 price and wage freezes, 11 stabilization plans, and 3 debt moratoriums, all over the past decade, have established Brazil's government as one of the most interventionist in the industrialized free world.

---

[3]S. J. Gray, "Towards a Theory of Cultural Influence on the Development of Accounting Systems Internationally," *Abacus* 24, no. 1 (1988), pp. 1–15.

At the beginning of 1995, Brazil's congress embarked on discussions to reform the country's constitution, first adopted in 1988. Breaking from 20 years of military rule, the authors of the constitution had sought to secure workers' rights and decentralize power, among other things. Many observers believe that the constitution's country-wide minimum wage, life-time employment guarantee for government employees, and huge payouts to the Brazilian states have hindered fiscal reform.[4] Informed observers of Brazil view the opportunity to simplify and reform its constitution as a prerequisite to the country's ability to develop fiscal discipline and national economic policies that work.

Government Debt.   By some accounts, Brazil has the developing world's largest foreign debt, estimated to be $123 billion as of mid-1993. Differences of opinion, domestic economic uncertainty, and a pending Brazilian presidential election led to the suspension of negotiations between Brazil and a committee of its creditors' representatives in June 1989. Talks resumed in October 1990 with Brazil's principal thrust being that debt repayments must be limited to its ability to pay and that it would not resume interest payments until a renegotiated agreement had been reached with its creditor banks. So much uncertainty existed surrounding just what Brazil's long-term ability to pay really was, however, that a negotiated agreement was deemed to be distant.

In June 1990, U.S. bank regulators required the banks under their jurisdiction to write down outstanding loans to Brazil by 20 percent ($2.2 billion). The U.S. banking industry was fearful that if these latest negotiations were to drag on too long, the industry would have to face another required write-down of similar proportions. Hard-line positions did change slightly, however, and by late November 1990, Brazil was approved for about $700 million in loans from the Inter-American Development Bank and the World Bank. This came in response to Brazil's concessions that it would be more flexible in the ongoing negotiations to restructure its existing indebtedness.

Indicative of the seriousness of the continuing debt problem and the groping for a compromise, in June 1990 then President Fernando Collor suggested that Brazil would consider trading part of its huge foreign debt for programs to preserve the Amazon—an environmental issue generating growing concern worldwide. Studies have indicated that the 2 million square mile Amazon could be totally destroyed in 50 to 100 years at current deforestation rates. Such a plan of debt for nature was never seriously considered. Progress has been made, however, in that $52 billion of debt, involving 750 banks, was restructured in the spring of 1994, in spite of the International Monetary Fund's lack of support. Such a restructuring is viewed by many as a major breakthrough and positive indicator for the future.

Individual Tax Law.   Under Brazilian tax law through 1992, net corporate earnings available for distribution to shareholders were subject to withholding at the corporate level. Public corporations were required to prepay to tax authorities 8 percent of net

---

[4]A. Foster, "Slow March Towards Reform," *Financial Times,* February 17, 1995, p. 19.

income on behalf of shareholders. Since domestic shareholders were taxed at a rate of 8 percent on dividends, corporate prepayment generally satisfied a domestic shareholder's tax liability for dividend income. Nonresident shareholders, however, were taxed at a 25 percent rate; hence, the 8 percent prepayment left them with a 17 percent tax liability. Beginning in 1993, the 8 percent corporate prepayment was no longer required, the taxability of dividend income to resident shareholders was revoked, and the 25 percent tax liability on dividend income to nonresident shareholders was reduced to 15 percent. Effective 1994, dividend income to resident shareholders likewise became subject to a 15 percent withholding tax. The highest marginal tax rate on individual income is 25 percent. Capital gains realized on the sale of shares issued by publicly traded companies are taxed at normal rates.

Corporate Tax Law.   With only limited differences, financial reporting in Brazil parallels tax reporting. Thus, any corporation that is subject to income tax is required to calculate its net income according to the accounting methods and principles deemed acceptable by Brazilian tax authorities. Of course, linking tax and financial reporting affects Brazilian financial statements in several important ways:

- Book and tax depreciation are the same. Each is calculated by the straight-line method over useful lives determined by statute without regard to economic judgment. Buildings are depreciated at 4 percent per year, vehicles at 20 percent per year, and all other fixed assets at 10 to 20 percent per year. The government may, in some cases, permit accelerated depreciation for investment in assets approved by the Industrial Development Council, an agency whose principal role is to oversee, and stimulate, the Brazilian economy. Property, plant, and equipment are generally restated annually to consider the effects of inflation. Depreciation is permitted on the adjusted balances.

- Inventories are valued at the lower of cost (determined by average purchase or production cost) or market. LIFO is not permitted by tax law. Write-downs for obsolescence are permitted only when the inventory is actually destroyed. A company without a cost accounting system may value work in progress at 150 percent of the cost of raw materials contained therein and finished goods at 80 percent of their sales price.

- Interest on financing for fixed assets in the preoperational stages of a business is normally deferred (i.e., capitalized) and amortized over the life of the related asset.

- Foreign currency exchange losses are included in income even if they are unrealized.

Of course, this list is by no means exhaustive, but it does highlight several likely aspects of the Brazilian tax law that impinge on financial reporting practices. Effective in 1994, the corporate tax rate was 25 percent plus a 10 percent surcharge (15 percent for financial institutions) on income over a certain amount. Companies are also required to pay a 10 percent social contribution tax (23 percent for financial institutions). The social contribution tax is based on pre-tax income and is deductible when calculating taxable income. Hence, the effective tax rate on income is approximately 42 percent (54 percent for financial institutions). Tax losses may be carried forward for up to four years.

Business Environment

Form of Business.   The business entity in Brazil analogous to a U.S. corporation is known as the *sociedade anônima* or *sociedade por ações,* commonly denoted by the abbreviation S.A. An S.A. may be privately or publicly held; most companies commence operations in private hands before making a public stock offering. A public offering of shares requires registration with the CVM. Brazilian law requires no minimum capital for corporations, except in the case of financial institutions, insurance companies, utilities, and export trading companies. However, the formation of an S.A. requires at least two shareholders.

Shareholders in an S.A. are entitled to receive an obligatory dividend stated in the bylaws; if the bylaws are silent, shareholders are entitled to receive 50 percent of current net income, adjusted for certain contingency and legal reserves. A privately owned corporation is not required to pay the obligatory dividend if all shareholders agree to forgo their right. A corporation, either private or public, may also avoid paying the obligatory dividend if it is financially unable to do so. If such is the case, the firm must place the dividend it would have paid in a reserve account. If the reserve is not used to offset a loss, the dividend must be paid from the reserve as soon as it is financially possible to do so.

The other main form of business in Brazil is the *sociedade por quotas de responsabilidade limitada,* known as the *limitada.* This entity resembles the private limited liability company in Great Britain and the closely held corporation in the United States. It is constituted as a partnership, with liability limited to the extent of the partners' capital. It also has no minimum capital requirement and must be formed by at least two quota holders. Although holdings may be of unequal value, the capital of a *limitada* is usually divided into quotas of equal par value.

Accounting and Audit Requirements.   All business enterprises are required to maintain and register accounting records appropriate to their size and activities. In addition, public corporations, banks, insurance companies, and other financial institutions must comply with the rules of the CVM and publish annual financial statements consisting of a balance sheet, an income statement, a statement of retained earnings or stockholders' equity, a statement of changes in financial position, and explanatory notes. These statements must be examined by an independent auditor. Private corporations and *limitadas* are not required to publish independently audited financial statements, but a growing number of them do so voluntarily.

Accounting Profession.   Professional accountants in Brazil fall into two categories: *contadores,* fully qualified professionals who have graduated from university accounting programs, and *técnicos de contabilidade,* accounting technicians whose professional activities are limited. There are approximately 50,000 *contadores* and 200,000 *técnicos* in Brazil. The **Instituto Brasileiro de Contadores** (IBC), analogous to the American Institute of Certified Public Accountants, is the main professional organization for Brazilian accountants. The laws governing the profession are interpreted and enforced by a system of federal and regional accounting councils responsible for arbitrating disputes and rendering judgment on cases of professional and ethical misconduct. Brazilian auditors must be qualified as *contadores* and must be registered with a regional accounting council. In addition, auditors of public corporations must also be registered with the CVM.

Inflation and Indexing.   The single most important influence on Brazil's system of accounting is the persistent, and at times devastating, inflation that has plagued the country for the last 40 years. (Since 1960, Brazilian prices have multiplied *22 billion times*.[5]) In response, the Brazilian government imposed in the early 1950s various systems of indexation to protect the economy from some of the worst effects of rapidly escalating prices. Although indexation was undoubtedly intended to be a temporary measure, the continuing high rates of inflation in Brazil have made it a more or less permanent fixture in the government's regulatory program, and some pundits assert that Brazilians ''are more preoccupied with having a good indexator than a low inflation rate.''[6]

In early 1986, the newly established democratic government under President José Sarney announced an end to indexation under the **Cruzado plan.** Among other measures, the Cruzado plan introduced a new monetary unit, the *cruzado,* to replace the heavily devalued prior monetary unit, the cruzeiro, at a rate of one cruzado to 1,000 cruzeiros. The government announced an increase in wages, immediately followed by an across-the-board freeze of both wages and prices, and it fixed the official exchange rate for the cruzado at Cz$13.8 per U.S.$1. Unfortunately, the plan failed within a year, and subsequent attempts to bring inflation under control fared no better. Inflation in 1988 ran at almost 1,000 percent; in December 31, 1988, a U.S.$1 purchased about Cz$760.

In January 1989, the Brazilian government introduced a *new cruzado,* worth 1,000 of the old ones. The creation of a new currency was a source of some confusion, especially since the government simply stamped *cruzados novos* on the old currency for use while it was printing the new, which meant that consumers had to remember to drop the last three zeroes themselves (i.e., a Cz$1,000 bill with a stamp on it was worth only 1 new cruzado). Some of the stamped old cruzado bills are still in circulation. As if that were not enough, when President Collor instituted yet another (considerably harsher) anti-inflation plan complete with a new currency, the *cruzeiro,* in March 1990, the government began stamping *cruzeiro* on the *new cruzado* bills while it was printing cruzeiro bills. Collor's bold plans (which included freezing 80 percent of Brazilian savings) did not work and, in fact, he was impeached for corruption in

---

[5]T. Kamm, ''Why Does Brazil Face Such Woes? Some See a Basic Ethical Lapse,'' *The Wall Street Journal,* January 4, 1994, pp. A1 and A5.

[6]Ibid., p. A5.

October 1992. At the end of 1993, inflation was on the rise (over 30 percent per month) and the cruzeiro was trading against the dollar at about 330 to 1 after another 1,000 to 1 devaluation in July 1993 by President Itamar Franco (the new currency was termed *cruzeiros reais,* the *real cruzeiro,* or simply *Cr*). Effective July 1994, the Brazilian government enacted yet another economic plan. Under this plan, the currency became known as the *real,* with R$1.00 equivalent to Cr$2,750. The plan's author, then-finance minister Fernando Cardoso, was heralded as having championed its passage and its key attribute, pegging R$1.00 to U.S.$1.00. In conjunction with the creation of the *real,* inflation went from a monthly rate of 50 percent to about 2 percent. Indeed, such a taming of inflation pushed Cardoso to a successful presidential campaign in October 1994. As of January 1, 1995, R$1.00 was equal to U.S.$.85, a significant *appreciation* of 15 percent in just six months.

As a consequence of the historical failure of numerous anti-inflation plans, Brazil has not yet escaped the need for a system of indexation. Although the details of Brazil's indexation system may change from time to time, the following description of the ***correçao monetaria*** (system of monetary correction) and its impact on financial reporting is indicative of the indexation process which is likely to remain applicable for the foreseeable future.

The basic idea underlying monetary correction is to improve the quality of information on the financial statements and to prevent decapitalization of a firm through the payment of dividends or taxes. In times of severe inflation, historical costs become less meaningful, and corporations can erode their capital base if they pay dividends or taxes on paper profits that have no basis in real wealth. To prevent these ill effects, Brazil's system of monetary correction requires companies to engage in two methods of restatement. The first method, prescribed for all companies organized as an S.A. by Brazilian corporate law, requires the original cost of certain balance sheet items to be adjusted to currency amounts reflecting *current purchasing power.*

> This is done by adjusting, or indexing, certain nonmonetary assets classified as permanent assets, such as fixed assets and related accumulated depreciation, investments and deferred costs, and shareholders' equity accounts. Inventories are not considered nonmonetary items. The index used to adjust permanent assets is defined in legislation as the index recognized by the federal government for measuring the devaluation of the local currency by adjusting the short-term federal government debt (treasury bills). The entry to adjust these accounts is recorded in income for the year in the monetary correction adjustment account.[7]

Exhibits 12–1 and 12–2 provide two examples of the basic procedures of price-level restatement as required by Brazilian corporate law. As these examples illustrate, the monetary correction adjustments are relatively straightforward and apply only to permanent assets and their related accounts (e.g., depreciation), as well as shareholders' equity. Inventory and monetary assets and liabilities are excluded. This simplicity has

---

[7]*International Accounting Summaries* (New York: John Wiley, 1993), p. B26; see also A. Alexandrou and T. Devins, ''Brazilian Monetary Correction and the Deemed Paid Foreign Tax Credit,'' *The CPA Journal,* June 1986, pp. 86–87.

EXHIBIT 12–1

Monetary Correction: Example 1

Assume a balance sheet as follows:

ABC Company
Balance Sheet
at January 1, 19X1

Cash	3,000	Notes payable	1,000
Land	10,000	Capital	12,000
Total	13,000	Total	13,000

During 19X1, the company generated revenues of 8,000 and expenses of 6,000. We assume that all revenues and expenses were realized in cash evenly throughout the year. Assuming an annual rate of inflation of 30 percent in 19X1, the monetary correction account realizes a net debit amount of 600.

Permanent assets—land	$10,000 \times 30\%$ =	3,000
Owners' equity—capital	$12,000 \times 30\%$ =	(3,600)
		(600)

The necessary journal entries are

Dr. Land	3,000	
Cr. Monetary Correction—to Income		3,000
Dr. Monetary Correction—to Income	3,600	
Cr. Special Capital Reserve		3,600

The income statement, ignoring taxes, appears as follows:

ABC Company
Monetary Correction Income Statement
19X1

Revenues	8,000
Expenses	6,000
Operating profit	2,000
Monetary correction	(600)
Net income	1,400

The net debit balance in the monetary correction account reduces operating profit by 600, resulting in a net income of 1,400. The balance sheet at December 31, 19X1, after monetary correction, is shown as

ABC Company
Monetary Correction Balance Sheet
at December 31, 19X1

Cash (3,000 + 8,000 − 6,000)	5,000
Land (10,000 + 3,000)	13,000
Total	18,000
Note payable	1,000
Capital	12,000
Special capital reserve	3,600
Retained earnings	1,400
Total	18,000

EXHIBIT 12–2

Monetary Correction: Example 2

Assume for this example an annual rate of inflation of 40 percent and that prices increased 20 percent by midyear. The following are comparative balance sheets and an income statement for 19X2 prepared under the system of monetary correction.

XYZ Company
Monetary Correction Balance Sheets

	12/31/X1	12/31/X2
Cash	500	1,000
Accounts receivable	2,000	2,500
Inventory	1,500	2,500
Fixed asset—including monetary correction	4,000	5,600
Accumulated depreciation—including monetary correction	(2,000)	(3,360)
Total	6,000	8,240
Accounts payable	700	1,100
Notes payable	500	700
Bond payable	2,300	2,300
Capital stock	2,000	2,000
Special capital reserve—monetary correction	—	800
Retained earnings—including monetary correction	500	1,340
Total	6,000	8,240

XYZ Company
Monetary Correction Income Statement
19X2

Sales		15,000
Cost of goods sold		
Inventory 1/1/X2	(1,500)	
Purchases 19X2	(13,000)	
Inventory 12/31/X2	2,500	(12,000)
Gross profit		3,000
Selling and administrative expenses	(1,000)	
Interest expense	(600)	
Depreciation expense	(480)	(2,080)
Operating profit		920
Monetary correction		(280)
Net income		640

Calculation of Specific Items

Brazilian law requires depreciation to be taken on the average corrected value of fixed assets rather than either the beginning or the ending balance. Assuming an average rate of inflation of 40 percent, the average value of fixed assets would be 4,000 + (4,000 × 40%)/2 = 4,800. Assuming that straight-line depreciation of 10 percent per annum is used, depreciation expense for the year becomes 4,800 × 10% = 480.

Monetary Correction		
Fixed asset	4,000 × 40%	1,600
Accumulated depreciation		
Initial balance	2,000 × 40%	(800)
19X2 depreciation expense	(480 × 20%)/120%	(80)*
Capital stock	2,000 × 40%	(800)
Retained earnings	500 × 40%	(200)
Reduction from operating profit		(280)

EXHIBIT 12–2 (continued)

	12/31/X1	*12/31/X2*
Accumulated Depreciation, 12/31/X2		
Initial balance		2,000
Correction of initial balance—40%		800
19X2 depreciation expense		480
Correction of 19X2 depreciation expense—20%		80 *
Total		3,360
Retained Earnings, 12/31/X2		
Initial balance		500
Correction—500 × 40%		200
19X2 net income		640
Total		1,340

---

*This calculation corrects depreciation for only one-half year, assuming that inflation grew at a rate of 40 percent compounded semiannually. To clarify, assume that the relevant price indexes were as follows: 100 at the beginning of the year, 140 at the end of the year, and 120 at midyear. Thus, $80 = 480 \times [(140 - 120)/120]$.

its disadvantages as well. Combining a variety of adjustments into one line on the income statement decreases the amount of information that the reader may draw from the statements and therefore prevents detailed analysis. Also, inventory is not adjusted, an omission that could cause serious distortion, depending on the nature of a company's business. Finally, critics have pointed out that the treasury bond index normally used as the basis for adjustment is not an accurate measure of inflation; studies have indicated that it tends to lag behind other indices of price changes.

The second method, required in addition to the first for companies listed with the CVM, requires the preparation of another complete set of financial statements denominated in *constant currency amounts.*

[A] government index must be used to adjust the financial statements into the functional currency. All transactions during the year are remeasured into the functional currency. At year-end, units of constant purchasing power are converted into units of nominal local currency using the published value of the index as of that date. Prior year financial statements are also converted from the units of constant purchasing power to nominal units of local currency at the latest year-end date.

In addition to remeasurement, the instructions for constant currency financial statements require that

• Inventory be considered a nonmonetary item and remeasured using the functional currency.

- Noninterest-bearing monetary items be discounted to their present value. Discounting reflects the inflationary gains and losses on monetary items in the proper reporting period on an accrual basis. The discounts reduce appropriate line items in the income statement. For example, a discount of trade accounts receivable is accounted for as a reduction of sales. A discount of accounts payable is accounted for as a reduction of the related balance sheet or income statement account.

- The adjustment of the balance sheet for inflation [in a fashion similar to that required by corporate law] is reclassified to the appropriate line items in the income statement. For example, the portion of the adjustment resulting from holding accounts receivable is reclassified as a reduction of sales. This adjustment is comparable to a gain or loss on the translation of financial statements of operations in high inflation countries.

- The accounting policies note should contain a summary of the methodology used to prepare the constant currency financial statements. The disclosure should include the functional currency used, classifications of discounts to present value, and reclassification of gains or losses from holding monetary items.[8]

The prescription of these two methods described—full indexation (per the Brazilian securities exchange commission) and correction of long-term accounts (per Brazilian corporate law)—has had the effect of requiring publicly traded corporations to prepare financial statements in two forms. Exhibit 12–3 presents an example of some of the explanatory footnotes contained in the 1991 annual report of Cruzeiro do Sul S.A., a Brazilian airline; Exhibit 12–4 presents the company's 1991 balance sheet and income statement. The notes suggest something of the complexity that inflation accounting has imposed on preparers and readers of Brazilian statements. Notice that Cruzeiro presents comparative financial statements according to the full indexation system required by the CVM while noting that "the net loss and shareholders' equity are the same as those determined [per corporate law]." (It should be noted that this need not be the case: in 1989, these amounts were different for Cruzeiro.) It is important to note also that some items (the Boeing 727 and 737 fleets) included in the long-term assets account were also revalued by independent appraisal in October 1988 before the account was restated to reflect general price-level increases. (The practice of revaluing specific assets is described later in the selected financial reporting practices section.) Thus, valuation for some assets can become an extremely complex matter under Brazilian accounting, involving historical cost conventions, two varieties of restatement for inflation, and revaluation of specific assets.

Stock Markets.   Of the nine stock market exchanges in Brazil, the two most important are located in Rio de Janeiro and São Paulo and together they account for over 90 percent of the total volume of transactions. The São Paulo Exchange, or **Bovespa** (short for *Bolsa de Valores de São Paulo*), generally handles more stock transactions, and its approximately 550 listed shares cover a broader range of industries than those on the Rio de Janeiro Exchange. Consequently, the Bovespa index, based on a selection of shares representing about 80 percent of the total volume of the Exchange, is widely

---

[8]*International Accounting Summaries,* pp. B–32, B–33.

Exhibit 12–3

Cruzeiro do Sul S.A.
1991 Selected Notes

Presentation of the financial statements

With the purpose of improving the quality of the information supplied to investors and to the general public, and in accordance with instructions from CVM (the Brazilian Securities and Exchange Commission), the Company is presenting only the "Fully Indexed Financial Statements" because the net loss and the shareholders' equity are the same as those determined in the Financial Statements Per Corporate Law.

The amounts presented in the Notes to financial statements were monetarily corrected to the currency of December 1991.

Summary of accounting practices

a)   **Inflationary effects**

The effects of the loss of currency purchasing power on the equity elements were recorded in the net result based on the BTNF (Daily National Treasury Bonds) variation for the month of January 1991 and, after that date, based on FAP (Equity Adjustment Factor), as established by the Law 8200/91 and complementary laws.

b)   **Monetary correction**

Current and long-term assets and liabilities, denominated in foreign currencies or according to internal indexes of price variation, are monetarily corrected based on the exchange rates and other indices in effect at the balance sheet date.

c)   **Allowance for doubtful accounts**

The allowance for doubtful accounts is based on historical experience and is considered sufficient to cover any losses expected upon realization.

d)   **Maintenance and operating supplies**

The Sundry Materials and Work in Process Inventories are stated at acquisition or production cost, monetarily corrected according to the variation of the indices used for recognition of the inflationary effects which is lower than replacement cost. The Imports in Progress are stated at the cost incurred until the balance sheet date.

e)   **Property and equipment**

Property and equipment are stated at monetarily corrected acquisition cost, except for flight equipment revalued in October 1988 and monetarily corrected from that date on. Depreciation is computed by the straight-line method at the rates shown without residual value.

f)   **Provisions**

The Provision for flight equipment overhaul is computed based on the hours flown and covers future flight equipment overhaul costs.

g)   **Adjustments to present value**

Receivables and payables which include inflationary expectations in their nominal value were adjusted to present value based on FAP (Equity Adjustment Factor) variation in December 1991 with contra entries to results of operations denominated "Present value adjustments."

Special monetary correction—Law 8200/91

Law 8200/91, governed by Decree 332/91, established procedures for recognition of monetary correction of the balance sheet, whose effects were adjusted in the financial statements according to the following criteria:

The Complementary monetary correction (article 3) of the Permanent assets and Shareholders' equity accounts for the year 1990 was calculated based on the IPC (Consumer Price Index) variation in comparison with the balance sheet as of 12.31.90, which on that date was monetarily corrected based on IGP-DI (General Price Index) variation. The net result was recorded in the Shareholders' equity, in the retained earnings account.

The Special monetary correction (article 2) of the property and equipment account was calculated based on the IGP-DI variation since the acquisition or revaluation date.

The Special reserves made by the subsidiaries and associated companies, in accordance with the criteria established by Law 8200/91-article 3, were charged directly to the Shareholders' equity in a capital reserve account denominated "Special monetary correction."

Exhibit 12–3 (continued)

Additional practices for full indexation

a) **Income statement**

Income statement items are monetarily corrected from the month recorded, based on average monthly variations of indices used for recognition of inflationary effects.

Present value adjustments, and the inflation gains and losses on monetary items were reclassified to the respective income items.

b) **Prior year financial statements**

For comparative purposes, the prior year financial statements were prepared in accordance with the full indexation criteria and adjusted to reflect the effects of the complementary monetary correction based on IPC-article 3 of this Law 8200/91, and monetarily corrected to the currency of December 31, 1991.

Property and equipment

	Thousands of cruzeiros				
	12.31.91		**12.31.90**		
	Monetarily corrected cost	*Accumulated Depreciation*	*Monetarily corrected cost*	*Accumulated depreciation*	*(a) Depreciation rates—% p.a. Jan/Dec*
Flight equipment					
B-727/100	33,074,826	(19,145,174)	33,074,826	(13,048,407)	20.0
B-737/200	67,596,296	(35,675,823)	72,758,427	(24,921,020)	16.6
Spare and repair parts	33,407,662	(28,659,379)	26,042,902	(20,752,220)	(b)
Ground equipment	7,190,724	(7,084,783)	6,453,936	(6,268,781)	10.0 to 20.0
Real estate	7,401,335	(4,173,830)	3,110,627	(1,692,185)	4.0
	148,670,843	(94,738,989)	141,440,718	(66,682,613)	

a) In accordance with the service life of the equipment which, in the case of flight equipment, was established based on an appraisal report of October 1988.

b) Depreciated at the same rates as the related equipment.

As a result of the flight equipment revaluation made in October 1988, depreciation expense and cost of goods written off were charged to results of operations in 1991 in the amounts of Cr$16,232,228 thousand and Cr$513,716 thousand, respectively. The amount of Cr$42,509,046 thousand remains in Property and equipment and will be recorded in the results of operations of future years when realized. The revaluation reserve made that year is Cr$7,017,432 thousand lower than the remaining balance in Property and equipment due to partial compensation with losses determined in prior years.

This year, in accordance with article 2 of Law 8200/91, a special monetary correction was calculated for the items classified in Property and equipment. The calculation was based on the IGP-DI (General Price Index) variation since the acquisition or revaluation date of the items through January 1991. The positive difference in relation to the individual value of each item was added to the cost of such item with contra entries to the Capital reserve denominated "Special monetary correction." Following are details of the composition of these amounts:

	Thousands of cruzeiros
Owned items	8,729,548
Depreciation	(6,101,763)
	2,627,785

On December 31, 1991, Cr$2,122,861 thousand remain in Property and equipment and will be recorded in results of operations in future years when realized through depreciation or sale.

EXHIBIT 12–3 (continued)

Shareholders' equity

a) Paid-in capital stock

Paid-in capital totals Cr$4,348,637,358.14 and is divided into 69,261,034 no-par value shares, of which 27,855,451 are common shares and the remaining 41,405,583 are preferred non-voting shares, distributed as follows:

Shareholders	*Common*	*Preferred*
Residing in Brazil	27,855,451	41,399,559
Residing abroad	—	6,024
	27,855,451	41,405,583

During this year the main corporate act was as follows:

On April 29, 1991 the shareholders approved a motion to increase capital stock from Cr$275,830,432.76 to Cr$4,348,637,358.14 through a capitalization of the reserve for monetary correction of capital stock, without issuance of new shares, thus maintaining the capital stock composed of 69,261,034 no-par value shares, of which 27,855,451 are common shares and the remaining 41,405,583 are preferred non-voting shares.

b) Reserves

The following reserves are recorded in agreement with the Companies Act and the Company's bylaws:

—Reserve for monetary correction of Capital stock, which may be capitalized by the Shareholders' Meeting;

—Reserve for special monetary correction recorded based on the amounts determined in Property and equipment;

—Cr$2,627,785 thousand (Note 5.2), investments in subsidiaries and associated companies—Cr$864,515 thousand (Note 4.2) and real estate classified in Investments—Cr$402,372 thousand, which may be capitalized by the Shareholders' Meeting.

c) Monetary correction—Law 8200/91

As established by the provisions of article 3 of Law 8200/91, a complementary monetary correction was calculated based on IPC for the year 1990. The difference in relation to the monetary correction based on IGP-DI was charged directly to the retained earnings account.

---

recognized as the best indicator of movements in the Brazilian stock market. In November 1990, the Bovespa hit its lowest level in 25 years, but within nine months, it had hit a record high of 20,817. As of the start of 1995, the index sat at 43,190.

The bodies responsible for regulating the stock exchanges are the Central Bank of Brazil and the CVM. A corporation must register with the CVM to make a public offering of securities or to have its securities traded on the exchanges (if they are listed) or over the counter (if they are unlisted). Registration with the CVM includes filing a feasibility study, proposed bylaws, and a prospectus.

The Brazilian government has made the development of the nation's stock markets a national priority and has accordingly encouraged investment in stocks by providing for the payment of obligatory dividends. Despite these incentives, however, securities markets have yet to play a major role in Brazilian financial reporting or as major sources of finance for the public or private sectors. The persistence of inflation in the Brazilian economy has made the exchanges vehicles for speculation instead of dependable avenues of financing. There are signs, however, that the markets may become more important. The Brazilian government has indicated its desire to increase the efficiency of the country's stock exchanges and attract more foreign participation in Brazilian equity

EXHIBIT 12–4

Cruzeiro do Sul S.A.
1991 Balance Sheet and Income Statement

	In currency of December 1991	
	---	---
Assets	*12.31.91*	*12.31.90*
Current assets		
Cash and cash equivalents	1,300,151	1,190,154
Accounts receivable		
Customers	1,731,965	1,552,676
Brazilian government	3,002,121	2,755,693
Other airlines	3,857,976	5,869,667
Subsidiaries and associated companies	127,582	85,789
Other receivables	1,132,836	729,043
Less: allowance for doubtful accounts	(25,980)	(23,290)
Total accounts receivable	9,826,500	10,969,578
Temporary investments	539,899	196,095
Maintenance and operating supplies	13,301,116	10,764,192
Prepaid expenses	96,201	97,671
Total current assets	25,063,867	23,217,690
Long-term assets		
Associated company	—	2,915,446
Other	111,989	139,915
Total long-term assets	111,989	3,055,361
Permanent assets		
Investments		
Subsidiaries	5,883,543	6,561,990
Other companies	69,110	69,110
Other investments	548,666	146,295
Total investments	6,501,319	6,777,395
Property and equipment		
Property and equipment	148,670,843	141,440,718
Less: accumulated depreciation	(94,738,989)	(66,682,613)
	53,931,854	74,758,105
Work in progress	773	207,536
Total property and equipment	53,932,627	74,965,641
Total permanent assets	60,433,946	81,743,036
Total assets	85,609,802	108,016,087

markets. In fact, as of the end of 1993, the value of Brazilian securities owned by foreigners equaled those owned by Brazilian pension funds.[9]

To create efficiencies in operations, the Rio de Janeiro and São Paulo exchanges merged in late 1990. To inspire confidence in the system, the CVM recently improved enforcement of the country's securities laws, particularly those involving insider trading. Moreover, the Central Bank's 1987 resolution allowing foreign creditors to

---

[9]"So Far, So Good," *The Economist,* April 2, 1994, p. 75.

EXHIBIT 12–4 (continued)

	In currency of December 1991	
Liabilities and Shareholders' Equity	*12.31.91*	*12.31.90*
Current liabilities		
Suppliers	3,774,029	5,442,805
Compulsory contributions	5,945,637	4,759,517
Accrued payroll	1,249,365	997,424
Short-term loans	132,864	94,012
Subsidiaries and associated companies	1,037,003	586,961
Payable to other airlines	120,684	4,901
Unearned transportation revenues	62,674	46,294
Social contribution	5,794	—
Accounts payable	4,388,261	5,378,096
Provisions for:		
Flight equipment overhaul	4,397,534	3,650,733
Vacation pay	3,701,004	2,823,097
Total current liabilities	24,814,849	23,783,840
Long-term liabilities		
Associated company	21,242,566	—
Total long-term liabilities	21,242,566	—
Shareholders' equity		
Paid-in capital stock	4,348,637	275,830
Monetary correction of capital stock	25,799,519	29,872,326
Total paid-in capital stock	30,148,156	30,148,156
Capital reserve		
Special monetary correction	3,894,672	—
Revaluation reserves		
Property and equipment	35,491,614	52,237,561
Investments	2,745,062	2,980,775
Total revaluation reserves	38,236,676	55,218,336
Accumulated losses	(32,727,117)	(1,134,245)
Total shareholders' equity	39,552,387	84,232,247
Total liabilities and shareholders' equity	85,609,802	108,016,087

exchange debt for equity securities has stirred interest among those international investors who are optimistic about Brazil's long-term prospects. Foreign investment bankers have set up Brazilian investment funds that are attracting money from institutional investors, and in May 1991, it was announced that the stock markets would be opened to direct foreign investment. The significance of these trends for Brazilian capital markets and, hence, for reporting requirements will depend on the government's willingness to continue to attract foreign investment and to privatize an estimated $200 billion worth of state-owned companies.

EXHIBIT 12–4 (continued)

Earnings

	In currency of December 1991	
	12.31.91	*12.31.90*
Gross operating revenues		
Flight revenue	312,065,196	367,120,648
Less: Value-added tax	(12,928,245)	(12,761,957)
Other	21,618,904	18,729,088
	320,755,855	373,087,779
Less: Taxes on revenues (PIS and Finsocial)	(2,761,746)	(2,375,231)
Net operating revenues	317,994,109	370,712,548
Operating costs		
Flight operations	(255,055,723)	(303,691,629)
Other operating costs	(561,347)	(96,317)
Depreciation	(23,176,171)	(24,652,093)
Adjustments to inventories and provisions	(2,657,364)	—
	(281,450,605)	(328,440,039)
Gross profit	36,543,504	42,272,509
Commercial expenses	(54,831,507)	(59,501,800)
General expenses		
Executive salaries	(297,959)	(599,241)
Administrative expenses	(17,305,338)	(32,594,883)
	(17,603,297)	(33,194,124)
Net financial income (expense)		
Financial income	4,620,909	1,586,612
Financial expenses	(17,301,566)	(2,299,387)
Gains (losses) on assets and liabilities in foreign currency	3,638,868	(525,561)
Interest on long-term debt for flight equipment	—	(46,821)
	(9,041,789)	(1,285,157)
Equity in subsidiaries	(1,434,554)	262,382
Adjustments of assets and liabilities to present value	(408,161)	(1,627,032)
Gains (losses) on non-interest monetary items	(1,097,291)	8,938,423
Operating loss	(47,873,095)	(44,134,799)
Nonoperating income		
Nonoperating income	689,470	25,976,239
Nonoperating expenses	(1,142,890)	(17,320,947)
	(453,420)	8,655,292
Loss for the year	(48,326,515)	(35,479,507)
Loss per share	(697.74)	(512.26)

Selected Financial Reporting Practices

Formulation of accounting and auditing standards is a multifaceted process in Brazil, with standards being issued from a variety of sources. The primary and most authoritative sources are the **Brazilian Commercial Code,** companies acts, and income tax laws (which affect all businesses), and the CVM, whose pronouncements apply only to publicly traded corporations. Supplementary guidelines are also issued from the Brazilian Accountants' Institute, which lacks the ability to enforce compliance, and the Central Bank (especially for financial institutions). The multiplicity of sources for reporting practices has sometimes had the effect of requiring companies to present information in more than one form.

In general, the accrual basis of accounting is used. Consistent with the revenue recognition practices in the United States, revenue is recorded when the earnings process is culminated and its collectibility is likely. In the income statement, costs are matched to the revenues they generated. In the balance sheet, assets and liabilities are reported in the order of their liquidity with property, plant, equipment, long-term investments, and deferred charges classified as *permanent assets.* Interim financial statements are generally prepared on a semiannual basis as opposed to a quarterly basis. Moreover, readers of Brazilian financial statements can count on extensive footnote disclosures intended to provide clarity, detail, and supplemental information.

The following review includes a number of Brazilian accounting practices that differ materially from U.S. GAAP. It is interesting to note that a recent survey found only seven Brazilian companies having been willing to restate their financial statements according to U.S. GAAP to list ADRs in the United States.[10]

Affiliation and Consolidation

Long-term investments are subject to price-level restatement as described. In addition, a significant investment in an affiliated company must be accounted for under the equity method. An *affiliate* is defined as a company in which the investor directly owns at least 10 percent of the capital but does not hold a controlling interest. An investment in an affiliate is considered to be *significant* if it equals 10 percent of the *investor's* equity. Smaller investments may be accounted for at cost-plus monetary correction.

Under Brazilian corporate law, a public corporation must prepare and publish consolidated statements if its investments in controlled companies exceed 30 percent of its own net worth. Control is defined functionally, without regard to the percentage of shares owned: it is deemed to exist if the investing company possesses the ability to elect or appoint a majority of the investee's officers. The CVM decides which companies should be included in the consolidated statements.

A controlled subsidiary normally does not need to be consolidated if *any* of the following conditions exist:

- Control by the parent company is temporary (i.e., sale of the subsidiary is pending).
- The subsidiary is undergoing a reorganization or is in bankruptcy.
- The financial statements of the subsidiary are sufficiently dissimilar in content to those of the parent that consolidation might be misleading (e.g., consolidation of a financing subsidiary with a manufacturing parent).

---

[10]Ibid.

The first two exceptions are consistent with the FASB's *SFAS No. 94;* the third is not. In the minds of many financial analysts, the third exception effectively creates a professionally approved form of off-balance-sheet financing.

Inventory

Inventories are valued at the lower of cost or market, principally on an item-by-item basis. Acceptable cost allocation methods include specific cost, average cost, FIFO, and LIFO, although LIFO is not acceptable for tax purposes and thus is not frequently used for external reporting. Under corporate law, inventories are generally not adjusted under the indexing process, and, consequently, the moving weighted-average cost method is preferred by most companies. As in the United States, published financial statements are prepared using absorption (or full) costing.

Revaluation of Assets

Certain assets (in practice, usually only fixed assets) may be written up above book value based on appraisal by an independent expert. These revaluations, which are optional and address the market value of specific assets, should not be confused with the mandatory restatement of certain account balances (described in the section on indexation) designed to show the effects of general price-level increases. The appraisal write-ups, if done, are also subject, however, to subsequent inflation adjustments. The offsetting credit created by the write-up is taken to a revaluation reserve account (Appraisal Reserve, or *Reserva de Reavaliacáo*), which is carried on the balance sheet under shareholders' equity. Depreciation is calculated on the reappraised value but creates a deferred tax liability since depreciation on the revaluation amount is not tax deductible. Annually, a portion of the appraisal reserve is transferred (on a net of tax basis) to retained earnings, reflecting the amortization of appraisal write-up.

Income Taxes

Because of the substantial overlap of book and taxable income, the use of deferred income tax accounting is largely unnecessary; however, when differences in book and taxable income arise, Brazilian GAAP provides that the liability method of deferred taxes be followed (i.e., that deferred income tax balances be adjusted for any subsequent tax rate changes).

Leases

Regardless of their economic substance, all leases are accounted for as operating leases by lessees. If the lessee is a publicly held company and accounts for a capital lease as an operating lease, footnote disclosure of the capitalizable-equivalent value of the leased asset and related liability is required. For lessors, only publicly held companies and leasing companies are required to account for leases on the basis of their economic substance; for all other entities, lease accounting remains undefined by existing GAAP.

Research and Development Costs

Companies may choose to expense research and development expenditures or carry them as a deferred charge. Expenditures for *new* products, however, are most commonly deferred when material in amount and expenditures relating to existing products or markets are principally expensed as incurred. When R&D is deferred, existing GAAP recommends disclosure of the nature and amount of capitalized expenditures, as well as the method and period of anticipated amortization.

Interest

Interest costs may be carried as a deferred charge (1) if incurred in the preoperating phase of long-term capital projects or (2) if the company is in a preoperating stage; otherwise, it is inappropriate to capitalize interest under Brazilian GAAP.

Shareholders' Equity

Brazilian corporate law segments shareholders' equity into four types: share capital and capital reserves, appraisal reserves, legal reserves, and profit reserves and retained earnings. Share capital includes both ordinary and preferred shares (which may be issued with or without par value); shareholder contributions in excess of par value are reflected in a capital reserve account. Treasury stock is accounted for at cost and reflected as a contra shareholders' equity account. An appraisal reserve results from the write-up of fixed assets to appraised market value; appraisal reserves are not eligible for distribution until the appraised asset is sold or retired or until the reserve is transferred to retained earnings.

Brazilian corporations are required to create and maintain a legal reserve by appropriating 5 percent of net income each year until the reserve equals 20 percent of share capital and capital reserves. The legal reserve is not available for distribution and may be used only to offset losses or increase share capital. Profit reserves represent the appropriation of retained earnings for specifically defined objectives. Dividends are payable from current net income, retained earnings, and profit reserves. As noted previously, Brazilian corporate law requires an annual dividend distribution of 50 percent of net income (adjusted for any contingency or legal reserves). Finally, shareholder equity accounts are adjusted for the effects of inflation.

Other Disclosure Requirements

Companies must disclose material investments in other companies, increases in asset values as a result of appraisals (as described), pledges of assets and contingent liabilities, prior year adjustments, and significant events subsequent to the balance sheet date. There are no requirements concerning segment disclosures or pension plans. Exhibit 12–5 presents a summary comparison of Brazilian and U.S. generally accepted accounting practices.

EXHIBIT 12–5

Comparison of Brazilian and U.S. Accounting and Reporting Standards

Item	*Brazil*	*United States*
Asset valuation	Historical cost, with revaluation adjustments permitted for specific fixed assets; in addition, permanent nonmonetary accounts (e.g., fixed assets and accumulated depreciation, investments and deferred costs, shareholder equity accounts) indexed for general price-level changes	Historical cost with selected revaluation (principally downward)
Inventory valuation	Principally moving weighted-average cost, although FIFO and LIFO permitted; LIFO not permitted for tax purposes and rarely used	Principally LIFO (because of tax considerations); also FIFO and average cost methods
Inventory: year-end	Lower of cost or replacement cost, principally applied on an item-by-item basis	Lower of cost or replacement cost
Depreciation	Principally straight-line, however, any method that systematically allocates an asset's carrying value is acceptable; if the asset is revalued, depreciation based on the revalued amount	Principally straight-line with accelerated and production-based methods permitted
Goodwill	Capitalized to the balance sheet and amortized over expected useful life; negative goodwill permitted	Capitalized to balance sheet, with amortization (principally straight-line) over a maximum of 40 years; negative goodwill not permitted
Research and development costs	Principally capitalized to the balance sheet if material and if involving new products; amortized over period of expected future benefit	Research costs expensed currently; development costs expensed currently except in certain industries (i.e., software, oil and gas)
Capitalized interest costs	Generally not permitted except when company is in preoperating state	Capitalization required for self-constructed assets
Intercorporate investments:		
Marketable securities (current asset trading)	Lower of monetarily adjusted cost or market	Market value (individual security basis), with *unrealized* gains and losses taken to income
Long-term investments:		
0–10% ownership (available for sale)	Lower of monetarily adjusted cost or market	Market value (individual security basis) with *unrealized* gains and losses taken to owners' equity
10–50% ownership	Equity method	Equity method
51–100% ownership	Consolidated (with exceptions), principally using purchase accounting; pooling permitted if the acquiror cannot be identified	Consolidated, using pooling or purchase accounting
Debt valuation	Valued at face value	Long-term debt (except deferred income taxes) valued at present value; current debt valued at face value
Leases	All leases, regardless of their economic substance, treated as operating leases	Capital leases reflected in balance sheet; operating leases disclosed in footnotes
Deferred income taxes	Generally unnecessary due to proximity of book and taxable income, but when appropriate, the liability method used	Computed under liability method
Pension liabilities	Company-sponsored plans not common in Brazil	Reflected on balance sheet

---

EXHIBIT 12–5 (continued)

Item	Brazil	United States
Discretionary reserves	Specific reserves for taxes, dividends, employee benefits, and future expenses (e.g., warranties) permitted	Restricted to identifiable operational losses
Statement of cash flows	Not required (but a statement of changes in financial position required)	Required

Analytical Considerations

From an analytical perspective, the key differences between Brazilian and U.S. accounting are found principally in four areas. First, as noted in Exhibit 12–5, Brazilian firms do not, as a general rule, present cash flow data, and thus analysts must be prepared to develop that information themselves. Second, unlike their U.S. counterparts, Brazilian firms are permitted to revalue upward their long-term assets and, when combined with the effects of indexing, may produce substantially higher asset values on the balance sheet and similarly higher depreciation charges on the income statement. Third, although U.S. firms value debt on the basis of its present value, Brazilian firms value debt at its face or settlement value. Financial statement discrepancies also arise because of the failure of Brazilian GAAP to consider the economic substance of certain debt-related transactions. For example, leases that are capitalized by U.S. firms are almost certainly treated as operating leases by Brazilian companies. Finally, considerable inconsistencies exist between the two countries in regard to the treatment of certain capitalizable costs. For example, in Brazil, research and development costs involving new products are principally capitalized; U.S. GAAP mandates current expensing. Similarly, although certain interest costs must be capitalized under U.S. GAAP, capitalization of interest is generally not practiced in Brazil (except under limited circumstances).

Considered in total, these differences are likely to produce a systematic upward biasing of balance sheet values for Brazilian companies as compared to U.S. firms. Because of the importance of indexing and revaluation of assets in hyperinflationary economies, these issues are considered further.

Revaluation. Under Brazilian corporate law, a company may revalue its specific assets (principally its fixed assets) upward to market value if a higher value is so indicated by a shareholder-approved independent appraisal. Under this process, market value is to be assessed on an asset-by-asset basis, and any write-up is recorded by an increase to the asset account and an increase to a special equity reserve account (i.e., Appraisal Reserve). Depreciation is then calculated on both the original asset carrying value and the revalued amount. An amount equivalent to the periodic depreciation

EXHIBIT 12–6

Petróles Brasileiro S.A.—Petrobrás
Financial Statement Disclosures

Panel A: Revaluation Reserve is established by Petrobrás in the amount of the revaluation increments of property, plant and equipment recorded by subsidiaries and/or affiliated companies based on appraisals by independent experts. As permitted by the Brazilian Securities and Exchange Commission (CVM) Decision No. 27, the realization of this reserve, proportional to the sale of the investments and the depreciation of the revaluated assets was: (i) credited to consolidated results of operations, classified in the account "Participation in the decrease in the net underlying assets of affiliated companies" in the amount "Per Integral Correction" of Cr$30,396 million—US$28,439 thousand— for reserves formed up to December 31, 1985 and (ii) transferred to retained earnings in the amount "Per Integral Correction" of Cr$141,315 million—US$132,218 thousand—for reserves constituted after that date.

Panel B: Price-Level Restatement Brazilian legislation requires companies to restate the carrying value of property, plant, and equipment and related accumulated depreciation, long-term investments, certain other assets, intercompany current accounts and stockholders' equity, based upon recognized quotation coefficients. The net result of this restatement is charged or credited to results of operations.

The monetary correction of the balance sheet, at December 31, 1991, is summarized as follows:

	Millions of cruzeiros
Permanent assets:	
Investments	3,677,542
Property, plant and equipment	6,737,003
Deferred charges	288,511
	10,703,056
Intercompany current accounts	63,323
Due to the controlling stockholder	1,191
Stockholders' equity	(10,474,992)
	292,578

charge taken on the revaluation figure is annually transferred from the appraisal reserve to retained earnings, net of any related tax effects. Following revaluation, the asset account and related accumulated depreciation account may then be indexed for general inflation (to which we turn shortly).

The effect of revaluation on Brazilian financial ratios varies by category. For example, the higher asset and equity balances that accompany revaluation tend to systematically (and correctly) depress such profitability measures as ROA, ROE, and ROS. Similarly, the higher asset and equity values also tend to result in somewhat lower leverage indicators (e.g., debt to assets and debt to equity), thereby suggesting an apparently superior solvency position. Clearly, the magnitude of these ratio distortions is directly tied to the amount and recency of the revaluation appraisal. To illustrate, consider the case of Petrobrás, Brazil's largest oil and gas company. As of year-end 1991, the company's revaluation reserve amounted to Cr$1,847,954 million, or approximately 15 percent of its total net worth of Cr$12,403,762 million. Exhibit 12–6 (panel A) reveals that during 1991, Petrobrás transferred an aggregate of Cr$171,711 million from this reserve, with Cr$30,396 million credited to consolidated income and

Cr$141,315 million credited to retained earnings. These latter amounts effectively offset the additional depreciation charged against the company's 1991 earnings resulting from the higher (reappraised) balance sheet values. If Petrobrás' had reported 1991 net earnings of, say, Cr$500,000 million—in fact, the company reported a loss— its ROE would have been 4 percent (500,000 ÷ 12,405,762). In the absence of revaluation, the company's ROE would have been approximately 4.7 percent (500,000 ÷ 10,555,808). And, based on actual total debt of Cr$6,889,724 million, Petrobrás' reported debt-to-equity ratio was 55.5 percent, whereas in the absence of revaluation, the debt-to-equity ratio would have been 65.3 percent. Thus, revaluation can be seen to systematically depress profitability measures while inflating solvency measures.

Indexing. Although historical cost is the initial basis of valuation for all assets, Brazil's chronically high inflation has necessitated a departure from the cost basis to ensure that the published financial statements are useful for shareholders, creditors, and other interested parties. Under the Brazilian system of indexation required for all publicly held companies, the historical cost basis is modified to express original cost in equivalent units of purchasing power as of the balance sheet date. This is accomplished by multiplying selected nonmonetary assets—principally fixed assets and accumulated depreciation, investments and deferred costs, and shareholders' equity accounts but excluding inventories (unless acquired more than 90 days before year-end)—by a government-approved price-deflator index. The offsetting entry to the indexing adjustment is taken directly to the income statement, reflecting an inflationary *gain* on the asset accounts or an inflationary *loss* on the shareholder's equity and other credit-balance accounts. Net inflationary losses are immediately deductible for tax purposes, whereas net inflationary gains need not be recognized for tax purposes until realized (i.e., the related asset is sold or retired).

Because Brazilian GAAP requires that the results of the indexing be disclosed in a company's footnotes (e.g., see Exhibit 12–6, panel B), it is possible to perform a ratio analysis of Brazilian financial statements with and without the effects of indexation. Consider again the case of Petrobrás. Exhibit 12–6 (panel B) reveals that the effect of price-level indexing as of December 31, 1991, was to increase the company's total assets by Cr$10,703,056 million, representing over 55 percent of total year-end assets values of Cr$19,293,486 million. The increase to shareholders' equity of Cr$10,474,992, on the other hand, represents nearly 85 percent of total year-end shareholders' equity of Cr$12,403,762 million. Based on the price-level restated values, Petrobrás' ratio of net worth to total assets is 64.3 percent; using unadjusted values, this ratio falls (substantially) to only 22.5 percent (1,928,770 ÷ 8,590,430). These ratio discrepancies raise the important question as to whether the analysis of companies in hyperinflationary economies should be conducted with or without price-level restatement. Our advice, and that of most professional analysts, is to use the indexed financial statement for analysis purposes, despite various limitations of these adjusted statements. A related consideration involves the across-company ratio comparisons that might occur when evaluating investments in Brazil and other less inflationary environments. Again, professional convention appears to favor the use of inflation-adjusted data.

Summary

The decade of the 1990s began with President Collor's optimistic and aggressive agenda to transition one of the world's most protected economies to an open trading system. The day after taking office in March 1990, he abolished a 15-year-old list of forbidden imports, drastically downsized the governmental trade bureaucracy, floated the currency, and eliminated many export subsidies. Such moves were aimed to do away with formidable trade barriers and the lack of global competitive forces that had greatly contributed to inefficient industrial processes and complacent managers who had been able to generate profits by simply charging ever-higher prices for their goods and services. The extent to which old ways were viewed as having to change was characterized by the fact that during its first two months in office, President Collor's government issued an average of eight new regulations every business day. (It must be noted that not all were well conceived and some were short lived.) These regulations were generally designed to tear down old practices and in some cases mandate new ones. Two and half years after taking office, Mr. Collor was impeached, achieving infamy as the world's first elected president to be impeached.

Some observers have noted the following:

> Brazil is really the capitalist equivalent of Russia—a vast, closed economy trying to open up through a mixture of exuberant Latin American *glasnost* and faltering *perestroika*.
>
> Despite its problems, Brazil is dismantling tariffs, privatizing firms, attracting foreign investment and generally getting on with things in its own shambolic way. Above all, as a huge country, rich in natural resources, and with relatively efficient export industries, it is well placed for continued economic growth.[11]

It is generally believed, though, that positive change is not likely to happen in the near term. The general ethos of those who could bring about change has been described as, in the best terms, a "culture of accommodation," and in more derogatory terms, "collective stupidity."[12] For those truly hopeful for positive reform, the three necessary ingredients of commitment, competence, and consensus are still lacking.[13] In short, the current government of President Franco has shown little in the way of competency; the Brazilian congress is comprised of members from 19 different parties; and for many of the non-poor citizenry, life is a series of adjustments and much skepticism.

> In a Rio supermarket an old lady stares at biscuits which have been cut in price to compete with Argentine imports. "There must be something wrong with them," she says, "normally they go up every week."[14]

---

[11]"Onwards and Downwards in Brazil," *The Economist,* November 13, 1993, Survey 19.
[12]Kamm, "Why Does Brazil Face Such Woes?" p. 1.
[13]"Onwards and Downwards in Brazil."
[14]*Financial Times,* September 21, 1990, p. 6.

Suggested Readings

"A Survey of Latin America." *The Economist,* November 13, 1993, Surveys 1–28.

"Brazil and Its Constitution." *Financial Times,* October 4, 1993, p. 11.

Brazil: Company Handbook. Pompano Beach, FL: International Co. Handbook Ltd., 1991.

Doing Business in Brazil. New York: Price Waterhouse, 1991.

Doupnik, T.S. "Indexation: Brazil's Response to Inflation." *The International Journal of Accounting,* Fall 1982, pp. 199–217.

Foster, A. "Fresh Feather in Their Caps." *Financial Times,* October 6, 1993, p. 14.

Hieronymus, B. "Stock Markets Attract International Interest." *Euromoney,* January 1988, pp. 60–61.

International Accounting Summaries. New York: Wiley, 1993.

Kamm, T. "Why Does Brazil Face Such Woes? Some See a Basic Ethical Lapse." *The Wall Street Journal,* January 4, 1994, pp. A1, A5.

Issues and Information for Further Inquiry

I.12.1   Foreign Direct Investment

An April 2, 1994 *Economist* article (p. 75), "So Far, So Good," noted that "Brazil is by far the most volatile of the emerging markets . . . [and] foreign investors in the Brazilian market are taking risks. [Moreover] American interest in Brazilian stocks [is likely to] grow as more Brazilian firms issue American Depositary Receipts. . . . Because of different accounting standards, only seven companies have so far issued ADRs."

Required:

Obtain a country analysis by any of the U.S. investment banks and summarize their current perspective on the Brazilian capital markets, noting the financial indicators they highlight for various companies.

I.12.2   Limited Shares to Trade

In a May 28, 1993 *Financial Times* article (p. 37), "Foreign Investors Drawn into Brazilian Equities," author B. Hinchberger notes that there is "no liquidity [in the market] because most companies have not issued stock in several years." Moreover, in a May 17, 1995 *Financial Times* article (p. 2), "Faith in the Markets," P. McCurry notes that in spite of the São Paulo stock market's recent growth, it "is still highly illiquid. About 70 percent of trading is concentrated in just five government-controlled companies . . . [and it] is also partly the result of a shortage of tradeable shares [due] to the reluctance of many family-owned companies to cede influence to outside shareholders."

Required:

(a) Research the reason that many companies have not issued stock in several years in Brazil.

(b) Report also on the disclosures required when a Brazilian company does have a stock offering.

EXERCISES

E.12.1   Your Management Promotion

You have just become the CEO of a Brazilian company engaged in manufacturing refrigerators, air conditioners, and freezers. The company was formed in 1950, and its shares have traded on the São Paulo and Rio de Janeiro Exchanges since 1976. There are about 1,100 stockholders and 7,500 employees. Sales and profits for the most recent fiscal year were approximately US$ 400 million and US$ 40 million, respectively. Ninety percent of sales are domestic. Export sales are to countries in Latin America, North America, Africa, the Middle East, and the Far East. You have spent the last 10 years as V.P.–Manufacturing for a U.S. company that produces similar products and is about the same size. Almost all of its sales were in the United States.

Required:

(a) Prepare a list of important *business issues* that you expect to have to deal with in Brazil that you did not encounter as manager of the U.S. company.

You have suddenly changed your mind and have decided not to become the CEO of the Brazilian Company. Instead you have accepted the position of CFO with the same Brazilian company.

Required:

(b) Prepare a list of important *financial reporting issues* that you expect to have to deal with that the CFO of your former company would not have encountered.

E.12.2   Brazilian Monetary Correction

Cafe Angelina S.A. is a Brazilian retailer that just completed its first year of operations. Exhibit 1 contains the financial statements prepared in nominal currency amounts and before the calculation of taxes, which are a function of income net of the monetary correction.

<u>**Exhibit 1**</u>

CAFE ANGELINA S.A.
Comparative Balance Sheets and Income Statement
For the Year Ended December 31, 1994

	1/1/94	*12/31/94*
Cash	100	171
Accounts receivable	—	300
Inventory	200	210
Plant and equipment	1,000	1,000
Accumulated depreciation	—	(100)
	1,300	1,581
Accounts payable	—	200
Bonds payable	200	200
Paid-in capital	1,100	1,100
Retained earnings	—	81
	1,300	1,581
Revenues		750
Cost of goods sold		400
Selling & administrative		140
Depreciation		100
Interest		20
Net income		90
Less: dividends		9
Change in retained earnings		81

Additional Information

- The appropriate index of price levels was 100 on January 1, 1994, and 140 on December 31, 1994. The index increased evenly throughout the year. For example, at midyear, the index stood at 120.
- Plant and equipment are depreciated at a rate of 10 percent per year.
- Inventory is accounted for on a FIFO basis. Purchases of inventory occurred evenly throughout the year.
- Dividends were declared and paid on December 31, 1994.

Required:

(a) Adjust the financial statements presented in Exhibit 1 to reflect Brazilian monetary correction procedures.

(b) What characteristics make the adjusted financial statements more or less informative than the unadjusted statements?

E.12.3   Brazilian Monetary Correction as a Measure of Purchasing Power Gains and Losses

Refer to Exhibits 12–1 and 12–2 in the chapter. It has been said that ''Brazilian monetary correction measures the loss in purchasing power on the initial net monetary asset position and the initial inventory position of a company.''

Required:

    (a) Use Exhibit 12–1 to explain this statement with respect to the net monetary asset position.

    (b) Use Exhibit 12–2 in respect to initial inventory position.

E.12.4   Complete Constant Currency Financial Statements

Companhia Zerio S.A., a Brazilian retailer, is a public company that issues financial statements that are fully adjusted for the effects of general inflation (see Exhibits 1 and 2). Since inflation during the most recent year was only 20 percent, the analyst desires to convert the unit of measurement to nominal currency.

Additional Information

    • The appropriate index of price levels was 100 on January 1, 1994, and 120 on December 31, 1994. The index increased evenly throughout the year. For example, at midyear, the index stood at 110.

    • Dividends were declared and paid on December 31, 1993 and 1994.

    • Inventory is measured at FIFO cost. Purchases of inventory occurred evenly throughout each year.

    • Additional plant and equipment were acquired on January 1, 1994. Plant and equipment are depreciated at a rate of 10 percent of historical cost.

Required:

    (a) Prepare an income statement and comparative balance sheets in nominal units of currency for Companhia Zerio.

    (b) The purchasing power adjustment for 1994 is a function of net monetary assets on January 1, 1994, and changes in net monetary assets that took place during 1994. Prepare a schedule that calculates the purchasing power adjustment for 1994. Compare the calculation of the purchasing power adjustment to the ''monetary correction'' under Brazil's system of monetary correction.

    (c) What characteristics make the nominal currency financial statements more or less desirable for financial analysis than the unadjusted statements?

EXHIBIT 1

COMPANHIA ZERIO S.A.
Comparative Balance Sheets
As of December 31, 1994 and 1995

	12/31/94	*12/31/95*
Cash	120.00	415.00
Accounts receivable	240.00	300.00
Inventory	240.00	252.00
Plant and equipment	1,200.00	1,440.00
Accumulated depreciation	(240.00)	(120.00)
	1,560.00	2,287.00
Accounts payable	180.00	200.00
Bonds payable	360.00	300.00
Paid-in capital	540.00	540.00
Retained earnings	480.00	1,247.00
	1,560.00	2,287.00

EXHIBIT 2

COMPANHIA ZERIO S.A.
Comparative Income Statements
Years Ended December 31, 1994 and 1995

	1994	*1995*
Revenues	2,160.00	2,181.82
Cost of goods sold	1,008.00	926.18
Selling & administrative	324.00	327.27
Depreciation	120.00	144.00
Interest	36.00	32.73
Operating income	672.00	751.64
Purchasing power adjustment	450.00	260.36
Net income	1,122.00	1,012.00
Less: dividends	200.00	245.00
Change in retained earnings	922.00	767.00

E.12.5   Interpreting the Accounting Disclosures of Cruzeiro do Sul S.A.

Refer to Cruzeiro do Sul's financial statements and accompanying notes in Exhibit 12–3 in the chapter.

Required:

(a) In the opening paragraph of the selected notes, it is stated that ''the Company is presenting only the 'Fully Indexed Financial Statement' because the net loss and the shareholders' equity are the same as those determined in the Financial Statements Per Corporate Law [i.e., the Brazilian system of monetary correction].'' How can it be that the two systems of adjusting for the effects of inflation yield the same net income and shareholders' equity?

(b) In the property and equipment schedule, referring to the B-727/100 aircraft:

  (1) The monetarily corrected cost of B-727/100 aircraft is the same as of 12/31/90 and 12/31/91. What is the likely explanation for this?

  (2) Do you think the ratio of accumulated depreciation to monetarily corrected cost of the B-727/100 is more or less informative than would be the same ratio calculated for a company reporting under U.S. accounting principles?

(c) Compare the measurement of current liabilities to the measurement of revenues. How is each measured?

(d) The concluding paragraphs of the property and equipment note describe a ''special monetary correction.''

  (1) What appears to be the purpose of this monetary correction, and what is its effects on the financial statements presented?

  (2) How will it affect financial statements of future years?

(e) (1) Why is it *not* possible to determine the rate of inflation recognized for 1991 in the financial statements of Cruzeiro do Sul?

  (2) How could it be determined, and would it be useful in an evaluation of Cruzeiro do Sul's financial performance for 1991?

(f) Explain how the following income statement items were measured for 1990 and 1991:

  (1) Gains (losses) on assets and liabilities in foreign currency.

  (2) Adjustments of assets and liabilities to present value.

  (3) Gains (losses) on noninterest monetary items.

E.12.6   Brazilian Consolidation Policy

In the United States, *SFAS No. 94* mandates the consolidation of all majority-owned subsidiaries. The apparent purpose of the statement is to eliminate certain "cosmetic" manipulations of financial statements by firms with relatively large unconsolidated subsidiaries. These manipulations generally have their greatest effect when the subsidiary is highly levered (e.g., the subsidiary was set up to perform banking or insurance-type services).

Brazilian accounting standards—and those of other countries such as Japan—are not as rigid in this respect. In Brazil, a company is not required to consolidate majority-owned subsidiaries whose financial statement structure is significantly dissimilar from the parent. Consolidated results in this case are presumed to be misleading.

The purpose of this exercise is to illustrate the systematic differences caused by varying consolidation policies. Consider the case of Companhia ABC, a diversified manufacturer of coffee, tobacco, and other consumer products. ABC is also the sole owner of a finance company (XYZ Finance) that it established several years ago. ABC accounts for its investment in XYZ using the equity method. Exhibit 1 presents condensed, side-by-side financial statements for the parent and its unconsolidated subsidiary.

EXHIBIT 1

COMPANHIA ABC
Side-by-Side Financial Statements
With Wholly Owned Subsidiary, XYZ

	ABC	*XYZ*
Current assets	100	20
Investment in XYZ	30	—
Other assets*	200	290
Total assets	330	310
Current liabilities	90	30
Long-term liabilities*	120	250
Paid-in capital	35	10
Retained earnings	85	20
	330	310
Revenues†	100	30
Operating expenses	50	6
Interest expense†	10	20
Equity in earnings of XYZ	3	—
Net income before taxes	43	4
Income tax expense	10	1
Net income	33	3
Dividends	15	2
Change in retained earnings	18	1

*Includes intercompany loan from XYZ to ABC of 20.
†Includes intercompany interest revenue/expense of 2.

Required:

    (a) Prepare statements for ABC that include the results of XYZ on a consolidated basis.

    (b) Compare the following financial statement amounts as originally presented and on a consolidated basis: total assets, total liabilities, total shareholders' equity, retained earnings, net income. Identify any systematic relationships between these amounts.

    (c) Compute the following ratios for ABC both with data as originally reported and using consolidated data:

        (1) Return on equity.

        (2) Unlevered ROA.

        (3) Capital structure leverage.

        (4) Common earnings leverage.

        (5) Unlevered profit margin.

        (6) Asset turnover.

        (7) Interest coverage.

        (8) Current ratio.

    (d) Identify any systematic relationships between these amounts. For example, is it possible to conclude that profit margin on a consolidated basis will always be less than profit margin as originally reported using the equity method? Assume a marginal tax rate for both companies of 25 percent.

CASES

CASE 12.1
REVENUE RECOGNITION FOR LESSORS

Alarmas Avançados S.A.

Rick Guzman, vice president of the investment banking firm that underwrote Alarmas Avançados' initial public offering of common stock in Brazil, knew he had a big problem. Aggressive accounting policies used by Alarmas Avançados for revenue recognition may now be coming home to roost. Alarmas Avançados has asked Rick's firm to explore ways of gaining access to U.S. capital markets. If Alarmas Avançados filed an initial registration statement with the U.S. SEC, would there be a significant downward restatement of net income in the reconciliation to U.S. GAAP?

Before attending a meeting with colleagues to discuss the situation, Rick decided to review what he knew about Alarmas Avançados and its accounting policies. Exhibit 1 presents the inflation-adjusted income statements and balance sheets of Alarmas Avançados for the two most recent years.

Company Background.   Alarmas Avançados began as a central station alarm-monitoring service 10 years ago with a handful of small accounts. The service provided was quite simple in concept and has remained relatively unchanged. Alarmas Avançados installs a monitoring system at a client's home, office, or store, and connects it to the central monitoring station. Upon a signal from the local system, which contains various types of electronic sensing devices, personnel at the central station would notify the proper authorities: local fire department or police, company officials, etc.

Alarmas Avançados grew rapidly through a combination of (1) cost-reducing efforts in central station monitoring systems relative to its competition in Brazil, (2) aggressive marketing toward small businesses and chain stores with geographically dispersed retail outlets, and (3) acquisition of other small competitors. By the date of the public stock offering, Alarmas Avançados' annual revenues were 14.5 million Brazilian reais (R$)[1] on 12,000 installations. Alarmas Avançados' own inflation-adjusted forecast of next year's sales is approximately R$23 million— a growth of 59 percent!

Although many of Alarmas Avançados' customers contracted for one or a small number of installations, chain stores accounted for a significant portion of sales. The three largest customer accounts have over 1,700 Alarmas Avançados systems installed in their retail outlets.

Approximately 80 percent of Alarmas Avançados' installations were in the form of leases. A customer (lessee) might be charged a R$1,000 installation fee payable upon contract signing and R$100 a month for the next 60 months. (The monthly rental would be pegged to the consumer price index.) All leases contained a bargain renewal option that allowed the customer to extend the lease term for an additional 36 months at a 10 percent reduction in monthly payments. The leased equipment is estimated to have an economic life of 10 years and would normally cost Alarmas Avançados R$1,200. Out-of-pocket installation costs, primarily labor, were R$300.

Lease Accounting.   In Brazil, lease transactions are generally accounted for as operating leases. That is, a lessor would recognize revenue over the life of the lease term as rental payments accrue to the lessor. Public companies in the leasing business are required, however, to account for the substance of lease transactions as opposed to their form. In general, for these lessors, classification is either as a capital lease or as an operating lease.

Alarmas Avançados interprets their current lease arrangements to qualify for capital lease accounting, principally because lease terms are expected to extend for substantially all of the

---

[1]The Brazilian government replaced the cruzeiro real (Cr$) with the real (the real plan), effective July 1, 1994. The conversion was made at R$1:Cr$2,750. Also under the real plan, R$1 was equal to US$1 on July 1, 1994. By December 31, 1994, the real had devalued about 15 percent against the dollar. All currency amounts in the case are expressed in terms of constant reais as of December 31, 1994.

EXHIBIT 1

ALARMAS AVANÇADOS, S.A.
Balance Sheets
At December 31, 1994 and 1993
(in thousands)

Assets	1994	1993
Cash and cash investments	R$ 390	R$1,047
Sales-type lease receivables	10,206	5,592
Accounts receivable	790	465
Inventory	888	375
Property and equipment, net of accumulated depreciation	1,635	882
Purchased rights to customer lists, net of accumulated amortization	2,424	1,406
Other assets	66	11
	R$16,399	R$9,778
Liabilities		
Accounts payable	R$ 849	R$ 342
Accrued wages, taxes and other	596	202
Notes payable	11,588	6,529
Total liabilities	R$13,033	R$7,073
Shareholders' Equity		
Common stock	R$ 1,430	R$1,430
Retained earnings	1,936	1,274
Total shareholders' equity	3,366	2,704
	R$16,399	R$9,777

Statements of Income
For the Years Ended December 31, 1994 and 1995
(in thousands)

	1994	1993
Revenues		
Equipment sales—lease	R$5,640	R$2,225
Equipment sales—direct	762	146
Service and monitoring fees	1,378	223
Interest earned on leases	1,011	345
Other	21	11
	R$8,812	R$2,950
Expenses		
Cost of equipment sold	R$1,612	R$ 591
Salaries and wages	2,551	694
Administrative and general	2,219	762
Interest	1,182	329
Depreciation	181	128
Amortization of purchased rights to customer lists	406	49
	R$8,151	R$2,553
Net income	R$ 661	R$ 397

EXHIBIT 1 (continued)

Notes to Financial Statements
(All amounts have been monetarily corrected to 12/31/94)

1. Sales-Type Lease Receivables
Sales-type lease receivables include equipment sales, service and monitoring and are generally due in monthly installments over a term of five years with a bargain renewal option for an additional three years. The bargain renewal option allows the lessee the option to renew at 10% less than the rental rate in effect at the expiration of the initial lease term. The Company believes there is reasonable assurance that its customers will exercise the bargain renewal option based upon the scheduled rent reduction, an industry average customer life of 10 to 13 years, and the ''penalty'' the customer would incur in the form of an installation fee to change to different equipment.

Interest ranging from 10% to 15% has been imputed on lease receivables based on an amount which normally approximates 2% in excess of the prime lending rate at the inception of the respective leases. Management believes such rates approximate the implicit interest rate based on the creditworthiness of the lessees. In each of the next five years approximately R$3,700,000 of the total minimum lease payments receivable matures with the balance of R$4,600,000 due after five years.

2. Operating Leases
Rentals and monitoring fees relating to operating leases, generally related to companies acquired, are recorded as billed on a monthly basis. If new lease terms are negotiated with customers of companies acquired, the new lease contract is converted from operating to capital lease status.

3. Income Recognition
Income is recognized on equipment sales when the equipment is delivered and installed. Income from service and monitoring is recognized as income on a straight-line basis over the term of the contract. Interest income on sales-type lease receivables is recognized over the lease term so as to produce a constant period rate of return on the sales-type lease receivables balance.

4. Property and Equipment
Property and equipment are stated on the basis of cost, net of accumulated depreciation computed on the straight-line method over the estimated useful lives. The cost, less related accumulated depreciation, of purchased alarm systems under contracts converted to sales-type leases is charged to cost of equipment sold at the date of conversion. The cost of systems remaining under operating leases is depreciated on the straight-line method over the estimated useful life.

5. Purchased Rights to Customer Lists
The excess of cost of purchased alarm system companies over the fair value of the tangible assets acquired is ascribed to the unexpired portion of lease contracts and the customer lists. Such costs are amortized over ninety-six months.

6. Notes Payable

	1994	*1993*
Lease loans, collateralized by certain sales-type leases, payable in monthly installments of R$29,760, plus interest at rates ranging from 10% to 20%, with maturities from September 1995 to December 2000	R$ 2,383,338	R$1,488,624
Acquisition loans, payable to former owners of purchased companies	2,358,248	1,066,652
Term loans collateralized by substantially all assets acquired in certain acquisitions, with interest at prime plus 2.5%	1,100,000	1,500,000
Line of credit for R$6,000,000 (R$3,000,000 in 1993) expiring in April 1995, collateralized by certain lease receivables and equipment at rates ranging from prime plus 2.5% to prime plus 5%	4,811,714	565,299
Other notes payable	934,332	1,908,432
	R$11,587,632	R$6,529,007

EXHIBIT 2
Illustration of Financial Statement Impact of Lease Accounting Method for One Hypothetical Lease*

	Operating	*Capital*
Income Statement for 1994		
Revenue		
Installation fee	R$1,000	R$1,000
Rental income	1,200	
Equipment sales—lease (equal to the present value of the lease payments)†		6,047
Interest earned on leases†		631
Total revenues	2,200	7,678
Cost of equipment sold		
Installation expense	300	300
Cost of equipment on capital lease‡		1,200
Depreciation§	120	
Impact on net income	R$1,780	R$6,178
Balance Sheet, 12/31/94		
Assets		
Cash	R$1,900	R$1,900
Equipment for lease or sale	(120)	(1,200)
Lease payments receivable		5,478
Impact on assets	R$1,780	R$6,178
Equities		
Retained earnings	R$1,780	R$6,178

*Lease contract assumed to have been signed on January 1, 1994, and monthly rental payments of R$100 begin on that date.
†Discount rate used for calculating present values was 1% per month.
‡Cost of equipment on lease has averaged approximately 20% of the present value of lease receivables.
§Amortization of R$1,200 for the first of 10-year economic life of the asset.

leased asset's estimated useful life. The attractiveness of the bargain renewal option in combination with the inconvenience and cost of switching systems makes the effective term of the lease a full eight years—80 percent of the estimated economic life of the installed system. In management's view, Alarmas Avançados is simultaneouly acting as an equipment dealer and performing the financing function—spreading the cost of the installation to the customer over 96 months.

Exhibit 2 summarizes the financial statement impact of the two prevalent methods of lease accounting for the lessor in the first full year of a lease contract: operating lease and capital lease. The currency amounts are based on the simple example described above. Under operating lease accounting, the lessor recognizes revenue in accordance with the schedule of lease payments. For the example above, that would mean that Alarmas Avançados would recognize R$1,000[2] of revenue in the first month, R$100 per month for the next 59 months, and R$90 per

---

[2]This represents one of many operating lease possibilities. For example, another alternative consistent with the operating lease method is to amortize the R$1,000 installation fee over the lease term.

month for the last 36 months (assuming that the lessee exercises the renewal option). Under Alarmas Avançados' method of accounting—capital lease treatment—substantially higher revenue is recognized in the first year of the lease contract. It therefore follows that substantially lower revenue (consisting only of interest earned on the outstanding balance of the lease receivable) is recognized in subsequent years.

Rick Guzman is concerned that Alarmas Avançados' lease accounting policies may not be in accordance with U.S. GAAP, which provides much more specific guidance in this area. *Statement of Financial Accounting Standards No. 13* (*SFAS 13*) is the principal source of U.S. GAAP as it relates to lease accounting. In accounting for the lease by the lessor, *SFAS 13* first makes the distinction between operating and capital leases. Capital leases are further classified into financing and sales-type arrangements.

SFAS 13 provides that if a lease meets any one of the following classification criteria, it is a capital lease:

- a. The lease transfers ownership of the property to the lessee by the end of the lease term.
- b. The lease contains an option to purchase the leased property at a bargain price.
- c. The lease term is equal to or greater than 75 percent of the estimated economic life of the leased property.
- d. The present value of rental and other minimum lease payments equals or exceeds 90 percent of the fair value of the leased property less any investment tax credit retained by the lessor.

Rick had only a few minutes left before the meeting and decided to use his time in trying to determine how Alarmas Avançados' financial statements would have appeared had the operating lease method been used in accounting for all leased systems.

Required:

The only data you need to answer the first two questions are from the hypothetical lease contract described in the case and in Exhibit 2. You do not need any information from the financial statements and notes that are contained in Exhibit 1.

- (a) Provide the first two months' journal entries for Alarmas Avançados, assuming the lease is accounted for as a sales-type lease. Although Exhibit 1 indicates that Alarmas Avançados' fiscal year is the calendar year, consider the fiscal year to end on the last day of February for the purpose of this question.

- (b) Prepare the journal entries for Alarmas Avançados, assuming that the lease is accounted for as an operating lease. Although Exhibit 1 indicates that Alarmas Avançados' fiscal year is the calendar year, consider the fiscal year to end on the last day of February for the purpose of this question.

- (c) Restate Alarmas Avançados' 1994 income statement and balance sheet under the assumption that all security system leases should have been accounted for as operating leases.

- (d) Evaluate Alarmas Avançados' method of accounting for its security system leases.

CASE 12.2
FINANCIAL ANALYSIS AND INFLATION

Aracruz Celulose S.A.

Aracruz Celulose S.A., headquartered in Rio de Janeiro with its production operations in the coastal state of Espirito Santo, is the world's largest producer of bleached eucalyptus kraft market pulp. Eucalyptus pulp is a high-quality hardwood pulp used by paper manufacturers to produce a wide range of products, including premium tissue, printing and writing papers, liquid packaging board, and specialty papers. Aracruz is the only Brazilian company listed on the New York Stock Exchange. The periodical *Global Finance* in 1994 designated Aracruz as one of approximately 40 ''world-class companies,'' selected for its global competitiveness and quality of management.

Exhibits 1, 2, and 3 contain comparative six-month financial statements for Aracruz. These financial statements, prepared on three different bases of accounting, were simultaneously released in one filing to the U.S. Securities and Exchange Commission:

- U.S. GAAP, constant R$ as of June 30, 1994. Effective July 1, 1994 the denomination of the Brazilian currency was changed from the cruzeiro real—(CR$)—to the real—(R$)—at the rate of CR$2,750 = R$1 = US$1.
- U.S. GAAP, nominal Brazilian currency units translated into U.S. dollars. As of June 30, 1994, approximately 63 percent of Aracruz's long-term debt (including current maturities) was denominated in currencies other than the real.
- Brazilian GAAP, constant purchasing power as of June 30, 1994. These data were reclassified by the case writer to conform as closely as possible with the presentation under U.S. GAAP.

The notes and other documents accompanying the financial statements contained the following information:

- The current portion of 1993 income tax expense relates principally to Aracruz's election to pay in advance at a reduced rate, rather than over a period of up to 20 years, the tax on the entire balance of inflationary income resulting from the partial price-level restatement of the Company's statutory financial statements.
- Worldwide pulp prices have been very volatile in recent years. On December 31, 1993, the price of Brazilian eucalyptus pulp delivered in the United States had declined to U.S. $410 per ton from the 1992 high of U.S. $550. In the first six months of 1994, Aracruz's shipments increased 4 percent, and prices of pulp have been recovering.
- The response of Aracruz to price declines in its product has been to aggressively seek ways to cut costs. The workforce has been trimmed by approximately 20 percent, and new pulp production processes have been implemented.

This case was prepared by Thomas I. Selling, American Graduate School of International Management. Copyright © 1995 by Thomas I. Selling. All rights reserved.

Exhibit 1

ARACRUZ CELULOSE S.A.
Condensed Consolidated Balance Sheets
(millions of currency units)
(Brazilian reals expressed in constant currency of June 30, 1994)

	U.S. GAAP				Brazilian GAAP
	R$	R$	US$	US$	R$
Assets	*12/31/93*	*6/30/94*	*12/31/94*	*6/30/94*	*6/30/94*
Current Assets					
Cash and cash equivalents	38.5	182.3	37.8	182.3	150.4
Accounts receivable	50.6	64.0	49.7	63.9	4.2
Short-term investments	3.2	3.6	3.2	3.6	
Inventories	62.9	62.6	69.3	70.1	49.1
Bank deposits for payment of supplier invoices	68.4	98.9	67.2	98.9	
Prepaid expenses, deposits and other current assets	5.6	15.0	6.4	16.5	12.0
Total	229.1	426.5	233.5	435.4	215.7
PP&E, net	1,986.1	1,932.9	1,906.7	1,874.1	1,838.3
Other Assets					
Deposits for tax assessments	46.1	17.7	45.2	17.7	
Investments in subsidiaries					70.4
PP&E held for sale, less allowance for loss	0.8	0.8	0.5	0.5	
Deferred income taxes, net			38.6	36.3	
Other	9.3	9.4	4.5	6.0	56.8
Total	56.2	27.9	88.8	60.5	127.2
Total	2,271.4	2,387.3	2,229.1	2,369.9	2,181.2
Liabilities and Stockholders' Equity					
Current Liabilities					
Suppliers	14.8	18.0	14.5	18.0	1.1
Payroll and related charges	8.3	9.3	8.1	9.3	9.2
Advance from customer	7.0	2.1	6.8	2.1	31.3
Short-term debt & current portion of long-term debt	477.0	577.6	468.2	577.6	348.6
Finance charges	27.7	29.3	27.2	29.3	
Other accruals and other liabilities	3.1	2.3	3.0	2.3	2.6
Total	537.9	638.6	527.9	638.6	392.8
Long-Term Liabilities					
Long-term debt	435.6	488.0	427.6	488.0	544.2
Deferred income taxes, net	38.9	64.7	44.7	16.7	
Tax assessments	45.5	16.7	—	—	16.7
Suppliers and other	8.6	8.4	7.6	7.6	11.2
Total	528.6	577.8	479.9	512.3	572.0
Stockholders' Equity					
Capital stock	727.1	727.1	683.0	683.0	926.1
Appropriated retained earnings	361.7	361.8	363.8	363.8	
Capital reserve	1.3	1.3	—	—	1.6
Retained earnings	115.1	81.0	174.7	172.4	288.9
Treasury stock	(0.2)	(0.2)	(0.1)	(0.1)	(0.1)
Total	1,205.0	1,170.9	1,221.3	1,219.1	1,216.5
Total	2,271.4	2,387.3	2,229.1	2,369.9	2,181.2

EXHIBIT 2

ARACRUZ CELULOSE S.A.
Condensed Consolidated Income Statements
For the Six-Month Periods Ended 12/31 and 6/30
(millions of currency units)
(Brazilian reals expressed in constant currency of June 30, 1994)

	U.S. GAAP				Brazilian GAAP	
	R$	R$	US$	US$	R$	R$
	6/30/93	*6/30/94*	*6/30/93*	*6/30/94*	*6/30/93*	*6/30/94*
Operating Revenues						
Sales of eucalyptus pulp						
Domestic	23.4	19.0	23.2	19.1	—	—
Export	154.1	196.7	154.2	194.0	—	—
Total	177.6	215.7	177.4	213.1	—	—
Value-added tax and other sales						
deductions	(11.5)	(11.0)	(11.1)	(10.7)	—	—
Net operating revenues	166.0	204.6	166.3	202.4	139.1	196.1
Operating Costs and Expenses						
Cost of sales	134.4	138.4	128.8	135.7	122.5	147.6
Selling	13.7	15.5	13.2	14.5	3.9	6.2
Administrative	28.5	28.6	23.3	23.1	31.6	26.4
Other, net	4.4	(6.1)	3.7	(10.4)		
Total	181.0	176.4	169.0	162.9	158.1	180.3
Operating income (loss)	(14.9)	28.3	(2.7)	39.5	(19.0)	15.9
Other Income (Expenses)						
Financial income	30.1	111.9	15.7	29.4	19.5	28.1
Financial expense	(469.8)	(521.5)	(41.9)	(46.4)	(18.7)	(66.7)
Foreign exchange loss, net	(755.7)	(1,280.0)	—	—	—	—
Purchasing power gain, net	1,172.7	1,654.5	—	—	—	—
Gains (losses) from currency						
remeasurement and transactions,						
net	—	—	2.4	(18.2)		
Other	(8.9)	1.0	(9.4)	(0.7)	(12.3)	1.6
Total	(31.6)	(34.1)	(33.2)	(36.0)	(11.5)	(37.0)
Income (loss) before income taxes	(46.5)	(5.9)	(35.8)	3.5	(30.5)	(21.1)
Income Taxes						
Current	11.6	(0.0)	11.2	(0.0)	(1.2)	(0.0)
Deferred	(38.5)	23.9	(23.4)	1.4	(39.0)	0.0
Total	(26.9)	23.9	(12.2)	1.4	(40.2)	0.0
Net income (loss)	(19.6)	(29.8)	(23.6)	2.1	9.7	(21.1)

EXHIBIT 3

ARACRUZ CELULOSE S.A.
Condensed Consolidated Statements of Cash Flows
For the Six-Month Periods Ended 12/31 and 6/30
(millions of currency units)
(Brazilian reals expressed in constant currency of June 30, 1994)

	U.S. GAAP			
	R$	**R$**	**US$**	**US$**
	6/30/93	*6/30/94*	*6/30/93*	*6/30/94*
Cash Flows from Operating Activities				
Net loss	(19.6)	(29.8)	(23.6)	2.1
Noncash items included in loss	44.2	117.2	42.1	90.3
Changes in operating working capital	(37.4)	(52.8)	(19.7)	(52.6)
Net cash provided by (used in) operating activities	(12.8)	34.5	(1.2)	39.8
Cash Flows from Investing Activities				
Additions to property, plant and equipment	(30.6)	(37.1)	(30.6)	(37.6)
Cash Flows from Financing Activities				
Short-term debt, net				
Related party	11.2	—	11.1	—
Other	(21.4)	115.4	(22.9)	117.2
Long-term Debt				
Issuances				
Related party	45.3	17.9	45.7	17.8
Other	1.7	142.7	1.3	141.1
Repayments				
Related parties	(31.1)	(50.9)	(31.2)	(50.6)
Other	(56.1)	(72.0)	(56.0)	(71.4)
Dividends	(5.1)	(4.2)	(4.6)	(4.3)
Net cash provided by (used in) financing activities	(55.5)	148.9	(56.6)	149.8
Effects of exchange variations on cash and cash equivalents of foreign subsidiaries	0.9	(2.5)	(9.7)	(7.4)
Increase (decrease) in cash and equivalents	(98.0)	143.9	(98.1)	144.6
Cash and equivalents, beginning of period	127.9	38.5	127.6	37.8
Cash and equivalents, end of period	29.8	182.3	29.5	182.3

Required:

(a) Identify material differences in the three sets of financial statements. To the extent permitted by the data, explain the differences.

(b) Evaluate the profitability, liquidity, and long-term solvency risk of Aracruz Celulose.

ANNUAL REPORT ANALYSIS

Varig

An interesting and important challenge for students of international financial reporting is to study the published annual reports of various companies from different countries. Your instructor will provide you with a recent copy of the Varig, a Brazilian airline, annual report. To facilitate your delving into this annual report, undertake the following endeavors.

Required:

    (a) List the key differences between the Varig annual report and what you would expect to see for a U.S. company like United Airlines.

    (b) Calculate the following ratios for Varig taking care to note the assumptions you found necessary to make and where you found the appropriate pieces of data in the annual report.

(1) Current ratio $= \dfrac{\text{Total current assets}}{\text{Total current liabilities}}$

(2) Quick ratio $= \dfrac{\text{Cash + Marketable securities + Accounts receivable}}{\text{Total current liabilities}}$

(3) Operating cash flow to current liabilities $= \dfrac{\text{Operating cash flow}}{\text{Average total current liabilities}}$

(4) Debt to equity ratio $= \dfrac{\text{Long-term debt}}{\text{Owners' equity}}$

(5) Debt to total capitalization ratio $= \dfrac{\text{Long-term debt}}{\text{Long-term debt + Owners' equity}}$

(6) Interest coverage ratio $= \dfrac{\text{Net income before interest \& income taxes}}{\text{Interest expense}}$

(7) Operating cash flow to interest charges $= \dfrac{\text{Operating cash flow}}{\text{Interest expense}}$

(8) Operating cash flow to total liabilities $= \dfrac{\text{Operating cash flow}}{\text{Average total liabilities}}$

(9) Receivables turnover ratio $= \dfrac{\text{Net sales}}{\text{Average accounts receivable}}$

(10) Inventory turnover $= \dfrac{\text{Cost of goods sold}}{\text{Average inventory}}$

(11) Asset turnover $= \dfrac{\text{Net sales}}{\text{Average total assets}}$

(12) Average collection period ratio $= \dfrac{\text{365 Days}}{\text{Receivables turnover ratio}}$

(13) Average number of days' inventory on hand ratio $= \dfrac{\text{365 Days}}{\text{Inventory turnover ratio}}$

(14) Return on assets (ROA)   = $\dfrac{\text{Net income}}{\text{Average total assets}}$

     OR   =   ROS × Asset turnover

(15) Return on equity (ROE)   = $\dfrac{\text{Net income}}{\text{Average total owners' equity}}$

     OR   =   ROA × Financial leverage

(16) Return on sales (ROS)   = $\dfrac{\text{Net income}}{\text{Net sales}}$

(17) Financial leverage   = $\dfrac{\text{Average liabilities} + \text{Average owners' equity}}{\text{Average owners' equity}}$

(18) Basic earnings per share   = $\dfrac{\text{NI applicable to common shareholders}}{\text{Weighted average common shares}}$

(19) Cash dividend yield   = $\dfrac{\text{Cash dividend per common share}}{\text{Market price per common share}}$

(20) Cash dividend payout   = $\dfrac{\text{Total cash dividend to common shareholders}}{\text{Net income}}$

(c) What do you conclude about the availability of the appropriate data in the annual report for calculating these ratios?

(d) What does this financial analysis tell you about Varig?

(e) What analytical metrics did Varig choose to report for itself? What do those choices say about the message the company is striving to tell and the audience it is addressing?

CHAPTER 13

Republic of South Korea

[In contrast to Great Britain and the United States but similar to Japan] Korea has a credit-based financial system with heavy involvement by the government or financial institutions.[1]

Corporate accounting does not give a clear picture of a [Korean chaebol's financial] position.[2]

Introduction

The Republic of South Korea, having emerged at the end of the 1980s as one of the fastest growing economies in the world, is entering a new stage of maturity that promises to transform the way in which the country does business. Historically, South Korea's prosperity has depended on exports and relatively low wages. Koreans have recently seen foreign demand for their products sag while domestic consumption rose, the result of unprecedented levels of wealth among the country's working and middle classes. Leading Korean multinationals, once content to provide low-cost products based on foreign technology and designs, are attempting to increase investments in research and development to develop their own reservoir of technical expertise and record of innovation. North American protectionism and steep increases in Korean labor costs have prompted Korean manufacturers to begin to move some of their operations overseas to ensure access to the North American market and to tap the less expensive labor pools available in eastern Europe and less developed areas of Asia.

The maturation of the Korean economy, as well as the nation's emergence into democracy, is certain to place new, more sophisticated demands on its financial markets

---

[1]C. Nobes, ''Accounting for Differences in the Far East: Are They Inscrutable?'' *Management Accounting* (London), October 1994, p. 36.

[2]''Down from the Mountains,'' *The Banker,* April 1990, p. 61.

and the role that financial reporting plays in those markets. Indeed, Korean financial reporting practices and disclosure requirements have remained considerably less developed than those in the Western economies, largely because of an underdeveloped securities market and the government taking a leading role in capital allocation by formally and informally directing bank loans to selected enterprises. In addition, foreign direct investment in Korea has historically been severely restricted: prior to January 1992, foreign investors were not allowed to trade directly on the Seoul stock exchange and even in 1995 they were allowed to do so to only a limited extent. Even more of a hindrance is the belief among corporate managers and bankers from around the world that Korea is

- The most nationalistic country in Asia.
- One of the most bureaucratic countries in Asia.
- An economy dominated by cartels and state-owned companies.
- The most protectionist nation in Asia.
- The Asian country with the highest potential for labor unrest.
- The country with the higher potential for social unrest than China.[3]

As Korean multinationals seek to develop new overseas markets and to tap new sources of financial capital and as the Korean government attempts to liberalize the nation's financial markets, the pressures for more detailed financial disclosure will undoubtedly guide Korean financial reporting into a new level of sophistication.

Environmental Factors

Cultural Environment

A variety of religions and world views exerts an influence on the South Korean people (20 percent of whom are Christian), making the country a complex mix of old and new that resists convenient generalization. Korean culture has been most deeply affected by the Confucian ethic, which became the officially sanctioned state philosophy in the late 14th century and has been dominant since. With its emphasis on hierarchy, conformity, and social cohesiveness, Confucianism teaches Koreans to depend on social and communal institutions, especially the family, for their sense of identity. This attitude has been labeled a *frame* orientation (as opposed to Americans' *attribute* orientation), in which the self is conceived primarily in terms of affiliations and loyalties rather than personal achievements and character traits. Such a frame is manifested by Korea's score of 18, one of the lowest recorded, on Hofstede's individualism (IDV) dimension. Not even Japan, traditionally viewed as one of the most collectivist societies, scored as low as Korea on the IDV dimension.

The sense of group membership, of who is an ''insider'' and who is an ''outsider,'' looms significantly in Korean culture and takes precedence over more abstract values

---

[3]P. Abrahams, ''Uphill Battle for Investors,'' *Financial Times,* June 23, 1994, p. III.

such as fairness. Outsiders may gradually earn only a small measure of acceptance, with proper introductions often being required for what an American would consider a casual interaction. Within the group, relationships (ideally, at least) are conducted on the basis of a scrupulous and finely honed sense of rank and a mutual trust that is less a sign of personal regard than a cultural norm. (This trust, of course, may be forfeited by serious misbehavior.) Each member is expected to subordinate his or her desires to the collective welfare of the group and the preservation of harmonious cooperation. The authority of the leader, who is usually something of a father figure in Korea, is not to be questioned (Koreans scored a relatively high 60 on the power-distance dimension); Koreans, unlike Americans, tend to place the prerogative of rulers above the desires and interests of the ruled. This Korean ideal of group consciousness not only permeates organizations and institutions within Korean society, including corporations, but also provides a model for society as a whole.

Social reality is inevitably more complex and ambiguous, however, than social ideology. The Confucian vision of harmony (a notion consistent with Korea's relatively high scores in uncertainty avoidance of 85 and long-term orientation of 75) and hierarchical order is being seriously challenged in Korea by the imperatives of capitalism, which generally celebrates individual freedom and views social control as unnecessarily restrictive and counterproductive. Moreover, capitalism sees society and social institutions in rather fluid terms as constantly evolving entities driven by conflicts and tensions. A free market economy, in traditional versions of capitalism, is less a harmonious household than a system of contending and dynamic forces that, given the space to operate properly, stimulates economic growth and provides the opportunity for social mobility.

The ideological tension between traditional Korean values and modern consumer capitalism has been aggravated by the material effects of the country's steep growth rate. Far from fulfilling the Confucian ideal of a harmonious society modeled after the patriarchal family, Korea's rapid industrialization has eroded traditional values and brought in its wake a number of social problems: severe labor unrest, housing shortages caused by urbanization and rampant land speculation, and widespread resentment over the concentration of wealth and the power of big business. Unlike other east Asian peoples, Koreans express anger openly and vociferously rather than masking it behind a facade of formality. After sharp drops in the Korean stock exchange in 1990, for example, gangs of investors—reportedly including middle-aged women—signified their displeasure by smashing furniture in brokerage offices. Strikes often turn violent, as do protests against government repression. While the inevitable dislocations of rapid growth have fueled dissension in Korean society, even its recent material success has caused problems as Koreans struggle to reconcile their newfound wealth with a traditional suspicion of luxury. Regardless of a people's cultural predispositions, the development of a full-fledged industrial economy does not occur without painful dislocations—both economic and ideological—and Korea is proving no exception to the rule.

Korean cultural values affect financial reporting practices and the economic environment in several ways. Confucianism tends to centralize authority in a single father figure or a small ruling elite, a pattern reflected in the pyramidal management structure of the 30 or so business groups (known as ***chaebol***) that dominate the economy. This penchant for autocratic power structures has posed something of a problem as the country struggles to transform itself from an underdeveloped nation with an authoritarian regime and a protected economy into a modern liberal democracy with open markets. Although a democratic constitution was adopted and free elections held in 1987, and the government promised to liberalize the financial markets by 1996, Koreans have found that old authoritarian habits die hard.

Likewise, the promulgation of financial reporting policy is a highly centralized process in Korea. Policy formation and reporting requirements are controlled by two agencies of the national government, the Securities Supervisory Board and the Ministry of Finance. The accounting profession has little influence on the standard-setting process other than assisting the board in formulating particular pronouncements. The Ministry of Finance is responsible for administering Korea's professional accounting examination, granting certificates, and regulating Korean CPAs, but it has delegated the authority to set auditing standards and procedures to the Korean Institute of Certified Public Accountants.

Education is highly valued for its own sake in the Confucian tradition, and Koreans also know that the quality of their training will affect their ability to compete in the world market. As a result, Korea boasts a well-trained workforce and a high rate of literacy. Korean education diverges from Western methods in its centralization—the textbooks and curriculum being dictated by the national government—and its greater emphasis on conformity, discipline, and technical training. In other words, Korean education stresses socialization and preparation for group membership rather than personal growth and development of independent judgment. Innovation, originality, and independence—the values on which British and American accounting professionals pride themselves—are not encouraged in Korea's educational system and may seem presumptuous and unnecessarily risky to a Korean. Individual initiative—and, hence, personal responsibility—takes a back seat to the needs of the group and the desire for consensus.

Westerners must also realize that the concept of accountability occupies a different place in the context of Korean group consciousness. In a homogeneous and tightly knit society in which most organizations are controlled centrally, "the public's right to know" carries considerably less weight than in the relatively open societies of the West. Financial data that are routinely shared with the press and the public in the United States may be considered company property in Korea and held in confidence. Given Koreans' habitual distrust of foreigners and their inexperience with international capital markets, Western investors and analysts seeking financial information from Korean enterprises should expect to meet with a degree of reticence, even suspicion, that may seem unreasonable by the standards to which Westerners are accustomed.

Even the largest, most sophisticated Korean firms release extremely sketchy financial data for overseas consumption, not because they are unaware of the benefits of global publicity but because they are cautious about giving potential weapons to outsiders. Convenience translations of recent annual reports for such companies as Sunkyong and Daewoo often include few or no footnotes even though such notes are required for domestic reporting. Exhibit 13–1, for example, presents the notes from

---

EXHIBIT 13–1

SUNKYONG, LTD.
Financial Notes

For the years ended December 31, 1992 and 1991

1. Summary of Significant Accounting Policies

The company maintains its books of account and prepares its financial statements in conformity with generally accepted financial accounting standards in Korea.

(1) Allowance for doubtful accounts

The losses estimated on the remaining receivables and other assets in a reasonable and objective manner are expensed currently by providing an allowance for doubtful accounts.

(2) Inventories

Inventories are stated at the weighted-average cost.

(3) Investments

Investments in affiliated companies are stated at cost using a moving-average method on an individual security basis.

(4) Tangible fixed assets and depreciation

Tangible fixed assets are stated at acquisition cost or at revaluation amount. The company computes depreciation using the straight-line method over the useful lives of depreciable assets in accordance with the Income Tax Law.

(5) Foreign currency translation

Monetary foreign currency assets and liabilities are translated into Korean won at the current rate of exchange at year-end. Nonmonetary foreign currency assets and liabilities are translated at historical rates. Exchange and translation gains or losses are credited or charged to income currently.

2. Basis of Translating Financial Statements

The financial statements are expressed in won and have been translated into U.S. dollars at the rate of W788.40 and W760.80 against US$1 at December 31, 1992 and 1991, respectively. These translations should not be construed as representations that all amounts shown could be converted into U.S. dollars.

3. Prior Period Adjustment

The Korean accounting standards require that prior period adjustments, which consisted principally of additionally paid or refunded income taxes, should be credited or charged to retained earnings.

4. Pledged Assets

The Company gave its assets as security for bank loans. Details of pledged assets at December 31, 1992, are as follows:

	Millions of Won	Thousands of U.S. Dollars (Note 2)
Cash (in banks)	610	774
Investments	28,874	36,624
Tangible fixed assets	6,674	8,465
	36,158	45,863

5. Investments

Major investments in subsidiaries and affiliated companies at December 31, 1992 and 1991, are summarized as follows:

	Millions of Won		Thousands of U.S. Dollars	
	1992	1991	1992	1991
Yukong Limited	88,881	78,221	112,736	102,814
Sunkyong Warehouse Limited	2,771	1,271	3,514	1,671
Others	57,832	54,198	73,354	71,238
	149,484	133,690	189,604	175,723

EXHIBIT 13–1 (continued)

6. Contingent Liabilities

Details of contingent liabilities at December 31, 1992 and 1991, are as follows:

	Million of Won		Thousands of U.S.Dollars	
	1992	*1991*	*1992*	*1991*
For guarantees of loans from bank to subsidiaries and affiliates	1,154,868	746,560	1,464,825	981,283
For repurchase of notes discounted and endorsed	56,288	64,357	71,395	84,591
	1,211,156	810,917	1,536,220	1,065,874

7. Legal Reserve

The Korean Commercial Code requires the Company to appropriate as a legal reserve an amount equal to at least 10 percent of cash dividends for each accounting period until the reserve equals 50 percent of stated capital. The legal reserve can be used only to reduce a deficit and it can be transferred to paid-in capital.

the English-language translation of the 1992 financial statements of Sunkyong, Ltd., the trading company for a large Korean petrochemical group. Although Sunkyong reports over $1.0 billion in assets and $3.0 billion in sales—making it a major company by anyone's standards—it includes only three brief pages of notes. Note the absence of extensive disclosures pertaining to inventories, liabilities, pensions, and so on. Eventually, the reluctance of Korean multinationals to share detailed data may be overcome as they begin to compete for foreign capital; in the meantime, however, U.S. investors must expect lower levels of disclosure than they are accustomed to in domestic company statements.

Legal and Political Environment

Tax Law—Individual Shareholders. In spite of its autocratic habits and its history of directing capital flows, the Korean government has recognized the importance of developing a vigorous domestic market for Korean equities and, consequently, has structured tax laws to encourage companies to list their shares on the Korea Stock Exchange and to encourage investors to buy them. As evidence of this, the amount of tax an individual shareholder pays on dividend income depends on whether the corporation paying the dividends is listed on the Korean Exchange or not. The basic tax provisions relating to listed versus unlisted companies include these provisions.

- *Listed corporations.* Recipients of cash dividends paid by companies listed on the Korea Stock Exchange are subject to a 20 percent tax rate plus a resident surtax of 7.5 percent of the income tax amount. This tax is withheld by the payor and the dividend income, in the case of minority shareholders, is not included in the calculation of individual income tax on other sources of income, such as wages. Majority shareholders, however, in addition to the withheld amount noted, must include the dividend income along with other forms of income (e.g., wages) in their calculation of personal income tax.

- *Unlisted corporations.* Recipients of cash dividends paid by unlisted companies are subject to a basic rate of 25 percent plus a 7.5 percent surtax of the income tax amount. In addition, all dividends received from unlisted corporations must be included in the calculation of the recipients' income taxes.

As if these rules were not complicated enough, the Korean tax code allows a tax credit amounting to 12 percent of the first W10 million (approximately $12,700) of an individual's dividend income and 6 percent of dividend income in excess of W10 million.[4] Capital gains on the sale of listed shares by a minority shareholder are exempt from taxation, an exemption that reflects the Korean government's desire to encourage small investors to trade on the Korean exchange. Dividends paid to resident corporations are exempt from these rules; they are simply included in the payee corporation's taxable income when declared by the payor corporation. The top individual income tax bracket is 50 percent.

Tax Law—Corporations.   Although book income is not required to equal taxable income in Korea, the former is materially affected by the latter in several respects. Inventory valuation, whether FIFO, LIFO, specific identification, or any other method permitted by tax law, must be the same for both financial and tax reporting. Likewise, tax law prescribes methods of depreciation (straight line or double declining balance in most cases) and useful lives for assets. Most companies claim the same amount of depreciation on both their financial statements and their tax returns, resulting in an overstatement of expenses and an understatement of net income on the financial statements. Moreover, special additional depreciation may be allowed by the tax authorities in the case of certain qualifying assets. Charging such depreciation against current income is acceptable under Korean GAAP and may be included in cost of goods sold or as an extraordinary loss on the financial statements.

Tax law also allows Korean companies to set up various tax-deductible reserves for a variety of purposes, such as overseas market development, export losses, and overseas investment. Although these reserves appear in the retained earnings section of the balance sheet, they do not affect book income, only taxable income. The note shown in Exhibit 13–2, taken from the 1993 financial statements of Daewoo Corporation, provides an illustration of these reserves and a characteristically laconic explanation.

The tax rates on corporate income are 20 percent on taxable income less than W100 million (about $127,000) and 34 percent on income exceeding W100 million. Corporations must also pay the 7.5 percent resident surtax on all corporate tax payments.

---

[4]The basic unit of currency in Korea is the **won,** denoted W, which was trading at about W788 = U.S.$1.00 as of January 1, 1995. This exchange rate has been retained throughout the chapter.

EXHIBIT 13–2

Daewoo Corporation Reserves Disclosures

Appropriated retained earnings as of December 31, 1993 and 1992, are summarized as follows:

	Millions of Won		Thousands of U.S. Dollars	
	1993	*1992*	*1993*	*1992*
Legal reserve	20,221	19,721	25,023	24,404
Reserve for business rationalization	51,470	38,470	63,693	47,606
Reserve for improvement of financial structure	68,709	60,709	85,025	75,126
Reserve for overseas market development	180,451	155,584	223,303	192,531
Reserve for export loss	44,367	36,667	54,903	45,374
Reserve for loss on overseas operations	14,500	16,500	17,943	20,418
Reserve for loss on overseas investments	26,750	21,750	33,102	26,915
Reserve for redemption of long-term debt	—	45,000	—	55,686
	406,468	394,401	502,992	488,060

(a) **Legal Reserve, Reserve for Business Rationalization, and Reserve for Improvement of Financial Structure**

The Korean Commercial Code requires the Company to appropriate as a legal reserve an amount equal to at least 10 percent of cash dividends for each accounting period until the reserve equals 50 percent of stated capital. Under the Tax Exemption and Reduction Control Law, the Company is allowed to make certain deductions from taxable income for overseas operations. The Company is, however, required to appropriate from retained earnings the amount of tax benefit obtained and transfer such amount into reserve for business rationalization. The Financial Control Regulations for listed companies require the company to appropriate as a reserve for improvement of financial structure an amount equal to at least 50 percent of the net gain on sale of property, plant, and equipment and 10 percent of the net earnings for each year until the company's net worth equals 30 percent of total assets. The above reserves may be used to reduce a deficit or they may be transferred to stated capital in connection with a free issue of shares.

(b) **Reserves Set Up for Tax Purposes**

Under the Tax Exemption and Reduction Control Law, the Company is allowed to make certain deductions from taxable income and set up reserves for overseas market development, export loss, loss on overseas operations and overseas investments, by appropriating retained earnings. The unused portion of the reserves is generally added back to taxable income over two to seven years after certain grace periods.

(c) **Voluntary Reserves (Reserve for redemption of long-term debt)**

The voluntary reserve included in the appropriated retained earnings was established by a stockholders' resolution for the purposes of redemption of long-term debt and may be restored to unappropriated retained earnings by a future stockholders' resolution.

Business Environment

Form of Business. The Korean Commercial Code recognizes four kinds of business entities: the limited partnership, the unlimited partnership, the limited liability company (similar to the GmbH in German company law, used for closely held businesses with 50 or fewer stockholders), and the joint stock company (known as the ***chusik hoesa***). A joint stock company may be formed by seven or more investors with a minimum capitalization of W50 million (about $63,500). It must also establish a legal reserve for the protection of shareholders and creditors by annually allocating a sum equal to 10 percent of annual cash dividends to the reserve account until it equals 50 percent of issued capital.

Every joint stock company must retain a statutory auditor who is directly elected by the shareholders and charged with reviewing the company's financial statements and general operations. Although the statutory auditor may not be an officer or director of the company, he or she is not required to be independent or professionally qualified to fill this role. In addition, joint stock companies with more than W500 million (about $635,000) of capital stock outstanding or with W3 billion (about $3.8 million) in total assets must be audited by an independent CPA. Companies listed on the Korea Stock Exchange or remitting dividends or royalties overseas must also have their statements independently audited.

Accounting Profession.   As mentioned, the accounting profession in Korea exerts relatively little influence on the formation of accounting policy. One reason is that it is relatively young; Korea's Certified Public Accountants Law was passed in 1950, and CPA examinations have been administered by the Ministry of Finance only since 1955. The profession remains small, consisting of approximately 2,000 licensed practitioners to serve a country of 44 million (one CPA per 22,000 citizens). The main professional association in Korea is the Korean Institute of Certified Public Accountants, which the Ministry of Finance has authorized to establish auditing guidelines.

Chaebol.   Korea's economy is dominated by 30 large, diversified conglomerates known as *chaebol*, whose ranks include such familiar names as Samsung, Hyundai, and Lucky-Goldstar, as well as lesser-known groups such as Sunkyong and Daewoo. Together, the combined sales of the 30 *chaebol* equal about 75 percent of Korea's GNP. These groups, like the Japanese *keiretsu*, are bound together by intricate and extensive cross-guarantees, cross-subsidies, and cross-holdings of stock among a large number of companies and usually include a general trading company as the flagship member.[5] Exhibit 13–3 provides information concerning some of Korea's larger *chaebol*.

The corporate structure of the *chaebol* tends to follow a brother-sister rather than a parent-subsidiary pattern, an arrangement that raises questions about the usefulness of Anglo-American consolidation rules in the Korean context. The Korean government has issued rules requiring consolidation of majority-owned subsidiaries, but implementation and enforcement of these requirements has been slow. Thus, it is not unusual to encounter annual reports that present financial statements for the flagship company only. For example, Daewoo Corporation's 1993 annual report states that "the financial statements include only the accounts of Daewoo Corporation. Investments in subsidiaries are accounted for on the cost basis." (The equity method is not required under Korean GAAP unless consolidated financial statements are prepared.) Although Sunkyong lists its major investments in subsidiaries and affiliates by company, it does not indicate its percentage of ownership of these enterprises, a common omission in Korean annual reports.

---

[5]L. Nakarmi, "A Flying Leap toward the 21st Century?" *Business Week,* March 20, 1995, pp. 78–80.

EXHIBIT 13–3

South Korea's Largest *Chaebol*

	Sales $bn	Net Profit $m	Total Debt $bn	Owners' Equity $bn
Samsung	35.6	348	27.8	4.4
Hyundai	31.8	445	26.6	6.6
Lucky-Goldstar	22.8	308	21.1	6.1
Daewoo	15.8	217	22.2	6.0
Sunkyong	10.6	90	7.3	1.8
Ssangyung	7.2	159	8.8	2.4
Kia	6.1	100	4.3	1.5
Lotte	4.9	142	8.1	2.5
Korea Explosives	4.0	64	7.1	1.7
Hanjin	3.8	4	7.1	1.3

Source: *The Economist,* June 8, 1991, p. 76.

For all their size and sophistication, the *chaebol* have not yet distinguished themselves for detailed and helpful financial reporting. In fact, their financial statements are notable primarily for their terseness. The 12 pages of notes accompanying Daewoo's 1993 financial statements appear rather adventuresome by Korean standards, although they seem quite reticent to the U.S. or British reader. The most immediate reason for this is the lack of an experienced and sophisticated investing public in Korea, one that needs and demands detailed financial information. Rather than depending on large numbers of individual investors, the *chaebol* have depended largely on government-guided loans from Korea's tightly controlled banking system to meet their capital needs, creating an altogether different sense of corporate accountability and disclosure than one expects from Ford or General Motors. At a time when small businesses were being charged interest rates of 30 percent on borrowed funds, the *chaebol* were receiving rates of around 18 percent. It is no wonder that they have tended to opt for borrowings rather than shareholder funds to fuel their diversification and growth. This phenomenon is attested to by the whopping 3.5 debt-to-owners' equity ratio for the average *chaebol*.[6] As a result of this extensive and favorable borrowing, capital has not been efficiently allocated across the Korean market, and, according to one noted expert, the large and powerful *chaebol* heavy debts ''have made hostages of the commercial banks.''[7]

Collectively, the *chaebol* exert an enormous influence over the Korean economy (too much, in fact, according to many Koreans who want a more equitable distribution of the nation's wealth). Many observers openly wonder whether the *chaebol* and the rest of Korea with them will be able to make the transition from cheap labor, low

---

[6]''Taming the *Chaebol,''* *The Economist,* January 22, 1994, p. 72.

[7]J. Burton, ''Industrial Empires Still Dominate,'' *Financial Times,* November 18, 1992, p. 14.

value-added manufacturing into the more capital-intensive and higher value-added industries in which they will achieve full citizenship in the global marketplace. To do so, they will have to attract enough money to raise their historically low levels of research and development expenditures and capital investment. To attract that money, they will have to broaden their ownership base and eventually will address the information demands of an increasingly sophisticated cadre of international equity investors.[8]

Toward these ends, the Korean government in late 1993 began allowing banks to charge small and large borrowers market interest rates,[9] thus creating the need for banks to become more sophisticated in credit analysis. Moreover, in January 1994, the government announced the agreement to its 1993 request that the *chaebol* prepare to restructure by concentrating on a limited number of core businesses. In particular, as part of its 1993–1997 economic plan, the Korean government requested the 10 largest *chaebol* to identify the three business sectors they wished to remain in (at the time of the request they were operating in an average of 11 sectors), and the next 20 largest *chaebol* were instructed to identify the two sectors they would remain in (a reduction from their average of seven). The government has promised continued favorable state-backed financing to those who reduce the diversity in their business activities and who also reduce the ownership interest of the controlling families. With such a move, the government has sparked a new era for business in Korea that aims to

- Encourage competition and foster small business.
- Wrestle power from the old industrial dynasties and hand it over to professional managers.
- Stem the ''octopus-like growth'' of the *chaebol* into unrelated areas.[10]

Although there is no clear notion of how and exactly when the restructuring will take place, all 30 *chaebol* have named their desired business sectors.

Whether the *chaebol* or Korean businesses at large are the focus of attention, it has been observed that

> Korean companies are characterized by extremely strong chief executives, who wield enormous power. Many firms are still run by their founders or the entrepreneurs who built them. Leaders are highly charismatic and intimately involved in all company affairs. They are bold and willing to invest aggressively. Companies are hierarchical and characterized by rigid discipline. [Historically,] Korean companies [have been] managed less for profitability than for growth. Company size is the key source of social recognition. A thirst for volume leads to [a] willingness to price aggressively, and cash flow to fund growth is more important than profitability.[11]

Capital Markets. Although the Korea Stock Exchange, located in Seoul, is among the 10 largest exchanges in the world with about 700 listed companies and a market

---

[8]J. Burton, ''Protection for a Tiger's Cubs,'' *Financial Times,* May 2, 1995, p. 15.

[9]''Role Reversal,'' *The Economist,* November 13, 1993, pp. 37–38.

[10]See ''Taming the *Chaebol*'' and Nakarmi, ''A Flying Leap toward the 21st Century?''

[11]M. E. Porter, *The Competitive Advantage of Nations* (New York: The Free Press, 1990), pp. 470–72.

capitalization in excess of $10 billion, many Korean companies are not accustomed to selling securities as a major avenue of financing. As mentioned, companies have traditionally depended on government-guided bank loans for their financial needs. In recent years, however, the government has sought to strengthen the market by requesting, under the Capital Market Development Law, nonpublicly held firms to list on the exchange after (1) accumulating paid-in capital of W5 billion (about $6.3 million) or net equity of W10 billion ($12.7 million); (2) operating, on a continuous basis, over three years; (3) achieving a debt-to-owners' equity ratio not more than 1.5 times the average for other listed companies in the same industry; and (4) achieving a ratio of profit to paid-in capital higher than the prevailing interest rate for one-year deposits. Listed firms are required to file an independently audited annual report with the Korean SEC no later than 60 days after the end of their fiscal year, and they must file unaudited interim statements at mid-year.

Foreign direct investment in Korean companies listed on the Seoul exchange was first allowed in January 1992. Such investment, however, remains restricted. Initially, foreign ownership was not allowed to exceed 10 percent of a company's shares.[12] Within weeks after this tentative step toward capital market liberalization, the 10 percent ceiling had been reached in 72 companies.[13]

> Once the ceiling is hit, a foreigner can buy stock only from another foreigner. The result is a two-tier market—one price for Koreans, another for foreigners. As an example, consider Korea Mobile Telecommunications, the country's cellular phone monopoly. For Koreans, it [traded] at W120,100 a share, only about 10 times 1993 earnings, while the average price/earnings ratio is 13. But, for foreigners, the price is W210,175, a 75 percent premium.[14]

The government has permitted the creation of *Korea funds,* investment trusts traded on major stock exchanges around the world. In addition, it has allowed a handful of Korean companies to issue convertible bonds on overseas markets, a move suggesting that foreign bondholders will at some point be allowed to hold equity shares. In fact, foreign participants in the first of these issues, floated by Samsung in 1985 and originally scheduled for conversion in 1987, were finally allowed to convert their bonds in early 1990. Thus, these investors became the first foreign owners of Korean equities with the right to sell them and purchase others with the proceeds. More bond conversions are likely to follow as the government attempts to pull the stock market out of a severe slump with infusions of foreign capital. The fact remains, however, that due to the government's history of allocating capital across corporate Korea, combined with the dominance of the *chaebol* in the Korean economy, there has not been the need for or development of efficient public capital markets.[15]

---

[12]For a select few companies, the ceiling is 25 percent. See "A Door Creaks Open," *The Economist,* January 4, 1992, p. 72; and P. Montagnon and J. Burton, "The Burden of Membership," *Financial Times,* May 29, 1995, p. 12. The 12 percent limit was scheduled to be raised to 15 percent in July 1995.

[13]"Past the Worst," *The Economist,* January 30, 1993, p. 71.

[14]D. Darlin, "A Half-Open Door," *Forbes,* February 5, 1993, pp. 188–90.

[15]Porter, *The Competitive Advantage of Nations.*

Selected Financial Reporting Practices

Korean GAAP is a mixture of decrees and regulations issued by the Ministry of Finance and the Securities and Exchange Commission as well as a blend of practices espoused by a variety of miscellaneous laws, tax principles, and general conventions. At a root level, the historic cost principle, with some exceptions, is one of the core concepts adhered to as is the accrual basis of accounting, the going-concern assumption, and the consistent application of GAAP. As Korea emerges from its isolationist financial markets cocoon and as the equity market, in particular, becomes a more viable and important source of domestic and international capital, Korean financial reports must become more illuminating of the financial position of the companies they purport to portray. For example, a fundamental issue pertaining to the definition of the most appropriate reporting entity is yet to be resolved. Moreover, Korean companies have historically had a government safety net that is now being withdrawn in some measure, thus giving rise to a recent local corporate and financial market challenge of understanding and assessing financial risk. With a strong historical role in government industrial and tax policy, Korean financial reporting practices are entering a new arena, the world stage. The following is a review of key Korean financial reporting practices and accounting principles. Exhibit 13–4 provides a comparison of Korean and U.S. GAAP. Where significant differences are noted to exist between Korean GAAP and that of other major financial markets, one must realize that enormous pressure exists for Korea to change as Korean companies search for global capital.

Valuation

Assets are generally valued at historical cost, with certain exceptions. Inventories, marketable equity securities, and passive long-term investments, for example, must be written down if market value has declined below cost. In the case of long-term investments that enable the company to exert significant influence (i.e., ownership of 20 percent or more of the investee's voting stock), the investment need not be written down, but a decline in value must be disclosed in the footnotes.

Under the provisions of the Asset Revaluation Law, certain tangible fixed assets may be written up to market value when the Bank of Korea wholesale price index has risen 25 percent from the date they were acquired (or from the date they were previously revalued). The amount of the revaluation is based on a certified appraisal of the assets, and the resultant gain is subject to a revaluation tax. The gain is not treated as income nor the tax as an expense; instead, the net amount of the two figures is shown as a separate capital reserve in the stockholders' equity section of the balance sheet. Although the revaluation reserve may not be appropriated for cash dividends, it may be used to issue stock dividends by transferring an amount equal to the par value of shares issued to the common stock account.

Depreciation

Depreciation rates and useful asset lives generally follow Korean income tax law and may not reflect the true business judgment of management. In certain cases, special

EXHIBIT 13–4
Comparison of South Korean and U.S. Accounting and Reporting Standards

Item	South Korea	United States
Asset valuation	Historical cost with selected revaluation (e.g., fixed assets under the asset revaluation law)	Historical cost with selected revaluation (principally downward)
Inventory valuation	Specific identification, FIFO, LIFO, weighted average, or "retail pricing"	Principally LIFO (because of tax considerations); also FIFO and average cost methods
Inventory: year-end	Lower-of-cost-or-market value on an item-by-item basis	Lower of cost or replacement cost
Depreciation	Straight-line, declining balance, or unit-of-production methods; additional depreciation permitted and separately identified	Principally straight line with accelerated and production-based methods permitted
Goodwill	Capitalized to the balance sheet, with amortization (principally straight line) over a maximum of 5 years; negative goodwill added to capital surplus on balance sheet	Capitalized to balance sheet with amortization (principally straight line) over a maximum of 40 years; negative goodwill not permitted
Research and development costs	Capitalized and amortized over expected useful life if (a) incurred in relation to a specific product or technology, (b) costs are clearly identifiable, and (c) future benefits are reasonably expected; otherwise, expensed as incurred	Research costs expensed currently; development costs expensed currently except in certain industries (i.e., software, oil and gas)
Capitalization of interest costs	Capitalization required for debt directly related to the manufacture, purchase, or construction of fixed assets	Capitalization required for self-constructed assets
Intercorporate investments:		
Marketable securities (current asset trading)	Lower of aggregate cost or market value	Market value (individual security basis only) with *unrealized* gains and losses taken to income
Long-term investments:		
0–20% ownership (i.e., available for sale)	Lower of cost or market value	Market value (individual security basis only) with *unrealized* gains and losses reported on balance sheet in owners' equity
20–50% ownership	Cost or equity method	Equity method
51–100% ownership	Consolidated (required after 1993), principally using purchase accounting (although some regulations require the use of pooling)	Consolidated, using pooling or purchase accounting
Debt valuation	All debt valued at face value unless present value is significantly different, in which case present value is used	Long-term debt (except deferred income taxes) valued at present value; current debt valued at face value
Leases	Financing leases capitalized (e.g., when ownership is transferred, lease contains a bargain buyout option or the lease term approximates the estimated life of the leased asset); operating leases disclosed in footnotes	Capital leases reflected in balance sheet; operating leases disclosed in footnotes
Deferred income taxes	Not accounted for; reported tax expense based on actual taxes due	Computed under liability method
Pension liabilities	Private pension plans rare, but when present and unfunded, liability reported on balance sheet	Reflected on balance sheet
Discretionary reserves	Provisions for future expenses not permitted, except for severance pay, repairs and maintenance, product warranties, and others that can be reasonably estimated	Restricted to identifiable operational losses
Statement of cash flows	Not required (although statement of changes in financial position required)	Required

depreciation in addition to normal depreciation may be charged against income on a company's financial statements. Special depreciation due to excess equipment usage is considered to be a manufacturing cost; special depreciation for any other reason is classified as an extraordinary loss.

Bad Debts

Reserves for doubtful accounts are generally calculated in accordance with Korean income tax law and may not reflect actual economic experience. A reserve of 1 percent (2 percent for financial institutions) is allowed under tax law. Estimating the allowance on the basis of prior years' experience is also permitted.

Goodwill

Purchased goodwill, or the excess of the acquisition price paid for a business over the fair market value of the net assets acquired, is capitalized and amortized over five years using the straight-line method. Negative goodwill, on the other hand, is treated as a "gain on business combination" and recorded as capital surplus on the balance sheet.

Income Taxes

The income tax expense shown in the financial statements reflects the actual tax due for operations during the year (i.e., the flow-thru approach). Although Korean tax law causes both timing and permanent differences between book and tax income, inter-period tax allocation is not required, nor is it commonly practiced. In addition, although Korean tax law permits the creation of a variety of tax-deductible reserves that appear on the balance sheet, amounts added to these reserves are not charged against income on the financial statements.

Leases

Korean GAAP provides for the classification of leases as either operating or financing leases. Because of differing criteria for classification, however, many leases that would be capitalized under U.S. GAAP are treated as operating leases. Under Korean GAAP, leases that meet the following criteria are considered to be financing leases: (1) title is transferred from lessor to lessee, (2) the lease contains a bargain buyout option, or (3) the lease life is approximately equal to the leased asset's remaining useful life.

In the case of a financing lease, the lessor reports a receivable on its balance sheet, with payments being divided between interest income and a reduction of the receivable. The lessee carries the asset at its fair market value at the time of its acquisition and discloses a capital liability, with payments being divided between interest expense and a reduction of the liability. In the case of an operating lease, the lessor may calculate depreciation based on the term of the lease rather than the asset's useful life. In general, the lessee must provide a description of the lease arrangements for both financing and operating leases in its financial statements.

Prior Period Adjustments

Changes in accounting method are applied only prospectively, not retroactively. Prior period adjustments are accounted for by adjusting the beginning balance of unappropriated retained earnings.

Capital and Reserves

Shareholders' equity is generally composed of four types of accounts: share capital, capital surplus, retained earnings, and capital adjustments. Share capital consists of the par value of any common or preferred shares issued. Capital surplus consists of Paid-in Capital in Excess of Par Value, the asset revaluation surplus account, and any other specific reserve accounts that may arise as a result of a gain on the retirement of share capital, a gain on business combination (i.e., negative goodwill), and various government subsidies. Retained earnings includes various legal reserves, discretionary reserves, and unappropriated retained earnings or undisposed deficit. Finally, capital adjustments include treasury stock, any discounts on share capital issued, prepaid dividends, and outstanding stock rights and warrants. Cash dividends may be declared only from unappropriated retained earnings; stock dividends, on the other hand, may be declared from unappropriated retained earnings, capital surplus, or any legal reserves.

Other Disclosure

Korean accounting principles do not require disclosure of industry segment information, nor are pension or postretirement liabilities required to be disclosed. Since 1990, earnings per share disclosures (based on the weighted-average number of common shares actually issued and outstanding) have been required; the potential dilution by outstanding convertible or exercisable securities on EPS should also be disclosed.

Analytical Considerations

Only in the last decade has the importance of South Korea as an economic entity become widely acknowledged. As a consequence, comparative financial data for Korea and the United States are somewhat limited. Nonetheless, the following country composite ratio data are quite revealing.[16]

---

[16]F. Choi, H. Hino, S. K. Min, S. O. Nam, J. Ujiie, and A. Stonehill, ''Analyzing Foreign Financial Statements: The Use and Misuse of International Ratio Analysis,'' *Journal of International Business Studies,* Spring 1983, pp. 113–31.

Financial Indicator	Korea	United States
Current ratio	1.13	1.94
Quick ratio	.46	1.10
Times-interest earned ratio	1.80×	6.50×
Inventory turnover ratio	6.60×	6.80×
Return on assets ratio	2.8%	7.4%
Return on equity ratio	13.1%	13.9%

These data present a relatively stark comparison of Korean and U.S. businesses: Korean companies appear less liquid, solvent, efficient, and profitable as compared to U.S. companies while also being more highly leveraged. This generalization is both a function of doing business in Korea and a consequence of the prevalent accounting and reporting practices of Korea.

A review of Exhibit 13–4 suggests that accepted practice in Korea is frequently more conservative than that commonly followed in the United States. Consider, for instance, the following:

- *Depreciation expense.* The revaluation of fixed assets produces higher levels of depreciation; in addition, additional special depreciation is permitted.

- *Amortization expense.* Intangible assets are generally amortized over no more than 5 years (versus 40 in the United States).

Offsetting these more conservative practices are the following more liberal practices:

- *Research and development costs.* R&D costs are frequently capitalized if the cost is identifiable, recoverable, and related to a specific product or technology.

- *Deferred income taxes.* Deferred income taxes are generally not recorded because the actual taxes paid flow-thru to a firm's financial statements; deferred taxes are also rarely needed because of the parallel between reported accounting income and taxable income.

Just how material these various differences in accounting practices may be can best be analyzed in relation to actual corporate data. For example, with respect to the revaluation of property, plant, and equipment, Daewoo Corporation reported that its 1992 total assets increased by approximately 10 percent while shareholders' equity increased by 8 percent relative to the values that would have been reported under U.S. GAAP.

Summary

As the mid-1990s draw to a close, Korea boasts of improving labor relations, the rise of an affluent middle class, its most democratic government effort ever to liberalize its economy, interest rates at a record low, a workforce at virtual full employment, and one of the world's highest personal savings rate.[17] All this good news has brought Korea to a crossroads: Can it take the next step to being a player in international financial markets, technology, and innovation? The Korean government has proposed to (1) diversify its markets away from the United States toward the EU and Asia, (2) establish off-shore manufacturing facilities to reduce costs and/or avoid trade barriers, (3) establish brand name merchandise to avoid original equipment manufacture sales, (4) increase R&D expenditures, and (5) shift production toward higher value-added products. Pressure for such changes are emanating from Korea's trading partners, the foreign exchange markets, and from a desire to become the 26th member of the Organization for Economic and Cooperative Development.[18] It remains to be seen whether Korea can successfully exploit its economic niche that currently lies between the low-cost producers such as Malaysia and the high-quality Japanese producers, or whether Korea will have to find a new niche. Moreover, as one renowned Korean economist recently noted:

> We think we are changing very rapidly because we only compare ourselves to our own past. What people don't realize is that the rest of the world is changing just as quickly, and we are in danger of being left out.[19]

Suggested Readings

"An Open and Shut Market." *Euromoney,* February 1992, pp. 62–64.

Choi, F. D. S. et al. "Analyzing Foreign Financial Statements: The Use and Misuse of International Ratio Analysis." *Journal of International Business Studies,* Spring 1983, pp. 113–31.

Darlin, D. "A Half-Open Door." *Forbes,* February 15, 1993, pp. 188–90.

Ford, M. "Down from the Mountains." *The Banker,* April 1990, pp. 60–62.

Han, D., and K. Ojah. "Evidence on Managers' Perceptions of Effects of Government Control of the Business Environment: A Study of the Republic of Korea." *International Executive,* January/February 1995, pp. 61–79.

Herd, R., and R. S. Jones. "Spotlight on Korea." *The OECD Observer,* June/July 1994, pp. 32–35.

"Korea: A Survey." *Financial Times,* June 3, 1993, pp. 25–28.

---

[17]See D. Darlin, "Seoul Angst," *Forbes,* December 21, 1992, pp. 48–50; J. Burton, "Enter More Dragons," *Financial Times,* February 23, 1994, p. 13; and "Not That Sort of Girl," *The Economist,* April 23, 1994, pp. 35–36.

[18]J. Burton, "South Korea Applies to Join Organization for Economic and Cooperative Development," *Financial Times,* March 30, 1995, p. 8.

[19]G. deJonquieres, "The Tigers Face a Challenge," *Financial Times,* October 17, 1994, p. 19.

Kraar, L. "Korea's Tigers Keep Roaring." *Fortune,* May 4, 1992, pp. 108–10.

Montagu-Pollock, M. "Overtaking the West." *Asian Business,* January 1990, pp. 48–51.

Nakarmi, L., and B. Einhorn. "Hyundai's Gutsy Gambit." *Business Week,* June 26, 1992, p. 48.

"South Korea." *The Wall Street Journal,* June 26, 1992, pp. B7–B9.

"South Korea." *The Times,* March 8, 1995, special report.

Issues and Information for Further Inquiry

I.13.1   *Chaebol* Changes

A January 26, 1995 *Wall Street Journal* news note (p. A10), "Korea Hopes to Tame Goliaths," reported that "South Korea's Fair Trade Commission unveiled regulations to dilute family ownership of conglomerates." In addition, it was reported that "Hyundai Group said it would pare its affiliates to 23 from 50."

Required:

   (a) Chronicle the changes being sought to the *chaebol.*
   (b) Detail the resulting changes we would see in Korean annual reports.

I.13.2   OECD Membership

In a November 11, 1994, *Financial Times* article (p. 6), "S. Korea to Apply to OECD," J. Burton reports that "Seoul [has the] goal of having its membership approved by June 1996 . . . [but] the negotiations are expected to be contentious, since the OECD is demanding that Korea accelerate its schedule for financial liberalization."

Required:

   (a) Research and summarize the financial market–related requirements a country must meet to join the Organization for Economic Cooperation and Development (OECD).
   (b) Which requirements are Korea most likely to have difficulty in meeting? Why?
   (c) Discuss the related financial reporting issues and/or impact.

EXERCISES

E.13.1 Accounting for Shareholders' Equity

The consolidated balance sheet of the Daewoo Corporation as of December 31, 1992, revealed the following balances in its shareholders' equity accounts.

Shareholders' Equity	*(₩, millions)*
Common stock, of ₩ 5,000 par value	
Authorized—200,000,000 shares	
Issued—88,056,964 shares	440,285
Capital surplus	418,267
Legal reserve	19,878
Equity adjustments from foreign currency translation	(23,733)
Unappropriated retained earnings	302,036
Total	1,156,733

The changes in these account balances in 1992 were described in the company's statement of shareholders' equity and related footnotes that follow.

Selected Footnote Information

During 1992 the Company issued convertible debentures amounting to ₩ 48,100 million ($61,010 thousand) and convertible debentures of ₩ 32,810 million ($41,616 thousand) were converted to common stock resulting in an increase in the stated capital of ₩ 12,116 million ($15,368 thousand) and an increase in capital surplus of ₩ 20,694 million ($26,248 thousand) (see note 11). The balance of convertible debentures at December 31, 1992 is ₩ 96,942 million ($122,960 thousand).

During the year ended December 31, 1992, the Company issued additional shares of par value ₩ 5,000 common stock as follows:

Common Stock Issued Upon	*Issued Shares*	*Issued Price per Share*	Won (millions) *Increase in Stated Capital*	*Additional Capital Surplus*	U.S. Dollars (thousands) *Increase in Stated Capital*	*Additional Capital Surplus*
Conversion of convertible		9,120 won–				
debentures	2,423,227	14,675 won	₩ 12,116	20,694	$ 15,368	26,248
Stock dividends	3,716,647	5,000 won	18,584	—	23,572	—
	6,139,874		₩ 30,700	20,694	$ 38,940	26,248

The Korean Commercial Code requires the Company and its domestic subsidiaries to appropriate as legal reserve an amount equal to at least 10% of cash dividends for each accounting period until the reserve equals 50% of stated capital. The legal reserve may be used to reduce a deficit or it may be transferred to stated capital.

The accompanying consolidated financial statements do not include any provision for the dividends (cash dividends 1%, stock dividends 5%) for the year ended December 31, 1992, aggregating ₩ 26,177 million ($33,203 thousand) to be proposed in February 1993 or for the appropriation to the legal reserve of ₩ 500 million ($634 thousand) based thereon.

DAEWOO CORPORATION
Consolidated Statement of Stockholders' Equity Year Ended December 31, 1992

	Won (millions)					
	Common Stock	Capital Surplus	Legal Reserve	Equity Adjustments from Foreign Currency Translation	Unappropriated Retained Earnings	Total
Balance at December 31, 1991	409,585	398,539	19,478	(16,928)	273,294	1,083,968
Net earnings for 1992	—	—	—	—	50,476	50,476
Cash and stock dividends (note 11)	18,584	—	—	—	(22,300)	(3,716)
Transfer to legal reserve (note 12)	—	—	400	—	(400)	—
Transfer to unappropriated retained earnings	—	(966)	—	—	966	—
Equity adjustments from foreign currency translation	—	—	—	(6,805)	—	(6,805)
Issuance of common stock for cash	—	—	—	—	—	—
Issuance of debentures with warrants	—	—	—	—	—	—
Conversion of convertible debentures (notes 9 and 11)	12,116	20,694	—		—	32,810
Balance at December 31, 1992	440,285	418,267	19,878	(23,733)	302,036	1,156,733

Required:

Using journal entries, explain the changes in Daewoo's shareholders' equity account from December 31, 1991, to year-end 1992.

E.13.2   Revaluation of Assets

Under the provisions of the Korean Asset Revaluation Law, corporations are permitted to revalue certain qualifying tangible assets above historical cost. For example, Daewoo Corporation's "summary of significant accounting principles" makes the following statement:

> The Company, and its domestic affiliated companies have, to some extent, recognized the loss of purchasing power of the won by upward restatement of the cost of property, plant and equipment with a corresponding credit to capital surplus. Revaluation taxes paid are offset against the revaluation surplus. Such surplus may be offset against exchange losses, a deficit, or may be transferred to stated capital in connection with a free distribution of shares.

In addition the company' footnotes revealed:

Had assets not been revalued, the consolidated financial statements would have been increased (decreased) as follows as of and for the year ended December 31, 1992:

Accounts	(Won, millions)
Net property, plant and equipment	(55,758)
Investments and advances	(65,034)
Common stock	(14,343)
Capital surplus	(37,290)
Retained earnings	(47,025)
Minority interest—surplus	(22,134)
Net earnings	1,665

The company's financial statements revealed the following data as of December 31, 1992:

Accounts	(Won, millions)
Net property, plant and equipment	2,124,752
Investments and advances	341,567
Common stock	440,285
Capital surplus	418,267
Retained earnings	302,036
Minority interests—surplus	(418,368)
Net earnings	50,476

Required:

(a) On the basis of the information contained in Daewoo's footnote, what journal entries were made in regard to the company's revaluation of assets? (Ignore amounts.)

(b) Assess the impact of the asset revaluation on Daewoo's 1992 financial results.

E.13.3   Accounting for Equity Reserves

Founded in 1967, the Daewoo Corporation is the parent company of the Daewoo Group, Korea's fourth largest *chaebol*. *Fortune* magazine rated Daewoo as the world's 45th largest industrial corporation.

Generally accepted accounting practice in Korea encourages eligible corporations to create tax-deductible reserves for a variety of qualifying purposes as a means to reduce otherwise taxable corporate earnings. The "qualifying purposes" usually reflect sectors of the Korean economy that the government desires to economically stimulate or to particular macrolevel economic objectives of Korea's Ministry of Finance.

Exhibit 13–2 in Chapter 13 lists the equity reserve accounts for the Daewoo Corporation as of December 31, 1993 and 1992.

Required:

    (a) Using journal entries, explain the change in each of Daewoo's eight reserves listed in Exhibit 13–2. Why do some reserves increase, while others decrease? Based on a statutory tax rate of 34 percent, how much income tax did the company save in 1993 under the system of tax-deductible reserves?

    (b) Compare and contrast Korea's system of tax reserves to that used in Japan (Chapter 10) and in Sweden (Chapter 11).

    (c) Write a one-sentence explanation regarding the role or purpose of each of Daewoo's equity reserves. What observations can you draw from your analysis?

E.13.4   Korean versus U.S. GAAP

The following is the summary of significant accounting policies footnote from the 1991 annual report of Hanil Synthetic Fiber Ind. Co., Ltd.

Required:

Review the accounting policies used by Hanil and indicate the accounting policy most likely used if the company had prepared its financial statements according to U.S. GAAP.

Hanil Synthetic Fiber Ind. Co., Ltd.
Selected Annual Report Excerpts

Summary of Significant Accounting Policies

  (a) Basis of Presenting Financial Statements
The Company maintains its books of account in conformity with generally accepted financial accounting standards in the Republic of South Korea, except for using where applicable, the accounting practices acceptable for tax purposes.

  (b) Marketable Securities and Investments
Marketable securities and investments are carried principally at cost plus incidental expenses, determined on the moving average method, less a reserve for losses. Commencing in the year ended March 31, 1991, the carrying values of invested companies over which the Company is able to exercise influence in operating and financial policies need not be written down. However, disclosure of any application valuation changes is made in the notes to the financial statements. Prior to April 1, 1990, the Company provided a reserve for losses for declines in market value or net equity in excess of 30% of the book value.

  (c) Inventories
Inventories are stated at lower of cost (moving average method) or market.

  (d) Property, Plant and Equipment
Property, plant and equipment were revalued in accordance with Republic of South Korea Asset Revaluation Law as of April 1, 1983. Property, plant and equipment which existed as of April 1, 1983, are stated at the net revalued amounts. Additions since that date are stated at

cost. Depreciation is computed on a straight-line basis over the estimated useful lives. Improvements that significantly expand the life of an asset or add to its productive capacity are capitalized. Expenditures for repairs and maintenance are charged to income as incurred.

(e) Leases

The company accounts for and classifies its lease transactions as operating leases in accordance with the Korean Lease Accounting Standards which became effective January 1, 1985.

(f) Amortization of Other Assets

Intangible assets are stated at cost, net of applicable amortization. Amortization is computed on a straight-line basis over the estimated useful lives.

Certain expenses relating to research and issuance of stocks and bonds are deferred and amortized by equal annual amounts over five years and three years, respectively.

(g) Income Taxes

Provision is not made in the accounts to reflect the inter-period allocation of income taxes resulting from certain income and expense items being treated differently for financial reporting purposes than tax computation purposes.

(h) Retirement and Severance Benefits

Employees who have been with the Company for more than one year are entitled to lump-sum payments based on current rates of pay and length of service when they leave the Company. A portion of the liability is covered by an insurance policy and the Company's estimated liability under the plan has been accrued in the accompanying financial statements at the amount which would be payable if all employees left at the balance sheet date.

(i) Foreign Currency Translation

Foreign currency items are translated into Korean won at current rates of exchange at year-end. Exchange adjustments are generally charged or credited to income as they occur.

(j) Losses on Industry Rationalization

In accordance with the Government's plan for industry rationalization, the Company acquired the stock of a majority shareholder of various former Kukje-ICC Group companies. These individual companies are Kukje Corporation, Nam Ju Development Co., Ltd., Shin Nam Development Co., Ltd., Woon Hyo Development Co., Ltd. and Union Mool San Co., Ltd.

Under the agreement with the credit bank group, the Company is obliged to assume certain debts of these companies on an installment basis. The amount of debt assumed is charged to operations as other deductions and credited to long-term debt.

(k) Net Loss per Common Share

Net loss per common share is computed by deducting preferred dividends from net loss in order to determine net loss attributable to common stockholders. This amount is then divided by the weighted average number of common shares outstanding during the year.

(l) Prior Year Adjustments

Generally accepted financial accounting standards in the Republic of South Korea allow for recognition as prior year adjustments the financial effects of certain adjustments occurring in the current year which are applicable to prior years' activity. Such adjustments have been reflected in the accompanying financial statements as direct adjustments to retained earnings at the beginning of the year.

(m) Reclassifications

Certain 1990 balances have been reclassified to conform to the 1991 presentation.

E.13.5   Statement of Cash Flows

Under Korean GAAP, the basic financial statements consist of a balance sheet, a statement of income, a statement of changes in financial position, and a statement of (proposed) appropriation of retained earnings; a statement of cash flows is not required.

The following is the statement of changes in financial position of Hanil Synthetic Fiber Ind. Co., Ltd. for the years ended March 31, 1991 and 1990. The company's balance sheet and statement of income are presented in Case 13.1.

Required:

Using Hanil's statement of changes in financial position as a starting point, prepare a statement of cash flows for 1991. What can you infer about the company's financial health from these data?

HANIL SYNTHETIC FIBER IND. CO., LTD.
Statement of Changes in Financial Position
For the Years Ended March 31, 1991 and 1990

	Won (millions)	
	1991	*1990*
Working capital provided by operations		
Net losses	(16,507)	(13,908)
Items which did not use (provide) working capital;		
Depreciation	9,482	15,142
Amortization of intangible and deferred assets	5,268	3,329
Amortization of discount on bonds issued	—	8
Provision for retirement and severance benefits	19,460	19,095
Losses on disposals of property, plant and equipment, net	(25,026)	(3,967)
Loss(gain) on valuation and disposition of investments, net	2,234	(4,690)
Provision for allowance for bad debts	96	154
Accrual of long-term interest expenses	5,810	5,810
Losses on industry rationalization	10,203	10,201
Unrealized exchange losses	417	363
Working capital provided by operating activities	11,437	31,537
Working capital provided by investing and financing activities		
Decrease in investments	12	7,240
Decrease in other assets	38,126	11,599
Proceeds from sale of property, plant and equipment	40,060	11,128
Increase in long-term debt	142,947	135,669
Issuance of common and preferred stock	17,008	6,400
Receipt of government subsidies	185	—
Gains on disposals of treasury stock	62	9
Prior year adjustments—gain	—	28
Working capital provided by investing and financing activities	238,400	172,073
Total	249,837	203,610
Working capital used for investing and financing activities		
Increase in investments	75,012	128,480
Increase in other assets	30,421	22,206
Acquisition of property, plant and equipment	48,186	29,774
Decrease in long-term debt	1,199	630
Current portion of long-term debt and other long-term liabilities	85,276	36,165
Retirement and severance benefits-payments	42,728	6,054
Dividends and directors' bonuses	3,198	4,749
Acquisition of treasury stock	68	—
Prior year adjustments—losses	695	813
Working capital used in investing and financing activities	286,783	228,871
Net increase in working capital	(36,946)	(25,261)

E.13.6   Analyzing Financial Trends

The following are the balance sheets and income statements for Sunkyong Industries for 1989 to 1991.

Required:

Prepare common-size financial statements for the three-year period and identify any significant financial trends of the company.

SUNKYONG INDUSTRIES
Income Statement

Revenue	Won (millions)		
	1991	*1990*	*1989*
Sales revenue	**578,637**	539,031	509,725
Nonoperating revenue	**34,976**	24,347	28,957
Interest income	**15,095**	8,578	10,593
Other nonoperating income	**19,881**	15,769	18,364
Total revenue	**613,613**	563,378	538,682
Expense			
Cost of sales	**469,202**	452,941	455,400
Selling & administrative expense	**57,726**	45,252	47,888
Nonoperating expense	**78,107**	63,320	31,956
Financial expense	**59,057**	48,045	23,618
Other expense	**19,050**	15,275	8,338
Total expense	**605,035**	561,513	535,244
Ordinary income	**8,578**	1,865	3,438
Extraordinary items	**244**	285	1,413
Net profit before tax	**8,822**	2,150	4,851
Income tax	**1,999**	415	2,216
Net profit after tax	**6,823**	1,735	2,635

SUNKYONG INDUSTRIES
Balance Sheets

Assets	Won (millions)		
	1991	*1990*	*1989*
Current assets			
Cash on hand & in banks	**159,436**	100,935	14,744
Marketable securities	**19,437**	19,548	18,193
Accounts receivable—trade	**101,345**	90,733	82,579
Accounts receivable—others	**8,118**	5,540	8,406
Finished goods	**48,734**	35,806	33,237
Work in process	**9,884**	9,240	8,746
Raw materials & supplies	**27,990**	21,614	30,431
Prepaid expense	**2,940**	2,945	2,846
Other current assets	**25,327**	27,745	45,853
Total current assets	**403,211**	314,106	245,035
Investment & other assets			
Investment assets	**42,636**	9,198	2,659
Other assets	**27,365**	32,461	25,780
Total investment & other assets	**70,001**	41,659	28,439
Fixed assets			
Land	**30,999**	29,506	29,790
Buildings & structure	**94,649**	92,494	60,851
Machinery & equipment	**308,136**	303,560	132,990
Construction in progress	**27,819**	66,427	214,810
Other tangible assets	**21,750**	40,625	90,956
Intangible assets	**629**	662	664
Total fixed assets	**483,982**	533,274	530,041
Deferred charges	**16,888**	9,742	2,092
Total assets	**974,082**	898,781	805,607

Liabilities			
Current liabilities			
Account payable—trade	**102,022**	80,338	96,714
Short-term borrowings	**245,974**	175,292	126,751
Accounts payable—others	**12,771**	16,872	31,470
Accrued expenses	**6,418**	5,122	7,167
Current portion of long-term debt	**66,982**	99,145	32,235
Other current liabilities	**4,572**	856	2,825
Total current liabilities	**438,739**	377,625	297,162
Long-term liabilities			
Long-term debt	**94,756**	162,463	184,433
Bonds	**227,653**	141,301	122,847
Reserve for retirement	**42,016**	38,709	34,080
Total long-term liabilities	**364,425**	342,473	341,360
Deferred liabilities	**1,365**	3,345	5,522
Total liabilities	**804,529**	723,443	644,044

SUNKYONG INDUSTRIES
Balance Sheets (continued)

	1991	*1990*	*1989*
Shareholders' Equity			
Total paid-in capital	**53,418**	50,440	43,992
Capital surplus	**88,978**	96,809	85,722
Retained earnings			
Reserve—legal & others	**19,293**	23,480	23,801
Other retained earnings	**1,041**	2,874	5,413
Net profit for the period	**6,823**	1,735	2,635
Total retained earnings	**27,157**	28,089	31,849
Total shareholders' equity	**169,553**	175,338	161,563
Total liabilities & shareholders' equity	**974,082**	898,781	805,607

E.13.7   Analyzing Cash Flows (Direct Method)

The following are selected financial data from The Lucky-Goldstar Group for 1989 and 1990.

Required:

(a) Using the available information, prepare a direct method statement of cash flows for 1990.

(b) What conclusions can you draw from these data about the company's financial health?

THE LUCKY-GOLDSTAR GROUP
Statements of Income
For the Years Ended December 31, 1990 and 1989

	Millions of Won	
	1990	*1989*
Revenue		
Export sales	**5,447,868**	4,763,580
Domestic sales	**9,720,814**	8,602,381
Other income	**1,030,244**	94,984
	16,198,926	13,460,945
Costs and expenses		
Costs, excluding items below	**13,253,947**	11,177,715
Depreciation	**540,181**	349,936
Accural of severance benefits	**141,244**	141,899
Selling, general and administrative expenses	**1,346,277**	1,119,311
	15,281,649	12,788,861
Operating income	**917,277**	672,084
Other expenses		
Interest expense, net of interest income	**480,685**	383,617
Others, net	**121,063**	(29,653)
	601,748	353,964
Income before income taxes	**315,529**	318,120
Income taxes currently payable	**155,557**	125,609
Net income	**159,972**	192,511

THE LUCKY-GOLDSTAR GROUP
Statement of Changes in Financial Position
For the Years Ended December 31, 1990 and 1989

	Millions of Won	
	1990	*1989*
Sources of working capital		
From operations		
Net income	₩159,972	₩192,511
Items not affecting working capital		
Depreciation and amortization	690,808	493,644
Accrual of severance benefits	141,244	141,899
Foreign exchange translation loss	26,501	118
Loss on valuation of investments and others	(33,708)	—
Working capital provided from operations	984,817	828,172
Increase in long-term debt	1,970,643	1,447,172
Disposition of property, plant and equipment	175,876	189,172
Issuance of capital stock for cash	633,426	971,475
Decrease in investments and other assets	330,771	280,638
Total sources of working capital	4,095,533	3,716,629
Uses of working capital		
Additions to property, plant and equipment	1,408,467	1,624,110
Current maturities of long-term debt	752,143	363,087
Decrease in long-term payables and other	89,460	189,787
Increase in investments and other assets	840,754	654,304
Cash dividends	81,508	87,971
Payment of severance benefits	40,304	33,605
Increase in deferred charges	194,903	104,126
Payment of revaluation tax and others	38,052	232
Total uses of working capital	3,445,591	3,057,222
Increase in working capital	₩649,942	₩659,407

THE LUCKY-GOLDSTAR GROUP
Statement of Changes in Financial Position
For the Years Ended December 31, 1990 and 1989

	Millions of Korean Won	
	1990	*1989*
Changes in components of working capital elements:		
Increase (decrease) in current assets:		
Cash and bank deposits	**64,121**	241,247
Marketable securities	**(300,744)**	401,043
Accounts and notes receivable	**930,634**	481,903
Inventories	**406,602**	137,014
Short-term loans	**474,925**	35,032
Advance payments	**59,051**	12,244
Other current assets	**1,153,392**	1,633,830
Increase in current assets	**2,787,981**	2,942,313
Increase (decrease) in current liabilities:		
Accounts and notes payable	**1,111,474**	384,062
Short-term borrowings	**950,079**	148,947
Current maturities of long-term debt	**365,622**	14,362
Income taxes payable	**17,609**	(5,040)
Advances received	**36,142**	2,062
Withholding taxes	**460,493**	12,695
Other current liabilities	**(803,380)**	1,725,818
Increase in current liabilities	**2,138,039**	2,282,906
Increase in working capital	**649,942**	659,407

E.13.8   Korean versus U.S. GAAP

The following is the summary of significant accounting principles footnote from the annual report of Sunkyong Industries:

Sunkyong Industries

1. Summary of Significant Accounting Policies

   The company maintains its books of account and prepares its financial statements in conformity with generally accepted financial accounting standards in Korea.

   (1) Allowance for doubtful accounts.

   The losses estimated on the remaining receivables and other assets on the basis of the analysis of prior period experience are expensed currently by providing an allowance for doubtful accounts.

   (2) Inventories

   Inventories are stated at the weighted average cost.

   (3) Investments

   Investments in affiliated companies are stated at cost using a moving average method on individual security basis.

   (4) Tangible fixed assets and depreciation

Tangible fixed assets are stated at acquisition cost or at revaluation amount. The company computes depreciation using the straight-line method over the useful lives of depreciable assets in accordance with the Income Tax Law.

(5) Foreign currency translation

Monetary foreign currency assets and liabilities are translated into Korean won at the current rate of exchange at year-end. Nonmonetary foreign currency assets and liabilities are translated at historical rates. Exchange and translation gains or losses are credited or charged to income currently.

Required:

Assume that Sunkyong was required to prepare its financial statements according to current U.S. GAAP. Which of these accounting policies would change, and what method would the company most likely utilize in their place?

CASES

CASE 13.1
ACCOUNTING VERSUS TAXABLE INCOME

Hanil Synthetic Fiber Ind. Co., Ltd.

Under generally accepted accounting practice in South Korea, the provision for income taxes reported on the publicly disclosed income statement is the actual taxes currently payable. This method is often called the *flow-thru* or *actual taxes payable* method. The taxes due, composed of the corporation tax and the resident tax surcharge, are calculated based on income according to Korean tax law and are then matched with income according to Korean GAAP. Under this system, no deferred income taxes are provided for those temporary differences between accounting and taxable income. This system dramatically differs from U.S. GAAP under which the provision for income taxes is based on reported accounting income, and a deferred income tax account is created to account for any tax effects related to temporary differences between accounting and taxable income. (Permanent differences between accounting and taxable income are ignored under both Korean and U.S. GAAP.)

The following selected financial information is from the 1991 annual report of Hanil Synthetic Fiber Co., Ltd., a publicly held Korean corporation.

Required:

    (a) Identify the primary differences in accounting for income under Korean GAAP versus Korean tax law. Estimate the company's taxable income for tax purposes.

    (b) Record the company's taxes assuming that interperiod tax allocation is generally practiced in Korea. What effect would this have on the company's reported income in 1991?

HANIL SYNTHETIC FIBER IND. CO., LTD
Balance Sheets
March 31, 1991 and 1990

	Won (millions)	
Assets	*1991*	*1990*
Current assets		
Cash and deposits (note 4)	234,562	201,844
Marketable securities (note 5)	7,257	21,685
Receivables		
Trade notes	18,430	14,021
Trade accounts	36,402	27,612
Other	55,593	35,331
	110,425	76,964
Less allowance for doubtful receivables	637	509
Net receivables	109,788	76,455
Inventories (note 6)	86,355	83,779
Prepaid expenses and other current assets	7,676	6,247
Total current assets	445,638	390,010
Investments (notes 3 and 7)	329,018	256,252
Property, plant and equipment, at cost (notes 3 and 9)	511,383	484,729
Less accumulated depreciation	293,706	290,722
Net property, plant and equipment	217,677	194,007
Other assets (notes 3 and 8)	32,271	45,340
	1,024,604	885,609

HANIL SYNTHETIC FIBER IND. CO., LTD
Balance Sheets (continued)
March 31, 1991 and 1990

	Won (millions)	
Liabilities and Stockholders' Equity	*1991*	*1990*
Current liabilities		
Short-term borrowings (notes 3 and 10)	91,878	72,418
Current portion of long-term debt and other long-term liabilities (notes 3 and 11)	85,276	36,165
Accounts and notes payable, trade	25,655	13,207
Other payables	8,391	3,884
Accrued expenses and other current liabilities	19,367	12,319
Total current liabilities	230,567	137,993
Long-term debt, excluding current portion (notes 3 and 11)	440,137	378,590
Retirement and severance benefits	38,531	61,799
Other long-term liabilities	26,285	23,845
Total liabilities	735,520	602,227
Stockholders' equity (note 12)		
Preferred stock, W5,000 par value		
Authorized and issued–4,383,500 shares in 1991 and 1,266,328 shares in 1990	21,917	6,332
Common stock, W5,000 par value		
Authorized–25,616,500 shares in 1991 and 28,733,672 shares in 1990		
Issued–11,250,705 shares in 1991 and 8,800,000 shares in 1990	56,253	44,000
Capital surplus	32,352	20,073
Revaluation surplus	143,379	157,395
Retained earnings		
Appropriated (note 14)	51,555	54,492
Unappropriated	(16,371)	1,092
	35,184	55,584
Capital adjustments—treasury stock	(1)	(2)
Total stockholders' equity	289,084	283,382
Commitments and contingencies (notes 11 and 18)		
	1,024,604	885,609

HANIL SYNTHETIC FIBER IND. CO., LTD
Statement of Operations
March 31, 1991 and 1990

	Won (millions)	
	1991	*1990*
Sales	356,223	388,108
Cost of goods sold	328,232	363,200
Gross profit	27,991	24,908
Selling, general and administrative expenses	38,904	33,393
Operating losses	(10,913)	(8,485)
Other income (deductions)		
Interest and dividend income	62,008	47,425
Interest expense	(62,916)	(46,242)
Foreign exchange gain (loss), net	(9,727)	1,163
Amortization of intangible and deferred assets	(5,268)	(3,329)
Donations	(1,248)	(1,645)
Gain (loss) on valuation and disposition of investments	(2,234)	4,690
Losses on industry rationalization (note 11)	(10,203)	(10,201)
Other, net	25,711	5,464
	(3,877)	(2,675)
Losses before income taxes	(14,790)	(11,160)
Income taxes (note 13)	1,717	2,748
Net losses (note 15)	(16,507)	(13,908)

HANIL SYNTHETIC FIBER IND. CO., LTD
Notes to Financial Statements
March 31, 1991 and 1990

(13) *Income Taxes*
The Company is subject to a number of taxes based on earnings which result in a normal tax rate of 36.55% in 1991 and 39.75% in 1990. The provision for income taxes at the normal tax rate differs from the actual provision for the following reasons:

	Won (millions)	
	1991	*1990*
Provision for income taxes at normal tax rate	(5,406)	(4,436)
Unrecorded tax effect of timing differences, primarily related to reserves for tax purposes, exchange loss and interest income	6,531	6,419
Permanent differences, primarily related to entertainment expenses and donations	920	269
Other, primarily related to investment tax credits	(328)	(404)
Additional taxes on capital gains on sale of land	—	900
Actual provision for income taxes per accompanying financial statements	1,717	2,748

CASE 13.2
KOREAN VERSUS U.S. GAAP

Daewoo Corporation

Daewoo Corporation is one of Korea's largest trading and construction companies. Established in 1967, the company now has operations in over 100 countries. As a trading company, Daewoo deals in more than 3,000 products for both export and import. In addition to its trading and construction activities, the company also has operations in energy, finance, and semiconductors.

The following are the company's income statements and balance sheets as of December 31, 1992 and 1993, as well as its summary of significant accounting policies and basis of presenting financial statements. According to these data, Daewoo prepares its financial statements in accordance with generally accepted accounting principles in the Republic of South Korea.

Required:

(a) Review Daewoo's accounting policies and basis of financial statement preparation. List those areas that differ from accepted practice under U.S. GAAP.

(b) Prepare a statement of cash flows for Daewoo for 1993.

Balance Sheets
December 31, 1993 and 1992

Assets	(Millions) Won		(Thousands) (Note 2) U.S. Dollars	
	1993	*1992*	*1993*	*1992*
Current assets				
Cash (note 4)	**473,961**	462,801	**586,513**	572,703
Marketable securities, at cost, which approximates market (note 4)	**170,338**	60,308	**210,788**	74,629
Trade notes and accounts receivable (note 16)	**2,060,341**	1,867,114	**2,549,611**	2,310,498
Less allowance for doubtful accounts	**6,034**	5,374	**7,467**	6,650
Net trade receivables	**2,054,307**	1,861,740	**1,542,144**	2,303,848
Other receivables	**159,834**	107,978	**197,790**	133,620
Inventories (notes 5 and 6)	**1,090,189**	1,091,090	**1,349,077**	1,350,192
Prepayments	**516,555**	465,097	**639,222**	575,544
Other current assets	**135,736**	110,689	**167,969**	136,974
Total current assets	**4,600,920**	4,159,703	**5,693,503**	5,147,510
Investments				
Affiliated companies (notes 4 and 7)	**1,126,290**	1,110,522	**1,393,751**	1,374,238
Other investments (note 4)	**6,755**	63,611	**82,607**	78,717
Total investments	**1,193,045**	1,174,133	**1,476,358**	1,452,955

Balance Sheets (continued)
December 31, 1993 and 1992

Assets	(Millions) Won		(Thousands) (Note 2) U.S. Dollars	
	1993	1992	1993	1992
Property, plant and equipment (notes 4, 6, and 10)				
Land	**78,065**	67,887	**96,604**	84,008
Buildings and structures	**132,799**	80,076	**164,335**	99,092
Machinery and equipment	**599,594**	527,915	**741,980**	653,279
Construction in progress	**6,951**	17,948	**8,601**	22,210
	817,409	693,826	**1,011,520**	858,589
Less accumulated depreciation	**447,563**	380,419	**553,846**	470,757
Net property, plant and equipment	**369,846**	313,407	**457,674**	387,832
Other assets (notes 4 and 8)	**499,421**	525,786	**618,019**	650,645
	6,663,232	6,173,029	**8,245,554**	7,638,942

Liabilities and Stockholders' Equity

	(Millions) Won		(Thousands) (Note 2) U.S. Dollars	
	1993	1992	1993	1992
Current liabilities				
Short-term loans (note 4)	**1,962,993**	1,557,387	**2,429,146**	1,927,221
Current portion of long-term debt (notes 4 and 9)	**114,231**	326,480	**141,358**	404,009
Trade notes and accounts payable	**1,035,300**	1,193,347	**1,281,153**	1,476,732
Other payables	**106,190**	127,077	**131,407**	157,254
Income taxes payable	**5,423**	3,453	**6,711**	4,273
Deposits and advance receipts	**229,632**	277,682	**284,163**	343,623
Accrued expenses and other current liabilities	**68,281**	87,444	**84,496**	108,210
Total current liabilities	**3,522,050**	3,572,870	**4,358,434**	4,421,322
Long-term debt, excluding current portion (notes 3, 4, 9 and 10)	**1,474,749**	973,233	**1,824,958**	1,204,347
Deposits and advance receipts—noncurrent (note 4)	**184,874**	291,046	**228,776**	360,161
Retirement and severance benefits	**101,537**	85,832	**125,649**	106,214
Total liabilities	**5,283,210**	4,922,981	**6,537,817**	6,092,044
Stockholders' equity (note 12):				
Common stock of ₩5,000 par value:				
Authorized–200,000,000 shares				
Issued–104,038,024 shares in 1993 88,056,964 shares in 1992	**520,190**	440,285	**643,720**	544,840
Capital surplus	**424,112**	371,845	**524,826**	460,147
Retained earnings				
Appropriated (note 13)	**406,468**	394,401	**502,992**	488,060
Unappropriated	**44,452**	40,994	**55,008**	50,729
Capital adjustments				
Compensation for conversion rights	**12,006**	2,523	**14,857**	3,122
Foreign-based operations translation (debit) credit	**(27,206)**	—	**(33,666)**	—
Total stockholders' equity	**1,380,022**	1,250,048	**1,707,737**	1,546,898
Commitments and contingencies (notes 3, 10, and 16)	**—**	—	**—**	—
	6,663,232	6,173,029	**8,245,554**	7,638,942

See accompanying notes to financial statements.

DAEWOO CORPORATION
Statements of Income
Years ended December 31, '93 and '92

	(Millions, Except Earnings per Share) Won		(Thousands, Except Earnings per Share) (Note 2) U.S. Dollars	
	1993	*1992*	*1993*	*1992*
Sales (note 7)	9,533,544	8,151,165	11,797,480	10,086,827
Cost of goods sold (note 7)	8,702,150	7,435,775	10,768,655	9,201,553
Gross profit	831,394	715,390	1,028,825	885,274
Selling, general and administrative expenses	340,974	348,481	421,945	431,235
Operating income	490,420	366,909	606,880	454,039
Other income (deductions):				
Interest income	94,440	94,497	116,867	116,937
Interest expense	(451,817)	(367,139)	(559,110)	(454,324)
Gain (loss) on sale of marketable securities and investments, net	7,479	(2,050)	9,255	(2,537)
Gain on disposition of property, plant and equipment, net	3,279	12,768	4,058	15,800
Exchange and translation loss, net	(17,310)	(16,753)	(21,421)	(20,731)
Dividends	3,838	4,587	4,749	5,676
Other, net	(62,482)	(39,305)	(77,319)	(48,638)
	(422,573)	(313,395)	(522,921)	(387,817)
Earnings before income taxes	67,847	53,514	83,959	66,222
Income taxes (note 11)	19,225	13,235	23,791	16,378
Net earnings	48,622	40,279	60,168	49,844
Earnings per share in won and U.S. dollars (note 17)	516.28	465.66	0.64	0.58

See accompanying notes to financial statements.

DAEWOO CORPORATION
Notes to Financial Statements
December 31, 1993 and 1992

1. Summary of Significant Accounting Policies and Basis of Presenting Financial Statements

(a) Basis of Presenting Financial Statements

Daewoo Corporation (the Company) maintains its books of account and prepares its financial statements in conformity with generally accepted financial accounting standards in the Republic of Korea. The financial statements include only the accounts of Daewoo Corporation. Investments in subsidiaries are accounted for on the cost basis.

(b) Allowance for Doubtful Accounts

The Company provides an allowance for doubtful receivables based on estimated uncollectible amounts as of the balance sheet date.

(c) Inventories

Inventories are principally stated at lower of cost or market, cost being determined substantially by the first-in, first-out method.

(d) Investments

Investments are carried principally at cost plus incidental expenses, determined by the moving average method. Beginning in 1991 under revised generally accepted financial accounting standards in the Republic of Korea, for invested companies over which the Company cannot exercise significant influence in operating and financial policies, investments in listed companies or unlisted companies are written down when the market value or the net equity per share, respectively, at the balance sheet date is less than the acquisition cost. Subsequent market value recoveries or increase in net equity of investments are recognized to the extent of any write-down previously made. However, write-downs of investments in listed companies are delayed until an accounting period to be designated in the future by Korea Securities and Exchange Commission. In the case of listed companies, disclosure of any applicable valuation change not recognized must be made in the notes to financial statements.

The carrying values of invested companies over which the Company is able to exercise significant influence in operating and financial policies need not be written down. However, disclosure of any applicable valuation change is made in the notes to the financial statements.

(e) Property, Plant and Equipment

As permitted under the Asset Revaluation Law of the Republic of Korea, the Company has, to some extent, recognized the loss in purchasing power of the won by upward restatement of the cost of property, plant and'equipment.

Property, plant and equipment are stated at the net revalued amounts at January 1, 1980. Additions since that date are stated at cost.

Depreciation is computed on the net revalued amounts by the declining balance method using rates based on the estimated useful lives of the related units of property.

Improvements that significantly expand the life of an asset or add to its productive capacity are capitalized. Expenditures for repairs and maintenance are charged to income as incurred.

Interest during the construction and installation period is capitalized as part of property, plant and equipment. Interest incurred of ₩3,032 million ($3,752 thousand) in 1993 and ₩2,944 million ($3,643 thousand) in 1992 have been capitalized.

(f) Other Assets

Debenture issuance costs are amortized on a straight line basis over periods up to three years.

(g) Income Taxes

Provision is not made in the accounts to reflect the interperiod allocation of income taxes resulting from certain income and expense items being treated differently for financial reporting purposes than for tax computation purposes.

(h) Retirement and Severance Benefits

Employees who have been with the Company for more than one year are entitled to lump-sum payments based on current rates of pay and length of service when they leave the Company. It is not the policy of the Company to fund completely the retirement and severance benefits accrued; however, provision has been made in the accompanying balance sheets for the estimated accrued liability under the parts. A portion of accrued retirement and severance benefits is covered by deposits with insurance companies included in other assets.

Under the national pension scheme of Korea, effective January 1, 1993, the Company is required to transfer a certain portion of retirement allowances of employees to National Pension Corporation. The amount transferred will reduce the retirement and severance benefits liability to be payable to the employees when they leave the Company and is reflected in the accompanying balance sheets.

Certain directors are not covered by the programs described above. Benefits paid to such directors are charged to earnings as paid since amounts vary with circumstances and it is not practicable to compute the liability for future payments.

According to these plans, the Company's total liabilities for employees' retirement and severance benefits as of December 31, 1993 and 1992 are ₩122,713 million ($151,854 thousand) and ₩106,899 million ($132,284 thousand), respectively. Beginning in 1991, the Company accrued its liability for employees' retirement and severance benefits at an amount equal to the net increase in total retirement and severance liability assuming all employees terminated as of the balance sheet date plus current year payments. The deficiency in its liability, ₩26,334 million ($32,587 thousand) at December 31, 1990 shall be accrued over ten years beginning in 1991 and shall be reflected in the accompanying financial statements as direct adjustments to retained earnings at the beginning of year. Such method is allowable under generally accepted financial accounting standards in the Republic of Korea. As such, the existing liability is understated by ₩18,433 million ($22,810 thousand) at December 31, 1993 from that which would be required assuming all employees terminated as of the balance sheet date.

(i) Long-Term Contracts

Long-term construction contracts are accounted for by the percentage-of-completion method of accounting for contract revenue and costs are recognized based on the percentage that work performed to date bears to total performance required by the contract.

(j) Foreign Currency Translation

Monetary assets and liabilities denominated in foreign currencies are translated into Korean won at current rates of exchange at the balance sheet date. Non-monetary assets and liabilities are translated at historical rates. Until 1992, unrealized exchange gains or losses on long-term foreign currency items were deferred and amortized over five years if such gains or losses exceeded 5 percent of capital in a year. Beginning in 1993 under revised accounting standards, unrealized exchange gains and losses on long-term foreign currency items are charged to income as incurred rather than deferred and amortized over five years.

Foreign currency assets and liabilities of foreign-based operations are first translated into local currency at current rates of exchange at the balance sheet date and the resultant gain or loss is reflected as exchange and translation gain/loss in the statement of income. Subsequently, in translating local currency financial statements into Korean Won (the reporting currency), the items of assets and liabilities in the balance sheet are translated at current rates of exchange at the balance sheet date while profit and loss items in the statement of income are translated at average rates. Translation gains on foreign-based operations are accumulated as a foreign currency translation gain to be offset against future translation losses on foreign-based operations. Translation losses on foreign-based operations are first offset against any foreign currency translation gains accumulated in prior years. Until 1992, the balance was amortized on a straight-line basis over 5 years, which amortization was reflected as exchange and translation gain/loss in the statement of income. Beginning in 1993 under revised accounting standards, the translation gains and losses on foreign based operations are offset and the balance is accumulated as capital adjustment-foreign based operation translation credit (debit) in the stockholders' equity section.

(k) Leases

The Company accounts for and classifies its lease transactions as operating leases or capital leases in accordance with Korean Lease Accounting Standards.

(l) Prior Year Adjustments

Generally accepted financial accounting standards in the Republic of Korea allow for recognition as prior year adjustments the financial effects of certain adjustments occurring in the current year which are applicable to prior years' activity. Such adjustments have been reflected in the accompanying financial statements as direct adjustments to retained earnings at the beginning of the year.

(m) Capital Adjustments for Conversion Rights and Stock Warrant Rights

When the Company is obliged to pay a redemption premium to the holders of convertible debentures who do not exercise their options to convert and hold the debentures until maturity or, in case of overseas issues, who exercised their option right to require the Company to redeem their debentures, the difference between the face value of debentures and the present value of the principal amounts payable at maturity or the expiration date of the option including coupon interest to be paid during the period, is considered compensation for conversion rights, which is deducted from long-term debt as conversion rights adjustment and credited to stockholders' equity as a capital adjustment for conversion rights.

The conversion rights adjustment is amortized over the terms of the debentures using the effective interest rate method and the amount amortized is recorded as interest expense on the debentures.

At the time of conversion, the conversion rights adjustment and the capital adjustment for conversion rights pertaining to the converted debentures are taken out of those accounts, with the difference, the amount amortized, being credited to capital surplus.

The above description relates to the terms of convertible debentures, similar accounting treatment would be applicable to debentures with warrants.

ANNUAL REPORT ANALYSIS

Hyundai

An interesting and important challenge for students of international financial reporting is to study the published annual reports of various companies from different countries. Your instructor will provide you with a recent copy of the Hyundai annual report. To facilitate your delving into this annual report, undertake the following endeavors.

Required:

(a) List the key differences between the Hyundai annual report and what you would expect to see for a U.S. company such as General Motors or Ford.

(b) Calculate the following ratios for Hyundai taking care to note the assumptions you found necessary to make and where you found the appropriate pieces of data in the annual report.

$$(1)\ \text{Current ratio} = \frac{\text{Total current assets}}{\text{Total current liabilities}}$$

$$(2)\ \text{Quick ratio} = \frac{\text{Cash + Marketable securities + Accts. rec.}}{\text{Total current liabilities}}$$

$$(3)\ \text{Operating cash flow to current liabilities} = \frac{\text{Operating cash flow}}{\text{Average total current liabilities}}$$

$$(4)\ \text{Debt-to-equity ratio} = \frac{\text{Long-term debt}}{\text{Owners' equity}}$$

$$(5)\ \text{Debt-to-total capitalization ratio} = \frac{\text{Long-term debt}}{\text{Long-term debt + Owners' equity}}$$

(6) Interest coverage ratio $= \dfrac{\text{Net income before interest \& income taxes}}{\text{Interest expense}}$

(7) Operating cash flow to interest charges $= \dfrac{\text{Operating cash flow}}{\text{Interest expense}}$

(8) Operating cash flow to total liabilities $= \dfrac{\text{Operating cash flow}}{\text{Average total liabilities}}$

(9) Receivables turnover ratio $= \dfrac{\text{Net sales}}{\text{Average accounts receivable}}$

(10) Inventory turnover $= \dfrac{\text{Cost of goods sold}}{\text{Average inventory}}$

(11) Asset turnover $= \dfrac{\text{Net sales}}{\text{Average total assets}}$

(12) Average collection period ratio $= \dfrac{\text{365 Days}}{\text{Receivables turnover ratio}}$

(13) Average number of days' inventory on hand ratio $= \dfrac{\text{365 Days}}{\text{Inventory turnover ratio}}$

(14) Return on assets (ROA) $= \dfrac{\text{Net income}}{\text{Average total assets}}$

              OR $= \text{ROS} \times \text{Asset turnover}$

(15) Return on equity (ROE) $= \dfrac{\text{Net income}}{\text{Average total owners' equity}}$

              OR $= \text{ROA} \times \text{Financial leverage}$

(16) Return on sales (ROS) $= \dfrac{\text{Net income}}{\text{Net sales}}$

(17) Financial everage $= \dfrac{\text{Average liabilities} + \text{Average owners' equity}}{\text{Average owners' equity}}$

(18) Basic earnings per share (EPS) $= \dfrac{\text{NI applicable to common shareholders}}{\text{Weighted average common shares}}$

(19) Cash dividend yield $= \dfrac{\text{Cash dividend per common share}}{\text{Market price per common share}}$

(20) Cash dividend payout $= \dfrac{\text{Total cash dividend to common shareholders}}{\text{Net income}}$

(c) What do you conclude about the availability of the appropriate data in the annual report for calculating these ratios?

(d) What does this financial analysis tell you about Hyundai?

(e) What analytical metrics did Hyundai choose to report for itself? What do those choices say about the message the company is striving to tell and the audience it is addressing?

CHAPTER 14

Italy

Inadequate disclosure requirements and insufficient safeguards for minority shareholders . . . may have slowed down the development of the securities market.[1]

Accounting in Italy is undergoing a period of major changes.[2]

Introduction

For a variety of reasons, some of them immediate and others more deeply rooted, Italy has found the going difficult as it attempts to harmonize its financial reporting standards with those of other European Union members. Despite being a founding member of the EU, Italy did not implement the Fourth and Seventh Directives until 1991. The immediate reasons for this delay include the magnitude of the required change and the lack of accounting experience and expertise on crucial topics such as consolidations. Among the more deeply rooted reasons are the relative insignificance of the country's equity markets, the prominence of family-controlled companies in the Italian economy, and the incentive to suppress or distort financial information caused by the traditional association of accounting income with tax collection. The former set of problems has confronted legislators and accounting professionals with procedural obstacles as they attempt to devise and implement changes; the latter raises serious questions about the purpose of financial reporting in Italy as the nation's economy moves from semi-industrialized insularity toward international integration.

Nevertheless, change is proceeding in Italy, regardless of how difficult and incremental the steps may be. The status of the accounting profession is increasing as government and business alike realize the necessity of a sophisticated corps of experts to

---

[1]A. Goldstein and G. Nicoletti, "Italy: Corporate Governance," *The OECD Observer,* February/March 1995, p. 48.

[2]S. Zambon and Saccon, "Accounting Change in Italy," *European Accounting Review,* September 1993, p. 245.

develop and operate financial reporting systems. During the 1970s, a new agency modeled on the U.S. Securities and Exchange Commission, the ***Commissione Nazionale per le Societa e la Borsa (CONSOB),*** was created to regulate Italy's securities markets (a process that was unfortunately delayed by bureaucratic resistance). And even though Italy does not have a formidable contingent of internationally traded companies resolutely leading the private sector toward international reporting (as Germany and Sweden do), high visibility firms such as Fiat and Pirelli are finding it necessary to adopt international accounting standards and to prepare consolidated statements. As a charter member of the EU, the world's fifth largest industrial power, and a nation whose economy depends on international trade, Italy has no intention of being left out as the rest of the industrialized world lays the groundwork for a new global economic order.

Environmental Factors

Cultural Environment

Generally speaking, the results of Hofstede's study of cultural attitudes suggests that groups of subjects scoring high in uncertainty avoidance can be found in countries with accounting systems based on statutory law: Germany, Japan, France, Brazil, and others. (It should be noted that Sweden provides a notable exception to this generalization for reasons that are discussed in the chapter on that country.) Because he is more concerned with organizational behavior than financial reporting practices, however, Hofstede never attempts to establish a correlation between national culture and financial reporting. Other researchers, though, have drawn on his research to do so. Gray, for example, advances the hypothesis that a country with high scores in uncertainty avoidance and power distance and a low score in individualism is likely to have a financial reporting environment characterized by uniformity (i.e., one that is legislated by a central power rather than negotiated by contending parties).[3]

Italy seems to bear out this tentative generalization, at least in part. Italian financial reporting is characterized by a high degree of legal prescription, and the Italian subjects surveyed in Hofstede's study scored high in uncertainty avoidance: a 75, compared to a 46 for the United States. This score, along with a score of 50 in power distance, places Italy in the organizational paradigm that Hofstede calls the ''pyramid of people.'' Hofstede describes this paradigm as hierarchical, held together by unity of command and adherence to rules. Employees operating under the pyramid paradigm are more likely to settle a disagreement by referral to higher authority than by negotiation. The strong appeal of hierarchical authority in Italian culture is evident in a number of the nation's traditional social structures such as the patriarchal structure of Italian families, the dominance of Roman Catholicism, and the influence of authoritarianism on the nation's political history and public discourse. (Although Italy and

---

[3]S. J. Gray, ''Towards a Theory of Cultural Influence on the Development of Accounting Systems Internationally,'' *Abacus* 24, no. 1 (1988), pp. 1–15.

the rest of Continental Europe have attempted to shed the heritage of fascism, splinter groups still garner more than token support. In the case of Italy, the neofascist party has been capturing a sizable percentage of the voters in recent national elections.) Even though the general tenor that Italian politics has taken since World War II could hardly be labeled authoritarian, it is still characterized by relatively strong central government initiatives and relatively weak local and regional control. Moreover, while political power in Italy is split among numerous parties, discipline within parties is strong, and voters do not change their allegiances easily.

Nevertheless, the reality of Italian organizational and political culture is predictably complex. It cannot be adequately described merely by appealing to the authoritarian and hierarchical elements mentioned. The Italians in Hofstede's survey also registered a high score in individualism (76), which suggests a very different side of the national character, one that is reflected in the popular stereotype of the passionate and rebellious Mediterranean temperament. If many Italians have been and continue to be attracted by the stability offered by hierarchical authority, others are repelled by the restrictions it places on individual freedom. More than 90 percent of the population calls itself Roman Catholic, but few actually attend worship services, and Italians are not noted for docile submission to papal pronouncements. Likewise, Italian families, both domestic and political, are justly reputed for the frequency and vehemence of their internal disagreements. Italians, it might be said, enjoy more than most societies the emotional support and emotional release that social structures such as family, religion, and regionalism may provide, but they do not necessarily want such institutions to assert excessive control over their personal actions.[4] As one veteran reporter recently observed, there is a ''battle which is waging perpetually in the Italian character between the forces of self-destructive irresponsibility and those of responsible pragmatism.''[5]

The peculiar ambivalence that marks the Italians' attitude toward authority results in notoriously inefficient social administration, a problem that affects financial accounting as well as other areas of Italian business. Although the rules governing Italian financial reporting practices are prescribed by a central authority, the resulting system is neither orderly nor particularly effective (at least by Anglo-American standards). Historically, a lack of coordination among tax law, company law, and securities law has created a plethora of rules and made compliance a nontrivial process. Businesses must exercise caution, lest in fulfilling one set of requirements, they violate another. Moreover, since 1991 ''virtually all of the previous regulation dealing with the technical and professional side of accounting has been swept away,''[6] introducing an era of new debate and a fresh focus on the purpose and role of financial reporting in Italy.

---

[4]See ''Vox Populi,'' *The Economist,* June 26, 1993, pp. Survey 6–12 and ''Great Expectations,'' *The Economist,* June 26, 1993, pp. Survey 21–22.

[5]J. Wyles, ''Dynamic but Deadlocked,'' *Financial Times,* April 17, 1990, p. I. Italy was not a part of Hofstede's studies involving the LTO cultural dimension and as a result, it is not discussed here. It is useful to note, however, that Italians have a relatively high savings rate, comparable to the Japanese, who score relatively high on the LTO dimension. See ''Northern Grit,'' *The Economist,* June 26, 1993, pp. Survey 12–15.

[6]S. Zambon and C. Saccon, ''Accounting Change in Italy,'' *European Accounting Review* 2 (1993), pp. 245–84.

Such a catalyst is needed if Italy is ever to address the informational needs of an international financial constituency.

Legal and Political Environment

EU Membership. The most effective impetus for change in Italian financial reporting is Italy's membership in the European Union. As mentioned in Chapter 3, the EU has issued two directives that bear directly on financial reporting: the Fourth Directive, concerning the format and content of financial statements, and the Seventh Directive, concerning the preparation of consolidated statements. The requirements of these directives do not impose a prefabricated system on member nations; rather, each country must revise its laws within a certain time period so that they conform to the directives in all essential points. (Some flexibility is built into the requirements of the directives.) Both directives have necessitated substantial change in Italian accounting practices.

In late 1991, Italy formally adopted both directives by revising its civil code. (All other EU members at the time had previously adopted and implemented the Fourth Directive.) The detailed principles being developed by the Italian accounting profession (discussed subsequently) are, for the most part, now fully consistent with the requirements of the directives. The Fourth Directive took effect for fiscal years ending December 31, 1993; the Seventh Directive's consolidation requirements took effect one year later.[7] Until the Seventh Directive took effect, only companies listed on stock exchanges were required to prepare and publish consolidated statements, and there was no formal requirement that such statements be independently audited (though in practice most large companies have this done). Now, consolidation accounts are required for groups meeting two of the following three size tests: (1) total assets of more than L10 billion ($6,165,000), (2) sales of more than L20 billion ($12,330,000), and (3) more than 250 employees.[8] For the years prior to the directives' implementation, the CONSOB directed companies to follow International Accounting Standards Committee (IASC) pronouncements, and that is why a company such as Fiat explicitly states in its annual report that it adhered to IASC standards when most large international companies from around the world make no reference to IASC standards.

Political Instability. The volatility of Italian politics is well known. Since World War II, Italy has experienced more than 50 governments, with few administrations lasting more than a year. The frequent changes can be attributed to the multiparty structure of Italian politics, because of which any single party is unlikely to achieve an outright parliamentary majority, much less maintain one. Thus, cabinets are forced to rely on coalitions (usually tenuous ones) to muster sufficient support to stay in

---

[7]C. Nobes and S. Zambon, "Piano, Piano: Italy Implements the Directives," *Accountancy,* July 1991, pp. 84–85.

[8]Zambon and Saccon, "Accounting Change in Italy." The Italian *lire* is often noted as Lit or L. As of January 1, 1995, US$1.00 = L1,622.

power. Administrations topple when disgruntled coalition members decide to switch allegiance or walk out. The advantage of such a system, of course, is that it allows considerable room for active dissent, and, consequently, minority groups often exercise real power. The disadvantage is equally obvious: achieving and maintaining effective governance is difficult. Indeed, corporate managers often lament, "We want stability. We need a government that can last long enough to make the changes that are needed."[9]

Paradoxically, the very volatility of this system has hampered accounting reform in Italy. Changing a nation's legal infrastructure requires deliberation, resolution, and, above all, a government strong enough to see the job through. Because Italian accounting practices are based on statutory law, the process of major reform is complex and beset with political pitfalls. Under Italy's parliamentary system, cabinets are simply too weak to initiate and push through reform measures by themselves. Although reform measures do not disappear when a cabinet is relieved of office, administrative shuffles routinely delay their approval and implementation by months or even years. Such delays are the reason that important stock exchange regulations have been bottled up in the Italian parliament (see the following discussion) and that Italy was among the last EU member nations to incorporate the requirements of the Fourth Directive in its company law.

Taxation of Shareholders.   Dividend and interest income are both taxed as ordinary income under Italian tax law. (Tax rates on individuals run from 10 percent to 51 percent. An additional "local" tax rate of 16.2 percent does not apply to dividends and interest.) Under the imputation system now in effect, however, recipients of dividends from Italian companies are entitled to a tax credit designed to provide at least partial relief from double taxation of corporate profits. The credit, available to corporate as well as individual shareholders, is currently set at 46 percent of dividend payments received, and the amount of the credit is included in income along with the amount of the dividend received.

Hence the recipient of L10,000,000 (US$6,165) in dividends from an Italian corporation also receives a tax credit of L4,600,000 ($2,836) and is required to show L14,600,000 ($9,001) of income on his or her tax return. If the taxpayer were in the 31.5 percent bracket, the dividend income would generate no extra tax liability (14,600,000 times 31.5 percent, less the credit of 4,600,000, equals zero). Of course, if the taxpayer were in a bracket higher than 31.5 percent, the marginal tax liability generated by the dividend income would exceed the tax credit. Because the basic national tax rate for corporations is 36 percent, the imputed credit is obviously designed to enable corporate shareholders to receive dividends substantially tax free.

Capital gains on the sale of shares are included in the ordinary income of business enterprises. Prior to September 1993, however, they were not taxable to individuals. Since that date, capital gains have been taxable to individuals at a preferential rate of 15 or 25 percent, depending on various parameters.

---

[9]B. Coleman, "Italy's Economic Backbone, the North, Is Heeded in Search for New Leadership," *The Wall Street Journal,* December 29, 1994, p. A6.

Corporate Tax Law.   As mentioned, the basic national corporate tax rate in Italy is 36 percent. Nondeductible regional taxes raise the effective tax rate to approximately 52 percent, however. Taxable income is calculated by adjusting book income to reflect tax law. Such adjustments generally include adding back expenses that are nondeductible for tax purposes or that exceed statutory allowances (such as excess depreciation, bad debt allowances, and maintenance costs) and applying tax losses carried forward from a previous period. Book income is not required to equal taxable income, although it frequently closely approximates it.

Because financial statements provide the basis for tax returns, tax rules do affect book income. Most costs and expenses are not deductible for tax purposes unless they are also shown on the income statement; hence, tax considerations often induce Italian corporate management to record a larger expense than is required under accepted financial accounting principles. For example, fixed assets with a unit cost of less than L1 million (about $616) may be fully written off for tax purposes but only if they are also fully written off for accounting purposes. Moreover, most companies adopt the maximum depreciation allowable for tax purposes as their depreciation expense on the financial statements. This propensity to conservatively measure reported earnings is commonly referred to as *fiscal bias* and creates a significant challenge for those analysts and investors interested in comparing the financial results of Italian companies with counterparts from other countries.

Most Italian companies accrue income taxes payable based on an estimate of their tax liability when the next return will be filed (i.e., a flow-thru approach). Although interperiod tax allocation is not widespread, some companies adopt a form of it in accordance with international accounting standards in which they account for deferred taxes only to the extent that an actual liability is expected to arise within the next three years. Accordingly, an Italian company can avoid a deferred tax charge if there is some conviction that the tax will not be payable within three years.[10] As might be expected, the deferred income taxes that are reported are relatively immaterial in amount.

Business Environment

Form of Business.   The business entity in Italy that most closely approximates the U.S. corporation is the joint stock company, or the *Società per Azioni (S.p.A.).* Italian law requires an S.p.A. to have minimum capital of L200 million ($123,305). An S.p.A. must create and maintain a legal reserve to which it allocates 5 percent of after-tax profits each year until the reserve equals 20 percent of paid-in capital. In addition, an S.p.A. must have more than one shareholder to be granted limited liability status under the law; owners of 100 percent of the stock of an S.p.A. are personally liable without limitation for all of the debts of the business. An S.p.A. may operate either under a single director or a board of directors, however. It is the preferred form of business for large enterprises.

---

[10]R. Khalaf, ''Buyer Beware,'' *Forbes,* June 20, 1994, pp. 204–5.

The *Società a Responsibilità Limitada (S.r.l.)* is the other major limited liability entity; it is often used to form small businesses and closely held concerns. An S.r.l. must possess minimum capital of only L20 million (about $12,330), which is represented not by shares but by quotas or parts held by investors. Quotas may differ in amount but may not be less than L1,000 (about 62¢). Quota holders are liable only to the extent of their capital contributions.

Italy's first antitrust law was passed in 1990 and applies to both state-owned and private companies. In general, it seeks to outlaw agreements that restrict free competition and abuses of dominant position, and it subjects all mergers of a certain size to scrutiny for their effect on competitive forces. Historically, Italian industry has been dominated by public and private conglomerates that enjoy close relations with certain banks, newspapers, and insurance companies. Skeptics believe the new antitrust law will do little to alter this scenario. It is expected, however, that the law will offer consumers and small businesses real opportunities for redress against abuses of the large industrial units' dominant positions, as well as to society at large, in hindering the corporate tendency to seek easy gain via alliances that thwart competition.

A particularly unique feature of the Italian business landscape is the preponderance, on the one hand, of relatively small companies and, on the other, of large state-owned conglomerates. For example, in the machine tools industry, Germany and Italy are prime competitors, yet German machine tool companies average 265 employees while Italy's average 71.[11] Moreover, Italy is the world's third largest machine tools manufacturer but it has only four companies ranked among Europe's 40 largest. Stated in a slightly more comprehensive manner, 39 percent of all Italian companies have less than 100 employees as compared to 21 percent in the United Kingdom.[12] Historically, Italian small businesses' only source of external financing has been short-term bank loans, with a real dearth of long-term loans and venture capital available.[13] At the other end of the spectrum, "of all Western economies, Italy still depends most heavily on state-owned entities that dominate whole [industrial] sectors."[14] These goliath-like conglomerates have not had to rely on an equities market for financing. Thus, given these two dominating features of the Italian business portfolio, there has been no real industrial demand for a broad, deep, sophisticated equity market and the business disclosures and governance that typically accompany such a market.

Audit and Reporting Requirements.   Every S.p.A. and every S.r.l with capital of more L100 million (about $61,652) must appoint a board of statutory auditors to monitor company management and ascertain that the company's books and financial statements conform to the requirements of the Italian civil code. These auditors must have some degree of independence: they may not be related to directors by blood or marriage and may not be employees of the corporation, but they may hold stock in it. At least

---

[11]J. Simkins, "Flexible and Resilient," *Financial Times,* October 13, 1993, p. 29.

[12]A. Hill, "The Small Imbroglio," *Financial Times,* May 9, 1995, p. 14.

[13]See "Change in the Heartland," *The Economist,* April 2, 1994, pp. 63–64, and J. Simkins, "Shift towards Bigger Units," *Financial Times,* October 13, 1993, p. 28.

[14]J. Valente, "Two Paths, Two Problems," *The Wall Street Journal,* September 30, 1994, p. R8.

one of the members must have certain business qualifications (not necessarily in auditing). In general, however, the role of the statutory auditor is not that of the trained independent auditor who undertakes the fairness attest function.

In addition to the largely formal oversight of statutory auditors, certain companies must submit their annual statements to an examination by an officially authorized auditing firm. (Independent audits were virtually unknown in Italy before 1975.) These companies include those listed on stock exchanges, those controlled or financed by the state, insurance companies, publishers with substantial income from periodicals, contractors bidding on large public construction projects, and several other types of enterprises. The agency that authorizes firms to perform independent audits is Italy's version of the SEC, the CONSOB According to a law passed in 1981, Italian firms may retain an auditor for a maximum of nine years, after which it must hire a new one. (This law applies even to very large companies.) Accountants and managers alike have complained bitterly about the hardships this measure entails on auditors and their clients.

The nature of an independent auditor's attestation has evolved during the 20th century. Prior to the 1942 code, S.p.A.s were required to file financial statements that depicted

> [w]ith straightforwardness and truth the financial situation and the economic results of the company. The 1942 Civil Code [set forth the concept that] the balance sheet and profit and loss account should present with clearness and precision a company's financial position and results. [Then a 1974 law establishing the CONSOB also established] the fundamental innovation of the introduction of compulsory external audit for listed companies. [A 1975 presidential decree further noted that] independent auditors had to verify whether the company's financial statements complied with both legal rules and correct accounting principles.[15]

The dual focus created in 1975 was not always compatible, and audit reports often went to great lengths to try to clarify the auditor's conclusions as they pertained to a particular focus. This situation was somewhat alleviated with the adoption of the EU's Fourth Directive, which became effective for fiscal years ending after April 1993. In its adoption of the Fourth Directive, Italy embraced the audit attestation objective of true and correct in contrast to the British notion of true and fair. Moreover, the clearness principle, a notion akin to the U.S. concern for full disclosure, was reiterated.

For nonresident readers of Italian financial statements, it is difficult to ascertain the appropriate level of comfort afforded by a true and correct assertion. Does *correct* suggest legal compliance or perhaps the correct application of an accounting practice or standard? Is *correct* synonymous with *fair?* Even in Italy, ''there is great concern as to how the 'true and correct representation' formula should be interpreted, and about the consequences of its introduction.''[16] Perhaps as a result of that confusion, contemporary Italian audit opinions are not yet uniform (as they would be in the United States

---

[15]Zambon and Saccon, ''Accounting Change in Italy,'' p. 247.
[16]Ibid., p. 251.

or Great Britain). Indeed, Exhibit 14–1 includes three different opinion statements, one each from three global accounting firms, all applicable to the same period of time.

Accounting Profession—Qualifications.   Italy's accounting profession includes two tiers of qualifications: the *dottore commercialista* (doctor of commerce) and the *ragioniere collegiato* (accountant and commercial expert). Requirements for the former include completing a four-year course of study at a university and three years of apprenticeship in addition to passing a special examination administered by the government, after which the candidate is admitted to membership in the *Ordine de Dottori Commercialisti*. Requirements for the *ragioniere collegiato* include graduating from a special five-year secondary school (a kind of advanced high school for business), obtaining a "short" three-year university degree, passing a national examination, and gaining three years of experience in public practice under the supervision of a *dottore commercialista* or a *ragioniere collegiato*. The candidate is then admitted into the *Collegio dei Ragionieri e Periti Commerciali*.

The distinction in titles has little or no effect on professional activities; a *ragioniere collegiato* is permitted to perform the same tasks as a *dottore commercialista*. Italy is served by approximately 50,000 accounting professionals, 60 percent of whom are in practice and half of whom are *dottore commercialistas*.[17] A shortage of professionals has presented particular problems because of the large amount of complex legislation in recent years covering various aspects of financial reporting.

As mentioned, the board of statutory auditors for an S.p.A. or an S.r.l. must include at least one member who is registered as a *revisore officiale dei conti* (official auditor of accounts). Registration requires five years of service in some professional capacity with a business that has at least L50 million (about $30,800) of capital stock. The experience requirement is shortened for an applicant who holds either the *dottore commercialista* or *ragioniere collegiato* designation.

Independent audits (as opposed to the examination made by statutory auditors) may be undertaken only by firms approved by CONSOB. For an accounting firm to obtain such approval, a majority of its partners must be certified as *dottori* or *ragionieri* and have five years of experience in auditing.

Accounting Profession—Policy Formation.   The creation of accounting policy in Italy is a complex and multilayered process. Although Italian accounting standards have traditionally been created by government legislation, the process of policy formation is becoming more a partnership between the accounting profession and the government. It must be understood, though, that the government is still clearly the senior partner. To that end, the civil code and tax law prescribe the contents of financial statements and set broad principles for valuing assets and liabilities. CONSOB, as the primary regulator of capital markets, oversees the enforcement of existing financial reporting standards and imposes rules of its own when necessary. To date, the accounting profession's role has been as a consultant to legislators and

---

[17]Ibid.

EXHIBIT 14–1

Excerpted Auditor Opinions in Italy

Panel A: Fiat

To the Board of Directors and Stockholders of Fiat S.p.A.:

• • •

In our opinion, based on our audits and the reports of other auditors, the consolidated financial statements referred to above present fairly, in all material respects, the financial position of Fiat S.p.A. and its subsidiaries as of December 31, 1993 and 1992, and the results of their operations and the changes in their financial position for each of the three years in the period ended December 31, 1993, in conformity with the accounting principles as recommended by International Accounting Standards Committee (IASC).

• • •

Price Waterhouse S.a.s.
Turin, Italy June 6, 1994

Panel B: Olivetti

To the Board of Directors of Olivetti S.p.A.:

• • •

In our opinion, on the basis of our examination and, as described in paragraph 2, the reports of other auditing firms, the above-mentioned consolidated financial statements present the consolidated financial position of the Olivetti Group as of December 31, 1993 and the consolidated result of its operations and the changes in its consolidated financial position for the year then ended, in conformity with correct accounting principles established or adopted (International Accounting Standards) by the Italian accounting profession within the limits described in the preceding paragraph.

Coopers & Lybrand S.a.s.
Turin (Italy), April 20, 1994

Panel C: ENI

To the Stockholders of ENI S.p.A.

• • •

In our opinion, the above-mentioned consolidated financial statements, taken as a whole, have been prepared clearly and give a true and fair view of the financial position of the ENI Group as of December 31, 1993, and the results of its operations for the year then ended, in accordance with the law related to consolidated financial statements referred to in the second paragraph.

Arthur Andersen & Co. S.a.s.
Rome, Italy
June 24, 1994

as a promulgator of accounting and auditing procedures that clarify and/or supplement the civil code's guidelines.

The Civil Code prescribes the content and format of the required balance sheet and income statement in quite some detail. The Alitalia financial statements in Exhibit 14–2 follow the prescribed forms. The following should be noted:

> The balance sheet is organized according to the German-based "destination principle," which leads to an apparently inappropriate application of the Anglo-Saxon financial approach based on items' liquidity. Balance sheet memorandum accounts have to [also] be disclosed. Their role is to point out future risks and obligations. As for the income statement, the implemented format is of the progressive type, and is based on the cost classification by nature rather than by destination. This German-derived model starts with the "value of production" and shows some intermediate results but unfortunately not the operating income. An attempt to overcome the problematic relationship between commercial law and fiscal rules has been made by trying to separate the influence of taxation from accounting profit calculation [in that] . . . the final section of the income statement include adjustments of valuations and provisions resulting purely from the application of the tax legislation [see the 5th and 6th lines from the end of Alitalia's income statement]. In this way . . . there has taken place an institutionalization of the linkage between commercial and tax accounting. . . . Only additional charges caused by tax allowances being greater than commercial accounting ones may be entered in these adjustment lines. Where the difference is the other way, the difference cannot be included in these two lines, and therefore the reconciliation between the tax profit and the commercial profit is one-sided and partial.[18]

The detail presented in Exhibit 14–2 is, at one level, overwhelming and perhaps more than one needs to make an investment decision. At another level, however, various company constituencies are likely to find various parts of the detail useful. As a set of financial statements for public consumption, it is out of step with the international norm. For this reason, most Italian companies that publish financial statements such as those in Exhibit 14–2 also publish a more succinct, more generally recognizable balance sheet and income statement. Indeed, Exhibit 14–3 presents such statements as provided by Alitalia. Moreover, some Italian companies (e.g., Olivetti) do not publish statements such as those in Exhibit 14–2 for general public use, instead using statements similar to those in Exhibit 14–3. For most investor analytical purposes, users of the Alitalia annual report are likely to find information presented in Exhibit 14–3 sufficient.

The accounting body with the most influence on policy formation is the *Consiglio Nazionale dei Dottori Commercialisti* (CNDC), a national association roughly analogous to the American Institute of CPAs. The CNDC not only advises the government on accounting legislation, but also has begun to issue guidelines delineating "good accounting practices" and standards for performing audits. (CONSOB has adopted all but one of the auditing standards promulgated by the CNDC and has given them the force of law.) The strengths of the CNDC standards are their attentiveness to international developments and their provision of detailed guidance. However, it will be some time before the CNDC can catch up with the need for agreed-upon interpretations of

---

[18]Ibid., pp. 252–56.

Exhibit 14–2

Alitalia Financial Statements
Prepared in Civil Code Format
(comparative years required but omitted here)

Panel A: Consolidated Balance Sheet as of December 31, 1993

ASSETS

Receivables from Shareholders as Outstanding Payments		–0–	–0–
FIXED ASSETS			
Intangible Fixed Assets			
Plant and expansion costs		2,030,147,423	
Research, development and advertising costs		19,141,382,838	
Royalties and copyright fees		230,422,400	
Franchise, license, trademark, and similar fees		705,048,348	
Goodwill		120,978,781	
Tangible fixed assets in course of construction and advance payments on tangible fixed assets		20,661,581,055	
Other costs		225,027,088,690	267,916,649,535
Tangible Fixed Assets			
Buildings and land		335,909,939,573	
Plant and machinery			
Fleet	2,390,182,567,179		
Other plant and machinery	122,953,510,701	2,513,136,077,880	
Other fixed operating assets		73,589,128,769	
Assets subject to transfer without charge		282,216,121,277	
Other assets		68,872,638,657	
Tangible fixed assets in course of construction and advance payments on tangible fixed assets		568,482,145,353	3,842,206,051,509
Financial Fixed Assets			
Participating interests in			
Subsidiary undertakings	685,110,379		
Associated undertakings	124,748,500,000		
Other undertakings	89,068,648,525	214,502,258,904	
Payments on account of participating interests	–0–		
Receivables*			
From subsidiary undertakings	3,474,413,191	3,474,413,191	
From others	1,431,042,989	22,786,583,405	26,260,996,596
Other investments		288,000,000	241,051,255,500
TOTAL FIXED ASSETS			4,361,173,956,544
WORKING CAPITAL			
Stocks			
Spares, other technical material and consumables		251,903,118,167	
Work in progress		2,806,943,867	
Work in progress under contract		83,272,175,172	
Finished goods and merchandise		12,023,378,837	
Advanced payments		10,436,080,298	360,441,706,341
Receivables†			
From customers	6,331,148,785	301,702,596,358	
From subsidiary undertakings		2,277,552,802	
From others			
Air navigation companies	154,587,250,260		
Travel agents	397,801,113,778		
Sundries	218,047,397,208	770,435,761,246	1,074,415,910,406

Exhibit 14–2 (continued)

Non-Fixed Financial Assets			
Securities		11,589,901,300	11,589,901,300
Cash at Bank and in Hand			
Cash at banks and post offices		89,586,583,997	
Cheques		507,195,236	
Cash and securities in hand		9,725,962,905	99,819,742,138
TOTAL WORKING CAPITAL			1,546,267,260,158
Accrued Income and Prepayments			
Prepaid loan charges		7,434,421,787	
Other accruals and prepayments		36,257,576,611	43,691,998,398
TOTAL ASSETS			5,941,133,215,127
LIABILITIES			
Shareholders' Equity			
Parent Company's share			
Issued Share Capital			975,000,000,000
Share Premium Account			16,167,406,789
Revaluation Reserves			
Revaluation reserves pursuant to law 413/91		14,703,766,000	
Revaluation reserves pursuant to law 72/83		41,689,855	14,745,456,855
Statutory Reserve			29,585,985,712
Other Reserves			
Extraordinary reserve		23,024,671,045	
Reserve created through grants-in-aid pursuant to law 181/89		27,847,087,600	
Profits set aside for reinvestment in Italy's south (D.P.R. 218/78)		–0–	
Consolidation reserve		28,154,613,151	79,026,371,796
Losses Carried Forward from Previous Years			(35,158,467,258)
Loss for the Year			(343,467,137,263)
Shareholders' equity in the Parent company			735,899,615,631
Minority Interests			
Capital and Reserves			53,369,255,770
Profit for the Year			6,592,830,467
Loss covered during the Year			–0–
Shareholders' equity—minority interests			59,962,066,237
			795,861,701,868
Provisions for Liabilities and Charges			
On account of taxes		33,805,154,510	
Other provisions			
Provision for exchange fluctuation	31,750,427,761		
Provision for discount coupons and price contests	6,682,337,348		
Provision for foreign exchange liabilities	81,968,528,610		
Sundries	88,868,509,210	209,269,802,929	243,074,957,439
Severance Pay			897,791,484,619
Payables†			
Payables to banks	973,214,283,619	1,849,246,855,422	
Payables to other lenders	50,984,333,334	216,591,104,297	
Advance payments	85,105,997,369	117,948,502,177	
Payables to suppliers	2,931,471,431	688,728,827,199	
Payables represented by instruments of credit		834,456,496	

EXHIBIT 14–2 (continued)

Payables to subsidiary undertakers				1,891,995,992
Payables to associated undertakings				4,829,835,936
Payables to holding companies				128,202,425,073
Taxes payable				117,934,056,658
Payables to social security institutions				157,704,942,226
Other payables				
Prepaid tickets		276,214,594,464		
Air navigation companies		84,525,913,574		
Travel agents		111,234,863,708		
Sundry payables	756,023,094	189,227,030,921	661,202,402,667	3,945,115,404,163
Accrued Liabilities and Deferred Expenses				59,289,667,038
TOTAL LIABILITIES				5,941,133,215,127

Panel B: Consolidated Memorandum Accounts as of December 31, 1993

PERSONAL SECURITIES GIVEN

SURETIES			
For subsidiary undertakings	–0–		
For associated undertakings	–0–		
For holding companies	–0–		
For undertakings controlled by the said holding companies	–0–		
For others	160,264,286,669	160,264,286,669	
ENDORSEMENTS			
For subsidiary undertakings	–0–		
For associated undertakings	–0–		
For holding companies	–0–		
For undertakings controlled by the said holding companies	–0–		
For others	–0–	–0–	
OTHER PERSONAL GUARANTIES			
For subsidiary undertakings	–0–		
For associated undertakings	–0–		
For holding companies	–0–		
For undertakings controlled by the said holding companies	–0–		
For others	121,210,000	121,210,000	160,385,496,669
COLLATERAL SECURITIES *FOR THIRD PARTIES'*			
OBLIGATIONS			
Of subsidiary undertakings	–0–		
Of associated undertakings	–0–		
Of holding companies	–0–		
Of undertakings controlled by the said holding companies	–0–		
Of others	–0–	–0–	
FOR OWN OBLIGATIONS OTHER THAN DEBTS FOR DEBTS			
ENTERED IN THE FINANCIAL STATEMENTS	–0–		
Fleet	473,536,530,303		
Buildings and land	470,460,000,000	943,996,530,303	
COMMITMENTS TO BUY AND TO SELL		5,190,979,642,907	
OTHER COMMITMENTS		2,464,382,094,115	
		8,759,743,763,994	

EXHIBIT 14–2 (continued)

Panel C: Consolidated Profit and Loss Account for 1993

VALUE PRODUCED

Sales		7,311,944,589,866
Variation in stocks relating to work in progress		2,290,763,000
Change in work-in-progress under contract		26,592,892,317
Increase in work performed for own purpose and capitalized		116,344,123,805
Other operating income		
Subsidies and grants-in-aid	13,600,025,024	
Capital gains on transfers	102,607,790,064	
Other operating income	137,239,650,142	253,447,465,230
TOTAL		7,710,619,834,218

COST OF PRODUCTION

On account of spares, other technical materials, fuel and consumables, and goods		(1,148,888,101,588)
On account of services		(2,806,404,885,479)
On account of use of third party property		(467,766,462,360)
Staff costs		
Wages and salaries	(1,803,668,552,762)	
Social security costs	(592,270,819,912)	
Severance pay	(144,159,838,408)	
Other staff costs	(19,206,490,367)	(2,559,305,701,449)
Depreciation and devaluation charges		
Depreciation of intangible fixed assets	(103,804,687,410)	
Depreciation of tangible fixed assets	(399,521,396,852)	
Other devaluation charges on fixed assets	(24,000,000)	
Extraordinary downward value adjustments in respect of receivables included among current assets, and of cash at bank and in hand	(18,268,566,343)	(521,618,650,605)
Variations in stocks of spares, other technical materials, and consumables		(15,072,508,304)
Provisions for liabilities		(11,270,488,492)
Other provisions		(78,141,570,023)
Sundry operating charges		(57,561,636,815)
TOTAL		(7,666,030,005,115)
Balancing difference between value produced and cost of production		(44,589,829,103)

FINANCIAL INCOME AND CHARGES

Income from participating interests		
Dividends from subsidiary undertakings	3,002,693,815	
Dividends from other undertakings	9,889,667,122	12,892,360,937
Income from other financial fixed assets		
From other receivables included among financial fixed assets	1,125,136,298	
From securities other than participating interests	21,540,604	
Other interest receivable and similar income	103,305,052,292	104,451,729,194
Interest payable and similar charges		
Interest and fees to subsidiary undertakings	(2,712,500)	
Interest and fees to holding companies	(16,872,913,559)	
Interest and fees to others and sundry charges	(417,140,792,133)	(434,016,418,192)
TOTAL		(316,672,328,061)

VALUE ADJUSTMENTS IN RESPECT OF FINANCIAL ASSETS

Revaluations		3,277,214,929
Devaluations		(14,324,761,609)
TOTAL		11,047,546,680

Exhibit 14–2 (continued)

EXTRAORDINARY REVENUES AND CHARGES

Revenues		
Capital gains on transfers	–0–	
Contingent assets and non-existent liabilities	45,966,985,193	45,966,985,193
Charges		
Capital losses on transfers	(1,397,500,000)	
Taxes for previous years	(33,300,029)	
Contingent liabilities and non-existent assets	(24,976,932,183)	
Grants-in-aid pursuant to L.64/86 and L.181/89	(18,425,617,600)	
Other charges	(25,788,379,483)	(70,621,729,295)
TOTAL		(24,654,744,102)
Operating profit or loss before taxation		(307,784,789,740)
Income tax for the year		(29,089,517,056)
Loss for the year		(336,874,306,796)
Value adjustments made only to comply with tax laws		–0–
Provisions made only to comply with tax laws		–0–
Loss for the year, including minority interest of which:		
Parent company share		(343,467,137,263)
Minority interest share		6,592,830,467
		(336,874,306,796)

*Amounts collectible within the following year.
†Amounts collectible after the following year.

the complex web of laws governing Italian financial reporting. In the meantime, beleaguered accountants and managers hope that implementation of the EU's Fourth Directive will reduce the intricacy and ambiguity with which they must struggle daily.

Banking. The 1990 Amato Law has been referred to as Italy's most important piece of financial legislation since the watershed Banking Law of 1936.[19] The law gives Italy's approximately 85 public sector banks the chance to privatize, listing up to 49 percent of their shares on the stock market. The intent of the law is to allow government-dominated banks to restructure to overcome their historical shortcomings of being too localized, too small, too numerous, and too inefficient to compete effectively with their larger international rivals. To encourage the restructuring, the law exempts banks from any tax on the capital gains associated with asset revaluations booked at the time of reorganization so that the total, real value of an institution's assets can be recorded. This provision has the effect of boosting a bank's capital base, providing room for subsequent loan growth and expansion. Recently, the Amato Law was viewed as having "failed miserably."[20]

[19]D. Lane, "Year of Profound Structural Change," *Financial Times,* November 19, 1990, p. II.
[20]"Half a Renaissance," *The Economist,* March 21, 1992, pp. 86–87.

EXHIBIT 14–3

ALITALIA FINANCIAL STATEMENTS
Prepared for Easier International Comparisons
(comparative years omitted here, in millions of lire)

Panel A: Consolidated balance sheet as of December 31, 1993

A. FIXED ASSETS		
Intangible assets		267,917
Tangible assets		3,842,206
Financial assets		241,051
		4,351,174
B. WORKING CAPITAL		
Goods on hand		360,442
Trade debtors		303,980
Other assets		794,193
Trade creditors		(812,999)
Provisions for liabilities and charges		(243,075)
Other liabilities		(995,756)
		(593,215)
C. TOTAL ASSETS, less current liabilities	(A + B)	3,757,989
D. SEVERANCE PAY FUND		897,791
E. TOTAL ASSETS less current liabilities and severance pay fund	(C − D)	2,860,168
F. SHAREHOLDERS' EQUITY		
Parent company share		735,900
Minority interests share		59,962
		795,862
G. MEDIUM LONG-TERM DEBT		1,577,444
H. NET SHORT-TERM FINANCIAL INDEBTEDNESS (CASH AND BANK BALANCES)		
Short-term debts		618,206
Cash and short-term credits		(131,344)
	(G + H)	2,064,306
I. TOTAL	(F + G + H)	2,860,168

Panel B: Consolidated Profit and Loss Account for 1993

A. SALES	7,352,138
Changes in work-in-progress and in stocks of finished goods	2,291
Work performed for own purpose and capitalized	116,344
B. VALUE PRODUCED THROUGH CORE BUSINESS	7,470,773
Cost of goods and services bought in	(4,438,554)
C. VALUE ADDED	3,032,219
Labour costs	(2,559,306)
D. GROSS OPERATING MARGIN	472,913
Depreciation charges	(503,326)
Other adjustment provisions	(18,293)
Provisions for liabilities and charges	(89,412)
Miscellaneous revenues and charges-credit balance	182,708
E. OPERATING PROFIT (LOSS)	(44,590)
Financial income and charges	(316,672)
Value adjustments on financial assets	(11,048)
F. PROFIT (LOSS) BEFORE TAXATION AND EXTRAORDINARY ITEMS	(283,130)
Extraordinary revenues and charges	(24,655)
G. PROFIT (LOSS) BEFORE TAXATION	(307,785)
Income taxes for the year	(29,090)
H. LOSS FOR THE YEAR of which:	(336,874)
Parent company share	(343,467)
Minority interest share	6,593

It may be, however, that Italy's recent adoption of the EU's second banking directive will become the real catalyst for change in a banking industry that is long overdue for one. Italian banks are now allowed to be shareholders in Italian companies, make long-term loans, and provide universal banking services.[21] Such changes, along with a planned privatization of the banking system and growing public sentiment to stop the practice of *lottizzazione* (appointing bank managers as part of the political reward system rather than based on qualifications), bode well for converting the banking industry to a more competitive, professionally managed basis on which credit risk might be assessed in regard to a company's cash-generating ability as opposed to the extent of its fixed-asset holdings.[22]

Capital Markets.   Of Italy's 10 stock exchanges, by far the most important is the ***Borsa Valori di Milano***—the Milan Bourse. It accounts for about 90 percent of the total daily trading volume in shares and about 80 percent of the total trading volume in fixed-income securities throughout Italy. As well as its regular market, the Bourse includes a second-tier unlisted market (known as *Il Mercato Ristretto*), which is open for trading one day a week. In addition, a largely unregulated over-the-counter market allows the trading of virtually any security.

CONSOB is the regulatory agency overseeing the Italian stock exchanges, and it was created in 1974 to improve the efficiency and fairness of Italian capital markets. Since then, it has established a number of requirements for listing on Italian exchanges, including the following:

- Net shareholder equity must be at least L50 billion (about $30.8 million) for banks and insurance companies and at least L10 billion (about $6.2 million) for other companies.
- The applicant must present financial statements showing a profit for the last three years. The most recent set of statements must have been audited by an authorized firm.
- A minimum of 25 percent of the company's outstanding shares must be publicly owned (as opposed to government owned).
- Bond offerings must be at least L10 billion (about $6.2 million), of which at least 25 percent must be offered for sale to the public.

---

[21]"Inching Forward," *The Economist,* June 5, 1993, pp. 90–91.
[22]See also "Unmasking Italian Banking," *The Economist,* February 12, 1994, pp. 77–78; and H. Simonian, "Italian Shares Boom on Shaky Foundations," *Financial Times,* September 17, 1993, p. 17.

Once listed, a company must furnish CONSOB with audited financial statements annually, directors' reports semiannually, and any other information the agency requests. Although fairly large by continental European standards, the Milan exchange is still far from becoming an international financial center. Only about 230 companies are currently listed on it, as compared to more than five or six times that many listings in New York, London, or Tokyo. Moreover, deposit requirements make trading in foreign equities on the Milan Bourse highly disadvantageous. Investors in foreign securities are required to deposit an amount equal to 15 percent of their purchase in a noninterest-bearing account in the Bank of Italy, to be held there until they sell the securities. Nonresidents are allowed to invest in Italian securities with few restrictions (although dividends paid to nonresidents are subject to a withholding tax of 32.4 percent).

Although exchange restrictions, most of which are in the process of being lifted, must bear some responsibility for scaring investors away from the Italian stock exchanges, a much larger problem involves the provinciality and lack of openness that characterize Italian bourses. The confidence of international investors has been dampened by the lack of liquidity and of an effective regulatory infrastructure to protect outsiders, minority interests, and small investors (e.g., insider trading was legal until the early 1990s). In addition, potential investors are wary of the closed structure of Italian stock markets: most companies listed on the Milan Bourse are controlled by a small circle of powerful business families. The five largest business groups in Italy, all controlled by families, account for 70 percent of the country's stock market capitalization. As a result of these problems, leading Italian equities are often traded more actively in London than in Milan.

In late 1990, stock market reform legislation was passed creating a new brand of financial institution, *Societa di Internediazione Mobiliare* (SIM). The new SIM law calls for all business in equities to go through a stock exchange, thus ending widespread prior practices among banks of matching buy-and-sell orders in-house. Estimates at the time of the SIM law put the level of ''off-floor'' trading at twice that done in the exchanges. As might be surmised, such a requirement has generated a flurry of activity in the banking industry to develop or acquire an SIM or enter into a joint venture with one to retain that phase of their business. Such reform, along with a 1991 prohibition on insider trading, suggests a concerted attempt to position the Milan Bourse as a major equities market for global and Italian investors. This comes at a time when historically ''fewer than 10 percent of Italian families hold shares—the lowest level among the industrialized countries [and] only 4 percent of household savings were held in shares and 36 percent in [government bonds].''[23] These facts have not gone unnoticed in Italy and, indeed, the further development of its capital markets is a main goal of the government.

---

[23]A. Hill, ''Equities for the Family,'' *Financial Times,* July 7, 1994, p. 28.

Selected Financial Reporting Practices

As particular Italian accounting conventions are discussed, remember that the general concepts undergirding its financial reporting are that (1) company taxable income, in principle, should be the same as that reported for external purposes and (2) certain expenses are not tax deductible unless reported in the external financial statements.[24] Springing from these premises, at least in part, has been an historical tendency for financial reporting conservatism and secrecy.

As an overview, consider that interim financial statements are on a semiannual basis and earnings per share data are not required. A cash flow statement is not required but is sometimes voluntarily provided. Footnotes are often extensive and quite detailed and provide analysis of changes to certain accounts. Lastly, audit opinions may not be qualified (i.e., they must be without reservation or totally negative).

It is also worth noting that whatever the state of Italian accounting practices, the world's modern-day standard of double-entry accounting was founded and has been practiced in Italy since the 14th century. Luca Pacioli, an Italian monk, is credited with preparing the first treatise on double-entry accounting. Also indicative of Italy's long-standing accounting tradition is the fact that the first professional society of accountants was formed in Venice in the 16th century.[25] Italy's modern-day practices have evolved from such roots.

Valuation

The Italian civil code requires the use of the historical cost convention as the basis of valuation for all assets. Specific laws passed in 1975, 1982, 1990, and 1991, however, permit the revaluation of certain fixed assets, using government specified indexes, if a company can show that the current economic value of an asset exceeds its proposed valuation. The offsetting credit is to a revaluation reserve account in the shareholders' equity section of the balance sheet. Over time, a revaluation reserve account may become quite substantial, thus indicating sizable holding gains likely to be recognized by the company sometime in the future. (In 1993, Olivetti's revaluation reserve equaled 18 percent of the company's consolidated owners' equity.)

Consolidation

Beginning in 1994, the Italian civil code required consolidated financial statements following the adoption of the EU's Fourth and Seventh Directives. In addition, CONSOB requires companies listed on stock exchanges to prepare and publish

---

[24]Zambon and Saccon, ''Accounting Change in Italy.''
[25]G. Mann, ''The Origins of Double-Entry,'' *Australian Accountant,* July 1994, pp. 17–21.

consolidated statements. As a consequence, all ''controlled'' subsidiaries are consolidated, except those whose line of business differs substantially from the principal business of the group, where control is temporary, or on grounds of immateriality. In such cases, the unconsolidated company is accounted for under the equity method.[26]

A firm is considered to be ''controlled'' if another company directly or indirectly controls a majority of its voting power (whether through stock ownership or some other means) or if another company exercises significant influence over it by virtue of special ties. A firm is considered to be an ''associate'' if another company holds more than 5 percent of its capital if it is listed on a stock exchange or more than 10 percent of its capital if it is not; investments in associate companies are often accounted for under the cost method for tax reasons, although the equity method is also permitted.

Investment Incentives

It is common for the Italian government to provide cash grants to companies to stimulate capital investment. These grants are usually carried in a special section of shareholders' equity without being included in income. Treatment may vary, however, according to the type of the grant and the accounting policy of a given company. For example, in the past Fiat has deferred such grants and credited them to income over the life of the related assets. Conversely, at other times, Fiat has credited them directly to an equity reserve account without including them in income.

Marketable Securities

Securities held as short-term investments are carried at cost or, in the case of listed securities, the lower of cost or market (on an individual security basis). Market value is determined by calculating the average daily market price of a security over the last three months of the financial year.

Inventories

Inventory must be carried at the lower of cost or market, calculated on an individual item basis. Common valuation methods include LIFO, FIFO, specific identification, and average cost (although standard cost is also acceptable if it approximates cost under one of the other methods). A version of LIFO is popular because it permits high tax deductions; other methods are allowable for both book and tax purposes so long as they do not result in a lower inventory value than LIFO.

---

[26]Under the Italian equity method, changes in the value of the investment account are also reflected in an undistributable reserve account in the shareholders' equity section of the balance sheet, thereby bypassing the income statement (and hence current income taxes).

Leases

Because Italian tax law does not provide for the capitalization of leases, long-term leases are generally accounted for as operating leases by both parties, regardless of the substance of the lease agreement.

Goodwill

Goodwill may be recorded only if it arises from the acquisition of a business. It is defined as the difference between the consideration given and the agreed upon value of identifiable net assets and is amortized over its estimated useful life (but rarely in excess of 10 years). The charge-to-equity method is also permitted. Negative goodwill may be capitalized to the balance sheet and systematically amortized to income or written off against the depreciable assets acquired, as in the United States.

Long-Term Contracts

Accounting for long-term contracts is dictated by Italian tax law, which permits both the completed contract method and the percentage of completion method, which is more commonly used. If a loss is anticipated, it is fully accrued currently but is not tax deductible until realized. If the percentage of completion method is used, a provision for contractual risks equaling 2 to 4 percent of expected revenues is permitted under Italian tax law.

Segment Reporting

With the recent integration of the EU's Fourth Directive into the Italian civil code, Italian companies are now required to report results by geographical area or by line of business. Few of them did so voluntarily prior to the implementation of the Fourth Directive.

Shareholders' Equity

Shareholders' equity consists of capital reserves, legal reserves, revaluation reserves, retained earnings, and various other reserves. Capital reserves include share capital—namely, the par or nominal value of shares issued—and share premium—or the excess of share price over par (or nominal) value. The share premium reserve is distributable to shareholders when the legal reserve (see the next paragraph) equals 20 percent or more of share capital. Treasury stock is carried as an asset, usually under the heading other long-term investments.

The legal reserve is a reserve representing the withholding of 5 percent of annual earnings. Withholding is required until the legal reserve equals 20 percent of share capital. The legal reserve may not be distributed. Revaluation reserves are created when noncurrent assets are revalued above original historical cost, as permitted or required by legislative action and when long-term investments accounted for under the equity method are revalued. Revaluation reserves are distributable. If retained earnings reflects a deficit, it may be carried on the debit side of the balance sheet.

Analytical Considerations

As illustrated by Exhibit 14–4, generally accepted accounting practice in Italy in many instances parallels U.S. GAAP. Significant differences, however, are noteworthy in the following areas:

- *Valuation of property, plant, and equipment.* Unlike U.S. companies, Italian corporations are permitted—and sometimes required—by special legislative action to revalue certain fixed assets in excess of historical cost using government-specified coefficients developed from Italian inflation statistics. The corresponding revaluation surplus is carried as part of consolidated shareholders' equity, and the revalued assets are depreciated over their normal remaining useful life. Annually, a portion of the revaluation reserve is transferred to retained earnings to reflect (i.e., offset) the excess depreciation taken on the revalued assets.
- *Goodwill.* Goodwill may be capitalized to the balance sheet (as in the United States) and then amortized against earnings or may be written off in total at the time of acquisition against shareholders' equity.
- *Debt valuation.* Unlike U.S. GAAP, all debt instruments are valued at their face or settlement value; in the United States, present value is the dominant valuation approach.
- *Lease accounting.* Italian law does not recognize the capitalization of lease agreements; consequently, regardless of a contract's inherent substance, all leases are treated as operating leases.
- *Research and development costs.* Unlike U.S. GAAP, accepted Italian accounting practice permits the capitalization of recoverable R&D expenditures that relate to new products, projects, or technologies. When such costs are capitalized, it is customary to amortize them over five years.
- *Treasury stock.* Under Italian GAAP, treasury stock may be carried as an asset (usually under long-term investments); in the United States, treasury stock is accounted for as a contra owners' equity account.
- *Deferred income taxes.* Under Italian GAAP, deferred income taxes for temporary differences between book and tax income are rarely recorded (or are relatively immaterial because of the short three-year time horizon used in assessing timing differences); the flow-thru approach is most common when the reported provision for income taxes is the actual taxes due and/or paid by a company.

EXHIBIT 14–4

Comparison of Italian and U.S. Accounting and Reporting Standards

Item	Italy	United States
Asset valuation	Historical cost with selected revaluation (e.g., property, plant, and equipment revaluations may be mandated by law [e.g., as was done in 1991])	Historical cost with selected revaluation (principally downward)
Inventory valuation	Specific identification, LIFO, FIFO (principally), and average cost	Principally LIFO (because of tax considerations); also FIFO and average cost methods
Inventory year-end	Lower of cost or market value (defined as replacement cost or net realizable value)	Lower of cost or replacement cost
Depreciation	Principally straight-line-method at rates permitted by tax law; "additional depreciation" during the first three years of an asset's life also frequently taken if permitted by tax law	Principally straight line with accelerated and production-based methods permitted
Goodwill	Principally capitalized and amortized over a 5- to 10-year period; immediate charge-to-equity method also permitted; negative goodwill written off immediately against the value of purchased assets or capitalized to the balance sheet and amortized to income	Capitalized to balance sheet with amortization (principally straight line) over a maximum of 40 years; negative goodwill not permitted (i.e., eliminated against long-term depreciable assets)
Research and development costs	Consistent with tax law, may be either expensed as incurred or capitalized and amortized over 5 years; must expense capitalized R&D judged to be nonrecoverable	Research costs expensed currently; development costs expensed currently except in certain industries (i.e., software, oil and gas)
Capitalized interest costs	Capitalization of interest during period of asset construction permitted (but required for tax purposes)	Capitalization required for self-constructed assets
Intercorporate investments:		
Marketable securities (current asset trading)	Lower of cost or market value on an individual investment basis	Mark to market (individual security basis) with unrealized gains and losses taken to income
Long-term-investments:		
0–20% ownership (available for sale)	Lower of cost or market value on an individual investment basis	Mark to market (individual security basis) with unrealized gains and losses reported on balance sheet (i.e., owners' equity)
20–50% ownership	Equity method	Equity method
51–100% ownership	Consolidated, unless a subsidiary's line of business differs substantially from the rest of the group (in which case, the equity method used); both pooling (merger) and purchase (acquisition) accounting permitted	Consolidated using pooling or purchase accounting
Debt valuation	All debt valued at face or settlement value	Long-term debt (except deferred income taxes) valued at present value; all other debt valued at face or settlement value

---

EXHIBIT 14–4 (continued)

Item	Italy	United States
Leases	All leases treated as operating leases	Capital leases reflected in balance sheet; operating leases disclosed in footnotes
Deferred income taxes	Generally unnecessary because tax law usually subjects the reported accounting income to taxation (hence tax and book income are equivalent); when deferred taxes present, the liability method used	Computed under liability method
Pension liabilities	Private pension plans rare but when present and unfunded, liability reported on balance sheet	Reflected on balance sheet
Discretionary reserves	Restricted to identifiable operational losses that are probable and can be reasonably estimated	Restricted to identifiable operational losses
Statement of cash flows	Permitted but not required	Required

The effects, in general, of these noted differences on the financial statements of Italian companies, as compared to their U.S. counterparts, can be summarized as follows:

Item	Financial Statement Impact
Revaluation of fixed assets	Total assets and shareholders' equity overstated with net earnings understated (due to excess depreciation on the revalued assets); hence, ROA and ROE relatively understated
Goodwill	Total assets and shareholders' equity understated (assuming the charge-to-equity approach) with net earnings overstated; hence, ROA and ROE relatively overstated
Lease accounting	Total assets and total debt understated by the present value of any capital leases; effect on net earnings not readily predictable
Capitalization of R&D	Total assets and current earnings overstated with future earnings relatively understated (due to the rear-end loading of R&D expenditures); ROS likely to be overstated with ROA and ROE not predictable
Treasury stock carried as asset	Total assets and shareholders' equity overstated; hence, ROA and ROE relatively understated
Deferred income taxes not reported	Net earnings and shareholders' equity overstated with total debt understated; hence, debt-to-equity ratio relatively overstated

To gain some sense of the relative financial effects attributable to these accounting differences on the reported earnings of one company, consider the case of Montedison S.p.A., a diversified conglomerate, headquartered in Milan, Italy. The company's 1992 unaudited financial statements revealed consolidated earnings of $1,093 million based on Italian GAAP. In addition, the company disclosed the magnitude (in millions) of the various accounting differences between Italian and U.S. GAAP as depicted in Exhibit 14–5.

EXHIBIT 14–5

Montedison S.p.A.
Reconciliation of Italian GAAP versus U.S. GAAP Net Earnings

Balance as reported in the consolidated profit and loss account	(1,093)
Items increasing (decreasing) reported net profit (loss)	
Reduction in depreciation of fixed assets and increase in net gains on disposal of fixed assets arising from revaluations	21
Adjustment to research and development and other deferred charges	(7)
Adjustment to share in earnings of associated companies	15
Sale of certain real estate	59
Change in provision for deferred taxes, including effect of the above adjustments	144
Capital tax and tax amnesty charges	(86)
Other, including goodwill amortization	(11)
Effect on minority interests of the above adjustments	(16)
Total net increase (decrease)	119
Balance in accordance with accounting principles generally accepted in the United States	(974)

On the basis of these limited data, drawing the generalization that the net earnings of all Italian companies under Italian GAAP are consistently understated relative to their earnings under U.S. GAAP is inappropriate. In 1990, for example, these same adjustments would have *lowered* Montedison's net earnings from $556 million under Italian GAAP to just $353 million under U.S. GAAP. Nonetheless, other evidence also exists to suggest that the Italian GAAP–based earnings of Italian companies are consistently and systematically understated, on average, as compared to those of U.S. companies.[27] Consider, for example, the following average price-earnings for 1993 and 1994:

	Average P/E Ratio	
	1993	*1994*
Italy*	33.0	24.6
United States†	24.1	17.7

*Source: *Reuter Textline,* "Japanese P/Es Exceed 'Bubble-era' Levels," June 28, 1993, and *The Wall Street Journal,* March 17, 1994, p. C1.
†For data for Standard and Poor's Industrials as of May 31, 1994 and 1995, see *Financial Times,* June 2, 1995, p. 35.

Assuming efficient world global markets, these data suggest a persistent biasing of reported earnings by Italian companies. Since security prices are thought to correctly

[27]M. Hagigi and A. Sponza, "Financial Statement Analysis of Italian Companies: Accounting Practices, Environmental Factors, and International Corporate Performance Comparisons," *International Journal of Accounting* 25, no. 4 (1990), pp. 234–51.

reflect all available information about a company, Italian and U.S. firms with equivalent earnings potential should be equivalently priced, *ceteris paribus.* Consequently, the higher price-earnings multiples afforded Italian companies in general numerically result from the understatement of reported earnings characteristic of those firms. Thus, this institutionalized fiscal biasing must be considered by analysts when making inter-firm comparisons involving Italian companies.

Summary

"The need to make its politicians accountable is perhaps the greatest challenge facing Italy which, if not confronted, may progressively weaken the nation's capacity to deal with its many other policy challenges."[28] Those other policy challenges include curbing government spending to eliminate its deficit, successfully overhauling an unwieldy and inefficient banking system, creating a better regulated stock market and an industry privatization program to stimulate growth of small and medium-sized companies, meeting the needs of an aging population, and overcoming extreme regional differences and loyalties. As East meets West and as the European Union becomes a reality, Italy may have the potential to be a key player. It must, however, seize the opportunity and instill confidence in its partner countries that it has finally set its own house in order. Many would claim that the recent insider trading, antitrust, and Amato laws along with budget cuts are all steps in the right direction. The key is whether these steps will mark the end or the beginning of change.

Suggested Readings

Buxbaum, P. "Italy: High Disposable Incomes and a Bias to Buy American." *Export Today,* June 1992, pp. 54–57.

Hagigi, M., and A. Sponza. "Financial Statement Analysis of Italian Companies: Accounting Practices, Environmental Factors, and International Corporate Performance Comparisons." *International Journal of Accounting* 25, no. 4 (1990), pp. 234–51.

"Italy—A Survey." *Financial Times,* June 30, 1993, pp. I–VI.

"Italy." *The Economist,* June 26, 1993, pp. Survey 1–22.

Khalaf, R. "Buyer Beware." *Forbes,* June 20, 1994, pp. 204–5.

Nobes, C., and S. Zambon. "Piano, Piano: Italy Implements the Directives." *Accountancy,* July 1991, pp. 84–85.

Valente, J. "Two Paths, Two Problems." *The Wall Street Journal,* September 30, 1994, p. R8.

Zambon, S., and C. Saccon. "Accounting Change in Italy." *European Accounting Review,* September 1993, pp. 245–84.

---

[28]J. Wyles, "Italy: Dynamic but Deadlocked," *Financial Times,* April 17, 1990, p. I.

ISSUES AND INFORMATION FOR FURTHER INQUIRY

I.14.1   Corporate Debt

In a February/March 1995 *OECD Observer* report (p. 47), "Italy: Corporate Governance," A. Goldstein and G. Nicoletti note that "for the vast majority of firms, debt-financing has mostly taken the form of short-term borrowing from a plethora of banks." Moreover, in a September 17, 1993 *Financial Times* article (p. 17), H. Simonian asserts that Italian banks have extended credit "too freely."

Required:

    (a) Report on the nature and extent of debt disclosures and discussions contained in an Italian corporate annual report of your choosing.

    (b) Compare and contrast what you find with the annual report from a U.S. company in the same industry.

I.14.2   Information Needs

In a July 7, 1994 *Financial Times* article (p. 28), "Equities for the Family," A. Hill asserts that "a more sophisticated personal and professional investor is emerging in Italy."

Required:

Assume this statement is true and that the equity market will become a more significant source of corporate capital in Italy. Identify and discuss at least three ways that trend would be reflected in the information desired from companies.

EXERCISES

E.14.1   Recapitalization

When a company is initially formed, it is said to be *capitalized* to the extent of the contributions made by its founders. In some sectors of the financial community, the concept of capitalization is given a broader interpretation to include not only the contributed shareholder capital of the firm but also its long-term debt.

    Some companies experience financial difficulties and, as a consequence, consume significant quantities of their capitalization just trying to stay in business. Frequently, such companies are characterized by a low or even negative balance in retained earnings (or its equivalent, the Profit and Loss Reserve account). When this occurs, several options (including shutting down the business) exist for the company: (1) reorganization, and (2) recapitalization.

A reorganization is an attempt to refocus a company on its core activities. It may involve the "restructuring" of various activities, such as the sale or liquidation of unsuccessful or unprofitable operations and assets; it may also involve a restructuring of its balance sheet, particularly when the balance in retained earnings is negative.

Either in conjunction with or instead of a reorganization, a struggling company may undertake a recapitalization. Like an initial public offering, the purpose of a recapitalization is to raise sufficient new equity capital to permit a company to place (or maintain) its core operations on a sound financial foundation.

Consider, for example, the case of Fiat, the Italian automaker, and Italy's largest private sector company. Poor economic conditions throughout Italy and Europe during the early 1990s, as well as declining sales in the U.S. automarket, put Fiat's core operations on shaky financial grounds. During the first half of 1993, for example, Fiat lost L966 billion on sales of L29.3 trillion. As a consequence of the reported losses, Fiat's shareholders' equity totaled only L20.3 trillion. Regrettably, the losses occurred at the middle of a massive capital investment program scheduled for completion in 1996.

To avoid taking on more debt, a cost that would only increase the automaker's losses, Fiat began a massive three-phase recapitalization program. Phase 1 involved the sale of 10 percent of the company to a consortium of financial institutions for L615 billion. Phase 2 involved the sale of 58 percent of Fiat's wholly owned Rinascente subsidiary (a supermarket chain) for L870 million. Phase 3 involved Italy's largest-ever share offering: a L3.2 trillion, 2-for-3 stock offering to investors, at a 40 percent discount from Fiat's prior share price. In total, Fiat hoped to raise L4.7 trillion (or approximately $2.94 billion in United States).

Required:

    (a) Assume that Fiat had a negative (debit) balance in retained earnings. If the company wanted to restructure its balance sheet, what actions would you propose?

    (b) Prepare the journal entries for Fiat's three-phased recapitalization program.

    (c) What specific effects would Fiat's recapitalization plan have on the company's balance sheet, if successful?

E.14.2   Privatization

In early 1994, the Italian government announced the sale of 69 percent of its state-controlled electrical equipment company, Nuovo Pignone, to an investment group led by General Electric Co. for $420 million. After the sale, ownership of the company would be distributed as follows:

Ownership Interest	Ownership
25%	General Electric Co.
12	Ingersoll-Rand Co.
12	Dresser Industries, Inc.
20	A consortium of Italian banks
20	Ente Nazionale Idrocarburi (the Italian state-controlled energy conglomerate)
11	Italian private investors
100%	

The sale of a controlling interest in Nuovo Pignone was part of Italy's continuing privatization effort.

Required:

(a) Based on the ownership interest data, what restrictions appear evident for foreign investors involved in italy's privatization program?

(b) Based on the available data, what value would you assign to GE's investment?

(c) How should GE, Dresser, and Ente Nazionale Idrocarburi account for their investments in Nuovo Pignone?

E.14.3   Statement of Cash Flows

Luxottica Group S.p.A. is an Italian-based corporation involved in the design, manufacture, distribution, and marketing of traditional and designer lines of frames for eyeglasses and sunglasses. The company's products are principally manufactured in Italy and are distributed worldwide by a variety of wholly owned foreign subsidiaries. The company's shares trade on the New York Stock Exchange via American depositary receipts under the symbol LUX.

The following are the company's balance sheets for the years ended December 31, 1992 and 1993 as they appeared in its 20-F filing with the SEC. The footnotes accompanying Luxottica's 20-F filing also revealed the following information for 1993 (in millions of lire):

- Net income of 91,914.
- Depreciation and amortization of 24,695.
- Dividends declared and paid of 27,030.
- Currency translation effects of 21,748 (relating to the translation of foreign subsidiary financial statements into the Italian lire, the functional currency), which was recorded directly in retained earnings.

Required:

Using the available data, prepare a statement of cash flows for 1993 for Luxottica and comment on the company's financial health vis-à-vis its cash flows.

LUXOTTICA GROUP S.p.A. AND SUBSIDIARIES
Consolidated Balance Sheets
December 31, 1992 and 1993

	(millions of lire)	
Assets	*1992*	*1993*
Current assets		
Cash	48,390	30,568
Marketable securities	16,741	77,373
Accounts receivable		
Less: Allowance for doubtful accounts, L 3,776 and L 4,565, respectively)	135,732	168,928
Sales and income taxes receivable	12,507	5,150
Inventories	88,345	88,870
Prepaid expenses and other	7,167	19,895
Deferred income tax benefits	10,488	8,142
Total current assets	319,370	398,926
Property, plant and equipment—net	122,335	139,449
Other assets		
Intangible assets-net	32,721	28,207
Investments	803	705
Security deposits and other	1,308	1,365
Sales and income taxes receivables	2,081	2,915
Total other assets	36,913	33,192
Total	478,618	571,567

LUXOTTICA GROUP S.p.A. AND SUBSIDIARIES (continued)
Consolidated Balance Sheets
December 31, 1992 and 1993

	(millions of lire)	
Liabilities and Shareholders' Equity	*1992*	*1993*
Current liabilities		
Bank overdrafts	54,138	39,341
Current portion of long-term debt	2,400	10,890
Accounts payable	35,381	59,669
Accrued expenses and other	36,557	40,847
Accrual for customers' right of return	5,148	6,791
Income taxes payable	24,008	5,881
Total current liabilities	157,632	163,419
Long-term debt	20,450	14,181
Liability for termination indemnities	17,553	21,100
Deferred income taxes	20,698	22,970
Minority interests in consolidated subsidiaries	3,078	5,695
Shareholders' equity		
Capital stock; par value L 1,000 − 45,050,000 ordinary shares		
authorized and issued, 44,584,500 shares outstanding	45,050	45,050
Surplus from monetary revaluations of assets	7,828	6,191
Retained earnings	223,788	310,420
Total	276,666	361,661
Less: Treasury shares at cost	17,459	17,459
Shareholders' equity	259,207	344,202
Total	478,618	571,567

E.14.4   Intangible Asset Amortization

Goodwill, an intangible asset, represents the excess purchase price paid in an acquisition of another company over the fair market value of identifiable assets acquired, less any liabilities assumed. Under Italian GAAP, purchased goodwill is recorded as an asset and amortized over a 5- to 10-year period. It is also permissible to immediately write off any goodwill incurred as a consequence of an acquisition against retained earnings.

Luxottica Group S.p.A. is one of the world's largest manufacturers and marketers of frames for eyeglasses and sunglasses. In recent years, the company had been active in the acquisition of competing companies. According to the company's December 31, 1992 and 1993 balance sheets, Luxottica had L32,721 million and L28,207 million, respectively, in intangible assets largely composed of goodwill (see following table and balance sheets in E.14.3). The company amortized this goodwill over a 10-year period.

The company's annual report revealed the following information about its intangible assets (amounts in millions of lire):

	December 31	
	1992	*1993*
Goodwill		
which arose in connection with the acquisition of the remaining 50% interest in Luxottica United Kingdom—net of amortization of L 300 million and L 450 million at December 31, 1992 and 1993, respectively.	1,197	1,047
Goodwill		
which arose in connection with the acquisition of Florence Line S.r.l.—net of accumulated amortization of L 3,237 million and L 4,316 million at December 31, 1992 and 1993, respectively.	7,554	6,475
Goodwill		
which arose in connection with the acquisition of Fidia S.p.A.—net of accumulated amortization of L 4,253 million and L 5,672 million at December 31, 1992 and 1993, respectively.	9,925	8,506
Goodwill		
which arose from the acquisition of the remaining 50% interest in Avant Garde Optics Inc. net of accumulated amortization of L 22,736 million and L 25,984 million at December 31, 1992 and 1993, respectively.	9,744	6,496
Other, principally trademarks		
net of accumulated amortization	4,301	5,683
Total	32,721	28,207

Required:

Using the income statement and balance sheet data from E.14.3 as well as the data in this table, restate Luxottica's 1993 net income and balance sheet assuming the following:

    (a) A 40-year amortization period for goodwill (as per U.S. GAAP).

    (b) The direct write-off of goodwill against retained earnings (as per British GAAP).

E.14.5   Accounting for Shareholder Reserves

Luxottica Group S.p.A. produces more than 700 traditional eyeglass frame styles and over 500 designer frame styles. Since Luxottica's shares trade over the NYSE as ADRs (1 ADR is equivalent to 1 ordinary Luxottica share, par value of L1,000), it files with the Securities and Exchange Commission form 20-F to report its annual financial results and form 6-K to report its quarterly financial results.

The company's 20-F reported the following data (in millions of lire) as of December 31, 1993:

Shareholders' Equity	1993	1992
Capital stock	45,050	45,050
Surplus from monetary revaluations of assets	6,191	7,828
Retained earnings	310,420	223,788
Total	361,661	276,666
Less: Treasury shares (at cost)	17,459	17,459
Total shareholders' equity	344,202	259,207

The company's SEC filing also disclosed the following footnote information:

- At the company's annual shareholders' meeting in April 1993, cash dividends of L27,030 million were approved and were subsequently paid in July. Italian civil code requires that 5 percent of net income be retained as a legal reserve until this reserve is equal to one-fifth of the issued share capital. (Net income in 1993 was L91,914 million.)

- Part of Luxottica's property, plant, and equipment (see E.14.3 for Luxottica's 1993 balance sheet) was revalued in accordance with the provisions of Italian Laws No. 576 as of December 2, 1975, No. 72 as of March 19, 1985, and No. 413 as of December 30, 1991. The revaluation was undertaken to partially account for the change in the purchasing power of money (i.e., monetary revaluation).

On December 31, 1991 (effective January 1, 1992), the Italian government passed a law requiring the compulsory revaluation of industrial buildings. This revaluation resulted in a net write-up of the carrying value of assets and, accordingly, an increased charge for depreciation over a building's remaining useful life, such lives approximating 15 years. For financial reporting purposes, building costs and accumulated depreciation were increased by a like amount, resulting in no net write-up to either fixed assets or shareholders' equity.

Required:

    (a) Calculate the required value of Luxottica's legal reserve. Where would you expect this reserve to be disclosed? Do you think that the legal reserve constrained Luxottica's ability to declare dividends?

    (b) Use journal entries to explain how the account Surplus from Monetary Revaluations of Assets was created and why it declined from 1992 to 1993.

E.14.6   Accounting for Commitments and Contingencies

Luxottica Group S.p.A. is an Italian designer and manufacturer of eyeglass and sunglass products. The frames manufactured by Luxottica in Italy are sold by distributors throughout the world.

The company's 1993 annual report revealed the following partial balance sheet data (in millions of lire):

	1992	*1993*
Current liabilities	157,632	163,419
Long-term debt	20,540	14,181*
Liability for termination indemnities	17,553	21,100
Deferred income taxes	20,698	22,970
Minority interest	3,078	5,695
Shareholders' equity	259,207	344,202
Total	478,618	571,567

*The long-term debt reflects notes payable to banks, with interest payable at 9 to 13 percent, depending on maturity and payable in installments through 2000.

The company's footnotes also revealed the following in regard to its commitments and contingencies:

The company is obligated under noncancelable distribution agreements with designers which expire at various dates through 2002. In accordance with the provisions of such agreements, the Company is required to pay royalty and advertising fees based on a percentage of sales with, in certain agreements, minimum guarantees of such payments in each year of the agreements. Minimum payments required in each of the years subsequent to December 31, 1993 aggregated Lire 17,207 million, Lire 17,907 million, Lire 12,863 million and Lire 10,360 million in each of 1994, 1995, 1996, and 1997 respectively.

A subsidiary of the Company leases factory and office space under an agreement which expires in 2005 and provides for minimum annual rentals of approximately Lire 603 million.

Years ending December 31,	
1994	603
1995–1998	2,411
1999–2005	4,149
TOTAL	7,163

Required:

(a) Based on the available information, calculate the present value of Luxottica's commitments under its (1) distribution agreements and (2) lease agreements.

(b) Assume that the noncancelable distribution and lease agreements should be capitalized to the company's balance sheet. Calculate Luxottica's long-term debt to equity both with and without capitalization of the commitments. Does capitalization materially affect the company's solvency?

E.14.7   Analyzing Research and Development Costs

Montedison S.p.A. is a diversified food product and pharmaceutical company headquartered in Milan, Italy. Because of the company's involvement in chemicals and pharmaceuticals, it has had significant expenditures for research and development (see the following data).

	(lire, in billions) Year Ended		
	12/31/91	*12/31/90*	*12/31/89*
Trademarks, licenses, and research	106	229	194
Deferred charges	485	164	159
Total	591	393	353
Annual amortization	166	170	106
Net income before tax	514	1,403	2,164
Shareholders' equity	5,363	5,312	2,120

According to the company's 1991 annual report, the accounting policy with respect to intangible assets and deferred charges was as follows:

Licenses, trademarks and know-how are recorded at acquisition or internal production cost. These intangible assets are amortized on a straight-line basis over their expected useful lives. Amortization is provided over five years when no contract exists or there is no other way of determining useful life.

Industrial technology patents are amortized over their expected useful lives or the duration of the related licenses, if shorter.

Pure research costs, those relating to pharmaceutical and pharmacological research and the development of improvements to existing products or production processes are expensed as incurred.

The cost of research into new products or processes (excluding pharmaceuticals) and related development is deferred only if it relates to projects that are expected to be profitable. Such costs are amortized on a straight-line basis over five years.

Deferred industrial research costs are written off in the year the research proves unsuccessful.

When research is completed successfully, the residual costs are reclassified as industrial technology patents.

Required:

(a) Compare and contrast Montedison's accounting policy for research and development costs with (1) *IAS No. 9* and (2) *SFAS No. 2.*

(b) Restate Montedison's (1) net income before tax and (2) shareholders' equity (assume a tax rate of 36 percent) for 1990 and 1991 assuming that all deferred charges and research and development costs are expensed as incurred.

(c) Calculate the company's return on equity both before and after your restatement.

(d) Do you agree with Montedison's R&D policy? If so, why? If not, why not?

E.14.8   Accounting for Treasury Stock

At the end of 1990, Montedison S.p.A. merged with and into Ferruzzi Agricola Finanziaria S.p.A., its controlling shareholder. The resulting company was renamed Montedison S.p.A. Today it maintains operations in such diverse products as sugar, starch and derivatives, consumer products, industrial oils, animal feeds, chemicals, pharmaceuticals, and energy. Following the merger, certain shares in the new company were repurchased, and under the Italian civil code, treasury shares may be carried as an asset. According to the footnotes to the company's 1991 annual report,

Long-Term Investment Securities

Long-term investment securities, amounting to Lire 1,202 billion, include shares of the parent company Ferruzzi Finanziaria S.p.A., acquired for Lire 200 billion, as well as treasury stock totaling Lire 267 billion. The treasury stock is not expected to be sold or canceled in the near future.

The company's balance sheet as of 31 December 1991 also revealed the following capitalization:

	Lire, in billions
Long-term debt	5,529
Shareholders' equity	
Share capital	2,917
Legal reserve	154
Additional paid-in capital	224
Retained earnings and other reserves	1,900
Net income	168
Total shareholders' equity	5,363
Total liabilities and shareholders' equity	27,704

Required:

    (a) Restate Montedison's shareholders' equity section on a basis consistent with U.S. GAAP.

    (b) Calculate Montedison's (1) long-term debt-to-shareholders' equity ratio and (2) shareholders' equity-to-total assets ratio, both before and after your restatement in part (a).

    (c) List arguments (1) supporting the classification of treasury stock as an asset and (2) arguments against the treatment of treasury stock as an asset.

E.14.9   Analyzing Changes in Shareholders' Equity

Benetton Group S.p.A. is a well-known manufacturer of casual apparel which it markets under the brand name The United Colors of Benetton. The company was founded in 1965 by the Benetton family in Ponzano Veneto, Italy, and became a public company in 1978. In 1989, the company made its first public offering of American depositary receipts, each representing two ordinary shares (par value L 500), which trade on the NYSE.

    Benetton's statement of changes in consolidated stockholders' equity for the years ended December 31, 1991, 1992, and 1993, is presented on p. 808 as it appeared in the company's 1993 20-F filing with the SEC. The company's footnotes to the 20-F report also revealed the following information about other reserves which were aggregated with retained earnings in the statement of changes in stockholders' equity:

Other Reserves are as follows (lire, in millions):

	31 December	
	1992	*1993*
Exchange fluctuation reserve	20,055	55,561
Risk reserve	14,210	7,099
Taxation reserve	—	7,580
Reserve for agents' termination indemnities	8,992	9,219
	43,257	79,459

The exchange fluctuation reserve reflects the net effect of adjusting foreign currency balances of payables and receivables of the Italian companies in the Group using year-end exchange rates.

The risk reserve prudently covers various business contingencies, including outstanding legal cases.

The taxation reserve prudently covers liabilities which may arise on the final settlement of outstanding tax disputes with the authorities.

Benetton Group S.p.A.
Statement of Changes in Consolidated Stockholders' Equity
For the Years ended December 31, 1991, 1992, and 1993
(in millions of lire)

	Capital Stock	Additional Paid-in Capital	Surplus from Monetary Revaluation of Assets	Other Reserves and Prior Years' Retained Earnings	New Income for the Year	Total
BALANCES AS OF DECEMBER 31, 1990	81,777	186,661	19,118	165,776	133,271	586,603
Allocation of 1990 net income to reserves	—	—	—	133,271	(133,271)	—
Dividends distributed, as approved at the stockholders' meeting of April 30, 1991	—	—	—	(40,888)	—	(40,888)
Effect of monetary revaluation	—	—	27,104	(23,074)	—	4,030
Differences arising from the translation of foreign currency financial statements	—	—	—	2,004	—	2,004
Net income for the year	—	—	—	—	164,783	164,783
BALANCES AS OF DECEMBER 31, 1991	81,777	186,661	46,222	237,089	164,783	716,532
Allocation of 1991 net income to reserves	—	—	—	164,783	(164,783)	—
Dividends distributed, as approved at the stockholders' meeting of April 29, 1992	—	—	—	(49,066)	—	(49,066)
Disposal of Prince Holdings Inc.: recovery of goodwill on acquisition previously charged against consolidation reserves	—	—	—	56,534	—	56,534
Differences arising from the translation of foreign currency financial statements	—	—	—	14,052	—	14,052
Net income for the year	—	—	—	—	184,709	184,709
BALANCES AS OF DECEMBER 31,1992	81,777	186,661	46,222	423,392	184,709	922,761
Allocation of 1992 net income to reserves	—	—	—	184,709	(184,709)	—
Dividends distributed, as approved at the stockholders' meeting held on April 29, 1993	—	—	—	(57,244)	—	(57,244)
Differences arising from the translation of foreign currency financial statements	—	—	—	(10,277)	—	(10,277)
Net income for the year	—	—	—	—	208,038	208,038
BALANCES OF DEC. 31, 1993	81,777	186,661	46,222	540,580	208,038	1,063,278

Required:

Using journal entries, explain the changes in Benetton's stockholders' equity accounts from year-end 1992 to year-end 1993.

E.14.10   Reconciling U.S. and Italian Net Income

The ADRs of Benetton Group S.p.A. trade on the NYSE, and, consequently, the company files a Form 20-F (annual report) with the SEC. A key component of that report is the reconciliation of generally accepted accounting principles in Italy and the United States. Excerpts from that report include the following:

Differences which have an effect on net income and stockholders' equity:

- Revaluation of Fixed Assets and Trademarks
  In 1991 and prior years, certain categories of property, plant and equipment and trademarks were revalued to amounts in excess of historical cost. This procedure, which was authorized by Italian law, was allowed under Italian accounting practice to give consideration to the effects of local inflation. Revaluations (totaling L46,222 million) were credited to stockholders' equity and revalued assets are depreciated over their remaining useful lives on a straight-line basis.

- Accounting for Goodwill
  In prior years, goodwill on investments acquired were charged or credited to stockholders' equity at the date of purchase. The adjustment in the accompanying reconciliation has been made to recognize the goodwill on acquisitions, originally amounting to L11,519 million. Goodwill is amortized over a 10 year period, corresponding to the estimated useful lives of the underlying assets acquired. The relevant decrease in 1992 is due to the sale of the company's interest in Prince Holdings, Inc., and the consequent reversal of the related goodwill.

	Year Ended December 31 (lire, millions)		
	1991	*1992*	*1993*
Net income, per Italian GAAP	164,783	184,709	208,038
Reduction in depreciation and amortization on revalued fixed assets and trademarks	2,067	2,575	3,134
Amortization of goodwill	(6,724)	(338)	(1,252)
Net income per U.S. GAAP	160,126	186,946	209,920
Stockholders' equity per Italian GAAP	716,532	922,761	1,063,278
Elimination of revaluations of fixed assets and trademarks	(19,494)	(16,919)	(13,785)
Reinstatement of goodwill previously written off	57,101	7,295	6,043
Stockholders' equity per U.S. GAAP	754,139	913,137	1,055,536

Required:

(a) Recreate the journal entries necessary to (1) revalue Benetton's fixed assets and trademarks and (2) write off purchased goodwill to stockholders' equity.

(b) Compare and contrast Benetton's return on equity under Italian GAAP with its return on equity under U.S. GAAP. What generalizations can you draw about the profitability of Italian companies under Italian GAAP versus U.S. companies under U.S. GAAP?

E.14.11 Italian versus U.S. GAAP

Benetton Group S.p.A. is a well-known, worldwide, manufacturer and distributor of clothing. The company's ADRs trade on the NYSE, and, consequently, the company files a 20-F (annual report) with the SEC. Presented below are excerpts from the footnotes to Benetton's 1993 20-F filing:

- **Form and content of consolidated financial statements**
  The financial statements conform to the accounting policies established by the Italian accounting profession, and are reclassified in accordance with the standards generally followed in international practice. In addition, the financial statements of minor subsidiaries located in highly inflationary countries are restated to reflect changes in the purchasing power of the local currencies in accordance with inflation accounting policies.

- **Consolidation policy**
  The difference between the cost and appropriate fair market value of stockholders' equity of subsidiary companies at the time they were acquired (goodwill) was recorded directly to consolidated equity.

- **Foreign Currency Translation policies**
  The financial statements of foreign subsidiaries, including those operating in countries with hyper-inflationary economies are translated into Italian lire using end-of-period exchange rates for balance sheet items and the average exchange rate for the period for income statement items. Any translation differences are reflected directly in consolidated stockholders' equity (i.e., the Exchange Fluctuation Reserve).

- **Marketable securities**
  Marketable securities are stated at lower-of-cost-or-market value at the balance sheet date. Securities subject to resale commitments are recorded at cost.

- **Inventories**
  Inventories are stated at the lowest of cost, on a weighted average basis, or net realizable value.

- **Investments**

  Investments of between 20% and 50% in associated companies are accounted for on an equity basis. Less significant investments are valued at cost.

- **Fixed assets**

  Fixed assets are recorded at either purchase or construction cost. Revaluation of the majority of those assets in accordance with Italian Law No. 72 of 19 March 1983 occurred as of 31 December 1983. Real estate holdings were revalued under Law No. 413 as of 31 December 1991. Depreciation is computed on a straight-line basis using rates that reflect the estimated useful lives of the assets.

- **Trademarks**

  Trademarks are stated at registration or purchase cost, revalued at 31 December 1983. The related revaluation surplus was credited to a specific stockholders' equity reserve.

- **Income taxes**

  Current income taxes are provided for on the basis of a reasonable estimate of the liability for the year. Deferred taxes, principally arising from the reversal of excess depreciation and from lease accounting adjustments, are also provided for.

- **Reserve for termination indemnities**

  The majority of the company's employees are covered by a plan required under Italian law and labor contracts which grant a termination indemnity based on compensation and years of service. As is normal in Italy, the Group has accrued the amount due to each employee as of year-end, but does not fund this liability.

- **Revenue recognition**

  Revenue from product sales are recognized at the time of shipment, which represents the moment when ownership passes.

- **Expense recognition**

  Expenses are recorded in accordance with the matching principle. Advertising costs are charged to income in the year in which they are incurred.

Required:

Review the accounting policies utilized by the Benetton Group and indicate where (and how) they differ from policies under U.S. GAAP.

E.14.12   Accounting for Shareholders' Equity

The Olivetti Group is one of Italy's leading company's in the information technology industry. The following are examples of the company's accomplishments:

- The leading European manufacturer of personal computers and printers.
- The leading supplier in Europe of printers for specialized banking applications.
- The leading European supplier of bank automation systems and self-service terminals.
- The leading European supplier of multivendor support services.
- The leading European supplier of services for intelligent building premises.

The company's annual report for the year ended December 31, 1993, revealed the following information about its shareholders' equity:

	(lire in millions)	
Shareholders' Equity	*31 December 1992*	*31 December 1993*
Share capital	604,575	1,264,416
Capital in excess of stated value	1,366,452	1,366,452
Treasury stock	(4,450)	(4,450)
Revaluation reserve	468,572	462,454
Retained earnings and other reserves	643,954	(47,570)
Cumulative translation adjustments	(68,062)	(26,259)
Net results for the year	(649,853)	(464,594)
Total shareholders' equity	2,361,188	2,550,449

The 1993 annual report also contained a statement of changes in consolidated shareholders' equity:

Olivetti Group
Statements of Changes in Consolidated Shareholders' Equity
For the Years Ended December 31, 1993 and 1992
(in millions of lire)
(Translation from original issued in Italian)

	Share Capital	Capital in Excess of Stated Value	Treasury Stock	Revaluation Reserve	Retained Earnings and other Reserves	Cumulative Translation Adjustments	Net Result for the Year	Total
Balances as of December 31, 1991	604,575	1,366,452	(4,450)	532,077	1,063,422	(18,763)	(459,771)	3,083,542
Utilization of reserves to cover net loss for the year 1991				(63,775)	(395,996)		459,771	—
Property revaluation during the year				270				270
Excess of acquisition cost over current value of net assets of companies acquired during the year					(7,080)			(7,080)
Translation adjustments						(49,299)		(49,299)
Taxes on shareholders' equity in accordance with Italian Law No. 461/92					(24,049)			(24,049)
Other					7,657			7,657
Net result for the year 1992							(649,853)	(649,853)
Balances as of December 31, 1992	604,575	1,366,452	(4,450)	468,572	643,954	(68,062)	(649,853)	2,361,188
Share capital increase	659,841							659,841
Utilization of reserves to cover net loss for the year 1992					(469,853)		649,853	—
Property revaluations during the year				1,066				1,066
Excess of acquisition cost over current value of net assets of companies acquired during the year					(24,554)			(24,554)
Translation adjustments						41,803		41,803
Taxes on shareholders' equity in accordance with Italian Law No. 461/92					(24,279)			(24,279)
Other				(7,184)	7,162			(22)
Net result for the year 1993							(464,594)	(464,594)
Balances as of December 31, 1993	1,264,416	1,366,452	(4,450)	462,454	(47,570)	(26,259)	(464,594)	2,550,449

Required:

Using this information, construct the journal entries necessary to explain the changes in the shareholders' equity accounts of the Olivetti Group for 1992 and 1993.

CASES

CASE 14.1
VALUATION AND REPORTING UNDER ITALIAN CIVIL CODE AND TAX LAW

Giordani Trading Company S.r.l.

The Giordani Trading Company (herafter GTC) is a small Italian trading company headquartered in Salerno. The following are financial data taken from the company's accounting records as of December 31, 1994. Exhibit 1 presents the ledger account balances for GTC as of December 31, 1994; Exhibits 2 and 3 are, respectively, the company's current balance sheet and income statement prepared according to articles 2424 and 2425 of the Italian civil code. In Italy, the civil code dictates the financial reporting practices that must be followed by a public company. Exhibit 4 presents the significant accounting policies used by the company in the preparation of its financial statements. Finally, Exhibit 5 details the reconciliation of GTC's reported income to its taxable income under the Italian Consolidation Act on Taxable Income.

Required:

    (a) Using the ledger account balances as of December 31, 1994, as presented in Exhibit 1, replicate GTC's income statement as presented in Exhibit 3.

    (b) Review Exhibits 2–4 and list the apparent accounting differences between Italian and U.S. GAAP reflected in them.

    (c) Comment on GTC's reconciliation of civil and taxable income as presented on Exhibit 5.

This case was prepared by Professor Gaetano Di Palo, The University of Salerno, and revised by Kenneth R. Ferris. Copyright © 1994 by Gaetano Di Palo and Kenneth R. Ferris. All rights reserved.

EXHIBIT 1

GIORDANI TRADING COMPANY S.r.l.
Ledger Account Balances* as of 31 December 1994
(in lire)

Accounts	Debit	Credit
Commercial real estate	481.500.000	–0–
Furniture	21.000.000	–0–
Motor vehicles	31.500.000	–0–
Capital expenditures	10.500.000	–0–
Office equipment	10.050.000	–0–
Credit toward customers	126.000.000	–0–
Advance payment to personnel	420.000	–0–
Foreign client receivables	3.450.000	–0–
Petty cash	2.700.000	–0–
Debts toward suppliers	–0–	98.100.000
V.A.T. debt	–0–	3.375.000
Passive loans	–0–	37.275.000
Severance pay fund	–0–	48.000.000
Capital stock	–0–	450.000.000
Bank account	28.500.000	–0–
Social security agency	–0–	7.275.000
Goods: Stock in trade	86.250.000	–0–
Goods: Purchase	678.000.000	–0–
Wages	84.000.000	–0–
Social security contributions	40.500.000	–0–
Transportation expenses	31.500.000	–0–
Utilities	3.450.000	–0–
Telephone expenses	5.850.000	–0–
Passive rents	11.100.000	–0–
Gasoline expenses	9.750.000	–0–
Sales expenses	1.230.000	–0–
Interest paid on loans	3.750.000	–0–
Returned goods	–0–	3.720.000
Discounts	–0–	1.770.000
Capital loss	480.000	–0–
Goods: Sales	–0–	1.020.000.000
Miscellaneous services	–0–	1.965.000
Abatements	5.100.000	–0–
Consulting fees	4.050.000	–0–
Commercial interests	–0–	1.800.000
Various proceeds	–0–	7.350.000
Total	1.680.630.000	1.680.630.000

*The ledger account balances do not include the end-of-year adjustments for amortization, severance pay, devaluation of receivables, and income taxes.

EXHIBIT 2

GIORDANI TRADING COMPANY S.r.l.
Balance Sheet as per Civil Code (Article 2424)
31 December 1994
(in lire)

Assets		Equities	
Fixed Assets:		Net Worth:	
Immaterial assets:		Capital stock	450.000.000
Cost of facilities and		Net profit	12.025.458
enlargement	8.490.000		
Material assets:		Total	462.025.458
Land and buildings	457.425.000		
Facilities and equipment	20.775.000		
Other goods	15.750.000	Reserves for expenses	68.492.273
Total fixed assets	502.440.000	Severance pay fund	55.127.269
Circulating Assets:		Debts:	
Stock in trade:		To banks	
Finished goods and		To suppliers	37.275.000
merchandise	80.160.000	To taxes	98.100.000
Credits:		To social security	9.675.000
To clients/customers	117.450.000	Total debts	7.275.000
To others	6.720.000		152.325.000
Cash balances:			
Bank deposits	28.500.000		
Vault cash	2.700.000		
Total circulating assets	235.530.000		
Total assets	737.970.000	Total equities	737.970.000

Explanatory Notes:

- ''Land and buildings'' represents commercial real estate.

- ''Facilities and equipment'' is composed of furniture (15.750.000) and office equipment (5.025.000).

- ''Other goods'' represent motor vehicles.

- ''Reserves for expenses'' includes the receivable devaluation fund (7.560.000), the exchange rate fluctuation fund (12.354), and corporate income taxes (60.919.919).

EXHIBIT 3

GIORDANI TRADING COMPANY S.r.l.
Income statement as per Civil Code (article 2425)
For the Year Ended 31 December 1994
(in lire)

Production value	1.019.895.000
Less: Cost of production	
For goods	674.280.000
services	4.050.000
third party goods	11.100.000
employees: salary and wages	124.500.000
pension plan	7.127.269
amortization and devaluation:	
immaterial assets	2.010.000
material assets	50.100.000
devaluation of receivables	19.572.354
miscellaneous costs of operations	51.780.000
Total cost of production	944.519.623
Difference between value and cost of production	75.375.377
Financial proceeds and expenses	
Other financial proceeds	1.800.000
Interest and financial expenses	(3.750.000)
Total	(1.950.000)
Extraordinary proceeds and expenses	
Capital loss	(480.000)
Total before taxes	72.945.377
Less: Taxes	(60.919.919)
Net profit	12.025.458

EXHIBIT 4

GIORDANI TRADING COMPANY S.r.l.
Summary of Significant Accounting Policies
(as per Italian Civil Code)

Material Assets

Article 2426 of the Civil Code provides that material assets be valued at their cost of purchase or of production. ''Purchase price'' shall include all costs incidental to purchase, whereas ''production cost'' shall include all costs directly associated with an asset's development (to include ''other costs for an amount reasonably ascribable to the product with reference to the period of manufacture and up to the point in which'' the asset can be placed in service). Thus, interest costs relating to asset production may also be included.

The capitalized value of material assets must be systematically amortized, and any modifications in the amortization policy must be explained in the accompanying notes.

In the event that an asset's value declines over time, the value should be written down to reflect this decline.

EXHIBIT 4 (continued)

GIORDANI TRADING COMPANY S.r.l.
Summary of Significant Accounting Policies
(as per Italian Civil Code)

On the basis of article 2426, the following amortization rates and amounts were utilized in 1994:

	Percent	*Amortization Amount*
Commercial real estate	5	24.075.000
Furniture	25	5.250.000
Motor vehicles	50	15.750.000
Office equipment	50	5.025.000
		50.100.000

Immaterial Assets

Article 2426 of the Civil Code provides that the cost of asset installation and enlargement, as well as the cost of research, development, and advertising with expected future useful lives, may be capitalized upon approval by the Board of Directors. Amortization of such assets may not exceed five years; and until such amortization is complete, dividends may be distributed only to the extent that existing reserves are sufficient to cover any remaining unamortized costs.

Purchased goodwill may be capitalized upon approval by the Board, but must be amortized over a five year period. Longer amortization periods are permitted, if justifiable, and if disclosed in the footnotes.

On the basis of article 2426, the following amortization rates and amounts were utilized in 1994:

	Percent	*Amortization Amount*
Capital expenditure for facilities and enlargement	20	2.010.000

Receivables

The Civil Code dictates that receivables (i.e., "credits to . . . ") be valued at their expected realizable value, requiring an analysis of actual and expected losses therefrom. Based on prior accounting data, GTC has forecasted uncollectible receivables amounting to 6 percent of those outstanding. The expected uncollectible balance is carried in the "receivable devaluation fund" account, and included in the "Reserve for expenses." Receivables from foreign clients/customers are exposed to exchange rate movements; a currency loss of L. 12.354 is anticipated as of 31 December 1994, and this amount is included in the "Reserve for expenses." The bad debt expense (i.e., "devaluation of receivables") charged against current period income amounted to L. 19.572.354:

Realized losses on receivables	12.000.000
Unrealized, but anticipated losses on receivables	7.560.000
Unrealized exchange rate losses	12.354

Severance Pay

The Civil Code provides that public companies must accrue on an annual basis severance pay for its employees. Calculation of the annual amount is obtained by dividing annual wages by 13.5 and then multiplying by a coefficient of correction. For 1994, this calculation amounted to L. 7.129.269.

Stock in Trade

Finished goods inventory and merchandise are valued at their cost of purchase, or their market value if less. The cost of stock in trade may be determined using an estimated average cost method, FIFO, or LIFO. GTC has determined that LIFO is appropriate for its purposes, in part because LIFO undervalues inventoried stock during periods of inflation, which is a prudent policy and allowed for tax purposes. At 31 December 1994, the LIFO value of stock was L. 80.160.000.

EXHIBIT 5

GIORDANI TRADING COMPANY S.r.l.
Reconciliation of Civil and Taxable Income

The following is a reconciliation of Civil Income (L. 72.945.377) to Taxable Income (L. 116.704.825):

Civil income (as per accounting records)	72.945.377
Nondeductible costs recovered for taxation:	
Excess amortization	24.825.000
Excess devaluation	18.934.448
Taxable income	116.704.825

Excess Amortization

Articles 67, 68, and 74 of the Italian Tax Code provide that material and immaterial assets may be amortized from their inception of use, but any deductions may not exceed the rate of amortization as provided by the Ministry of Finance (MOF). Any asset whose cost is less than one million lire may be deducted in full in the year of purchase.

GTC's 1994 excess amortization was:

Asset	Civil Code Amortization Rate (%)	Amortization per Books	MOF Amortization Rate (%)	MOF Amortization	Excess Amortization
Commercial real estate	5	24.075.000	3	14.445.000	9.630.000
Furniture	25	5.250.000	12	2.520.000	2.730.000
Motor vehicles	50	15.750.000	20	6.300.000	9.450.000
Office equipment	50	5.025.000	20	2.010.000	3.015.000
Capital expenditures for facilities and enlargement	20	2.010.000	20	2.010.000	—0—
					24.825.000

Excess Devaluation

Articles 66 and 71 of the Italian Tax Code provide that receivable writedowns are tax deductible to the extent that they are documented and if the debtor is already subject to bankruptcy proceedings.

Estimated uncollectible accounts may be deducted up to an amount equal to 0.5% of the receivable value carried on the balance sheet (but can be increased to 0.75% for specific industrial sectors or for certain creditors).

EXHIBIT 5 (continued)

GIORDANI TRADING COMPANY S.r.l.
Reconciliation of Civil and Taxable Income

Article 72 of the Italian Tax Code provides that foreign currency exchange losses on receivables may be deducted to the extent provided using the Ministry of Finance's decreed exchange rates (e.g., the average for the period rather than the specific rate in effect or expected to be in effect at the time of account settlement).

GTC's 1994 excess devaluation was:

Receivable	Devaluation Permitted under Civil Code		Devaluation Permitted under MOF decree		Excess Devaluation
Realized losses on receivables written-off		12.000.000		0*	12.000.000
Estimated but unrealized receivable write-offs	6%	7.560.000	0.5%	630.000	6.930.000
Unrealized exchange rate losses		12.354		7.906**	4.448

Calculation of Income Taxes	
Income before taxes as per Civil Code	72.945.377
Income before taxes as per Tax Code	116.704.825
Regional corporate tax (16.20%)	18.906.182
Corporate tax (36%)	42.013.737
Total income taxes	60.919.919
Income after tax as per Civil Code	12.025.485

*Debtor not yet subject to bankruptcy proceedings.
**Calculated using MOF decreed average exchange rate for the period rather than the exchange rate at 31 December 1994.

CASE 14.2
RESTATEMENT AND ANALYSIS

Napoli Can Manufacturing Company S.r.l.

The Napoli Can Manufacturing Company S.r.l. (hereafter NCM) is a limited liability but private company headquartered in Naples, Italy. The company, founded in 1991, specializes in the manufacture of aluminum and tin cans. A significant portion of NCM's production is sold to a U.S. company, which also holds a 15 percent shareholding in NCM. Although the U.S. investor's shareholding in NCM was principally undertaken to control and protect a key source of inputs to its operations, the U.S. investor is nonetheless interested in the financial health and performance of NCM as a stand-alone investment. Depending on NCM's profitability, for example, executives of the minority U.S. investor company have discussed increasing their investment in NCM, possibly to as much as 49 percent.

Unfortunately, the format of NCM's financial statements and some of the accounting principles it uses in the preparation of its statements are not consistent with either U.S. or international accounting standards. Under the Italian civil code, companies must adopt the decreed statement format, and deviations from the accepted layout are not permitted unless they improve the statement's comprehensibility and adhere to providing a true and fair view of the company's financial results. Thus, the U.S. investor company is neither legally entitled nor actually able to obtain a U.S. GAAP or IASC version of NCM's financial statements. This situation is of some concern to executives of the U.S. investor since they are aware that NCM's statements are almost certainly "fiscally biased." Italian civil code permits adoption of valuation methods that intentionally understate asset values and reported earnings, so long as the fiscal bias is declared and quantified in the footnotes.

Presented in Exhibits 1 and 2 are NCM's balance sheet and income statement prepared according to Italian civil code standards. Exhibit 3 presents the explanatory footnotes to NCM's financial statements.

Required:

Executives of the minority U.S. investor company have retained you to assist with the preparation of IASC consistent financial statements for NCM. Consequently, review NCM's Italian GAAP statements and complete the following:

(a) List the accounting inconsistencies.

(b) Reformat and/or restate NCM's Italian financial statements on a basis consistent with IASC standards.

(c) Prepare a financial analysis of the restated statements and be prepared to offer advice to the executives as to whether they should (or should not) increase their shareholding in NCM.

This case was prepared by Michele Pizzo, Universita Di Napoli, and revised by Kenneth R. Ferris. Copyright © 1994 by Michele Pizzo and Kenneth R. Ferris. All rights reserved.

EXHIBIT 1

NAPOLI CAN MANUFACTURING COMPANY S.r.l.
Balance Sheet as per Civil Code

Assets	31.12.94	31.12.93
A) CALLED-UP SHARE CAPITAL NOT PAID	450.000.000	450.000.000
B) FIXED ASSETS:		
I-INTANGIBLE ASSETS		
1) preliminary expenses	3.240.000	4.320.000
2) research and development, publicity costs		
3) patents		
4) concessions, licenses, trademarks, and similar rights and assets		
5) goodwill;		
6) intangible assets in course of construction and payment on account		
7) other assets;		
TOTAL	3.240.000	4.320.000
II-TANGIBLE ASSETS		
1) land and buildings	583.972.500	658.023.750
2) plant and machinery	660.000.000	1.020.000.000
3) industrial and commercial fixtures, fittings, tools and equipment	60.000.000	90.000.000
4) other assets	223.563.000	280.584.000
5) assets in course of construction and payments on account		
TOTAL	1.527.535.500	2.048.607.750
III-INVESTMENTS		
1) shares in:		
a) subsidiaries	525.000.000	450.000.000
b) associate companies		
c) other companies		
2) loans:		
a) to subsidiaries		
b) to associate companies		
c) to holding companies		
d) other loans		
3) other investments other than loans		
4) own shares		
TOTAL	525.000.000	450.000.000
TOTAL FIXED ASSETS	2.055.775.500	2.502.927.750
C) CURRENT ASSETS		
I-STOCKS		
1) raw materials and consumables	165.000.000	162.900.000
2) work in progress	120.000.000	114.000.000
3) contract work in progress		
4) finished goods and goods for resale	222.000.000	202.500.000
5) payments on account		
TOTAL	507.000.000	479.400.000

Exhibit 1 (continued)

NAPOLI CAN MANUFACTURING COMPANY S.r.l.
Balance Sheet as per Civil Code

Assets	*31.12.94*	*31.12.93*
II-DEBTORS		
1) trade debtors		
-amounts falling due within one year	1.696.548.600	1.173.150.000
-amounts falling due after one year		
2) amounts owed by subsidiaries		
3) amounts owed by associated companies		
4) amounts owed by holding companies		
5) other debtors	29.532.000	133.278.750
TOTAL	1.726.080.600	1.306.428.750
III-INVESTMENTS		
1) shares in subsidiaries		
2) shares in associated companies		
3) shares in other companies		
4) own shares		
5) other investments	24.000.000	30.000.000
TOTAL	24.000.000	30.000.000
IV-CASH AT BANK AND IN HAND		
1) bank and postal accounts	398.552.250	
2) cheques		
3) cash	4.629.750	1.661.250
TOTAL	403.152.000	1.661.250
TOTAL CURRENT ASSETS	2.660.232.600	1.817.490.000
D) PREPAYMENTS AND ACCRUED INCOME		
-accrued income	900.000	900.000
-prepayments	3.750.000	3.750.000
-premium on bonds	9.000.000	10.125.000
TOTAL	13.650.000	14.775.000
TOTAL ASSETS (A+B+C+D)	5.179.658.100	4.785.192.750
MEMORANDUM ACCOUNTS: LEASE		
COMMITMENTS	2.540.583.600	2.964.014.200

Liabilities		
A) CAPITAL AND RESERVES		
I-CALLED UP SHARE CAPITAL	1.500.000.000	1.500.000.000
II-SHARE PREMIUM ACCOUNT		
III-REVALUATION RESERVE		
IV-LEGAL RESERVE	13.194.000	
V-RESERVE FOR OWN SHARES		
VI-RESERVE PROVIDED FOR BY THE ARTICLES		
VII-OTHER RESERVES	325.679.250	
VIII-PRIOR YEAR INCOME (LOSS)		
XI-PROFIT AND LOSS ACCOUNT	275.386.350	263.873.250
TOTAL	2.114.250.600	1.763.873.250
B) PROVISIONS FOR LIABILITIES AND		
CHARGES		
1) pensions and similar obligations		
2) deferred taxation and tax litigations		
3) other provisions		
TOTAL		

EXHIBIT 1 (continued)

NAPOLI CAN MANUFACTURING COMPANY S.r.l.
Balance Sheet as per Civil Code

Liabilities (continued)	*31.12.94*	*31.12.93*
C) STAFF CREDITORS FOR DISMISSAL WAGES	100.500.000	45.000.000
D) CREDITORS		
1) debenture bonds:		
-amounts falling due within one year	75.000.000	75.000.000
-amounts falling due after one year	525.000.000	600.000.000
2) convertible bonds		
3) bank loans and overdraft:		
-amounts falling due within one year		1.680.270.000
-amounts falling due after one year		
4) other loans		
5) payments received on account		
6) trade creditors:		
-amounts falling due within one year	895.395.000	532.200.000
-amounts falling due after one year		
7) bills of exchange payable:		
-amounts falling due within one year	450.000.000	
-amounts falling due after one year		
8) amounts owed to subsidiaries		
9) amounts owed to associated companies		
10) amounts owed to holding companies		
11) tax debts	917.503.500	23.599.500
12) social security debts		
13) other creditors		
TOTAL	2.862.898.500	2.911.069.500
E) ACCRUALS AND DEFERRED INCOME		
-accruals	102.000.000	65.250.000
-deferred income		
TOTAL	102.000.000	65.250.000
TOTAL LIABILITIES (A+B+C+D+E)	5.179.568.100	4.785.192.750
MEMORANDUM ACCOUNTS: LEASE		
COMMITMENTS	2.540.583.600	2.964.014.200

EXHIBIT 2

NAPOLI CAN MANUFACTURING COMPANY S.r.l.
Income Statement as per Civil Code

Profit and Loss Account	*31.12.94*	*31.12.93*
A) PRODUCT OF THE FINANCIAL YEAR		
1) turnover	4.041.430.600	2.385.430.600
2) change in stocks of finished goods and in work progress	25.500.000	316.500.000
3) change in contract work in progress		
4) own work capitalized	90.000.000	150.000.000
5) other operating income	52.500.000	30.000.000
TOTAL	4.209.430.600	2.881.930.600

EXHIBIT 2 (continued)

NAPOLI CAN MANUFACTURING COMPANY S.r.l.
Income Statement as per Civil Code

	31.12.94	*31.12.93*
B) COSTS OF THE PRODUCT OF THE FINANCIAL YEAR		
6) raw materials and consumables	−942.000.000	−637.500.000
7) services	−71.175.000	−58.500.000
8) rentals	−423.430.600	−423.430.600
9) staff costs		
a) wages and salaries	−802.500.000	−727.500.000
b) social security costs	−390.000.000	−360.000.000
c) accrued charges for staff post-retirement benefits	−55.500.000	−45.000.000
d) other pension costs		
e) other costs		
10) depreciation and other amounts written off		
a) intangible assets depreciation	−1.080.000	−1.080.000
b) tangible assets depreciation	−480.572.250	−300.497.250
c) exceptional amounts written off fixed assets		
d) exceptional amounts written off debtors and cash at bank and in hand	−8.381.400	−4.500.000
11) change in stocks of raw materials, consumables and goods for resale	2.100.000	162.900.000
12) provisions for liabilities and charges		
13) other provisions		
14) other operating charges	−76.350.000	−31.125.000
TOTAL B	−3.248.889.250	−2.426.232.850
DIFFERENCE BETWEEN A) AND B)	960.541.350	455.697.750
C) FINANCIAL EXPENSES AND REVENUES		
15) income from shares in a group companies	82.032.000	
16) other financial income		
a) from loans		
b) from investments other than shares included among fixed assets		
c) from investments other than shares included among current assets		
d) other revenues	1.800.000	1.800.000
17) interest payable and similar charges	−226.875.000	−171.375.000
TOTAL (15+16−17)	−143.043.000	−169.575.000
D) AMOUNTS WRITTEN OFF INVESTMENTS AND REVALUATIONS		
18) revaluations		
a) shares		
b) investments other than shares included among fixed assets		
c) investments other than shares included among current assets		
19) amounts written off		
a) shares		
b) investments other than shares included among fixed assets		
c) investments other than shares included among current assets	−6.000.000	
TOTAL (18−19)	−6.000.000	
E) EXTRAORDINARY ITEMS		
20) income	7.500.000	1.350.000
21) charges		
TOTAL EXTRAORDINARY ITEMS	7.500.000	1.350.000
PROFIT OR LOSS BEFORE TAX	818.998.350	287.472.750
22) tax on profit or loss	−543.612.000	−23.599.500
23) profit loss for the financial year	275.386.350	263.873.250

EXHIBIT 3

Napoli Can Manufacturing Company S.r.l.
Significant Accounting Policies

Preliminary expenses: Legal and administrative expenses for the company's incorporation and the issue of shares; usually capitalized and amortized within five years on a straight-line basis.

Tangible assets: Valued at purchase cost.[1] Own work capitalized includes direct costs, a share of the general expenses, and the cost of borrowed capital financing the construction up to completion. The sale of a building for 145.500.000 has resulted in a gain of 7.500.000, which is included among extraordinary items.

Shares in subsidiaries: A 60% shareholding accounted for by the equity method. The figure allows for the share of the investor's earnings accrued during 1994 (75.000.000), but this amount is not included in the calculation of net profit by the investor; it is allocated to a nondistributable reserve[2] as long as it is not realized (by means of a dividend or shareholding sale).

Raw materials and consumables: Valued according to a tax method similar to LIFO.[3] The replacement cost (approximately 245.250.000 for 1994 and 241.650.000 for 1993) substantially differs from the accounting figure, the resulting difference between taxable income and accounting income being permanent.

Work in progress, finished goods, and goods for resale: Valued at production cost.

Trade debtors: Written off, for tax purposes, as 4.500.000 (1993) and 8.381.400 (1994).[4]

Other investments: Fixed interest bonds. The purchase cost has been written off owing to a decrease in market value.[5]

Premium on bonds: This refers to the debenture bonds issued and is amortized on a straight-line basis according to the bond's period of maturity (10 years).

Lease commitments: Financial leases are not capitalized because the asset is not legally owned and, for tax purposes, they must be accounted for as operating leases.[6] The following items show the fixed rentals due for a financial lease on an industrial building (1/1/93–1/1/2002;[7] internal rate 14.49% equal to current market rates; semiannual payments).

---

[1]Revaluations are not allowed unless within the amount written off over previous years.

[2]In practice, an equity accounting solution is applied.

[3]First year: weighted average purchase price for that year. Following year:
  a) increase in quantity: first year quantity at the same value plus each added quantity valued at the weighted purchase price for that year.
  b) decrease in quantity: previous year amount less the change in quantity valued at the weighted average purchase price for each previous year, working backward from the year immediately preceding.

[4]For tax purposes, trade debtors can be written off each year as 0.5% of their nominal value, but the global provision cannot be greater than 5% of trade debtors.

[5]Cost or market is applied for investments included among current assets, whichever is the lower.

[6]Otherwise rentals would not be allowed as tax expenses.

[7]A minimum term required by tax legislation.

EXHIBIT 3 (continued)

Napoli Can Manufacturing Company S.r.l.
Significant Accounting Policies

Legal reserve: The Civil Code requires the allocation of 5% of net profit to this undistributable reserve up to 20% of called-up share capital.

Other reserves: This includes retained profit and the earnings (75.000.000) on a shareholding accounted for by the equity method.

Staff creditors for dismissal wages: Italian companies do not usually have any pension obligation, but they have to pay a lump sum when the employee retires or is dismissed, the amount being calculated on the basis of the number of years of employment.

Debenture bonds: Original value 675.000.000, annual reimbursement 75.000.000.

Bills of exchange payable: These refer to trade purchases.

Tax debts: These include a debt for value-added tax (373.891.500) and a provision for taxes payable (543.612.000), calculated by applying a rate of 52.2% to the taxable income.

Own work capitalized: Deferred costs for the improvement of buildings.

Other operating income: Revenue for ancillary services such as packing and transportation.[8]

Services: Costs for energy, insurance, maintenance, telephone.[9]

Rentals: Lease rentals.

Staff costs: accrued charges for dismissal wages: Amount accrued for the lump-sum obligation the company has toward employees when they retire or are dismissed.

Tangible assets depreciation: The straight-line method is applied. The amount is the same as the tax allowance for depreciation and accelerated depreciation.[10] During the first year of the asset's life, the rate is reduced by 50%.[11] Accelerated depreciation for plant and machinery (90.000.000 in 1993 and 180.000.000 in 1994) represents a fiscal bias, while for the remaining tangible assets it is consistent with useful life. (See table below.)

Exceptional amounts written off debtors . . . . : This is a provision for doubtful accounts. It is 0.5% of the nominal amount for trade debtors and is recognized only to obtain tax relief as a reduction of the item trade debtors.

Other operating charges: Remuneration for members of the Board of Directors, appointed auditors' fees, stationery costs, etc.

Income from shares in a group of companies: Dividends plus tax relief to avoid double taxation on them.

Other revenues: Interest accrued on purchased bonds. Interest payable and similar charges: interest on bank account and issued bonds, premium on bond amortization and other financial charges.

Extraordinary items: Income: Capital gain on the sale of a building.

Tax on profit: Provision for the amount of taxes payable with reference to the taxable income for the period considered. Although mandatory, deferred taxation is not included, except in the case of listed companies.

---

[8]If it includes state subsidies for costs incurred, the amount must be shown separately here and not among extraordinary items.

[9]It can also include technical, administrative, consulting costs.

[10]According to civil code, it should be calculated according to the foreseen useful life, but, in practice, tax rates are used.

[11]It is a fiscal rule but is widely applied also for simplicity, as it avoids a time-consuming calculation of the months during which the asset is actually used.

EXHIBIT 3 (continued)

Napoli Can Manufacturing Company S.r.l.
Significant Accounting Policies

Tangible Assets	Purchase Cost	Previous Years' Depreciation	Net Book Value at 1/1/94	Purchases	Own Work Capitalized	Sales	Disposals	Amount Written Off	Financial Year Depreciation	Accelerated Depreciation	Net Book Value at: 31/12/94
Land and buildings	678.375.000	−20.351.250	658.023.750		90.000.000	−145.500.000			−18.551.250		583.972.500
Plant and machinery	1.200.000.000	−180.000.000	1.020.00.000						−180.000.000	−180.000.000	660.000.000
Industrial and commercial fixtures	120.000.000	−30.000.000	90.000.000						−30.000.000		60.000.000
Other assets	350.730.000	−70.146.000	280.584.000	15.000.000					−72.021.000		223.563.000
Total tangible assets	2.349.105.000	−300.497.250	2.048.607.750	15.000.000	90.000.000	−145.500.000			−300.572.250	−180.000.000	1.527.535.500

ANNUAL REPORT ANALYSIS

Fiat

An interesting and important challenge for students of international financial reporting is to study the published annual reports of various companies from different countries. Your instructor will provide you with a recent copy of the Fiat annual report. To facilitate your delving into this annual report, undertake the following endeavors.

Required:

    (a) List the key differences between the Fiat annual report and what you would expect to see for a U.S. company such as General Motors.

    (b) Calculate the following ratios for Fiat taking care to note the assumptions you found necessary to make and where you found the appropriate pieces of data in the annual report.

$$(1)\ \text{Current ratio} = \frac{\text{Total current assets}}{\text{Total current liabilities}}$$

$$(2)\ \text{Quick ratio} = \frac{\text{Cash} + \text{Marketable securities} + \text{Accounts receivable}}{\text{Total current liabilities}}$$

$$(3)\ \text{Operating cash flow to current liabilities} = \frac{\text{Operating cash flow}}{\text{Average total current liabilities}}$$

$$(4)\ \text{Debt-to-equity ratio} = \frac{\text{Long-term debt}}{\text{Owners' equity}}$$

$$(5)\ \text{Debt-to-total capitalization ratio} = \frac{\text{Long-term debt}}{\text{Long-term debt} + \text{Owners' equity}}$$

$$(6)\ \text{Interest coverage ratio} = \frac{\text{Net income before interest \& income taxes}}{\text{Interest expense}}$$

$$(7)\ \text{Operating cash flow to interest charges} = \frac{\text{Operating cash flow}}{\text{Interest expense}}$$

$$(8)\ \text{Operating cash flow to total liabilities} = \frac{\text{Operating cash flow}}{\text{Average total liabilities}}$$

$$(9)\ \text{Receivables turnover ratio} = \frac{\text{Net sales}}{\text{Average accounts receivable}}$$

$$(10)\ \text{Inventory turnover} = \frac{\text{Costs of goods sold}}{\text{Average inventory}}$$

$$(11)\ \text{Asset turnover} = \frac{\text{Net sales}}{\text{Average total assets}}$$

(12) Average collection period
ratio
$$= \frac{\text{365 Days}}{\text{Receivables turnover ratio}}$$

(13) Average number of days'
inventory on hand ratio
$$= \frac{\text{365 Days}}{\text{Inventory turnover ratio}}$$

(14) Return on assets (ROA)
$$= \frac{\text{Net income}}{\text{Average total assets}}$$

OR $= \text{ROS} \times \text{Asset turnover}$

(15) Return on equity (ROE)
$$= \frac{\text{Net income}}{\text{Average total owners' equity}}$$

OR $= \text{ROA} \times \text{Financial leverage}$

(16) Return on Sales (ROS)
$$= \frac{\text{Net income}}{\text{Net sales}}$$

(17) Financial leverage
$$= \frac{\text{Average liabilities} + \text{Average owners' equity}}{\text{Average owners' equity}}$$

(18) Basic earnings per share
(EPS)
$$= \frac{\text{NI applicable to common shareholders}}{\text{Weighted average common shares}}$$

(19) Cash dividend yield
$$= \frac{\text{Cash dividend per common share}}{\text{Market price per common share}}$$

(20) Cash dividend payout
$$= \frac{\text{Total cash dividend to common shareholders}}{\text{Net income}}$$

(c) What do you conclude about the availability of the appropriate data in the annual report for calculating these ratios?

(d) What does this financial analysis tell you about Fiat?

(e) What analytical metrics did Fiat choose to report for itself? What do those choices say about the message the company is striving to tell and the audience it is addressing?

PART IV

Harmonization of International Accounting and Reporting Standards Revisited

The topic of harmonization was first presented in this text prior to the financial-analysis chapters and the country-specific chapters. At that juncture, perhaps a true appreciation for the difficulties and shortcomings of harmonization were not apparent. Since so many voices in the marketplace continue to tout the goal of harmonization, the topic is raised again in this last chapter and is done so as a capstone to the book. Mr. Arthur Wyatt, past chair of the IASC, offers further food for thought for those who now bring to the listening the ideas and learnings sparked by the preceding 14 chapters.

Harmonization's Future

The impact of [the] International Accounting Standards Committee will not be revolutionary or immediate. The impact will be . . . of dominating importance in the presentation of financial statements by about the year 2000.[1]

Introduction

What follows are excerpts from a February 1995 presentation by Mr. Arthur Wyatt at the University of Virginia. Mr. Wyatt is past chairman of the International Accounting Standards Committee (IASC), past president of the American Accounting Association, former member of the Financial Accounting Standards Board, and past member and chairman of the American Institute of CPAs' Accounting Standards Executive Committee. He recently retired as a partner from the international accounting firm of Arthur Andersen & Company, where he served in its Accounting Principles Group. He is a member of the AICPA and a past member of its board of directors. He is a professor of accountancy at the University of Illinois. Mr. Wyatt's insights are pertinent in that for the past 25 years, he has been at the epicenter of accounting debate, policy setting, practice, and education.

. . .

There are many reasons why accounting standards are different in different countries. Not only are there differences in accounting, but also in many other aspects of life. There are differences in legal systems, customs, business practices, capital structures and, of course, differences in the stages of economic development. Most of the countries in Africa, for example, really do not need accounting standards that deal with manufacturing enterprises. They are much more interested in standards that deal with agricultural, forestation, and mining activities.

---

[1]A quote attributed to Sir Henry Benson, founder of the IASC, noted in "Lord Benson—IASC's Creator," *IASC Insight,* March 1995, p.1.

In the United Kingdom, it is generally thought that everything in accounting is accepted unless it is prohibited. However, in Germany, the prevailing view is that everything is prohibited unless it is accepted. Alternatively, if you go to Romania, everything is prohibited even if it is accepted. And then if you go to Italy, everything is accepted especially if it is prohibited. Such is the context in which I have seen IASC members debate issues.

Over the last 10 years, there has been increasing interest in accounting harmonization and in reducing global accounting diversity. More specifically, harmonization is the ultimate goal; reducing diversity is a step-by-step process intended to lead to harmonization. If you were an investment banker or even a commercial banker in Frankfurt or Zurich or any place on the Continent, in the course of a given month you would probably get requests for loans from a dozen or more companies from a dozen or more countries. You would receive their financial statements and they would look alike in some ways, but you would not want to compare them with each other and conclude that you were comparing like kinds of items. If you were in the lending business, you would throw back your head and say, "Why can't we do better? Why can't we have the accounting be similar in each country because that would make my job easier?" Investment bankers are no different from anybody else—everybody is looking for a way to make their job easier and reducing the diversity in accounting standards around the world would make their jobs easier. Thus, there is considerable interest on the part of the capital markets in harmonization.

There is also some interest on the part of securities regulators. They have essentially the same problem. Securities regulators are charged with the responsibility of trying to make the markets in their country a fair game for the residents of their country. One of the ways that they monitor this is to require companies that register securities with them to file financial statements. Every so often a securities regulator in country A will get a request from a company in country B to enter country A's capital markets. The regulator then has to decide whether the financial statements are fairly presented in accordance with something and, the regulator finds we've got different rules in Germany from those in the United States. Hence, the securities regulator's job would be easier if accounting standards were less diverse.

Finally, I think we have to get some kind of an overview of what is the role that accounting plays in business? What does accounting contribute to the process? Some of you may say, "Not very much," or "I haven't been able to figure that out yet," but the fact is, if we contribute anything as accountants it is to try to make the business system run more efficiently. That is what accounting is about—trying to provide information that will assist those who make decisions to make better decisions, more efficient decisions. So, to the extent that we have differences in accounting amongst different countries and to the extent this causes dis-economies in the capital market process, we have not done as good a job with meeting the efficiency objective as we might have.

We have, as you know, an entity that has as its mission the reduction of this diversity and that is the International Accounting Standards Committee (IASC). It was formed in 1973 which also happens to be the year the FASB was formed (but that is purely an historical accident). The IASC is based in London. It has a very small staff or secretariat, four or five people. The members of IASC are professional bodies of accounting in about 80 countries and there are about 105 such bodies. The board members of IASC—the board being the body that issues international accounting standards—currently consists of 14 members—representatives from 13 countries and the International Association of Financial Analysts. There are currently three additional empty seats on the board. One seat is reserved for the Financial Executives' worldwide body. Another seat is reserved for the International Chamber of Commerce, while the last is reserved for an international banking organization. These organizations have not yet developed a framework within which their representative could act as a representative of their international community and so they have not utilized their seats.

Of the 14 members, 11 votes are necessary to issue a standard. That is a pretty high hurdle. Four dissents out of 14 means that no standard is issued. The IASC follows certain due process procedures in the sense that before a standard is issued there is an exposure draft and there is an invitation for anybody who is interested to submit their written comments. We have had some public hearings—not quite as an elaborate a due process as the FASB has, but somewhat similar in nature.

Until 1990, I think it is fair to say that the IASC standards—27 or so of them at that time—were characterized by the ''acceptability of alternatives.'' Now, think about it—How good a standard is a standard if it lets you do something more than one way? It is sort of like having a standard for driving your car which says you can drive on the right or you can drive on the left. That would produce chaos. In accounting you can get some rather chaotic answers if you apply alternatives and the user of the statement does not understand that the numbers were derived by following different rules. And so, the IASC was, I think, viewed by most of the world as a group of people who met in three nice places a year and were treated very nicely and ended up issuing standards that were the result of compromises, and if they eliminated one or two practices, they still retained at least two for most issues.

In 1988, the Board undertook a project called their Improvements Project and the objective was to eliminate as many alternatives as possible. Maybe there were 38 or so when they started and the project did eliminate 23 or 24—that's a pretty big chunk but it also means that even today there are some 12 to 14 alternatives that are accepted in the revised standards.

Now, let me give you an example of how this worked and how the Board works. It is different at the IASC and the FASB. At the FASB you see the same people that you are working with as fellow board members every day. At the IASC, we only meet three times a year. We meet for four days at a time and it is possible that, in the interval between Board meetings there may be some task force meetings and you may see a subset of the members, but you do not really get to know the members as well as—in my case—as well as I would have liked. I like getting to know people, figuring out what it is that motivates them and makes them tick. Then I can figure out how to deal with them effectively and persuading them that my answer is the right answer, especially on accounting standards.

We had progressed fairly well along in the Improvements Project and we were coming to some road blocks. Certain countries had agreed that they would accept a limitation which would eliminate a practice that had been acceptable in their country for years. But it seemed that it was the same countries that were giving in each time and the feeling was growing that the United States was not participating in any of the compromises and the UK was not participating in very many. We were finding it increasingly difficult taking up a proposal to get the practice that had been embedded in a certain society for a while to be eliminated. When our focus shifted to inventories, there were some sharp words that flew back and forth and one country representative said in one portion of the meeting, "The U.S. will never give up on LIFO." It is important to note that the IASC conceptual framework does not embrace the LIFO approach. LIFO leads to outdated numbers in the balance sheet. It leads to eliminating certain inflation effects in the income statement, but not all of them, and so you get an income statement number that is partially adjusted for the effects of inflation and to the extent that it is not really very pure, it is partial.

So after lobbying, consulting a bit with each other, the United States representatives stated that the United States was ready to give up on LIFO. The United States would vote to eliminate LIFO and permit as acceptable accounting only FIFO or average cost. Well, that stunned the group. The feeling amongst the other countries had been that LIFO was not something the United States would ever concede. We also told them, of course, that we—the two United States representatives—did not have the power to do this but that we would deal with the FASB and the SEC and urge the SEC to deal with Congress because LIFO exists in the United States, at least in part, because the Treasury Department and Congress enacted a rule that if you want to use LIFO for tax purposes, you must use it for accounting purposes as well. The LIFO conformity rule is a big hurdle in the United States to getting rid of LIFO.

So, the IASC had a discussion and we took a vote and there were two countries that voted to retain LIFO even with the United States giving it up; and, I cannot remember which two, but Japan was one of them and, I think, Korea was the other. So we left the meeting and LIFO was a done deal. I got back to the States and I went down to see the people at the SEC and the people at the FASB. Time goes by and we have another IASC meeting—you never really decide things at one meeting. Losers always reintroduce the issue, and hence we reconsidered LIFO; and, low and behold, Italy and Germany announced that in recent months their countries had adopted LIFO as a part of their tax code and in each of those countries a company's financial statements must agree with its tax return. So, all of a sudden now we have Japan, Korea, Italy and Germany against eliminating LIFO, and as a consequence, we were unable to eliminate LIFO. That is how it happens.

In the case of LIFO, it was not the result of lobbying; it was the result of certain countries going home and finding out that they had voted in favor of something that was no longer a policy of their country's standard-setting group. And so, LIFO remains in the IASC standard as an alternative. Whether it will be eliminated in the next set of meetings, nobody knows. There are now about 12 to 14 acceptable alternatives. I suspect that there will have to be more elimination of alternatives before we make substantially greater progress than we have at the present time.

Let me talk now for a moment about the role of securities regulators. There is another organization not related to IASC called IOSCO. It is the International Organization of Securities Commissioners. Its membership is comprised of representatives from countries that have securities regulation. In the United States that is the Securities and Exchange Commission. In other countries it may be the stock exchange which both manages the markets and does the regulation. IOSCO is an organization that meets from time to time and it has work groups that develop its various programs and policies. During the process of the IASC Improvements Project, IOSCO representatives were present at all meetings. They did not have a vote but, obviously, they could participate in the discussion and they knew what was going on.

As I mentioned earlier, the present system makes the work of securities regulators more difficult. Our SEC requires a company from outside the United States that wishes to raise money in this country to file financial statements in accordance with United States standards or that are reconciled to United States accounting standards. That is a slap in the face to the professions of all the other countries. It is, in effect, telling them, ''Your standards aren't good enough for the United States.'' It is a problem. But other countries have a policy of accepting financial statements coming to them as long as they have been audited by a reputable firm of public accountants and they do not put a barrier up with regard to what set of standards have been followed.

In other countries, I presume that the regulators have a group of people that, if they get a set of financial statements from the United States, would undo those numbers and recast them in accordance with that country's accounting standards. I do not know that, but somehow they have to get the information into a framework that users will be able to understand and make comparisons with. The reason for all the interest at this time is the result of what has evolved during your lifetimes in the areas of communications and technology. People poke fun at a little town near where I live, Peoria, Illinois. But if you have a business in Peoria and you want to raise money, you may be able to raise it in Dusseldorf, Germany. All you need is a good lawyer and a good accountant—somebody that can point you in the right direction and almost instantaneously you can send them information and you get a decision back. But the decision maker needs to be able to evaluate the financial information. The pace of that kind of cross-border financing inquiries has multiplied many, many times and is continuing to multiply; and, unless you think that we are going to roll back technology and communication developments, it is going to continue to grow. So securities regulators have a problem in meeting the requirements of their particular country. They are interested in making their jobs a little easier.

Even with IOSCO, however, nationalism raises its head. Each country thinks that what it does is pretty darned good. It is very difficult, particularly for the Germans, to agree to do something the way the United States does it. It is even more difficult for them to agree to do something the way the UK does it even though they are part of the European Union. So, the IOSCO representatives have the same problem that the IASC has—each of them is trying to promote their own national policies but they are doing it in an arena where the overall objective is to reduce diversity—not a real easy arena to work in. IOSCO has been extremely supportive of the IASC work until recently when, about a year ago IOSCO decided that it was going to delay officially embracing the IASC revisions in their existing statements until the IASC had approved a specific package of what IOSCO referred to as ''core standards.'' In other words, up until that point, IOSCO had approved the things that IASC had done. Now they have said, ''No more. We're not going to do it piece meal. We want to see the whole package and when you get done with the whole package, if it's good enough, we'll approve it.''

Now, why did that happen? Well, I suspect that all of a sudden the people at IOSCO came to the realization that they had given up a lot of control over accounting standards to IASC and that is not really what they wanted to do. After all, IOSCO are government people, representatives of government agencies, and the IASC is a private sector body; the government conceding decision making to a private sector body is not common here or anywhere else. And so, I think, IOSCO realized that this was going pretty far, and that we better take a time out and check our signals to see what is going to happen.

Alternatives to IASC

There are some alternatives to the IASC. One alternative is to reduce diversity by having regional agreements. We already have that on the European continent with the EU. They have a number of accounting directives, and two are important: the fourth directive which sets accounting rules and the seventh directive which provides guidance on consolidated statements. Hence, the European Union, at least on the surface, is following one set of rules.

We have in North America recent agreements with Mexico and Canada on trade, and the FASB currently has two or three projects that they are working on jointly with the Canadian Institute of Chartered Accountants and the Mexican Institute of CPAs to come up with standards that would be uniform for the three countries. And there certainly is a possibility that the Southeast Asian countries, which already have an organization, would get together and set their own standards. The question is, ''Would it be advantageous to have three major regional bodies or would that impose new barriers to having harmonization?'' I believe that it is likely to move in that direction. The United States is joining with Canada and Mexico, and if Brazil and Argentina should ever figure out how to make real economic progress, they would probably join in that agreement as well.

Another approach is called ''mutual recognition.'' We could go to Canada and say, ''Look. You've got some companies that would like to raise capital in the United States. We've got some companies that would like to raise capital in Canada. We'll accept your financial statements without having any reconciliation if you'll accept ours without having any reconciliation.'' Try to envision how long it would take for the United States to work out mutual recognition pacts with each of the countries in the world with which we trade. The world will come to an end before Germany and the United States would ever agree. They have two fundamentally different approaches. Mutual recognition may be inefficient to start with, and not very fruitful.

Another possibility is to have the new IASC standards be applicable only to multinational companies or only to consolidated financial statements that are used in international trade and permit all other companies in a country to continue to use their local standards. I suspect that we may evolve that way because if we make some changes for international purposes, the small corner grocery store—if there still is such a thing—would not have any particular need to do anything any different from what they are doing presently.

I suppose one other alternative is to create a substitute for the IASC that is comprised of standard setters from 13 countries. One of the down sides of that is—suppose you were the United States representative and you had just voted this week in the United States to adopt a particular standard and now you go to the IASC—how can you possibly vote other than the way you just voted? Such an approach hardens positions, making it more difficult to work out compromises. So, in my view, I would keep the standard setters out of the picture. They have got enough to do in the home court.

The Outlook

What is the outlook? Well, first of all, I think, we ought to recognize that the process that we are embarking on within the IASC is somewhat unusual. It is hard to find parallels where international agreement is obtained at the initiative of a private sector body. Most of our international agreements are worked through governments, and so, what the IASC is trying to do does not have a great deal of precedence behind it. The politics of effecting change, not just in accounting but in any facet of our society, are difficult. In accounting standard setting we are asking many people in many countries to give up positions that they have lived with for years. It is just not an easy process; it takes a lot of time and effort.

How powerful is the force of international capital markets? That is a question that we will have to evaluate. If this is a passing phenomenon, then the move toward harmonization is likely to go away. If it is not, then the pressure is likely to continue until we find out we cannot do it or we do a better job. I happen to believe that the IASC can do the job and I think it will continue to drive the process. I suspect that it will announce, perhaps in 1996, that it is undertaking a new Improvements Project— a second iteration in which it will attack the 14 or so existing acceptable alternatives to try to get the number remaining down to, say, 4 or 5. I think we can live with 4 or 5 because we could then report in the footnotes what the effects of adopting the other alternative would be and there would not be so much noise in the disclosure that the reader would be turned off. I think that it will take them five years at the minimum to eliminate 8 to 10 alternatives. Remember that, to date, they have picked off all the easy ones. The ones that are left are the ones they could not get agreement on the first time around. I think that IOSCO will gradually feel the pressure to buy into the progress that IASC has made.

In the United States you should recognize that the SEC today is under enormous pressure from the New York Stock Exchange to have the United States loosen its standards. The New York Stock Exchange would love to be able to trade the shares of Siemens, BMW, and German companies other than Daimler Benz. That is profit for the Exchange. They are driving the SEC. The SEC gets its money from Congress. That is the way the system works, so the pressures will continue to mount and I would guess that as soon as it is apparent that the IASC is, in fact, going to be able to eliminate 8 to 10 of the remaining alternatives, IOSCO will make a positive move forward and say, "We are going to be supportive of this." I suspect that the initial support will make this applicable to multinationals who have cross-border capital dealings. And that, probably, will take place in 2005 to 2010.

And then, I suspect, that once the multinationals move in this direction, there will be considerable pressure in various countries for all companies to do things the way the "big boys" do them. Nobody likes to be characterized as following "second class standards." And, if the IBMs, Minnesota Minings, and Mercks of the world are following one set of accounting, the smaller domestic companies will say, "We want to follow the same standards. If we don't, our prices in the market will be negatively affected because we are viewed as following less desirable standards."

And so, over a period running into the 2030s or so, there will be a gradual evolution such that students that start college a hundred years from the time I started college, will not be worried so much about what the United States policies are, they will really be focusing on the international standards. Now, that is the horizon that I see which is, of course, subject to a lot of caveats; one—no world wars, and two—no major depressions. In other words, it is important for things to keep going like they are with nothing coming along, unrelated to accounting, that would cause this level of cooperation which we have at the present time among countries to diminish. This process is an evolving one. Change comes. The change that I've seen in my life is substantial and you have already seen a lot of change because the pace of change is faster now than it used to be.

I think the private sector will react more effectively to these changing needs than any governmental body would. That is a bias that I have. I just happen to think that the private sector will be more responsive, on a more timely basis, and will do things that will have less aberrations in them than will a body of governmental regulators, or even a body of representative national standard setters.

Question and Answers

Question: Does harmonization require that financial and tax accounting be separate or not?

Mr. Wyatt: Harmonization does not address that question. Harmonization deals only with financial accounting. Tax provisions are a national issue. There is no effort that I am aware of to have each country follow the same tax code. In places like Germany and Italy, for example, the tax law drives the accounting rules. In the United States, other than for LIFO where, if you adopt LIFO for tax purposes, you have to follow it for accounting purposes as well, we have no other provision in our tax law which says that "if you do this for tax purposes, you have to do it for accounting." So, they really are separate issues and the IASC has not dealt at all with the tax part of it.

Question: You mentioned that the United States is willing to compromise on LIFO. Are there any specific issues that the United States is not willing to compromise on?

Mr. Wyatt: Oh, I think there would be a lot. I do not think the United States would be willing to compromise in moving away from accrual accounting toward cash-basis accounting. I do not think the United States would be willing to compromise on omitting depreciation accounting. I doubt very seriously at this time that the FASB would be willing to compromise on moving pension accounting back to the cash basis. So there are a lot of things that would be considered so crucial to fair accounting, fair reporting that we would not compromise on them. But, you see, if you analyze LIFO in the context of the FASB's conceptual framework or anybody else's conceptual framework, it does not fit. It is an aberration. I am not saying it does not do good things. I'm just saying that it does not fit the conceptual framework. Remember, that the FASB's conceptual framework focuses on the real things—the assets and liabilities. For a company to report their asset inventory containing 1950 prices, is to report something with zero information content. So, it was easy—at least for me—for us in the United States to agree to give LIFO up because it did not fit the framework that we were supposed to be working in. I think that there are other things that the United States would give on. For example, the FASB has a current project jointly with IASC on revisiting how earnings per share are calculated. Now, we can argue whether that is an accounting problem or not, but the fact is that we will probably simplify markedly our approach to calculating earnings per share because nobody else does it the way we do it.

Question: The developed countries seem to have a lot of influence over many of the world's organizations. Is that any different in the IASC?

Mr. Wyatt: That's a great question and I wish I had a great answer. Let me talk about it.

When the IASC was constituted, one of its missions was to be responsive to the needs of developing countries (DCs). As the work at the IASC progressed, the issues brought to the IASC have been issues brought by the DCs primarily. The IASC has, at any given time, amongst the 14 Board members, 3 from developing countries. For example, Korea was included as a developing country, although Korea did not like the label. Jordan is on the Board currently as a developing country and so is South Africa. Now those hardly fit our normal idea of a developing country.

The basic problem is that we do not have a very good package of accounting standards yet for the developed countries. That is where the high visibility is. The IASC does not have the time in its standard setting process to devote to the developing countries. On the other hand, the IASC Secretary General visits at least a dozen developing countries in a year, talks to their professional bodies, meets with them, facilitates their getting access to the work that IASC is doing, and gets a feel for the kinds of questions that they have.

There are a number of the developing countries that use IASC standards as their own, Zimbabwe, Zambia, Singapore, several others—Malaysia has in the past and may still be. What they do is take the standards, put their own cover on it and it becomes the standard in their country, which I think is wonderful because of the limited resources that they have for dealing with their local accounting challenges and problems.

So, the developing countries are a part of—an important part of the IASC mission and mandate but—they do get short shrift. I think that is gradually going to change. Individual developed countries provide significant help to the developing countries in the accounting arena.

Question: What is the likelihood of regional standards? It seems that if culture affects taxes and taxes affect the accounting standards, then it would be more likely for regional standards to develop than IASC standards. Do you think that is going to happen?

Mr. Wyatt: Well, it happened in Europe but not because of accounting. The European Union came into being for reasons a little bit more significant than debits and credits, and accounting had to follow because accounting is an important ingredient to the economic process. I think that the governing body in Brussels for the European Union is not about to embark on writing additional accounting standards. It was all they could do to get the ones they have adopted. After all, Italy did not adopt them until about two years ago and trying to get any major changes adopted is not going to be easy. So, I do not really think that we are going to see great efforts in this regional area. The European Union is the only other party that attends IASC meetings that is not a member other than the FASB.

Question: Cultural dimensions are one of the many reasons behind the differences in national GAAP. How does the IASC deal with these kinds of issues?

Mr. Wyatt: Well, the IASC is not trying to change the cultural aspects of any country. In the accounting arena, the major basis for the differences that we have in accounting has to do with what is called "transparency." How much openness should a company have to its national affairs? Our whole system in the United States is based upon a high degree of disclosure, a high degree of openness. In other cultures there is no need for that. In both Japan and Germany, for example, the bulk of the finance to the major companies is provided by a limited number of banks. They can get whatever information they want, or the company does not get its money—it is pretty simple. They have not had the capital markets with individual stockholders playing any significant role.

The change in Germany will arise, at least in part, because the demands on the German financial system for capital are going to far exceed the ability of the six big, German banks to provide it. Germany is going to finance former East Germany. It is going to be a heavy financier of Romania, Bulgaria, even probably, some of the former Soviet Union states. That is going to call on far more capital than the German system can provide so the German companies are going to say—"Hey, we have great demands that will keep our interest rates up. We can go to the United States. We can go to France. We can get money cheaper. We are going to get it from people who do not know us. They are going to tell us that they want to know more about us."

I think the same thing will evolve in Japan and with the rest of Southeast Asia. Japan is going to be the banker. Japan is going to be a principal financier for a lot of the development that will take place in other parts of Southeast Asia. That is going to put burdens on their capital system and their companies are going to look elsewhere. The Japanese have been far more adaptable than the Germans. We have had a number of Japanese companies trading on the New York Stock Exchange for years.

What is going to happen is that gradually the culture will change and I believe that the German society and the Japanese society will become more open with regard to financial disclosures because companies will have to in order to get the capital they need. That is what will break the barrier—the demand for openness and the reaction to it.

The cultural change that I see is going to permit international accounting standards to evolve is the change that will arise in some countries to make their financial affairs more open, more transparent. That is what the markets will demand and that will be very difficult in the short run but, as time goes by, I think companies will find that the more that they tell about themselves, the fairer the market will treat them. The more information that the market has about a company, the fairer their prices in the market will be.

Question: It seems like the principal goal of harmonization is for comparison purposes? In light of all the differences between the companies (e.g., tolerance for debt), are these statements even under similar standards going to be all that comparable?

Mr. Wyatt: Yes. I think that if we had the ideal accounting situation where everybody is accounting in the same way—and that is not even going to happen if we get an excellent set of international standards, because there will be interpretations and nuances that would permit an evaluation by the lender of whether they want to lend to an entity that has 80 percent debt as opposed to a company in another country that has 50 percent debt—they would then have to evaluate the fact that there is a higher tolerance for risk in certain countries than in others. Without a level ground for comparison, we have that kind of a judgment having to be made without knowing for sure what the numbers should be that we are comparing. I am not saying—and do not think that if we get uniform or harmonized accounting that all companies in the same industries will look the same around the world—there are certain countries that are more liberal in terms of financing than others and they are used to that and they are comfortable with that and that will continue to exist. Probably at the extremes there will be some move toward the middle but not uniformly.

Question: One of the reasons that a trade organization such as the Asia-Pacific Economic Cooperation (Org.) (APEC) is being resisted by Asian countries is because of the role the United States is playing. Do you think that the U.S.'s leadership role in IASC will cause some of the countries to resist harmonization?

Mr. Wyatt: My former colleagues at the IASC would chuckle at the description of the United States having the leadership role. We just happened to have the chairman's seat for two and a half years. I succeeded a Frenchman, the Japanese succeeded me, an Australian succeeded the Japanese and the new chairman will be from Denmark. So the United States really does not have a particular leadership role. The chairman has no vote. All I was was a traffic director. I called on people who put their hands up. The fact that the standards that are evolving seem to be moving toward the United States system is not because it is the United States system. It is moving that way because that is the direction of the movement in most of the countries of the world. As capital demands increase, the demands for openness increases. It happens that our system is the one that is the most open system. So, I do not really think that the IASC is viewed around the world as being an entity that is directed by the United States. But I understand the basis for your question and I think it is legitimate. There is evidence in history that the United States gets its hands on something and they try to take it over. I think we have worked hard in the IASC to prevent that from happening because it won't work. It simply will not work and if we have been unsuccessful and the perception around the world is that IASC is a United States entity then what I've talked about will not fly. We have worked hard not to let that happen.

Question: Is harmonization worth the time and the money that is being put into it? Is it that important?

Mr. Wyatt: I happen to think it is, but that is a judgment call. It is not something I can prove. It is true that there would be differences, but those differences would be differences of fact rather then differences that some bookkeeper created by making a decision to use FIFO rather than LIFO. That is what we are really trying to get down to in accounting—the reporting of economic facts about business decisions. When we have accounting alternatives, we are obfuscating that by layering on some other stuff. I would like to get rid of that other stuff.

ISSUES AND INFORMATION FOR FURTHER INQUIRY

I.15.1 A Contrarian View

In a December 13, 1994 *Financial Times* editorial (p. 16), "High Cost of Liquidity," A. Bhide opines that "the worldwide scramble to mandate accurate and complete disclosure, incarcerate insider traders, and eliminate shady trading practices will likely benefit stockbrokers rather than stockholders." Moreover, "the SEC's enforcement of accurate disclosure facilitates the trading of claims on companies that neither buyer nor seller has personally examined."

Required:

With these quotes as a stimulus, prepare an essay that supports either a pro or con position on the following statement:

The harmonization of international accounting standards will contribute to a deterioration of a company's potential competitive advantage in obtaining scarce international financial resources.

I.15.2   Harmonization Progress

In a May 6, 1993 *Financial Times* article (p. 10), ''Still Too Many Variations for Global Harmonization,'' A. Jack reports that there is ''little prospect of harmonization among accounting standards setters and international accounting standards . . . [the pertinent groups are] looking inwards and [are] not ready for any serious attempts at global harmonisation.''

Required:

Do you believe that significant progress will occur in the next 10 years in the harmonization of international accounting standards? Why or why not?

APPENDIX I
COMPARATIVE ACCOUNTING AND REPORTING PRACTICES AROUND THE WORLD

Item	Australia
Asset valuation	Principally historical cost with selected revaluation (i.e., noncurrent assets at revalued amount; inventory and marketable securities at LCM)
Inventory valuation	Principally FIFO or average cost, but specific identification and standard cost methods permitted; LIFO, base stock, and other current cost methods not permitted
Inventory: year-end	Lower of cost or net realizable value
Depreciation	Principally straight-line and declining balance methods
Goodwill	Purchased goodwill capitalized as a noncurrent intangible asset and amortized to income over the expected period of benefit but not to exceed 20 years; negative goodwill not permitted (i.e., charged off against nonmonetary assets acquired until eliminated)
Research and development costs	Generally expensed as incurred; however, costs possibly deferred if recoverability is beyond a reasonable doubt; amortization of deferred costs match recoverability or receipt of related benefits
Capitalized interest costs	Generally permitted if interest costs clearly associated with bringing related asset to revenue-producing state
Intercorporate Investments:	
Marketable securities	Stated at lower of cost or net realizable value (on an individual basis); unrealized gains and losses taken into income
Long-term investments:	
0–20% ownership	Stated at cost, with revaluation permitted; revaluation amounts taken to revaluation reserve
20–50% ownership	Equity method
51–100% ownership	Consolidated, using purchase accounting; pooling of interests not permitted
Debt valuation	Long-term debt valued at present value; all other debt valued at face value
Leases	Finance leases capitalized to balance sheet; operating leases disclosed in footnotes
Deferred income taxes	Computed under liability method
Pension liabilities	Reflected on balance sheet; underfunding measured as projected benefit obligation less fair value of plan assets
Discretionary reserves	Permitted if authorized by board of directors
Statement of cash flows	Required

APPENDIX I *(continued)*
COMPARATIVE ACCOUNTING AND REPORTING
PRACTICES AROUND THE WORLD

Item	Canada
Asset valuation	Principally historical cost with selected revaluation (principally downward)
Inventory valuation	Principally average cost and FIFO, although specific cost and standard cost also permitted; LIFO not permitted for tax purposes, hence rarely used for reporting purposes
Inventory: year-end	Lower of cost or market with market approximated by replacement cost or net realizable value
Depreciation	Principally straight line, but unit-of-production and declining balance methods also permitted
Goodwill	Purchased goodwill is capitalized to balance sheet and amortized to income (straight-line basis) over expected life, but not to exceed 40 years; negative goodwill not permitted (i.e., eliminated against nonmonetary assets)
Research and development costs	Research costs expensed as incurred; development costs must be deferred and amortized if (a) product/process clearly defined, (b) technical feasibility established, (c) clear intent to produce and market the product, (d) the future market is clearly defined
Capitalized interest costs	Capitalization of interest on constructed assets permitted but not required
Intercorporate investments:	
Marketable securities	Lower of cost or market, applied individually or on a portfolio basis; unrealized gains and losses taken to earnings
Long-term investments:	
0–20% ownership	Principally at cost, adjusted for permanent value declines. Write-downs taken directly to earnings
20–50% ownership	Equity method
51–100% ownership	Consolidated, principally using purchase accounting; pooling of interest permitted if acquirer cannot be identified
Debt valuation	Long-term debt valued at present value; all other debt valued at face value
Leases	Finance leases capitalized to balance sheet; operating leases disclosed in footnotes
Deferred income taxes	Computed under deferral method
Pension liabilities	Reflected on balance sheet; both pension liability and asset disclosure required
Discretionary reserves	Generally not permitted (except for specific losses or liabilities)
Statement of cash flows	Permitted but not required (if statement of changes in financial position presented instead)

APPENDIX I   *(continued)*

COMPARATIVE ACCOUNTING AND REPORTING PRACTICES AROUND THE WORLD

Item	*China**
Asset valuation	Principally historical cost
Inventory valuation	Principally FIFO, LIFO, and weighted average; other methods (e.g., standard cost) also permitted
Inventory: year-end	Lower of cost or net realizable value
Depreciation	Principally straight line, production-based methods also permitted; accelerated methods less common but permitted
Goodwill	Treatment of purchased goodwill not currently addressed by Ministry of Finance's accounting regulations
Research and development costs	Treatment of research and development costs not currently addressed by Ministry of Finance's accounting regulations
Capitalized interest costs	Interest directly related to the acquisition or construction of an asset capitalized
Intercorporate investments:	
Marketable securities	Historical cost on individual security basis
Long-term investments:	
0–20% ownership	Historical cost on individual security basis
20–50% ownership	Principally historical cost
51–100% ownership	Consolidated, unless unconsolidated (i.e., equity method) accounting is approved by Ministry of Finance, usually on grounds of nonhomogeneity of operations
Debt valuation	All liabilities valued at face or settlement value
Leases	The treatment of leases not currently addressed by Ministry of Finance's accounting regulations
Deferred income taxes	Treatment not addressed by Ministry of Finance's accounting regulations
Pension liabilities	Not an issue in PRC because foreign investment enterprises do not maintain pensions for their employees; foreign investment enterprises do pay retirement insurance premiums according to national labor laws
Discretionary reserves	Generally not permitted (except for specific losses or liabilities)
Statement of cash flows	Not required, although statement of changes in financial position required on an annual basis

---

*The accounting principles listed here apply to foreign investment enterprises and need not apply to state or collective enterprises or to joint stock limited companies.

APPENDIX I *(continued)*
COMPARATIVE ACCOUNTING AND REPORTING PRACTICES AROUND THE WORLD

Item	Denmark
Asset valuation	Principally historical cost; revaluation permitted
Inventory valuation	Principally FIFO, specific identification, or standard cost; average cost also permitted; LIFO not recommended
Inventory: year-end	Lower of cost or net realizable value
Depreciation	Principally straight line and declining balance methods
Goodwill	Principally charged to equity at time of acquisition; capitalization and amortization (although not in excess of 5 years) also permitted
Research and development costs	Principally expensed as incurred; deferral permitted if clear relation exists between expenditure and future earnings; maximum amortization period of 5 years if capitalized
Capitalized interest costs	Permitted but not widely practiced
Intercorporate investments:	
Marketable securities	Lower of cost or net realizable value on an individual security basis; unrealized losses to income and unrealized gains to revaluation reserve (unless a prior unrealized loss is reversed)
Long-term investments:	
0–20% ownership	Mark to market, on individual security basis; write-ups taken to revaluation reserve unless a prior write-down taken to income reversed
20–50% ownership	Equity method
51–100% ownership	Principally consolidated; nonconsolidation permitted if disclosed; principally purchase accounting, although pooling of interests permitted
Debt valuation	All liabilities valued at face value
Leases	Generally, all leases treated as operating leases; companies increasingly adopting *IAS No. 17*
Deferred income taxes	Principally calculated under liability method; deferral method also permitted
Pension liabilities	Disclosed in balance sheet if underfunded
Discretionary reserves	Generally not permitted except for specific losses or liabilities
Statement of cash flows	Not required

APPENDIX I   *(continued)*
COMPARATIVE ACCOUNTING AND REPORTING PRACTICES AROUND THE WORLD

Item	*France*
Asset valuation	Principally historical cost, with revaluation of property, plant, equipment, and investments permitted
Inventory valuation	Principally FIFO and weighted-average cost; LIFO may be used in consolidated statements
Inventory: year-end	Lower of cost or replacement cost
Depreciation	Principally straight line and declining balance methods; excess depreciation to reduce a company's tax liability also permitted (accumulated excess depreciation classified under shareholders' equity)
Goodwill	Purchased goodwill (and negative goodwill) capitalized to balance sheet; amortization over a period of expected benefit, with no maximum period specified
Research and development costs	Generally expensed as incurred but may be deferred if feasibility of product is established and costs clearly identifiable; maximum amortization period of 5 years
Capitalized interest costs	May be capitalized but not required
Intercorporate investments:	
Marketable securities	Lower of cost or net realizable value on either an individual or portfolio basis; unrealized gains and losses to income statement
Long-term investments:	
0–20% ownership	Lower of cost or assumed (by management) value on an individual basis; revaluations taken to revaluation reserve in shareholders' equity
20–50% ownership	Equity method
51–100% ownership	Consolidated except when (1) operations of parent and subsidiary nonhomogeneous, (2) control temporary or impaired, (3) subsidiary immaterial to the group as a whole; pooling of interests not permitted, hence purchase accounting only
Debt valuation	All debt valued at face amount
Leases	For consolidated statements, finance leases generally capitalized to the balance sheet; in statutory statements, all leases accounted for as operating leases
Deferred income taxes	For consolidated statements, computed using either the deferral method or the liability method; not required in statutory financial statements
Pension liabilities	Reflected in balance sheet if unfunded
Discretionary reserves	Generally not permitted except for liabilities and losses reasonably estimated
Statement of cash flows	Not required but recommended

APPENDIX I *(continued)*
COMPARATIVE ACCOUNTING AND REPORTING PRACTICES AROUND THE WORLD

Item	*Hong Kong*
Asset valuation	Principally historical cost with revaluation of noncurrent assets permitted
Inventory valuation	Principally FIFO and average cost
Inventory: year-end	Lower of cost or net realizable value
Depreciation	Principally straight line and declining balance methods; other methods permitted
Goodwill	Charge to equity and capitalization/amortization permitted; negative goodwill is credited to shareholder reserves
Research and development costs	Currently no prescribed accounting standard
Capitalized interest costs	Capitalization generally recommended for significant interest costs
Intercorporate investments:	
Marketable securities	Lower of cost or net realizable value on either individual or portfolio basis; unrealized gains and losses to income statement
Long-term investments:	
0–20% ownership	Principally cost with revaluation permitted; revaluation adjustments taken to shareholders' reserve
20–50% ownership	Equity method
51–100% ownership	Principally consolidated; many exceptions for excluding subsidiaries; principally purchase accounting; pooling of interests permitted
Debt valuation	All debt valued at face value except capitalized leases
Leases	Finance leases capitalized to the balance sheet; operating leases disclosed in footnotes
Deferred income taxes	Computed under the liability method
Pension liabilities	Currently no prescribed accounting standard
Discretionary reserves	Made at the discretion of management
Statement of cash flows	Required using either direct or indirect method

APPENDIX I   *(continued)*
COMPARATIVE ACCOUNTING AND REPORTING PRACTICES AROUND THE WORLD

Item	*India*
Asset valuation	Principally historical cost with selected revaluation (i.e., fixed assets) usually on basis of independent appraisal
Inventory valuation	Principally FIFO, average cost, or LIFO; specific identification and standard cost methods permitted
Inventory: year-end	Lower of cost or net realizable value
Depreciation	Principally straight line and declining balance methods; excess depreciation due to revaluation recovered from the revaluation reserve
Goodwill	Purchased goodwill capitalized and amortized over the expected period of benefit or charged against any available capital reserve account
Research and development costs	Charged to expense as incurred, except costs associated with products for which (1) costs clearly identified, (2) technical feasibility demonstrated, (3) management intent to produce and market, (4) costs likely to be recovered, and (5) resources exist to produce and market
Capitalized interest costs	Actual interest costs incurred on construction or installation of fixed assets capitalized
Intercorporate investments:	
Marketable securities	Lower of cost or net realizable value on an individual security basis
Long-term investments:	
0–20% ownership	Principally cost adjusted for any permanent declines
20–50% ownership	Equity method permitted but not required
51–100% ownership	Consolidation permitted but not required
Debt valuation	Principally valued at face value
Leases	Generally all leases accounted for as operating leases
Deferred income taxes	Generally the flow-thru approach used when no deferred taxes arise; liability method recommended
Pension liabilities	Disclosed on balance sheet if unfunded; rare since most currently funded for tax consideration
Discretionary reserves	Generally not permitted unless loss probable and reasonably estimable
Statement of cash flows	Permitted but not required

APPENDIX I *(continued)*
COMPARATIVE ACCOUNTING AND REPORTING PRACTICES AROUND THE WORLD

Item	*Mexico*
Asset valuation	Principally current value based on inflation accounting; replacement cost required (public companies); choice of general price-level accounting values or replacement costs (private companies)
Inventory valuation	Principally LIFO, FIFO, and average cost; other methods also permitted
Inventory: year-end	Restated to replacement cost (public companies) or general price-level-adjustment cost (private companies)
Depreciation	Principally straight line based on restated values
Goodwill	Purchased goodwill capitalized and amortized to income over expected period of benefit not to exceed 20 years; negative goodwill capitalized and amortized to income over 5 years
Research and development costs	Expensed as incurred
Capitalized interest costs	Financing costs during period of fixed asset construction or installation may be capitalized
Intercorporate investments:	
Marketable securities	Net realizable value
Long-term investments:	
0–20% ownership	Lower of cost or net realizable value
20–50% ownership	Equity method
51–100% ownership	Consolidated, except subsidiaries in bankruptcy or foreign subsidiaries subject to blocked funds (i.e., repatriation restrictions) using the purchase method
Debt valuation	All debt valued at face value except finance leases
Leases	Finance leases capitalized to the balance sheet; operating leases disclosed in footnotes
Deferred income taxes	Calculated using the liability method
Pension liabilities	Disclosed on balance sheet if underfunded on basis comparable to *SFAS No. 87*
Discretionary reserves	Generally not permitted
Statement of cash flows	Not required; statement of changes in financial position required

APPENDIX I   *(continued)*
COMPARATIVE ACCOUNTING AND REPORTING PRACTICES AROUND THE WORLD

Item	*New Zealand*
Asset valuation	Principally historical cost with selected revaluation of fixed assets either annually or at least every 3 years
Inventory valuation	Principally FIFO, weighted average, or specific identification; LIFO and base stock not permitted
Inventory: year-end	Lower-of-cost or net realizable value
Depreciation	Principally straight line method; others permitted
Goodwill	Purchased goodwill capitalized and amortized usually over a 10–20 year period; negative goodwill eliminated against nonmonetary assets
Research and development costs	Research expensed as incurred; development outlays capitalized if (1) costs of products clearly identifiable, (2) technical feasibility demonstrated, (3) management intends to manufacture and sell product, (4) future market exists, and (5) resources ensure project completion
Capitalized interest costs	Permitted but not generally practiced
Intercorporate investments:	
Marketable securities	Principally lower of cost or market
Long-term investments:	
0–20% ownership	Either cost (adjusted for any permanent impairment) or market value
20–50% ownership	Equity method
51–100% ownership	Principally consolidated; subsidiaries excluded if immaterial to group, if resulting consolidated data misleading, or if substantially nonhomogeneous; principally purchase accounting, although pooling of interests permitted if acquirer cannot be identified
Debt valuation	Generally valued at face value; present value permitted
Leases	Finance leases capitalized at the lower of the fair value of the asset or present value; operating leases disclosed in footnotes
Deferred income taxes	Calculated using liability method
Pension liabilities	Generally disclosed if unfunded but not required
Discretionary reserves	Generally not permitted except for reasonable future estimable costs
Statement of cash flows	Generally presented principally using direct method

APPENDIX I *(continued)*
COMPARATIVE ACCOUNTING AND REPORTING PRACTICES AROUND THE WORLD

Item	*Spain*
Asset valuation	Principally historical cost; periodic revaluation (or "actualization") of fixed assets required by legislation using specified coefficients
Inventory valuation	Principally weighted average or specific identification; FIFO and LIFO also permitted
Inventory: year-end	Lower-of-cost-or-market value
Depreciation	Principally straight line method; declining balance also permitted
Goodwill	Purchased goodwill capitalized and amortized over 5–10 years; negative goodwill capitalized and amortized only to offset anticipated losses associated with acquired business
Research and development costs	Principally expensed as incurred but may be capitalized if (1) costs clearly identifiable and (2) recoverability relatively certain
Capitalized interest costs	Permitted for fixed assets purchased or constructed
Intercorporate investments:	
Marketable securities	Lower-of-cost-or-market value with unrealized losses taken to income
Long-term investments:	
0–20% ownership	Lower-of-cost-or-market value with unrealized losses taken to income
20–50% ownership	Equity method
51–100% ownership	Generally consolidated using purchase accounting except for subsidiaries (1) with pending sale, (2) immaterial value, (3) with nonhomogeneous principal business, or (4) with restricted control due to bankruptcy filing
Debt valuation	All liabilities valued at settlement value
Leases	Finance leases capitalized to balance sheet; operating leases disclosed in footnotes
Deferred income taxes	Calculated using liability method
Pension liabilities	Disclosed on balance sheet if underfunded
Discretionary reserves	Restricted to specific, probable and estimable losses
Statement of cash flows	Not presented, although statement of sources and uses of funds is frequently disclosed

APPENDIX I *(continued)*
COMPARATIVE ACCOUNTING AND REPORTING PRACTICES AROUND THE WORLD

Item	*Switzerland*
Asset valuation	Principally historical cost; current or replacement cost of fixed assets also permitted
Inventory valuation	FIFO, specific identification, average cost, standard cost
Inventory: year-end	Lower-of-cost-or-market value (i.e., replacement cost or net realizable value)
Depreciation	Straight line or declining balance methods
Goodwill	Not separately disclosed; no required amortization
Research and development costs	Normally expensed as incurred, but capitalization permitted if recoverability highly certain
Capitalized interest costs	Permitted but not generally practiced
Intercorporate investments:	
Marketable securities	Cost or current market value applied either on individual or portfolio basis
Long-term investments:	
0–20% ownership	Cost or current market value applied either on individual or portfolio basis
20–50% ownership	Cost or equity method
51–100% ownership	Generally consolidated with few standards as to procedures
Debt valuation	All debt valued at face value
Leases	All leases treated as operating leases
Deferred income taxes	Generally unnecessary due to consistency between tax and publicly reported data
Pension liabilities	Disclosed in balance sheet if underfunded; disclosure rare due to conformity of tax and book statements
Discretionary reserves	Fully permitted
Statement of cash flows	Not required; usually not presented

Glossary

accelerated depreciation A cost allocation method in which depreciation deductions are largest in an asset's earlier years but decrease over time.

accounting A language used by businesspeople to communicate the financial status of their enterprise to interested parties.

accounting exposure (risk) The hazard of recognizing and reporting foreign exchange gains (losses) in the income statement for a given period.

accounting period The time, usually a quarter or one year, to which accounting reports are related.

accounting policies The specific accounting principles and practices adopted by a company to report its financial results.

Accounting Principles Board (APB) An organization of the AICPA that established U.S. GAAP during the period 1957–1973; some of the APB's opinions remain in force today.

Accounting Standards Committee (ASC) The principal accounting standards-setting organization in Great Britain (and the U.K.) until 1990; issued statements of standard accounting practice or SSAPs.

accounts receivable An asset representing the future receipt of cash (or other assets), usually as a consequence of a sale of goods or services; see also *debtors*.

accounts receivable turnover ratio A measure of the effectiveness of receivable management calculated as net credit sales for the period divided by the average balance in accounts receivable.

accrual concept (accrual basis of accounting) An accounting measurement system that records the financial effects of transactions when a business transaction occurs without regard to the timing of the cash effects of the transaction.

active investment An intercorporate investment by an investor company that allows the investor to exercise influence or control over the operations of the investee-company.

additional paid-in-capital Amounts paid by shareholders in excess of the minimum amount required for the shares to be fully paid (e.g., par or stated value); also known as *paid-in capital in excess of par value* and *share premium reserve*.

Advance Corporation Tax (ACT) A British tax set at 25 percent in 1995 and paid by corporations based on the level of dividends expected to be distributed to shareholders.

affiliated company A company in which an investor company holds an equity investment in excess of 20 percent of the voting capital stock.

aging of accounts receivables A method of accounting for uncollectible trade receivables by which an estimate of the bad debts expense is determined by classifying the specific receivable balances into age categories and then applying probability estimates of noncollection.

Aktiebolag (AB)   A limited liability company in Sweden.

Aktiengesellschaft (AG)   A publicly held corporation in Germany.

all-current method   A method of translating foreign financial statements by which all assets and liabilities are translated at the current (i.e., as of the statement preparation date) exchange rate; also called *current method.*

American depositary receipt (ADR)   A security issued by a bank or other recognized trustee representing an actual shareholding in a foreign company; these beneficial ownership shares are issued to avoid problems relating to the collection of dividends denominated in a foreign currency and to facilitate rapid ownership transfer; also referred to as *stock depositary receipts.*

amortization   A cost allocation process that spreads the cost of an intangible asset over its expected useful life.

annual report   The report prepared by a company at year-end for its shareholders and other interested parties that frequently includes a letter to the shareholders from the chairperson of the board, management's discussion and analysis of financial performance, and a variety of financial highlights in addition to the basic financial statements; it also includes the auditor's report in which the independent auditors express an opinion as to the fairness of the financial data presented in the financial statements.

asset management   The effective utilization of a company's revenue-producing assets; a measure of management's ability to effectively utilize a company's assets to produce income.

asset turnover   The rate at which sales (or revenues) are generated from a given level of assets; a measure of a company's effectiveness in generating revenues from the assets at its disposal, calculated as net sales divided by average total assets.

assets   Tangible and intangible resources of an enterprise that are expected to provide it future economic benefits.

associated company   One that is not a legal subsidiary of another company (i.e., control is less than 50+ percent) but in which the other company exercises significant influence (i.e., presumably at least a 20 percent shareholding).

audit   A process of investigating the adequacy of a company's system of internal controls, its consistent use of generally accepted accounting principles, and the presence of material errors or mistakes in its accounting data.

auditor's opinion   A report to a company's shareholders and the board of directors issued by an independent auditor summarizing his or her findings with regard to the company's financial statements; the four types of opinions are clean or unqualified, qualified, adverse, and disclaimer.

authorized shares   The total number of shares of capital stock authorized to be sold under a company's charter of incorporation.

average cost method   An inventory cost-flow method that assigns the average cost of available finished goods to units sold and, thus, to cost of goods sold.

average number of days' inventory on hand ratio   A measure of the effectiveness of inventory management, calculated as 365 days divided by the inventory turnover ratio; a measure of the appropriateness of current inventory levels given current sales volume.

average receivable collection period ratio   A measure of the effectiveness of accounts receivable management, calculated by dividing the receivable turnover ratio into 365 days.

balance sheet (statement of financial position)   An accounting statement describing, as of a specific date, the assets, liabilities, and shareholders' equity of an enterprise.

blocked funds risk   The hazard that a government will restrict the flow of funds either into or out of a given locale.

book value (per share)   The dollar amount of the net assets of a company on a per share of common (ordinary) share basis; calculated as total assets minus total liabilities divided by the number of outstanding shares of ordinary or common shares.

book value (of an asset)   The original cost of an asset less any accumulated depreciation (depletion or amortization) taken to date; also known as *carrying value.*

Borsa Valori di Milano   The Italian stock exchange in Milan, Italy.

Bovespa   The São Paulo stock exchange, the largest stock exchange in Brazil (i.e., Bolsa de Valores de São Paulo).

Brazilian commercial code   A principal source of accounting and auditing standards in Brazil along with income tax laws and the CVM.

business combination   The purchase of one or more businesses that are merged together as one accounting entity but not necessarily into one legal entity.

capital expenditure   An expenditure for the purchase of a noncurrent asset, usually property, plant, or equipment.

capital intensity ratio   A measure of a company's operating leverage calculated as fixed assets divided by total assets.

capitalization   The process of assigning value to a balance sheet account, such as a capitalized asset (e.g., a leased asset) or a capitalized liability (e.g., a lease liability).

capitalization (of a company)   The composition of a company's long-term financing, specifically, shareholders' equity and long-term debt.

capital lease   A noncancelable lease obligation accounted for as a liability on the balance sheet; a lease agreement in which the risks and rewards of asset ownership pass (either formally or informally) to the lessee.

cash dividend payout   A measure of the cash return to common shareholders, calculated as the cash dividend per common share divided by the basic earnings per share.

cash dividend yield   A measure of the cash return to common shareholders calculated as the cash dividend per common share divided by the average market price per common share.

cash equivalents   Bank deposits usually in the form of short-term certificates of deposit and short-term investments in relatively risk-free securities (e.g., U.S. government securities).

cash flow adequacy ratio   A cash flow ratio calculated as the cash flow from operations divided by the sum of capital expenditures, dividends paid, and long-term debt repayment; indicates the extent to which cash flows from operations are sufficient to cover asset replacement and capital carrying costs.

cash flow from operations (CFFO)   A measure of the net cash flows from transactions involving sales of goods or services and the acquisition of inputs used to provide the goods or services sold; the excess of cash receipts over cash disbursements relating to the operations of a company for a given period; net income calculated on a cash basis.

CFFO to current liabilities ratio   A measure of firm liquidity calculated as the cash flow from operations (CFFO) divided by average current liabilities; reflects the short-term debt coverage provided by current cash flows from operations.

CFFO to interest charges ratio   A measure of solvency calculated as the cash flow from operations divided by interest charges; reflects the extent to which interest charges are covered by current cash flows from operations.

CFFO to total liabilities ratio   A measure of solvency calculated as the cash flow from operations divided by average total liabilities; reflects the extent to which current cash flow from operations is sufficient to satisfy both long-term and short-term obligations.

chaebol   Korean business conglomerates (similar to Japan's *keiretsu*), numbering approximately 30, which dominate that country's economy (e.g., Samsung, Hyundai, Lucky Goldstar, and Daewoo).

chartered accountant (CA)   A certified public accountant in Great Britain (and elsewhere).

classified balance sheet   A balance sheet that delineates the assets and liabilities as current and noncurrent.

Chusik Hoesa   A Korean joint-stock company formed by seven or more investors with a minimum capitalization of W50 million (approximately $62,000).

collateral   The value of various assets used as security for various debts, usually bank borrowings, that will be transferred to a creditor if the obligation is not fully paid.

collectivism   The extent to which the societal ties between individuals are strongly coupled; the opposite of individualism.

Cmmercial Code of Japan   Dates to 1899, provides general rules for the valuation of assets and liabilities, provision of reserves, and the accounting for legal and capital reserves.

Comissao de Valores Mobiliários (CVM)   The securities and exchange commission of Brazil.

Commissione Nazionale per le Societa e la Borsa (CONSOB)   The Italian equivalent of the U.S. Securities and Exchange Commission; regulates listing requirements and accounting disclosures for publicly held Italian companies.

commitment   A type of contingent liability in which the value of the future obligation is known but that is not currently an obligation because various future events or conditions have not transpired or are currently satisfied.

common-size balance sheet   A balance sheet in which all account balances are expressed as a percentage of total assets or total equities.

common-size financial statements   Financial statements in which the dollar amounts are expressed as a percentage of some common statement item (e.g., a common-size income statement might express all items as a percentage of sales).

common-size income statement   An income statement in which all revenue and expense items are expressed as a percentage of net sales.

common equity share of operating earnings (CSOE)   A measure of the proportion of a company's operating earnings allocable to common shareholders.

common shareholders' capital structure leverage ratio (CSL)   A measure of a company's financial leverage calculated as average total assets divided by average common equity.

common stock (shares)   A form of capital stock (shares) that usually carries the right to vote on corporate issues; a senior equity security; see also *ordinary shares.*

common stock equivalents   A subset of convertible securities, for example stock options and stock warrants, that enable the holder to become a common shareholder by exercising various rights.

Companies Act of 1985   Current British regulation governing the formation of corporations in that country.

compensating balances   The percentage of a line of credit or of a loan that a bank requires a borrower to keep on deposit at the bank; the amount increases the effective interest rate of any amount borrowed.

consolidated financial statements   Financial statements prepared to reflect the operations and financial condition of a parent company and its wholly or majority-owned subsidiaries.

consolidated reporting   A reporting approach in which the financial statements of the parent and subsidiary companies are combined to form one set of financial statements.

contingent asset   An asset that may arise in the future if certain events occur.

contingent liability   A liability that may arise in the future if certain events occur.

contributed capital   The sum of the capital stock accounts and the capital in excess of par (or stated) value accounts.

convenience statement   A set of foreign financial statements translated into the language and the currency of another country.

convenience translation   A set of foreign financial statements translated into the language (not currency) of another country.

correçao monetaria   A system of monetary correction in Brazil designed to reflect the hyperinflationary effects of that country in reported financial statements.

countertrade   A trade practice equivalent to barter or the exchange of goods and/or services for other goods and services (i.e., no currency is exchanged); typically occurs as a consequence of restrictive currency laws.

country risk analysis   A process of identifying the various types of risks associated with investing or doing business in a given country.

cross-sectional analysis   A process of analyzing financial data between or among firms in the same industry, or between a firm and industry averages, to identify comparative financial strengths and weaknesses.

currency risk   See *foreign exchange risk.*

Cruzado Plan   Instituted in 1986, an attempt to rectify the hyperinflationary environment of Brazil; the heavily devalued cruzeiro was replaced by the cruzado as the primary monetary unit of Brazil.

current asset   Resources of an enterprise, such as cash, accounts receivable, inventory, or prepaid expenses, whose consumption or use is expected to occur within the current operating cycle.

current cost accounting   A method of accounting in which financial data are expressed in terms of current rather than historical cost.

current liability   An obligation of an enterprise whose settlement requires the use of current assets or the creation of other current liabilities, usually within one year.

current maturity of long-term debt The portion of a long-term obligation payable within the next operating cycle or one year.

current rate method A method of restating foreign financial statements in which assets and liabilities are restated using the current exchange rate at the balance sheet date, and revenues and expenses are translated at a weighted average rate for the period.

current ratio A measure of liquidity and short-term solvency calculated as current assets divided by current liabilities.

debt-to-equity ratio A measure of solvency calculated as long-term debt divided by total shareholders' equity.

debt-to-total capitalization ratio A measure of solvency, calculated as long-term debt divided by the sum of total shareholders' equity and long-term debt.

debtors An alternative designation for accounts and notes receivables, principally used in the financial statements of Great Britain and other Commonwealth companies.

declining balance method A method to depreciate the cost of a tangible asset in which the allocated cost is higher in the early periods of the asset's life (i.e., an accelerated method).

default risk The probability (or hazard) that a company will be unable to meet its short-term or long-term obligations.

defeasance A method of early retirement of debt in which risk-free securities are purchased and then placed in a trust account (i.e., sinking fund) to be used to retire the outstanding debt at its maturity.

deferral A postponement in the recognition of an expense (i.e., Prepaid Insurance) or a revenue (i.e., Unearned Rent) account.

deferred charge An asset that represents an expenditure whose related expense will not be recognized in the income statement until a future period; prepaid rent is an example.

deferred income taxes The portion of a company's income tax expense not currently payable; postponed because of differences in the accounting policies adopted for financial statement purposes versus those policies used for tax reporting purposes.

deficit An accumulated loss in the retained earnings or profit and loss reserve account; a debit balance in Retained Earnings.

depreciation A systematic allocation process that allocates the acquisition cost of a long-lived asset over the expected productive life of the asset.

devaluation A material downward adjustment of the exchange rate between two currencies.

direct financing type lease A capital lease in which the lessor receives income only from financing the ''purchase'' of the leased asset.

discretionary cash flows A measure of a company's cash flows from operations that are available to finance such discretionary corporate activities as the acquisition of another company, the early retirement of debt or equity, or some form of capital asset expansion; also referred to as *free cash flows.*

dividend yield A measure of the level of cash actually distributed to common (ordinary) shareholders calculated as the cash dividend per common (ordinary) share divided by the market price per common (ordinary) share.

double-declining-balance depreciation A method of calculating depreciation by which a percentage equal to twice the straight-line percentage is multiplied by the declining book value to determine the depreciation expense for the period; salvage value ignored when calculating it.

Du Pont formula An overall indicator of corporate performance obtained by multiplying a company's asset turnover by its profit margin; equivalent to ROA or ROI.

earned surplus A term synonymous with *retained earnings* or *profit and loss reserve.*

earnings per share A standardized measure of performance calculated as net income after taxes, less preferred dividends, divided by the weighted-average number of common (ordinary) shares outstanding during an accounting period; also known as *basic EPS.*

economic exposure (risk) The risk of experiencing a real gain (loss) in purchasing power as a consequence of foreign exchange rate fluctuations.

efficient market hypothesis A theory to explain the functioning of capital markets in which share and bond prices always reflect all publicly available information, and any new information is quickly impounded in security prices.

equity in earnings of investee   An income statement account representing an investor company's percentage ownership of an investee's (or subsidiary's) net earnings.

equity method   A method to value intercorporate equity investments by adjusting the investor's cost basis for the percentage ownership in the investee's earnings (or losses) and for any dividends paid by the investee.

European Union (EU)   An organization of politically independent European nations (currently numbering 15), united to act as a single economic (i.e., trading) entity (or bloc); includes three cooperative alliances intended to improve the efficiency and competitive ability of its member-nations: the European Coal and Steel Community, the European Atomic Energy Commission, and the European Economic Community.

European currency unit (ECU)   A currency intended to be used by all European Union members when conducting trade.

European exchange rate mechanism (ERM)   A system created by the EU to stabilize the rate of exchange of currency between EU member-nations.

exchange   Currency or legal tender used to facilitate trade between parties.

exchange rate   The rate at which one unit of currency may be purchased by another unit of currency.

executory contracts   A category of legal agreements requiring some type of future performance.

expense   An expenditure whose revenue-producing value has been fully consumed and thus has no future revenue-producing value.

expropriation exposure (risk)   The likelihood that a company's assets located in a foreign domain will be involuntarily appropriated by the local government, with or without compensation.

extraordinary item   A loss or gain that, according to U.S. GAAP, is both unusual in nature and infrequent in occurrence.

face amount (maturity value)   The value of a security as stated on the instrument itself; see also *settlement value*.

Financial Accounting Standards Board (FASB)   An independent, private sector organization responsible for establishing U.S. generally accepted accounting principles.

Financial Reporting Council (FRC)   An accounting standard-setting organization in the United Kingdom founded in 1990 that succeeded the Accounting Standards Committee; issues financial reporting standards.

financial reporting standard (FRS)   An official accounting pronouncement issued by the Financial Reporting Council of the United Kingdom.

financial statement analysis   The process of reviewing, analyzing, and interpreting the basic financial statements to assess a company's operating performance and/or financial health.

first-in, first-out (FIFO)   An inventory cost-flow method that assigns the first cost value in finished goods inventory to the first unit sold and thus to cost of goods sold.

fiscal year   Any continuous 12-month period, usually beginning after a natural business peak.

footnotes   Written information by management designed to supplement the numerical data presented in a company's financial statement.

foreign currency option contract   A contract providing the right to buy or sell a set quantity of foreign currency at a preset exchange rate within a specified future time frame; typically used to hedge foreign exchange risk exposure and often thought of as *currency insurance.*

foreign currency translation adjustment   A shareholders' equity account measuring the change in value of a company's net assets held in a foreign country attributable to changes in the exchange rate of the foreign currency as compared to the U.S. dollar; arises under the current rate method.

foreign exchange   Any currency other than the one in which a company prepares its basic financial statements.

foreign exchange exposure (risk)   The risk associated with changes in exchange rates between the U.S. dollar and foreign currencies when a company maintains operations in a foreign country.

Form 8-K   A special SEC filing required when a material event or transaction occurs between Form 10-Q filing dates. Events usually necessitating the filing of Form 8-K: a change in control or ownership of an enterprise, the acquisition or disposition of a significant amount of assets, a bankruptcy declaration, the resignation of an executive or director of an enterprise, or a change in the independent external auditor.

Form 10-K   The annual financial report filing with the SEC required of all publicly held enterprises in the U.S.

Form 10-Q   The quarterly financial report filing with the SEC required of all publicly held enterprises in the United States; filed only for the first three quarters of a fiscal year.

Form 20-F   The annual financial report filing with the SEC required of all foreign companies whose debt or equity capital is available for purchase/sale on a U.S. exchange.

forward exchange contract   A contract providing for the payment (receipt) of a foreign currency at a future date at a specified exchange rate; typically used to hedge foreign exchange risk exposure.

forward exchange rate   An exchange rate between two currencies quoted for 30, 60, 90, or 180 days in the future; a rate quoted currently for the exchange of currency at some future specified date.

Fourth Directive   A European Union agreement, adopted in 1978, to (1) eliminate legal and bureaucratic obstacles to economic activity between EU member-nations and (2) establish the basic reporting requirements and financial statement formats (i.e., comparability) for companies operating in EU member-nations.

free cash flows   See *discretionary cash flows*.

front-end loading   An accounting process by which revenues (expenses) are recognized for income statement purposes before they have been earned (incurred).

fully diluted earnings per share   A standardized measure of performance calculated as net income applicable to common (ordinary) shares divided by the weighted-average number of common (ordinary) shares outstanding plus common (ordinary) stock equivalents and any other potentially dilutive securities.

functional currency   The currency of the primary business environment (i.e., country) of a company's operations.

generally accepted accounting principles (GAAP)   Methods identified by authoritative bodies (i.e., APB, FASB, SEC) as being acceptable for use in the preparation of external accounting reports.

generally accepted auditing standards (GAAS)   Auditing practices and procedures established in the U.S. by the AICPA (or other comparable professional organizations in other countries) and used by CPAs to evaluate a company's accounting system and financial results.

Gesellschaft mit beschränkter Haftung (GmbH)   A privately held corporation in Germany.

goodwill   An intangible asset representing the excess of the purchase price of acquired net assets over their fair market value.

gross profit (gross margin)   A measure of a company's profit on sales calculated as net sales minus the cost of goods or services sold.

gross profit margin ratio   A measure of profitability that assesses the percentage of each sales dollar that is recognized as gross profit (i.e., after deducting the cost of goods sold) and that is available to cover other operating expenses (e.g., selling, administrative, interest, and taxes).

harmonization   The attempt by various organizations (e.g., the IASC, the EU, IOSCO) to establish a common set of international accounting and reporting standards.

hedge   A process of buying or selling commodities, forward contracts, or options for the explicit purpose of reducing or eliminating foreign exchange risk.

hedged items   Those accounts (assets, liabilities, revenues) or contracts for which an artificial or natural hedge exists.

hedging instrument   A forward exchange contract or option contract acquired to hedge some type of exposure (e.g., currency risk, expropriation risk, political risk).

highest-in, first-out (HIFO)   An inventory cost-flow method that assigns the highest cost value available in finished goods inventory to the first unit sold and thus cost of goods sold.

historical cost concept   An accounting concept that stipulates that all economic transactions be recorded using the dollar value incurred at the time of the transaction.

holding company (parent company)   A company that owns a majority of the voting capital shares of another company.

impairment   A temporary or permanent reduction in asset value; usually necessitates a write-down in the asset's balance sheet value.

income   A generic term used to indicate revenue from miscellaneous sources (e.g., interest income or rent income) or the excess of revenue over expenses for product sales or services.

income smoothing An accounting practice that implicitly or explicitly attempts to present a stable (but growing) measure of net income (e.g., straight-line depreciation).

income statement (profit and loss statement) An accounting statement describing the revenues earned and expenses incurred by an enterprise for a given period.

independent auditor A professionally trained individual whose responsibilities include the objective review of a company's financial statements prepared for external distribution.

individualism The extent to which the societal ties between individuals are loosely coupled; the opposite of collectivism.

inflation A phenomenon of generally rising prices.

initial public offering (IPO) The first or initial sale of voting stock to the general market by a previously privately held concern.

insolvent (bankrupt) A condition in which a company is unable to pay its current obligations as they come due.

Instituto Brasileiro de Contadores (IBC) The professional society of certified public accountants in Brazil.

intangible assets The resources of an enterprise, such as goodwill, trademarks, or trade names, that lack an identifiable physical presence.

intercompany profit The profit resulting when one related company sells to another related company; removed from the financial statements when consolidated financial statements are prepared.

intercorporate investments Investments in the shares and bonds of one company by another.

interest coverage ratio See *times-interest-earned ratio.*

interim financial statements Financial statements prepared on a monthly or quarterly basis, usually unaudited.

internal control The policies and procedures implemented by management to safeguard a company's assets and its accounting system against misapplication or misuse.

international accounting standards (IAS) The accounting and reporting standards adopted and promulgated by the IASC.

International Accounting Standards Committee (IASC) An organization established in 1973 by the leading professional accounting groups of the major industrial countries; goals: (1) to formulate, publish, and promote the worldwide acceptance and observance of international accounting standards and (2) to harmonize the accounting standards and procedures relating to the presentation of financial statements on a worldwide basis.

International Federation of Accountants (IFAC) An association of professional accounting organizations from more than 70 nations founded in 1977; largely concerned with developing international guidelines for the accounting profession in the areas of auditing, ethics, and education.

International Organization of Securities Commissions and Similar Organizations (IOSCO) An organization of securities regulatory agencies representing various member-countries, whose goal is to assist in the creation and regulation of orderly international capital markets.

International Stock Exchange (ISE) The largest securities exchange in the United Kingdom.

interperiod tax allocation The process of allocating the actual taxes paid by a company over the periods in which the taxes are recognized for accounting purposes.

inventory The aggregate cost of salable goods and merchandise available to meet customer sales; sometimes referred to as *stocks.*

inventory turnover A measure of the rate of inventory sales.

inventory turnover ratio A measure of the effectiveness of inventory management calculated as the cost of goods sold for a period divided by the average inventory held during that period.

investment ratio A cash flow ratio calculated as capital expenditures divided by the sum of depreciation and proceeds from the sale of assets; indicates the relative change in a company's investment in productive assets.

investment tax credit A reduction in a company's current income taxes payable earned through the purchase of various applicable assets.

investor company A company that holds an equity investment in another company (the investee company).

issued shares The authorized shares of capital stock sold to shareholders less any shares repurchased *and* retired.

Japanese Securities and Exchange Law of 1948   Based largely on the U.S. securities laws of 1933 and 1934; requires companies issuing securities to the public to file financial statements (*zaimushohyo*) audited by an independent auditor with the Ministry of Finance; also known as *shokentorihikiho.*

keiretsu   An association of Japanese companies with interlocking shareholdings that provide economic support to one another; literally interpreted as ''headless combines.''

krona   The basic unit of currency in Sweden.

last-in, first-out (LIFO)   An inventory cost-flow method that assigns the last cost value in finished goods inventory to the first unit sold and thus to cost of goods sold.

lease   An agreement to buy or rent an asset.

lessee   An individual or company who leases an asset.

lessor   The maker of a lease agreement; an individual or company that leases an asset *to* another individual or company.

leverage   The extent to which a company's long-term capital structure includes debt financing; a measure of a company's dependency on debt; a company with large quantities of debt is said to be *highly leveraged;* sometimes referred to as *gearing.*

liabilities   A company's obligations to repay moneys loaned to it, to pay for goods or services received by it, or to fulfill commitments made by it.

life cycle   The cycle that an enterprise normally follows throughout its existence: introduction, growth, maturity, decline; see *product life cycle.*

LIFO liquidation   The sale of inventory units acquired or manufactured in a prior period at a lower cost; results when the level of LIFO inventory is reduced below its beginning-of-period level.

LIFO reserve   An amount presented in the footnotes to the financial statements of companies employing the LIFO method of inventory valuation; calculated as the current cost of ending inventory minus the LIFO cost of ending inventory.

limited company (Ltd)   A limited liability but privately held company in the United Kingdom having no minimum capital requirement.

limited liability   The concept that shareholders in a corporation are not held personally liable for its losses or debts.

line of credit   An agreement with a bank (or other financial institution) by which an organization obtains authorization for short-term borrowings up to a specified amount.

liquid assets   Current assets, such as cash, cash equivalents, or short-term investments, that either are in cash form or can be readily converted to cash.

liquidating dividend   A cash dividend representing a return of invested capital and, hence, a liquidation of a previous investment.

liquidation   The process of selling off the assets of a business, paying any outstanding debts, and distributing any remaining cash to the owners.

liquidity   The short-term debt repayment ability of a company; a measure of a company's cash position relative to currently maturing obligations.

listed company   A company whose shares or bonds have been accepted for trading on a recognized securities exchange (e.g., NYSE).

lire   The basic unit of currency in Italy.

long-term liabilities (noncurrent liabilities)   A company's obligations payable after more than one year.

long-term orientation   A societal inclination for the long-term and one that values persistence and thrift.

lower of cost or market   A method to value inventories and marketable securities (both current and long term); the lower of an asset's cost basis or current market value used to value the asset accounts for balance sheet purposes.

market price   The current fair value of an asset as established by an arm's-length transaction between a buyer and a seller.

marketable securities   Short- or long-term investments in the stocks or bonds of other corporations.

matching principle   A fundamental accounting concept stipulating that all expenses incurred to generate a given level of revenues should be matched with those revenues in the same accounting period in which the revenues are recognized on the financial statements.

merger   A combination of one or more companies into a single corporate entity.

minority interest   An account that reflects the percentage ownership in the net assets of a subsidiary held by investors other than the parent company.

monetary assets   Resources of an enterprise, such as cash and marketable securities, whose principal characteristic is its monetary denomination.

multinational corporation (MNC)   A for-profit organization with operations in two or more countries.

multinational enterprise (MNE)   A for-profit or not-for-profit organization with operations in two or more countries (e.g., a multinational corporation).

multiple reporting   Reporting by a company that requires the preparation of multiple sets of financial statements in the language and currency of another country.

natural hedge   A hedging instrument that exists as a consequence of the normal course of business.

negative goodwill   The excess of the net book value of an acquired company over the consideration paid for it.

net assets   Total assets minus total liabilities; equivalent to shareholders' equity.

net current assets   Current assets minus current liabilities; working capital.

net income (net earnings)   The difference between the aggregate revenues and aggregate expenses of an enterprise for a given accounting period; referred to as *net loss* when aggregate expenses exceed aggregate revenues; sometimes referred to as *profit*.

net realizable value   The amount of funds expected to be received upon the sale or liquidation of an asset.

net worth (of an enterprise)   Total assets minus total liabilities; the value of owners' equity; also known as the *book value* of an enterprise.

noncurrent assets   The long-lived resources of an enterprise, such as property, plant, and equipment, whose consumption or use is *not* expected to be completed within the current operating cycle.

noncurrent asset turnover ratio   A measure of the effectiveness of noncurrent asset management; calculated as net sales for the period divided by the average balance of noncurrent assets.

noncurrent liability   An obligation of an enterprise whose settlement is not expected within one year.

nondiversifiable risk   Unique, nonsystematic risk associated with an investment that cannot be effectively hedged (e.g., through portfolio diversification).

nonmonetary assets   Resources of an enterprise, such as inventory or equipment, whose principal characteristic is other than its monetary denomination or value.

off-balance sheet debt   Economic obligations that are not reported on the face of the balance sheet (e.g., operating leases).

operating cycle   The average length of time between the investment in inventory and the subsequent collection of cash from the sale of that inventory.

operating funds index   A cash flow ratio calculated as net income divided by cash flow from operations that indicates the portion of operating cash flow provided by net income.

operating lease   A lease agreement in which the risks and rewards of asset ownership are retained by the lessor.

operating leverage   The extent to which a company operates with a high proportion of fixed costs.

operational risk   The probability that unforeseen or unexpected events will occur and consequently reduce or impair the revenue, earnings, and cash flow streams of a company.

option contract   Usually used for hedging purposes to grant one party to it the right to choose whether (and sometimes when) a currency exchange will actually take place.

Organization for Economic Cooperation and Development (OECD)   Formed in 1960, an association of representatives from various countries whose purpose is to promote economic cooperation among nations.

outstanding shares   The number of authorized shares of capital stock sold to shareholders that are currently in the possession of shareholders; the number of issued shares less the shares held in treasury.

owners' equity (shareholders' equity)   The dollar value of the owners' (or shareholders') investment in an enterprise; may take two forms—the purchase of shares of stock or the retention of earnings in the enterprise for future use.

paid-in capital in excess of par value (contributed capital in excess of par value)   An owners' equity account reflecting the proceeds from the sale of capital stock in excess of the par value (or stated value) of the capital stock; sometimes referred to as *capital surplus reserve* or *premium.*

par value   A legal value assigned to a share of capital stock that must be considered in recording the proceeds received from the sale of the stock; see also *stated value.*

passive investment   An intercorporate investment in which the investor cannot (or does not) attempt to influence the operations of the investee company.

payback period   The time required to recover the cash outlay for an asset or other investment.

permanent difference   A difference in reported income or expenses between a company's tax return and its financial statements that will never reverse (i.e., the difference is permanent).

permanent earnings (cash flows)   The recurring earnings (cash flows) of a company; earnings (cash flows) expected to recur in future periods.

pledging   Using assets as collateral for a bank loan.

political exposure (risk)   The degree of stability (or lack thereof) among political groups and the established government in a given country.

pooling of interests   A consolidation method that combines the financial results of a parent company and its subsidiary on the basis of existing book values.

power distance   A cultural concept pertaining to the extent members of an institution or a society expect and accept that power is distributed unequally.

preferred stock   A (usually) nonvoting form of capital stock whose claims to the dividends and assets of a company precede those of common shareholders; also known as *preference shares.*

premium   An amount paid in excess of the face value of a security or debt instrument.

present value   The value today of a future stream of cash flows calculated by discounting the cash flows at a given rate of interest.

price-earnings (P-E) ratio   A market-based measure of the investment potential of a security calculated as the market price per share divided by the earnings per share; also known as *P-E multiple.*

price-level-adjusted financial statements   Financial statements in which the account balances have been restated to reflect changes in price levels due to inflation.

primary earnings per share   A standardized measure of performance calculated as net income applicable to common shares (i.e., net income after tax minus preferred share dividends) divided by the weighted-average number of common shares outstanding plus common share equivalents.

prior period adjustment   An accounting adjustment that does not affect the current period's earnings but instead is reflected as an adjustment to beginning retained earnings (or profit and loss reserve).

private placement   The sale, or "placement," of a significant number of stocks or bonds to a limited group of buyers (i.e., the securities are not offered for sale to the general marketplace).

privatization   The sale of all or part of a previously state-controlled entity to the general public.

product life cycle   The cycle of introduction, growth, maturity, and decline that all products and their companies are assumed to pass through in a natural evolutionary fashion.

productivity index   A cash flow ratio calculated as the cash flow from operations divided by the capital investment; indicates the relative cash productivity of a company's capital investments.

profit   The excess of revenues over expenses.

profit and loss reserve   The amount of retained earnings of a company; see *retained earnings.*

profit margin   The excess (or insufficiency) of operating revenues over operating expenses; a measure of a company's ability to generate profits from a given level of revenues; calculated as net income after tax divided by net sales; also known as the *return on sales.*

profitability   The relative success of a company's operations; a measure of the extent to which accomplishment exceeded effort.

pro forma financial statement   A forecasted or projected financial statement for a future accounting period.

proportionate consolidation   A method of consolidating the financial results of a parent company and its subsidiary in which only the proportion of net assets owned by the parent are consolidated; as a consequence there is no need for a minority interest account.

proprietary company   A label used in some countries to describe a privately held (or nonpublic) company.

prospectus   A document describing the nature of a business and its recent financial history, usually prepared in conjunction with an offer to sell capital stock or bonds by a company.

proxy   A legal document granting another person or company the right to vote for a shareholder on matters involving a shareholder vote.

prudence   The criterion used under German GAAP to establish the appropriateness and necessity of recognizing a loss contingency.

public company   One whose voting shares are listed for trading on a recognized securities exchange or are otherwise available for purchase (sale) by public investors.

public limited company (Plc)   A limited liability publicly held company in the United Kingdom; must have share capital of at least £50,000.

purchase accounting   A consolidation method in which the financial results of a parent company and its subsidiary are combined using the fair market value of the subsidiary's net worth.

qualified opinion   Issued by an independent auditor indicating that the financial statements of a company are fairly presented on a consistent basis and use generally accepted accounting principles but for which some concern or exception has been noted.

quick assets   Highly liquid, short-term assets such as cash, cash equivalents, short-term investments, and receivables.

quick ratio (acid test ratio)   A measure of liquidity and short-term solvency calculated as quick assets divided by current liabilities.

ratio   A financial indicator (e.g., the current ratio) formed by comparing two account balances (e.g., Current Assets and current liabilities).

ratio analysis   The process of analyzing and interpreting the ratios formed from two or more financial statement numbers.

raw (basic) earnings per share (EPS)   A measure of EPS calculated as net income after taxes minus preferred dividends, divided by the weighted average number of common (or ordinary) shares outstanding.

realized loss (gain)   The amount recognized in the financial statements usually due to the sale of an asset.

rear-end loading   An accounting process by which expenses (revenues) are deferred for income statement purposes despite being incurred (earned).

receivable turnover   A measure of the rate of collections on sales.

receivable turnover ratio   A measure of the rate of collections on sales, calculated as net sales divided by the average receivable balance; the rate at which a company's receivables are converted to cash.

reconciliation report   A statement or report reconciling the financial statements of a foreign entity to the accepted or prevailing accounting practice of another country.

registrar   An independent agent, normally a bank or a trust company, that maintains a record of the number of a company's shares of capital stock that have been issued and to whom.

reorganization   A process of changing the ownership structure of a company, usually as a direct result of a deficit in retained earnings.

replacement cost   The cost to reproduce or repurchase a given asset (e.g., a unit of inventory).

reporting currency   The currency used to measure and report a company's net assets (i.e., the "local" currency).

reserve   An owners' equity account including the profit and loss reserve (i.e., retained earnings), revaluation reserve, capital reserve, or share premium reserve (i.e., paid-in-capital in excess of par value), and legal reserves (those mandated by a given country's laws of incorporation).

retained earnings   Earnings of an enterprise that have been retained in the enterprise (i.e., have not been paid out as dividends) for future corporate use; see *profit and loss reserve*.

retained earnings—appropriated   The amount of total retained earnings that has been allocated for specific corporate objectives, such as the redemption of debt or capital stock.

retained earnings—restricted   The amount of total retained earnings that is legally restricted from being paid out as dividends to shareholders usually because of a borrowing agreement with a bank or other financial institution.

return on common equity (ROCE) ratio   A measure of profitability calculated as the net income available to common shareholders divided by average total common equity for the period.

return on owners' equity (ROE) ratio   A measure of profitability; a measure of the relative effectiveness of a company in utilizing the assets provided by the owners to generate net income; calculated as net income after tax divided by average shareholders' equity.

return on sales ratio (net profit margin ratio)   A measure of profitability calculated as the percentage of each sales dollar earned as net income (i.e., net income after tax divided by net sales).

return on total assets (ROA)   A measure of profitability that assesses the relative effectiveness of a company in using available resources to generate net income; also called *return on investment* (ROI); calculated as net income after tax divided by average total assets.

revaluation   A material upward adjustment of the exchange rate between two currencies; an upward adjustment in asset value, usually undertaken to reflect the economic effects of inflation.

revenues   The inflow of assets, the reduction in liabilities, or both, from transactions involving an enterprise's principal business activity (e.g., sales of products or services); also referred to as *turnover or total trading transactions*.

sales-type lease   A capital lease that generates two income streams: (1) from the "sale" of the asset and (2) from financing the "purchase" of the asset.

salvage value (residual value)   The amount expected to be recovered when an asset is retired, removed from active use, and sold.

self-sustaining foreign operation   A foreign entity financially and operationally independent of its parent company.

sensitivity analysis   A process by which the effect of a change in a given assumption is assessed (i.e., as in a pro forma analysis).

Seventh Directive   A European Union agreement adopted in 1983 governing the preparation of consolidated financial statements for companies operating in EU member-nations.

short-term orientation   A societal inclination that values personal stability, protecting "face," and respect for tradition.

Società per Azioni (S.p.A.)   A publicly held (joint stock) company in Italy.

Società a Responsibilità Limitada (S.r.l.)   A closely held, limited liability entity in Italy.

solvency   The long-term debt repayment ability of a company; a measure of a company's long-term liquidity.

specific identification   An inventory cost-flow method that assigns the actual cost of producing a specific unit to that unit; the only inventory method that matches exactly the cost flow and physical flow.

spot rate   The prevailing exchange rate between two currencies on a given date.

stated value   The recorded accounting value of capital stock; see also *par value*.

statement of cash flows   An accounting statement describing the sources and uses of cash flows for an enterprise for a given period.

statement of changes in financial position   An accounting statement describing the inflows and outflows of a company's funds or working capital.

statement of fund flows   An accounting statement describing a company's inflows and outflows of funds over a given period; *funds* defined with reference to a company's cash, liquid assets, or working capital.

statement of owners' equity (statement of shareholders' equity)   An accounting statement describing the principal transactions affecting the owners' (or shareholders') interests in an enterprise for a given period.

statement of retained earnings   An accounting statement describing the beginning and ending balances in retained earnings and the major changes to the retained earnings account (e.g., dividends and net income).

Statement of Standard Accounting Practice (SSAPs)   Official accounting pronouncements issued by the Accounting Standards Committee of the United Kingdom.

stock depositary receipt (SDR)   A beneficial ownership share in a foreign entity held by a trustee (e.g., a bank or brokerage firm) on behalf of the investor; see *American depositary receipt*.

stockholders' equity   The owners' equity of a corporation; comprises paid-in capital and retained earnings, as well as any reserve accounts; also known as *shareholders' equity*.

straight-line method   A method to depreciate the cost of a tangible asset or to amortize the cost of an intangible asset in which the allocated cost is constant over the life of the asset.

strategic business units (SBUs)   Autonomous business segments of a company that could be managed and run as viable isolated entities.

subsidiary   A company in which an investor company (the parent) holds an equity investment in excess of 50 percent of the voting shares of the investee company.

sum-of-the-years'-digits method   A method to depreciate the cost of a tangible asset in which the allocated cost is higher in the early periods of the asset's life (i.e., an accelerated method).

take-or-pay contract   An executory contract by which one party agrees to pay for certain inventory (or other products) regardless of whether the inventory is physically received or not.

tangible asset   Resources of an enterprise, such as property, plant, and equipment, that possess physical characteristics or have a physical presence.

temporal method   A method of translating foreign financial statements in which cash, receivables, and payables are translated at the exchange rate in effect at the balance sheet date; other assets and liabilities translated at historical rates; revenues and expenses translated at the weighted-average rate for the period.

times-interest-earned (interest coverage) ratio   A measure of solvency and leverage calculated as net income before income taxes plus interest charges divided by interest charges; a measure of the extent to which current interest payments are covered by current earnings.

time value of money   The concept that money can always be invested at a bank to earn interest for the period it is on deposit.

total asset turnover ratio   A measure of asset management effectiveness reflecting the rate at which sales are generated from a company's investment in assets; calculated as net sales divided by average total assets.

total debt-to-total assets ratio   A measure of solvency or long-term liquidity calculated as total debt divided by total assets.

transaction exposure (risk)   A source of foreign exchange risk resulting from exchange rate fluctuations between the date on which a contract is signed or goods delivered and the date of payment.

transitory earnings (cash flows)   The nonrecurring earnings (cash flows) of a company; earnings (cash flows) that are not expected to reoccur in future periods.

translation exposure (risk)   A source of foreign exchange risk resulting from the restatement of foreign financial statements denominated in a foreign currency into U.S. dollar equivalents; also known as *accounting exposure*.

treasury stock   Outstanding capital stock that has been repurchased but not retired and usually held to be reissued at some future date.

trend analysis   The analysis of ratios or account balances over one or more accounting periods to identify the direction or trend of a company's financial health.

true and fair view   The current standard of precision required of all audited financial data in the EU; analogous to the "fairly presented" standard used in the United States.

turnover   A measure of the rate of sales of goods or services; in the United Kingdom, a measure of net sales or net revenues.

uncertainty avoidance   The extent to which the members of a society feel threatened by uncertain or unknown situations; the opposite of uncertainty acceptance.

unleveraged ROA (UROA)   A refinement of the return on assets (ROA) ratio obtained by restating net income to include interest charges on an after-tax basis (i.e., net income plus interest expense net of tax benefits).

unrealized loss (gain)   A loss (gain) recognized in the financial statements but not associated with an asset sale; usually involves a revaluation of an asset value.

useful life   The estimated productive life of a noncurrent asset.

value-added statement   A financial statement prepared by some foreign companies reflecting a measure of the wealth created by the operations of the company and the distribution of that wealth among its major constituents (e.g., employees, investors, and the government).

value-added tax   A tax levied at each stage in the production and distribution chain on the basis of the value that is added to a product as it passes through a given stage.

weighted-average cost method   An inventory cost-flow method that assigns the average cost of available finished goods, weighted by the number of units available at each price, to a unit sold and thus cost of goods sold, and to ending inventory.

Wirtschaftsprüfer (WP)   A certified public accountant in Germany.

won   The basic unit of currency in Korea.

working capital   A measure of liquidity or short-term solvency calculated as total current assets minus total current liabilities.

working capital maintenance agreement   An executory contract by which one entity guarantees to maintain the level of working capital of a second entity; usually arises as a consequence of a borrowing agreement by the second entity for which the first party becomes a guarantor.

world standards report   A set of financial statements prepared according to IASC accounting standards.

zaibatsu   Japanese industrial conglomerates that existed prior to World War II but were disbanded and have been subsequently replaced by *keiretsu*.

Index